“Destined to Fail”

"Destined to Fail"

Carl Seashore's World of Eugenics, Psychology, Education, and Music

Julia Eklund Koza

University of Michigan Press
Ann Arbor

Published in the United States of America by
the University of Michigan Press
Manufactured in the United States of America
Printed on acid-free paper

First published August 2021

A CIP catalog record for this book is available from the British Library.

ISBN 978-0-472-13260-7 (hardcover : alk. paper)

ISBN 978-0-472-12911-9 (ebook)

To my beloved husband, Jim,
who has been at my side every step of the way

The race is not always to the swift but to those who keep on running.
—Author unknown

Contents

Digital materials related to this title can be found on the Fulcrum platform via the following citable URL https://doi.org/10.3998/mpub.11865737

Acknowledgments

A village helped make this book possible. I thank those who gave me access to archival materials, including archivist David McCartney and library assistant Kathryn Hodson at the University of Iowa, as well as special collections technician Charles Scott and special collections coordinator Mary Bennett at the State Historical Society of Iowa. I also thank reference librarian Steven Baumgart, at UW–Madison's Memorial Library, for helping me track down multiple versions of the Seashore Tests, as well as Charlene Simms, the genealogy and special collections librarian in the Pueblo City-County District, who generously sent me an obscure article from the *Pueblo Chieftain*. Adrianna Darden, the archives collections and records manager at Gustavus Adolphus College, located an elusive obituary and sent me information about Seashore's graduating class. Barry Atkins at the Carnegie Library of Pittsburgh provided me with an article from a hard-to-find edition of the *New Pittsburgh Courier*. Michael Frost, a library services assistant at Yale University's Sterling Library, tracked down a letter I needed from the Robert Yerkes papers. Katherine Koza and Kate Wellenstein were able assistants when I initially examined archival materials at the University of Iowa in 2010. During the 2020 COVID-19 pandemic, Katherine Koza saved the day when she stepped in as an excellent and invaluable project assistant. She and I created, by hand, every endnote in this book (more than 3,000 of them) when RefWorks proved unequal to the task. Adam G. Harry, an assistant professor in the School of Music at the University of Iowa, generously rescanned and emailed an important item after the copy I made during my 2019 visit to the Iowa archives mysteriously vanished into cyberspace. Elham Milani and Melanie Stege gave me excellent administrative support. Jeanne Swack, Charles James, and Christine Otterstatter were helpful in translating and interpreting the Mjøen studies, published in German. Jay Lesseig, the senior technical support specialist for RefWorks, and Jim Jonas, the information and instructional services librarian at UW–Madison's MERIT Library, helped me solve a host of database management problems. Susan Lauter, creative director at the DNA Learning Center of the Cold Spring Harbor Laboratory, provided guidance on citing items from the Image Archive on the American Eugenics Movement. The Department of Curriculum and Instruction, in addition to granting me the two sabbaticals that I devoted to this project, also partially funded a part-time project assistant, Tracy Carolan, in 2018–19. Tracy tirelessly helped with formatting; checking the accuracy of quotes, paraphrases, and citations; and boosting morale. Over the years, graduate students in two courses, Education and the American Eugenics Movement; and Histories of the Present: Eugenics and Global Education Reform, Past and Present, provided invaluable suggestions and feedback. I thank two wonderful friends who always have shown me kindness and support: Thomas Popkewitz, with whom I have had many lively conversations about salvation, cosmopolitanism, and eugenics; and Gloria Ladson-Billings, who transformed our department—and my thinking—with her brilliance. I am grateful for the superb editors at the University of Michigan Press—Daniel Otis, Marcia LaBrenz, and Elizabeth Demers—and thank them for their wisdom, guidance, and support. Elspeth Tupelo at Twin Oaks Indexing deserves a round of applause for her meticulous work. Finally, I thank my loving family, especially my dear husband, Jim, for cheering me on when it seemed like I would never finish this long race, and for patiently listening to my endless musings about Carl Emil Seashore and eugenics. Jim, I will try not to mention him to you again. I promise.

One

Setting the Stage

This project began with a hunch. In 2003, Steven Selden, a renowned expert on eugenics and education, spoke at UW–Madison about the better baby and fitter family contests held at state and county fairs throughout the Midwest during the early twentieth century. Just as livestock were judged in the barns, babies and whole families were judged in nearby tents, the fittest being awarded medals. Selden reported that these contests were sponsored by the American Eugenics Society. He was a member of the editorial advisory panel for the recently created website, Image Archive on the American Eugenics Movement, and he showed archival pictures of the contests.

I was in the audience at that talk, and one name kept popping into my head: Carl Emil Seashore (1866–1949). I had first learned about Seashore in 1982 when I was a doctoral student in music education at the University of Minnesota, but I had never heard a word that linked him to eugenics. I knew that he was an experimental psychologist, a pioneer in the field of the psychology of music, and a professor and later dean of the graduate school at the University of Iowa.[1] I knew he was a Mendelian hereditarian who believed that musical talent is biologically inheritable, differentially bestowed, and immutable. I also knew that he had developed the first standardized tests of musical talent (tests of what he called "musical capacities"). I knew all this because in my first year of doctoral study, I had to give a seminar presentation on "nature versus nurture" in musical ability; I was to discuss Seashore's work as representative of the nature camp and James Mursell's as representing the opposing view. I understood that at least some of Seashore's contemporaries were critical of his work, including Mursell; that his critics had questioned the validity of the Seashore Tests; and that some portions of the tests had been found unreliable. I also knew that portions of the tests were still in use in the 1980s. In 1983, one of my jobs as a teaching assistant was to administer

Edwin Gordon's Musical Aptitude Profile (MAP), a second-generation standardized test of musical aptitude, to undergraduate music education majors. Troubled by Seashore's views and their potential for excluding some children from music classrooms, I revised the seminar assignment by adding Shinichi Suzuki's *Nurtured by Love* to the list of books I discussed.

I was aware that although he had critics, Seashore was something of a rock star among music education researchers, such that when the Seashore Tests lost credibility, rather than abandoning the idea of developing standardized measures of musical ability, his successors just set out to build better ones. Thus, his ideas and his research set the tone and helped establish the parameters of legitimate music education research for much of the twentieth century. This research was positivistic and focused on psychometrics, perceptual studies, and standardized test development. In short, many considered Seashore to be a titanic founding father in music education and other fields. This assessment continues to the present.

Nevertheless, many questions came to mind during that 2003 Selden lecture. Was musical talent being tested at the fitter family contests and used as a criterion for determining which families were fittest? If so, how was it assessed? Were the Seashore Tests ever used? Could Seashore himself have been involved in better baby contests or the American Eugenics Society that sponsored them? I saw many potential connections between him and eugenics—primarily his belief that talent is biologically inherited, but also the shared time period (the early twentieth century) and the geographical location (the US Midwest). I checked a number of standard sources and found nothing connecting him to eugenics. Time went by, and faced with other projects and administrative responsibilities, I relegated the Seashore question to the back burner.

The following year, the Committee on Institutional Cooperation (now known as the Big Ten Academic Alliance) held its annual meeting of music education researchers at Northwestern University. That year the event was something of a love-fest for the fathers of music education, living and dead. I ended up in a breakout session with a group of men, members of a whole new generation of scholars, who were singing Seashore's praises and talking about how their work continued along the intellectual path he had created. By that point in my career, I had grown weary of "great man" narratives, and as the accolade-filled minutes ticked by, my blood pressure rose. Finally, in a brash moment I blurted, "*Well*, at Wisconsin, we are looking into the possibility that he was a eugenicist." This was not a lie; I had done a cursory investigation, and although I hadn't found anything yet, I felt I was onto something. I left myself an out by saying this was only a hypothesis. The room went silent and stayed that way for what felt like an eternity—enough time for me to ponder what the silence meant. Were these men shocked or shamed by the possibility that one of the titans of music education had some skeletons in his closet? Was this an angry silence—were they mad at me for saying anything negative about someone they clearly admired? Was it an ignorant silence—was it possible that people in my field had never heard of eugenics and did not know what to make of my comment?

Having opened my mouth at the conference, I knew I had to follow up on my hunch, and having exhausted more conventional research routes, I decided to use what at that time was an unconventional one: the internet. I googled "Seashore" and "better baby contests" and got one hit, a shred of evidence from the image archive that Selden had helped establish. It was an undated letter from the American Eugenics Society (AES) to fair associations; written on AES letterhead, it requested free exhibit space.[2] The letterhead named a long list of prominent individuals serving on the AES Advisory Council—ranging from the White supremacist Madison Grant and the superintendent of the Eugenics Record Office, Harry H. Laughlin, to psychologist Edward L. Thorndike. Seashore's name was nested among them! It was not much to go on, and I did not know precisely what the presence of his name on that letterhead meant, but I knew I had a story.

The Project and Its Significance

The mere presence of Seashore's name on a letterhead told me little; in the United States and elsewhere, eugenics was a large, popular tent during the early twentieth century. In it camped a diverse array of individuals who gathered there for a variety of reasons and who had somewhat different goals and projects. Initially, I wanted to know what had brought Seashore to that tent, the extent and nature of his involvement, which specific tenets of eugenics appealed to him, what benefits he may have derived from his involvement, and what role eugenics may have played in his ideas about musical ability and in his music-related research. I also wondered why I had never been told about this part of Seashore's career and whether other scholars were aware of it.

This book addresses these matters. As I investigated further, I realized that Seashore was, as he described himself, an "indescribably complex bundle of elements," as was his work.[3] As I looked at sources outside of music education, I realized that he was a titan in a host of other areas as well, known for his significant contributions to fields ranging from audiology to aesthetics. Furthermore, he was a champion of specific types of education reform, both in K–12 schools and in higher education. He served a term as president of the American Psychological Association and was the seventh psychologist to be elected to the National Academy of Sciences. Because he had his fingers in so many pots, this story is bigger and has broader implications than I initially imagined.

These implications apply not just to music education, but to schooling overall as it is conceptualized and practiced in the United States. Thus, what began as a simple search for evidence to confirm what I only vaguely suspected, evolved into the biggest research project of my life, a project that has consumed more than half of my academic career.

This book is, in part, an analysis of the life and work of one eugenicist. In addition to documenting Seashore's involvement in the American eugenics movement, I map out the precise nature of his engagement. Recognizing that he and others who supported eugenics viewed themselves as being in the right and as virtuously striving for the good, I took into account historian Tzvetan Todorov's comment that noble ideals can be perceived by others as "a mere mask for self-serving objectives, be they material or political."[4] Todorov was referring to the tendency of powers such as the United States to impose "virtue" on other countries, but his statement prompted me to consider Seashore's vested interests, as well as the benefits he may have derived from marching under this particular banner of virtue.

I conducted a close reading of Seashore's writings not only to determine whether he explicitly endorsed eugenics and euthenics, but to situate him within eugenics thought—to ascertain the degree to which his ideas and beliefs were consistent with pillars of eugenical thought and core eugenical beliefs. Thus, this book both is and is not about him, in the sense that it also explores an assemblage in which he was but one element. I am not suggesting that it is possible to understand the whole assemblage, nor have I attempted to; furthermore, Seashore is not a metonym for all eugenicists of the early twentieth century. He was, however, a central element.

I explore the intellectual worlds in which he traveled, as well as his engagement with the systems of reasoning that constitute the dynamic assemblage called "eugenics." Specifically, I examine how his eugenically informed ideas about race, ability, disability, and gender worked in concert to shape his music-related research, to color his views about musical ability, and perhaps most importantly, to undergird his efforts to institute broad education reform both in K–12 settings and in higher education.

This is not a biography. Walter R. Miles wrote a lengthy one in 1956,[5] but significantly, he did not talk about Seashore's involvement in eugenics, even though his list of Seashore's publications documents that he was aware of at least some of it.[6] Recognizing that eugenics is vast and neither static nor monovocal, that it has had somewhat different contours in different places and times, and that not all eugenicists subscribed to the same eugenics precepts, I focused on an individual—one data point—as an anchor. Thus, this project is about how power inserted itself into one individual. It is a case study of embodied discourse—of how the systems of reasoning that informed and constituted eugenics were embodied in Seashore, informing and constituting him as well.

A vast body of critical scholarship exists both on eugenics generally and on eugenics in education; furthermore, interest in the topic has grown dramatically since I began this project in 2004. Several stories are missing from this vast literature, however. First, extant research on education and eugenics has overlooked both music education and Carl Seashore. Second, when I began this project, music education researchers had given no attention to eugenics or its impact on the field. Third, although a great deal had been written about Seashore, his contributions, and his favored projects—including the formation of the Iowa Child Welfare Research Station—eugenics had not been part of that conversation. Thus, at the outset (and largely to the present), I took up a topic that had not been mentioned in published or unpublished work on either eugenics or Seashore—not in biographies, obituaries, or published or unpublished comments by his former students and protégés. One early exception was a few passing references to Seashore in Barry Mehler's dissertation on the history of the American Eugenics Society (AES).[7] In the more than fifteen years since I began this work, only three other studies have focused on Seashore, music, and eugenics. In 2016, Alexander W. Cowan completed a master's thesis at King's College, "Music Psychology and the American Eugenics Movement in the Early Twentieth Century," which focused on music and eugenics at the Eastman School of Music.[8] Currently a doctoral student in musicology at Harvard University, he is researching the rhetoric of musicality as it threads through the writings of hereditarians from Francis Galton to Charles Murray.[9] In 2018, Adria Hoffman published a chapter in the *Palgrave Handbook of Race and the Arts in Education* that briefly discusses Seashore and eugenics in the context of musical aptitude testing and race.[10] Finally, in 2019, Johanna Devaney published an article in the *American Music Review* that examines the relationship between Carl Seashore's work on talent testing and eugenics.[11] Even though I had finished the relevant parts of my book when these three studies appeared, I consider them vital; in addition to spreading the word about Seashore, music, and eugenics, they may signal a critical sea change in music-related fields.

The considerable literature on Seashore and his work often has been disciplinarily specific, focusing narrowly, for example, on his work in psychology, higher education administration, education reform, gifted and talented education, aesthetics, or music education. Discussions within the field of music similarly have demonstrated this specificity, tending to look exclusively at what he said or did concerning music, or even more narrowly at only one dimension of his musical contributions: aesthetics, vibrato, musical talent, or the standardized testing of musical capacities. Furthermore, scholars in music and music education have tended not to read across disciplines when researching Seashore. This narrowness is a shortcoming. The passing mention of Seashore in Mehler's dissertation, where he is referenced as one of the many presidents of the American Psychological Association who also were members of the AES, seems to have been overlooked by scholars in many disciplines; in particular, Mehler's dissertation is an unlikely read for music education researchers.

Thus, one goal of this book is to bring eugenics into the Seashore story, and by doing this, to make eugenics part of stories of music education and education more generally. Another goal is to bring Seashore and music education into discussions of eugenics, particularly those concerning education. To accomplish this, I look across disciplines at what Seashore said not only about music, education, and music education but about a variety of other seemingly unrelated topics, and I nest his contributions to education and music education within that broader context. Finally, this book addresses some of the implications of his involvement for the present—why this involvement matters.

Although I introduce information that has not been talked about much, my goal is not to "set the record straight." Rather, it is to tell a different story, one that may affect how his work in music, education, and music education is read and received—as well as how work patterned after his is understood. The ideas and practices Seashore and his colleagues promulgated in eugenics have long arms, so in multiple ways, this project is a critical case study of intersections and resemblances, including resemblances between past and present.

I have concluded that Seashore was engaged in eugenics activities and associated with a host of eugenicists because he was a true believer in the fundamental planks of the official eugenics platform promulgated by organizations in the United States. Knowing this helps us make sense of his writing in a different way. As I reread his work knowing that he was a eugenicist, I realized that signs of this involvement had been present all along, even when he did not mention the subject; previously, I had not had eyes to notice most of them, however.

What I learned from this project transformed my understanding of Seashore, his work, and work modeled after his. It also transformed my thinking about a number of related education-reform initiatives, past and present. For example, I have concluded that racism was foundational to these projects in ways that do not readily meet the eye, intricately threading its way through a host of discourses and discursive practices. It is critical to keep this point in mind when considering the significance of my project, especially when recognizing the not-coincidental resemblances between eugenics discourses and practice of the early twentieth century and some education discourse and practice today. Seeing these resemblances reaffirms the importance of mapping out the contours of these discourses and practices, past and present, inside and outside of music education.

Conceptualizing Historical Inquiry, Its Goals, and Its Potential Outcomes in Relation to This Study

Having witnessed firsthand the birth of the "new musicology" when I was a doctoral student studying with musicologist Susan McClary, I recognize that there are many culturally and temporally bounded conceptualizations of history, and a multiplicity of views on the purposes and processes of historical inquiry. I saw tectonic plates shift as the positivistic German musicological traditions in which I had been schooled early in my studies gave up ground to more postmodern conceptions of what is commonly and often problematically called "the past." "The past" conjures up a monolithic, unitary, universally agreed-on narrative, but I posit that "the past" is a dynamic construct created and recreated in the present. When I refer to "the past" in this book, I rely on a definition that underscores multiplicity and fluidity. Finally, I feel compelled to situate my work within the multiplicity of possible conceptualizations, and although I am hesitant to assign a label to this work or to myself, I am drawn to the purposes and processes of what some have called postmodern historical inquiry.

In conceptualizing historical inquiry, I am reminded of Kim Stanley Robinson's observation that there are similarities between theory building and writing science fiction: "It's always a story that you tell, that you make up, from a limited amount of data."[12] In the context of historical inquiry, "making up" does not mean lying, but acknowledging that conducting historical inquiry is a fluid, dynamic, contentious, politically invested interpretive process of storytelling based on a limited amount of data. Furthermore, even what counts as "data" is contested territory. Conducting historical inquiry involves examining what is said and recorded, and also considering what is not. Thus, my goal is not to arrive at a once-and-for all "truth" about the past, but to offer a different evidence-based version.

My research on Seashore and eugenics revisits the past, focusing on the silences and absences in current understandings of the history of education, music education in particular. It reveals how eugenics provided impetus for and served as a kind of connecting tissue within early-twentieth-century education-reform discourse and practice, recognizing that at least some of that discourse and practice shapes the field today. Rather than attempting to remember what has been forgotten, I aim for a different way of remembering, acknowledging, as Todorov observed, "The choice that we have is not between remembering and forgetting; because forgetting can't be done by an act of the will. . . . The choice is between different ways of remembering."[13]

My definition of historical inquiry, its processes, and its purposes is culturally situated, even down to the choice of the term "history" to describe this kind of activity. For example, it is culturally situated in that it is based on the construct "time" and on assumptions about this construct—that in addition to being segmentable into equal-sized portions called hours, days, or years, time is linear and composed of three parts—past, present, and future. The length of past and present, and the very existence of a phantasm called future, which may or may not ever occur, are culturally constructed and bounded as well.

Even the concept of "now" is fluid, a fluidity captured by a mural on the side of an abandoned building in Berlin, which asks, "How Long Is Now?" The mural's query is applicable to a conception developed by philosopher Michel Foucault: how long is the "present" Foucault imagined when he spoke of a history of the present? In the deep time encompassing the formation of the universe and the planet, could "the past" of 70–100 years ago, the period about which I write in this book, still legitimately be considered "now?" Perhaps. Similarly, my historical work is culturally and temporally situated in its assumptions about the relationship between past, present, and future. Metaphorically speaking, the understanding of history I employ assumes that the future lies ahead and that the past is behind us. According to this metaphor, we who are living in the present look to the future. By contrast, according to traditional Māori thought, we walk backward into the future, because we cannot see what lies ahead.

Finally, I recognize that the sense I do or do not make from reading texts retrospectively is bounded by my situatedness. Thus, I recognize that because

I am positioned in time, place, and discursive space, my version of the past is contextual and partial. I acknowledge that my reading and analysis of the evidence I examined are neither the only nor the definitive ones.

Strictly speaking, my project may not be what Foucault called a "genealogy" or a "history of the present," but it is informed by some dimensions of Foucauldian thought. For example, I concern myself with operations of power as conceptualized in specific ways—how particular ideas and actions are rationalized, naturalized, and instituted. Recognizing that politics are about power, my analysis underscores the intensely political nature of education discourse and practice, inside and outside of music education. In particular, I examine relations between power, knowledge, and the body. Informed by Foucault's assertion that bodies are "totally imprinted by history,"[14] I examine the body politics of education, especially music education, at a specific historical moment in a given place: how the categories that construct bodies as sexed/gendered, abled, and raced, are themselves constructed and deployed; how these constructions are mobilized to systematically include some while excluding others, and to manufacture hierarchies; and how they can help form a rationale for inequitable treatment.

Furthermore, from Foucault's discussion of genealogy, I have adopted his assertion that historical research should have a critical dimension, and his assessment of the relationship between past and present. According to David Garland, genealogies "begin with a certain puzzlement or discomfiture about practices or institutions that others take for granted."[15] This discomfiture is not merely about past practices and institutions, however. Garland describes Foucault as "using history as a means of critical engagement with the present":[16]

> [Genealogy is a] way of using historical materials to bring about a "revaluing of values" in the present day. Genealogical analysis traces how contemporary practices and institutions emerged out of specific struggles, conflicts, alliances, and exercises of power, many of which are nowadays forgotten. It thereby enables the genealogist to suggest . . . that institutions and practices we value and take for granted today are actually more problematic or more "dangerous" than they otherwise appear.[17]

Foucault himself wrote of resemblances between past and present, and about the use of historical inquiry for critiquing or "diagnosing" the present:

> I was interested in [phenomena of the past] . . . because I saw in them ways of thinking and behaving that are still with us. I try to show, based upon their historical establishment and formation, those systems which are still ours today and within which we are trapped. It is a question, basically, of presenting a critique of our own time, based upon retrospective analyses.[18]

Garland also discusses Foucault's reasons for conducting genealogical inquiry and his quite revolutionary understanding of the relationship between past and present:

> The idea is not to connect the present-day phenomenon to its origins, as if one were showing a building resting on its foundations, a building solidly rooted in the past and confidently projected into the future. The idea, instead, is to trace the erratic and discontinuous process whereby the past became the present: an often aleatory path of descent and emergence that suggests the contingency of the present and the openness of the future. Genealogy is, in that sense, "effective history" because its intent is to problematize the present by revealing the power relations upon which it depends and the contingent processes that have brought it into being.[19]

In *Marking the Mind: A History of Memory*, Kurt Danziger speaks of various ways of conceptualizing relationships between past and present, and of the resultant truth claims:

> One way [to conceptualize the relationship between past and present] is to take the present as representing the truth, so that the past becomes the story of how this truth triumphed and error was defeated. However, there is another way of using the present as a starting-point. Instead of equating the present with the truth, one can trace back its certainties so as to demonstrate their historical contingency. One can turn to the past in order to interrogate the present about the stuff out of which it was constructed.[20]

In my case, recognizing that current dominant school discourse and practices are neither natural nor inevitable, I wanted to investigate how and when it became possible, reasonable, and "normal" to think about students, teachers, learning, and schools in the particular ways that dominate in the United

States today—especially the ways that, in effect, perpetuate inequity. In particular, my discomfiture concerned discourses and practices that construct similarities and differences, that use those constructions to sort and order people, and that then mobilize difference to rationalize inequitable treatment in schools that is not understood as such. I wanted to understand how the particular dominant discourses and practices that justify and perpetuate inequities came to be understood not merely as commonsensical but as sound, fair, and humane, recognizing that there has never been consensus about them. Thus, my work is indebted to Foucault in the sense that I considered relationships between past and present to conduct a "diagnosis" of the present.

As I delved into primary sources, I noticed many resemblances between eugenical discourse and practice of the early twentieth century, and current educational discourse and practice. One goal of this project is to point out and analyze these resemblances. By recognizing them, I am not suggesting that resemblances mean history repeats itself or that the present is a mere replica of the past. I am mindful of Todorov's warning against "making the past trivial by likening present events to past ones too easily, trawling it [the past] for facile solutions to current issues."[21] Furthermore, I am not suggesting that current thought and practice necessarily originated with eugenics. Rather, past and present may be bound together by shared systems of reasoning,[22] many of which predated eugenics; these systems of reasoning made eugenics appear rational and reasonable rather than outrageous or even unimaginable. In other words, I argue that eugenics did not necessarily represent a rupture in dominant thought.

Finally, my goal in undertaking this historical project was not to dethrone or discredit Seashore. Rather, I place him under the microscope to stimulate critical thought about the ideas he promoted and the practices he engaged in, especially those that resemble patterns of popular thought and practice in the present. I sought to destabilize remembering to provide an avenue to rethink matters of the present.

The productive processes of creating history and of conducting historical inquiry produce things—including possibilities for the present and the future. As such, they are acts of power. Re-visioning the past has the potential to foster particular kinds of change in the present and future. If the past is understood to be dynamic rather than monolithic and static, then its "lessons for the present" are dynamic as well. Disrupting the supposedly natural and normal can open up different ways to think about the present and future in education, music education in particular. It can also open up different avenues for action. But different is not necessarily and universally better; every way of thinking has possibilities, limitations, and diverse consequences. When considering various ways of thinking, a critical question is what possibilities, limitations, and consequences they present, and for whom. Thus, in its diverse, partial, and dynamic multiplicity, the past matters. Engaging with the past is important because it creates possibilities for different understandings of the present, which in turn create the possibility of different futures.

On Responsibility as an Ethical Demand

Although ethics should always be a critical consideration in scholarly inquiry, I maintain that this project made extraordinary ethical demands on me. Judith Butler defines ethics as "relational practice that responds to an obligation that originates outside the subject."[23] One obligation I acutely felt was responsibility as conceptualized by Emmanuel Levinas. Levinas described responsibility as "the essential, primary and fundamental structure of subjectivity,"[24] and he added, "Responsibility is what is incumbent on me exclusively, and what, *humanly*, I cannot refuse [emphasis in original]."[25] Butler claims this responsibility is limitless.[26]

In his discussion of responsibility, Levinas used the face as a representation of the other. For example, in "Ethics as First Philosophy," he maintained, "In the face of the other man I am inescapably responsible."[27] According to him, the face does not merely recommend, it demands: "The face orders and ordains me."[28] In her commentary on Levinas, Judith Butler elaborates on this face, claiming that it captures what is human and injurable in others; she states that violence becomes more possible—more reasonable—when the other is rendered faceless:

> The Levinasian face is not precisely or exclusively a human face, although it communicates what is human, what is precarious, what is injurable. . . . Those who remain faceless or whose faces are presented to us as so many symbols of evil, authorize us to become senseless before those lives we have eradicated, and whose grievability is indefinitely postponed.[29]

Thus, one of my ethical responsibilities in this project has been to keep the face of the other, the full humanity of the other, ever before me; doing so, according to Butler, both reveals and reminds me of my own capacity for violence:

> Thus, in the face of the other, one is aware of the vulnerability of that other, that the other's life is precarious, exposed, and subject to death; but one is *also* aware of one's own violence, one's own capacity to cause the death of the other, to be the agent who could expose the Other to his dissolution. Thus the face signifies the precariousness of the Other, and so also a damage that can be caused by my own violence; it signifies as well the interdiction against violence that produces a fear in me of my own violence [emphasis in original].[30]

One's own fear of this violence, Butler maintains, helps keep it in check.[31] According to her, the face prohibits violence;[32] similarly, Levinas wrote, "The face is what forbids us to kill."[33] Metaphorically speaking, slaughtering the father—the king—to ensconce oneself as the new sovereign is a fairly common academic project. It is not my project here.

Obviously, the potential violence of this project is not physical, but the impulse and potential to harm are real, and I decided to heed the demand not to kill. In this scholarly project, whose are the faces to whom I have responsibility? I argue that the responsibility is to all. On the surface at least, this may seem like an impossible demand, or at least it may seem impossible to meet ethical responsibilities to some without harming others.

The faces of those wronged by Seashore and by other eugenicists loom large as I consider to whom I am responsible. I have a responsibility to keep those faces before me and to try to do no harm. Thus, I have a responsibility to speak, to bring this story to light, to break the silence that has surrounded it for far too long, especially in music education, and to hold nothing back. To remain silent would perpetuate violence and harm.

Much of this book is a response to these particular ethical demands; this is a huge responsibility, but it is not the only one. The ethical demands that have weighed heavy on me have concerned not so much whether to tell the story, but how. It is especially in this regard that I have a responsibility to Seashore. Some may find this assertion ridiculous given that he has been dead for more than seventy years. His death does not absolve me, however. Another way to try to dodge this responsibility is to argue that my book focuses less on him and more on the systems of reasoning to which he subscribed, the intellectual worlds in which he lived, and the real, material effects of the discourses that constituted them. I find this argument disingenuous. Systems of reasoning and discourses live somewhere, they are embodied, and they require bodies to survive. In this book, they are embodied by Seashore. Thus, my responsibility to him still stands, and the fact that he is dead does not change matters.

Perhaps greater still, however, is my ethical responsibility to my readers. How I tell this story—how I navigate my responsibilities to those harmed and to Seashore—shapes how my remarks are likely to be taken up and used by readers. By taking seriously my responsibility to those harmed, and to Seashore, I take seriously my responsibility to my readers as well.

In my telling of this story, I have a responsibility to acknowledge and respect Seashore's full humanity, and a responsibility to check my own violent impulses. By keeping his face and the faces of other eugenicists before me, I have attempted to resist the tendency to dehumanize him and other eugenicists, recognizing that rendering others faceless opens the door to their abjection and annihilation.

What I found in my research is deeply disturbing, and my discoveries left me angry and discouraged. Especially since it comes at the end of my career, I have found this to be a deeply troubling project. I was not merely disappointed with Seashore and his cohort but ashamed of my profession and of academe generally. Seashore and his eugenics allies profoundly shaped the intellectual trajectory of my field; US academics—people like me—were involved in eugenical violence. Part of me has wanted to pulverize him by writing a scathing exposé. The views on eugenics that currently dominate in the United States give me a powerful weapon, because although this has not always been the case, "eugenics" is now a loaded term, a topic that lends itself to sensationalism. The recent significant uptick in scholarship on eugenics (a phenomenon that itself merits consideration) has increased the heat of the limelight, and today identifying someone as a eugenicist has a negative potency that was largely absent 100 years ago. In this context, although I chafe at my responsibility to Seashore and others who provided the intellectual framework that helped rationalize the senseless murder of six million Jews (to mention but one of the devastating effects of the systems of reasoning that scaffold eugenics), I acknowledge it, nevertheless. It is a difficult ethical demand. In a discussion of Levinas, Butler captures this difficulty: "For Levinas, there are situations in which responding to the 'face' of the other feels horrible, impossible, and where even the desire for murderous revenge feels overwhelming and irresistible."[34]

Similarly, as part of my responsibility, I have attempted to avoid a dichotomous treatment that constructs people as either heroes or villains. Dichotomous thinking contributed to the largely heroic, positive past portrayals of Seashore, and also to the portrayal of the United States as a heroic champion of the good in World War II.

Keeping Seashore's face before me reminded me that he was neither a monster nor a villain. Like all people, he was complicated, multifaceted, and flawed. As I discuss at length in chapter 3, he made notable contributions to a wide array of fields; many of his ideas and inventions were quite revolutionary and had positive outcomes, whether it was suggesting that disciplinary experts be consulted to make movies more realistic or devising technology to monitor and improve the performance of elite athletes. He championed adequate health care for children, suggested that children needed to spend more time outdoors, supported learning many languages, and decried boring teaching. In the United States at least, many of the projects he proposed would still widely be considered "progressive" and "good." Thus, rather than being an either/or story, this is a "yes, and" story. Throughout my research, I was haunted by the question of why such an interesting, complicated, and successful man would be drawn to eugenics. Over time, I realized it made a particular kind of sense.

Some of the archival materials I examined helped keep Seashore's face before me, and after having worked on this project for more than fifteen years, I got to know him quite well. I sifted through place cards for dinner parties that he held in his home, the cards bearing the names of his graduate students. I saw pictures of his house in Iowa City, and drove by it. I read his description of the tragic death of his young son, who drowned while trying to rescue other swimmers, and examined a sad Christmas letter to Robert Mearns Yerkes in which a very elderly Seashore talked about the death of his beloved wife (just months before his own death). During this process I sometimes wondered whether I had developed a researcher's case of Stockholm syndrome. I located information about his children and grandchildren—at least one grandchild was still living when I started this project. Seashore's grandson Charles, a psychologist, was one of the founding directors of the Lewin Center, which is dedicated to social change and social justice. This information tempered me and gave Seashore the human face that was critical for me to see. It helped me realize that while a screed about Grandpa Seashore might sell, it would disregard my responsibility to him, would not meet my responsibilities to those wronged by eugenics, and would not meet my responsibility to my readers.

The Productivity of Responsibility

Although my responsibility to Seashore has been a terrible ethical demand, I was determined to take it seriously for important reasons, not all of them stemming from the assertion that all humans, including Seashore, should be regarded respectfully. Butler, quoting Levinas, warns of the danger of becoming the "persecutor in reverse"; this was a real danger in my project.[35] I realized that if I did not see Seashore's face, I could fall into the same trap that eugenicists did; denying the full humanity of people, othering, abjecting, villainizing—all were available to me. These are the very practices for which eugenicists can justifiably be faulted.

Furthermore, I concluded that I had a responsibility to keep Seashore's face *close* to mine. As Zygmunt Bauman wrote in *Modernity and the Holocaust*, "With the growth of distance, responsibility for the other shrivels, moral dimensions of the object blur, till both reach the vanishing point and disappear from view."[36] Othering and villainizing can be effective strategies of distancing, containment, and quarantine. These strategies are useful and productive in a Foucauldian sense, allowing certain things to be thought or to happen while disallowing others.

In discussions of Seashore specifically, and of eugenics generally, distance and dichotomizing can be used to contain and quarantine eugenics. Gulfs between we and they, now and then, hero and villain, and good and bad can help insulate the "we," "now," and "good," protecting some, but not all, from interrogation and critique. In his observations about the perpetrators of the Holocaust—which can also apply to eugenicists—Bauman spoke of the blindness that distancing produces:

> The implication that the perpetrators of the Holocaust were a wound or a malady of our civilization—rather than its horrifying, yet legitimate product—results not only in the moral comfort of self-exculpation, but also in the dire threat of moral and political disarmament. It all happened "out there"—in another time, another country. The more "they" are to blame, the more the rest of "us" are safe, and the less we have to do to defend this safety. Once the allocation of guilt is implied to be equivalent to the location of causes, the innocence and sanity of the way of life of which we are so proud need not be cast in doubt.[37]

Furthermore, creating distance by speaking of eugenics retrospectively as "bad science" obscures the reality that eugenics represented and was shored up by a fairly substantial body of science considered solid by many in its day. The then/now dichotomy may intimate that, according to a linear model of progress, science is "better" today than it was 100 years ago. This dichotomy may hide the possibility that at least some of what passes for solid, "good science" today should merit just as much ethical interrogation as eugenics should have been subjected to (but often was not)—not to mention the possibility that, ethical considerations aside, some current science is downright shoddy. Thus, I have attempted not to place Seashore or eugenics in quarantine, in an isolation that could prevent our contamination—that is, the contamination of White, twenty-first-century academics like me, who constitute at least part of my imagined audience. I also recognize that denunciation has tactical productivity. As Butler observes, "Moralistic denunciation provides immediate gratification, and even has the effect of temporarily cleansing the speaker of all proximity to guilt through the act of self-righteous denunciation itself."[38]

Keeping Seashore close, looking at his face, enabled me to see what distance can veil, the sometimes unsettling and not-coincidental resemblances between the eugenical discourse and practice of nearly a century ago, and current discourse and practice both in education broadly and in music education specifically. Furthermore, it enabled me to see resemblances between Seashore and *me*. Seashore's face "communicates what is human";[39] his face resembles mine. Indeed, Butler takes Levinas's argument one step further by challenging the self/other dichotomy:

> The Levinasian position assumes . . . that this other is already me, not assimilated as a "part" of me, but inassimilable as that which interrupts my own continuity and makes impossible an "autonomous" self at some distance from an "autonomous" other. Indeed, the Levinasian position, taken seriously, would defeat [Martin] Buber's philosophical notion of dialogue.[40]

She thus claims that the other constitutes me and consequently, I am responsible; in this research project, I count Seashore among the others that constitute me:

> I am responsible for what the other has done, which does not mean that I have done it; it means that I suffer it and, in suffering, assume responsibility for it. I no longer occupy my own place. I have assumed the place of the other, but, more important, the other has assumed my place, usurped me, taken me hostage. . . . The other is not "over there" . . . beyond me, but constitutes me fundamentally. The other does not just constitute me—it *interrupts* me, establishes this interruption at the heart of the ipseity that I am [emphasis in original].[41]

Finally, although I acknowledge my responsibility to Seashore, I do not intend to be his protector or apologist. Seashore, too, was responsible, and as Levinas wrote, "I am responsible even for the Other's responsibility."[42] The claim that Seashore was simply a man of his times does not get him (or me) off the hook, either. Other options were available to him; he did not choose them.

Thus, one challenge of this project was how to tell this story without slipping into reductive dichotomies, without villainizing Seashore, and without distancing him from me and from current intellectual projects in education. Acknowledging his humanity and keeping his face close to me helped me to better understand some of the ways that eugenics is about today, and about me. Paradoxically, keeping him close enough to see resemblances and honoring my responsibility to him helped me to honor my responsibility to those wronged by eugenicists and by many of the ideas and practices they promulgated. As I stated earlier, I considered this course of action to be part of my responsibility to my readers.

Two

On Eugenics

Those who are destined to fail should be eliminated early.[1]
—Carl E. Seashore, 1922

A Google search using the term "eugenics" produces more than sixteen million hits (a number that has more than quadrupled since I began working on this project); even Wikipedia has a lengthy and substantive entry. These facts illustrate the magnitude of current interest in eugenics. They also demonstrate the impossibility of reviewing all the scholarly literature on the subject. As recently as the 1980s, however, there was little interest in the topic—at least among historians—although a few scholars produced key sources. Two early classics are Daniel Kevles's book *In the Name of Eugenics: Genetics and the Uses of Human Heredity*, published in 1985,[2] and Barry Mehler's groundbreaking 1988 dissertation on the history of the American Eugenics Society.[3] In the early 2000s, scholarly interest in the topic increased dramatically. For example, Edwin Black, an investigative reporter with the *New York Times*, with his team of more than fifty researchers, examined more than 50,000 documents to produce his 2003 book *War against the Weak: Eugenics and America's Campaign to Create a Master Race.*[4] In 2010, Alison Bashford and Philippa Levine published *The Oxford Handbook of the History of Eugenics*, which examines how eugenics was taken up in various locations throughout the world.[5] In education, paleontologist Stephen Jay Gould, who published *The Mismeasure of Man* in 1981,[6] and Steven Selden, whose pioneering research includes the 1999 book *Inheriting Shame: The Story of Eugenics and Racism in America*, helped ignite the recent interest in eugenics.[7]

The Dynamic and Diverse Slipperiness of Eugenics

Consulting a sampling of primary and secondary sources reveals that eugenics has been called, among other things, a science, a pseudoscience, a social theory, a type of scientific racism, a movement with clear edges and distinct contours, a new religion, a doctrine, a philosophy, a policy, a set of beliefs and practices, and (vividly, by Alexandra Minna Stern) "a plastic and sprawling phenomenon."[8] Just as there is no consensus in the scholarly community about what eugenics is, there is also debate about whether it is dead. The death question is germane to my project because one of my goals is to consider relationships between past and present. As I read arguments on both sides of the death question, I realized that the answer depends, at least in part, on how eugenics is conceptualized.

Throughout the book, I use the term "eugenicist" to refer to individuals who had (or have) documented formal affiliations with eugenics organizations or who openly describe themselves as eugenicists. Labeling Seashore a eugenicist and discussing his involvement in eugenics required that I grapple with what this term might mean, and consider at least some past and present conceptualizations. I quickly realized that this is a difficult, treacherous project. Eugenics is slippery in part because it is dynamic and somewhat diverse. Martin S. Pernick alludes to this when he states that eugenics "encompassed a large and shifting constellation of meanings."[9] Although attempts were made to codify an official eugenics platform, including a book that some have referred to as the eugenics catechism—Ellsworth Huntington's *Tomorrow's Children: The Goal of Eugenics*, which even has the structural format of a catechism[10]—there was no unanimity of thought within eugenics organizations, as evidence from the journals *Eugenics* and *Eugenical News* shows. Despite this variation in thought, there also was considerable coalescing.

The activities spawned by eugenics were somewhat diverse as well. For example, according to Allan Chase, in England and the United States there was a "free-love wing of the world's eugenics movement" that supported free procreation among the ostensibly fittest; Chase says that this understanding essentially served as "scientific license for wholesale lechery."[11] Free love was not at all the message promulgated by the official eugenics publications, however; the free-love wing is an example of how eugenics was taken up locally in a particular but not broadly accepted way. Recognizing the difficulty of capturing how eugenics was conceptualized across time and place, throughout this project I attempt to situate Seashore by comparing his observations to the prevalent views in the "official" texts, notably the publications of contemporaneous organizations such as the American Eugenics Society and the Eugenics Research Association. When I say that Seashore's ideas or practices were consistent with eugenics, I mean that they aligned with dominant "official" views appearing in these publications or with statements expressed by prominent leaders in the movement.

The Commonsensicality of Eugenics

Another reason it is difficult to conceptualize early-twentieth-century eugenics is that in many ways, it was consistent with prevalent commonsense thinking of the day that was not labeled eugenic. Indeed, to become acceptable or popular, eugenics had to pass what I call the sniff test, a concept that stems from a statement my daughter, Katie, made when she was a tiny girl. She often would nuzzle up to me and say, "Mmmm. You smell like Mama!" Once I asked her whether I still smelled like mama after I had returned from getting my hair cut at a salon that used a different brand of shampoo. She replied thoughtfully, "You smell sufficiently like Mama not to be rejected as an imposter." When I say eugenics had to pass the sniff test, I mean it needed to smell sufficiently familiar not to be rejected as an imposter—not deemed crazy, outrageous, or unimaginable.

Eugenics circulated in various places around the globe, and eugenical ideas were taken up in a variety of ways when they landed—they "hybridized" as they interacted with local cultural conditions. Significantly, while they grew in some places, they failed to thrive in others; for example, according to Hans Pols, they did not have broad appeal in the Netherlands.[12] This invites consideration of why they were taken up differently or not at all in some places, and suggests that conditions had to be "right" for eugenics to seem sufficiently "good," sensible, and reasonable to be taken up.

Thus, the people who formally affiliated with eugenics and openly promoted eugenical projects were not the only individuals and who supported the ideas, projects, and "reforms" I discuss in this book. The many consistencies between eugenics and other prevalent thinking of the day give rise to thorny questions: what, if anything, makes eugenics distinct? For example, what makes eugenics different from the racist discourses and practices that predated, surrounded, and followed it? What conditions made it both possible and reasonable for Seashore, other US academics, and a host of Americans who were not in the academy to take up eugenics in the way they did?

It is beyond the scope of this study to examine what conditions made eugenics possible or to map out all of its so-called "roots." Nevertheless, I recognize that many of the ideas on which eugenics was premised predate the early twentieth century; Ann Winfield is among the scholars to point out that "the programs and policies of the eugenics movement" were rooted "in streams of intellectual history long preceding the 20th century."[13] Consider, for example, the views of Thomas Malthus (1766–1834) on population, poverty, scarcity, and disease; or those of Arthur de Gobineau (1816–82) on the Aryan master race; or those of Herbert Spencer (1820–1903) on education, the "undeserving" poor, evolution, and society; or those of Cesare Lombroso (1835–1909), who developed a theory of anthropological criminality; or even those of John Humphrey Noyes (1811–86) on what he called "stirpiculture"—the selective breeding of humans.[14] Thus, what came to be known as eugenics emerged from a whole constellation of preexisting beliefs, values, and ideas that collectively helped form and make possible a particular logic. The confluence of these ideas made a particular version of eugenics possible in the United States during the early twentieth century.

Philippa Levine and Alison Bashford ask not merely what made eugenics possible, but what made it appealing and *popular*: "What made eugenics so attractive, so powerful a pull for policy-makers in the early decades of the twentieth century, and in such different locations?"[15] These are important questions, but answering them is a larger project than mine.

The Slippery, Shifting Terminology of Eugenics

The dynamism of terminology commonly used both by eugenicists and in subsequent discussions of eugenics is another dimension of its slipperiness. Not only were new words invented but extant terms took on new meanings, such as "heredity," "genetics," "environment," "moron," "ability," and "race." For instance, the term "gene" was used for the first time in 1909,[16] in the middle of Seashore's career. Furthermore, Seashore was a Mendelian hereditarian, but as Carolyn Beans notes, inheritance as understood today is far more complex than Mendel's conception of it.[17] Thus, when wading into the morass, it is not sufficient simply to examine what "eugenics" can variously mean; it is important to remember that the terms associated with it also have histories and spaciotemporal contexts. One part of the dynamism of terms and their meanings is the widespread shift in attitudes toward eugenics over the past 100 years. Labeling has productive power, and given the more universally negative connotations associated with the term today, calling someone a eugenicist probably produces different outcomes than it would have 100 years ago. Nikolas Rose issued the important reminder that in its day, "eugenics was not disreputable or marginal: it defined one dimension of mainstream thinking about the responsibilities of politicians, professionals, scientists, and individuals in the modern world."[18] For the most part, in the early twentieth century, the label "eugenicist" was not condemnatory.

Some Early Eugenicists on Eugenics

Francis Galton

Rather than providing a comprehensive view of eugenics, I present a series of snapshots, beginning with a few from eugenicists themselves. The first are of Sir Francis Galton (1822–1911) and his use of the term. Galton was an English anthropologist known for his contributions to a host of fields, including statistics. "Eugenics" comes from Greek words meaning well-born; Galton reportedly was the first person to use the term, the *Oxford English Dictionary* dating it to 1883 and citing a source Galton wrote.[19]

In a talk given to the Sociological Society, which met in the School of Economics in London University in 1904, Galton called eugenics a science: "Eugenics is the science which deals with all influences that improve the inborn qualities of a race; also with those that develop them to the utmost advantage."[20] Although we do not know for sure—texts of this period are quite unclear—"race" in this context presumably referred to humanity as an aggregate, that is, the human race. As Levine and Bashford point out, however, "race" was variously used to refer to quite different things: "In English-speaking contexts, race was a slippery concept, sometimes meaning 'White people,' sometimes 'English-speaking peoples of the world,' but also sometimes 'human species.'"[21]

Much subsequent scholarship on eugenics has focused on the first half of Galton's sentence: improving the supposedly inborn qualities of humanity as a race. Note, however, that his definition has two parts, even though his 1904 talk focused exclusively on the first. The second part, pertaining to the influences that develop inborn qualities, refers to what some eugenicists subsequently called "euthenics." Thus, from the outset, eugenics and euthenics were entwined.

Galton's work exemplifies the kind of thinking that predated the formation of eugenics organizations in the United States and helped make eugenics as understood in these organizations seem reasonable and sensible. For example, his essay "Hereditary Talent and Character," published in 1865, and his book *Hereditary Genius: An Inquiry into Its Law and Consequences*, published in 1869, helped promulgate the idea that mental ability is biologically inheritable.[22] In his human pedigree studies, he used "eminence" as the criterion for determining extraordinary ability, and he concluded that ability is biologically inheritable because eminence can be demonstrated by members of multiple generations of the same family. However, many factors help determine why members of multiple generations of a family do or do not become eminent, including definitions of what is praiseworthy.

Significantly, Galton claimed that eugenics prevents suffering by replacing natural selection with a more merciful process; the two goals he identified informed many of eugenics' central projects in the United States:

> Its first object is to check the birth-rate of the Unfit, instead of allowing them to come into being, though doomed in large numbers to perish prematurely. The second object is the improvement of the race by furthering the productivity of the Fit by early marriages and healthful rearing of their children. Natural Selection rests upon excessive production and wholesale destruction; Eugenics on bringing no more individuals into the world than can be properly cared for, and those only of the best stock.[23]

His claim that benevolence and compassion motivate eugenics is threaded through eugenical thought throughout the period I examined.

Significantly, many of the ideas associated with eugenics predated Galton. For example, according to a number of scholars, he was heavily influenced by the work of Thomas Malthus and reportedly based eugenics on Malthus's Natural Laws.[24]

The Eugenics Tree Logo

The tree logo used by the Second International Congress of Eugenics, held in 1921, provides another snapshot of how mainstream eugenicists of the early part of the twentieth century conceptualized eugenics. Two statements appeared on the image. The first was "Eugenics is the self direction of human evolution." The second alluded to the roots of eugenics: "Like a tree, eugenics draws its materials from many sources and organizes them into an harmonious entity." The name of each "source" is printed on a root of the flourishing eugenics tree, and a variety of fields are represented: anatomy, biology, physiology, genetics, psychology, mental testing, anthropometry, history, geology, anthropology, archaeology, ethnology, geography, law, statistics, politics, economics, biography, genealogy, education, sociology, religion, medicine, surgery, and psychiatry.[25]

The logo was redesigned for the Third International Congress of Eugenics, held in 1932. Among the changes was the addition of more roots, including some labeled "mate selection," "race crossing," "family-stock study," and "migration."[26] Eugenicists' choice of a tree as the logo is significant given their interest in and frequent reference to family trees—that is, to blood line and pedigree.

One reading of the tree logo is that eugenics comes from everywhere. This seems like a grandiose overstatement, but in my attempt to conceptualize eugenics, I realized that it is somewhat accurate. Even though it did not come from or go everywhere, eugenics had its roots—and its branches—in many places.

As illustrative as the eugenics tree may be, even the expanded 1932 version fails to capture the concept in a number of respects; it doesn't reflect all of the topics and fields that fed into or grew from eugenics. For example, animal husbandry, which is a taproot of eugenics, was not listed. Prior to the formation of the Eugenics Research Association and the American Eugenics Society, the American Breeders Association, which was founded in 1903, had a standing committee, established in 1906, that focused on eugenics. Two key figures in the American eugenics movement, Charles Davenport and Henry Laughlin, reportedly forged their relationship at the Association's fifth annual meeting.[27] It may not have been their first meeting, however; Black says that Laughlin wrote to Davenport two years earlier asking to attend a biology course at Cold Spring Harbor and that the application was immediately approved. It is not clear whether the two met at the course, but it is clear that Laughlin had ties to Cold Spring Harbor early on.[28]

Furthermore, the tree did not mention philosophy—even though other supposedly nonscientific disciplines such as history were allotted a root. The absence of philosophy is curious, given that the fledgling field of psychology, which was given a prominent root on the images, was initally entwined with philosophy. It is highly likely that at the end of the nineteenth and in the early twentieth century, many of the first psychologists in their newly minted field had extensive backgrounds in philosophy. For example, G. Stanley Hall's doctorate from Harvard in 1878 was awarded in philosophy. Carl Seashore began doctoral studies in philosophy at Yale at a time when the department was first offering "the new branch of Experimental Psychology";[29] he quickly focused on psychology. The absence of a root for philosophy is especially noteworthy given that some scholars, including Ann Winfield and Christine Rosen, trace eugenics to philosophical thought, including the writings of Aristotle and Plato; Winfield calls it a "strain of a deeply held philosophical maxim in Western thought."[30]

Thus, eugenics is about everything mentioned on the tree logo and more. In the United States, eugenics of the early twentieth century was about reproduction—involuntary sterilization, and antimiscegenation laws, and baby bonuses; it also was about nation building, and race, and social class, and disease, and disability, and immigration. Germane to my study is the fact that according to the tree logo, eugenics of the early twentieth century was about *education*.

A second shortcoming of the tree image is its inability to reflect intricate interconnections among the various roots, as well as interconnections among the branches—what scholars today might call "intersections." Finally, although a tree is living and organic, the tree image does not reflect eugenics' shape-shifting dynamism.

Philippa Levine and Alison Bashford on Eugenics

An especially helpful recent discussion of eugenics and its history appears in Philippa Levine and Alison Bashford's introductory chapter to *The Oxford Handbook of the History of Eugenics*. Like many other scholars, Levine and Bashford place reproduction at the core of their conceptualization.[31] Their description of the major goals and practices of eugenics movements focuses on what philosopher Michel Foucault calls the "calculated management of life" that characterizes modernity[32]; they write:

> The aim of most eugenics movements was to affect reproductive practice through the application of theories of heredity. Eugenic practice sometimes aimed to prevent life (sterilization, contraception, segregation, abortion in some instances); it aimed to bring about fitter life (environmental reforms, puériculture focused on the training and rearing of children, public health); it aimed to generate more life (pronatalist interventions, treatment of infertility, "eutelegenesis"). And at its most extreme, it ended life (the so-called euthanasia of the disabled, the non-treatment of neonates).[33]

Significantly, when referring to eugenics movements, Levine and Bashford use the past tense, which is consistent with locating these movements in the past, and especially in the first half of the twentieth century.

They state that Galton envisioned eugenics as rational planning, and that it actually "materialized both as individuals managing their own reproduction and as state and expert interventions into people's reproductive lives and choices."[34] Like Nikolas Rose, Levine and Bashford claim that eugenics was more concerned with populations than with individuals:

> Eugenic advocates typically had population-level aims firmly in sight, and were concerned less with making individuals happier, healthier, or fitter for their own sake (although for many, this was a perfectly desirable side effect) than with making a significant difference to the physical constitution of future generations. Yet the materialization of the population-level change necessarily entailed intervention into individual lives, mostly though not exclusively managed or promoted by the modern or modernizing state, whether directly or indirectly.[35]

They note that there was an "evaluative logic" at the core of eugenics: "Some human life was of more value—to the state, the nation, the race, future generations—than other human life, and thus its advocates sought to implement these practices differentially."[36] Elsewhere they describe eugenics as "an evaluative project for the classification of humans."[37]

Eugenics, Degeneracy, and Degeneration

Part of eugenicists' human betterment project was to eliminate all types of what they viewed as degeneracy and degeneration. While acknowledging that racism is a companion and component of eugenics, Levine and Bashford argue that it is too simplistic to claim that racism and eugenics are interchangeable.[38] They point out that the "objects of intervention" typically were "degenerates"—"marginalized insiders whose very existence threatened national and class ideals"—and they note that those perceived to be degenerate included people of color and *others*.[39] For example, urban poor and rural people, as well as people with illnesses and disabilities, also were targets.[40] Thus, race is an element and racism a key component of a larger project, a war on supposed degeneracy.

Eugenics and Modernity

Levine and Bashford call eugenics a modern project and say that it "became a signal for, and almost a symbol of, modernization."[41] They include Frank

Dikötter's statement that "eugenics was not so much a clear set of scientific principles as a 'modern' way of talking about social problems in biologizing terms."[42] They discuss some of eugenics' distinctly modern conditions of possibility: "The emergence of widespread nationalism, important technological changes, and new ways of thinking about populations as a citizenry, as a labor force, and as the generator of future fitness combined to produce an environment sympathetic to claims that preceded Francis Galton."[43]

According to Levine and Bashford, the formation of nation-states, "and in particular the focus on their population's potential at a biological level," are essential elements of modernity.[44] Thus, the formation of such states was among the conditions of possibility for eugenics. They observe that even though eugenical measures were not invariably initiated by the state, eugenics' "presuppositions and premises frequently did feed state policy."[45] Noting that eugenics was simultaneously concerned with projects of "improvement" and "impairment," Levine and Bashford point out that "duality" is characteristic not only of eugenics but of modernity in general.[46]

In his book *Modernity and the Holocaust*, Zygmunt Bauman argued that the Holocaust was both a product and a failure of modernity, adding that it was the "rational world of modern civilization that made the Holocaust thinkable."[47] The modern conditions of possibility that he implicated similarly helped make eugenics seem reasonable and rational:

> The bureaucratic culture which prompts us to view society as an object of administration, as a collection of so many "problems" to be solved, as "nature" to be "controlled," "mastered" and "improved" or "remade," as a legitimate target for "social engineering," and in general a garden to be designed and kept in the planned shape by force (the gardening posture divides vegetation into "cultured plants" to be taken care of, and weeds to be exterminated), was the very atmosphere in which the idea of the Holocaust could be conceived, slowly yet consistently developed, and brought to its conclusion. And I also suggest that it was the spirit of instrumental rationality, and its modern, bureaucratic form of institutionalization, which had made the Holocaust-style solutions not only possible, but eminently "reasonable"—and increased the probability of their choice.[48]

Bauman's other observations on the modern similarly apply to eugenics:

> Like everything else done in the modern—rational, planned, scientifically informed, expert, efficiently managed, co-ordinated—way, the

> Holocaust left behind and put to shame all its alleged pre-modern equivalents, exposing them as primitive, wasteful and ineffective by comparison. Like everything else in our modern society, the Holocaust was an accomplishment in every respect superior, if measured by the standards that this society has preached and institutionalized.[49]

He rejected the idea that the Holocaust was an aberrant wound or malady of modern civilization:[50] "Every 'ingredient' of the Holocaust—all those many things that rendered it possible—was normal; 'normal' not in the sense of the familiar . . . but in the sense of being fully in keeping with everything we know about our civilization, its guiding spirit, its priorities, its immanent vision of the world."[51]

Eugenics' Optimistic Dual Focus on Past and Future

Another dual focus of eugenics that Levine and Bashford discuss is the simultaneous concern with both past and future.[52] They further note that eugenics' future orientation was infused with optimism: "[Eugenics was] about the optimistic possibilities of planning future generations. There was a power in eugenic promise—perfectibility, improvement, the benefits that would accrue from rational planning."[53] Part of that optimism was a confidence in science, specifically the confidence that science could "help" evolution along.

Of course, optimistic eugenical planning for the future is based on a host of potentially questionable assumptions—that the future is plannable; that "the good" is knowable now, is good for all, is agreed upon, and is unchangeable; and that the good knowable now will continue to be similarly good in the future. Another way to conceptualize good and bad is to see them as effects of power. Historian Tzvetan Todorov's comments about the optimistic but conditional promises of totalitarianism are applicable to eugenics, too, and this similarity raises questions about other parallels between totalitarianism and eugemics. He wrote, "Totalitarianism promises happiness for all—but only when all who are not worthy of it (enemy classes, inferior races) have been wiped out. . . . It accepts the sacrifice of the individual in the service of revolution, ideal society, or cleansed humanity."[54]

As they consider the conditions of possibility and situate eugenics temporally, Levine and Bashford point out that although today eugenics typically is associated with World War II and Nazi atrocities, it is every bit as much about "the years around World War I, and the major new political configurations of people and territory it precipitated."[55] Finally, they report that while early historians of eugenics viewed it "through the lens of the history of science," more recent scholars claim that eugenics is "primarily concerned with the nation and nationalism of the modern period."[56]

Nikolas Rose on Eugenics

A related contemporary take on eugenics comes from sociologist Nikolas Rose, who works primarily in the field of biomedicine. Rose has written extensively on the relationship between eugenics and the "new biopolitics." He conceptualizes eugenics (which, significantly, he refers to in the past tense) as a collection of strategies:

> [Eugenics] comprised a whole set of strategies, which had in common the presupposition that it was desirable, legitimate, and indeed necessary to secure the future welfare of the nation by acting upon the differential rates of reproduction of specific portions of the population, so as to encourage the best to procreate and to limit the procreation of those thought to be of lower, inferior, defective, or diseased stock.[57]

Rose claims that four terms delineate eugenics: population, quality, territory, and nation.[58] He states that eugenics "sought to maximize the fitness of the population" and did so by privileging one site—reproduction.[59] Employing Foucault's concept of biopower, Rose claims that eugenics exemplifies both biopower and biopolitics:

> Biopower is more a perspective than a concept: it brings into view a whole range of more or less rationalized attempts by different authorities to intervene upon the vital characteristics of human existence—human beings, individually and collectively, as living creatures who are born, mature, inhabit a body that can be trained and augmented, and then sicken and die. Given the intrinsic connections between the management of populations and their characteristics, and the government of bodies and their conducts, I will use the term "biopolitics" to refer to the specific strategies brought into view from this perspective.[60]

Thus, Rose is among the scholars who assert that power infuses eugenics discourse and practice. I would add that eugenicists advocated for pastoral exercise of power in some instances, and for more forceful, juridical exercise in others.

He also is among the contemporary scholars who claim that eugenics has unique margins and contours that distinguish it from the "new biopolitics," that is, from more recent discourses and practices. Finally, even though he claims that eugenics and the new biopolitics are not the same, he considers both to be examples of biopower.

Who Openly Embraced Eugenics and Who Did Not?

As many scholars have noted, during the first part of the twentieth century in the United States, eugenics had broad appeal.[61] Furthermore, the ideas on which eugenics is grounded, as well as the movement itself, received considerable support from individuals who today might be considered unlikely bedfellows—people from both sides of the many divides that differentiate and separate people into groups. Membership lists for eugenics organizations read like a who's who of luminaries of the day.[62] It was popular among intellectuals and social and political elites.[63] Edwin Black comments on the popularity of eugenics among academics: "Eugenics rocketed through academia, becoming an institution virtually overnight. By 1914, some forty-four major institutions offered eugenic instruction. Within a decade, that number would swell to hundreds, reaching some 20,000 students annually."[64] In particular, Ivy League schools and other elite colleges and universities were breeding grounds for eugenical thought.

Eugenics was consonant with progressivism and progressive ideals as they were articulated during this period; Levine and Bashford report that part of its appeal to liberals and progressives was its optimism.[65] That said, it was popular among the middle class, not solely with elites, and not just with liberals and progressives, but with some conservatives.[66] Daniel J. Kevles claims that it appealed largely to the middle and upper-middle class—not to the American aristocracy, who, he opines, may not have suffered from the social insecurities that made eugenics attractive to others.[67] He states that eugenics' chief supporters were White Protestants.[68] Christine Rosen claims that the religious scope of interest was broader, saying that "during the first few decades of the twentieth century, eugenics flourished in the liberal Protestant, Catholic, and Jewish mainstream."[69] It also was taken up by people who held no religious beliefs; for example, the famous atheist activist Joseph L. Lewis owned the Eugenics Publishing Company.[70] In a discussion of the diverse membership of the American Eugenics Society, Barry Mehler writes, "Many of the elite of the American Eugenics Society came from old American stock. Some were socialist while others were conservatives. The eugenics movement was not monolithic. It was held together by a fear of degeneracy and a dream of a better world. All eugenicists considered themselves 'progressive' in the sense that eugenics was a great social-scientific movement to improve the human species."[71] Thus, as I said earlier, as we consider what it means to call someone a eugenicist today, it is important to remember that eugenics was quite mainstream a century ago, and to label someone a eugenicist at that time did not necessarily carry the extraordinarily negative weight that it tends to today.

Even in the early part of the twentieth century, however, eugenics had its critics, a band of individuals and groups that grew rapidly as the century proceeded.[72] Edwin Black reports that original Galtonian eugenicists in Great Britain were "horrified by the sham science" taking hold there and in the United States; he states that one of them, David Heron, "publicly excoriated the American eugenics of Davenport, Laughlin, and the Eugenics Record Office."[73] This is especially interesting given that American eugenics was very much in alignment with what Galton professed.

Critics of eugenics often came from the same roots that, according to the eugenics tree image, were feeding eugenics. Catholics and conservative Protestants tended to take a rather dim view of it;[74] the Catholic Church's official denunciation of eugenics appeared in Pope Pius XI's encyclical *Casti Connubii*, which was issued in 1930.[75] Ann Marie Ryan and Alan Stoskopf point out that skepticism among Catholic educators about IQ testing, an education initiative strongly supported by eugenicists, stemmed in part from "resistance to the eugenics movement by Catholics in general."[76]

The Global Circulation of Eugenics

In this book, I look almost exclusively at eugenics in the United States. Eugenics is commonly associated with Nazi Germany in the United States today, even though it was a global phenomenon in the early twentieth century. Ann Winfield discusses both the global reach of eugenics and its connections to the Shoah: "The programs and policies of the eugenics movement . . . were evident across the globe and were ultimately responsible for the Holocaust and other genocidal events."[77] Attendance at the First International Congress of Eugenics, held in 1912, illustrates this broad reach. According to Edwin Black, representatives hailed from the United States, Belgium, England, France, Germany, Italy, Japan, Spain, and Norway.[78] Significantly, US eugenics journals were publishing work from eugenicists in these countries as well.

Having been born in the United States only seven years after the end of World War II, as a child I was taught a particular, dichotomous history of that war, one in which the United States and other powers of good fought valiantly against the forces of evil—Germany and the other Axis powers. Adolph Hitler was portrayed as evil personified. Subsequent scholarship indicates, however, that the history I was taught is inadequate and inaccurate. As Edwin Black demonstrates, eugenics flourished in Germany *and* the United States long before Hitler's time; during the early twentieth century, German eugenicists read the work of US eugenicists just as US eugenicists devoured the work of their counterparts in Germany and elsewhere. For example, in 1934, *Eugenical News*—the official organ of the Eugenics Research Association—printed Wilhelm Frick's speech "German Population and Race Politics," which Frick had given in Berlin the previous year to "the first meeting of the expert council for population- and race-politics."[79] Written in Germany by a German, the speech referred to virtually every topic of concern and promoted every plank in official eugenics policy as forwarded in the United States, including the degeneracy of the population, the danger of this degeneracy to the nation, the need to increase the numbers of "valuable stocks," the threat of deterioration due to the ostensibly high birthrates of ostensibly inferior immigrants, the perils of "race-mixture," and the economic burden of caring for the unfit.[80] Frick served on Hitler's cabinet from 1933 to 1945; after the war, he was tried at Nuremburg, convicted of war crimes, and hanged.

The same issue of *Eugenical News* included a letter from the French anthropologist and eugenicist Count Georges Vacher de Lapouge (1854–1936) to American eugenicist Madison Grant. Like Frick, Lapouge decried immigration and predicted "the end of a great people"—in this case, the French: "The end of a great people, that yellow and black races are preparing to colonize, and whose territory will pass into the hands of foreigners from all parts of the world."[81] In addition to stating his concerns about the immigration of large numbers of "Africans and Asiatics," he added as an additional complaint that "it is 'raining' German Jews."[82] He called German activity "a splendid example of an attempt at solution" and proudly claimed that German law was based on his writings, even though he warned that due to Germans' "belligerent instincts," these very activities might lead to the extermination of the German people.[83] Finally, he encouraged the entire world to read Frick's speech, gave his stamp of approval to Frick's activities, and ended on a familiar note of optimistic eugenical hope:

> Frick has been with us since the beginning. We owe him the creation of Guenther's chair for Anthropology at the University of Jena. This

> is no longer a question of theoretic desiderata, but of an entire legislation concerning selection, realized through decrees to be applied, and designed to rapidly extinguish undesirable stocks and to perfect the eugenical strains. It is the birth of a new civilization, replacing in Germany and soon in the entire world—so we hope—the political ideals and the classic and religious morals, the breakdown of which has upset the social life of all peoples.[84]

In September of the same year, *Eugenical News* published an article that first appeared in *Rassenpolitische Auslands-Korrespondenz*, which praised German efforts to reduce the number of Jewish physicians in Berlin, and called these efforts logical: "The city of Berlin quite logically is trying to reduce the number of its Jewish physicians, which is not in keeping with the racial composition of the general population."[85] The article claimed, "The excitement caused by the German racial legislation and the adoption of measures directed against Jewish physicians in Germany was, after all, rather ungrounded if we realize that the large German cities were literally swamped by these physicians and that, in spite of careful attempts to limit the Jewish contingent, their numbers actually were but slightly reduced."[86] This article referred to one component of a larger body of legal measures adopted in Germany starting in 1933 that aimed to curtail the activities of Jewish lawyers and physicians, deny Jewish students access to German universities, and bar Jews from civil service jobs; among these was a German law that denied national insurance coverage to patients who were treated by non-Aryan doctors.

I combed subsequent issues of *Eugenical News* appearing in 1934 and into 1935 for evidence of a published outcry—for criticism or complaints about these articles—but I found none. Significantly, Seashore was on the Advisory Council of the American Eugenics Society and a member of the Eugenics Research Association throughout this period, a time when articles such as the three I have just described appeared regularly in US eugenics journals and elsewhere in the United States. For example, two years earlier, *Eugenical News* published "Hitler and Race Pride," which included laudatory quotes from the *Atlantic Monthly* and the *New York Times* on "the racial purification of Germany."[87]

Black reports that Hitler and his Nazi followers were familiar with eugenics as it was understood in the United States: "Hitler openly displayed his eugenic orientation and thorough knowledge of American eugenics in much of his writing and conversation."[88] Hitler reportedly expressed great admiration for *The Passing of the Great Race*, a classic eugenics tome by the American attorney Madison Grant.[89] Black asserts that pointing a finger solely at Hitler effectively erases what was actually happening in the United States, Germany, and elsewhere: "For decades, Hitler's bloody regime, the Holocaust and the Second World War would be perceived as merely the outgrowth of the unfathomable madness and blind hatred of one man and his movement. But in fact, Hitler's hatred was not blind; it was sharply focused on an obsessive eugenic vision. The war against the weak had graduated from America's slogans, index cards and surgical blades to Nazi decrees, ghettos and gas chambers."[90] Thus, rather than claiming that Nazi Germany imported eugenics from the United States or that it invented eugenics while the United States as a whole abhorred it, it is more accurate to state that long before the rise of Nazism in Germany, eugenics was circulating widely, with ideas flowing back and forth—feeding off of each other—between the many locales where it was thriving.[91]

To say that eugenics was circulating widely in the first part of the twentieth century is not to suggest that it was identical in all places. Various iterations were appearing throughout the world (but not everywhere), they were influencing each other to varying degrees, and they had distinctive characteristics in various locales. The distinctiveness of circulating eugenical discourses in the early twentieth century may be analogous to the effects of growing grapes under different conditions. When a grape variety is brought to a new location, conditions must be favorable for it to grow, and conditions affect how it grows and whether it flourishes. Grapes of the same variety will look and taste different depending on local growing conditions—the terroir. Terroir also refers to the unique flavor and qualities produced by those particular conditions. Thus, a grape variety imported from Italy and grown in California is not likely to produce grapes, or wines, that taste identical to those grown in Italy. Indeed, it is terroir that makes grapes from particular regions so prized by winemakers.

Similarly, conditions must be favorable for *discourses* that travel, including eugenics discourses, to take root. *If* they take root and grow, they take on something of a life and personality of their own as they are shaped by local growing conditions.

Recognizing the differences that terroir makes, however, it is safe to say that grape varieties imported from Italy and grown in California, if they grow at all, will still produce grapes, not watermelons, and the grapes grown in California are likely to *resemble* those grown in Italy. Similarly, it is inaccurate to say that eugenics in the United States in the early twentieth century was completely different from eugenics in Norway or Germany. There were "families" of ideas and actions: there were resemblances.

Throughout this book, I use the term "resemblances" to describe the similarities I notice—for example, similarities between eugenics as conceptualized by Seashore and eugenics as articulated by the official publications of organizations such as the American Eugenics Society and the Eugenics Research Association. In the final chapter, I look across time to examine how eugenically informed education, as conceptualized and practiced in the early twentieth century, bears not-coincidental resemblances to some current educational discourse and practices. To focus on resemblances is not to suggest sameness or discount differences, however. Furthermore, I recognize that identifying resemblances necessarily involves comparisons, and that resemblances are part of a double gesture that implicitly or explicitly invokes differences. Recognizing that resemblances are part of such a double gesture, I made a strategic decision to focus largely on that part of the double gesture. Focusing on differences can effectively and strategically create distance; focusing on resemblances and similarities can lessen it, which is one of my goals.

Categories, Classification, Bodies, Power, and Eugenics

Sorting and ordering humans was central to eugenics; eugenicists, as well as most others in the United States at the time, considered sex, race, ability, and the categories that construct them to be, to borrow a phrase from John Marshall, "'real' entities."[92] By and large, these entities were assumed to merely reflect scientifically verifiable biological facts. The sorting and ordering of bodies that pervaded eugenical thought was consistent with and based on hallmark activities of modern science, notably the development of taxonomies and the classification and ordering of things—including humans—based on similarities and differences. Rather than being seen as effects of power, the classifications promulgated by eugenicists were premised on similarities and differences assumed to be real. In other words, early-twentieth-century eugenicists assumed that these entities reflected biological realities residing in bodies and were fertile territory for discovery and study. That idea has never disappeared.

Some categories eugenicists used to sort bodies long predated both modern science and eugenics. For example, eugenicists accepted without question the idea that there are two (and only two) radically dimorphic sexes. The two-sex model has deep roots in Christian thought, appearing, for example, in the creation story as found in the book of Genesis; it says that humans, created by God and in the image of God, were made in two types: male and female (Genesis 1:27). When eugenicists accepted without question the two-sex model, however, they cited science, not the Bible, as the authority. Although the concept that there are only two sexes is deeply entrenched in Judeo-Christian thought, since ancient times and throughout the world, other, more fluid and pluralistic conceptualizations have existed. The exclusion of these possibilities from eugenical thought is significant.

As was the case with sex, eugenicists similarly assumed that the existence of race and of distinct races was scientific fact supported by biological evidence. Historians have challenged these assumptions by mapping the emergence of race as a concept, arguing that it is associated with specific times and places rather than being a universally circulating idea. For example, in his 1996 book *Race: The History of an Idea in the West*, Ivan Hannaford traced the development of the concept of race to its antecedents in ancient times to support his thesis that race is a historically situated invention and that the modern concept of race is a relatively recent creation: "The idea of race does not lie dormant in every society on all occasions and at all times, simply waiting to be discovered. The idea of race has a historical pedigree and authenticity *sui generis* that may be traced by careful exegesis of what people were thinking about when they acquired the postulates, suppositions, and dispositions to divide the world in a racial way."[93] Hannaford further argued that "there is very little evidence of a conscious idea of race until after the Reformation [1517]"[94] and that the concept was not fully formed until after the French and American Revolutions.[95] Significantly, the *Oxford English Dictionary* states that the first known use of the term "race" meaning "a group of people belonging to the same family and descended from a common ancestor" appeared in 1547, and the first known use meaning "an ethnic group, regarded as showing a common origin and descent" appeared in 1572.[96]

Hannaford acknowledged that the modern concept of race has many antecedents, and that differences between people have been recognized since ancient times. For example, he reported that Aristotle distinguished between Greek and barbarian, as well as between freeman and slave.[97] According to Hannaford, however, ancient differentiations were based on very different criteria than those imputed by translators and textual interpreters writing in the late eighteenth and early nineteenth centuries.[98]

More recently, in his 2016 book *Stamped from the Beginning: The Definitive History of Racist Ideas in America*, Ibram X. Kendi documents the role of the Aristotelian concept of human hierarchy in the formation of the modern conception of race. Kendi quotes Aristotle in support of the claim that he *equated* Greeks with masters and barbarians with enslaved people: "'Humanity is divided into two: the masters and the slaves; or, if one prefers it, the Greeks and the Barbarians, those who have the right to command; and those who are born to obey.'"[99] In accord with Hannaford's conclusion, Kendi writes that although prejudice was present in ancient times, the modern idea of race was not: "Ethnic and religious and color prejudice existed in the ancient world. Constructions of *races*—White Europe, Black Africa, for instance—did not, and therefore racist ideas did not. But crucially, the foundations of race and racist ideas were laid. And so were the foundations for egalitarianism, antiracism, and antislavery [emphasis in original]."[100] According to Kendi, the Aristotelian human hierarchy was imported into colonial America, in part via the curriculum adopted by the earliest colonial universities, including Harvard; modeling their curriculum after Cambridge University's, the new colonial schools relied heavily on Latin and Greek texts.[101]

Kendi describes other ideas and practices similarly imported to colonial America by the British, and he dates the early development of the modern concept of race to approximately the same period as Hannaford does.[102] He reports that early in the fifteenth century, Prince Henry convinced his father, King John of Portugal, to raid and plunder the riches of Africa, starting with Ceuta in Morocco.[103] After the battle, the Portuguese continued to sail the African coast, transporting enslaved Africans to Europe; Kendi reports that Portugal thus became the first European nation to venture beyond Cape Bojador to engage in the African slave trade.[104] According to a 1444 account, the skin color of the enslaved people ran the gamut, ranging from white to black, and yet all of those who were enslaved were collectively regarded as "one inferior people."[105] Kendi also describes the importation of slavery to early colonial America by the British, citing a 1638 document indicating that ships were arriving in Boston carrying enslaved "Negroes."[106] Thus, he directly ties modern conceptions of race to empire building at a particular historical moment and to the enslavement that stemmed from and contributed to that empire building.

Historical narratives such as those of Kendi and Hannaford push back at the assumption that race is an ahistorical, static, biological given. Furthermore, Kendi's analysis ties modern conceptions of race directly to hegemonic power.

A quick perusal of eugenics publications from the early twentieth century reveals that although race was assumed to be real, racial categories were shifting and amorphous. The number of races varied from source to source, as did the defining characteristics of the categories. For example, at various points in the literature, Nordics, Germans, Alpines, Hawaiians, American Indians, "Gypsies," Mongolians, West African "Negroes," and Slavs—among many other groups—were called distinct races. Throughout this project, I struggled with language and word choice when writing about the racial categories eugenicists employed—how could I write in a respectful way when the primary sources I examined used language that is not merely obsolete but offensive? I also struggled with offensive and obsolete terms referring to disability. For the sake of historical accuracy, I have retained the original race and ability terminology in my discussions of primary sources, and I have placed quotation marks around terms such as "Negro," "colored," and "gypsy." Racially coded terms such as "savage" and "primitive" also frequently appeared in the primary sources, and although I do not support the authors' word choice or characterizations, I did not place quotation marks around them. The primary sources overflowed with terms that are obsolete and widely viewed as offensive today. In some cases, I chose race terms in use today, but these are fraught, too, and using them did not solve every problem. For example, their use did not change the fact that I am referring to racial categories, nor the reality that invocations of racial categories tend to perpetuate them. Their use may contribute to forgetting that race is a dynamic social construction—that despite their real, material, and differential effects, all racial categories, including White, are historically contingent, shape-shifting, power-laden phantasms. Using racial terms that have been in continuous use for the past 100 years was not without its problems, either. For example, even though "White" has been in continuous use, the criteria for determining "White" and the boundaries defining who counts as "White" have shifted somewhat; what has not changed, however, is that in the United States, the use of "White" helps create distinctions, simultaneously qualifying some while disqualifying others.

The racial categories eugenicists employed had histories long predating the early twentieth century. Hannaford, for example, attributed the idea of national character, which contributed to the designation of nationalities as races, to Emmanuel Kant (1724–1804), and to a lesser degree to David Hume (1711–1776).[107] Eugenicists called at least one religious/cultural group a race—Jews—a practice that has a similarly long history. Johann Blumenbach did so, for example, in his 1775 treatise *De Generis Humani Varietate Nativa Liber* (On the Natural Variety of Mankind).[108] Importing this labeling to eugenics, Francis Galton referred to Jews as a race in his 1865 treatise "Hereditary Talent and Character."[109] Galton also described Hindus as a race.[110] Although eugenicists did not similarly describe Catholics as a race, they nonetheless tended to view this group as a threat.

The shifting amorphousness of eugenicists' conceptions of racial categories is evident in eugenicist Paul Popenoe and Roswell Johnson's comment that the US census classifications in 1910 were "Native White of Native Parentage, Native White of Foreign Parentage or of Mixed Parentage, Foreign-born White, and Negro."[111] Beneath these many amorphous categories and classifications sat a fundamental dichotomy, however: White and non-White, and as Charles Mills notes, "The Racial Contract evolves not merely by altering the relations between whites and nonwhites but by shifting the criteria for who *counts* as white and nonwhite [emphasis in original]."[112] What did not shift and remained largely unquestioned was the assertion that races existed, grounded in biological realities of the body—and were articulated in terms of in-group similarities and out-group differences; regardless of how the racial categories were articulated, they established a we/they dichotomy such that those who were not Northern European and White were labeled as inferior. Mills calls this inferior label "subpersonhood" and describes how it is inextricably bound up with whiteness: "The terms of the Racial Contract mean that *nonwhite subpersonhood is enshrined simultaneously with white personhood* [emphasis in original]."[113]

Reinforcement of racial categories and classificatory systems came from the loudest voices in the room, but in the United States and elsewhere, there were counternarratives. For example, in an article published in 1928 in the *Annals of the American Academy of Political and Social Science*, W. E. B. Du Bois invoked science as the bearer of a different truth, presciently stating that the concept of races has no scientific basis.[114] He spoke critically of the ongoing research on race that ignored the facts: "Notwithstanding these facts, and indeed, in the very face of them, we have serious discussions of race in the United States and of race relations; scientific investigations, based on race measurements; and widespread assumption among intelligent people that there are between certain large groups of men ineradicable, and, for all practicable purposes, unchangeable racial differences."[115] In an uncannily prophetic voice, he warned that a nation would face dire consequences by ignoring the facts:

> When, now, a nation of reasonable human beings faces such a contradiction and paradox, the danger to their development and culture is great. The greatest danger lies not in the so-called "problems" of race, but rather in the integrity of national thinking and in the ethics of national conduct. Such a nation, if it persists in its logical contradictions, is bound to develop fools and hypocrites: fools, who in the presence of plain facts, cannot think straight; and hypocrites, who in

the face of clear duty, refuse to do the right thing and yet pretend to do it.[116]

Du Bois's statements appeared in the same issue as—and cheek by jowl with—a host of articles that unquestioningly accepted race and racial differences as scientific fact. These articles included, for example, eugenicist Carl Seashore's "Three New Approaches to the Study of Negro Music,"[117] Yale Nathanson's "The Musical Ability of the Negro,"[118] and Joseph Peterson's "Methods of Investigating Comparative Abilities in Races."[119] Du Bois's voice was marginalized, however, drowned out for generations by the "facts" of those who ignored the facts he reported.

Butler, Bodies, and Normative Phantasms

In the past 100 years, the categorizations that were foundational to eugenics have been challenged as different ways of thinking about race, sex, and ability have come into wider circulation. Drawing on some of this recent scholarship, I conceptualize race, sex, and ability as dynamic inventions with histories—a very different understanding than that forwarded by eugenicists. Consequently, although throughout this book I use many of the same terms that eugenicists did, I do not assign the same meanings to them that they did. I follow in the footsteps of Du Bois and others, acknowledging that these concepts are socially and culturally constructed, historically situated, and temporally bounded. For example, I draw on the work of Judith Butler, who challenges the distinction drawn by some twentieth-century feminists between sex and gender; Butler asserts that sex, like gender, is a socially constructed "normative phantasm";[120] she describes construction as "a process of materialization that stabilizes over time to produce the effect of boundary, fixity, and surface we call matter."[121] Calling sex a "regulatory ideal," meaning that it "not only functions as a norm, but is part of a regulatory practice that produces the bodies it governs,"[122] she argues that through performativity, which she describes as "the reiterative and citational practice by which discourse produces the effects that it names," bodies are materialized as sexed.[123] She states that in addition to considering "how and to what end bodies are constructed," we also should think about "how and to what end bodies are *not* constructed [emphasis in original]."[124]

Butler argues that bodies that challenge the adequacy of dominant sex discourse too often are abjected—viewed as pathological and in need of remediation or elimination. She describes an exterior, "a domain of abjected bodies, a field of deformation, which, in failing to qualify as the fully human, fortifies those regulatory norms,"[125] and she also points to the potential of this exterior domain to *disrupt* and *rearticulate* "what qualifies as bodies that matter:"[126] "It is not enough to claim that human subjects are constructed, for the construction of the human is a differential operation that produces the more and the less 'human,' the inhuman, the humanly unthinkable. These excluded sites come to bound the 'human' as its constitutive outside, and to haunt those boundaries as the persistent possibility of their disruption and rearticulation."[127] In speaking of sex as a regulatory norm that is materialized through "certain highly regulated practices," Butler ties the processes that materialize sex to power, specifically to hegemony; she conceptualizes power as a "reiterated acting" and views sex as an effect of power.[128] She does not, as some critics have argued, deny the materiality of the body. Rather, she interrogates how that materiality comes to have meaning, recognizing the connections between these processes and power relations.

Expanding on Butler's theory concerning sex, I claim that race and ability also can be viewed as regulatory hegemonic effects. To view them as such does not deny that there are variations in bodies. Furthermore, this is not to suggest that claims about race, sex, and ability are one and the same; although they are related, each of these dynamic constructs has its own history, trajectory, consequences, and implications. Furthermore, claiming them to be discursively produced does not deny or negate the real, material effects—including suffering—that they produce. Rather, I assert that what constitutes a similarity or difference is a hegemonic effect of power, as are the criteria on which categorization relies; the categories that constitute race, ability, and sex; the labels assigned to individuals, groups of people, and states of being; and the differential value of constructed similarities and differences. Recognizing the productivity of power, it is important to consider what the constructs of sex, race, and ability did or did not produce when deployed by eugenicists.

Ian Hacking on Making Up People

When conceptualizing sex, race, ability, and the body, I also draw on Ian Hacking's theory of dynamic nominalism, specifically his discussion of a process of categorization that he calls "making up people."[129] Hacking argues that official statistics projects in the early nineteenth century produced an avalanche of numbers and a concomitant array of classifications; in particular, these projects were obsessed with what he calls "*analyse morale*," or the statistics of deviance.[130] He reports that there was a proliferation of classifications of types of deviance and the creation of new classes "in which to fit and enumerate people."[131] He points out, for example, that heterosexual and homosexual as kinds of people came into being in the late nineteenth century.[132] Thus, Hacking, building on the work of Arnold Davidson, argues that perversion, the pervert, deviance, and types of deviance were, in effect, invented by a process that labeled particular people, groups, or practices as such.[133] He calls this process "dynamic nominalism" and argues that it creates, or makes up, people: "The claim of dynamic nominalism is not that there was a kind of person who came increasingly to be recognized by bureaucrats or by students of human nature but rather that a kind of person came into being at the same time as the kind itself was being invented. In some cases, that is, our classifications and our classes conspire to emerge hand in hand, each egging the other on."[134] Elsewhere, Hacking restates his case, arguing that "numerous kinds of human beings and human acts come into being hand in hand with our invention of the categories labeling them."[135] He describes the provenance of the idea that "social reality is conditioned, stabilized, or even created by the labels we apply to people, actions, and communities," crediting a 1968 journal article by Mary MacIntosh and other contemporaneous work published in *Social Problems* for formulating the idea.[136] According to Hacking, the proliferation of labels in the nineteenth century produced a proliferation of kinds of people—perhaps "vastly more kinds of people than the world had ever known before."[137] Stating that there is no "general story to be told about making up people," he reminds us that "each category [of people] has its own history."[138] He further argues that the creation of "new categories of people" also created "new ways for people [i.e., individuals] to be."[139] "Making up people," Hacking writes, "changes the space of possibilities for personhood."[140]

He links making up people to power, and specifically to a process of control that both creates and limits what is possible for individuals and groups: "Is making up people intimately linked to control? Is making up people itself of recent origin? The answer to both questions might conceivably be yes. We may be observing a particular medico-forensic-political language of individual and social control."[141] Especially germane to a discussion of the categorizing in which eugenics participated is Hacking's assertion that one vector of making up people involves "labeling from above, from a community of experts who create a 'reality' that some people make their own."[142]

Making Up People, Statistics, and Eugenics

Hacking's discussion of the central role of statistics in nineteenth-century projects of making up people, and of statistics' shift in focus, is applicable to eugenics. Gathering data about populations—for example, census taking—dates back to ancient times; in the United States, the practice of collecting agricultural statistics to monitor crop yields, land values, and livestock prices, existed in the late eighteenth century, in the earliest days of the nation.[143] Sometimes called the father of eugenics, Francis Galton also is widely recognized for his contributions to statistics, and he has been described as the founder of biostatistics and biometry; through Galton's work, eugenics and the fledgling field of modern statistics became entwined.[144] Statistics were foundational to much eugenical thought, and eugenicists, including Seashore, frequently relied on them as evidence.[145] The normal curve, which was developed by Abraham De Moive in the early eighteenth century, was rediscovered by eugenicist Karl Pearson in the early twentieth century. It contributed to particular meanings of the terms "norm" and "normal," both of which appeared frequently in works by eugenicists. These particular meanings stand in contrast to Georges Canguilhem's assessment that normal is "'a judgment of value'" and that normal cannot be objectively measured.[146]

When considering some of the reasons eugenics seemed sensible to Seashore, it is important to remember that statistics and animal husbandry, which played central roles in eugenical thought, both have deep agrarian roots. Thus, in the agrarian contexts of the day, these discourses would have been familiar and sensible, especially to someone like Seashore, who grew up on a farm and spent nearly all of his life in the farm states of Iowa and Minnesota.

Hierarchies, Personhood, and Eugenics

In addition to sorting people, the eugenical process of making up people involved ordering individuals and groups. The underlying assumption was that some individuals and groups are, by "nature," more human, more worthy, or somehow better than others. To eugenicists and others, science provided the evidence, the "facts"—statistical facts, in particular—to support such ordering.

Ann Gibson Winfield claims that "hierarchical models of human worth can be traced throughout intellectual history."[147] For example, the hierarchical ordering of races was underway long before the period I examined. It appeared, for instance, in physician Charles White's treatise *An Account of the*

Regular Gradation in Man, which was published in England in 1799. White claimed that Africans were the lowest humans on the hierarchical ladder of human beings, "nearer to the brute creation than any other of the human species";[148] he insisted that his scientific work was unrelated to the slave trade, which he said he abhorred.[149]

In his discussion of ideas that contributed to the concept of race, philosopher Charles Mills refers to the long-standing existence of a hierarchical divide between the human and less-human, the latter having often been labeled as savage or barbarian.[150] According to Mills, non-White races became equated with the latter,[151] the ancient Romans having set the precedent for the idea that "*only Europeans were human* [emphasis in original]."[152] In his discussion of personhood and the subperson, he details race-based processes of ordering people and the effects of this ordering. Central to what he calls the Racial Contract is differential privileging; all people categorized as White are considered to be full persons, while all other humans are categorized as subpersons of subordinate standing.[153] The category of "subperson" is deployed to rationalize inequitable treatment and to assure hegemony, resulting in "the differential privileging of the whites as a group with respect to the nonwhites as a group," as well as "the exploitation of their [the subpersons'] bodies, land, and resources, and the denial of equal socioeconomic opportunities to them."[154] Mills describes the power relations inherent in race and racial hierarchies when he asserts, "*Whiteness is not really a color at all, but a set of power relations* [emphasis in original]."[155]

Expanding on the assertion made by critical race theorists that whiteness is property, and pointing out that understandings of race and intelligence are intertwined historically and up to the present in the United States, Zeus Leonardo and Alicia Broderick explore intersections between whiteness and disability.[156] They conclude that both whiteness and smartness can be considered property. Although it does not discuss eugenics, their work is helpful in conceptualizing intersectionally the ordering of individuals and groups that characterizes eugenics.

Quality, Double Gestures, and Eugenics

In conceptualizing eugenics and the process that Hacking calls making up people, it is also useful to consider what Thomas Popkewitz calls the double gestures of cosmopolitanism,[157] especially those that accomplish simultaneous and intertwined inclusion and exclusion.[158] According to Popkewitz, the "rationality of cosmopolitanism instantiated *comparative* [emphasis mine] distinctions that differentiated, divided, and abjected groups and individual[s] *not* 'civilized' and hence not qualitied for participation [emphasis in original]."[159] His reference to quality is key: eugenical discourse and practice assumed that not all individuals or groups were of the same quality, they claimed that differences in quality were inherent, and they promoted the idea of inclusion or exclusion based on the supposed inherent quality of that individual or group.

Eugenicists asserted that differences in quality are natural results of evolution, evidence that some humans and groups of humans are more evolved than others. Claiming that human intervention had upset "natural" evolutionary processes, which resulted in a reduction in the quality of the human race, they maintained that eugenics would set things right and even help accelerate evolution: it would improve *quality*. It is important to remember that establishing the criteria to be used when determining the quality of individuals or groups is a power process: quality is, in effect, both a commentary on values and an effect of power. Furthermore, quality invariably involves comparison.

As I discuss in later chapters, for eugenicists, the quality of an individual or group was determined by measuring ostensibly biologically inheritable and immutable characteristics or traits. They considered three broad categories of traits: physical, mental, and moral. Mental traits were conceptualized as either general intelligence or a variety of specific intelligences, and moral traits were demonstrated by, among other things, alcohol use or abuse, criminality, and sexual practices. Given that three domains or categories were being considered and there were a plethora of characteristics within each category, many processes of sorting and ordering were underway simultaneously, each holding the double-gesture potential for inclusion and threat of exclusion. Eugenicists frequently used two double-gesture quality categories: fit, which was good, and unfit, which was not.

As I have indicated, the processes on which qualifying and disqualifying relied were based on a particular logic and set of assumptions. For example, eugenicists deemed it logical, reasonable, and valuable to measure people. They assumed that humans possess traits that should be grouped into categories, that the characteristics comprising these categories are not present in equal amounts in all people, and that they should be measured.

Often an examination by an "expert" was the means eugenicists used to measure individuals and groups and assess quality. Foucault underscored the qualitative dimension of the examination when he described it as "a normalizing gaze, a surveillance that makes it possible to qualify, to classify and to punish. It establishes over individuals a visibility through which one differentiates them and judges them."[160] In this passage, Foucault observed that the examination makes it possible to include and exclude simultaneously, and in this sense, the examination exemplifies what Popkewitz calls a double gesture. Significantly, Foucault also considered such examinations to be "at the heart of the procedures of discipline."[161]

Some eugenical measuring processes, but certainly not all, were based on establishing populational norms and making statistical comparisons. These ostensibly scientific and neutral quantitative exercises were simultaneously qualitative; whether or not eugenicists recognized it, they are studies in values. When eugenicists used the term "normal," and they often did, they necessarily were relying on a comparison. To deploy "normal" and its double-gesture twin, "abnormal," was to make a commentary on quality. In some cases (but not all), when eugenicists spoke of normal, they were referencing the vast space between the two tails on a Gaussian curve. Significantly, however, they paid a great deal of attention to individuals or groups in the tails. Both tails of a bell curve are abnormal in the sense that they do not constitute the statistical norm. Qualitatively speaking, however, for eugenicists each tail was a vastly different space. Eugenicists criticized the individuals and groups located in both tails, but it was a different kind of criticism in each case, and only one tail was an uninhabitable zone of abjection. They drew very different conclusions about the quality of the abnormal individuals and groups in each of the tails, and only one tail was the realm of low quality.

Although the term "normal" implies sufficiently high quality and safety from intervention, as I document in subsequent chapters, Seashore did not necessarily see normal or average as good enough: one of his goals was to increase the average. Certainly, lopping off the bottom tail would create a new higher average, but the new average would still be average, presumably subject to further intervention in an endless, Sisyphean project of so-called quality improvement.

If quality "creates" value and worth, then the process of establishing quality creates an opportunity to calculate worth.[162] To eugenicists, not all germ plasm was of equal quality, and thus not all individuals or groups were of equal quality; the assumption that people or groups are of different quality—that people, like butter or eggs, can and should be assigned grades—undergirded the assertion that individuals or groups of people are of different value or worth. Although their proponents often claim that school grades reflect achievement, variations in achievement also are mapped onto bodies to create kinds of people—the "A" student, the "B" student, the failing student, and so on. In this context Canguilhem's claim that normal is a "'judgment of value'" bears consideration.[163]

One limitation of viewing the project of establishing quality and worth as a double-gesture exercise is that eugenicists did not always view these dimensions dichotomously. There were gradations or degrees of quality, fitness, and worthiness: in addition to the worthy, there were those who were by degrees less worthy, and others who were worthless.

Eugenical discourses on quality and worth demonstrate that eugenics aimed to make up *particular* kinds of people, people deemed to be of higher quality and consequently of greater worth to society, the nation, and the world. The ideal person was a global citizen only in the sense that the ideal was the same kind of person everywhere. The imagined society, nation, and world were to be filled with particular kinds of people—and not with others. Examining how eugenicists imagined quality—what constituted fit and unfit—and which kinds of people or groups served as exemplars, is a study in both values and power relations.

For eugenicists, supposed quality and worth rationalized double gestures of inclusion or exclusion. In a discussion of calculating the value of each life, Rose speaks of actions that follow judgments of worth: "To judge the worth of life is to judge some *less* worthy and to act accordingly [emphasis mine]."[164] The eugenical actions toward those included focused on increasing, promoting, and enhancing; the actions toward those excluded aimed to reduce, demote, or eliminate. The included were to be advantaged and the excluded disadvantaged. As a double gesture, advantaging some but not all simultaneously and automatically placed others at a disadvantage. Again, as with quality and worth, rather than invariably being a dichotomous double gesture, inclusion and exclusion were on a spectrum. That said, there were cutoff points, although they were movable and moving. Those who were worth less could become worthless if the cutoff point moved.

For eugenicists, the double gestures inhering in specific discourses about quality and worth helped rationalize the double gesture of inclusion and exclusion. This line of thinking often served as justification for unequal and inequitable resource allocation. Thus, the inclusion and exclusion double gesture is grounded in and related to other double gestures evident in eugenical systems of reasoning, all of which have real, material effects. Systems of reasoning are dynamic assemblages composed of a host of intersecting and often mutually supportive discourses and discursive practices; they also encompass the cohering logic that connects these discourses to each other and helps them seem reasonable and rational. Examining them can help explain how it becomes possible and reasonable to think and act in particular ways.

Eugenics' Double Gestures of Hope and Fear

In addition to describing the cosmopolitan double gesture of inclusion and exclusion, Popkewitz discusses another double gesture—hope and fear—which I argue is similarly present in eugenical discourse and systems of reasoning.[165] In addition to being optimistic, eugenics of the early twentieth century traded in hope, especially hope for the future. For example, in his address to the 1921 Second International Congress of Eugenics, Leonard Darwin, the son of Charles Darwin and then-president of England's Eugenics Education Society, spoke of the hope and the promise of eugenics: "Eugenics has been called a dismal science, but it should rather be described as an untried policy. Eugenics indicates a new method of striving for human welfare which, if combined with an equal striving for improvements in human surroundings, more truly justifies a hopeful outlook than anything which has yet been tried in the whole history of the world."[166]

Hope, however, is only one component of this eugenical pairing. Eugenics also mobilizes and propagates fear. The hope/fear pairing is one way that eugenics discourse demonstrates the duality that Levine and Bashford argue characterizes modernity.[167] Along with the hope expressed by Leonard Darwin and others is fear stemming from claims of degeneracy and eugenicists' assertion that society, the nation, or the whole world is facing destruction. These claims include the assertion that human intervention has tampered with "natural" evolutionary processes and that disaster is inevitable without scientific intervention. In short, eugenicists claimed that we were "on the eve of destruction."

The productivity of this fear merits further consideration. In *State of Exception*, philosopher Giorgio Agamben discusses several instances when broad expansion of government power and the abrogation of human rights have been rationalized by claims that the state is facing an emergency of such magnitude that such acts are justified.[168] In addition to interrogating the productivity of state-of-emergency discourses, Agamben claims that "the voluntary creation of a permanent state of emergency . . . has become one of the essential practices of contemporary states, including so-called democratic ones."[169] He observes that the state of exception has become a "technique of government."[170] I recognize that in the United States, eugenics was not specifically initiated by the state, although President Theodore Roosevelt was instrumental in promulgating the idea of race suicide, and eugenicists expected the state to legislate the reforms they envisioned. Nevertheless, I find Agamben's model, and particularly his argument that the state of exception has become a technique of government, to be a useful way to think about the fear component of the hope/fear double gesture of eugenics. I argue that eugenics is based on a state-of-emergency mentality: eugenicists' claim that the society, nation, or world is under threat generated and mobilized fear; in the face of this fear and in response to this supposed state of emergency, eugenicists call for a radical course of action to remediate the problem. Conveniently, eugenicists had devised both the problem and the course of action to remediate. In these circumstances, what might have seemed irrational or even unthinkable seems logical, necessary, and good.

When considering the relationship between eugenics, fear, and the state in the United States, it is important to remember that to fully operationalize eugenics, both an expansion of state powers and an abrogation of at least some people's rights were necessary, and in the early twentieth century, eugenicists called on the state to do precisely that. Significantly, Agamben calls the Third Reich, which clearly fostered and was fed by eugenics, "a state of exception that lasted twelve years."[171] In addition, it is useful to view the mobilization of the double gesture of hope and fear as a pastoral governing practice.

The conceptions of bodies and persons I have employed in this project were probably unimaginable to eugenicists of the day and to many other people in the cultures from which eugenics sprang. It is these more recent conceptualizations, however, that permit me to describe and analyze what eugenicists said about race, sex, and ability while simultaneously historicizing and deconstructing these very categories. Thus, they helped me denaturalize the supposedly natural and deconstruct what eugenicists accepted as unquestioned, irrefutable fact. Perhaps most importantly, they helped link eugenical processes of sorting and ordering, and of qualifying and disqualifying, to power relations—hegemony, in particular. I acknowledge that having access to these more recent conceptualizations situates me, historically, temporally, and culturally, and I recognize that just as there was not unanimity of thought in the first half of the twentieth century—not among eugenicists, and not among all people everywhere—there is not unanimity of thought about these matters today.

On Religion, Predestination, Salvation, and Eugenics

Both the 1921 and the 1932 versions of the eugenics logo tree include a root labeled "religion," which indicates that those who represented the official voice of the American eugenics movement believed that eugenics grew out of and was fed by religion.[172] Galton himself referred to eugenics as a "new religion," but he did not elaborate on whether it was to supplement or supplant established ones.[173] In her study of Catholic, Jewish, and Protestant religious leaders who supported eugenics during the first decades of the twentieth century, Christine Rosen writes that "eugenics flourished in the liberal Protestant, Catholic, and Jewish mainstream; clerics, rabbis, and lay leaders wrote books and articles about eugenics, joined eugenics organizations, and lobbied for eugenics legislation."[174] In her account of why the religious leaders who supported it were drawn to eugenics, she states that it tended to align with their charity goals; it offered solutions to the social problems they were eager to solve in their communities, including poverty.[175] Religious leaders who supported eugenics tended to be progressives who were attempting to embrace science and incorporate it into their belief systems; invested in the Enlightenment claim of the perfectibility of human life, they were drawn to the possibilities that eugenics ostensibly offered.[176] Rosen notes that "Protestants proved the most enthusiastic and numerically powerful group of religious participants in the eugenics movement."[177] In short, eugenics tended to be consonant with a Social Gospel reform mentality and goals.

In my attempts to conceptualize eugenics, I examined one discursive link between eugenics and religion: potential connections between eugenical thought and some forms of predestination and salvation doctrine. The title of my book, "*Destined to Fail*," which comes from a statement Seashore made in a 1922 *School and Society* article, hints at this possible link. The article championed the classification of students according to supposed native ability and the sectioning of classes accordingly, and Seashore asserted, "Those who are destined to fail should be eliminated early."[178] When stripped of context, the quote seems quite monstrous, the reference to elimination eerily presaging the Nazi genocide. Seashore was not talking about genocide or even physical death, however; rather, consistent with his education philosophy, he was directing teachers and administrators to increase school effectiveness and efficiency by instituting tracked sections of courses, a system that he claimed would quickly weed out students destined to fail on account of their supposedly insufficient "native" intelligence. As a Mendelian hereditarian who believed that intelligence and other mental capacities were biologically inheritable, differentially bestowed, and immutable, he maintained that the germ cell set a student's destiny, at least for those destined to fail. For those destined to succeed, the picture was more complicated. In addition to possessing "native intelligence," if they were to develop their full potential, students destined for success needed the kind of environment that euthenics would provide, and it was society's responsibility to provide it. Society apparently had little or no responsibility to develop the potential of those destined to fail—or at least no responsibility to prevent them from failing by *assisting them*: failure was their destiny; it was perhaps society's role to point out and accelerate that fate. Although it may seem dishonest to strip the quote of its original context, doing so reveals that it is part of the same eugenical discourse that rationalized the Holocaust. The quote indicates that directly or indirectly, Seashore, too, advocated a necessary death of sorts, a death of educational opportunity, a death of dreams, perhaps even the death of a much-hoped-for future. This death was justified by invoking supposedly native, immutable differences in intelligence.

Calvinism, Double Predestination and Eugenics

Seashore's use of the term "destined" invites consideration of the assertion that eugenics derives, at least in part, from particular forms of Christian thought concerning salvation—specifically, the matter of destiny as articulated in the Calvinist doctrine of double predestination. "Calvinists" is an umbrella term referring to members of a number of evangelical, reformed Protestant denominations, most notably Presbyterians and Congregationalists. The basic premise of double predestination is that God has chosen a select number of elect who will be saved and has foreordained the rest to reprobation, often called damnation. Double predestination is spelled out in the portion of the 1646 Westminster Confession called "Of God's Eternal Decree":

> By the decree of God, for the manifestation of His glory, some men and angels are predestinated unto everlasting life; and others foreordained to everlasting death.
>
> These angels and men, thus predestinated, and foreordained, are particularly and unchangeably designed, and their number so certain and definite, that it cannot be either increased or diminished. . . .
>
> Wherefore, they who are elected, being fallen in Adam, are redeemed by Christ. . . . Neither are any other redeemed by Christ, effectually called, justified, adopted, sanctified, and saved, but the elect only.[179]

Today, not all Congregationalists and Presbyterians subscribe to this belief. Translated into the language used by eugenicists, double predestination means that the germ plasm foreordains which individuals and groups are destined to succeed or to fail.

Eugenicists themselves occasionally talked about whether eugenics was a form of predestination. For example, in a 1930 article appearing in the journal *Eugenics*, three eugenicists—Albert Edward Wiggam, Frederick Osborn, and Leon F. Whitney—were asked to respond to two questions: "Is Eugenics 'Scientific Calvinism'? Is It Biological Predestination?"[180] Wiggam replied that environmentalists are the true predestinarians because if environment is the only determining factor, then environment alone predestines the course of people's lives.[181] Osborn wriggled out of answering the question by stating that if eugenical aims are followed, future generations will be "predestined to better lives."[182] Whitney, however, answered solidly in the affirmative and added:

> But what of it? If the admission surprises or frightens some of the sentimentalists who have wished to believe in complete equality as between man and man, certainly eugenics can't help that. If what eugenics teaches is the truth, and if what eugenics teaches is based on truth, persons who are intellectually honest with themselves and with others will accept it, no matter how it may hurt their preconceptions in other directions. Whether it is "gloomy" or not, it must be faced.[183]

In a 1922 critique of intelligence testing and of those who believe intelligence is "innate, hereditary, and predetermined," Walter Lippmann similarly referred to these beliefs as a form of predestination:

> Most of the more prominent testers . . . claim not only that they are really measuring intelligence, but that intelligence is innate, hereditary, and predetermined. They believe that they are measuring the capacity of a human being for all time and that this capacity is fatally fixed by the child's heredity. Intelligence testing in the hands of men who hold this dogma could not but lead to an intellectual caste system in which the task of education had given way to the doctrine of predestination and infant damnation.[184]

More than eighty years later, John White similarly argued that specific religious beliefs figured heavily in eugenical thought. In his article "Puritan Intelligence: The Ideological Background to IQ," he describes parallels between the notion of intelligence as innate and the thought-world of Puritans, notably the "ideas of predestination, the elect, salvation, vocation, and intellectual education."[185] White also observes that the terms "talent" and "gift" are of religious origin.[186] He maps the faith pedigree of several prominent early supporters of the concept of innate intelligence and the practice of intelligence testing. Among others, he discusses Henry Goddard, Lewis Terman, and Francis Galton, all of whom he identifies as eugenicists.[187] White's faith-pedigree map includes the denominational affiliations of the individuals he discusses and of their progenitors, and he concludes that Puritan/Calvinist thought played a central role in their logic.[188] He elaborates on predestination by quoting from one of his earlier publications:

> "The proposition that all men have genetically determined intelligence is not unlike the Calvinist belief that for all of us our future state is predestined by God. . . .
>
> The official doctrine of intelligence is a modern re-edition of an older Puritanism. Nature has replaced God; an élite, the elect; Mensa the community of the saved; and intelligence testers, the Puritan high priests. It is time we shook such primitive notions [*sic*] out of our minds."[189]

As thought-provoking as White's argument may be, especially given that Seashore—whom White does not mention—reportedly converted from Lutheranism to Congregationalism,[190] it is too simplistic on multiple levels and inaccurate in a number of ways. For example, in support of his claim of Puritan influence, White states that several of the individuals he discusses were Anglicans.[191] Global pronouncements about members of any denomination are dangerous, but it is safe to say that few if any Anglicans would call themselves Calvinists, because these are considered distinct groups with different theologies. In addition, White is not always specific about which Protestant groups are contributing which concepts to the thought-world of the proponents of intelligence testing. For example, he states that Goddard and Goddard's parents were Quakers.[192] Quakers may have been similar to Calvinists in viewing themselves as "the elect," but the notion of election is not unique to Calvinists or Quakers (nor is it unique to Christians), and Quakers are neither Puritans nor Calvinists. They are not predestinarians, either; even White himself acknowledges that Quakers jettisoned the concept.[193] Furthermore, although many Quakers consider themselves Christians, some do not.

In another instance of reductiveness to the point of inaccuracy, White states that Lewis Terman came from "Protestant stock,"[194] a global designation; Puritans/Calvinists constitute one subset of Protestants, but Puritans/

Calvinists and Protestants are not one and the same, and the beliefs of Puritans/Calvinists, if they can be neatly categorized at all, do not represent the beliefs of all Protestants or Christians. Thus, the distinctions and differences, both large and small, that are critical to forming a strong argument on these matters, are lost in White's universalizing pronouncements.

Some Shortcomings of Global Pronouncements

Clearly, many dimensions of Christian thought have shaped US public schooling since its inception, and have influenced many other US institutions as well. That said, when speaking about Christian ideas of salvation in general and the concept of predestination in particular, there is a danger of being reductive and consequently erroneous, as White's article demonstrates. As I stated earlier, one danger is ascribing to the whole the beliefs and practices only of some, when in actuality there is both across-group and within-group variation. Christianity has a rich history, particularly within Protestantism, of multiple, diverse positions—not to mention fights and schisms—concerning a host of issues, including predestination. The danger of being reductive is present not only when discussing Christians, but also Protestants as a group, and even denominations such as Lutherans. Historically and up to the present, Lutherans have splintered over many topics, predestination among them. Because Christian soteriology is a complex field, global pronouncements are treacherous. For example, other types of predestination are promulgated by Christians in addition to double predestination, one of them being single predestination, which confirms election but rejects categorical reprobation. Furthermore, some Christian groups and individual Christians reject both predestination and reprobation altogether.

To further complicate matters, some Christians reject the existence of hierarchies—or even differences—when conceptualizing human ontology, and would therefore argue that the sorting and ordering of humans on which eugenics is based is distinctly unchristian. Consider, for example, the potentially antihierarchical implications of the doctrine of original sin. According to historian James Boyce, this doctrine was formulated by Augustine[195] and was a product of the breakup of the Roman Empire in the fifth century.[196] Boyce states that although this doctrine has been highly influential in Western Christendom, it is not and has never been universally accepted by all Christians, including Eastern Christians.[197] He asserts that Calvinism, and particularly the concept of original sin, had a powerful influence on early political thought in the United States and on the formation of early political institutions.[198] He points out, however, that there is a "radical equality" in the doctrine of original sin that was appealing to the creators of these institutions because it asserts that "the king of England is just as much a sinner in the eyes of God as a struggling farmer . . . the poorest person is spiritually equal to the most politically powerful."[199] In this sense, the doctrine of original sin is a great equalizer, one that, in theory at least, would run counter to eugenical thought.

The Diversity of Christian Salvation Discourses

Beliefs about predestination are related to Christian positions on salvation or deliverance, which once again are diverse, especially when considered across time and place, and when eschatology—including understandings of "end times"—is brought into the mix. Once again, because of this diversity, sweeping generalizations are perilous. Some differences stem from whether particular Christian individuals and groups are scriptural literalists. Salvation discourse *tends* to focus on the effects of Christ's actions on what happens to people after they die. Among the points of disagreement is whether reprobation—sometimes referred to as damnation or going to hell—is a possibility (or even a certainty), at least for some individuals and groups, even after deliverance was effected by Christ. Among the Christians who view reprobation as a possibility (or certainty), there is not consensus about for whom.

I say Christians *tend* to focus on what happens to humans after their physical death because some, but certainly not all, believe in the millennium, an end-times thousand-year period of peace and justice on *earth* that is ostensibly to precede the end of the earth. Furthermore, there are at least two types of millennialists: premillennialists, who believe that Christ will return to earth and *usher in* the millennium, and postmillennialists, who believe that Christ will return to the earth at the *end* of the millennium. Rosen notes that religious leaders who supported eugenics tended to be postmillennialists:

> Postmillennialists believed that the millennium would come through human effort. . . . [They] viewed the world as a place to change for the better to create the Kingdom of God on earth, and so reform was a vital part of their Christianity. . . . Their opponents were usually premillennialists. Premillennialists saw hubris in the assumption that human beings could usher in the Kingdom through their own efforts.[200]

Thus, only a particular type of salvation trope aims to create a state of perfection, wholeness, and restoration—or at the very least, improvement—here on earth. Using biblical imagery, in this salvation trope, the Garden of Eden returns, and earth is restored to a prelapsarian state. However, according to many if not most Christians, salvation is not the same as and is unrelated to returning the earth to a prelapsarian state. Indeed, Tzvetan Todorov claimed (perhaps somewhat erroneously) that Christianity and secular humanism are grounded on the tenet that "this world is irremediably imperfect (humans are tainted by original sin; their existence is an 'imperfect garden'), and that no definitive triumph over evil can ever be achieved."[201] Significantly, he added, "Only millenarist heretics and revolutionary utopians have ever maintained such an illusion [of the achievability of perfection]."[202] In contrast to millenarists and utopians, Todorov maintained that "we shall achieve a perfect world only by turning into another species."[203]

Another complicating factor in soteriological matters is the debated issue of whether humans are agentic in salvation or deliverance, and if they are, what constitutes their role. Christians do not agree on whether belief in God is necessary for salvation; among those who say it is, no consensus exists about whether there must be a conscious, formal acceptance of this faith—as decision theology asserts is imperative—or even about whether faith must be augmented by good works or good morals as preconditions for salvation. Some Christians assert that salvation is solely in God's domain and has already been brought about by God; they say that good works are important but are responsorial—a good unto themselves—rather than conditional. Others claim that although it is brought about by God, individual salvation is conditional on individual human buy-in or other human action. These differing positions are captured by what has been called "monkey versus cat" theologies; monkey theology asserts that baby monkeys (humans) must cling to their mother (God)—they must do something—if they are to be close to their mother. Cat theology states that mother cats pick up their babies by the scruff of the neck, and the babies need to do nothing but enjoy the ride.

As I mentioned earlier, some Christian groups and individual Christians reject both predestination and postdeath reprobation, including damnation. Among these are universal reconciliationists, who believe that salvation is both universal and unconditional, already having been brought about by Christ. Although apparently it has been a minority position, belief in universal salvation has been a part of Christian thought since ancient times. In her 2013 book *The Christian Doctrine of Apokatastasis: A Critical Assessment from the New Testament to Eriugena*, theologian Illaria Ramelli systematically documents the claim that *apokatastasis,* which she defines as "eventual universal salvation," is an ancient, scripture-based "Christian, or Jewish-Christian, doctrine."[204] She states that it "is found, from the New Testament to Eriugena [c. 815–77], in many Christian texts and Patristic authors."[205] Edward T. Oakes, while acknowledging the prevalence in medieval times of the Christian belief in hell, asserts that there were dissenters, including women mystics.[206] Theologian Gregory MacDonald (aka Robin Parry) indicates that Augustine (354–430), in his stated support of the doctrine of eternal punishment, also acknowledged the prevalence of a contrary view: "'Very many, moan over the eternal punishment, and perpetual, uninterrupted torments of the lost, and say that they do not believe it shall be so.'"[207]

Several scholars note that beginning in the nineteenth century (and I note, well before Seashore's time), many Christian theologians gradually abandoned the concept of eternal punishment.[208] Richard Bauckham discusses this sea change while also asserting that a respectable minority rejected the concept of eternal punishment early on:

> The history of the [Christian] doctrine of universal salvation (or *apokatastasis*) is a remarkable one. Until the nineteenth century almost all Christian theologians taught the reality of eternal torment in hell. Here and there, outside the theological mainstream, were some who believed that the wicked would be finally annihilated (in its commonest form, this is the doctrine of "conditional immortality"). Even fewer were the advocates of universal salvation, *though these few included some major theologians of the early church*. . . . Since 1800 this situation has entirely changed, and no traditional Christian doctrine has been so widely abandoned as that of eternal punishment. Its advocates among theologians today must be fewer than ever before. The alternative interpretation of hell as annihilation seems to have prevailed even among many of the more conservative theologians. Among the less conservative, universal salvation, either as hope or as dogma, is now so widely accepted that many theologians assume it virtually without argument [emphasis mine].[209]

MacDonald considers universal salvation to be one of the *theologoumena*: "*Theologoumena* are pious opinions that are consistent with Christian dogmas. They are neither required nor forbidden."[210] Thus, he concludes that universal salvation is "an issue about which Christians can legitimately disagree within the boundaries of orthodox Christianity."[211] Presumably this means that belief in selective salvation, with double and single predestination being examples, similarly falls in the realm of *theologoumena*. Ironically, universal reconciliation may be considered a form of predestination, one that does not include what Popkewitz calls double gestures of simultaneous inclusion and exclusion.[212] Instead, all are included in an after-death future that is promised to be good.

The Tactical Productivity of Eugenical Destiny Discourse

In considering the influence of Protestant doctrine on eugenics, yet another complicating factor is that, according to those who follow Luther's strain of reformation theology, individual conscience can trump official authority, including official teachings of the church. Seashore himself exercised this right (or responsibility) when he expressed opposition to what he called "factional dogma, outmoded doctrines, and unbelievable religious fictions."[213] He did not specify which dogma, doctrines, and fictions he had in mind. Thus, although eugenics clearly was popular among Protestants, and although the specific eugenic tenets of inherent ability and inability resembled and may have been modeled after the Calvinist doctrine of double predestination, on matters of salvation there were and always have been many other theologically sound, doctrinally acceptable positions available to Christians, including Protestant Christians. In short, there is not and never has been a unified salvation narrative in Christianity or even in Protestantism. Rosen refers to the "pliable compendiums" that constituted the theologies of many ministers of the early twentieth century.[214] I maintain that such theological pliability was not limited to clerics. Thus, being a Christian in no way predestined, or even necessarily predisposed, an individual to being a eugenicist or a predestinarian.

Furthermore, blaming their religious pedigree does not get eugenicists off the ethical hook. As I stated earlier in the chapter, staunch opposition to eugenics came from the ranks of Christians, including Catholics and Protestants—conservative Protestants, in particular.[215]

Rather than being an exercise in apologetics, recognizing the multiplicity and diversity of roads available to Christians invites consideration of the reasoning behind the roads that *were* taken both by Christians who embraced eugenics and by eugenicists who adopted ideas resembling double predestination. I am referring to what Foucault called the tactical productivity and strategical integration of discourse: "We must question them [discourses] on the two levels of their tactical productivity (what reciprocal effects of power and knowledge they ensure) and their strategical integration (what conjunction and what force relationship make their utilization necessary in a given episode)."[216] A double-gestures salvation/damnation model of inclusion and exclusion is productive in ways that a universal reconciliation model is not, and vice versa. What was the appeal of the double gestures inherent in double predestination? What fears did they quell and what desires did they mobilize that universal reconciliation did not? What projects became not merely imaginable, but logical, sensible, reasonable, and good? What became outrageous or unimaginable? Of course, these questions are applicable to eugenics discourse regardless of whether it is rooted in religious beliefs, and these are questions I return to later in the book.

Eugenics as a Rescue Trope

Although I stop short of calling eugenics a salvation trope necessarily derived from Christianity, I acknowledge that eugenics trades in heroic rescue tropes. In such tropes, the hero has the power to rescue an endangered and ostensibly helpless individual or group. A child who has fallen into a lake, cannot swim, and is in danger of drowning is an object of rescue. That child is marked not only as imperiled but as incapable, weak, and powerless—doomed. Enter the rescuer who, by contrast, is capable, knowledgeable, and powerful; the rescuer exercises that power by intervening and attempting a rescue. If the rescue is successful (or sometimes even if it is not), the glory goes to the rescuer, whose picture may appear on the front page of the newspaper. Thus, the rescuer "saved" the person in the lake, but the narrative does not necessarily have religious overtones.

Rescue tropes abound in discourse in the United States and elsewhere, "damsel in distress" melodramas being but one example. They can appear outside of Christian thought, and they predate it. Consider, for instance, the ancient Greek myth describing Orpheus's foray into the underworld to rescue his dead wife, Eurydice. His attempt was unsuccessful, but his failure did not tarnish his heroic reputation. Many ancient and modern heroic rescue tropes construct, legitimize, and reinforce power differentials and unequal power relations (e.g., male/female, adult/child, rich/poor). They are double gestures that construct some individuals or groups as having and others as lacking.

Finally, some may claim that certain flavors of Christian soteriology constitute a particular type of rescue trope; this may be an accurate claim in some cases, but many Christians would counter that salvation is not a heroic rescue narrative at all but rather a story of suffering, loss, compassion, humility, and sacrifice; the prevailing message is not about human heroes but about God's unconditional love. In eugenics rescue tropes, however, science and the scientist are the heroic rescuers that promise to save an imperiled and powerless humanity (or at least a particular race or nation), which without intervention cannot save itself from an ostensibly terrible fate. When the rescue is accomplished, the glory goes to the scientist.

Eugenics as Utopian Discourse

Social Gospel precepts are just a few of eugenics' many intellectual scaffolds, and although discussing all of these scaffolds would require a multivolume book, I will briefly mention another: utopianism. In his 1865 essay "Hereditary Talent and Character," Galton used the term "utopia" to describe the bright future he envisioned; this essay was written decades before the first known time he used the word "eugenics" in print.[217]

One commonality between eugenics and other types of utopian thought is the presence of hope, optimism, and a future focus; this presence, in turn, feeds the shared belief that humanity is, if not perfectible, at least improvable. In his book *Hope and Memory: Reflections on the Twentieth Century*, Todorov identified a second group, in addition to millenarist heretics, that he claimed holds the "strange world view" that the world is perfectible: revolutionary utopians.[218]

Utopianism has a long, venerable presence in the United States. In the nineteenth century, some individuals and groups claimed that the United States—New England in particular—would be the site of the New Jerusalem, a replication of the Garden of Eden.[219] A number of utopian communities sprang up in the United States in the nineteenth century, especially in the Midwest. Iowa, where Seashore spent most of his life, was home to at least two of them, the Amana Colonies and an Icarian community. Not all utopian communities were Christian or even faith-based. Regardless, the goals of these groups indicate that aiming to create a better world, a better life on earth, and more perfect humans was neither new nor unique to eugenics.

Thus, rather than being an aberration, eugenics as conceptualized and practiced in the early twentieth century resembles and is consistent with utopian impulses that predated it. It is a particular manifestation of utopian thought, and although it has unique contours, it continues and builds on earlier ideas, rather than being a diversion away from them. Eugenicists maintained that science, and scientifically informed public policy, would help shorten the road to a promised better future, a state of perfection.

There is a direct and perhaps unique link between eugenics and the utopian millenarist Oneida Community in New York (1848–80): the promotion of selective human breeding. Beginning in the 1860s, the Oneidans practiced what community founder John Humphrey Noyes reportedly called stirpiculture—the selective breeding of humans. According to an unsigned 1865 article in the community's weekly newspaper (attributed by others to Noyes), the characteristics to be cultivated via selective breeding of humans are "Receptivity to inspiration, and Obedience."[220] Retrospectively, stirpiculture has been called eugenics.[221] Although some sources claim that the practice of stirpiculture began after Noyes read works by Charles Darwin and Francis Galton, Laurence Karp argues that Noyes was promoting the idea of selective human breeding more than a decade before either Darwin or Galton had published their seminal works.[222] To situate the Oneidans and the practice of stirpiculture chronologically, the community ceased operations in 1880, when Seashore was only fourteen years old; thus, early on, stirpiculture was an element in the systems of reasoning that made twentieth-century eugenics seem reasonable, logical, and familiar.

The Centrality of Education to Eugenical Thought

Although eugenical goals sometimes were to be achieved via legislation and coercion, in the United States during the early twentieth century, eugenicists also assigned a prominent role to pastoral strategies such as education. For example, an education root appeared on both the 1921 and the 1932 eugenics tree logos. Education initiatives were among the tree's many fruits as well.

Education was viewed as an essential vehicle for spreading the word about the precepts, aims, and projects of eugenics. As Barry Mehler notes, when the Eugenics Committee that eventually became the American Eugenics Society was formed by the Executive Committee of the Second International Congress, it had a distinctly different mission and focus than existing eugenics organizations. Education was central to that mission: "Where the new Eugenics Committee would differ from the ERA, Galton Society, and ERO was that the Committee would emphasize political and educational goals rather than research and information exchange among professionals."[223]

In his speech to the Second International Congress, Leonard Darwin described three directions in which eugenics should advance, and the first of these was education, the aim being to disseminate information: "In the first place the public should be made to realize more and more fully what a potent influence heredity has on the fate of all nations."[224] He later stated that eugenics societies should "formulate a sound eugenic policy based on existing genetic knowledge, and then . . . promote the translation of every advance in eugenic theory into general practice."[225] Teachers, Darwin maintained, are essential to the project of disseminating eugenics: "No class of the community is more important to interest in racial problems than teachers of all grades; because the ideas of the youth of to-morrow will depend so largely on the opinions of the teachers of to-day."[226] He spoke of the importance of adequately educating teachers and claimed that to be properly educated, all teachers should take a biology class.[227] He underscored his message by adding, "Eugenics has a long struggle before it, and all these methods of laying educational foundations for future progress should certainly come within the scope of the efforts of eugenical societies."[228]

Events such as the better baby contests were part of eugenics' broad educational mission. When education is more narrowly conceptualized as what happens in schools, however, it is clear that eugenics had a powerful presence. Especially during the first half of the twentieth century, eugenics was expressly discussed and promoted in a host of curricular areas; for example, in the United States it shaped the content of high school biology and social studies textbooks, home economics curricula, and health education programs.[229] Furthermore, it was instrumental in the development of a new school subject: sex education. In *Eugenics, Race and Intelligence in Education*, Clyde Chitty argues that "popular eugenic theories actually *acquired* their popularity through the official knowledge sponsored by the state [emphasis in original]"; he uses the presence of eugenical discourse in textbooks as an example of how it achieved its popularity.[230]

In addition, some eugenicists believed that education as a whole needed a massive, eugenically informed overhaul. Such education reform would be a mechanism for building the better society and world they envisioned. As I will demonstrate in subsequent chapters, Seashore was among them.

Eugenics as a Dynamic Assemblage

I struggled with the issue of how to adequately address the dynamism, complexity, and intersectionality that I observed in the materials on eugenics I examined. Speaking provisionally—I am only referring to eugenics in the United States in the early part of the twentieth century—I decided to conceptualize it as a complex, dynamic, and cohering assemblage of interrelated and mutually supportive discourses and discursive practices. Among the elements I examined in this assemblage are ideas, people, and activities, as well as the mutually supportive relationships and intersections among them. I imagine eugenics three-dimensionally, because when elements are represented multidimensionally, they can appear closer to one another than they would when represented one-dimensionally; in a multidimensional representation, it is easier for all of the elements to touch and overlap with one another. Like the subject itself, my conceptualization is messy and disorderly; its edges, and the edges of its many elements, are fuzzy and overlapping. Furthermore, in my conceptualization, the elements of eugenics are moving, but like the components of an atom, they are not moving everywhere, and they cohere, more or less. I view Seashore as one tiny element in this massive, messy, moving assemblage.

In an attempt to demonstrate the breadth and complexity of eugenics, I decided that rather than adopting one extant conceptualization to the exclusion of others, I would draw elements simultaneously from many of them. Thus, I have taken a "yes, and" approach: yes, it is this, and yes, it is this. Yes, it is an example of biopower; and yes, it is about reproduction; and yes, it is about whiteness; and yes, it is a collection of organizations and activities; and yes, it is about national planning, and yes, it is about human-race planning, and yes, it is about individual planning. Finally, yes, it also is about intersections among all of these. Eugenics is complex, in part, because of its intersectionality, which has prompted me to analyze it intersectionally. The concept of intersectionality was developed by critical race theorist Kimberlé Crenshaw, who pointed out the shortcomings of a "single-axis framework"; her research, by contrast, attends to the "interaction of race and gender."[231] Typically, when contemporary scholars speak of intersectionality, they are referring to intersections between race, class, gender, sexuality, and ability. I respond, "Yes, and in the case of eugenics, intersectionality is even bigger; eugenics is about, among other things, intersections among all of these and such seemingly disparate subjects as immigration, and nation, and religion, and schooling, and quality." It is about how all of these elements—and more—play off of and work with one another.

I do not claim that my conceptualization "captures" eugenics. Nevertheless, looking outside of the boundaries of education and music education and grappling with this messy, dynamic complexity informed and enriched my understanding of eugenics in the smaller realms of education and music education. I noticed broader intersections and connections that I otherwise might not have seen.

Researching Seashore and Eugenics: Investigative Processes, Sources, and Limitations

Investigative Processes

Taking a "yes, and" approach, I identified and analyzed four distinct yet related types of evidence of Seashore's investment in eugenics. Recognizing that each has strengths and weakness, I decided that one type of evidence alone was insufficient:

- *Formal participation and length of participation.* The major indicators of participation were membership in organizations such as the American Eugenics Society (AES) and the Eugenics Research Association (ERA), attending or presenting papers at conferences sponsored by eugenics organizations, or publishing in journals sponsored by such organizations. I also looked at length of membership.

  Formal participation is strong, straightforward evidence, and some may argue that it alone is sufficient. I concluded, however, that it offers a limited picture. Consider, for example, the shortcomings of relying solely on organizational membership. Given that many intellectuals of the day, psychologists in particular, held memberships in the AES or the ERA, I questioned how much weight I could give to Seashore's membership. People join organizations for many reasons, and sometimes they are members in name only. Membership may be a matter of professional expediency; the networking potential in eugenics organizations was considerable. Membership can be more a product of a sense of professional duty than a sign of commitment. Not belonging to an influential organization or resigning from it due to disagreement with its goals and activities can be costly professionally, especially when other prominent members of a field retain their membership. I viewed the length of Seashore's participation as a measure of the strength of his commitment, and it informed my understanding of why he belonged. I also wanted to know whether he changed his mind or distanced himself from the movement during or after World War II.

  In addition, formal participation has limits as evidence because members may not necessarily agree with all or most of the official platform (if one exists), all of the organization's practices, or the views of most other members. Sometimes disagreeing members may choose to "work from within" rather than resign. Thus, there are degrees of participation in and agreement with organizations and their activities. Evidence of participation was useful in situating Seashore's involvement on a spectrum of agreement. That said, quite a few academics and others subscribed to discourses and engaged in practices consonant with eugenics even though they did not formally belong or participate. Formal participation is a strong indicator, but limiting the label of "eugenicist" only to those who participated in the formal activities of eugenics organizations grossly underreports eugenics' scope and influence during the first half of the twentieth century in the United States.

- *Seashore's home in eugenics: the relationship network that he established with other eugenicists.* As additional evidence, I turned to the company Seashore kept—the people with whom he associated, attending to his professional and in some cases personal relationships, and to the *network* of relationships created by these individual relationships. I focused in particular on evidence of relationships with those who have been identified as prominent figures in the eugenics movement—insiders. In choosing to examine this kind of evidence and to call it "Seashore's home," I was influenced by the work of anthropologists such as Michael Jackson, author of *At Home in the World*, who claims that although "home" can be conceptualized as a place, it can also be understood as a "mode of activity,"[232] or, germane to this project, a "group of *people* without whom your life would cease to have meaning [emphasis in original]."[233] He refers to a "social universe . . . made up of skeins of relationships,"[234] and in his explanation of possible conceptions of home, he quotes Tennessee Williams's *The Night of the Iguana:* "'I don't mean what other people mean when they speak of a home . . . as a place. . . . I think of a home as being a thing that two people have between them in which each can . . . nest—rest—live . . .'"[235]

If I conceptualize eugenics as consisting, at least in part, of dynamic and complex skeins of personal relationships, then situating Seashore within that network not only provides partial evidence of his involvement but sheds light on the degree of his involvement. Taking the home-and-family analogy one step further, I hoped that by studying relationships, I could better discern whether the eugenics family viewed Seashore as a favored child or something of an outsider. Furthermore, recognizing the potential power of connections, I wanted to know what Seashore and others in the eugenics relationships network were *saying to* each other and *doing for* each other. To this end, I examined correspondence, as well as evidence of formal and informal meetings, interactions, and visits.

Although useful in providing a richer picture, mapping out Seashore's home also has limitations. Simply having friends and colleagues who were eugenicists could not alone be definitive proof that Seashore was one, especially given the large number of psychologists of the day who were eugenicists. Seashore inevitably would have rubbed elbows with eugenicists simply because he was a psychologist. That said, not all psychologists—nor all academics—were eugenicists, and some volubly came out against it.

- *Explicit mentioning, discussion, and endorsement of eugenics and euthenics in published or unpublished documents.* This category of evidence consists of instances when Seashore used the terms *eugenics* or *euthenics* in his writing. I sought instances not only of endorsement but of criticism. Like formal participation, the presence of such references is a strong indicator, but to limit my textual analysis to these particular references would prevent me from discussing texts that do not mention these terms but that nevertheless promulgate eugenical ideas.
- *The presence in Seashore's writings of ideas, beliefs, and values that are consistent with eugenics, and the degree to which his writings are consistent with dominant eugenical discourse.* Perhaps the richest source of information about Seashore is his writings. The bulk of my inquiry focused on understanding what he thought by examining what he said in published or unpublished documents, and on establishing the extent to which he promulgated ideas, beliefs, values, and practices that were consistent with eugenics *even when he did not mention eugenics or euthenics.* I gathered this fourth type of evidence by closely reading all of Seashore's published and unpublished writings that seemed even remotely related to my project. I have attempted to use his own words whenever possible and have referenced his autobiography extensively, recognizing that a retrospective such as an autobiography, however hyperbolic it may be, represents the way an author *wants* to be remembered.

Recognizing, as other scholars have argued, that race talk occurs without the word *race* ever being uttered,[236] I chose to examine this kind of evidence because I maintain that eugenics talk can operate similarly. Like the other kinds of evidence, however, this type has limitations. First, as I have already indicated, many of the ideas central to eugenics predated eugenics if it is defined as a group of organizations and activities or as a specific social philosophy. They were accepted elements of discourse circulating outside of eugenical circles at the time—taken up not solely by eugenicists but by others as well. As I have already argued, rather than being an aberration, eugenics tapped into familiar "commonsensical" ideas.

Because there was not unanimity of thought within eugenics organizations, part of my project was to map out with nuance and specificity where Seashore was situated—which aspects of eugenical thought, which versions, and which positions he did or did not embrace. I learned, for example, that he supported promotion of the fittest through educational programs for students labeled gifted or talented, as well as the early elimination of students deemed unfit from particular kinds of educational opportunities and settings. These ideas, and even the terms he used in describing them, link him directly to eugenics. Did this mean, however, that he also supported involuntary sterilization or the actual murder of the ostensibly unfit?

Because Seashore was a prolific writer, a large body of published materials was available to me. However, a good portion of his unpublished materials and papers were destroyed in a 1946 fire in the psychology section of the University of Iowa's East Hall (later called Seashore Hall).[237] Handwritten notes in the archival materials at the University of Iowa indicate that Seashore family members were contacted by previous scholars on more than one occasion and asked whether they had anything else; the notes state that the family has repeatedly said they have nothing more. The loss of archival materials in the 1946 fire required that I be creative in my search for evidence beyond his publications.

Types of Sources

I examined two broad categories of materials: (1) primary and secondary sources on eugenics, and (2) and primary and secondary sources on Seashore. When examining the eugenics sources, I looked for any references to Seashore or his research. In addition to providing information about him, these sources helped me to understand the general eugenics landscape and to place my findings on Seashore in context.

I examined a host of primary sources in the first category, concentrating on publications of the American Eugenics Society and its near relative, the Eugenics Research Association. Specifically, I examined all issues of the journals *Eugenics* and *Eugenical News*, looking for references to Seashore or his work, articles or comments penned by him, and even advertisements for the Seashore Tests. I also examined key books published or endorsed by the AES and ERA, as well as eugenics conference proceedings.

I examined some archival eugenics materials, including the correspondence of select prominent eugenicists, notably Robert Mearns Yerkes, whose papers are at Yale University, and Charles Davenport, whose papers are at the American Philosophical Society in Philadelphia. In particular, I focused on correspondence between these individuals and Seashore, the correspondence between Yerkes and Seashore spanning nearly four decades.

Secondary sources that discuss eugenics, in addition to broadening my understanding of the topic, helped me determine what prior discussion of Seashore and eugenics exists. As with the primary source materials, I focused largely on secondary sources that discuss eugenics in the United States, and more specifically, the activities of the AES, ERA, and the AES Advisory Council.

I also consulted and analyzed what I call primary and secondary Seashore sources, looking in particular for links to eugenics. Among the primary sources were Seashore's publications, including his 1930 autobiography, and a number of unpublished archival materials, including those in the Seashore Papers at the University of Iowa and Gustavus Adolphus College. I also looked for references to Seashore or eugenics in the President's Correspondence Collection at the University of Iowa.

Seashore and his work have been discussed in a wide range of fields, and the category I call secondary Seashore sources encompassed what was written about him during his lifetime and down to the present, including published articles and doctoral dissertations that either focus on or mention him. In these secondary sources, I looked specifically for anything pertaining to eugenics. A notable secondary source was Walter Miles's 1956 biography of Seashore,[238] but I examined a host of others, as well—including obituaries—that provided biographical information.

Limitations

I acknowledge that this study has many limitations, one of them being my limited perspective. Mine is a situated retrospective reading conducted by only one person. I have produced one possible reading of these materials, and I do not claim that it is the only viable one. The discursive "tools" I have access to, and the systems of reasoning with which I am or am not familiar, shaped and limited what I could or could not "see" in what I examined. Thus, I acknowledge that this project is limited by my blind spots, which I know are present even though I cannot precisely locate them.

In addition, limited physical resources limited the study. For example, like all historians, I only have what is left. In this case, what is left are published works and a scattering of unpublished material. The fire at the University of Iowa, which destroyed what apparently was a substantial portion of the archival materials, forced me to be creative and to gather unpublished materials through indirect routes. Locating all of the correspondence between Seashore and all known or even all prominent eugenicists was beyond the scope of this study, however.

Finally, time and staffing limits compelled me to limit the scope of my inquiry. Unlike Edwin Black, who had a staff of more than fifty to assist him in researching *War against the Weak*, I worked alone—albeit with invaluable help from a part-time project assistant during my final year of writing and the assistance of those I mentioned in the acknowledgments. Internet access to archival collections has been a boon, but it also has been a curse because of the staggering amount of material available to scour. I do not claim that I have analyzed every extant reference to Seashore, let alone every reference to eugenics. Thus, although it has been exhausting, this project is not exhaustive.

Despite its limitations, I am confident that my research is of sufficient breadth and depth to support the conclusions I reach—more confident than I have been about any of my previous work. My most valuable resource has been the time I have devoted to this research; like preparing slow food, working on this project for more than fifteen years has produced food for thought with a depth of flavor I never could have achieved if I had only spent a year or two with Carl Seashore.

Three

The Faces of Carl Emil Seashore

When I found the first shred of evidence that Carl Seashore was a eugenicist, I wanted to know not only the extent of his involvement and how it related to his work, but who else knew this information and whether anyone had written about it. I read everything I could find about him, including biographies, his autobiography, and a host of other sources, ranging from studies in scholarly journals to obituaries. Throughout this process, I learned about his contributions and influence, and also about how he has been received. In addition to looking for references to eugenics in these sources, I wanted to know whether his reception, whether positive or negative, stemmed from his involvement in eugenics. This chapter examines some of the faces of Seashore that I found. Although Seashore himself was forthright about his involvement in eugenics, portrayals of him by most other scholars have not been. I open with what has been said, and then present what has not been said.

To provide background and context, I begin with a brief introduction to Seashore's life and accomplishments as reported elsewhere. His autobiography and the biography written by Walter Miles were valuable sources. Next, I discuss his contributions, focusing in particular on his influence and his reception, the former being considerable and the latter positive, overall. Throughout, I attend to what has and what *has not* been said by others. In the third section, I confirm what most previous scholars have not reported or discussed—Seashore's involvement in eugenics as evidenced by his organizational membership, conference participation, and presence in eugenics publications. Fourth, I verify his involvement by reporting on his explicit and overt support of eugenics in published and unpublished sources. Fifth, I ascertain his involvement by examining a sampling of the relationships he established with other eugenicists, and I describe the kinds of mutual benefits that were derived from them. Finally, I acknowledge and discuss the rare instances where scholars broke the silence surrounding Seashore and eugenics.

My synopsis of what has previously been reported about Seashore is brief because I never set out to write a new biography, and space does not allow me to repeat everything that already has been said. I found it daunting to wade through the vast sea of extant information and difficult to decide what to include. Summarizing Seashore, I discovered, is like trying to capture lightning in a bottle. The biographical information I have included, in addition to introducing Seashore to those unfamiliar with him, provides chronological guideposts, situating him in time and place. This situating, in turn, may help explain why some discourses and discursive practices made sense to him, while others seemed outrageous, and still others were simply unimaginable even though they were circulating elsewhere at that time. I situate him within a particular time and place, not to excuse or dismiss his beliefs and practices, but rather in an attempt to better understand how local and global contextual factors—matters of time and place—came into play in shaping his subjectivity.

Seashore's Life

Carl Emil Seashore was born on January 28, 1866, in Mörlunda, Sweden. His family immigrated to the United States when he was three years old. They settled in Boone County, Iowa, west of Des Moines, where they purchased and farmed an eighty-acre plot. He attended singing school as a child, had music lessons, and at the age of fourteen, became a church organist.[1] He attended the preparatory academy and college at Gustavus Adolphus College, a small, private, coeducational school in St. Peter, Minnesota, and he was valedictorian of both his high school and college classes.[2] He was a member of Gustavus College's second graduating class, the class of 1891; although there were four women and twenty-one men in his freshman class, the women left after their first year, and only four of the remaining men graduated.[3] He studied a variety of subjects as an undergraduate, and although he did not major in music, he served as organist and choir director at a church in nearby Mankato, Minnesota;[4] in his autobiography, he also mentioned that he continued to sing.[5]

He entered Yale University as a graduate student in philosophy, Seashore reporting that he began his studies on the day that the Yale Psychology Laboratory first opened, and on the advice of his advisor, he enrolled in the laboratory class.[6] His advisor was the philosopher and psychologist George Trumbull Ladd. At that time, psychology and philosophy were not separate departments. Seashore was one of four students to take the first course offered by the lab.[7] Edward Wheeler Scripture, the lab's founder, taught the course. Scripture was a student of Wilhelm Wundt and a cofounder with G. Stanley Hall of the American Psychological Association. Although he remained an advisee of Ladd's, Seashore quickly shifted his focus to psychology, and he stated that all of his dissertation work was done under and approved by Scripture.[8] He completed doctoral studies in 1895; he then went abroad for a summer, visiting laboratories in Germany and France.[9] When he returned, he became a postdoctoral fellow at Yale, a post he held for two years; in 1897, he accepted a job as an assistant professor of philosophy and head of the Psychology Laboratory at the State University of Iowa (that is, the University of Iowa).[10] Seashore was hired by George T. W. Patrick, a student of G. Stanley Hall, who had founded the lab at Iowa in 1887.[11]

In 1900, he married Mary Roberta Holmes ("Roberta"), who had received two degrees from the University of Iowa (BPh 1891, MA 1893).[12] According to Carl Seashore, Roberta majored in classics, was elected to Phi Beta Kappa, and studied philosophy in graduate school.[13] They had four children, all sons.

The University of Iowa credits Seashore for founding its Department of Psychology.[14] He became chair of the Philosophy and Psychology Department in 1905, and in 1908, he became dean of the Graduate College. He held both of these positions (chairing the Psychology Department when it became a separate entity in 1927) until his first retirement in 1937, at which point he was seventy-one years old.[15] In 1942, in the midst of World War II, he was called out of retirement to resume temporarily the role of dean of the Graduate College, a position he relinquished for the last time in 1946. Seashore was eighty years old. He died three years later, on October 16, 1949.

The Seashores' son Robert became a psychologist. He received his doctorate from the University of Iowa, where his father served as his dissertation adviser, and he was a postdoctoral fellow at Stanford University under the guidance of Carl Seashore's biographer, Walter Miles.[16] He was a professor at the University of Oregon, and according to his father, at the University of Southern California; he later became chair of the psychology department at Northwestern University.[17] Their son Carl Gustaf received a degree in civil engineering, worked for the White Motor Company, and became a professor of engineering (the Associate Director of Safety Education) in the extension division at Pennsylvania State.[18] Their third son, Marion, was a lifeguard at a boys' camp in Maine during the summer following his junior year at Harvard University, and he died in a swimming accident while rescuing two friends.[19] Their fourth son, Sigfrid, became an attorney.[20] Carl's grandson (Robert's son) Charles N. Seashore was a psychologist and a founding member of the board of directors of the Lewin Center, which is dedicated to promoting equity and social justice.[21] Carl's nephew Harold, whose doctoral advisor was his Uncle Carl, became a president of the Psychological Corporation (which merged into what is known today as Pearson plc); Carl's nephew Stanley was a psychology professor at the University of Michigan.[22]

Seashore's Contributions and Reception

Seashore made contributions in many disciplines, and he published more than 240 books and articles on a wide range of topics.[23] His work has been cited frequently, and quite a bit has been written about him, including entire dissertations, and biographies large and small. In general, he and his work have been well received and the reviews have been highly complimentary.

Seashore and Psychology

He is perhaps best known for his contributions to psychology, music psychology in particular. His work in this field had a major impact both at the national level and more locally at the University of Iowa. Terms such as "titan," "giant," and "pioneer" have been used to describe him.[24] Seashore himself used the concept of "pioneering" to characterize his work and the work of other early psychologists.[25]

Early in his career, he focused on sensory perception and conducted research on such phenomena as "visual accommodation time, perception of pressure and weight, and the laws determining illusions and hallucinations."[26] He published on "psychological" topics ranging from mental fatigue[27] to the value of a midday nap.[28] A fan of machines, technology, and gadgets, he designed, built, and improved on scientific instruments, especially those measuring sensory perception.[29] Some of his early research examined pitch and time or rhythm discrimination.[30]

The Psychology of Music

During his lifetime and to the present, Seashore has been recognized as an early leader in empirical and applied music psychology. In 1946, Lloyd F. Sunderman, editor of the journal *Education*, heaped praise on Seashore for these contributions: "For over half a century his inquiring, penetrative, and scientific scholarship has pervaded psychological circles. It is safe to say that no man in America has contributed so much research in the field of applied music psychology."[31]

Some of his contributions in this domain were in psychometrics, where he created the first standardized test of musical ability, the Seashore Measures of Musical Talent. Convinced that musicality includes a combination of biologically inheritable perceptual capacities, he developed a battery of tests that use pairs of sounds to measure an individual's ability to discriminate differences in five (and later six) domains: pitch, intensity, time, consonance, tonal memory, and (later) rhythm. According to Seashore, the early testing apparatus was cumbersome, making widespread use of the tests in schools unfeasible.[32] The practicality factor changed when Seashore, ever enamored with gadgetry, came up with the idea of recording the test sounds on a phonographic disc; the recording project was undertaken by the Columbia Graphophone Company, which began marketing the battery in 1919.[33] In his 1942 book *Pioneering in Psychology*, Seashore commented on the longevity and impact of his tests: "It is rather remarkable that these measures stood up for twenty years without revision and with continually increasing use for many purposes."[34]

I will discuss the Seashore Tests in greater depth in chapters 6 and 7. Suffice it to say here that despite questions about the validity and reliability of the battery, or at least of some subtests, Seashore was accurate about their durability. Over the years, all or parts of the battery have been put to a variety of uses within and outside of music contexts. During World War II, they were employed to select sound operators on submarines.[35] Portions of the battery have been used in extramusical studies of sound perception, as well as in medical diagnostics, an example being a 2006 study of sound perception among individuals who had suffered head injuries.[36] A 2010 study concluded that the rhythm portion of the Seashore Tests is effective in diagnosing neurocognitive dysfunction due to traumatic brain injury,[37] and a more recent rhythm test modeled after Seashore's was used in a 2013 study of linguistic and musical rhythm perception.[38] Finally, the rhythm portion of the Seashore Tests was used to demonstrate the construct validity of the auditory portion of the Test of Variables of Attention (TOVA), which is used today to diagnose attention deficits, including attention-deficit/hyperactivity disorder.[39]

His National Presence in Psychology

He held a number of prestigious leadership positions in psychology. In 1911, he became the president of the American Psychological Association. He was a member of the National Research Council (NRC), and from 1921 to 1922, he chaired the NRC's Division of Anthropology and Psychology.[40] He was elected to the National Academy of Sciences in 1922—the seventh psychologist to receive this honor,[41] and from 1933 to 1939 he was chair of the Division of Anthropology and Psychology of the National Academy of Sciences.[42]

He authored textbooks, was a journal editor, and helped establish a flourishing corporation. Forty-six years after the publication of Seashore's textbook *Psychology of Music*, R. W. Lundin called the work a classic.[43] Notably, Seashore was a coeditor of the *Journal of Educational Psychology* in 1916 when a historic special series on standardized intelligence testing appeared. He also was a collaborator when James McKeen Cattell established the Psychological Corporation, one of the entities comprising what is known today as Pearson plc.[44]

His Contributions to Psychology at the University of Iowa

Seashore had an enormous impact on psychology at the University of Iowa, and his contributions there were recognized both during and after his lifetime.[45] For example, in the preface to Seashore's 1942 book *Pioneering in Psychology*, his former student George D. Stoddard spoke of that impact: "Among all of the University of Iowa's 'lengthened shadows,' Seashore's is the longest and the most enduring."[46] Stoddard's imagery was employed again nearly fifty years later by Ernest R. Hilgard in his assessment that Seashore's "long shadow falls on all aspects of the history of psychology at Iowa."[47] Seashore built up the psychology program to a level such that 100 years later, in a centennial retrospective on psychology at the University of Iowa, Howard H. Kendler characterized the program Seashore helped develop as "topnotch."[48] Kendler also praised Seashore for helping make psychology a respected field: "By the force of the scientific standards he set and the scientific goals he achieved, Carl Seashore was able to earn psychology a privileged status at the University of Iowa, no mean achievement considering the suspicion, if not outright antagonism, with which the new science of psychology was viewed by traditional academics."[49]

He was instrumental in establishing the child psychology clinic at Iowa—only the second in an American university, according to Miles[50]—and in creating the Iowa Child Welfare Research Station.[51] Today the psychology clinic at the University of Iowa is named after him.

More Accolades in Psychology

Among the countless references to Seashore's contributions to psychology is mention of him by Harvard University professor Edwin G. Boring in the classic 1929 tome *A History of Experimental Psychology*.[52] Fifty-five years later, the *Encyclopedia of Psychology*, published in 1984, included an entry on him.[53] One of the more unusual recent accolades was naming the online newsletter published by the Psychology Department at Seashore's alma mater, Gustavus Adolphus College, after him. It is called *Emil's Epilogue*, a reference to his middle name, and the Gustavus archives contain copies of the newsletter dating from as recently as 2012.[54] Among the many published discussions of Seashore's contributions to psychology is James V. Hinrichs's 2006 summary, which illustrates Seashore's long-lasting reach and the reach of psychology into other fields:

> Like all aspects of the man, Seashore's psychological interests were both broad and deep. Seashore liked to demonstrate the scope of the field of psychology by pointing to his own career, which led him to associations in a wide variety of fields. In medicine, he consulted on the diseases of the ear; in architecture, the acoustic qualities of rooms; in defense, personnel selection and training; in biology, inheritance of hearing and measurement of hearing ability in animals; in anthropology, individual differences in hearing ability. In speech, he was a leader in the field, as he was in education. He essentially founded the discipline of psychoacoustics and was present at the birth of speech pathology. . . . Seashore pioneered hearing testing of children and made it a component of the early training of clinical psychologists. Although not a clinician himself, he was instrumental in the founding of the second psychological clinic for children in the country. All this without mentioning music![55]

Seashore and Music Education

In music education, Seashore is best known for his conceptions of musical ability and his development of the Seashore Tests. Among the ways his work became known to musicians, music scholars, and music educators was through his publications in music-related periodicals. His first publication on a music-related subject, an article on pitch discrimination, appeared in 1899 in a psychology monograph series that he later edited (from 1905 to 1926), the *University of Iowa Studies in Psychology*.[56] Two other articles, one on rhythm and time perception and the other on the voice tonoscope, were published in the same journal in 1899 and 1902, respectively.[57]

The migration of his work to music-related venues began a few years later; his first publication to appear in a journal designed specifically for musicians was a 1906 article in *The Musician* on the use of the tonoscope in voice training.[58] From then on, his music-related articles were published in journals from multiple disciplines, including *Annals of the American Academy of Political and Social Science*, the *Journal of Educational Psychology*, and *Science*; and in periodicals for musicians, such as the *Musical Quarterly* (1915) and *Etude* (1917). His 1915 article in *Musical Quarterly*, which appeared in the very first issue of this highly respected scholarly journal, opened with a description of the nature of musical talent as Seashore understood it and then described his early efforts to measure the components of musical talent in the laboratory.[59] The *Etude* article, entitled "How Psychology Can Help the Musician," is similar in content.[60] From 1916 on, articles by Seashore appeared in the *Music Supervisors' Journal* (later known as the *Music Educators Journal (MSJ/MEJ)*, a key journal for school music educators. The first article, "Scientific Procedure in the Discovery of Musical Talent in the Public Schools," discussed how his tests of musical capacities could be used in schools.[61] In time, his articles became a regular fixture in the *MEJ*. According to my count, between January 1916 and April 1945, the *MSJ/MEJ* published thirty-seven, most of them in the 1930s. This astonishing number does not take into account reviews of his books, notices of revisions of the Seashore Tests, or discussions of his work written by others. His *MSJ/MEJ* articles addressed topics ranging from violin intonation[62] to age-related hearing loss.[63]

Thus, his many articles indicate that over time, he became very visible to the music teachers reading the journal, especially when considered along with the other ways he received attention. He served as a member of the *MEJ* editorial board,[64] and on his death was honored with an obituary in *MEJ*.[65] At the time, any activity that might be construed as research was uncommon in music education. Thus, being identified as a scientific researcher set Seashore apart from the readers and from most contributors to *MSJ/MEJ*. It probably accorded him high status.

The music-related periodicals that published Seashore's work reached somewhat different but often overlapping audiences, which indicates that by appearing in all of these venues, his work had a wide reach in the musical world. For example, the *Musical Quarterly* is read by music scholars, musicians, and "discerning general readers."[66] *Etude* was designed for any musician, from beginner to professional, and the *Music Supervisors' Journal* was intended for school music teachers.

Seashore and Music Teaching Practices

Another sign of Seashore's entry into school music education was his appearance at the annual meeting of the Music Supervisors' National Conference in St. Louis in the spring of 1919.[67] Known today as the National Association for Music Education (NAfME) (and before that for a time as the Music Educators National Conference [MENC]), the Music Supervisors' National Conference was and remains the major professional organization of school music teachers; it publishes the *MSJ/MEJ*. In the early twentieth century, these conferences typically included observation tours of local school music classrooms, teaching demonstrations, music performances by local school groups and professional ensembles, mass concerts performed by the music teachers attending the conference, and lectures on topics ranging from practical methods of teaching music to music and morals. True to form, the 1919 meeting included these activities, but what made it different from its predecessors was the visibility of psychology and psychologists. Nearly one full day of the five-day event was devoted to presentations by and discussions of the work of psychologists, including Seashore. According to the preliminary program, Walter Van Dyke Bingham, a professor of psychology at the Carnegie Institute of Technology, was to have delivered a talk entitled "The Practical Possibilities of Applied Psychology as Exemplified in the Building of an Army."[68] This was an unusual topic for a music teachers' conference even as World War I came to a close. Bingham was the author of the 1910 book *Studies in Melody*, and in 1916, he had given a talk at the annual meeting of the Music Supervisors' National Conference on psychological aspects of teaching music.[69] As far as I can determine, the earlier talk was the first and only time prior to 1919 that a psychologist had presented at these meetings. Bingham also was a key figure in the army testing movement, and along with Charles Davenport, Edward Thorndike, and Clark Wissler, he was on the advisory committee for the study described in the book *Race Crossing in Jamaica*.[70] Bingham apparently sent someone to deliver the talk in his stead, the conference proceedings listing the speaker as Reuel H. Sylvester from the army's educational service.[71] Sylvester was a clinical psychologist with ties to Iowa; he received a degree from the University of Iowa in 1908 and by 1922 was employed by the Des Moines Health Center.[72] Sylvester spoke exclusively about applying psychology to army efforts—specifically, about Army intelligence testing—and did not say a word about music.[73]

After Sylvester's talk, much of the rest of the day belonged to Seashore, who demonstrated his tests of musical capacities using a class of schoolchildren, and then administered other portions of the battery to the conference attendees.[74] Next, he gave a lecture on procedures for identifying musical talent in public schools; conference programs state that this was to be followed by scholarly presentations related to the tests, one of them by his student Hazel Stanton, but the proceedings do not report on these presentations, if they were given.[75] Finally, there was a general discussion entitled "Discriminations Based on Differences of Music Capacity."[76]

Seashore and psychological thought had made small inroads into music education conferences and discourse prior to 1919, but the St. Louis program provides clear early evidence of a shift in thinking such that it had become reasonable to invite psychologists to a national meeting of music teachers.[77] What previously might have been considered as outrageous as a performance by trained seals had become not merely acceptable, but a major component. Knowing what came after and reading retrospectively, I view Seashore's presence at this conference as significant not only because it illustrates his growing visibility among music educators, but because it signals the direction of change in music education. It is also clear that this "new" thinking and these new thinkers bore some resemblances to the "old." For example, in his conference lecture, Seashore stated that music instills moral values; this belief was consistent with his larger views about morality and education, which informed his ostensibly scientifically neutral research in the area of experimental psychology.[78]

In 1916, Seashore also spoke at a meeting of the Music Teachers' National Association (MTNA), another major music teachers' organization. His topic was the use of the tonoscope in vocal training.[79] Today MTNA membership consists primarily of studio music teachers while NAfME membership consists of school music teachers, but in the early part of the twentieth century, this distinction was far less clear.[80]

Thus, as was the case with his publications, Seashore's conference appearances indicate that he was reaching a wide swath of individuals associated with music teaching, including music teachers of various stripes. Furthermore, what he promulgated was not merely the Seashore Tests, but perhaps more importantly, what Ian Hacking calls particular "styles of reasoning" or Thomas Popkewitz calls "systems of reasoning," which were bearing specific kinds of fruit at that time.[81]

Part of Seashore's reach into the ideas and practices that have shaped K–12 school music in the United States was his provision of ostensibly scientific evidence to support the assertion that musical talent is biologically inheritable, differentially bestowed, and immutable. Another part of that reach was the introduction of standardized tests of musical talent, and as we have seen, he often had direct access to music teachers. The Seashore Tests and others of a similar ilk were used in many US schools for much of the twentieth century. Especially early in my career, I met many individuals who remembered taking either the Seashore Tests or a test like it in their public school music classes. In 1947, James Mainwaring, a British music educator and fellow of the British Psychological Society, described the Seashore Tests as "still probably the best known and most widely used tests of their kind."[82] In the 1959 edition of their classic tome *Foundations and Principles of Music Education*, Charles Leonhard and Robert House discussed the debate surrounding standardized tests of music talent and spoke favorably of an instance of the use of the Seashore Tests: "The Rochester, New York, public schools have for the past twenty-five years used the *Seashore Measures of Musical Talent*, teachers' estimates of musical excellence, average grades, and other factors to identify pupils with musical talent. [Ruth C.] Larson believes that the program has resulted in a high level of performance achievement for gifted pupils and a saving in time and energy of pupils, teachers, and parents."[83]

In 1963, Frank W. Pinkerton published results of his survey of the use of music aptitude tests by "prominent music educators" in K–12 instrumental music programs.[84] Pinkerton stated that 62.5 percent of respondents were using a test of musical talent, with respondents reporting a variety of purposes for these tests, including screening and placement.[85] The Seashore Tests and "teacher-devised" tests were the most frequently used instruments, each having an equal number of responses.[86] In addition, the study's subjects were asked to rate the quality of fourteen standardized tests of musical aptitude; the Seashore Tests received the highest number of "excellent" and "good" ratings.[87] Pinkerton stated that among those not currently using such tests, "many declared their intention to begin a testing program, but had not yet determined the best means of procedure."[88] He closed by encouraging more music teachers to become familiar with standardized musical aptitude tests, calling for more opportunities for music teachers to become familiar with the psychology of musical talent, and asserting that although the tests provide valuable information, this information should be only one of several factors to consider when selecting students for participation.[89] The Seashore Tests were used in higher education, too. For example, for a period beginning in 1923, test scores were a criterion for admission to the Eastman School of Music.[90]

In 1969, fifty years after Seashore demonstrated the tests at the 1919 meeting in St. Louis, Paul Lehman published the observation that in recent years there had been a "sharp and persistent decline in interest" in measuring musical aptitude in the United States.[91] Lehman contrasted that decline with the flurry of interest that preceded it, his comment alluding both to widespread prior interest in music aptitude tests and to Seashore's role: "The reduced status of aptitude testing in music at present is particularly noteworthy because it stands in such marked contrast to the intense activity of earlier decades of this century, beginning with the publication of Carl Seashore's test battery in 1919."[92] Lehman maintained that there had been a recent decline both in standardized test creation and in *use*, although he admitted he did not have hard data to back up the latter observation.[93] He also said that publishers were claiming the opposite, that sales of tests actually were increasing; Lehman speculated that the increase may have be due to a number of factors, one being increased use of the tests for research rather than instructional purposes.[94] Lehman also made what has proven to be a startlingly prophetic observation about the future of standardized music testing:

> The decline in interest in aptitude testing I have reported has been accompanied recently by an increased interest in achievement testing. The net result is that there seems to be more interest in music testing now than ever before, but it is in achievement testing rather than in aptitude testing, and it is as concerned or more concerned with the evaluation of instructional programs than with the evaluation of the learning of individuals. I believe that this development will represent the major thrust in music testing within the next few years.[95]

Lehman was wrong on one count: the focus on norm-referenced standardized tests of musical achievement would last far longer than just a few years. It continues to the present, at least in the area of music teacher certification.

Seashore and Scholarly Inquiry in Music Education

Seashore and his work figure prominently in music education scholarly inquiry and have had a profound impact on the field. As the twentieth century progressed, a period when being both scientific and a researcher gained currency in music education, the nascent field of music education research, having neither an extensive research tradition nor many individuals who identified themselves as researchers, adopted as models experimental psychology generally and Seashore's work in particular. This adoption established a scholarly agenda that has lasted to the present. Specific types of research questions and particular processes for finding answers became not merely reasonable and acceptable, but the gold standard as Seashore-influenced schools of thought grew and flourished.

These were not the only models in music education research, but I maintain that their ascendency probably came at the expense of other ways of thinking, types of questions, and investigative processes. A brief perusal of the articles appearing in the *Journal of Research in Music Education* (*JRME*) during the first few decades after its inception in 1953 indicates that by that time, a mixed bag of scholarship—ranging from historical studies to reports on the development of new teaching methods—was being conducted. Many of these studies did not resemble Seashore's work and did not appear to be based on his ideas. Thus, it would be inaccurate to say that all music education scholars followed Seashore's lead. Nevertheless, a number of types of scholarly inquiry that were popular throughout the twentieth century in music education stemmed directly from Seashore and his work. The first is psychometrics, specifically, the development and implementation of standardized tests of musical talent or achievement. The Seashore Tests were used extensively by music education researchers and served as a model for subsequent generations of test creators. Critiques of the Seashore Tests' reliability and validity did not diminish psychometricians' enthusiasm for tests. Rather, it spurred other music psychometricians to develop what they hoped would be better tests. Thus, when Seashore's mousetrap was found wanting, the race was on to build a better one, but the value of mousetraps remained largely unquestioned, at least by the psychometricians. A number of music education researchers entered that race, producing successive generations of tests of musical talent and achievement. One participant was Edwin Gordon, who created tests of musical aptitude and musical achievement that are still sold and used today. Gordon claimed that Seashore "established the guidelines" for subsequent research on the nature and measurement of musical aptitude.[96] Indeed, the Seashore Tests have been used in some recent studies of the inheritability of musical ability, one example being Finnish research published in 2008.[97] Furthermore, media coverage of these recent studies tends to pop up on the internet.[98]

Another sign of Seashore's influence on scholarly inquiry in music education is the proliferation of auditory perceptual studies, and a third is the popularity of experimental methods. Finally, Seashore's development and use of instrumentation and his promotion of new technologies helped set the stage as successive generations of music education researchers tried out gadgets and technologies ranging from tachistoscopes for improving sight singing to X-rays for examining the tongue position of trumpet and clarinet players. One measure of the impact of Seashore's work is the presence of more than 100 *JRME* articles that use or refer to his work. This statistic is quite remarkable given that *JRME* did not exist until four years after Seashore's death. Furthermore, this number does not take into account the many articles that refer to subsequent research modeled after Seashore's.

Even some scholarship that does not seem to be directly related to Seashore's reflects the growing popularity of quantitative methods of analysis during the twentieth century, one example being the use of statistical procedures in surveys of music preferences. As interest in specific kinds of research grew in music education, courses on music psychometrics became central to graduate study at many institutions in the United States. Some institutions still offer such courses, and some of the courses still talk about Seashore. For example, a graduate course offered at the University of Arkansas, "Tests and Measurement in Music," promises to critically analyze existing music tests, and it lists the Seashore Tests among those to be examined.[99] Thus, critical or not, discussions of Seashore and of psychometrics generally still are in the news in graduate music education today.

Reception and Honors in Music Education

In summary, Seashore's work has been used, cited, and extensively discussed in music education, in published sources ranging from histories of music education to refereed articles in research journals. In addition, praise, recognition of his contributions to the field, and bestowed honors abound, beginning during his lifetime and continuing to the present; critique of him and his work, if present, typically focuses on the adequacy of his concept of musical ability or on the validity and reliability of the Seashore Tests.[100]

Seashore even was inducted into what is known today as the Music Educators Hall of Fame. In 1983, *MEJ* published a speech by Russell P. Getz, president of MENC (today's NAfME), in which he called for "a roll of honor that should be inscribed on the halls of MENC as well as in our hearts"; Getz named those who should appear, Seashore among them.[101] Shortly thereafter, MENC created the Music Education Hall of Fame, which "recognizes and honors those music educators who, by virtue of their contributions, are of such significant stature that they are considered to be among the most highly regarded professional leaders in American music education."[102] The first recipients were inducted in 1986, and Seashore was in that first group.

He also was featured as a member of the Music Education Hall of Fame in a lengthy retrospective on the first 150 years of school music, published in *MEJ* in 1988.[103]

One piece of evidence indicating he has achieved something akin to rock star status is the presence of an entry about him in the venerable *Grove Music Online*; the entry calls Seashore a pioneer.[104] It is highly unusual for anyone associated with music education, living or dead, to appear in this prestigious publication.

Accolades continue to the present. In 2006 and in conjunction with its 100th anniversary, the School of Music at the University of Iowa hosted the Seashore Symposium, which featured papers about him and his contributions (as well as others on musicality in general). The University of Iowa published proceedings from the symposium.[105] As is the case elsewhere, the symposium papers were largely laudatory, with critique again focusing largely on Seashore's conception of musical ability or on the tests.[106]

One way Seashore was honored posthumously was by the creation of the Carl E. Seashore Chair for Research in Music Education at Temple University. This chair was held by Edwin Gordon from 1979 until his retirement in 1997. Gordon developed the Musical Aptitude Test, a second-generation standardized test of musical ability, and he selected the name for the endowed chair.[107]

Contributions and Recognition in Other Domains

The Arts

Although Seashore is probably best known and praised among musicians for his contributions to music education, he was involved in other areas of music as well. He was a member of the American Musicological Society (AMS) and has been recognized for his pioneering work in quantitative studies in musicology and ethnomusicology.[108] In 1937, he ran for vice president of the AMS but lost to composer Howard Hanson of the Eastman School of Music.[109]

Fascinated by "musical anthropology," he researched and wrote about what he termed "primitive," "folk," and "Negro" music, and he even attempted to convince the Motion Picture Academy to undertake a project involving the use of "scientifically and artistically true" field-recorded music in films.[110]

He also is known for his contributions to aesthetics, including the measurement of emotion in music, and to studies of vibrato; furthermore, he was the codeveloper of the Meier-Seashore Art Judgment Test.[111] An obituary by Francis P. Robinson, which appeared in *Educational Forum*, said that Seashore was "internationally known as a leader in the scientific approach to aesthetics."[112] Kathryn Kucsan's 1995 doctoral dissertation focused on the approaches to aesthetics of two psychologists, Seashore and Vernon Lee.[113]

Education

One of the fields to which Seashore brought psychology was education, and in education, too, he has been called a pioneer.[114] As I discuss in greater depth in chapter 5, on the national stage, he was a champion of education reform—a promoter of the widespread use of tracking and sectioning by ability, of the development of special programs for students identified as gifted and talented, and of the use of norm-referenced standardized college examinations.

As dean of the Graduate College for thirty-three years, he had a significant impact on education at the University of Iowa.[115] An entry on Seashore that appears in *The Biographical Dictionary of Iowa* describes him as "the most important figure in the history of the University of Iowa, more than any president or collegiate dean."[116] The entry credits him with establishing one of the first graduate fine arts programs in the nation, and it is among the sources that praise him for his support of the arts.[117] A 1939 *Life* magazine article, replete with photographs, similarly credited Seashore for establishing the University of Iowa's innovative graduate program in fine arts, stating that unlike programs at institutions such as Yale, which emphasized history and theory, Iowa's program focused on studio art.[118] Seashore apparently broke the mold by allowing students to substitute portfolios of artistic work for graduate theses.[119] Grant Wood was among the program's early artists-in-residence, and the famous Writers' Workshop is among the program's continuing successes. An entire dissertation has been written on Seashore's contributions to fine arts at Iowa.[120] According to Leslie B. Sims, former dean of the Graduate College at the University of Iowa, Seashore was a visionary and pioneer, in part because he was an early proponent of interdisciplinary graduate programs; he adds, "As you can imagine, this idea of 'interdisciplinarity' was not readily embraced nor has it survived at Iowa, and probably not elsewhere."[121]

Thus, Seashore was widely known as an educator,[122] and the entry on him in *The Biographical Dictionary of Iowa* lists "educator" as the first descriptor and "scientist" as the second.[123] In education, as is the case elsewhere, his impact on the field is evident in the appearance of death notices in prominent venues.[124]

Speech Therapy, Hearing, and Reading

Seashore has been called a pioneer for his research on hearing and speech,[125] and his interest in this field may have stemmed from the studies of stuttering conducted by Scripture, under whom he studied at Yale. At the University of Iowa, he helped develop an exploratory program to study and correct stammering, which led to the establishment of a speech clinic and a speech pathology program there.[126] In 1944, he received national recognition from the American Speech Correction Association for his contributions to the field.[127] In a similar vein, at his suggestion, a reading clinic designed to study reading disabilities was established at Iowa.[128]

His Students as "Living Memorials"

Seashore's students and their scholarship have been listed among his praiseworthy contributions. For example, in a death notice appearing in the *Educational Forum*, Francis P. Robinson stated that Seashore left behind three living memorials, "his writing, his students and the institutions that he developed during his lifetime."[129] Sources indicate that with Seashore at the helm, the psychology program at the University of Iowa churned out a large number of advanced degrees in psychology. Between 1919 and 1928, Iowa conferred 45 doctorates in psychology, the third-largest number in the nation, and from 1929 to 1938 it conferred 120, the largest number.[130] Many of Seashore's students went on to establish illustrious careers. Among his many notable advisees was George D. Stoddard, who became a professor of psychology, dean of the graduate school, and director of the Iowa Child Welfare Research Station at the University of Iowa; president of the University of Illinois; and chancellor of New York University. Another notable advisee was Walter R. Miles, who became a psychology professor at Stanford and Yale, and president of the APA. Hazel Stanton became the first music psychologist at the Eastman School of Music and a professor of psychology at the University of Rochester. Jacob Kwalwasser became the chair of music education at the University of Iowa, professor of music education at Syracuse University, and codeveloper of the Kwalwasser-Dykema Music Tests.

A number of sources, including obituaries, described Seashore as a kind man, a humanitarian who cared deeply for people—students in particular.[131] One obituary claimed, "No student ever had a better friend."[132] Seashore's biographer and former student, Walter Miles, stated that when he was a graduate student, he lived across the street from the Seashores and sometimes babysat their children; he spoke glowingly of his fond memories of the Seashore family.[133]

Part of this "people legacy" are the many individuals who have followed in Seashore's footsteps and have used his research as an exemplar even though they were not his students. One of them was Edwin E. Gordon, who held the Carl E. Seashore Chair for Research in Music Education at Temple University; Gordon also taught at the University of Iowa, SUNY Buffalo, and the University of South Carolina. The Gordon Institute for Music Learning, which currently has six regional chapters, bears his name.[134]

Accolades and Praise Befitting a Hero

Thus, in general, Seashore had (and has) rock star status in a number of fields, as is reflected in the many honors and accolades bestowed on him. He was awarded seven honorary doctorates, including one from his alma mater, Yale University.[135] In 1939 a bronze bust of Seashore, donated by the Philosophical Club, was placed in Memorial Union at the University of Iowa, and in 1981, Iowa named a campus building after him.[136] When the building was slated for demolition in late 2017, an alumni publication lionized Seashore in an article about Seashore Hall's history and name.[137]

Sifting through honors heaped on Seashore, I found a few unusual ones, including a published poem, "Dean Carl Seashore," by Minnesota poet laureate Margarette Ball Dickson, which celebrates Seashore's dedication to promoting gifted students:

His was a new philosophy of life:

To help the student with the brilliant mind . . .
The skillful fingers, one whose brain was rife
With bridges to be built . . . with roads that wind
To unmapped regions . . . goals not yet achieved;
Inventions unperfected . . . other scope
For time and talent, hardly yet believed;
Goals visualized by men of flaming hope!
To give materials, the leisure . . . means
That genius may work out unhampered ends;
Like Medici of old, to lend the scenes
Where talent, fostered, ultimately bends
The hidden forces . . . gives that phase to art
That smolders, dreamlike, first, within the heart.[138]

Another unusual sprinkle of stardust is a 1935 photograph of Seashore and a handful of other distinguished psychologists posing with the famous child star Shirley Temple on the set of the film *Captain January*.[139]

Seashore's Critics

Although Seashore's reception in music education and elsewhere has been largely laudatory, the accolades and praise showered on him befitting a hero, he and his work did not escape critique, some published, some not, some from his contemporaries, and some from subsequent generations of scholars. A large cluster of criticism focuses on his concept of musical ability and on his tests of musical capacities, notably their validity and reliability.[140] Some of these critics were not opposed to musical talent testing per se but simply to Seashore's tests, and they developed tests of their own, which they claimed were better.[141] James Mursell was perhaps Seashore's most outspoken contemporaneous critic, and their debates were heated. Samuel Flueckiger described the fierce back and forth in his 1939 essay on trends in music education, published in the *Music Educators Journal*; Flueckiger appears to have been more sympathetic to the testing camp than to its critics, despite the fact that Mursell sat on the *MEJ* editorial board at the time:

> Those who believe in music tests without reservation were a bit shocked to read Dr. James L. Mursell's dogmatic statement against their value in the October-November, 1937, issue of the MUSIC EDUCATORS JOURNAL, but were comforted by the tactful and scholarly reply by Dr. Carl E. Seashore in December. The controversy raged on during the entire year, with various degrees of heat being displayed by most of the parties concerned, especially Dr. Jacob Kwalwasser. One fears that the methods employed by the protagonists of the music tests, as well as their antagonists, were in a small way reminiscent of P. T. Barnum or his modern counterpart, Grover Whalen. But it would be obviously unfair to condemn as unworthy the careful research which has been done in music and music education, including the various types of tests, by such institutions as the State University of Iowa, the Eastman School of Music, the Peabody Conservatory, and many others. Is it not possible that this handful of careful investigators may yet be the leaven that will eventually change our ideas about the entire content and procedure in music

> education, if not its basic philosophy? Or is it sportsmanlike for us to belittle the as yet tentative results of the tests and measurements movement unless we ourselves have found, after reasonable personal experiment, that the use of the various tests in our work does not produce better results?[142]

Seashore has had more recent critics. In 1969, Shinichi Suzuki criticized his assertions about musical ability and described the Seashore Tests as "outdated."[143] In 1991, Patricia Shehan Campbell pointed out Seashore's potentially negative impact on music education, stating that his views on the immutability of rhythmic capacity resulted in a reduction of rhythmic activities and movement in school music curricula.[144] In 2006, Estelle Jorgensen enumerated a number of limitations in Seashore's thought, including its grounding in the Western classical music tradition, its focus on mental constructs and not the body as a whole, and its absence of definitional rigor.[145] Perhaps the most disquieting statement about Seashore and his tests comes from an unlikely source, his staunch supporter Edwin Gordon. As part of her 1987 dissertation on the controversy surrounding musical aptitude tests and Seashore's testing research, Penelope Nichols-Rothe interviewed Gordon, who stated that Seashore had ordered the suppression of disconfirming—and potentially damning—evidence:

> "Now that was a case where he [Seashore] buried data. You see, that study of the Seashore test, the ten year longitudinal study [Eastman School of Music study conducted by Hazel Stanton], and it came up with zero predictability. And he had Stanton bury the data. Now that's the one thing Carl Seashore did that I'm aware of that tells me he wasn't a true scholar. But you see, at that time he was being so bugged by Mursell that he had to prove he was right. And I have a feeling had Mursell not been bugging him, I don't know what other words to use, not been disturbing him, I don't think Seashore would have done that, I think he did it out of desperation. But that ten year study is a fright. All the necessary information is buried and at Iowa that data does not exist. It was all gone out of the file cabinets, everything. It was almost like a purge in the Watergate. What a shame. Because that data would have been invaluable and when I went through the files there was nothing, the Stanton file was an empty folder, except for the written report, no raw data."[146]

Gordon did not indicate how he learned that Seashore had ordered Stanton to suppress data; after reading Nichols-Rothe, I phoned Gordon, and he again refused to reveal his sources. He carried the secret to his grave.

Some sources, mostly unpublished, report that Seashore lacked interpersonal skills in his role as an administrator, and treated colleagues and students poorly, women students in particular. Scholar Hamilton Cravens described Seashore as domineering, obstinate, autocratic, imperialistic, and imperious.[147] Gordon called him an egomaniac who did not entertain the possibility of being wrong.[148] A number of sources refer to strained relations between Seashore and his colleague Edwin Starbuck, a professor of philosophy; there is evidence that these tensions had deleterious effects on students.[149] For example, in a letter about his decision to leave the University of Iowa, a student of Starbuck's spoke frankly of what he called Seashore's "uncompromising meanness" toward Starbuck and its impact on the student's academic life: "I was not willing to any longer bear the brunt of the strife going on between you and Dean Seashore. I am very sorry that he has shown such an unappreciative and unethical attitude toward you personally simply because he did not two years ago land me in the department of psychology. Personally I feel that his attitude toward you is wholly immoral."[150]

In his dissertation on Seashore's views on graduate education, Lewis Lester Jones stated that Starbuck accused Seashore of stealing students, and Jones mentioned other issues: "The list of charges leveled against Seashore [by Starbuck] was formidable. Seashore was accused of antagonizing faculty, subverting the counseling process, intimidating students, and influencing them against their will to change career interests."[151] Significantly, Jones defended Seashore's actions, claiming that they were motivated by concern for students: "The Seashore-Starbuck controversy illustrated that the Dean was willing to risk charges of departmental interference, if he assumed that graduate students were receiving inadequate counseling from their mentors as well as doing poor research. His criticism of Starbuck probably emerged from an intense concern that Starbuck was doing poor psychology under the guise of philosophy."[152]

The accusation that Seashore scorned philosophers and the field of philosophy—that he tried to convince students to leave philosophy in favor of psychology—is common in sources pertaining to the Seashore/Starbuck conflict.[153] In a letter to Starbuck, Seashore defended himself against such allegations; he appeared to deny all charges and promised to be "impartial" in the future:

> Let me, therefore, assure you with all humility and realization of my own shortcomings, that in the future as in the past I shall do everything I can to maintain an impartial attitude as regards the relations between philosophy and psychology and between you and myself in whatever capacity you and I may continue in the University. So long as I am Dean I must scrutinize subjects and confer fearlessly with both students and professor, but if in this I do any injustice may you bring the case to my immediate attention for correction.[154]

Partiality toward psychology would not be surprising given that Seashore quickly moved in the direction of that fledgling field after having been admitted as a philosophy student at Yale.

His attitudes toward women were mentioned in a 1926 letter of complaint that Starbuck sent to University of Iowa president Walter A. Jessup;[155] at least three other recent sources address this topic as well.[156] For example, one of the appendices in the published proceedings of the 2006 symposium held in Seashore's honor at the University of Iowa includes personal reflections by Himie Voxman, a colleague of Seashore's at Iowa who later became the director of the School of Music there. Voxman spoke of Seashore's bias against women graduate students and of his authoritarian approach to colleagues and students.[157] Some of the harshest criticism of Seashore on any subject other than musical ability appeared in Jones's dissertation, which discussed at some length Seashore's sexist attitudes toward women;[158] yet, as in his treatment of the Seashore/Starbuck conflict, Jones painted Seashore in a favorable light, claiming that he was a man of his times and concluding, "To expect that Seashore would have possessed a more enlightened attitude toward women may be unrealistic."[159]

More evidence of concern about Seashore's treatment of some students appeared in a 1944 letter University of Iowa president Virgil M. Hancher sent to him asking him to comment on the allegation that Seashore had given poor, racially discriminatory advice to an African American graduate student, Alvin Rose. As I will discuss in chapter 5, the comments Seashore allegedly made were consistent with a published statement he made about African Americans and education.

What is noticeably absent in nearly all discussions of Seashore, whether or not they are critical, is mention of his participation in eugenics. It did not show up in his biographies, or in lists of his memberships, in dissertations focusing on him and his work, or even in his obituaries.[160] I turn next to that absent presence, and I begin by documenting his participation in eugenics activities.

Seashore's Involvement in Eugenics

Membership in Organizations

One indicator of participation in eugenics is membership in eugenics organizations, and the first of the eugenics-related organizations to which Seashore belonged was the Eugenics Research Association (ERA).[161] According to a history of the eugenics movement published in 1929 by the superintendent of the Eugenics Record Office (ERO), Harry H. Laughlin, the ERA was born at the ERO in Cold Spring Harbor, New York; it was "the immediate outgrowth of the series of conferences of field workers of the Eugenics Record Office that began in 1911 and that overlapped, for a few years, the meetings of the Eugenics Research Association."[162] The purpose of the ERA was to foster eugenics research, and Seashore was elected to the group in 1920 as an active member.[163] A 1921 article in *Eugenical News* explained that there were four classes of membership with different rights and membership fees—active, associate, supporting, and patron.[164] Active members had voting rights while other categories did not, and, significantly, Seashore belonged to the highest class.[165] At the time of his election, he was fifty-four years old and well established in his career. Seashore's age and career stage suggest that he did not necessarily need such membership to advance his career.

The second such organization was the Eugenics Society of the United States, later known as the American Eugenics Society (AES). AES was a product of the Second International Congress of Eugenics held at the American Museum of Natural History in New York in 1921.[166] While the ERA was designed to support eugenics research and discussion among researchers, the AES was to focus on popularizing eugenics and meeting political and educational goals.[167] Seashore was listed as a charter member of the AES in the April 1923 issue of *Eugenical News*.[168] Many members were overt and virulent racists, Nazi sympathizers, or both.[169] Historian Barry Mehler calls the AES the "key networking organization within the eugenics movement,"[170] stating that it was an active group that did not experience a membership decline until the early 1940s.[171] Mehler notes that philanthropists George Eastman and John D. Rockefeller Jr. were major contributors to the AES.[172]

The same issue of *Eugenical News* that mentioned Seashore's charter membership in the AES listed him as one of ninety-six members of the newly formed Advisory Council of the AES.[173] Mehler calls the Advisory Council a "highly select" and elite group, noting that membership was by invitation only.[174] Stating that the Advisory Council constituted the "core membership of the movement," he reports that the group consisted of the "most active and committed members."[175] He describes the constitution of the Council and notes that members came from a variety of backgrounds:

> They were prominent in all fields of endeavor including business, academia, and politics. The advisory council of the AES included wealthy bankers, financiers, and manufacturers. Among its politicians were senators, congressmen, and governors. Among its religious leaders were nationally and internationally known figures. Its membership included influential leaders of major philanthropic foundations. And among its professors were the elite of America's social scientists.[176]

Charles W. Eliot (one-time president of Harvard University), John H. Kellogg (the inventor of cornflakes and founder of the Race Betterment Foundation), Paul Popenoe, Lewis Terman, Edward L. Thorndike, and Clark Wissler (an anthropologist) were among the other members of the Advisory Council in 1923. As Mehler notes, many members of the Advisory Council held degrees from such elite schools as Harvard, Columbia, and Johns Hopkins.[177] Names of Advisory Council members appeared on AES letterhead, Seashore's among them.[178] Furthermore, the names of all Advisory Council members, including Seashore's, appeared at the beginning of what some have called the catechism of eugenics, Ellsworth Huntington's *Tomorrow's Children: The Goal of Eugenics*.[179] Seashore's name also appeared on the inside cover of every issue of the AES journal *Eugenics*. Mehler states that members of the Advisory Council were often asked to play an active role in the AES: "The AES Advisory Council was clearly not constituted to serve merely as an impressive letterhead. Members of the council were constantly being called upon to read and comment on society literature, join committees and attend meetings."[180] *Organized Eugenics*, a booklet published by the AES in 1931, spelled out the history and aims of eugenics and stated that advisory council membership shifted somewhat annually, "so that it represents persons who can give the attention needed and *who are in thorough sympathy with the eugenics movement.* Certain authoritative counsel is needed from time to time and the Council is consulted concerning matters of policy and any important projects [emphasis mine]."[181] The Advisory Council dissolved in 1935, a casualty of organizational restructuring,[182] but Seashore remained a member—an insider—to the end.

Conference Participation

Perhaps the most significant evidence of Seashore's attendance at eugenics conferences was his delivery of a paper, "Individual and Racial Inheritance of Musical Traits," at the Second International Congress of Eugenics (1921).[183] Laughlin called the congress one of the two high points in the history of eugenics activities in the United States.[184] Several scholars of eugenics have stated that speakers were carefully vetted in an attempt to keep out what organizers called "crackpots."[185] Seashore apparently passed muster, as did his student Hazel Stanton, who delivered a paper entitled "An Experimental Investigation of Musical Inheritance."[186] Bird T. Baldwin, Seashore's colleague and director of the Iowa Child Welfare Research Station, also spoke.[187] The papers given at the congress were published as a book that was organized by a committee of eugenics notables: Charles B. Davenport, Henry Fairfield Osborn, Clark Wissler, and Henry H. Laughlin; the preface claimed that work found in one section of the book represented "the results of some of the most advanced and best known investigators in genetics."[188] Seashore's paper appeared in that section.

In a discussion of the tenor of the congress, and specifically the views expressed on race, Mehler writes, "The [Ku Klux] Klan's views on race were similar, though less scientific, than the eugenicists."[189] He notes, however, that newspapers treated the two movements differently: "Although the Klan's position on racial issues did not differ significantly from that of the eugenicists, the newspaper treatment of the Klan is in marked contrast to the treatment of eugenics. The Klan schemes were a 'menace' and 'moral idiocy'. . . . Statements on race made by the leaders of the Eugenics Congress, on the other hand, were seen as 'scientific' and therefore not racist."[190]

Seashore's Appearance in Print Sources Sponsored by Eugenics Organizations

In addition to publishing a paper in the proceedings of what many consider to be one of the most important gatherings in the history of eugenics in the United States, Seashore was published or mentioned in other AES and ERA publications as well, including the two monthly journals, *Eugenical News* (published from 1916 until 1954, when it became *Eugenics Quarterly*) and *Eugenics* (published from 1928 to 1931). Sometimes these articles had been solicited. For example, in 1948, AES president Frederick Osborn gave an address, published in *Eugenical News*, that stated that mental fitness, not physical fitness, should be the concern of eugenicists:

> "I would not emphasize physical health as a direct objective of the eugenic effort. People of sound mind who lack physical characteristics worthy of survival are not as likely as others to have four, five, six or more children. Nor are people of sound mind likely to increase a serious hereditary defect, if their doctors are sufficiently trained to advise them.
>
> Physical factors will take care of themselves. People not capable of sound thinking should be reduced in number as rapidly as possible. That would take care of their physical characteristics at the same time.
>
> Our practical program of eugenics needs then to be concerned only with mental qualities."[191]

The address apparently met with harsh criticism from AES members, and Seashore was among the twenty active members whose opinion was sought. The article reporting on this address and its aftermath stated that all respondents agreed on the importance of mental factors and that all respondents who were scientists or physicians warned against neglecting physical factors.[192] Stating that all who disagreed with Osborn were scientists or physicians may have given the opposing view greater weight. As a member of the esteemed group called scientists, Seashore took issue with Osborn, arguing that the scope of eugenics should be *wider* than Osborn suggested: "'The mental factors should, of course, be emphasized; but the physical factors will not take care of themselves.'"[193] Notably, Seashore gave this opinion three years after the end of World War II and apparently did not see connections between events in Nazi Germany and the eugenics he was promoting at home. Much earlier, in 1929, *Eugenics* had published solicited views on eugenics from "nationally recognized leaders in academic and professional circles," and Seashore's response was among those that appeared; the article was entitled "In Praise of Eugenics."[194]

Eugenics journals also served as venues for disseminating information about Seashore and his research, the Seashore Tests of musical capacities, and multiple test-related music projects—proposed or underway—of interest to or sponsored by the eugenics societies.[195] For example, a 1928 article in *Eugenics* sang the praises of the Seashore Tests and underscored their eugenical value:

> A new activity for the Committee on Popular Education of the American Eugenics Society is now under discussion which it is believed will help to educate large numbers of people in the facts of heredity. This is the giving of Seashore Music Tests to children and their parents.

> Thousands of dollars are wasted each year on musical education of children who are incapable of profiting by it to any extent. At the same time there are large numbers of children with high innate musical ability who should be educated musically.
>
> The tests, in order to bring out the eugenics lesson, will have to be given to the whole family. . . . Present plans include enlisting the cooperation of leading music stores in principal cities, whose managers will sponsor the contests, advertize [*sic*] them and handle all details. From a preliminary survey it is apparent that school boards will also render assistance both in helping with the education and in the advertizement [*sic*] of the contests.[196]

The *Journal of Heredity* (originally the *American Breeders Magazine*), which was edited by eugenicist Paul Popenoe from 1913 to 1921, included similar references.[197]

Some of the projects discussed in these journals involved the Eugenics Record Office, where Seashore's student Hazel Stanton was conducting genealogical analyses of innate musical ability. In addition to reporting on Stanton's pedigree studies[198] and on her combining the traditional pedigree research method with the Seashore Tests,[199] the journals mentioned ERO studies and activities on which Seashore himself collaborated. For instance, a 1926 *Eugenical News* article provided a brief summary of Seashore's book *The Psychology of Musical Talent*[200] and then described a collaborative project underway at the ERO that appears to have been an early example of an education/business partnership: "With the collaboration of Professor Seashore and the Columbia Phonograph Company, who manufacture the disks for running the tests already made quantitative, the Eugenics Record Office has recently issued a new schedule for recording the family distribution of quantitatively measured factors of musical talent. The special instruction schedule is called the 'Family-Tree Folder' designed especially for . . . the Genetical Study of Musical Talent."[201]

Interested parties would receive copies of a family tree chart, which they were to complete; an instruction guide for administering the Seashore Tests; and one test sheet for each family member. These materials were free, but families had to pay for the phonograph and the six Columbia recordings of the tests. They were to send one copy of the test results to the ERO in Cold Spring Harbor and retain one copy for themselves.[202] The journals also included discussions of studies of race differences in innate musical ability that had been conducted using the Seashore Tests.[203]

Finally, Seashore was cited as an authority on the question of the inheritability of musical ability: "Learned investigators (Seashore, Stanton, Davenport, *et al.*) have shown that musical talents are family property, a capacity that readily passes from father to son, from generation to generation."[204] Notably, this statement about inheriting "family property" did not mention mothers or daughters.

Seashore's Overt Support of Eugenics

Another type of evidence is Seashore's overt support of eugenics in published and unpublished sources, specifically, instances in which he used the term. The earliest usage I located came in the 1911 article "The Consulting Psychologist," which appeared in *Popular Science Monthly*, a journal edited and published by eugenicist James McKeen Cattell.[205] A call for the use of consulting psychologists, whom Seashore described as scientific specialists, the article stated that these experts would be useful in four domains: mental pathology, education, technical arts, and eugenics.[206] Describing eugenics as an applied science and a promising field belonging to the future, he enumerated its goals: "The improvement of the race, direction in the choice and preparation for a vocation, social adjustment, the scientific reduction of crime, and the increase in the sources of human happiness."[207] Another early reference appeared in his 1914 book *Psychology in Daily Life*; in a section on mental health, Seashore discussed at length the need for eugenical planning.[208] He also spoke enthusiastically and optimistically of a triumvirate of "great movements" that would usher in a bright and carefully controlled future; eugenics was one of them:

> Here, then, are three great movements looking toward the increase of human efficiency; namely, preventive medicine, eugenics, and scientific management. More has been done in all of these in the last decade than in the century before. In the light of these facts the generation of to-day is living in a new world of possibilities and responsibilities. The present awakening of civic consciousness and conscience moves man to have regard not only for his own immediate personal well-being, both present and future, but also for that of his neighbor; and the whole world is now one neighborhood.
>
> Conserve your energies . . . by taking hold of the agencies of modern discovery in deliberate and far-sighted self-control.[209]

Echoing Francis Galton, he claimed that eugenics was concerned with more than merely being well born: "Eugenics is not only the science of being well-born, but also the science of well-being—not only of physical, but yet more significantly of mental well-being. With a common purpose preventive medicine affects the home, the school, and the civic organization, enlightens the individual and society in regard to private and public sanitation, and concentrates forces of economic, moral, and religious institutions in the common struggle for the one great goal—health."[210]

In an article appearing in the journal *Science* in 1941, the year the United States entered World War II, he described eugenics as "a happy term" and then spelled out subbranches of the field: "Within the area of eugenics we recognize various segments; such as individual eugenics and racial eugenics, and various areas pertaining to controlling factors; such as eugenic birth control, eugenic climate and eugenic legislation."[211] Much earlier, in his outline of proposed activities at the Iowa Child Welfare Research Station, he had spoken of eugenics' potential: "But modern eugenics is hopeful and aggressive, and is not satisfied with warding off evil; it bids us proclaim those conditions which will enhance the birthright of the child above the present normal level."[212]

He spoke positively about eugenics in his autobiography, saying that his family history is interesting from the perspective of eugenics, and claiming that Swedish primogeniture practices constitute a type of eugenics.[213] Consistent with eugenical practice, he also gave a short pedigree report on his wife and her family.[214]

Interestingly, in 1943, at the height of World War II, the *Journal of Higher Education* published an article by Seashore entitled "The Sunny Side of Graduate Work for the Duration"; in it, he clearly distanced himself and the Allied nations from Germany, portraying the allies as heroic defenders of civilization: "We are in this war not as criminals debauching the powers of science, but as defenders of civilization who must match weapons with the destroyers of civilization."[215] He appears to have seen no connection, however, between Nazi activities and eugenics in the United States.

The last reference to eugenics I located appeared in 1949, the year of Seashore's death, in an article published in the journal *Mental Hygiene*: "The term eugenics, meaning well born, is a well-established concept, denoting those aspects of all sciences and arts which have a bearing on improvement of the individual or the group through the medium of the germ cell."[216] This definition of eugenics is virtually identical to one he published a year earlier in *Educational Forum*.[217] As in a number of other instances, Seashore followed his definition with a discussion of its relationship to its companion, euthenics. These late references are notable because they appeared after World War II, at a time when many scholars were distancing themselves from eugenics, at least overtly.

"The Men I Have Known": The Company Seashore Kept

Reading eugenics literature from the first half of the twentieth century is a mind-boggling study in networking. It is true that eugenics was popular during this period; that said, tracing names and examining with whom eugenicists interacted reveals a complex and tight-knit skein or web of relationships. If we conceptualize eugenics as consisting, at least in part, of a dynamic skein of relationships among like-minded individuals, then another way to measure Seashore's involvement is to consider his place in this network.

Seashore knew people in a wide array of fields, and clearly not all of his relationships were with eugenicists. He was proud of the relationships he cultivated and even stated that it would have been a pleasure to write his autobiography from the standpoint of "the men I have known."[218] Some of these relationships resulted from his ground-level position when psychology as a field was forming in the United States, a position that prompted him to write, "There was a time when I had visited all the psychological laboratories in the world, was familiar with practically all existing psychological instruments and special methods . . . and had met practically all the then living psychologists of any consequence."[219] As I have already mentioned, he had many interests in addition to psychology and played a variety of roles in a host of other fields. Each of these roles enabled him to cultivate a somewhat different array of relationships.

When mapping his relationships, in some cases I found it difficult to decide who was or was not a eugenicist and what was or was not a eugenical influence. Nevertheless, the map of his relationships with known, avowed eugenicists reveals that he was deeply ensconced in the eugenics network and connected to a host of prominent figures in the movement. It is also clear that eugenicists offered each other many forms of assistance and support. One example is providing publishing venues; Seashore published a plethora of articles in the journals *School and Society*, *Science*, and *Popular Science Monthly*, all of which were owned and edited by eugenicist James McKeen Cattell.[220] Clearly, the existence of a network and Seashore's position as an *insider* assured him many kinds of help.

Every individual who formally affiliated with either the AES or the ERA was signing on to a deeply troubling platform grounded in racism. Many were overt White supremacists, Nazi sympathizers, or both. Mapping all of Seashore's relationships with eugenicists is beyond the scope of this study, and selecting which relationships to highlight was difficult. I decided to focus narrowly on a few representative examples of his interactions with individuals in the inner core of the eugenicist network and to provide only bare-bones information about these individuals, recognizing that other scholars have already published extensive research about these figures. This extant research helps to confirm the import and gravity of Seashore's more-than-passing interactions with these people.

My decision to focus only on Seashore's relationships with select core members may not do justice to the magnitude and influence of the eugenics network or to his position in it, however. Furthermore, it may occlude some of the complexities involved in determining what constitutes a eugenics relationship, who was or was not a eugenicist, and what does or does not constitute eugenical influence. For example, earlier in this chapter I reported that Walter Van Dyke Bingham and Seashore were among the first psychologists to speak at meetings of the Music Supervisors' National Conference. I found no evidence that Bingham was a member of a eugenics organization or subsequently has been identified as a eugenicist. That said, however, he was deeply involved with standardized army testing during World War I, which was a pet project of eugenicists. Furthermore, he was on the advisory committee for the study of race crossing in Jamaica conducted by eugenicists Charles Davenport and Morris Steggerda (see chapter 7). Thus, according to my criteria, Bingham was not formally a member of the eugenics network, but he was working on some of the same eugenically motivated testing and measurement projects that Seashore was.[221]

Recognizing that eugenicists—insiders in particular—took very good care of each other, I turn next to a few representative examples and consider the fruits of these relationships. These consequences assisted eugenicists and their careers, were consistent with eugenical values, and supported progress toward eugenical goals. One way ideas travel is through relationships. Thus, because Seashore "lived" in so many places intellectually and developed so many relationships in these various places, he helped foster the spread of eugenical ideas across disciplines.

Also, before discussing examples of Seashore's associations with specific eugenicists, I want to make a few general observations about the web of relationships that helped constitute eugenics. First, eugenicists had an imposing presence in a host of venues, including a number of organizations and activities that did not appear on the surface to be associated with eugenics. Mehler points out this presence, stating that five early presidents of the American Psychology Association were members of the AES Advisory Council and that a number of members of the Council were journal editors and prolific authors.[222] However, leadership in the APA, publishing books, and editing scholarly journals constitute only the tip of the influence iceberg; eugenicists were using their positional power in diverse contexts, often to effect eugenically informed policies and practices. In other words, noneugenics organizations were promoting eugenics-approved projects because eugenicists were involved in these organizations and promoting eugenics through them.

Fitting this pattern, Seashore's activities placed him in elite circles with individuals who were or would become famous, only some of whom were eugenicists. For example, he was in the select group that attended the now-famous by-invitation-only Clark University psychology conference held in September 1909, and he even chaired one of the sessions. G. Stanley Hall, a founder of the child study movement, eugenicist, and president of Clark, organized the event, which has become famous in part because it was the site of a series of lectures given by the then-little-known neurologist Sigmund Freud. These were the only lectures Freud gave in the Western Hemisphere and are credited with helping launch his career.[223] A photograph of those attending the Clark conference features forty-two White men, including not only Freud, Hall, and Seashore but Carl Jung, William James, Henry Goddard, E. B. Titchener, and Franz Boas.[224] Some of these individuals—Boas, for example—rejected eugenics. A host of others, however, belonged to and embraced eugenics organizations—or at the very least were sympathetic to the movement.

My second observation is that there was a familiar lineup—a core of eugenicists—whose names popped up repeatedly in diverse contexts. Furthermore, in addition to being part of a eugenics network, these core eugenicists, like Seashore, were members of and "worked" other networks as they promoted eugenically motivated policies and practices. For example, other scholars have pointed out that many eugenicists had connections to Ivy League institutions or to a handful of other prestigious colleges and universities.[225] Seashore is a prime example, having received his doctorate from Yale. In addition to perhaps indicating that the systems of reasoning promulgated at these institutions during this period were consonant with eugenics and that these institutions tended to attract individuals whose thinking was consonant with eugenics, this pattern may also document that eugenicists relied on other extant networks when promulgating their ideas, including networks that they had established as students or faculty members at these institutions. Being a member of the American Psychological Association and serving on the National Research Council are a few other examples of ostensibly "non-eugenics" networking opportunities that eugenicists capitalized on, including Seashore.

Third, because eugenicists came from a wide array of backgrounds and intellectual disciplines, belonging to formal eugenics organizations gave members like Seashore opportunities to forge relationships with people from a larger galaxy than psychology. Although many psychologists were eugenicists, many eugenicists hailed from other fields; for example, Charles Davenport was a biologist, Ellsworth Huntington a geographer, and Vernon Kellogg an entomologist. The eugenics galaxy was larger than the social sciences, the sciences, or even academe generally, however. People ranging from clergy members to stupendously wealthy philanthropists such as George Eastman affiliated with the movement and its organizations. Thus, Seashore's membership in the AES and the ERA widened his relationship sphere considerably. When attending an event such as the Second International Congress of Eugenics, he hobnobbed with prominent eugenicists from throughout the world, including such notables as Leonard Darwin, Georges Vacher de Lapouge, Jon Alfred Mjøen, Henry Fairfield Osborn, and Charles Davenport.

Fourth, in addition to being a close-knit group, eugenicists took very good care of each other in a multiplicity of ways. Seashore was no exception.

"My Dear Yerkes": Seashore's Relationship with Robert M. Yerkes and Friends

To illustrate the company he kept and the benefits derived, I begin with Seashore's interactions with Robert Mearns Yerkes (1876–1956), with whom he had a long-standing and cordial relationship. The evidence I present comes largely from correspondence that spans nearly forty years and is found in the Robert Mearns Yerkes Papers at Yale University.

Yerkes was a psychologist, primatologist, eugenicist, and professor at Harvard and Yale. Like Seashore, he was among the eugenicists who served as an early president of the American Psychological Association, he was elected to the National Academy of Sciences, and he had close ties to the Eugenics Record Office in Cold Spring Harbor, New York. Like Seashore, he was on the Advisory Council of the AES. For a time, he was an employee of the

National Research Council (NRC). From 1922 to 1924, he was chair of the NRC's Committee on Scientific Problems of Human Migration, and from 1921 to 1947, he chaired the NRC's Committee for Research in Problems of Sex.[226] Both of these committees were deeply involved in eugenics projects. As we have seen, Seashore also was involved in the NRC and served as a division chair from 1921 to 1922.

Yerkes is perhaps best known for his work in intelligence testing, notably the development of the Army Alpha and Beta intelligence tests. In addition, in 1939, he established a primate laboratory at Yale with funding from the Rockefeller Foundation; he also founded what came to be called the Yale Laboratories of Primate Biology in Orange Park, Florida. Known today as the Yerkes National Primate Research Center, it currently is affiliated with Emory University.[227]

Visits and Meetings

Correspondence indicates that over the course of many years, Seashore and Yerkes arranged to meet on a host of occasions in many locations and that they both attended many meetings of organizations as well.[228] For example, Seashore apparently visited Yerkes's labs at Yale and in Orange Park, Florida,[229] and Seashore entertained Yerkes in his home when Yerkes was in Iowa City to deliver a lecture.[230]

Furthermore, important things happened during at least some of these meetings. For instance, in 1917, at Yerkes's invitation, Seashore attended a meeting at Columbia University where the proposal to develop the Army Mental Tests was adopted.[231] Both Yerkes and Seashore attended the National Research Council's 1921 conference on sex research, which was organized by Earl Zinn with support from Yerkes. According to Wade Pickren, the conference was funded by the Bureau of Social Hygiene, which in turn was sponsored by John D. Rockefeller Jr. Participants discussed a number of eugenically informed possible studies of sex and recommended the formation of the NRC's Committee for Research on Problems of Sex, which Yerkes chaired from 1921 to 1947.[232]

Several pieces of correspondence indicate that in 1922, during the period when Seashore chaired the NRC's Division of Anthropology and Psychology and Yerkes was employed by the NRC, Yerkes visited the University of Iowa to determine whether it was a suitable location for an unnamed "institution." Seashore apparently considered Yerkes's visit so important that he informed University of Iowa president Walter A. Jessup of it and asked Jessup to meet with Yerkes.[233] The paper trail ended abruptly, suggesting that the institute never materialized, at least not at Iowa. Nevertheless, this cluster of correspondence confirms that powerful relationship networks were mobilized by eugenicists, who used face-to-face meetings to bring about the outcomes they sought.

Committees and Appointments

Correspondence indicates that one way Yerkes and Seashore supported each other was by appointing one another to powerful committees and important leadership positions. For example, in 1911, the year Seashore was elected president of the APA, he placed Yerkes on an APA committee focusing on teaching experiments; he also nominated, among others, Edward L. Thorndike and Guy M. Whipple—both eugenicists.[234] In turn, in an undated letter from circa 1916 or 1917 (in 1917 Yerkes was elected president of the APA), Yerkes appointed Seashore as chair of a subcommittee on "scales for mental measurement"; he promised that both Seashore and Yerkes, who also would sit on the committee, would be able to associate with "[Guy M.] Whipple, [Lewis] Terman, [Helen Thompson] Woolley, [Augusta Fox] Broner [*sic*], [Henry H.] Goddard, and [J. E. Wallace] Wallin."[235] In addition to being prominent psychologists, nearly all of those named in Yerkes's letter are eugenicists.[236]

Scholarly Consultation and Critique

Research was among the many matters on which Seashore and Yerkes consulted, specifically asking each other for critique and suggestions. For example, in 1916, Yerkes and Seashore corresponded about the development of intelligence tests. In the first of these letters, Seashore told Yerkes that he did not think it would be a good idea to attempt to standardize "the Binet tests." Rather, he recommended that a committee be formed to develop a similar test based on a point scale that Yerkes apparently had suggested.[237] Yerkes sent a lengthy response in which he proposed various age-based scales for children, and he discussed his own research, which involved developing a separate scale for adults. He proposed the abandonment of "all forms of the Binet Scale except some such as the Stanford Revision."[238] In February, Seashore wrote that Yerkes's previous letter was "extremely stimulating" and asked to publish it in the *Journal of Educational Psychology*.[239] Seashore was an editor of that journal at the time. In March 1916, he published Yerkes's letter, along with an open invitation for scholars to respond.[240] Serving as commentator, in three subsequent months he published a host of responses, the majority of which were from eugenicists.[241] Thus, in this case, consultation between Yerkes and Seashore resulted in published promulgation and promotion of Yerkes's ideas and work.

In different correspondence from the same year, Yerkes wrote again about the point-scale test of adult intelligence that he was developing and asked Seashore to "try out, perfect, and obtain norms for the scale" by administering 100 tests.[242] Seashore found a professor at Iowa who agreed to do this.[243]

Requests for feedback went in both directions, and in 1921 Seashore asked Yerkes to critique a rating scale he had developed, Seashore stating that he planned to use it in a NRC national project to determine "talent for research" among college students.[244] Yerkes complied.[245]

Consultation went beyond the topics of intelligence scales or talent ratings. For example, Seashore offered to help Yerkes with class experiments;[246] he asked him for feedback on a manuscript he was writing on euthenics, which Yerkes proffered;[247] and he sought Yerkes's counsel on the advisability of approaching the NRC with a plan to create a new academic status, "visiting professor," to be offered to select retired faculty interested in continuing to conduct research.[248] Yerkes strongly supported the retirement proposal.[249]

In one instance, Seashore even gave Yerkes career advice. In a 1916 letter, Yerkes reported that he had been offered a position at the University of Minnesota and had not decided whether to take it.[250] Seashore responded that he would be happy to have Yerkes as a neighbor but thought it would be unfortunate if accepting the offer would end Yerkes's dreams for a research station, dreams Yerkes apparently had shared with Seashore the previous winter.[251] Yerkes took the Minnesota position and held it in absentia for two years.

Promotion and Praise

Seashore's publication of Yerkes's letter in the *Journal of Educational Psychology* is but one example of the many ways that these men both publicly and privately promoted and praised each other's ideas and work.[252] In 1925 Seashore reported to Yerkes that he had "just read your book in one whiff"—*Almost Human*, which was published that year.[253] Yerkes thanked Seashore for his "delightful reaction" and stated that Seashore "sized up the book almost perfectly."[254] In 1942, Seashore sent Yerkes a copy of his new book *Pioneering in Psychology*, which mentioned Yerkes several times.[255] Yerkes responded with praise not only for the book but for Seashore: "I am full of memories of things which we did together and I am sorry that our ways did not enable us more often to fuse our pioneering efforts, thus achieving greater impetus. . . . You have done a great work at Iowa for your institution, state, and science, also for the common welfare, and in congratulating you on a life wonderfully spent both personally and professionally I give you also my warm thanks."[256] In other correspondence, Yerkes praised other publications by Seashore, including *The Junior College Movement*,[257] a discussion of academic business that appeared in *School and Society*,[258] the "Educational Decalogue,"[259] and *A Preview to College and Life*—which Yerkes called a masterpiece.[260] In 1947, Seashore's publisher sent Yerkes a copy of *In Search of Beauty in Music* and asked for a response that could be used to publicize the book.[261] Yerkes provided a complimentary statement.[262]

Seashore even attempted to protect and defend Yerkes when he thought another scholar had misused Yerkes's work. In a 1933 letter, he asked whether Yerkes had read H. M. Parshley's recent article in *Scientific American*, "Sexual Abstinence as a Biological Question." Alerting Yerkes to the fact that his research had been cited and calling the article raw, Seashore stated that, with Yerkes's permission, he would write a letter of concern to the journal's editor, whom he called a sensation monger.[263] Apparently without waiting for a response, Seashore fired off a heated letter to the editor; he identified himself as "one of the men who have been actively interested in the organization of sex research" and stated that Parshley's attitude was not the "attitude of science."[264] Claiming that Parshley "falls down completely," he enumerated flaws, arguing that Parshley cited "such excellent work as that of Yerkes, and then he makes the ridiculous leap of applying this to man, without taking into account that this is one respect in which man is higher than the lower animals."[265] He accused the journal of engaging in sensationalism, claimed the article would do "untold harm in this age of rebellion," and closed by opining that the article had done "almost irreparable injury" to morals and science.[266]

Parshley's article asserted that humans engage in essentially the same sexual behavior as other primates and that sexual repression, including sexual abstinence, is neither normal nor healthy.[267] In the meantime, Yerkes responded to Seashore, saying he had read Parshley's article and found nothing seriously objectionable about it.[268]

The correspondence surrounding Parshley's article demonstrates that Seashore supported and willingly defended his colleague and fellow eugenicist, Yerkes, even if the defense was neither wanted nor needed. In addition, Seashore clearly was upset by what Parshley wrote. It is true that Seashore was interested in the "organization of sex research"—as I discuss in chapter

4, some of his work on the National Research Council involved the organization, promotion, and (probably) regulation of the nascent field of sex research. However, the NRC's conception of appropriate sex research was heavily informed by eugenics, and it emphasized abstinence and careful mate choice. Thus, Parshley's promotion of "free love" was antithetical to the goals Seashore and other eugenicists on the NRC had in mind; Seashore's reference to "this age of rebellion" was laced with anxiety. Interestingly, however, Yerkes was not similarly incensed, even though he, too, was involved in the NRC's organization and regulation of sex research.

A final example of praise and promotion is Seashore's 1930 request for an autographed photo of Yerkes to be displayed with pictures of other "distinguished psychologists" at the dedication of the University of Iowa's new psychology laboratory.[269] These dedication ceremonies were held in conjunction with the annual meeting of the APA, which convened in Iowa City that year. Yerkes sent Seashore a photo and said he wanted to attend the meeting.[270]

Supporting the Careers and Career Advancement of Others in the Eugenics Network

Seashore and Yerkes also relied on their relationship to support and promote the careers of other colleagues, notably other eugenicists. For instance, Yerkes recommended eugenicist Bird T. Baldwin for the directorship of the Iowa Child Welfare Research Station.[271]

Handwritten correspondence from Seashore to University of Iowa president Walter A. Jessup indicates that in about 1920, Seashore tried to recruit Yerkes's collaborator Carl Campbell Brigham (1890–1943) for a position in psychiatry and psychology at the University of Iowa; Seashore stated, "I think we can get him."[272] Apparently, Iowa could not, but Seashore vigorously attempted to do so, opining, "I think he is the man that can put the psychological clinic on a strong basis for state service. [Bird T.] Baldwin can tell you about him."[273]

Brigham was a eugenicist and a member of the AES's Advisory Council.[274] Recipient of a PhD from Princeton and later a faculty member there, he worked with Yerkes on the development of the Army Mental Tests; he also is known for adapting the Army Alpha test for use as a college entrance exam, and for developing a similar test known today as the SAT.[275]

Brigham published the results of his work on the Army Mental Tests in the 1923 book *A Study of American Intelligence*, which includes a foreword by Yerkes. In the book, Brigham claimed that racial differences in intelligence exist, with Nordics demonstrating intellectual superiority.[276] He attributed the higher IQ scores of African Americans in the North in part to the presence of larger amounts of White blood.[277] In the acknowledgments, he stated that he relied heavily on *The Passing of the Great Race, or The Racial Basis of European History*, by Madison Grant. Grant, too, was a eugenicist and White supremacist.[278]

In 1930, Brigham published a formal retraction, stating that race-based comparisons in intelligence could not be made using extant tests, including his own, and he admitted that the study on which his 1923 book was based was groundless.[279] In the retraction, he rejected the use of a combined scale score, which he admitted is what he employed in his own study, and he added, "As this method was used by the writer in his earlier analysis of the army tests as applied to samples of foreign born in the draft, that study with its entire hypothetical superstructure of racial differences *collapses completely* [emphasis mine]."[280]

In his discussion of Brigham's retraction, Andrew Heinze pointed out that it came too late, the damage already having been done.[281] Edwin Black states that by the time Brigham changed his mind, the book had become a widely circulated "scientific standard."[282] Furthermore, it is somewhat unclear precisely what Brigham retracted and why. Despite the retraction, Brigham remained a member of the AES Advisory Council, his name appearing on the Advisory Council list in the January 1931 issue of *Eugenics*, the last issue published. Mehler states that Brigham served on the Council until 1935.[283]

Friendship

Many of the business letters between Seashore and Yerkes included personal news, indicating that they and their families were friends. For example, there were references to a car purchase, golfing, vacations, Seashore's forthcoming retirement, and health issues.[284] There often were greetings to, inquiries about, and reports on spouses, children, and, later on, grandchildren.[285] For example, in 1945, Yerkes wrote that his son David was back from the war; he sent good wishes to Roberta and the Seashore children and grandchildren, and he said he wished the families lived closer.[286]

The salutations often read "My Dear Yerkes" and "My Dear Seashore,"[287] but it was not until 1944, thirty-four years after the date of the first correspondence in the collection, that they decided to call each other by their first names. Yerkes asked whether it would be acceptable for them to do this, and Seashore quickly replied that he would be delighted, noting that their "habits" had been established before using first names became commonplace.[288] Seashore added that he wished the two could engage in the Swedish tradition of *duskol* (which I assume is a friendship toast involving a shot of aquavit or some other alcoholic beverage) and said, "From now on between you and me it shall be first names with all the warmth of friendship that goes with that."[289]

Letters continued after Seashore's second retirement, and by 1947, some of them contained no business. There are two chatty Christmas letters from 1947 and 1948 filled with Seashore family news, the later one mentioning that Carl had suffered a slight stroke.[290] The final piece of correspondence is a heartbreaking letter Seashore sent to friends describing the last days of Roberta's life and her death on August 17, 1949.[291] A hand-written note in the letter's margin stated that Yerkes sent condolences.[292] The letter also indicated that Seashore had sold his home in Iowa City and moved in with his son in Lewiston, Idaho; Seashore mentioned plans to go to Florida in December.[293] However, on October 16, 1949, less than two months after Roberta's death, he died at his son's home. The Yerkes papers include a copy of Seashore's obituary on which Yerkes wrote "1949."[294] Seashore and Yerkes were friends to the end.

The many indicators of friendship point to the depth of the relationship between Yerkes and Seashore. If, indeed, we are judged by the company we keep, however, then it is significant that Seashore kept company with an array of staunch eugenicists, some of whom were not merely colleagues but also personal friends.

All Roads Lead to Charles Davenport and the Eugenics Record Office

Seashore also kept company with Harvard-educated biologist Charles Benedict Davenport (1866–1944), a key figure in the American eugenics movement. Active in the newly founded American Breeders Association and interested in human heredity, in 1898 Davenport became the director of the Biological Laboratory at Cold Spring Harbor, New York. Heavily influenced by the work of Francis Galton and Karl Pearson, he negotiated with the Carnegie Institution of Washington, DC, for funding to establish a second research institute at Cold Spring Harbor;[295] thus, in 1904, the Station for Experimental Evolution was born with Davenport serving as director.[296]

Next, Davenport approached philanthropist Mary Harriman, widow of railroad tycoon E. H. Harriman, for additional funding, which he used in

1910 to establish another unit at the Cold Spring Harbor compound, the Eugenics Record Office (ERO).[297] Harriman served on the AES Advisory Council until her death in 1934.[298] In time, the Carnegie Institution provided some funding for the ERO, as did John D. Rockefeller and John H. Kellogg.[299]

The ERO has been described as the "epicenter of the American eugenics movement."[300] For example, the Eugenics Research Association (ERA) was an outgrowth of a 1913 meeting held at the ERO, and it held its annual meetings there.[301] Davenport steered the ERA and also served on the board of directors of the AES.[302] When the ERO opened in 1910, Davenport chose Princeton University alumnus and Nazi sympathizer Harry Laughlin to be its superintendent, a position Laughlin held until it closed in 1939. Laughlin was a staunch supporter of compulsory sterilization legislation and testified before a committee of the US Congress in support of immigration restriction.

It is clear that Seashore knew Davenport, was familiar with and supported his work, and had a variety of contacts with him over many years. Among the contacts is correspondence from January 1919, in which Seashore asked Davenport for advice on how Seashore's student Hazel Stanton might conduct a quantitative research study into the inheritance of musical talent.[303] Stanton was a eugenicist who completed her master's degree with Seashore in 1918 and a doctorate with him in 1921. The study Seashore discussed in the January 1919 letter set out to measure six musical capacities in students in the Des Moines public schools, and Seashore asked for a prompt response from Davenport, indicating that the research was scheduled to begin in ten days.[304] Three months later, Davenport replied, apologizing for the fact that Seashore's letter had been misplaced, and characterizing the proposed work as "of the greatest possible importance."[305] Davenport stated that the ERO was studying musical families, but not quantitatively, and said he would be happy to cooperate with Seashore on the study. He invited Stanton to come to Cold Spring Harbor during the summer to examine the records on musical inheritance stored there. He also suggested that Stanton might look for a correlation between musical and mathematical capacity.[306] Seashore responded promptly, introducing Stanton to Davenport more formally and attesting to her seriousness and capability as a researcher. Seashore indicated that Stanton would come to Cold Spring Harbor in the summer to discuss the resources available at the ERO, and he stated that she needed funding. He also said he wanted to visit the ERO during his next trip east.[307] Davenport indicated he was willing to appoint Stanton as an "investigator" at the ERO; he stated that the ERO had data on about 100 musical families, he advised Stanton to personally interview families, he said the ERO might have field-travel funding for Stanton but nothing more, and he warmly welcomed Seashore to the ERO.[308] A number of letters followed that discussed Stanton's work and the details of her visit to the ERO, Seashore stating that he hoped the project would be an undertaking on "a fairly large scale."[309] Davenport gave Seashore and Stanton advice about how the study should be conducted,[310] and Stanton apparently began her work at the ERO in January 1920.[311] In April 1920, Seashore wrote to Davenport asking whether the ERO could fund Stanton for another year or two and describing an alternate plan if the ERO could not: Seashore would appeal to the NRC for money.[312] Davenport replied that the ERO had already allotted $1,500 (about $19,000 in 2019 dollars) to Stanton; he indicated that no additional funding was available for 1920 and that funding for future years was highly unlikely; he urged Seashore to tap the NRC.[313] By mid-April, Seashore apparently had decided that the NRC would not be a good source of future funding, so Stanton was to continue her research until the ERO money ran out.[314] As I will discuss a bit later, by 1921 Stanton had landed a job at the newly formed Eastman School of Music.

In the summer of 1921, *Eugenical News* published abstracts of nine research presentations given at the ninth annual meeting of the Eugenics Research Association, which was chaired by Davenport. One of these abstracts, which appears to have been written by Davenport himself, stated that he had discussed Stanton's field investigations at the meeting; it indicated that Stanton had used the Seashore Tests to measure the musical capacities of eighty-five family members and then reported in classic Mendelian form on how many children were musical in the following conditions: if both parents were musical, if one was musical and the other not, and if no parents were musical. Davenport claimed that the Seashore Test scores cannot be altered by environmental factors and thus reflect biologically inheritable capacities; he described Stanton's method as interesting.[315] Correspondence between Davenport and Seashore about Stanton continued in 1922, several letters indicating that the ERO ordered 650 copies of a publication by Stanton that appeared in *Psychological Monographs*, presumably the article "The Inheritance of Specific Musical Capacities."[316] In the monograph's acknowledgments, Stanton mentioned both Seashore and Davenport, stating that Davenport was "personally instrumental in effecting this study." She added, "Their constructive suggestions and sustained interest throughout the study were most helpful."[317]

Thus, this constellation of correspondence illustrates that eugenicists capitalized on their relationships with other eugenicists to support each other's students and research agendas and to promote each other's work. In this case, the student given assistance was also a eugenicist, and the support included money, scholarly advice, and publicity—the dissemination of research results.

The interactions between Seashore and Davenport apparently included both written correspondence and face-to face meetings. For example, early correspondence confirms that Seashore visited the ERO in October 1919;[318] a letter from a decade later in which Davenport requested that Seashore attend a Cold Spring Harbor meeting of the AES Advisory Council is evidence that invitations to meet and actual meetings continued.[319]

Some of these interactions involved consultation and support. For example, one letter indicated that the two men discussed a conference that Seashore was proposing on the inheritance of musical talent.[320] In another letter, Seashore asked Davenport for advice about the eugenics professorship and possible eugenics projects at the Iowa Child Welfare Research Station;[321] Davenport proffered his suggestions.[322] As late as 1942, Seashore turned to Davenport for information, in this case for details about the origin of the term "eugenics."[323] Finally, another important cluster of correspondence between Seashore and Davenport occurred between 1926 and 1929, and involved the research that culminated in the book *Race Crossing in Jamaica*. I will discuss this research at some length in chapter 7; suffice it to say here that the Jamaica project involved not only Davenport and Seashore but also Edward Thorndike, Clark Wissler, Walter Van Dyke Bingham, and Morris Steggerda—familiar figures in the eugenics world.[324]

Henry H. Goddard and the Vineland Training School

Another example of the company Seashore kept is his long-standing relationship with psychologist and eugenicist Henry H. Goddard (1866–1957). Goddard was a student of G. Stanley Hall's at Clark University, the author of the 1912 book *The Kallikak Family: A Study in the Heredity of Feeble-Mindedness*, and the research director at the Vineland Training School in Vineland, NJ, where early studies of cognitive disability were conducted. He is credited with coining the term "moron," which Seashore adopted.[325] He brought the Binet-Simon intelligence tests to the United States,[326] he was a member of the Advisory Council of the American Eugenics Society,[327] and he collaborated with Charles Davenport (among many other eugenicists).[328] Described by Leila Zenderland as an old friend of Goddard's, Seashore reportedly supported Goddard and his work in 1942 during a period when *The Kallikak Family* was being heavily criticized; Zenderland stated that earlier, in 1940, the book had been pronounced scientifically dead.[329] In turn, in 1943, Goddard favorably reviewed Seashore's book *Pioneering in Psychology*.[330]

Furthermore, in an article appearing in *School and Society* in 1949, Seashore paid tribute to Goddard, citing his key role in the development of his own (often-repeated) educational philosophy: "'Keep each individual busy at his highest normal level of successful achievement that he may be happy, useful, and good.'"[331] Seashore said that about forty years earlier (c. 1908 or 1909), he had made a week-long observational visit to Vineland, which had transformed his thinking.[332] Seashore explained, "Goddard's theory was this: Examine each individual and find out what remnant capacities he may have; make a job analysis of all the things in which these children can help; then assign each child to do a job in which he can show competence and gain selfrespect [*sic*] as a successful individual."[333] He also described the long-term widespread impact of what he observed:

> On my return I reported to the Governor, elaborating this key to the treatment of the feeble minded. The head of our institution for the feeble minded, Dr. Mobridge, immediately recognized the significance of the policy and put it into operation in his institution. But even more significantly, this principle had widespread reverberations which are felt throughout the state to this day, in realization of its profound social and educational significance in care for the dependent, criminal, and otherwise socially, educationally, and economically maladjusted individuals.[334]

Walter Miles, Seashore's biographer, claimed that the visit to Vineland occurred as Seashore "was considering the opportunity and need for a psychological clinic at Iowa."[335] Seashore was among those who founded the Iowa clinic in 1908.

The length and nature of Seashore's relationship with Goddard also are evident in a series of four published discussions of intelligence testing that Seashore helped moderate, which appeared in the *Journal of Educational Psychology* beginning in March 1916.[336] Seashore was a coeditor of the journal at the time (and had been since its inception in 1910), and he stated that he had received and published both solicited and unsolicited correspondence on the topic.[337] In April, he published excerpts of what he described as a personal letter from Goddard, in which Goddard discussed his own use of the Binet test with the feeble-minded.[338] In May, he published Goddard's lengthy discussion of those portions of a Cleveland school survey pertaining to persons with cognitive disabilities—a condition that was called "feeble-mindedness" at the time. Goddard stated that most of the report, which advocated segregation and institutionalization of persons deemed "socially incompetent," was excellent; his primary criticism was his disagreement with the survey author's assertion that the Binet test is not in itself sufficient for identifying "the defectives."[339]

Thus, Goddard and Seashore had a long-standing, cordial relationship. They mutually supported and promulgated each other's work and views; among the benefits Seashore gained from this relationship were ideas that shaped his educational philosophy, as well as a model of how to put that philosophy into practice. Black states that "Goddard eventually abandoned the eugenic creed entirely, at least publicly."[340] I found no evidence that Seashore did likewise.

Vernon Kellogg and the National Research Council

Another of the eugenicists with whom Seashore affiliated was Vernon Lyman Kellogg (1867–1937), an entomology professor at Stanford University who studied insect genetics. He also was one of the founding organizers of the National Research Council (NRC). Some call the NRC the "working arm" of the United States National Academies, which today also include the National Academy of Sciences, the National Academy of Engineering, and the National Academy of Medicine.[341] In 1919, Kellogg became the first permanent secretary of the NRC, a post he held until 1931. Like Seashore, he was a eugenicist who served on the AES Advisory Council.[342]

In his autobiography, Seashore claimed that he, too, was instrumental in the "organization and early development of the National Research Council and was made Chairman of the Division of Anthropology and Psychology in the third year."[343] He served as chair from 1921 to 1922, assuming that post after previously having served as vice-chair.[344] Cravens stated that during this period, Seashore also served as chair of the division's Committee on Child Welfare.[345]

During his time as division chair, Seashore developed and launched the Gifted Student Project, an endeavor illustrating both his relationship with Kellogg and the benefits he derived from it. In his autobiography, he reported that the project received sponsorship and financial support from the NRC, provided by Kellogg: "The Division of Educational Relations under the leadership of Professor Vernon Kellogg joined the Division of Anthropology and Psychology in sponsoring this project and secured funds for its conduct."[346] Seashore said that the purpose of the project was to establish "working relationships between the National Research Council and the colleges and universities of the country, in particular in the interest of helping students who should look forward to a learned career."[347]

For five years of the six-year project, Seashore traveled to colleges and universities throughout the United States championing special learning opportunities for gifted students.[348] He mentioned that he visited more than 140 colleges and universities,[349] and he sent his 1927 progress report to none other than Kellogg.[350]

In 1925, Kellogg sent supportive correspondence to Iowa president Walter A. Jessup describing an upcoming honors conference to be held at the University of Iowa and sponsored by the NRC.[351] Kellogg reported that as an expert in the field of gifted education, Seashore would be a paper respondent.[352] Kellogg and Seashore also corresponded with each other about the conference.[353] Thus, by collaborating with eugenicist Kellogg, who was in a powerful position at the NRC, Seashore received the support he needed to disseminate his ideas widely and to implement a project for gifted students that by all accounts was consistent with eugenical goals.

Another example of this support appeared in correspondence from the same year between Kellogg and University of Iowa president Jessup indicating that the NRC committee chaired by Kellogg was responsible for distributing thousands of copies of a pamphlet Seashore had penned:

> For two or three years the Division of Educational Relations of the National Research Council has sent out each spring several thousand copies of the enclosed "Open Letter to College Seniors" to colleges and universities for distribution to upper classmen. Expressions of appreciation of this pamphlet which have been returned have prompted us to make the pamphlet available again this year. It was originally prepared by Dean Seashore for the purpose of stimulating serious-minded students in the University of Iowa to take definite steps to make the most of their capabilities.
>
> If you should wish to distribute this "Open Letter" this spring to upper classmen in your institution we shall be glad to send you as many of these pamphlets as you think you can profitably use.[354]

The NRC's commitment to eugenics was clear during this period and took many forms. For example, according to Barry Mehler, in 1922, Yerkes and Davenport created the Committee on Scientific Problems of Human Migration, which was under the auspices of the National Research Council's

Division of Anthropology and Psychology. Mehler states, "The Committee believed that it was 'urgent' to study the biological consequences of racial intermixture."[355]

"We're in the Money": George Eastman and the Eastman Study

George Eastman (1854–1932) was another eugenicist who assisted Seashore and his projects. Founder of the Eastman Kodak Company, in 1921 he established the Eastman School of Music at the University of Rochester. In addition, he used some of his considerable wealth to help fund the American Eugenics Society.[356] Seashore reported that when he was looking for a site to study the Seashore Tests, the newly formed Eastman School of Music expressed interest and asked him to be in charge of the experiment; Seashore sent his personal assistant and doctoral student Hazel Stanton to head up the study in his stead.[357] Stanton, a eugenicist who by this time had worked at the ERO conducting studies on the inheritance of musical ability using the Seashore Tests[358] and had delivered a paper at the Second International Congress of Eugenics,[359] was appointed as Eastman's music psychologist in 1921.

Eugenicists publicized these events. For example, in 1922, *Eugenical News* stated that Stanton was organizing a research department in music psychology at the Eastman School.[360] From time to time, *Eugenical News* also reported and discussed results of the various studies that Stanton published on musical ability.[361]

Seashore stated that Stanton's project at the Eastman School, which he said lasted more than ten years, was supported in multiple ways—including financing—by George Eastman; in 1935, he wrote, "Mr. George Eastman sponsored the project, authorized it, and took a deep personal interest in its furtherance up to the very last days of his life."[362] Miles stated that the Seashore Tests were used as predictive measures at Eastman, and "the results proved to be so useful to the administration and faculty that the examination was made a regular part of the entrance requirements for the school."[363] Seashore also said that results of the Stanton experiments became a basis for admission to Eastman.[364]

Seashore and Eastman spoke or corresponded with one another about the project, Seashore reporting in his biography that Eastman claimed the tests had saved the school large sums of money and that Eastman appealed to Seashore to find other uses for the tests—for what Eastman calls a "positive procedure"—to stand along with the negative procedure, which presumably consisted of denying some students admission to the school; Seashore quoted a statement of Eastman's:

> "You have saved us vast sums of money and undoubtedly you have prevented much human suffering by the introduction of this procedure. But that is all negative. Can you not inaugurate a positive procedure?" My answer was, of course, "Yes," and as a result experimental units are now operating in certain public school systems where a psychologist is employed for the sole purpose of discovering and motivating those children who are musically talented. This is a positive procedure and, in the spread of measurement which now prevails in the public school systems, it is destined to play a very large rôle in the future.[365]

This passage, in addition to documenting connections between Seashore and Eastman, speaks the language of eugenics by claiming that the measures taken eliminated human suffering, by relying on cost-saving and efficiency as rationales for action, and by promoting both positive and negative measures (that is, promotion and elimination).

Eastman was so pleased with the results of the Stanton project at the Eastman School that in 1927 he rewarded Seashore with research fellowships to be used at the University of Iowa. In a letter to Seashore, he offered details:

> I am so well satisfied with the results that the Eastman School of Music has been getting from the "Seashore Tests" in the selection and grading of students, and have acquired such confidence in your methods, that I am willing to adopt the suggestion which came to me through Dr. Hanson that I establish three Research Fellowships in the University of Iowa to work on the development of improved methods in teaching the fundamentals of music; the Fellowships to be $800.00, $1,200.00 and $1,600.00 per year, beginning next June, for one year.[366]

In 2019 dollars, the total value of the fellowships given by Eastman is about $52,500.

Thus, Seashore's relationship with eugenicist Eastman gave him a venue to conduct research and multiple forms of support, including money. It helped launch the career of one of Seashore's doctoral students, also a eugenicist, who conducted research consistent with eugenical goals. It even resulted in a gift of fellowship support that would fund the kinds of research Seashore was undertaking, research that also was consistent with eugenical goals.

Finally, in April 1921, Seashore corresponded with University of Iowa president Walter Jessup on NRC letterhead about a rather vague study of measurements of music and speech that Seashore was proposing, which he wanted to conduct at Iowa.[367] In this letter, he claimed that he had a possible source of funding in mind, an unnamed "certain party in New York." The research proposal asked for $27,000 over a period of three years, which in 2019 dollars would be more than $383,000.[368] He also stated that he hoped his division of the NRC would approve the project and help secure funding.[369] I was unable to identify that unnamed party, but it may have been Eastman or even Davenport at the ERO.

International Connections

As I stated earlier, the web of eugenicists with whom Seashore kept company was international in scope. One person whose work Seashore praised was the prominent Norwegian eugenicist Jon Alfred Mjøen (1860–1939), founder of the Vinderin Biological Laboratory in Oslo.[370] Influenced by the German Nazi eugenicist Alfred Ploetz, Mjøen was a leader in promoting race hygiene in Norway; an article appearing in *Eugenics Review* in 1935 claimed that Mjøen's cousin was responsible for introducing sterilization laws there.[371] Mjøen vehemently opposed race crossing,[372] Edwin Black reporting that Mjøen claimed it was responsible for the spread of tuberculosis in Norway.[373] Mjøen also authored the article "The Masculine Education of Women and Its Dangers," which I will discuss in chapter 4.[374] According to *Eugenics Review*, Mjøen's research interests included the effects of race crossing and the inheritance of intellectual capacity, notably musical capacity.[375] The article elaborated on the latter interest:

> Dr. Mjøen selected music as the chief subject of his psychological research, the first task being conceived as the isolation of basic faculties. . . . A thousand families or groups of relatives covering two to four generations have now been investigated from the Winderen [*sic*] Laboratory, running to more than ten thousand individuals. The work has demonstrated the course of each particular faculty measured, so that the study does not merely demonstrate inheritance of musical ability in general, but the type of inheritance for each of this considerable number of factorial capacities.[376]

Seashore clearly shared Mjøen's research interests, and in at least two published sources, he praised Mjøen's work, as well as that of Mjøen's son

Fridtjof, a biologist and actor. For a period in the 1920s, Fridtjof Mjøen conducted research at Vinderin that focused on the inheritance of musical talent. In his 1938 book *Psychology of Music*, Seashore reviewed research literature on race differences in musical talent and referred to studies conducted by both Mjøens.[377] Later, Seashore mentioned what he called Mjøen's "notable contributions to studies in race heredity in various European countries."[378] In a 1940 article on the inheritability of musicality, Seashore spoke positively of work being done at the Vinderin Laboratory without specifically mentioning the Mjøens; in the same source, he also stated that in the United States, confidential records about musical families were housed at the ERO in Cold Spring Harbor.[379]

Just as Seashore cited and discussed Mjøen's work, Mjøen returned the favor by citing and discussing Seashore's research, Stanton's research, and the Seashore Tests.[380] Mjøen's son Fridtjof similarly discussed Seashore and Stanton.[381]

Like Seashore, Mjøen presented a paper at the Second International Congress of Eugenics, which was entitled "Harmonic and Disharmonic Racecrossings."[382] In his opening address of welcome to the congress, Henry Fairfield Osborn praised Mjøen for his leadership, specifically mentioning his contributions to increasing appreciation of the value of the Nordic race and his role in sounding the alarm that the race "must not be too severely depleted by emigration."[383] It was Mjøen who proposed the formation of the American Eugenics Society at that historic congress.[384] Given that both Seashore and Mjøen attended the congress, it is possible that they met, but I did not find concrete evidence that this happened.

Thus, Seashore's home was a tight-knit network of eugenicists who took care of each other and of each other's friends and students. Seashore and other eugenicists engaged in many of the networking activities promoted today as effective means of advancing a professional career. I am not suggesting that networking is inherently wrong; rather, I am pointing out the productivity of networking in this particular case—the productivity of inclusion. Despite its disciplinary and geographical breadth, the network of relationships created by eugenicists also excluded, however, and these exclusions resulted in insularity. Networking produced a community of like-minded individuals who celebrated each other and their shared ideas while summarily dismissing detractors and critique. Convinced of the rightness of a particular system of reasoning, eugenicists apparently engaged with detractors only to ridicule them or reject them as wrong.

Breaks in the Silence

As I stated earlier, I scoured extant discussions of Seashore and concluded that in addition to being largely laudatory, they *almost* never mentioned, let alone critiqued, his involvement in eugenics. This was true whether the sources were written by his contemporaries or by subsequent scholars, and this was the case despite the fact that at least some of his contemporaries, including his main biographer and former student, Walter Miles, were aware of his involvement. The Miles biography included a list of Seashore's publications, one of which is the published paper Seashore delivered at the Second International Congress of Eugenics.[385] Nevertheless, Miles did not mention Seashore's memberships in the ERA, AES, or the AES Advisory Council. Lewis Lester Jones mentioned Seashore's debt to Goddard but did not say a word that would link Goddard or Seashore to eugenics.[386]

The silence is especially thick in music education, and until recently, the few notable breaks have come from outside of the field. The first appeared in 1926 when social psychologist J. B. Eggen, an outspoken critic of eugenics, published the essay "The Fallacy of Eugenics"; he argued that eugenical thinking is based on the mistaken assumption that acquired characteristics are inherited. Eggen cited Seashore's work on musical ability as an example of such erroneous thinking.[387] In 1988, Barry Mehler broke many silences with his groundbreaking dissertation, "A History of the American Eugenics Society, 1921–1940." In a discussion of prominent psychologists who were members of the AES, Mehler talked briefly about Seashore, noting that he was one of no fewer than five members of the AES Advisory Council who also served as presidents of the American Psychological Association.[388] He stated that Seashore was one of the tremendously influential AES psychologists who authored a host of publications and edited many important journals.[389] He also mentioned the close association between Seashore and Charles Davenport, which included collaboration on a research project.[390] In a 1984 article on the Iowa Child Welfare Research Station that Seashore helped establish, Harry L. Minton briefly mentioned eugenics but distanced Seashore from it by arguing, erroneously, that Seashore was an environmentalist.[391] In a later discussion of the station, published in 2006, author Alice Boardman Smuts made a similar argument;[392] as I will discuss in chapter 4, these authors' distancing of Seashore from eugenics is not supported by evidence. Seashore's name appeared in 2005 on an online list of eugenicists published by EugenicsWatch.[393] Finally, as I stated in chapter 1, three recent scholarly works have made some inroads into this silence.[394] In chapter 9, I will reflect on this silence.

As I have demonstrated in this chapter, Seashore's involvement in eugenics is documented through organizational membership, participation in activities, explicit references to the term, and his network of relationships. However, his writings themselves provide the strongest evidence of his ways of thinking, whether or not he explicitly used the term "eugenics." His writings help shed light on why he acted as he did—why he was deeply involved in these organizations and their activities.

Knowing that Seashore was deeply involved in eugenics changed how I read his work; this knowledge attuned me to subtle clues and cues that I might otherwise have missed. Like one of those reversible-figure optical illusions, in which, for example, what at first appears to be a goblet can also be seen as two faces looking at each other, his writings suddenly revealed another face, and I was able to see for the first time what had been hidden in plain sight. It is to Seashore's writings, his ways of thinking, and the actions that stemmed from them, that I turn in the next chapters.

Four

The "Charm of an Educated Woman"

Women, Education, Sexuality, and Eugenics

As dean of the Graduate School at the University of Iowa for thirty-three years, Carl Seashore had ample opportunity to advise students. By all accounts, he freely dispensed advice—some of which eventually was published—and some of the published advice was directed at girls and women. I begin this chapter by summarizing Seashore's statements about and to women and girls, focusing in particular on his views on education in relation to marriage, fertility, and career. Next, I review dominant eugenics discourse and practice concerning these subjects, underscoring their grounding in eugenicists' fears of race suicide. Third, I map out the not-coincidental resemblances between Seashore's views and dominant eugenics discourse. I examine his position on various negative and positive eugenics policies and practices, and, recognizing that there was some diversity of opinion among eugenicists, I demonstrate that his views aligned closely with dominant, hard-line voices. I concur with previous scholarship that argues that Seashore's views on women were sexist, and in addition, I claim that they also were informed by dominant eugenical beliefs about race, specifically fear of race suicide. Bringing eugenics into a picture that appears on the surface to be almost exclusively about gender makes explicit what might otherwise remain hidden: how Seashore's views on women and girls were grounded in and supported racism, even though he said little or nothing about race.

To most people living in the United States during the early twentieth century, regardless of whether they were eugenicists, the ostensibly biologically determined two-sex model was a received truth. A related common belief was that each sex exhibits distinct behaviors or states of mind, which were often described as "natural." Questioning the unquestionable is not easy, and the most difficult concepts to challenge may be those that have gained widespread acceptance as being commonsensical, "natural," or scientifically factual. As I read retrospectively, I noticed the absence of challenges to these received truths about sex, and I concluded that this absence, combined with frequent *repetition* of received sex truths, played powerful roles in perpetuating this construct. Furthermore, even though I consider "woman," "girl," and "sex" to be social constructs rather than unassailable biological facts, I found it easy as a reader to be lulled into accepting them as Seashore and most others saw them. Thus, one of my challenges was to resist this tendency.

Although I focus primarily on sex/gender in this chapter, I aim to address the topic intersectionally. The texts themselves provided evidence of the limitations of focusing exclusively on sex/gender and the need for an intersectional approach that addresses race and other elements as well. For example, because the two-sex model was so prevalent, I was surprised to find a section in a popular eugenics sex education textbook that seemed to question the unquestionable by asking, "Is There a Third Sex?"[1] Perhaps more surprising was the answer: there is. According to the textbook, the third sex is homosexual. Thus, to the author of this 1933 textbook, sex and sexuality were entangled, and in my analysis, I attend to a number of such intersectional entanglements.

Women, Higher Education, and Marriage

Consistent with his position as a professor and dean, in nearly all extant sources Seashore's discussions of women and education focused on higher education. He supported schooling for girls and women, including higher education, but the level of support depended on both the kind of higher education under discussion and the purposes of that education. He believed that at least some women should go to college to earn two- or four-year degrees. A champion of creating a wide variety of post–high school educational opportunities, including junior colleges and training schools, he mapped out a hierarchy of higher education institutions, categorizing and ranking types of institutions according to their goals and target populations. Significantly, he categorically approved of women attending junior colleges and training schools—the institutions on the lowest rung of this institutional ladder.[2]

His support for women undertaking any form of post–high school study was qualified by his understanding of the purposes of educating women. To him, a woman's ultimate career goals ought to be marriage and motherhood, with all education plans developed and adjusted accordingly. For example, he praised women who possess musical skill, claiming that it makes them more attractive as wives as long as they don't pursue music as an all-consuming career: "A woman skilled in music is, as a rule, especially admired and sought in marriage; and marriage, as a career in itself, then invites music as an avocation and not as a fierce, all-demanding, time-consuming goal of composition."[3] He also believed that trouble lies ahead when all education roads for women do not lead to the altar.

He freely gave students advice on marriage, women in particular. For example, his book on musical aesthetics included a chapter, "Why No Great Women Composers?" that broached the topic of marriage. He asserted that for women, marriage is "a career in itself."[4] In an unpublished manuscript he stated it was "'the most universal, the most laudable, and the most desirable career for a normal woman.'"[5] Elsewhere, he claimed that women would probably not compete with men for jobs because "the normal woman tends to marry and thereby take on a full-time job" as wife and mother.[6] In these statements and elsewhere, his use of the term "normal," a word frequently employed by psychologists and eugenicists, to describe women who set marriage and family as their ultimate life goals, helped draw the boundaries of acceptable behavior, marking women who did not have these priorities and goals as abnormal and pathological. Seashore's chapter on women composers also stated that bearing children will "add to normal development of a woman" and claimed that although "married women may not have produced great compositions . . . they have produced great composers."[7] Thus, being a composer's mother, in Seashore's estimation, was every bit as worthwhile as being a composer, his statement serving as further evidence that he viewed breeding and brooding as a woman's most important functions.

The idea that men and women have different roles and spheres, with the home being the appropriate sphere for women, also was evident in a speech Seashore gave to high school students at Iowa's thirteenth annual Brain Derby, held in June 1941. He opened the speech by congratulating students for being Iowa's brightest and best, and then he issued a call to duty, "Your Country Calls You." Delivered shortly before the United States entered World War II, the speech spoke of patriotic duties and the group's need to exhibit intellectual leadership. He told the boys that they might be called on to fight for their country; he told the girls that rather than making bundles for Britain, their patriotic duty would be to keep the home fires burning.[8] Bundles for Britain was a humanitarian effort that provided nonmilitary supplies to Great Britain, including hand-knit sweaters. Thus, Seashore was telling the girls that the best thing they could do to support the war effort while the boys were off fighting was to stay home and take care of their homes and families.

Some of Seashore's most telling remarks on women, education, and marriage appeared in a 1940 book chapter, "The Aesthetics of Marriage," which he coauthored with his wife, Roberta. Filled with advice ostensibly to be read by men and women alike, the bulk of the Seashores' chapter is for or about women; marriage was thus positioned as a women's topic, a positioning supported by the fact that Seashore's wife wrote most of the chapter. As Carl stated in the introduction, when he was too busy to write an invited lecture on marriage, he asked his wife whether she would do it—if he would deliver it; he claimed that she knew more about the topic than he did.[9] Even though the bulk of the ten-page chapter was written by Roberta—with Carl contributing only the two introductory paragraphs and a two-page conclusion—Carl was listed as first author. Even if he viewed marriage as a topic to which women are specially attuned, he claimed top billing. He clearly agreed with everything Roberta said: "I have read this lecture to this notable class for three years now and have always given credit for the authorship with the statement that, while it in no sense represents co-operative writing, it does represent shared experiences. I wish to say that the reaction of students to this lecture has convinced me that professors' wives should do more of the writing of lectures for their husbands who hold the platform."[10] Notably, wives were to write their professorial husbands' lectures—not become professors themselves.

Roberta's advice directed at men tended to focus on the desirable attributes of a good wife. For example, she told a story about a medieval knight who was forced to choose between his three wives, one who was wealthy, one who bore his children, and a third who "brought him beauty and entertainment." The knight chose the third wife, a decision Roberta considered wise only because the knight already had children; Roberta added, "The supreme reason for marriage is children."[11]

Her advice for women quickly turned to education and career in relation to marriage and children. Roberta quoted Arthur Morgan, a former president of Antioch College, who spoke of the value of a college education for a particular woman—a homemaker—who thanked her college degree for helping her prepare for her career as a wife, mother, and community leader. According to Roberta, a college education enabled this homemaker to "make her marriage a beautiful experience."[12] In other words, for women, a college education elevated homemaking to an art, a beautiful aesthetic experience.

Roberta also discussed women and careers, stating that combining marriage and career may be possible for a few extraordinary women, but for most women, marriage and children should be the only career, and the noblest; too often, she opined, a woman's attempt to combine career and marriage comes at the price of personal happiness and marital harmony:

> I doubt if there is a woman alive today who has not wished that she might be happily married, but of a hundred women, more than half also wish that they may have a successful career. What kind of career? Oh, writing, the stage, the arts, a profession, business, teaching, or what have you? Well, I would suggest marriage itself as a career, exacting in its demands upon a woman as a wife, a mother, a citizen interested in improving the environment of her children, a friend and gracious hostess to all who enter her home. Solomon has said that her price is above rubies, and I believe that happiness and inner fulfillment come to her more often than to a woman who tries to combine marriage and a career. I know, however, that it is possible for a woman to tackle two full-sized jobs if she has twice the ordinary physical and emotional vigor and balance.[13]

Roberta enumerated the many supposed "hazards" to a marriage that a woman's career creates, arguing that it limits the number of children born, contributes to the neglect of children and husband, and fosters a sense of inferiority in the husband. She stated that if a woman has a career, it should be an avocation so that it does not come before her family.[14] She added, "Fine children are a greater satisfaction and asset both to the parents and to the state than a hundred mediocre career products forgotten in a month and gone with the wind."[15] Carl chimed in at the end with an anecdote about women, marriage, and graduate study that similarly positioned marriage as a more honorable goal for a woman than an advanced degree or a career outside the home.[16] Nowhere, not in this article or elsewhere, did issues of conflict between marriage, education, and career appear in Seashore's advice to men. The only related advice he gave to men was to choose a mate wisely, which he advised women and men alike to do.

Seashore's support for specific kinds of post–high school educational experiences for women also is evident in his 1927 *School and Society* article on junior colleges. Notably, *School and Society* was founded and (during this period) edited by eugenicist James McKeen Cattell. Seashore described training schools as ideal institutions for teaching women to be fit mothers and better homemakers. He recommended the revitalization of two-year normal schools to educate elementary school teachers (most of whom presumably would be women)[17] and the creation of two-year home economics institutes for girls:

> A course in the arts of home-keeping, not for the preparation of teachers or specialists, but purely a home training in the school in which vital interests, such as child welfare, heredity and euthenics, will play an important rôle so that a girl who wants a general education for home life will get out of the training in that course a more effective education for her purpose than is ordinarily gotten out of the four-year course in which there is no objective. In addition to the specific training in the home arts it will cultivate for her a love for home life, a feeling for culture and an interest in reading and travel.[18]

In his book on the junior college movement, he supported a junior college education for women from farming communities:

> In the community as a whole [an imagined agricultural community in the Midwest] there are as many women as men who are intelligent and willing leaders of the community and the home. And their responsibilities are more than fully equal to the responsibilities of the men for the rearing of families, the conducting of an efficient and attractive home, and leadership in social, educational, and health-generating activities of the farm community. How many of these could have profited by a small amount of higher education especially adapted to their needs?[19]

As important as Seashore may have considered them to be for women, however, junior colleges were low on his hierarchy of post–high school educational opportunities. Thus, although according to Seashore, homemaking was important women's work, it was not as important as the knowledge taught at more prestigious institutions. He did not recommend creating training institutes to make men better fathers.

"Is There Danger of Becoming a Neurotic Old Maid?" The Perils of Graduate Study

Seashore generally supported an undergraduate education for *some* women, but he took a dimmer view of women undertaking graduate study. Some evidence of this comes from people who knew and worked with him. For example, in a series of personal reflections published in 2006, his colleague, Himie Voxman, a former director of the School of Music at the University of Iowa, mentioned Seashore's bias against graduate study for women.[20] Bessie Rasmus Peterson, a former student of Seashore's, was interviewed by Lewis Lester Jones for a 1978 doctoral dissertation; Peterson stated, "'Seashore did not believe in graduate education for women,'" adding, "'He was not opposed to women doing graduate work generally, but he considered it a waste of time if the women would eventually get married. . . . He did not block women from enrolling in the graduate college. However, he was more reluctant to offer fellowship money to women than to men. He had nothing personal against women but thought they might not employ the training gained in graduate study.'"[21]

The strongest evidence of Seashore's views comes from Seashore himself, and to better understand his at-best-lukewarm support of women attending graduate school, it is important to consider his views on the purposes and status of graduate study in general.

If training institutes and junior colleges were at the bottom of Seashore's hierarchy of institutions of higher education, graduate schools were at the top. For example, according to his published speech "Graduate Study: An Address Delivered to the Students in the Colleges of Iowa in 1909," graduate work prepares students for "high places," and for greatness—for a career as a professor, clergyman, attorney, statesman, banker, pharmacist, physician, or researcher.[22] He stated that thanks to educational progress, graduate study is required for a host of professions, including some that previously did not require advanced degrees, and he methodically described why it is required for each.[23] His comments indicate that he viewed the professions, the institutions that prepare students for the professions, and the students enrolled at these institutions as representing the best of the best. However, referring to a pyramid of human achievement, he warned that all cannot be at the top,[24] which raises the question of whom he imagined could or should be there. In every case in this speech, his discussions of preparation for the professions referred exclusively to men. Many of these discussions were followed by remarks directed at women. For example, after a section on the need for high school teachers to hold a graduate degree, Seashore stated, "The girl who expects to marry the high school teacher has to wait five years longer than her mother did, and probably needs those five years to prepare herself for her social position."[25] After a section on preparing to become a professor, Seashore again addressed women: "The girl who is preparing to be a professor's wife must have the virtue of constancy if she has to wait faithfully all these years; but boys, do not worry; she will wait, because, to fill her position in the home, she needs a fairly corresponding time of preparation."[26] After a section on preparing for the ministry, Seashore added, "And his wife must be his complement in learning."[27] Following a section on preparing for a career in medicine, he talked about the rigorous preparation required of doctors, including clinical work in foreign countries, and then opined, "It is hard for the girl at home to wait while he goes through college, and through the medical school . . . but her patience will be repaid. And if she is to be a mate to such a man she must keep busy every minute of the time that she is waiting."[28]

Seashore most explicitly spelled out his views on women and graduate study in the book chapter "The Aesthetics of Marriage," published in 1940, and in "An Open Letter: Addressed to Women in Graduate Schools," which was published in the *Journal of Higher Education* in 1942. The latter article includes excerpts from and slight revisions of materials from the 1940 book chapter. In "An Open Letter: Addressed to Women," Seashore claimed that as dean of the Graduate School at the University of Iowa, he had the opportunity to counsel thousands of women students, and he stated that this article presented his convictions, which were based on his advising.[29]

The article offered some support for women attending graduate school; for example, it opened with an optimistic progress trope—praise for the increase during his lifetime in the number of women graduate students.[30] Seashore continued the progress theme later in the article, claiming that at that point nearly every profession was open to women. He asserted that graduate schools were admitting women on an equal basis with men and had the same goals and objectives for all.[31] He stated that if a woman pursues graduate study, she should by all means engage in research or other forms of original scholarship, arguing that this constitutes the most important reason for attending graduate school.[32] Finally, he closed by celebrating the new opportunities open to women in learned fields.[33]

Despite these sunny remarks, however, the article is not supportive of women overall; his advice is once again colored by his views on what women's roles in the world ought to be—specifically, that all roads should lead to marriage and having children. His advice is filled with warnings, caveats, and cautions. He included a list of questions women often ask about graduate study, many of which could rightly be asked by any graduate student; one was, "What is to be my real objective or goal in this study?"[34] Other questions alluded to issues that apparently needn't similarly trouble men, including career prospects. Some questions are based on a different imagined relationship for women between education, career, and marriage than that imagined for men; they referred to what were portrayed as the negative, abnormal or pathological outcomes for women of pursuing graduate study: "What shall be my attitude toward marriage? Is there danger of becoming a neurotic old maid? What is the effect of intensive study on physical health? . . . Does graduate training make a woman mannish?"[35] Even the article's closing celebratory remarks included cautions, talking about the "great responsibility" women have to plan carefully and to seriously apply themselves to their studies when presented with the new opportunities open to them.[36]

In "An Open Letter: Addressed to Women," Seashore divided women into three categories according to their reasons for undertaking graduate study, and he bestowed or withheld approval accordingly. In the first group, he placed women who have a clear and "practical" professional, semiprofessional, or technical job in mind. Women who want certification to teach high school fall into that category, and he approved of these women and their goals.[37]

The second group consisted of women who seek marriage to a man in a learned career and who are pursuing graduate study to find and keep pace with such a husband—to be a "fit helpmate" for him.[38] Seashore stated, for example, that a woman who is planning to marry a physician "needs time and opportunities to prepare herself" for that role; he added that later her graduate study could be used avocationally.[39] Seashore approved of these women and their goals.

He did not similarly praise women in the third category, "distinctly career-minded women" who seek a learned career "whether married or not."[40] Seashore noted, "It is these women who confront the most serious problems of orientation and need the most helpful guidance."[41] In "The Aesthetics of Marriage," he similarly described the "career woman" as a problem—the biggest concern he faced as a dean: "When I was Dean of the Graduate College, the problem which caused me the greatest concern for twenty-five years was the career woman as she actually is when psychologized and psychoanalyzed."[42]

One of the perils of undertaking graduate study, Seashore claimed, is the possibility that a woman will become an old maid—potentially a neurotic one:

> The calamity of becoming an old maid is often overlooked. The real and wise intention of most normal women undertaking graduate work is to prepare for being happily married to a scholarly and cultured

> man. Indeed, this is the purpose most often achieved in graduate residence, which has often been spoken of as a match factory. But it would be utterly foolish for a girl to substitute the profession of this objective for that of a career in her announcements from the house tops.
>
> Preparation for a career is often the best way of reaching other goals in that it gives a woman a sense of independence. If necessary she can pursue her technical work before marriage, and in case of adverse circumstances she will have something to fall back upon. But in my judgment the chief reason for favoring the career attitude is that the type of occupation chosen for a woman can be of as high cultural value for the higher life of a woman as general training can be when pursued without some such objective.[43]

Seashore used his wife, Roberta, whom he noted had done graduate work in classics and philosophy, as an example of how a woman should use graduate study; he quoted at length the same statements about marriage and career that had appeared earlier in "The Aesthetics of Marriage."[44] He said that Roberta had been asked in a survey from a "national woman's organization" what she had achieved in her career, and she had replied, "'I have reared four sons.'"[45] Thus, Roberta epitomized the type of woman graduate student whom Seashore elsewhere called the queen of the hearth.[46]

As I stated earlier, according to Seashore, if a woman undertakes graduate study, it must be "practical," and his definition of practicality was narrow, typically focusing on a woman's future role as wife and mother. For example, he related a few discussions he had had with women about the advisability of their graduate school plans. He described one such advisee as "a fine normal girl" who had been elected to Phi Beta Kappa and was considering an advanced degree in mathematics. Seashore asked her why she wanted the degree and she replied that she wanted to teach. When she admitted that she only planned to teach for two or three years, Seashore advised her to select a more practical subject, arguing that mathematics would probably not improve her home or social environment.[47]

In another instance, a woman doctoral student approached him to talk about her career after completing her degree. He advised her not to think about that, stating he figured she would be getting married soon anyway. She went away angry. As proof of the accuracy of his hunch and the wisdom of his advice, he reported that she married within six weeks of commencement and six years later had shown no interest in a career in her chosen field. He said that her doctoral study was "a superior preparation for the life she is now leading in her place in society"; presumably, that place was wife and mother.[48]

In a third case, Seashore asked a woman who was considering whether to pursue a doctorate to make a list of the pros and cons of such a move. After doing so, she apparently decided against doctoral study, her primary reason being that if she pursued a doctorate, she had an "obligation to put into practice the technical training obtained; that if she did not take up a learned career the University might count her a loss."[49] Seashore praised this woman's use of such a balance sheet and supported her decision. Of course this "obligation," if it exists, should hold for all students, but apparently it was not an issue that needed to be broached with male students; it was simply assumed that they would put their training into practice and that marriage and family would not impede their ability to do so.

The message that women who give up their careers to marry are ultimately the happiest is underscored in a story that Seashore told in "The Aesthetics of Marriage" about a woman who had received a doctorate, become a psychology instructor, advanced in her career, and kept a young man waiting for marriage for seventeen years. Seashore reported that the woman finally agreed to give up her career and marry her fiancé, adding, "About a year after that, she wrote me a very interesting analysis of the move, the gist of which was expressed in these words: 'Even the happiest and most successful teaching is a poor substitute for a happy marriage.'"[50]

Seashore's section on marriage in his chapter "Why No Great Women Composers?" also veered onto the subject of doctoral study:

> In the graduate school I have observed that when a woman of marked achievement and fine personality is invested with the doctor's hood, there is a young man around the corner: we hear the wedding march, love's goal is reached, and the promising Ph.D. settles down and gets fat. We find no fault with that; but to the career-minded woman, it is often a tragedy. Yet it need not be and should offer no true alibi. The bearing of one or more children should add to normal development of a woman, and marriage under favorable circumstances occasionally brings to the wife more freedom for self-expression in achievement than the husband—the breadwinner—enjoys.[51]

Although in some cases he claimed that doctoral study is not wasted when a woman stays home and raises children, elsewhere he talked about the expense institutions incur when educating graduate students[52] and underscored the difficulties women with advanced degrees encounter when seeking jobs in the professions. For example, in "An Open Letter: Addressed to Women," Seashore reworked a statement that first appeared in "The Aesthetics of Marriage" about the costs and rewards of giving women graduate students stipends, stating that as the graduate dean, he favored distributing stipends "without discrimination on the basis of sex."[53] He then discussed a survey of students who had completed graduate degrees at the University of Iowa and had been out at least five years, reporting that most jobs had gone to men; he claimed that although the "career woman" might find such a trend distressing, he, the educator, did not:

> During the fifteen years thus surveyed, there were more than forty men who had achieved marked distinction by becoming leaders in their professions, filling chairs of presidents, deans, directors, and heads of divisions, and leaders in other types of learned careers. Yet from the same period, covering an approximately equal number of stipend holders, the highest academic achievement of any woman was that of assistant professor. From the point of view of the career woman, this seemed almost unbelievable and distressing; but to the educator it was not necessarily so, because the great majority of women had found themselves in avenues of life in which the investment of the university had born rich fruit.[54]

Dismissing the distress of women facing the glass ceiling, he did not elaborate on what other avenues he had in mind. "The Aesthetics of Marriage" specifically referred to the difficulties women with graduate degrees encountered when seeking positions in the professorate. He mentioned an unnamed dean at an unnamed leading women's college who was "eating fire about the impossibility for a woman to get a professorship."[55] His reflection on the dean's complaint showed little sympathy for the plight of graduate women and blamed the problem on the women's college: "I regret to say that the attitude at this college was a bitter-end attitude of encouraging the woman to fight for a career with men. Some of these forty women [who had not been able to get a job] of outstanding ability had scorned marriage; others had been disappointed in love."[56]

One of Seashore's concerns was that too many women graduate students fail to cultivate their social natures, which he claimed constitute the very "charm of an educated woman."[57] He thus advised the woman professional not to "sacrifice the development of her personality as a cultured woman."[58] Stating that graduate work is tailor-made for men, he also warned women graduate students not to be mannish in their attitudes or approach toward it.[59] Together with references to the improved marriage prospects of "attractive" educated women, Seashore's comment about the charm of an educated woman indicates that in his estimation, the worth of a woman should be measured in terms of her physical and intellectual allure to men.[60]

Support for the assertion that Seashore emphasized a particular kind of practicality when advising women graduate students appeared in an unpublished letter of complaint from Seashore's colleague, Professor Edwin Starbuck, to University of Iowa president Walter A. Jessup.[61] The letter alleged, among other things, that in September of 1926, Seashore approved of two men enrolling in a graduate-level philosophy course but advised a third student, a woman, not to do so, arguing that it was not practical. Starbuck claimed that Seashore had advised the student to "change her major to Psychology. Philosophy, he claimed, led to nothing practical, particularly for a woman."[62]

Thus, graduate school, which stood at the pinnacle of his hierarchy of post–high school educational opportunities, was the place Seashore was least willing to open to women. At one point he called graduate study "liberal culture" and prophesied that a time was coming when undergraduate study would not be a liberal education but merely a preparation for the true liberal culture to be experienced in graduate school.[63] In effect he was claiming that the academic rigor, exciting opportunities to study abroad, pathways to high-status professional careers, and experiences with the ultimate in liberal culture are privileges rightfully belonging, by and large, to men.

Education, Career, and Women's Health

Another of Seashore's concerns was that education, career, or a combination of both might be too taxing and damaging to a woman's health. He warned men and women alike of the health perils of too much studying, but women's health was of special concern; his assertions were based on and reinforced the assumption that women are the weaker sex. For example, in "An Open Letter: Addressed to Women," he stated that his biggest concern is that women graduate students maintain their physical and mental health, adding, "Many girls come with high credentials from colleges where their one distinction was scholarly record at the sacrifice of physical and mental health. They tend to take their graduate work so seriously that nothing matters except success in their studies."[64] He advocated exercise and sports for all students, and then claimed that he often asked brilliant women, "Are you going to be a dictionary grind or a laboratory rat? The grand rush for a degree or other measure of academic success threatens a brilliant student with the deterioration of physical and mental health."[65] Significantly, he said that health maintenance among graduate student women had become a moral issue, an assertion I explore further a little later.

Another link between education and women's health appeared in his autobiography, where he attributed the untimely death of his sister, who died at age twenty-three, to too much energy spent on intellectual interests and community activities.[66] Furthermore, in his book *Psychology in Daily Life*, he argued that the leap directly from college graduation to the rigors of high school teaching is too great for many women, leading to loss of beauty and mental illness.[67] The problem, according to him, is that high school teaching is too demanding for women fresh out of college, especially for those who have their minds on something else (marriage?) and have no intention to make teaching a lifelong career. For women foolish enough to follow this "extravagant course," he recommended a graduated high school teaching load, with a full load achieved in the fourth year and salaries adjusted accordingly:

> In this country many girls go directly into high-school teaching upon graduation from college; and this is a common story; too severe nervous strain—deteriorating health and beauty—[no] rest to recuperate—a neurotic wife and mother. . . . A large portion of the young women who do not intend to make teaching a profession for life, but teach for five consecutive years in the high school, acquire some marked tendencies to nervous breakdown. If only ten per cent of them suffered in this respect the sacrifice would be too great, but the percentage is much higher. Teaching is now a profession, and ordinarily it is not good mental economy to follow this profession temporarily while the mind is bent on something else. But assuming that the young woman is going to take this extravagant course, wasting precious life-energies in establishing herself in a skilled occupation which she does not intend to pursue permanently (and she can show many reasons for so doing), the condition might be met by allowing her to undertake about two-thirds of the usual service for the first year, three-fourths for the second, four-fifths for the third, and assume full work in the fourth year, with corresponding advances in salary. By such a system the progressive adaptation would prepare for a gradual increase in application and lessen the strain involved.[68]

Significantly, his concern was with the leap to high school teaching, a field dominated by men, and not to elementary teaching, a pink-collar domain; he made no suggestions to men about this transition, which again implied that women are of weaker physical and mental constitution than men.

Language and Seashore's Imagined Student

Even though he was talking to and about the generic student in his discussions of education, Seashore frequently used language suggesting that his imagined student was male, whether the topic was undergraduate or graduate education. Some may argue that in the early twentieth century, "man" variously referred to males or to all humans, making Seashore's intended meaning unclear. That said, in case after case he really was talking about males. For example, in a 1921 letter, Seashore asked eugenicist and psychologist Robert Mearns Yerkes to comment on a rating system designed to identify college students who show potential for conducting research; Seashore referred to the college student as "the man."[69] In a 1927 letter to eugenicist and secretary of the National Research Council Vernon Kellogg, Seashore talked about a dearth of "students of the best quality" entering scientific research, and he said the problem was occurring because "the best men graduating from the colleges" are finding jobs elsewhere.[70] One example of Seashore's gendered word choice also confirmed his belief in women and men having different roles and goals in life—with woman serving as a "counter image" to man and having marriage at the top of her must-do list. In the bulletin *A Preview to College and Life*, published in 1938, Seashore included a chapter, "Open Letter to a Freshman," that is filled with references to boys and men.[71] In the section "I Shall Be a Man," Seashore talked about a man's physique, a man's intellect, a man's moral nature, and so on.[72] In a footnote, he stated that the letter is addressed to men but is useful for women, too.[73] However, he suggested that women should substitute the word "have" for "be" so that the section reads, "I Shall Have a Man," and should use the reading as a means of "reciprocal self-analysis."[74] He did acknowledge in this footnote that college life has many commonalities for women and men.[75] The bulletin is a reprint of an essay that first appeared in 1927 in *Learning and Living in College*, and the footnote in the original essay, although substantially the same as the later version, stated, "If addressing a girl, the author would modify the content of the message very materially," without providing details about the modifications.[76] It also included another explanation of his suggested word substitution: "The girl who reads this chapter with that substitution will find no difficulty in building from it a challenge to herself—the counter image of that man."[77]

Although few US students, male or female, attended college or graduate school during the early twentieth century, Seashore's focus on males apparently is *inconsistent* with the demographics of the population that did attend. It is true that most Ivy League institutions, including Yale, Seashore's doctoral alma mater, did not officially open their doors to women until quite some time after his death. It is also true that even though Seashore's undergraduate alma mater, Gustavus Adolphus College, was a coeducational institution, there were no women among the four students in his graduating class, the class of 1891.[78] Nevertheless, Claudia Goldin et al. report that between 1900 and 1930 there *was* gender parity in the United States among undergraduates.[79] Significantly, there were gender differences in the *type* of undergraduate institution attended. Goldin et al. state that women were more likely than men to attend two-year colleges, while men were more likely to attend four-year colleges; about 30 percent of these women were enrolled in teacher training schools.[80] Furthermore, even though Seashore placed marriage at the top of a woman's must-do list, Goldin et al. report that "a substantial fraction of the women who graduated in these early classes never married and did enter the labor force. Those who did marry were far more likely to marry a college-educated man."[81] The researchers also report that in 1925, half of all college students were enrolled in public colleges and universities, and that 55 percent of college *women* were attending these types of schools; the latter statistic dispels the perception that the only women attending college at the time were enrolled at elite institutions and were daughters of affluent parents.[82] Thus, Seashore's language not only points to his gendered preferences but also erases women from the picture, obliterating the reality that they were attending college about as often as men were.

Women, Intellectual Capacity, and the Eternal Feminine

Seashore assumed that women and men are intellectual equals. In both "An Open Letter: Addressed to Women" and "The Aesthetics of Marriage," he used "brilliant" to describe women graduate students, and in the latter publication, he stated that on the whole the women applying for scholarships and fellowships were as brilliant as the men.[83] He also believed that women and men had equal musical capacity. In seeking answers to the question "Why No Great Women Composers?" he systematically rejected gender differences in native talent,[84] general and musical intelligence,[85] musical temperament,[86] creative imagination,[87] musical precocity,[88] education,[89] and endurance.[90] He stated, for example, that all evidence indicates that boys and girls "inherit musical talent in approximately the same degree, of the same kind, and equally diversified."[91] After rejecting both heredity and environment as causes, Seashore alluded to the Jungian notion of the eternal feminine in the psychological explanation he proposed, arguing that the absence of great women composers is due to fundamentally different and "distinctive male and female urges":

> Woman's fundamental urge is to be beautiful, loved, and adored as a person; man's urge is to provide and achieve in a career. There are exceptions; but from these two theories arise the countless forms of differential selection in the choice and pursuit of a goal for life. Education, environment, motivation, obligations, and utilization of resources, often regarded as determinants in themselves, are but incidental modes for the outcropping of these two distinctive male and female urges. They make the eternal feminine and the persistent masculine type. It is the goal that accounts for the difference. Men and women both have their choice and both can take pride in their achievements.[92]

Seashore had met Jung many years earlier, having chaired sessions on psychology and higher education at the Psychology, Pedagogy and School Hygiene conference G. Stanley Hall organized at Clark University in 1909; there, American psychologists had met and heard talks by Sigmund Freud, Carl Jung, and Ernest Jones, among others.[93]

Thus, although he viewed women and men as intellectual equals, he argued that differences in fundamental urges, notably a woman's urge to be beautiful, cherished, and adored, lead to different life goals, and different but equally meritorious uses of their capacities. Furthermore, according to his logic, it was contrary to her fundamental urges for a woman to want a career. Whether the elite, fit women Seashore idealized can be considered the equals of their male counterparts hinges on whether *separate* ever constitutes *equal*.

Familiar Tropes Recycled

Few of Seashore's views about women and education were new. He was recycling familiar tropes that could just as easily have come from a mid-nineteenth-century women's magazine such as *Godey's Lady's Book*. For example, among those who supported women's education, the notion that women have equal intellect to men but should put it to different purposes was a standard strand of thought in the second half of the nineteenth century in the United States.[94] Other standard tropes were the desirability of women cultivating music as an ornamental amateur activity and the need for a modicum of music education to make them more desirable mates. The doctrine of separate spheres and the cult of domesticity, as manifest in the ideas of the "angel in the house" and the "queen of the hearth," factored heavily into nineteenth-century logic about the importance of education in making women fit wives and mothers. Seashore's attitudes about women and careers, notably that jobs outside the home are acceptable but only until marriage, and that true happiness cannot be found in a career outside the home, similarly are throwbacks to popular nineteenth-century middle-class views. His assumptions that there are only two sexes and that heterosexuality is a given were nothing new. Even his anxieties about the potentially deleterious effects of education on women's health had nineteenth-century roots. For example, as the nineteenth century progressed, some in the United States were concerned about declining birth rates of the White middle class; some experts identified the ostensibly deleterious effects of education on a woman's health as a potential cause of this decline. In 1873, Harvard physician Edward H. Clarke published *Sex in Education; or, A Fair Chance for the Girls*—a popular tome that went through multiple editions—which claimed that the mental rigors of schooling deemed appropriate for boys were too taxing on girls. These intellectual demands, Clarke argued, diverted energy away from girls' reproductive development, resulting in mental illness, including hysteria, and reproductive pathology. He recommended a different kind of education for girls, specifically one that included reduced workloads during menstruation.[95]

Previous scholars have discussed Seashore's attitudes about women, education, marriage, and fertility; in one instance, they were defended as typical of the times.[96] His views are unabashedly sexist, have been critiqued as such, and have been dismissed by some, including music psychologist Paul Farnsworth; in 1997, University of Iowa law professor Marc Linder called Seashore a "male chauvinist pig" and questioned the prudence of naming a building after him.[97] What previous scholars have not considered, however, is how eugenics—and by extension racism—informed his views. In addition to circulating outside the eugenics movement, the old tropes evident in Seashore's remarks were appropriated and repurposed by some eugenicists. Knowledge of Seashore's involvement in eugenics places his views on women, specifically on women and education, in a somewhat different light, prompting a different reading; central to this re-reading is an understanding of the eugenical perspective sometimes termed "race suicide."

Eugenics and the Specter of Race Suicide

"Race suicide" is a term coined in 1901 by sociologist Edward Alsworth Ross, describing what eugenicists perceived to be a serious threat not only to the future of the nation but the future of the whole human race: the dying out of the ostensibly fit coupled with the unbridled proliferation of the ostensibly unfit.[98] Mehler states that the concept of race suicide was quickly adopted and popularized by progressives, including President Theodore Roosevelt.[99] Rooted in a fear/hope double gesture, race suicide discourse and the practices that stemmed from it circulated among eugenicists in the United States and flourished abroad as well. Anxieties about race suicide were omnipresent in the journals published by the ERA and AES. The concept appeared, for example, in a chilling address by Nazi interior minister Wilhelm Frick, published in 1934 in the American journal *Eugenical News*.[100] Eugenics journals also referred to racial degeneration, racial decay, or racial decadence, which allegedly were spreading across Europe and the United States like a plague.[101]

Eugenicists called groups of people "stock," a term derived from animal husbandry, and the word reflects the eugenics movement's roots in the American Breeders Association. For example, in 1936, *Eugenical News* published an article by American eugenicist and Nazi sympathizer C. G. Campbell defending Nazi actions in Germany; his article used the terms "stocks" and "breeding": "This national policy seeks to attain the greater purity of racial stocks by selective endogamous mating and breeding, with a clear conception and conviction as to its beneficial effects upon its racial quality and its culture; the increased proportionate reproduction of the more competent eugenic stocks; and the proportionate decrease of the incompetent and undesirable dysgenic stocks."[102]

Like discussions of other issues that concerned eugenicists, conversation about the causes of and solutions to race suicide was framed by a good/bad, fit/unfit dichotomy. The traits that relegated some individuals and groups to the fit category and others to the unfit were considered biologically inheritable, immutable, and unequally distributed. Although which individuals and groups were placed in the good or bad category varied somewhat from source to source, the presence of the categories—fit and unfit—did not; race, social class, nationality, and immigrant status figured heavily in constructions of the two categories. Sometimes "race" referred to the whole human race, but in reality race suicide was not about a supposed decline in numbers of the "best" people of all races; rather, it was concerned with the supposed decrease in the *best* examples of the ostensibly *best* race: White people. It is a virulently racist concept. For example, a 1935 *Eugenical News* article asked, "Are the White

People Dying Out?" It concluded that if they were not at the time, they would be in twenty or thirty years:

> Life means growth and progress and the white people seem to have lost their courage to live and to develop—not so the colored races.
>
> Certainly these questions are not determined by numbers only but also by quality. Here again the study of heredity reveals the disastrous effects of counter-selection which not only reduces the population quantitatively but also qualitatively—the most valuable and desirable elements of the population being most affected by the low birth-rate. When the racial constituents of a nation are changed by differential fecundity or by immigration, it follows that its cultural level also must change.[103]

The article concluded with a call to action: "It is up to the white nations of the Western hemisphere to decide whether they will let themselves drift towards ruin or whether they will put up a vigorous fight for survival."[104] Race suicide also had a social class component; rather than calling for the proliferation of all White people, eugenicists focused on the proliferation of White people from specific social classes, sometimes derogatorily referring to poor White people as "White trash";[105] some eugenicists referred to what they called *class* suicide.[106]

Who Were the Fit and How Were They Contributing to Race Suicide?

A frequently cited cause of race suicide was declining birth rates among the ostensibly fit. This cause was identified, for example, in the 1920 book *Applied Eugenics*, by Paul Popenoe and Roswell Hill Johnson; the authors provided a typical eugenical definition of the fit: "old American stock"—so-called "Native Whites."[107] A 1920 *Eugenical News* article entitled "Non-fecundity of the Fit" added professional status to the list of attributes of the superior-but-imperiled fit; the demise of the affluent, the article further warned, would assure national decay and loss of prosperity: "'The lowest fertility rates of all are those of the professional classes. . . . If any criterion of success—the imperfect one of worldly prosperity, which we now employ, or some better one yet to be devised—is in practice always correlated with relative sterility, ultimate national decadence would seem to be assured.'"[108] Applying criteria Francis Galton had employed many years earlier, Popenoe and Johnson used eminence and accomplishments as evidence that old American stock is superior:

> The old American stock has produced a vastly greater proportion of eminence, has accomplished a great deal more proportionately, in modern times, than has other any [*sic*] stock whose representatives have been coming in large numbers as immigrants to these shores during the last generation. It is, therefore, likely to continue to surpass them, unless it declines too greatly in numbers. For this reason, we feel justified in concluding that the decline of the birth-rate in the old American stock represents a decline in the birth-rate of a superior element.[109]

Like Popenoe and Johnson, Henry Fairfield Osborn sounded the imperilment alarm; in his opening address to the Second International Congress of Eugenics, held in 1921, he decried declining birth rates among the purest New England stock, whom he claimed had established the foundations of the nation: "In New England a century has witnessed the passage of a many-child family to a one-child family. The purest New England stock is not holding its own. The next stage is the no-child marriage and the extinction of the stock which laid the foundations of the republican institutions of this country."[110]

Why Was the Birth Rate Declining?

Eugenicists blamed poor choices, moral decay, liberal attitudes about gender roles, the education of women, and widespread use of contraception for declining birth rates among the most fit. Some eugenics sources specifically blamed the graduates of colleges and universities, as well as the institutions that educated them, particularly elite Ivy League and Seven Sister schools such as Harvard, Vassar, and Yale; the problem, according to a summary of addresses delivered at the ERA's ninth annual meeting in 1921, is that the education system destroys the very beliefs and values needed for the human race to survive and flourish: "At present then our educational system seems to be destroying the very material on which it works! Colleges seem to be engines for the mental suicide of the human race!"[111]

In a discussion of birth rates among various groups in the United States, Popenoe and Johnson stated that even though the overall birth rate of Native Whites of Native Parentage was increasing, the birth rate was decreasing in a specific, ostensibly superior subgroup: college-educated women.[112] Popenoe and Johnson, among others, blamed declining birth rates among the fittest on college-educated women's decisions to delay marriage or never to marry: "The best educated young women (and to a less extent young men) of the United States, who for many reasons may be considered superior, are in many cases avoiding marriage altogether, and in other cases postponing it longer than is desirable. The women in the separate colleges of the East have the worst record in this respect, but that of the women graduates of some of the coeducational schools leaves much to be desired."[113]

After praising the National Socialistic movement under the leadership of Adolph Hitler, in his address published in *Eugenical News* in 1934, Nazi interior minister Wilhelm Frick blamed declining birth rates in Germany on the moral decay of the people, which he claimed was caused by the deleterious influence of Marxism and communism.[114] Decay was precipitated, Frick claimed, by liberal attitudes that destroy domestic life and desire for parenthood:

> Its [the people's] soul had been poisoned by the liberalistic spirit, which also destroyed its domestic life and its desire for parenthood. This spiritual and structural change has been accompanied by a transformation of our home life. Husband and wife go to work and to their respective occupations, both striving for education on the one hand and for work and a share in the economic life on the other. Thus man and woman became estranged to the family, while they believed to have found equality in an unrestrained independence of sexes. Publicity glorifies the masculine woman in sports and professions, but no one has a word for the mother of a large family.[115]

Some eugenics sources argued that overuse of contraceptives by the fittest was contributing to birth-rate reduction in that group,[116] Frick arguing that it was the primary cause of national suicide in Germany.[117] Overall, whether contraceptive use was viewed favorably by eugenicists tended to depend on who was using them. For example, an abstract of Irving Fisher's 1921 presidential address to the Eugenics Research Association mapped out the potential effects of birth control, only one of which he perceived to be beneficial:

> Where will birth control really take us? There are three possibilities: (1) it may cause depopulation and ultimately bring about the extinction of the human race; (2) it may reduce the reproduction of the prudent and intelligent and the economically and socially ambitious, leaving

> the future race to be bred from imprudent, unintelligent and happy-go-lucky people, thus resulting in race degeneration, or (3) it may cut off the strain of the silly and selfish, the weak and inefficient who will dispense with children for the very good reason that they lack physical stamina or ability to support a large family.[118]

Thus, it was not contraceptive use per se that eugenicists opposed. For example, Margaret Sanger, the founder of Planned Parenthood, strongly supported birth control and was also a staunch eugenicist. Rather, eugenicists tended to criticize what they perceived to be contraceptive *overuse* among the ostensibly *fittest*.

In addition to blaming reduced fecundity for declining numbers of the ostensibly fittest, eugenicists also blamed war, especially World War I.[119] Osborn wrote, "Europe, in patriotic self-sacrifice on both sides of the World War, has lost much of the heritage of centuries of civilization which never can be regained. In certain parts of Europe the worst elements of society have gained the ascendancy and threaten the destruction of the best."[120]

Who Were the Unfit and How Were They Contributing to Race Suicide?

If the contribution of the fit to race suicide was declining birth rates, one contribution of the ostensibly unfit, according to eugenicists, was profligate fertility. Popenoe and Johnson provided a typical definition of which groups were considered unfit, too fecund, and unwisely "preserved" through social welfare programs: the insane; epileptics; "physical, mental, and moral cripples"; the feeble-minded; inefficients; wastrels; criminals; "Negroes"; and non-Nordic immigrants, to name a few.[121] Popenoe and Johnson considered poor people, immigrants in particular, to be problematically prolific; the authors cited birth rates in Pittsburgh to support their claim that the poor and unfit were outstripping the affluent fit:

> Taking into account all the wards of the city, it is found that the birth-rate *rises* as one considers the wards which are marked by a large foreign population, illiteracy, poverty and a high death-rate. On the other hand, the birth-rate *falls* as one passes to the wards that have most native-born residents, most education, most prosperity—and, to some extent, education and prosperity denote efficiency and eugenic value [emphasis in original].[122]

They elaborated on this point, arguing that fecundity is inversely related to intelligence and that the future of the city would be imperiled if population trends continued:

> Pittsburgh, like probably all large cities in civilized countries, breeds from the bottom. The lower a class is in the scale of intelligence, the greater is its reproductive contribution. Recalling that intelligence is inherited, that like begets like in this respect, one can hardly feel encouraged over the quality of the population of Pittsburgh, a few generations hence. . . .
>
> Taken as a whole, it can hardly be supposed that the fecund stocks of Pittsburgh, with their illiteracy, squalor and tuberculosis, their high death-rates, their economic straits, are as good eugenic material as the families that are dying out in the more substantial residence section which their fathers created in the eastern part of the city.[123]

They stated that if the US birth rate appeared acceptable, it was only because immigrant women are fecund, a situation they found unacceptable.[124] They further argued that programs to assist the poor subvert natural selection and enable unfits to produce even more of their own kind: "The inefficients, the wastrels, the physical, mental, and moral cripples are carefully preserved at public expense. The criminal is turned out on parole after a few years, to become *the father of a family* [emphasis mine]."[125]

Arguments that linked decline of the nation to the unfettered fecundity of the unfit surfaced in British eugenicist Leonard Darwin's address to the Second International Congress of Eugenics. Darwin warned of the "danger of national deterioration resulting from the unchecked multiplication of inferior types."[126] The address given by Nazi Wilhelm Frick similarly stated as "fact" that the unfit are unusually fecund: "The feebleminded and inferior persons multiply at a rate greatly exceeding the average. Deplorable as it sounds, the healthy German family of today hardly produces an average of two children—while we find that just the feebleminded and inferior produce twice and even three times as many children, on the average."[127]

It was not simply a particular nation that was at risk, however; it was the future of the human race. A 1917 *Eugenical News* article reported, for example, that if "the more worthless, incapable, and anti-social individuals are so prolific, while the more gifted tend to become sterile, the human race will degenerate."[128]

In addition to being concerned about the future of the nation and of all humanity, eugenicists talked about the extraordinary and wasteful economic cost to society of supporting the unfit[129]—resources that could be put to better use promoting the fittest. Frick called for reallocation of state resources, stating it was "our duty to reduce the expenditures for the antisocial, inferior and those suffering from hopeless hereditary diseases and to prevent reproduction by hereditary defective persons."[130] Eugenicists argued that without state support, the unfit would be eliminated by natural selection—weeded out; in essence, and ironically, they criticized social policy for tampering with the so-called natural order of things.

Other than claiming that welfare policies and medical advances were allowing the unfit to live and reproduce when they would otherwise die, sources said little about why they had concluded that the unfit would be more prolific than other groups. However, racialized discourses that long predated the American eugenics movement associated persons of color, who often were the objects of eugenic intervention, with hypersexuality, fecundity, easy parturition, and early sexual maturity. For example, British physician Charles White's 1799 treatise comparing Africans, Europeans, and apes on a number of physical characteristics claimed that the typical penile size of Africans was midway between that of Europeans and apes—longer than the European's but shorter than the ape's.[131] Whether or not the claim could be substantiated, this size hierarchy placed Africans in a position that marked them as more sexual, fertile, and bestial than Europeans. White also claimed that parturition is easier among native women of Africa, America, Asia, and the West Indies than it is for Europeans, theorizing that having "large and capacious pelvises" and "living nearly in a state of nature" may explain this difference.[132] Finally, he argued that African children achieve sexual maturity earlier than European children do.[133] These discourses, or variants, bear strong resemblance to the eugenical assertion that persons of color, as well as others marked as abject or less fully human, had a biological or "natural" fecundity advantage.

Discrimination against Catholics—Catholic immigrants in particular—long predated the early twentieth century, and the perception that they would proliferate due to the Catholic Church's opposition to contraceptives doubtless played a role in their relegation to the abject-and-profligate unfit category. Ann Marie Ryan and Alan Stoskopf point out that as a large and diverse immigrant population, Catholics were targeted by eugenicists for sterilization, birth control programs, and immigration restriction; Sharon Mara Leon describes opposition to eugenics by the Catholic leadership.[134] Fear of Catholics extended beyond concerns about their fertility, however.

For example, in a 1947 letter to Seashore, Robert Yerkes complained that "the Catholic church is making studied and determined effort to gain control of our public school system."[135]

Eugenicists frequently identified the absence of laws regulating immigration as contributing to race suicide. Their concern was not so much with immigration per se but with immigration of people of specific races and ethnicities. In his 1916 book *The Passing of the Great Race*, eugenicist Madison Grant complained that unlike previous immigration waves, which were composed of members of the Nordic race, new waves coming to the United States contained too many unfits; Grant claimed that European governments were "sweeping" their jails and asylums,[136] resulting in "a large and increasing number of the weak, the broken, and the mentally crippled of all races drawn from the lowest stratum of the Mediterranean basin and the Balkans, together with hordes of the wretched, submerged populations of the Polish Ghettos."[137] Popenoe and Johnson listed some unwanted immigrant groups: "Italians, Slavs, Poles, Magyars, East European Hebrews, Finns, Portuguese, Greeks, [and] Roumanians [*sic*]" followed by "Syrians, Armenians, and other inhabitants of Asiatic Turkey. Beyond this region lie the great nations of Asia, 'oversaturated' with population. So far there has been little more than the threat of their overflow, but the threat is certain to become a reality within a few years unless prevented by legal restriction."[138] Eugenicists' concern about immigration from Asia was shared by G. Stanley Hall, among others. According to Daniel Kevles, in a 1911 publication, Hall had "raised the specter of 'the yellow and Oriental peril.'"[139]

Popenoe and Johnson cited Edward Alsworth Ross in their discussion of the woes that would befall the United States if immigration were not better regulated: a decrease in natural ability, morality, height, and good looks; coupled with this decline would be a dramatic increase in fecundity.[140] Charles Davenport took a similarly dim view of many immigrant groups and discussed at length the relative strengths and weaknesses of a whole host of groups he called "races."[141] Among the racial groups that Davenport named and criticized were Jews, especially Jewish immigrants from Russia.[142] In parallel fashion, in his 1934 discussion of race suicide in Germany, Frick mentioned Jewish immigrants.[143]

Positive and Negative Eugenical Solutions

Just as eugenicists described the nature of the degeneration problem dichotomously, they approached proposed solutions dichotomously, one set of solutions being known as positive eugenics and the other as negative. After sorting and ordering individuals and groups, identifying them as fit or unfit, the next step was to promote the fit and eliminate the unfit through a host of strategies. These so-called solutions were effected by juridical and pastoral means; the goal was called race "betterment"[144] or "race hygiene." The choice of the term "hygiene" is interesting given that it can mean the establishment and maintenance of health, as well as practices conducive to health, such as cleanliness and cleansing. The latter meaning, in particular, hints at purges. According to Edwin Black, in 1923 Charles Davenport and Harry Laughlin added a subtitle to the name of the journal *Eugenical News*, which thereafter was called *Eugenical News: Current Record of Race Hygiene*; Black reports that "race hygiene" was the phrase used by Germans for eugenics, and its addition to the journal's title was a way for American eugenicists to acknowledge activities underway in Germany.[145]

Leonard Darwin, in his speech delivered at the Second International Congress of Eugenics, stated that one of the goals of eugenics was "increasing the rate of multiplication of stocks above the average in heritable qualities, and . . . decreasing that rate in the case of stocks below the average."[146] Popenoe and Johnson echoed this sentiment by articulating the problem as manifold: *more* superior persons need to have children, superior persons need to have *more* children, and inferior persons need to have fewer children or none at all.[147] In a statement supporting eugenics legislation to achieve ostensibly optimal numbers, Harry Laughlin called for the establishment of eugenical ideals:

> Every nation, community and every family should have its own eugenical ideals. These apply to race, to optimum numbers, and, within race and numbers, to hereditary physical, mental and moral qualities. It is within the range of practical achievement for families, communities and nations with eugenical ideals to exercise much greater control than has hitherto been possible over the principal forces and agencies which determine eugenical fortunes."[148]

Dominant Eugenical Views on Positive Solutions

The positive eugenics goal of increasing the fecundity of the ostensibly fittest was to be reached in part by education, specifically by spreading word of the need for and value of the fittest reproducing at higher rates. Barry Mehler writes that a distinguishing characteristic of the Eugenics Committee (out of which emerged the AES) was its goal of promoting eugenics outside of the eugenics research community; specifically, it was to "emphasize political and educational goals rather than research and information exchange among professionals."[149] Edward Alsworth Ross, among others, argued that the requisite number of children was four.[150] Although it may have been a coincidence, the Seashores had four children.

Eugenicists often framed their appeals to reproduce in terms of moral responsibility or duty, stating that it was morally reprehensible for the fittest to limit family size. For example, Leonard Darwin argued, "Again it is even more important that it should be widely felt that it is morally wrong to limit unduly the size of the family when parents are up to 'standard' in all respects; for it is essential for the welfare of mankind that the seed of this good stock should not be lost to posterity."[151]

Because they considered so many characteristics to be biologically inheritable, many eugenicists viewed individual mate choice and decisions about whether to have children as critical to achieving positive eugenics goals. For example, in his book *Tomorrow's Children: The Goal of Eugenics*, Ellsworth Huntington strongly supported what he called "selective mating."[152]

Competitions and bonuses to identify and reward the fittest individuals and families, including better baby and fitter family contests, were among the incentive programs eugenicists promoted. Furthermore, individual institutions and legislatures were encouraged to promote fecundity through financial incentives, including family allowances and tax breaks.[153] Edward Alsworth Ross stated that universities should implement such allowances:

> From my observations I am inclined to expect that general acquaintance with contraceptive measures will have the effect, in the better educated groups at least, of reducing the average number of births to less than the four births per couple necessary to avert eventual extinction of the group in question. Since society will not consent to sit with folded hands while its more energetic and gifted breeds die out, we may be sure that the system of family allowances which already applies to at least ten million heads of families in the Old World and Australia, will soon make its appearance in this country. In no place could the first step toward this mode of compensation be taken with better grounds than in our universities.[154]

Women, Education Reform, and the Threat of Race Suicide

Eugenicists' fear of race suicide and their aspirations to avert it shaped hardline views on women and education; this is exemplified in the article "The

Masculine Education of Women and Its Dangers," by the Norwegian eugenicist Jon Alfred Mjøen. Appearing in a 1930 issue of the American journal *Eugenics*, "The Masculine Education" opened with Mjøen quoting himself in opposition to suffrage in Norway and stating that education reforms proposed by women leaders were destroying the family:

> "We have no reason . . . for doubling our voters; we have enough of them, but what we need is a *new view* in regard to bettering the world. . . . By the methods of education which women leaders propose to impose upon women, new standards of culture are praised, new ambitions are created which would destroy the ties which bind to family and home. In these methods of education the ideals of marriage and home are neglected and subordinated to the cult of personality. Women should not be led to think, feel or be inspired as is man. The present educational requirements are built upon knowledge and branches of sciences created in the long run, by men for men. It has never been intended that this sort of knowledge should, by a compulsory act, be transferred to women."[155]

Mjøen made conflicting assertions about whether women and men have equal intellect. He acknowledged that women can do well in the current curriculum; he then backtracked: "But a natural love or aptitude for these studies cannot be crammed in nor a deeper understanding of their inherent nature. In physical geography, in theoretical science and the dead languages, in technical engineering and statecraft she will always stand behind man—far behind. And she need not be ashamed—on the contrary."[156] After denouncing those who make dim assessments of women's capacities, he listed a variety of realms in which women's capacities are *inferior*, asserting that women have a different kind of intellect to be put to different purposes, and finally arguing that a good education for women will include race hygiene:

> But I do admit the inferiority of woman in all tasks requiring physical strength and perseverance. . . . Her inferiority in professions calling for abstract reasoning, ability of observation and combination, is also generally admitted. Her imitative abilities, however, her talent for reproduction in art and music, her patience, sensibility and maternal affection, can—properly directed—be of inestimable value, not only in her home, but also to the State and the Community. She has not a lower mentality, but another. We have no right to measure woman

> with a man's measure. There is no common standard. Woman has her own tasks and her own measures. And should some of the most energetic female types desire doctoral degrees or examination-proofs at any price, the biological, physiological and hygienic sciences will give them scope enough. These are sciences which will direct the mind towards home and family.
>
> There are hardly any better subjects for teaching and training than biology, biochemistry and hygiene. Nor will anything be a greater help to the country in its future campaign against the ravaging diseases of the race than homes well trained in race hygiene.[157]

A proper education for a woman, Mjøen claimed, will lead her to home and hearth:

> She must know that marriage and the founding of a family is not only a question of love and economy. . . . She must know that sound and healthy offspring only can be expected from a genetically sound and healthy stock. . . . She must be filled with enthusiasm for the sacredness of motherhood and for the idea that to give life to healthy and numerous offspring and to rear them is the most important of all human undertakings.[158]

According to him, education should impress on women their moral obligation to procreate: "Above all, the young woman ought to be instructed about the serious responsibility in connection with procreation and its conformity to natural law."[159] He closed by proclaiming that women have a duty, a "divine calling," to be protector and savior of the race.[160]

Not all contributors to AES and ERA journals subscribed to the views expressed by Mjøen or Frick about women, education, and careers. For example, in the 1931 *Eugenics* article "When Wives Go to Business: Is It Eugenically Helpful?" feminist activist Chase Going Woodhouse concluded that working wives probably *are* eugenically helpful.[161] She pointed out that married women often need paid work out of economic necessity, and she decried forcing women to make a choice between marriage and intellectual interests.[162] In the same issue, feminist activist Anna Garlin Spencer supported married working women, arguing that "racial progress . . . cannot be secured by old methods of denying women either the education that leads to broad choice of vocational service or by asserting their incapacity to excel in anything outside of the older careers of the housemother."[163] Spencer also criticized Mjøen's view on women's capacities.[164] I did not find evidence that the women featured in the 1931 articles were formally affiliated with eugenics organizations, but all of them were White; historian Alexandra Stern points out that almost invariably, the women who took up eugenics were White.[165] Spencer was an early member of the general committee of the National Association for the Advancement of Colored People (NAACP);[166] that said, I did not find evidence that eugenicists fighting for women's rights critiqued the idea of racial progress or the fear of race suicide, or that they made connections between gender and race politics.

Seeing Eugenics in Seashore's Views on Women, Education, Marriage, and Fertility

Keeping eugenical attitudes about race suicide in mind, let us return to Seashore's statements about women, education, marriage, and fertility. As a trusted and long-standing member of the ERA and AES, he was well acquainted with eugenics discourse, and in particular with the concept of race suicide. Discussion of race suicide was omnipresent in the journals published by the ERA and AES, as was support of policies and practices designed to avert it. Seashore explicitly used the term in his autobiography and referenced Theodore Roosevelt's popularization of it; stating that his father was one of eight children and his mother one of nine, he explained that these impressive figures were typical of the time that predated the "Rooseveltian war on race suicide."[167] Seashore was a featured speaker at the Second International Congress of Eugenics—as were a number of the eugenicists I quoted in my discussion of race suicide. The opening address at that congress was given by Henry Fairfield Osborn, who talked about the importance of race betterment, the loss of "the heritage of centuries of civilization which never can be regained," and the ascendancy of the "worst elements of society" who threaten the best.[168] Osborn called on science to "enlighten government in the prevention of the spread and multiplication of worthless members of society, the spread of feeble-mindedness, of idiocy, and of all moral and intellectual as well as physical diseases."[169] Leonard Darwin[170] and Charles Davenport were among the other speakers making similar appeals.[171]

Like other eugenicists, Seashore used the term "stock" to describe groups of people. He stated, for instance, that students at his undergraduate alma mater, Gustavus Adolphus College, "were of Swedish descent, a sound, sturdy stock, which has constituted so many wholesome ingredients in the melting-pot of the North Central States," and he also called them "the most virile stock."[172] Just as a horse breeder might recite the heritage of a prized animal, Seashore described his wife's pedigree and again used the term "stock": "On her father's side she comes of the same family stock as Oliver Wendell Holmes and William Holmes, director of the Smithsonian, and through her mother, her ancestry through the Bodley and Dubois families is traced back to early Dutch and French sources."[173] Like Galton and other eugenicists, Seashore used ancestral eminence as an indicator of superiority. At a speech he delivered to high school students participating in a program for gifted students, he likened the participants to well-bred horses, suggesting that gifted students constitute the best stock.[174] Furthermore, in his 1938 book *Psychology of Music*, Seashore used "stock" in a discussion of studies of the inheritability of musical talent: "Tentative conclusions from these studies are that musical parents from musical stock on one or both sides tend to have musical children; nonmusical parents from nonmusical stock tend to have nonmusical children; parents, one of whom is musical from musical stock, the other of whom is nonmusical from nonmusical stock, tend to have both musical and nonmusical children."[175] The *Eugenical News* announcement of the formation of the Advisory Council and of Seashore's membership on it illustrates eugenicists' widespread use of the term "stock"; it stated that its members were interested in eugenics research and "in the practical application of the principles of eugenics to the conservation of family stocks in America."[176]

Seashore's writings about women, education, marriage, career, and fertility—in addition to being undeniably sexist—may accurately be viewed as efforts to promote positive eugenics. They are rooted in the specter of race suicide, the anxieties that fueled it, and the positive eugenics goals that ostensibly would avert it. For example, in every respect except for a slight difference in attitude about women and intelligence, his statements resembled those made by hard-line eugenicist Mjøen.

Much of Seashore's advice was to college women, a group that eugenicists identified as inherently superior and yet exhibiting unsatisfactory fertility rates—a group supposedly contributing to race suicide. Seashore framed college women who did not place marriage and family first as misguided and in need of wise counsel, however, not as constitutionally unfit. Consistent with a broad eugenical plan to educate for a better tomorrow, he aimed to achieve positive eugenical goals by disseminating freely given expert advice; by directing his advice at women in higher education, he was targeting the women he deemed fittest. Threadbare nineteenth-century tropes derived from the cult of domesticity and separate-spheres discourse were repurposed by Seashore, Mjøen, and others, given new life as they were tied to the future of the nation, the White race, and all of humanity. For Seashore and many other eugenicists, the return of ostensibly superior women to hearth and home—to their role as breeders and brooders—was a positive eugenics measure to be enthusiastically promoted. The women graduate students who most troubled Seashore, those who sought to be educated for a career other than motherhood, were misguided, not unfit, and needed to be made aware of the consequences if they foolishly squandered their birthright.

Not all eugenicists agreed with Seashore's view that women did not belong in the professions, but hard-liners like Mjøen did. Women entering the professions, from a hard-liner's perspective, were not simply a threat to the men holding those jobs or to the patriarchy; they were precipitating the dysgenic decay of the social order and the end of civilization. Similarly, even the question of whether married women should work outside the home evoked negative responses from some. For example, in the 1931 article "When Wives Go to Business: Is It Eugenically Helpful?" David Snedden, a professor at Columbia University, restated stock race suicide fears concerning the fittest and concluded:

> He [referring to himself] applauds as sound social policy the exclusion of married women from teaching and other gainful public service employments, notwithstanding the injustice of such policies in a few individual cases. He would urge similar policies upon all public-spirited private employers. And he would suggest to all agencies concerned with the schooling of adolescent girls and of young women that, in spite of their much talk about the "social values" of the educations they give, that they re-examine their fundamental scales of values in the light of modern insight and the principles of the "greatest good to the greatest number in the *long run* [emphasis in original]."[177]

The best kind of education for the "best" women did not simply point them in the direction of domesticity; it also schooled them in race hygiene. The assertion, prevalent in the nineteenth century in the United States, that women, especially affluent White women, were culture bearers and conservators of civilization was repurposed and given a heightened sense of urgency. In the fear/hope dichotomy on which eugenics was grounded, hope for the race rested with affluent White women who cheerfully accepted their position as brooders and breeders. Even Seashore's comments about college women maintaining their health tied him not only to past tropes about the imperiled health of educated women but also to eugenics; in stating that a fit college woman has a moral responsibility to maintain her health, he echoed other eugenicists' claims that preventing race suicide was a moral duty to be taken seriously by the fittest, women in particular. Thus, knowing that Seashore was a eugenicist permits a somewhat different reading of his comments about women, education, marriage, career, and fertility.

Seashore was a renaissance man, but his primary research focus was music psychology, so it may seem puzzling that he was considered enough of an expert to be invited to write about marriage and fecundity, and that he agreed to address these subjects in chapters such as "The Aesthetics of Marriage." His holding forth is not puzzling, however, if we recognize that marriage and fecundity were important subjects to eugenicists and that Seashore was a eugenicist very much in agreement with dominant eugenical thought.

Seashore, Sex Research, and Eugenics

Seashore's eugenically informed scholarly projects regarding sex and marriage were not limited to writing about women and education. He was one of twelve invited participants at a conference organized in 1921 by Earl Zinn, a former student of G. Stanley Hall's, who set out to drum up interest in sex research among members of the National Research Council.[178] According to Philip Pauly, the conference report named many potential research topics, including "eugenic concerns about population and race."[179] Wade Pickren writes that the participants advocated the study of sex in all kinds of human beings, including "'infrahuman species, savages, primitive peoples, and normal and pathological human beings at different ages.'"[180] He also states that all of the participants agreed that practical applications of sex research should be given top priority.[181] Pickren and Pauly report that sexual continence, abstinence, and finding ways to control sexuality were among the conference's overarching themes.[182]

Seashore on Other Positive Solutions

In keeping with the overall optimistic tone of his work, Seashore spoke primarily about positive solutions, and advising college women to breed and brood was only one of his fertility-related positive eugenics activities. He also suggested creating incentives to encourage professors to reproduce. In the December 1930 issue of *Eugenics*, six male eugenicists were asked to respond to the question, "The Faculty Birth Rate: Should It Be Increased?" One of them was Seashore. A note preceding the article described the intent of this query: "In order to develop thought upon the general question of stimulating, by family allowances, the birth rates of groups considered superior, *Eugenics* has arranged this discussion of the proposal as applied to college faculties."[183] Although not all respondents believed that family allowances are a good idea, a majority did, and Seashore was among them. He mentioned a practice of the National Research Council as a possible model (and also appeared to assume that all faculty members are male):

> According to the best present American standards a man should reach his doctorate about the middle of his twenties and should, as a rule, be free from family responsibilities up to that time. Eugenically and socially, however, the principal reason for this deferment lies in the importance of selecting a mate after his character, tastes and responsibilities have been cultivated through the graduate work so that he may choose a mate who has corresponding preparation for life and will be for him a fit mate.
>
> On the other hand, we welcome any tendency which will favor the possibility of marriage and of having children soon after a man has completed his formal training for a learned career. One example of such encouragement is found in the practice of the Biological Fellowship Board of the National Research Council of allowing a bonus for a child that is born during the period of the Fellowship. This, together with a differential allowance for a married man represents a very wholesome type of encouragement of well-born children.[184]

Formed in 1916, the National Research Council engaged in a number of eugenics projects during this period, and baby bonuses for the well-born was just one of them. In his autobiography, Seashore again mentioned the NRC Fellowship Board's decision (he was a board member) and waxed nostalgic about it: "I recall one incident in the Biological Fellowship Board which gave me much pleasure and that was the adoption of the rule providing a bonus for a child that should come to a National Research Fellow."[185]

The article on family allowances for faculty members also included views from J. Russell Smith of Columbia University, who, like Seashore, supported them; Smith's comments are typical of eugenical discourse on race suicide: civilization is endangered, the birth rates of the best are falling, miseducation is contributing to the problem, and action must be taken if civilization is to be rescued:

> The job of a college or university is to help civilization. We once thought that education made civilization. Now it is quite clear to me that proper procreation is even more important if we are to *keep* civilization. The upkeep of civilization requires good human stock, persons with brains and character. At present the college faculty is a carefully selected strain of established utility to society.
>
> Education is proving to be a great fatality to the present generation—witness the birth rates in families of the alumnae. If the college cannot save its alumni from destruction, perhaps it can render its greatest eventual service by saving or even increasing the blood of the faculty. Why should we bother to learn about the laws of heredity if they are to be used only on horses, cows, pigs, dogs and chickens? Are not the professors of America worth more than many chickens?[186]

Setting aside for a moment the question of whether America's professors are worth more than chickens, let us place Seashore's proposal in a broader eugenics context. As I stated earlier, many eugenicists supported incentives to encourage the fittest to reproduce; Seashore's incentives model was similar to other such programs. For example, Douglas Blackmon reports that one of the first projects of the Pioneer Fund, founded by White supremacist and eugenicist Wickliffe Draper, was "a program to encourage officers of the all-white U.S. Army Air Corps . . . to have more children. Mr. Draper and other directors of the foundation believed that the Pioneer Fund should encourage a higher birth rate among the best of the white race."[187] According to anthropologist Michael G. Kenny, Draper established an endowment that would provide college scholarships as incentives for the fittest to reproduce.[188]

Educating young people about wise mate choice was another positive eugenics project that Seashore supported. In 1916, when attempting to establish the Iowa Child Welfare Research Station, he spoke promisingly of the work that could be done there; the education of young people on mate choice was one of his proposed projects. If young people are aware of "Mendel's law" and consider how its facts apply to their mate choice, he claimed, they will make a better choice:

> As regards the larger questions of mating and forethought in procreation, much is to be gained by the cultivation of a sentiment in favor of intelligent parenthood. . . . For, after all, there are few matters that young persons give so much forethought to as the selecting of a partner for life. They grope in despair for help from friends, physicians,

> and science. Furnish them the facts! Without the facts they are not free to choose. . . .
>
> Young people are entitled to know, for instance, that if, according to Mendel's law, a neurotic girl marries a neurotic boy, it is almost a complete certainty that their children will be neurotic, and much more so than the parents, because we are mating a weakness to a weakness. The same would be true of every other heritable disease. On the other hand, if a sound girl marries a neurotic or a tubercular boy, or *vice versa*, the soundness may possibly be "dominant" and the illness would then be "recessive," *i.e.*, there is a tendency for the disease to disappear, provided favorable conditions of hygiene prevail. In this way by a little forethought it is practically possible to eliminate certain dreaded hereditary taints without forbidding the marriage of those suffering [italics in original].[189]

Significantly, he did not suggest that the boy and girl not marry, merely that they not marry each other.

In late 1919 and early 1920, Seashore and Charles Davenport, the director of the Eugenics Record Office, corresponded about possible eugenics projects that could be undertaken by the station.[190] Davenport opined that one such positive eugenics project would be to "develop in young unmarried people an interest in Eugenics"; he described how this could be accomplished: "By encouraging them [young, unmarried people] to use the services of some informed central agency (as for instance, the Eugenics Record Office), as to the prospective marriage, especially if there were any doubt as to the desirability of a given marriage. It might be of interest and perhaps an effective experiment to offer a prize for the best organized eugenical inquiry on the part of both members of any pair before marriage during the year 1920."[191]

Marriage choice also was mentioned in a 1921 report on the activities of the station. The report included a section on eugenics, which stated that eugenics involves studying how heredity and environment contribute to the "conservation and betterment of normal children"; it reported that eugenical studies examine how "physical health, superior mentality and moral development" affect selection in marriage.[192] Although not named as the author of the report, Seashore was listed as a collaborator.[193] In a discussion of the value of scientific inquiry into the inheritability of musical traits, Seashore again referred to mate choice, arguing that knowledge of whether a potential mate is likely to carry musical traits can help people make important decisions based on conscious selection.[194]

Seashore, Eugenics, and the Sorting and Ordering of Women

Classification was a common practice among early modern scientists and eugenicists, including Seashore. For example, he sorted and ordered bodies into two sexes, he sorted women seeking post–high school education into several categories, and he further sorted and ordered women graduate students according to their goals for seeking an advanced degree. In accordance with eugenical precepts, he also sorted and ordered women into types, and into the categories of fit and unfit. Fit women might not cultivate their potential, but that was different from being born without it. Nevertheless, fit women had a *moral obligation* to maintain their fitness. Seashore portrayed college women who decided not to marry or not to have children, and women graduate students who acted "mannish," as misguided and miseducated—traitors to the superior stocks. Arguably, however, they still were not in the same league as unfit women, who were perceived to have nothing to squander in the first place.

If extant sources are accurate indicators, Seashore focused primarily on the ostensibly *fittest* women, devoting most of his attention to fostering positive eugenics initiatives. These were college-bound women who would probably have a husband to support them. They could afford to quit working outside the home when they married, they had the financial resources to raise children full time, they could view their education as a resource to fall back on in times of adversity, and they had the luxury of pursuing higher education solely for the purpose of cultivating a "higher life."[195] Although he did not explicitly refer to race, Seashore presumably had White women in mind. These were the women who needed to be encouraged to reproduce, maintain good health, avoid activities that would prevent reproduction, and meet the moral imperative of preventing race suicide.

When he referred to a woman as a fit helpmate for her husband, however, he also reinforced the abject category of unfit woman. His reference exemplifies what Thomas Popkewitz calls double gestures of simultaneous inclusion and exclusion.[196] Including and promoting some women, in effect, excluded and demoted others.

A Panoply of Negative Solutions

Seashore's attention to positive eugenics and his focus on women ostensibly in the top tail of the Gaussian curve invites consideration of what, if anything, he said about the other tail and about negative eugenics. Which women were placed in the unfit category and what actions toward them did he support? Before examining Seashore's views, let us consider dominant negative eugenical solutions, specifically those pertaining to fertility.

Negative eugenics was concerned with reducing in number or totally eliminating the ostensibly unfit. Eugenicist Madison Grant called for the elimination of the least desirable 10 percent of "the community," describing them as the "unemployed and unemployable human residuum."[197] The unfit were a somewhat amorphous group, and they were targeted for possessing a similarly amorphous array of ostensibly biologically inheritable negative characteristics. Cognitive disability, often called feeble-mindedness, was invariably included on the list, as was mental illness. Intelligence was one characteristic that eugenicists assumed was biologically inheritable, but it was not the only one. For example, in his preface to Madison Grant's book *The Passing of the Great Race*, eugenicist Henry Fairfield Osborn posited that "moral, social, and intellectual characteristics and traits" are inherited.[198] Harry Laughlin presented a slightly different list, claiming that physical, mental, and moral characteristics are biologically inheritable.[199] The assumption that moral behavior is biologically inherited and variable among individuals and groups resulted in studies of race differences in moral traits;[200] as we will see a bit later, this assumption also played a critical role in negative eugenics initiatives directed at women. Eugenicists considered moral defects to be forms of biologically inheritable *cognitive* defectiveness. Moral defect was deemed a form of *mental deficiency*, and it manifested itself in criminal behavior, "chronic dependency,"[201] and disregard for moral norms—specifically sexual norms—particularly when women disregarded them. These assumptions led eugenicists to create and assign such labels as "moral imbecile."[202]

Negative eugenics goals were to be achieved in various ways, including decreased public financial support for the unfit; in the United States, standard negative eugenics policies promoted contraceptive use, voluntary or involuntary sterilization, segregated institutionalization to prevent reproduction, immigration restriction, and marriage restriction. Negative and positive eugenics goals were to be achieved through *voluntary* compliance and education. When they focused on the unfit, however, eugenicists also supported legislation and other involuntary, externally imposed actions; the unfit typically were deemed incapable of acting "responsibly" on their own.

Sources such as *Tomorrow's Children: The Goal of Eugenics*, by Yale University geography professor Ellsworth Huntington,[203] and *The Passing of the Great Race, or The Racial Basis of European History*, by attorney and Yale University alumnus Madison Grant,[204] spelled out the planks of the negative eugenics platform. Published in 1935 during the period when Huntington was president of the board of directors of the American Eugenics Society (1934–38), *Tomorrow's Children* has been called the catechism of eugenics.[205] It has been described as such not only because it systematically articulates doctrinal planks in the eugenics platform, but because it is organized in the question-and-answer style typically used in catechisms. Written by a founder of the American Eugenics Society and published in 1916, *The Passing of the Great Race* was favorably reviewed in a 1917 issue of *Eugenical News*;[206] it was referenced by the same journal as a canonical source in a 1920 discussion of Lothrop Stoddard's *The Rising Tide of Color against White World-Supremacy*;[207] and it was cited as solid evidence in Popenoe and Johnson's classic tome, *Applied Eugenics*.[208] According to William Tucker, *The Passing of the Great Race* was read by Adolph Hitler, who reportedly called it "'his Bible'" and thanked Grant for writing it.[209]

One eugenically approved method of eliminating the unfit was birth control. For example, Huntington's catechism discussed and promoted birth control among the unfit, which was to be accomplished via "marital continence [that is, married people abstaining from intercourse], contraception, and the restriction of marital intercourse to the so-called 'safe period.'"[210] He defined contraception as mechanical or chemical methods of preventing pregnancy and argued that most religious bodies, including the Roman Catholic Church, approved of some method of pregnancy prevention.[211]

Second, a host of eugenicists in the United States and elsewhere supported sterilization of the unfit, which was a standard topic of discussion in eugenics publications. For example, Huntington argued that voluntary birth control would not be enough to reduce the proliferation of the unfit, and he advocated sterilization as another means of meeting negative eugenics goals. Sterilization initiatives were to target the "least intelligent elements of society, and . . . those with least self-control."[212] He spelled out three positive outcomes of sterilization: alleviation of misery, reducing the need for charity, and reducing taxes.[213] He further argued that sterilization is a protective rather than a punitive measure.[214] He supported both voluntary and involuntary sterilization; in the latter case, according to Huntington, decisions about who was to be sterilized should be governed by state statutes and should be made by "a committee of experts, by the trustees of the institution in which the patient is confined, by the State Board of Charities and Correction, by the State Board of Eugenics, or by some similar body."[215]

Grant, too, was among the many eugenicists who supported state-controlled sterilization: "The individual himself can be nourished, educated, and protected by the community during his lifetime, but the state through sterilization must see to it that his line stops with him, or else future generations will be cursed with an ever increasing load of victims of misguided sentimentalism."[216] Invoking what he called the laws of nature and drawing a very circumscribed picture of the valuable life, he dismissed what he called the "sentimental belief in the sanctity of human life," arguing that it erroneously tends "to prevent both the elimination of defective infants and the sterilization of such adults as are themselves of no value to the community. The laws of nature require the obliteration of the unfit, and human life is valuable only when it is of use to the community or race."[217]

Primary eugenics sources from a number of countries discussed and supported involuntary sterilization, and *Eugenical News* reported on various states' sterilization legislation in the United States. For example, a 1918 issue described Wisconsin's 1913 sterilization law and its 1917 revisions, noting that the legislation permitted the "sterilization of criminals, insane, feeble-minded and epileptic individuals."[218] The journal also kept abreast of sterilization efforts throughout the world; in 1935, it reported the following about activities in Germany: "Sterilization of the slightly feeble-minded is to be included in the Nazi program of a national 'purge.' The code for sterilization of criminal and insane offenders has been in force for some time. Early in February it was estimated that over 180,000 have been sterilized in Germany. A periodically insane musical genius was, however, saved from sterilization, as the passer-on of a potentially valuable heredity trait."[219] An article entitled "German Sterilization Progress" appeared in 1934 in *Eugenical News* on the same page as Frick's essay "German Population and Race Politics." Quoting snippets appearing in the *New York Times* in 1933, the article included a prediction that between 200,000 and 300,000 persons would be sterilized in Germany within a few years.[220] The journal *Eugenics* included advertisements for E. S. Gosney and Paul Popenoe's 1929 book *Sterilization for Human Betterment: A Summary of Results of 6,000 Operations in California, 1909–1929*.[221] Journals published abroad similarly featured news about sterilization policies and practices. For example, *Eugenics Review*, which was published by the Galton Institute based in the United Kingdom, reported in 1935 on Norway's sterilization law that reportedly was introduced by a cousin of eugenicist Jon Alfred Mjøen.[222]

Institutionalization was another negative measure promoted by the official eugenics platform. Like many other eugenicists, Huntington recommended segregation of the "socially inadequate" via institutionalization for the express purpose of preventing reproduction, and he enumerated the types of institutions he had in mind: "insane asylums, homes for feeble-minded, reformatories, and the like, *where the inmates of the two sexes are kept separate* [emphasis mine]."[223] Grant similarly discussed segregation as an effective negative measure.[224]

Imposed and Voluntary Restrictions

Another popular plank of the negative eugenics platform was immigration restriction through legislation. Both Huntington and Grant favored it, Huntington arguing that if immigration is permitted, the quality of those admitted should be considered and regulated by the state.[225] Influenced by Grant, eugenicists Popenoe and Johnson, among others, similarly favored immigration restriction.[226] As I stated earlier, immigration was a fertility issue because the groups of immigrants deemed unfit also were thought to be too fecund. Immigrants' supposed fecundity was far from the only concern eugenicists expressed, however. For example, Popenoe and Johnson warned that immigrants would take jobs away from "old" Americans, depress wages, and have a deleterious effect on farming.[227] According to Barry Mehler, not only did eugenicists play a key role in passing the Johnson-Reed Immigration Restriction Act of 1924, they "campaigned persistently for the extension of the quota system to the Western Hemisphere in the period 1924 to 1940."[228]

Eugenicists also favored restrictions on sexual intercourse and marriage, whether voluntary or imposed, as ways to prevent the proliferation of the unfit. Although eugenicists opposed the reproduction of all ostensibly unfit groups and individuals, they especially railed against what they called miscegenation and race crossing—sexual intercourse between and offspring from people of different races. I discuss race crossing at length in chapter 7; suffice it to say here that race crossing was assumed to produce inferior offspring, and preventing race crossing was assumed to reduce the number of unfit humans. This goal was to be achieved largely through legislation. Although in most cases, the goal was preventing *marriages* involving one or more unfits, some eugenicists took matters a step farther by suggesting that all sexual intercourse involving unfits should also be outlawed.

Popenoe and Johnson spelled out their recommendations for prohibiting race crossing, which they claimed were in the best interest of the nation; significantly, they mentioned prohibitions—taboos and legal restrictions—both on marriage and on sexual intercourse:

1. We hold that it is to the interests of the United States . . . to prevent further Negro-white amalgamation.

2. The taboo of public opinion is not sufficient in all cases to prevent intermarriage, and should be supplemented by law, . . .
3. But to prevent intermarriage is only a small part of the solution, since most mulattoes come from extramarital miscegenation. The only solution of this, which is compatible with the requirements of eugenics, is . . . an extension of the taboo, and an extension of the laws, to prohibit all sexual intercourse between the two races.[229]

Popenoe and Johnson indicated that four states—Louisiana, Nevada, South Dakota, and Alabama—had passed such laws; they opined that all states should follow suit so that the law would be uniform throughout the nation, and they emphasized that the laws should be enforced.[230] African Americans were not the only group targeted in discussions of race crossing. In 1930, *Eugenics* published a portion of a letter by Herbert Spencer, written in 1892, that offered advice to a Japanese statesman:

> There is abundant proof, alike furnished by the intermarriages of human races and by the interbreeding of animals, that when the varieties mingled diverge beyond a certain slight degree *the result is inevitably a bad one* in the long run. . . . [He refers to problems arising from breeding livestock.] And the same thing happens among human beings—the Eurasians in India, the halfbreeds in America, show this. . . . By all means therefore, peremptorily interdict marriages of Japanese with foreigners [emphasis in original].[231]

In his book *War against the Weak: Eugenics and America's Campaign to Create a Master Race*, Edwin Black argues that early on, many ideas and projects forming the foundation of Nazism in Germany were imported from the United States, marriage restriction laws among them:

> From 1895 to 1900, German physician Gustav Boeters worked as a ship's doctor in the United States and traveled throughout the country. He learned of America's castrations, sterilizations and numerous marriage restriction laws. When Boeters returned to Germany, he spent the next three decades writing newspaper articles, drafting proposed legislation and clamoring to anyone who would listen to inaugurate eugenic sterilization. Constantly citing American precedents, from its state marriage restriction statutes to sterilization laws from Iowa to Oregon, Boeters passionately argued for Germany to follow suit.[232]

Most of the time eugenicists in the United States focused (at least openly) on preventing future generations of the unfit, rather than physically eliminating those already living; however, not all of them tiptoed around physical elimination. Popenoe and Johnson, for example, spoke quite favorably about execution as a means of maintaining "the standard of the race," while also acknowledging that it was not consistent with the "spirit of the times":

> The means of restriction can be divided into coercive and non-coercive. We shall discuss the former first, interpreting the word "coercive" very broadly.
>
> From an historical point of view, the first method which presents itself is execution. This has been used since the beginning of the race, very probably, although rarely with a distinct understanding of its eugenic effect; and its value in keeping up the standard of the race should not be underestimated. It is a method the use of which prevents the rectification of mistakes. There are arguments against it on other grounds, which need not be discussed here, since it suffices to say that to put to death defectives or delinquents is wholly out of accord with the spirit of the times, and is not seriously considered by the eugenics movement.[233]

Finally, physical annihilation is but one type of elimination among many possible forms, and although killing was not generally discussed by the US sources I examined, other forms of elimination figured prominently in eugenics discourse of the early twentieth century. I will illustrate this prominence in chapter 5, which examines Seashore's education reform plans.

Which Women? Negative Eugenics, Fertility, and Targeting Patterns

As I have stated, patterns emerged in which individuals and groups were targeted for both positive and negative eugenics interventions surrounding reproduction. Gender, race, social class, immigrant status, and religious affiliation were among the factors that determined who was or was not targeted.[234] Whereas fit women were urged to reproduce, ostensibly unfit women were forcibly denied the right to do so. In her book *Killing the Black Body: Race, Reproduction, and the Meaning of Liberty*, Dorothy Roberts discusses one element of this pattern, stating that eugenics was a source of the idea that African American women's fertility and fecundity should be externally regulated and curbed; Roberts states that this idea persists to the present.[235] In her article "Policing the 'Wayward Woman': Eugenics in Wisconsin's Involuntary Sterilization Program," Phyllis E. Reske similarly points out that gender and class played a role in who advocated for or was victimized by negative eugenics measures.[236] She states that in Wisconsin, as in the United States as a whole, the majority of people involuntarily sterilized were women.[237] Significantly, eugenicists used moral defect, which was considered a biologically inheritable mental deficiency that manifested itself as disregard for societal sexual norms, as a rationale for involuntary sterilization. Reske points out that those who were involuntarily sterilized tended to be poor or working-class women who had engaged in sexual behavior that was deemed immoral—at least immoral for women.[238] Immoral behavior could include having multiple sex partners;[239] giving birth out of wedlock;[240] engaging in sodomy;[241] having sex with Indians, Italians, or "Negroes";[242] having sexual intercourse "'readily, cunningly, and frequently'"; or even running after men.[243] She describes the case of a sex worker arrested in Madison, Wisconsin, who was committed to a custodial institution in the northern part of the state and then involuntarily sterilized shortly before being released three years later; when she was admitted to the institution, she reported that her husband had brought home other men to have sex with her.[244] Reske also relates the case of an incest victim who had given birth to three children fathered by her father. Having committed no crime, she, too, was involuntarily sterilized.[245]

Thus, many women were sterilized on the grounds that they were "promiscuous," a term having distinctly negative connotations; the *Oxford English Dictionary* says "promiscuous" refers to a person who frequently changes sexual partners or is indiscriminate in sexual relations.[246] So, there were patterns in the *rationales* used for intervening with various individuals and groups. Women who disregarded gendered double standards concerning sexual morals and norms, and whose activities and beliefs more closely resembled those of men (who were not similarly stigmatized), were deemed unfit and were targeted for negative eugenics interventions, especially if they were poor, from the working class, or not White.

In the summary of his history of the American Eugenics Society, Mehler speaks of the constancy over time of the planks of the negative eugenics platform, and one of them was eugenic sterilization:

> Eugenicists' advocacy of immigration restriction, anti-miscegenation, and eugenic sterilization remained remarkably constant even as the rationale for these positions was adjusted to suit changed social conditions and more sophisticated genetics. Thus, the belief in "inferior-

ity" of identifiable sub-populations remained constant even if sophisticated readers of the genetics literature realized that the "genetic" component of "inferiority" could not be positively identified. Where the genetic arguments began to falter, sociological arguments could be brought in to bolster the case.[247]

Seashore and Negative Eugenics

Without a doubt Seashore supported eugenics generally and positive eugenics in particular. Documenting his views on negative eugenics policies and practices is more difficult, largely because I found few explicit statements from him on the topic. The negative eugenics planks described above dominated eugenical discourse both in the United States and elsewhere, however. Discussions of negative eugenics pervaded the AES and the ERA, the journals these organizations published—*Eugenics* and *Eugenical News*, the books they promoted, and the conferences they sponsored. These organizations were vigorous and relentless in their support of both positive and negative measures. Seashore belonged to both of these organizations and was a charter member of the AES; given the pervasiveness of support for negative eugenics in the organizations to which he belonged, it would have been impossible for him to be unaware of these policies and practices. As Barry Mehler states, the very purpose for formation of the committee that would evolve into the AES was to achieve political and educational goals rather than research goals, and those goals focused on preventing race suicide.[248] Mehler discusses and quotes from an AES letter soliciting members:

> "The time is ripe for a strong public movement to stem the tide of threatened racial degeneracy. . . . America needs to protect herself against indiscriminate immigration, criminal degenerates, and . . . race suicide." [Mehler continues] The letter called for resistance to the threatened "complete destruction" of the "white race." It stated that eugenics was the only movement which stood "against the forces . . . [of] racial deterioration and for progressive improvement in the vigor, intelligence, and moral fiber of the human race."[249]

Mehler also points out that in 1922, eugenicists Charles Davenport and Robert Yerkes formed the Committee on Scientific Problems of Human Migration, which was under the auspices of the National Research Council's Division of Anthropology and Psychology; the objective of the committee was to "study the biological consequences of racial intermixture."[250] Seashore was chairman of the NRC's Division of Anthropology and Psychology in 1921 and 1922.

Consider, too, the contents of the journals *Eugenics* and *Eugenical News*, two official organs of the AES and the ERA. Articles spelling out planks of the negative eugenics platform appeared even before Seashore became a member of the ERA, and they continued throughout the full run of these journals. Members of the AES Advisory Council are listed at the beginning of every issue of *Eugenics*, and Seashore's name appears on every list; he was a charter member of the Advisory Council.[251] I have deliberately cited many articles from these journals in my discussion of sterilization (and throughout this book) as evidence that the eugenics positions I am describing come directly from the organizations to which Seashore belonged and that he implicitly endorsed them in a variety of ways, including the presence of his name on the list of Advisory Council members. He was a member of these organizations, for example, in 1934 when *Eugenical News* published Wilhelm Frick's speech, discussed earlier; his name appeared as a member of the Advisory Council in the same issues of *Eugenics* that advertised Gosney and Popenoe's book *Sterilization for Human Betterment*.[252] His activities, tests, and research were mentioned a number of times in these journals, and on some occasions, his solicited opinions on various topics were published.[253]

He also would have been familiar with this official platform through the conferences he attended or at which he presented papers. For example, he was a speaker at the Second International Congress of Eugenics, where plans for the AES began taking shape. Henry Fairfield Osborn, who argued that the government must be enlightened about how to prevent "the spread and multiplication of worthless members of society," was another speaker at that conference.[254]

In addition to being listed as a member of the AES Advisory Council on every issue of *Eugenics*, Seashore was named on the same list as it appeared at the beginning of Huntington's *Tomorrow's Children: The Goal of Eugenics*, the eugenics catechism I quoted extensively earlier in the chapter. As I documented earlier, sterilization, segregation, and immigration restriction were among the actions supported in the catechism.

Evidence that he was aware of the eugenical argument that unfit people need to be segregated via institutionalization to prevent reproduction appeared in a 1920 letter to Seashore from Davenport, which included suggested eugenics activities that could be undertaken at the Iowa Child Welfare Research Station; Cora Bussey Hillis and Seashore had helped found the station. Davenport lobbied for "cacogenic investigations" that would result in "the segregation of feeble-minded and feebly controlled men and women during the whole of the reproductive period."[255]

The appearance of a scholar's name on an advisory board for an organization or journal, or the presentation of a paper at a particular scholarly conference, although it indicates overall support for the endeavor, does not necessarily mean the scholar approves of every view expressed. Keeping that in mind, let us consider what, if anything, Seashore said about specific negative eugenics measures.

As I discuss at length in chapter 5, Seashore supported the general concept of segregation by innate ability, especially as it applied to education settings. Tracking and other forms of segregation based on supposed innate ability were foundations of his proposed education reforms. He praised Henry Goddard's work at the Vineland Training School for Feeble-Minded Girls and Boys, claiming that his visit to Vineland served as the inspiration for his philosophy of education.[256] I found no evidence explicitly indicating that he supported segregation for the explicit purpose of *preventing reproduction*, and I did not find statements from him in support of immigration restriction or physical elimination, either. He was a consultant and provided technical advice to Morris Steggerda, who studied race crossing in Jamaica, but I located no comment about whether Seashore disapproved of race crossing.[257]

That said, he made a number of somewhat cryptic statements that appear to support negative eugenics measures. For example, in his proposal to establish the Iowa Child Welfare Research Station, he came out in support of legal restrictions to prevent ill-born children; he did not spell out which legal restrictions he had in mind, but certainly marriage restrictions or sterilization laws, and perhaps even immigration restrictions, are the most logical possibilities. The proposal opened with a section entitled "Heredity and Prenatal Care" that discussed the prevention of what he considered to be hereditary diseases:

> The first step . . . is to investigate, classify, and make common, knowledge of the conditions which produce ill-born children in Iowa. Among such, the most dreaded are the hereditary diseases such as all forms of degeneracy, venereal and other forms of heritable disease. The effects of these can be reduced very materially by general education about the facts and their consequences, and *further by legal restrictions*. Intemperance in all forms including abuse of drink, drugs, food, sex, and physical and mental strain, represent an enormous drain of energy

> from the vitality of the coming child. But a large part of the inborn weakness of a child is due to ignorance and neglect by parents in little, common things which affect their vitality, and indirectly the vitality of the child [emphasis mine].[258]

In the above passage, he lobbied for education as a measure to prevent degeneracy, but he did not specify what needed to be taught—in particular, whether education about wise mate choice was what was needed. Furthermore, he appeared to suggest that through education and wise parental action, "inborn weakness" is preventable, at least in some cases. However, in the next portion of this excerpt, he implied that once inborn weakness occurs, even if it is the result of poor prenatal decisions by the parents, it is automatically *inherited* by subsequent generations; he also referenced a familiar eugenics argument: one unfit person can produce large numbers of unfit descendants who will be a great burden to the state:

> Let the people see a modern family tree of the 400 or 500 descendants of a single feebleminded girl, practically all degenerates and charges of the state, and they will take notice. Let them know the actual facts of alcohol, drug habits, and other forms of intemperance, and they can no longer hide their heads in blissful ignorance like the proverbial ostrich.[259]

In a 1914 discussion of the merits of eugenics, Seashore spoke optimistically of the role that scientific forethought and preventive medicine could play in eliminating degeneracy and promoting health. He again referred to prevention and to "precautionary measures," as well as to "scientific check," without spelling out precisely what he meant by these terms, but he clearly indicated that applying to humans what had been learned from animal breeding would be a valuable contribution of eugenics:

> Scientific forethought by the individual and society will in the near future very materially reduce the dreaded mental diseases, such as epilepsy, idiocy, imbecility, and insanity, by precautionary measures. For these are no longer regarded as scourges of blind fate, but are known to be due to natural and traceable causes, explicable in scientific terms, and often preventable.
>
> The possibility of dealing successfully with these grossest types of disease is proof that the countless lesser human ills are being brought

> under scientific check; and the lesser ills are the more significant because they are so many and so common. We are and should be more concerned about the warding off of inceptive nervousness, for example, than of insanity.
>
> Modern biological experiments in inheritance have demonstrated the possibility of preventing deterioration, eradicating congenital weaknesses, improving the species, and in other ways modifying animals. Horses, chickens, cats, and dogs are being improved systematically under the directing forethought of the breeder, and in such transformations in animals a mental trait may be quite as radically modified as a physical trait.
>
> The coming science of eugenics is making a survey of the principles of inheritance applicable to human life. It is taking an inventory of the forces in the environment that make for weal or for woe of man, and is tracing them back to their sources, which are fast being put under control. Eugenics is not only the science of being well-born, but also the science of well-being—not only of physical, but yet more significantly of mental well-being. With a common purpose preventive medicine affects the home, the school, and the civic organization, enlightens the individual and society in regard to private and public sanitation, and concentrates forces of economic, moral, and religious institutions in the common struggle for the one great goal—health.[260]

Perhaps the strongest evidence that Seashore promoted negative eugenics is the presence of his name on the Advisory Council list published in Huntington's eugenics catechism, *Tomorrow's Children: The Goal of Eugenics*. Huntington stated that the book was created in consultation with members of the Advisory Council and that the galley proofs were reviewed by some members: "This book has also been improved by suggestions from members of the Advisory Council of the American Eugenics Society. So far as they could be reached the galley proof was submitted to all of the members, and great gratitude is due to the many who were able to read it."[261] In his description of how the catechism came into being, Mehler indicates that it was a long process in which Council members were deeply involved; he further asserts that the book represented group consensus:

> Although Ellsworth Huntington was credited as the author "in conjunction with the Directors of the American Eugenics Society," *Tomorrow's Children* may be said to represent the collective view of

> eugenics worked out by the Board of Directors *and the Advisory Council of the American Eugenics Society* over a period of more than a decade of debate and discussion. . . .
>
> The final version of the manuscript went through seven drafts. . . . The final catechism represented the consensus of the group. . . . To make it entirely clear the verso of the copyright page lists the entire one hundred and ten members of the Board and Advisory Council of the Society. Virtually all these members had belonged to the Society for five years or more. Sixty-three of them had belonged to the group since at least 1923 [Seashore was among the sixty-three] and thus had participated in the many discussions that had taken place in the process of hammering out this final collective catechism of American Eugenics [emphasis mine].[262]

While alluding to possible minor disagreement, Huntington stated that the group agreed on major points:

> All who have shared in the preparation of this book agree that everything possible should be done to encourage large families in the right kinds of homes *and to discourage them in undesirable homes*. They are also agreed as to the main outlines of the program here set forth. As is natural among any such group of thoughtful people, there are many diverse points of view as to lesser, but nevertheless important matters. In such cases the author has done his best to express the general sentiment of the group as a whole [emphasis mine].[263]

Two scholars have claimed that Seashore rejected sterilization, selective breeding, and physical elimination. In his 1984 article about the debate in the late 1930s and 1940s on the role of nature versus nurture in intelligence, Henry L. Minton stated that the Iowa Child Welfare Research Station and its director George D. Stoddard weighed in on the side of nurture, challenging the hereditarian position.[264] Minton claimed that institutional context helped create and support the station's environmentalist position, and as evidence of this, he rightly stated that Seashore, one of the station's founders, was among those claiming that both nature and nurture play a role in child development.[265] Acknowledging that Seashore supported the eugenic goal of racial improvement, Minton asserted that Seashore "stressed the role of nurture and specifically dismissed such eugenic measures as sterilization and selective breeding."[266] He included a quote from Seashore to support this assertion: "'There are countless possibilities for improving the human child as he now is, not by destroying the unfit or selecting the most desirable, but by discovering, verifying, and popularizing facts about how to provide such favorable conditions for child life as shall result in greater physical and mental strength, higher efficiency, and a more beautiful life.'"[267] Seashore's comment is cryptic; although he supported ways to improve the human child other than destroying the unfit and selecting the most desirable, the comment did not categorically rule out the latter options; elsewhere, for example, he explicitly supported careful mate choice—selective breeding—to produce desirable, ostensibly biologically inheritable traits. Furthermore, most eugenicists in the United States did not support destroying the unfit—at least not openly. Third, although it is true that over time, the station became known for challenging hereditarian positions, ample evidence indicates that as Seashore originally conceived it, the station was to foster both eugenics and euthenics; he viewed them as mutually supportive companions and not as antithetical to each another. I will discuss this companionate relationship at greater length in chapter 8.

Minton further stated that Seashore's preference for using the term "euthenics" in the research station's title was consistent with Seashore's interest in nurture and environment.[268] Without a doubt, Seashore was interested in these topics, but he also was interested in and deeply committed to eugenics and heredity. His own discussion of the naming decision does not suggest he supported euthenics more than eugenics. Rather, he stated that "euthenics" was jettisoned in favor of "child welfare" based on the assumption that the public would more easily understand the latter term, which would better foster public approval of the project.[269] Ample evidence from Seashore himself indicates that he supported both eugenics and euthenics; supporting both was consistent with dominant eugenical thought in the United States and elsewhere.

Using a close paraphrase of the Seashore quotation found in Minton, in 2006 Alice Boardman Smuts made a similar assessment of Seashore's views on negative eugenics: "There were countless opportunities for improving the human child, he [Seashore] declared, not by destroying the unfit or selecting the most desirable, but rather by discovering and popularizing information about improving conditions for children."[270] To support this claim, Smuts cited a 1915 article by Cora Bussey Hillis published in an unidentified newspaper.[271] The Hillis article cited by Smuts said nothing about destroying the unfit, and certainly nothing about Seashore's views on destroying the unfit; indeed, it did not mention Seashore at all. It may well be that Smuts was referring to the same quote Minton had cited more than twenty years earlier.

Thus, although Seashore explicitly supported eugenics generally and positive eugenics specifically, his statements about negative eugenics are somewhat cryptic and his views are discernable only indirectly. That said, the evidence I found did not support the assertions that he categorically opposed negative eugenics or that he favored euthenics over eugenics. The possible asymmetry in his views raises the question of whether positive eugenics can be subscribed to without simultaneously explicitly or implicitly supporting negative eugenics. Through the process of selection, positive eugenics policies and practices simultaneously included some while excluding others. Unless all are promoted, identifying and marking those to be promoted necessarily involves identifying and marking those who are not to receive such favorable treatment. Not being selected for promotion has negative effects that may not be as easy to pinpoint as the effects of involuntary sterilization, but they exist, nonetheless.

Perhaps the most powerful evidence in support of the assertion that Seashore approved of negative eugenics was his silence. Amply aware of the general eugenics platform, including its negative components, he did not speak out against it, nor did he resign from the AES or the ERA. If he disapproved, he did not voice this disapproval. His silence, under these circumstances, constituted complicity.

Seashore on the Other Women

Having taken a journey abroad, let us return to the topic of Seashore's views on women. Although he commented at length about the fittest women, he did not say much about the rest—women who were not finishing or even attending high school, let alone college or graduate school, women who were not White, who were not from the upper class, or who refused to be contained. As Wendy Kline notes, however, in the eyes of eugenicists, "the woman adrift represented the dysgenic threat."[272] These women are ghosts, invisible in Seashore's writings, but they are absent presences; for many of them, the effects of negative eugenics were devastating.

Seashore made a few disparaging—potentially anxiety-ridden—remarks about "emancipated women" and flappers; these statements may or may not provide glimpses of his views on abject women and their characteristics. In his discussion of the absence of great women composers, for example, he enumerated the activities of the emancipated woman, someone he clearly held in low regard: "Will the emancipated woman who smokes, dons mannish attire and manners, takes marital obligations lightly, is athletic, and competes freely with men in business, politics, and professions, pave the way for great composers?"[273] In this passage, he portrayed the emancipated woman as an impediment to a bright future filled with great composers, presumably all of whom would be male.

In the publication *Learning and Living in College*, which appeared in 1927, he portrayed flappers in a similarly unfavorable manner. Advocating for tracked educational opportunities, he compared each track to a different mode of transportation, ranging from the fastest, the airplane, to the slowest, the ox cart. He also talked about the kinds of people who take each mode: flappers, along with other ne'er-do-wells, are found in the covered wagon—the vehicle one step above the ox cart. He enumerated flappers' negative qualities:

> With this group there is persistently a group of adventurers. When they are of the male sex, we call them loafers; of the female sex, we call them flappers. They are not willing to pay for the comforts of more desirable classes, but they submissively take the punishment and live, like tramps, from day to day. There is a philosophy of the road which cheers them up, keeps them companionable, and enables them to live in intellectual poverty.[274]

Seashore stated that colleges must make room for flappers and loafers but warned that these types of people must not be allowed to "contaminate good students."[275]

According to the *Oxford English Dictionary* (*OED*), flappers tended to want the vote, and the dictionary cites a 1936 source reporting that a flapper was wearing a scandalous piece of apparel—slacks—while riding a *man's* bicycle.[276] Perhaps more importantly, however, the word "flapper" carried a judgment about a woman's sexual activity, which in turn, was a prime determinant of whether she was considered a moral person. The *OED* indicates, for example, that "flapper" was a slang term used as early as the 1880s to refer to a very young female prostitute or to a young and very immoral girl.[277] Thus, to call a woman a flapper was not merely to mark her as an emancipated woman but also to subtly degrade her by intimating that she was sexually active while not married, and consequently immoral. In the above passage, Seashore likened flappers to tramps, a word that, to the present, has negative connotations, and when it is applied to a woman, it links her morality to her sexual practices.[278]

By speaking disparagingly of flappers and other emancipated women, was

Seashore signaling that they were constitutionally and inherently unfit? On the one hand, perhaps he did deem them so, not on intellectual grounds but on moral ones, destined to fail due to inherent moral defect. On the other hand, perhaps in Seashore's estimation flappers and emancipated women were more akin to wayward women graduate students, fit sheep who had gone astray but could be redeemed through education. Behaving in a manner that *resembled* the hereditarily unfit was a sign that a fit woman had gone astray. Significantly, emancipated women and flappers may have held the same views and engaged in many of the same activities that Reske claims were grounds for the involuntary sterilization of women deemed inherently morally unfit. I found no evidence, however, that despite his criticism, Seashore supported using negative eugenics measures on flappers and emancipated women, any more than he was suggesting that problematic women graduate students should be sterilized or subjected to marriage restrictions. Rather, their race and class were protecting these women. Perhaps he would have offered flappers the same advice that he gave to women graduate students: come to your senses, go home, get married, and start having babies. This was not the advice eugenicists were giving to those labeled constitutionally unfit, however. Not only should women deemed unfit—whether because of race, economic status, morals, or intelligence—not be staying home with their children, they should not be having children at all. Fecundity was encouraged only for the fit.

So, it appears that women who were marked as hereditarily superior and destined to succeed had a choice, they had free will; they could choose to succeed or fail, the argument being similar to one that appeared in some Christian predestinarian tropes: although salvation is available to God's elect, free will means it can be lost through human choice. In Seashore's mind, education was key to helping the fittest maintain their fitness, make good choices, and avoid bad ones. Some women had the choice to be unfit while others were constitutionally unfit, denied any choice in the matter. Perhaps being marked as having the ability to choose, in addition to having a different array of choices available, was a prime factor distinguishing fit from unfit women.

Women, Containment, and Control

Although it is not clear whether Seashore deemed flappers and emancipated women unfit or simply misguided, it is clear that these were uncontained women, and Seashore was critical of them. He spoke positively of the charm of an educated woman; "charm" suggests allure and attractiveness but also implies a kind of mild and controlled sexuality. Charm is a dash of black pepper, not a whole jalapeño. Flappers and emancipated women, by contrast, were dishing out whole jalapeños, too spicy and too excessive for Seashore's taste.

When considering Seashore's views and influence concerning women's sexual activity, it is important to note that he was a member of the select group, several of whom were eugenicists, that attended Earl Zinn's sex research conference in 1921. In his analysis of the conference, Wade Pickren states that one overarching theme was the need to "impose control" over sexual behavior.[279] Seashore's participation in this conference is evidence that his views were probably consonant with those the conference promoted. For the fittest (especially the fittest women), sexual activity was to be reserved for marriage, and especially for the purpose of reproducing; for the unfit, sex, if it was to be had at all, was to be controlled and contained in its outcome either by contraception or sterilization. Thus, although Allan Chase notes that a "free-love wing of the world's eugenics movement" existed, which promoted sexual license and free procreation among the fittest—prompting Chase to call eugenics "scientific license for wholesale lechery"—Seashore does not appear to have lived in that wing.[280] In his autobiography, however, he talked about taking girls on sleigh rides when he was young and added in a rather wink-and-a-nod manner, "We learned more than spelling in those schools."[281] He did not elaborate on who constituted the "we" or what constituted the learning; however, sleigh rides tended to be associated with sexual adventures—however mild. It is possible that when it came to fit boys, Seashore looked the other way as they sowed their wild oats.

Imposing control in a host of arenas, including sexual activity, was a popular goal of eugenicists. Huntington's catechism supported state legislation (i.e., state control) that would effect the sterilization of those who lack self-control.[282] Of course, discourse and practice aimed at controlling women's sexual activity was ubiquitous outside of eugenics, evident, for example, in the prevalence of what some have called the virgin/whore dichotomy. It probably factored into Seashore's assessment of types of women, and it may also have made the containment discourses that flourished in eugenics seems sensible rather than outrageous.

The Third Sex, Eugenics, and Compulsory Heterosexuality

The plot thickens when sexuality is considered. Seashore did not explicitly discuss sexuality, although all of his comments about women and marriage were heteronormative. Other eugenicists addressed it head on, however. Kline details the role of eugenicists such as Lewis Terman and Paul Popenoe in constructing and perpetuating discourses of sexual maladjustment; in particular, she describes Terman's development of a test to "weed out homosexuals."[283] Ian Hacking argues that the homosexual as a "kind of person" came into being in the latter part of the nineteenth century, so even thinking about people as homosexuals was a relatively new phenomenon in the early twentieth century.[284]

According to Kline, twenty years after his work on the Stanford-Binet scale, Terman, with co-creator Catherine Miles, set out to "standardize male and female behavior just as he had standardized intelligence, thereby providing a mechanism to weed out both mental and sexual 'deviants.'"[285] Terman's masculinity-femininity test was based on the assumptions that there are two biologically determined sexes and that in "normal" individuals, a person's interests and activities align closely with stereotypical conceptions of what is appropriate for that person's sex assigned at birth. Kline states that the "test provided evidence that gender-inappropriate behavior was the key to the 'problem' of homosexuality."[286] Thus, venturing across the divide between what were considered masculine or feminine interests and activities became a marker of sexual deviance. In light of this information, Seashore's criticism of "mannish" women may have been an oblique reference to ostensibly deviant sexuality.

Kline observes that one similarity between Terman's tests of intelligence and of sexuality was their capacity to produce anxiety, which stemmed, in part, from the short distance between normalcy and deviance, and from the fear of being labeled one of *those* kinds of people: "Just as the Stanford-Binet test raised anxiety that only a few degrees separated 'feeblemindedness' from 'normal' mentality (it would be easy, in other words, to 'slip' into such a state), the M-F test provided evidence that only a simple deviation from masculinity or femininity separated the 'healthy heterosexual' from the 'homosexual invert.'"[287] Terman's sex test both reflected and reinforced the understanding that a line of distinction exists between two and only two possible sexuality categories: heterosexual and homosexual; similarly, his intelligence test was based on the assumption that clear lines of distinction exist between categories of intelligence: normal intelligence, giftedness, and feeble-mindedness.

There are other resemblances between these two projects. Both of them played a role in making up kinds of people. Both used psychometrics to help identify, sort, and order individuals, placing them in groups based on supposed similarities and differences; both simultaneously qualified some and disqualified others; and both used group placement to help justify different kinds of actions toward individuals. In each case, the sorting and order process constructed what Judith Butler calls a zone of abjection to which bodies that do not matter are relegated.[288]

Terman believed that homosexuality was a pathology, a characteristic of a particular kind of person—the homosexual—and his test ostensibly diagnosed the pathology, after which intervention could follow. Kline observes, "By either weeding out or 'curing' homosexuality, Terman believed he could stabilize the American family and thereby strengthen the race."[289] Citing Michael Kimmel, she reports that Terman's test was used in some school districts into the 1960s.[290] She also notes that eugenicist and marriage counselor Paul Popenoe, who rose to fame through his *Ladies' Home Journal* series "Can This Marriage Be Saved?," held similarly dim views of homosexuality; according to Kline, Popenoe, like Terman, viewed it "as a pathological condition that threatened marital stability and eugenic purity."[291]

Overall, the eugenics sources I examined were largely silent about sexuality, but this does not mean that the topic was of no interest to eugenicists; rather, my choice of sources may at least partially explain this absence. If I had read medical—specifically psychiatric—literature, my findings probably would have been different. That said, I found one eugenics source not directly related to Seashore, Herman Rubin's popular book *Eugenics and Sex Harmony: The Sexes, Their Relations and Problems*, that presented a more favorable, albeit mixed, view of homosexuality than that described by Kline. Rubin was a member of both the American Eugenics Society and the Eugenics Research Association. By the time the 1947 version I examined was published, the book, which first appeared in 1933, had gone through nineteen printings (and a revised edition in 1942).[292]

The Rubin textbook illustrates that there were at least a few degrees of freedom and some variance of opinion among eugenicists concerning sexuality. For example, to the somewhat outside-the-box question, "Is There a Third Sex?," Rubin responded that there is: homosexuals.[293] His brief discussion of homosexuals and homosexuality is relatively celebratory and supportive. First, he posited that homosexuality is very common. He stated that in the United States "sexual relations between women . . . are *extraordinarily* common [my emphasis]."[294] He claimed that homosexual activity is similarly "extraordinarily common" and "exceedingly prevalent" in boarding schools, prisons, the military, and lumber and mining camps.[295] He noted that the percentage of homosexuals was "very large" in particular professions, notably theater and musical comedy.[296] He described homosexuality as being on the increase in the United States and "even more flagrant in such capitals as Berlin, Paris, London, and Vienna."[297] Aside from the use of the word "flagrant," his commonality assertions did not necessarily suggest that homosexuality being common is problematic.

Next, he appeared supportive by pointing out that homosexuals have been major contributors to society at large and to a host of fields, as "splendid musicians, capable writers, adept hairdressers, and designers, and perhaps the best of all interior decorators."[298] Of course, by listing these particular ostensibly "feminine" fields, and later mentioning actors, Rubin reinforced stereotypes that persist to the present concerning males in these fields; that said, Rubin nevertheless praised the contributions of homosexuals.

Continuing the supportive and celebratory tone, he pushed back at the assertion that homosexuality is a physical or mental disease, stating it should not necessarily be viewed as "psychical degeneration, or even as a manifestation of disease."[299] He further asserted that homosexuality (and presumably he was referring to male homosexuality) is not associated with "marked decline in physical powers,"[300] and he quoted the Austro-German psychiatrist Richard von Krafft-Ebing, who claimed, "'Variations of the sexual life may actually be associated with mental superiority'";[301] Krafft-Ebing backed up this claim by pointing out that prominent men, including "'authors, poets, leaders of armies, and statesmen'" have been gay.[302] Rubin may have cherry-picked his citations, however, because Krafft-Ebing is better known for his assertion that homosexuality is a pathology. Rubin, again quoting Krafft-Ebing, went so far as to say that homosexuality is not "'necessarily a vicious self-surrender to the immoral,'"[303] and he even appeared to have proffered a eugenical seal of approval, stating that it is general opinion (Rubin citing sexologist Magnus Hirschfeld to support this) that there is "no definite stigmata of degeneration among these individuals. *Nor do they inherit any tendency toward hereditary taint* [emphasis mine]."[304] Again citing Hirschfield, Rubin further stated that there is no evidence that homosexuality is caused by interbreeding or by parental alcoholism, syphilis, or mental disorders.[305]

Even in this more celebratory text, however, the messages were mixed. Common is not synonymous with normal, and in the space of three pages, Rubin referred to the abnormality of homosexuality thirteen times;[306] in one instance, he called it "trouble."[307] He said that some people take pride in their "un-normality."[308]

Hints of pathology are evident even in his discussion of the prevalence of homosexuality and its early signs. For example, he claimed that homosexuality was on the increase and listed a number of conditions contributing to this, none of which were positive factors: increased wealth and leisure time, the departure of "hundreds of thousands of people from the old fashioned domestic life,"[309] being away from parental influence at boarding school,[310] and living in a state of heterosexual deprivation (e.g., prison).[311] Consistent with Terman's thinking, Rubin provided possible early signs of homosexuality, including cross-dressing and engaging in activities not deemed appropriate for a child assigned to a particular sex. According to Rubin, when these activities continue at puberty, the child should be examined by a doctor with the goal of possibly correcting the abnormality:

> For, not infrequently, the entire trouble may be absolutely corrected by merely aiding the thymus gland to regress normally, and allow normal development of the sexual organs of the boy or the girl to be completed.
>
> In which event, all traces of abnormal yearnings for those of his or her own sex will be removed, and the true heterosexual function will be restored.[312]

Thus, he applied the pathology-diagnosis-intervention-cure model; to Rubin, the homosexual is a pathological body in need of a cure.

The primary-source eugenics literature is vast, and I do not know how representative the slightly more liberal views expressed in Rubin's popular textbook were. Nevertheless, his book is evidence that there were a few small degrees of freedom within eugenics discourse concerning sexuality. Given that this was the case, where did Seashore stand? Although I found no explicit reference in Seashore's texts, I argue that like race, sexuality is an absent presence in his work. A complex, symbiotic, mutually supportive relationship existed among discourses about sex, gender, sexuality, race, and social class. If, as Gayle Rubin argues, compulsory heterosexuality is a glue that holds sex/gender systems together, then this absent presence is a critical part of the systems of reasoning that made eugenics sensible.[313] Thus, in his discussions of women and higher education, Seashore supported what Kline calls "white womanhood,"[314] a race- and class-based set of ideas and practices that also trade in and shore up heteronormativity.

Can silence constitute a stance? In the case of Seashore's silence on sexuality, I argue that it can. In the absence of evidence to the contrary, specifically any evidence that Seashore spoke out against the dominant views of hard-line eugenicists such as Terman and Popenoe, I maintain that given how deeply ensconced Seashore was in eugenics, his silence indicates that his views were consistent with the dominant perspectives held by hard-liners.

Thus, although eugenicists, including Seashore, tended to support control and containment of women generally, especially sexual containment, they promoted different kinds of intervention for different groups of women. The process of categorization, whether into races, social classes, sexes, sexualities, religions, or immigrant groups, was instrumental in effecting different forms of containment and in producing vastly different outcomes for different groups of women, even though containment of all women was an overarching theme. In addition to the existence of different rules for different types of women concerning sexual activity, reproduction, and marriage, there were gendered double standards, overall.

Maintaining White Supremacy: Reading the Charm of an Educated Woman Intersectionally

Acknowledging that Seashore was an avowed eugenicist and bringing eugenics into an analysis of his statements about women makes visible connections and intersections that might otherwise remain hidden. One such connection is how his views on women, education, marriage, fertility, and career were grounded in and integrally related to the White supremacist discourse on race that was foundational to eugenics. Seashore did not mention race in the references to women that I examined, but it always was hovering in the wings, an absent and yet powerful presence. Just beneath the surface lie racialized anxieties. Other eugenicists, however, robustly expressed White supremacist views and conveyed high levels of White anxiety in journals and books sponsored by the organization to which Seashore belonged, and in eugenics publications where Seashore's work also appeared. Seashore's sexist statements are connected to discourses that sort and order people and groups into races, classes, abilities, sexualities, and citizenship categories. The 1921 eugenics tree logo stated that eugenics "draws its materials from many sources and organizes them into an harmonious entity."[315] Seashore's views on women constituted one such source that combined with many others to effectively benefit a few at the expense of most.

Amid the limited diversity of viewpoints in the eugenics universe, Seashore's beliefs nested him close to the hard-liners, and consequently to the racist fears on which eugenics was grounded. Why were White, college-educated women wanted at home? For eugenicists such as Seashore, one reason was to maintain the birth rate of so-called superiors—presumably all of whom were White; without this, eugenicists warned, superiors would be washed away by degenerates and inferiors. Viewed in this light, Seashore's call for faculty family allowances was not mere advocacy of family-friendly policies in academe. It was a xenophobic, classed, and racialized response to a call to arms; the alleged peril was the potential annihilation of the supposedly superior forms of the human race. Were Seashore's statements aimed at preserving the patriarchy, or shoring up compulsory heterosexuality, or maintaining class distinctions, or upholding the Racial Contract? The answer is yes on all counts.

Five

Mental Ability, Testing, and the Pedagogical Production of Destinies

One of Seashore's career goals was to apply psychology to a host of disciplines, including education.[1] He believed, for example, that psychological knowledge could be used to identify and solve what he perceived to be education's problems. He was intensely interested in human mental ability, which he maintained was governed by innate, biologically inheritable capacity; this interest animated his scholarly work, and it was shared by other prominent psychologists who were eugenicists. Thus, it is not surprising that his perception of the problems of education and his proposed solutions often focused on how mental ability was understood and addressed in education. He became identified with a number of wide-ranging education interventions and reforms. This chapter focuses on what he perceived to be education's ability-related problems and solutions.

I begin by examining his beliefs about mental ability—intelligence, in particular—and by discussing his participation in nascent intelligence testing initiatives. Next, I describe his role in creating, promoting, and using a wide array of standardized mental tests, including college admissions and placement tests, occupational fitness tests, and tests of artistic ability. I also discuss his role in making Iowa a hotbed in the burgeoning standardized testing movement. In the second half of the chapter, I examine his proposed education reforms, most of which were predicated on the administration of standardized tests. I describe and analyze his educational philosophy, focusing on what he believed the goals of education should be and on his perceptions of the shortcomings that prevented those goals from being achieved. I detail several of his proposed reforms, including the establishment of a hierarchy of institutions of higher education, the institution of sectioning by ability, and the creation of special programs and opportunities for students identified as gifted. Finally, I analyze Seashore's claims and promises about what his proposed reforms would accomplish. Throughout the chapter, I demonstrate how eugenics informed and infused his thought and activities. Specifically, I argue that his focus on what was assumed to be biologically inheritable capacity, his goals for education, his beliefs about what was problematic about education, his proposed education interventions, and his reform claims and promises, all were consistent with and steeped in eugenics. Finally, I maintain that the education reform he envisioned and helped to implement, which involved systematic identification and differentiation based on presumed innate capacity, followed by segregation, promotion, and elimination, is a eugenics blueprint that situates him firmly in the thick of the movement, in the company of some of the most hardcore eugenicists of his time.

I decided to use the word "ability" to describe the focus of Seashore's research interests that I discuss in this chapter. I maintain that mental ability and many related concepts—including talent, intelligence, and gift—are social constructs, and I recognize that these terms are polysemic—replete with messy, ever-shifting, and sometimes overlapping meanings. I chose "ability" both because it is broad and because it can refer simply to having the means or skill to do something. The term can be agnostic about why that something can be done, and it is broad in the sense that the kinds of things that can be done are manifold. I selected it, in part, as a signal that I do not subscribe, for the most part, to Seashore's understandings of why people can or cannot do things. Nevertheless, I recognize that choosing this term—especially to describe his work on intelligence and talent—has its problems. I suspect that if he were alive, he might quarrel with me, arguing that "capacity" would be a more accurate descriptor of intelligence or talent. Indeed, in one of his publications, he drew a distinction between capacity and ability, defining capacity as "inborn or native power," and ability as acquired skill.[2] According to this distinction, intelligence is a type of innate capacity and musical talent is another type; having ability is premised on having innate capacity. In his conception, someone does not become intelligent or talented—someone either is or is not; this state of being, in turn, determines whether one can become able. Therefore, ability, according to Seashore, even though it is distinct from capacity, is governed by biologically determined, innate, inherited capacity. In his estimation, capacity cannot grow; it can only be allowed to flourish into ability. Furthermore, according to this logic, having or not having capacity is not simply a characteristic of a person or a state of being; rather, it constructs a kind of person: the gifted child, the genius, or the unfit. A second reason I decided not to abide by Seashore's distinction is that he did not consistently abide by it; he tended to use terms loosely and sometimes conflated capacity and ability. For example, he referred to "natural ability," but if ability is an acquired skill, then natural ability is an oxymoron.[3] Elsewhere he advocated comparing students' accomplishments to their ability.[4] Once again, if he had abided by the ability-capacity distinction, he would have used the word "capacity."

Unlike those who reserve "gift" for high academic ability and "talent" for high artistic ability, Seashore used the word "gift" to describe both high intellectual and high musical capacity, and he made the same assumptions about both concerning their provenance. Unlike those who view genius as a more distilled and potent form of talent, he saw genius as somewhat distinct from it and more highly prized; he assumed that genius, too, is grounded in biologically inherited innate capacity. "Gift" is an interesting term to describe high ability because a gift is, by definition, something freely given to someone. A gift is not earned; the recipient does not contribute and has no further obligation—other than perhaps to be grateful for the gift or to use it wisely. Thus, according to Seashore, high intelligence and talent cannot be acquired through work; they are simply freely given gifts.

I employ the terms "inherited," and "biologically inheritable" in the circumscribed way that early-twentieth-century eugenicists such as Seashore used them—meaning transmissible according to Mendelian understandings of genetics. I recognize that the word "genetics" was not used in a biological sense until well into Seashore's career and that biological inheritability may involve more than genetics. I also recognize that theirs is a narrow, partial, and situated understanding of these terms. "Inherit," which from earliest times has meant to come into possession by descent, dates to the fifteenth century and in its earliest usage, referred to the transfer of material goods, title, or privilege.[5] Sometime thereafter, it began to refer to the familial transmission of a physical, mental, or personality characteristic. For example, in 1600, William Shakespeare used the term in this manner in *Henry IV* when he stated, "The cold blood he did naturally inherite of his father."[6] As Stefan Willer argues, however, these early usages were different from Francis Galton's deployment of the term and from biological understandings of inheritance generally.[7] Thus, when I talk about Seashore's belief that ability is "inheritable," I am referring to the Galtonian meaning, which claimed that ability is transmissible via a specific biological process.

Identifying Ability

Natural Ability, Fitness, and Quality

A basic tenet of eugenics is that mental capacity or talent—sometimes called natural ability—is biologically inheritable and immutable. By extension, quality—or its supposed lack—is similarly assumed to be based in biological heredity, and high or low innate ability (sometimes called capacity) as measured by some predetermined metric is considered to be a marker of innate high or low quality. Although Seashore sometimes mentioned the needs of society when discussing the types of education that should be made available to individuals and groups, he, like other eugenicists, assumed that ability—and hence quality—resides in the body rather than being a cultural construction reflecting a society's needs, values, desires, and fears.

The terms "fit," "fitness," "unfit," and "unfitness" were elements in the eugenics lexicon, and they appeared quite frequently in Seashore's writings. For example, he supported entrance exams to sort and order students who may be interested in attending college, hailing tests as an aid in determining whether a student has "a college brain": "This will discourage the unfit and encourage the fit, which is our main objective, before the great risk of the college venture has been taken. It will improve our college timber and reduce college failures."[8] This usage may have stemmed from the concept of survival of the fittest, which was derived from Darwinian evolutionary theory.

Eugenicists conceptualized three broad domains in which quality or fitness can be manifest: physical, mental, and moral. The fittest of the fit were of high quality in all three domains. *Capacity* was understood to be biologically inheritable and immutable, but *fitness*, which was grounded in heredity, needed to be maintained. Capacity needed to be accessed and cultivated to maintain fitness. The use of "fit" and "unfit" was loose, however, sometimes referring to innate, constitutional characteristics and at other times to acquired characteristics. Thus, quality was to be maintained by maintaining fitness. The Boy Scout Oath, in which boys promise to *keep* themselves "physically strong, mentally awake, and morally straight," came to mind as I considered eugenicists' tripartite conception of the fitness of the supposedly superior. I subsequently found evidence suggesting that the resemblance is not coincidental. In his book *The Rhetoric of Eugenics in Anglo-American Thought*, Marouf Arif Hasian Jr. reports that eugenicists strongly supported the Boy Scout movement.[9] He quotes the British eugenicist Caleb Saleeby, who maintained that scouting was a boon to eugenics: "'If national eugenics is ever to be achieved in Great Britain it will come through the Boy Scouts and the Girl Guides, who almost alone, of all our young people, are being made ready, by 'training in citizenship, character, discipline, and patriotism,' for education for parenthood, which must be the beginning of national eugenics. This movement is what national education in Great Britain has tried and failed to be for forty years.'"[10]

The original Scout Promise was created by the founder of the Scouts, Robert Baden-Powell, who was British. According to Hasian Jr., the US version of the Promise was written by hereditarian Jeremiah Jenks;[11] this version added the phrase "physically strong, mentally awake, and morally straight." Jenks was an economist at Cornell University whose research on race and immigration and work on the Dillingham Commission played a key role in developing restrictive immigration policies and laws in the early twentieth century. Eugenicists lobbied for these policies and laws.

Seashore's writings focus largely on mental ability and fitness—as well as on their double-gesture twins, mental disability and unfitness—and particularly on intelligence or its lack. That said, he sometimes used a wider lens and discussed characteristics of the whole person,[12] and he also commented on physical and moral fitness. For example, he advised graduate students, women especially, to develop and maintain excellent physical and mental health, and not to allow studying to destroy either;[13] he added, "The recognition of the possibilities and the significance of physical fitness is an achievement of modern science. It is a matter of intellectual economy and scientific morality. The scholar is now not only expected to show good judgment in regard to matters of physical health; but, in the culture of today, the maintenance of health has become a moral question."[14] His comment that maintaining physical health is a moral question for scholars is puzzling until eugenicists' fear of race suicide is considered.[15] The fittest have a moral obligation to maintain their health in order to survive and reproduce. Another example of his concern about morality is found in an address to high school students attending a Brain Derby at the University of Iowa in 1941; he spoke of their duties as the brightest of the bright, one of them being to maintain their moral health.[16]

Seashore on Intelligence

Like his forebear eugenicist Francis Galton, Seashore staunchly subscribed to and promulgated eugenical inheritability claims concerning intelligence. As evidenced in his references to Gregor Mendel, he was a Mendelian hereditarian.[17] Furthermore, in his autobiography, he called himself a Darwinian evolutionist and mentioned his abandonment of Alfred Russel Wallace's position on the evolution of the "mental life" in favor of Darwin's: "The first year [of doctoral study at Yale] I undertook to defend Wallace's point of view in opposition to Darwin's, namely, that while evolution holds sway in all organic life, it does not apply to mental life. The conclusion stated as a result of my year's work was that Wallace was wrong and Darwin was right, just the opposite of what I had started to prove."[18] It is not clear from this passage whether "mental life" referred narrowly to intelligence or whether it included other elements—mental health, for example.

He maintained that in populations, mental capacity or intelligence is normally distributed,[19] and he referred to what he called "natural laws," including the "law of the distribution of mental capacity";[20] elsewhere he called it the "law of distribution of brains."[21] Significantly, although he used a normal curve to describe the distribution of intelligence in populations, in a 1909 address to undergraduates in the colleges of Iowa, he used a pyramid—not a curve—to describe human *achievement*. In doing so, he mapped out gradations, or a hierarchy—even within the top of the achievement pyramid: "The pyramid of human achievement is like every other pyramid; it tapers toward the top and the top would be useless without the broad expanding base and all intervening strata."[22] Unlike a normal curve, which tapers at both ends, a pyramid is largest at its base, at the bottom. What is similar about a normal intelligence curve and Seashore's achievement pyramid, however, is the limited space at the top. When he claimed that all gradations below the top are needed, he was addressing college students, all of whom he would place at the top of the pyramid. Thus, he was describing the need for gradations within the top, gradations within a *segment* of the pyramid; he also was calling for identification, sorting, and ordering within that segment. Notably, Seashore considered supporting the top to be a primary and appropriate purpose of whoever is seated below.

As Leila Zenderland discusses in her book *Measuring Minds: Henry Herbert Goddard and the Origins of American Intelligence Testing*, there was lack of consensus among psychologists in the early twentieth century about the nature of intelligence and how it might best be measured.[23] Regardless of the debate among psychologists about its nature, Seashore and other eugenicists prized high intelligence, however it was conceived. For many eugenicists, statements such as eugenicist and White supremacist Madison Grant's—"breed from the best, or . . . eliminate the worst by segregation or sterilization"[24]—were calls for selective human breeding for intelligence even though intelligence was determined by shifting criteria.

Part of the legacy of Galton and his like-minded contemporaries was the assumption that eminence is an indicator of intelligence, as was the belief that high intelligence is a characteristic of the best. Another part of that legacy was the use of human pedigree studies as evidence of the biological inheritability of talent; in a pedigree study, the investigator examines multiple generations of a family for examples of individuals demonstrating eminence in a particular field. A third component of the legacy was keen research interest among eugenicists in the biological inheritability of mental ability and in selective breeding for intelligence. Consider, for example, Ernst Kretschmer's article "The Breeding of the Mental Endowments of Genius," which appeared in the journal *Eugenics* in 1931. Kretschmer, a psychiatrist at the University of Marburg, opened with the oft-stated claim that heredity is responsible for talent and genius: "That heredity and not environmental factors constitutes the fundamental cause for the achievements of great talent may be considered as definitely established at the present stage of our knowledge."[25] Presumably, the qualifier "fundamental" was a nod to the need for a fertile environment if inherent ability is to grow and flourish; acknowledging this is consistent with eugenicists' advocacy of euthenics. As was typical of work appearing in eugenics publications in the early twentieth century, the article cited a host of eminence pedigree studies, including Galton's work, as proof of the biological inheritability of talent and genius.[26] It described two groups of geniuses whose pedigrees had been studied: the first consisted of artists and musicians, and the second of scholars, ministers, poets, military leaders, and politicians.[27] The article closed with a discussion of the effects of human hybridization on intelligence.[28] As Daniel Kevles notes, "Like Francis Galton . . . eugenicists identified human worth with the qualities they presumed *themselves* to possess—the sort that facilitated passage through schools, universities, and professional training. They tended to equate merit with intelligence, particularly of the academic sort [emphasis mine]."[29]

Intellectuals, Especially Academics, Among the Best

Seashore's writings indicate that he counted intellectuals—particularly academics, including himself—among the best and fittest. For example, in an article entitled "Academic Business," which first appeared in *School and Society* in 1945, he stated that the university's "primary business interest is the faculty and the students—select and superior minds, experts, and specialists; its personnel problem is that of selecting, promoting, improving, and satisfying a superior lot of human beings on humanistic and idealistic principles for the vitalizing of learning."[30] Elsewhere, in praise of the scholar and the scholarly life, he claimed that scholars are accorded an immortality not available to those engaged in "lower orders of service," the mere mortals: "But the scholarly life has another characteristic, in reality a phase of immortality, in the fact that, unlike work in the lower orders of service, his life work may continue for generations and ages after his death."[31] In "Academic Business," he mentioned a question he had fielded from an immigrant grocer after having delivered a speech at a commercial club event. Imitating the grocer's accent, he revealed his own belief in the superiority of academics—and perhaps nonimmigrants—as well as his attitude toward those he presumed to be lesser beings. According to Seashore, the grocer remarked, "'Dat vas a nice talk by the professor; but vot dos he know about beesness?'"[32] Seashore reported that the chairman of the event came to Seashore's "rescue" by pointing out that the grocer probably handled $20,000 per year, but that as dean of the Graduate School, Seashore was the administrator of an annual budget of between two and three million dollars.[33] In the face of the magnitude of Seashore's importance as a dean, the grocer was diminished and became the butt of a joke to be retold in a scholarly journal.

Furthermore, Seashore publicly counted himself among the fittest. In his autobiography, he described himself as a successful man—Galton probably would have used the term "eminent"—and he thanked good fortune, including the good luck of having a good pedigree, for his success: "I have been a lucky man—lucky in the place and race of my nativity, in the 'choice' of my parents, in my education, in my jobs, in my travels, in my marriage and children, in success and recognition beyond my fondest expectations."[34]

Other Types of Mental Ability and Disability

Seashore was interested in other varieties of mental ability or disability in addition to intelligence. Evidence supporting this claim appeared in his autobiographical description of his contributions to clinical psychology and psychiatry; he wrote about his involvement in establishing the University of Iowa's Psychological Clinic (in 1908) and the Institute of Mental Health. Speaking of a need for diagnosis and treatment, he lumped together criminals and those he called "mental defectives" in his description of the people for whom these institutions were intended: "For many years inquiries came to me in regard to the availability of a psychiatrist to treat mental patients, and I had to say that there was no one in Iowa. Cases were, therefore, referred to the heads of hospitals for the insane who, except in one or two cases, were primarily business managers. No adequate provision was made for the examination, not to mention treatment, of mental defectives and criminals."[35] In an early discussion of the practical applications of psychology and the need for consulting psychologists, he stated that mental pathology was among the domains where such expertise would be useful, and he listed various conditions comprising it:

> [Mental pathology] embraces all institutions for those who deviate from the normal condition of the mind; such as insane asylums, schools for the sensory defective, institutions for moral delinquents, homes for the feeble-minded, epileptic colonies, the provision for the abnormally retarded and mentally defective in the public schools, and special schools, clinics, foundations, laboratories or retreats for the study and treatment of mental deviation.[36]

Thus, psychological clinics were to be big tents designed for people with intellectual disabilities and a host of other conditions, including mental illness. Walter Miles reported that Seashore went on a fact-finding mission to Henry Goddard's training school for the feeble-minded in Vineland, New Jersey, during the period when he was considering the formation of the Psychology Clinic at Iowa.[37] He further reported that Seashore was instrumental in creating a psychological clinic for children, which he said was established in about 1910; he claimed that it was only the second such clinic at a US university and stated that "it dealt primarily with the problems of feeble-mindedness and retarded development."[38]

Seashore said that one goal of the Institute of Mental Health was the "early discovery of mental defects and the organization of specific treatment for each."[39] He listed projects in speech pathology and reading disabilities as examples of the work done there.[40] Stuttering, apparently, was considered a form of unfitness, a treatable mental pathology.

Seashore also championed the creation of the Psychopathic Hospital at the University of Iowa, which he stated was established in 1915.[41] Miles reported that the idea for the hospital came to Seashore after he had attended G. Stanley Hall's famous 1909 psychologists' conference at Clark University; Carl Jung and Sigmund Freud also attended.[42] Seashore claimed that "Iowa was therefore one of the first states to take this step of providing a research center for mental diseases at the University."[43] Residential institutions that warehoused people labeled "insane" existed long before the formation of the Psychopathic Hospital at Iowa; the Iowa hospital was different, however, in that it focused on research and treatment. In a 1944 letter to University of Iowa president Virgil M. Hancher, Seashore urged Hancher to consider building a similar hospital for children—a "hospital for the experimental treatment of mental and behavioral disorders of children": "Fundamentally it involves taking the children from the Out-Patient Service of the Psychopathic Hospital and the Psychological Clinic and providing for them the housing and treatment now accorded to adult patients in the Psychopathic Hospital."[44]

Seashore's interest in varieties of mental ability and disability other than intelligence is evident in his description of how he fostered coordination and cooperation between psychology and psychiatry at Iowa.[45] He also mentioned the fruits of these efforts in a 1923 letter to University of Iowa president W. A. Jessup, using them as evidence of the university's dedication to "scientific investigation for the advancement of the welfare of humanity."[46] Seashore described a number of coordinated, associated projects designed to study and treat all aspects of the child:

> Practically every angle of child life is touched by experts in their respective fields; the specialization in medicine is well known; our child welfare station is the best organized scientific station of this kind in the country; our psychological clinic for the study of borderline and defective children is unique in that it is associated with the child welfare station for the study of the normal child, with the psychopathic hospital for the study of mental defects, and with the psychological laboratory for general scientific investigations bearing on child life.[47]

Miles stated that in the early twentieth century, both psychiatry and psychology were relatively new fields and that "to most doctors then [psychiatry] represented a new-fangled fad with which they would have nothing to do"; he noted that early relations between clinical psychology and psychiatry were "hazardous."[48] According to Miles, not only did Seashore build bridges at Iowa, he attempted to foster cooperation and coordination between psychology and psychiatry at the national level during the period when he was vice-chairman of the Division of Anthropology and Psychology of the National Research Council (NRC).[49]

Finally, further evidence of Seashore's interest in mental phenomena other than intelligence is found in Miles's description of a course in abnormal psychology that Seashore "offered in his department."[50] According to Miles, the course "gave major attention to the more curious examples of mental behavior: dreams, hallucinations, automatic writing, hypnotism, alternating personalities, and other phenomena, classified under psychical research."[51]

Seashore's comments regarding these various mental phenomena confirm that although in some cases, eugenical intervention involved totally eliminating the individual or group, in other cases, it aimed to eliminate the supposed pathology that rendered individuals or groups unfit or defective. Thus, to at least some eugenicists, some forms of unfitness, even though they were deemed pathological, were also considered correctable or treatable, and at least some eugenicists thought it acceptable and worthwhile to apply these corrections. Seashore was among them.

In such discussions, Seashore adopted an interventional medical model that included identification, diagnosis, and when possible, treatment or even prevention of disease or pathology. For example, he wrote that the purpose of the Iowa Institute of Mental Hygiene was "scientific investigation, treatment, and prevention of mental disorders."[52] In describing coordinated efforts between the Institute, the Psychiatric Hospital, and the Psychological Clinic, he similarly used language consistent with discourses of interventional medicine:

> [At the Institute] emphasis is placed upon the early discovery of mental defects and the organization of specific treatment for each. . . . Another unit which is being formulated is the development of a systematic psychiatric survey with corrective treatment in the hope of discovering inceptive maladjustments in young school children when they are most amenable to treatment.
>
> Thus, the program of the Institute is a program of preventive medicine on the mental side joined to the continual treatment in the Psychiatric Hospital and the Psychological Clinic.[53]

Finally, Seashore was interested in mental *abnormality*; this interest is consistent with eugenicists' tendency to focus on the two tails rather than the middle of the normal curve. Hamilton Cravens, in his book on the formation of the Iowa Child Welfare Research Station, an institution that conducted research on the normal child, writes that initially Seashore was the station's strongest opponent because he wanted instead "a clinic or hospital for *problem* children within the university medical college [emphasis mine]."[54] Seashore eventually changed his views about the value of the station and in his autobiography took at least partial credit for its formation.[55] Thus, both the normal and its double-gesture twin, the abnormal, were of interest to Seashore and were under study at the University of Iowa.

"Testing, Testing, One, Two, Three": Identifying and Measuring Innate Mental Ability, Differentiating, and Assigning Worth

Testing for Intelligence

Like many other eugenicists, Seashore was a proponent of using intelligence tests in a variety of contexts to identify ability and fitness. In *Pioneering in Psychology*, published in 1942, he retrospectively described discussions he had had early in his career with Alfred Binet and Theodore Simon, and he mentioned the impact of these discussions on his research interests: "In 1895 I spent some time with Binet and Simon in Paris, discussing the possible nature and purpose of the now-famous Binet tests. With this began my growing interest in the possibilities of differential psychology and the extension of measurements beyond the walls of the laboratory."[56] In his autobiography, he reported that after he completed his doctorate at Yale in 1895, he went abroad during the summer; the meeting with Binet and Simon occurred at that time.[57] The above quotation links the young Seashore to the very beginnings of intelligence testing and to the creators of the first intelligence test—to an early period prior to the test's importation to the United States. His meeting with Binet and Simon occurred more than a decade before the Binet test was picked up and reworked by American psychologists such as Lewis Terman and Henry Goddard. Neither Binet nor Simon was a eugenicist, but many of the American psychologists who favored IQ testing were, including Terman and Goddard. In addition to placing Seashore in the thick of the intelligence testing movement early on, the passage indicates that late in life, he remained proud to stand on the shoulders of the movement's founding fathers and to trace his intellectual lineage back to them.

Zenderland notes that during this period, lack of consensus about the nature of intelligence spilled over into discussions of intelligence testing.[58] In his role as editor of the *Journal of Educational Psychology*, Seashore contributed to the burgeoning intelligence movement by facilitating published discussions of this subject. Zenderland explains: "Still anxious to achieve a broader and more meaningful professional consensus, in early 1916 [eugenicist Robert Mearns] Yerkes conferred with Carl Seashore, one of the editors of the *Journal of Educational Psychology*. It was time to ground intelligence testing in some basic psychological principles, he insisted, while also calling professional attention to its 'dangerous developments.' In response, Seashore proposed using the pages of his journal for a symposium."[59] Yerkes did not explicitly state what he considered the "dangerous developments" to be, but he clearly opposed the use of age scales.[60] Among such developments may have been some widely publicized and heavily ridiculed deployments of intelligence tests that had put psychologists on the defensive; these deployments prompted psychologists to circle the wagons and argue that only psychologists should be administering the tests.[61]

Yerkes's support for a committee to hash out these matters (the committee ultimately took the form of a symposium) appeared in a letter he sent to Seashore in February 1916; Seashore published most of Yerkes's letter in the March issue of the *Journal of Educational Psychology*.[62] Yerkes stated that he and Seashore were "'in perfect agreement as to the direction for further work'"; the two men also appeared to agree on the kind of scale to be used in intelligence tests.[63] In addition to publishing Yerkes's letter, Seashore responded to Yerkes's request for a symposium by issuing an invitation to "workers in this field of testing" to join the discussion by writing letters that would present their views and offer suggestions on next steps in intelligence testing.[64] He listed ten problems that he believed should be addressed, including what such tests should be called, what "traits" should be tested, what scales should be used, and how to train test administrators in light of the American Psychological Association's recent vote that only qualified psychologists should be allowed to administer the Binet tests.[65] In a subsequent issue, he stated that in addition to the global invitation, he also had solicited responses from a few select individuals.[66] The result was a collection of letters that appeared in 1916 in three successive issues of the *Journal of Psychology*; the majority were written by eugenicists, including Lewis Terman, James R. Angell (who later became the president of Yale University), Harry Levi Hollingworth, Thomas H. Haines, Clara Harrison Town, John Edward Wallace Wallin, Guy M. Whipple, and Henry Goddard; Seashore published two letters from Goddard, the second ending with a strong defense of the Binet scale.[67] In addition, between January and May of 1916, Seashore and Yerkes corresponded back and forth on the topic of intelligence test scales, and in one of these letters, Yerkes invited Seashore to chair a subcommittee addressing the question of scales; the correspondence also indicates that Seashore and Yerkes met face-to-face during this period.[68] Seashore's role as facilitator and editor of this published symposium, and his back-and-forth correspondence with Yerkes concerning test scales, place him and a host of other prominent eugenicists in the center of discussions about intelligence testing; they indicate that he was well aware of the issues and controversies surrounding this testing and how to conceptualize intelligence.

Seashore also was party to the creation of the Army Alpha and Beta tests.

These intelligence tests were designed by psychologists, including eugenicists Lewis Terman and Robert Mearns Yerkes, and were to be used by the US military to select and position US Army recruits during World War I.[69] In an excerpt from *Pioneering in Psychology*, Seashore again placed himself at the center of the nascent intelligence movement—a center thickly populated by eugenicists—stating that as an ex-president of the American Psychological Association, he attended a historic by-invitation-only meeting where psychologists decided that they could help the war effort by developing an intelligence test:

> The day we entered the first World War [April 6, 1917], President Wilson asked the American Psychological Association for an immediate report on what psychology could do in selecting and developing an efficient personnel. Professor Yerkes, then president of the association, called the living ex-presidents of the association to a meeting the following day. We met for dinner in the faculty club of Columbia University and by nine o'clock had passed a resolution to organize the now-famous Army Mental Tests. After the resolution had been passed, we sat around the table discussing the project until two o'clock when practically all of us felt uncertain about the possibilities implied; but as we had already caught the spirit of war psychology, no one was willing to prove a slacker by moving reconsideration. Immediate steps were taken to set a staff of psychologists to work on the development of the tests, now generally known as mental tests.[70]

Seashore's admission that "practically all of us felt uncertain" but nobody asked for reconsideration of the resolution because they had "caught the spirit of war psychology" is thought provoking. Although he implied that he was among the "practically all of us" who were uncertain, he did not elaborate on the nature of this uncertainty. Seashore's biographer, Walter Miles, indicated that Seashore supported the Army tests early on, however: "He believed in their probable usefulness and later saw this faith fully justified."[71]

Seashore discussed the value of the Army Alpha and Beta tests elsewhere as well, describing them as part of a well-oiled personnel machine that effectively sorted and ordered, promoting the fittest and eliminating the unfit:

> In World War I, this personnel work began with the then famous Army mental tests which were designed specifically to eliminate the mentally unfit. From such a beginning the [military] service devel-

> oped rapidly into positive machinery for effective sorting on the basis of tests and case histories and assigning to particular branches of the service. The resultant specialization in emergency training replaced the old pervading practice of promotion on seniority and set up criteria for selection and promotion in terms of achievement records.[72]

According to him, merit as measured by the tests—whether it was innate or achieved—would rightly trump seniority as the determinant of selection and career promotion in the military. During World War II, Seashore wrote again about the well-oiled military selection machine, and significantly, in a draft version of the publication, he stated that careful sorting and ordering keeps the fittest men *off* the battlefield (that is, out of harm's way):

> Never before has there been such deliberate and well planned procedure through personnel service in the selection and organization of a particular fitness through natural ability and training as is operating at the present time at headquarters, in every camp and at the front. Our enlisted chemists, physicists, physicians, dentists, engineers, mathematicians, historians, artists, educators, psychologists, economists and philosophers, are not used as cannon fodder, but, as a rule, are set to work in technical investigation and professional and technical services, each within his particular field of competence.[73]

Thus, protection from death in battle appears to have been one of the privileges that Seashore felt should rightly be given to the elite; this belief probably had its roots, at least in part, in eugenics. One concern eugenicists raised shortly after World War I was that the war had killed too many of the fittest men, and in so doing had contributed to race suicide. Seashore was probably aware of this concern; his claim that careful sorting and ordering were keeping the fittest out of harm's way may have been an assurance that measures were in place to prevent another dysgenic catastrophe. Significantly, in one published version of the article, he changed one sentence in this passage, perhaps after recognizing that at least some of those he deemed to be the fittest *were* in combat; he may also have realized that the original wording insulted everyone who went into battle by implying that they were less fit: "Our enlisted chemists, physicists, physicians, dentists, engineers, mathematicians, historians, artists, educators, psychologists, and economists are not necessarily used as cannon fodder, although many prefer to take the risk."[74] Thus, the high value that Seashore placed on the elite was on display in the *draft* of this article whereas it was masked somewhat in the final version.

The Army Alpha and Beta tests were administered to about 1.5 million recruits during World War I, and Mott Linn credits these tests, which he describes as objective, with helping to popularize examinations of this kind.[75] After World War I, the Army Alpha was put to use in contexts other than selecting and placing war recruits. For example, it was among the tests administered to subjects in Charles Davenport and Morris Steggerda's famous eugenics study, which is described in their 1929 book *Race Crossing in Jamaica*.[76]

Standardized College Qualifying Tests

Perhaps the most significant repurposing of the Army Alpha test was undertaken by Carl Brigham, a psychologist and eugenicist who had helped Yerkes administer the Army Mental Tests during World War I. After the war, he joined the faculty of Princeton University and in 1922 authored the book *A Study of American Intelligence*. Edwin Black describes this particular contribution to racist eugenical discourse and practice:

> A radical raceologist, Brigham analyzed Yerkes's findings for the world at large, casting them as eugenic evidence of Nordic supremacy and the racial inferiority of virtually everyone else. Brigham's 1922 book, *A Study of American Intelligence*, published by no less than Princeton University Press, openly conceded that the volume was based on two earlier raceological books, Madison Grant's virulently racist *Passing of the Great Race*, and William Ripley's equally biased *Races of Europe*.[77]

Brigham modified the Army Alpha test for use as an entrance examination designed to determine who was fit to enroll in college. A similar test Brigham helped design was adopted and first administered by the College Entrance Examination Board in 1926 and was called the Scholastic Aptitude Test (SAT). Black explains:

> Quickly, *A Study of American Intelligence* became a scientific standard. Shortly after its publication, Brigham adapted the Army Alpha test for use as a college entrance exam. It was first administered to Princeton freshmen and applicants to Cooper Union. Later the College Board asked Brigham to head a committee to create a qualifying

test for other private colleges in the Northeast and eventually across the country. Brigham's effort produced the Scholastic Aptitude Test, administered mainly to upper middle-class white students.[78]

In their histories of college entrance examinations and selective college admission, Harold Wechsler and Mott Linn indicate that entrance exams of some kind have existed in the United States for a long time, Linn dating them to colonial times.[79] Linn states that in the earliest days, college presidents typically did the examining, and that the exam usually included oral and written components.[80] Wechsler reports that each institution had its own exam; initially these were oral exams, but by the late nineteenth century, they had become written tests.[81] According to Linn, in the 1800s, professors "began to take control of colleges' entrance examinations," each university and in some cases each professor having specific requirements.[82] He states that by the 1890s, some educators, including Charles W. Eliot, had begun agitating for standardized college entrance requirements;[83] out of this agitation, in 1899 the College Entrance Examination Board (CEEB) was born.[84] The first CEEB exams consisted of essay questions.[85] Wechsler reports, however, that these exams were not used much during the first decade of the twentieth century.[86]

Thus, the college entrance examination was not new to the early twentieth century. What was different, however, especially by the early 1920s, were the use of the same standardized test by many schools; the format of the test, notably the abandoning of the essay; and the fact that psychologists, not college presidents or faculty members from the schools or departments, were developing and administering them. The SAT—which grew out of the Army Alpha and was developed by a eugenicist whose work subsequently has been called virulently racist—epitomized this new type of entrance examination.

Carl Brigham was not the only eugenicist busying himself after World War I with the development of standardized college or university qualifying examinations; at the University of Iowa, Seashore was at it, too, describing such exams as the first step in a larger process aimed at "*the progressive elimination, selection and motivation of the individual* [emphasis in original]."[87] He variously called such tests qualifying examinations, entrance examinations, or admissions tests. When attempting to understand the purposes and uses of these tests, it is important to keep in mind that, as Seashore reported, at the University of Iowa, students who had graduated from high school could not be denied admission. Wechsler states that the University of Michigan had a similar policy that only applied to in-state students.[88] In these instances, the tests could be required, but they could not be used as a criterion for admission.

In his autobiography, Seashore described the beginnings of standardized qualifying testing at Iowa. He recalled that the president of the University of Iowa (Walter Jessup, whom Seashore did not name) asked him to solve the problem of having 273 applicants to the Dental College but only 125 spaces. Seashore reported that after he had agreed to help, he quickly realized he had a problem because the University of Iowa could not deny college admission to any high school graduate.[89] He described how he solved the problem, a solution that included a new, soon-to-be-standardized intelligence test:

> We immediately took the Thorndike Intelligence Test, which was then just out, and designed a number of specific tests sampling the type of skill involved in dental work and gave the examination in the spring in Sioux City, Des Moines, and Iowa City, and repeated it for late-comers in the fall in Iowa City. The result was that a large number of the applicants were scared away by the idea of having to take an examination, and a considerable number of those who took it and were advised of low standing accepted the warning and withdrew voluntarily without discussion. After this winnowing there were only 137 who claimed the right to be admitted and of these there were twelve that we had slated for discard. Eight of these yielded to advice in personal conference, and the remaining four were admitted into the College of Liberal Arts instead of the Dental College which then took students direct from high school. These all failed during the first semester and were dropped.
>
> Apparently the administration was pleased with the way in which this situation was handled, for the President called me in and said "I will give you ten years in which to develop a qualifying examination on the basis of which we may eliminate candidates for lack of ability."[90]

In *Pioneering in Psychology*, Seashore claimed that in the summer of 1923[91] and with the assistance of Jessup, he managed to mandate the administration of qualifying tests without getting approval from the faculty:

> After the war, interest in the possibilities of this type of test for organizing student personnel spread fast and often furiously. President Jessup charged me with the responsibility of introducing this service as a means of analyzing the freshman class in the University of Iowa. This

> was in the summer of 1923 when the faculty was not in session, and he took advantage of that by making the recommendation an executive order, well knowing that if it were laid before the faculty, it would certainly not have carried. Accordingly, he charged me with the responsibility of rendering a service by providing and administering an intelligence test to every entering freshman as a psychological experiment.
>
> We had already been experimenting with the Thorndike intelligence test, which was largely an out-growth of the Army Alpha; as it was the best available at that time, we organized the freshmen in army fashion in the Armory and followed the army technique developed for the administration of a three-hour examination. The ordeal was shocking and baffling to many freshmen, and the occasion for gross misinterpretation by students and faculty. I was out of town at the time of the first faculty meeting following this performance. Upon my return my friends intimated that my absence had been fortunate because the faculty had wanted to burn me at the stake. It was reported that one of the most distinguished professors wept copiously as he reported the ordeal to which the freshmen had been subjected![92]

He also claimed that faculty skepticism evaporated when he produced evidence that test scores accurately predicted the first-semester grades of the top and bottom 10 percent of test takers; Seashore added, "This was probably one of the first times a report of this nature had been made to an academic faculty on such a devastating scale."[93] He admitted that despite the faculty's change of heart, his findings "did not meet with popular approval in the state."[94]

The above quotations are significant, in part because they link intelligence testing to qualifying examinations at Iowa, and in doing so they connect Iowa's qualifying examinations to eugenicists and eugenical goals. Seashore reported that the Thorndike test was derived largely from the Army Alpha, which confirms that the eugenical reach of the Army Alpha into the realm of qualifying examinations was longer and broader than merely the creation of the SAT. Like Terman, Yerkes, and Brigham, Edward Thorndike was a eugenicist. The passages also confirm that in 1923, three years prior to the creation of the SAT, the University of Iowa was using its own standardized qualifying exam, at least a portion of which traces its lineage back to the Army Alpha. The passage describing the dental exam indicates that some of the qualifying examinations consisted of an intelligence test stitched onto other test components designed to measure knowledge or achievement rather than ostensibly innate intelligence.[95] Third, the passages explain how qualifying examinations could effectively eliminate students even when denying them admission outright was not possible: taking the tests was sufficiently terrifying, or receiving the test results was sufficiently discouraging, that a number of students simply withdrew. Wendy Kline notes that a similarity between IQ and sexuality tests is their capacity to induce anxiety.[96] Seashore unapologetically admitted that qualifying tests effectively mobilized anxiety and led to self-selected elimination. Guidance from professionals helped students make the "right" decision. Given the claim that such tests reveal truth, it also is possible that the testing experience generated persistent and encumbering anxieties among low scorers who did enroll, especially those who were struggling with stereotype threat. Their scores could have, in effect, sparked an avoidable self-fulfilling prophecy of failure. Thus, these passages indicate that early on, qualifying examinations helped create a double-gesture culture: encouragement and promotion of some, those who were labeled the fittest, and discouragement or outright elimination of others. As such, they were entirely consistent with eugenical goals.

Correspondence in 1924 from Seashore to the director of the American Council on Education, Charles Riborg Mann, indicates that Seashore approved of new national efforts to standardize college entrance examinations even though Iowa had opted out of the national effort. In his rationale for declining to participate in the national activities, Seashore described the entrance examination Iowa was using at that time; his description indicates that by 1924, the Iowa qualifying examination consisted of the Thorndike intelligence test plus two other tests developed in-house:

> I wish to express our approval and appreciation of this effort to secure cooperation in the standardizing of an entrance test. This is the first that we have known of this movement and we are therefore not in a position to cooperate immediately. We have our own college entrance examination with which we have been experimenting now for some years, and since it has proved satisfactory, we shall continue to use it, in the meantime publishing results from our progressive studies of its workings. . . .
>
> For the purpose of information for your office, I am enclosing herewith a copy of two parts of our test; namely, the Ruch Content Examination and the Iowa Comprehension Test. The third part is one part of the Thorndike Intelligence Test.[97]

Seashore devised the Iowa Comprehension Test mentioned above, which was to measure reading comprehension, and Giles M. Ruch, a psychology professor at the University of Iowa, developed the Ruch High School Content Examination.[98] According to Ruch, his test measured achievement in four content areas: English and literature, mathematics, science, and social studies and history.[99] Thus, the above passage indicates that Seashore believed college admissions should take achievement, in addition to innate intelligence, into account. He also stated that careful examination of cases where students failed during the first semester revealed that extenuating life circumstances sometimes play a role.[100] In other words, Seashore admitted that in some circumscribed instances, life circumstances can explain why the innately fittest sometimes fail.

In Seashore's plan, college qualifying examinations were to be adapted so that they could be administered in high school, where they would serve as predictors of students' future academic success.[101] Test results, he claimed, would give students information to help them make wise decisions and avoid life-planning mistakes:

> One aspect of this college qualifying examination is the adaptation of it for use in the high schools in order that the student may have the information about his fitness for college before he leaves home or burns his bridges behind him with the decision to go to college. This examination which has now been conducted for a period of eight years [i.e., since about 1922], yielding predictions for from 1500 to 2000 high school students a year, and follow-up work tracing the performance of these students in college has fully demonstrated the validity of the procedure and its great usefulness.[102]

He stated that George Stoddard had done the work on tests for prospective students in Iowa.[103] Elsewhere, he underscored the value of providing prospective students with test information and with professional guidance on how to interpret and act in response to that information:

> The giving out of the results of the examination will be accompanied by a service of carefully prepared material for interpretation and guidance. . . . [This process will help teach the community that] it makes a difference whether a youth has or has not a college brain. . . . This will discourage the unfit and encourage the fit, which is our main objective, before the great risk of the college venture has been taken. It will improve our college timber and reduce college failures.[104]

College Placement Examinations

After the administration of qualifying examinations, the next step in Seashore's plan to systematically sort and order incoming college students involved more testing: placement exams.[105] In a 1924 *School and Society* article, he called them "the natural sequel to intelligence tests at college entrance."[106] Elsewhere, he called them "the next stage of this sorting process."[107] He stated that he had become a supporter of such examinations while working on the National Research Council's Gifted Student Project. He also said that he asked Ruch and Stoddard to develop the instruments to be used at the University of Iowa, which were called the Iowa Placement Examinations.[108]

These placement examinations were single-subject tests in a variety of areas that were to be administered to freshmen during the first two hours of class at the beginning of the term.[109] According to Seashore, one purpose of the exam was to remind students of prerequisite knowledge.[110] In a published paper he delivered to the National Academy of Sciences in 1925, he identified another central purpose: classifying students according to their test scores, which was to be followed by their placement in ability-tracked sections.[111] He used the English placement examination as an example, stating that it was composed of two parts, the first of which was "a highly standardized test of training for English"; Seashore continued:

> The second hour is devoted to an analysis and measurement of Language ability and particularly to aptitude for command of English. Both examinations are of the objective type and may be scored over night, so that at the opening of the third day all of the students in English are classified in the order of percentile rank on two scores, (1) training, and (2) aptitude for work in English.[112]

He indicated that similar tests were administered to freshmen in all subject areas at Iowa,[113] and in the 1924 *School and Society* article, he detailed the specific topics covered in the first edition of examinations in four subject areas: English, French, mathematics, and chemistry.[114] He suggested that over time, such tests could be standardized, that test results could be used to develop statistical norms, and that they could form the basis of research.[115]

In a paper he gave to the Engineering Society and that he shared with Iowa president Walter A. Jessup in the summer of 1924, Seashore championed placement exams and described what they were intended to show:

"When the student enters the Engineering School, he should be required to take a placement examination in each of the first year subjects, such as English, chemistry, mathematics. This examination, administered by each of the departments independently, is designed to show: first, the degree of natural aptitude for the particular subject; and, second, the character of preparation in that subject."[116] He also underscored their value in helping set the pace at which a student was to work: "The use of such placement examination is absolutely essential if we shall start our student rightly at his natural level for achievement, taking into account natural aptitude and character of preparation in the subject as a basis for determining the pace at which he shall be set to work and the character of his task."[117]

He did not come up with the idea of the subject-specific placement examination, but he was an early adopter. In addition, he used his positional power and national visibility to champion its implementation at other institutions. For example, in his autobiography, he noted that he was an advisor to the Board of Investigation of Engineering Education and was asked what recommendations psychology could make concerning the "organization of incoming students"; his first recommendation was to institute placement examinations.[118] Miles reported that in the fall of 1924, a number of other institutions tried an engineering placement exam developed at Iowa by Ruch and Stoddard.[119]

In his 1924 *School and Society* article, Seashore wrote that the University of Iowa was selling trial editions of the Iowa Placement Examinations to other institutions at cost, stating that Iowa would not make a profit on the examinations during the "experimental" period; he also said that future profits would go toward research:

> The department of psychology in the State University of Iowa has organized what is known as "The Iowa Placement Examinations" and has, up to date, issued four of these in trial editions, namely, English, French, mathematics and chemistry. Others are in preparation. In the interest of the educational experiment, the participants have rendered their services free and the Extension Division of the University of Iowa has undertaken to publish and sell this edition at actual cost of production to all institutions that wish to participate in experiments with these examinations for the current year. It is planned that any profit that may accrue from later sales . . . shall be used for research purposes within this field.[120]

Other Tests of Talent and Fitness

Tests of Occupational Talent and Fitness

Seashore promoted other types of tests, in addition to intelligence, college entrance, and placement exams, to be used in a variety of sorting and ordering projects. In some cases, he developed these tests himself. For example, he favored tests that would give vocational and career guidance by assessing whether a student had the natural ability to succeed in a particular job or career. In *A Preview to College and Life*, an essay directed at college students, he described various factors that should go into making a career choice. He advised students that they should do a careful and somewhat "scientific analysis of the way in which [they] differ from other people in natural capacities and abilities" and described what he called a "fundamental psychological rule": "Other things being equal, choose that career for which you have the highest natural resources for a good and successful life; and, second, within that career choose that level of activity which is most nearly at your personal highest level of achievement. Do not aim above or below your natural level in the pursuit of a specific career. If your forte is in manual activities and not in intellectual activities, by all means choose the former."[121] In other words, Seashore saw natural ability as a prerequisite for occupational success, and mindful of their natural ability, students were to select their optimal location on the achievement pyramid, not aiming too high or too low. Aiming too high was a recipe for failure and a waste of resources; aiming too low was a waste of natural talent. Other factors that he believed should be taken into account included an individual's wants, emotional drives, and urges.[122]

As we saw earlier in his discussion of entrance examinations in the Dental College, in Seashore's grand plan, a test would inform students—and their teachers—of whether they had the "natural resources" needed for a particular job. In an editorial entitled "From Vocational Selection to Vocational Guidance," which appeared in 1917 in the *Journal of Educational Psychology*, Seashore called for standardized vocational tests created by educational psychologists, and one of his selling points was that such fitness tests would prevent the waste of tax dollars:

> When a youth knocks at the door of professional industry, questions will be asked as to his fitness. If a vocational school prepares for the various crafts, arts, and other forms of skillful activity in a large city, the tax payer has a right to know whether or not the children who enter upon a course of training are by nature fitted for the occupation

> to which it will lead. Thus, the purely economic issue, quite regardless of interest in the child, will force upon as applied psychology [*sic*] in the determination of fitness for occupations in the early stages of vocational training. The educational psychologists, therefore, face a very specific issue for the next few years, namely, that of standardizing tests for specific occupations.[123]

He suggested that the development of a fitness test for stenography would be a good starting point.[124]

Significantly, in these passages and elsewhere, he tended to draw a distinction between careers and vocations, with vocations being lower on the achievement pyramid. Nevertheless, he claimed that occupational testing would be useful for all who aspire to a paid job, and for those who would teach or employ them, too.

Seashore also alluded to a form of vocational testing in his comment that one of his contributions during World War I was to develop "techniques" for determining which college students were the fittest to receive "special training for scientific war service."[125] Later, he was part of a national project conducted by the National Research Council to assess an individual's "talent for research."[126] In a 1921 letter to Robert Yerkes, he enclosed a rating system that was being used at Iowa, and he recommended that it be used in this national project in conjunction with an intelligence test and other "evidences"; the other evidences could include honors, a "record of leadership," productivity, etc.[127] Seashore asked Yerkes for "careful constructive criticism," requested advice on what items to change, and invited Yerkes to recommend a different system.[128] Five teachers were to give each student a percentile rating in twelve areas, including creative imagination, serviceable memory, emotional stability, perseverance, intellectual honesty, moral attitude ("solid and wholesome moral standards and ideals"), and physical health.[129] Yerkes replied that not being an expert in "subjective ratings," he was hesitant to criticize.[130] His one suggestion was that Seashore use a fixed scale, and he referred him to the work of "Scott" and "Ruml," presumably Walter D. Scott and Beardsley Ruml, whom Yerkes claimed had had extensive relevant experience in both the military and industry.[131]

Talent Tests and Fitness in the Arts

Seashore's portfolio of projects to measure fitness included the development of more than one test designed to measure talent in the arts. In chapter 6, I will discuss his tests of musical ability, but a second example is the Meier-

Seashore Art Judgment Test. He claimed that this test objectively and scientifically measures artistic talent[132]—or at least one dimension of it. He partnered with Norman Meier to develop the tests, which were published in 1929; Meier himself acknowledged that artistic talent is complex and that aesthetic judgment, the ability measured by the test, is but one element of it: "Talent in graphic art may be regarded as a complex function having its basis in inborn capacities, aesthetic responsiveness or judgment, and constructive ability or inventiveness. Talent in art is, however, not completely accounted for by these larger general aspects; a full appraisal would probably include particular items such as the following: color sense and color memory; sense of balance, stability, and symmetry."[133]

Test takers are given 125 pairs of drawings, and one picture in each pair is altered slightly; the test taker is asked to focus on the element that has been changed and decide which image is better.[134] There is a right and wrong answer to each question, and according to Meier, the right answer is the version an artist had selected:[135] "The criterion of rightness herein adopted is that of the master's own judgment. The absolute criterion would be the massed judgment of all experts; but in the judgment of the master artist there is a corroborating social judgment in the approval of critics and the sanction of art patrons, teachers of art, students of aesthetic structure, and the public generally."[136]

One purpose of this test, according to Seashore, is to discover innate talent; it was designed to be used in the public schools, specifically on eighth graders, although Seashore claimed it could be used in other grades as well: "[The Meier-Seashore Test is] to be used as a dragnet to discover art talent primarily in the eighth grade of the public-school system; and, secondly, the organization of a program of research on the analysis of the development of art talent in pre-school children."[137] He also suggested that such talent testing should be expanded into other domains, including sports and athletics.[138]

Seashore and Testing in K–12 Schools

Seashore's work on the Meier-Seashore Art Judgment Test is evidence that his testing activities sometimes focused on K–12 schoolchildren; evidence abounds further documenting his work on various types of testing and measurement of children. For example, in "Suggestions for Tests on School Children," which appeared in *Educational Review* in 1901, he said he had helped develop a battery of testing instruments for the Iowa Child-Study Society, which had set out to test all schoolchildren; according to Seashore, the tests measured physical characteristics and habits, muscle fatigue, vision, hearing, pitch discrimination, and mental capacity.[139] In his autobiography, he stated that he was involved in mental testing from early on and said he was conducting testing experiments at Iowa City High School starting in 1899; he also said that for two years beginning in 1900, he conducted "an experimental class in the local high school, making measurements on individual differences of children. This was one of the first movements of the kind."[140]

Tenure as a Talent or Fitness Test

Seashore even viewed tenure as a kind of systematic merit-based fitness test that would help identify and promote the fittest while eliminating the unfit. In "An Open Letter to a Professor," which was published in *School and Society* in 1938, he argued that the same principles of elimination and advancement should apply to faculty members and college students alike:

> The encouragement of the competent and the elimination of the incompetent student is conditioned upon the application of the same principles of elimination and advancement to the faculty. There must be a progressive selective process at work with emphasis upon early action for the sympathetic adjustment of the person concerned.
>
> From the point of view of the administration and, therefore, from the point of view of all helpful members of the faculty, one of the greatest problems of education is that of progressively eliminating members of the staff who, after fair and sympathetic trial, have shown clearly that they lack capacity for their work and interest in their job in relation to the aims and objectives of the institution. There has grown up in America a sort of squatter claim which makes it difficult to dismiss a teacher for incompetence.[141]

Although he underscored the importance of academic freedom, calling it a treasured privilege,[142] he also complained that tenure was devolving into protection of the incompetent:

> Every true educator will demand freedom of investigation, speech and writing within the field of his competence. In so far as the seeking and teaching of truth is concerned, he should be supported at every turn. But a halo of this protection of academic freedom has radiated into a vicious practice of protecting the incompetent, the instructor who has

> no growth in him, whose intellectual life is stale and sterile, who has become more or less a robot on his job.[143]

He added that fast action regarding the fitness of faculty members is essential: "Rapid promotion on merit is quite as important as early elimination of the incompetent."[144]

Seashore's Pioneering Role in Making Iowa a Hotbed in the Standardized Testing Movement

Seashore played a major role in making Iowa a hotbed in the standardized testing movement. Both Seashore and his biographer, Walter Miles, proudly described Iowa as a *leader* in developing and implementing standardized qualifying examinations, and Miles credited Seashore for this: "The state of Iowa under Seashore's general guidance was one of the first to experiment with qualifying examinations."[145] In a 1941 letter to University of Iowa president Virgil Hancher, Seashore proudly boasted that Iowa had kept abreast of the best movements in education, saying that his own recommendations and actions concerning qualifying and placement examinations, "a state-wide testing program, intelligence tests, [and] measurement of talent," exemplified this bold approach.[146] In *Pioneering in Psychology*, he claimed that the University of Iowa was among the first institutions to use the "objective examination," saying the practice had begun in about 1910 with the employment of true-false questions.[147] Furthermore, in an earlier letter to University of Iowa president Walter A. Jessup, Seashore called Iowa a pioneer in conceptualizing "controllable procedure within the field of educational personnel"; entrance tests, qualifying tests in the high school, and tests to provide vocational guidance to music students appeared on his list of notable achievements.[148] He described Iowa as having "attained a position of leadership," and added that "the effect upon college education is almost beyond the power of present conception."[149]

Iowa remained at the forefront of the burgeoning testing movement long after Seashore's death. For example, in 1925, the University of Iowa hired Everet Franklin Lindquist as a graduate assistant, and on completion of his doctorate in 1927, he joined the faculty. Lindquist developed the first Iowa Tests of Basic Skills and the first National Merit Scholarship Qualifying Test; in 1959, he cofounded the American College Testing Program and developed the first versions of the ACTs.[150]

"We're in the Money": Testing and Profit

As I mentioned earlier, there was money to be made from the development and sale of standardized tests. Although profit probably was not the primary motivator of those creating and distributing them, it is a factor to keep in mind when considering the goals and benefits of standardized test development and administration. Seashore's connection to corporate test construction was mentioned briefly in an undated manuscript, "Life in the Seashore Family," written sometime after 1980 by his son Carl G. Seashore. The manuscript tantalizingly stated that Seashore was "one of the originators of the Psychological Corporation, organized as a Test Construction Agency for Psychologists."[151]

The Psychological Corporation was founded in 1921 by the psychologist and eugenicist James McKeen Cattell (1860–1944). While enrolled at Johns Hopkins University, he studied under G. Stanley Hall and was a classmate of John Dewey; it was Cattell who reportedly later convinced Dewey to join the faculty at Columbia University.[152] Cattell also studied with experimental psychologist Wilhelm Wundt at Leipzig University. His ties to eugenics were strong. He met Galton in 1886; early in his career, and prior to joining the faculty at Columbia, he worked in Galton's research laboratory at Cambridge University.[153] In 1914, he served as president of the Eugenics Research Association.[154]

According to Cattell, Seashore became one of the elected directors of the Psychological Corporation on its incorporation.[155] Cattell was president, and Walter Dill Scott and Lewis Terman were the corporation's vice presidents.[156] Shortly after the corporation's formation, it established branches in ten states throughout the United States, one of them at the University of Iowa; two executive directors, Seashore and Bird T. Baldwin, were placed at the helm of the Iowa branch.[157] According to Cattell, the purpose of the corporation was to advance psychological research, and all profits were to be used to that end.[158] I mention this particular corporate connection because the Psychological Corporation lives on: although it floundered initially, it eventually thrived and in 1970, became a subsidiary of Harcourt, which was acquired by Reed Elsevier. In 2007, the British corporation Pearson plc acquired the assessment branch of Harcourt from Reed Elsevier. Today, Pearson plc is the world's largest education company, known in part for publishing standardized tests.

Seashore was aware of the financial gain that could come from test development. In October 1924, he sent a letter to Iowa president Walter Jessup that spelled out some of the potential financial benefits. Stating that test development had received little funding from the university, he urged Jessup to bring Iowa into the game by providing financial support, and he mentioned the profits that tests can generate for individuals and the institution:

> We are now facing a most strategic economic issue in these matters. There has been a rapidly growing tradition for investigators to design, copyright and sell personally new test procedures, *often with very satisfactory financial returns*, but generally with some of the drawbacks attendant upon the commercializing of scientific material. At the present time the Extension Division has entered into an agreement with a committee of which Dr. Ruch is chairman, for the production and distribution of test material on two different bases: one, that of a personal contract with the author for royalty; and the other that of a service of the University without royalty to the authors [emphasis mine].[159]

Seashore focused on the second "base." He asked Jessup for funding to hire a graduate student, George Stoddard, to edit test materials; these were to be sold by the university with profits going to the Graduate College "and distributed for research purposes within the field most nearly represented by the earnings" (presumably psychology).[160] I do not know whether Jessup honored Seashore's request, but Stoddard completed his doctorate at Iowa in 1925, immediately joined the psychology faculty there, and eventually succeeded Seashore as the dean of the Graduate School. The above passage is significant because it confirms that Seashore was aware of the substantial money individual test developers were making from their work, that he was aware of the money that universities could make from test development, and that he wanted Iowa to be on board. In the next chapter, I discuss the financial benefits he derived from his musical talent tests and from the corporate connections that made the test possible. Regardless of what was being measured, profit appears to have been a factor in a number of assessment-related ventures that he and the University of Iowa undertook.

Seashore's Deep Investment

The evidence I have just presented indicates that Seashore was a central player in the standardized testing movement writ large, and confirms that his participation was informed by eugenics. His public statements confirm that he was involved in testing and measurement precisely because these practices, and the beliefs that undergirded them, were consistent with his eugenical beliefs and could accomplish his valued eugenical goals. Identification of the fit and unfit through ostensibly objective and scientific measurement was foundational to eugenical intervention; this was precisely what the standardized tests he helped develop and promote were to accomplish.

Some may argue that he engaged in this research simply because he was an early-twentieth-century psychologist, and intelligence testing was a hot topic in psychology at the time. However, not all early psychologists were eugenicists, nor were all of them engaged in testing and measurement. The standardized testing movement's deep roots in eugenics have been confirmed and widely discussed by other scholars. Seashore was among the many eugenicists so engaged, and my work adds more evidence tying standardized testing and measurement to eugenics. In addition, the evidence I have just presented provides a context for understanding Seashore's beliefs about musical talent and his work on music-related psychometrics. As I discuss in the next chapter, these beliefs and this work were similarly grounded in eugenical thought.

All Men Are Not Created Equal: Segregation, Promotion, and Elimination

Seashore on the Goals and Shortcomings of Education

As we have seen, innate ability was a topic of intense interest to eugenicists, including those who were psychologists. Seashore was among them. Creating and administering standardized tests to identify and to draw distinctions were merely precursors to a host of eugenically informed education reforms and interventions focusing on ostensibly innate ability. Consistent with widely circulating eugenical tenets, the education-related reforms Seashore promoted and implemented involved segregation, selective promotion, and selective elimination based on innate ability. Before examining specific reforms, I will consider some of the broad education goals he advanced, recognizing that they were foundational to his conception of the problems of education and to his ideas about how to solve them.

First, Seashore viewed education as a valuable tool to be used in orchestrated efforts to improve society. He claimed that psychologists were providing vital information about the "nature and evolution of man, aiming to project its future,"[161] and he imagined psychology as working hand in glove with education to effect that future. In his autobiography, he described himself as an "educator interested in the conscious direction of the evolution of future society," and in so doing, he implied that such conscious direction is a rightful role of educators.[162] This description occurred in a passage discussing biological "frailties" that had popped up in his family in recent generations; one of them was bad teeth, which he attributed to fast living.[163] He suggested that lessons could be learned by studying this degeneration, "lessons which may help to stem the tide of this rushing, overheating response to new opportunities by bringing future generations closer to Nature and closer to God."[164] Thus, the bright future that conscious direction of evolution by educators (and presumably others) would help effect would be closer to God.

A draft and three published versions exist of "The Sunny Side of Graduate Work for the Duration," an article he wrote late in his life, during the middle of World War II. Every version spoke of the role that education and educated people would play in the creation of a new world order, and all of them spelled out the multiple ways that war is an invaluable learning experience for graduate students.[165] "The war is a school," Seashore stated.[166] He claimed, for example, that practicing medicine at the front is a superior learning experience to a medical internship at home; he further claimed that by being given the opportunity to travel, graduate students "are being trained for world citizenship"; he predicted that equipped with knowledge learned from their war experiences, students would be "called upon in large numbers to shape a new world order" when they returned from the trenches to "civilization."[167] Thus, in addition to describing new learning opportunities as being part of the "sunny side to the war," a phrase he did not use in the final version of the article,[168] Seashore underscored the role that he believed learning and education in multiple forms could play in creating a new and better world order. "New world order" is a phrase sometimes associated with conspiracy theorists today, who perceive it to be a threat, but Seashore envisioned a shining new world order brimming with hope for a bright future.

The future orientation of these particular education goals, the assumption that the world and the people who occupy it are not satisfactory as they are and are improvable, the belief that experts know the good and are capable of effectively intervening, and the conviction that improvement is achievable via broad-scale conscious direction of evolution, all are consistent with utopian thought, and more specifically with eugenics as a particular manifestation of that thought. Significantly, all are consistent with Seashore's explicit statements about what eugenics is, what it can accomplish, and how.

Although he occasionally discussed education goals aimed at improving the population and society overall, he tended to focus on the education of the individual, and his goals aimed at *broad-scale* development and improvement of society went hand in hand with those aimed at *individual* development and improvement. For example, in his autobiography he quoted radio broadcaster Graham McNamee, who described three new goals of education—the three Cs; in his reflection on the quotation, Seashore confirmed his belief that consciously directed *individual* development should go hand in hand with consciously directed *social* evolution: "'Our fundamental aims in education used to be the three R's; now we have a new ideal. It is the three C's: character, culture, and citizenship.' . . . Individual development, like social evolution, is now more consciously directed than ever before."[169] Thus, McNamee's three C's tied the individual to the group, and in so doing, they tied individual goals to group goals. Education is to improve society or the world by helping to make up particular kinds of improved individuals: cultured citizens of high character. Education is to rely on scientific experts to help consciously direct both individual and group development.

Nikolas Rose argues that the new biopolitics in biomedicine are not eugenics, and he says that one of the differences is eugenics' focus on population; in the new biopolitics, he claims, concern for and intervention into the quality of the population has been replaced by concern for and intervention into individual health and quality.[170] Seashore's writings are evidence that for at least some eugenicists, this distinction did not apply. He was concerned both about populational quality and about individual quality, and he aimed to improve both through education. Thus, he adopted a "yes, and" rather than an "either, or" approach. The goal is to improve society by improving individuals and to improve individuals by improving society—to the degree that individuals are improvable. What is good for the individual is good for the society, state, and whole world, especially *if* the scientific expert, not the individual, is defining the good. In turn, what is good for the society, state, and whole world is good for the individual if, once again, the scientific expert is at the helm. Even when he focused on broad populational and societal improvement goals, he still saw the individual as the site of intervention and as a recipient of at least some of the benefits derived from this intervention. Because it was the individual making the choices, his proposed improvement projects were buffered from the criticism that they represented governmental overreach.

According to Seashore, a major flaw of education in a democratic society is that it rarely takes into account the nature of ability as it is accurately understood by psychologists; instead, it is grounded in an equality fallacy, the mistaken belief that natural ability is equally distributed. Acting in accord with this fallacy, he argued, educators foolishly and wastefully attempt the impossible: to achieve equality among the constitutionally unequal, who have been created unequal by God (or evolution). In a 1922 article in *School and Society*, he stated that new knowledge of the mental profile confirms the futility of educators' attempts to make equal those who are constitutionally unequal:

> This new knowledge cuts at the root of one of the most pernicious theories of educational systems, namely, the assumption that where the great Creator failed to make all human beings equal, it is the business of the school to make them equal.
>
> To justify this procedure, the school men have found cover in the notion that this task works toward a democratic idea; that it represents the rights of individuals; that it is necessary for the successful operation of educational machinery; that it is good for the lowly individual; that the procedure is justified by results. Each of these alibis represents a fundamental error and misconception of fact in educational procedure.[171]

He repeated this claim elsewhere,[172] typically in reference to higher education: "There are . . . large bodies of educators who maintain that where nature made individuals different, it is the function of the college to make them alike; and in this, they have had remarkable success because it is comparatively easy to hold the entire class down to a dull, drab, mediocre level."[173] He continued by complaining that "some educators still act as if they believed that all men are created equal," asserting that this clearly is not true, at least not as far as natural ability is concerned.[174]

In a true democracy, Seashore claimed, education should be provided in proportion to innate ability: "The democratic ideal in education, as everywhere else in life, is not equal distribution to all, but equal opportunity in proportion to capacity. The genius and the moron do not have quantitatively the same rights to knowledge; they have equal rights in proportion to their capacities (quantitative and qualitative), and one should be as insistent upon his rights as the other."[175] Thus, according to Seashore, in a democracy, education should be quantitatively and qualitatively different for people with different amounts of native ability.

These ideas about education in a democracy can be traced directly to eugenics, echoing beliefs expressed by eugenicist Henry Fairfield Osborn in his address to the Second International Congress of Eugenics in 1921:

> We are engaged in a serious struggle to maintain our historic republican institutions through barring the entrance of those who are unfit to share the duties and responsibilities of our well-founded government. The true spirit of American democracy that *all men are born with equal rights and duties* has been confused with the political sophistry that *all men are born with equal character and ability to govern themselves and others*, and with the educational sophistry that education and environment will offset the handicap of heredity [emphasis in original].[176]

Seashore was another of the featured speakers at the Second Congress, and his first published discussions of the equality fallacy appeared in 1922, less than one year after the congress.

Madison Grant similarly discussed what he perceived to be the fallacies of contemporary democratic thought on human equality. In his introduction to his 1916 book *The Passing of the Great Race*, he mentioned misunderstandings of equality, democracy, and ability. He argued that especially given their attitudes toward Indians and enslaved African Americans, the nation's founders did not really mean all men when they stated that "all men are created equal":

> Democratic theories of government in their modern form are based on dogmas of equality formulated some hundred and fifty years ago, and rest upon the [mistaken] assumption that environment and not heredity is the controlling factor in human development. . . . The men who wrote the words, "we hold these truths to be self-evident, that all men are created equal," were themselves the owners of slaves, and despised Indians as something less than human. Equality in their minds meant merely that they were just as good Englishmen as their brothers across the sea.[177]

As I have already mentioned, Grant was a virulently racist eugenicist whose book influenced Carl Brigham, the creator of the SATs. In addition, Hitler read *The Passing of the Great Race* and reportedly referred to it as his Bible.[178] Allan Chase states that Francis Galton himself viewed democracy as a menace;[179] in *Hereditary Genius*, Galton wrote, "It is in the most unqualified manner that I object to the pretensions of natural equality."[180]

Education Reform Inspired by Henry Goddard

Ever proclaiming the scientific expert as the purveyor of truth, Seashore envisioned vast reforms that could be effected by applying the new field of psychology to education; in particular, he favored applying scientific management to schooling.[181] Just as eugenics shaped Seashore's views on what was wrong with education, it undergirded the solutions he proposed. For example, he claimed that a central tenet of his education philosophy was inspired by the work of Henry Goddard, a eugenicist.[182] He distilled this tenet into a motto that he repeated many times over the course of his career: "Keep each individual busy at his highest normal level of successful achievement that he may be happy, useful, and good."[183] In 1949, shortly before his death, he told his oft-repeated story of how he came up with this motto:

> I wish to pay tribute to Henry H. Goddard for having inspired it. About forty years ago the Governor of Iowa asked me to visit institutions for the feeble minded in the United States and report what recommendations could be made for the treatment of the feeble-minded children in Iowa. The first place I went to was the Training School at Vineland, N. J., where Goddard had inaugurated an experiment which was a masterpiece of basic and enduring significance in applied psychology. I spent a week there observing the operations. Here were 465 feeble-minded children among whom more than the upper half proved to be a colony of happy, successful, useful, and good individuals. This was, to me, a grand revelation.
>
> Goddard's theory was this: Examine each individual and find out what remnant capacities he may have; make a job analysis of all the things in which these children can help; then assign each child to do a job in which he can show competence and gain selfrespect [*sic*] as a successful individual.[184]

According to Seashore, Goddard's philosophy and practices at Vineland had transformed the useless, unhappy, and bad into a good, happy, and productive work force:

> In a certain institution for the feeble minded, the morons were happy, useful, and good. Many of these children had been sent from good homes because they were unhappy, useless, and bad; but the institution had brought about this marvelous transformation by proceeding on

> the theory that feeble-minded children, as a rule, possess fragmentary capacities in which they may become good and valuable workers if rightly placed. The institution had taken an inventory of each child's capacity and organized the work of the colony so that each child was employed at his best, where he could be successful and receive approbation.[185]

Seashore envisioned broad application of Goddard's education philosophy and practices, including in higher education, public schools, the home, and the community.[186] He also claimed that just as it worked with students at the bottom of the intelligence spectrum, it also would work with students who are highly talented in music, art, history, or science.[187] Late in his life, he underscored the profound impact on Iowa of his widely disseminated motto.[188]

Goddard was director of research at Vineland from 1906 to 1918. A student of G. Stanley Hall, he brought the Binet intelligence tests to the United States, served on the team that developed the Army Alpha tests, invented a system of classifying people with cognitive disabilities, instituted the use of the term "moron" as a label for one of these categories, and in 1912 published his widely read book *The Kallikak Family: A Study in the Heredity of Feeble-Mindedness*. His work was followed, cited, and supported by a host of prominent eugenicists including Paul Popenoe, an author of *Sterilization for Human Betterment*.[189] Like Seashore, Charles Davenport, the director of the Eugenics Record Office at Cold Spring Harbor, New York, consulted with Goddard.[190] Even Seashore's scholarly foe, James Mursell, who was not a eugenicist and was skeptical of many of Seashore's ideas, referenced Goddard's Kallikak study as an example of the type of research absent but needed in music: studies of the absence of ability.[191] Edwin Black states that later in life, Goddard "recanted his whole life's work," abandoning his earlier positions on the biological inheritability of intelligence and on eugenics, but this change came long after Seashore's visit.[192]

Vineland was a residential facility, and the kind of educational opportunities Goddard created were ability-segregated because the institutions themselves were designed to segregate those deemed less able from the rest of society. For eugenicists, however, institutionalization as a segregating practice had less to do with providing a sound educational environment than it did with preventing reproduction. As Charles Davenport stated in a 1920 letter to Seashore that discussed possible candidates for a eugenics professorship at the Iowa Child Welfare Research Station, "The result of . . . cacogenic investigations should be the segregation of feeble-minded and feebly controlled men and women during the whole of the reproductive period."[193] In their book *Applied Eugenics*, Paul Popenoe and Roswell Johnson described people with cognitive disabilities as an economic liability to the state.[194] One of their management suggestions was to place at least some people with cognitive disabilities in segregated classes in regular schools until they reach sexual maturity, at which point they were to be institutionalized; Popenoe and Johnson quoted E. R. Johnstone, superintendent of the Vineland School:

> "There are idiots, imbeciles, morons and backward children. The morons and the backward children are found in the public schools in large numbers. Goddard's studies showed twelve per cent. of an entire school district below the high school to be two or three years behind their grades, and three per cent. four or more years behind.
>
> It is difficult for the expert to draw the line between these two classes, and parents and teachers are loth [*sic*] to admit that the morons are defective. This problem can best be solved by the establishment of special classes in the public schools for all who lag more than one year behind. If for no other reason, the normal children should be relieved of the drag of these backward pupils. The special classes will become the clearing houses. The training should be largely manual and industrial and as practical as possible. As the number of classes in any school district increases, the classification will sift out those who are merely backward and a little coaching and special attention will return them to the grades. The others—the morons—will remain and as long as they are not dangerous to society (sexually or otherwise) they may live at home and attend the special classes. As they grow older they will be transferred to proper custodial institutions. In the city districts, where there are many classes, this will occur between twelve and sixteen years of age. In the country districts it will occur earlier."[195]

The timing mentioned by Johnstone indicates that sexual maturation was the trigger leading to institutionalization, at least for those identified as having less severe disabilities. Perhaps those with more severe disabilities—the people labeled "idiots" and "imbeciles"—were to be institutionalized much earlier in life. Popenoe also championed sterilization, and he and Johnson mentioned total elimination as another possibility, but they claimed that eugenicists were not seriously considering it because "to put to death defectives or delinquents is wholly out of accord with the spirit of the times."[196]

Madison Grant, by contrast, claimed that the laws of nature demanded wholesale elimination of the unfit; he dismissed what he called "a sentimental belief in the sanctity of human life . . . [that tends] to prevent both the elimination of defective infants and the sterilization of such adults as are themselves of no value to the community. The laws of nature require the obliteration of the unfit, and human life is valuable only when it is of use to the community or race."[197]

In his discussion of Goddard's advocacy of institutionalization of the feeble-minded in sex-segregated settings "until they were past breeding age," Allan Chase indicates that Goddard preferred segregation over sterilization primarily because he feared that sterilization would lead to sexual license and debauchery; Chase quotes from *The Kallikak Family*: "'What will be the effect upon the community in the spread of debauchery and disease through having within it a group of people who are thus free to gratify their instincts without fear of consequences in the form of children?'"[198] Public opposition was the other so-called practical difficulty that Goddard mentioned in his discussion of why it was problematic to use sterilization to solve "the problem" of people with disabilities.[199]

The fingerprints of eugenics are on Seashore's motto even if the influence of Goddard is not considered. For example, his emphasis on making useful and good people is consistent with and informed by eugenics. Goodness is a commentary on morality, and the fittest people, according to eugenicists, are both useful and moral.

Hierarchical Educational Opportunities to Make Happy, Useful, and Good People

Seashore's Action Plan

Basing his plan for education reform on the philosophy and practices he gleaned from Goddard, and armed with a motto, Seashore proposed a hierarchical range of educational opportunities that would match a hierarchy of people established by the identificatory process of standardized testing. The hierarchy of educational opportunities was premised on the assumption that there is not—and should not be—room at the top for all. In most cases, when discussing the most appropriate placement of people on his hierarchical education opportunity ladder, Seashore talked about fitting education to the individual, but in a few instances he also mentioned fitting education to groups. The environmental focus of his plan to provide educational opportunities that would permit individuals (and groups) to reach their "highest natural level of successful achievement"[200] was consistent with the goals of euthenics, the companion of eugenics.

The education reforms he championed combined providing a hierarchical range of segregated, differentiated learning opportunities with a systematic process of placement that involved selection, early and rapid promotion of the ostensibly fittest, and early and rapid elimination of others. As Seashore stated in reference to one of his proposed projects, "Those who are destined to fail should be eliminated early."[201] Promotion is to be based on merit, and like elimination, it is to be swift: "Rapid promotion on merit is quite as important as early elimination of the incompetent."[202] As we have seen, eugenicists frequently mentioned systematic promotion of the fittest and elimination of the unfit as solutions to the problem of degeneration.

Before discussing specific education projects that Seashore developed based on his motto, let us consider four elements of his views on quality education, focusing on how they are linked to eugenics. First, his philosophy and motto were forged at Vineland, a segregated residential institution directed by eugenicists and organized in a manner consistent with the eugenical goal of segregating those deemed unfit. Seashore championed many types of native-ability-segregated education opportunities, firmly believing that people learn best in homogenous groupings surrounded by others just like themselves.

Second, Seashore's philosophy and education action plan underscored the individual or group's usefulness, especially to society and employers. As I stated earlier, eugenicist Madison Grant claimed that life only has value if it is of use to the community or race, and he called for the elimination of the useless.[203] Goddard's Vineland, which served as Seashore's template, attempted to transform at least some of those deemed useless into useful, productive employees. In a discussion of Edward Alsworth Ross's conception of social control, Thomas Popkewitz states that productivity within a circumscribed social role was a characteristic of the kind of person that Ross sought to create through education: "The individual was to learn to be productive within his or her assigned role as a future citizen."[204] Ross founded the Sociology and Anthropology Department at the University of Wisconsin–Madison, and like Seashore, he was a eugenicist. Not coincidentally, he and Seashore shared views on productivity, social control, and assigned roles for future citizens.

Third, not only were the education opportunities that Seashore envisioned differentiated, they were hierarchical. This is evidenced, for example, by his frequent use of the term "levels," a word that appears in his motto and in many other references to ability: "It should be clearly understood among the students: that each will be kept busy at his highest natural level of successful achievement; that there are very great differences in the capacity for achievement; that each will be praised or blamed according as he achieves on the basis of his natural capacity; and that we have frankly given up the idea of bringing them all to the same level."[205] In addition to speaking of different levels of innate ability, he also placed the educational opportunities he championed on levels of a hierarchy. Thus, he did not merely talk about different kinds of educational opportunities for different kinds of individuals and groups; rather, he placed these opportunities on a ladder having higher and lower rungs. The assumptions that humanity naturally lives on a hierarchical ladder and that society should be structured accordingly are fundamental tenets of eugenics. Seashore's plan is thus consonant with eugenics.

Fourth, his education philosophy called for keeping *each* individual busy at his natural level of achievement, which may appear to be an appeal for global inclusion, but appearances can be deceiving. He wanted to keep people busy, including the unfit—not to annihilate them—which indicates that he may not have been in league with radicals such as Popenoe and Grant, the small minority of US eugenicists who openly supported the immediate elimination of the unfit. Nevertheless, this view keeps him well within the boundaries of accepted eugenical thought. To many US eugenicists, improving the race by eliminating degeneracy through strategies such as eugenics education, immigration limitation, and sterilization was a gradual process, and they supported what they perceived to be more socially palatable intermediary interventions targeting the unfit, especially if these interventions made the abject individuals more useful to society and less of a financial liability.

In Seashore's plan, education would transform at least some of the abject unfit into useful, productive, good citizens. Education could assure the formerly useless a spot at the base of the achievement pyramid, the base being a critical component of the infrastructure supporting the top. Spaces on the achievement pyramid were reserved for those who are productive, and to say that education would make people useful, productive, and good suggests that it would move them out of a place where they were neither useful nor productive, and therefore, not good. The available space was at the *bottom* of the achievement pyramid, but the bottom was still safer than any location not on the pyramid at all.

Like eugenical thought generally, Seashore's education plan exhibited a double gesture of inclusion and exclusion. Inclusion on the achievement pyramid was conditional, assured only to the educable. It is not clear whether he believed that every individual is educable in at least some domain—capable of achievement, potentially useful for something, and therefore eligible to become good. Furthermore, if he believed that some individuals were completely useless, it is unclear from his education plan what he believed the future of those useless individuals would or should be. Did he assume that because they were not useful, they could not be happy? Did he assume that because they were at their highest level of achievement, they were good even if they were not useful? Seashore was silent on these matters. Thus, despite his reference to "each individual," it is unclear whether the inclusion he promoted was selective or universal, and whether "each individual" really did mean all. Seashore stated that at Vineland, approximately the *upper half* of the residents qualified for education; [206] by extension, it appears that only the upper half qualified to be happy, useful, and good. Whatever the case, according to Seashore, operating at one's highest level of ability is a moral imperative that makes a person good, while failing to do so makes a person bad.

A Hierarchy of Institutions

In addition to promoting the accurate, systematic, and broad-scale identification of ostensibly innate ability through testing, Seashore proposed to solve education's ability-related problems via a host of practices that established and maintained segregated ability hierarchies, and that aimed to promote the fittest while eliminating the unfit. First, he supported the existence of different kinds of institutions of higher education, each type constituting a component of an institutional hierarchy. The hierarchy materializes, in part, through Seashore's use of words such as "higher" and "lower" to describe various types of institutions. Such variety, Seashore argued, is central to education in a democracy, the various levels of institutions being tailored to students exhibiting different levels of innate ability.[207] Some institutions were to be reserved for the education of a superior class; others were the proper place for students with less ability and for those from a different, and lower, "level" or class of society. A college education was to be a privilege provided in proportion to a student's capacity to personally benefit, and to the probability that society would benefit: "The higher education of a superior class is absolutely essential to democracy, but with it there must go a fair program of continuity reaching all levels of society. . . . The principle applied, in so far as circumstances permit, should mean education for every American in proportion to his capacity to profit thereby personally and give adequate returns in service."[208]

At the Top of the Top: Universities and Elite Four-Year Colleges

Institutions that serve graduate students sat at the top of his institutional hierarchy, with elite four-year colleges not far below them. Seashore favored the education that he claimed was provided largely by "the best colleges and universities;" these schools, he stated, are the "bulwark of higher education"—their approaches to education necessary for the "maintenance of democracy."[209] The purpose of these superior institutions is to educate superior minds. In reference to students and faculty alike, Seashore wrote that universities faced the problem of finding and promoting *superior humans*.[210] One sign that graduate students and the institutions that educated them constituted the top was a proposal to give baby bonuses to National Research Fellows, Seashore reporting that as a board member he was pleased when the Biological Fellowship Board of the National Research Council approved the plan.[211] As I discussed in chapter 4, baby-bonus programs to support the proliferation of the fittest were popular with some eugenicists, including the White supremacist Wickliffe Draper.

Not far below graduate institutions came four-year colleges, notably elite Ivy League schools. Four-year colleges were the crucibles from which graduate students emerged, and they were to be reserved for an elite few—again, those with innately superior minds. Seashore noted, for example, that "college-educated men and women constitute a very small fraction of any normal community,"[212] and he further claimed that fewer than 5 percent of people in the United States would benefit from an education at a four-year college.[213]

He viewed four-year college students as born leaders, and he stated that the ability to lead is based on many factors—intelligence, first and foremost:

> A natural leader is born a leader and leads from the cradle to the grave. College men are or should be selected leaders. The ability of a leader depends, first of all, upon his intelligence and knowledge of his opportunity; but with these he may fail utterly if he has not acquired, through persistent practice, habits of confidence in himself, confidence in the other fellow, mastery of his body and mind in meeting the other fellow, readiness in the rules of the game of life, charm of personality, and the ability to inspire loyalty.[214]

It is not clear whether he included women in his multiple references to the college men who should rightly lead, but most of the graduates emerging from the colleges at Ivy League institutions, which Seashore held up as models, were White males.

According to Seashore, democracies rightly are to be led by the fittest: the fittest are the smartest, and the smartest should attend, at a minimum, a four-year college. His support of an intellectual aristocracy appeared, for example, in his discussion of the growth of higher education. He stated that higher education was expanding both downward and upward, the upward movement being the development of specialized graduate and professional programs; this upward movement, which was "resting basically upon the four-year college, [would provide education] for the intellectual aristocracy or democracy in the Jeffersonian sense. . . . It will be taken for granted that we favor 'education for aristocracy' in the good sense of the term, as represented in large part by the best colleges and universities of our day."[215] However others may understand Jeffersonian democracy, Seashore clearly saw it as rule by an aristocratic intellectual elite, and college was to prepare leaders to take their rightful place in the intellectual aristocracy he favored.

The idea that democracies should be led by an elite aristocracy did not originate with eugenics, but it was popular with eugenicists such as White supremacist Madison Grant, who in 1916—long before Seashore made his observations—expressed similar views about flawed thinking concerning leadership in a democracy. Allowing average rather than aristocratic people to lead is a mistake, Grant stated, which "from a racial point of view . . . will inevitably increase the preponderance of the lower types and cause a corresponding loss of efficiency in the community as a whole."[216] He claimed that mankind's emergence from "savagery and barbarism" was due to enlightened selective leadership, and he maintained that such leaders constitute "a minute fraction of the whole."[217] Enlightened leaders, Grant asserted, rightly use the "brute strength of the unthinking herd as part of their own force," the unthinking herd being composed of "slaves, peasants, or lower classes."[218]

The intellectual aristocracy that Seashore favored is meritocratic, even though the term was not coined until years after his death: individuals and groups gain membership into the ranks of the elite, and concomitant access to leadership opportunities, by virtue of their high worth, which they possess at birth and perhaps augment through hard work. The theories of Zeus Leonardo and Alicia Broderick came to mind as I considered some of the privileges that Seashore reserved for the highly intelligent, one of them being the opportunity to lead. In their article "Smartness as Property: A Critical Exploration of Intersections between Whiteness and Disability Studies," Leonardo and Broderick problematize the smartness construct, which they claim "intersects both race and ability as ideological systems."[219] Transferring Critical Race Theory's conception of whiteness as property onto the construct of smartness, they argue that "smartness works as a form of property, with all the advantages that come with membership in the group."[220] They discuss some of the "spoils" available only to the smart in belief systems grounded in particular understandings of smartness. Clearly, in the minds of Grant and Seashore, the most elite leadership opportunities are among the spoils to be reserved for the supposedly smartest: college-educated White men.

According to Seashore, one job of four-year colleges and graduate schools is to prepare the fittest men for positions in the professions, and by 1927, he was proclaiming that a previous crisis—a shortage of "the right kind" of men to occupy these positions—would soon be replaced by a new "tragic" crisis: a supply of educated individuals that exceeded demand.[221] In a 1927 article appearing in *School and Society*, he stated, "At the present time we have about as many engineers, lawyers, doctors, teachers, preachers and other professionally trained men as the community needs and will support adequately."[222] He warned that "there may be a serious danger ahead for the intellectual aristocracy" and predicted that the looming surplus would "bring about cut-throat competition and a consequent moral, political and social crisis."[223] He claimed that too many students were attending college with the intention of entering a "learned profession" when there was room for only a few: "It has been estimated that 60% of the high school graduates who go to college go for the purpose of entering a learned profession; but the traditionally learned professions are not open to more than a very small fraction of these aspirants."[224] Furthermore, due to this error, he stated, young people were wrongly being drawn away from farming, grade-school teaching, and rural living.[225]

He opined that the new crisis had been created by a dramatic increase in college admissions, arguing that colleges were admitting and graduating too many students: "The shortage of men in the learned professions and scientific careers has been so great that there has been reason for encouraging every person who enters college to continue throughout the four years; and the outlook for jobs has continued to be good. This situation is now changed by the large increase in admissions to college, creating the danger of oversupply at the top."[226] He stated that professional schools were doing the same: "The rate of increase in the output from professional schools has led to the doubling of the number of professional men in short periods of time and is destined to continue until the crisis will be upon us—the overproduction of white-collar men."[227]

Furthermore, he claimed that demand for an education at a four-year college or graduate school was reaching or exceeding the capacity of institutions of higher education to meet it. According to Seashore, colleges were being overwhelmed, and students and institutions alike were suffering: "The surging waves of increasing demands for higher education roll against the walls of the halls of learning. These walls are bulging and trembling under the pressure of mass education."[228]

The problem, according to him, was not just that too many students were being admitted, but that too many of those admitted were unfit for college: "Many graduates have been floundering in college. . . . These are, as a rule, the people who never should have been in a four-year college, whose educational life should not have been cast in the mold of higher scholarship."[229] Seashore claimed that the problem of admitting too many students unfit for college should be blamed on a misunderstanding of "education for democracy," a misunderstanding that was resulting in the elimination of up to fifty percent of freshmen in the first year.[230] Elsewhere, in a passage discussing four-year colleges, he stated that individuals should not be called "unfit" but rather "college unfitted."[231]

In Seashore's view, part of the problem of such misguided "education for democracy" was that four-year colleges were trying to do the impossible. They were faced with the foolish, wasteful, and ultimately futile task of making fit the naturally unfit. These attempts, he claimed, were violations of a fundamental natural law, "the law of the distribution of mental capacity."[232] He criticized "a blind belief in the efficacy of education in spite of the absence of natural equipment."[233] Colleges, he argued, could not and should not even attempt to make equal those whom God or evolution had created fundamentally and constitutionally unequal. He underscored this at one point by telling professors that they should not attempt to "make gold out of iron."[234] This may have been an allusion to Plato's myth of the metals, which appeared in *The Republic*. This myth is part of the "noble lie" that Plato claimed rulers should promulgate to assure leadership by only the best: different people are born constitutionally different, some made of gold, some of silver, and some of brass or iron; in most cases, children are of the same metal as their parents, and people made of gold are at the top of hierarchy.[235] In Plato's hierarchy, only the gold should rightly rule, and he warned that "the state shall then be overthrown when the man of iron or brass is its guardian."[236] The myth of the metals is a famous section in the *Republic*, which Seashore, well schooled in philosophy, had undoubtedly read. Furthermore, in the early twentieth century, some scholars were linking ancient philosophers to the modern eugenics movement. For example, in *Ancient Eugenics*, which won Oxford University's Arnold Prize in 1913, Allen G. Roper described the ideas of a number of ancient philosophers, including Plato, as "ancient eugenics."[237]

The practice of admitting too many students, and particularly too many unfit students, had serious consequences for them, Seashore claimed, including frustration and "serious unrest" among those who did not belong in a four-year college.[238] He described failing at college as a disgrace: "These students are sent back to home and community disgraced and disheartened, and constitute not only an economic waste, but a gross maladjustment of human energies, hopes and ambitions."[239]

In addition, he argued that the practice was harming at least some institutions by reducing academic standards: "The attempt of the college to meet this influx has resulted in a considerable demoralization of academic standards on the part of some institutions."[240] In short, his objections to admissions policies were based at least in part on the fear that a supposedly massive influx of the less fit was dragging down and polluting four-year colleges and graduate schools, leading to institutional degeneration and loss of quality. Fear of degeneration and of loss of quality was central to eugenics discourse.

Who were the college-unfit who were inundating and ostensibly overwhelming overextended four-year colleges and graduate schools? I found no mention of the poor or the working class; instead, Seashore referenced the *upper-middle class*. For example, he claimed that college expansion was coming from "a constituency of a different order from that which filled the standard college a few years ago. It is the upper middle class which is demanding education for practical life rather than scholarly erudition."[241]

Never short on advice, Seashore made a series of recommendations for solving the surplus enrollment problem and the related issue of excessive numbers of unfit, dissatisfied students. He stated that actions on the part of four-year colleges and universities should be guided by "two fundamental natural laws": the "law of the distribution of mental capacity and the law of supply and demand for men in learned careers."[242] These laws were to guide a lengthy, progressive process of selection and elimination that was to begin at the high school: "If we are to educate reasonably for democracy, the candidates from the secondary schools up through the post-doctorate period must pass through a progressive process of selection and elimination."[243] Furthermore, the laws were to be applied in service of the purposes of institutions of higher education: "To give a higher education to each individual among American youth somewhat in proportion to his capacity, and to provide higher education for every occupation to the extent that the expenditure can be justified in terms of the needs of the community, both economic and cultural."[244]

One solution Seashore proposed to the surplus-and-unfit enrollment problem was for institutions to monitor, control, and restrict enrollment through the use of standardized entrance and qualifying examinations.[245] Elsewhere, he suggested limiting higher education capacity by limiting the number of four-year colleges in existence: "The four-year undergraduate college patterned after Harvard, Yale, and Princeton is in sight of a natural ceiling."[246] The context of this statement suggests that, rather than merely championing enrollment limits at these schools, he was further arguing that no more four-year colleges should be created. The "natural ceiling" was to be respected to prevent a top-heavy aristocracy and a consequent crisis. Thus, he maintained that creating scarcity by limiting the number of four-year colleges and institutions in existence, as well as the number of students admitted, was both right and necessary. The supply of some kinds of institutions of higher education should be limited even if it does not meet student demand because institutional supply should align with occupational demand and students' natural capacity. In Seashore's estimation, room at the top, in the top schools at the top of his institutional hierarchy, rightly should be carefully limited because the number of people who belong at the top is, by nature, limited.

The Next Level Down: Junior Colleges

Universities and four-year colleges were at the top of Seashore's hierarchy of institutions of higher education, but he did not confine his attention to them. Speaking of a need to fill an institutional gap between high schools and four-year colleges, he also championed junior colleges,[247] and an obituary written by George Stoddard claimed that Seashore probably was the first psychologist to wholeheartedly support them.[248] Seashore promoted junior colleges, for example, in an article that appeared in *School and Society* in 1927 (as well as in *Learning and Living in College*); thirteen years later, he wrote an entire book on the topic, *The Junior College Movement*.[249] There are many similarities between the book and the article, and in some cases, he borrowed book material directly from the article; that said, the subtle differences between the two documents may indicate subtle shifts in his thinking over time. For example, the dangers of "overproduction" in the four-year college, which figured prominently in the early article, were relegated to a paragraph in the 1940 publication, where they were accompanied by a host of other reasons why junior colleges were needed, especially in the period after World War I.[250]

Junior colleges occupied a niche on Seashore's hierarchy, but that niche was on a lower rung than the one occupied by four-year colleges. That they were to be not merely different from four-year colleges but also *lower* on the institutional hierarchy is apparent in the language he used to describe the expansion of higher education. As I indicated above, he stated that the upward expansion of higher education was in the direction of graduate study; by contrast, he used the term "downward" rather than "lateral" to describe the expansion consisting of "the wider opening of college opportunities for terminal courses in the first two years of the college."[251] Seashore underscored that junior colleges and the opportunities they would provide contributed to "education for democracy"; they would help maintain the "dignity of skilled labor" while raising the level of "patriotic citizenship" among those attending.[252] He stated that unlike four-year colleges, which were to provide education for an intellectual aristocracy, junior colleges were to dispense "education for citizenship" for a different class of people.[253] Graduates would be leaders in the arts and crafts, and they would lead through "intelligent and competent living."[254] One major difference between the two types of institutions was that junior colleges were to provide a practical rather than a scholarly education; significantly, at one point he indicated that students from both types of institutions were equally intelligent.[255] According to Seashore, junior colleges were to educate between two and five times as many students as the four-year colleges did.[256]

He supported two types of junior colleges, the academic and the technical (what he called "technological"),[257] and he described two types of academic junior college curricula—the regular academic program, which would be comparable to the first two years at a four-year college and could conceivably enable a student to transfer to a four-year school, and the "junior academic" program, which would be more general and would lead instead to "intelligent citizenship."[258] The other type of junior college would offer specialized post–high school "technological or semi-vocational" programs: his list of two-year technical junior colleges included business colleges and revitalized normal schools for elementary school teachers, as well as institutes devoted to home economics; music; art; and applied science, including carpentry, plumbing, and electrical work.[259] Only in rare cases were two-year terminal programs to be provided by four-year colleges or universities; rather, junior colleges were to be separate and distinct institutions.[260]

Although Seashore spoke of an absence or a gap needing to be filled, by the time his 1927 article appeared, junior colleges, including public junior colleges, had been around for some time. In the United States, two-year normal schools and other types of private two-year colleges date back to the nineteenth century; Joliet Junior College, the first public junior college in the United States, was founded in 1901. That said, the number of junior colleges grew exponentially in the early twentieth century, and Seashore fully supported this growth. He mentioned that "a disgraceful shadow" had fallen over two-year normal school degrees, the shadow being a loss of status, and he argued that the degree should once again be given a "dignified status."[261] Even though he claimed it merited dignity, he did not place it on a par with a four-year degree.

He staunchly maintained that four-year colleges were not for everyone and that junior colleges were for some of those who didn't belong. Who was to be educated at a junior college? Calling them the "People's College," he claimed that they should be for "the people"[262]—members of the upper-middle class, he stated.[263] Elsewhere he said that junior colleges are for "the intelligent middle class."[264] Significantly, he distinguished between the upper-middle class and the superior class that constitutes the intellectual aristocracy in a democracy.[265] As I mentioned earlier, in his discussion of the problem of overpopulation at four-year colleges, he identified the upper-middle class as the new group that was inundating four-year schools and contributing to a loss of academic quality. Thus, for Seashore, solving the problem of overpopulation at four-year schools was to be one of the functions of junior colleges. His message was that although they were unfit for four-year colleges, the students for whom junior colleges were intended were fit for at least some kind of post–high school education and for important, but presumably less prestigious, occupations. Seashore noted that a few junior college students successfully transferred to four-year schools; he explained that this "comparatively surprising fact" was possible because "adequate" junior colleges carefully screened their students and recommended a transfer only to the few who had a good chance of succeeding at a four-year school.[266] Like their more prestigious four-year counterparts, junior colleges were to engage in sorting, ordering, promoting, and eliminating. Seashore recommended, for example, that they use qualifying examinations.[267]

In addition to being for the upper-middle class, junior colleges, Seashore maintained, should be for those "types of students" who are not in college at all, saying that he envisioned "a new type of student body of a distinctly American origin and character."[268] Among the groups that would be well suited for junior colleges were farmers and their wives.[269] (It apparently did not occur to him that women could be farmers.) A junior college education that included information about farming and homemaking, he claimed, could reverse the flight from farming that was producing a "very rapid deterioration of the country population";[270] it could help turn the tide that had resulted in too many farming communities being "drained of their ablest citizens" and the consequent tendency for farms to fall into the hands of "white trash."[271] Although the 1940 book is different from the 1927 article in many respects, Seashore mentioned farmers and White trash in both publications. The book even included his definition of White trash: "persons who have no ambition, no resources, no motives for the making of a good farm and a beautiful home."[272] According to the *Oxford English Dictionary*, the first known reference to "White trash" appeared in 1821; the *OED* states that White trash are "poor white people of low social status, especially when regarded as uneducated or uncultured."[273]

According to Matt Wray, author of *Not Quite White: White Trash and the Boundaries of Whiteness*, "White trash" emphasizes moral failings in addition to poverty.[274] In her book *White Trash: The Eugenic Family Studies, 1877–1919*, Nicole Hahn Rafter connects the concept of White trash directly to eugenics, claiming that the supposed degenerates studied by eugenicists—including Goddard's Kallikak family—exemplified White trash.[275] From Seashore's passages on farmers and the junior college, it appears that he did not regard White trash as good candidates for a two-year college education.

In these two texts on junior colleges, he also singled out women as a group. For example, he mentioned them as good potential students for two-year home economics institutes, which would focus solely on "home training" rather than on education for a paid job.[276] In the 1927 article, the coursework Seashore suggested had a distinctly eugenical flavor:

> Child welfare, heredity and euthenics, will play an important rôle so that a girl who wants a general education for home life will get out of the training in that course a more effective education for her purpose than is ordinarily gotten out of the four-year course in which there is no objective. In addition to the specific training in the home arts it will cultivate for her a love for home life, a feeling for culture and an interest in reading and travel.[277]

Like his mention of farmers, his discussion of girls and home economics institutes appeared in both the book and the article.[278] In the 1940 book, however, Seashore replaced heredity and euthenics with other possible curricular subjects, ranging from chemistry to interior decorating.[279] Both the article and book mentioned revitalized normal institutes, and in the book, girls were specifically identified as the potential students.[280] Furthermore, he singled out women when discussing the role that junior colleges can play in developing community and home leadership in rural areas.[281]

African Americans from the South constituted yet another group he identified as a potential population for junior colleges. In his 1927 discussion of technical schools that educate skilled workmen, he stated, "Hampton Institute, for the colored people of the South, is a splendid example of this kind of institution."[282] In the 1940 book, he reported that the burgeoning junior college movement "takes many forms well adapted to the education of Negroes in the South."[283] He supported this statement with a quote from Nick A. Ford that appeared in a 1936 issue of the *Journal of Negro Education*:

> "There are three obvious advantages of the junior college over its more sophisticated senior. If there is any group of people such an institution can benefit more than any other, certainly that group is the Negro in the South. In the first place, few Negro families during these times of depression are able to send their children to expensive senior colleges, which in many cases are more than a hundred miles distant from their homes. Junior colleges draw largely upon neighboring districts and thus give opportunity for further training to hundreds of youth who find it impossible to leave their immediate localities."[284]

In the sentence following the Ford quotation, Seashore commented on what he called a strange phenomenon: not only are junior colleges "suitable for pioneering education in more or less backward countries," they also are popular in the most progressive nations, including countries in Scandinavia.[285] The placement of this observation is significant: even though he acknowledged that junior colleges are embraced by ostensibly progressive countries, his first comment was that they are suitable for backward ones; the context implies that he believed the people in the United States he had just discussed—"Negroes" in the South—are similarly backward. Furthermore, he did not explain why he would find it strange for an education institution to be effective for all people.

In the above quotation, Ford alluded to a hierarchy of institutions of higher education when he said that four-year colleges are more "sophisticated" than junior colleges; significantly, he pointed African Americans in the direction of the ostensibly less-sophisticated institutions. Ford cited poverty as a reason for his recommendation, but Seashore's rather curious multiple references to "Negroes in the South" may have an explanation that has more to do with eugenics than with poverty. According to Stephen Jay Gould, eugenicist Robert Yerkes had reported that Blacks from the North scored higher on the Army Alpha test than Blacks from the South.[286] In his 1923 book *A Study of American Intelligence*, Carl Brigham claimed that this difference has three causes; two of them alluded to innate intelligence:

> The superior intelligence measurements of the northern negro are due to three factors: first, the greater amount of educational opportunity, which does affect, to some extent, scores on our present intelligence tests; second, the greater amount of admixture of white blood; and, third, the operation of economic and social forces, such as higher wages, better living conditions, identical school privileges, and a less complete social ostracism, tending to draw the more intelligent negro to the North. It is impossible to dissect out of this complex of forces the relative weight of each factor. No psychologist would maintain that the mental tests he is now using do not measure educational opportunity *to some extent*. On the other hand, it is absurd to attribute all differences found between northern and southern negroes to superior educational opportunities in the North, for differences are found between groups of the same schooling [emphasis mine].[287]

In the next paragraph, to bolster his argument, Brigham added, "The intellectual superiority of our Nordic group over the Alpine, Mediterranean, and negro groups has been demonstrated."[288]

Even though Seashore had a great deal to say about African American music and musicians, and expressed interest in race differences in musical ability—topics I will discuss in chapter 7—I found almost no mention of African Americans in his statements about general ability, intelligence testing, or education, even though the eugenics community as a whole was on fire about race. I found no evidence that he challenged prevailing White supremacist eugenical views on race, and so I interpret Seashore's silence as tacit agreement.

Along with the brief references I have just described, I found an archival item that may shed more light on his views about the "rightful" place for African Americans on his institutional hierarchy. The item is a letter from University of Iowa president Virgil Hancher to Seashore, dated August 3, 1944, describing an encounter Seashore had with an African American graduate student, Alvin W. Rose. President Hancher quoted from a written complaint he had received from Edward B. Reuter, a professor in the Sociology Department. Reuter conducted research on race; he wrote the complaint the same summer he retired from Iowa and accepted a professorship at Fisk University. Hancher wrote:

> The following is an excerpt from a letter which I received this morning from Professor Reuter:
>
> "Some months ago Mr. Alvin Rose, a Negro student, was given an appointment by the Graduate College to continue graduate work at the University of Iowa. On Friday of last week, Professor Seashore called Mr. Rose into his office and notified him that he had cancelled the appointment. When pressed for an explanation of this arbitrary procedure, he stated among other reasons that 'Negroes should have "special" rather than academic education' and that Mr. Rose should quit school and get a manual labor job."
>
> "Is this to be a policy of the University? If so, is there any reason why it should not be given general publicity?"
>
> I shall be pleased to have your comments.[289]

Rose went elsewhere for his doctorate and became a prominent sociologist. Born in New Haven, Missouri,[290] he received a master's degree from the University of Iowa in 1943 and a doctorate in sociology from the University of Chicago in 1947.[291] After completing his doctorate, he did postdoctoral work at the Sorbonne.[292] He was a United Nations senior advisor to the Congo in social affairs in the early 1960s,[293] as well as a sociology professor at a number of institutions, including St. Louis University, North Carolina College, and Wayne State University.[294] He joined the sociology faculty at the University of Miami in 1972, and in 1976, he became that institution's first African American department chair.[295] Today, the department gives the Alvin W. Rose Award annually to its most outstanding sociology major.[296]

I found no other information about the exchange between Seashore and Rose, and so I do not know whether and how Seashore responded to Hancher's request for comment. That said, the remarks Seashore reportedly made to Rose were in line with his belief that junior colleges—institutions lower on his higher education hierarchy—were especially well suited for African Americans, at least for those from the South. It is conceivable that Seashore viewed Missouri, Rose's birthplace, as part of the South.

As we have seen, not only were people to be sorted and ordered, but institutions of higher education were to exist on a hierarchy that matched up with people of varying levels of fitness. The net effect was a tracked system where institutions had different ranks or standings, and where the gold and iron surely would not mix. By intent or effect, Seashore's institutional hierarchy was racially segregated. The Carnegie Classification of Institutions of Higher Education, which was created in 1970 and remains in use to the present, may reflect earlier hierarchical classificatory impulses such as Seashore's. In the current Carnegie Classification lineup, associate's colleges are listed below baccalaureate colleges; significantly, however, tribal colleges are listed last, at the very bottom.[297]

Sectioning by Ability

In Seashore's education reform plan, after students had been sorted, ordered, promoted, or eliminated by entrance and qualifying exams, and had been slotted into an institution that sat on a particular level on an institutional hierarchy, yet more sorting, ordering, promoting, and eliminating awaited those who remained: a form of progressive selection and elimination that Seashore called sectioning by ability. According to him, just as societies are hierarchical, reflecting a supposedly natural hierarchy of human capacity and quality, learning opportunities should be similarly hierarchal and structured to reflect presumably biologically innate capacity or talent. Sectioning by ability was a type of tracking that involved creating multiple ability-segregated sections of the same course; the quantity and quality of work assigned would vary from section to section on the hierarchy.[298] He stated that sectioning by ability was an old practice that had fallen into disuse, in one source claiming it had begun 100 years earlier, and in another dating it back two generations.[299] As evidence of the soundness of the practice, he said that it had been in use in the best colleges in the nation, and specifically named Ivy League schools: "Yale, Harvard, Dartmouth and other good colleges."[300] He asserted that he was one of the first to revive the practice, and his biographer, Walter Miles, further claimed that Seashore improved upon it.[301] Seashore recalled that he had begun "pioneer experiments" with sectioning by ability in 1907 in one of his psychology courses.[302] Over the years, he used his positional power to try to convince other institutions to adopt the practice. For example, he promoted its revival in a 1921 paper he read before a division of the National Research Council, claiming that it improves both motivation and efficiency.[303] These efforts were part of his larger plan to encourage other academics and schools to engage in a variety of teaching experiments, and they typify his use of influential platforms to promote his plans. Another instance of this use of platforms occurred in 1911 when he, as president of the American Psychological Association, created an APA committee on teaching experiments and appointed Robert Mearns Yerkes, Guy Whipple, Edward Thorndike, Margaret Washburn, and James Angell to serve on it.[304]

According to Seashore, as a result of a resurgence in interest, by 1924 approximately half of "the leading colleges and universities in the country" were using sectioning by ability in one or more departments.[305] In the same year, he also claimed that sectioning by ability had been endorsed by the National Research Council, the Association of University Professors, and the Association of Land Grant Colleges.[306] By 1927, he had added the Board of Investigation of Engineering Education and "numerous other agencies" to his list of endorsers.[307] In a discussion of these endorsements, Walter Miles gave Seashore partial credit for the revival of this practice.[308]

Seashore believed that sectioning by ability was well suited for "elementary" college courses,[309] and he maintained that the college system should be modeled after practices in the best elementary and secondary schools in the country.[310] Miles stated, however, that Seashore found public school sectioning, which relied on merely two or three sections per grade, to be inadequate and unsatisfactory.[311] Although in one source Seashore described a system composed of three sections,[312] elsewhere he advocated for as many sections as feasible, claiming that five different levels of the same course was ideal in large departments.[313] He described in minute detail how his plan should work. As part of his broader strategy for the "progressive elimination, selection and motivation of the individual," at the beginning of the term, faculty members were to administer a "competitive test of capacity" to all students enrolled; test results were to determine students' section placement.[314]

He also discussed how grading would work across the multiple sections of the course, with students' grades reflecting the *section level* to which they had been assigned; it is in this context that he spoke of early elimination of those destined to fail: "If the competition has been fair and well conducted throughout the year, the students in the high section should have either the highest or next highest grade; those in the middle sections should have something approximating the middle grade; and those in the low section should have either the lowest or the next higher grade, if they pass. Those who are destined to fail should be eliminated early."[315] Thus, a single grading curve would be applied across all sections, and students relegated to the lowest section would probably—and rightly, in Seashore's estimation—receive the lowest grades. Those in the lower sections had a slight chance to escape from their allotted section by proving themselves worthier than their assigned placement indicated, but given that the sections were to differ both in quality and quantity of content, it is hard to imagine how section transfers could be navigated easily and successfully. Thus, Seashore clearly believed that sectioning by ability reflected rather than created students' destinies, which were played out within a hierarchical scale of ability-determined sections.

Sectioning in the Name of Freedom, Fairness, Benevolence, and Justice

Sectioning by ability, Seashore claimed, helps institutions discover and encourage the superior student,[316] and it benefits all by successfully breaking "the lockstep of the unsegregated class."[317] As a consequence, the best students are liberated, freed to soar: "The cutting of the leash which has traditionally held the good student to the level of mediocrity, forces the enlargement of the scope of reasonable assignment for the good student in each course."[318] Sectioning released the best students from "a dead load," presumably the rest of the students, and propelled them toward self-actualization: "To the gifted student it is a means of finding himself and being motivated by effective competition, freedom from a dead load, stimulation of initiative, and the joy of achievement."[319] Liberating gifted students—the fittest—and enabling them to soar, unfettered by the drag of the unfit, is a stock eugenics goal. The unfit as a burden on the fit is a common trope in eugenics discourse.

Elsewhere, when enumerating the benefits that all students would derive from the system, he mentioned some of what Leonardo and Broderick might call the spoils of smartness, notably innovative curricular approaches; significantly, he devoted the most space to benefits that should be given to the best:

> The high students can go fast and take long lessons, can do a better quality of work, and can acquire a more genuine understanding and first hand grasp of the situation. As to content, they can consider topics which are entirely beyond the reach of the low students, and the method of conducting the class can be entirely different, particularly in taking advantage of the capacity for discussion, extensive reference work, freedom of initiative, and experiments. On the other hand, the low students, with equally hard work, should cover a limited territory on a lower standards [*sic*] of quality; they should, therefore, be limited to such content as is within their reach and should work by such methods as will meet their peculiar needs.[320]

Another benefit of sectioning by ability, according to Seashore, is that it separates students from others with whom they ostensibly have nothing in common:

> Thus the man who comes with good heredity to freshman English from a good home, where he has used good English, read good books, has been trained in a good school and has acquired good habits of study and will to work, is for the first time charged with the responsibility of investing all his talents, and the man at the other extreme of endowment and training for the first time is treated with respect and trained efficiently at his own level. *They have nothing in common* [emphasis mine].[321]

As we have seen from other passages, however, although Seashore may have argued that the "man at the other extreme"—the man with low endowment—would be treated with respect, that man also would be at heightened risk of swift and early elimination. His call for segregation via sectioning by ability is consistent with eugenicists' claims that separation will help prevent contamination of the fit by the unfit.

In addition to enumerating benefits for the good student, Seashore discussed why sectioning is good for the poor student, one claim being that it is fairer than heterogeneous grouping because it gives the poor student a chance; he stated, for example, that sectioning "means kindness, comfort, justice, and relative efficiency for the poor student. It gives the poor student a fair chance, which the old system does not."[322] Arguing that high- and low-ability students suffer different kinds of injustice in heterogeneous groupings, he claimed that one injustice poor students suffer is being expected to accomplish the impossible: "In the present system we do injustice to the high student by accepting from him mediocre work; we do injustice to the low student by blaming him for not coming up to a standard which lies entirely beyond his capacity."[323] Elsewhere, in addition to underscoring sectioning's fairness, Seashore added morale boosting to his list of the benefits of sectioning: "Such sectioning establishes a fair basis for praise and blame, introduces fair standards of achievement, and creates a morale in the class. To the poor student it means kindness, comfort, justice and opportunity for relative efficiency and approbation."[324] He maintained that the success of sectioning hinges on convincing students—and faculty—that such segregation is both fair and in their own best interest: "The advantages of segregation will not be gained unless the spirit of the organization is such as to win the adherence of the students. All the students must be led to a realization of the fact that the plan is fair to all; and each serious student, regardless of level, must be convinced that the segregation is an advantage to him."[325] Finally, in his discussion of possible objections to sectioning, he addressed the argument that it is not democratic; in his rebuttal, he admitted that his true ideal is ranking as it ostensibly naturally occurs outside of school: "There is a peculiar cogency to this argument [that it is not democratic] in that it points out the weakness of this plan as a compromise requiring classification. Our real ideal is the socialized class, so that the ranking on the basis of ability would be taken care of automatically, as it is socially, intellectually, and industrially in daily life."[326]

Gifted Education for Gifted Students

For Those of Highest Quality and Greatest Worth

The gifted student was the focus of another constellation of Seashore's proposed education reforms. "Gifted" was a special category of person, and the gift was an unusually high level of innate capacity or talent. Giftedness had long been a subject of research interest to eugenicists, Galton having set the course in 1869 with the publication of his book *Hereditary Genius*; gifted education was a hot topic in the early part of the twentieth century as well, especially among eugenicists. The lineup of pioneers in the gifted education movement in the United States reads like a eugenics who's who; Stanford University professor Lewis Terman, sometimes called the father of the United States gifted education movement, was among them. Terman et al. claimed that systematic studies of gifted children—identified as such through IQ testing—had begun at Stanford University in around 1911, three years after the Binet scale had been published in the United States.[327] Among Terman's early contributions on the topic were "The Mental Hygiene of Exceptional Children," published in 1915,[328] and his series Genetic Studies of Genius; the first volume in the series, *Mental and Physical Traits of a Thousand Gifted Children*, was published in 1925.[329] Other prominent eugenicists in the gifted education movement included Leta Hollingworth, who published *Gifted Children: Their Nature and Nurture* in 1926;[330] Henry Goddard, who studied gifted education in Cleveland's public schools and published *School Training of Gifted Children* in 1928;[331] and Bird T. Baldwin, the first director of another of Seashore's pet projects, the Iowa Child Welfare Research Station, which was founded in 1917. For eugenicists, special education initiatives for the smartest students were consistent with the eugenical goal of promoting the fittest.

The dates of Seashore's publications on identifying and educating gifted children confirm that he was a pioneer in the field. Although he stated that his efforts to identify gifted men for special service in World War I were the springboard for some of his gifted education initiatives, he mentioned the identification and education of gifted children even prior to the war. He discussed it, for example, in a 1915 article on musical talent,[332] and in a 1916 article on the role that the Iowa Child Welfare Research Station could play in providing parental education for the rearing of three distinct types of children: the "sub-normal, normal, and gifted."[333]

Like other eugenicists, Seashore premised his gifted education action plan on specific assumptions concerning intelligence: residing in the body, it is measurable via a standardized test, biologically inheritable, and normally distributed. He presented these views as scientific fact. Furthermore, he considered the gifted to be the students of highest quality or worth.[334] This belief was consistent with views of such eugenicists as Lewis Terman, who considered the gifted to be a national treasure essential to building and preserving the nation. Terman opened the first volume of the Genetic Studies of Genius series by asserting, "It should go without saying that a nation's resources of intellectual talent are among the most precious it will ever have."[335] Like other eugenicists, both Seashore and Terman assumed that this precious resource also is scarce—present in only a small minority of the population.

The Neglect of the Gifted Student

Seashore assumed that gifted students were being neglected; he identified this supposed neglect as a problem and attempted to address it throughout his career.[336] He blamed this neglect on leveling practices in schools that "retarded" the natural growth of the gifted student. For example, in *Learning and Living in College*, he wrote that the intelligent boy whose intelligence has been cultivated by a good environment typically is placed in the same class as the boy who lacks both native intelligence and a good background, the result being that the gifted student is held back: "On account of the success of traditional leveling influences of the college, such differences [in inherited ability and background] are ordinarily ignored and often not recognized. The good student has been forced to tread in lockstep with the inferior—a degrading and deteriorating process. It has been well said that the gifted student is the retarded student."[337] He argued that equal treatment in education, in effect, makes the inherently unequal equal and damages the superior student in the process: "The claim that the traditional procedure is justified by results presents a specious element of truth in the fact that the school actually often succeeds in discouraging initiative, cutting the wings of imagination, lowering ideals, and recognizing inferior standards, so that the superior student comes out from the system not much different from the inferior."[338] The idea that the gifted student is the retarded student did not originate with and was not unique to either Seashore or eugenicists. For example, in 1910 Frederick G. Bonser wrote, "Perhaps the worst type of retardation in the schools is the withholding appropriate promotion from those pupils who are the most gifted, therefore of most significance as social capital. Are these pupils utilizing their abilities in the healthful measure possible for their best development?"[339]

W. H. Holmes later quoted Bonser in a 1912 *Journal of Education* article entitled "Promotion Classes for Gifted Pupils."[340] Holmes, a school superintendent, opened his article with the statement, "Democracy should not keep talent in the quarantine of mediocrity"; he then argued that extant education systems were erroneously geared toward the average child and consequently were ill-suited for "subnormal" and "supernormal" students.[341] Citing the German psychologist William Stern, he stated that "society cannot afford to neglect the supernormal, or gifted, children."[342] Holmes was promoting ability grouping here, but he was associated with the Batavia System of Individual Instruction, which, rather than categorizing students by age or ability, eliminated grade levels and ability-tracked groupings altogether. In a strict application of the Batavia System, the gifted child would be best served by a school where all children study independently at their own pace. As we shall see shortly, independent study was an education privilege that Seashore felt should be reserved only for the fittest.

The claim that the fittest were being neglected resonated with eugenicists. They frequently warned that in a host of realms, the fittest were being held back both by the unfit and by policies and practices benefitting the unfit; they also complained that the fittest were not receiving the privileges and rewards rightly due them. They spoke often of the dire consequences in store for a nation or for a whole race that held back the fittest. Eugenicist Madison Grant, for example, decried the eradication of privilege in the United States, including the "privilege of intellect," and he mentioned the destruction of the right of the privileged to have a solid education:

> In America we have nearly succeeded in destroying the privilege of birth; that is, the intellectual and moral advantage a man of good stock brings into the world with him. We are now engaged in destroying the privilege of wealth; that is, the reward of successful intelligence and industry, and in some quarters there is developing a tendency to attack the privilege of intellect and to deprive a man of the advantages of an early and thorough education.[343]

Eugenicist Paul Popenoe, who later penned a popular *Ladies' Home Journal* column, "Can This Marriage Be Saved?" and was the "father" of marriage counseling, mentioned (with coauthor Roswell Johnson) the deleterious effects of the unfit on the education prospects of the normal (and presumably the supernormal): "The feeble-minded child is painfully 'educated,' often at the expense of his normal brother or sister. In short, the undesirables of the race, with whom the bloody hand of natural selection would have made short work early in life, are now nursed along to old age."[344]

In his autobiography, Seashore mentioned a speech he had given at Harvard in support of neglected gifted students and indicated that Harvard's president shared his concerns: "Speaking at Harvard, I said, 'We ask only that the faculty should do as much for the encouragement of the good student as it does for the poor student. This is not being done.' President Lowell spoke up with vim, saying, 'That is true. Harvard never has done as well by the good student as by the poor student.' And by that he meant that no institution had done it."[345] Seashore was referring to A. Lawrence Lowell, a strong supporter of eugenics; according to Adam S. Cohen, Lowell favored strict immigration restrictions, and "worked to impose a quota on Jewish students and to keep black students from living in the Yard."[346] Seashore sought to "liberate" the gifted student through higher education reform, freeing him to work at his "natural level" and enabling him to experience the joys of intrinsic motivation:

> If we once liberate the good student, give him facilities and encouragement to work at his natural level of successful achievement, formal and outward marks of distinction will be of little consequence as compared with the deep satisfaction in doing this kind of work. To make this enjoyable, many institutions must, however, change their atmosphere so that both students and faculties will hail the superior student with approbation, instead of looking upon him as a "grade-getter" or a union scale breaker.[347]

Seashore's Gifted Student Project

One of Seashore's most significant and far-reaching education reform initiatives, the Gifted Student Project, was designed to help solve the problem of underservice to the fittest. It was a national, multi-year undertaking of the National Research Council (NRC). In her chapter on the role of the National Research Council in addressing the problem of the gifted student, Jane Robbins calls Seashore the project's "missionary leader."[348] Among the places where Seashore detailed the history and purposes of this project was his final report to eugenicist Vernon Kellogg, the first permanent secretary of the National Research Council and a former professor at Stanford University.[349] Seashore reported that the project had its roots in a World War I venture designed to address a shortage of fit college graduates suitable for scientific, technical positions in war service.[350] The National Research Council was charged with locating the most promising men to fill the gap;[351] Walter Miles reported that colleges recommended the top 10 percent of their seniors to an NRC committee.[352] Seashore chaired that committee, which selected candidates from those the colleges had nominated.[353] He claimed that it was a popular project[354] and that after the war, it served as a template for his proposed solution to a new problem: colleges, inundated with students, were delivering a mass education that was ill-suited to the fittest.[355] In his report to Kellogg, he asserted that attending to those wounded in the war, admitting poor students, and employing mediocre faculty were having a deleterious effect on those he considered to be brightest and fittest: "After the war colleges and universities discovered that they were engaged in mass production by methods suitable for primitive conditions; that the first concern of all institutions was to take care of its 'cripples'; that the bright student was held in leash by the poor student and by a mediocre faculty."[356] He stated that in the face of an overproduction of college students, institutions needed to rethink the aims of higher education,[357] and he set out to design a peacetime project that would "discover and motivate the youth who give promise of fitness for a learned career."[358] Because the NRC wartime project was his idea, he also led the new initiative, which began when he chaired the NRC's Division of Anthropology and Psychology.[359] Two NRC divisions sponsored the project, the Division of Anthropology and Psychology and the Division of Educational Relations.[360] Kellogg secured foundation funding,[361] Robbins stating that the money came from the Commonwealth Fund, the General Education Board, and the NRC itself.[362]

Seashore claimed that colleges were clamoring for information on new education trends, especially concerning the education of gifted students.[363] To set the education reform wheels in motion, he sought to establish working relationships between the NRC and colleges and universities.[364] His plan involved campus visits by a representative from the NRC.[365] During the period when Seashore was at his NRC post in Washington, DC, these visits were conducted by his University of Iowa colleague, Professor George W. Stewart, and for five years after that, Seashore made the visits himself.[366] Seashore's visits came in conjunction with what was called an NRC Day or a Gifted Student Day.[367] He met with faculty, students, and administrators during these all-day events, which involved a variety of activities focusing on gifted students,[368] and he also gave a speech. Thus, he claimed that rather than setting out to inspect schools and identify what was wrong, he was a goodwill messenger bearing good tidings in the form of sound advice.[369]

He said that he had given a great deal of thought to how colleges should be reorganized to keep each individual busy and to acknowledge differences,[370] and that he had collected information on incipient reform movements.[371] Using this material, he wrote a stock speech that distilled his advice into fourteen points, admitting that as something of a stunt, he had used President Woodrow Wilson's Fourteen Points as a model.[372] His recommendations were based on his motto, "Keep each individual busy at his highest natural level of successful achievement":[373]

1) An advisory college qualifying examination, differentiating natural aptitude for college work from training, to be given at the end of the high school course.
2) Departmental placement examinations for the orientation of the student within the department and for the furnishing of a general profile of student capacity to the administration.
3) Sectioning of classes on the basis of ability.
4) Organization of instruction on the basis of individual, group, or project methods, permitting free progress of the individual at his natural level for competition and progress.
5) Honors systems, including honors courses and other forms of free and competitive work for distinction.
6) Honor credit, or the gaining of time on the basis of superior work.
7) Elimination of competitive introductory courses and the organization of single basic courses in which different levels of progress are recognized.
8) Placing the ablest teacher in the department in charge of the basic course.
9) Initiatory, orientation, and final survey courses.
10) Facilities for giving intellectual comradeship to the ablest students among themselves and with the faculty.
11) Development of a system of character record and the motivation of character as such.
12) Development of adequate educational personnel service.

13) Technological training with a natural finishing place in the junior college for students of applied science and art.
14) Differentiation of the functions of institutions.[374]

Having already discussed a number of these points, I want to underscore that Seashore was mobilizing the concept of individual difference to advocate for more advantages for the fittest. Furthermore, his broad education reform plan as spelled out in his Fourteen Points was directly connected to and emerged from his goal of addressing the neglect of the gifted. Once again, his emphasis on the fittest, and on freeing them from encumberment caused by the unfit, is one of the many ways that his reform plans and activities were linked to and consistent with eugenics.

Seashore claimed to have visited 140 campuses directly and 15 more indirectly as part of the Gifted Student Project,[375] his travels taking him everywhere from the University of Washington to Harvard.[376] He also mentioned Bloomington, Indiana;[377] Purdue;[378] Dartmouth, Williams, and Amherst Colleges;[379] and Wesleyan, Mount Holyoke, Smith, Amherst, and Wellesley.[380] He described a grueling, exhausting travel schedule, claiming at one point that he had delivered forty-seven after-dinner speeches in forty-six days.[381] He was a man on a mission and he stated as much.[382]

He remarked that his visits were met with enthusiasm and support,[383] and he claimed that the timing was good for his message, which, he argued, effectively addressed the different needs of different institutions:

> The country was at this time just awakening to a recognition of the significance of individual differences, and a testing program and service putting out dragnets to discover gifted students in the senior class, in the freshman class, and in the high schools came to be a popular movement. It was at this time that institutions like Dartmouth, Williams, and Amherst were being thoroughly revamped so as to come out entirely different from their traditional character in many respects. The institutions of the Mid-West and Far West were perhaps at that time at the peak of growing pains and therefore receptive to my mission.[384]

In 1927 as the project drew to a close, he recommended that the NRC hire a permanent employee to continue the visits,[385] but he later reported that the NRC could find no one willing to replace him,[386] and so the initiative ended. Nevertheless, the Gifted Student Project bore much fruit, including a host of publications. For example, Seashore said that his book *Learning and Living in College* was a report on the Gifted Student Project and its outcomes.[387] In addition, the NRC took on the far-reaching project of widely circulating Seashore's *An Open Letter to College Seniors*; Seashore claimed that this circulation also was a result of the Gifted Student Project:

> One of the by-products of this Gifted Student Project was the adoption of my *Open Letter to a College Senior* [*sic*] as an annual message to every senior graduating from a liberal arts college. This letter was circulated for a number of years by the Council [i.e., the NRC] and at other times by other national agencies, while several universities and colleges printed their own editions from time to time, so that this bulletin has been circulated for twenty years in some form or other and has served a unique purpose.[388]

Kellogg spearheaded the effort.[389] Miles wrote that "perhaps no other single pamphlet having to do with higher education has had a wider circulation in this country."[390]

Another important outgrowth of the Gifted Student Project was burgeoning interest in college honors courses and programs. Seashore was a staunch proponent, the fifth of his Fourteen Points focusing on them. Robbins claims that the best-known publication to come out the Gifted Student Project was Swarthmore College president Frank Aydelotte's 1924 report *Honors Courses in American Colleges and Universities*.[391] She notes that college honors programs predate Seashore, stating that the University of Missouri had established one in 1912, but she credits Seashore for their spread.[392] In 1927, Seashore stated that in the United States, there had been a marked increase in recent years in interest in honors courses modeled after the "English system," and he praised Aydelotte's report.[393] He also claimed that about ninety institutions offered such courses but remarked that most courses were of poor quality because faculty did not know how to teach them properly.[394]

In 1925, the NRC hosted a national conference on honors courses, which was held at the University of Iowa.[395] Seashore, Aydelotte, and Kellogg were among the members of the conference committee,[396] and Seashore and Aydelotte were paper respondents.[397] Robbins states that the event was attended by representatives of forty-one colleges and universities.[398] All but two of the thirty-seven institutions appearing on a list found in the papers of University of Iowa president Walter Jessup are located in the Midwest, the list including such notable liberal arts institutions as Carleton and Macalester Colleges, as well as a host of Midwestern universities.[399]

Finally, Seashore claimed that in addition to playing out on a national scale, the Gifted Student Project had had an impact on education policy and practice at the University of Iowa. He noted that the faculty had formally adopted eleven of his fourteen recommended points.[400]

He stated that the Gifted Student Project represented his largest influence as an educator,[401] and he opined that nobody else had met as many faculties as he had in the interest of higher education.[402] Miles called the project the capstone of Seashore's many accomplishments as an educator, writing, "College deans and departmental chairmen gave more attention to this subject [the gifted student] per semester during this five-year program than had probably taken place in any previous twenty-year period."[403] Thus, even though the Gifted Student Project ended, Seashore had helped set a massive machine in motion that altered the national higher education landscape. According to Robbins, although momentum slowed after the NRC withdrew its leadership, the gifted education movement never came to a complete halt and picked up steam again in the 1950s and 1960s.[404]

More Privileges and Perks

Seashore's list of privileges for the academically fittest did not end with honors courses and programs; it also included independent study. In his autobiography, he reported that he came to recognize sectioning by ability as a "compromise," the ideal being independent work: "My next step was to substitute for it [sectioning by ability] the project method by which each individual student works for himself, under ideal library and experimental conditions, and no one is hampered in the least by the quality or rate of work of his associates."[405] In a discussion of reforms to engineering education, he argued that individual instruction would "enable the student to finish his course in a time somewhat proportionate to his capacity for work."[406]

In particular, he championed independent study for graduate students, at one point claiming that the new, truly liberal education was to be found in graduate study, not in the four-year college.[407] Thus, the perk of conducting independent study was the rightful property of the best of the best who lived at the top of his hierarchy of education institutions and opportunities. Seashore held a generally dim view of women graduate students; thus, this perk was, in effect if not by design, largely out of reach for women and African American men, among others. A 1929 University of Iowa news bulletin detailed the recent adoption of radical changes to graduate study at Iowa that aimed to "accelerate the progress of capable students in routine study in order that the time thus gained may be used for acquisition of a cultural background and attainment of greater perfection in chosen fields of learning."[408] The bulletin credited Seashore with formulating this radical plan and stated that the changes enabled graduate students to engage in independent study, a new practice that it claimed is consistent with democratic ideals: "Individual graduate study, though new in this country, is in harmony with the tradition of democracy in education and with the current tendency to eliminate mass methods from higher education."[409] Another feature of the newly adopted plan was to excuse graduate students from class attendance, course examinations, and "accumulation of credits."[410]

In his discussion of college entrance examinations, Seashore mentioned another privilege to be accorded to the fittest: special counseling for the top 10 percent of scorers,[411] and in his Fourteen Points, he listed yet another: special facilities and opportunities that would allow the fittest to mingle with each other and to meet faculty members.[412] In his discussion of sectioning by ability, he recommended giving the highest-performing students additional credit and excusing them from examinations altogether.[413] As I mentioned earlier, in a clear nod to eugenics, when he was a member of the Biological Fellowship Board of the NRC, he supported the policy they adopted of giving baby bonuses to National Research Fellows.

He also advocated public identification and recognition of the fittest individuals via honors and awards.[414] According to Seashore, such honors should reflect and be bestowed in proportion to the various levels of achievement; for example, in a chapter entitled "Honors and Awards," he stated that "the oxcart, the covered wagon, the day coach, the pullman express, and the airplane division, are splendidly descriptive of the grades of distinction and honors involved."[415] Airplanes and Pullman cars are the first-class modes of luxurious transportation rightly reserved for the elite: "A passenger in the pullman express travels with speed and comfort in the company of men of means and men of influence; he takes first-class accommodations at hotels and clubs and does business on a big scale, enjoys rich contacts in social life, engages in creative enterprises, secures preferred entrée wherever he goes in companionship with his fellow passengers, and feels that he is a part of a going concern."[416] The average person travels on the day coach, which is democratic and functional but not luxurious, and it is lower on the transportation hierarchy.[417] It lacks "comfort, distinction and speed," and after his journey, the day coach traveler "may get into good company and secure better privileges of living; but, in general, the habits acquired in the day coach are indelibly impressed upon his character as shown by industry, initiative, self-respect, and ambition throughout life."[418] At the bottom, in the covered wagons and oxcarts, there is only poverty, struggle, and death—no honors or awards: "At this end there is no reward—it is just the operation of natural law under most charitable conditions in the grim, bitter struggle for existence. . . . Many a wooden cross is set up along the way; many a traveler is crippled for life as a nervous wreck; some make their destination only to be disillusioned about the dreamland promises for which they had lived."[419] To Seashore, this hierarchical transportation analogy reflects the natural order of things and illustrates the inevitable consequences of natural law. One of these consequences is that for some, there will be no honors or awards.

For others, however, the awards were to be legion, including the conferral of Latin and departmental honors at graduation. Latin honors—the various levels of cum laude—had been used by Harvard and other US institutions for many years; in addition to supporting them, however, Seashore set a high bar for their bestowal. The honor of summa cum laude was to be given to 2 percent of the graduating class, magna cum laude to 4 percent, and cum laude to about 8 percent.[420] He said that sectioning by ability could help decide who would receive departmental honors.[421] Significantly, he indicated elsewhere that other factors, in addition to good grades, should be taken into account when conferring departmental honors; he mentioned "a scholarly attitude"; a "balance of activities, representing health, socialization and academic life"; and a good personality.[422]

Opportunities to Compete

Perhaps following in the path of Herbert Spencer or Darwinian evolutionary theory, Seashore supported using competition as a motivator in school settings, especially competitions designed for the fittest. For example, he saw competition as the means by which students could change their appointed slot on his hierarchy of ability-determined sections. He provided a statement that professors could read to the class when initial section placements were announced, and he underscored the value of competition in such settings: "'Your preliminary showing is that you qualify for reciting in section X; but this is accepted in a tentative way, and it now remains for you to show where you belong. This injection of the competitive element, and a clean-cut provision for rapid promotion or demotion is a most wholesome influence in the conduct of the class.'"[423] In a *School and Society* article published in 1928, he promoted formal intercollegiate academic competitions, which he claimed would motivate "the work of superior students."[424] He reported that he had developed a plan for such competitions in response to a request from the

Harvard chapter of Phi Beta Kappa, which was looking for a way to raise the organization's eligibility bar and identify superior ability early in the college program.[425] He proposed that schools create teams that would go to meets where they would take examinations and receive team scores.[426] These competitions were to use written examinations. He suggested awarding "medals, badges, prizes, or other insignia" to individual participants and giving cups to teams.[427] He stated that such competitions should be modeled after school athletics and organized around existing athletic conferences such as the Big Ten.[428] In many ways, the meets Seashore envisioned resemble *College Bowl*, a radio (and later, television) series that first aired in 1953 and had grown out of USO entertainment in World War II.

Seashore also supported the Iowa Academic Meet, a high school academic competition sometimes known as the Brain Derby. The University of Iowa began this academic contest, which was based on standardized tests developed by Everet F. Lindquist, in 1929. The tests were administered in Iowa high schools, local winners advanced to district contests, and winners of district contests—approximately 1,000 of the highest scorers—advanced to the state contest, which was held at the University of Iowa.[429] The top scorers at the state contest received awards.[430] For example, in 1937, Lois Jeanne Mayhew made the front page of the *Daily Iowan* for being "Iowa's 'brainiest,'" the top overall scorer; the article reported that she received a jeweled key for her efforts.[431] By 1937 seventeen academic divisions or areas were tested, and the top ten students in each division had their names published in the *Daily Iowan*.[432]

Seashore described the Brain Derby as "a clean sport, vigorous as an athletic contest, with far-reaching practical results," and he supported it, in part, because it allowed each superior individual to achieve "at his natural level."[433] Lois Quinn reports that within three years, more than half of Iowa's high school students were participating in the Brain Derby.[434]

A number of sources credit the Brain Derby to Lindquist, who developed the tests, although Seashore stated that Thomas J. Kirby, a professor in the College of Education at Iowa, organized it and that Lindquist led it.[435] It is also widely recognized that with Lindquist at the helm, these tests morphed into the Iowa Tests of Educational Development.[436] Late in life, Seashore implied that the Derby had been his own brainchild. He stated that the intercollegiate plan he described in his 1928 *School and Society* article was modeled after one he had developed for high school competitions, and he added that his high school plan was "practically the same system which was put into operation by the college of education [where Lindquist and Kirby were on the faculty] for the State of Iowa in 1928 [*sic*, wrong year]."[437]

Regardless of who got there first, it is clear that there were a lot of like-minded thinkers at the University of the Iowa and also that Seashore strongly supported the Derby, which he called an "epoch-making event";[438] furthermore, he praised Lindquist's leadership.[439] I found no evidence that Lindquist was associated with eugenics organizations or that he publicly supported eugenics. Thus, his research on standardized testing, his promotion of these tests, and his support for gifted and talented programs illustrate that the systems of reasoning that made eugenics logical and sensible were circulating outside the formal bounds of eugenics as well. As I said in chapter 2, this reality contributes to the slipperiness of eugenics' boundaries.

In June 1941, six months before the United States entered World War II, Seashore addressed the students attending the thirteenth and last annual Derby.[440] Standing in for President Virgil Hancher, he congratulated the finalists on having won this distinction and told them that they were famous; he stated that they represented the highest 1 percent or even half-percent of all students in Iowa, adding that because they were highest in achievement, they were probably also highest in intelligence.[441] He said that he was issuing them a call to duty in light of the fact that President Franklin Roosevelt had declared a national state of emergency the previous week. Seashore listed five duties, the first of which was to intelligent leadership, and in a nod to eugenics, he described the Derby participants as the most valuable—from the best stock: "In the famous English derby races, the horses that qualify are very valuable; they come from good stock and are well trained for the winning of races. In our now nationally famous brain derby, those of you who have qualified for entry are very valuable boys and girls, selected and trained for intellectual achievement."[442] Next, he called participants to social action, asking them whether they would work for a better world order at home and abroad. Third, he called them to action in patriotic service and arming for peace; he stated that the boys might be called to carry guns and the girls to keep the home fires burning. Recalling my mother's heart-rending description of her 1943 high school graduation—of throngs of uniformed boys heading off the next day to a war from which many of them would not return—I was chilled by Seashore's call, especially because it came from a seventy-five-year-old man who had never served in a war. He continued, "We are *destined* to have a hand in the building for peace [emphasis mine]."[443] He called on participants to be courageous and finally to maintain moral health, stating that the "basis for morality is an attitude toward God which results in a progressive realization of truth, goodness, and beauty in your life."[444] Thus, Seashore told these students, who had performed well on standardized tests and whom he assumed had done well because of inherited ability, that they were destined for leadership and greatness, and he asked them whether they would heed the call.

School competitions were not new—activities such as spelling bees and essay contests long predate the twentieth century—and the Derby was not the first large-scale academic contest, although it may have been the first to be based on statewide written testing. What is significant is that Seashore supported them and that he did so because he saw them as an effective means of liberating, motivating, and improving the fittest. He also supported competition in other school domains, proudly reporting that, based on the same principles that informed the Derby, the University of Iowa had developed similar state contests in music, speech, visual arts, and drama.[445] According to Seashore, the state music contest plan "vastly improved the status of musical organizations in the high schools, has given an opportunity for progressive selection and differentiation of musical abilities and achievements, and has effectively motivated musically gifted students in the serious pursuit of their subjects."[446] He also said that a choir and an orchestra composed of students "discovered by this dragnet" had been created at Iowa; selected high school students came to campus during the summer to perform.[447] Reporting on one of the concerts, Seashore remarked that "every participant was highly talented."[448] In an update, he said that the state music festival had become too large for one site and had been replaced with regional festivals.[449] High school solo and ensemble music festivals continue to thrive in many states to the present, including Wisconsin, and although "festival" has replaced the word "contest," these events are still informally referred to as contests. Similarly, in some states, honors bands, choirs, and orchestras still flourish.

Although not new, a focus on contests and competitions—the better baby and fitter family contests, for example—is entirely consistent with eugenics. Influenced perhaps by the writings of Thomas Malthus, eugenics accepts as a foundational assumption the scarcity of resources. Competitions are similarly premised on scarcity, notably scant room at the top, and they promote the fittest while necessarily eliminating all others. In a world swept clean of misguided efforts to support the constitutionally unfit and where scarce resources would no longer be wasted on hopeless causes, the fittest would survive through competition, taking their rightful place at the top by beating out the others. Furthermore, competition among the fittest would keep their survival skills well honed.

Thus, Seashore strongly believed that the fittest should be given what he called special advantages or privileges,[450] and although in his chapter on honors and awards, he claimed that the highest honor the scholarly world can accord is the opportunity for a student to be at his highest "natural level" of achievement,[451] he did not believe the awards should end there. Some may counter that it is only sensible to reward hard work and a job well done, but I maintain that it also is sensible to view these many privileges as examples of what critics Leonardo and Broderick call the spoils of smartness, and to recognize the combinative effects of cumulative advantage.

Many elements in Seashore's grand plan of sorting, ordering, promoting, and eliminating were based on the fundamental eugenical assumption that the fittest are being threatened by the unfit, shortchanged, and denied their fair share; his plan for redress involved providing more advantages to those who already were variously and substantially advantaged. Gifted education programs were consistent with the goals of positive eugenics and were strongly supported by eugenicists. Seashore's beliefs and his proposed reforms were consistent with eugenics and promulgated by eugenicists who called for an intellectual elite to lead and rescue the nation and the human race; implicitly or explicitly, it was the White race that eugenicists claimed needed rescuing. It became possible and reasonable to give more time, attention, and resources to students who arguably already had more than most by invoking the stock eugenics claim: the gifted few are the rescuers—the hope and the future of the nation or the human race. Denying them extra opportunities would contribute to degeneration. Thus, although Seashore's plans for gifted education appear sunny, optimistic, and positive, it is important to remember that they are laced with eugenic fear of threat, degeneration, and loss.

Justifying Education Reform: Seashore's Claims and Promises

Seashore justified the cluster of reforms he proposed by making claims and promises, some of which involved the ostensibly less fit or unfit student. He never discussed the potential costs of these reforms, asserting instead that they would benefit all and were in the best interest of all. By "all" he meant not only the fittest individuals and "all" as a group, but also each unfit individual slated for elimination. For example, under the heading "Early Sympathetic Elimination and Adjustment," he declared that the early elimination of the poor student is for the student's own good—in addition to being good for the institution: "I have told the entering student that he will be met by sympathetic educators who will deal with him on the basis of his personal needs and qualifications. If he is eliminated by failing to qualify, he is not eliminated merely for the good of the institution but primarily for his own good, because there are countless areas of training in which he can meet with success that he could not get through college."[452] His reference to the institution indicated that the promised benefits would be enjoyed by more parties than just students, however.

Significantly, he described different kinds of benefits for different kinds of students. He constructed elimination of the ostensibly unfit student as reasonable and good by claiming that the reforms would spare that individual injustice, humiliation, disappointment, suffering, failure, and loss. He also claimed that the reforms were *fair* to the *less fit*.[453] In his rejoinders to potential critics, he constructed the reforms as righting the wrongs of a flawed system that harmed less-fit students. He stated that proponents of the then-current system, while charitable in intent toward the less-fit or unfit student, were, in effect, supporting unfairness. For example, in a discussion of the benefits of tracking, he maintained that equal treatment is not good for the "lowly individual," and he argued that a lower, segregated placement for poor students protects them from humiliation and injustice: "With a glow of charitable sentiment the instructor says, 'It is good for the poor student to hear the good student recite.' The fact is, it is not good: often heartrending; the facts recited, if at the level of the good student, are beyond his comprehension, and the movement of the recitation is far beyond his pace; it is gross injustice."[454] He further countered potential criticism by promising better things for the ostensibly less fit or unfit: kindness, comfort, and an opportunity for a fair chance. For example, according to Seashore, rather than being a "hardship" for the abject student, sectioning by ability is a "kindness."[455]

Just as the benefits of reform were to be different for different individual students and groups, the motivations for Seashore's reforms were different, as well. Even when the ostensibly less-fit or unfit student was under discussion, Seashore mentioned benevolence, compassion, caring, and sympathy, suggesting that his reforms were grounded in altruism and only the noblest motivations. The truly charitable figures are not the well-intentioned-but-ill-informed old-school instructors, but rather the new "sympathetic educators" who offer guidance and wise counsel. His claims concerning benevolence and compassion echoed those made by other eugenicists, including Galton. For instance, after stating that eugenics attends to charity, Galton wrote, "Man is gifted with pity and other kindly feelings; he has also the power of preventing many kinds of suffering. I conceive it to fall well within his province to replace Natural Selection by other processes that are more merciful and not less effective."[456]

The tone and affect of Seashore's discourse may have contributed to the allure and palatability of his messages, particularly those focusing on the ostensibly less fit or unfit. The writings of many eugenicists of the early twentieth century drip with fear, but that was not the case with Seashore's oeuvre. Calling himself "somewhat of an optimist," he proposed his education reforms cheerfully and enthusiastically;[457] like other eugenicists, he spoke of his beliefs and reforms with unwavering confidence in their soundness and his rightness. His tone of confident optimism may have contributed to the power of his recommendations, making them at least as effective as the gloom-and-doom jeremiads of other eugenicists. In addition, his optimism about a brighter future was consistent with eugenical thought overall. Thus, promises of good and fair outcomes for everyone, declarations of noble motives, and a cheerful, positive, and confident tone worked together to make even exclusion and elimination look reasonable, sensible, and sound. Seashore's proposed reforms—even though they accomplished exclusion and elimination as well as inclusion and promotion—were bathed in a glow of goodness and light.

In the same happy and optimistic tone, he told many of those in a lower place on his achievement pyramid that their work is noble, and he advised them to be content with their lot. For example, underscoring the nobility of the work of those whose "calling" is on a lower, humbler, plainer, more ordinary plane, he advised all to be satisfied with their place in the order of things—including professors who merely teach rather than advancing science by conducting research:

> We need teachers in all the grades from the lowest to the highest. We need college professors who are satisfied to teach and do not hang around heart-broken because they have no opportunity to advance science. We need the preacher who is indeed a minister in humbler walks of life. . . . We need physicians who can handle the plain cases and are conscientious enough to send the serious cases to the proper specialist. . . . We need the humble citizen in public affairs at home.
>
> But in all these lines we need a few at the top, and these we give special advantages, and hold responsible for greater results.[458]

He told the humble teacher, whom he identified as "she," that her work is as noble as that of the professor's: "The nobility of work and calling may be just as great at one plane in the pyramid as at another. The primary teacher may very well carry her head as high as the college professor. She may rightly regard her mission in the world as one well worth while."[459] Elsewhere, he emphasized the "dignity of honest and effective labor in all the walks of life."[460] In Seashore's view, labor makes people useful, valuable, dignified, and noble, and his beliefs about work serve as reminders that early-twentieth-century eugenics was as much about optimism and hope for the future—at least for some—as it was about fear. Trading in hope for the future also is one resemblance between eugenics and other kinds of utopian discourse.

Seashore also valued economy and efficiency—which variously referred to saving time, optimally distributing resources in a society, or optimizing mental capacity—and significantly, he hailed eugenics as one of the three great movements that were increasing human efficiency.[461] Economy and efficiency also appeared on his list of the pluses of his education reforms. In some cases, his claim was that the reforms would save the student time and money. For example, he stated that going to college and dropping out is a waste of a student's money.[462] At other times, other entities would reap the benefits of economy and efficiency. For example, he promoted increased class size by stating that it saves faculty members' time.[463] He claimed that sectioning by ability is efficient and prevents wasted teaching.[464] He opined that education policy in the United States should keep the economic and cultural *needs* of the community in view, which suggests that education policy should keep the *economic benefits* to the community in mind.[465]

Economy, efficiency, and keeping the best interest of society in view figured prominently in eugenics discourse writ large. Editorials appearing in a 1910 issue of *American Breeders Magazine* supported maintaining records of the "efficiency" of school students, their future success, and the potency with which parents infuse "efficiency" into their children, in an effort to increase the more efficient human blood strains and decrease the less efficient ones.[466] Madison Grant railed against democratic forms of government that "inevitably increase the preponderance of the lower types and cause a corresponding loss of efficiency in the community as a whole."[467] Popenoe and Johnson complained, "The inefficients, the wastrels, the physical, mental, and moral cripples are carefully preserved at public expense,"[468] and they later warned that the financial costs to society of caring for the "socially inadequate" are huge:

> At such prices, each state maintains hundreds, sometimes thousands, of feeble-minded, and the number is growing each year. In the near future the expenditures must grow much more rapidly, for public sentiment is beginning to demand that the defectives and delinquents of the community be properly cared for. The financial burden is becom-

> ing a heavy one; it will become a crushing one unless steps are taken to make the feeble-minded productive . . . and an intangible "sinking fund" at the same time created to reduce the burden gradually by preventing the production of those who make it up. The burden can never be wholly obliterated, but it can be largely reduced by a restriction of the reproduction of those who are themselves socially inadequate.[469]

In his argument that the norms and institutions of modernity made the Holocaust not merely feasible but predictable, Zygmunt Bauman stated that bureaucratic preoccupation with efficiency and saving money was emblematic of the genocide and also was among the conditions that made it possible.[470] In addition, he described the bureaucratic pursuit of efficiency as "ethically blind."[471] Motivations that subsequent scholars would deem ethically blind were deployed by eugenicists such as Seashore to promote change that he, and others, cheerfully touted as noble and altruistic.

Concluding Thoughts

Thus, to Seashore and like-minded eugenicists, education in a democracy did not mean rich and equal opportunities for all. Rather, the allocation of opportunities and resources was to be in proportion to the individual or group's supposedly innate ability—taken in combination with achieved fitness—as measured by a standardized test. This allocation logic was premised on the assumption that opportunities and resources are necessarily and inevitably limited or even scarce. Eliminating the unfit did not mean total annihilation in all cases: those who are fit but unfit for college, for example, would be fit for a lower spot on Seashore's achievement pyramid and would be candidates for an education designed for those destined to occupy a lower spot. Although there would be resources and opportunities for those in a lowlier place, most perks would go to the few at the top. Such a system, Seashore maintained, was humane, efficient, economical, and fair.

Ideal education, to Seashore, was a massive and efficient machine, systematically identifying, measuring, sorting, ordering, segregating, promoting, and eliminating individuals and groups. The higher elevations of the achievement pyramid, where space was limited, were the rightful place of White men, especially those from the best families. African Americans from the South and women, among others, rightfully belonged farther down, where they were advised to accept their humble role without complaint, knowing that even lowly contributions were noble and necessary supports for the top.

In Seashore's mind, all "men," and all groups of "men," clearly were not equal. Education was to help assure that a differentiated natural destiny would be fulfilled in all cases. Systematically and efficiently identifying who was or was not fit, segregating the fittest from the less fit and unfit, promoting the fittest, and eliminating the unfit were consistent with eugenicists' beliefs and goals. They were at the heart of Seashore's education reform goals, and the reach of eugenics into his beliefs and practices was broad and deep.

Six

Making Musical Destinies

Talent, Testing, and Music Education Reform

Although Seashore had many music-related research interests, including aesthetics, vibrato, and the pianist's touch, he focused primarily on musical ability.[1] His discussions of musical talent and ability-related music education reform bear a striking resemblance to his discourse on general ability as manifested in intelligence and on broad education reform. Continuities and parallel contours emerge in his assumptions, understandings, arguments, identified problems, and suggested solutions. Seashore recycled not only the same ideas and concepts but also, in some cases, the same quotations and illustrations. The resemblances are so close that in many cases, he merely substituted the phrase "musical talent" for "intelligence." These parallels are not coincidental; the similarities stem from their common roots, one root being the discourses that informed and were promulgated by eugenics.

I begin this chapter by examining Seashore's conception of musical talent—what he called "capacities"—focusing on his assertion that it is biologically inheritable, immutable, and normally distributed in populations. I describe his attempts to measure musical talent, from his earliest efforts through his development and dissemination of the recorded standardized Seashore Tests. I discuss his recommendations about how the Seashore Tests could be used, both in basic research, such as in studies of the biological inheritability of musical talent, and in applied settings, such as to facilitate selective human breeding and to solve musicians' technical problems. In particular, I describe and analyze his suggested practical applications of the music tests in school settings: to identify the presence or absence of talent and to sort and order students accordingly, to discover and promote the musically gifted child, to eliminate the unfit, to facilitate wise vocational and avocational choices, and to improve institutions' admissions processes. Next, I examine his philosophy of music education and his proposed music education reforms, including his rationale for those reforms. I briefly discuss profit as one unspoken motive. Finally, I revisit his reception and influence in music education, and as part of that revisiting, I examine his role in the evolution of music education's "slogan of the century": "Music for Every Child; Every Child for Music."

I demonstrate in this chapter that Seashore's ideas about musical ability and his recommended reforms for music education are entirely consistent with and strikingly similar to his broader views on ability—intelligence in particular—and on education reform. I argued in the previous chapter that his general perspectives are steeped in eugenics; by extension, the parallel contours, continuities, and resemblances I identify in this chapter indicate that his ideas about musical ability and his recommended music education reforms are similarly steeped in eugenics. Because I discussed in the previous chapter how eugenics informed and grounded Seashore's ideas about ability and education as a whole, I will not repeat all of the similar links to eugenics here. Nevertheless, when this chapter is considered in conjunction with the previous one, the evidence overwhelmingly indicates that eugenics was foundational to his thought in all of these domains.

On Musical Talent

Science as the Bringer of Truth to Music and Music Education

Seashore was confident that science could make major contributions to knowledge about music, musicians, and music pedagogy. For example, in the essay "Music," published posthumously in 1950, he listed contributions of various sciences, closing with a plug for the new field of psychology:

> Biology gives a theory and verified facts about the nature, extent, and laws of heredity. Musical anthropology gives a history of the evolution of music from primitive times to the present. Genetics deals with the evolution of music in the race and the development of music in the individual. Psychiatry deals with deviations from the normal, such as type of temperament and musical genius. Psychology contributes the fundamental scientific interpretation of human experience and behavior.[2]

He was especially enthusiastic about the potential contributions and applications of psychology; indeed, the "Music" essay appeared in an edited collection entitled *Handbook of Applied Psychology*.[3] His enthusiasm was longstanding; as early as 1915, in the very first issue of the now-venerable journal *Musical Quarterly*, he explained to musicians the reach of music psychology and mentioned three possible domains: "the psychology of individual talent, the psychology of aesthetic feeling in musical appreciation and expression, and the psychology of the pedagogy of music."[4] Although he did not claim to have conducted research in all music-related areas of psychology, in his autobiography, he proudly enumerated contributions that psychological research had made to music during the first quarter of the twentieth century; his lengthy list included "the development of the musical mind in early childhood, anthropological studies of racial types, and the evolution of music in primitive peoples," as well as experimental studies of aesthetics.[5]

Seashore on Talent: Musical Capacities

Musical talent was a subject of particular research interest to Seashore, and among the resemblances between his work in this domain and his work on general ability was a similar focus on a systematic process of identifying ability, measuring it in individuals or groups, sorting and ordering them, and finally selectively promoting or eliminating them. He claimed that science could provide information to assist with intelligent decision-making concerning musical talent. Furthermore, in his 1921 address to the Second International Congress of Eugenics, he drew direct connections between eugenics and his approach to research on musical talent, describing the study of musical talent as comprising five tasks:

> The approach to the problem of inheritance of musical talent, from the point of view of eugenics, divides itself naturally into five stages or tasks: (1) the analysis of what constitutes musical talent and the isolation of measurable factors; (2) the development and standardization of methods of measurement and rating of each of these talents under control; (3) the actual field work of measuring sufficiently large numbers of generations in selected family groups; (4) the interpretation of such results in terms of biological principles of heritable factors; and (5) interpretation and dissemination of established information for eugenic guidance.[6]

Thus, at the historic conference that precipitated the formation of the American Eugenics Society, Seashore described his research pertaining to musical talent as a massive eugenics project.

Throughout his career, even though he referred to musical talent in the singular, he regularly underscored his belief that musical talent is not a single, unitary thing but rather an assemblage, a combination of many isolable, measurable talents or components.[7] Arguing that the mind and body are indivisible, he described musical talent and the components constituting it as complex psychophysical phenomena.[8] He variously called the components of musical talent "capacities," "traits," "elements," or "factors."[9] True to form as a modern scientist and eugenicist, he set out to systematically identify, classify, and order these components; in a few instances, he published detailed tables that listed and grouped them.[10] For example, in his 1919 book *The Psychology of Musical Talent*, he made an "inventory" of the musical mind, which he reported was based on two "coördinate bases of classification: first, the attributes of sound; and, second, the generally recognized powers of the human mind."[11] He listed five overarching "factors of the musical mind": musical sensitivity, musical action, musical memory and imagination, musical intellect, and musical feeling. Beneath the factors, he listed subgroups of talent, twenty-five in all. For example, "musical sensitivity" consisted of four "simple forms of impression": sense of pitch, sense of intensity, sense of time, and sense of extensity; and four "complex forms of appreciation": sense of rhythm, sense of timbre, sense of consonance, and sense of volume.[12] "Musical feeling," by contrast, consisted of more ineffable elements: "musical taste," "emotional reaction to music," and "emotional self-expression in music."[13] Foundational to musical talent, however, was what Seashore called the "responsive" ear, which consisted of the physical ear and the "nervous system through which it functions."[14]

He conceptualized musical talent as being related to general intelligence, several of his inventories listing general intelligence as one element of musical talent;[15] signaling the importance of general intelligence, in one of these sources, he called it a "far-reaching element in musical merit."[16] In his address to the Second International Congress of Eugenics, he stated that general intelligence is a factor that "determines the degree of intelligence that may be exhibited in the musical talent of an individual."[17] Elsewhere, in a call for the use of an IQ test as a partial measure of musical talent, he claimed that "the character of the musician is determined largely by the character of his general intelligence."[18] He also asserted that general intelligence is not related to some capacities comprising musical talent, notably sensory capacities: "The physiological limit for the sense of pitch does not vary significantly with intelligence. The moron may have as keen a sense of pitch as the philosopher. Measurements on children and adults in which pitch discrimination is compared with intelligence show no significant correlation."[19] He claimed that other components of musical talent are not necessarily related to each other, either, stating, "There is no reason for assuming that there is any necessary relationship between, for example, sense of pitch and sense of time."[20]

His talent inventories varied somewhat from publication to publication both in the number of components and in how the talent groups were labeled and described. For example, although the above inventory from *The Psychology of Musical Talent* is similar to statements he made four years earlier in his 1915 *Musical Quarterly* article, there are important differences, including different numbers of fundamental capacities and subtalents; in the *MQ* article, for instance, he listed thirty-six measurable capacities:[21]

> It is quite possible to make a fairly exhaustive classification of the essential traits of musical talent. This may be done by considering, first, the characteristics of sound which constitute music and, second, the mental powers which are needed for the appreciation of musical sounds.
>
> The elements of musical sound are really three, namely: pitch, time and intensity. The fourth attribute of sound, extensity, which represents the spatial character, is negligible for the present purpose. Pitch is the quality, the essence of a sound. Timbre, usually spoken of as quality, is merely a pitch complex. Consonance, harmony, and clang fusions are also pitch-complexes. Rhythm represents aspects of time and intensity. This classification of the fundamental aspects of musical sounds gives us a basis for the classification of musical talents into the ability to appreciate and the ability to express respectively, pitch, time, and intensity of tone. Each of these may, of course, be subdivided in great detail.
>
> Turning then to the human side of music, we find that the capacity for the appreciation and expression of music may be divided, for convenience, into four fundamental capacities; namely, sensory, the ability to hear music; motor, the ability to express music; associational, the ability to understand music; and affective, the ability to feel music and express feeling in music. By combining these two classifications—the elements of musical sounds and the capacity of the human individual—we shall obtain the principal groups of musical talent.[22]

In a 1917 article appearing in *Etude*, he listed the same five broad talent factors that appeared in *The Psychology of Musical Talent*, but in the *Etude* article, he identified twenty-two measurable capacities.[23] In the paper he delivered to the Second International Congress of Eugenics in 1921, he listed four overarching talent factors: sensory capacities; motor capacities; representative capacities, which included imagery, memory, and imagination; and general capacities, which included intelligence quotient and emotional type.[24] There were categories of talent within each of these factors, and subgroups within each of the categories—a total of twenty-six measurable capacities.[25] Once again, although this inventory resembled the other two in some respects—for example, in its emphasis on sensory capacities—in other ways it was quite different, notably in which talents were listed, what they were named, how many were listed, and how they were organized in the inventory.

In a *Scientific Monthly* article appearing in 1940, he described two levels of measurable psychophysical capacities, the simple or elemental, and the complex. The elemental capacities included sense of pitch, loudness, time, and timbre. He stated that complex capacities involve the "cooperative functions of the elemental capacities," and he described the ability to hear rhythm, consonance, volume, and sonance as complex capacities; he also suggested that because complex capacities are difficult to deal with, psychological study should focus primarily on the four elemental or basic capacities. According to Seashore, excellence in the elemental capacities helps produce "ear-mindedness."[26] He also mentioned motor control of four elements of sound—frequency, amplitude, duration, and form.[27] Although he suggested in this article that hereditary studies should most "properly" focus on elementary capacities, he acknowledged the existence of a host of other "general traits," which he said are similarly biologically inheritable: "musical intelligence, creative imagination and the artistic temperament, or facilities for specific skills, such as sight reading and the memorizing of repertoires."[28]

To support his claim that musical talent is complex and composed of multiple elements, in at least one instance he asserted that there are "scores" or even "hundreds of fairly distinguishable capacities," all of which potentially are measurable.[29] In the 1940 article, he took his argument one step further, suggesting that musical talent consists of an *infinite* hierarchy of measurable capacities: "Musicality is not one specific human trait but an infinite hierarchy of traits running through the entire gamut of the psychophysical musical organism."[30]

Although one might argue that the differences I have described reflect changes and refinements in his conception of musical talent over time, the nature and timing of the changes may indicate instead that despite his invocation of empiricism, science, and rigorous experimental procedures, his conception of musical talent was, and remained, diffuse, vague, and confusing. His changes were quite substantive—this was not merely a matter of adding a capacity or two—and they dramatically changed the contours of his conception of musical talent. These changes conceivably could have had widespread implications and consequences for the individuals and groups whose talent was under scrutiny. Furthermore, as I have argued elsewhere concerning bodies and music, categories are neither natural nor inevitable, and the act of creating categories—what I call binning—is an act of power: "Establishing bins, naming them, determining the number of bins that will apply, . . . creating the criteria that will distinguish one bin from another, determining whether the bins will be discrete, and deciding how to proceed when bodies do not clearly fit into established bins are acts of power."[31] Germane to this discussion is the understanding that changing the musical talent categories—their names, number, characteristics, boundaries, and so on—similarly is an act of power that had a profound impact on people. Seashore freely exercised that power.

A Hierarchy of Musical Capacities

In addition to claiming that different kinds of musical elements or capacities constitute musical talent, he further asserted that these capacities comprise a hierarchy.[32] He likened this hierarchy to a tree: "Musical talent is not one, but a hierarchy of talents, branching out along certain trunk lines into the rich arborization, foliage, and fruitage of the tree, which we call the 'musical mind.'"[33] The hierarchy moved from the simple to the complex.

Furthermore, his hierarchical classification of musical capacities—his sorting and ordering of them—sorted and ordered people as well, including musicians. The quality and value of an individual or group are determined both by which capacities the individual or group does or does not possess and where these capacities are located in the musical talent hierarchy. For example, in a discussion of intelligence as a musical capacity, he spoke of small and large musicianship and claimed that "great" musicians are on a different intellectual plane than other musicians.[34] Describing how the presence or absence of capacities may affect a musician's achievement, he also indicated that the capacities of intelligence and reflective thinking are at the top of the musical talent hierarchy while sensorimotor capacity is at the bottom:

> The type and the degree of intelligence may characterize or set limits for the musical achievement. The great composer, the great conductor, the great interpreter live in large intellectual movements. They have the power of sustained thought, a great store of organized information, and the ability to elaborate and control their creative work at a high intellectual level. At the other extreme are the various kinds of small musicianship in which reflective thinking does not function; the experience and the performance are on a sensorimotor level. . . . Between these extremes we may sort musicianships into markedly different qualities and levels in terms of some sort of intelligence quotient—a hypothetical musical intelligence quotient.[35]

Thus, consistent with a hierarchical aesthetic trope of the day, Seashore claimed that capacities such as intelligent thought sit higher on the talent hierarchy than the base, elemental sensory capacities. Furthermore, he stated that the musician whose musical intelligence capacities are larger than those of other musicians—including those who merely possess elemental sensory capacities—derives far greater *satisfaction* from music; in stating this, he positioned the musician who "thinks intelligently" firmly at the top of the hierarchy:

> This classification of sensory capacities is probably complete, because it is based upon the known attributes of the sound wave. It must be borne in mind that the sound wave is the only medium through which music as such is conveyed from the performer to the listener; everything that is rendered as music or heard as music may be expressed in terms of the concepts of the sound wave. . . . The lover of flowers may derive deep pleasure from flowers through his senses without knowledge or thought of the physics or chemistry of their structure. So it is possible to enjoy and perform music without insight or knowledge of its true nature; but the musician who knows his medium and *thinks intelligently about it* has a vastly greater satisfaction than the one who does not [emphasis mine].[36]

As part of his hierarchical sorting and ordering of people, Seashore distinguished the musical genius from the merely musically talented individual:

> We should distinguish between the talented person and the genius. The most distinctive trait of the musical genius is that fact that he

> finds in music a dominant interest, is driven to it by an impulse, burns to express himself in music. He is driven by an instinctive impulse or craving for music which results in supreme devotion to its realization. The talented person, on the other hand, gives evidence of unusual powers which may or may not be motivated by an instinctive impulse. The talented person tends to manifest specific skills while genius actually generalizes, creates, thinks in a large whole. To view genius merely as a talent is to view the waterfall in terms of measures of water or height, instead of regarding it as water in action, falling, working, entrancing.[37]

Although grounded in talent, genius, in his mind, is broader, grander, and more dynamic than talent; the words "merely as a talent" position talent—and the talented musician—lower on the hierarchy, beneath the exalted musical genius. Drawing a distinction between talent and genius, citing creativity or originality as a distinguishing characteristic of genius, and exalting the genius at the expense of the merely talented are familiar tropes dating back at least to the mid-nineteenth century in the United States.[38] Seashore's reliance on these discourses indicates that his hierarchies of musical talent and musicians displayed both old and new elements.

The Elemental Capacities and the Primacy of Auditory Perception

Regardless of how multidimensional and complex his various inventories of musical talent were, and irrespective of his claim that an infinite number of measurable musical capacities exist, Seashore concerned himself largely with only a handful of elements, particularly four elemental capacities: the sense of pitch, the sense of loudness, the sense of time, and the sense of timbre.[39] These capacities loomed large in all of his inventories, indicating that auditory perception was central to his conception of musical talent. His focus on sensory and perceptual processes may reflect his educational pedigree. As a doctoral student at Yale, he worked in the laboratory of Edward Scripture, who was a student of Wilhelm Wundt; Seashore visited Wundt's laboratory during his trip to Europe in the summer of 1895.[40] Wundt was a founding father of psychology, known for perceptual and sensory studies. An observation made about Wundt, appearing in Kurt Danziger's *Constructing the Subject: Historical Origins of Psychological Research*, may shed light on Seashore's predilection for perceptual and sensory studies: "At one extreme are problems for which the experimental method provides an excellent source of valid data, at the other extreme are problems that are quite unsuitable for experimental investigation. Wundt consistently assigns problems in the areas of sensation and perception to the top end of this quasi scale and problems in the areas of thinking, affect, voluntary activity, and social psychology to the bottom end."[41] Thus, according to Danziger, in the relatively new field of psychology, sensory and perceptual problems were considered ideally suited for the experimental method. Seashore's focus on sensory and perceptual studies placed him squarely in the camp of his educational "ancestors," who were among the founders of the field. Finally, during the summer of 1895, Seashore also visited the laboratory of the German psychologist Carl Stumpf; according to Johanna Devaney, Stumpf published the very first tests of musical talent in 1883.[42] Stumpf's tests focused primarily on auditory perception.

The Nature of Musical Destinies

Musical Talent is Biologically Inheritable

Seashore joined the ranks of psychologists of his day who assumed that *intelligence* is biologically inheritable, immutable, and variable among individuals—and many of these psychologists, but not all, were avowed eugenicists. He similarly asserted that *musical talent* is biologically inheritable, immutable, and variable. He confidently made this claim throughout his career, one assertion appearing in his 1915 *Musical Quarterly* article, a passage also illustrating that he sometimes used "talent" and "natural ability" interchangeably: "Musical talent, like all other talent, is a gift of nature—inherited, not acquired; in so far as a musician has natural ability in music, he has been born with it."[43] He made a similar statement in his 1919 book *The Psychology of Musical Talent*, and as in the *Musical Quarterly* article, he called musical talent a gift: "Musical talent is a gift bestowed very unequally upon individuals. Not only is the gift of music itself inborn, but it is inborn in specific types. These types can be detected early in life, before time for beginning serious musical education."[44] Consistent with his complaint that extant conceptions of musical inheritance were unitary when musical talent actually consists of many things, he argued for the existence of multiple musical gifts: "We must at once abandon the idea that a person is either musical or not musical, that the gift of music is one gift or one talent."[45]

He relied on a Mendelian understanding of heredity to explain how these gifts are passed from generation to generation: "We may accept as a general working basis the Mendelian hypothesis and proceed to ascertain what determiners in the germ plasm function for musical talent; which are dominant and which recessive; which musical dispositions are carried on the same determiner, and which are carried on determiners charged with nonmusical factors, etc."[46] In his discussion of how to determine the laws of inheritance of musical talent, he even referred to Mendel's classic study of the hereditability of pea blossom color:

> Granting that we know what we wish to measure and how to measure it, the staging of an experiment to determine the laws of the inheritance of musical talent in human beings is not different from the staging of an experiment on the inheritance of color in peas, the milk-producing quality in cows, or speed in race horses, except that there are more factors to take into account and the experiment will take longer.[47]

Although Seashore repeated his supposedly airtight inheritability claim many times throughout his career, in a few instances—perhaps when he was addressing an audience of scientists—he spoke somewhat more cautiously, and in a few cases, even appeared to contradict himself. For example, he opened his 1921 address to the Second International Congress of Eugenics with the statement that after many years of rigorous experimentation, he could confidently assert that "musical talent is resolvable into a number of inborn natural capacities which may be isolated and measured or rated adequately for statistical or experimental purposes."[48] Later in the talk, however, he said that the inheritance facts had not been gathered yet, although he expressed confidence that they could be gathered and would be applicable:

> The eugenicist might rightly expect me to recite established facts on the inheritance of musical talent and present arguments showing that they should be applied. But the time is not yet ripe for either. The object of this paper is merely to present a point of view, showing that such facts can be gathered; and this is done in the anticipation that, once established, the desirability of their application will be taken for granted by those who are interested in this phase of eugenics.[49]

Moments later, when describing the elements that comprise musical talent, he again seemed somewhat cautious: "Is the sense of pitch, is the sense of time, is auditory imagery, is musical imagination, is a voice of large volume, is a voice possessing a given tone quality, heritable? . . . As to the reference of these elements of musical talent to biological factors, determiners, or carriers in the mechanism, we are only in a position to assert that it *may be* feasible [emphasis mine]."[50] This passage is vague, however. It is not clear whether Seashore remained unsure about precisely which elements constitute musical talent, or about whether these elements are biologically inheritable, or about the feasibility of experiments to determine whether these elements are biologically inheritable.

Another qualified statement appeared in the article "Musical Inheritance," published in *Scientific Monthly* in 1940. Seashore opened with "some fundamental assumptions upon which probably all competent investigators agree," one of them being that the germ cell carries chromosomes, which are "chains of genes," and that "heritage" is transmitted by genes.[51] He concluded this segment with the statement, "We may assume that superior musical talent is determined *in large part* by superior musical heredity, and that inferior musical talent or lack of talent may be determined in large part by a correspondingly defective heredity [emphasis mine]."[52] In this passage, it is not clear what Seashore meant by musical talent—whether, for example, he was equating it with musical ability, which on one occasion he defined as the combination of innate capacity and the cultivation of that capacity. What is clear, however, is that in a few instances, he admitted that there was a shortage of facts to support the assertion that musical talent is completely or even largely biologically inheritable. It is also clear that he believed that the facts, once gathered, would support the biological inheritability claim. He told readers that psychologists faced "high barriers" if they were to scientifically determine the laws of musical inheritance and prove what is common knowledge, namely that musical ability is biologically inheritable: "Common observation and reasoning convince us without question that musicality is inherited in some mysterious way and this follows also from general considerations of current theories of biological inheritance."[53]

Thus, despite the fact that Seashore's conception of musical talent is slippery—a shape-shifting and potentially infinitely large conglomeration of elements—he nevertheless asserted that at least some of these components—and potentially all of them—are biologically inheritable. At the very least, he considered the fundamental or elemental capacities to be inborn: "On the basis of our experiments in measuring these sensory capacities, we find that the basic capacities, the sense of pitch, the sense of time, the sense of loudness, and the sense of timbre are elemental, by which we mean that they are largely inborn and function from early childhood."[54] He did not limit his inheritability assumption solely to the elemental capacities, however. For example, in his address to the Second International Congress of Eugenics, he listed twenty-six "isolable factors of musical talent that may be inherited";[55] in addition to elemental capacities—including a sense of pitch, timbre, and time—he also listed more ineffable factors, including imagination type, creative imagination, and emotional type.[56]

Musical Talent is Immutable

Another characteristic of musical talent, according to Seashore, is that it is immutable, meaning that it cannot be improved through education or practice.[57] Perhaps once again alluding to Plato's myth of the metals, or even to the foolishness and futility of alchemy, he warned—as he did in his discussion of general intelligence—that no one, certainly not educators, can make gold out of iron: "Education can do wonders but it cannot make gold out of iron, or a musician out of one who is not *born* with a musical mind and body [emphasis in original]."[58]

When Seashore stated that talent is immutable, he was not saying that environment is inconsequential, however. He believed that heredity and environment are companionate; in the case of musical ability, as with other supposedly inheritable mental qualities, the role of the environment is to act on what is biologically inheritable and immutable: to develop inborn musical talent. The environment, like soil, plays a critical part, determining whether the good seed will grow and flourish. In a passage that nods to euthenics, Seashore underscored the importance of both heredity and the environment, referencing classic genetic research—studies of fruit flies—to argue that focusing solely on heredity is insufficient:

> If we would gain a true and comprehensive insight into the nature and extent of role [*sic*] of environment in musical life, we must start with some established facts or reasonable assumptions of what is "given" for environment to act upon. The heritage is the capital fund which the environment invests or squanders. Only by knowing the hereditary contributions can we appraise the environmental contributions. In the study of the fruitfly, for example, the revelations of factors which must be regarded as environmental are quite as significant and essential as the revelations about the original organization of genes. The determination of the limits of heredity is the best means for revealing the functions and possibilities of environment. The music geneticist will therefore learn fully as much about environmental influences as he will about hereditary influences in studying heredity.[59]

Musical Talent Is Variable among Individuals and Normally Distributed in Populations

In addition, Seashore made several claims about musical talent's variability, including the assertion that this endowment or gift is universally understood to be variably or unequally bestowed among individuals.[60] He used terms such as "extraordinary" and "striking" to describe this variability. For example, in his 1917 essay "Avocational Guidance in Music," which appeared in the *Journal of Applied Psychology*, he wrote, "Music is universally recognized as a gift bestowed upon different individuals in extraordinarily unequal degree."[61] In other words, he said it is found in varying degrees in different individuals, some people having little or none and others having considerable amounts. He had similarly asserted this in a monograph that had appeared a year earlier, *Vocational Guidance in Music*: "Talent for music is a 'gift' bestowed by nature upon different persons very unequally. We recognized this by speaking of some persons as musical and others as not musical in various degrees."[62] While holding firm to his view of the variability of musical talent, he also opined that high ability may be more prevalent than is commonly understood, the problem being that it has not been identified or cultivated: "Perhaps natural ability of a high order is not so very rare, for modern psychology has demonstrated that a surprisingly small portion of our talents are allowed to develop and to come to fruitage, and thus has given great reinforcement to the dictum that many men 'die with all their music in them.'"[63]

Seashore's next variability claim was that within one individual, the various elements that constitute talent—the capacities—are present in different amounts, this variability being found even in musicians. He stated that it is unlikely that any musician has equally superior talent in all of the capacities comprising it:

> The gifts of music are diverse. Perhaps no musician possesses all of those listed above [that is, the elements of musical talent] in high degree. One musician gets along with one little group of talents and a smattering of some of the rest, while another musician employs another group. This is the reason that musicians differ, and the result of differences in musicians is differences in music. It is by the relative prominence or absence of one or more of these fundamental capacities that we characterize a musician.[64]

Elsewhere, he maintained that although the "distinctly musical mind" will be superior in all four of the main sensory capacities, "great musical achievement" nevertheless can be attained by a musician who has as little as average talent in *one* of the four groups: "Generalizing on the basis of all types of record available we may say that, so far as the sensory capacities are concerned, a balanced and distinctly gifted musical mind will in these capacities measure in the highest 10 per cent of the normal community. But great musical achievement may be attained by persons who may have as low as average sensory capacity in one of these four main lines."[65]

The Normal Musical Mind

One of Seashore's oft-repeated assertions about musical talent was that "the musical mind is first of all a normal mind"; this phrase and the term "normal" may have meant different things in his various deployments, however.[66] Sometimes he employed "normal" as it would be used in psychoanalytic or developmental theory, as when, for example, he yoked "normal" to "well-balanced" in describing a mind capable of development.[67] A similar understanding appeared in *The Psychology of Musical Talent* in a passage referring to a normal personality: "Indeed, the normal mind is musical to the extent that it is normal. . . . We must take it for granted that the musical mind is an aspect of a normal personality with endowments for a general mental life, and we must also take the general psychology of such mental life for granted."[68] He also indicated in the above passage that the *musical* mind is premised on a mind that is normal, overall.[69] "Normal" in these contexts suggested healthy or undamaged. As the professor of a course on abnormal psychology, he would have been acquainted with this conception of normal and with its opposite—especially the pathologically abnormal. Notably, in his discussion of the contributions of science to music, he indicated that the supernormal is a deviation from the normal, stating that psychiatry deals with one such deviation: the musical genius.[70]

Seashore also used "normal" in the statistical sense, claiming that musical talent and the capacities comprising it are normally distributed in populations. For example, he referred to the normal distribution of pitch discrimination among university students,[71] and his article "Talent," which appeared in *School and Society*, described a Gaussian distribution:

> We may define talent as the *native capacity for exceptional achievement in various degrees*, and lack of talent as *exceptional native limitations on the possibilities of development in a particular line of achievement*. These two extremes are exceptions to the balanced distribution of capacities in a given population; between these lies the wide range of "average"

> capacities of the normal child. Such is the normal range and distribution of human "soil" which may be cultivated by the environment and brought to fruitage through a process of maturation [emphases in original].[72]

He even spoke of the most musically talented as falling in the "highest 10 per cent of the normal community."[73] His use of "average" further ties some of his discussions of normal to statistics. He alluded to both the psychoanalytical/developmental and the statistical meaning of normal in the following passage:

> Again we must remember that the musical mind is first of all a normal mind. . . . What we shall look for then in a psychophysical organism is the imminence of certain resources especially favorable or especially unfavorable to the normal functioning of the musical mind. We may assume that an average capacity present in the genetic constitution may be adequate for musical purposes but that exceptionally gifted persons require these traits in a correspondingly exceptional degree and that exceptionally unmusical individuals lack essential elements.[74]

Like many other eugenicists, Seashore was not primarily concerned with the normal or average, however, necessary as this middle ground was to the existence of abnormal, subnormal, or supernormal. Rather, he focused on the two Gaussian tails, and in the case of musical talent, he concentrated, in particular, on the high tail.

Seashore, the Nature of Musical Talent, and Eugenics

The resemblances between Seashore's position on general intelligence and his view on musical talent are striking. Among the similarities is the assumption that musical ability, like general intelligence, ostensibly resides in the body. Like other contemporaneous psychologists who researched general intelligence, Seashore valued a particular conception of ability, and he exercised the power to define what constitutes ability, including musical ability. He believed that in the realm of musical talent, as in general intelligence, all people are not created equal. In his estimation, musical inequality, like inequality in general intelligence, is determined and governed by biological heredity, which bestows or withholds gifts. He assumed that musical inheritance, like inherited general intelligence, is variable among individuals, normally distributed in populations, and immutable. He maintained that there was a need to sort and order individuals according to musical ability, just as he saw a need to sort and order individuals according to general intelligence. As with general intelligence, he equated differences in musical capacity with differences in quality. One difference between his views on musical talent and on intelligence, however, is that he conceptualized musical ability as a constellation of capacities as opposed to a single entity that could be measured by an IQ test.

In addition to attending to individual differences, Seashore was concerned with group differences in musical talent. For example, as I discussed in chapter 4, he claimed that there were no significant differences between boys and girls in inherent musical talent. In addition, in his address to the Second International Congress of Eugenics, he opened the door to the "scientific" study of race differences in musical talent, a topic I discuss further in chapter 7.

According to Seashore, inherited musical potential shapes and limits the musical destiny of us all, an assertion that is virtually identical to what he said about general ability. Not only are people innately, fundamentally, and constitutionally musically different from one another, but when compared to one another, some people are innately, fundamentally, and constitutionally *better* than others: by degrees, some are constitutionally superior musicians, while by degrees others are constitutionally inferior. As we have seen, belief in inherited, immutable differences in ability—and consequent differences in quality and value—were among the stock messages of eugenics, and as was the case with Seashore's statements about general ability, his beliefs about musical talent situated him deeply within the eugenics fold.

Scholars discussed the nature of musical talent and its prevalence in particular families long before Seashore's time. For example, in his analysis of pre-Galtonian discussions of heredity and genius, cultural historian Stefan Willer reports that in 1802, Nikolaus Forkel, an early biographer of J. S. Bach, commented on the Bach family's "'predisposition'" for music, Forkel describing this predisposition as "'inheritable.'"[75] As Willer reports, the first chapter of the biography describes six generations of the Bach family in language "rooted in the vocabulary of a genealogical tree with extensively outspread 'branches' and 'limbs.'"[76] Willer also points out that "innate" was used to describe genius throughout the second half of the eighteenth century; he offers evidence from Immanuel Kant's *Critique of Judgment*, published in 1790: "'Since talent, as an innate productive faculty of the artist, belongs itself to nature, we may put it this way: *Genius* is the innate mental aptitude (*ingenium*) *through which* nature gives the rule to art [emphasis in original].'"[77] However, according to Willer, the understanding of heredity that informed Forkel's discussion of Bach is quite different from Galton's biological and scientific conception, Forkel exemplifying "an ancient narrative model, which had testified to the relative constancy of traits from generation to generation long before that constancy was a scientific issue of heredity."[78] Willer further asserts that Forkel's biography "perpetuated the early modern nondistinction of heredity and environment ('nature and nurture')."[79] According to Willer, "Only in the late nineteenth century did questions of whether or not genius is hereditary, whether it can be passed on to one's descendants, and whether there are familial predispositions that make the birth of a genius probable, become the object of systematic and coherent discussion."[80] He states that late-nineteenth-century understandings "can be ascribed, with relative accuracy" to eugenicist Francis Galton.[81] Indeed, Galton devoted a chapter of *Hereditary Genius* (1869) to musicians and included "pedigree" or family-tree charts of several eminent musical families.[82] Thus, Seashore inherited his concept of the biological inheritability of musical talent from Galton, a eugenicist, and although Galton, in turn, had reconceptualized heredity, he did so by employing redefined, repurposed elements of long-standing discourses and practice. Notably, Jere Humphreys reports that Galton's first psychometric experiments were tests of auditory perception, and he states that in many ways, Galton's work heavily influenced later musical testing.[83] This indicates that Galton's handprints were on Seashore's work in multiple respects.

As Galton's works indicate, the biological inheritability of music ability was of interest to eugenicists from early on. Support for gathering family pedigrees to study this phenomenon is evident in early US eugenics sources. For example, in 1910, its first year of publication, the *American Breeders Magazine* included not only discussions of corn and horse breeding—and the announcement that family records were being collected by Charles Davenport in Cold Spring Harbor, New York—but also an editorial, "Efficiency Records of People," that underscored the value of collecting human family histories. According to the author, W. M. Hays, these pedigree studies were to encourage the proliferation of the "more efficient races, families, and individuals"—especially those most likely to produce geniuses—while simultaneously discouraging reproduction among the "less efficient races and strains."[84] Hays, who was a founder of the American Breeders Association and had been appointed US assistant secretary of agriculture in 1904, provided a list of those positive and negative characteristics that may be in at least some degree "subject to the Mendelian laws of segregation, dominance, and recombination."[85] Negative characteristics included dishonesty, licentiousness, drunkenness, and mental defect, while musical talent numbered among the positive traits.[86]

At about the same time, the Eugenics Section of the American Breeders Association was using pedigree charts in studies of the biological inheritance of musical talent. Explanatory notes accompanying the data collection form described music as a complex ability, the data collector being instructed not only to gather information on its various components—including "'the ability to discriminate between good and common music and to thoroly [*sic*] enjoy good music'"—but also to carefully distinguish between characteristics that were inherited and those acquired through learning.[87] Raters were to assess each participant's ability to appreciate music, sing, play a musical instrument, etc., on a scale of one to five, and participants also were given an overall ability score.[88] Such studies were mentioned in a 1910 letter from Davenport to benefactor Mrs. E. H. Harriman, which was written on letterhead from the American Breeders Association.[89] These references predate the first mention of eugenics by Seashore that I was able to locate (1911), as well as his first publication on the inheritability of musical talent.

Fitter family contests, which were supported by the American Eugenics Society, similarly collected musical talent pedigree data from participants. These contests began at the Kansas State Fair in 1920 and were the brainchild of Mary T. Watts and Florence Brown Sherbon.[90] In 1911, Watts and Sherbon had brought the better baby contests, which Mary DeGarmo had founded in Louisiana in 1908, to the Iowa State Fair.[91] One source reported that the winning Iowa babies were part of a million-dollar livestock parade and "rode in an automobile with a runner on the side proclaiming them to be 'Iowa's Best Crop.'"[92] A report of the Eugenics Department of the Kansas Free Fair from the early 1920s stated that the baby contest examiners used judging methods derived from the livestock judges, who reportedly "always took inheritance into consideration in judging."[93]

At the fitter family contests, judges took musical talent into account when determining whether a family was fit. Examination forms from the mid-1920s included a column labeled "Special talents, gifts, tastes, or superior qualities,"[94] or a question about "special tastes, gifts or peculiarities of mind or body."[95] Hand-written or typed comments about musical talent or taste sometimes appeared in these locations, family members and their progenitors being variously described as singers, musical, fond of music, loving to play good music, etc.[96] Generosity, business skills, athleticism, physical beauty, and literary and math talent were among the other attributes mentioned in these places on the form. Like the earlier pedigree studies described above, the fitter family examinations relied on self-report. I did not find evidence that the Seashore Tests were administered at these contests, but that does not rule out the possibility that they were used.

These sources confirm that Seashore was not the only eugenicist interested in the biological inheritability of musical ability. Rather, eugenical interest in musical talent pedigree studies predated him and was evidenced by other eugenicists throughout Seashore's life. Thus, his work fits into a larger eugenical pattern of thought and scholarship.[97]

Discussion of the reasons for the existence of musical ability also was underway among Seashore's contemporaries who were critical of eugenics. For example, Alfred Russel Wallace, who co-developed the concept of natural selection, argued that mathematical and musical "faculties" could not be explained by natural selection.[98]

On Measuring Musical Talent

Seashore's Early Measurement Efforts

Starting in around 1915, Seashore began criticizing extant musical talent pedigree studies, claiming that they were merely anecdotal—neither systematic nor scientific—and therefore, not dependable. He warned against relying on "biographical material in naive form" rather than on statistical data that could be gathered through measurement.[99] In 1919, he similarly claimed that "the comparatively large, though scattered, literature on the inheritance of musical genius is of little value because it does not deal with tangible fact."[100] He further criticized this corpus of scholarship on the grounds that it focused on musical talent as a whole.[101] Two years later when he addressed the Second International Congress of Eugenics, he advocated jettisoning prior scholarship on the subject altogether: "We must discard the literature on musical inheritance now extant, because it is not based on scientific conceptions of the musical mind."[102] He also called for making "a fresh start in the study of inheritance of musical genius."[103] This fresh start, as he asserted for the remainder of his career, was to be based on the "isolation of specific factors which can be measured" and on "rigidly conducted measurements which can be described, interpreted and verified."[104] In his autobiography, he used medical language—"diagnosing of musical talent"—to describe his forays into such measurement.[105] Thus, he articulated a particular conception of science that he claimed trumped all; his job, as he saw it, was to replace naïve myth, ignorance, and uncertainty with what he firmly believed science could deliver: truth, knowledge, and certainty.

Coupled with his criticism of prior scholarship was his assertion in 1917 that music is the easiest of all talents to accurately analyze and evaluate.[106] In Seashore's estimation, just as there are many musical capacities, there are many measurements to be made, and he attributed the ability to make reliable and "fairly complete measurements of the fundamental capacities" to the "wonderful development of modern psychology."[107]

He regularly used terms such as "elemental" and "basic" to describe not merely musical capacities but also the examinations he designed to measure these capacities. In a 1917 article, he said that his tests measured three elemental capacities—sense of pitch, sense of time, and sense of intensity—as well as the sense of consonance, auditory memory span, and imaginal type.[108] By 1940, he claimed that the measurements were of four capacities: pitch, loudness, time, and timbre.[109] In his 1917 description of the measurement process, he reported that each capacity was measured separately with each capacity test consisting of two half-hour exercises.[110] He added that the test scores were augmented by "statistics about musical education, musical ratings by teachers, the general mental ability, and artistic aims and aspirations of pupils and parents," and that "all the records are reduced to percental rank and interpreted in terms of established norms."[111] In a contemporaneous study of pitch discrimination in people who are blind, Seashore said that a test is elemental when test scores cannot be improved with practice, and he stated that it has been "abundantly proved" that his test of pitch discrimination is elemental.[112] Elsewhere he added age and intelligence to the list of factors that do not affect the results of an elemental test.[113] He also clearly stated that his tests do not measure achievement—only capacities.[114] In 1940, late in his career, he described two orders of measurements of musical capacities. First-order measurements are of anatomical structure, physiological function, and "endocrines, which are in large part the determinants of musical emotionality."[115] Second-order measurements, according to Seashore, are "psychophysical," and he claimed there are two levels of second-order measurements, simple and complex; in this source he described measurements of four (not three) elemental capacities.[116]

He claimed that measurement of musical talent, starting with studies of pitch discrimination, began at the University of Iowa in 1901, and that he conceived of the idea of a standardized battery of measurements in about 1910.[117] The early measurements were made in a laboratory.[118] Seashore stated that he first demonstrated the use and interpretation of his measures of musical talent to a Des Moines women's club in 1912 and that he measured all the fifth graders and eighth graders in Charles City, Iowa, shortly thereafter.[119] He explained his choice of fifth graders as subjects: "The fifth grade is chosen because that is the earliest period at which the tests can be applied with safety as mass tests and because it is early enough to start the musical education of those who have been neglected up to that time."[120]

He apprised music teachers of his early work in a 1916 article appearing in the *Music Supervisors' Journal*, stating that although most measurements had to be made on one individual at a time, many could also be made on an entire classroom of 500 students in one sitting.[121] He reported that he currently was taking measurements of 300 university students and planned to use the tests to measure Iowa schoolchildren the following semester;[122] he claimed that he was striving to simplify the measurement instruments and process so that the tests soon could be placed in the hands of music teachers.[123] In the same year, Seashore reported elsewhere that he would be using the tests to conduct vocational surveys in several schools in Iowa cities in the coming year, and in 1917, he stated that his tests had been administered in three Iowa cities—Red Oak, Charles City, and Sioux City—as well as in St. Louis.[124]

Seashore admitted that the early classroom tests were "somewhat crude and incomplete" but maintained, nevertheless, that they were suitable for "preliminary sifting."[125] His early forays into the schools led him to conclude many years later that the "apparatus was expensive and bunglesome and we saw no hope for making it generally available for school surveys."[126]

His 1915 *Musical Quarterly* article sheds light on the early measurement processes. He was fascinated by scientific apparatuses and gadgets, and the article included pictures of some of the measurement instruments he used: a box of tuning forks and a resonator.[127] In *The Psychology of Musical Talent*, which came out in 1919, he published photographs and illustrations of other measurement apparatuses—pitch range audiometers and a time-sense apparatus on a synchronous motor.[128]

Among the many charts and graphs littering in the *MQ* article are visual profiles summarizing the varying capacities of six individuals, one of them having "extraordinary musical talent," another having "poor musical talent," and the rest having good capacity in some areas and poor capacity in others.[129] The charts recorded individuals' percentile rankings for thirteen different types of measurements, Seashore reporting that these were the only measurements for which "adequate norms" had been established.[130] Some of the measurements were of auditory perceptual capacity and were made using instruments such as the box of tuning forks, but three other capacities—vocal training, instrumental training, and musical appreciation—were measured using a questionnaire.[131] The graphs were accompanied by commentary; for example, the profile of the individual with extraordinary musical talent, a twenty-year-old man, included the comment, "Would have been encouraged for a musical career if discovered early enough."[132] The individual characterized as having "poor musical talent" also was described as "intellectually bright" but nevertheless was "advised to discontinue intensive training in music."[133] One individual with "good musical talent" also was deemed "shiftless and poor in other studies."[134] Thus, some but not all of the data collected consisted of numerical measurements gathered with gadgetry.

In 1916 and 1917, Seashore published graphs of individuals' percentile rankings for measurements of nineteen different elements of musical talent, and by 1919, the graphs included percentile rankings for as many as thirty items.[135] Even within the same article, however, the graphs did not necessarily include the same number of elements for each individual discussed.[136]

Seashore argued that different kinds of musicians—for example, singers versus pianists—would need different kinds of musical talent[137] and also claimed that the talent profiles for various kinds of musicians would look different. He stated, for instance, that a violinist would need a different capacity set (and presumably would exhibit a different capacity profile) than a pianist would.[138] In addition, he recommended the measurement of somewhat different capacities for different kinds of musicians.[139] In other words, the list of measurements to be taken was to be adapted according to the kind of musician—singer, violinist, or pianist—being measured.

These early articles indicate that Seashore was measuring some—but clearly not all—of the musical capacities he had previously identified. Furthermore, in the *Etude* article, the items measured and reported on the graphs of individuals' percentile rankings did not invariably map neatly onto the inventory of talents appearing earlier in the article.[140]

Modern Technology Takes Measurement to a New Level

It was a relatively new gadget—the phonograph—that launched a new phase in Seashore's career of measuring musical talent.[141] Walter Miles, Seashore's biographer, reported that Seashore collaborated with "Columbia Phonograph Laboratories";[142] in 1919, the Columbia Graphophone Company published Seashore's *Measures of Musical Talent*.[143] Edwin Gordon, a Seashore aficionado, stated that with the 1919 release of these recordings, Seashore became the first person to publish a standardized battery of "music aptitude tests."[144]

Measures of Musical Talent as published in 1919 consisted of five 78 RPM records containing tests of pitch, intensity, time, consonance, and tonal memory, along with a manual describing the administration and interpretation of the tests. The pitch test consisted of 100 pairs of tones, and test takers were to identify whether the second tone in each pair was higher or lower than the first.[145] The distance between the tones in each pair decreased as the test progressed, and thus the test items became progressively more difficult. The intensity test similarly consisted of 100 pairs of tones, and test takers were to report whether the second tone in each pair was louder or softer than the first.[146] Each of the 100 questions on the time test consisted of three clicks with silence between them, and the test taker was to report whether the second silence was longer or shorter than the first.[147] The consonance test involved fifty pairs of two-tone clusters, and the test taker was to report whether the second cluster in each pair "sounded better" (or worse) than the first, better being described as smooth and blending well together.[148] Seashore apparently did not entertain the possibility that consonance, including what sounds "better," arguably is culturally determined. Finally, the tonal memory test included fifty, five-note pairs with one note changed in the second five-note pattern, and the test taker was to identify which of the five notes had changed.[149]

The manual included norms for three age categories: adults, eighth graders, and fifth graders, and for each of these groups, the percent of correct answers on a test resulted in a different percentile ranking. For example, getting 68 percent of the answers right on the pitch test placed an adult in the twelfth percentile, an eighth grader in the twenty-seventh percentile, and a fifth grader in the fifty-third percentile.[150] The manual also explained how to estimate ranks for all other ages and grade levels.[151] Seashore reported elsewhere, "We make up for age differences by having a different norm for each age."[152] For him, the need for different norms for different age and grade levels did not indicate that musical talent can improve. Rather, he explained that the age differences showed up in mass administrations of the tests but not in individual administrations, and he claimed that such differences were due to age-related differences in students' ability to concentrate, especially in a setting such as mass administration of a test.[153] He chose fifth grade because he deemed children of that age to be old enough to take the test seriously and eighth grade because vocational decisions were on the horizon for students of that age.[154]

Different versions of the test manual from this period exist, some containing five subtests and some six; one version bearing a 1919 copyright date has the handwritten name of a sixth test listed in the table of contents and is longer than the original 1919 manual because it includes a printed section describing this the sixth test—rhythm; by around 1923 or 1924, the rhythm subtest was an official part of the Seashore Tests.[155] The rhythm test consisted of fifty pairs of rhythm patterns, and the test taker was to determine whether the second pattern was the same as or different from the first.[156]

The test officially was revised in 1939; both the original test and the 1939 revision consisted of two series, labeled "A" and "B." According to Gordon, the only difference between the two series was that the content of the B series was more difficult; he further reported that the B series eventually was discontinued, without explanation.[157]

Those who have taken the Seashore Tests tend to generally agree that they are boring. Seashore may have overestimated their appeal when he stated in the instruction manual that they could be the source of "scientific entertainment" at home: "Taking one test each evening, this outfit provides material for five evenings of delightful entertainment in the form of a competitive game."[158]

Thus, phonograph technology enabled Seashore to record his tests, thereby eliminating the need to provide test administrators with the "expensive and bunglesome" apparatuses that had previously made mass administration of the tests so difficult. He praised the "wonderful reproduction of the modern phonograph" and claimed that recordings made it easier to accurately standardize musical talent test material.[159] Furthermore, it was the phonograph and the subsequent mass dissemination of quite readily available recordings that dramatically increased the influence of his ideas, as well as the number and scope of studies of musical talent. Although Seashore tended to use the term "measure" rather than "test," he sometimes employed these words interchangeably, and in common usage, the 1919 recordings came to be known as the Seashore Tests (or Test). According to Miles, it was this recorded test that Seashore demonstrated at the 1919 meeting of the Music Supervisors' National Conference (MSNC) in St. Louis.[160] The conference proceedings stated that Seashore had planned to demonstrate six capacities tests, not five, the sixth being a measure of music imagery; the final test was to be administered "without the use of instruments," that is, presumably, without the use of the recorded tests.[161] The proceedings reported that Seashore did not have time to administer the fifth or sixth test, however; most significantly, the manual accompanying the recorded tests did not mention a sixth, music imagery, test.[162] Regardless of the number or types of measurements he originally envisioned, the Seashore Tests merely consisted of the five (or later, six) tests included on the recording.

Seashore's presentation at the 1919 music teachers' convention was a sortie by a man on a mission who was eager to demonstrate the practical applications of science and to enlist others—in this case, teachers—as partners on this mission. Among the attractants were promises of what good science—science when properly undertaken, science as he understood it—ostensibly would deliver: truth, knowledge, and certainty.

Furthermore, his recorded test made its way to the Eugenics Record Office (ERO), where it was used in studies of the biological inheritability of musical ability. For example, in a discussion of studies of family pedigree that were underway at the ERO, a 1926 announcement in the journal *Eugenical News* mentioned the recorded test and Seashore's collaboration with the Colombia Phonograph Company.[163]

The Seashore Tests focused on a small fraction of the components that Seashore viewed as constituting musical talent, and he acknowledged that the five measures comprising the Seashore Tests "do not constitute a complete survey of musical talent."[164] In *The Psychology of Musical Talent*, which was published in the same year as the Seashore Tests, he discussed some components of musical talent that are not measured by the Seashore Tests,[165] and he championed other tests for these other components. For example, he described two test series, one being the Seashore Tests and the second consisting of motor tests.[166] He recommended a different array of gadgets for administering the second series, which focused on measuring "timed action, rhythmic action, motility, singing in pitch, and other tests."[167] He claimed that unlike the first series, which could be administered to large groups, the second could only be administered to one individual at a time.[168]

Especially when faced with critics who challenged the validity and reliability of his tests, Seashore argued that his tests were a time-saving compromise that only measured what he called elsewhere the fundamental capacities.[169] Regardless of the number of musical capacities Seashore conceptualized or the number of possible tests he wanted to disseminate to measure them, the Seashore Tests rapidly became a standard measure of music talent, due in part to their widespread availability and ease of administration. Seashore's caveats notwithstanding, the recorded Seashore Tests, in effect, reduced musical talent to the capacities measured. The test was not called *A Subset of Musical Measures*, even though even Seashore viewed it as such; furthermore, aside from the consonance test, which measured familiarity with arguably culturally contingent notions of consonance and dissonance, the Seashore Tests measured auditory discrimination. Thus, the process of making up kinds of people—of sorting and ordering them, of marking some as musically talented and others as not, and of qualifying some while disqualifying others—was efficiently accomplished with a handful of measurements of a small number of perceptual capacities.

Arguing that musical preferences are determined by musical talent, Seashore claimed that measurements of musical talent can explain individuals' tastes. In his 1917 *Etude* article he wrote, "We can understand the limitation to ragtime or capacity for symphony only as we know what fundamental talents are present."[170] This passage relied on and invoked a musical hierarchy to which Seashore clearly subscribed that considered ragtime to be a lower form of music and symphony to be among the highest forms. According to Seashore, talent could limit an individual's taste to lower forms of music or enable an individual to appreciate the finest music. Thus, individuals' tastes were not culturally formed but preordained—predestined—by biologically determined innate musical talent.

Another of his claims was that the Seashore Tests were durable because they were grounded in systematic scientific research and had been subjected to extensive scientific scrutiny prior to their release. In his 1930 autobiography he stated, "I should perhaps claim credit for the fact that these measures have stood the fire of criticism for these many years due to the fact that each one was the result of very extended preliminary experimentation in the laboratory."[171]

The Role of the Scientific Expert in Measuring Musical Talent

Seashore's confidence in science (as he understood it) was unshakable, and his praise of the new scientific expert—the psychologist—was unwavering, whether the domain was intelligence and intelligence testing or musical talent and musical talent testing. Only the scientific expert armed with modern technology could identify musical talent and measure its presence or absence with any precision. Only the scientific expert could develop and interpret a valid and reliable test of musical talent. In the early years, only a scientific expert could *administer* such a test. Only a standardized test created by a scientific expert could measure the musical *quality* of an individual.

Seashore called for the creation of "a new specialist," the "consulting psychologist in music," who would be trained in both psychology and music.[172] Using proselytic language, he claimed that this new specialist would have a "mission."[173] The Psychology of Music Studio at the University of Iowa reflected a team approach, Seashore stating that it was headed by a psychologist and a musician.[174] He explained that at the studio, trained assistants under the supervision of the heads administered the tests.[175] He also envisioned training musicians in psychology, suggesting, for example, that such musicians could use the scientific data gathered from the music tests to advise and guide test takers.[176] He underscored the importance of psychological expertise in a comment that subtly compared music psychologists to physicians—a warning that music tests, like drugs, "should only be used by those who can use them safely."[177] If "concrete and accurate knowledge" of musical talent is to be obtained from the tests, he maintained, those "in charge"—the scientific experts—need to make sure that they interpret the test results carefully.[178]

Seashore did not believe that musicians could accurately identify or assess musical talent without the assistance of psychologists and psychological testing. In his 1915 *Musical Quarterly* article, he underscored the elite, exclusive nature of psychological knowledge when he told musicians flat out that they were incapable of administering his tests: "This system of measurements, if it may be called a system, is unfortunately not adapted for general use by musicians themselves. It presupposes a technique, an equipment, and a skill in psychological analysis which the musician does not possess. It requires a specialist trained in music and psychology."[179] Elsewhere, he stated that musicians should not be blamed for their inability to accurately identify and measure musical talent because the expert knowledge was new and only available to an elite few: "It is no fault of the musician that he has not been able to analyze and measure musical talents technically, for that is a recent achievement in laboratory psychology, and the procedure is not generally available."[180]

While elevating the expert knowledge of the scientist, he undercut the legitimacy of music teachers' expertise by claiming that the selection processes used by schools for participation in music did not correlate with students' actual musical talent. This claim intimated that in the absence of psychologists and their expertise, music teachers could not identify or did not take into account students' innate musical talent: "Surveys of public schools show clearly that very little correlation exists between the possession of musical talent and the selection of children for musical education; and records of the extent of children's musical education show no close relationship to the possession of talent."[181]

An article appearing in a 1924 issue of *Eugenical News* reported that Seashore's former student Hazel Stanton had studied music teachers' estimates of students' musical ability and had compared these ratings to students' scores on the Seashore Tests. In addition to claiming that the Seashore Tests are reliable, the article underscored the potential unreliability of teachers' assessments: "This brings out vividly the difference in the rigor of rating exercised by the different teachers. The groups of pupils run, as would be expected, tolerably uniform in the tests, but the ratings applied to these students by the teachers vary tenfold from the strictest to the most liberal of the teachers. It appears that the teachers of the violin are, for some reason, more nearly uniform in their judgements than those of the piano."[182]

Even though he limited the identification of talent and the development of measures of musical talent to psychologists, by 1916 he was envisioning a simple test that could be placed in the hands of any music teacher or music supervisor.[183] Seashore used the term "simplified" to describe the transformation of the testing process into a form that teachers could use, which indicates that he did not believe that teachers could handle scientific complexity.[184] By the time the Seashore Tests were published in 1919—and thanks to the phonograph—he was trusting teachers to administer the tests, the instruction manual containing explicit directions written for teachers.[185] However, in this case, teachers played a role similar to that assigned previously to the lab assistants: scientific experts identified musical talent and created the means of measuring it, while underlings administered the tests.

Not only did he question whether music teachers could accurately identify musical talent in students, he sometimes cast aspersions on teachers' musical ability. For example, he recollected "several amusing incidents" that occurred when he demonstrated the Seashore Tests at the 1919 meeting of the Music Supervisors' National Conference.[186] The demonstration, which happened in conjunction with a speech that borrowed heavily (and often verbatim) from his new book *The Psychology of Musical Talent*, consisted of administering the tests to teachers attending the conference and to a group of seventh graders.[187] He stated that a music supervisor from one of the largest cities in the Midwest did poorly; the supervisor used this performance as evidence that the Seashore Tests were of questionable validity, the teacher publicly challenging the test and its creator.[188] Holding back no punches, Seashore responded by mocking and shaming the supervisor, calling into question his musical ability and pronouncing him incompetent:

> He [the music supervisor] then rose and, fully conscious of the dignity of his job and adulating himself on having his convictions verified, announced that he now had objective proof that these measures did not mean anything because he, a successful music supervisor, had made a very poor record. I then asked what instrument he played, and he said that he did not regard himself as a virtuoso on any instrument.

> I asked if he were a composer; no, he was not. I asked if he were a conductor; no, he was not. Then he volunteered, "I am a supervisor of music." "Ah," I replied, "that explains it. You are a business man, and business men do not necessarily rate high on musical talent." This did much to swing the audience to my side.[189]

Although Seashore told it as a joke, the anecdote was derisive, dismissive, and degrading, which raises the question of who would find it amusing. If enlisting new followers was the goal of Seashore's sortie, then publicly demeaning and discrediting a conference attendee would seem to be an odd way of achieving it. How might he have met his goal through this action? It is possible that even though he was successful overall, this incident did not help his cause and may even have done damage. It is also possible, however, that regimes of truth may gain ascendancy, may "win," by active, simultaneous discrediting of competing regimes, and woe be it to those who stand in the way of change. If regimes of truth are not deemed capable of coexisting, the ideas to be replaced may be marked as wrong, and those who continue to subscribe to them, rather than merely being deemed wrong, may be marked as abject.

In addition to being a cautionary tale about what might befall those who question the scientific expert, the above passage elevated the scientist, placing the scientific expert on the interior while simultaneously marking an exterior to which others were relegated, including the music teacher who resisted. Seashore's comments thus had a double-gesture effect. Furthermore, Seashore placed school teaching beneath other professions (including his own) on his status hierarchy, which was a disadvantaging position. His message that lowly work is noble work did not change the message that lowly work is lowly. The music teachers themselves were probably familiar with this status hierarchy—which was not unique to Seashore—and with their lower position. In the above passage, Seashore also cemented this lowly status by referencing a status hierarchy *within* music: he compared the lowly teacher to composers and virtuosi, people whose jobs were associated with greater eminence and status. The teacher, by admitting (or confessing) his limitations, was found wanting, according to Seashore's criteria. More than merely being marked as less competent, he was deemed so unqualified as to not even count as a musician.

Wendy Kline's observation that standardized tests can produce anxiety due to test takers' fears of being labeled deviant also applies to the Seashore Tests and may help explain why Seashore successfully recruited joiners through a process that included abjection.[190] Perhaps a combination of fear and desire fueled the actions of other music teachers in the audience, who may have been afraid that they, too, would be measured and found wanting. Perhaps they hoped to increase their own status or the status of their profession by aligning with elite professionals and with what was being presented as elite, high-status knowledge. For whatever reasons, few teachers appear to have pushed back, at least openly; they did not challenge Seashore's assumption that virtuosity and the ability to compose are signs of quality and necessary qualifications for being a high-quality music teacher. If Seashore's telling of the incident is accurate, they cast their lot with the scientific expert. They did so, however, at the expense of the truth regime to which they had previously subscribed and the knowledge of one of their own. This observation is not a criticism of the teachers but rather a speculation on how enlistment was effectively accomplished; despite the naysayers, Seashore met his enlistment goal.

The anecdote may reflect the creation of an alliance of experts, or the displacement of one kind of expert by another, or perhaps both. That said, although scientists and teachers may have forged alliances in this project to replace myth with truth and uncertainty with certainty, Seashore clearly did not view teachers as equal partners. Like the assistants who administered the Seashore Tests in laboratory settings, teachers were relegated to the position of mere implementers.

Finally, according to conference proceedings, one of the seventh graders tested as part of the Seashore demonstration scored in the first percentile on the pitch test.[191] The proceedings did not indicate whether the child was informed of this score or whether the audience was told which child had received it. A national conference on music education would be a particularly difficult and embarrassing place to receive such news.

Seashore's elevation of the scientific expert and his insistence that scientific experts must be at the helm of music talent testing may reflect conditions that Kurt Danziger discusses in his analysis of what many early American psychologists were marketing in first part of the twentieth century. According to Danziger, they were selling more than a material commodity—psychological tests: "Clearly, what the psychologists were marketing were their own skills and their own special competence of which the test materials were merely the external mark. The product that their society valued was *professional expertise* [emphasis in original]."[192] Thus, Danziger maintains, these psychologists faced multiple challenges, not only establishing psychology as a legitimate science and developing research practices "whose products would answer to the immediate needs of socially important markets," but marketing themselves as the possessors of professional expertise.[193]

Especially after the publication of the recorded tests, Seashore was identified as the quintessential scientific expert he prized and praised—at least on the subject of musical talent—by people both within and outside of eugenics circles. As I mentioned in chapter 3, eugenics publications helped spread the word about his work and tests, and unpublished correspondence generated by the ERO similarly referenced Seashore as an expert on musical talent.[194] Among the signs of the global scope of Seashore's influence on the study of the ostensibly biological inheritability of musical ability are discussions and citations of Seashore's work by Jon Alfred Mjøen and Mjøen's son, Fridtjof, at the Vinderin Laboratory in Norway, along with Fridtjof's use of Seashore's testing method.[195]

Uses for the Seashore Tests: Basic Research on the Hereditability of Musical Talent

Seashore claimed that the tests were invaluable for conducting various kinds of basic research, particularly studies of the biological inheritability of musical talent. He promoted family history pedigree studies with an added scientific component: administration of the Seashore Tests. This was precisely the kind of research his student Hazel Stanton undertook at the Eugenics Record Office; in her study of six prominent musical families, she used four sections of the Seashore Tests in combination with qualitative data, including individual case histories.[196] One source from the ERO described Stanton as Seashore's assistant.[197] Seashore praised Stanton's work and reported that all of the records she collected were on file at the ERO.[198] Even after Stanton left the ERO, the "Pedigree of Music Capacity" materials distributed by the ERO for the "genetical study of musical capacity" continued to use results from the Seashore Tests to map out the presence or absence of musical talent in families.[199]

At the Second International Congress of Eugenics and elsewhere, Seashore offered descriptions of and advice about the conduct of such studies. He mentioned studies of musical families;[200] an eminent musician, plus the musician's ancestors, progeny, and mate;[201] musically precocious children;[202] large numbers of families with children regardless of whether members had been identified as musical;[203] and newly married couples, their eventual children, and their children's mates for successive generations.[204] He likened the studies of newly married couples to research on plants and animals in which scientists "select a colony and breed successive generations under observation."[205]

In what perhaps was an allusion to the ERO and the work done there, he stated that at least some of his endorsed longitudinal studies of musical inheritance were of such magnitude that only large, well-endowed entities could attempt them: "The laws of the inheritance of musical traits must ultimately be determined by actual experiment on carefully selected matings in which the measurements may be repeated for successive generations. Such an undertaking can be fostered only by an agency heavily endowed, of a nation-wide or international scope, adopting a thoroughly standardized procedure which can be sustained for many years."[206] Significantly, he pragmatically suggested that scientists could use data collected through musical talent testing in schools as a starting point for inheritability research: "The most promising immediate approach is, however, to utilize material now available in the test programs of public schools by selecting marked cases of talent or absence of specific talent among children and working back from them to their parents, brothers and sisters, and other near blood relatives."[207]

He prefaced a description of the kinds of research that might be conducted with an acknowledgment that some of the selective breeding processes used successfully on plants and animals are not feasible for studies of humans, noting that in the case of humans, "we cannot breed successive generations" for a particular trait.[208] However, he opined that this "restriction" is not an insurmountable obstacle, claiming that the alternative processes he advocated, which involved volunteers, would not infringe on "reasonable sensibilities":

> We can adopt the device of selecting from volunteers, in which the factor under control is mated in a known way, and examine them and their children and their children's mates in successive generations. Ratings through systematic observations and case histories may be kept quite complete. This is undoubtedly the method of the future. It involves not the slightest infringement upon reasonable sensibilities or proprieties; on the contrary, it should constitute a most fascinating cooperative search for truth.[209]

With knowledge of the past and present, Seashore claimed, scientific experts would be able to predict—and perhaps even manage—the future; in this case, what could be predicted and potentially managed was the presence, absence, and amounts of musical talent.[210]

Seashore supported the use of measures of auditory perception for other types of basic research as well, including various comparative studies of groups. For example, prior to the introduction of the recorded tests, he described a study undertaken by Tsoerum Ling at the Iowa Psychological Laboratory to determine whether blind people have better hearing than sighted people do. The study measured sound-direction and intensity-discrimination capacities. Seashore reported that contrary to popular opinion, blind people do not have significantly better hearing.[211] The previous year he had reported that pitch discrimination "does not vary appreciably by sex."[212] Late in his life, he reiterated the claim that there are no sex differences in inherent musical talent in the book chapter "Why No Great Women Composers?"[213] In the earlier publication, he admitted that the test scores of preadolescent girls *were superior* to those of boys and claimed that this phenomenon had everything to do with boys' attitudes toward music and nothing to do with inherited musical talent:

> Records of school girls are ordinarily superior to the records of school boys, but this is due to the common aloofness of the preadolescent boy toward music. The boys in the American schools investigated, often regard music as a frill for girls and therefore do not enter the test with the same zeal and fervor as do the girls. It is significant that this difference in favor of girls disappears at the university age notwithstanding the fact that there is still more interest in music among young women and they have, on the whole, had more advantages of musical training than the university men.[214]

Thus, in some cases, Seashore attributed differences in test scores to factors other than biology, yet he claimed that biology ultimately prevailed. As I discuss in chapter 7, he used his presentation at the Second International Congress of Eugenics to promote the employment of the Seashore Tests in studies of race differences in musical talent.[215] His adherents produced a plethora of studies that did so. Although some subsequent studies focused on race differences (with races variously defined), others examined talent differences between urban and rural people. For example, one study compared the ostensibly outstanding musical talent of US "mountain" children to the talent exhibited by other populations of US children; another compared Japanese children from the country to Japanese children from the city.[216]

More Uses for the Seashore Tests: Practical Applications of Music Psychology

Just as he staunchly advocated for practical applications of the knowledge generated by the new field of psychology, Seashore similarly advocated for practical applications of one of its new subfields: music psychology.[217] He described the path of applied psychology in music as difficult, besieged, and fettered by primitive views: "In music the way of applied psychology is still desperately obstructed by the underbrush of primitive views of mind and the barbed-wire entanglements of the warfare of uncritical theories and self-interests."[218] Nevertheless, he spoke glowingly of the promise of this new field, claiming for example in his 1915 *Musical Quarterly* article, "The psychology of music is a new field, quite unworked, but full of promise and fascinating possibilities."[219]

In a discussion of US universities' rapid acceptance of new fields such as psychology—applied psychology, in particular—Kurt Danziger argues that new fields faced different tribunals in the United States than they did in Europe, where universities tended to be headed by philosophers—members of an "entrenched German philosophical establishment."[220] In Europe, it was administrators schooled in philosophy who needed to be convinced of the value of psychology; in the United States, by contrast, universities tended to be governed by "scientific—or, more properly, scientistic—dogma," with "ultimate control of university appointments and professional opportunities . . . vested in businessmen and their appointees, in politicians and in men engaged in practical professional activity."[221] In the minds of academic leaders in the United States, Danziger maintains, research needed to be "relevant to managerial concerns," capable of providing data that could be used to make immediate decisions, and applicable to solving "circumscribed problems."[222] Danziger states that Seashore was among the "fairly traditional experimentalists" who were quickly drawn to the new field of applied psychology.[223]

Selective Breeding of Humans

One of Seashore's suggested practical applications of the Seashore Tests was to selectively breed humans for musical talent. His advocacy was consistent with larger conversations among eugenicists concerning selective human breeding for the traits of talent and genius. For example, Ernst Kretschmer's 1931 article "The Breeding of the Mental Endowments of Genius," which appeared in the journal *Eugenics*, claimed that selective family breeding produces talent clans, as evidenced in royal families such as the House of Orange and in nations such as Germany.[224] He cited artists and musicians, as well as their families, as examples of the fruits of the breeding of German genius.[225] He referred to this process as "the piling up of talent through breeding," and although he admitted that genius sometimes appears through "happy accidental combinations . . . they [happy accidents] could not suffice to supply a whole nation with leaders. On the contrary, we find that in the breeding of talent and genius by any nation, certain families and professional groups among which a blood relationship exists, play a greater rôle than the rest of the people."[226]

Seashore believed that musical talent overall was a positive trait and that knowledge of the laws of inheritance, coupled with knowledge of whether individuals do or do not have musical talent, could be used to help conserve positive musical traits and eliminate negative ones; he likened the process to the way traits are enhanced or eliminated in plants and animals through selective breeding:

> If it should prove possible to identify heritable musical traits, as we believe it is, and if the laws of the operation of this inheritance should become common knowledge, it is conceivable that the gain for the development of artistic resources would be as far-reaching in consequence for musical art as knowledge of such laws is proving to be in conservation of favorable traits and the elimination of unfavorable traits in animals and plants. And this may all come about without any eugenic infringements of the rights and finer sensibilities of esthetic man in human evolution.[227]

Although women were scarcely mentioned in Galton or Kretschmer's discussions of genius, Seashore reported that mothers can carry and transmit musical genius to their *sons*, and he admitted that the innate talent of the genius's mother might never be discovered: "The male musical genius has often come from a mother whose extraordinary talent has passed undiscovered until it appeared in the career of a son."[228]

According to Seashore, selective breeding for musical talent would be accomplished without infringing on "the rights and finer sensibilities of esthetic man" by ensconcing scientific fact into commonsense thinking; the music psychologist, through a scientific test, would provide concrete information to guide individuals in making informed, voluntary decisions:

> Suppose a youth is endowed with a wonderful musical mind and imbued with a deep desire to have children endowed with the same precious gift. Would it be an advantage to have definite knowledge and insight in the predictions on the basis of family history, for each of the factors I have described, such as, the sense of pitch, musical

> imagination, and quality of voice and be able to say that the chances are 10 to 1, 1 to 1, 1 to 2, 1 to 5, 1 to 10, or 1 to 100 that this factor shall be reproduced? If youth enters into wedlock in possession of this knowledge, will that not tend to a deepening of love to the extent that it carries with it confidence of great promise? The opponents of eugenics fail to realize that scientific facts when well established become a part of common sense and a basis of intuitive reactions. My proposition is that if certain musical talents are heritable, as we believe them to be, it is quite within the power of future generations to enhance the quality and degree of a musical talent by conscious selection. The great significance for eugenics, however, lies not in the development of a system of artificial and formal eugenic guidance, but rather in the popular assimilation of well established facts in the common sense of the age and the naive projection of this common sense in natural reaction in courtship and mating.[229]

Thus, Seashore's selective human breeding implementation plan demonstrates the productivity of power and exemplifies pastoral governance in the sense that it promised much, capitalized on desire, and called for voluntary rather than coerced action. This plan is also infused with eugenics, eugenicists arguing that the positive eugenical measure of breeding for talent could play a key role in attenuating the threat of degeneration and fostering the proliferation of the fittest, who were destined to rescue the nation or the human race.

Solving Professional Musicians' Technical Problems

According to Seashore, another practical application of musical testing was in the diagnosis and sometimes solving of technical problems that professional musicians and "serious" music students experience.[230] He acknowledged that most professional musicians have handicaps and stated that capacities tests can provide information about the precise nature of these problems:

> This inventory also serves to explain experiences of the past which may not have been understood. If the singer has had defeat, it will show exactly why. If she has been misguided in musical training, it may show the nature of the error and its results. If the singer is conscious of lack in some capacity, the record shows the nature of this lack, and may even suggest a remedy, if such there is. Even among the best musicians it is rare to find one who does not have some kind

> of difficulty. Indeed, the difficulties of the singer are unquestionably great.[231]

Capacities tests, he claimed, could be used for diagnosis and remediation, in teaching settings and elsewhere.[232] He apparently assumed that musicians were ill equipped to solve these problems without scientific assistance, and he also stated that thanks to the "versatility and the plasticity of the human organism," many musical handicaps could be overcome.[233] He specified, for example, that flatting can be corrected if the problem *is not innate*: "A girl who flats in singing is immediately set into an intensive training series in which this defect which might follow her through life is eradicated in a few exercises of intensive drill with objective control, *provided it does not rest upon innate incapacity* [emphasis mine]."[234] This passage clearly indicates that Seashore viewed the presence of innate problems as an altogether different issue, and according to him, the capacities tests can help a musician determine whether the problem at hand can be overcome by training.[235]

The Pedagogical Production of Destinies: Music Testing Goes to School

Science in the Interest of Intelligent Decision-Making

As part of his campaign to underscore the practical value of psychology, Seashore stated scientific knowledge was needed in the music classroom. This knowledge, he argued, was beneficial to students and teachers alike: "No student of music can afford to go far in the field without taking account of scientifically established procedures about how best to learn music, and no teacher is prepared to teach or supervise music without a practical knowledge of such psychology of music."[236] He made various promises about what talent testing would accomplish and who it would benefit. For example, in addition to being useful to students and teachers, it would help stimulate community interest in music:

> It [the Seashore Tests] will stimulate an interest in the search for talent and efforts in the conservation of talent on the part of all concerned, particularly the teachers. Among the pupils it will cause a wholesome awakening to a recognition of their particular talents. For teachers of music it will stimulate the recognition of responsibility for the talented children of the community. It will be a part of the coming

> system of vocational and avocational advice, and should be a potent instrument in the development of community interest in music.[237]

Skillful interpretation of musical talent measures, he stated, provides "concrete and accurate knowledge"—facts—that can form the basis of intelligent decision-making.[238] He enumerated some of the decisions test results can facilitate: "On the basis of such concrete facts in hand, the parent and teacher can decide intelligently whether or not to give this child a musical education, how extensive the plans for a musical career ought to be, and what type of music to undertake in order to use natural equipment to the best advantage."[239] He underscored that the tests enable a music teacher to "render *a disinterested decision on well-founded and accurate information* [emphasis in original]."[240] He noted that the measurement of musical capacities can lead to the construction of individual student profiles,[241] and the Seashore Tests enabled him to realize his dream of producing vast numbers of these profiles through mass administration of music capacities tests to children in school.

Although he focused primarily on testing young people, he also favored the use of musical talent inventories on adults.[242] He supported the testing of adults by stating that musicians had warned of a threat—an onslaught by the musically unfit on vulnerable society—that had been created by music teachers. Seashore wrote, "There is no reason for limiting inventories of musical talent to children, because musicians tell us that, in this vast army of music teachers, society has but little protection against the unfit."[243] This statement was tinged with eugenical fear, as it referenced the negative impact on society of the ostensibly unfit and the need to protect society by eliminating the threat.

Constructing, Sorting, and Ordering Kinds of People

In addition to helping create and solidify a particular understanding of musical ability, the Seashore Tests helped construct qualitative categories of *ability* and of *people*—individuals and groups. They helped create an array of types of people, ranging from the talented musician to the musically deficient or disabled—as well as various types of people in between. For example, Seashore claimed that genetic studies had identified different *types* of color blindness, and he stated that different *types* of genetically governed musical ability or defect similarly could be identified: "As in genetic studies of the inheritance of color-blindness it has been possible to identify types, so in musical hearing we may look forward to the identification of types of defect and types of superiority deviating markedly from the normal."[244] The type of defect or superiority exhibited by an individual qualitatively marked that person as a type of musical (or unmusical) being: genius, gifted, talented, naturally endowed, normal, "unusually bad," or even "helplessly unmusical."[245] Judith Butler's conceptualization of sex as a normative regulatory ideal may be applicable to Seashore's conception of musical talent and to his views on the role that standardized testing should play in its identification.[246] If musical talent is a normative regulatory ideal, then identifying a child as talented both constructs that child as talented—as a particular kind of musical being—and also constructs, through citation or reinforcement, the concept of talent. Whether the regulatory ideal is sex or talent, however, such normative discourses tend to pathologize bodies that do not fit, relegating them to what Butler describes as a zone of uninhabitability and abjection; they become bodies that do not matter.[247]

Seashore used the term "diagnose," a word often associated with pathology in medical discourse, to describe a function of musical talent testing.[248] He also said that "sorting of pupils," presumably based on diagnosis, was among the possible uses of musical talent tests.[249] For example, he described how the tests could be employed in elementary classrooms—once again relying on the language of medical pathology in his choice of the word "treatment"; significantly, in the following passage, he referred to types—or classes—of people, and he called those classes deemed to be without musical ability the "bad": "Certain of the few most fundamental tests can and will be used as group tests, for the purpose of a rough preliminary sifting in the schoolroom. This will reveal the unusually bad as well as the unusually good; and both of these classes deserve individual treatment."[250]

After students had been sorted, they were to be rank-ordered according to musical talent, and hence according to quality. Seashore wrote, "The very good and the very poor will be identified with considerable certainty and all will be ranked roughly in the order of their natural ability. The results will be discussed with teachers and parents and due caution will be exercised in preventing hasty conclusions."[251] Rather than merely *scoring* well or poorly, the students *become* the very good or the very poor. The final statement in the passage is curious. If his tests were inerrant, what was the purpose of discussion with teachers and parents? It is not clear whether Seashore was suggesting that these discussions might elicit changes in the ranking of particular students or whether the hasty conclusions to be avoided were from teachers and parents.

Seashore's views about music testing in schools parallel those about testing in education writ large. For example, schools were to be in the business of determining how much inherent ability—and hence, quality—individuals have, and of sorting, ordering, qualifying, and disqualifying students accordingly. The means of determining ability and quality were necessarily standardized, and standardized testing was to be at the core of plans to achieve organizational and managerial goals. Furthermore, the introduction of standardized testing into schools was a foundational reform on which a host of other educational reforms were to be based.

"Finding Gold in the Dross"

Seashore was especially enthusiastic about the potential of standardized musical talent tests to *discover* talent—to identify which children are talented or gifted.[252] The eugenic claim that gifted children are being neglected, which appeared in his writings on general intelligence, surfaced again in his discussion of musical talent.[253] Another of his central tenets was that innate musical talent too often remains hidden: "Musical talent is a gift but like many of the gifts of nature it often remains concealed and a natural musical genius may 'die with all the music in him.'"[254] Elsewhere, in a discussion of the musically talented top 10 percent, he similarly argued that too many gifted students have no awareness of their gift.[255] The Seashore Tests, he claimed, were ideal for discovering hidden "unsuspected and latent talent."[256] Those with hidden talent were to be discovered through what he called "dragnets," and the ideal place for conducting a dragnet, he claimed, was the public school.[257] Broad-scale musical testing in the schools, he promised, would successfully separate the best from the rest: "Their [his early tests of musical capacities] real value is in finding the gold in the dross. One gifted child found early, investigated, and encouraged, is a great reward."[258] He reported that fewer than half of all musically gifted students in a given community had been discovered and given a "fair chance of a musical education."[259]

Seashore underscored that his tests helped discover talent that had been overlooked by others, including teachers. For example, in his 1919 book *The Psychology of Musical Talent*, he described two cases drawn from testing 2,500 schoolchildren.[260] One of the girls, Viola, had been identified as musically talented prior to the administration of the tests; her high test scores affirmed her as a musician and reinforced her decision to continue to pursue music. The other girl, Jean, was a "discovery"; Seashore reported that unlike Viola, Jean came from a poor family and had "enjoyed no musical advantages"; however, she had received the highest score in her grade in her town.[261] He noted that teachers had rated Jean higher in singing ability than they had rated Viola,[262] but he nevertheless claimed that prior to the tests, Jean had been ignored; the discovery of her talent through standardized testing opened the door to rescue and an intervention effected, in part, by philanthropy:

> Jean . . . was clearly a discovery. While the teachers reported, *after she had been found*, that she had been singing unusually well in school, no one had paid any attention to her as a musically talented girl. The report went not only to her parents, but, through the superintendent, to a woman's club which expressed its willingness to guarantee that Jean should have the opportunity of trying herself in a musical education. . . . It is no sacrifice for a music teacher to foster a charity pupil of that caliber [emphasis mine].[263]

Seashore spoke of undiscovered musical talent in terms of loss, waste, or what was being missed.[264] What was wasted was talent, and what was lost or missed was opportunity. For example, he warned that teens may grow into adulthood oblivious to what they are missing because their musical talent has not been discovered: "Unfortunately, large numbers of youth naturally endowed with the power of enjoying music have not even been discovered up to this time, either by themselves or by others, and they may pass through this last stage of opportunity [the teen years] without being discovered and often without realizing what they are missing."[265] Discovery of innate musical talent opened the door to opportunities to promote the fittest, cultivate talent, and guide or channel it.[266] Furthermore, Seashore claimed that being identified as musically talented would serve as a powerful motivator if the student were currently not participating in school music. The promised benefits of the Seashore Tests would not be experienced solely by the talented students. School music programs also would get a boost: being identified as musically gifted would motivate students to join orchestras, glee clubs, or choruses.[267]

He sometimes used terms such as "saving" and "conservation" to describe the purposes of test-based talent dragnets; for example, he wrote, "The applied psychology of music leads to a conservation movement. Indeed, it is not out of place to speak of the saving of life by the discovery and encouragement of unknown genuine talent in such a way as to lead to achievement in the art."[268] Rescue and conservation tropes were central to eugenics discourse of the day. President Theodore Roosevelt, a staunch supporter of eugenics and a key figure in popularizing the phrase "race suicide," is sometimes called the Conservation President or the Father of Conservation; he is identified as such in light of his efforts to establish national parks. Michael G. Kenny writes that Madison Grant was both an environmental and a racial conservationist who drew links between these two activities.[269] Thus, while eugenicists Roosevelt and Grant were promoting the conservation of the best lands and people in the United States, eugenicist Seashore, in a parallel gesture and using similar logic, was promoting the rescue and conservation of another national treasure that otherwise would be wasted or lost: the best musical minds.

It is true that Seashore mentioned girls in his case studies of undiscovered talent, and he also claimed that there weren't sex differences in musical ability. That said, it is possible that his discussion of discovering hidden talent was gendered. Music educators of the early twentieth century were concerned about the perception that music is not an appropriately masculine activity, and about the relative dearth of boys participating in school music.[270] Sources dating at least as far back as the 1830s indicate that in the United States, the perception that music is a feminine activity and the disproportionately large representation of girls in musical activities long predated the early twentieth century.[271] Given this context, although a goal of Seashore's dragnets may have been to snag all musically talented people, boys may have been particularly sought and prized. Undiscovered talent may have been viewed as a problem more likely to affect boys, while the useless waste of music lessons on the hopelessly unmusical may have been seen as a problem most likely to affect girls. Seashore decried the "craze"—the expectation—that all girls should play the piano.[272] A hint that gender dynamics were in play appeared in one of his case studies predating the Seashore Tests; the discussion focused on one of his discoveries, a male university student with little musical training but an impressive musical talent profile: "Figure 1 [this man's musical talent profile] is a record of a young man, a sophomore in the University, who has always wanted to study music but has been discouraged by his father, while his two sisters who do not care for music, or achieve any marked success, have always been encouraged by the father."[273]

Consistent with eugenicists' views on scarcity, Seashore maintained that musical giftedness, like high intelligence, was scarce and that such scarcity was both natural and inevitable. Furthermore, his intense interest in identifying the musically gifted was shared by other eugenicists, just as the nature of music talent was a topic of special interest to them. Eugenicists were not alone in their interest in these subjects; nevertheless, the fact that Seashore was drawn to them and addressed them in particular ways helps situate him squarely in the eugenics camp.

Testing to Eliminate the Musically Unfit

Although Seashore focused primarily on the positive eugenical value of standardized tests of musical talent—their centrality to discovering hidden gold—he also talked about the identification of those who lacked it—the exceptionally or helplessly unmusical; furthermore, he promoted the identification and ordering of everyone falling between the two tails.[274] Teachers were to use test scores in a process that qualified and promoted some students while simultaneously disqualifying and eliminating others. Test scores would tell teachers at the outset which students would or would not benefit from music instruction, and would help them decide who should or should not participate in school music. For example, in a discussion of the uses of musical talent tests in elementary schools, Seashore wrote, "Such tests may *eliminate* the helplessly unmusical and save them from an intolerable imposition of musical requirements [emphasis mine]."[275]

Elsewhere, in the article "Avocational Guidance in Music," he denied that experts in the psychology of musical talent were looking for the absence of talent, and he further claimed that test scores should not be used to discourage even students who scored in the twenty-fifth percentile:[276] Rather, he advised teachers to encourage students in proportion to innate talent:

> Special care [should be] . . . taken to encourage wherever justified and stimulate musical interest in proportion to apparent ability of the pupil. Thus, even a person who ranks 25% from the bottom is not discouraged from participating in ordinary singing and other musical exercises; but those of average ability are heartily encouraged, and those of superior ability are encouraged with enthusiasm.[277]

He claimed that the role of the scientific guide is to push back at societal—specifically parental—pressure on children who lack innate talent to pursue music. The scientific guide is to throw a floodlight on possible obstacles to becoming a good, successful musician so that children will not be tripped up without having been given advance warning. According to Seashore, the role of the scientific guide is analogous to that of a physician who attempts to ward off deterioration and disease.[278]

His procedures for identifying talent—and for sorting and ordering—had back doors—ways to allow some people to enter even if their test scores were low. For example, in a passage that may have engendered hope, he stated that some people can beat the odds and overcome some handicaps; however, he ended by saying that those with handicaps will have been forewarned by the psychologist:

> We must not forget the enormous resourcefulness of the human will, and the possession of latent powers. A one-legged man may become a rope dancer, a blind man a guide, a man with wretched voice an orator. . . . A singer may be permanently lacking in some fundamental capacity and yet have such merits in other respects, or have such exceptional ability in covering faults, that he may be successful in spite of an overt handicap. But even then psychology has warned and explained.[279]

He also patently believed that some handicaps or deficits could not be overcome; he stated that the talent tests should eliminate at least some students, not merely those on a career track in music who are unfit to succeed, but those some who are unfit to enjoy it as an avocation. In a passage supporting elimination, he also created a back door by asserting that the selection-and-elimination process should not discourage those who enjoy music:

> Unfortunately, as in academic subjects, the real elimination of the unfit is not accomplished effectively, and there are masses of music students dribbling along with at best a low mediocrity as the destination in sight. Since music, to be of service in later life, must be either professional or eminently satisfying as an avocation after advanced work in the subject, the necessity of making discriminating and wise eliminations before a youth is of age cannot be stressed too strongly. A wise selection and guidance at this stage should, however, in no way discourage those who get a genuine satisfaction out of music and are wisely motivated, especially for the keeping of an avocational interest alive with a modest degree of attainment.[280]

Discouragement, Seashore argued, is not the "mission" of the psychologist—except in "serious cases."[281] In serious cases, however, to discourage and eliminate was precisely the goal. For example, he told teachers that talent tests should be used to eliminate at least some students—the untalented tenth, or even more: "Among the poorest ten per cent *or more* one is likely to find those who are by nature totally unfit for musical appreciation or production and who might, for that reason, be excused from the school exercises which are not adapted to them [emphasis mine]."[282] It is hard to imagine how being relegated to the bottom 10 percent would not be discouraging for anyone; for a student aspiring to a career in music, being average, rather than in the top 10 percent, might have a similarly dampening effect.

Other Uses of the Tests in School

In addition to helping teachers decide which students should or should not participate in music instruction, the Seashore Tests, Seashore indicated, could help direct and govern the futures of those deemed fit to study music. Ever promoting practical applications of psychology, he advocated the use of musical talent tests in decision-making about the kinds of instruction and educational opportunities that should be provided to students who qualified for music. For example, he claimed that the tests could help teachers assign instruments to students and place them in ensembles.[283] He also said they could be used to check whether students are achieving at a level commensurate with their innate ability.[284] He even suggested that the tests could be used for drill and practice, and for teaching music appreciation.[285] The latter suggestions seem odd if musical ability is innate and immutable, but Seashore explained by saying that these drills would help in bringing up "laggards who have a musical ear and for some reason have failed to exercise it."[286] Ample evidence that teachers took his advice and used his tests comes not merely from Seashore himself but also from music education journals of the day.

Test-Based Vocational and Avocational Guidance

Mirroring his views that standardized tests could help with vocational planning in a host of fields, Seashore maintained that his standardized music test could be used for vocational and avocational guidance and counseling in music. He emphasized in particular that test-based guidance would lead to wise decision-making.[287] In addition to ascertaining an individual's potential, test scores could predict the "the probable extent of achievement and rate of progress."[288] In 1919, the year the Seashore Tests were published, he commented that scientific vocational guidance in music was still a dream rather than a reality, and he also stated that music was the most promising of all fields for the use of scientific procedures in vocational guidance: "In no other field does vocational guidance give so great promise of becoming scientific as in music."[289] He gave many reasons why he considered it the most promising:

> Among the reasons are these: music requires specific talents; these talents can be identified and rated by psychological methods; to a certain

> extent they are essential to happiness and success in the art; musical education is expensive; misguided talent may entail a chain of grievous misfortunes; and, other things being equal, musical advantages should be conferred in proportion to the degree of talent.[290]

Significantly, his list included the expense of training for a musical career, which he may have assumed would be greater than the cost of preparing for other careers. This was not the first time he had mentioned the expense of becoming a professional musician, however.[291] Three years earlier, in an article published in the *Music Supervisors' Journal*, he called a professional music education a large investment; presumably, he was referring to the investment of both money and time: "A professional musical education is a very large investment and it is a small matter to go to a little expense for the purpose of making a psychological inventory of the musical capacities so that the pupil may know exactly what capital he or she may have to invest."[292]

High test scores would assure fledgling professional musicians that their investment would pay off.[293] For those possessing the "gift," early testing could "serve as a guide in the selection and planning of a musical career"; this planning would be shaped by the musical strengths and weaknesses discovered by the tests.[294] Once again referring to investment—this time the investment of a life in music—Seashore promoted the value of testing to identify the "specific nature" and "possibilities" of a future professional musician's talent.[295] According to him, different career paths in music—for example playing different musical instruments—required different kinds of musical talent.[296] Test scores constituted "concrete and accurate knowledge" that would help tailor the career path to the talent.[297] Viewing vocational guidance in music as highly specialized,[298] he stated that the individual providing such guidance was to be an expert—"a technically trained psychologist who is also an artist in music and devotes himself professionally to this highly specialized task."[299] In 1919, he warned music teachers that unqualified "quacks and sharks"—fake experts disseminating fake information and charging high fees—might abound in the coming years.[300]

Seashore also claimed that places at the professional musician table were few and should be reserved only for an elite handful. Using music as a "tool for bread earning," he told music teachers at their 1919 national meeting, "is only for the few."[301] This speech also supported talent discovery to promote music as an avocation, which could become the "glory" of the student's life, but he qualified this support by saying that music should be an avocation only to the degree that the individual is "musical by nature."[302] As we have seen, he did not believe that all people are qualified to participate even as amateurs. In a discussion of the use of pitch-discrimination test scores in vocational guidance, he described the strength of the encouragement to be given to a test taker, which was to be based on test score percentile rank:

> Best 10 per cent: stimulate enthusiastically.
> Next 20 per cent: encourage freely.
> Next 40 per cent: encourage.
> Next 20 per cent: question.
> Next 10 per cent: discourage.[303]

In the same discussion, he stated that those with the very lowest scores "should have nothing to do with music."[304] That said, his discussions of testing for avocational and vocational guidance alluded to back doors. For example, immediately after charting out how much encouragement should be given to which students based on test-score percentile rankings, Seashore warned that those offering guidance should never look solely at one factor but "must always take the whole into account."[305] In his article "Avocational Guidance in Music," which appeared in the *Journal of Applied Psychology*, he spelled out some factors to consider other than test scores: statistics about musical training, music teacher ratings, general intelligence, and the "artistic aims and aspirations of pupils and parents."[306] Elsewhere, he added the will to achieve, family economic status, "aspirations for a career in other directions," and health to his list of factors.[307] According to Seashore, all of these factors must be "reduced to percental rank and interpreted in terms of established norms so that the records on all points are in the same terms, namely, rank expressed in per cent from 0 to 100."[308] Thus, in his estimation, even the most potentially subjective evaluations could and should be reduced to numbers and percentile ranks.

Testing and Music School Admissions

Convinced that scores from his tests had predictive value,[309] Seashore promoted their employment as an admissions criterion for music schools—or as a means of immediately weeding out the unfit who had been admitted erroneously.[310] For example, he reported that the Eastman School of Music, with assistance from his former student Hazel Stanton, was using his test for this purpose; he claimed that admission to Eastman was based *mainly* upon an individual's scores on the Seashore Tests:

> One of the most fortunate opportunities for the development of this applied psychology of music has been the situation offered in the Eastman School of Music. Through the work of Dr. Hazel Stanton this institution carried on a seven-year program for the purpose of validating my six measures of musical talent as a means of selection for admission to the Eastman School. The recently published reports from that institution are extremely gratifying, showing statistically that the institution is justified in basing admission of students mainly upon this musical profile.[311]

In an article published in the *Music Supervisors' Journal*, Stanton told music teachers that in 1923–24, Eastman dropped students from the school because of their test scores, and that in 1924–25, "the faculty of the school voted unanimously to admit only those who measured above a certain score."[312]

Elsewhere, he suggested that test taking could be an admissions requirement, in which case, the individual student—not the institution—would make a prudent decision to enroll (or not) based on supposedly scientific information about the likelihood of success.[313] This strategy resembled one he supported (and implemented) for college admissions generally.

The Seashore Tests were used by institutions of higher education other than Eastman and for far longer than the 1920s. For example, a fall 1945 article in the *Gustavian*, the school newspaper of Seashore's undergraduate alma mater, announced the upcoming administration of the Seashore Tests to freshman and any interested upperclassmen.[314]

According to Seashore, schools could use the Seashore Tests both to decide who would be admitted and to raise school standards by restricting access; a school's consequent high quality, in turn, could be widely advertised.[315] Through this suggestion, Seashore again signaled that professional music training was to be, by design, a scarce commodity reserved for a small, elite group: the fittest.

Parallel Eugenical Contours: Testing in Education and Music Education

Seashore's views on standardized testing in music education and on standardized testing in general were virtually identical. Tests were to be used to determine who was worthy to participate—who was to be admitted to a school of music, who could participate in a musical ensemble, or who could play a particular instrument. Standardized tests would determine who would be promoted and who would be eliminated. All of these actions were premised on the assumptions that all are not worthy to do these things—not all are fit—and that fitness and unfitness are dictated by biological inheritance. Eliminating the unfit shielded the fit from contamination and eliminated the threat of degeneration. As I stated in the previous chapter, in his broader discussions of education, Seashore did not describe the shadowy fate of those not fit to be educated. In the case of the musically unfit, however, the path was clearer: they were to be eliminated. Of course, he did not suggest that they should be killed—although he did discuss selective voluntary breeding to increase the number of musically fit—but they were to be administered a milder dose of the eugenics poison: killed off from music and shipped elsewhere, to a class for which they supposedly were better suited. When considering Seashore's strong support for using musical talent tests to identify and measure talent, and to sort, order, promote, and eliminate individuals based on test scores, it is important to keep in mind that these discourses and practices were entirely consistent with and central not only to his views about education generally, but to eugenics.

Seashore's Music Education Philosophy and Plan for Music Education Reform

The Goals and Problems of Music Education

Seashore's discussions of music education share many resemblances and parallel contours with his analyses of education overall. His philosophy of music education, his list of music education's problems, and his proposed solutions were virtually identical to the views he expressed in his writings on education in general. In some cases, he used the same examples almost verbatim. For example, in an article entitled "Youth and Music," published in the *School Review* in 1940, he again identified the overabundance of unfit students as an education problem stemming from a lack of effort to rightly eliminate them, and he described this as a problem affecting both higher education and music education:

> Youth is the dominant educational period. Those who in this period qualify for higher education can and should continue their studies with organized effort and with confidence in success; but, on account of the American popular demand for higher and higher education,

> many of those who should be eliminated during this period float on, ill-motivated, ill-directed, floundering through college or professional education without regard to the worth-whileness of the procedure. Unfortunately, American education has not made adequate provision for the diversifying of training especially in the practical outlets at this age. This educational dominance of the period of the teens is particularly true for music.[316]

Another resemblance is his assertion that misguided notions of democracy, specifically the idea that all should be treated equally, were harming education. Once again, he underscored that equal is neither democratic nor fair; this is an assertion that many educators would make today, but most of today's educators would find equal far fairer that what Seashore proposed. His words about music education in a democracy sound familiar both to those who have read Seashore's publications outside of music education and to those familiar with the writings of eugenicists such as Madison Grant. Consider, for example, the strikingly eugenical statement Seashore made in *The Psychology of Musical Talent*, under the heading "The Corruption of Democracy":

> The doctrine of democracy often results in great educational corruption. From certain universally admitted declarations of equality we derive the maxim: Treat all alike. From this the educator takes his cue and imposes upon the community the education doctrine: Make all alike. This doctrine finds great following because it can be administered by smooth and conventional machinery. But it is vicious because it results in decadence and suppression of the best forces in society.[317]

In his writings on music education, his oft-repeated education motto—which he coined in response to his visit to eugenicist Henry Goddard's Vineland—morphed into "Keep the child busy at his highest level of achievement *in music* and he will be happy, useful, and good [emphasis mine]."[318] Without naming Goddard or Vineland, in *The Psychology of Musical Talent*, he referenced his visit to Vineland and even described the miraculous effects of this philosophy—its ability to transform the abject other, the "mentally bereaved," who had been made "unhappy, useless, and vicious":

> In studying, a few years ago, the provision for the care of the higher grade of feeble-minded the author found a certain institution in

which it could be said that the children were happy, useful, and good. An inquiry into the organization of that institution revealed that it was because each child was kept at his highest level of achievement. Many of these mentally bereaved children had come from good homes in which they had been made unhappy, useless, and vicious because they had not been kept busy or because unreasonable tasks had been imposed upon them; but in this institution the capacities of each child had been determined as a basis for the assignment of tasks and privileges. This principle for the care of the defective child applies with more force to the normal child in an art. Keep the child busy at his highest level of achievement in music and he will be happy, useful, and good.[319]

A Hierarchical Solution: Sectioning by Musical Ability

Another parallel between Seashore's views on education and on music education was his support for creating a hierarchy of educational opportunities and for instituting ability-segregated tracking. To Seashore, tracking—which he claimed he was instrumental in reviving—was an excellent way to differentiate instruction, especially when working with large numbers of students. It was the new approach, and in his view, it was far superior to, and should rightfully replace, what he called the "old method" that only sorted students by age.[320] Because students exhibited different levels of ostensibly natural musical ability, they were to be slotted into a music education program that similarly was structured into levels; musical talent test scores were foundational to students' placement on the hierarchy.[321] He spelled out a possible tracking plan for music classrooms:

> The real purpose [of a tracked music program] should be to bring together, as nearly as possible, those of the same degree of natural musical ability. The true solution . . . may be gained by carrying, either for each grade, or preferably for a small group of grades, three divisions, roughly as follows: the superior twenty-five per cent, the middle fifty per cent, and the inferior twenty-five per cent, with continual shifting from one division to another as merit may warrant. This, with free promotion or demotion, would make a happy solution.[322]

Mirroring his discussions of tracking in other education settings, Seashore's plans for tracked music classes included provisions for changing tracks.[323]

Such changes presumably would occur if an underachieving, naturally talented student began tapping that unused talent. Seashore also supported what he called a "flexible" music curriculum. Arguing that music students should not be tethered to their same-grade peers, he declared that a flexible curriculum would allow them to move one or more grades up or down for music class, the goal being to align educational opportunities with natural talent.[324] He stated, for example, that it might be appropriate for some third graders to sing with the fourth graders and for some fourth graders to be placed with first graders.[325] He apparently did not believe that what many might view as a demotion would bother or harm the fourth graders placed in a first grade music class. To the contrary, he maintained that selective promotions, demotions, and eliminations were beneficial for all students; by contrast, in his view, settings in which students were untracked were universally harmful. Just as he had enumerated the deleterious effects of untracked college classes, he spelled out the negative effects of untracked music classes:

> The old [equal, untracked] method . . . has a demoralizing effect upon talented and untalented child alike. All admit that it is not good for a child who is superior in singing to be held in leash by an artificial classification [as in, classifying by age]. It is not so generally known, but it can be demonstrated beyond question, that psychologically the effect of such alignment is always bad for the child of inferior musical endowment. If the training is above his level, it creates a feeling of self-depreciation and disgust, and it fails to give the child that musical stimulus which can reach him. The old argument that it is good for the inferior singer to be trained with the superior singer is false.[326]

According to Seashore, untracked schooling in music was not only unwise and ineffective, but unjust. The students who ostensibly were treated most unjustly in such untracked classrooms were those at the two ends of the talent curve. In a passage that identified a one-size-fits-all curriculum as the enemy, he mapped out a normal curve when describing who was or was not suffering abuse and injustice:

> A visitor to one of the middle grades will find that one fourth of the pupils are beyond the stage of instruction of the class and the exercise serves as a deadening of the best sensibilities and enthusiasms. One fourth of the class are not capable of comprehending or performing the task in hand, but sit listless and helpless and rightly regard them-

> selves as unjustly abused. The members of the remaining one half of the class represent a variety of conditions, but most of them are capable of profiting to some extent by the exercises. The future musicians are all in the upper quarter of the class and suffer injustice musically in proportion to the actual magnitude of their musical talents.[327]

Music Education for the Musically Gifted Child

Seashore's tracking plan for music classes was based on the eugenically informed premise that resources, including what he sometimes called musical advantages, should rightly be provided in proportion to natural talent.[328] This was the same resource allocation claim he made when discussing other education settings, notably higher education. In particular, those with more talent deserved more resources, he argued, and once again, he reserved the most and best for gifted students. In fact, in addition to calling for music education adapted to the individual, Seashore even claimed that allocations for the gifted student should be *more than proportional* to innate talent; musically untalented students, by contrast, should rightly receive even *less than their proportional share*:

> First, that the pupil in music has a right to expect that the instruction and training shall be adapted to his personal nature, which we have called . . . his personal equation; second that, other things equal, a musically talented person should have musical advantages proportional to his talent. The affirmative answer does not go so far as to affirm what many of us believe, that musical advantages should be more than proportional to the magnitude of the talent of the highly gifted, and that those who are markedly delinquent in musical capacities might be better off with less than proportional training.[329]

Significantly, in the above passage, Seashore used the term "delinquent" to describe the student lacking musical talent. This label has moral connotations, suggesting criminality or a failure to fulfill an obligation, and thus this usage marked the untalented pupil not merely as lacking and deficient, but as bad. Finally, he argued not only that tracking is just, but that disproportionate resource allocation, with the most going to the best, is similarly just.[330]

One special advantage he mentioned is the employment by public schools of a psychologist whose sole job is to identify and motivate musically gifted students. Recounting a conversation he had had with eugenicist George Eastman, he reported that Eastman had asked whether the Seashore Tests, which Eastman claimed had been very helpful at his conservatory, could be part of a "positive procedure"; Eastman called test usage at the Eastman School a negative procedure.[331] Seashore reported that they could. He described an experiment underway in public schools that included employing such a psychologist, who also could help increase the use of music psychometrics; he predicted that this "positive procedure" was destined to be very influential in the future:

> Experimental units are now operating in certain public school systems where a psychologist is employed for the sole purpose of discovering and motivating those children who are musically talented. This is a positive procedure and, in the spread of measurement which now prevails in the public school systems, it is destined to play a very large rôle in the future.[332]

It is unlikely that many (or any) public schools hired music psychologists once the experiment had ended. Nevertheless, it is abundantly clear that even without a music psychologist, the Seashore Tests were a game changer, and they were entirely consistent with eugenical goals. Finally, Eastman's reference to negative and positive measures came straight out of dominant eugenics discourse of the day, and this use in a conversation between two eugenicists is yet another fingerprint marking the omnipresence of eugenics in this discourse.

Thus, consistent with his general discussions of education and hearkening back to eugenicists such as Goddard, Seashore's advocacy of musical sectioning by ability was based on the assumption that humans can be sorted and ordered along a hierarchy and that schooling should reflect that hierarchy. Once again, he identified the problem as the assumption that humans are the same and that the solution was pedagogical differentiation. He again saw integration as a problem for which segregation is a solution, a solution that, among other things, prevents the fittest from being contaminated by the unfit. Another parallel contour is Seashore's insistence that special educational opportunities—the spoils of smartness—should be reserved for musically gifted children, and he again described these spoils as justly and rightfully belonging exclusively to them. He again assumed that only the fittest would benefit from special programs and rich resources, and once again, he justified the allocation of extra resources for the musically gifted on the grounds that it is wasteful not to do so. In Seashore's estimation, both high musical talent and educational resources inevitably are scarce. Differential allocation of resources is prudent, he again claimed, because of "scientifically" proven differences in biologically inherited capacity, and once again, he equated human capacity with human quality.

Even though promoting the fittest via special learning opportunities for children identified as musically talented was popular among eugenicists, other individuals and groups aimed to do this as well. For example, a preliminary schedule for the 1919 meeting of the Music Supervisors' National Conference listed an address by Mr. E. W. Pearson, director of music for the Philadelphia Public Schools, entitled "Opportunities Which the Schools Should Offer the Child of Exceptional Musical Talent."[333] Pearson specialized in vocal sight-singing and became the first director of music for the Philadelphia schools when the position was created in 1897.[334] He apparently was a no-show at the conference, however, the proceedings only reporting on the general discussion that replaced his talk.[335] That discussion, which sounds surprisingly contemporary, focused on augmenting standard music curricular fare with new course offerings. The innovative courses discussed included harmony, history of music, music appreciation, and private lessons on instruments, including the piano; the standard offerings were choir, orchestra, and the relatively new kid on the block—band.[336] Significantly, the discussion was all about new or existing courses and not about gifted children or rationales for providing them with special opportunities.

The Neglect of the Musically Gifted Child

Seashore's preoccupation with the fittest extended to people identified as musically gifted, and his discussions of the musically gifted parallel those about the highly intelligent. For example, according to him, the musically gifted child is among those who suffer most in untracked music classrooms.[337] It is the musically gifted child who, due to neglect, is truly the retarded child, held back by a barren, stultifying environment:

> The bright child is the "retarded." The spirit of the Good Samaritan goes out rightly to help those who are in distress, those who are popularly regarded as retarded. But who is the retarded child? [G. D.] Strayer well says it is the bright child. The retarded child in public school music is the musically brilliant child who is entitled to instruction and association with those who are musical, but who is being held back and deprived of the stimulus which comes from the keenest social competition.[338]

In the above passage, he argued that gifted children are even more neglected than children at the other end of the normal curve, and that they are unjustly denied an entitlement. Significantly, that entitlement is not merely the opportunity to receive appropriate instruction, but the chance to *associate* and *compete* with others who are similarly musically gifted. Keeping musically gifted children busy at their highest natural level of achievement liberates them from the mediocre, freeing them to grow. Seashore declared, "Our appeal, however, is not for the lessening of instruction to the mediocre, but for the freeing of the musically talented into a musical atmosphere in which they can grow and grow with joy in the comradeship of art."[339] Consistent with dominant eugenics discourse, he maintained that just as the intellectually unfit were bearers of degeneracy and a drag on the highly intelligent, so too were the *musically* unfit a threat to the most musically talented, wastefully draining precious resources. His focus on those that his tests identified as most talented was consistent with his eugenical belief that the most gifted were the hope of the future.

Opportunities for the Gifted to Compete with Each Other

Like other eugenicists, Seashore believed that competition should play a key role in achieving eugenics goals; competition also had a central place in his vision of good schooling. His fondness for competition—especially among the gifted—extended to school music contests, which he claimed were destined to become "a clearinghouse."[340] He likened music contests to football games, claiming that they would generate enthusiasm equal to that engendered by sports:

> Educators used to think that football was the only thing that would arouse enthusiastic support in the field of avocational activities for youth; but, as I have witnessed the attitude of high-school pupils in training for musical contests, heard reports of the attitudes of the parents and the backers, and watched the culmination of enthusiasm at the annual contest, I can say that there can be, for youth, as substantial enthusiasm in contests of music as there is in football.[341]

As I discussed in chapter 3, eugenics publications helped promote both Seashore's research and the Seashore Tests, and consistent with a larger pattern of supporting contests to help educate the public about eugenics, they even mentioned the possibility of creating music contests based on the tests.[342] For example, in an article appearing in 1928 in the journal *Eugenics*, an unnamed author (very possibly Charles Davenport or even Seashore, himself) reported that the Committee on Popular Education of the American Eugenics Society was discussing possible ways to administer the Seashore Tests on a broad scale. After stating that the tests must be given to entire families "to bring out the eugenics lesson," the article reported on a suggestion that today might be called a school/business partnership: collaboration between school boards and music stores in large cities to organize, advertise, and promote music ability contests that used the Seashore Tests.[343]

Seashore's Claims and Promises about His Proposed Music Education Reforms

Music Education Reform in the Interest of Benevolence, Humanitarianism, and the Prevention of Suffering

Seashore's music education reform plan was virtually identical to his general education plan in the sense that once again, benevolence, humanitarianism, and the elimination of suffering were his justifications for identifying ability, segregating by ability, and eliminating the unfit.[344] For example, he quoted eugenicist George Eastman's claim that the Seashore Tests had prevented much human suffering.[345] Not only are untracked music settings pedagogically ineffective, Seashore argued, they are universally demoralizing.[346] Just as untracked music settings create suffering for the fit who are held back, they also ostensibly have adverse effects on the unfit, and Seashore used the language of psychological diagnostics and pathology to explain these effects.[347] Elsewhere, he stated that the less able child is "humiliated and discouraged by enforced association" with musically able children.[348] Children lacking musical ability—those in the bottom quarter of the class—have "the heart taken out of them" by a placement that does not take into account their natural level of musical ability, Seashore argued.[349] He maintained that in music settings, it is only humane to release an unfit child from unrealistic expectations: "We must have the good sense not to hold him responsible for, or attempt to force upon him, powers with which nature has not endowed him."[350] Eliminating the helplessly unmusical *rescues* them from imposed music requirements.[351] Testing for musical talent helps free the "non-talented from the curse of maladjusted effort."[352] Guidance saves the life of the unmusical youth who is rescued from the "torture" of a failed career in music.[353]

Music Education Reform in the Interest of Efficiency and Economy

As in his discussions of education reform overall, in his treatises on music education reform, Seashore cited efficiency and economy as reasons to institute change; as I already have indicated, this rationale is entirely consistent with eugenics.[354] Money and time typically are the resources that he claimed would be conserved; students, parents, teachers, and institutions would be the beneficiaries. Seashore told parents that the cost of individual musical talent testing was inconsequential compared to the expense involved in getting a professional music education.[355] In a comment decrying fiscal extravagance and excess, he argued that spending money on music lessons can be even worse than wasting it (although he did not explain what that worse use might be): "It is safe to say that a very large portion of the enormous sum of money spent on musical instruction is worse than wasted, because spent on persons who have no adequate musical talent."[356] Seashore preceded this statement with a quote from the president of the Music Teachers' National Association, who claimed that Americans were spending four times as much money annually on music lessons as on all public high schools and almost three times as much as on colleges and universities.[357] Eugenics publications promoting the Seashore Tests echoed the theme of waste, similarly claiming that large amounts of money were being squandered on music lessons for "children who are incapable of profiting by it to any extent."[358] Institutions could save money, too, Seashore maintained. For example, he quoted Eastman's claim that the Seashore Tests had saved the Eastman School of Music "'vast sums of money.'"[359] Responding to the concern that conservatories would lose tuition money if they were to "weed out the unfit," Seashore countered that such elimination would signal higher institutional standards, which would in turn increase institutional status; as a result, better students would be attracted to the school, and their tuition would more than compensate for the initial loss.[360]

Energy and time are other resources not to be wasted.[361] Seashore claimed, for example, that studying music is a waste of energy for the nongifted student.[362] Once again alluding to Plato's myth of the metals, he referred to the futility—the waste—of trying to make a "precious metal out of a base one," of attempting to transform an unmusical child into a musical one.[363] In a statement steeped in moral judgment, he commented that untracked music classes are "shamefully wasteful in time."[364] Thus, according to him, economy is a virtue, untracked settings are pedagogically unsound because they waste time, and any activity that is deemed a waste of time is morally wrong. In response to critics, he admitted that his tests provide "short-cut and snapshot samplings," adding that every test is a compromise designed to provide fair results "in a minimum time."[365] He viewed tracking as a solution to wasting time, and in the same breath he also spoke of efficient musical *achievement*.[366] The goal of vocational guidance in music, he maintained, is "efficiency in the profession,"[367] and "the demand for efficiency" is, in his view, an outstanding feature of this guidance.[368]

Music Education Reform in the Name of Individuality, Merit, Justice, and Fairness

The arguments that Seashore used to support a music education reform plan that included and promoted some students while eliminating others intricately interwove discourses of individuality, merit, and individual choice with claims of justice and fairness. First, Seashore's focus was on the individual: the individual's needs and differences between individuals needed more attention, he claimed. This focus is evident in his statement that the goal of avocational guidance in music is self-realization.[369] He assumed that individual differences in musical ability exist, are important, and can be identified via standardized testing.[370] He also argued that once identified, these individual differences should be addressed by providing individualized learning opportunities.[371] He stated that child study had morphed into "child adaptation," and he spoke of a student's *right* to receive instruction "adapted to his personal nature" and "proportional to his talent."[372] He also spoke of the wrongness of treating all alike and the impossibility of making all alike.[373] Testing, he claimed, is an informational tool that enables *individuals* to make wise choices; for the unfit, the wise choice is to pull out. In his 1919 speech at the St. Louis conference of music educators, he even claimed that the gates of the conservatory were to be open to all and that test scores—rather than barring anyone from admission or the opportunity to achieve—were to be merely informational; this claim placed responsibility for making a wise choice squarely on the individual: "The gates are open to you, but this is your chart; this is the capital which you have to invest."[374] The "but" in the above sentence suggests that Seashore had the musically unfit in mind: individuals are free to make their own choices, *but* test results have forewarned the unfit of their dim prospects. Thus, participation or elimination is not invariably imposed by an external force but is to be decided by the individual who, armed with good information, makes a free "choice." It is through individuals and their better choices that projects of improvement, whether of an institution, a nation, or the human race, would be accomplished. As we have already seen, however, Seashore did not leave decisions about participation or elimination solely in the hands of the individual. According to him, teachers and institutions also have the right and responsibility to decide who should be included or excluded, and some teachers and institutions clearly used the Seashore Tests to shape the destiny of others. Perhaps Seashore believed that teachers and institutions should exercise their power as a second line of defense when the ostensibly musically unfit fail to exercise good judgment by failing to withdraw voluntarily.

Another element in Seashore's discourses on individuality is his call for selection processes based on individual merit, with merit defined largely (but not solely) by musical ability as determined by his standardized tests. Furthermore, using individual merit as a rationale for giving disproportionately more to those deemed to have the most and disproportionately less to those deemed to have the least, he buttressed his claims by asserting that such processes are only just and fair. For example, he maintained that in a tracked music education system, placing the "dull child" and the "brilliant child" at different levels is fair to both of them.[375] According to Seashore, if decisions about who is to receive education privileges—including admission to a music school—are to be fair, they must be based on *individual* quality or merit. His tests, he claimed, can help determine who has ability and, thus, who merits privileges. He wrote, "Judge him [the musician] on his merits. This is of vital importance for musical pedagogy, particularly in the directing of the young, because we shall not make satisfactory progress unless we find the child in a field in which we can justly encourage him."[376] He suggested that using standardized test scores—whether of musical ability or general intelligence—is fundamental to merit-based decisions and contributes to a fairer admissions process than what was used in most institutions: "So in music, the music school of any consequence in the future, like a few rare examples at the present time, will extend its privileges, not in the order of application, nor at the rate of willingness to pay, but on the basis of merit; and one far-reaching element in musical merit is the general level of intelligence."[377]

Without interrogating the potential unfairness of the processes and reforms he promoted, he appealed to claims of justice by arguing that having money or influence should not govern access to music education. Indeed, justice and fairness were recurring themes in his discussion of why reforms must be made to music education.[378]

Finally, as with his proposed reforms for general and higher education,

Seashore's plans for change in music education were imbued with promise, optimism, and positivity. His descriptions were downright cheerful. Eliminating the musically unfit, he claimed, "is not a negative process" if accompanied by a search for other talents that the student may possess.[379] In his mind, his solutions are happy ones that help produce happy children.[380] As in his discussions of general education reforms, when he peddled reform in music education, the positivity of his delivery may have contributed to the appeal of his plans; furthermore, as I discussed in previous chapters, this positivity—at least optimism about the future—was emblematic of eugenics.

Music Education Reform in the Name of Profit

When considering Seashore's rationale and motives for instituting his proposed reforms in music education, it is important to remember that his plans involved for-profit ventures from which he stood to reap financial gain: neither he nor the Columbia Graphophone Company (later RCA) was giving away either the Seashore Tests or the phonographs needed to administer them.[381] Not only were his tests for sale, but official eugenics publications were among the places that promoted their sale.[382] Advertising for the tests also appeared in the first issue of the *Music Supervisors' Journal* published after the 1919 convention in St. Louis; the price for the recordings and the test instruction manual was $7.50 ($109.58 in 2019 dollars).[383] The advertisement also featured a photograph of a relatively new piece of technology, the Columbia School Grafonola with Pushmobile, a record player on a cart, which could be ordered in either oak or mahogany; the ad stated that this device was being offered to schools at a special price.[384] Earlier issues of the *Music Supervisors' Journal* were peppered with advertisements for phonographs and recordings, including music appreciation series, so advertising the Seashore Tests was consistent with the journal's established practices.[385] There also is evidence that companies making record players and recordings had exhibits at the national conferences.[386] That said, advertisements for the Seashore Tests confirm that Seashore, too, was participating in a marketing bonanza, and they document the entrepreneurial dimension of musical talent testing.

I mentioned in chapter 5 that Seashore was in on the ground floor when the Psychological Corporation—which eventually became a vast, highly profitable business—was formed in 1921. Significantly, while in 1919 the Columbia Graphophone Company was selling the Seashore Tests, by 1939 RCA was the publisher, and by 1957 the publisher was none other than the Psychological Corporation. I did not investigate in detail Seashore's profits from the sale of the tests, and I do not know whether he enjoyed additional financial benefits from his affiliation with the Psychological Corporation, but it is safe to say that he or his heirs profited in some way from these ventures. Toward the end of his life, he donated at least some of the royalties from his books and tests to the University of Iowa, in one instance to be used in any way the university wished, and in another, through the Carl E. Seashore Memorial Fund, to support the University of Iowa School of Religion.[387]

He or the University of Iowa could make a little money from his musical talent testing in other ways as well. For example, Seashore charged a registration fee for musical talent consultation services provided by the University of Iowa; he stated that the services themselves were free to citizens of the state and claimed that the registration fee would have been ten times higher if the services had not been provided by a public institution.[388] Third, he unapologetically promoted his newly published book and the Seashore Tests at the 1919 St. Louis convention of music educators.[389] He stood to gain financially from such self-promotion.

Music for Every Child?
A Slogan, a Philosophy, and Seashore's Critics

Having discussed Seashore's general reception and impact in chapter 3, I want to revisit these topics, focusing narrowly on the reception of his ideas about musical ability and of his standardized musical talent tests. As I indicated earlier, Seashore had critics; in particular, he received a mixed reception from music educators, and in some cases, he faced outright resistance. For example, I have already mentioned that at least one music educator openly challenged him at the 1919 convention in St. Louis; in addition, Seashore opened his address by stating that an attendee had asked him why he had not made the tests musical, and he countered that it had never been his goal to make them musical, merely psychological.[390] In his biography, he admitted that he was the "butt of criticism from the musical profession," but added that he had learned from his scientific career "never to stop and count noses."[391] He then described himself as being "utterly callous to criticism based upon lack of knowledge."[392] He typically dismissed critics by claiming that they were uninformed and flat-out wrong. A close look at a claim he made about his influence on music education may indicate that he received at least some pushback from leadership in the Music Supervisors' National Conference. The claim is Seashore's assertion that he played a role in the evolution of what Lauren Heidingsfelder calls music education's "slogan of the century":

"Music for Every Child; Every Child for Music."[393] Heidingsfelder is among the scholars who attribute the slogan to Karl Gehrkens, a professor at the Oberlin Conservatory of Music; she states that Gehrkens coined the slogan for the presidential address he delivered at the 1923 meeting of the Music Supervisors' National Conference in Cleveland.[394] She also quotes Gehrkens's claim that the slogan was the theme of the entire 1923 conference,[395] and she accurately states that in 1933 Gehrkens penned an article with the slogan as its title.[396] The 1933 article by Gehrkens is prefaced with a note saying that he devised the slogan shortly after he was elected president in 1922.[397] In the body of the article, Gehrkens said the 1923 conference program was developed based on ideas he expressed in his presidential speech that were consistent with the slogan.[398] Elsewhere, he was more cautious, however, not claiming "credit for the idea behind 'Music for Every Child,'" and saying instead that the concept came from a founder of public school music in the United States, Lowell Mason (1792–1872).[399]

It may be true that Gehrkens shaped the slogan into its most famous and enduring form, and it is clear that he embraced both the slogan and the philosophy it represented. However, he did not use the slogan in his 1923 presidential address, "Some Questions," as published in the conference proceedings, although he spoke positively about what he called a new trend: educating all students in all subjects.[400] Furthermore, although "Music for Every Child; Every Child for Music" may indeed have been the basis of the 1923 convention, advanced advertising for the conference appearing in the *Music Supervisors' Journal* did not mention the slogan, nor did the official program as it appeared in the proceedings.[401] Regardless, by 1924, the slogan was quoted verbatim in discussions of that year's national convention held in Cincinnati, one source reporting, for example, that the 1924 conference contributed to the goal of music for every child, and every child for music.[402]

All that said, portions and versions of the slogan had been floating around for quite some time prior to 1923, and Seashore laid claim to one of the earlier versions. In describing his impact on music education thought and practice, he proudly stated that he had precipitated an early change not only in the philosophy but in the official slogan of the Music Supervisors' National Conference. In 1942, he described his presentation at the 1919 national convention:

> On the whole, the afternoon was a success. Up to that time the association had carried as a legend on its stationery, "Music for every child in the United States at public expense." But, as a result of the showing that afternoon, the executive committee changed it for some time to,

> "Music for every child *in proportion to his capacity* at public expense." Before that music teachers had been fighting for a recognition of music among the three R's in the public schools and were *shockingly ignorant of individual differences* and their significance in musical education, vigorously militant for what they called "democracy." That session in St. Louis was perhaps the first organized awakening of music teachers to a recognition of the significance of individual differences in musical talent. Since that day great progress has been made in this respect [emphasis mine].[403]

In the above passage, Seashore unapologetically took credit for helping to thwart a growing movement to add music to the list of core subjects taught in US public schools, subjects accessible to all and perhaps even required of all. In another description of his influence on this national organization of music educators, he stated that music teachers changed their slogan after "realizing the futility of making every child musical."[404]

Proceedings from the 1919 conference confirm that Seashore told the audience, "Every child should have music as an avocation in so far as he is musical by nature," the proceedings reporting that the statement was greeted with applause.[405] A series of brief snapshots of the conference published in the *Music Supervisors' Journal* included that particular quote and similarly reported that it was applauded.[406]

Elsewhere, Seashore did not hide the fact that he opposed universal music education. For example, in 1916 he described the money being wasted on music lessons for the innately talentless as an economic problem and stated, "We are in the midst of a campaign to universalize musical education. This campaign, be it based on educational theory, social fad or fancy, or the mere performance of the newly-rich [*sic*], forces music upon larger and larger numbers of those who are unfit, and at the same time makes us unconscious of the neglect of the gifted."[407] In other words, Seashore argued that universal music education runs contrary to the desired goals of promoting the fittest and eliminating the unfit—of what he called the process of "selective admission and elimination."[408] These are fundamentally eugenical goals and processes.

Conference proceedings and conference snapshots published in the *Music Supervisors' Journal* reveal some of the points on which other speakers agreed or disagreed with Seashore. For example, Osbourne McConathy, a professor at Northwestern University and president of the Music Supervisors' National Conference, addressed the conference shortly before Seashore demonstrated the tests and spoke; McConathy summarized his own philosophy in words that closely resembled those that Seashore would utter later in the day: "Every child should be educated in music according to his natural capacities, at public expense, and his studies should function in the musical life of the community."[409] He spoke positively of Seashore's research and of the discovery and measurement of musical talent; he supported the classification of students into three categories according to musical ability: musical, average, and unmusical.[410] He, too, called for differentiated educational opportunities based on ability classification, and he supported providing this education at public expense.[411] He parted from Seashore on one count, however: in McConathy's plan, no child would be excluded from music instruction.[412] He further claimed that a segment of the 1919 conference would focus on developing educational opportunities for students in the first and third of his categories, that is, the most musical and those lacking talent.[413] Music appreciation, he stated, is to be for all three categories of students, and he specifically supported creating more music appreciation curricular offerings for the unmusical.[414] The excerpts from McConathy's talk published in the *Music Supervisors' Journal* included his "Every child" quote and his calls for differentiated music education. Significantly, however, they did not include his message that no students should be excluded.[415]

Perhaps the speaker to express views most different from Seashore's was W. Otto Miessner, the director of the Music Department at the State Normal School in Milwaukee (known today as the University of Wisconsin–Milwaukee). According to the conference program, two days after Seashore's and McConathy's speeches, Miessner was scheduled to lead singing followed by an address entitled "Opportunities Which the School Should Offer the Child of Exception [*sic*] Musical Talent"; I do not know whether he led singing, but the speech he actually delivered was entitled "Music Democratized."[416] Miessner presented views contrary to Seashore's, saying that music should be as universal as the three Rs.[417] Marching under the banner of democracy, he further claimed that there is no such thing as an unmusical child[418] and that the presumably unmusical child can become musical.[419] Third, unlike Seashore, he called for equal musical advantages for all. Conceptualizing access as being governed by ability to pay, he said that the advantages should be available regardless of whether people are rich or poor.[420] Despite these views, he, too, tipped his hat to Seashore, acknowledging that the Seashore Tests may help teachers meet the needs of each child.[421] The *Music Supervisors' Journal* summary of his talk emphasized, among other things, democracy and making music education available to all.[422]

Miessner may have planned to deliver the "Music Democratized" speech all along; it is also possible that he modified his remarks in light of what he had heard earlier at the conference from Seashore and McConathy. However, even Miessner's vision of democratic universal music education did not challenge the belief that there are hierarchies of people to whom a hierarchy of educational opportunities should be available; he, too, imagined educational opportunities in music that were tracked and ability based. He identified four hierarchical classes of students, and musical geniuses who have "demonstrated musical talent" populated the class at the top.[423] His next class included the child with a strong liking for music, who would become the future amateur; the third class was for "the future layman" who shows only a passive interest in music; and the fourth class was composed of students who show no interest in music.[424] Significantly, what set members of the top class apart from the others was the presence of *talent*; what differentiated members of the three lowest classes was level of *interest*. He also supported differentiated music instruction for individuals and groups, including different kinds of musical opportunities for different classes of students, ranging from specialized training for members of the top class, down to activities for students in the lowest class that would transform them from being unmusical people into individuals interested in music.[425] In addition to references to democracy, the excerpts of Miessner's speech published in the *Music Supervisors' Journal* included his claims that students should be divided into four classes, that educators have overlooked the individual child, and that instruction should be individually differentiated.[426]

Miessner, like Seashore, was not immune to the allure of the money and fame to be had from selling music products to schools, however. In addition to holding a post at the State Normal School in Milwaukee, he was head of the Milwaukee-based Miessner Piano Company, which sold instruments to schools and advertised in the *Music Supervisors' Journal*.[427]

An examination of slogans appearing on the cover of the *Music Supervisors' Journal* during this period confirms that Seashore was accurate in stating that the Music Supervisors' National Conference adopted his recommended modification to their slogan, at least temporarily. The March 1919 cover of the *Music Supervisors' Journal* included the following quotation: "Every child should be educated in music in accordance with his natural capacities, at public expense, and his musical development should function in the life of the community."[428] This wording is almost identical to what Osbourne McConathy would say shortly thereafter at the 1919 national conference; significantly, it contains Seashore's recommended capacities caveat. Quotes first appeared on the journal's cover in September 1918, and the three issues featuring slogans prior to March 1919 included two quotes about war; one of them was from President Woodrow Wilson and the other was "A singing army is a fighting army."[429] The war quotations were eliminated shortly after the end of World War I and immediately replaced by the McConathy quote. The executive committee may have officially changed the slogan in response to Seashore's talk, but unless the journal came out late, Seashore must have spoken to the organization's leadership *prior* to the convention—to MSNC president McConathy or journal editor Peter Dykema, from the University of Wisconsin at Madison—because the March 1919 publication date was *before* the convention had been held. However, the slogan only appeared on *one* issue of the journal, and it was replaced in the next issue by, "Publicly supported, socially functioning, adequate musical training for all children."[430] Significantly, *Seashore's capacities caveat had disappeared.* The new version of the slogan appeared on the journal's cover for several years, then for a period quotes disappeared altogether from the front cover, and finally, in May 1924, the final iteration of the slogan—"Music for Every Child; Every Child for Music"—appeared on the cover for the first time.[431]

Thus, changes in the slogans appearing on the journal covers, the organization's final iteration of the slogan—"Music for Every Child; Every Child for Music," and the decision to make the final slogan the philosophical basis of the 1923 convention may indicate that at least some powerful figures associated with the organization disagreed with at least parts of Seashore's philosophy, and with some of his proposed pedagogical practices. It is also important to remember, however, that even the most inclusive of the organization's several iterations of the slogan did not necessarily translate into having equally high expectations of all students or equally rich and challenging musical opportunities for all.

To this day, residuals persist and resemblances exist between the Seashore Way and discourse and practice in music education. In the United States, music is not a compulsory subject in most schools, at least not at the secondary level. Furthermore, hierarchies in the music curriculum persist, with ability-based hierarchical performing ensembles anchoring most secondary school music programs. A divide has remained between these highly valued performing groups designed for those who are perceived to have musical ability and other, less-valued curricular offerings for those perceived to be less musically able—if other courses are offered at all. Finally, the commitment to educate those perceived to have little musical talent arguably continues to be weak compared to interest in educating those perceived to have more. Although exclusionary music discourses and practices were not unique to eugenicists, eugenicists promoted them; in Seashore's case, they were promoted by a eugenicist using the philosophy and even the language of eugenics.

Impact Redux: Seashore, Musical Ability, and Talent Testing

Seashore wanted to effect change. He spoke at music education conferences and published in music education journals in an attempt to get the word out—to reform music teachers' ideas and transform their pedagogical practices. He unquestionably shaped music educators' discourse and practice, and his reach within the field was wide. An event such as the 1919 convention of the Music Supervisors' National Conference created multiple opportunities for all of the speakers I have just discussed to reach a large audience. Music educators who did not attend could read the proceedings or at least peruse the brief summaries that appeared in the *Music Supervisors' Journal*. Furthermore, public school music educators constituted only one of the many music-related audiences that Seashore approached with his message about musical talent and talent testing. He reached not only members of the Music Supervisors' National Conference but also those who belonged to the much older Music Teachers' National Association (MTNA); unlike the MSNC, which was designed primarily for public school music teachers, MTNA was composed of a wide range of music pedagogues, including independent studio music teachers. Through journals such as *Etude* and the *Musical Quarterly*, he reached yet other audiences; *Etude* was designed for all musicians, not just teachers, and the *Musical Quarterly* was the first scholarly music journal in the United States. The combined readership of these journals included professional performers, music scholars, composers, and devoted dilettantes, in addition to public school music teachers and private studio pedagogues. Furthermore, he spread his ideas about musical talent and promoted talent testing in venues outside of music and music education, including journals from the fields of psychology, educational psychology, and applied psychology. Significantly, as I documented in a previous chapter, his music-related work also was published, discussed, and promoted by eugenicists in eugenics journals and elsewhere. By his own admission, virtually all of his research on musical ability and all of his proposed music education reforms were consistent with eugenics.

Although at least some music educators may already have been under the sway of "science" and particularly of psychology, Seashore helped nudge teachers and the field as a whole in that direction—the national conferences morphing into an odd mixture of sing-alongs, visits to schools, performances by school groups, and addresses by research experts in psychology. Moreover, he was among those who helped pull a fledgling activity—conducting music education research—in particular directions, toward perceptual studies and psychometrics. Movement in these directions came at the expense of other possible scholarly activities in music education, however.

Typically, the question among music education researchers was not whether to test for musical talent, but which test series was best. For example, in an article appearing in *Teachers College Record* in 1932, Mary Whitley compared the Seashore Tests to a new series, published in 1930, created by Jacob Kwalwasser (1894–1977) and Peter Dykema (1873–1951).[432] Seashore was Kwalwasser's doctoral advisor at the University of Iowa,[433] and Kwalwasser's accomplishments included serving as head of the music education department at the University of Iowa and, later, as a professor and head of music education at Syracuse University. In his book *The Social Psychology of Music*, Paul Farnsworth called Kwalwasser a "staunch hereditarian."[434] Peter W. Dykema, in addition to serving as the first editor of the *Music Supervisors' Journal* (originally called the *Music Supervisors' Bulletin*), was a professor at the University of Wisconsin at Madison, and later at Columbia University. The Kwalwasser-Dykema tests, which were published in 1930, had been preceded by the Kwalwasser-Ruch Test of Musical Accomplishment, published in 1924. Although these competitors existed, the Seashore Tests reigned supreme, Whitley reporting somewhat inaccurately in 1932 that Seashore had been the sole player in the musical talent testing game for quite some time: "Until recently the six Seashore music tests have had an uncontested field. They were the only ones available for the educator who wished to apply a standardized group test for music capacity, or musicality."[435] Whitley put both test series—Seashore's and the Kwalwasser-Dykema—to the test, and after describing the strengths and weaknesses of each, she called for new tests that would combine the best features of both.[436]

Significantly, even one of Seashore's harshest critics, James Mursell, valued music psychometrics. He opened his 1937 article "What about Music Tests?" by stating that although reputable psychologists had criticized musical talent tests, most people were unaware of this critique. The public at large and music educators in particular were being bamboozled, he argued—"treated to a barrage of claims of the brashest and most misleading kind."[437] He stated that tests should measure what they purport to measure and warned that some test titles are as worthless as the "label on a quart bottle of Doc Whoosis's Herbal Remedy, guaranteed to cure rheumatism, paresis, lumbago, and cancer."[438] He discussed two tests—Seashore's and the Kwalwasser-Dykema—and slammed both. He said that evidence of the validity of the Seashore Tests was lacking, that Stanton's work at the Eastman School did not validate them, and that there was little relationship between test scores and musical competence.[439] Referring to the Seashore Tests, he added, "It seems incredible to me that an instrument with such a flimsy underpinning could be seriously considered as an adequate agency for significant research and guidance."[440] Despite all this, however, he made it clear that his quarrel was with extant tests, not with musical talent testing per se: "I understand that in certain quarters I am regarded as 'hostile' to music tests. This is not true. On the contrary I would enthusiastically welcome a *good* music test. It would be a research instrument which we sorely need, and also an invaluable agency for educational guidance. But I am not convinced that any such exist, although I believe that they could be developed."[441] Thus, for music education researchers, the problem was not with the idea of mousetraps but with extant mousetraps, and even one of Seashore's harshest critics called for the building of better ones.

Concluding Thoughts

As I have demonstrated throughout this chapter, Seashore's statements about musical talent and music education reform are virtually identical to what he said about intelligence and education reform writ large. Among the commonalities are the processes by which they make up "kinds of people," construct educational opportunities and pedagogical practices that assume the existence of kinds of people, and create very different destinies for different individuals and groups. In effect, the discourses that Seashore promulgated systematically built a hierarchical constellation of destinies, each destiny appearing to be largely foreordained, immutable, and inevitable.

The parallel contours I have described in this chapter and the previous one are not coincidental. Furthermore, they demonstrate that his statements about musical ability and music education reform were as informed by and infused with eugenics as his statements about general ability and education reform. Eugenicists believed it was their duty to shape public thought, policy, and practice; Seashore saw one of his jobs as shaping public thought, policy, and practice in education *and* music education. His education reform projects in both arenas are eminently eugenical in logic and form, right down to a focus on the tails of the "normal curve." Through his work in these domains, he actively advanced eugenics, and, reciprocally, he and his work were actively supported by eugenicists. He lived largely, but not exclusively, in the realm of positive eugenics, but that realm did not extend sunny, optimistic, positivity to all.

When considering Seashore's "novel" approaches to education and music education, it is important to remember that eugenics passed the sniff test; it had to be "thinkable" and sufficiently familiar not to be rejected as outrageous. In light of this, as I reflected on his statements and actions, I was reminded of Zygmunt Bauman's critical analysis of modernity. I see striking similarities between Seashore's ideas about how things should be done and the list Bauman provided of how things—including the Holocaust—are and have been done in modern civilizations; modern actions, he claimed, are "rational, planned, scientifically informed, expert, efficiently managed, [and] co-ordinated."[442] His critique of modernity's bureaucratic culture, specifically of its view that society should be an object of administration and a garden to be tended, easily could have been written about Seashore's statements on ability and school reform—or about eugenics, which played a major role in providing a rationale for the Holocaust.[443]

Thus, Bauman argued that the Holocaust should be regarded as a "horrifying, yet legitimate product" of modernity,[444] and I maintain that Seashore's statements and actions concerning education, as well as eugenical thought and action more globally, may be viewed as similarly troubling products. For example, as microcosms of society, schools are among the gardens where cultured plants are to be nurtured and weeds culled out. Obviously, the effects of Seashore's proposed reforms were not as catastrophic as the effects of the Holocaust, but both "reform" agendas are linked to each other by eugenics. Viewing Seashore's educational beliefs and practices in this way identifies a problem that is much larger than his impact or even the impact of the eugenics movement. It is a problem that did not disappear when Seashore and the eugenics organizations to which he belonged died.

Finally, Seashore's leadership role was somewhat different in education reform overall than it was in music education reform. Although he was an early investor in such projects as standardized intelligence testing, standardized college admissions tests, sectioning by ability, the establishment of junior colleges, and the creation of gifted and talented programs, he was not the first person to suggest them. That does not mean, however, that he was not a leader. Rather, he was what Derek Sivers calls a "first follower," and according to Sivers, first followers play a critical leadership role in creating movements. He states that first followers are essential to a movement because without them, there is no movement—only a "lone nut" leader.[445] Especially given the many powerful platforms to which Seashore had access, his leadership contributions as a first follower in early-twentieth-century education reform should not be underestimated. What is different about his leadership position in music and music education, however, is that he *was* the "lone nut" leader, the Pied Piper. Although Carl Stumpf had developed the first tests of musical talent, and individuals such as James McKeen Cattell, Livingston Farrand, and Clark Wissler had made forays into tests of auditory perception and discrimination, Seashore was the first person in the world to develop a *standardized* test of musical talent, and together with his first followers, he created a movement.[446] What the followers who continue in the tradition of Seashore today may not realize, however, is that the Pied Piper was a eugenicist whose movement was grounded in eugenics. This reality should give those of us in music education or music psychology pause.

Seven

In Defense of Whiteness

Music, Musical Ability, and Racism

Departing from his pattern of largely remaining silent about race, Carl Seashore talked about it from time to time in his writings on music, culture, and musical ability. He conducted and supported research on musical styles and performance practices associated with racial groups other than Whites, championed the recording and preservation of this music, and was interested in whether races exhibited significant innate differences in musical talent. In the 1920s and '30s, the Seashore Tests were the instrument of choice for studying race differences in musical talent. In at least three publications appearing late in his life (between 1938 and 1942), he reported that this research revealed little or no difference between racial groups.[1] This claim echoed statements made by other scholars, including Thomas Garth in his 1931 book *Race Psychology: A Study of Racial Mental Differences*.[2]

On the surface, Seashore's no-race-differences conclusion appears to be an equal-opportunity claim that confirms the fundamental equality of all people; it could mean, for example, that if musical talent, including genius, is biologically inheritable, then all races are capable of producing geniuses. Some scholars of the day used his no-race-differences conclusion to challenge hereditarian race-deficit theses. For example, a 1933 review of Garth's book appearing in the *Journal of Negro Education* reported that research using the Seashore Tests had found no race differences in musical talent.[3] Pointing out that race differences had appeared only in results of *intelligence* tests, the reviewer stated that Garth had challenged the "organic heredity" explanation of race differences in standardized test scores.[4] If Seashore's statement was intended to support universal human equality, however, it departed significantly from dominant discourse among eugenicists. In particular, it stood in stark contrast to grim assertions about innate race differences in *intelligence*, which had been bolstered by studies that used standardized intelligence tests.

Subsequent scholarship on Seashore appears to have interpreted his no-race-differences assertion as a sign of his egalitarianism. For example, Ruth Zinar's laudatory 1984 article on Seashore's contributions to music education described his position on race and musical ability in equal-opportunity language, reporting that he viewed musical talent as "an inherent ability, unrelated to age, intelligence, training, culture, or racial origin."[5] Placing the no-race-differences claim in the context of his other statements on race, culture, and music creates a more complicated picture, however, and has led me to introduce a different possible interpretation.

In the first section of this chapter, I offer glimpses of dominant discourse among early-twentieth-century eugenicists concerning race and race differences. These snapshots provide context for Seashore's work and for studies of race differences in musical talent. I examine prevalent eugenical views on the existence of race differences, the relationship between evolution and a hierarchy of races, the effects of race crossing, and connections between cultural progress and a race hierarchy. Next, I examine the infiltration of these ideas into racialized discussions of music, musical genres, aesthetics, and taste, focusing in particular on Seashore's statements. I end this section by examining his statements about people whom he considered to be fascinating, exotic, and primitive "others." I focus on two kinds of projects: his phonophotographic studies and his proposed collaboration with the motion picture industry to create ostensibly scientifically accurate representations of what he called primitive people and primitive music.

In the second part of the chapter, I review research from the 1920s and 1930s that attempted to determine if there are biologically innate race differences in musical talent. I begin with an in-depth examination of the research of Charles Davenport and Morris Steggerda as reported in their book *Race Crossing in Jamaica*. Next, I examine every study that Seashore cited in support of his no-race-differences claim, and I review contemporaneous research that he did not mention. The results of these studies indicate that his no-race-differences conclusion was not accurate.

In the final section of the chapter, I look at Seashore's no-race-differences-in-musical-talent conclusion and discuss possible reasons why he made this claim despite evidence to the contrary—data that researchers had gathered using the Seashore Tests. These were flimsy tests—of questionable validity and reliability—but Seashore believed that they were purveyors of truth; in the case of the race-differences-in-musical-talent research, however, he apparently turned a blind eye to the results they produced. Why? I maintain that Seashore's conclusion is not an indication that he was a race egalitarian. Rather, I argue that his assertion constituted damage control—he may have made it to protect the reputation of the Seashore Tests. More importantly, however, he may have made it because it was the best defense of whiteness that a White supremacist could mount under the circumstances.

Snapshots of Eugenicists' Understandings of Race

Eugenicists on Race Differences

Seashore's relative silence on the topic of race was unusual for a eugenicist. Evidence from eugenics publications of the day documents that eugenicists assumed races were biological realities and that eugenicists displayed both an intense interest in race and deep racism. Although space does not permit me to review even a fraction of the extant scholarship on eugenics and race, I look briefly at two assertions regularly made by eugenicists that are foundational to my argument about Seashore. The first is that there are biologically inherent physical, mental, and moral race differences; the second is that racial *hierarchies* exist that are based on these inherent differences. These assertions long predated the early twentieth century, and they circulated inside and outside of eugenics organizations and discourses. For example, according to Allan Chase, in the mid-nineteenth century, Joseph Arthur de Gobineau's claim that there are inherent differences in races was taken up by White supremacists, used to support enslavement in the United States, and cited to justify British imperialism in Asia and Africa.[6] More than fifty years later, the same claim sat at the core of race research conducted by eugenicists, and it was littered through eugenics publications.[7] Henry Fairfield Osborn discussed the existence of race differences and the distinctive characteristics of various races in his welcoming address to the Second International Congress of Eugenics; he asserted, for example, that "education and environment do not fundamentally alter racial values."[8] In the preface to Madison Grant's 1916 book *The Passing of the Great Race, or The Racial Basis of European History*, Osborn claimed that "highly distinctive racial traits date back many thousands of years."[9] According to "The Great Nordic Race," a favorable review of *The Passing of the Great Race*, one of Grant's major contributions was his conclusion that behavior is largely determined by the distinctive characteristics of various races.[10] In 1920, *Eugenical News* published a similarly favorable review of Lothrop

Stoddard's *The Rising Tide of Color against White World-Supremacy*; entitled "The Color-Races," it warned that "America can no longer remain blind to the existence of racial differences."[11]

Francis Galton had drawn on the idea of innate race differences, especially on what eugenicists called mental and moral differences.[12] In his 1865 essay "Hereditary Talent and Character," he first described inherited *individual* differences in physical features and temperament and then launched into a commentary on *race* differences:

> Still more strongly marked than these [inherited individual differences], are the typical features and characters of different races of men. The Mongolians, Jews, Negroes, Gipsies, and American Indians; severally propagate their kinds; and each kind differs in character and intellect, as well as in colour and shape, from the other four. They, and a vast number of other races, form a class of instances worthy of close investigation, in which peculiarities of character are invariably transmitted from the parents to the offspring.[13]

He stated, for example, that American Indians are "naturally cold, melancholic, patient, and taciturn," while the West African "Negro" is "warm-hearted, loving towards his master's children, and idolised by the children in return"; according to Galton, the "Negro" also is impulsive; gregarious; "always jabbering, quarrelling, tom-tom-ing, or dancing"; passionate; and has "neither patience, reticence, nor dignity."[14] Other eugenicists, including Charles Davenport, followed in Galton's steps by ascribing distinguishing characteristics to various races.[15]

The importance of preserving the ostensibly distinctive characteristics of each race was a common trope in eugenics texts. For instance, Harry Laughlin called for each race to "strive for its own development" and for the conservation of its best characteristics—its "best race values": "The world has need for many races and many cultures, each of which, besides having a cosmopolitan interest, should possess and treasure its own hereditary endowment and special culture."[16] The article "Race-matters," which appeared in *Eugenical News* in 1934, called for policies to help each race or nation achieve its biological ideals; each race or "human group," it stated, should "strive to eliminate its own degenerate strains, and to breed most abundantly from those stocks which most nearly approach its own race-ideals."[17] Despite calls such as Laughlin's for the preservation of the best traits of each race, eugenicists clearly tended to believe that some races had far fewer beneficial hereditary endowments than others did. Seashore doubtless was acquainted with these discourses: he attended the eugenics congress where Osborn gave his address.

Eugenicists on Evolution and a Hierarchy of Races

Consistent with thought dating back at least to the eighteenth century as demonstrated in Charles White's 1799 essay on the gradations of man, early-twentieth-century American eugenicists claimed not merely that races existed and exhibited different physical and mental characteristics, but that various races, and the people comprising them, occupied different "natural" positions on a human hierarchy.[18] The concept of racial hierarchy predated Charles Darwin, but eugenicists pointed to evolution and natural selection to explain the hierarchy's existence; they claimed that some races are more evolved than others, and they referred to higher and lower as well as to superior and inferior races.[19] Galton himself spoke of lower races, but some of his contemporaries who did not identify with eugenics did as well; one of them was Alfred Russel Wallace, who developed his own theory of evolution contemporaneously to Darwin.[20]

Eugenicists layered a "civilized" versus "primitive" dichotomy over the racial hierarchy, sometimes referring to people of particular races as "savage" or "barbaric" as well as primitive.[21] Galton referred to savages and barbarism, and Wallace used the civilized/savage dichotomy as well, placing savages one rung above animals on the human hierarchy.[22] Fear of race suicide, a central driver of eugenics, was premised on the assumption that a hierarchy of races exists.

White people sat at the top of eugenicists' racial hierarchy, with Nordics or Aryans at the top of the top. In his discussion of racism among eugenicists, Edwin Black describes gradations *within* the White race:

> The racism of America's first eugenic intellectuals was more than just a movement of whites against nonwhites. They believed that Germans and Nordics comprised the supreme race, and a typical lament among eugenic leaders such as Lothrop Stoddard was that Nordic populations were decreasing. In *The Rising Tide of Color Against White World-Supremacy*, Stoddard wrote that the Industrial Revolution had attracted squalid Mediterranean peoples who quickly outnumbered the more desirable Nordics.[23]

Echoing a taxonomy established by William Z. Ripley in his 1899 book *The Races of Europe*, in *The Passing of the Great Race*, Grant drew distinctions among Whites and described three White European races: Nordic, Mediterranean, and Alpine.[24] He also defined the ideal human: "In general the Nordic race in its purity has an absolutely fair skin, and is consequently the *Homo albus*, the white man par excellence."[25] In a point-counterpoint article appearing in *Eugenics* in 1929, John M. Cooper admitted, "That [in America] the organized eugenics movement has been and is still steeped in the doctrine of superior races, particularly in the doctrine of superior Nordics, few would bother to deny."[26] Paul Popenoe and Roswell Johnson described Native Whites of Native Parentage as the racial group "probably of greater eugenic worth";[27] relying on Galton's criterion of eminence, they also praised "old American stock" (and they clearly were not talking about American Indians) for making exceptional contributions:

> The old American stock has produced a vastly greater proportion of eminence, has accomplished a great deal more proportionately, in modern times, than has other any [*sic*] stock whose representatives have been coming in large numbers as immigrants to these shores during the last generation. . . . We feel justified in concluding that the decline of the birth-rate in the old American stock represents a decline in the birth-rate of a superior element.[28]

As with other racial precepts fundamental to eugenics, the idea of White supremacy with the White race further subdivided into hierarchical subraces predated the early twentieth century, Chase reporting that Gobineau believed "Teutons were the most superior of all the master Aryan racial strains."[29] Although people identified as White-but-Mediterranean were not at the top of eugenicists' racial hierarchy, they were quite a distance from the bottom. Rather, people identified as "Negroes"—whether living in the United States or elsewhere—were placed in or near that bottom space, as were, in some cases, American Indians. Popenoe and Johnson discussed the low position of "the Negro" on the racial hierarchy:

> No matter how much one may admire some of the Negro's individual traits, one must admit that his development of group traits is primitive, and suggests a mental development which is also primitive. . . . The following historical considerations suggest that in comparison with

some other races the Negro race is germinally lacking in the higher developments of intelligence:

1. That the Negro race in Africa has never, by its own initiative, risen much above barbarism, although it has been exposed to a considerable range of environments and has had abundant time in which to bring to expression any inherited traits it may possess.
2. That when transplanted to a new environment—say, Haiti—and left to its own resources, the Negro race has shown the same inability to rise; it has there, indeed, lost most of what it had acquired from the superior civilization of the French.
3. That when placed side by side with the white race, the Negro race again fails to come up to their standard, or indeed to come anywhere near it.[30]

Invoking civilization and progress, they said that their conclusions were especially true when the "Negro" race was "tested by the requirements of modern civilization and progress, with particular reference to North America."[31]

After quoting at length from Popenoe and Johnson, Reginald G. Harris came to a similar conclusion in his 1922 *Eugenical News* article "Eugenics in South America."[32] Harris, who would later become a prominent figure in the eugenics world, was a lecturer at Brown University at the time, and he used data from South America to support the thesis that the inferiority of some races is a global phenomenon: "It has been seen that the several races, white, Negro, and Indian, were not all at the same degree of development; that the Negro and Indian races have been drastically acted upon by lethal factors of natural selection. From various kinds of evidence . . . it is concluded that both the Indian and Negro races, as represented in South America, are inferior to the white race."[33]

Eugenics sources repeatedly underscored the low position of "Negroes" on eugenicists' racial hierarchy. For example, Earnest Sevier Cox's *White America: The American Racial Problem as Seen in a Worldwide Perspective* was favorably reviewed in *Eugenical News* in 1924, and the review stated, "The worst thing that ever happened to the area of the present United States was the bringing of large numbers of the Negroes, nearly the lowest of races, to our shores."[34] Historian Barry Mehler reports that there was a complaint about the review, but he does not elaborate on the nature of the complaint.[35] The accusation that eugenics was racist tended not to come from eugenicists. That said, racist views were widespread among White people, and racism ran deep in the

United States outside of eugenics circles. Daniel Kevles notes that the racist, anti-Black attitudes of eugenicists such as Charles Davenport "conformed for the most part to the standard racism of the day."[36]

Popenoe and Johnson, among many other eugenicists, similarly described the people they identified as "Negro" in deficit terms, as lacking in positive qualities and abounding in negative ones. They reported that the deficit was most pronounced in "'higher' mental functions," and they cited age of entering high school, school grades, presence of retardation, and IQ scores to support their thesis of innate inferiority.[37] They claimed that there were also deficiencies in areas other than intelligence. "The Negro," they maintained, lacked competitiveness, foresight, wisdom, persistence, initiative, and organizational skills; they also said that "his sexual impulses are strongly developed and inhibitions lacking" and clearly viewed the latter "traits" as problematic.[38]

The middle section of the racial hierarchy was muddier. Davenport described the middle ground in his 1911 book *Heredity in Relation to Eugenics*; he stated that it is populated with "Hebrews" (Jews)—whom he placed below Swedes, Germans, and Bohemians but above Serbians and Greeks—and a variety of immigrant groups whom he identified by geographical location or nationality.[39] He placed Southeastern Europeans on a lower rung than other Europeans, and he even distinguished between Northern and Southern Italians, placing Southern Italians lower on the hierarchy; noting that they were "darker" than Northern Italians, he opined that they probably had more Greek and North African blood.[40] Where the Portuguese fell on his hierarchy similarly depended on their skin color—described as white or dark—and he spoke more favorably about lighter-skinned Portuguese people.[41] According to Davenport, the value of immigrants ultimately depended on whether they had good or bad blood, and he clearly associated bad blood with darker skin color.[42] Asians also occupied the middle ground—probably on the lower levels of the ladder. In 1892, Herbert Spencer had expressed opposition to Japanese and Chinese immigration, and *Eugenics* reprinted his views in 1930.[43]

As with their descriptions of "Negroes" and American Indians, eugenicists' statements about specific groups of immigrants were largely negative, deficiencies-focused, and race-based. Citing Edward Alsworth Ross, Popenoe and Johnson warned that unregulated immigration of people from specific races would result in an American population that was uglier, shorter, less moral, less intelligent, and more fertile.[44] New waves of immigration, they warned, had too many of "the 'three D's'—defectives, delinquents, and dependents."[45]

One claim eugenicists made about the races they placed low on the hierarchy was that they demonstrated arrested development. For example, in *The Passing of the Great Race*, Grant concluded that "Negro" people, as a "species," are incapable of improving: "Negroes have demonstrated throughout recorded time that they are a stationary species, and that they do not possess the potentiality of progress or initiative from within."[46] Lower races, eugenicists asserted, also displayed an early precocity that preceded developmental arrest. Galton was among the eugenicists who made this claim:

> Savages seem incapable of progress after the first few years of their life. The average children of all races are much on a par. Occasionally, those of the lower races are more precocious than the Anglo-Saxons; as a brute beast of a few weeks old is certainly more apt and forward than a child of the same age. But, as the years go by, the higher races continue to progress, while the lower ones gradually stop. They remain children in mind, with the passions of grown men.[47]

In *Race Crossing in Jamaica*, Charles Davenport and Morris Steggerda alluded to assumptions of early precocity and arrested development in their discussion of the mental capacities of "Brown" (or what they called mulatto) and Black children: "The fact that youthful Browns sometimes score higher than youthful Blacks or Whites suggests the conclusion that Brown children develop in some mental capacities precociously; and then fall behind in development. The brightness of 'negro' school children in the States has often been commented on."[48] Their comment about the brightness of "Negro" children contrasted with their dim assessment of the intelligence of adults in that racial category, however, and they used their precocity statement to support their arrested development claim.

Eugenicists invoked their claims about the lower status of some races to justify abrogating rights and limiting opportunities. For example, in the introduction to Lothrop Stoddard's book *The Rising Tide of Color against White World-Supremacy*, Grant argued that it was "amazing folly" for White people to entrust democratic ideals to people of all colors: "Democratic ideals among an homogeneous population of Nordic blood, as in England or America, is one thing, but it is quite another for the white man to share his blood with, or intrust [*sic*] his ideals to, brown, yellow, black, or red men. This is suicide pure and simple, and the first victim of this amazing folly will be the white man himself."[49] Stoddard's book was favorably reviewed in *Eugenical News*, the reviewer including the above quote from Grant.[50]

Eugenicists on Race Mixing

Eugenicists frequently expressed a fear of the loss of racial purity; Grant and many others had nothing positive to say about the offspring of people who crossed race lines to engage in what eugenicists variously called race mixing, race crossing, hybridization, crossbreeding, miscegenation, or mongrelization.[51] Race crossing, they warned, contributed to race suicide. In 1916, Grant detailed the perils of race mixing, stating that the dangers of a "mongrel race" were only beginning to be understood.[52] He complained that the deficiencies of the Polish Jew were "being engrafted upon the stock of the nation," and he spelled out these deficiencies: "dwarf stature, peculiar mentality, and ruthless concentration on self-interest."[53] Race mixing was dangerous because of the threat of reversion, he claimed, and explained that the characteristics of superior races are unstable and vulnerable, easily diluted or exterminated when superior and inferior races mix: "It must be borne in mind that the specializations which characterize the higher races are of relatively recent development, are highly unstable and when mixed with generalized or primitive characters, tend to disappear. Whether we like to admit it or not, the result of the mixture of two races, in the long run, gives us a race reverting to the more ancient, generalized and lower type."[54] In a comment that referenced not just one but three White European races, he asserted that due to reversion, the offspring of a member of any of these White European races and a Jew would be a Jew.[55]

Grant and others talked about race crossing in terms of blood, specifically, the degradation that resulted from the mixing of *pure* blood. For example, in his address to the Second International Congress of Eugenics in 1921, Osborn argued that the positive qualities of each race could only be perpetuated by keeping racial blood "pure"; the melting-pot theory, he claimed, held little promise:

> The 500,000 years of human evolution, under widely different environmental conditions, have impressed certain distinctive virtues as well as faults on each race. In the matter of racial virtues, my opinion is that from biological principles there is little promise in the "melting pot" theory. Put three races together, you are as likely to unite the vices of all three as the virtues. . . . For the world's work, give me a pure-blooded Negro, a pure-blooded Mongol, a pure-blooded Slav, a pure-blooded Nordic, and ascertain through observation and experiment what each race is best fitted to accomplish in the world's economy.[56]

Wilhelm Frick, a Nazi whose speech was published in *Eugenical News* in 1934, spoke of the threat to German blood of race mixing, the dire consequences of race mixing, and the need to maintain racial purity: "It is up to the educated youth to recognize the value of the German hereditary constitution, to preserve race-purity and to strive toward improvement of their own family-stocks by suitable matings. Miscegenation must be labelled what it is: namely, the foundation for mental and spiritual degeneration and alienation from the native stock."[57]

Popenoe and Johnson weighed in on race crossing in their summary of the history of the United States. Drawing distinctions as Grant did between three races of White Europeans, they stated that the earliest immigrants were Nordics who mated with each other and maintained "racial homogeneity."[58] They observed that recent White immigrants, by contrast, were more likely to have come from the Mediterranean or Alpine races; this shift, they stated, raised the specter of crossbreeding and its evil effects, which increased proportionally as the racial quality of the immigrant population declined:

> Even if these immigrants were superior on the average to the older population, it is clear that their assimilation would not be an unmixed blessing, for the evil of crossbreeding would partly offset the advantage of the addition of valuable new traits. If, on the other hand, the average of the new immigration is inferior in quality, or in so far as it is inferior in quality, it is evident that it must represent biologically an almost unmixed evil; it not only brings in new undesirable traits, but injures the desirable ones already here.[59]

They said that in cases of miscegenation between Whites and "Negroes," the White race loses and the "Negro" gains, but the gains are minimal; in the end, they argued, it is most beneficial to all if White purity is maintained: "If the level of the white race be lowered, it will hurt that race and be of little help to the Negro. If the white race be kept at such a level that its productivity of men of talent will be at a maximum, everyone will progress; for the Negro benefits just as the white does from every forward step in science and art, in industry and politics."[60]

Eugenicists claimed that one had only to look at locations around the globe where race crossing was prevalent to see its deleterious effects. For example, in "Eugenics in South America," Harris claimed that race crossing was impeding progress on that continent:

> Indeed anyone who is interested in rapid and permanent progress in South America, especially in those countries where crossing between the races already mentioned has been great, and where the hybrid class, or the inferior race, is greater in number than the white race, must often despair of the realization of his hope. Eugenically, the crossing of widely different human races, viz., Indians, Negroes, and whites, in South America has not been successful, and its continuance is undesirable.[61]

In a *Eugenics* article that appeared in 1931, Ernst Kretschmer painted a somewhat rosier picture of some types of race mixing. Race mixing between inbred and what he called "highly talented" races, he claimed, sometimes results in an "almost explosive production of a large number of geniuses."[62] He, noted, however, that even in instances with such favorable outcomes, mixing has its costs. He reported that the mixing of differences that occurs in hybridization produces instability and tension, which in turn create a predisposition toward pathology, specifically insanity: "Hybridization produces internal contrasts and conflicts, affect-tensions, highly strung and uncompensated passions and a spiritual lability; it consequently creates a predisposition to genius—but also to psychopathological complications. Thus, the research on hybridization becomes closely interwoven with old familiar questions, leading us back to the problem: 'Genius and Insanity.'"[63]

Osborn was among the eugenicists to claim that the state has the right "to safeguard the character and integrity of the race or races."[64] Popenoe and Johnson expressed a similar view. Arguing that it was in the best interest of the nation, they recommended strict antimiscegenation laws to support extant social taboos such that all sexual intercourse between Whites and "Negroes" would be illegal; they expressed particular concern about the actions of recent White immigrants, including Italians, whom they claimed lacked strong social taboos concerning intermarriage:

> 1. We hold that it is to the interests of the United States, for the reasons given in this chapter, to prevent further Negro-white amalgamation.
> 2. The taboo of public opinion is not sufficient in all cases to prevent intermarriage, and should be supplemented by law, particularly as the United States have of late years received many white immigrants from other countries (e.g., Italy) where the taboo is weak because the problem has never been pressing.

3. But to prevent intermarriage is only a small part of the solution, since most mulattoes come from extramarital miscegenation. The only solution of this, which is compatible with the requirements of eugenics, is not that of *laissez faire*, suggested by the National Association, but an extension of the taboo, and an extension of the laws, to prohibit all sexual intercourse between the two races.[65]

Popenoe and Johnson concluded their chapter with a weak call for the "Negro" race to be treated kindly, but also said that the welfare of the state was of ultimate importance, and that race crossing does not promote this welfare:

> We favor, therefore, the support of the taboo which society has placed on these mixed marriages, as well as any legal action which can practicably be taken to make miscegenation between white and black impossible. Justice requires that the Negro race be treated as kindly and considerately as possible, with every economic and political concession that is consistent with the continued welfare of the nation. Such social equality and intercourse as might lead to marriage are not compatible with this welfare.[66]

Scholars had discussed race mixture long before the eugenics movement gathered steam in the early twentieth century, and some of these discussions may have been laced with what would later be called fear of race suicide. For example, in his 1799 essay, Charles White published a table of race mixtures that gave the names "mulatto," "quadroon," "samboe," etc., to various degrees of mixture. A person who was deemed 1/2 Black and 1/2 White was called a mulatto; someone who was 7/8 Black and 1/8 White, or 7/8 White and 1/8 Black, was a quinteron; and a person who was 15/16 White was a White.[67] Later in the treatise, he discussed the potential long-term effects of race mixing, claiming that if there were indiscriminate mating of equal numbers of Whites and Blacks in a given population, within three centuries, less than 1 percent of the population would be White.[68]

About 100 years later, in his 1892 letter discussing the dangers of immigration from Asia—an excerpt of which was published in *Eugenics* in 1930—Herbert Spencer talked about human interbreeding and interracial marriage, both of which he strongly opposed: "It should be positively forbidden. . . . There is abundant proof, alike furnished by the intermarriages of human races and by the interbreeding of animals, that when the varieties mingled diverge beyond a certain slight degree *the result is inevitably a bad one* in the long run [emphasis in original]."[69] After stating that interbreeding widely disparate varieties of livestock produces inferior offspring, he continued:

> And the same thing happens among human beings—the Eurasians in India, the halfbreeds in America, show this. . . . By all means therefore, peremptorily interdict marriages of Japanese with foreigners.
>
> I have for the reasons indicated entirely approved of the regulations which have been established in America for restraining the Chinese immigration, and had I the power I would restrict them to the smallest possible amount, my reasons for this decision being that one of two things must happen. If the Chinese are allowed to settle extensively in America, they must either, if they remain unmixed, form a subject race standing in the position, if not of slaves, yet of a class approaching to slaves; or if they mix they must form a bad hybrid. In either case, supposing the immigration to be large, immense social mischief must arise, and eventually social disorganization. The same thing will happen if there should be any considerable mixture of European or American races with the Japanese.[70]

In Seashore's time, a host of White scholars who were not eugenicists opposed race crossing, including Katharine Murdoch. Murdoch, who conducted research of interest to eugenicists, reported that intelligence and morality test scores of mixed-race people were between what she called superior and inferior races but closer to the inferior race; in an article published in *School and Society* in 1925, she stated that her findings did not support race crossing: "On the whole, what light this research throws upon the results of race crossing are not encouraging, the crossed races being in every case more like the inferior than the superior race of the two from which they have sprung."[71]

Race scholar Edward B. Reuter, the University of Iowa sociology professor who wrote a complaint to Iowa president Virgil Hancher about Seashore's alleged poor treatment of Alvin Rose, was not a eugenicist and probably was one of the more progressive White intellectuals of his time.[72] Following his retirement from Iowa in 1944, he joined the faculty at historically Black Fisk University. Nevertheless, some of the same assumptions and "facts" concerning race crossing that eugenicists used to support their racist agenda also appeared in his article "The American Mulatto." Published in the *Annals of the American Academy of Political and Social Science* in 1928, the article described the past, present, and future status of the American mulatto, often by drawing comparisons between mulattoes and pure-blooded "Negroes." He observed that in the United States, there was a high percentage of mulattoes in upper social classes and professional occupations; by contrast most unmixed "Negroes" were in the lower social classes.[73] He stated that "Negro" men who have become famous in the United States have "in nearly all cases been of bi-racial ancestry"; to back this assertion, he listed names of famous men, described at length the superior qualities and activities of mulattoes, and reported that standardized test scores increased as White intermixture increased.[74] He rejected the assumption—which he described as commonsensical but unproven—that these phenomena were due to innate racial superiority of mulattoes over unmixed "Negroes," and he forwarded an alternative explanation: a plethora of cultural factors had advantaged mulattoes.[75] Delving into psychological realms, he stated that well-adjusted "normal" *mulattoes* were those who identified as "*Negroes*" and who accepted the status of "Negroes" in American culture; by contrast, he said, mulattoes became unadjusted when they refused to identify with "Negroes," viewed "Negroes" as inferior, and also were deemed not-White themselves by Whites.[76] Reuter claimed that because of race mixture, the "Negro" population was growing whiter—was becoming "contaminated"—and the White stock was growing darker. He reported that a small percentage of "octoroons" passed as White, the ability to pass increasing as the percentage of "Negro" blood decreased.[77] Perhaps to allay White anxiety, he added that passing was a rare occurrence, and thus, the amount of "Negro" blood introduced into the White race due to passing was negligible.[78] According to Reuter, a major factor affecting the physical characteristics of Americans was the influx of "mixed-blood and dark-skinned" immigrants from Southern and Eastern Europe, Mexico, and French-speaking provinces in Canada. Some of the new European immigrants, he claimed, had been "modified in the direction of the negroid type by a large but long-forgotten infusion of Negro blood."[79] He noted that the new immigrants contrasted sharply with "original white stock."[80] This influx of new and different immigrants, he claimed, "blurs the line of division between the Negro and the white and makes it easier for the light colored mulattoes to leave the race."[81] He predicted that this blurring would continue: "The mulattoes will presently displace the Negroes and ultimately the mulattoes, because of further bleaching and because of continued contamination of the lower orders of the whites, will merge with the general white population."[82] Reuter also predicted that mulattoes' superiority in "the world of color" would decline as "Negroes" as a group advanced. Stating that "Negroes" were advancing rapidly, he predicted that equalizing opportunity and reducing racial prejudice would hasten this advancement; one marker of advancement, he claimed, would be increased numbers of men of eminence.[83] He also said, however, that "Negroes'" *internalized* perception of their inferiority was a major obstacle to their advancement, and that advancement would proceed in proportion to "Negroes'" self-respect and confidence in their own ability.[84] According to Reuter, "external obstacles," although present, were removable and less significant barriers than "Negroes'" own sense of inferiority: "So long as the Negro remained psychologically inferior—so long as he accepted the mental status assigned him by the mulattoes and the whites—little advance was possible. As the Negroes overcome their sense of inferiority there will be a decline in the percentage of mulattoes in the leadership of the race."[85]

Compared to many other articles on race written by White intellectuals of the period, Reuter's seemed progressive. Space does not permit me to analyze in depth his complex and sometimes contradictory assertions, but I will address a few to underscore that regardless of whether they approved of race crossing, and regardless of whether they were eugenicists, many White intellectuals of the day based their race thinking on a number of stock assumptions. For example, although Reuter championed racial equality and did not appear to oppose race crossing or the new immigration patterns, he nevertheless accepted races and a racial hierarchy as givens. He even subdivided Whites to the degree that he referred to lower orders of Whites. When he discussed race mixtures, he shared terminology with eugenicists, referring to "mulatto," "octoroon," "stocks," "pure blood," and "hybrids." He assumed that race was a biological reality and described this reality in terms of blood; this assumption led him to state, for example, that pure blood can become "contaminated." Although Reuter clearly intended to support mulattoes, he placed them in juxtaposition with "pure-blood" "Negroes," whom he characterized as both different from and inferior to mulattoes; in effect if not in intent, he thereby reinforced the idea that White blood effected racial improvement in "Negroes." Like eugenicists, he talked about race crossing and immigration in the same breath. Furthermore, deficiency and inferiority figured heavily in his descriptions of "Negroes," despite the fact that he said that culture was to blame; significantly, he did not rule out the possibility that blood played a role. His statement that the "Negro masses" were rapidly advancing also signaled that they were not advanced, at least not according to a specific set of criteria. Galton's gold standard, eminence, was among Reuter's gold standards. Perhaps most astonishingly, he attributed lack of advancement to the actions or thoughts of the "Negro," placing far more blame on the internal psychological state of individual "Negroes" than on "external obstacles"; he dismissed the latter quite lightly. Finally, in a gesture that distinguished and distanced intellectuals from others, Reuter said that although racial inequality had been discredited in scholarship, it remained "firmly fixed" in American popular thought.[86] Somewhat ironically, he apparently did not see its presence in his own work.

For the most part, eugenicists tended to deflect or flat-out reject any suggestion that eugenics was about White supremacy or racism. For example, in his introduction to Grant's *The Passing of the Great Race*, Osborn denied that eugenics was about race pride or racial prejudice, declaring instead that it was about love of country.[87] In a *Eugenics* article appearing in 1929, Leon F. Whitney and John M. Cooper gave somewhat conflicting opinions about whether eugenics was racial snobbery. Cooper asked, "Is there any connection between eugenics and the doctrine of superior races?"[88] He answered his question by saying that there currently was but should not be; after admitting that the organized movement was "steeped in the doctrine of superior races," he stated that many American eugenicists were steering away from the movement for that very reason.[89] He asserted that "differences in racial level" are probable but had yet to be proven, and that to date, no research had confirmed the superiority of Nordics or any other group.[90] He called for eugenics to base its theories and agenda on facts.[91] Cooper's admission that the organized movement was steeped in White supremacy implicated Seashore, even though he was not named in the article. Not only was he a member of the official organizations at the time, he was serving on the Advisory Council.

Whitney, by contrast, opened by saying that eugenicists had been falsely accused of demonstrating racial superiority leanings. He explained that the accusations had stemmed from eugenicists lobbying Congress for immigration restrictions, and he said that rather than race, the issue was which immigrants would "tend to raise the quality of the national germ plasm."[92] Because test scores of Northern Europeans were higher than those of Southern Europeans, it was only natural, he argued, for eugenicists to favor immigration restrictions that would only "bring the best here."[93] He closed by saying that because eugenics was about improving the whole human race, and most particularly the American people, eugenicists would welcome any who would help achieve that goal, "*even* if they were Chinese [emphasis mine]."[94]

Seashore on Race

Having mapped out some general contours of dominant eugenical discourse on race in the United States in the early twentieth century, I turn next to

Seashore's references to race. Like other authors of the day, he used the term loosely, sometimes to refer to the whole human race and at other times to speak of "different" races. It is not always clear which meaning he had in mind in specific instances.[95] Thus, when late in his career he referred to "racial eugenics" and "racial euthenics," it is unclear whether the racial improvement he had in mind involved promoting or eliminating specific races.[96] Similarly, when he stated that "play preserves the racial inheritance," he presumably was referring to the whole human race, but again his meaning is unclear.[97] In other instances, he specifically spoke about "human races," which indicates not only that he believed in the existence of multiple races but that in any of the ambiguous cases, he may indeed have been referring to subgroups of humans.[98]

Although explicit references to race were scarce, Seashore's publications included evidence that he believed not only in levels of kinds of humans, but in a racial hierarchy. For example, he spoke of what he believed were ceilings on what specific culture groups or races could learn or accomplish, which led him to call for "environmental restriction" for some children: "One of the advantages of environmental restriction in development is that it makes it possible for the child to adjust himself to the restricted spheres of life which operate at his culture level or in his racial group."[99] This source also indicates that he was an evolutionist who subscribed to the notion of the survival of the fittest, Seashore referring to a necessary "radical process of selection" and culling that would prevent "chaotic and self-destructive conditions arising from attempted overdevelopment."[100] Elsewhere, in a sentence about human races, he referred to the existence of "various culture levels of civilized people," which suggests not only that he assumed that some people were uncivilized, but that a hierarchy of *civilized* people existed.[101] That he placed Nordics on a high rung of the racial hierarchy is evident in his statement that he (a White man born in Sweden) was lucky in the "place and race" of his birth.[102]

An evolutionist, he believed that some races were more evolved than others, and like other eugenicists, he overlaid his discussions of racial hierarchy with a primitive-versus-civilized dichotomy. He described a past primitive man who had emerged in an early stage of human evolution,[103] and he also referred to living individuals, races, and communities as primitive or civilized.[104] For example, he referenced primitive races and primitive man, past and present, when he opined:

> In all primitive races color names [that is, names given to wavelengths on the color spectrum] have arisen gradually. . . . Untutored people confuse color and brightness. Red is the color which first attracts the

> attention of primitive man. . . . The ability to use names of colors is gradually acquired by persistent education of the race. The common man of to-day has far to go in this respect.[105]

He also referred to living individuals and groups as savages, a term he equated with primitives.[106] For instance, he spoke of the "savage orgie dances" in Indian religious feasts.[107] In a discussion of musical talent, he described South Sea Islanders as primitive and stated that the distribution of talent among them was equal to that of "the families of the social register," a group he apparently believed was the antithesis of primitive.[108] He also described an American Indian woman's trading and business practices as primitive.[109] Elsewhere, he stated that the "racial life" of the American "Negro" and Indian are "not necessarily primitive"; from the context of the statement, however, he clearly saw them as falling somewhere below the top of the hierarchy.[110] Poor, urban immigrants living in settlement houses also apparently were on a lower rung of his hierarchy, Seashore claiming, for example, that it would be difficult for settlement workers to avoid becoming debased when surrounded by the evils of settlement houses; he apparently assumed that the "fallen and stricken" living in settlement houses were morally inferior to the settlement workers, and that the evil was contagious.[111] He described the potential for debasement: "Like the surgeon who looks upon a wound under control as a beautiful wound, this worker may feel that the slums constitute a most promising field for rich returns, and that to draw humanity from the depths of suffering and despair is a great privilege. Yet, in such a reaction the tinge [of debasement] may be traceable, for example, in the callousness of professional attitude."[112] Although he did not mention this, the workers in danger of moral infection presumably were middle-class White women who were not recent immigrants.

Seashore's descriptions of how past primitive man lived provide insights into the characteristics he ascribed to present *primitive* man, the man who was different from present *civilized* man. For example, in a discussion of the importance of play in the life of "cultured man," he stated that primitive man, like the child, was a "playing animal" who lived a simple, childlike existence, free from care, a sense of responsibility, and a felt need to advance; civilized man, by contrast, displayed other characteristics:

> Primitive man lived relatively free from thoughtful care; the child, though endowed with a keen imagination, is disposed to tread in the footsteps of his distant ancestors. Civilization has modified this ten-

> dency in two ways: it has established a sense of responsibility, a prudent forethought in the division of labor, and a sympathetic effort to make advancement. . . . While primitive man was essentially a playing animal, cultured man has vastly more play interests than had his remote ancestor.[113]

Stating that play has not disappeared from civilized life, that cultured man has *more* play interests than primitive man ever had, and that play is part of greatness and a strenuous life, he pointed out that President Theodore Roosevelt had used Africa and the courts of Europe as a "continuous, fascinating playground in which he played with all his heart."[114] Thus, although playing linked primitive man and civilized man, civilized man's *wider variety* of play interests separated the two groups. He also stated that red was the first color to which primitive man was attracted;[115] describing red as primal may be telling, given that in European-influenced cultures, red often is associated with emotion and passion. In "Cooperation with the Film Industries in the Study of Primitive Music," published in *Science* in 1942, he described present primitive communities as "conservative"—presumably meaning reticent about engaging with outsiders—but interested in "all forms of magic."[116] He called on researchers to capitalize on this primitive interest in order to gather accurate data on the "true life of the people"; he said that gadgets such as cameras could stir this interest.[117] Thus, in Seashore's estimation, characteristics such as a preference for passionate colors and a fascination with magic helped distinguish primitive man from his opposite, civilized man.

Seashore was not the only music education researcher to refer to a racialized primitive-versus-civilized dichotomy, or to ascribe different characteristics to different racial groups. Furthermore, eugenicists were not the only people using these constructs. For example, Thomas Garth and Sarah Isbell invoked the primitive/civilized dichotomy in their research on the musical talent of American Indians, and in a statement perhaps illustrative of the concept of "noble savage," they described the American Indian as "that perennial romancer, always . . . an object of interest to the white man."[118]

Measuring Race Differences

Perhaps in response to Galton's 1865 suggestion that the distinctive features and characteristics of various races were "worthy of close investigation," many early-twentieth-century US psychologists, particularly eugenicists, set out to perform such investigations.[119] Describing it as a strictly scientific endeavor, they frequently used standardized tests in their studies. Their efforts were supported by White supremacists intent on proving not merely the existence of innate race differences but also the superiority of White people.

As I discussed in chapter 3, Carl Brigham was among the influential eugenicists to claim that standardized intelligence tests—including the Army Mental Tests—revealed the innate intellectual superiority of White people over "Negroes."[120] He further stated that his analysis disproved the popular belief that Jews are highly intelligent, and he even reported significant differences in intelligence when the three White racial categories were compared, with Nordics outscoring Alpines and Mediterraneans.[121]

Another representative example of race-differences research from the period is Bird T. Baldwin's 1913 *Journal of Educational Psychology* article that found race differences in the learning capacities of delinquent girls; Baldwin concluded that Black girls' learning capacities, overall, were inferior to White girls'.[122] Significantly, a few years after the article was published, Baldwin became the first director of the Iowa Child Welfare Research Station, one of Seashore's pet projects.

In an article appearing in the *Annals of the American Academy of Political and Social Science* in 1928, Morris S. Viteles reviewed a host of studies of the mental status of the "Negro" and reported that in most cases, "Negroes" scored lower than Whites on intelligence tests. To support this conclusion, he included a number of studies that used the Army Mental Tests, including Brigham's.[123] However, he also cited a study by E. B. Reuter that stated, "'The negro may be the intellectual inferior of the white racial stock, but to date no one has marshalled in proof of the position any body of evidence that has scientific validity.'"[124] Viteles warned readers to exercise "extreme caution" in generalizing from extant studies and remarked that if racial differences exist, the question of whether patterns are due to nature or nurture had not yet been answered.[125] Like Viteles, Joseph Peterson was skeptical of extant research that concluded there were innate racial differences in intelligence: "Much of the work in this line has been premature and untrustworthy; nevertheless many testers have been ready with conclusions. A number of workers in this field have naïvely assumed that all differences of race medians are innate differences."[126] He warned researchers that inadequate methods and hasty decisions were universally damaging, and he advised researchers to put "the emphasis on the perfecting of methods and technique and in deferring hasty conclusions and evaluations of aptitudes, which have every prospect of being not only erroneous but damaging both to the 'superior' and the 'inferior' race or national groups."[127] Significantly, Peterson's quarrel was not with intelligence testing as such, or with the idea of testing for race differences in intelligence; rather, he argued for improvement in methods and technique.

Music education researchers other than Seashore were aware of psychological discourse concerning innate racial differences, the measurement of differences, and hierarchies. For example, in a 1926 *Music Supervisors' Journal* article, Jacob Kwalwasser—who had been a student of Seashore's—invoked the arrested-development premise when he referred to G. Stanley Hall's belief that White and "colored" children are of equal intelligence until the age of twelve, at which time the White child "shoots ahead"; he also cited James Bardin, Edward Thorndike, and Gustave LeBon to support the assertion that the "Negro" is inferior to the White person in mental capacity and imagination.[128] Significantly, drawing on a mind/body dichotomy, Kwalwasser also cited sources that claimed "Negroes" were superior to Whites at "automatic action" and at responding to "auditory, visual and electric stimulation."[129] Because eugenicists tended to prize intellectual activity most highly, however, this assessment placed "Negro" people lower on the racial hierarchy; these assertions probably supported and justified the exclusion of "Negroes" from intellectual opportunities, as well as their relegation by Whites to physical, manual activity.

Although racism was inescapably pervasive in the United States during the early twentieth century, not all scholars of the day concluded that there were innate race differences in intelligence or a "natural" racial hierarchy. The countervailing voices tended to come from sources outside of eugenics, however, and the conclusion they typically proffered was that differences in intelligence test scores and school achievement were due to differences in environment, social advantages, and educational opportunities—not to biology. For example, an article by Howard University professor Charles H. Thompson, which appeared in the same issue of the *Annals of the American Academy of Political and Social Sciences* as an article by Seashore on the "Negro" singing voice, debunked the idea of the innate inferiority of "Negro" people and concluded that environment is the culprit:

> 1. That the doctrine of an inherent mental inferiority of the Negro is a myth unfounded by the most logical interpretation of the scientific facts on the subject produced to date.
> 2. That the mental and scholastic achievements of Negro children, as with white children, are, in the main, a direct function of their environmental and school opportunities rather than a function of some inherent difference in mental ability.
> 3. That a philosophy of education based upon the current unwar-

> ranted interpretations of achievement differences between white and Negro children, as due to inherent racial mental inferiority of the Negro, is not only UNJUST, but a little short of disastrous, especially in view of the many other disabilities the Negro has to undergo in this country.[130]

In a discussion of the status of "Negroes" in elementary schools in the North, E. George Payne, a professor and assistant dean at New York University, went one step further, not only pointing out that equal opportunity was not present in the North but concluding that intractable White supremacy was the source of the "race problem" in the United States: "The solution of the race problem will remain impossible, as long as the white race assumes that the Negro comprises an inferior group and that he must remain the ward of the white man. This fact may postpone the solution indefinitely."[131] What largely went unquestioned even among critics, however, were the soundness of existing conceptions of intelligence, the robustness of extant intelligence tests, and the value of measuring whatever it was that the tests were measuring.

Race Hierarchies and Cultural Progress

A Hierarchy of Cultures

Consistent with what was common practice among many White US intellectuals during the early twentieth century, eugenicists mapped a cultural evolutionary hierarchy onto a racialized human evolutionary hierarchy such that, like individuals and groups, cultures and cultural expressions were situated on various rungs of a ladder. Each rung on the cultural hierarchy conferred differential status and reflected prevalent conceptions of quality and worth. Julia J. Chybowski notes, for example, that the widely circulating tropes of cultural progress and evolution informed music appreciation textbook content during this period.[132] A substantial body of research similar to hers confirms that these discourses were not limited to eugenics; nevertheless, they thrived among eugenicists. For example, alluding to a racialized cultural hierarchy, eugenicists Popenoe and Johnson spoke of levels of "social heritage" and stated that globally and in the United States, the social heritage of "Negroes" was on a much lower level than that of Whites: "An elementary knowledge of the history of Africa, or the more recent and much-quoted example of Haiti, is sufficient to prove that the Negro's own social heritage is at a level *far below* that of the whites among whom he is living in the United States [emphasis mine]."[133]

Using "original contributions" as their criterion, they argued that "Negroes"—as a race—had contributed virtually nothing to world civilization: "If the number of original contributions which it has made to the world's civilization is any fair criterion of the relative value of a race, then the Negro race must be placed very near zero on the scale."[134] They asserted that the low position of "Negroes" on the social hierarchy is inevitable given their low position on the evolutionary racial and cultural hierarchy:

> It is certain that, at the present time in this country, no Negro can take a place in the upper ranks of society, which are and will long remain white. The fact that *this situation is inevitable* makes it no less unfortunate for both Negro and white races; consolation can only be found in the thought that it is less of a danger than the opposite condition would be [emphasis mine].[135]

Using the language of threat, they reached a conclusion that rendered White people blameless for the low status of "Negroes" in the United States. Their reference to "an elementary knowledge of the history of Africa" is bitterly ironic given their own visible lack of such knowledge.

A Hierarchy of Cultural Activities

In addition to referring to primitive and civilized cultures, eugenicists spoke of primitive and civilized cultural activities. Significantly, Popenoe and Johnson considered music to be a primitive activity and used that supposition as evidence that "Negroes" were low on the evolutionary ladder: "The Negro's contribution has perhaps been most noteworthy in music. This does not necessarily show advanced evolution; August Weismann long ago pointed out that music is a primitive accomplishment."[136]

Music was not typically considered a "primitive accomplishment," however; the more common understanding was that some kinds of art and artistic activities—including kinds of music and musical activities—are more evolved than others, with art reflecting the evolutionary status of the racial group from which the artist had sprung. Consider, for example, Reginald Harris's article "Negro Art as an Indication of Racial Development," which appeared in *Eugenical News* in 1923. Harris was a biologist and eugenicist who received a PhD from Brown University in 1924; he had first studied at the Cold Spring Harbor Laboratory as an undergraduate. In 1922, he married Charles Davenport's daughter, and his career in the eugenics world quickly blossomed. In 1923, he was appointed acting director of the Biological Laboratory at Cold Spring Harbor, and that year he also traveled with his wife to study eugenics in North Africa. In 1924, when control of the lab was transferred to the Long Island Biological Association, he was elected its permanent director.[137] Thus, details of Harris's biography confirm both that he was deeply ensconced in Cold Spring Harbor eugenics and that his education was in biology, not art.

He opened the article with the claim that two indicators of racial development are the ability to compete successfully with other races, and the presence and quality of cultural accomplishments.[138] He stated that the failure of the "Negro" to compete with White races was one indication of the inferiority of the "Negro" race. In reference to the second indicator, he admitted that the inferiority of "Negro" cultural accomplishments recently had been questioned, acknowledging that some schools of modern art, as well as many *nonprofessionals*, maintained that "Negro" art demonstrates "a very high development among Negroes."[139] He set out to test this assertion by assessing the worth of "Negro" art and, by extension, determining through art the racial development of the "Negro." The developmental stage of "Negroes" as a race, he claimed, could be ascertained by studying the collections of "Negro" art in European museums.[140]

After a brief description of the kinds of art created by African "Negroes," he launched into an assessment of its worth. Harris's choice of descriptors is telling; calling a mask from the Congo region charming, he asserted that it was appealing due to its "exotic character," "primitiveness of line," "general simplicity," and the creator's "skill of execution"; all of these factors, he claimed, made the mask "immediately agreeable."[141] Those who do not like "Negro" art, he observed, may find it jolting, unfamiliar, "rude," and "primitive," viewing it merely as an "ethnographical specimen rather than as a thing of beauty"—that is, as an object of scholarly interest but not a work of art.[142] Noting that modern music and art can elicit similar critical responses, he set out to compare "Negro" art to modern art. He did so by first comparing two types of artists—the modern artist and the "Negro," noting what distinguished one type from the other. The modern artist, Harris claimed, "seeks freedom" and wants to make "strange, exotic, imaginative, creative," unconventional work. Modern art, Harris claimed, is "the *intelligent* attempt of a *reasoning* individual to employ form and color in an imaginative, creative way [emphases mine]."[143] He added that it is the freedom and imagination of "Negro" art that appeals to the modern artist.[144]

Next, he stated that the best way to compare art is to consider the "mental attitude of its representatives"—the artists—and it is there, according to Harris, that all resemblances between the modern artist and the "Negro" artist cease. He argued that in contrast to the intelligent and reasoned approach of the modern artist, "the mental approach of the Negro artist to his subject is that of a primitive individual."[145] He continued, "Negro art is not the result of an intelligent attempt of the artist to disregard conventional representation in order that his work may possess the more satisfying qualities of imagination, well-chosen form and color. It is not comparable with modern art in its motives. *It is not intellectual* [emphasis mine]."[146]

According to Harris, "Negro" art is "as free from intellectuality as it is from imposed traditions" because its creator is not intellectual; it is based, instead, in nature. He maintained that because nature is incomprehensible to primitive people, their artwork springs from the artist's mysticism and is consequently "impregnated with the supernatural."[147] Sex organs in "Negro" art are disproportionately large, Harris claimed, because the artwork is "the reaction of the Negro artist to a phenomenon of nature which he does not understand, viz., reproduction"—and cannot understand.[148] "Negro" art may be pleasing, Harris noted, and it portrays "the reactions of the race," but these "reactions remain primitive, intellectually immature."[149] He opined that "Negro" art reflects the primitive and "natural" state of the "Negro" artist, and he concluded that "Negro art, judged by the mental attitude of the artist, can not be considered as an indication of very high racial development."[150] Thus, according to him, "Negro" art cannot successfully compete against the art forms of other races; it is primitive, not intellectual, and not on a par with modern art because the mental attitude of artists of different races is different.[151] He theorized that it might be fair to conclude, based on their art, that the "Negro" race once was highly developed but has degenerated, and he stated that it may be possible for the race to advance again if conditions are favorable.[152] Nevertheless, he maintained that regardless of environment, "Negroes" are incapable of making art of as high quality as that made by members of the White race: "It is safe to conclude that in art, as well as in other expressions of racial development, the Negro race has manifested, and continues to demonstrate, its inferiority to the white race."[153]

In his address of welcome to the Second International Congress of Eugenics, Osborn mentioned the artistic contributions of the Japanese and Chinese in his comments about the distinctive contributions that "pure-blooded" members of various races make to "the world's economy."[154] After stating that if the "Negro" fails in government he may succeed as a mechanic or farmer, he claimed that the Japanese and Chinese have demonstrated a "range of ability in art, literature, and industry *quite equal to our own* in certain arts [emphasis mine]."[155] He then acknowledged that the artistic ability of the Japanese and Chinese is "greatly superior to our own in other arts, like ceramics."[156]

Significantly, Osborn's discussion of the career prospects of the "Negro" reflected a status hierarchy—farming and government were not of equal status—and intimated that the "Negro" rightly belonged on a lower rung. His comments indicated that other races were to be measured against what he assumed was a gold standard—the abilities described as "ours," presumably referring to White people. Furthermore, because the comments occurred in a segment praising pure-blooded races, Osborn undoubtedly assumed that the superiority or inferiority of a racial group's artistic ability was due to racial "blood" inheritance rather than to the cultural transmission of specific artistic skills, techniques, or preferences.

Seashore on the Evolution of Music and Musical Activity

Seashore's discourse on musical activities resembled Harris's statements about visual art. He subscribed to a hierarchical, developmental, evolutionary understanding of music and musical activity, claiming that it evolved as humans evolved.[157] Calling the evolution of music "orderly," he described the history of music as a study of the "principal rungs in the tottering ladder" of music's evolution.[158] Each of these rungs, he claimed, provides a "vantage ground from which larger and larger horizons developed in the rise of civilization and culture."[159] In his estimation, climbing the ladder rung by rung, humanity has been rewarded with an improved and enlarged view at each step of the ascent. He referred to the "rise" of man as a million-year process and stated that the concurrent progress of the evolution of music is contingent on the evolutionary progress—the "level"—of human and societal evolution.[160] Relying on the primitive-versus-civilized dichotomy, he placed the "primitive" at the beginning of his progress model; the end was an ever-moving target—the civilized present. His pronouncements about the evolution of music and musical activity reflected broader social values, mapping out what was—or was not—considered civilized. For example, in the lower animals that preceded early man, he claimed, musical behavior was "instinctive" whereas starting with early man, it "gradually became rational and deliberative," characterized by "deliberate and feelingful pursuit of musical goals," the "attachment of *meaning* to musical sounds [emphasis mine]," and a desire to control life.[161]

Seashore's grand narratives about the evolution of music were littered with the word "primitive"; he spoke of primitive past times filled with primitive people creating primitive cultures and making primitive music. Although he set the present apart from the primitive past in his statement that musical anthropology's scientific contribution to music is to provide the history of music's evolution "from primitive times to the present," he also understood the primitive to live on in the present.[162] This understanding was based on the assumption that because not all races, nationalities, and culture groups had evolved at an equal pace, some living groups were more primitive than others; as a consequence, he concluded, the cultural activities—including music—of these various groups, displayed different levels of evolutionary development. Thus, the so-called "primitive" characteristics of some kinds of music of the present ostensibly reflected the less-evolved state of those who had created it.[163]

Significantly, in a slightly different description of the role of anthropologists, he said that they traced "the evolution of the progressive development of music in races and nations," once again suggesting that this musical development differs depending on the development of the racial group or nation from which it had emerged.[164] Another statement about musical anthropology—that it traces the unfolding progress of music in "rising racial cultures"—similarly suggested that different racial groups demonstrate different rates of progress.[165] Seashore maintained that the anthropologist who studies "the most significant aspect of musical culture in a selected group" will see that it "represents a definite culture stage" in the development of various components of music, these components ranging from melody to musical instruments.[166] According to Seashore, "modern music" is the full flower of music's development from its rudimentary beginnings.[167]

In a few discussions of primitive music, Seashore referenced race. For example, he described "Negro," American Indian, Hawaiian, and Filipino music as primitive types that could be found and then collected via recording.[168] In the chapter "Primitive Music," which appeared in his 1938 book *Psychology of Music*, he stated that "Negro" and American Indian music were primitive types that could be collected at home—that is, in the United States.[169] The chapter included a section entitled "Negro Songs."[170] In a report on the use of sound recording in the study of primitive music, he included a graphical recording of an American Indian singer whom he described as a member of the Sioux Tribe.[171]

Seashore on Music as an Indicator of Evolutionary Stage

Seashore claimed that the purposes of music—or its lack of purpose—indicate its evolutionary-stage level. His statements changed slightly over time, however. In a source published in 1938, he emphasized the practicality of the arts, claiming that the fine arts, including music, serve a purpose.[172] In a 1947 publication, however, he argued that functionless music was more evolved and refined than music from early stages of development, when it was intended "to serve a purpose rather than to give pleasure."[173] Early functions of music, he said, included appealing "to the gods"; serving as a kind of magic between the individual and the gods; facilitating rhythmic movements and engendering "emotional drives" for military purposes; and, when used in conjunction with magic, hastening healing.[174] He maintained that from the beginning, music has been the expression of ideals and urges—including sexual urges—and of emotional life "not reducible to logical language."[175] Stating that expressing love has been one function of music throughout time, he noted that this use has been progressively *refined* over time.[176] Only later, he claimed, did music become a leisure activity that facilitated social bonding—after which time folk music emerged—and he concluded that "it is only in comparatively recent times that music has been cultivated as art for art's sake."[177] Echoing prevalent aesthetic theory of the time, he concluded that this cultivation was a glorious capstone of the evolutionary process: "While the earlier function of music as of life preserving value has not diminished, the capstone of musical achievement even today lies largely in its purely artistic aspect—in music as a form of play with no ulterior purpose, as art for art's sake."[178]

The Distinguishing Characteristics of Primitive Music and Musicians, Past and Present

Relying on the primitive-versus-civilized dichotomy, Seashore described several distinguishing characteristics of primitive music and musicians that set them apart from their civilized counterparts. He presented his highly speculative assertions as fact. Primitive music of the past, he declared, was filled with "mysterious and powerful noises." It lacked formal elements such as melody, as well as sounds having "specific meaning."[179] Early on, it consisted of individual expression and only later evolved into organized group action.[180] He stated that past-primitive song was not "exclusively a method of conveying meaning"; rather, some primitive song set out merely to enrich sound with feeling.[181] He used chant as an example, stating that it "might consist of the continuous repetition of two or more words for their euphonic value."[182] This description was consistent with his other comments about primitive music in that it emphasized repetition and focused on the value of emotion and sheer sound.

Significantly, he assigned many of the same characteristics to present-primitive music as he did to past-primitive music. For example, he argued that primitive music of the present displays the same emphasis on repetition and sheer sound rather than storyline: "This characteristic is well represented even in the primitive music of today, where a song is not the telling of a story but a repeated play upon certain key words which have symbolic meaning and euphonic power."[183]

His description of the characteristics of a primitive singer of the present provides further insight into his construction of primitive musicians and musical activities, past and present. He opened by comparing the comprehension of gardening of a "home-loving peasant woman" to that of a botanist. The garden may be "thrillingly beautiful" to the woman, he acknowledged, but unlike the botanist, the peasant woman has limited vision because she lacks critical knowledge of the garden.[184] The primitive singer, he wrote, analogously sings without *understanding* and specifically without knowledge of the scientific nomenclature that makes analysis and discriminative evaluation of music—true understanding—possible:

> The primitive singer may sing in true pitch, but he may not know what pitch is. He may show artistic deviation from true pitch, but he has no name for it, and he may not know of its existence. The fundamental contribution of science to music is the laying of foundations for exact, permanent, and verifiable terminology which is the basis for analysis and discriminative evaluation of beauty or ugliness in music.[185]

Seashore also believed that the primitive *mind* lived on in the present, exhibiting the same characteristics as it had in the past. For example, after stating that music has its roots in "the most primitive savage life and has evolved through countless culture strata," Seashore added that "throughout the ages the untutored primitive mind" has asked the same questions about music.[186] Thus, the primitive mind—the antithesis of the civilized mind—has persisted, asking the same questions throughout the ages.

Seashore described another cultural activity in evolutionary, developmental, and hierarchical terms: religion. In his 1914 book *Psychology in Daily Life*, he argued that religions on all levels of the evolutionary hierarchy demonstrate an element of play; terms such as "crude," "primitive," "highest," and "refined" signaled the evolutionary level he assigned to the religions he discussed:

> While crude ceremonials are conspicuous in primitive religion, the same play elements continue in a refined form in progressively evolving higher forms of religion. Indeed, the highest type of religion is that which is characterized by the noble play attitude. Mass is celebrated; celebration, from the singing of the gospel hymns to the rendition of the sacred oratorio, is an expression of the play-motif of freedom, exultation, and faith.[187]

Notably, like Harris in his essay on visual art, in the above passage, Seashore associated the "primitive" with freedom; he maintained that the element of playful freedom is still evident in more evolved "higher forms" of religion. He also maintained that like play, religion preserves the "racial inheritance," although here, as often was the case, he was not clear about whether he was referring to the whole human race or to different races.[188] He also differentiated between "negative" and "positive" religions, joy and self-expression being the characteristics of positive ones; according to Seashore, the progressively higher forms of religion displayed more of the "positive element."[189]

The Fine and Not-So-Fine Arts

The construct of evolutionary levels of art, with primitive art at the bottom, created and reinforced a dichotomy between fine arts—great music, for example—and the opposite, what I call the "not-so-fine" arts. This dichotomy, which existed both inside and outside of eugenics, tended to be racialized; the people creating and enjoying the not-so-fine arts were marked as lesser. For example, in "The Musical Ability of the Negro," a 1928 article that appeared in the *Annals of the American Academy of Political and Social Science*, University of Pennsylvania psychologist Yale Nathanson indicated that the creation of "great" music had eluded "Negroes," and he explained why. Nathanson—who did not appear to have ties to eugenics—argued that this void was due to the "Negro attitude," or personality, and he attributed both the absence of great music and the enslavement of "Negroes" to their docility. In a derisive portrayal suggesting that a generic African leader had engaged in less-than-fully-human activity, he argued that enslavement had resulted from the actions of African leadership and was the fault of African people; furthermore, comparing "Negro" music to that of American Indians and "Asiatics," he found it inferior and wanting:

> Great lasting music which should have resulted from the atrocities and hardships of slavery does not exist, because essentially the Negro atti-

> tude is such that he is docile, as proved by the fact that cases of organized rebellion have been indeed rare. It is this very trait or absence of this positive characteristic which made slavery possible. The African chieftain sold off a given number of his subjects and their children, or decapitated them as a sacrifice to a deity which appeared in his previous night's dream, his slumbers having been disturbed by gastronomic indiscretions. The lack of fiery resistance robbed the Negro music of a dynamic theme common to the Indian War Dance, or the stirring religious compositions and exotic melodies of the Asiatic. The Negro song contribution is of the song-fest type, the easy, pleasing expression of a peaceful people.[190]

Notably, Nathanson stated that "Negro" docility is due to cultural rather than biological factors, but he viewed it as a deficiency, nevertheless.[191] Furthermore, unlike eugenicists, he claimed that "the handicaps of poverty and racial prejudice" had excluded the "Negro" from the educational opportunities necessary to produce "fine, artistic" music.[192] He also employed the exceptionality trope and quoted from E. B. Reuter's list of "Negroes" who had overcome disadvantage to become successful musicians.[193] Similarly, Guy Benton Johnson alluded to the role of social class in defining the parameters of greatness when he opined that "when the Negro race acquires more wealth, leisure, and cultural background, it may be motivated to produce some of the world's greatest musicians."[194] Nevertheless, if Johnson had intended to support the "Negro" race by suggesting that all people could become great musicians, his comments fell short, not only because he did not recognize that all kinds of music can be great (however defined) and that musicians creating and performing all styles of music can be great, but because he implied that the supposed absence of "Negroes" from the halls of musical greatness was due to the race's collective lack of motivation.

Eugenicists also drew distinctions between the fine and not-so-fine arts. Just as having musical ability was considered a positive trait, liking good or great music was seen as a sign of superiority. The assessment forms used in the fitter family contests included a column for hand-written notes about a participant's special abilities or qualities; comments such as "loved and played good music" sometimes appeared in this column.[195] Seashore, too, drew distinctions between the fine and not-so-fine arts. He claimed that exposure to art affects the character of the mind, and although the effect presumably would be different depending on whether the art was fine or not-so-fine, in the passage in question he was referring to the positive influences of presumably fine art: "Daily contact with the beauty of nature, or with works of art, or noble deeds, will invariably result in some sort of reflection of the traces of these in the character of the mind."[196] He also distinguished the fine arts from other arts in his descriptions of the characteristics of each. Creativity, he stated, is a characteristic of fine art.[197] By contrast, he associated free expression of rhythmic instinct with "all stages of primitive life" and claimed that this free expression tends to be "attenuated or repressed" by culture—subdued but present in the "refined arts."[198] Significantly, Seashore stated that freedom—specifically, free use of intonation—is a characteristic of "Negro" spirituals.[199]

As I mentioned in chapter 3, Seashore has been credited with instituting the University of Iowa's innovative graduate program in the fine arts. His support of this initiative indicates that he was a staunch proponent of the arts labeled "fine"; he also was deeply interested in some of the music not labeled "fine." Whether an art form had a place in the academy, and how it was approached if given a place, signaled whether it was considered fine. For example, in Seashore's innovative fine arts graduate program at the University of Iowa, creating and performing the arts deemed fine were legitimate academic pursuits, as was the study of the history and theory of these arts. By contrast, as I demonstrate shortly, at Iowa the not-so-fine arts generated objects—curiosities—to be scientifically scrutinized and dissected by musical anthropologists, including Seashore. Some not-so-fine arts were not deemed sufficiently worthy to be given any place at the university.

A Racialized Hierarchy of Musical Genres that Assigned and Reflected Worth and Value

Whether or not they came from eugenicists, statements about "great" or the "best" music reflected the belief that different *genres* of music are of different quality and worth; such beliefs were premised on the existence of a hierarchy of musical genres that was shaped by race, social class, and nationality. Assuming that music had progressively evolved, those who subscribed to the concept of a hierarchy of musical genres maintained that the various genres reflected the evolutionary state of the cultures and people that had created them.[200] Once again, a civilized-versus-primitive dichotomy was layered onto this hierarchy, with various genres described as civilized or as more or less primitive. European classical or high art music—sometimes called "great" or the "best" music—sat at the top of the heap. Chybowski notes that symphonic and operatic genres "stood unquestionably as intellectually viable in their 'whiteness.'"[201] "Folk" music sat somewhere below high art music, but not at the very bottom of the ladder. Chybowski reports that although folk music was considered a less-evolved genre, music educators promoted its use with children and amateur musicians, and viewed it as a steppingstone toward "better intellectual forms of music."[202]

Some sources from this period called "Negro" music, especially songs, folk music. For example, in his study of musical talent and the "Negro," Johnson wrote, "Historically speaking, the Negro *in America* has built his musical reputation on his folk singing [emphasis mine]."[203] Nathanson similarly claimed that the "Negro's" greatest musical contributions to American music are folk songs—what Nathanson called "America's only indigenous music."[204] Despite this praise, however, in a comment that indirectly mapped out the characteristics of great music, he described "Negro" folk songs in deficit terms, signaling that he did not place them at the top of the musical-style hierarchy: "These [Negro] songs are relatively simple, with a highly restricted musical span, endless repetition, devoid of specific theme, childish, unfinished."[205] Although he did not view them as worthless, Nathanson considered "Negro" folk songs to be less evolved and worth less. Regardless of the race of the people making it, folk music commonly was considered less evolved and lowlier than high art music.

Like folk music, popular music was below high art music on the genre hierarchy, and it may very possibly have been relegated to a rung below folk music. Folk music was considered acceptable for schoolchildren, which was not necessarily the case for popular music. By the early twentieth century, "popular" referred to a constellation of music genres other than high art—not, as was the case in earlier times, to music that was widely liked regardless of its genre. Music scholars' disapproval of popular music often was palpable even though the music was wildly popular with the public. Chybowski notes, for example, that authors of early-twentieth-century music appreciation textbooks classified popular music—especially ragtime and jazz—as primitive.[206] Nathanson did so, quoting E. B. Reuter in his claim that ragtime and jazz are "'primitive rather than African in origin'"; he spoke quite disparagingly of these popular styles, adding that the "Negro" had been inaccurately and unfairly associated with this bad music.[207] Although he may have considered both African and popular music to be primitive, he may have placed some African music on a slightly higher rung than some American popular music. Just as there ostensibly were "trashy" people, including those whom Seashore disparagingly called "White trash," there also was trashy music, "primitive" music that threatened to effect the downfall of civilization. Eugenics sources associated ragtime and jazz with degeneracy, and they considered dislike of jazz and ragtime to be a positive trait. A fitter family assessment form described a family member positively based on the music she did or did not enjoy: "Loved and played good music but disliked rag time or jazz."[208]

Seashore subscribed to this genre hierarchy of value and worth, too. For example, he spoke of the "limitations" of jazz and swing, two genres he described as boring.[209] Even though he mentioned ragtime and dance music as cruder forms that the masses should not be discouraged from listening to, elsewhere he spoke of musical ability in terms of "limitation to ragtime or capacity for symphony."[210] It is not clear whether he was referring to the capacity to perform these genres, to enjoy them, or both; what is clear, however, is that he believed innate capacity governed access to some musical genres, with access to the "best" being possible only for an elite few.

His comments about the location of "Negro" music on the genre hierarchy are somewhat puzzling; what is unclear is whether he viewed folk and primitive music to be distinct genres or whether he considered folk music to be a type of primitive music. He sometimes called "Negro" music a kind of folk music,[211] and elsewhere, as I have discussed, he called it primitive music. To further confuse matters, in one article he described "Negro" music as not being necessarily primitive. This article detailed his proposal to film primitive music in situ, and the hypothetical group he described was "savage" people of the South Sea Islands; in a footnote, he recommended using the same filming process in other studies of "racial characteristics of music": "The same principle would apply to the filming of racial characteristics of music or racial life in general, *not necessarily primitive*, such as the music of the American Negro or Indian or any *clean-cut national type* of folk music [emphases mine]."[212] Even though Seashore's genre hierarchy was murkier below the top, without question, jazz, swing, ragtime, folk, and "primitive" were genres that did not measure up to the top—albeit to varying degrees; according to him, some types of primitive music were more primitive than others.

Aesthetics, Taste, and Race

Seashore on the Beautiful

Aesthetics was among Seashore's special interests; one of his obituaries described him as having been "internationally known as a leader in the scientific approach to aesthetics."[213] His 1947 book *In Search of Beauty in Music: A Scientific Approach to Musical Esthetics* is but one of his many publications on this topic.[214] He called aesthetics a "normative *science*" [emphasis mine] and supported "the coming musical esthetics," which he claimed was based on experimental science.[215] Science, he claimed, can objectively document and measure the features of music deemed beautiful or ugly, thereby providing insight into expressive emotion.[216] The scientific investigator, he stated, can make precise measurements and use this data in an attempt to "formulate principles of beauty and ugliness in music in permanent language and in verifiable terms."[217] He also was convinced that aesthetic judgment could be objectively measured, an assertion based on the assumption that the good and beautiful can be objectively determined.

These understandings undergirded a project that he and University of Iowa faculty associate (and later, professor) in psychology Norman C. Meier undertook to develop a standardized visual art judgment test. In a published discussion of the test, Meier stated that aesthetic judgment is a crucial and measurable component of artistic talent.[218] Claiming that there are principles governing artistic choices, and that there is consensus among experts about what constitute good and bad choices in visual art, Seashore and Meier assigned the "master artist" the role of aesthetic arbiter.[219] Like Meier, Seashore assumed that there is consensus—at least among those who count—about what constitutes the good and beautiful; in a few cases, he revealed who counted: educated, thinking people. For instance, in a *Music Educators Journal* article that appeared in 1941, he called for beautiful poetry that can serve as the basis of beautiful religious music for public school choirs, and for "poetic expression of the universal sentiments of truth, goodness and beauty in the spiritual life about which *educated people all* agree [emphasis mine]."[220] He also claimed that the religious emphasis that appeals to "all *thinking* people is on the truth, goodness, and beauty of religious life [emphasis mine]."[221] Continuing the universalizing theme, he said that the needed beautiful poetry should stem from "universal religious truths."[222]

The Beautiful Vibrato

Seashore's ideas about aesthetics informed, and sometimes surfaced in, his statements about fine and not-so-fine music, governing his map of the landscape of the beautiful and good in art. For example, he displayed elite views in his 1925 article on vibrato. Coauthored with Milton Metfessel and published in the *Proceedings of the National Academy of Sciences*, the article reported on the authors' study of the vibrato of twelve vocalists, at least eleven of whom were famous, White, opera singers.[223] The researchers' goal was to scientifically capture and codify the distinctive characteristics of beautiful vibrato. Metfessel was a professor of psychology and speech at the University of Iowa; he joined the faculty after having completed a master's degree and a doctorate there (in 1924 and 1925 respectively). He left Iowa in 1929 to chair the psychology department at the University of Southern California. Although he shared many research interests with Seashore, I found no evidence that he was a eugenicist.

Seashore and Metfessel opened the article with a discussion of beautiful music, describing it in universal terms and assuming that it displayed the same characteristics at all times and in all contexts. They stated that in music, deviation from the true, pure, and exact creates the beautiful and is the means by which emotion is expressed.[224] However, they claimed that deviation creates the beautiful only if it is intentional; unintentional deviation, by contrast, is ugly, as is the absence of deviation, which results in cold, restricted, and unemotional music.[225] They maintained that the musician must know and master the true and exact before engaging in a "flirtation" with it, that is, before deviating from it.[226]

The study itself began with "photographing sound waves" produced by the twelve singers; this was followed by an "objective portrayal or description of the expression of emotion in music," which was based on the data collected via sound wave photography.[227] They focused on one among many possible deviations, vibrato, which they described as a regulated departure from true pitch. Basing their conclusions on their measurements of the vibrato of the twelve singers, they stated that good vibrato is "a highly refined trembling," and they explained its features using technical acoustic language.[228] They contrasted good vibrato, which they characterized as slight, controlled deviation, with tremolo, which they said was excessive, uncontrolled deviation. Unlike good vibrato, they stated, tremolo is ugly.[229] At the end of the article, they briefly discussed temporal deviations—performers' liberties in time, tempo, and rhythm— restating their thesis that the beautiful is the result of a "flirtation" with the exact, such deviation being "an assertion of freedom which is but the affirmation of law."[230] They concluded that the new technology they were using opened the door to objective measurement of emotional expression in music.[231] Their goal was to demystify emotion by comprehending it. One of the epistemic assumptions guiding them was that scientific dissection and analysis are the best, and perhaps the only, routes to the highest forms of knowing and understanding. If knowledge is indeed power, Seashore and Metfessel set out to govern by knowing—by anatomizing vocal production to reveal emotion's technologies.

To Seashore and Metfessel, a universal characteristic of the beautiful is the presence of small deviations introduced by a *comprehending* musician who knows and has mastered the rules before attempting to "flirt" with them. If the music is to be beautiful, the deviations must be controlled and not excessive; excess, by contrast, produces ugliness and bad music. They not only promoted the idea that universal conceptions of the good and beautiful exist, they selected this particular group as the gold standard. Accordingly, the vibrato of these opera singers was to be emulated by all singers of all styles of music; whether singing was of high quality was to be judged by assessing whether it was *as good as* that of the twelve. That the researchers chose operatic singers exclusively (or almost exclusively) is notable in light of Chybowski's observation that operatic and symphonic music, safely in the fine art fold, was conspicuously White. Without mentioning people of color, the article by Seashore and Metfessel confirms Ruth Gustafson's observation that Seashore's projects to quantify scientifically the aesthetic qualities of music were deeply racialized.[232]

Taste and Race

Discussions linking aesthetics, taste, and race were not new to the early twentieth century, nor were they unique to eugenicists. Chybowski notes, for example, that authors of early-twentieth-century music appreciation textbooks assumed that musical taste in individuals and racial groups, like music generally, evolved developmentally, with different races exhibiting different stages of development.[233] In individuals, musical taste started with a preference for primitive music, which in some individuals could develop into a taste for high art.[234] She also states that the textbook authors believed that some people were incapable of acquiring good musical taste, and saw race as factoring into this inability:

> They [textbook authors] identified race as the most significant inhibitor. Music appreciation taught implicitly and explicitly that science and intellect were exclusive to certain Americans, part of a construction of whiteness that stood for many as a racial category. Predisposed to experience music from the elementary stages of rhythm and physicality, Africans and African Americans were more susceptible to the power of music, which hindered the possibility for their intellectual mastery over the music.[235]

Chybowski reports that authors assumed that the music at the top of the genre hierarchy—European high art music—was inaccessible to African American listeners and musicians, who were presumed to be incapable of appreciating this music due to the less evolved state of their race.[236] Although he did not use the word "race," in his 1891 book *Darwinism: An Exposition of the Theory of Natural Selection with Some of Its Applications*, Alfred Russel Wallace discussed in racially coded terms the evolutionary development of artistic faculties and of appreciation for music. Wallace considered mathematical and musical ability to be faculties of "civilized" man, and he argued that musical faculty evolved in humans in a way that paralleled the evolution of the mathematical faculty.[237] Wallace supported his thesis by claiming that in savages, the music faculty is less evolved, and that as groups collectively rise in intellect, appreciation for music rises concomitantly: "Among the lower savages music, as we understand it, hardly exists, though they all delight in rude musical sounds, as of drums, tom-toms, or gongs; and they also sing in monotonous chants. Almost exactly as they advance in general intellect, and in the arts of social life, their appreciation of music appears to rise in proportion."[238]

These racially infused beliefs and assumptions figured heavily in eugenics discourse; even prior to Seashore's forays into aesthetics and taste, eugenicists had identified taste as a component of biologically innate musical ability and had studied the possible existence of innate racial differences in taste. For example, Galton considered taste to be both a component of musical aptitude and a sign of fitness. In survey instructions he wrote for a study of race differences in "innate character and intelligence," he directed the interviewers to gather a wide array of data, ranging from whether participants observed the Sabbath to whether they had strongly developed "sexual affection"; one survey question focused on the possession of "special aptitudes," including musical taste.[239] Similarly, questionnaire instructions for a pedigree study conducted by the Eugenics Section of the American Breeders Association at about the same time as Galton's study (circa 1909 and 1910) directed questioners to collect data about the participants' music appreciation abilities.[240] The appreciation question had two parts. First, interviewers were to note the participant's "ability to discriminate between good and common music and to thoroly [*sic*] enjoy good music."[241] Next, in an attempt to distinguish the respective roles of heredity and environment, interviewers were to ask how much musical training the participant had had. The instructions provided a sample answer: the child had studied music for several years but still was unable to "discriminate between good and common music."[242] Presumably, such a response would indicate that the child was inherently incapable of developing good taste.

Reinforcing distinctions not only between fine and not-so-fine music but also between elite and mass taste, in his 1940 *School Review* article "Youth and Music," Seashore held forth on the developmental characteristics of teenagers; in his discussion of teenagers and music, he associated what he called the "cruder forms of music" with the masses.[243] He said, however, that interest in these cruder forms should not be discouraged, because "high brow" music is enjoyed by few—even in the highest echelons of society.[244] Thanks to the phonograph and radio, he reported, America had wide access for the first time to music "good, bad, and indifferent";[245] he praised this technology for bringing "good music" to the masses and for raising the level of American music appreciation.[246] He responded to critics who sneered at the phonograph and radio—those who complained that the quality of performance and type of music recorded and broadcast were wanting—by countering that these technologies merely offered what people wanted.[247] He added that "to a great extent what people really want is what is good for them."[248] He also reported that in Copenhagen, people of all classes were enjoying opera because it had been "brought down to their level."[249] In this statement, Seashore situated opera music in the stratosphere and reported on Copenhagen's successful effort to lower it to a level where it could easily be digested by a lower level of people—the masses. Recalling Chybowski's observation that whiteness is a fundamental element of early-twentieth-century discourse concerning high art music, I argue that Seashore's commentary on taste is replete with both classism and racial coding.

Encounters with the Fascinating and Exotic Primitive Other

Even though they degraded it and marked it as less than fine, inside and outside of eugenics, White people were fascinated by the "other" music they labeled exotic, "primitive," less evolved, and ostensibly dangerous. Garth demonstrated this fascination, for example, in his description of a recording of an American Indian war dance, and of the even greater thrill of observing the primitive "other" in situ:

> Who has not listened to a phonograph record of the "White Dog" war dance of the Blackfeet Indians with some thrills absolutely indescribable, a subjective experience which remains subjective and never becomes successfully objectified? Still more is this the effect if one observes the actual performance of the dance on the reservation with fitting setting of campfire and the shadows of darkness, broken by the reflection of the light upon the faces of silent spectators.[250]

If civilization is rational, the "primitive" in the dichotomy undergirding Garth's description is the opposite—wild, unbridled, emotional, fascinating, and magical. Constructing this encounter with the "primitive" music of the American Indian as the antithesis of the rational, Garth warned that the artistry of this type of musical experience is "violated" by analysis.[251] As I will demonstrate shortly, Seashore disagreed with Garth on this point.

Seashore's Phonophotographic Studies of the "Negro" Singer

Seashore was fascinated by music of the exotic other; the array of studies of ostensibly primitive music that he conducted or supported reflects this fascination, as well as his enthrallment with new recording technologies. Beginning in about 1921, he made claims about the critical role that various types of recording technology could play in the important task of collecting, preserving, and transcribing the primitive music of primitive cultures.[252] He studied or supported the study of the music of American "Negroes," American Indians, South Sea Islanders, and other ostensibly primitive people and cultures from around the globe. He called his work musical anthropology. Although he considered popular genres such as jazz and ragtime to be in some sense primitive, he did not focus on them.

Preservation, Seashore claimed, was a critical function of recording projects involving primitive music. He warned that due to encounters with and contamination by civilization, what he called authentic primitive cultures and pure primitive music were in danger of extinction. Ironically, the much-heralded march of progress, as well as attempts to accelerate the evolutionary advancement of the ostensibly uncivilized, played unacknowledged roles in endangering so-called primitive cultures. Seashore supported recording projects that would capture and document what he described as rapidly vanishing primitive music and cultures: if they could not survive as living entities, then vestiges could be preserved through scientific documentation. In this preservation plan, cultural artifacts such as music would be conserved as museum pieces, taking their place next to stuffed carrier pigeons—documentary proof of the once-living extinct. He reported that dwindling pockets of primitive cultures remained that had not yet been changed by outside influences. He stated, for example, that in the United States, small colonies of "Negroes" remained that had been "relatively little affected by other music," and he promoted scientific projects that would capture the pure music of these groups.[253] In his introduction to Milton Metfessel's 1928 book *Phonophotography in Folk Music: American Negro Songs in New Notation*, Seashore described this race against time:

> In this age of extraordinary spread of civilization into the remotest parts of the earth, primitive folk traits are being obliterated and lost at an amazing pace. Shall we preserve the native songs of our Indians, our Negroes, our Hawaiians, our Filipinos? Shall the scientific collection of the songs of the most primitive peoples be taken seriously, together with other anthropological collecting? Let us hope that the present trial of instruments and methods of collecting songs in the field may arouse investigators to a recognition of the great value of this type of collections [*sic*] and the necessity of doing it at an early date, unless we shall forever lose the opportunity of recording permanently some of the most interesting expressions of folk life which are now being wiped out by the march of civilization.[254]

He also voiced support for studies of music of what he considered to be cultured, civilized people but warned that projects involving primitive music were more urgent. Juxtaposing the eternal with the transitory, he claimed that "artistic singing," the singing of "cultured people," would always be available for study because it "will always be with us"; this was not the case with primitive singing, he warned.[255] The "purest of primitive types of songs" needed to be preserved immediately, he said.[256] Ironically, although Seashore blamed the encroachment of civilization for the obliteration of pure primitive cultures, it apparently did not occur to him that his preservation proposal constituted precisely such encroachment. Furthermore, his conception of cultural authenticity failed to recognize that cultures, however conceptualized, are not static; he apparently did not take into account the problematic cultural politics of attempting to freeze what is, by definition, living and dynamic. What Seashore apparently did not consider was the fact that recorded music and stuffed pigeons are artifactual residua; frozen in time, they can no longer live, breathe, grow, or change.

Merely preserving the primitive using recording technology was not Seashore's primary goal, however. Rather, he aimed to use such recordings in controlled anthropological studies; he believed that primitive music could best be understood by dissecting and analyzing it as a scientist would dissect and analyze natural specimens. In a discussion of the study of "Negro" songs, he described some shortcomings of early attempts to collect and analyze musical specimens. Prior to the phonograph, he stated, collectors had no other option than to listen to live performances and notate what they heard as best they could.[257] He said that while the phonograph had improved the collection process, problems remained, especially if the data collected were to be used in scientific research.[258] For example, transcribers could listen to recordings repeatedly, but in the case of primitive music, conventional notation was inadequate for capturing what they were hearing; he also stated that recordings deteriorated with use.[259] He maintained that although large collections of primitive music already existed, they were virtually worthless because the recording and transcribing processes were incomplete and inaccurate.[260]

In his introduction to the Metfessel book, Seashore praised what he saw as the solution to these problems: phonophotography, a new technology involving the substitution of a camera for the phonograph, such that sound waves could be photographed.[261] This appears to have been the same technology Seashore had used in his earlier study of the famous opera singers, and his Metfessel introduction included phonophotographs of the opera singers, much of the same discussion of vibrato that had appeared in his study of operatic vibrato, and even his description of vibrato's "flirtation" with the exact.[262] He also repeated his message that new technology enabled scientists to objectively study and evaluate emotion, in this case, the emotional components of primitive song and singing.[263]

As the title of the book indicates, the purpose of the Metfessel study was to use phonophotography to dissect and analyze "Negro" singing. As Gustafson notes, the study was premised on the assumption that "the grain of the 'Negro' voice would be clarified through scientific analysis."[264] The book consisted of phonophotographic representations of a host of song examples, many of them field recordings, along with frames from moving pictures of some of the singers and detailed technical descriptions of the phonophotographs. The Metfessel study apparently was something of a group project, and it is unclear exactly what role Seashore played. In his acknowledgments, Metfessel said that Seashore had planned the study; he also thanked H. W. Odum and Guy Benton Johnson from the University of North Carolina for supplying the songs and singers, and for serving as project managers.[265] He further noted that the study was a collaboration between the University of Iowa and the University of North Carolina.[266] Curiously, even though the Metfessel book listed a single author and Seashore identified Metfessel as sole author in several citations, Seashore also wrote several articles based on data collected in the study and used the pronoun "we" in these articles to describe the researchers.[267]

An early mention of the Metfessel study appeared in Seashore's 1928 article "Three New Approaches to the Study of Negro Music," which was published in a special issue of the *Annals of the American Academy of Political and Social Science*; the special issue focused on the "American Negro." Published in the same year as Metfessel's book, Seashore's brief article championed the use of phonophotography to collect and acoustically analyze "Negro" music, which he described as a type of folk music.[268]

Ten years later, he again discussed the Metfessel study in *Psychology of Music*, devoting a section of the chapter "Primitive Music" to "Negro" songs. This section focused narrowly on phonophotographic representations of three songs plus an example of a "Negro" laugh. These four examples had appeared previously in Metfessel's book. The phonophotographic charts were identical to those in Metfessel, but the commentary on the charts was Seashore's.[269]

Seashore's first phonophotographic example was a representation of a recording of "On Ma Journey." He provided the label number—20013-B from Victor's enormously popular black label series—but not the singer's name; Metfessel had named the singer, however—Paul Robeson.[270] Seashore gave a brief note-by-note commentary on the phonophotographic representation, sometimes pointing out what he described as distinctive characteristics of "Negro" singing.[271] His commentary is somewhat similar to Metfessel's descriptions, although not as detailed.

In his second example, he analyzed a rendition of "All My Days" sung by "the famous bass of the Hampton quartet," whom he did not name.[272] Unlike Metfessel, Seashore described the singer; the description implied that Seashore was among the researchers present at the recording session, but he may simply have watched the movie or talked with the research team: "While this singer has appeared before learned audiences and thrilled musicians, he is still ignorant and sings by his primitive impulses with a most charming abandon. He was so lazy that it was difficult to keep him awake for the recording. The words of the song seem appropriate to the character. His singing is characterized by a very deep voice, lazy legato movement."[273] Seashore's descriptors are telling. First, he used "lazy" twice in the span of three sentences, saying that both the musician and the singing were lazy. Significantly, he attributed the singer's sleepiness to laziness rather than to other possible causes. Next, he apparently assumed that the singer was incapable of singing the song the same way twice, and he ascribed variability in the singer's performances to musical ignorance rather than to a conscious decision to improvise and embellish.[274] His assumption that variability was unintentional and due to ignorance constructed the singer as less competent. Like Harris's, Seashore's base assumption was that "Negro" artists did not understand their art and consequently were deficient. Thus, in his estimation, even if the music was pleasing or beautiful, it was not at the same level as music made by a knowing and understanding musician. Furthermore, his conception of "knowing" was narrow and culturally and temporally specific. Third, he used the phrase "primitive impulses" to describe what governed this musician's singing; this phrase signaled the position of this musician and his music on music's evolutionary hierarchy. Seashore relegated the music to a lower rung, beneath that created by musicians who acted with understanding and out of conscious intent rather than impulse. Fourth, he spoke of the singer's "charming abandon." As we have seen, unbridled freedom was a characteristic often ascribed to what were considered less evolved, less refined music and musicians.[275] Seashore's choice of the term "charming" is interesting; although it sometimes has positive connotations, it also is associated with spells—with control achieved by magic. Finally, even though the singer was famous, Seashore denied him recognition by failing to name him.

Despite Seashore's unflattering description of the Hampton bass and his statements about peculiar characteristics of the singing—despite a portrayal that rendered the bass less than fully evolved and less than fully human—Seashore raved about what he heard: "His rendition keeps ringing in my ears, even to this day, as one of the most beautiful tone pictures I have ever heard."[276] He apparently had been charmed by the irresistible, magical music of the exotic other. Nevertheless, his fascination and professed love was mixed with race-based disdain.

According to Metfessel, the Hampton Quartet hailed from the Hampton Normal and Agricultural Institute, and was famous.[277] Known today as Hampton University, in the 1920s this historically Black institution had become widely known for its outstanding choir and for the Hampton Quartet. The quartet traveled the world, giving "highly acclaimed performances in London, Vienna, Zurich, Berlin, Geneva, and Paris."[278] Given that Hampton was a trade and normal school, Seashore's assessment that the singer was ignorant clearly was incorrect. Given that the group toured extensively, it is possible that the singer was exhausted from a grueling performance schedule, or from intense study or work demands. Seashore did not give the singer the benefit of the doubt.

His third phonophotographic example was the song "You Ketch Dis Train"; he reported that it was sung by a worker, hoe in hand, in a field of corn; once again, he provided commentary not offered by Metfessel:

> One must see the dreamy attitude of the singer in order to realize that his spirit is more in the singing than in the eradication of weeds. He did not know that his singing was recorded. He was aware that a moving picture was being taken but apparently was not much distracted by it. In his song, the rhythm is, of course, the conspicuous element,

> with a marked breaking up of short phrases, each ending with a grunt, "Huh!"[279]

Once again, Seashore characterized the singer as lazy (dreamily singing rather than working), ignorant (lacking the understanding that he was being recorded), and primitive (ending phrases with a grunt). His statement about what was "of course" the most distinctive feature of the singing stereotypically tied the "Negro" to what Seashore and others considered the most primitive element of music: rhythm.

Seashore's final example was a "Negro" laugh, which he said he had included because laughter plays an important role in "the jovial Negro song."[280] He stated that he believed it was the first recorded example of a "hearty laugh in Negro style."[281] Invoking and perpetuating a trope of difference that served to separate and segregate, he pointed to even a small detail such as laughter to support the idea that "Negroes" are constitutionally different from White people.

He opened his summary of the Metfessel study's findings with a section entitled "The Feelingful Abandon," in which he described researchers' surprise at the "wildness" of the singing of the "Negroes" and Indians they recorded and phonophotographed.[282] The researchers decided to compare their phonophotographs to those made of "our best artists," and to their surprise, the best artists also took many liberties. According to Seashore, this revelation made the researchers "more charitable toward the untutored savage."[283] "Charity" is an interesting word choice because charity is an act of giving by those who have to those who do not; regardless of his avowed intent, he still assumed that the singers in this study were untutored savages, people not equal to him. After acknowledging similarities in liberty taking, Seashore continued to mark differences, stating that the "Negro" "indulges most lavishly in various forms of license"; he argued that even if the "Negro" knew conventions such as a diatonic scale, he would shun them because license in rhythm, syncopation, and ornamentation is what he does in "his natural habitat."[284] "Natural habitat" would not have been the phrase used to describe an operatic singer's environment. Continuing the theme of license and liberty, he concluded that "Negro" singers deviate freely from pitch and conventional intervals. He noted that some authors had claimed "Negro" singers were incapable of singing intervals precisely, and he countered that measures of "Negro" hearing had refuted this claim.[285] He acknowledged, "He sings in his own way and likes it. The present vogue of Negro singing and the imitation of it in the music of the whites might suggest that there are other people who like the same kind of freedom and that fixed intervals are not the goal of all music."[286]

In his discussion of musical ornamentation and embellishments, he included a quotation from Metfessel, who had said that the musical ornamentation of primitives now could be placed on exhibit in museums alongside visual artifacts, including personal ornamentation.[287] Seashore also quoted Metfessel as having said that good tone quality is rarely found in "Negro" folk singing and that subtlety is lacking: "'He [the singer] is interested in the more *obvious* embellishments and rhythmical devices rather than in the subtle effects of beauty resulting from the relatively regular vibrato of artistic singing [emphasis mine].'"[288] These researchers—these arbiters of taste—decided not only what was or was not beautiful but also what was or was not excessive and obvious. Metfessel's conclusion that "Negro" singers' vocal embellishments and rhythmic devices are obvious or conspicuous is potent when subtlety is the marker of artistic beauty and when all excess—excessive emotion, excessive embellishments, etc.—is met with disapproval and disdain.[289]

Seashore walked back slightly from Metfessel's claim about "Negro" vibrato, stating that in the best of the songs, the vibrato of the "Negro" singers was as good as that of "artistic singers."[290] This walk-back was consistent with a statement he had made in the 1927 article "A Base for the Approach to Quantitative Studies in the Aesthetics of Music." This article included his usual claims about the value of experimental aesthetics, its ability to produce concrete knowledge of the beautiful and ugly, and the role of deviation in creating the beautiful and ugly.[291] He used the vocal embellishments that are "characteristic of Negro singing" as an example of artistic deviation. By and large, however, his aesthetic evaluation of "Negro" singing was hardly glowing even though it clearly fascinated him.

In several articles about the Metfessel study, Seashore wrote in dialect when naming songs or quoting lyrics, and in *Psychology of Music* he commented on "Negro" dialect. The singers' pronunciations, he concluded, were "not mere ignorant dialect or affectation," but rather intentional gravitations toward "musical" vowels.[292] Although his statement mildly supported the "Negro's" use of dialect, Seashore's dialect spellings signaled primitivism, especially to the likely readers of his book. His allusion to "ignorant dialect" brought ignorance onto the stage, and his choice of the word "mere" is significant; although it was not *solely* ignorant dialect, the dialect was ignorant nevertheless. Furthermore, in his discussions of operatic singers, he did not mention their gravitation toward musical vowels, nor did he use invented spellings to capture their pronunciations, even though many classically trained singers customarily adjust vowels and modify consonants to their vocal advantage.

At the end of the chapter, Seashore represented himself as an apologist for "Negro" music and musicians. He stated that he hoped his research would help create a "sympathetic attitude" toward what the "Negro" singer is trying to do, recognizing that what he is trying to do "may be hampered by the cultured music of his day."[293] Even in his role as apologist, however, he clung to the cultured-versus-uncultured dichotomy that marked the "Negro" singer as a lesser. Seashore described the "Negro" singer as primitive and uncultured, and said he did not produce good tone quality. The singer traded in excess and the obvious rather than in the subtly beautiful, he was governed by primitive rhythm, and he communicated in thick dialect. That singer may have created vibrato as good as that of someone Seashore deemed an artist, but the "Negro" singer was not, in Seashore's estimation, an artist. He did not deny that the music he called "Negro" was beautiful, but his descriptions were filled with qualifiers. It was not as beautiful as the gold standard because it was excessive or displayed too many irregularities compared to what he considered the best. Most significantly, it was not the gold standard because it was not produced by a comprehending musician, as defined by Seashore. Finally, he did not name any of the singers discussed in his articles on primitive singing, not even the famous bassist of the Hampton Quartet. By contrast, all twelve of the singers in the opera study were named. If naming is a form of recognition and a way to acknowledge the status of a musician, then Seashore denied that honor to the ostensibly primitive singers he studied. He closed by saying that no song—including "Negro" song—is mysterious; rather, it can be demystified by scientific research that relies on "concrete, observable, and recordable facts."[294] In other words, science can transform the ineffable—even the exotic, fascinating "Negro" song—into the knowable. If to know is to conquer and govern, then Seashore had declared victory over primitive music.

In his 1947 book *In Search of Beauty in Music*, nearly ten years after *Psychology of Music* was published and near the end of his life, Seashore once again discussed the Metfessel study. He included six phonophotographic charts taken directly from Metfessel—different examples than he had included in his 1938 book.[295] He provided little commentary on the phonophotographs, but unlike Metfessel, he included some behind-the-scenes glimpses of how data were collected. Reporting that the singers had been recorded in their "natural setting,"[296] he indicated that the researchers tricked the singers, ostensibly to prevent them from feeling embarrassed.[297] He apparently did not find this problematic, and the fact that he talked about it in his book indicates that he found deception to be an acceptable research practice—at least in research on people he considered primitive. Stating that the field recordings had been made before movies with sound were in use in scientific research, he reported that the researchers had hidden the sound-recording equipment in a suitcase, which falsely led participants to believe that only visual recordings were being made:

> In order to camouflage it, the [phonophotographic] camera was built into a suitcase which was represented as being a moving picture camera. This was to keep the singers unaware of the fact that their singing would be recorded. The Negro workers in the field were delighted to have their pictures taken, but they might have been embarrassed had they suspected that their voices were being recorded.[298]

Seashore did not elaborate on why the researchers assumed the singers might have been embarrassed if they had learned that their voices were being recorded; perhaps the researchers assumed that the singers considered their own singing to be inferior. Although ethical standards for conducting human subjects research were slim to nil in the early twentieth century, the practices Seashore described stand out, partly because the researchers assumed that the "Negro" singer was childlike, naïve, and therefore easily tricked. Significantly, the researchers used their assumption as grounds to proceed with the deception. I found no evidence of whether the participants were aware that they were being tricked, probably because none exists.

In a 1934 article promoting phonophotography, Carl Seashore and his nephew Harold discussed its use in their study of the singing of a Sioux Indian woman. They did not name the singer but stated that she was "exhibited" at the "Century of Progress."[299] A Century of Progress International Exposition was the official name of the 1933–34 World's Fair, which was held in Chicago. The overarching theme of the fair was progress, and technological innovation figured prominently. In addition, an exhibit of five Indian villages was part of a social science cluster called "The Stirring Story of Mankind's Rise."[300] According to the official fair guidebook, North American Indians lived in the villages during the fair "in as close an approximation of their native life as it is possible to attain."[301] It is telling that the Seashores chose to say the Sioux Indian singer "was exhibited," not that she sang. It is possible that she lived in and was part of one of the Indian village exhibits; it also is possible that she performed as part of a demonstration of the use of recording technology to capture the primitive. In either case, Carl and Harold Seashore described her as a specimen on exhibit.

The article stated that the recording that Carl and Harold Seashore phonophotographed had been sent to the Iowa Laboratory by Frances Densmore.[302] Densmore was a Minnesota-born anthropologist and ethnomusicologist who spent her life recording the music of a host of American Indian tribes, at times with the assistance of the Smithsonian Institution. Much of the Seashores' article was devoted to explaining how to read the phonophotographic chart. They briefly discussed characteristics of the singing, however:

> One is struck at once with the futility of trying to convey an adequate description of the pitch performance in terms of the conventional musical notation as based on auditory transcription. The presence of a fairly normal and beautiful vibrato is confirmed and quantified as to extent and rate. Other tonal ornaments allied to those discussed by Metfessel in Negro singing are shown in certain characteristic flights and dips. Apart from irregularity and lack of rigidity, the deviations from recognized tonal intervals are matters of great interest. The whole tonal movement reveals the characteristic abandon in the legato style which calls for interpretation into musical significance.[303]

In this passage, they focused on the magnitude of the singer's deviation from pitch and conventional tonal intervals; their description was filled with references to freedom, abandon, and irregularity—a freedom that defied and could not be captured by conventional notation. They compared the vibrato of the Sioux singer to a "normal" and beautiful standard, presumably the standard set by operatic singers, and the Sioux singer's vibrato was found to be acceptable because it was similar to the operatic norm. Seashore and Seashore said that the technical "ornaments" resembled those noted in Metfessel's study of "Negro" music,[304] suggesting that different types of primitive singing shared characteristics that linked them together while simultaneously separating them from so-called civilized music. Although Carl Seashore considered deviation from the exact and pure to be a characteristic of the beautiful, it is not clear whether he found the deviations in the Sioux woman's singing to be beautiful or ugly; if he deemed them ugly, he probably would have judged them as such by claiming that they were too extreme. He did find them unusual. After acknowledging that the technology was imperfect and produced errors, Carl and Harold Seashore remarked on how detailed a picture the phonophotograph provided, noting that it recorded fine-grained features of the singing, including "numerous devices for ornamentation and, of course, many manifest faults."[305] This technology would have recorded many faults in all singing, but Seashore did not note this in his discussion of the graphs of operatic singing. Furthermore, the "of course" comment is cryptic. Were the authors saying that of course faults appeared because all singers exhibit them, or that of course many manifest faults showed up because this was primitive Indian singing? Carl and Harold Seashore were not clear.

Seashore's Proposed Collaboration with the Motion Picture Industry

Seashore discussed the fascinating and exotic—but primitive—other in a second cluster of publications and archival documents, all of which pertained to a project that never got off the ground: a collaboration between music anthropologists and Hollywood movie producers to create films featuring scientifically accurate representations of primitive people and primitive music.[306] Aware of the educational potential of recording technology, he marveled at the ability of new technologies to make the life and music of distant, exotic cultures available for local viewing; technology, he claimed, was making the world smaller:

> The coming in of methods of recording and reproducing sounds from a film is one of the marvels of the present century. It enables us to live in a new world situation. When we can sit down in a theater or private studio and see the primitive savage in his native haunts at work and play, in ceremonial dance and song, the world is made smaller. Concrete situations, as seen and heard, are brought to us from all parts of the globe, regardless of distance, and may be preserved for all time.
>
> We have marveled at the exhibition feature, at the entertainment which we enjoy in the theater, and at the possibility of collecting data for all kinds of historical purposes by this extraordinary means; but very few have realized anything of the unlimited possibilities of a scientific character that this movement introduces for music.[307]

Seashore's plan resembled trophy hunting; exotic cultures and music could be captured, preserved, and brought home for display thanks to recording technology. Ever seeking practical applications of new scientific research, he identified a problem with commercial films that he believed scientists could solve: such films, he claimed, were not scientifically factual in their representation of primitive music and cultures.[308] He noted, for example, that extant movies did not accurately represent local primitive music, specifically the "Negro" and American Indian music that had not been "spoiled by contact with our own."[309] He proposed to solve the problem of inaccuracy through a collaboration that he claimed would benefit both movie producers and researchers. The final product would be field-recorded footage that could be used both for research and to create entertaining Hollywood movies.[310] He said that the footage would capture scientific data that could facilitate the study of "the origin and development of racial music";[311] in addition, it would be the raw material from which Hollywood producers could create entertaining commercial films.[312] He also suggested that Hollywood could use the strictly scientific footage as film shorts.[313] Not only would Hollywood movies be more scientifically accurate, Seashore argued, but the moviegoers attending them would be both entertained and educated;[314] he variously described these commercial movies as "educational entertainment"[315] or "semi-educational entertainment."[316] He said that scientists did not have enough funding to undertake such field expeditions and that through collaboration, the movie industry could advance scientific research.[317] He also said that scientists would provide a service to the film industry: just as pure science had useful applications in industry, it had useful applications in "the advancement of the art of educational entertainment."[318]

Seashore claimed retrospectively that he had first approached the film industry when the feature film *Trader Horn* came out, and he said that the industry had been excited about his proposal.[319] Nominated for an Academy Award for best picture, *Trader Horn* was a fictional rendition of the life of a real-life ivory trader, Alfred Aloysius Smith. Most of the movie was filmed in Africa. *Trader Horn* (1931) was an early talking movie, coming out just a few years after the first talking feature film, *The Jazz Singer*, which appeared in 1927.

By 1938, he was promoting his movie collaboration in a published article, stating that the movie industry was ready to enter a partnership that would make their films more educational.[320] He also described his plan in other publications, two of which appeared in 1942.[321] In these publications, he explained how the collaboration would work; one article mapped out a hypothetical plan that began with "penetration into a primitive community"[322] to make a film representing "the primitive culture of a relatively pure strain of savage people in one of the South Sea islands."[323] In a footnote to this discussion, Seashore added that the same process could be used to film the "not necessarily primitive" music of American "Negroes" and Indians.[324] Significantly, earlier, in his 1938 publication, Seashore had described "Negro" music as primitive; by 1942, he called it folk music but not necessarily primitive.[325]

The first step in his plan was to send a music anthropologist into the field for a period of one or two years.[326] This person would be a knowledgeable expert, Seashore said, who would cultivate good will and win the trust of primitive people to gain access to homes, ceremonies, etc.[327] The music anthropologist would use primitive people's interest in magic to cultivate "responses which shall reveal the true life of the people"; another job of the anthropologist would be to make primitive people comfortable with recording devices.[328] During this period, the music anthropologist would decide what constituted the most significant aspects of the culture while also noting what would have the most entertainment value:

> The first step that is necessary to take in this cooperation is to employ a musical anthropologist to go into the field as a scout and apply existing knowledge of the situation in a survey of available material. This will take two forms. First will be the determination of what is anthropologically the most significant aspect of musical culture in a selected group. The anthropologist will probably find that it represents a definite culture stage in the development of melody, accompaniment, musical instruments, ceremonial value, echo of environment, and a number of other issues fundamental to the history of music. He may then select from these the features which should be illustrated in order to show the most characteristic and significant elements in the situation. These elements may be of as good entertainment value as the hodge-podge ordinarily assembled by the professional photographer in the interests of stage playing.[329]

In anticipation of the arrival of the filmmakers, the music anthropologist also would select the "actors" to perform in the film, "organize performing units," and conduct rehearsals.[330] Although Seashore did not discuss this, I speculate that these "actors" would not be paid. The music anthropologist would consider all aspects of the cultural experience with an eye toward discerning their ethical and aesthetic significance: "The scientist should exercise insight into the various types of affiliates with music; such as dance, speech and mimicry, and try to reveal the ethical and esthetical significance of the entire setting at the culture level of this particular group."[331] Thus, the music anthropologist would serve as an advance project manager; he would have laid the groundwork and have "paved the way for the organization of amusement features."[332] Seashore maintained that this scientific approach to the filming process would not interfere with the entertainment value of the footage because "patrons of the movies would be quick to discover that in such cases truth may be stranger than fiction."[333]

He also said that the music anthropologist would "lead a sort of heroic life by introducing into their [primitive people's] play life a pattern which is in harmony with their culture level and will lead to self-forgetfulness and revealing self-expression in all performances."[334] It is not clear why Seashore described this role as heroic, but he may have meant that the anthropologist would become a trusted leader who would guide participants into producing what the anthropologist and filmmakers were looking for. His word choice, however, invoked the idea of the heroic quest, and his movie plan did contain elements of the heroic literary template: heeding the call to adventure, the music anthropologist would leave home destined for exotic and distant locales. On arrival, he would discern who could or could not be trusted or useful, would identify and overcome a series of challenges, and heroically return home with a prize—the data—and stories to tell.

In 1942 he again stated that his movie proposal was being considered by Hollywood producers,[335] but correspondence from 1943 revealed its ultimate fate. In May 1943, at the height of World War II, Seashore wrote to the Motion Picture Academy saying that he had found "a splendid investigator" well suited to the movie project.[336] This investigator, Seashore reported, had already successfully done fieldwork on primitive music and was currently working on a project in conjunction with the Library of Congress. He stated that the investigator was interested in devoting two years to helping make a motion picture that would "represent negro music in a way which would be entertaining and at the same time scientifically and artistically true and of educational value."[337] According to Seashore, the investigator was seeking communities "representing the most characteristic negro music in the various activities of daily life."[338] Seashore reiterated his familiar account of how the research would be undertaken, and he noted that the film industry could advertise that the film had "approved scientific and artistic backing"; he further claimed that such a film would garner international interest.[339] On the same day, he sent a letter to poet and playwright Archibald MacLeish, who was the Librarian of Congress at that time. Seashore stated that he had contacted MacLeish about the movie project because he knew that the Library of Congress was interested in "Negro" music; he enclosed an article about the project and stated that "Dr. Bach" was prepared to undertake it:

> With Dr. Bach in an undertaking of this kind I see the possibility of securing a critical sampling of negro spirituals and should like to see

> the project limited to this particular music. There are in this country small colonies of negroes who have been relatively little affected by other music. If we can get the assurance of a producer and be given free hands, the first step would, of course, be to organize cooperation with the various agencies now interested and active in the study of this racial music.[340]

Seashore apparently was referring to Marcus Bach. Born in Wisconsin, Bach studied music at the University of Wisconsin, was ordained, received a Rockefeller Fellowship, became a playwright, and (in 1942) completed a doctorate from the University of Iowa's School of Religion.[341] He later became a professor at the University of Iowa (from 1945–64). MacLeish replied promptly, saying that the Library of Congress was very interested in the project and confirming that the library had been collecting "Negro" music for a decade.[342] He also said that the library wanted to add moving pictures to its collection, and he referred Seashore to Alan Lomax, who had made most of the recordings of "Negro" music that the library owned.[343] MacLeish indicated that Lomax had recently left the library to work for Columbia Broadcasting.[344] What MacLeish could not have known is that in the years that followed, Lomax would become a legendary ethnomusicologist, widely known for his field recordings of twentieth-century American folk music.

On June 9, 1943, Seashore was sent a response from the Academy of Motion Picture Arts and Sciences. Mrs. Donald Gledhill, executive secretary at the Academy, reported that she was filling in for her husband while he was serving in the army, and she stated that although Seashore's proposal was interesting, the Academy could not help because the industry was experiencing severe shortages of materials and staff due to the war. She suggested revisiting the idea when the war was over.[345] Prior to 1943, Donald Gledhill had been the executive secretary of the Academy of Motion Picture Arts and Sciences; when he joined the army during World War II, his wife, Margaret Gledhill (later Herrick), was chosen to serve as acting executive secretary. She became the permanent executive secretary in 1945, [346] and she held that position until 1971. The Academy's famous film library is named in her honor.

A few days later, Seashore replied to Gledhill saying that the two-year project with Dr. Bach at the helm would move ahead despite lack of financial support from Hollywood.[347] In fact, from 1943 to 1945, Bach recorded interviews with clergy and examples of congregational singing from a host of groups and denominations, including African Americans. The project was sponsored by the University of Iowa's School of Religion, and the recordings,

"Preserving Iowa's Religious Heritage," are held by the Library of Congress. Thus, even though Seashore's Hollywood-sponsored movie project did not pan out, an anthropological study emerged from it. Significantly, Bach did not single out African Americans as exotic others; instead, he recorded and preserved sacred singing from a wide variety of groups, African Americans among them.

In many ways, the racialized contours of Seashore's discussions of his Hollywood-movie proposal resemble those of his anthropological studies of "primitive" musical cultures. A distinguishing element of the movie proposal, however, was the idea of using "primitive" cultures and people as entertainment for what presumably would be White, middle-class audiences in the United States—regardless of the meaning, intent, or significance that the culture-bearers themselves ascribed to the activities filmed. Whether the goal was to educate or to entertain, however, Seashore did not find objectification or voyeurism problematic—at least not when the object of the gaze was deemed primitive.

On the one hand, Seashore was prescient. Accuracy of representation in entertainment movies would be of greater concern to filmmakers in the latter twentieth century than it was in the days of *Trader Horn*. On the other hand, Seashore's answers to questions about what constitutes accuracy, who decides what is accurate, why accuracy is important, and who benefits from it reveal that the people being filmed were conspicuously missing. The anthropologist decided what constituted accurate, valuable knowledge and which people were valuable; the anthropologist, filmmakers, and audiences stood to gain from this knowledge. Seashore never mentioned whether or how the "primitive" people featured in the films would benefit from the project, monetarily or otherwise. As I indicated earlier, although he referred to members of culture groups as "actors," he did not indicate that they would be paid.

Seashore's characterizations of "primitive" people brought to my mind Toni Morrison's description of what she called an Africanist persona. In her 1992 book *Playing in the Dark: Whiteness and the Literary Imagination*, Morrison said that it is a fabrication or invention found in American fiction written by White authors. Significantly, she stated that an Africanist persona is "reflexive; an extraordinary meditation on the self; a powerful exploration of the fears and desires that reside in the writerly conscious. It is an astonishing revelation of longing, of terror, of perplexity, of shame, of magnanimity."[348] Even though Seashore claimed that his work lived in the realm of factual, scientific objectivity, I argue that it nevertheless contains racialized fabrications that resemble Morrison's conception of an

Africanist persona. If Seashore's fabrications are reflexive, then they offer glimpses of the tangled web of desires and fears that motivated him, other eugenicists, and all who subscribed to these inventions, viewing them as blood-based facts. According to Morrison, an Africanist persona—and particularly its association with raw savagery—serves as a "staging ground and arena for the elaboration of the quintessential American identity."[349] In a commentary on Morrison's concept, Alex Lubin writes, "Through the spectral image of blackness, the nation constructs itself as white."[350] I maintain that her observations also apply to the fabrications Seashore employed, which may have been especially potent because they were presented as scientific fact. Furthermore, not only did these fabrications construct the nation as White, they constructed the nation as *superior because it was White.*

Standardized Testing of Race Differences in Musical Ability

The discursive landscape I have briefly sketched helps provide context for a particular type of research that emerged in the 1920s: studies that employed standardized tests to determine if there were race differences in musical ability. In September 1921, two years after the Seashore Tests had been published, Seashore delivered the paper "Individual and Racial Inheritance of Musical Traits" at the Second International Congress of Eugenics. He devoted nearly all of it to his standard messages about the nature of musical ability, the merits of standardized measures of musical talent, the types of research underway that were germane to eugenics, and potential practical applications of this research, including the use of test scores in mate selection.[351] He only mentioned race twice, once in the title of the talk and the second time in a single sentence describing one of the many possible eugenical tasks that could be accomplished using standardized tests of musical talent: "I wish here especially to call attention to their [standardized tests'] availability in the study of racial differences as well as the study of individual differences in the experimental investigation of the inheritance of musical talent. The relation of these to eugenics is self-evident."[352]

On that day, Seashore flung open a door, and through it walked a stream of scholars intent on doing precisely what he had suggested. Although Seashore did not conduct his own research on race differences in musical talent, he played a key role in the work of others, sometimes serving as an advisor or consultant. Significantly, early studies of race differences used the Seashore Tests exclusively, while later studies employed them along with other similar standardized tests. Because Seashore claimed that his tests measured innate capacities, the results of these race-differences studies were assumed to reveal innate biological characteristics regardless of whether race differences were found. He helped disseminate the results of these studies; when he cited them, he also, in effect, promoted his tests. Seventeen years later, he continued to claim that measuring racial differences was a suitable component of anthropological study, and he called for the enlargement and refinement of this kind of research.[353]

Race Crossing in Jamaica

The Project

Charles Davenport and Morris Steggerda conducted one of the early landmark studies of race differences in musical ability. In September 1926, they sailed to Jamaica to conduct research on the effects of race crossing on a wide array of mental and physical characteristics of three groups of Jamaicans, whom they described as pure-blooded "Negroes," Whites, and "the crosses between the two."[354] The researchers sometimes called the third category of people "mulattoes," "Browns," or "hybrids."[355] In a report to the Galton Society on preparations for the study, Davenport indicated that after having considered St. John's of the Virgin Islands, the researchers chose Jamaica because it was geographically accessible, had populations of Blacks and Browns to study, and had been the site of prior research on "skin color."[356]

A key figure in the American eugenics movement, Davenport had been intensely interested in and vehemently opposed to race crossing for quite some time. In 1921, he had described race crossing as an "extremely alluring" and little-researched field, and he had suggested that New York City would be an excellent site for conducting such studies.[357] During the early 1920s, he played a major role both in organizing the Second International Congress of Eugenics and in publishing congress proceedings.[358] A long-time director of the Eugenics Record Office (ERO), when the ERO and the Station for Experimental Evolution combined in 1921 to form the Department of Genetics of the Carnegie Institution of Washington, DC, he was chosen as its head.

Steggerda was a doctoral student in zoology at the University of Illinois, and he was described in the study's report as having had "excellent training in genetics and psychology."[359] In an article appearing when the study was under way, *Eugenical News* reported that Steggerda was "favorably known" for the many genetics records he had contributed to the Eugenics Record

Office.[360] He would later join that journal's editorial team.[361] His dissertation, which he completed in 1928, examined the physical characteristics of "negro-white hybrids" in Jamaica.[362]

The Jamaica study's advisory committee consisted of Walter Van Dyke Bingham, Edward Thorndike, Clark Wissler, and Davenport.[363] Like Davenport, Thorndike and Wissler were eugenicists, Thorndike having served with Seashore on the AES Advisory Council and Wissler having served with Davenport on the publication team for the proceedings of the Second International Congress of Eugenics. Bingham had been on Yerkes's team that developed the Army intelligence tests.

Prior to departing for Jamaica, Steggerda trained for two or three months in Cold Spring Harbor, the location of Davenport's eugenics operations.[364] After accompanying Steggerda to Jamaica and getting the project started in the fall of 1926, Davenport returned to the United States and Steggerda stayed on, returning to Cold Spring Harbor in December and consulting with the study's advisory committee in New York City.[365] He went back to Jamaica in January 1927 and stayed until October.[366] The study's findings were published in 1929 in the book *Race Crossing in Jamaica*.

The *Race Crossing* study had many components, including comparisons of "developmental anthropometry, basal metabolism, blood groups, and intelligence."[367] The researchers reported that they concentrated on psychological differences, notably differences in intelligence and sensory capacities.[368] Their hypothesis was that constitutional differences exist between races:

> It is often held that, while physical differences between races are beyond dispute, it has never been shown that there is such a thing as racial differentiation in mentality. Those who look at matters broadly were inclined, on *a priori* grounds, to think such difference in mentality and instincts to be probable. Dogs, for example, differ not only in their form, but also in their instincts, such as the mammal-killing instinct of the fox-terrier, the herding instinct of the collie, the instincts of pointing, retrieving, etc.
>
> In humans there has seemed to be a nomadic instinct in Gypsies and Bedouins, a trading instinct in Arabs and Jews, an instinct for industry in the Chinese, for tracking in Australian aborigines, for hunting in Indians, and for life on the sea in Norwegians and many English. These differences in behavior have been ascribed by the doubters to tradition, to early training, to opportunity. There has been no satisfactory evidence of innate, constitutional differences.

> To test the hypothesis that such constitutional differences in the intellectual and sensory spheres exist, special attention was directed toward psychological tests to be made on our three groups of people from Jamaica.[369]

They administered all or portions of a host of tests, including the Army Alpha, the Knox Moron, the Knox Cube Imitation, and the Binet-Simon Measuring Scale for Intelligence; participants were tested on form discrimination, geometric figures copying, figure drawing, reconstruction of a manikin, folded and notched paper shape recognition, form substitution, repetition of seven numbers, criticism of absurd sentences, *and musical capacity*.[370] As historian William H. Tucker notes, the researchers also took seventy-eight anthropometric and physiological measurements, including some of tongue furrows.[371]

The Funding and the Funder

The advisory committee for the *Race Crossing* study had been formed after the Carnegie Institution of Washington, DC, received a special gift of $10,000 ($143,000 in 2019 dollars) that, according to Davenport, was earmarked for the "study of the adaptability of negroes and mulattoes for civilization. A comparative study of negroes, mulattoes and whites was to be made in some tropical country, with special reference to their comparative social adjustability."[372] In the introduction to *Race Crossing*, Davenport and Steggerda indicated that the benefactor was concerned about the impact of race crossing on the future of a nation; the study was undertaken by the Department of Genetics, which Davenport directed.[373] The project also received additional support from the Eugenics Research Association.[374] Part of the funding went to providing Steggerda with a "native assistant and a Ford car."[375]

The project's benefactor was Col. Wickliffe Preston Draper (1891–1972),[376] a wealthy heir to a textile fortune who devoted his life and money to furthering White supremacy. In "Toward a Racial Abyss: Eugenics, Wickliffe Draper, and the Origins of the Pioneer Fund," Michael G. Kenny states that Draper approached Davenport in 1923 proposing an endowment of $1 million or $1.5 million ($22.2 or $22.4 million in 2019 dollars) to support the advancement of eugenics.[377] Kenny quotes from a March 23, 1923, letter Davenport sent to Draper that summarized the benefactor's goal: to support work that "'would preserve in the population a high proportion of the excellent Nordic traits by a proper selection of immigrants and by securing desirable matings (the repression of undesirable ones) in the population already in America.'"[378]

According to Kenny, Davenport suggested several possible research topics, including race crossing, but Draper initially gave very little money. Kenny states that a few years later, Davenport suggested a study of the inheritability of musical ability, which did not capture Draper's interest, but Draper responded with a proposal for a study of the effects of race crossing in a country such as Brazil or Haiti.[379] William H. Tucker reports that Davenport was delighted with Draper's idea, which culminated in Davenport and Steggerda's study of race crossing in Jamaica.[380]

Throughout his life, Draper funded a host of other White-supremacist causes in addition to eugenics, often funneling donations anonymously through a private banking unit of J. P. Morgan.[381] For example, Kenny reports that in 1928, Draper approached Davenport about establishing an essay competition focusing on the fecundity of Nordics and non-Nordics.[382] Tucker states that in the years that followed, Draper funded three contests, two on topics related to his original proposal to Davenport and one on the inheritability of mental disorders; according to Tucker, Draper was not named as the benefactor in the contest announcements.[383]

In 1936, Draper paid for the printing of 1,000 copies of Earnest Sevier Cox's book *White America: The American Racial Problem as Seen in a World-wide Perspective*, which supported the repatriation of American "Negroes" to Africa, and he instructed Cox to decide to whom the books should be given; according to Tucker, Cox sent them to members of Congress and to legislators in North Carolina and Mississippi.[384]

Draper's most far-reaching philanthropic initiative was the formation of the Pioneer Fund, a foundation that still operates today; it had two initial purposes: (1) to support the education of children whose parents were of "unusual value as citizens," and (2) to support the "study and research into the problems of heredity and eugenics in the human race."[385] Legal historian Paul A. Lombardo writes that Draper created the fund in 1937, not long after he had served as an official delegate representing the American Eugenics Research Association at the International Congress for the Scientific Investigation of Population Problems, a Nazi-led eugenics conference held in Berlin in 1935.[386] The honorary president of the congress was none other than Wilhelm Frick, Hitler's Reichsminister of the Interior.[387] Reporting that Draper was excited about attending the congress, Lombardo traces a tangle of connections between Draper, Laughlin, and the German Nazi movement.[388]

Laughlin served as the Pioneer Fund's first president and established its early goals,[389] which Kenny describes:

> Whatever Pioneer's goals may be now, "human" race betterment was most certainly not its aim in the early years. The historical record unequivocally shows that the Fund was established to provide a scientific basis for projects to defend the American white race against degeneration from within and contamination from without. These were Wickliffe Draper's primary and passionate concerns. . . . All research and political activity with which Draper himself had anything to do was in the service of an agenda aimed at forestalling America's genetic decline through positive and negative eugenics. Any other conclusion is obfuscation bordering on whitewash.[390]

One of the earliest of the fund's many grants went to an aviator project that included a study of the fertility of aviation officers and an incentives program that encouraged pilots to reproduce.[391] Lombardo reports that pilots were considered "prime eugenical specimens"[392] and notes that the project was modeled after similar initiatives in Germany.[393] The incentives program consisted of scholarship funding for a fourth child born in 1940 to aviators' families that already had three children.[394]

Draper bequeathed $3.3 million ($20.2 million in 2019 dollars) to the Pioneer Fund,[395] and Tucker states that by the time of Draper's death in 1972, the Fund had become "the most important and perhaps the world's only funding source for scientists who still believed that white racial purity was essential for social progress."[396] Among the many recipients of Pioneer Fund grants are Arthur Jensen (1923–2012), described by the Southern Poverty Law Center as the "father of modern academic racism";[397] J. Phillipe Rushton (1943–2012), who headed the Pioneer Fund from 2002 to 2012 and whose writings were published by the White supremacist think tank American Renaissance;[398] William Shockley (1910–89), who developed the Bonus Sterilization Plan and promoted the idea that American "Negroes" are hereditarily inferior;[399] and Roger Pearson (1927–), the anti-Semitic editor of the journal the *New Patriot*, who after World II established the Northern League, a neo-Nazi organization, in Britain.[400]

Significantly, sixteen researchers receiving Pioneer funding were cited in the 1994 book *The Bell Curve: Intelligence and Class Structure in American Life*, by Richard J. Herrnstein and Charles Murray.[401] This book, which was described in an op-ed piece by *New York Times* columnist Bob Herbert as "a scabrous piece of racial pornography masquerading as serious scholarship," reportedly has experienced a resurgence of popularity in recent years.[402]

In 2003, the Southern Poverty Law Center called the Pioneer Fund a hate group, and it currently designates it as a White nationalist extremist group.[403]

Although creating the Pioneer Fund was Draper's most influential project, until his death he funded a host of other White supremacist causes, including research in the 1950s on "racial blood-type incompatibilities."[404] According to Douglas A. Blackmon, in the 1960s, Draper anonymously gave about $300,000 (nearly $2.5 million in 2019 dollars) to the Mississippi State Sovereignty Commission, which had been established to oppose civil rights legislation and integration; among its many activities were lobbying Congress and distributing more than 1.4 million pamphlets and mailings in opposition to the Civil Rights Act.[405] Blackmon states that in the wake of the Act's passage, Draper helped fund private, segregated White academies that served White families "fleeing newly integrated public schools."[406]

Race Crossing's *Army Alpha Test Results*

The Army Alpha test is among the standardized measures the *Race Crossing* researchers administered, and if Draper and Davenport had hoped that results of the intelligence tests would resoundingly support White supremacist views, they did not get what they wanted. Blacks outscored Whites on four of the eight sections of the test, and Whites outscored Blacks on the other four. Whites were the lowest-scoring group in three of the eight sections of the test, having been outscored both by Blacks and Browns, and Browns were the lowest scoring group in the other five sections.[407] Using the researchers' criterion for statistical significance, in four sections, Whites' scores were significantly higher than Blacks' scores, and in two sections, Blacks' scores were significantly higher than Whites'. In the remaining two sections, Blacks outscored Whites but the differences were not statistically significant. These results did not support across-the-board White superiority. Nevertheless, and perhaps in deference to Draper, Davenport and Steggerda concluded, "In the Army Alpha test the highest adult standing goes to the Whites, the lowest to the Browns."[408] In the final chapter of the book, Davenport and Steggerda summarized all of the study's findings, including the Army Alpha test results, and they reported group results in *rank order*; although they stated that not all of the Army Alpha findings were statistically significant, they did not report which findings were or were not.[409] They also claimed that there were greater mental disharmonies among Browns,[410] which led Davenport to conclude, "A population of hybrids will be a population carrying an excessively large number of intellectually incompetent persons."[411]

Kenny reports that Draper got what he had paid for, stating that Davenport sent a copy of the book to Draper and urged him to read the conclusion; according to Kenny, Davenport also said that he believed Draper would be pleased with the outcome of the study.[412] Tucker states, however, that the study's results must have been a disappointment to Davenport and Draper:

> Given the high expectations for some definitive evidence of both black inferiority and miscegenation's additional disadvantage, the results must have been a major disappointment for Davenport, and especially for his patron. Although white subjects attained higher average scores on a number of the mental tests, blacks performed better than whites at "complicated directions for doing things" as well as "in simple mental arithmetic and with numerical series," a result for which Davenport offered an interesting explanation: "The more complicated a brain, the more numerous its 'association fibers,' the less satisfactorily it performs the simple numerical calculations which a calculating machine does so quickly and accurately." The data collected on "hybrids" also failed to reveal any significant intellectual disharmonies caused by miscegenation despite Davenport's creative efforts at interpretation.[413]

Tucker reports that in the wake of a "meager return on his investment," Draper channeled his money to projects other than "the fruitless study of miscegenation."[414]

Seashore's Role in the Race Crossing *Study*

The *Race Crossing* study is widely known and has been discussed by many scholars of eugenics. Less widely known, however, is that as part of the study, Davenport and Steggerda measured musical capacities and used the Seashore Tests to do so. In addition, they consulted with Seashore prior to and after data collection.

This was not the first time that Seashore and Davenport had collaborated. Mehler reports, for example, that between 1921 and 1930, the two had worked together to study the inheritance of musical ability; as I discussed in chapter 6, the Eugenics Record Office employed Seashore's graduate student, Hazel Stanton, and used the Seashore Tests to collect data during this period.[415] Mehler describes Seashore as "a close associate" of Davenport's.[416]

In a letter dated March 25, 1926, Davenport introduced Steggerda to Seashore and described the planned research. He stated that the study's purpose was to examine the effects of race crossing; he also said that Steggerda was planning to study "special capacities" and welcomed up-to-the-minute information from Seashore about methods—presumably ways of measuring musical capacities.[417] As the book documents, at some point between June and September 1926, Steggerda traveled to Iowa City to confer with Seashore about "technical matters."[418] A letter from Davenport to Seashore dated September 22, 1926—a response to Seashore's request for a copy of Steggerda's project proposal—documents that the two men were in contact at the launch of the study; this letter also described an element of the research method, indicating that some of the "examinations" would be given to groups and others to individuals.[419]

The Findings about Musical Talent

The researchers administered the Seashore Tests to 90 adults and about 300 children; the children were divided into two, equal-sized groups: younger children, aged ten to twelve, and teenagers aged thirteen to fifteen.[420] The researchers decided that the ranking charts in Seashore's test manual produced "curiously irregular" distributions and were unsuitable for the study at hand because Seashore's data had come from White children in the United States; they consulted with Thorndike and Robert S. Woodworth—not Seashore—and came up with a different way to tabulate and report test scores.[421] Using the same three race categories that were employed throughout the larger study—White, Brown, and Black—and the three age categories I have just described, the researchers reported race by age means and standard deviations for each of the six parts of the Seashore Tests: pitch, intensity, time, harmony, tonal memory, and rhythm.[422]

If the data from the other mental and psychological tests were something of a disappointment to Davenport and Draper, then the results of the Seashore Tests were probably a big shock. Davenport and Steggerda summarized their conclusions: "In musical capacity, in general, the Blacks stand first and the Whites last."[423] They also gave a synopsis of findings for each of the six parts of the tests:

> In general . . . musical capacity, as measured by the Seashore tests, is more highly developed in Blacks than Whites. This superiority is most marked in time, rhythm, intensity and pitch. In sense of consonance the races do not differ significantly. In tonal memory the Whites seem to be slightly superior to the Blacks.

> The Browns are generally intermediate between Blacks and Whites in musical discrimination. In two tests applied to the adolescents the Browns have slightly, but not significantly, higher grades than either of the other two groups. In the six adult groups the average of the Browns never significantly exceeds that of the other two groups.[424]

They reported that tonal discrimination was the only subtest where "Whites *came near to* excelling [emphasis mine]."[425] In a statement that clearly reflected their hope of proving unequivocal White superiority, Davenport and Steggerda used the word "disappointing" to describe the test performance of Whites from Seaford Town and Grand Cayman: "The musical record of the Whites of Seaford Town and Grand Cayman is disappointing. Their worst failure is discrimination of pitch where the mean of the Whites is 14 per cent below that of the Blacks. Also in discrimination of time and in rhythm the Whites are markedly inferior to the Blacks."[426]

They sometimes reported subtest results by stating which group had done best and which had done worst based on mean percentages of correct responses; for example, they stated that Blacks had done best and Whites worst on the pitch test.[427] If they had reported every music subtest test result in terms of rank order of mean percentages of correct responses, then Whites would have been best six times and worst eleven times; Browns would have been best four times and worst two times, and Blacks would have been best eight times and worst five times. These results would not have sat well with White supremacist eugenicists. In some instances, the researchers appear to have attempted to downplay the superior performance of Blacks; for example, after reporting that "the colored groups" were superior to Whites in pitch discrimination, they added that none of the Jamaican groups, regardless of race or age, did particularly well compared to the fifth graders Seashore tested.[428]

Near the end of the book, Davenport and Steggerda listed all of the traits "that differ so strikingly between Whites and Blacks as to render it probable that they are genetically distinct in the two races."[429] They reported results of four Seashore subtests—pitch, intensity, time, and rhythm; Blacks had excelled in all of them.[430]

In a single-authored *Scientific Monthly* article, "Race Crossing in Jamaica," which appeared a year before the book was published, Davenport reported on many of the study's findings, including the superior performance of Blacks on the Seashore Tests. Toward the end of the article, he stated that given the English race's poor musical endowment, hybridization with "Negroes" might increase musical capacity. He warned, however, that without controlled selective breeding, hybridization would be a slow process that might introduce undesirable traits, and he closed with a call to maintain homogenous, racially segregated populations.[431]

A 1929 letter indicated that Davenport had sent Seashore a copy of *Race Crossing* shortly after it was published. Seashore thanked him for the book and, significantly, expressed appreciation for "the *splendid way in which you have handled the data* based upon the use of my Measures of Musical Talent [emphasis mine]."[432] The letter began some back-and-forth speculation between the two men about the findings of the music portion of the study. These findings sent Seashore and Davenport scrambling for an explanation other than the most obvious one, given their previous assumptions about the validity and reliability of the Seashore Tests: "Negroes" had routed Whites due to innately superior musical talent. Innate biological difference was precisely how Seashore explained *individual* differences in musical talent scores. Pointing to innate biological differences when Blacks outscored Whites would have been unpopular among White-supremacist eugenicists, however, who may have deemed it impossible for "Negroes" to be superior to Whites at anything.

Seashore stated that he was very interested in what might have caused race differences in test scores, and in a quite uncharacteristic move, he—the staunch Mendelian hereditarian—opined that "a social factor," motivation, may have come into play. He said that he had observed a potentially comparable situation: at some age levels, boys outscored girls on one portion of the test, and at a different age level, girls outscored boys. This difference, he claimed, was probably due to boys' lack of interest in music at a particular age:

> The girls excel in the grades because at that time a large number of boys take a rebellious attitude toward music and, therefore, do not throw themselves so heartily into testing competition; whereas, later in the high school, the boys excel not only because the original inhibition has ceased to function, but also because at that age boys develop more interest in objective measurements.[433]

In other words, if girls outscored boys or "Negroes" outscored Whites, Seashore attributed the differences to factors other than heredity. By contrast, eugenicists, including Seashore, were not saying that race differences in IQ scores were due to environmental factors.

Seashore also said that as research using the Seashore Tests continued, the role of motivation in creating "small differences" might be better understood.[434] "Small" is an imprecise term that minimized the differences reported in the *Race Crossing* study; regardless of what "small" might mean, however, at least some of the study's findings were statistically significant. Finally, he said that if the study's race differences could not be adequately attributed to differences in motivation, then "it should be our business to find an explanation in more deep-lying racial habits."[435] In other words, biological heredity should be entertained only after all possible environmental explanations have been ruled out. This comment ran contrary to Seashore's general practice, which was to look to heredity first and foremost in matters of musical ability.

A few days later, Davenport responded to Seashore by hinting that sampling error may have been the cause of the unexpected finding: "Certainly one of the greatest difficulties that a student of race differences has, is to secure a random sample of each race that shall be, as far as possible, unbiased by special environmental and training influences or other selective factors."[436]

Elsewhere, in *Race Crossing*, Davenport and Steggerda stated that there might have been a sampling problem involving the entire study; they conjectured that it was possible that their White participants were less fit than, and therefore not representative of, Jamaican Whites as a whole, a problem they felt was less likely to have occurred in their selection of "Negro" participants:

> There are great inherent difficulties in selecting personnel for the three groups that will be strictly comparable, as representing random samples of the respective groups. First of all it was decided that all three groups should belong to the prevailing agricultural class and that the Whites of the governing class and the white merchants of Kingston should be excluded. A difficulty arises in this, that just those Whites who are satisfied to live as agriculturalists in the midst of the island are hardly as representative of the more ambitious and intellectually endowed Whites as the agricultural Blacks are of the run of the Black population. It is possible that in choosing non-urban Whites we have selected farther below the average of Whites than in selecting non-urban negroes we have selected below the average of negroes.[437]

Davenport closed the November 1929 letter to Seashore by saying that he did not have a good explanation for the study's findings concerning musical capacity, and he suggested that structural, biological differences, specifically differences in the organ of Corti, may explain the results.[438] Seashore replied that although the idea of organic differences is interesting, the easiest approach is one of "experimental analysis and separation of factors that enter into any testing program."[439] Seashore's comment was vague, but in context, I interpret it to mean that scientists should look first at testing conditions and other factors—including motivation—that affect test performance before resorting to biology. Again, this was an atypical comment for him.

Seashore's interest in the effects of race crossing was broader than learning the results of the *Race Crossing* study. Late in his life, in his 1942 book *Pioneering in Psychology*, he provided a proud retrospective on the formation of the Iowa Child Welfare Research Station and described the station's current activities regarding genetic psychology; he reported that it was providing answers to a number of important questions in "genetic psychology," including the effects of race mixtures.[440]

Eugenicists Talked About Race Crossing

Eugenics venues covered the *Race Crossing* study while it was underway and after it had ended.[441] Norwegian eugenicist Jon Alfred Mjøen mentioned it in a publication,[442] as did Seashore;[443] neither of them reported the study's results, however. In one instance, Seashore talked about numerous studies of race differences in musical ability, including studies of "different degrees of race mixture," but in that case, he did not cite the Davenport and Steggerda study and concluded instead that when capacities are "adequately measured" there are no race differences.[444] Even Davenport retrospectively talked about the study, but he did not mention the results of the musical talent portion. Rather, he played a familiar eugenics tune by railing against race crossing. He reported that in *most* cases, Whites scored higher than Blacks did on the mental tests and added his familiar claim that hybridization produces greater mental disharmony and mental confusion:

> On the mental side sure evidence of a disharmony in hybrids between Negroes and Europeans has been secured in a study of ours made in the island of Jamaica. Using a variety of mental tests we found that in *most of them* the whites scored higher than the blacks; while the browns secured an intermediate score. But a study of the distribution of grades showed, in many cases, this remarkable fact: that about 5 per cent of the browns received lower scores than any of the blacks or whites. . . . Among the various browns are some individuals who find themselves quite unable to make even a beginning on certain mental tests. . . .

> The conclusion may be drawn that the hybridization of two races that differ distinctly in mentality results in an excess of individuals that are characterized by mental confusion. In so far the crossing of such distinct races is not good for the community in which the hybrids dwell. In general, we have enough evidence of disharmony in human hybrids to urge that it is on the whole bad when wide crosses are involved. Valuable new combinations might possibly arise through hybridization; but society has not yet worked out a plan by which such better combinations may be encouraged to reproduce, while the worse combinations should remain sterile. Until it does race crossing is not to be encouraged [emphasis mine].[445]

Other Studies of Race Differences in Musical Talent

The Research of Zaid Lenoir

This was not the first study of race differences in musical ability that used the Seashore Tests and reported that Blacks outscored Whites on some portions. Seashore knew this. In 1925, a master's student at the University of Iowa, Zaid Lenoir, compared the average test scores of "colored" students and White students on all six sections of the Seashore Tests, the Kwalwasser-Ruch Test of Musical Accomplishment, and the Stanford Achievement Test. In the preface to his thesis, he thanked three people for helping him with various aspects of the study: Carl Seashore, George Stoddard, and Giles M. Ruch; Ruch appears to have been Lenoir's advisor, and the other men presumably rounded out his committee.[446] Lenoir's subjects were fifth graders from Gary, Indiana.[447] There were 191 "colored" and 191 White subjects for the Seashore Tests, and 122 "colored" and 120 White subjects for the Kwalwasser-Ruch Test.[448] Lenoir stated that "colored" children conclusively were "superior to the white children in Sense of Time and in the Sense of Rhythm," adding that there was "a very noticeable difference in the superiority of the colored children in the native ability in the Sense of Rhythm over that of the white children."[449] He stated that "it is conclusive" that White children were superior in sense of pitch, intensity, and consonance, saying that "in the sense of consonance the difference is so pronounced that there is no chance of its not being significant."[450] He reported no significant differences in mean scores on the tonal memory portion of the Seashore Tests.[451] Lenoir stated that on the Kwalwasser-Ruch Test, there were not significant differences between "colored" and White children in detection of pitch errors, knowledge of key signatures, knowledge of note values, knowledge of musical symbols, and knowledge of rest values.[452] He said that there were significant differences, with White children being superior to "colored" children, in recognition of syllable names, detection of time errors, and recognition of pitch names.[453] Notably, he also said that there were significant differences, with "colored" children being superior to Whites, in recognition of time signatures, and "very much superior [to Whites] in Recognition of Familiar Melodies from Notation."[454] Lenoir calculated composite scores for the Kwalwasser-Ruch Test and concluded, "While the white children scores show superiority in particular exercises of the tests, the colored show a superiority [of] ability in music as a whole."[455]

Lenoir was African American, and after he had completed his master's degree at Iowa, he became a civics teacher at Vashon High School, in St. Louis, Missouri.[456] He was active in and honored by Phi Beta Sigma, a collegiate and professional fraternity founded at Howard University in 1914, and some sources state that he became a Baptist minister.[457]

Lenoir also was Lloyd Lionel Gaines's high school teacher; Gaines was a brilliant African American student who, on graduating from college, sought admission to the University of Missouri's law school, which did not admit Black students.[458] Lenoir, a member of the NAACP, reportedly urged Gaines to challenge the law school's admissions policy and accompanied Gaines to an initial meeting with Sidney Redmond, an NAACP lawyer who became a member of the team that represented Gaines in the suit.[459] The US Supreme Court ruled in favor of Gaines in this landmark civil rights case, although the response from the state of Missouri was to establish a separate law school for Black students. Shortly thereafter, however, Gaines disappeared, and to this day there are no clear answers to the question of what happened to him.

The Studies Seashore Cited in a Discussion of His "No-race-differences" Conclusion

In one source where Seashore claimed that there are no race differences in musical talent, he cited seven studies but did not report any of the studies' results; Lenoir's research was not among them.[460] Results from these seven studies paint a complex picture that does not support a no-race-differences conclusion, however. Davenport and Steggerda's *Race Crossing* research was among the seven, and, as we have seen, it concluded that "Negroes" clearly outperformed Whites. Seashore called it the most interesting of the seven—without stating the study's results.[461]

Guy Benton Johnson's Research

The second source Seashore cited in his discussions of race differences was Guy Benton Johnson's article "The Negro and Musical Talent," published in the *Southern Workman* in 1927.[462] The article was based on Johnson's doctoral dissertation in sociology, which he completed at the University of North Carolina at Chapel Hill in 1927; the dissertation also served as the basis of an article that appeared in the *Music Supervisors' Journal* in 1928.[463] Johnson became a noted sociologist and anthropologist specializing in southern Black culture; considered a pioneer in race equity, he was a faculty member at the University of North Carolina for almost his entire career.[464] In the preface to his dissertation, Johnson stated that he had collaborated with Metfessel on the vibrato study, as well as with Seashore and Metfessel on the phonophotographic study of "Negro" songs (both of which are described earlier in this chapter).[465]

Johnson opened the *Southern Workman* article with praise for Seashore—whom he described as having pioneered in the application of "scientific methods to the study of musical talent"—and with a description of the Seashore Tests.[466] In his dissertation, he called musical talent an endowment.[467] Claiming that Seashore had developed the test norms for Whites, Johnson set out to determine whether there were race differences in this endowment; he aimed to accomplish this by administering the Seashore Tests to "Negroes" and then comparing median scores to the norms developed by Seashore.[468] His subjects were "about 3500" fifth-grade, eighth-grade, and college students from North Carolina, South Carolina, and Virginia.[469] The dissertation listed 3,300 participants, and the *Music Supervisors' Journal* article reported 3,350.[470] He used five portions of the Seashore Tests but excluded consonance, reporting that the ability to determine harmony or dissonance was a product of learning whereas the other sections of the Tests measured inborn capacities.[471] He concluded that there were "*no significant differences in the basic sensory musical capacities between whites and Negroes* [emphasis in original]"; this was the same conclusion he reported in the *Music Supervisors' Journal* article.[472] This was not exactly the conclusion he had reached in his dissertation, however; the same statement appeared in his dissertation, but it ended with the tag "except in the case of rhythm."[473] In the data analysis section of his dissertation, Johnson reported that "Negroes" were clearly superior to Whites in rhythm at all three age levels—most markedly at the fifth-grade level—and he predicted that retesting would reveal an even *greater* superiority: "For sense of rhythm, the Negroes consistently excelled the white norms, their order being, fifth grade, eighth grade, adults. In view of the fact that the low scores are not thoroughly reliable, re-testing should increase the Negro's superior showing on the rhythm test."[474] He also mentioned that even though he did not administer the consonance test to all of his subjects, he gave it to 100 "Negro" adults at Shaw University and North Carolina State College for Negroes at Durham, and he found a distribution of scores that was identical to the norms Seashore had reported.[475]

At the end of the *Southern Workman* article, he noted that the Seashore Tests only measured sensory capacities and acknowledged that other factors, including motivation, play a role in the making of a musician. He also stated that the average "Negro" voice is superior to the White voice; he said that this superiority is due to anatomical differences in vocal structure, not to inborn race differences in talent.[476]

University of Pennsylvania psychologist Yale Nathanson critiqued Johnson's study, echoing the criticism expressed by others that sentiment rather than fact too often governed race psychology; he expressed concern that tests of musical ability failed to take into account the unique characteristics of various races. He began the essay by arguing that defenders of the "Negro" were as guilty as Nordics in making biased claims about the superiority of one race over the other.[477] After describing the "Negro" as simian and as a cousin to apes, he warned researchers against allowing sentiment and appeals for justice to "swerve" them from the truth:

> The Negro, too, has his defenders, and when the anthropometrist points out the physical characteristics, so simian in the Negro's make-up, his protagonist points to the Negro's heavy lips, so completely lacking in his agile animal cousin. The necessity for truth in these matters of racial differences is obvious and appeals to our sense of justice, it is in fact this very attitude that swerves many a conscientious investigator from the intellectually "straight and narrow." For in an attempt to insure absolute fairness in the interpretation of his findings, to offset a suspected prejudice, he grants a trifle more consideration, enough latitude often to invalidate his results.[478]

He called an unnamed anthropologist a pseudoscientist in response to the anthropologist's claim that because the "Negro" has music in his heart, the race must never die; he called the latter anthropologist's statement "ballyhoo."[479]

His primary complaint about extant methods of measuring musical talent was that the instruments were assumed to be equally suited for all races, and he stated that fair tests would take into account the different evolutionary paths of the races:

> There must ever be, at least as long as there is maintained as much racial identity as at present, a specific phylogenetic background which must be measured by special instruments, just as one would expect the veterinarian to employ a different type of scalpel in performing abdominal surgery on a cow or a canary. Then again if the races, Caucasian and Negro, are different because of phylogenetic background, how much more difference are we to expect in terms of ontogenetic variations. But the present method seems to insist that a rod be calibrated and all who come in its reach measured.[480]

He called extant methods unsatisfactory and unfair, and after quoting at length from Johnson's study, he claimed that it exemplified this unfairness: "The Negro is not seen in an advantageous light when thus bludgeoned with a measuring rod constructed for other races."[481] As I discussed earlier in this chapter, however, Nathanson himself did not portray "Negroes" in a particularly favorable way. At one point, he stated that there was a tendency among the "philanthropically inclined" of other races to overrate the talent of "Negroes" of "rather ordinary ability," and he closed the essay with the assertion that there is no evidence to suggest that the musical talent of the "Negro" is either superior or inferior to that of the Caucasian.[482]

Research by Joseph Peterson and Lyle H. Lanier

The third source Seashore cited was *Studies in the Comparative Abilities of Whites and Negroes*, a monograph by Joseph Peterson and Lyle H. Lanier. Their study examined race differences in the intelligence of children, the mechanical ability of adults, and the musical talent of adults. Peterson was a psychology professor at George Peabody College for Teachers in Nashville, Tennessee. Historian Graham Richards describes him as one of the most prolific race-differences researchers in the interwar period.[483] Lanier was on the faculty at Vanderbilt University when the study was published; later in his career, he became vice president and provost of the University of Illinois at Urbana-Champaign.

In a preliminary test, Peterson and John Lewis administered the pitch and consonance portions of the Seashore Tests twice to students at George Peabody College and Fisk University.[484] On the first administration, "Negroes" outscored Whites on both tests, the researchers reporting that the differences were "reliable" only for the consonance test; on the second administration, "Negroes" outscored Whites on the pitch test and Whites outscored "Negroes" on the consonance test, but the researchers reported that the differences were not reliable.[485] In the study, itself, the "Negro" group consisted of students from the Agricultural and Industrial Normal College in Nashville; the White group was drawn from students at Middle Tennessee State Teachers College at Murfreesboro.[486] The researchers administered all six portions of the Seashore Tests and concluded that Whites showed "statistically reliable superiority" in all portions except for rhythm, where "Negroes" outscored Whites but not by a reliable amount.[487] They also reported that results for both groups were far below Seashore's norms.[488] They stated that their findings could not "safely be interpreted as showing an *innate* race difference [emphasis mine]," and yet, curiously, they ended by reiterating that in the main study, Whites significantly outscored "Negroes" on all portions of the test except rhythm.[489]

Thomas Garth's Research

Fourth, Seashore cited Thomas Garth's 1931 book *Race Psychology*, which included a slightly expanded version of a study Garth and Sarah Rachel Isbell had published in the *Music Supervisors' Journal* in 1929. Garth received a doctorate from Columbia University and was head of the Department of Education at the University of Denver; historian Graham Richards describes him as the "single most prolific researcher on race differences during the inter-war period."[490] Isbell completed a master's degree from the University of Denver and was a high school mathematics teacher.[491]

In the *Music Supervisors' Journal* article, Garth and Isbell reported that they administered the Seashore Tests to 769 students enrolled in Indian schools in four locations: Chilocco, Oklahoma; Rapid City, South Dakota; Santa Fe, New Mexico; and Albuquerque, New Mexico. The students were categorized as full bloods or mixed bloods, and their median scores were compared to those of "Whites of their respective communities."[492] For the fifth graders tested, the researchers also examined possible correlations between degrees of White blood and test scores.[493] The researchers concluded that there were no significant differences between races on test performance and that there was no correlation between degree of blood and test performance.[494] Nevertheless, the data Garth and Isbell reported indicated that based on their own definition—that an overlap of 25 percent or less constituted a significant difference—mixed-bloods and full-bloods significantly underperformed

Whites on the pitch and memory tests.[495] The researchers attributed some differences to Indians having reached their "cognitive limit."[496] Although the total number of subjects Garth reported in his *Race Psychology* findings was slightly different from that in the *Music Supervisors' Journal* article, and the explanation of the study was more detailed, the results and conclusions in both sources were identical.[497] In *Race Psychology*, however, Garth took the earlier study one step further by comparing the median scores of Indians to the medians of Southern "Negroes" as reported by Johnson. In this comparison, full-blooded Indians significantly underperformed "Negroes" on the pitch section of the test, and again, Garth attributed the difference to Indians having reached their "cognitive limit."[498] Once again, Garth concluded that there were no innate race differences in musical talent.[499]

Historian Graham Richards states that during the course of his career, Garth changed his mind about the existence of innate race differences. According to Richards, after having initially held the view that innate race differences were self-evident and having worked unstintingly throughout the 1920s on race-differences research, by 1930, Garth had concluded that claims of innate race differences were "bunk."[500] Richards says that with *Race Psychology*, Garth "finally threw in the towel" on the innate-race-differences thesis, and Richards (rather inaccurately) calls the book the "swan song of race psychology."[501] He states that although opponents of race psychology, including Otto Klineberg, frequently cited *Race Psychology* and Garth's other work of this period, it also attracted the attention and fomented the wrath of proponents, including Nazi psychologist Bruno Petermann.[502]

One of Garth's critics was Lanier, a coauthor of one of the race-differences studies that Seashore cited. Lanier wrote a scathing review of *Race Psychology*, dismissing it as flimsy science. His grounds for panning the book included Garth's trusting attitude toward the Seashore Tests; Lanier described the tests as "notorious for their low reliability."[503] Significantly, however, Lanier had used portions of the Seashore Tests in his own study. He further claimed that Garth presented data sketchily and did a poor job of analyzing it. According to Lanier, Garth was too eager to accept study results at face value, had reached unjustified conclusions, and was prejudiced "in favor of a nurtural explanation of observed race differences in performance."[504] Lanier decried the "backwash of sociological theorizing which has captivated the imagination of the 'tenderminded' during the past decade" and called for "the proper scientific attitude" in the field of race differences: agnosticism.[505] He claimed that an "'environmentalistic' uplift attitude" had caused many psychologists to "abandon the scientific point of view," and he closed with the reminder that there was not solid evidence to support either an environmentalist or a hereditarian explanation of race differences.[506] Notably, Lanier's claims—that the environmentalist position was leading psychologists to abandon scientific agnosticism and that Garth was biased—were not accompanied by similar criticisms of researchers in the hereditarian camp, even though similar critique would have been equally applicable to them. Lanier's statement that psychologists had abandoned scientific agnosticism suggested both that such agnosticism exists and that it had prevailed prior to 1933, the year his review was published. I recognize that the focus of Lanier's review was Garth's book, not research from the opposing camp; nevertheless, given the direction of Garth's change in heart, the asymmetry of Lanier's criticism is noteworthy.

Katharine Murdoch's Research

Seashore also mentioned a multipronged study conducted by psychologist Katharine Murdoch.[507] Presented as a paper in 1923 at a meeting of the American Psychological Association and published in *School and Society* in 1925, the Murdoch study examined race differences in intelligence, morality, and musical talent in twelve-year-old children from Honolulu, Hawaii, and its environs.[508] Murdoch reported on eleven racial groups using the same racial categories employed by the department of public instruction in the territory of Hawaii: Anglo-Saxon, Anglo-Saxon-Hawaiian, Chinese, Japanese, Portuguese, Korean, Chinese-Hawaiian, Hawaiian, Country Japanese, Puerto Rican, and Filipino.[509] She concluded, "Anglo-Saxons *clearly* excel all the other races in general intelligence measures, *except the Orientals*. Here the distinction is not so marked in non-verbal tests, the Japanese particularly showing up well in these [emphasis mine]."[510]

Murdoch also measured moral traits. To do this, she administered a modified version of a standardized test of honesty.[511] She also used teacher-generated estimates of students' moral traits, as well as measurements stemming from a questionnaire she administered to faculty members at the University of Hawaii and to prominent Honolulu social workers; the questionnaire asked these experts to report their opinions on what differences existed between the racial groups present in Honolulu.[512] The other moral traits she examined were ambition, perseverance, trustworthiness, self-assertion, sensitiveness to public opinion, and control of emotions. She reported results in terms of overlap with Anglo-Saxon medians,[513] and she stated that on most measures, the Chinese excelled and the Portuguese fared worst: "The Chinese, however, stand in the most enviable position of all. Out of the fifteen [moral] traits the Chinese stand highest in eight, including the school mark and Citizenship Scale, two of the least subjective of our measures."[514] Anglo-Saxons stood "supreme" (her word) only in self-assertion.[515]

In the third portion of her study, she examined race differences in musical talent, again basing her conclusions on teachers' estimates, measurements based on the experts' questionnaire, and results of the pitch discrimination portion of the Seashore Tests. She said that she had administered several sections of the Seashore Tests, which she did not name, but only reported the pitch discrimination results because "it seemed probable that the scores were greatly affected by the low intelligence of some of the pupils."[516] She stated that although teachers' estimates and the experts' questionnaire results concluded that Hawaiians were very musical, the pitch discrimination results did not show "marked ability in this trait" in either pure or part-Hawaiian groups. Chinese-Hawaiians constituted the only group to outscore Anglo-Saxons on the pitch discrimination test, and the Portuguese had the lowest scores.[517] Murdoch left it up to the reader to decide whether the differences she reported in all portions of her study were innate.[518] In *Race Psychology*, Garth reported on the musical talent portion of the Murdoch study and claimed that the racial group sizes were too small for her to make valid claims about significant differences between the groups.[519]

Research by Jon Alfred and Fridtjof Mjøen

Finally, Seashore stated that two studies—both of which he attributed to Jon Alfred Mjøen, even though Mjøen's son Fridtjof conducted one of them—"made interesting comparisons between Lapps and Nordics in the Scandinavian countries and other races in central Europe."[520] Both studies referenced the work of Seashore and Stanton, but neither of them matched Seashore's description. Fridtjof Mjøen's study, published in 1926, focused on pitch perception and used Seashore's work as a template; it probably used the recorded Seashore Tests, but F. Mjøen was not clear about this.[521] He studied 1,276 youths of unreported race and nationality, probably Norwegians.[522] In some cases, he discussed whether his findings were consistent with assertions made by Seashore, but he did not appear to have compared his study's data to Seashore's norms.[523] Within the group he studied, Mjøen examined correlations between pitch capacity and a variety of other factors, including students' gender, whether they played musical instruments, whether they played by ear, whether they studied German in school, and how they scored on measures of their capacities in the areas of tone, intensity, time, consonance, and memory.[524] He did not appear to have compared races within his group or to have compared his results directly to results of studies of other races or nationalities.

The other Norwegian research that Seashore cited was a pedigree study published by Jon Alfred Mjøen in 1934. Although it discussed a variety of prior studies, the article was devoted primarily to describing pedigree data collected from questionnaires sent to 10,000 musicians from Germany, Scandinavia, and the United States—students as well as performers in such groups as the Jenny Lind Chorus, the United States Scandinavian Singers, and the Thomaner-Chor of Leipzig, among others.[525] He also included a few pedigree charts for famous musicians (and for one poet).[526] J. Mjøen mentioned research by Seashore and Stanton, but I could find no evidence that he used the Seashore Tests in his study; as far as I could determine, his was not a comparative study of race differences, not even within the various White races that eugenicists sometimes discussed.[527] Thus, although other sources indicated that race-crossing research was being conducted at Mjøen's Vinderen Laboratory, the two articles Seashore cited did not discuss either race crossing or race differences in musical ability.[528]

Studies Seashore Did Not Cite

Research by C. T. Gray and C. W. Bingham

Consider, however, other studies in addition to Lenoir's that Seashore did not include on his list, all of which used the Seashore Tests or portions of it. In some of these studies, researchers reported that Whites outscored Blacks. For example, C. T. Gray and C. W. Bingham administered the Seashore Tests to 258 "colored" and 219 White children from public schools in select cities in Texas; they used three race categories: Whites, mulattoes, and "coloreds," the third category composed of "Negroes" and mulattoes.[529] They concluded that "the superiority of the whites when compared with either mulattoes or negroes seems apparent in most comparisons made."[530] They stated that the median score of Whites exceeded that of "colored" children on the pitch, intensity, time, and memory portions of the tests and that the median score of "colored" children slightly exceeded that of Whites on the consonance test: "In this, the colored pupils have a median of 32.5 while the white pupils have one of 31.9, a difference of only .6. All of the differences seem valid except that for consonance and here the chances are four out of five that the difference would be greater than zero in favor of the colored pupils."[531] They did not mention a rhythm section of the tests, which indicates that they used the original 1919 version.

Raymond Willis Porter's Research

In his doctoral research conducted at the University of Chicago and completed in 1931, Raymond Willis Porter set out to answer the question, "How musical are Chinese?"[532] He studied all 120 available Chinese elementary and secondary students enrolled in the Chicago Public Schools, his subjects ranging in age from eight to thirty-two.[533] Porter administered three tests designed to measure various aspects of musical ability. One of the three was the six-section version of the Seashore Tests; he compared the scores of Chinese students to those of White classmates and to Seashore's norms.[534] Using Seashore's norms as the basis for comparison, he concluded, "This particular group of Chinese subjects possesses less than 'average' musical talent as measured by these tests."[535] He also stated that they "have practically an even chance to do no worse than . . . non-Chinese of the same school in these tests. They even do sufficiently well in the test of discrimination of intensity of sounds to surpass this particular group of white subjects."[536] He also said that Chinese subjects were inferior to Whites in tonal memory and discriminating consonance.[537] He added that although the Chinese subjects were a representative sampling of the Chinese population of Chicago, the White subjects were from families of "appreciably low social status"; this comment intimated that he attributed the respectable performance of the Chinese subjects relative to their peers to a sampling error—that the Whites tested were not representative of the White population overall.[538]

Kenneth L. Bean's Research

A few studies concluded that Whites had more musical capacity even though the data they reported painted a more complex picture. In 1936, Kenneth L. Bean published a study of the musical talent of southern "Negroes." Stating that crossings with Whites had occurred "here and there for over a century," he claimed that the Gulf States were home to the largest proportion of "pure blacks"; thus he chose Baton Rouge, Louisiana, as the site of his study.[539] Consistent with the broader perceptions I discussed in chapter 5, he believed that northern "Negroes" were constitutionally different from and superior to southern "Negroes": "The colored people who migrated to the North were, as a rule, the ambitious ones who were capable of more skilled work than was required of them on the plantations in the South. Therefore, studies of these people in the North involve a select group rather than a group typical of the race such as can easily be found in Louisiana."[540]

In the first part of the study, Bean administered the pitch, intensity, time, consonance, and memory portions of the Seashore Tests to 119 students attending a "Negro" high school in Baton Rouge.[541] He compared the *median* scores of the Baton Rouge students to the *median*s and *means* reported by Gray and Bingham, Johnson, and Peterson and Lanier; he concluded that the Baton Rouge subjects were "inferior."[542] In the second part of the study, he administered the same subtests plus the rhythm subtest to forty students studying music at Southern University, a historically Black college known for its music program.[543] He compared the *means* of the Southern University students to the *medians* reported by Peterson and Lanier and concluded that the Southern University students' means were above the medians reported by Peterson and Lanier for "Negroes" and above Peterson and Lanier's medians for Whites in all cases except intensity.[544] He also noted that the Southern University students demonstrated "marked excellence in Rhythm," adding that they probably were "superior negroes as a group."[545] These findings led Bean to conclude that "this race ["Negroes"] is definitely inferior to *our own* in musical capacities, with the probable exception of Rhythm, in which they are at least equal if not superior to white people [emphasis mine]."[546] He closed by alluding to precocity, stating that "Negroes" were equal to or superior to Whites as children but, unlike Whites, stopped developing in adolescence.[547]

Research by Lester and Viola Wheeler

Lester and Viola Wheeler set out to test the perception that mountain people have "remarkable" musical ability; they tested 456 mountain children from East Tennessee[548] and compared their test scores to Seashore's norms for six subtests. The Wheelers did not report the race of the mountain children, but I surmise that they probably were White based on the Wheelers' reference not only to the Appalachian Southern Highlands but to the importation of songs from England.[549] The Wheelers stated that the mountain children scored "significantly below the norms in pitch and tonal memory, but with less differences in the other measures."[550] Noting that other scholars had found Seashore's norms to be high compared to results of other studies, they also compared their results to revised Seashore norms developed by Ruth Larson; they stated that mountain children's scores were statistically lower than Larson's norms as well.[551] They compared mountain children's scores to the scores of "Negro" children as reported by Johnson and concluded that "Negro" children were *superior* to mountain children "in practically all measures of the test,"[552] They stated, "The Negroes appear superior to the mountain children in all measures except those of intensity and time in Grade VIII.

The greatest differences appear in pitch and tonal memory."[553] They reported, however, that they could not determine statistical significance, and then they raised questions about the soundness of Johnson's data:

> The indications are that the Negroes are probably above the mountain children in most of the measures, but as to the statistical significance we are unable to say. The scores reported by Johnson in this study are above the Seashore-Larson norms in a number of measures. *These are the highest scores we have found in any of the investigations*. It is unfortunate that we could not obtain reliability measures for Johnson's data in order to make accurate comparisons. We are inclined to believe that his data are rather high for Negro children [emphasis mine].[554]

In other words, when "Negro" children scored similarly to (or outperformed) White children in Johnson's study, and Johnson reported scores that the Wheelers said were the highest they had found in any study, the Wheelers questioned the soundness of Johnson's data.

According to the Wheelers, when mountain children's scores were compared to scores of full-blooded Indians as reported by Garth, there was a "significant difference in favor of the mountain children."[555] Curiously, they reported that they decided not to use Garth's data on mixed-blood Indians because Garth had reported no significant race differences for that group.[556]

Mountain children's scores, the Wheelers stated, were "superior" to those of the children (whose race was not specified) from San José, California, who had been studied by Paul Farnsworth and N. Church, and significantly better than or "above" those of children of unspecified race studied by W. S. Larson and Ruth Larson.[557] The Wheelers stated that mountain children's scores also were "above" those of the White and "Negro" children in Gray and Bingham's study.[558] Earlier in their study, however, the Wheelers had acknowledged that when compared to data reported by Gray and Bingham, mountain children were above "Negroes" on the intensity, consonance, and tonal memory tests, and *below* them on pitch and time "with smaller differences."[559] They reported, "Even without the reliability measures for these comparisons, the differences appear such that we can say that the mountain children compare favorably with the white children . . . [and] are probably superior to the colored children in most of the measures."[560] These findings led Wheeler and Wheeler to conclude, "We feel fairly safe in saying that the mountain children compare favorably in musical talent with the normal for the country at large."[561] In drawing this conclusion, however, they appear to have overlooked at least some of their data.

Helen Sanderson's Research

Using the three sections of the Seashore Tests that she claimed had the highest reliability—pitch, intensity, and memory—in 1933, Helen Sanderson published a study of race differences in the musical ability of 550 teenagers of various races and nationalities from the Chicago Public Schools.[562] The race/nationality categories she selected were Polish, "Negro," Italian, German, and Jewish.[563] Jewish participants outperformed every other group on every section of the Seashore Tests, with differences being statistically significant in many cases.[564] She also administered the Kwalwasser-Dykema music tests; Jewish subjects again performed well, but subtest results were mixed. For example, "Negroes" outscored all other groups on the Kwalwasser-Dykema rhythm-discrimination test; Sanderson reported that the differences were statistically significant in favor of "Negroes" when their scores were compared to those of Italians, Germans, and Poles.[565] She concluded that there were significant differences between "various racial and nativity groups" and that "the Jewish group shows a *marked* superiority to all other groups except the German, which ranks a close second [emphasis mine]."[566] She also concluded that the Polish group demonstrated a marked inferiority and the "Negro" group a definite inferiority except in rhythmic discrimination.[567] Sanderson did not explain why she chose these particular groups to study, and the inclusion of Germans is puzzling. All of the groups she chose faced discrimination in the United States during the early twentieth century, and all of them except Germans were the objects of criticism from eugenicists. Did her inclusion of Germans reflect her pattern of focusing on those perceived to be inferior, or was she testing the hypothesis, expressed by eugenicists, that Germans were predisposed to producing individuals of exceptionally high musical talent? Sanderson provided no answers.

Richard A. C. Oliver's Research

Among the studies of race differences in musical talent that reported mixed results was one published in 1932 by Richard A. C. Oliver, who later became the Sarah Fielden Professor of Education at the University of Manchester. He administered the Seashore Tests to ninety Kenyan students and compared mean scores with those reported by Seashore for American seventh graders.[568] Oliver concluded that the Kenyan students were superior to Americans on the intensity, time, and rhythm tests and inferior to them on the pitch, consonance, and memory tests.[569]

Jacob Kwalwasser's Research

Another cluster of studies of race differences reported generally superior performances by "colored" students. In 1926, Jacob Kwalwasser, who had completed a PhD at the University of Iowa with Seashore serving as his advisor, published an article in the *Music Supervisors' Journal* praising the scientific testing of musical talent, enumerating its many benefits and championing its use in determining race differences. Revealing race differences, he claimed, would enable teachers to adjust their practices to "race requirements."[570] He reported results from a study he had conducted of 200 "colored" and 200 White fifth graders from Gary, Indiana; from this study, he concluded that many significant race differences exist.[571] "Colored" students outperformed White students on the time and rhythm sections of the Seashore Tests, while White students outperformed "colored" students on the pitch and intensity sections.[572] He also administered the Kwalwasser-Ruch Test of Musical Accomplishment and again noted significant differences in achievement between these groups. He stated, "The negro is superior to the white child in his ability to translate musical notation into sound," adding that on the song recognition portion of the test, the average score for the "colored" child was 37, compared to an average of 14 for the White child.[573] He continued: "Comparing the two races in general, musical accomplishment on the basis of this test, we find that the negro is one grade in advance of the fifth grade white child in Gary, and 1.6 grades in advance of the norm for the fifth grade found in the manual."[574]

After citing a number of scholars from outside of music who had concluded that race differences exist, including G. Stanley Hall, and asserting that "differences between the two races, regardless of advantage is conceded by all authorities," Kwalwasser criticized music teachers for teaching as if all races are musically equal.[575] Stating that the equal-treatment approach is damaging to students, he urged teachers to abandon traditional pedagogies in favor of those tailored to each race.[576] He called this new, differentiated, race-based practice "scientific pedagogy."[577]

Elsewhere, in response to an attack by Mursell, Kwalwasser claimed that no fewer than six studies in addition to his own had confirmed Lenoir's initial findings of "Negro" superiority:

> Aside from the fact that a half-dozen other investigations have confirmed the original study by Zaid Lenoire [*sic*], using both the Sea-

> shore and the Kwalwasser-Dykema rhythm tests with different groups of children numbering thousands, I made the generalization of superiority of the Negro over the Whites only after I had applied the established statistical techniques.[578]

He did not cite these six studies, but unless one of them was *Race Crossing*, Seashore did not cite any of them, either.

Research by Rosalind Streep

In a study published in 1931, Rosalind Streep tested 1,315 "Negro" and White children from the New York City public schools using the rhythm and consonance portions of the Seashore Tests.[579] She reported that on both portions, the median scores of "Negro" children exceeded the scores of White children "to a small degree."[580] Streep concluded, "These results would seem to indicate a very slight but, nevertheless, consistent superiority of negro children over white children in regard to the phases of musical ability tested."[581]

Research by Dorothy van Alstyne and Emily Osborne

In 1937 Dorothy van Alstyne and Emily Osborne administered Williams's adaptation of the Seashore Tests to 483 preschoolers; the adaptation focused on rhythm-pattern reproduction.[582] The researchers compared the scores of White subjects to those of "Negro" subjects and concluded that "Negro" preschoolers were superior to White children in rhythmic ability.[583] Clearly believing that musical talent is inherited, the authors closed by reporting that many of the "Negro" children had White blood, and they raised the question of whether the scores of "Negro" children would have been even higher if they had had no White blood.[584]

General Observations about These Race-Differences Studies

Taken as a whole, these studies, most of which were not conducted by researchers documented to be eugenicists, are a bewildering blizzard; it would be foolhardy for anyone to use them to draw sound general conclusions. They tend to share a number of flaws, the first of which is that they used a flawed instrument, the Seashore Tests, or a modification of it. The validity and reliability of the Seashore Tests had been under fire from the beginning; some authors of the race-differences studies themselves raised questions about the tests even though they used them. Of course, Seashore stood behind his tests, claiming that they were sound, scientific, and accurate indicators of innate characteristics. To make matters worse, different studies used different versions of the battery—the five-subtest version in some cases and the six-subtest version in others. Furthermore, some of the studies used just one or two portions of the tests, not all five (or six), and yet the researchers nevertheless made pronouncements about overall musical talent. Third, the studies were riddled with other design flaws, weak analyses, and unsupported conclusions. For example, not all researchers reported whether differences between groups were statistically significant. Fourth, even if races were scientific facts and not social constructions, the fuzziness and variability of the racial categories used from study to study should have rendered any general conclusions invalid. These race categories form a bizarre potpourri that is itself worthy of a study; they ranged from "country Japanese" to more conventional formulations. "Negro" and White, notably, served as pedal points. Some references to Whites were coded; for example, "mountain children" was a descriptor of poor, rural, White children from the South. In addition, sometimes studies subdivided Whites, reflecting a hierarchy that included Poles, Italians, Germans, and other groups. To their credit, the studies tended to use large numbers of subjects, but that alone did not make them sound.

In 1931, Farnsworth reviewed a sampling of studies of race differences in musical talent and reported that the data were "too confused to form bases for generalizations."[585] His conclusion was on point, not merely for the studies he reviewed but for those I examined. But this was not Seashore's conclusion.

I have described these various studies, not because they have reliable knowledge to offer, but because they form the research landscape from which Seashore drew his conclusions (or could have drawn them in the case of the studies he did not cite). Significantly, if we ignore the quality of the research—perhaps by arguing that it was fairly representative of psychological research of the period—and just look at the data, the research still does not support Seashore's "no-race-differences" conclusion. Rather, if the research results are taken at face value, the accurate conclusion should be that the studies produced mixed results.

Unpacking Seashore's No-Race-Differences Conclusion

What would lead Seashore to state, in the face of evidence to the contrary, that the studies had found no significant race differences in musical talent? Why would he ignore the findings of Davenport and Steggerda's *Race Crossing* study, as well as research by Zaid Lenoir and Jacob Kwalwasser—students with whom he had worked at Iowa? What about the six unnamed studies that, according to Kwalwasser, confirmed Lenoir's conclusion that "Negroes" have superior innate musical talent?

Seashore did not exactly say that there were no differences. Rather, he hedged a bit, in one source saying there was "little difference" without explaining what "little" meant.[586] In another source, he said that "normal individuals in different racial groups or on different cultural levels *probably* do not differ markedly [emphasis mine]" in basic musical capacities, but he did not explain what would constitute a marked difference.[587] In a third source, he reported a more nuanced conclusion, stating that there were "no distinctly significant differences in racial groups" in sense of pitch, loudness, and time when these capacities were "adequately measured"; he then added that "in many cases" this was also true for sense of rhythm and tonal memory.[588] He may have hedged slightly to protect himself from being accused of lying.

Race-Laced Themes

The Myth-Busting Frame

I can only speculate about why Seashore chose to inaccurately report the aggregate conclusions of these studies. I suggest that racism played a role, and statements by some authors of these studies—particularly those that Seashore cited—support my argument. Consider, first, how the researchers often posed the research question. Guy Benton Johnson, for example, opened the introduction to his dissertation by asking whether the popular belief that "Negroes" are innately *superior* musicians is based in fact:

> Much has been said by lovers of Negro music about the superior musical endowment of the race. How often have we heard the Negro characterized as "naturally very musical," "a born harmonizer," "instinctively good at rhythm," or having a "keen ear"! Do these popular ideas rest upon a factual basis? Are there any measurable differences in the musical endowments of white people and Negroes? If there are differences, what are they and how are they to be explained? If there are no differences, how account for the obvious fact that the Negro does enjoy an unusual prestige in the field of folk music?[589]

Earlier, in the dissertation's preface, Johnson similarly asked, "Would objective measurement verify the popular notion that the Negro is gifted with superior musical endowments?"[590] He posed the question in the same way in both of the published articles based on his dissertation.[591] Not only did he acknowledge the popularity of the belief, he stated that "Negroes" were, in fact, outstanding musicians, although the reference to folk music attenuated his praise. In the *Music Supervisors' Journal* article, he further claimed that belief in the natural musical superiority of "Negroes" was long-standing: "There has *long* existed a popular belief to the effect that the Negro has an unusual natural talent for music. Does this belief rest on facts [emphasis mine]?"[592]

Thus, Johnson chose a myth-busting framing of the research question and ended with the punchline, "But is it true?" Elements of this framing were common in the studies of race differences in musical talent that I examined; not only were there references to what the authors called "the popular belief" that "Negroes" have innately superior musical talent, there was the recommendation to put that belief to the scientific test.[593] For example, when reporting Johnson's research results—no significant race differences in musical talent—Garth, too, referred to this popular "opinion": "This [no-race-differences finding] is in spite of the fact that popular opinion would accord to the Negro a high degree of musical ability from his musical habits and from the famed Negro spiritual."[594] Notably, the myth-busters discourse even came from scholars such as Johnson and Garth who were not eugenicists and are remembered today as champions of race equity. Usually, but not always, the answer to "But is it true?" was a resounding "No!"[595] Streep, however, used the myth-busters framing and concluded that "Negroes" did, indeed, have innately superior talent, at least in the two capacities she measured—rhythm and consonance.[596] Johnson, after having reported that the myth was not true, offered an opinion as to why it existed and then claimed that debunking the myth would in no way detract from "Negroes'" future prospects in music:

> At any rate, singing has become one of the race's strongest points, and this fact has no doubt been largely responsible for the notion that the Negro is naturally endowed with a superior talent for music. If this notion has been proved to be erroneous, as it now appears to have been, nothing is subtracted from the beauty of Negro folk songs or from the possibility of the Negro's achieving future greatness in music.[597]

Johnson's dismissive claim that nothing was subtracted by the discovery of these scientific "facts" reflected an apparent blindness to what had been taken away—a small place in the sun at a time when "Negroes" were generally deemed by US Whites to be inferior in every other way. Busting this particular myth without taking a hammer to the many other racist myths that immeasurably harmed "Negroes" in the United States can be viewed more as a strategic buttressing of whiteness—or as an attack on "Negroes"—than as a step toward race equity. The "But is it true?" framing posed the question as a challenge and delivered an answer that can be viewed as a jab, even if that was not the author's intention.

In these studies, myth busting was the scientific interrogation of an alluring belief about an exotic, fascinating other. Science, the bringer of unbiased truth, ostensibly was setting the record straight. Similarly, after having described the American Indian as "that perennial romancer," and having waxed eloquently about the indescribable thrill of the Indian war dance, Garth presented science's hard facts: no race differences.[598]

The myth-busting frame was used most often in reference to the musical talent of "Negroes," but it also was employed by Wheeler and Wheeler in their study of poor, White, rural children from the South. In that instance, however, the Wheelers concluded that scientific evidence *supported* a myth: mountain children did demonstrate superior musical talent.[599] In a slight variation on this theme, Kwalwasser posed related questions about Jews—a group often viewed as generally inferior but superior at music:

> At present we are hopelessly ignorant of the significance of race in the study of music. We have all observed that certain races prefer certain instruments to the exclusion of others. Why should the violin, more than any other instrument appeal to the Jews? Why should they be superior in their command of the instrument? No attempt has ever been made to analyze their fondness for the instrument and their skill in manipulating it. Yet the psychological traits which manifest themselves so magnetically are both present and measurable.[600]

Examining how the comparisons of groups were constructed in these studies provides more evidence of the insidious but powerful racist assumptions that informed this research. White competence was the unquestioned baseline. Not only had White people developed the tests, the scores achieved by Whites were the point of reference to which all other groups were compared. Researchers sought to determine whether other groups measured up, and they asked, "Is the Negro (or other group) mentally *equal* to the White?"[601] Lenoir was among the scholars who used this framing, which placed "Negroes" and all other groups similarly positioned on the defensive.[602] Significantly, the researchers did not ask whether Whites were equal to Blacks. Eugenicists and most other race psychologists apparently did not question why anyone would assume that humans are not constitutionally equal; as I have discussed in previous chapters, they simply assumed that all were not.

Structuring of the Inquiry

This manner of structuring the inquiry, combined with a tendency to refer to "our own" in a we/they dichotomy, not only helped construct a wall of segregation but marked Whites—and the White intellectuals who developed these studies—as the in-group who possessed the best or most of whatever element of musical talent was under discussion. Not only did these practices stamp all others as different, but they marked these others as inferior until proven otherwise.

Racist Assumptions

Recurring themes in these studies' discussions of "Negroes" and other abjected groups offer further insight into the racial landscape. First, there were statements about the cognitive limits and limited attention span of "Negroes" and members of other non-White groups; these typically appeared in discussions of why average test scores on some measures of musical talent were low. For example, Garth reported that in his study of the musical talent of full-blood and mixed-blood Indians, "in many cases the 'cognitive limit' and not the physiological limit was the one reached by these students."[603] In his discussion of the low average scores of his participants on the pitch portion of the Seashore Tests, Garth claimed that the "temporary cognitive limit" of the test takers had been reached.[604] Similarly, Johnson suggested that the test scores of "Negroes" on the time portion of the Seashore Tests might have been higher if the test had not been so long.[605] The suggestion that test length might affect one racial group, "Negroes," but not others assumed some kind of cognitive deficiency that was present in the "Negro" but not in members of other races.

One claim threading through these studies is that preadolescent "Negro" or "Brown" youth are precocious, but experience arrested development at adolescence. Johnson was among those who mentioned the precocity element of this trope; in his literature review, Lenoir quoted G. Stanley Hall at length on the arrested development of "Negro" adolescents.[606]

Yet another theme was increased within-group score variability for groups other than Whites. For instance, Johnson commented on variability in the data he collected on "Negroes" and remarked that his findings were consistent with variability reported in other studies:

> They [the data] do reveal a greater variation from individual to individual on the part of Negroes, and it is this variability within the Negro race itself which needs to be explained. This same thing has been found by others who have given tests of various kinds to Negroes, but at present I know of no satisfactory explanation of this phenomenon.[607]

He emphasized that saying "Negroes" exhibit greater variability is "quite a different thing" from reporting that "Negroes" as a whole have superior musical talent.[608]

Garth similarly discussed within-group score variability in his analysis of the musical talent data he collected on mixed-blood and full-blood Indians.[609] When dominant discourses constructed stability, predictability, and reliability as positive attributes, variability may well have had negative connotations. Notably, because these tests ostensibly measured innate characteristics, researchers apparently assumed that variability in score results reflected an innate (and potentially undesirable) biological variability present in some races but not in others.

Racist assumptions clearly were not the exclusive domain of eugenicists or of proponents of studies of race differences. For example, they seeped into a critique of research on race differences in musical talent written by James Mursell, one of Seashore's staunchest opponents. In his 1937 book *The Psychology of Music*, Mursell opened the section on musicality and race by stating that no extant study had "satisfactorily demonstrated" race differences; however, his complaint was with these studies' faulty *methodology*: "The methodology of these studies is so defective that any results would be valueless, even admitting the validity of the testing instrument."[610] He reported the results of several studies of race differences, including Lenoir's: "He [Lenoir] found the Negroes somewhat superior to the whites in rhythm and tonal memory, and not inferior in the other tests."[611] Mursell dismissed Lenoir's conclusions on the grounds that Seashore's fifth-grade norms were "open to question" and on the inaccurate claim that Lenoir's results had not been corroborated by "more extensive investigations."[612] Thus, his first complaint was that the studies were flimsy because the test itself was flimsy. Notably, however, the only study that Mursell singled out for critique—even though all of the others had used the same flimsy tests—was Lenoir's, which was also the only study he named that reported higher scores for "Negroes" than for Whites.

The pervasiveness of racist assumptions also was on display in Mursell's list of what he called "very serious technical objections" that tended to invalidate the race-differences studies' results.[613] His first objection was the failure of the researchers to take racial purity into account. He warned, "Obviously unless we are definitely sure of the degree of blood intermixture in the group with which we are dealing, the obtained differences mean absolutely nothing so far as racial characteristics are concerned."[614] His second objection was researchers' failure to use representative samples: "A group of Negroes in a public school system may represent an entirely different segment of the race from an equally large group of whites, and the same holds true of all other ethnic groups."[615] His third objection was the same as Nathanson's, Mursell claiming that tests that had been standardized using one race produced invalid results when administered to other races.[616] He maintained that this reality had already been recognized by experts studying intelligence tests, and he ended with a dig at race psychologists in *music*: "Apparently this information has not yet penetrated the minds of certain 'experts' on musical measurement, and they continue to utter sophomoric pronunciamentoes which reveal nothing but their ignorance of facts and problems which they ought to have known long since."[617]

Thus, even as Mursell attempted to discredit research on race differences in musical talent, he left other planks in the racial platform untouched. In another publication that came out in the same year, he again attacked the Seashore Tests, focusing specifically on Kwalwasser's research, which he criticized for citing Lenoir's work;[618] he made it abundantly clear that he thought the Seashore Tests were nonsense.[619] What is significant about this article, however, is that although he could have cited and critiqued a plethora of studies that used the Seashore Tests, most of which did not examine race differences, he mentioned only three; two of the three—Kwalwasser's and Lenoir's—were among the race studies to conclude that "Negroes" demonstrated innately superior talent:

> Kwalwasser . . . cites the unpublished study by Lenoire [*sic*] who gave the Seashore tests to 191 white and 191 Negro fifth-grade children. According to Kwalwasser the Negro child "was found far superior to the white child in rhythm. . . ." And this is offered as a scientific tid-bit to the unsuspecting music supervisor. Well, we may not be scientific experts, but still we can count; so let us ask just how superior was the Negro child? Here we have it! "The colored child averaged 65.69 in rhythm, whereas the white child averaged only 61.48." A difference of 4.21 entire points! Copernicus and Darwin had nothing on this. One does seem to have heard that the rhythm test is one of the two least reliable of the battery.[620]

Years later, in his 1958 book *The Social Psychology of Music*, Paul Farnsworth provided a brief overview of research on race differences in musical talent and reported that studies continued to be conducted into the 1930s.[621] Although he rejected the "racial determinists'" assumption that some races are innately musically superior to others and called these assertions racist, he also made statements that underscored the ongoing resilience of the construct of race, at least among White academics.[622] After mentioning general debate about what constitutes race, Farnsworth noted that anthropologists were in the process of discarding the term—"*except, perhaps*" in the use of the categories of "Caucasians, Mongoloids, and Negroids [emphasis mine]."[623] Again alluding to racial categories, he concluded that "research in music testing has proved of little worth for 'racial' assessments, even for the comparisons of whites and Negroes."[624]

Seashore's Responses to Unexpected Results

Seashore's speculations about study results that did not favor White subjects provides more support for my theory about why he drew inaccurate conclusions. As I discussed earlier, when Davenport and Steggerda concluded that "Negroes" demonstrated innately superior musical talent, Seashore scrambled for other explanations of the study's results—as did Davenport and Steggerda when they mentioned that sampling error may have favored "Negroes." Seashore suggested that perhaps the White subjects simply were not motivated or not paying attention.[625] In one discussion of race differences studies, he admitted that in some cases, "measurements in a given environment do bring up significant differences," but he quickly added that social and environmental factors should be examined before these differences are attributed to innate biological capacity.[626]

In his comment that there were no differences when particular capacities were "adequately measured," he introduced the possibility that studies reporting race differences had methodological problems, but I argue that all of these studies tended to have methodological problems, regardless of their conclusions.[627] It is possible that his caveat was a subtle critique of the *Race Crossing* study, but in a 1929 letter to Davenport, Seashore reported that he was pleased with the "splendid way" the research team had handled data.[628]

What is clear from his speculation is that he did not publicly raise questions about the quality of the Seashore Tests. His were not good tests, but he refused to entertain the possibility that either their validity or their reliability was flawed. Furthermore, he firmly believed that what they measured was innate and biologically inheritable. He did describe *limits* of the tests, however, and he did so in ways that helped maintain a racialized understanding of musical ability. As I discussed in chapter 6, Seashore drew an analogy between musical talent and the trunk and branches of a tree. The basic capacities, he stated, formed the trunk (or trunks). He used this analogy, for example, in a discussion of the musical mind, which appeared in his 1928 article "Three New Approaches to the Study of Negro Music":

> The accumulating experimental evidence has resulted in an analysis of the musical mind, the building of a sort of musical family tree composed of all the branches of the three fundamental trunks; namely, the tonal talents, the temporal talents, and the dynamic talents. Each of these trunks radiates into more and more refined classifications of capacities, including those from the lowest sensori-motor responses up to the most attenuated aspects of musical feeling and intelligence.[629]

It also appeared in his 1938 book *Psychology of Music*:

> Musical talent is not one, but a hierarchy of talents, branching out along certain trunk lines into the rich arborization, foliage, and fruitage of the tree, which we call the "musical mind." The normal musical mind is first of all a normal mind. What makes it musical is the possession, in a serviceable degree, of those capacities which are essential for the hearing, the feeling, the understanding, and ordinarily, for some form of expression of music, with a resulting drive or urge toward music.[630]

The movement upward on his hierarchical tree was from simple to complex.

In *Psychology of Music*, he gave the "family tree of musicality" four trunks: the tonal, the dynamic, the temporal, and the qualitative.[631] His tests, he claimed, only measured these trunks—the simplest, lowest, fundamental, crude, primal, elemental sensory-motor capacities. Because his tests only measured elemental capacities, his no-race-differences claim similarly applied solely to these elemental capacities: "It has been found that in the human races of the world to-day and in the various culture levels of civilized people, there is but little difference in the average of the *elemental capacities* for musical hearing [emphasis mine]."[632] Thus, when he added that "there is as wide a distribution of the gift of music among the primitive South Sea Islanders as there is in the families of the social register," by distinguishing between trunks and branches, he was able to maintain a distinction between what he considered to be less evolved humans and the families of the social register.[633] He accomplished this by adding the caveat that his tests merely measured the trunks of the tree, not the high and lofty branches, thereby supporting a kind of racial segregation that marked the upper branches of the tree as exclusive territory populated almost entirely by White people. Furthermore, the tree analogy helped draw and maintain distinctions not merely between different kinds of talent, but between different kinds of people.

According to Richards, by the 1930s, the tide was turning in favor of no-race-differences conclusions.[634] In the face of this potential sea change, Seashore's claim that the Seashore Tests only measured *basic* capacities created space for this new no-race-differences conclusion while simultaneously reserving the upper mental echelons of musical ability for Whites only.

Rhythm, Race, and the Family Tree of Musicality

Seashore's discussions of one of these basic capacities, rhythm, demonstrated another way that his family tree of musicality was racialized, his statements about rhythm laying the groundwork for the construction of this hierarchical, racialized tree. Between 1918 and 1938, he published three versions of an essay on rhythm. First was an article appearing in the *Musical Quarterly* in 1918, next a chapter in his 1919 book *The Psychology of Musical Talent*, and finally a chapter in his 1938 book *Psychology of Music*. He described the 1919 book chapter as appearing "essentially as printed in *The Musical Quarterly*,"[635] but it was not a verbatim reprint, and although he repeated large sections of the 1919 book chapter in the 1938 chapter, he added sections and comments. In all versions, he departed from the relatively straightforward reportage style he had used in his descriptions of the other elemental musical capacities to wax eloquent about rhythm. This curious change in register may reflect his assumptions about this capacity, and statements he recycled in the various versions shed more light on these assumptions.

Four clusters of statements illuminate Seashore's thinking about rhythm and its relationship to race. First, he used the term "instinctive" to describe a sense of rhythm and responses to rhythm. In one version, he said flat out that rhythm is instinctive, and in all three versions he described rhythm as an instinctive disposition to group.[636] He also said that rhythmic periodicity is instinctive[637] and that an "instinctive craving for the experience of rhythm results in play."[638] Rhythm was the only elemental capacity that he described as such; tying rhythm to instinct cemented its position as a less evolved capacity.

Next, in the later two versions, he said that "all rhythm is primarily a projection of personality."[639] This description departed from his standard explanation of capacities as the ability to perceive acoustical phenomena. This understanding aligned rhythm with temperament and the spirit rather than with cognition.

Third, he described rhythm in organic, visceral terms, stating that it affects the whole body, is associated with emotions, and arouses agreeable feelings. In a statement similarly worded in all three versions, he even claimed that rhythm is the physical manifestation of emotion:

> Indirectly it affects the circulation, respiration, and all the secretions of the body in such a way as to arouse agreeable feeling. Herein we find the groundwork of emotion; for rhythm, whether in perception or action, is emotional when highly developed, and results in response of the whole organism to its pulsations. Such organic pulsations and secretions are the physical counterpart of emotion. Thus, when we listen to the dashing billows or the trickling raindrops, when we see the swaying of the trees in the wind, the waving of the wheat fields, we respond to these, we feel ourselves into them, and there is rhythm everywhere.[640]

Fourth, he claimed that rhythm both stimulates and lulls; he associated it with unbridled sensuality and noted that it can be an intoxicant. In a passage appearing in all versions of the essay, he described the effects of rhythm on the body and the brain:

> It [rhythm] stimulates and lulls, contradictory as this may seem. Pronounced rhythm brings on a feeling of elation which not infrequently results in a mild form of ecstasy or absent-mindedness, a loss of consciousness of the environment. It excites, and it makes us insensible to the excitation, giving the feeling of being lulled. This is well illustrated in the case of dancing. Seated in comfort and enjoyment in pleasant conversation, the striking up of a waltz is a call which excites to action. It starts the organic, rhythmic movements of the body the moment it is heard, and one is drawn, as it were, enticingly into the conventional movements of the dance. But no sooner is this done, in the true enjoyment of the dance, than one becomes oblivious to intellectual pursuits, launches himself, as it were, upon the carrying measures, feels the satisfaction of congenial partnership, graceful step, freedom of

> movement—action without any object other than the pleasure in the action itself. There comes a sort of autointoxication from the stimulating effect of the music and the successful self-expression in balanced movements sustained by that music and its associations.
>
> The same is true of the march. When the march is struck up it stimulates tension of every muscle of the body. The solder straightens up, takes a firmer step, observes more keenly, and is all attention; but as he gets into the march, all this passes into its opposite, a state of passivity, obliviousness to environment, and obliviousness to effort and action. The marked time and accent of the band music swing the movements of all parts of the body into happy adjustment. He can march farther in better form and with less fatigue.[641]

Thus, Seashore associated rhythm with the body side of the mind/body dichotomy and with the emotional side of the rational/emotional opposition. His references to stimulation, pleasure, ecstasy, and satisfaction—in combination with his earlier comments about pulsation and secretions—connected rhythm not merely to the body, sensuality, and emotion, but to the erotic. Significantly, he claimed that rhythm can hijack or circumvent the brain, and furthermore, that movement such as dancing plays a role in these takeovers.

The idea that music, specifically the waltz, can be an intoxicant capable of shutting down the intellect was not new. In the nineteenth century and earlier, some critics viewed all dancing as immoral; others considered specific dances and the music associated with them to be lewd. Although Seashore reveled in the sensuality of rhythm and dancing, he nevertheless invoked familiar moralistic tropes, especially by mentioning the waltz. It was a wildly popular dance in the nineteenth century, and it also had the reputation of being a dirty one. It gained that reputation early on because couples were partnered, they stood close to one another and face-to-face, and they held hands. Waltzing's dirty-dancing reputation spread to the music itself. The belief that music could intoxicate the hapless listener factored into nineteenth-century stories about the downfall of the fallen woman, the woman who had foolishly succumbed to the sexual overtures of some rake after the strains of a waltz had addled her brain.[642] The associations between waltzing and debauchery had largely disappeared by the early twentieth century; nevertheless, Seashore's description of the effects of dancing and of waltz music could just as easily have appeared in a morality tale published in a mid-nineteenth-century women's magazine.

Significantly, he referred to the intoxicating effects of rhythm and dancing in two other publications, and in both cases, he did so in discussions of play. In both cases, the passage ended on a cautionary note, with a warning about the dangers of overindulging in mental intoxicants:

> It [play] attracts, engages, and holds the individual in a state tending toward elation. This tendency, when it is real play and not mere social labor or conformity, carries the dancer away in so far as he falls into a state of diffused and dreamy consciousness, intoxicated by the sense of pleasure, lulled by the *rhythmic movements*, and soothed by the melodious and measured flow of music. This element of ardent fascination and elation may be seen in some degree in all play—in the romping of the infant, in the adolescent mating plays, in the sport and adventure of youth, in speculation and gambling, or the recreation of the adult. Indeed, in this fascination lies a grave danger—the danger of overindulgence [emphasis mine].[643]

Thus, even though he sang the praises of rhythm and dance, he promoted contained pleasure and warned about the dangers of excess. Not only was rhythm powerful and intoxicating, it was potentially dangerous. Belief in rhythm's power to intoxicate or colonize may have tapped into and reflected the desires and fears of the White intellectuals who promulgated these beliefs.

Seashore's essay was part of a larger corpus of scholarly work from this period that focused on rhythm. In his essay "'Im Anfang war der Rhythmus': Rhythmic Incubations in Discourses of Mind, Body, and Race from 1850–1944," Michael Golston points out that between 1890 and 1940, theories of rhythm and experiments involving rhythm abounded in the United States and Europe.[644] He maintains that discourses and developments in a host of fields, including psychology and eugenics, helped form a "complex equation" that linked rhythm, music, blood, and the organized modern state and its subjects.[645] Golston analyzes ideas that Thaddeus Bolton forwarded in his 1904 essay "Rhythm," one of which was that specific groups of people—notably the lower classes, children, and those considered uncivilized—were especially susceptible or responsive to the influence of rhythm; according to Golston, rhythmic susceptibility became both an object of study and a marker of social, national, or ethnic identity—and difference.[646] Golston states that this component of Bolton's theory led to studies of race differences in rhythmic susceptibility, which were related to studies of innate race differences in musical ability.[647] Bolton also claimed that rhythm's power included the capacity to induce both ecstasy and catalepsy; Golston reports that belief in rhythm's ability to control figured prominently in Fascist projects of individual and group regulation during this period.[648] Thus, Seashore's commentary on rhythm and its powers was in many ways consonant with general theorizing of the day, particularly with Bolton's work. Evidence of this includes his claim of the dual potential of rhythm to stimulate and lull, which appeared in the dancing example, and his allusion to rhythm's potential to regulate or control, which occurred in his description of the marching soldier.

Finally, Seashore associated rhythm with children and "Negroes," two groups that some assumed were primitive and less evolved. In his 1938 essay on rhythm, he said that the instinctual rhythmic responses of children to music were characteristic of all stages of primitive life, and that these responses were attenuated by maturation; significantly, he associated such primitive responses with spirituals and revival singing, which he claimed exhibited a primal emotional freedom not present in mainline worship:

> We see [in children] this sort of exhibition in response to music, which is a form of inceptive dance, in all stages of primitive life. The free expression of this sort tends to be attenuated or repressed through the forces of maturation and culture. It is the outstanding characteristic of spirituals and revival singing but is thoroughly suppressed in the more dignified church service.[649]

Although the topic was children and rhythm, this passage contained thinly veiled allusions to race and social class. Even though spirituals spanned the race divide in the United States, they tended to be associated with African Americans, and although revivalism often has been described as a White movement, theology professor Estrelda Y. Alexander argues that this characterization is inaccurate. In *Black Fire: One Hundred Years of African American Pentecostalism*, she states that revivalism has been understood as a White phenomenon because White scholars wrote African Americans out of history, overlooking the early and substantial involvement of African Americans in revival activities, including in the Pentecostal and Holiness movements.[650] She notes, for example, that the 1906 Azusa Street Revival, a watershed moment in the growth of Pentecostalism in the United States, was led by an African American pastor, William J. Seymour.[651] She also points out that the earliest Pentecostals embraced racial inclusivity and interracial leadership; she states that although over time, segregated congregations became the norm, some revivalist groups continued the early tradition of unprecedented inclusivity.[652] Noting that these groups came under fire for many reasons, she states that race mixing was among the criticisms leveled against them; critics of the Azusa Street Revival condemned it in part because of free intermingling of Whites, Blacks, and Latinos.[653] Alexander also reports that members of Pentecostal revivalist groups, who typically came from lower social classes, were stereotyped by academics and members of mainline denominations as "uncouth, overemotional and ignorant."[654] Her research sheds light on Seashore's comments. The primitive people singing primitive spirituals and revival songs were very probably African Americans or lower-class White people who fraternized with African Americans; regardless of their race, however, they were marked as crude.

In a 1991 article describing the gradual infusion of rhythmic activities into the music curriculum for young children, Patricia Shehan Campbell claims that the child study movement, and specifically the views of G. Stanley Hall, contributed to increased use of rhythm activities and folk songs in late-nineteenth- and early-twentieth-century classrooms. She describes Hall's understanding of the relationship between rhythm, young children, and evolution: "Rhythm, the fundamental element in all primitive music, was to be emphasized during the first three stages of childhood development, which corresponded to the 'primitive' stage in the evolutionary process."[655] Thus, Hall and other key figures in the child study movement helped to cement connections between rhythm, children, and the primal.

In addition to associating rhythm with children, Seashore also associated it with "Negroes." In all three versions of his rhythm essay, he chose a "plantation melody," with its name written in dialect spelling, to exemplify the instinctive tendency to place sounds into groups:

> A good illustration of this [instinctive tendency to group] is found in a very crude way when one is lying in a Pullman sleeper and the successive beats coming from the crossing of rail joints set up a time which carries tunes that come into one's head. The rails seem, as it were, to beat the time emphatically into measures. The writer recalls once being haunted by the plantation melody, "What kind o' a crown you gwine to wear? Golden crown?" As he allowed the imagery of the melody to flow, the accentuation of the click of the rails became very prominent and satisfying as rhythm.[656]

His description of rhythm as "instinctive" and of his illustration as "crude" in a discussion of a melody coded as "Negro" fortified a racialized discourse that marked the "Negro" and "Negro music" as less evolved. Elsewhere in the 1938 essay, in a description of the singing of the work song "You Ketch Dis Train," he stated that rhythm is "of course" the conspicuous element in

"Negro" singing without explaining why that would be obvious.[657] He closed the 1938 version with a new statement underscoring that rhythm is the backbone of many things, even the "humdrum of the common laborer"; his common laborer was a "Negro" rhythmically chopping wood or "working on the railroad" while singing to the time of his work.[658] In yet another passage that connected rhythm to the "Negro," Seashore maintained that the "Negro" singer was more interested in obvious rhythmic "devices" than in beautiful, subtle singing.[659]

He was not alone in making these associations and holding these views. In a comment reminiscent of Bolton's assertions about race differences in susceptibility to rhythm, Nathanson stated that the "Negro" allegedly finds rhythm irresistible; after acknowledging that this belief may be based in fact, he countered that this tendency also is found in young children and apes—in other words, in other less-evolved groups: "The Negro cannot resist the rhythm of music, it is alleged; perhaps this is true, but likewise is it true that the young of all races react to the rhythm of music, and not only do all human infants respond to music but the Chimpanzee, as well, nods and sways in accompaniment to the note of bow or trumpet."[660] Thus, children, "Negroes," rhythm, and chimpanzees made appearances in discussions of the primitive, and in the above passage, Nathanson gave all of these players a role.[661]

In addition to frequent references to the popular belief that "Negroes" have superior innate musical talent overall, the race-differences sources I examined included comments about "Negroes'" innate talent in *rhythm*. Johnson opened his dissertation chapter on the rhythmic capacity of "Negroes" with the statement that the "Negro" is widely known for his capacity for rhythm, and like Nathanson, he mentioned "Negroes," rhythm, and apes in the same breath:

> If there is one thing for which the Negro is known more than for any other it is his capacity for rhythmic action. In his spirituals, his blues, his jazz, and his dances he has demonstrated his ability to behave rhythmically. It will be especially interesting, therefore, to see how the Negro compares with the white man in the sense of rhythm as measured by the Seashore test.[662]

He then reported that sense of rhythm is based on many factors, "most of which are very probably a part of man's innate equipment."[663] In a footnote he referred readers to Wolfgang Köhler's discussion of the rhythmic actions of apes, which appeared in *The Mentality of Apes*.[664] Although Köhler's work challenged the existence of a divide between humans and animals, it is not clear that Johnson's comments did. Rather, reporting on a trait for which "Negroes" ostensibly were best known, Johnson noted that this trait was present both in humans and in animals. His reference to apes placed rhythmic capacity so low on the evolutionary ladder that it spanned the divide that was believed to exist between humans and animals.[665] Associating "Negroes" with rhythm—going so far as to say that it was the thing for which they were best known—tied them to this low spot on the evolutionary ladder. In the summary of his dissertation research appearing in the *Southern Workman*, Johnson again mentioned the perception that rhythm is the "Negro's" "long suit" and then engaged in myth busting, reporting that his subjects did not show a clear superiority on the rhythm section of the Seashore Tests.[666] Nathanson, too, spoke of the "Negro's" adeptness at rhythm in his discussion of ragtime and jazz, claiming that both styles had been attributed erroneously to the "Negro," "perhaps because the Negro is adept at the peculiar gliding syncopations introduced with this new music or his slurring indistinguishable drawl."[667] The fact that "Negroes" often did well on the rhythm section of the Seashore Tests may have fueled the belief that there was a unique, *innate* biological connection between "Negroes" and rhythm.

Thus, Seashore considered rhythmic capacity to be the lowest and most primitive of the elemental, base capacities that comprised the trunk of his family tree of musicality. Furthermore, he and other race psychologists who used his tests helped construct and reinforce an assemblage that bundled together this lowest of capacities, "Negroes" (and other groups not considered White), unbridled emotion, the body, sensuality, instinct, primitivism, and danger. This bundling marked "Negroes" as inferior, and it helps explain why Seashore's trunks-and-branches description of music ability was not merely hierarchical but also racialized. When rhythmic capacity—described as the basest capacity comprising the base or trunk—was associated with "Negroes," then "Negroes" and what was believed to be their innate musical talent similarly were relegated to the lowest positions.

Damage Control

Protecting the Seashore Tests

I suggest two possible reasons why Seashore made his no-race-differences-in-musical-capacities claim. The first is that he ignored inconsistencies and differences in study results because he wanted to protect the reputation of the Seashore Tests. He believed that the tests were objective, scientific purveyors of truth, and that what they measured was a universal, hard-wired phenomenon. He was deeply invested in them in multiple ways, including financially.

These tests were based on problematic assumptions, and critics had long questioned not merely their validity but their reliability. Seashore summarily dismissed these critics, even though they asked the same questions that should be asked about all standardized instruments: what do they measure, and do they consistently measure what they claim to? Significantly, even Davenport and Steggerda expressed skepticism about the validity of at least a few questions found in another standardized test they used in the *Race Crossing* study: the Army Alpha intelligence test. For example, they mentioned the unfairness of one section of the test when administered to Jamaicans; in this section, one question asked whether the Pierce-Arrow (a car) was manufactured in Buffalo, Detroit, Toledo, or Flint.[668] (The correct answer is Buffalo.)

Seashore made his no-race-differences claim during a period when his tests were under intense fire. For example, Penelope Nichols-Rothe uses an article by Seashore that appeared in the *Music Educators Journal* in 1937 as evidence that he was on the defensive.[669] In it, he countered the criticism that the tests had low reliability.[670] Nichols-Rothe states that during this period, Seashore fended off attacks from James Mursell, among others, and notes that he went so far as to potentially alienate his allies to defend the tests; she speculates that this may have been the period when, as some have alleged, he ordered the destruction of damning data from the Stanton study at the Eastman School:

> Seashore has tried to shift the focus of the controversy off of his tests specifically and on to the relative merits of the two theories of music research. He tries to distance himself from any taint of "unscientific" behavior even to the point of alienating his own group: "The Lord protect me from my friends. . . ." It brings to mind the question of when (if at all) he actually destroyed the data from the Stanton study. Could it have been at this time?[671]

The mixed and variable results that emerged from the race differences studies may have cast more doubt on the validity and reliability of the Seashore Tests, as well as raising questions about whether what the tests purported to measure was *innate*. Problems with validity and reliability are (or should be) the death knell of any standardized test, as Seashore probably knew. Furthermore, inconsistencies in test results could have called into question the overall soundness of research in the fledgling field, psychology, in which Seashore was deeply invested.

Upholding the Racial Contract

Another compelling explanation of Seashore's decision to report no race differences is that, given the options, it was the conclusion most consonant with his White supremacist beliefs. Results from the race differences studies did not in all cases confirm White superiority. Not only were Whites not superior or even equal to other races, in some cases they were markedly inferior, according to tests that ostensibly measured innate capacities. Reporting mixed results would have openly acknowledged this, and no race differences was a less dangerous conclusion for Whites. Although Seashore and his White hereditarian peers steadfastly clung to the idea that ability is inherited, they would probably have been resistant to the idea that "Negroes" could be inherently superior to Whites at any mental activity. The idea of "Negro" superiority ran contrary to the fundamental beliefs that grounded their racialized evolutionary human hierarchy. Evidence that Seashore subscribed to this racialized hierarchy even appeared in one of his no-race-differences discussions; he spoke of the presence of musical talent in "all *levels* of man now living [emphasis mine]."[672]

Reporting as scientific fact the "natural" superiority of African Americans, American Indians, or other groups not considered White would have been earth-shattering to any fear-filled White supremacist. Such a conclusion could have effected a seismic shift in the political landscape. What might come from such natural superiority if Blacks, American Indians, and others were afforded equal opportunities? As I noted earlier in the chapter, gradations of Whiteness already rendered some White people more fit than other Whites, but data indicating "Negro" superiority rendered White people *as a whole* less fit, and, consequently, as potential targets for whole-group negative eugenical intervention. This was a possibility that eugenicists such as Seashore would not entertain. By contrast, the "no-race differences" conclusion helped to maintain the status quo, offering a measure of protection to White supremacy; in effect, it tore down "Negroes" by declaring that science had proven that a popular perception, which had placed them in a positive light, was false. Seashore and other elite White intellectuals claimed that scientific evidence had determined that "Negroes" were not more musically talented. As much as possible given the data reported in the race-differences studies from the 1920s and 1930s, "no race differences" kept Black people "in their place" by denying them innate superiority at any mental activity; at a time when the presumed innate superiority of some and the inferiority of others were claimed to govern destinies, this denial had momentous consequences.

The "no-race-differences" conclusion, whether reached by Seashore or others, was variously interpreted as proof of innate racial equality or as proof that Blacks lacked superiority in music. It should not be interpreted as a sign that Seashore was a race egalitarian, however. As his writings clearly indicate, he did not subscribe to egalitarianism on many fronts, and the no-race-differences conclusion was inconsistent with other statements he made throughout his career. He did not see all races as equals any more than he saw women and men as equals. The first section of this chapter documented his distinctly nonegalitarian views on race, music, and culture. When his tests, which he and many other researchers claimed produced scientific fact, revealed differences that supported nonegalitarian theses, he unquestioningly accepted the data and attributed the differences to a presumably stable factor: biological heredity. In the case of research on race and gender differences in musical talent, however, when test results did not favor the dominant group, he changed tack and pointed instead to the environment. Significantly, in the case of some race-differences research, he simply ignored the data.

Some eugenicists changed their minds and denounced both eugenics and the idea of race differences in mental ability. For example, Edwin Black reports that Carl Brigham eventually rejected all scholarship, including his own, that claimed there were innate race differences in intelligence.[673] Seashore cannot be numbered in this group, however. To claim that he was a race egalitarian ignores the fact that he was an inner-circle member of organizations headed and populated by White supremacists and Nazi sympathizers, as well as the reality that he remained a staunch supporter of eugenics throughout and after World War II—right up to his death in 1949. Moreover, it ignores what he said elsewhere in his writings.

Mehler says that the eugenics movement was held together not only by fear but by a desire to improve the human race: "All eugenicists considered themselves 'progressive' in the sense that eugenics was a great social-scientific movement to improve the human species."[674] In a parallel gesture, in his biography of Seashore, Walter Miles reported on Seashore's desire to improve humanity. He quoted from a commendation written by a member of the Iowa State Board of Education at the time of Seashore's second retirement in 1946: "'He retires from active duty at fourscore years . . . interested in anything that promises better things for the human race—revered, beloved, and honored is this man of letters and achievement.'"[675] Seashore's writings suggest that he believed that whiteness was best for the human race; throughout his life and in many arenas, he supported eugenical interventions that reinforced and assured the continuation of a human hierarchy with elite White intellectuals at the top. If Seashore and other eugenicists genuinely had been concerned about the welfare and improvement (however defined) of the whole human race, they would have embraced superiority (however defined) regardless of who demonstrated it, but that did not take place—not for Seashore or for most of the race psychologists who used his tests.

In his book *The Racial Contract*, Charles Mills describes a "cognitive and moral economy psychically required for conquest, colonization, and enslavement."[676] One element of that moral economy, he claims, is White self-deception on matters of race.[677] He also states that "structured blindnesses and opacities" are necessary to establish and maintain White supremacy.[678] I have no doubt but that Seashore thought of himself as a moral person, and yet the moral economy that Mills describes undoubtedly steered Seashore's beliefs and actions. Furthermore, I doubt that Seashore consciously decided to uphold the Racial Contract. Rather, I suspect that structured blindness prevented him from seeing—made it impossible for him to imagine—any alternatives. This blindness did not diminish his moral responsibility or reduce his culpability. It merely may serve as a possible explanation of how it was possible for him to act as he did.

In summary, Seashore may have made the no-race-differences claim both because he sought to preserve the reputation of his tests, and because, like many other White academics, he was so deeply invested in White supremacy and what Gloria Ladson-Billings calls the full social funding of race that he could not or would not see evidence leading to a different conclusion.[679] Especially given the context, his seemingly egalitarian proclamation may have been nothing more than White apologism.

Returning to Zeus Leonardo and Alicia Broderick's concept of smartness as property, I argue that in this context, the "no-race-differences" claim disqualified people not identified as White from having more property—more musical smartness—than White people did. For Seashore to have asserted otherwise would have upset the White-supremacist apple cart. He ignored data that upended White-supremacist theses—data from the same flimsy tests that had led him to draw many nonegalitarian conclusions about musical ability and difference, data collected, in some cases, by his own students or under his supervision. Ironically, his "no-race-differences" conclusion helped preserve White supremacy even as race egalitarians simultaneously deployed this conclusion and praised it. "No race differences" constituted damage control, however, and it was the best defense of whiteness that a White supremacist could muster under the circumstances.

"And the Beat Goes On"

Graham Richards claims that Thomas Garth's 1931 book *Race Psychology* was the swan song of race psychology. Richards was not completely accurate, for the reach of racial determinism is long and extends to the present. Research on race differences in *musical talent* continues, and some of it uses the Seashore Tests. Consider, for example, the work of Richard Lynn (1930–). Described by the Southern Poverty Law Center as an "unapologetic" eugenicist at the forefront of scientific racism, he is the author of the 2001 book *Eugenics: A Reassessment* (which he acknowledges was made possible by financial support from the Pioneer Fund).[680] The book documents the history, objectives, and implementation of what Lynn calls "classical" eugenics.[681] Throughout it, he supports eugenics and its goals on grounds that are virtually identical to those forwarded by eugenicists of a century ago, and he uses similar arguments. Acknowledging that classical eugenics (regrettably, in his mind) will never be widely accepted in the future, he is optimistic that new eugenics—with genetic bioengineering playing a central role—will meet the same goals.[682] Lynn has been the president of the Pioneer Fund since 2012 and has received "hundreds of thousands of dollars" in grants from the fund.[683] This is the same Pioneer Fund that Wickliffe Draper, the benefactor of the *Race Crossing* study, established in 1937. Prior to his retirement, Lynn was a psychology professor at the University of Ulster. In April 2018, the BBC reported that the university had "withdrawn" Lynn's emeritus title in response to accusations that his work is racist and sexist.[684] He currently serves as an assistant editor of *Mankind Quarterly*, which, according to the Southern Poverty Law Center, primarily publishes "racist pseudoscience."[685]

Among Lynn's publications is his 2006 book *Race Differences in Intelligence: An Evolutionary Analysis*, which was published by Washington Summit and is, according to its title page, a National Policy Institute book.[686] The Southern Poverty Law Center calls Washington Summit Publishers a White nationalist hate group.[687] Washington Summit also published Lynn's 2008 book *The Global Bell Curve: Race, IQ, and Inequality Worldwide*. In its carefully and strategically worded description, the National Policy Institute's website claims that it is "an independent organization dedicated to the heritage, identity, and future of people of European descent in the United States and around the world."[688] As recently as 2010, however, the Institute was blunter about its mission. In that year, the Southern Poverty Law Center published a quote from the Institute's mission statement: "'To elevate the consciousness of whites, ensure our biological and cultural continuity, and protect our civil rights. The institute . . . will study the consequences of the ongoing influx that non-Western populations pose to our national identity.'"[689] According to Michael Wines and Stephanie Saul, reporting for the *New York Times*, the National Policy Institute has received money from the Pioneer Fund.[690]

The current president of the National Policy Institute and head of Washington Summit Publishers is Richard Spencer, a White nationalist who popularized the term "alt-right." He made the national news shortly after the election of Donald J. Trump for having made a Nazi salute at a National Policy Institute conference in Washington, DC, while shouting, "Hail Trump, hail our people, hail victory."[691] On May 13, 2017, he led torch-carrying White nationalist demonstrators in a protest against the proposed removal of a statue of Robert E. Lee in Charlottesville, Virginia; furthermore, the *Washington Post* identified Spencer as a leader of the August 2017 "Unite the Right" rally in Charlottesville that ended in violence.[692]

Although much of Lynn's 2006 book is an attempt to defend the concept of races and to "prove" the role of genetics in race differences in intelligence, it includes two sections that review research on innate race differences in *musical* ability.[693] In many respects, these sections resemble race-differences literature from the early twentieth century. For example, his discussion of a global racial category he calls "Africans" opens with the familiar trope that popular belief ascribes exceptional innate musical ability, especially rhythmic ability, to this group: "It has often been considered that Africans have good musical abilities and a particularly strong sense of rhythm. The conclusion appears to have been first suggested in the fourteenth century by the Arab writer Ibn Butlan [*sic*] who wrote that if an African 'were to fall from heaven to earth he would beat time as he goes down.'"[694] The quote from Buṭlān is, indeed, evidence that Africans long have been known as musicians (although Buṭlān lived in the eleventh century, not the fourteenth), but it says nothing about innate ability. Next, Lynn asks the same but-is-it-true question that race psychologists had posed eighty years earlier: "Musical abilities are associated with intelligence, so it is interesting to consider whether Africans have the good musical abilities often attributed to them, or poor musical abilities consistent with the low IQs they obtain on intelligence tests."[695] His description of how musical ability is measured resembles Seashore's; he refers to tests of pitch discrimination, melodic memory, chord-note number identification, and detection of rhythmic differences.[696] He summarizes an article he coauthored that reported results of two studies, both of which had found an "association" between musical ability and intelligence.[697] Each study used a second-generation test of musical talent—Herbert Wing's Standardised Tests of Musical Intelligence in one instance, and Bentley's Measures of Musical Abilities in the other.[698]

His literature review of research on African Americans' musical talent includes five studies conducted between 1928 and 1981; among them are Johnson's dissertation study, as described in the 1928 *Music Supervisors' Journal* article, and Peterson and Lanier's 1929 research. Lynn reports that four of the five studies used the Seashore Tests.[699] He aggregates results of these studies and summarizes his findings:

> The general outcome of these studies is that African Americans perform less well than Europeans on tests of musical abilities of pitch discrimination, tone discrimination, and memory, but they perform about the same as Europeans on tests of rhythm. To show this pattern of musical abilities, the results of these studies have been aggregated to give a Musical Quotient (MQ) derived from tests of musical ability other than rhythm, and a Rhythm Quotient (RQ). . . . All the studies show that African Americans have Rhythm IQs substantially greater than general Musical IQs by about 15 IQ points. There appears to be no change in the musical abilities of Africans over the period of approximately half a century from the 1920s to the late 1970s. . . . The relatively high rhythm ability of Africans is expressed in their music in which a strong rhythmic element is frequently present. This is notably the case in the hymns sung by congregations in African and African-American churches. It also appears in jazz, which was first developed by African Americans in New Orleans in the early years of the twentieth century, and in its subsequent development in "swing," with its strong syncopated rhythms.[700]

Thus, like his predecessors in race psychology, Lynn links African Americans to rhythmic ability and concludes that musical ability is a stable entity rooted in biology. He further claims that this innate ability shapes competence in various musical styles. Throughout the section, Lynn uses "Africans" and "African Americans" interchangeably, even though all of the studies he discusses were conducted in the United States. This usage strips the studies' participants of their citizenship while it simultaneously constructs a global phantasm, a transnational "African." Although his assertion is more qualified than Seashore's, Lynn nonetheless makes a heritability claim: "Heritabilities of this magnitude make it likely that the low general musical abilities and the high rhythm ability of Africans have some genetic basis."[701] His use of "some" acknowledges that rhythmic ability is influenced by other factors, environment presumably being one. However, nodding to environment was quite common among US eugenicists of the early twentieth century. Finally, in a statement reminiscent of Galton's eminence criterion, he suggests that the low scores of Africans on standardized tests of musical talent go hand in hand with their lack of eminence in classical music: "There are no African composers, conductors, or instrumentalists of the first rank and it is rare to see African players in the leading symphony orchestras."[702]

In an effort to determine whether Native Americans have low musical ability consistent with their low IQ scores, Lynn developed a Musical Quotient (MQ) using Garth's research results from 1931. Lynn concludes that on the pitch identification and tonal memory subtests of the Seashore battery (the latter of which Lynn calls "memory-for-tunes"), Native Americans' MQ scores were somewhat higher than their IQ scores, and he notes that Native Americans had a higher MQ in rhythm than White students did.[703] Appearing to contradict a statement he had made earlier that attributed race differences in musical talent at least somewhat to genetics, he says that there is "no apparent explanation for this [rhythm] aptitude in Native Americans and Africans."[704]

Thus, Lynn cites some of the same research from the 1920s that I have discussed in this chapter and continues to make some connections between African Americans and rhythm that do not address cultural factors. He not only asks a question that Seashore invited the scholars attending the Second International Congress of Eugenics in 1921 to investigate—whether there are innate race differences in musical talent—but he relies, in part, on the Seashore Tests to answer it.

Eight

"And All the Children Are Above Average"

Euthenics, Eugenics, and the Iowa Child Welfare Research Station

For decades, the classic radio program *A Prairie Home Companion* regularly included news from a fictitious small town in Minnesota named Lake Wobegon. In a poignant commentary on small-town life in the Upper Midwest, all of the news reports ended with the sign-off, "And that's the news from Lake Wobegon, where all the women are strong, all the men are good looking, and all the children are above average." A gentle poke at the quiet pride displayed by residents of small Midwestern towns, this statement is witty in part because it asserts the impossible: given the statistical definition of average, all children cannot be above it—unless, of course, the average in question comes from a population larger than Lake Wobegon. Living in a community filled with above-average children was a point of pride for parents and the community. As I read Carl Seashore's statements on euthenics, I recalled Lake Wobegon and realized that a world in which all the children are above average was precisely what he had in mind—or perhaps he imagined an endless process of creating new and higher averages, which also created an endless stream of new bottom tails to be endlessly pruned.

Today the term "euthenics" is not well known, and the concept has received less scholarly attention than its companion, eugenics, perhaps because it is deemed less controversial. Nevertheless, analyzing euthenics and examining its relationship to eugenics provide insight into the systems of reasoning that rationalized eugenics. Drawing primarily from Seashore's writings, I begin this chapter with an introduction to euthenics and its goals. Next, I explore relationships between euthenics and eugenics, basing my analysis primarily on sources discussing the formation of the Iowa Child Welfare Research Station. Seashore helped establish and develop the station, the creation of which he and others have called one of his major career achievements. In a number of sources, Seashore claimed that "euthenics" would have been the most accurate term to use in the station's name, and it was the descriptor that he preferred over "child welfare."[1] This statement confirms that euthenics was central to Seashore's vision of the station's mission, and his remarks about the station offer insights into his views on the value and role of euthenics. He classified euthenic interventions into types, all of which were grounded on the assumption that the scientific expert is best qualified to determine the good—for "the child," the state, and ultimately, the human race. My third project in this chapter is to analyze several types of interventions he associated with the station. Some were intended to improve the individual or group by improving parenting and home life, and others were to improve conditions in the community or state. Later in the chapter, I discuss another type of euthenical intervention he proposed: self-improvement to be taught in schools. Throughout the chapter, I argue that Seashore valued euthenics and eugenics equally, and that he viewed the two concepts as companionate, not antithetical. Recognizing that there are clear differences between these concepts, I submit that there are significant, not-coincidental resemblances stemming from shared discourses and systems of reasoning. I argue that Seashore's proposed *euthenical* interventions, like his eugenical interventions, illustrate both juridical and pastoral forms of governance. Finally, I maintain that the evidence I have gathered does not support the assertion made by some previous scholars that Seashore exhibited an "environmental bias."

Conceptualizing Euthenics

The *Oxford English Dictionary* (*OED*) states that euthenics is "the science and art of improving the well-being of man by the betterment of the conditions of life."[2] Bettering the conditions of life frequently is understood to mean improving "the environment," a term often appearing in discussions of euthenics. Note, however, that according to the *OED*'s tracing of usage, the earliest appearance of "euthenics," a 1905 quotation by E. H. Richards (Ellen Henrietta Swallow Richards), did not mention improving either *conditions* of life or the *environment*. Richards, who helped found the field of home economics, simply said that euthenics is the "science of *better* living [emphasis in original]."[3] Two later *OED* usage quotations refer to environment, however, and one of them is from Richards, who wrote in 1910 that euthenics is "the science of controllable environment; a plea for better living conditions as a first step toward higher human efficiency."[4] Notably, the scope of the earliest definition is broader than that of the later ones. A "science of better living" would involve more elements than simply improving the environment, especially if the environment is conceptualized as whatever surrounds and is external to the individual or group. For example, doing yoga or meditating could be part of a "science of better living," but it involves internal change rather than changes to environment.

Seashore defined, described, and praised euthenics in a number of sources, sometimes using the earliest broad understanding of the term and at other times referencing the later environmentally focused one. For example, in a 1949 *Mental Hygiene* article, "The Scope and Function of Euthenics," he stated, "The term euthenics is derived from the Greek word, *euthenia*, which means well-being, and may be defined generally as the science and art of welfare."[5] "Welfare" in this passage is synonymous with well-being, and the statement harkens back to the earliest definition of euthenics. In the same source, however, he referred to improving the individual or group via improvements to the environment, saying that euthenics "denotes those aspects of all sciences and arts which have a bearing on the improvement of the individual or the group through the medium of the objective or the subjective environment."[6] This article also spelled out his vision of the function of euthenics (while simultaneously exhibiting his preoccupation with classifying, sorting, and ordering): "The general function of euthenics is to organize and supervise all welfare interests and activities by comprehensive classification and blueprints for projects in welfare. The issues, needs, techniques, and theories in welfare fall into orderly genera, species, and varieties biologically."[7] Characterizing it as a fledgling field that had recently come into its own, he claimed that euthenics had gained acceptance in a number of fields: "It [euthenics] has found approval and implementation in anthropology, genetics, comparative psychology, child welfare, and race betterment, and has found some recognition in the fields of social, educational, and medical welfare."[8] Among the several sources in which he supported euthenics was his 1930 autobiography.[9]

Eugenicists on the Relationship between Eugenics and Euthenics

Seashore differentiated eugenics from euthenics by saying that "the one has to do with heredity; the other, with the environment."[10] His distinction between heredity and environment raises questions about the relative importance he gave to each, and about his views on the relationship between eugenics and euthenics. Like many other eugenicists, he considered them to be compatible and equally valuable. In 1929, C. G. Campbell, the first president of the Eugenics Research Association (ERA) and a Nazi sympathizer, articulated the companionate view:

> It is to be regretted . . . that there should be any necessity of upholding euthenics as against eugenics. Galton's definition of eugenics as the study of all the agencies under social control which may affect the inborn qualities of future generations of man, plainly embraces euthenics. And that euthenics should be regarded as a separate field would indicate that eugenicists have neglected an essential branch of their subject.[11]

Campbell spoke of constant interplay between heredity and environment and warned eugenicists not to belittle environmental influences.[12] He said that eugenics is about heredity, the "raw material out of which humanity is fashioned,"[13] and that euthenics "is concerned with keeping this physical material in the best functional condition."[14] Thus, the role of the environment—and consequently euthenics—is to provide fertile conditions in which the inherited seed might grow. Eugenics Record Office (ERO) director Charles Davenport dismissed the question of the relative importance of heredity and environment, adding, "It seems to me that we should not formulate the problem in this manner. There is no heredity without environment and few environmental effects which are not dependent also upon heredity."[15]

Consistent with other prominent eugenicists, Seashore understood the relationship between eugenics and euthenics to be both/and rather than either/or. In some sources, he called them companions[16] and coordinates;[17] in others, he called euthenics the logical *sequence*[18] or the logical *sequel* to eugenics.[19] Rather, than praising one and discounting the other, he praised both, claiming that both are about the business of improvement: "Both are adequate carry-alls or clearing houses for a vastly expanding group of approaches to betterment or welfare."[20]

Seashore reported that Davenport was one the first Americans to use the term "euthenics," and he wrote to Davenport asking for information about the history of the word; Davenport correctly attributed it to the aforementioned "Mrs. Ellen H. Richards."[21] Seashore's turning to a well-known eugenicist such as Davenport for information about euthenics indicates that euthenics was in the lexicon of eugenics insiders, that Davenport was considered a knowledgeable and reliable supplier of information on the topic, and that Davenport was sufficiently supportive of euthenics to make him a trustworthy source for Seashore to consult.

Correspondence between Seashore and eugenicist Robert M. Yerkes provides more evidence that prominent eugenicists supported euthenics. In one letter, Seashore asked Yerkes for feedback on a draft manuscript that later was published as the article "Euthenics, A Design for Living."[22] Yerkes praised the manuscript, said it was a pleasure to read, and claimed that he had tried to use both eugenics and euthenics with his students at Harvard nearly forty years earlier (that is, in 1907).[23] As was the case when Seashore conferred with Davenport, if eugenics and euthenics had been antithetical to each other, either Seashore would not have asked Yerkes for feedback, or Yerkes would not have offered praise. Seashore's article presented a proposal for teaching euthenics in high schools; here and in other sources where he promoted teaching euthenics in schools, he envisioned it being taught along with eugenics and heredity.[24]

Eugenicists' understandings of the relationship between euthenics and eugenics also are evident in their claims about what euthenics could or could not do. It could cultivate and improve, but only to the degree that heredity permitted. Thus, the possibilities of euthenics were limited. For example, linking euthenics to a phrase he used often throughout his life, Seashore stated, "Euthenics can now say: Keep each individual busy at his highest natural level of successful achievement."[25] "Natural level" is a nod to eugenics, indicating that capacities are inherited; the purpose of euthenics is to optimize whatever those inherited capacities might be.

Given that eugenicists viewed euthenics and eugenics as companions, it may appear that eugenicists made contradictory statements about the value of social interventions and social welfare. On the one hand, they blamed human social intervention for the proliferation of the unfit; on the other hand, they called for improvements in the environment. For example, Campbell's article in support of euthenics also included the claim that modern health work is dysgenic, a disruption of the natural order:

> No one wishes to deprecate the efforts that are made to attain sanitary conditions of living, to prevent and cure disease, to relieve suffering, and to patch up individuals who are afflicted with disabilities of one kind and another. But we should recognize with our eyes wide open that such action, by preserving individuals who would otherwise succumb, tends to lower the general standard of vitality and resistance, not to mention the general standard of efficiency and accomplish-

ment. And these standards are still further lowered by the degree in which such individuals produce offspring.[26]

How could eugenicists support euthenical practices while simultaneously blaming them for the proliferation of the unfit? The answer is found in Campbell's conclusion: environmental interventions could only be supported if they were matched with what he called "compensating eugenic measures."[27] He ended the article with a call for "selective eugenic breeding."[28] Because eugenics and euthenics were thus coupled, it was possible and quite likely that an individual could be both a eugenicist and a euthenicist. Seashore, like many other eugenicists, was both.

The Iowa Child Welfare Research Station: Intelligent Care and Forethought

The Station's Formation and Goals

Keeping this coupling in mind, let us turn to the formation of the Iowa Child Welfare Research Station and Seashore's contributions to its establishment and growth.[29] The station was the brainchild of Cora Bussey Hillis, an Iowa activist involved in the child study movement, who envisioned a station that would disseminate scientific information about children to assist parents in child rearing.[30] After unsuccessful attempts to generate interest in her project elsewhere, she approached the University of Iowa. According to historian Hamilton Cravens, Seashore initially opposed the project because he was more interested in establishing a clinic or hospital for "problem" children.[31] Cravens states that Seashore agreed to support Hillis when University of Iowa president Thomas MacBride sweetened the pot, offering to help Seashore establish a psychopathic hospital in conjunction with the medical school in exchange for his assistance with the station.[32] Seashore chaired the university committee that helped formulate the project, but in 1915, the state legislature failed to pass the bill approving it. By 1917, Hillis had garnered enough support that a bill passed. Henry Minton, in assessing the scope of influence of the station, calls its establishment groundbreaking and claims that it served as a national model.[33] The station was consistent with early-twentieth-century progressive thought and with the goals of the growing child welfare movement; it also was quite similar in focus to the US Children's Bureau, which had been established in 1912 but had been endorsed many years earlier by President Theodore Roosevelt, a staunch supporter of eugenics.[34]

Seashore was a powerful figure—instrumental in the growth of the station—and one of his roles was chairman of the board.[35] In his autobiography, he spoke proudly of his involvement; his biographer, Walter Miles, did, too.[36] A number of Seashore's obituaries credited him for its creation and success,[37] an obituary by George Stoddard even claiming it was Seashore's greatest lifetime achievement.[38] Long after his death, he continued to receive accolades for his contributions to its establishment and growth.[39]

The 1915 bill that proposed the establishment of the station to the Iowa state legislature included a purpose statement: "'The investigation of the best scientific methods of conserving and developing the normal child, the dissemination of the information acquired by such investigation, and the training of students for work in that field.'"[40] In his autobiography, published in 1930, Seashore reflected on the campaign to establish the station, and the operative word was "improvement": "We used the argument that, since Iowa has improved its corn, its hogs, its horses, and its sheep very greatly through the scientific studies at the agricultural college, the State might well ask its university to see what it could do to improve the normal child or at least improve the conditions of the normal child."[41]

Several elements in his reflection merit further consideration. First, here and elsewhere, Seashore used the term "the child," which has different connotations than "children" does; his word choice suggested that, despite his belief in what he called individual differences, he also assumed that a kind of generic, knowable sameness exists among the many individuals comprising the category "children." Second, he identified two targets for improvement: the child and "the conditions of the normal child"—that is, the environment. This statement suggested that improving the environment, although important, was but one component of a larger improvement project. Third, he stated that the station's focus was the "normal" child. Of course, establishing norms and studying the "normal" were central to the child study movement, and "normal" was a commonly used concept among psychologists of the day. Seashore used the word frequently in a variety of contexts in reference to both individuals and groups.[42] However, by specifying that the station studied the "normal" child, he also spelled out which children it did not study or serve. Significantly, Seashore stated elsewhere that the station was concerned with the "conservation and development" of normal and *superior* children.[43] Thus, if he was concerned with the study, conservation, and development of so-called "subnormal" children, work in this regard was to be conducted elsewhere, presumably in a segregated setting.

In a 1923 letter to University of Iowa president W. A. Jessup, Seashore indicated where some of the research on the "subnormal" child was being undertaken. The letter described the many ways that the university's scientific research and expert knowledge were advancing human welfare, Seashore specifically pointing to the university's "interest in the study and care for the child."[44] Claiming that the university was researching almost every aspect of child life, he reported that the station focused on the normal child, indicating that other children were studied elsewhere, including at the psychological clinic and the psychopathic hospital:

> Practically every angle of child life is touched by experts in their respective fields; the specialization in medicine is well known; our child welfare station is the best organized scientific station of this kind in the country; our psychological clinic for the study of borderland and defective children is unique in that it is associated with the child welfare station for the study of the normal child, with the psychopathic hospital for the study of mental defects, and with the psychological laboratory for general scientific investigations bearing on child life.[45]

In the wake of the Iowa legislature's initial failure to pass legislation approving and funding the station, and in preparation for another attempt to pass such a bill, in 1916 Seashore published a proposal summarizing what he envisioned to be the station's scope and focus. He listed six categories of inquiry and activity: heredity and prenatal care, nutrition of the child, preventive medicine, social surveys and social policy, education and morals, and applied psychology.[46] The proposal included a variety of legislative, data collection, and education projects. The types of euthenical interventions he described sought to improve conditions external to the individual—in the community and home. Seashore apparently assumed that quite a bit of parenting was not merely unscientific but subpar, because many euthenical education initiatives focused on improving the child by improving home conditions and parenting. All reforms were to be approved by scientific experts who had pronounced them good, Seashore apparently believing that what is good for the state is good for the individual—or rather, good, scientifically approved reform is good for the state and the individual. The state was to be actor and funder in some cases, while in other instances, parents—mothers, in particular—were to shoulder these responsibilities.

The 1916 proposal clearly indicated that Seashore wanted the station to promote research in both euthenics and eugenics. It opened with a discussion of heredity and a nod to eugenics, Seashore stating that the station would make scientific inquiry into the conditions that produce ill-born children in Iowa. He called hereditary disease the most dreaded of these conditions, and he specifically listed degeneracy and venereal disease as forms of inheritable disease; later, he added feeble-mindedness, tuberculosis, and neuroticism to his list.[47] He argued that inheritable diseases could be reduced by education initiatives that disseminate "the facts and their consequences" *and by legal restrictions*.[48] He also claimed that parental intemperance and neglect can damage "the coming child," and he warned that "abuse of drink, drugs, food, sex, and physical and mental strain" all can have deleterious effects on the unborn child.[49] Thus, he appeared to conclude that prenatal environmental factors—such as alcohol consumption—could result in ill-born children. However, he also seemed to believe that ill-born children pass degeneracy along to future generations even if the damage is due to environmental factors. He included the frequently stated eugenics argument that one defective child can produce a proliferation of unfits in subsequent generations.[50] This assertion closely resembled those made by eugenicist Henry H. Goddard in his 1912 book *The Kallikak Family*. Next, Seashore promoted *eugenics*, claiming that it aims not merely to ward off evil, but to attend to conditions that will "enhance the birthright of the child above the present normal level."[51] He stated that the station would undertake scientific inquiry into the conditions that produce well-born children.

Under the same heading, "Heredity and Prenatal Care," he supported education focusing on what he called "intelligent parenthood," which he defined as good mate choice and "forethought in procreation"—standard topics of interest to eugenicists.[52] He referred to Mendel's laws of biological inheritability in an example he gave in support of parent hygiene education, claiming that, armed with the "facts" about inheritance, young people can make wise, informed choices.[53] One theme throughout this section is that better living is achievable through science and education, specifically by teaching both "the science of heredity and the hygiene of prenatal care."[54]

Nutrition was his second proposed area of inquiry. One again, he championed improvement and scientific expertise, arguing that just as scientific knowledge of what to feed cattle can improve cattle, scientific knowledge about what and how much to feed children can improve children.[55] The first step in this process, Seashore claimed, is to gather data about the nutritional value of the food Iowa children eat and about what nutrients children need. He suggested studying the differential effects on children of giving them breast milk, cow's milk, or other commercially available products.[56] Claiming that the poor spend too much money on food, he supported education that would teach tenement mothers how to plan nutritious meals for a fraction of the cost they currently were spending: "Special surveys have shown that the poor, in the majority of cases, spend twice as much for food as would be necessary in order to produce the same result. In other words, the nutrition nurse could often show the tenement mother how to get better results for her children for half the money that she now is spending."[57]

Claiming that although the nutritional "sins" mothers had committed in the past are forgivable because past mothers did not have the advantage of scientific information to guide them, Seashore warned that future mothers would not be similarly excused.[58] He closed the section by saying that today's mothers are responsible for knowing about good nutrition, and that the state is responsible for teaching them the requisite knowledge.[59]

In the section on preventive medicine, Seashore once again promoted scientific knowledge, intelligent forethought, intervention, and improvement: "Let us realize that we are emerging from a blind sort of animal existence guided by the universal instincts for the protection of life, and we are beginning to take intelligent care and forethought, largely because science has placed at our disposal new means of care and higher ideals of achievement."[60] For example, he called for a reduction in infant mortality, which he suggested could be accomplished, at least in part, by improving sanitation at home.[61] He also called for such interventions as wellness checkups and preventive dental and eye care; he claimed that physical norms did not exist for children, and consistent with goals of the child study movement, he called for the collection of the data necessary to establish them.[62] Establishing norms, Seashore argued, also would create a felt need to meet them—"to measure up to standards"; norms would motivate and thus contribute to the ever-upward motion of improvement.[63]

Merely keeping children well, however, was not sufficient in Seashore's estimation, nor was simply maintaining the current norms. The ultimate goal was to make even the "normal" better and superior, the new standards being derived from the supernormal:

> We must remember that the goal of preventive medicine is not merely to ward off disease, but rather to set those conditions by which beneficent nature may have free sway to make more of the human being than has been done before. The aim is not only to keep well, but to rise to a superior physique. We must not be misled to think that the so-called normal child is the standard and the goal. The normal is merely the average and a large number of very poor specimens drag

> this average down to a low level. Rather should we seek our standard from among those who have achieved superior excellence, remembering that even the best of those have fallen far short.[64]

Thus, recognizing that "average" is a shifting marker, Seashore envisioned a future better time when all the children would be above the current average. They would be taller, smarter, more musically talented, more moral, and "better" in every way.

In the section entitled "Social Surveys and Social Policy," Seashore claimed that the station would be involved in projects such as birth registration to gather vital statistics concerning birth rates and infant mortality. He called for a constructive and aggressive attitude that would result in the kinds of legal code that would augment "preventative legislation"; he described the latter as "merely a defensive measure."[65] His examples of "preventive legislation" included codes that would create playgrounds for children and would incentivize cities to attend to other physical conditions that would improve child welfare.[66] Seashore maintained that establishing the station would be another example of such policy.[67] He stated that there was a need for surveys of child life at home and for the intervention of economists, who were to educate families on how to avoid wasteful spending.[68] Using the language of disease, he championed studies of the working conditions of mothers, arguing that "crime and vice are epidemic and contagious" and that knowledge of "social infection" could reduce crime: "A social survey may locate the source of physical and mental contagion, and, in many cases, it may be possible to intercept this contagion at the very source."[69]

In the section on the potential contributions of the station to education and morals, Seashore stated that moral and character development occur early in a child's life, and for that reason, the station would hire a scientist who specialized in early childhood. In a brief nod to the subnormal child, he claimed that this scientist would give parents guiding principles on "training" "sub-normal, normal, and gifted children."[70] Arguing that home conditions and mothers were interfering with "nature's ways," he stated, "Common conditions of home life interfere with nature's ways and prevent a reasonable development of the human mind."[71] A specialist, specifically one "trained in the science of the mind and its education," would sort out what impedes nature's ways and would offer expert advice on remediation.[72] Character building and moral training would be among this specialist's areas of expertise; the specialist's initiatives would "help in the making of manhood and womanhood for the state."[73] He closed this section with yet another appeal for scientific intervention into the home: "Let all those who say that all good begins in the home demand that the light of science and modern information shall penetrate into home life!"[74]

In the section on applied psychology, Seashore praised child study, and then he extolled the virtues of "enlightened parenthood," claiming that research and interventions conducted by psychologists would open up vast reservoirs of natural resources—of untapped latent talent:

> The limited mental power of the average man is merely a question of undeveloped resources. To say that the average man has not developed one-tenth of his natural mental resources is making a very conservative estimate. . . . What has been said about latent resources in intellectual capacities is equally true of social power, of moral sense, of the sense of the beautiful, and of the religious life.[75]

Child study, according to Seashore, provided the fertile ground that enabled nature to have its way.[76] It allowed for the optimal development of differentially bestowed natural ability.

He closed the bulletin by calling the station "a preventive measure" and by claiming that in addition to being the most precious thing in a home, the child is also "the most valuable resource of the State."[77] Given that one of his goals was to convince skeptical legislators—who had already vetoed the project once—of the merits of the proposed station, in this passage, Seashore clearly was talking about the state of Iowa.

Improvement and Power

Let us consider the station proposal in light of philosopher Michel Foucault's observations about governmentality and technologies of power in the modern state. Seashore's intervention plan vividly exemplifies the technologies of power, and the kinds of discourse and practice that Foucault associated with power relations in modern times. For example, Seashore embraced what some scholars have called scientific motherhood.[78] He meticulously mapped out intervention by the state—via science and the scientific expert—into the everyday lives and homes of parents of young children. These proposed interventions were broad in scope, involving all aspects of a child's life—physical, mental, moral, and religious; they even were to encompass a child's concept of beauty and "the good." As he said in the proposal's section on morals, he wanted the light of science to "penetrate" home life, and he claimed that all who want good in the home should demand this. In addition to being local, these interventions also were intimate, involving parental decisions and actions that previously were considered private and outside of the purview of the state; the decision of whether to breastfeed is one example. In his conceptualization of good parenting, simply loving young children, feeding them, and letting them play is not sufficient. Rather, parents are to participate in creating a particular kind of child—the designed child—using practices and standards planned by scientific experts acting in the service of the state. The making of this generic "good" child was to be guided by a particular set of standardized values, which were presumed to be universally accepted as good. An overarching theme throughout was the need for scientific expertise and carefully planning, what Seashore called "intelligent forethought." Foucault asserted that one characteristic of modernity is a different form of governing, one taken up with the pastoral disciplining and management of the docile body. He described the body as entering a "machinery of power,"[79] and he stated that power "reaches into the very grain of individuals, touches their bodies and inserts itself into their actions and attitudes, their discourses, learning processes and everyday lives."[80]

The goals Seashore established were to be met through education and laws, what Foucault called pastoral and juridical means of governance. Consistent with Foucault's conception of the modern apparatuses of power, however, Seashore's plan relied heavily on pastoral governance and voluntary compliance, with education playing a critical role.

The station proposal also illustrates that, as Foucault argued, power is not invariably repressive or negative. Rather, power produces things,[81] and it can function through desire. Seashore's proposal promised much fruit; optimistic, upbeat, and energetic, it was fueled by promise, desire, and hope—hope for a better child, a better state, a better nation, and a better world.

Finally, although the proposal spoke largely in universal terms, and Seashore claimed that the interventions were directed at all parents (at least all parents of normal and supernormal children), it simultaneously sorted and ordered, qualifying some and disqualifying others. For example, although his goal ostensibly was to improve bad parenting—he used the terms "parent" or "parenting" thirteen times—his primary focus was mothering. He referred to mothers or mothering twenty times, and he never mentioned fathers. The gender dynamics are further complicated by his presumption that the scientific experts, the psychologists proffering advice, are male. The abject body in need of intervention and remediation is the mother, and the fact that he specifically singled out mothers who had few financial resources—stating that they needed to improve their nutritional practices and learn to keep a budget—suggests that he believed mothers living in poverty need more improvement than others. Thus, whether intended or not, it is likely that the plans Seashore proposed had differential effects that reflected existing hegemonic power relations.

Eugenics at the Station

A Eugenicist at the Helm

Without a doubt, one function of the Iowa Child Welfare Research Station was to promote euthenics-related and "environment"-focused research, policies, and practices. However, at least in its conception and early years, the station also was dedicated to and actively promoted eugenics. One sign of this was the person chosen to lead it. The first director was the eugenicist Bird T. Baldwin, a graduate of Harvard University, who led the station from 1917 until his untimely death in 1928. Historian Hamilton Cravens states that Baldwin was recommended to Seashore by Seashore's good friend Robert Yerkes.[82] As we have seen, Yerkes was a eugenicist. Baldwin, like Seashore and a host of other prominent eugenicists, presented a paper at the Second International Congress of Eugenics in 1921, which was published in the volume *Eugenics in Race and State*.[83] Other indications of his involvement in the eugenics movement include his election to the Eugenics Research Association in 1922,[84] and the review of one of his publications in the journal *Eugenics Review*.[85] Some of his research published by the station used the Stanford-Binet IQ test to measure mental *growth* in children.[86] That his research measured intellectual *growth* does not mean, however, that he eschewed eugenics. Rather, these studies recorded the blossoming of what apparently was perceived to be innate intelligence. One of the studies categorized students from early on as being of average or superior intelligence and then mapped the trajectory of each group's mental growth over time.[87] Baldwin's successor to the directorship was George D. Stoddard, whom Cravens describes as an architect of the Iowa Placement Tests and a protégé of Seashore.[88]

A Professorship in Eugenics

The station's establishment of a Department of Eugenics to study "problems of heredity and racial betterment," and of a professorship of eugenics,[89] is further evidence of its commitment to eugenics, as is the list of people consulted in the process of filling the professorship. A 1920 letter from eugenicist

Charles Davenport to Seashore talked about the establishment of the professorship, Davenport stating that Baldwin had consulted with him about possible candidates for the job.[90] Correspondence also indicates that Seashore informed eugenicist Harry H. Laughlin, a protégé of Davenport's, about the creation this chair and asked Laughlin to suggest good candidates.[91] According to Cravens's history of the station, Baldwin rejected all of Laughlin's suggestions after concluding that Laughlin's scientific standards were subpar.[92] In 1921, Phineas Wescott Whiting, a graduate of Harvard University and the University of Pennsylvania, was hired for the job, his title being Research Associate Professor of Eugenics.

Eugenics Research and Projects

The bulletin series "Aims and Progress of Research" published multiple versions of *Administration and Scope of the Iowa Child Welfare Research Station*, including one appearing in 1921 and another in 1924, which described activities underway at the station; both of the versions I examined indicate that eugenics research was being undertaken there, and both contained a section entitled "Eugenics."[93] Some versions listed Baldwin as the author, others listed none; in any case, Seashore was listed as a station collaborator[94] or a member of the Advisory Council.[95]

The 1921 version of the "Eugenics" section mentioned the station's research on how heredity and environment contribute to the betterment of normal children; it explicitly referred to a favorite topic of eugenicists, wise mate choice, stating that the station was studying "the influence of physical health, superior mentality and moral development as affecting selection in marriage and the relative distribution in the state of normal as compared with inferior children."[96]

The 1924 version of the same section was modified somewhat. Whereas the earlier version referred to the role that "conditions of heredity and environment" play, the later one added "chance conditions" to the list of influences on child development.[97] The 1924 version also spoke of specific eugenics research projects underway, including heredity studies that involved breeding insects and dogs.[98] A 1922 memorandum to Seashore from Baldwin and Whiting offered details on the dog research, stating that its focus was on the genetic transmission of dogs' "psychical and physical traits."[99] Seashore shared this memorandum with eugenicist John C. Merriam, president of the Carnegie Institute, this sharing being one of the many ways that the station involved eugenicists.[100] Subsequent correspondence from Samuel T. Orton to

University of Iowa president W. A. Jessup on the progress of the dog research indicates that Whiting was conducting the genetic studies, and with his resignation, the genetic work ground to a halt.[101] Orton claimed, however, that his own work was continuing on the effects of various interventions—what others might call environmental factors—on the brain development of dogs. He expressed interest in additional funding to study the effects of poisons, starvation, and vitamin deficiencies on dog brain development, the proposed research focusing on pregnant dogs and their offspring.[102]

The 1924 version spoke of proposed station research on identical twins, a popular object of study for eugenicists,[103] the bulletin using distinctly eugenical language to describe the purposes of heredity studies: "The study of the inheritance of defective traits such as feeble-mindedness and especially the investigation of the inheritance of superior traits such as good physique, musical ability, moral qualities and the like is fundamental for the improvement of the human stock."[104] It also talked about the station's study of migration patterns into and out of Iowa, and a study of fecundity rates; the stated rationale for these studies clearly alluded to fears of race suicide: "Both [studies] show the danger to the future stock of the state, resulting from migration west and to the cities, and from the tendency of the better educated and more successful to have fewer children than have the less desirable elements of the population."[105]

One difference between the two versions of the bulletin is that in 1921, the purpose of the station spoke of stemming a rising tide of degeneracy. The passage adopted language often used by eugenicists, even though eugenical measures were not specifically mentioned: "Recognizing the presence in every community of increasing numbers of defectives, delinquents, degenerates, derelicts and social misfits, the energies of the Station are turned to the constructive problem of materially reducing this social and economic waste by preventive means."[106] In the 1924 version, this statement was removed.

Other sources written by Seashore similarly confirm the presence of eugenics activities at the station. For example, a chapter on the formation of the station, which appeared in his book *Pioneering in Psychology*, was titled "Genetic Psychology: The Iowa Child Welfare Research Station."[107] In this chapter, he stated that research was conducted at the station on the effects of race mixtures.[108] Finally, the fact that eugenics was on the station's agenda and on Seashore's mind is evident in a 1919 letter he wrote to Davenport, stating that the station had received a $50,000 grant (nearly $735,000 in 2019 dollars) to be devoted to eugenics; Seashore sought counsel from Davenport about possible scientific projects.[109] Davenport sent suggestions; the first project he proposed would identify "cacogenic communities," especially those in rural and semirural areas of the state, the outcome being the "segregation of feeble-minded and feebly controlled men and women during the whole of the reproduction period."[110] As positive eugenics research, Davenport suggested a project that would instill interest in eugenics in young unmarried people, invite them to map out their family history using materials from the Eugenics Record Office, and encourage them to use an agency such as the ERO to determine the advisability of a prospective marriage.[111] Davenport even suggested that as a part of this project, a prize would be awarded to the couple with the "best organized eugenical inquiry."[112]

Building the Self to Build the Nation and Lead the World: Another Type of Euthenics Project

The Iowa Child Welfare Research Station was not the only euthenics project that Seashore envisioned. For example, in the 1948 *Educational Forum* article "Euthenics, A Design for Living," he published a plan for euthenics workshops to be conducted in high schools; like the station, the workshops were to focus on improvement, but they were to have somewhat different contours than those he proposed for the station. As I stated earlier, two related meanings of euthenics were in circulation, the dominant one referring to the word "environment" or the conditions of life, and the other referring broadly to well-being, or to living well. In his proposal for high school euthenics workshops, Seashore relied on the broader meaning, claiming that euthenics "deals with the science and art of living well"; he called it a "unified normative science and art pertaining to the good life."[113] He posited this definition in support of a proposal that had more to do with self-improvement directed by the scientific expert—and with group or national improvement via self-improvement—than with improving the home environment, the larger environment, or living conditions conceived broadly.

Seashore opened the article with the claim that the civilized world, including the United States, was revamping education to enable its citizens to become world leaders, and he stated that courses in euthenics should be a critical component of the revamping.[114] Enthusiastically recommending the introduction of euthenics courses and workshops into high schools, he said that a goal should be to teach individuals "a commonsense and habitual view of the good life."[115] Realization of truth and beauty, he stated, is a sign that euthenics values have been learned: "Progressive realization of truth, goodness, and beauty in life is the evidence of euthenic values."[116] This comment on truth and beauty is similar to other statements he made about taste and aesthetics, which I discussed in chapter 7.

He outlined both what might be taught in euthenics workshops and how it might be taught.[117] Euthenics, Seashore claimed, encompasses a range of topics, including mental and physical hygiene, citizenship, health, and morality.[118] The workshops he proposed were to focus on personality and character building;[119] they were to foster ambition and cultivate good taste.[120] They also were to advance self-knowledge and self-guidance, which were to be enhanced by data gleaned from standardized assessments of ability, aptitude, achievement, skills, and personality.[121] As recommended readings, he suggested a series of Public Affairs Committee pamphlets that focused on a wide range of topics: "Food, Money, Education, Health, Marriage, Eugenics, Children, Vitamins, The Blue Cross, The community, Veteran's guide, The races of mankind, The census, Jobs, Labor, Freedom, The American way, Public health, Sanity, Alcoholism, Life insurance, Wings over America"[122] [capitalization as in the original]. Linking self-improvement to national strength, he also recommended a series called Building America.[123]

Thus, in the workshop proposal, Seashore supported the cultivation of a particular kind of person—a particular kind of citizen—who has learned what constitutes "the good life," has developed self-knowledge, and has engaged in self-improvement, not merely to lead "the good life" but to bolster the position of the "civilized" United States as a global leader. That he referred to "the good life" and not to "a good life" suggests that he held, and sought to disseminate through education, a fairly circumscribed understanding of what constitutes living well and being well. Like the euthenical interventions directed outward and at others, Seashore's self-improvement project, which was directed inward, proposed the creation of a state of constant, continuous, and endless quality improvement. Euthenics aimed not merely to create more high-quality individuals, but to raise quality within the already-high-quality individual. Thus, it appears that he conceptualized euthenics as involving multiple related projects, some of which focused on understanding and improving the environment, community, and home, while others involved understanding and improving the self. All of these were ultimately aimed at constantly improving humanity, the nation, and the world.

Resemblances between Euthenics and Eugenics

On the surface, euthenics and eugenics can appear to be antithetical, reflecting the oft-used phrase "heredity versus environment." As we have seen, however, many individuals, Seashore among them, subscribed to both, which suggests that they were compatible. How and why they might be so becomes clearer if we examine the mentality, discourses, and assumptions on which euthenics and eugenics were based. At that level, there are many resemblances, suggesting that they are bound together by a shared mentality or system of reasoning. When discussing either euthenics or eugenics, I recognize that assuming they were monolithic and static leads to reductive overgeneralizations. They were not. *Both* were complex, slippery, and dynamic. How they were conceptualized, taken up, and implemented varied over time and place and even from one individual to another. Recognizing the dangerousness of making reductive assertions when examining such resemblances, I qualify my assertions by cautioning that they only apply to the texts I examined, which appeared in the first half of the twentieth century in the United States. These texts were written by authors with ties to the American eugenics movement, and in particular the American Eugenics Society and the Eugenics Research Association. Many were written by Seashore himself.

Seashore's writings indicate that he saw well-being as one of the shared goals of euthenics and eugenics. Eugenics and eugenics also shared assumptions, one of which was that the status quo—the current state of affairs—was deficient and in crisis. There were shared claims that a serious problem existed, whether it was the ostensibly deficient parenting practices that were to be addressed at the Iowa Child Welfare Research Station, or the birthrate patterns that eugenicists assumed could be altered by segregation of the supposedly unfit. There was a shared belief that due to this serious problem, someone or something was under threat. In eugenics and euthenics discourse alike, the threat was manifest on a host of levels, affecting the individual, the state, the nation, and even the whole human race. In both cases, the threat or problem was to be managed or solved though social engineering.

The next shared assumption was that reform was the solution to the problem—the key to eliminating the threat. In response to the ostensible crisis, there was a shared call for interventions that would effect a crescendo of improvement on multiple scales. For example, in the case of the euthenics projects conducted at the station, improvement of the individual child would result in improvement of the state, the nation, and all humanity. Interventions were described in terms suggesting rescue or small "s" salvation. Of course, reform and improvement discourse did not originate either with eugenicists or euthenicists; nevertheless, they shared and also expanded upon this extant discourse.

A third shared assumption was that "the good" can be and has been consensually agreed upon; as a consequence, "the good" was assumed to be universally applicable. Furthermore, eugenics and euthenics were grounded on the assumption that science has determined (or will determine) the good. Not only do right answers and solutions exist, but scientific experts have found them (or will in the future). Eminence was considered a sign of inherent worth, and thus what the eminent did was considered better, and worthy to serve as a model for the rest. Both eugenics and euthenics supported intervention of the scientific expert, as guardian of the welfare of the individual and the state, into matters not previously seen as within the state's purview. Discussions of these reforms and interventions were laced with paternalism and couched in terms of benevolence, the expert knowing what is good and best for all.

Foresight, planning, and control were assumed to be good, whether demonstrated by individuals, groups, or nations. Furthermore, both euthenics and eugenics were future oriented, sharing the utopic dream of building not merely a better present but also, and perhaps more importantly, a better future. Utopic visions were not new; euthenicists and eugenicists were building on extant discourse, and in this case, the imagined better world would be carefully designed and orchestrated by the scientific expert. Forethought and intelligent care—with intelligence presumably provided by the scientific expert—were the keys to this better future. An emphasis on planning for the future is based on the assumption, shared by eugenics and euthenics, that the future is sufficiently knowable and predictable.

Improvement and reform were to be accomplished using a both/and approach, employing both juridical and pastoral means. In particular, Seashore favored education as a pastoral means, whether the project was eugenical or euthenical. That said, in his discussions of both eugenics and euthenics, he also supported legislative measures.

Another shared underlying assumption was that qualitative differences exist between individuals and between groups. The categories of subnormal, normal, and supernormal were part of a shared language. Measurement, assessment, and evaluation, all of which establish similarities and differences and assist in sorting and ordering individuals and groups, were considered to be useful. Norms and standards were deemed valuable, and establishing norms and standards was understood to be a worthwhile activity. Numbers, statistics in particular, were accepted as the best evidence, and assessment, evaluation, and differentiation were assumed to be best accomplished using large-scale standardized measures.

Yet another resemblance was a deep concern about the morality of people identified as needing eugenical or euthenical intervention, coupled with an apparent absence of reflection about the ethics of the eugenical or euthenical projects themselves. Both eugenics and euthenics are grounded on the assumption that subscribers to these concepts, and the activities they engaged in, were above reproof, unquestionably right, moral, and ethical. The ethics of eugenical activities have been critiqued by a host of scholars; euthenical activities equally merit critique. For example, Orton's dog research, which was euthenical in the sense that it studied the effects of environment, involved subjecting pregnant dogs to starvation and poisons. It could have raised ethical questions similar to those that could have been posed about eugenics activities, but the questions appear to have gone unasked, at least among adherents. Thus, the ethical assumptions grounding euthenics were similar to those grounding eugenics, and all roads seem to have led to the same conclusion: the ends justify the means.

The euthenics texts I examined in this chapter resemble the eugenics texts I analyzed concerning women (see chapter 4) in at least one important respect: the existence of absent presences. Social class, gender, race, and ability played key roles in the strategic and selective application of both euthenics and eugenics, even when Seashore did not explicitly say a word about these topics. Differential targeting and differential effects are among the other absent presences.

Finally, whether the topic was eugenics or euthenics, Seashore's tone was positive, cheerful, and optimistic. The sun was always shining in his world; in 1943, in the middle of World War II, he even wrote about what he called the sunny side of war (although in published versions of the manuscript, he removed the reference).[124] In discussions of euthenics and eugenics alike, Seashore's sweet glaze of enthusiastic optimism was omnipresent, a seductive and effective deflector. It contributed to the appeal of his proposals and may have contributed to their success. It also obscured what may have rested underneath, at least some of which is troubling regarding both euthenical and eugenical projects. This positivity may seem ironic given eugenics' and euthenics' shared assumption that all is not well with the world. However, throughout, Seashore's was the expert voice of assurance and comfort: even if all was not well, it would be well in the future—*if* scientific expertise were the guide.

On Claims of Seashore's "Environmental Bias"

The Iowa Child Welfare Research Station, one of Seashore's most notable achievements, engaged in many projects that were considered euthenical and that have come to be associated with liberal, progressive, environmentalist positions. The station reflected and supported the child study movement and scientific motherhood, the emergence of home economics, and the growth of social work as a field. It gained national prominence and is widely recognized today for its pioneering work in child development and child psychology. It cast a long shadow of influence, remaining in existence until 1974 (although under a different name starting in 1963). Alice Smuts observes that historians point to the establishment of the station as the "prelude" to questioning during the 1940s of the constancy of IQ scores.[125] Minton is one such historian; however, as he points out, neither side in the 1940s debate about the role of heredity versus environment questioned the assumption that heredity played a role in intellectual ability, adding, "The real issue in the debate was the *degree* to which environmental stimulation could improve intellectual performance [emphasis mine]."[126] The evidence I have gathered and presented—here and in previous chapters on general ability and musical ability—*does not support* Minton and Smut's assertion that Seashore displayed an "environmental bias."[127] Daniel Kevles writes that by the late 1930s, researchers at the station had gathered substantial data to support the environmental thesis, specifically the idea that environment could substantially affect IQ scores.[128] I argue, however, that if the station leaned in a more distinctly environmental direction, it did so later, when it was led by Stoddard—not at its inception. It is accurate to claim that Seashore supported euthenics; it is also accurate to claim that he valued euthenics' companion, eugenics. Finally, it is accurate to state that as Seashore envisioned them, eugenics and euthenics were grounded on systems of reasoning that closely resembled one another—and may have been largely the same. Hand in hand, Seashore believed, the improvement companions called eugenics and euthenics would work in concert to produce a better future—a world where all the children WOULD be above average.

Nine

What Should We Tell the Children?

Silences, Secrets, Erasures, and the Full Social Funding of Race

> *There is not one but many silences, and they are an integral part of the strategies that underlie and permeate discourses.*[1]
> —Michel Foucault

In her 2010 book *The Grace of Silence: A Memoir*, National Public Radio host Michele Norris chronicles some of her family's experiences of racism and reflects on the silences and erasures surrounding them. For example, Norris, who is African American, learned that shortly after returning home from honorably serving his country during World War II, her father was harassed by a White police officer in Birmingham, Alabama. When he refused to submit to the harassment, the officer pointed a gun at her father's chest. In the scuffle that ensued, the gun accidentally discharged, wounding her father in his leg.[2] He walked with a limp for the rest of his life. Norris heard nothing of her father's story until after his death, and only when she began asking family members about race. She was haunted by the silence surrounding this incident and wondered, "Why would he hide it from his children?"[3] She also learned that her maternal grandmother had dressed up as Aunt Jemima and traveled throughout the Midwest selling pancake mix to White people.[4] Stunned, Norris wanted to know why her family had not told her these things before.[5] She further discovered that three family members spanning three post-1960 generations had been told by teachers or guidance counselors that they lacked the ability to attend college or the college of their choice.

Two of the three had been counseled to consider junior college, and all three had subsequently succeeded at prestigious institutions, Stanford University among them. For years, all three family members kept secret the shameful advice they had been given.[6] Reflecting on the secrets that had almost gone untold in her family, Norris wondered, "How would I have been different without their complex grace of silence? And what's been more corrosive to the dialogue on race in America over the last half century or so, things said or unsaid?"[7] Next, she in essence asked, "What should we tell the children?"[8]

The title of Norris's book intrigued me as I thought about the multiple silences, secrets, and erasures I encountered when conducting this research. I wondered whether there was grace in the silences I had found, and if there was, on whom it had been showered. From whom had these silences withheld grace, and why? As I launched into Norris's book, I realized that in their context, rationale, and intent, the silences she discussed were different in many ways from those I was seeing in the materials I examined in my research. Nevertheless, in complex ways, all of these silences were related. One resemblance was that racism was at the heart of all of them. Although eugenics is about many things, virulent, unvarnished racism is at its core, so silences about eugenics inevitably are race silences. Second, in both instances, at least some of the silences were secrets. A secret is a particular kind of silence created by deliberately withholding information. Third, in both instances, literal or metaphorical "children" were among those from whom information was withheld. Furthermore, in both instances the reasons for the silence merit consideration because, secrets or not, these silences and erasures shaped how subsequent generations could construct not only past but present.

In this chapter I analyze the silences, secrets, gaps, and erasures surrounding Seashore and eugenics. I begin with a brief general discussion of silences, and then turn to Seashore's silence, specifically reflecting not only on what he did not say and why he did not say it, but on the tactical productivity of his silence. Next, I turn to the silences of his contemporaries, again discussing the reasons for them, as well as their effects. Third, I nest all these silences within the broader race silences that tend to characterize music education research discourse down to the present. I argue that Seashore's silences, those of his contemporaries, and those of subsequent scholars are part of larger silences that contribute to the *continued* full social funding of race. Critical race theorist Gloria Ladson-Billings has discussed the concept of the social funding of race as it applies to schooling; the effects of this funding are devastating for large segments of the US population.[9] Given this continuation, I am ethically required to end these silences; to do otherwise would constitute complicity. I close by posing the question that Norris, in essence, asked: "What should we tell the children?"

About Silences

Like Foucault, I assert that are many kinds of silences. In recognition of this multiplicity—of the complex, dynamic, polysemic nature of silences—I speak of them in the plural. I also posit that silences are integral components of discourse, and that, as Foucault claimed, they function alongside and in relation to what is said:

> Silence itself—the things one declines to say, or is forbidden to name, the discretion that is required between different speakers—is less the absolute limit of discourse, the other side from which it is separated by a strict boundary, than an element that functions alongside the things said, with them and in relation to them within over-all strategies. There is no binary division to be made between what one says and what one does not say; we must try to determine the different ways of not saying such things, how those who can and those who cannot speak of them are distributed, which type of discourse is authorized, or which form of discretion is required in either case.[10]

Next, as José Medina (paraphrasing Foucault) states, silences are "situated speech acts,"[11] suggesting that making meaning of what is *not* said is contextual, dynamic, time- and space-specific, and shaped and bounded by discursive communities. Summarizing Alice Crary, Medina writes, "Meaningful silences are always internal to a discursive practice: only internal silences are interpretable, for it is only within a language-game that we can attribute a tacit meaning to a silence."[12]

Even within a particular discursive practice, there is an interpretive openness to silences (to what is not said and not done). Furthermore, in different cultures, times, and contexts, silences are not only open to different meanings but are held in different regard. For example, in some discursive communities, silences are valued and read as signs of wisdom; in others, they are generally read negatively—as signs of inadequacy, inferiority, or ignorance. Silences may or may not come from not knowing. They may or may not come from forgetting.

Third, recognizing that silences are integral components of discourse, I assert that they should be subjected to the same questions that Foucault posed concerning all discourses: "We must question them [discourses] on the two levels of their tactical productivity (what reciprocal effects of power and knowledge they ensure) and their strategical integration (what conjunction and what force relationship make their utilization necessary in a given episode of the various confrontations that occur)."[13] Put slightly differently, if discourses are productive, what might the silences and gaps I have located produce or allow? What effects of power and knowledge do they ensure?

Having said this, I acknowledge that I am speculating about the silences surrounding Seashore. I present only a few possible interpretations and do not claim they are "correct," comprehensive, or definitive. Furthermore, I do not claim to fully map out the tactical productivity or strategical integration of these silences. Rather, my goal is merely to acknowledge the presence of these layers of silences and by so doing, to open the door to further conversation about their effects.

Seashore's Silences

Seashore's silences and inaction constitute the first layer of silences, and they should be considered in conjunction with his statements and actions. The organizations to which he belonged, their publications, and their members said and did many troubling things "in the name of eugenics," to quote Daniel Kevles. What is significant here is what Seashore, *as a member of these organizations*, did not say or do. First, he did not speak by resigning. Sometimes members choose to remain in organizations to effect change from within. I found no evidence, however, that he attempted speak critically from within—to critique the discourses and practices the organizations officially endorsed. He did not write letters of protest to eugenics journals; he did not publish critiques in eugenics publications or any other published or extant unpublished source. It is possible that he did not agree with every point of the official platform of the American Eugenics Society (AES) or with every statement made by the AES and the Eugenics Research Association (ERA), but if he had reservations, I found virtually no evidence of them. He didn't renounce the movement or even distance himself from it as some eugenicists did, before, during, or after World War II.[14] In fact, he remained a supporter to his death. One of his final publications, which appeared in 1949—four years after the end of World War II and the year Seashore died—praised eugenics.

There also is the matter of what is not said in Seashore's writings but is an absent presence, nevertheless: race is one such absent presence. For example,

Seashore did not speak about race in his discussions of women and education, but this was not an empty silence. It exemplifies, as Michael Omi and Howard Winant put it, how racial domination can be accomplished without ever explicitly referring to race.[15]

The evidence I examined indicates that Seashore remained silent because he unapologetically supported enough of what eugenicists were saying and doing to go along with it. He may not have seen a need to offer critique; it may not even have occurred to him to question. Of course, it is possible that he had reservations, but we only have what remains, and what remains suggests that the reason for his silences is the same as the reason for his speech and actions.

Seashore's silences thus were both effective and productive. They fostered—or at least did not hinder—the proliferation of eugenical ideas and practices, producing many benefits and harms that were differentially bestowed on specific individuals and groups. His silences, in addition to his words, produced careers and good reputations; they enabled the unfettered growth of psychology as a field and of psychological discourse. Wittingly or unwittingly, however, Seashore's silences were a form of complicity, and they contributed in complex ways to the full social funding of race.[16]

Silences about Seashore

In addition to Seashore's silences, there are the silences of his contemporaries who wrote about him. These include at least two related silences. One is that Seashore's involvement in eugenics is not mentioned in contemporaneous texts, including obituaries, biographies, and other discussions of his life and work. Coupled with this is a second silence, the absence of critique of this involvement. How might these silences be explained? It is possible that some of the contemporaries who wrote about him were unaware of his involvement, whether or not they would have considered it problematic. Seashore made no secret of his involvement or his views, however, and a number of those who wrote about him were his former students, colleagues, or both—including Francis P. Robinson, George Stoddard, Joseph Tiffin, and most notably his biographer, Walter R. Miles. At least one of his contemporaries, Miles, was aware of Seashore's involvement but said nothing. In a lengthy list of Seashore's publications that Miles included at the end of the Seashore biography is a citation for the published paper he delivered at the Second International Congress of Eugenics.[17] The body of the biography did not mention Seashore's eugenics memberships, activities, or views, however. It is possible that although Miles and others were aware of this involvement, they did not consider it problematic, and simply deemed it not newsworthy—too inconsequential to be discussed. If this is the case, their silences reflect the norms and cultural politics of the selective tradition. However, a number of these contemporaneous sources included quite exhaustive lists of Seashore's other accomplishments, so it is notable that his participation on the AES Advisory Council and his memberships in the AES and ERA are conspicuously absent.

It is also possible that Miles and others said nothing because they did not want this information known, having deemed it too embarrassing or incriminating. Seashore's biography was published in 1956, nine years after the end of World War II. By that point, eugenics' stock had plunged. To know but to choose not to tell is a particular kind of silence; it is the making of a secret, a specific form of erasure. Miles may have decided to keep a secret.

Consistent with philosophical idealism and the conventions of constructing heroic tropes, it was quite common in the mid-twentieth century to keep secrets about prominent figures by focusing on what was considered positive and by strategically leaving out the negative. Idealism tended to construct larger-than-life heroes who were portrayed as incapable of doing wrong, or whose mistakes could be justifiably minimized or erased in the interest of protecting a particular image or acknowledging overall contributions. Some silences may reflect conventions surrounding obituaries and death notices, notably adherence to the ancient advice *De mortuis nihil nisi bonum* (do not speak ill of the dead). By 1949, the year of Seashore's death, discussing his involvement in eugenics may have been a forbidden breach of protocol tantamount to hauling skeletons out of the closet.

Taken collectively, however, the silences of his knowing contemporaries scrubbed Seashore's reputation clean. If silences produce things, among the many things these silences produced was protection. If acknowledging Seashore's involvement would have been damning or at least embarrassing to Seashore or his followers, then keeping secrets was an act of grace that preserved both his reputation and his legacy. These silences were signs and benefits of privilege—classed, White, male privilege. This protection came (and comes) at the expense of others, however.

Withholding incriminating information has consequences and effects. As was the case with Seashore's silences, the silences of his contemporaries enabled psychological discourse, the field of psychology, and specific school-reform initiatives to flourish largely unfettered. It preserved and promoted not only Seashore's career and reputation but the careers and reputations of those who followed him. If his contemporaries knew of his involvement and hoped to control damage by remaining silent, then their silences constitute complicity. These silences shaped subsequent discourses and practices, what was imaginable and what was deemed possible. Because eugenics is about race, the silences of Seashore's contemporaries wittingly or unwittingly contributed in complex ways to the full social funding of race.

The Silence of More Recent Scholars

The third layer of silences consists of those by more recent scholars in music education. This silence was broken briefly in 2018 by Adria Hoffman, who published a handbook chapter on musical aptitude, race, and equity that talked about Seashore and eugenics.[18] Her chapter appeared in a collection focusing on arts generally—not in a music education source. Silences about eugenics were broken long ago in fields other than music education. For example, there is a bit of research on Seashore and eugenics, notably Barry Mehler's 1988 dissertation on the American Eugenics Society. Other recent breaks in the silence have been made by musicologist Alexander Cowan and sonic arts scholar Johanna Devaney.[19] In music-related fields, however, the research contributions of Hoffman, Cowan, and Devaney are very recent and isolated developments.

Steven Selden in education and Barry Mehler in history were lone voices thirty years ago, but especially during the past decade, eugenics has become a hot topic in a host of fields. Students who were in my eugenics seminars and researchers who have attended the talks I have given since 2008 are adding to a new corpus of scholarship focusing on eugenics and education. This work includes, for example, Tracey Hunter-Doniger's 2017 article on eugenics and art education; Bethsaida Nieves's research on education and eugenics in Puerto Rico; Peter Woods's work on eugenics and aesthetics; and Brandon Singleton's dissertation on Edward Thorndike, mathematics education, and eugenics.[20]

Given this burgeoning interest in eugenics, what might explain the continued near-total silence in music education?[21] I posit that it results, in part, from dominant understandings of what music education research should be about—what kinds of questions may legitimately be asked and what kinds of investigative processes are acceptable. In Seashore's time and until fairly recently, music education research consisted primarily of positivistic experimental studies, a research paradigm largely dictated by experimental psychology. More recently, qualitative studies, particularly ethnographies, have gained acceptance. Historical research, while long present in some form, has always sat on the sidelines; furthermore, most historical studies are acritical and descriptive rather than analytical.

In addition, what is or is not said in music education scholarship continues to be shaped by the long-standing convention that controversy and critique are to be avoided, ostensibly in the interest of distanced, presumably achievable, scholarly neutrality. With few exceptions, one of them being the famous disagreements between Seashore and James Mursell over the nature of musical ability, discourse in music education has been marked by a tendency not to ruffle feathers, critique, or debate, at least not publicly.

Disciplinary compartmentalization and the practice of not reading widely across disciplines may also partially explain why the scant research on Seashore and eugenics that exists in other disciplines has not filtered into music education. Music education researchers tend to be educated quite insularly in schools of music; coursework tends to focus on a narrow array of topics. In these contexts, scholarly interests similarly have tended to be narrow. Consequently, extant music education scholarship on Seashore has confined its scope to his views on musical capacities and music psychometrics. His publications that are not specific to music or music education are more revelatory of his eugenical views, however, and reading them provides context for his music-related work. Thus, the tendency in music education to bore narrowly rather than to sample broadly has, in effect, created gaps, silences, and erasures.

It is likely that silences in music education occur because race issues and race equity are subjects that a substantial number of researchers in the field do not want to talk or think about. In the United States, the vast majority of music education research is conducted at historically (and currently) White colleges and universities by individuals whose race has advantaged them and who do not see their racial privilege as problematic. This segregated insularity has helped determine what questions have or have not been deemed worthy of investigation.

Research agendas set in contexts such as these have a racial politics of their own. Race issues and equity too often are viewed as other people's problems. For example, in 2010, the Music Education Area at the University of Wisconsin–Madison hosted two research conferences concomitantly, one sponsored by the Consortium for Research on Equity in Music Education (CRÈME), an international group dedicated to research on equity issues, and the other by the Committee on Institutional Cooperation (CIC, now called the Big Ten Academic Alliance, BTAA). CIC/BTAA is a consortium of the Big Ten institutions and a handful of other universities. For more than fifty years, music education researchers from the historically (and currently) White institutions that comprise the CIC/BTAA have met annually. Although there was some membership overlap between CRÈME and CIC, hosting both conferences at the same time created a rare opportunity to bring together somewhat different groups. The topic of the joint conference was race issues in music education, and the keynote speakers were pedagogical theorist Gloria Ladson-Billings, sociologist Eduardo Bonilla-Silva, and the African American studies specialist Cameron McCarthy. The conference was well received overall, but some members of the CIC consciously changed the focus for the next year's event to move the conversation back to more traditional music education territory. This decision reminded me of a comment made by an attendee at an earlier CIC conference focusing on equity: "That's enough about politics; let's get back to talking about music."[22] The program at these historic conferences did not fit some—perhaps many—researchers' conceptions of what music education should be about. The critic who used the word "politics" invoked the no-politics convention and was expressing disapproval of what had taken place.[23]

Silences and erasures continue today in what textbooks tell our children about psychology. In the summer of 2010, my daughter brought home the high school textbook to be used in her AP psychology course, a popular publication by David G. Myers that was in its eighth edition.[24] Knee-deep in my research on Seashore and eugenics, I was curious to know what the textbook said about the early history of psychology. I opened to a timeline, "The Story of Psychology," which portrayed an impressive, progressive march, and I quickly noticed the names of people I knew were eugenicists: Francis Galton, Leta Hollingworth, Edward L. Thorndike, and Robert Mearns Yerkes.[25] When I examined the textbook's contents, I realized that eugenics and scientific racism were almost totally erased from its rendition of the illustrious history of the field. Although the index contained no reference to eugenics, the book did feature several chapters on intelligence, including one on its assessment. In that chapter, I found a few paragraphs pertaining to Lewis Terman's contributions to the concept of IQ:

> In sympathy with eugenics—a much-criticized nineteenth-century movement that proposed measuring human traits and using the results to encourage only smart and fit people to reproduce—Terman envisioned that the use of intelligence tests would "ultimately result in curtailing the reproduction of feeble-mindedness and in the elimination of an enormous amount of crime, pauperism, and industrial inefficiency."[26]

The textbook then described the use of the Army Alpha tests to restrict immigration from specific regions, claiming that Binet would have been horrified by this usage[27] and stating that in the end, even Terman changed his views.

The section closed with the statement, "Abuses of the early intelligence tests serve to remind us that science *can be* value-laden. Behind a screen of scientific objectivity, ideology *sometimes* lurks" [emphases mine].[28] In addition to being brief, this passage is notable for its construction of eugenical thinking and its deleterious consequences as past embarrassments. To say that science *can* be value laden suggests that sometimes it is not. This construction is productive in that it distances eugenics from the present and erases the possibility that all science is culturally and politically invested. Rather than continuing to inform contemporary discourse, eugenics becomes a past mistake that can teach valuable lessons about the importance of maintaining scientific neutrality and objectivity. Invoking a good/bad dichotomy, it places Terman's work in the bad, abject bin.

The textbook used in 2019–20 in the same AP psychology course is the third edition of *Myers' Psychology for the AP Course*, published in 2018. Myers coauthored this book, and despite a new title and publication date, it includes a timeline of the history of psychology featuring the same eugenicists who appeared in Myers's earlier book.[29] Furthermore, the new textbook's statements about Terman and eugenics are virtually identical to those found in the textbook my daughter's class used in 2010.[30] One difference is that the new textbook removes some references to the work of the White supremacists Richard Lynn, Richard Herrnstein, Charles Murray, and J. Philippe Rushton.[31]

Because much early research in music education borrowed its epistemic traditions from psychology, psychology's silences and erasures are also music education's. Returning to Foucault's assertion that discourse should be questioned in terms of its tactical productivity, the music education community should consider the tactical productivity—the effects—of maintaining the larger silences, of consciously or dysconsciously keeping race secrets. What questions are not askable as a result of these silences?

Some silences and erasures are double gestures, simultaneously acts of exclusion and violence as well as inclusion and protection. The complex multilayered silences I found in this research are prime examples of double gestures. To omit a substantive discussion of eugenics and scientific racism from a psychology textbook or to erase Seashore's deep involvement in eugenics is an act of symbolic violence and of protection.

Music education's race silences and secrets, including those pertaining to Seashore and eugenics, are part of a history that is not glorious, but according to David Blight, the director of the Center for the Study of Slavery, Resistance and Abolition at Yale University, glorious is precisely what most Americans want.[32] In a 2013 National Public Radio interview about enslavement, Blight stated, "Most Americans want their history to be essentially progressive and triumphal. They want it to be a pleasing story. And if you go back to this story [of enslavement in the United States], it's not always going to please you."[33] Blight also observed, "We love being the country that freed the slaves [but] . . . we're not so fond of being the country that had the biggest slave system on the planet."[34] Of course, Blight's comments raise questions about which Americans constitute the "most" and "we" he referenced; by and large, music education researchers may be among them. Nevertheless, not telling stories that many Americans do not want to hear comes at a great cost, not only to those who have been directly harmed by the ideas and actions not being discussed, but also to those who do not *want* to hear the stories but *need* to.

Another reason why silences persist is because some race stories and secrets remain too dangerous to tell. In one instance, a source shared a painful personal race secret with me that was related to this research; in the end, the source did not grant me permission to publish it. Now, it is my secret, too, and I mention it only because it serves as a powerful reminder and corrective: for many, it is unsafe to hold nothing back; the option of holding nothing back is a privilege only available to an elite few.

Breaking the Silence

Reflecting on the title *The Grace of Silence*, I have concluded that Seashore has been extended considerable grace via silences, whether I conceptualize grace as protection or as forgiveness, and I scoured Norris's book for an explanation of how silence about racism can possibly be grace-filled except toward those who continue to fully fund it. Norris posits that her parents believed there was grace in sparing children the burden of painful stories. She writes, "You can't keep your eye on the prize if your sight is clouded by tears. How can you soar if you're freighted down by the anger of your ancestors?"[35] Thus, grace in this context involves protection. Norris maintains, however, that her parents' silence weighed her down even if it was well intended, and it was problematic because of "the consequence of silence on matters of race."[36] She concludes, nevertheless, that there is a grace in silence, at least in the graceful silence of listening "to that which, more often than not, was left unsaid."[37]

The grace in silence of which Norris speaks is not the grace that shielded Seashore during or after his life, however. Rather, it is the grace shown by listening to what has been untold, withheld, or erased. Norris's grace is the honoring act of respectful listening. Although grace conceptualized as forgiveness or exoneration may need to be part of the race story in the United States, it is not what Norris had in mind. The cultural politics of grace, whether conceptualized as forgiveness or protection, are complex, as are their differential effects.[38]

I am haunted by the question, "What should we tell the children?" It eludes simple answers because the what, why, how, and who of telling and not telling are dynamic and deeply invested in power; the complexity of telling matches the complexity of silences. The community that constitutes Norris's family is not the music education research community or the education community generally, and each community has different secrets and different reasons to remain silent, as well as to speak. Nevertheless, these communities are bound together by the presence of race secrets. For example, Norris's story about family members who were pointed to junior colleges by their guidance counselors is related to Seashore's rationale for establishing junior colleges—institutions he placed low on his prestige ladder and considered ideal for "Negros in the South."[39] It is also related to the advice Seashore reportedly gave to Alvin Rose, an African American graduate student at the University of Iowa, to quit school and get a manual labor job.[40] Like Norris's relatives, as I reported in chapter 5, Rose succeeded despite the deep racism to which he was subjected.

What is erased or kept secret in one family may be common knowledge in another. Eugenics stories may be race secrets in the predominantly White music education research community, but may come as no surprise or even be well known in other communities, especially those that have experienced eugenics' most devastating effects. The question of what we should tell the children is salient. When Norris asks how she would have been different if the silences in her family had been broken, I ask how I, and the education research communities into which I was inducted, might have been different if race secrets had been told. I am persuaded by Norris's assertions that keeping silent on race secrets may benefit a few but is damaging, overall, and that there is much to be learned in the graceful silence of listening to that which has usually been left unsaid.

Finally, in the United States, there are many different kinds of race secrets in music education, the academy, and elsewhere. Recognizing that silences are part of the collective process of remembering called history, and acknowledging that eugenics is about race, I decided that I had a responsibility to speak about the race secrets I learned throughout this project. To remain silent would be complicity, a perpetuation of a tradition of protecting some at great cost to others. I hope that the story I have told will be received with the graceful silence of listening.

Ten

Resemblances

Why, Carl, Why?

As I have demonstrated, Carl Seashore was deeply involved in the American eugenics movement during the first half of the twentieth century; he was a member of an elite, tight-knit inner circle of eugenicists who supported each other and each other's work, and he explicitly and staunchly advocated for eugenics to the end of his life—even though other US intellectuals distanced themselves from eugenics, especially during and after World War II. All the types of evidence I examined—participation, mentioning, skeins of relationships, and discourses—overwhelmingly support the conclusion that he was in deep. As my project enveloped ever larger chunks of my life, my family began referring to it as "Carl." ("Mom is spending time with Carl today.") Sometimes when I studied his portrait and looked into his eyes, I imagined conversations with his ghost. I had questions and speculated on how he would answer them. Would he protest my project, claiming that I had miserably misread and misunderstood him? Would he argue that time will vindicate him, and that genetics does indeed govern destinies in ways yet unimagined? Having studied him for many years, I feel like I am on a first-name basis with him, familiarity placing his face near mine. For a long time, I puzzled over the question, "Why, Carl, why?" Why was he drawn to eugenics, why did he belong to these organizations, and why did he stick with eugenics to the very end? The more I read his writings, however, the more I realized that I did not need to ask his ghost, because Seashore answered most of my questions through his work. His writings make it clear that he was a true believer. Eugenics made perfect sense to him. He subscribed not only to the planks of the official eugenics platform, but also to the systems of reasoning that made eugenics seem sensible. Eugenicists used extant concepts for their own purposes and wove them together into a remarkably cohesive whole. Seashore's statements on diverse topics similarly were remarkably consistent, supporting each other to form a coherent logic. Furthermore, like his writings, the projects he promoted were grounded in central tenets of eugenics. His membership in eugenics organizations was not a pragmatic convenience or merely an effort to further his academic career and research agenda. When he first wrote about eugenics in 1911, Seashore was forty-five years old; he had been a professor for fourteen years and a dean for three. His were not the actions of a young, unknown-but-eager upstart. His successful academic career was well established, and he was well on in years—fifty-four years old—when he was elected to the Eugenics Research Association in 1920; by that time, he had served a term as president of the American Psychological Association. Given his fame and success, his presence on the American Eugenics Society's Advisory Council in 1923 and the appearance of his name on the society's letterhead gave the *organization* legitimacy. The *depth* of his involvement in eugenics supports the claim that this was not merely a pragmatic arrangement.

The organization's journals repeatedly reported on planks in the official eugenics platform; this ostensibly "reasonable" discourse was rife with racism, virulent White supremacy, anti-Semitism, xenophobia, sexism, classism, and horrifying attitudes toward people with disabilities. Why would Seashore find this platform appealing? Recognizing that membership in an organization does not constitute unqualified endorsement, I initially wondered if he was fully aware of the beliefs and goals of the eugenics organizations to which he belonged. The evidence indicates that he was, and he did not cancel his subscriptions or memberships. Furthermore, as I indicated in chapter 9, I found no evidence that he disagreed with particular planks of the platform or that he remained affiliated with eugenics in an attempt to effect change from within.

Not only was he a full signatory, he also was a promoter and a conduit, bringing eugenical ideas and practices to the University of Iowa, to colleges and universities throughout the nation, and to a host of disciplinary areas other than music and psychology. As I have demonstrated, his work circulated among like-minded eugenicists globally; thus, Carl Seashore's world of eugenics, psychology education, and music truly was vast.

Why was he a true believer? Eugenics had to make sense to him; what made sense to him was governed by the systems of reasoning to which he had access and to which he subscribed. Time and place tend to play a role in which discourses are available to whom, as well as which discourses are dominant. These realities do not get him off the hook, however. His apologists may argue that it is neither scholarly nor fair to fault him merely for being a "product of his times." Although it is true that eugenics discourses were widespread, and that a great many people in powerful positions supported eugenics and the ideas from which it sprang, it also is true that quite a number of people did not—certainly not to the degree that Seashore did. Discourses inevitably constrain us all, and dominant discourses have an overdetermined way of seeping into every crack and crevice; that said, other discourses and positions were circulating at the time. For example, as I reported in chapter 2, Seashore's work appeared in the same issue of a journal as W. E. B. Du Bois's assertion that race has no scientific basis. Seashore could not have missed it.

There were eugenicists who changed their minds, issued full or partial retractions, or at least publicly distanced themselves from eugenics. For example, Barry Mehler states that James McKeen Cattell resigned from the eugenics committee that helped create the American Eugenics Society after receiving a letter describing the intent of the organization.[1] Although Thomas Garth may not have been an official member of a eugenics organization, he promoted eugenics, and the concept of race differences in intelligence, early on; after many years of researching the subject, however, he publicly admitted that his early understandings were wrong.[2] According to Edwin Black, even Henry Goddard changed his mind, Black reporting that Goddard "eventually abandoned the eugenic creed entirely, at least publicly."[3] In addition, a host of prominent intellectuals from an array of fields openly criticized and opposed eugenics from the outset. According to contemporary scholars Daniel Kevles, Philippa Levine, and Alison Bashford, these critics included Franz Boas, Otto Klineberg, J. B. S. Haldane, Julian Huxley, Herbert S. Jennings, Lancelot Hogben, L. T. Hobhouse, G. K. Chesterton, Bertrand Russell, Clarence Darrow, Hermann J. Muller, Raymond Pearl, and William Bateson.[4] Either Seashore was not listening to or was not buying their critique. Although contemporary music education researcher Carlos X. Rodriguez did not mention eugenics, he speculated on whether Seashore might have thought differently if he had engaged substantively with a different group of scholars of his day:

> Carl Seashore's views on musicality were most certainly influenced by the most potent scientific movements of his time. Imagine, however, if he had also enjoyed lively debates with ethnomusicologists such as [A. H. Fox] Strangways, [Jaap] Kunst, and others who redefined music and musicality as a result of observations of diverse cultures from around our planet.[5]

Kunst's ideas were different in some ways from Seashore's—for example, he argued that "exotic" music is not inferior—but their resemblances indicate that both men were drawing somewhat from a shared discursive well. Like Seashore, Kunst referred to primitive and civilized cultures (although Kunst prefaced "primitive" with "so-called"), and to higher and lower forms of music.[6] They both described similar processes of gaining access to "primitive" people and to information about primitivism,[7] both were fans of using recording technology to preserve and analyze the music of the exotic other, and both proceeded on the assumption that dissection and systematic analysis are central to musical knowing.[8] Furthermore, both were White men studying "exotic" other people whose skin was not white. Nevertheless, Rodriguez's invitation to conjecture about what might have been also is an invitation to considering how change occurs both in individuals and in groups.

So What?

Why should anybody care about this history? Why does it matter that a man who has been dead for more than seventy years—who was lionized long after his death but whose name is slowly slipping into the shadows—was a eugenicist? At the very least, this knowledge invites different readings of his work, his legacy, and subsequent research modeled after his. But this matters for other reasons, too. The double-gesture discourses and practices taken up by prominent White "progressive" academics like Seashore were fueled by selective love and hate, the hate taking the form of racism, classism, ableism, anti-Semitism, xenophobia, and sexism. The ideas and practices that emerged from eugenics had devastating effects on a host of individuals and groups while simultaneously and systematically advantaging those identified as fittest. Most importantly, this history matters because it is not simply past: the past lives on in the present. Thus, just as my findings invite a different reading of Seashore, they invite a different reading of the present.

Throughout the time I have worked on this project, and especially in the years since Donald Trump was elected president, I have seen startling resemblances between eugenics as conceptualized and practiced in the United States during the early twentieth century and present discourse and practice in a host of domains, including education. If others do not notice resemblances, I wonder why. Is it because silences have led to lack of awareness? Is it a conscious choice not to notice? Although others may dismiss these resemblances or argue that things are different now—and I agree that in some ways they are—I see enduring handprints of eugenics everywhere, sometimes in rather unlikely places. For example, I recently spent an afternoon at the National Gallery of Art in Washington, DC. I love this beautiful museum, and on this visit, I wandered into the Impressionist art section. As I was studying Van Gogh's *Roses*, I noticed that the painting was a gift from Pamela Harriman in memory of W. Averell Harriman. The Harriman name sounded familiar, and eugenics immediately came to mind. I remembered that Mrs. E. H. Harriman, the wealthy widow of a railroad executive, had given a substantial gift to help establish the Eugenics Record Office in Cold Spring Harbor, New York. I googled "W. Averell Harriman" on the spot and learned that he was the *son* of Mary Williamson Averell Harriman, that is, of Mrs. E. H. Harriman. W. Averell Harriman was a Democrat who served as secretary of commerce under President Harry Truman; he also was governor of New York from 1955 to 1958. Wikipedia told me he graduated from Yale University, inherited one of the largest fortunes in America, and was a recipient of the Presidential Medal of Freedom. The internet also said that Harriman and his second wife, Mary Norton Whitney, collected Impressionist art and donated many pieces to the National Gallery of Art. Pamela Harriman, the donor of *Roses*, was W. Averell Harriman's third wife.

That was only the beginning. As I worked my way around the room, I noticed that the W. Averell Harriman Foundation had donated Gauguin's *Parau na te Varua ino* (*Words of the Devil*), which is a nearly full-frontal portrait of a nude woman of color. Nearby was Gauguin's *Te Pape Nave Nave* (*Delectable Waters*), which features at least four nearly nude women of color. In other words, thanks to the Harriman inheritance, the public (including me, and before that the Harrimans) could engage in what bell hooks calls "eating the other," entertaining White guests with "the naked image of Otherness."[9] I looked away. I was not ashamed of the bodies but of the gazing. No longer paying attention to the artwork, I noticed that the donors of other pieces by Gauguin were Mr. and Mrs. Paul Mellon. Once again, the name set my eugenics bells ringing, and once again, Google assisted. Paul Mellon was Andrew W. Mellon's son; Cordelia Scaife May was Andrew W. Mellon's grandniece. I recognized Cordelia May's name because she contributed to White supremacist causes that I will discuss shortly. Cordelia May's grandfather, Richard B. Mellon, and Paul's father, Andrew W. Mellon, were brothers. I learned that in addition to being fabulously rich, Andrew W. Mellon helped establish the National Gallery of Art. Not caring much about the art anymore, I spent the rest of the afternoon looking at the names of the donors. These were "great" artworks, but I was haunted by questions about the fortunes and the politics of those who donated the pieces I was viewing.

At the most granular level, racism and whiteness were on full display at the National Gallery of Art—but only to those who know something about Mrs. E. H. Harriman or Cordelia Scaife May. Of course, Cordelia May and Paul Mellon were not the same people, and the politics of each may have been very different; truth be told, I would not want to be judged by the politics of some of my relatives. Thus, my problem is not necessarily with these particular heirs, these gifts to the museum, or with the National Gallery of Art. My problem is coming to terms with the reality that people who shared a family name, regardless of their politics, also inherited and kept the fortune; some who amassed that money were virulent racists, and at least portions of the fortune went to racist causes. Regardless of their politics, these benefactors of the National Gallery share both a racist and a monetary inheritance. In a similar fashion, as I look at Carl Seashore, I see that he is my "relative" and that eugenics is part of my inheritance. Applying more broadly what Charles Mills observed about Whites and the Racial Contract, even though I am not a signatory, I am a beneficiary.[10] After having worked on this project for nearly half of my life in academia, I see my inheritance—whether it is eugenics or the racialized discourse of which eugenics is an element—everywhere. The haunting question is, what to do with it?

Is Eugenics Dead?

Some contemporary scholars view eugenics as a past phenomenon. One way they signal this is by using the past tense when discussing it.[11] These scholars tend to conceptualize eugenics narrowly, however—describing it as a temporally bounded "movement," a constellation of now-defunct organizations, or a group of long-dead people. For example, sociologist Nikolas Rose uses the past tense in his argument that eugenics and contemporary biopolitics are distinct.[12] Because I see resemblances everywhere in the present, I examined his rationale for declaring eugenics to be something largely different from ideas and events of the present.

Nikolas Rose on Eugenics and Contemporary Biopolitics

Rose views eugenics of the early twentieth century as a form of biopolitics that is different from contemporary biopolitics as manifested in biomedicine—so different that the latter should not justifiably be called eugenics: "History is not repeating itself. Even as we try to choose one kind of life over another, to give birth to a child free of illness or disorder rather than one afflicted, we are not on the verge of a new eugenics, or even a revived biological determinism."[13] Positioning himself as an originalist, he promotes definitional specificity:

> If the term "eugenic" is not to become an all purpose and analytically meaningless rhetorical device, we should retain it for those biopolitical strategies that partook of its original sense. Our contemporary biopolitics is no less problematic, no less entangled with relations of power and judgments of the differential worth of different forms of life, the nature of suffering, and our individual and collective obligations to the future, but it deserves to be analyzed on its own terms.[14]

Rose points out that some scholars invoke eugenics to connect past to present, while others do so to distinguish past from present.[15] He places himself in the latter camp, stating that "the troubles of our own times are not reactivations of the past."[16] Reactivation, however, presupposes inactivation. This framing helps cut past off from present.

Like others who relegate eugenics to the past, Rose forwards a narrow understanding of it:

> Eugenics . . . comprised a whole set of strategies, which had in common the presupposition that it was desirable, legitimate, and indeed necessary to secure the future welfare of the nation by acting upon the differential rates of reproduction of specific portions of the population, so as to encourage the best to procreate and to limit the procreation of those thought to be of lower, inferior, defective, or diseased stock.[17]

Elsewhere, he states that eugenics is (or rather, was) a "nationally organized and politically directed program to improve the quality of the national stock and eliminate taints or weaknesses."[18]

He argues that four constructs, as well as links between them, characterized eugenics: population, quality, territory, and nation; in some passages, he adds race to his list.[19] One of the salient characteristics of eugenics, he maintains, is that it focused on the population as a whole—specifically on wholesale population management; its goal was improving stock—improving the *quality of the population*—through rational planning and state intervention.[20] According to Rose, the state was the judge of value, and quality was conceptualized as fitness.[21] He also states that in eugenics discourse, the nation (or state) was the unit required to act,[22] the project being "taking charge of the lives of each in the name of the destiny of all."[23] Its assignment was to fend off threats to populational fitness coming from "within and without."[24] The beneficiary of these actions was society.[25] He describes a eugenical strategy of nationalizing "the corporeality of its subjects into a body politic on which it works *en masse*, in relation to the body politics of other states *competing* in similar terms [emphasis mine]."[26] Reproduction is central to his definition, Rose stating, for example, that in its emphasis on increasing population fitness, eugenics "privileged one site—that of reproduction."[27] Furthermore, he claims that a discourse of "insectification" circulated in Nazi Germany, some individuals and groups being viewed as parasites to be eliminated or cleansed from the population.[28]

Rose maintains that contemporary biopolitics do not operate in the same problem space that characterized eugenics of the early twentieth century: "Individual substitutes for population, quality is no longer evolutionary fitness but quality of life, the political territory of society gives way to the domesticated spaces of family and community, and responsibility now falls not on those who govern a nation in a field of international competition but on those who are responsible for a family and its members."[29] Contemporary liberal politics, he claims, are no longer concerned with the "quality of the race and the survival of the fittest."[30] He also maintains that contemporary biopolitics are unlike the biopolitics of eugenics in that today, the vitality of the nation, population, or race is only rarely used to justify interventions into the lives of individuals.[31] Vitality, he claims, is now the realm of entities such as pharmaceutical companies and the food industry.[32]

He also asserts that contemporary biopolitical projects focus on improving the quality of *individual* life by improving *individual* health, which is to be accomplished through interventions at the molecular level.[33] He points out that after World War II, there were concerted efforts to decouple concerns about *individual* genetic health from those about *populational* health.[34] I suggest that these efforts may have been deliberate attempts to distance genetic research from eugenics, to protect the interests of those who wanted genetics to move forward unsullied by eugenics' tarnished reputation. Once again drawing distinctions between eugenics and contemporary biopolitics, Rose argues that although in the latter, the value of life continues to be judged, the judgments are not being made by "a state managing the population en masse"; furthermore, he claims that the state is no longer the judge of value.[35] He says that although pastoral power remains evident in the present, it is no longer "organized or administered" by the state and is not concerned with the "flock as a whole."[36] Instead, he argues, pastoral governance is accomplished by plural, diverse entities, including self-governance "imposed by the obligations of choice, the desire for self-fulfillment, and the wish of parents for the best lives for their children."[37] The new territory—the new beneficiaries—are family and community.[38] He further maintains that the contemporary state no longer employs the eugenical strategy of nationalizing the body politic in order to act on it collectively and compare it to the body politics of competing states.[39] He also argues that classifying, identifying, promoting, and eliminating no longer are undertaken in the name of the fitness of population or nation, but rather in the name of managing risk:

> It is no longer a question of seeking to classify, identify, and eliminate or constrain those individuals bearing a defective constitution or to promote the reproduction of those whose biological characteristics are most desirable, in the name of the overall fitness of the population, nation, or race. Rather, it consists in a variety of strategies that try to identify, treat, manage, or administer those individuals, groups, or localities where risk is seen to be high.[40]

According to Rose, eugenics' politics of populational quality are not the same as contemporary politics of risk management.[41] Stating that an organizing principle of eugenics is the normal/pathological binary, he claims that in contemporary biopolitics, this binary is enfolded into strategies for governing risk.[42] He further claims that eugenics' goal—"to maximize racial fitness in the service of a biological struggle between nation-states"—is very different from such no-less-problematic contemporary goals as limiting population size for economic reasons.[43] In his discussion of the dilemmas surrounding the use of contemporary reproductive technologies to prevent health conditions of genetic origin, he claims that insectification is not present: "There is nothing analogous to Nazi insectification here, or remotely similar to the view that those who are born afflicted by any of these conditions are of less worth than others."[44]

He draws other distinctions between past and present as well. For example, he states that eugenicists viewed biology as destiny, but in contemporary biomedicine, biology has become opportunity because opportunities are created to improve on, reform, or repair biology: "To discover the biological basis of an illness, of infertility, of an adverse drug reaction . . . is not to resign oneself to fate but to open oneself to hope. The nonimplantation of a potentially afflicted embryo is not to condemn a defective or inferior person to death."[45] Significantly, Rose maintains that contemporary biopolitics is a "government of *life*" marked by "logics of vitality," not death,[46] and he argues that while biopower today is engaged in letting die, it is not about making die [emphasis in original].[47] In context, his assertions suggest that eugenics operated otherwise.

Dissecting Rose's Claims

As important as it is to heed Rose's advice about avoiding meaningless rhetorical devices, it is every bit as important to consider the limitations of his conceptualizations and arguments. First, his definition of early twentieth-century eugenics is so narrow that it obscures the complexity of eugenics as Seashore and others of his day understood it. His assertion that eugenicists privileged one site, reproduction, exemplifies this narrowness. Eugenicists did privilege reproduction, and it was at the core of early definitions, but there were many other privileged sites, as well. Seashore said relatively little about reproduction, but he said plenty about eugenics. For example, he described his work on musical ability and ability testing as a massive eugenics project, and yet reproduction was not the sole or even the leading element in his project.[48] Furthermore, as I discussed in chapter 2, he claimed that eugenics was not merely the science of being well born, but also the science of *well-being*.[49] Seashore was not alone in envisioning eugenics broadly. Over time, the self-direction of human evolution mentioned on the eugenics tree logo came to involve more undertakings than just managing reproduction.[50] For example, immigration restriction was a major goal of eugenics organizations, and although eugenicists sometimes mentioned reproduction in their anti-immigration arguments, their project was much larger. Eugenics was also engaged in asserting and maintaining White dominance. Thus, I maintain that there was no single "glue" holding eugenics together, no single privileged site. Rather, it was held together by many glues, each with distinct properties and characteristics; the diversity of glues may have added strength to eugenics as it was conceptualized in the United States during the early twentieth century.

Another problem with Rose's definition, which again stems from its narrowness, is the distinction it draws between eugenics and other early-twentieth-century biopolitical strategies. Some eugenicists considered these other strategies to be a part of eugenics, or at the very least, inseparable companions of eugenics—stemming from the same logics and systems of reasoning.[51]

A third shortcoming is his reliance on reductive either/or dichotomies. For example, his assertion that eugenics' ultimate goal was to improve populational quality rather than individual quality is grounded on a false dichotomy. According to this line of thinking, intervention at the individual level was to serve the ultimate purpose of bringing good to the population. Seashore took a somewhat different, "yes, and" approach; he focused on interventions that would improve the population, the individual, and other entities—including colleges and universities—without suggesting that all interventions ultimately were aimed at improving the population. Consider, for example, his motto, "Keep each individual busy at his highest normal level of successful achievement that he may be happy, useful, and good." The goals of being useful and good may indeed have been linked to the perceived needs of the state and the construction of a particular kind of population—what Ian Hacking calls making up kinds of people. Furthermore, the politics of what constitutes "happy" "useful" and "good" may have been complex and colonized, but Seashore's writings suggest that he viewed the good life—however defined—as a good unto itself. The individual is to be kept busy that *he* may be *happy*. In other words, Seashore supported management of life, and he supported it in the name of the well-being of the institution and of the individual without asserting that the latter was ultimately to serve the former. Unlike Rose's characterization, in eugenics as Seashore applied it to education, attention to the quality of each and of all was to be managed in service to all and to each.

Similarly, Seashore was obsessed with classifying, identifying, eliminating, constraining, and promoting people, but not solely (or even necessarily primarily) for the benefit of the population, nation, society, or race. For example, he claimed that these activities benefitted institutions such as colleges and universities as well as individuals. He supported eliminating some students from music study—not for the benefit of the nation, but to improve the reputation of the school, to save parents money, to prevent other students from being held back, and even to preserve the self-esteem of those eliminated. Furthermore, in the United States, eugenicists such as Seashore did not invariably view contemporary pastoral power as being organized solely or even primarily by the state. Once again, this was not an either/or proposition. Although he supported the juridical and pastoral power of the state, he viewed the scientific expert as sovereign as well; he did not necessarily consider the scientific expert to be an instrument of the state. Rose himself mentions that eugenics was about the responsibilities of a host of entities, including scientists.[52] Thus, it is reductive to say that placing responsibility on diffuse entities other than the state is a distinguishing characteristic of contemporary biopolitics that sets them apart from eugenics of the early twentieth century.

Another limitation of Rose's argument is that his conceptualization of contemporary biopolitics is derived from biomedicine. He sometimes refers broadly to contemporary biopolitics when he actually is focusing narrowly on contemporary molecular biopolitics or on the biopolitics of biomedicine. Because of this conflation and intermingling, it is unclear whether the entire conversation is about molecular biopolitics or whether some points apply more broadly to contemporary biopolitics. Because contemporary biopolitics at the molecular level and the biopolitics of biomedicine do not represent all contemporary biopolitics, Rose's conceptualizations and distinctions may not apply outside of contemporary biomedicine.

Finally, when drawing distinctions between past and present, Rose maintains that contemporary biopolitics are concerned with government of life and are a politics of life, not death; because he states this in the context of distinguishing it from eugenics, he intimates that eugenics was different. Seashore's conception of eugenics was not that it was solely a politics of death. Rather it was characterized by a logic of vitality—it was a politics of life, and like other pastoral forms of modern governance, it involved managing life. It was not an either/or proposition, however; it also involved involuntary elimination. Few early-twentieth-century US eugenicists openly supported causing physical death, and consistent with the broader pattern, Seashore did not talk about physical death; rather, his "softer" eugenics involved figurative rather than literal death, including exclusion, removal, and elimination. For example, it was a politics of "making die" in the sense that scores from standardized tests were used to cull out—forcibly eliminate—some students, and it was a politics of "allowing to die" in the sense that test scores were to empower individuals to make the informed "choice" to voluntarily self-eliminate. It was a politics of "allowing to live" in the sense that particular test scores allowed inclusion and participation, and it was a politics of "fostering life" in the sense that those identified by standardized tests as being gifted and talented were to be given special privileges, opportunities, and advantages. It normalized abjectification, exclusion, and elimination, and it normalized structuring schools on a double-gestures logic of inclusion and exclusion. According to Rose, Zygmunt Bauman and Giorgio Agamben argue that the administration of life and the administration of death are inextricably linked; their assertion also applies to the double gestures that characterized the "softer" eugenics practiced and espoused in the United States during the early twentieth century.[53] Thus, Seashore's eugenics was a politics of the government of life, and it was a politics of the government of figurative, if not literal, death.

Eugenics may be pronounced dead when Rose's narrow definition is applied, and when eugenics is compared to contemporary *molecular* biopolitics and to biomedicine, but his definitions and distinctions come up short in domains such as some forms of contemporary *education* discourse and practice. It is not accurate to claim that the four pillars of eugenics—population, quality, territory, and nation—no longer define the problem space of contemporary biopolitics in *education*. Furthermore, just as it is reductive to say that eugenics of the early twentieth century was a problem space defined by these four pillars, as I will argue shortly, it is similarly reductive to think that these elements and the relationships among them have disappeared today.

Thus, it appears that whether or not one can pronounce eugenics dead hinges on how it is conceptualized. Eugenics may not be an accurate descriptor of current biopolitics in biomedicine, but that does not mean it is inapplicable everywhere—especially when a different and broader definition is used. By adopting a narrow and somewhat reductive conception of early-twentieth-century eugenics, by defining it such that reproduction becomes the primary focus, by making generalizations about contemporary biopolitics based on its manifestations in biomedicine, and by concentrating almost exclusively on differences between past and present, Rose misses a bigger and potentially more troubling story about resemblances and commonalities.

In his acknowledgment that other conceptions of eugenics exist, Rose states that those in the camp that links past to present point to the existence of commonalities despite differences. He summarizes one argument made by members of this camp: "Despite its differences, contemporary biomedicine, in combination with genetics, still judges human life and worth, insofar as it intervenes upon the chances of life in order to eliminate differences coded as defects."[54] I argue that inside and outside of education, debating whether contemporary discourses and practices should be called eugenics misses the point; history may not repeat itself, but if it rhymes, it is important to consider why. Some resemblances may be striking and others subtle, but I contend that these resemblances are not coincidental. Recognizing that eugenics is a slippery construct, and acknowledging that past and present are not the same—that history is not merely repeating itself—I maintain that examining resemblances between past and present plays a key role in diagnosing the present. That resemblances between past and present exist is more important than whether or not we call contemporary biopolitics eugenics.

Eugenics and Schooling Today

Signs of the influence of early-twentieth-century eugenics abound in education policy and practice in the United States today, both on the K–12 level and in higher education. This is so, in part, because the eugenically informed policies and practices that Seashore and other eugenicists proposed or supported caught on. They became part of standard operating procedure, and they remain so to the present. These structural residua are part of a living eugenics legacy; like glacial erratics, they are what remain. The eugenic roots of these firmly ensconced taken-for-granted current policies and practices are not necessarily obvious, however, and their connections to eugenics may be largely unknown today. For this reason, to many (perhaps most), they no longer are material reminders of what came before. Because eugenically informed early-twentieth-century education reforms were successfully implemented and have endured, schooling in the United States is one space where eugenics never was inactivated.

An obvious remnant of eugenically informed education reform efforts of the early twentieth century is standardized testing, which continues to govern students, teachers, and schooling. Seashore and other eugenicists of his day helped usher in a new era marked by use of this type of assessment—tests that are standardized, norm-referenced, designed for large-scale administration, and produced by for-profit entities. Today's repertoire of standardized tests is remarkably similar to that of a century ago and includes, among others, intelligence tests, achievement tests, admissions tests, and entrance examinations. As I discussed in chapter 5, Seashore was instrumental in establishing Iowa as a hotbed of standardized test creation and distribution, a reputation that continues today. American College Testing (ACT) has an international reach, and its headquarters are still in Iowa City. The use of standardized testing has increased exponentially since Seashore's time, and the creation and sale of standardized tests has become a gargantuan, highly profitable enterprise. Pearson plc, the largest of the many test corporations in existence today, reportedly sees annual profits of about $9 billion.[55] Profits come not merely from the tests themselves, but from a host of peripherals, including standards-aligned textbooks and test-preparation services. In 2015, the *Washington Post* reported that annual *parental* spending on test preparation, tutoring, and counseling services was $13.1 billion.[56] At the graduate-school level alone, a bewildering, daunting, and expensive array of tests exists, including the Graduate Record Examinations, the Law School Admission Test, the Medical College Admission Test, and the Test of English as a Foreign Language.

Standardized testing of musical ability continues, too. For example, advertisements for the Musical Aptitude Profile (MAP)—a latter-generation test of musical ability developed by Seashore's protégé Edwin Gordon—appeared in the 2018 music education catalog from GIA Publications.[57] The complete MAP kit, which includes "manual, compact discs, 5 class record sheets, 50 answer sheets, and 50 profile cards, scoring masks, introduction to testing booklet, and four research monographs," costs $140.[58] The GIA website describes MAP as "the world standard in music aptitude testing," and it includes a quotation from Plato that also could have come straight from Carl Seashore: "There is nothing so unequal as the equal treatment of students of unequal ability."[59] Although Seashore and his compatriots are dead—as is Edwin Gordon—their acolytes are not, and in music education, they carry on intellectual traditions and pedagogical practices that began with Seashore.

Furthermore, standardized tests are used today precisely as Seashore and other eugenicists intended them to be—as part of what is (and was) described as a systematic, efficient, and ostensibly "scientific" process of identifying and measuring ability. They play a key role in the continued obsessive sorting and ordering of students in schools. Just as Seashore imagined them to, test scores are used to justify systematic, double-gestured inclusion and exclusion—that is, to selectively qualify and promote, and to selectively disqualify and eliminate. Their use continues to be accompanied by both the promise of reward and the threat of punishment; thus, testing and test scores have powerful governing effects on students, teachers, and schools. They are strong gatekeepers, which is precisely what Seashore wanted them to be.

Another remnant is a system of tracked, ability-segregated educational opportunities ostensibly designed to "fit" hierarchically sorted bodies. Reminiscent of Goddard's Vineland, segregated special education classrooms persist and may be experiencing a revival, although an initial justification—preventing reproduction—is not used anymore. Like Seashore, proponents of segregation by ability tend to argue that it is in the best interest of each individual. In school music programs, students continue to be sorted and ordered based on their ability, and then placed accordingly into ability-based hierarchies of ensembles. In school bands and orchestras, chair seating and chair challenges rank and order musicians in the ensemble according to the quality of their playing; in some ensembles, a hierarchy of sections exists within ensembles. For example, second violin is not merely a specific part of an orchestral work. Musicians in the second violin section (those playing second fiddle) often are assumed to be less proficient than those in the first violin section, their playing presumed to be of lower quality. Furthermore, the least proficient players within a first or second violin section tend to be seated farthest from the front. Thus, seating plans in traditional instrumental school ensembles often reflect a hierarchy of quality, and they mark the position of individuals within that hierarchy. Inside and outside of music classrooms, competition continues to structure schooling and to be viewed as pedagogically worthwhile. Chair challenges, a type of competition in the music classroom, confirm the existence of hierarchies within sections while simultaneously offering individual musicians a chance to change their position within the hierarchy.

In higher education, a hierarchy of educational institutions persists that strongly resembles the one Seashore envisioned. This hierarchy is maintained, in part, through mechanisms such as *US News and World Report*'s annual rank-ordering of colleges and universities. High status on this institutional hierarchy tends to be associated with low rates of admission—that is, with high rates of exclusion. This arrangement supports the idea that the highest-quality educational opportunities are and should be scarce.

Gifted and talented programs, which remain popular and continue to be lauded by some academics, are another remnant of eugenically informed education reform of the early twentieth century.[60] They sit at the top of a tracked, ability-segregated structural hierarchy of programs and course offerings in schools. One such out-of-school program is UW–Madison's Wisconsin Center for Academically Talented Youth (WCATY), which until quite recently occupied an office down the hall from mine. WCATY offers a series of Saturday and summer courses for children in grades 1–12, and its website says WCATY is "an inclusive community of academically talented youth."[61] The irony of this statement apparently eludes WCATY: because it specifies that youth must be academically talented, WCATY can never be a fully inclusive community. The website does not provide a definition of academic talent, but the eligibility documentation that must be submitted with the application provides insight into who decides who is talented, what constitutes talent, and how admissions decisions are made. The amount and types of eligibility documentation vary depending on the age of the applicant, but the overall list includes grades, scores on national or local standardized tests, letters of recommendation from a teacher or counselor, and samples of coursework.[62] Attending WCATY is expensive, and although the website states that financial aid is available, applying to the program and applying for financial aid are quite daunting, far more challenging than simply attending a nearby school that enriches and challenges all students.

In addition to programs that explicitly state they are for gifted and talented students, veiled examples of tracking of the ostensibly fittest also exist. For example, districts may say that they do not track students and yet accomplish precisely this by offering Advanced Placement or International Baccalaureate classes that are not open to all students.

Seashore's ideas about offering special opportunities and awards to a select few have taken root and flourished. A wide range of ostensibly merit-based award systems exist in education today—from collegiate departmental honors to merit pay for teachers. These award systems are double gestures of inclusion and exclusion, however, that selectively eliminate and promote; in the course of giving to some, they withhold from others. Based on the assumption that overt or covert competition with clear winners and losers is an essential part of schooling—an assumption held by Seashore—these systems inevitably mark some (or typically most) as less fit, unfit, or unqualified while simultaneously elevating a select few. Letter grading is one such award system; grading assigns worth not merely to a student's academic work but also, too often, to the student. Grades are used to justify selective promotion and elimination. Finally, awards systems are one example of how contemporary biopolitics in education are a politics of life, of managing life, and of *eliminating* life—not simply of "allowing" the elimination of life.

Thus, although the term "eugenics" is not commonly used in current education discourse—at least not in reference to the present—eugenically informed education reform of the early twentieth century has left behind a host of policies and practices, glacial erratics dotting the education landscape. Just as erratics do not shout "glacier" to most who observe them, these policies and practices do not shout "eugenics" to most people. Their connections to eugenics are no longer obvious, not widely discussed, and perhaps not widely known. Clearly, the reforms I have just discussed have advantaged some students, teachers, administrators, and parents, who consequently may have difficulty seeing what is problematic about them. However, too often these reforms have advantaged some at the expense of many, and for the many students, past and present, who have been harmed by them, the happy, hopeful, and shining eugenic utopia Seashore envisioned has been a devastating and deadly dystopia. It is staggering to consider the number of students who have been harmed by these policies and practices—denied educational opportunities and excluded from learning experiences that could very well have benefited them. The harm done to them has harmed society as well, and the costs in terms of human life and potential are incalculable. As contemporary educators consider the wisdom of continuing these supposedly sound, commonsense policies and practices, it is crucial to remember that these glacial erratics were grounded in racism, sexism, and ableism; their continuing existence in our schools may perpetuate these deleterious social forces. These erratics were part of plans to systematically, deliberately, and selectively include some while simultaneously excluding or eliminating many others from educational opportunities. These plans have been coldly and cruelly successful. The plans were premised on distinctly undemocratic ideas, and their continuance may make our educational spaces less democratic.

School policies and practices are more dynamic than glacial erratics. Perhaps the logic and rationales that initially undergirded eugenically informed reform initiatives have disappeared and over time been replaced by new ones. If the initial rationales and logic have indeed gone away, what new ones have replaced them? In what ways does the new resemble or differ from the old? In what ways is the new consonant with or contrary to visions of democratic schooling that aim to achieve fairness and social justice? It is beyond the scope of my study to answer these questions or to suggest alternatives to eugenically informed policies and practices, but doing so would be a valuable part of diagnosing the present.

Resilient Systems of Reasoning

I have taught two different graduate courses on eugenics and education over the years, and the assigned readings have included many primary-source materials written by eugenicists of the early twentieth century. These texts have titles such as *The Passing of the Great Race, or The Racial Basis of European History* and *Sterilization for Human Betterment: A Summary of Results of 6,000 Operations in California, 1909–1929*. White students have told me that when they read these materials on the bus or in other public places, they hide the covers because they are concerned about how they themselves might be read. Concern among White students reflects their awareness that White-supremacist discourses remain in circulation today. Their title hiding is an acknowledgment that some people, and the chances are excellent that in the United States nearly all of them are White, still subscribe either to eugenics or to the systems of reasoning that made eugenics seem reasonable. My students do not want to be associated with these living systems of reasoning—at least not publicly.

Thus, a second reason why I see resemblances everywhere is that the very systems of reasoning that made eugenics seem reasonable and rational are resilient and endure to the present. Broad systems of reasoning created conditions that made both eugenics and education as it was conceptualized and practiced in the early twentieth century possible. I am not suggesting that these systems of reasoning are omnipotent or omnipresent today, merely that they often continue to rationalize education discourse and practice. While I acknowledge that ideas have beginnings, I maintain that the ideas and practices that coalesced into eugenics did not necessarily originate there, nor did they end when eugenics organizations folded and the membership died. Broad systems of reasoning that circulate outside schools flow into schools, and they shape and govern school philosophy and practice; these systems of reasoning encompass intersecting ideas about many things—not just about people and schools.

The systems of reasoning from which eugenics sprang were not the exclusive property of either conservatives or liberals, and these resilient systems of reasoning tend to be present in liberal and conservative thought today. Particular aspects of modern thought were the crucible from which eugenics "logically" emerged; in some respects, Seashore was a quintessentially modern thinker and eugenics a quintessentially modern idea. When Bauman stated that genocide was a predictable outcome of modern thought, he could have said the same about eugenics. He did not maintain that genocide was an inevitable outcome, however, and the same may be said about eugenics. For example, significantly and perhaps ironically, early studies indicating that environmental conditions can increase IQ scores were conducted at the Iowa Welfare Child Research Station, one of Seashore's pet projects and an early stronghold of eugenics.[63] Furthermore, Seashore's grandson, Charles N. Seashore, a psychologist like his grandfather, was a founder and director of the Lewin Center for Social Change, Action, and Research; the center's mission is to further social justice.[64] Finally, it is important to remember that modern thought is neither monovocal nor monolithic, and it does not omnipotently dictate outcomes and destinies with an iron fist.

Identifying and analyzing all of the elements of the broad systems of reasoning that tie eugenics of the past to schooling in the United States at the present is a project well beyond the scope of this book, and so I will focus on a small sampling—specifically, some ideas and assumptions about bodies, knowledge, and schooling.

Not All Humans Are Fully Human or Equal

Two resilient ideas are that not all humans are fully human, and that a hierarchy of humans exists, with those who are most fully human at the top—the ostensibly fittest, most "evolved" individual humans and groups of humans. Rather than being understood as a human construction, this hierarchy has been and continues to be represented as a descriptor and a reflection of innate and biologically inheritable "natural" variations in degrees of humanity. A related assumption is that not all are sufficiently human to count as human.

According to this line of thinking, due to ostensibly biological differences in capacity or fitness, not all humans are of equal quality; thus, differences in human *worth* are seen as "natural" effects of "natural" differences in human quality. On the human hierarchy, gradations of the human align with gradations of fitness; rather than *constructing* quality and worth, the hierarchy is assumed to *reflect* quality and worth. This thinking hearkens back to eugenics. For example, the 1931 booklet *Organized Eugenics* opened with a statement of the official position of the American Eugenics Society, which attributed inequality to heredity:

> All men are not created equal. Many a person is tragically destined to be mediocre or even degenerate, in *spite* of exceptional training and opportunity. Others become constructive leaders in the community, often in *spite* of extreme environmental difficulties. Varied and complex are all of the influences explaining why individuals differ in make-up and achievement, but *one* of the most important factors undoubtedly is heredity [emphases in original].[65]

Nikolas Rose claims that one of modernity's links with sovereignty is the belief that "life itself is subject to a judgment of worth."[66] His assertion indicates that this belief predated eugenics; I maintain that it persists to the present in education and elsewhere. It is still considered reasonable, rational, valuable, and necessary to assess the quality of life and to sort humans according to quality and worth. It is still considered reasonable to assume that because not all humans are of the same quality, not all humans qualify to be treated with dignity and the same amount of respect. Broad-scale assessment of quality is premised on the assumption that a working definition of quality can be established and agreed on. I argue that up to the present, what students know or are believed to know tends to establish their quality, worth, and value; standardized testing plays a central role in this determination process. Finally, some continue to assume that this process of creating hierarchies also is useful when considering humans' artistic creations, including music.

On hierarchies such as the one described by the late-eighteenth-century physician Charles White, the rung beneath those occupied by gradations of humans is occupied by nonhumans, including animals.[67] The people who do not meet specific "criteria" fall out of the human category altogether; they are abjectified and described as animals or monsters. Although Rose may be accurate in claiming that the particularly potent form of abjectification that he calls insectification is not present in current discussions of preventing disease, as I demonstrate later in this chapter, it has not disappeared everywhere. When such discourses circulate outside of schools, they inevitably seep into and are overtly or covertly present in schools, as well.

There Are Kinds of People

It remains reasonable to assume that distinct types or "kinds" of people exist and that these kinds are described by, rather than created by, the categories that materialize them. Sorting and ordering according to the similarities and differences that demarcate these kinds of people similarly are still considered reasonable actions. Thus, similarities and differences continue to be understood as residing in the body rather than being constructed effects of power. In education in the United States, some still consider it reasonable to assume that a multiplicity of biologically determined similarities and differences exist that can and should serve as the basis for drawing distinctions and making comparisons. What people ostensibly have been given as a biological inheritance, including intelligence or musical ability, which supposedly governs what they are capable of knowing, continues to determine what category individuals and groups are placed in. It remains reasonable to assume that education is a comparative project and that comparing humans is a necessary component of schooling; it also remains reasonable to compare the performance not merely of individuals but of groups and nations.

The practice of making up kinds of people by creating categories of people, a process described by Ian Hacking, persists, and it, too, predates eugenics. The assumption that ability, disability, sex, and race are biological "realities" rather than normative regulatory ideals and effects of power persists inside and outside of school. The systems of reasoning that make racism, sexism, and xenophobia possible persist, as does schooling's participation in their perpetuation. Creating categories and hierarchies is neither a natural nor an inevitable activity, however. For such processes to persist, they must be deemed reasonable and rational.

Enduring Understandings about Ability

Enduring ideas about ability account for some resemblances between past and present. Categories with such labels as "gifted," "fit," "normal," "abnormal," and so on, continue to construct kinds of people who are differentiated from one another on the basis of a historically and culturally constructed concept—mental ability—and on the basis of particular ideas about what this ability supposedly entails. One resilient idea is that humans and groups of humans are not only born with unequal physical, mental, and moral capacity, but that capacity in these domains is normally distributed in populations. In this line of thinking, excellence and competence are anchored goalposts rather than mobile, humanly constructed effects of power. A related resilient idea is that the capacity to be musically able is not merely biologically innate but differentially bestowed—normally distributed in populations such that only an elite few have the most.

The writings of Edwin Gordon exemplify the resilience of Seashore's ideas about musical ability and music education. First, Gordon's understanding of what constitutes music aptitude closely resembled Seashore's conception of musical capacities, and like Seashore, Gordon believed that music aptitude is the inborn capacity to learn music.[68] Unlike Seashore, Gordon believed that a person's inborn music ability is malleable and can increase—but only until the age of nine.[69] Like Seashore, Gordon claimed that music aptitude is not innately present in equal amounts in all people but is normally distributed in populations.[70] Drawing a distinction between music aptitude and music achievement, Gordon, like Seashore, claimed that music aptitude determines what an individual is capable of achieving.[71] Like Seashore, Gordon was a proponent of standardized tests of musical ability; Gordon stated that without such tests, it was almost impossible for teachers to objectively determine whether students have talent.[72] Although Gordon parted ways with Seashore by saying that nobody should be excluded from music instruction due to low test scores, his reasons for undertaking such testing were otherwise identical to Seashore's—diagnosing students' strengths and weaknesses, identifying students with high ability, adapting instruction, maximizing potential, and correcting teachers' misjudgments.[73] Like Seashore, Gordon not only advocated differentiated instruction based on students' music aptitude, he claimed that all students, regardless of their aptitude, benefit from such instruction.[74] Echoing Seashore and other eugenicists, Gordon maintained that equal treatment of the innately unequal is unfair. He spoke about the inequality of equal treatment of students with unequal aptitude.[75] He articulated these views in *Learning Sequences in Music: Skill, Content, and Patterns*, which has gone through multiple editions and remains in print today:

> Because all students do not have the same aptitude to achieve in music, instruction is most beneficial when it is adapted to students' individual musical differences. When taught in terms of their individual musical needs, students with below average music aptitude do

> not become frustrated and students with above average music aptitude do not become bored with the music instruction that they are receiving. It has been said that there is nothing more unequal than the equal treatment of students with unequal aptitudes. . . .
>
> When a group of students is taught as if all of the students in the group have average music aptitude, mediocrity is the result.[76]

Although Gordon opposed using test scores to exclude, many other educators and policymakers still consider it reasonable to use the results of the comparative project of standardized testing as sound evidence to justify qualifying and disqualifying, including and excluding. As a result, students' academic destinies continue to be constructed, governed, and rationalized by standardized tests. It is still considered reasonable to use standardized tests to determine not only what students know or don't know, who does or does not know, and who is or is not of high quality, but also who does or does not qualify. Just as Seashore argued that high ability, as determined at least in part by test scores, should justify extra resource allocation, some educators and policymakers today justify extra allocation on the same grounds.

As in Seashore and Galton's time, discussion of the source of ability continues to rely on a nature/nurture dichotomy in which these two elements are conceptualized as discrete but necessary entities, not as constructed elements of a reductive model that fails to capture complex phenomena. In addition, the construct of "normal" continues to serve as a regulatory ideal in conceptions of ability and states of physical, mental, and moral being.[77] It does so both when it is used to describe the middle range of a Gaussian distribution and when it is deployed in normal/abnormal binaries. For example, even as he distinguishes the present from eugenics of the past, Rose makes language choices, notably his references to disorders and afflictions, that are part of a discourse of normalcy and pathology that binds together past and present.

Thus, like eugenical interventions of the early twentieth century, current interventions in biomedicine and education continue to be premised on the culturally constructed phantasms of normalcy and quality. The presence of these phantasms in contemporary conversations about humans links past and present.

Another resilient idea connecting past to present is that general intelligence exists and is measurable by an IQ test. Although Howard Gardner's theory of multiple intelligences, which emerged in the 1980s and has been described as a more "capacious" conception of human intellect, ostensibly challenged this resilient idea, it echoes earlier voices in long-standing debates among psychologists about intelligence and intelligence testing.[78] Furthermore, Gardner's theory shares problematic assumptions with the concept it critiques. For example, rather than viewing multiple intelligences as particular sets of constructs reflecting the desires and fears of the culture that created them, or as effects of power, Gardner (and his coauthor Thomas Hatch) assume that they are products of evolution—"capacities" or gifts that reside in the body. They claim that multiple intelligences are products of a combination of biological heredity and environment, and like eugenicists of Seashore's time, they view heredity and environment as distinct but interrelated entities.[79] Like Seashore, they assume that these capacities or gifts are not given to all in equal quantity.[80] Music is one of the seven intelligences appearing in Gardner's original model; significantly, Gardner and Hatch's description of the characteristics of musical intelligence—"abilities to produce and appreciate rhythm, pitch, and timbre; appreciation of the forms of musical expressiveness"[81]—is remarkably similar to Seashore's. This description not only links Gardner to Seashore, it binds them both to the particular temporal, cultural, and discursive space they share, reflecting the assumptions about music and musicians that have prevailed in that space; like Seashore, Gardner and Hatch present their description as a universal truth. Thus, although even Seashore acknowledged that musical ability is a complex phenomenon, many of the reductive, ethnocentric conceptions of what constitutes it—the same conceptions that informed the Seashore Tests—persist to the present.

Resemblances between early eugenics and the present exist because of the resilience of particular ideas about how people become (or do not become) able. The idea that biology governs destinies by setting different limits on what is musically possible for different people is resilient. It continues to inform students', parents', and teachers' understandings of why some students achieve and others do not. For example, a recent study by Adam G. Harry indicates that the belief that musical ability or talent is innate continues to inform students' understandings of themselves and others.[82] Harry interviewed high school students enrolled in an instrumental music class, asking them to describe their conceptions of musical ability or talent. He concluded that although students drew their conceptions from a complex mix of sometimes competing discursive strands, they all subscribed to some degree to the idea of unequally distributed "natural talent": "Despite emphasizing the role of effort and practice in the development of musical skills, all participants invested in notions of natural talent."[83]

In the later twentieth century, Japanese violinist and educator Shinichi Suzuki challenged the notion that musical talent is normally distributed. He criticized Seashore's work, calling the Seashore Tests "the psychology of the last century."[84] Countering Seashore's claims, he argued that the potential for musical talent is a universal birthright: "Any child has the possibility to be musically inclined. Talent will sprout according to how the children are raised."[85] Suzuki's theory was grounded on the assumption that, like tires on a car, the potential for musical talent is standard equipment on all models. Rather than superseding the views of eugenicists such as Seashore, however, today Suzuki's claims about how people become musically able coexist along with Seashore's views.

Resilient Beliefs about the Purposes and Practices of Schooling

Resilient ideas that informed eugenics in the early twentieth century continue to inform ideas about the purposes and practices of schooling. For example, standardized measurement of ability, including musical ability, and comparison of individuals and groups using standardized instruments continue to be deemed worthwhile, at least by some. As in Seashore's time, standardized assessment is justified by arguing that it helps educators address differences in individual needs, and it continues to be part of a project of individuation in the service of standardized ends and goals. Furthermore, dominant contemporary education discourse continues to suggest that it is reasonable and rational to rank students according to their mental quality as measured by standardized tests, and to qualify or disqualify—to promote or eliminate—according to quality or worth as determined by the test.

The Effects of Standardization on Conceptions of Quality and Ability

The narrowing and standardization of conceptions of quality and ability through the use of standardized tests continues today, and voices in opposition remain on the margins. The argument that standardized testing helps produce narrow, standardized thinking has difficulty gaining traction given the power of dominant discourses—and the power of voices that have a financial interest in the continued use of these tests. When I was considering how standardized instruments such as the Seashore Tests can narrow and standardize conceptions of ability and quality, I was reminded of a lecture musicologist Susan McClary gave decades ago on how recording technology transformed orchestral sound in the first part of the twentieth century. According to McClary, before recording devices were invented, each orchestra had a distinctive sound and a somewhat individualistic style of performing. The dissemination of recordings reduced these distinctions and individual differences, and what emerged was a more standardized conception of quality sound and performance. As orchestras began sounding more and more alike, the ideal musician was no longer an individual whose style matched a particular orchestra, but a musician whose style and sound were standardized to such a degree that, like an interchangeable machine part, they could seamlessly fit into any orchestra.

Significantly, it was recording technology and widely distributed recordings that narrowed and standardized conceptions of musical talent (via the Seashore Tests) *and* conceptions of the ideal orchestra sound. In both instances, one effect of standardization was the production of a narrow, standardized vision, not merely of quality music, but of quality musicians.

Valuing Usefulness

Seashore's education goal of making people who are useful was consistent with eugenicists' values, and it was grounded on the assumption that usefulness determines quality. This resilient assumption predated eugenics, was shared by others of Seashore's time who were not eugenicists, and persists to the present. Usefulness is used as a yardstick not only when the quality of people is being measured, but when the quality of knowledge is being gauged. Then and now, usefulness tends to be conceptualized in narrow ways that associate it with specific understandings of productivity; furthermore, today as in Seashore's time, the cultural politics of conceptions of present and future usefulness often remain uninterrogated. The usefulness yardstick used in Seashore's time was odd, however, in that in some contexts, uselessness was the mark of low quality, while in others it was a goal and a characteristic of the highest quality. For example, according to a strand of twentieth-century aesthetics philosophy that was popular with many White intellectual elites, functionlessness was a characteristic of the best and highest forms of art. In this discourse, the highest art is unfettered by the mundane strictures of functionality; ironically, the same idea was not present in discussions of people, their usefulness, and their quality. The same fluctuating yardstick continues to be used in some contexts today.

Segregating by Ability: Gifted Programs and Tracking

Tracking continues in schools because it is still considered reasonable best practice to organize educational opportunities hierarchically and to segregate by ability. Like Seashore, some educators continue to rationalize ability segregation by arguing that it is a benevolent and fair practice—in the best interest not only of the targeted individual or group, but of everyone.

Thus, concepts such as innate giftedness remain in circulation, and resemblances between past and present include not merely the continued *presence* of gifted-and-talented programs but the continuing *mentality* that rationalizes their presence. One resilient idea is that there is a kind—or category—of person who is superior or best; another is that there is value in determining who is the best (or the most gifted); a third is that, by definition, not everyone—only a few—can be the best; a fourth is that the best merit special treatment; and a fifth is that only a few—the best—benefit from such special treatment.

Yet another resilient but potentially anxiety-inducing idea is Seashore's contention that gifted children are not being well educated in school. This idea surfaced, for example, in psychologist Ellen Winner's 1996 article "The Miseducation of Our Gifted Children."[86] She warned that schools are failing gifted children, and she used results derived from an IQ test, an instrument developed and lauded by eugenicists, to establish a hierarchy among the gifted. Distinguishing between the moderately gifted, who have an IQ of about 130, and the profoundly gifted, "whose IQs are far higher," she maintained that the profoundly gifted are the students most profoundly disserved in United States schools.[87]

In their 2015 book *Failing Our Brightest Kids: The Global Challenge of Educating High-Ability Students*, Chester E. Finn Jr. and Brandon L. Wright claim that neglect of gifted children in United States schools is imperiling the nation's ability to compete in a global economic market.[88] Apparently assuming that education policies and practices should be based on global-scale comparative projects involving standardized tests, they pointed out that the percentage of US students scoring in the highest tiers on international standardized tests, notably the Program for International Student Assessment (PISA) tests in mathematics and science, is lower than that of students from other nations in the Organization for Economic Cooperation and Development (OECD).[89] According to them, the nation's future leaders and innovators will come from the top-performing tier of students; gifted students, they claim, are key to improving the lives of all Americans.[90] In other words, in the face of national threat, gifted students—a select, elite, few—are the nation's hope for the future. These claims are strikingly similar to Seashore's; furthermore, one of the authors' definitions of giftedness uses potential for eminence as a criterion for inclusion in gifted programs.[91] This criterion ties this contemporary text directly to eugenicist Francis Galton's definition of genius.

Discursive resemblances to eugenics of the past also are evident in "What Works in Gifted Education: Documenting the Effects of an Integrated Curricular/Instructional Model for Gifted Students," an article published in the *American Educational Research Journal* (*AERJ*) in 2015.[92] Like eugenicists of a century ago, the authors assume the following: (1) giftedness resides in the body thus labeled; (2) US schools are not adequately serving "gifted" students because they are not sufficiently challenging them; (3) "gifted" children need special treatment; and (4) ability-segregated, pull-out programs are the best solution to what is described as a problem in education—the failure of "gifted" children to achieve "their full potential."[93] They also apparently assume that the special treatment and interventions to be provided in an ability-segregated setting for gifted children would not be beneficial for all children. The negative effects of tracking on students with disabilities have been widely discussed in contemporary literature, but as is quite typical of the recent giftedness discourse that resembles eugenics of a century ago, the authors of the *AERJ* do not mention the potential negative effects on gifted students of ability-segregated programs. For example, they do not consider how the label "gifted" might distance students from others, or how being surrounded by others similarly labeled might shape students' perceptions of themselves and the broader world in potentially harmful ways. They do not address how being in an ability-segregated setting may deleteriously affect "gifted" students' ability to interact in a world where not everyone has been described as such. Finally, they do not talk about how the presence of gifted and talented programs may negatively affect students *not* selected to participate.

Similarly, hierarchies of educational institutions and rankings of institutions persist because it is deemed reasonable to establish a narrow, specific definition of institutional quality and to rank institutions accordingly, in effect, placing schools in competition with each other for particular "kinds" of students. It is also assumed to be reasonable that only a few institutions and students are deemed the best, however best is defined.

Resources Are Scarce and Competition Is Important

A scarcity myth persists in and out of schools, a myth similar to that which informed both Thomas Malthus's thought and, later, eugenics. Eugenicists believed that great talent was scarce, and they also assumed that material resources are necessarily and inevitably limited; the latter assumption undergirded a supposed need for fiscal economy. Scarcity is still used to justify the absence of high-quality educational opportunities for all. To some, scarcity is necessary and rationalizes a need for competition.

Schooling in the United States continues to exhibit multiple manifestations of competition because competition in schooling continues to be deemed reasonable, rational, and valuable. The use of competitions as proving grounds where the fittest and those of the highest quality are identified has been normalized. The belief that it is acceptable to use competitions to promote some (or a few) at the expense of others (or most) is considered common sense today, as it was by Seashore. Then and now, the prevailing system of reasoning suggests it is both inevitable and acceptable to have winners and losers in life and in school.

Pedagogical practices such as holding concerto competitions and singing contests remain popular because it is considered reasonable and rational to use competitions between students to assess and rank the quality of their performances. Finally, structuring musical learning opportunities in hierarchical ways and using competition to place students in these hierarchies continue because systems of reasoning deem them to be rational and good.

Rose claims that the contemporary state does not think in terms of a body politic in competition with the body politics of other states.[94] In response, I maintain that a populational mentality and competitive comparative projects continue to characterize education discourse and practice in the United States today. Finn and Wright's assertion that the United States is failing in an international competition to produce the brightest students is evidence that Rose's assertion does not invariably hold true in education discourse today.

Discourses of Improvement

Today, as in the past, schooling focuses on improving both the individual and the collective body, and it engages in practices of comparison and improvement at multiple levels. Standardized tests do not merely measure the individual; populational statistics gathered via standardized testing also are used to compare schools, school districts, states, and nations. The focus is not just on individual improvement or "progress," but on group or population improvement. Scores on standardized tests, which are reported for individual schools, districts, and states, are published in newspapers like the results of Friday night football.

Contrary to what Rose asserts about contemporary biopolitics,[95] in some strands of contemporary education discourse, the vitality of the nation is used as a rationale for compulsory interventions into individual lives. The landmark 1983 report *A Nation at Risk*[96] is about national risk, not risk or risk management at the individual level. Furthermore, contemporary education discourses concerning risk and quality are not framed in terms of either population or individuals: the nation, individuals, and groups are all being surveilled. Risk is cited as a rationale for intervention, planning, and management in the name of the nation, groups, and individuals. The object of improvement can be the nation, a particular school, specific individuals, or all of these. Whatever the focus, the underlying assumption is that there is always room for improvement—improvement of test scores, of prospects in life, and so forth. Finally, although the politics of risk management may not be the same as the politics of populational quality, concern about a supposed lack of quality manifests itself in many ways in education discourse today just as it did in Seashore's eugenically informed discourse.

Resilient Ideas about Success, Failure, and the Distribution of Resources

Resilient ideas about success and failure that were foundational to early-twentieth-century eugenics continue to hold sway inside and outside of schools. One enduring element is ascribing success to a combination of inherent ability and the cultivation of that ability through hard work. Galton's use of eminence as an indicator of genius indicates that he subscribed to particular understandings of what constitutes success and of how and why people become successful. Another element is the assumption that success is earned and deserved, a sign that a particular promised and promising destiny has been realized rather than remaining tragically unfulfilled. As was the case with usefulness, the cultural politics of conceptions of success often remain uninterrogated today. Furthermore, although some aspects of Seashore's visions of success may seem anachronistic to many, they continue to inform complex and often conflicting contemporary understandings. For example, some still judge a woman's success in accord with Seashore's conception: she is married to a husband who supports her, and she stays home to raise the four children that eugenicists believed White middle-class families ought to have. To others, however, the model that Seashore exalted represents failure—failure of ambition or failure to fully develop one's potential.

Specific ideas about failure that were foundational to eugenical thought persist to the present as well. These ideas concern not only what constitutes failure and why people fail, but also the perceived relationship between failing and a person's quality of being. In his 2005 book *Born Losers: A History of Failure in America*, Scott Sandage reports that a transformation in thought about failure occurred in the United States in the nineteenth century, which he described as a shift "from ordeal to identity."[97] Rather than being an unfortunate consequence of trying something new or taking risks—a potentially valuable teacher—failure began to be understood as something people *became* as a result of failing. In an interview with Anne Strainchamps, Sandage explained that this new conception was an outgrowth of an early- to mid-nineteenth-century obsession with success; prior to that time, he stated, failure was not considered a personal failing. He claimed that this shift to conflating failing with being a failure has led to intense shame, stating that failing has become "the worst crime an American can commit." He added that "there is [now] almost no way in the American language to acknowledge that you can fail and still be a good person."[98]

The title of Sandage's book, *Born Losers*, captures the sentiment of Seashore's much-earlier statement about eliminating students who are "destined to fail." Counternarratives about failure—including, for example, the idea that failure can result from a culture or society's failure toward an individual or group—circulate today, but they coexist with and have not supplanted the ideas about failure that informed eugenics.

Resilient ideas about how resources and rewards should be distributed inside and outside of school persist, including those labeled "meritocratic." One persistent idea is that meritocracies are reasonable and result in the just and fair distribution of resources and rewards.

The Resilience of the Will to Exclude or Eliminate

Yet another resemblance between past and present is the enduring strength of the will to exclude or eliminate. Discourses of inclusion, rather than being narratives of universal belonging, tend to be part of a double gesture that also involves exclusion on the basis of ability, nationality, citizenship, or a host of other factors, including the presence or absence of whatever have been defined as the characteristics of quality. In the early twentieth century, Seashore's statement that those who are destined to fail should be eliminated early helped normalize exclusion in schools and classrooms; it reinforced the assumption that not only is failing preordained for some, but that it should lead to exclusion and elimination. Elimination and exclusion remain pervasive in US schools today because particular systems of reasoning have normalized them, deeming them *necessary, reasonable, and inevitable.* Processes of exclusion and elimination can range from auditions that determine which students are allowed to participate in music ensembles to college entrance examinations. Although Seashore claimed that standardized tests merely indicate whether students are sufficiently fit to be included in particular activities, he also apparently believed that some people are fit for nothing—for example, the abject "lower" group living at Goddard's Vineland, who apparently did not even qualify to become happy, useful, or good.[99] In schooling today, being "unfit" to participate in particular activities can also mean being unfit for anything anywhere—except possibly for prison or another form of institutionalization.

Inclusive schooling still tends to refer to policies and practices pertaining to students with disabilities—students who already have been marked as not merely different but as abnormal or subnormal in some way; it tends not to be seen as standard practice for all students. Furthermore, rather than being accepted as the most reasonable way to structure schools in a democratic and fair society, full inclusion remains in a defensive position; its advocates have to prove, using a very narrow gauge, that it is more effective for all students than the baseline, which is selective, stratified schooling. Furthermore, school processes of elimination and exclusion, including expulsion, in effect increase the likelihood of students' physical annihilation in places outside of schools, including prisons and on the street. Agamben wrote that every society decides which lives can be eliminated without punishment for those doing the eliminating;[100] I maintain that US schools are among the places where this takes place. Agamben also states that "in modern biopolitics, sovereign is he who decides on the value or the nonvalue of life as such."[101] If this is the case, then schooling and the scientific "experts" who construct the governing mechanisms employed by schools serve as modern sovereigns.

Systems of Reasoning, Modern Genocides, and Schooling

Resemblances between past and present may be due to the resilience of the systems of reasoning that make modern genocide—a particular form of exclusion and elimination—possible, and recurring. Some scholars claim that modern genocides occur in the United States today, and I maintain that these genocides may be products of the same systems of reasoning that made eugenics reasonable. For example, the award-winning 2012 documentary *The House I Live In* chronicles the devastating effects of the war on drugs in the United States, and it describes the race- and class-based differential effects of this war. The film was made by Eugene Jarecki, whose Jewish father fled Nazi Germany as a child, and one of its themes is resemblances between the war on drugs and other modern genocides. In the documentary, journalist and MacArthur Fellow David Simon states that "the drug war is a Holocaust in slow motion."[102] Jarecki also interviewed historian Richard Lawrence Miller, who outlines five links in a "chain of destruction" that characterizes genocides:

- Identification. Identification is a beginning phase "in which the group of people is identified as a cause for problems in a society." Members of the group are fellow citizens who come to be viewed as bad or evil, their lives deemed worthless.
- Ostracism. In this phase, people learn how to hate members of the identified group, "how to take their jobs away, how to make it harder for them to survive. People lose their place to live; often they are forced into ghettos" or otherwise separated from society.
- Confiscation. People lose their rights and civil liberties; laws change to make it easier to target members of the group and take away their property.
- Concentration. Concentration occurs when people are placed in facilities such as camps and prisons where their employment can be systemically exploited and their rights systematically abrogated.
- Annihilation. Although annihilation can be intentional killing, it can also include *indirect* ways of elimination, such as withholding medical care.[103]

Miller states that the US war on drugs exhibits all of the links of a chain of destruction. He notes that his concept was influenced by the work of the famous Holocaust scholar Raul Hilberg; Miller connects the war on drugs to the Holocaust by looking at resemblances.[104] In an extension of his claims, I maintain that the links in Miller's chain of destruction were also part of the early-twentieth-century *eugenics* discourse and practice that helped make the Holocaust possible. Some contemporary education scholars have studied what has been called the school-to-prison pipeline, but more scholarly attention needs to be paid to schooling's participation in a chain of destruction that, in effect if not intent, results in race- and class-based genocide in the United States. This chain of destruction connects the current school-to-prison pipeline to eugenics, as well.

Knowledge, Quality, Schools, and Power

Some of the same assumptions about *knowledge* that characterized eugenics discourse of a century ago thrive today, including in schools. Seashore's enthusiastic embracing of the new field of psychology reflects a much larger trend toward the "hard" sciences and away from the kinds of knowledge that the arts and humanities offer—including ethics. The evidence required when evidence-based school practices are mandated today—numerical data and statistics—is the same kind of evidence that governed eugenicists' conceptions of truth. The assumption that a particular iteration of science is the final arbiter of truth, and the assertion that it stands in contrast to and apart from mere belief, continue to shield science from fierce interrogations of the multiple ways that it is a diverse, socially constructed, and socially entangled way of thinking about the world.

Many still consider it reasonable to assess the quality of musical works, styles of music, and musical performances. Inside and outside of schooling, a race- and class-based knowledge hierarchy persists, shaping and reflecting particular conceptions of which musical works and styles are of the highest quality. One sign of the resilience of this hierarchy is the continued use of terms such as "fine arts" and "high art." It is possible that staid concert venues have broadened their programming in recent times because they have revisited and democratized their conceptions of quality music; it is perhaps more likely that they have made changes for more pragmatic reasons: few people listen to classical music anymore. Season schedules consisting largely or solely of performances of classical music at a time when the infirmities of age are rapidly thinning the already-miniscule ranks of classical music fans are a recipe for financial ruin. Thus, rather than adopting a broader conception of the "good" and of "quality," venue programmers may remain unmoved in their views, plugging their noses as they make programmatic changes, regarding them as unfortunate but necessary actions reflecting the subpar musical tastes of the public at large. Significantly, in a 1992 discussion of race suicide that appeared in the magazine *American Renaissance*, White supremacist Arthur Jensen mourned the potential loss of appreciation for European high art music: "My fear would be a nation that devolved to the point where the great things of Western civilization would be lost. I'd hate to think that Beethoven would be lost to all except some small elite. . . . I like the idea of having an opera house where I can go and see Wagner, Verdi, and Puccini."[105]

The belief that the musical tastes of the masses need improvement surfaced in Seashore's work, but it long predated the early twentieth century. For example, throughout the nineteenth century, improving musical taste figured prominently in the goals of public school music programs. Today, preservice music teachers may be advised to teach "good" music, but few are asked to consider the cultural politics of conceptions of musical quality or to interrogate prevalent assumptions about the "good." The continued reliance on the band/choir/orchestra structural model in US school music programs reflects particular understandings of what is good and of high quality; this model not only governs the styles of music that can be performed in schools today, it reflects and governs conceptions of *good* school music. Courses focusing on other styles of music and on different musical practices occasionally are part of the school music curriculum, but they tend to occupy the fringe of the program, not the core. Decisions about which courses will be taught and which will be at the core of the program reflect particular understandings about quality and "the good" in music, but the cultural politics of conceptions of valuable knowledge tend to be unplumbed in teacher preparation programs and elsewhere.

A Managerial Mentality and the Bureaucracies It Produces

The managerial mentality that undergirded Seashore's proposed education reforms continues to shape ideas about schooling and school reform today. This mentality assumes that control and management are achievable and desirable. Efficiency and economy, defined in terms of saving time and money, are high priorities: faster and cheaper are better. Today, as in the past, planning plays a central role in this managerial mentality. The planning that eugenicists promised would produce a better future, also in effect narrowed future possibilities. The question of how managerial models in education that focus heavily on planning similarly narrow imaginaries and limit future possibilities continues to be unasked.

I have already argued that what Zygmunt Bauman described as characteristics of the modern—rational, planned, scientifically informed, expert, efficiently managed, and coordinated—and what he claimed made the Holocaust not only reasonable but predictable, similarly made eugenics of a century ago seem reasonable.[106] Arguably, the same managerial mentality currently leads to viewing students as objects of administration, as projects for improvement, and as plants in society's garden to be cultivated and tended—or weeded out.[107] It renders systematic, large-scale school projects of identifying, measuring, labeling, sorting, ordering, segregating, selectively promoting, and selectively eliminating seem reasonable, rational, necessary, and good. Such projects can range from merit pay programs for teachers, which Seashore would have applauded, to the use of letter grades; they can, in effect, construct kinds of people and powerfully shape their life paths.

Bauman further claimed that modern *bureaucracy* helped create the conditions of possibility for the Holocaust. He pointed out, for example, that the decision to exterminate people at Auschwitz was the product of "*routine bureaucratic procedures*: means-ends calculus, budget balancing, universal rule application [emphasis in original]."[108] The bureaucratic culture of modernity, he argued, "prompts us to view society as an object of administration."[109]

Overall, US schools are bureaucratic institutions in multiple ways, albeit to varying degrees; consequently, it is useful to apply Bauman's critique of bureaucracies to US schools. He maintained, for example, that the distance that characterizes bureaucracies allows "functionaries of the bureaucratic hierarchy [to] . . . give commands without full knowledge of their effects."[110] This comment brought to my mind the policymakers and the test manufacturers who have effected widespread education "reform" in the United States, especially in the past twenty-five years, such that schooling revolves around and is governed by standardized testing. I wonder whether they have ever seen the faces of the students most harmed by these reforms, and of those whose lives are governed by test results. In his discussion of the dehumanization of the objects of bureaucratic administration, Bauman warned that reducing people to numbers is one manifestation of dehumanization: "Dehumanization starts at the point when . . . the objects at which the bureaucratic operation is aimed can [be], and are, reduced to a set of quantitative measures."[111] He stated that individuals, in effect, lose their distinctiveness under these conditions.[112] These statements once again brought standardized testing to my mind and have led me to conclude that pervasive standardized testing is a *dehumanizing* product of the same systems of reasoning that spawned eugenics and the Holocaust.

Modern bureaucracies are by definition hierarchical, and Bauman discussed the relationship between hierarchical organizational structures and the potential for cruelty. According to him, cruelty correlates very strongly "*with the relationship of authority and subordination*, with our normal, daily encountered, structure of power and obedience [emphasis in original]."[113] This comment brought to my mind the potential role that hierarchical school bureaucracies play in the prevalence of cruelty in schools, including bullying. In their 2003 study of bullying in Japanese schools, Shoko Yoneyama and Asao Naito concluded that a number of school climate factors are associated with higher rates of bullying: "authoritarian, hierarchical, and power-dominant human relationships, alienating modes of learning, high levels of regimentation, dehumanising methods of discipline, and highly interventionist human relationships in an excessively group-oriented social environment."[114] In a 2016 study of workplace bullying in Korea, researchers Yuseon An and Jiyeon Kang found that hierarchical organizational structures are associated with significant increases in the likelihood of being bullied.[115] Both of these studies suggest that Bauman's assertions are applicable in a variety of contemporary contexts, including schools.

Thus, resemblances between past and present exist at least in part because the characteristics that Bauman ascribed to modernity remain in play today inside and outside of schools. In drawing these parallels, I am not suggesting that modern thought is monolithic or univocal, or that its effects are invariably negative; furthermore, I am not saying that bureaucracies inevitably produce destructive results. Rather, I argue that when considering the resemblances between past and present, and the productivity of particular aspects of modern thought, it is important to consider the whole spectrum of actual or potential effects, not just those that currently are regarded as positive.

Mobilizing a Fear and Hope Double Gesture

Some resemblances between eugenics of 100 years ago and the present may be due to the continued use of double gestures of fear and hope as motivating strategies, especially in efforts to effect particular kinds of school reform. For example, some strains of current education-reform discourse claim that US schools are failing, unfit, and in need of sweeping improvements, but they typically do not offer nuanced or detailed explanations of how schools are failing, who they are failing, why they are failing, or whether proposed interventions—"reforms"—will solve problems, or at least not exacerbate them. A commonly cited indicator of failure is the test scores of US students compared to those of students in other countries. Finn and Wright's failure claim and their use of test scores as a failure indicator echoed the 1983 report *A Nation at Risk*. This failure discourse, whether it is used in discussions of schooling or elsewhere, tends to construct and mobilize selective fear, colonize individual and collective fear, and work in concert with claims of inadequacy and threat. The list of ostensible threats articulated in this threat discourse tends to remain similarly selective today for too many people; the immigration of particular groups, voter fraud, and the academic performance of students in Singapore are considered threats, but not climate change or incompetent leadership. As was the case with eugenicists, the people to be feared today tend to be those marked in some way as outsiders or abject, and the fear elicited typically is neither justified nor well-grounded. The nation remains an organizing device foundational to this discourse and to decisions about inclusion or exclusion. Thus, fear is mobilized by claims of threats from without, and what ostensibly is at stake is the future, particularly the future of the nation. It remains reasonable to mobilize not merely fear, but also, as Miller discussed in his description of the chain of destruction, hatred.

As I discussed in chapter 2, Agamben has demonstrated how the modern state has used claims of threat or emergency to abrogate human rights, and to engage in activities that might be deemed illegal or unacceptable; he has further argued that the modern state is in a permanent state of exception or emergency.[116] I argue that a permanent state-of-exception mentality is similarly employed to justify specific school reforms in US schools today.

The mobilization of hope is the second element of the dichotomy that links early-twentieth-century eugenics discourse to some contemporary discussions of education reform in the United States. Then and now, hope ostensibly lies in particular improvement plans (but not in others); what constitutes improvement and "the good" are assumed to be universal, knowable, and consensual. Then and now, a select and elite "we,"—the insiders, the "experts," the defenders of the nation or civilization—decide what is good and what represents improvement. This "we" attempts to impose that vision on others, the "they." As historian Tzvetan Todorov observed, however, "A virtue that is imposed on others ceases to be a virtue."[117] Seashore used this we/they or insider/outsider dichotomy in his 1943 article "The Sunny Side of Graduate Work for the Duration," which discussed the application of science to the war effort during World War II: "We are in this war not as criminals debauching the powers of science, but as defenders of civilization who must match weapons with the destroyers of civilization."[118] Later in the article, he proudly underscored the benefits of deliberate scientific planning and organization: "Never before has there been such deliberate planning and such effective organization for the accurate placement of men through appraisal of their natural ability and training as is now operating at headquarters, in every camp, and at the front."[119]

Shades of utopianism and a rescue mentality, both of which were characteristic of eugenical thought, similarly pervade many current discussions of education reform. Claims of good intentions link eugenically informed education reforms to the contemporary reforms I have mentioned here, yet in both cases, good intentions have not precluded selective and wide-ranging damaging results for some, as well as selective and wide-ranging benefits for others.

Today, as in Seashore's time, it remains reasonable to view schooling as productive in a for-profit sense, and for the funding of academic research to come from sources that have stakes in some particular outcomes—but not in others. In the latter case, disclosure requirements make vested interests more visible today, but as public funding of academic research has decreased, reliance on private sources has increased. The privatization of public K-12 education has increased, too. What vested interests drive specific education reforms and education research agendas? Today, as was the case in Seashore's time, the vested interests of those who march under the banner of virtue can include personal or corporate financial gain. Given this reality, Todorov's warning about noble ideals masking self-serving objectives is just as applicable to the motives behind school actions and reforms today as it is to Seashore's motives.[120]

In summary, particular contemporary reforms are grounded in the same systems of reasoning that grounded eugenics; these systems help support and further projects established and promoted by eugenicists such as Seashore. In education, it is not accurate to speak of a reactivation of discourses and practices because there never was a deactivation; rather, the contemporary "reforms" I have mentioned constitute accelerations.

The Conditions of Possibility for Imagining Different Possibilities

I have examined only a few elements of the systems of reasoning that tie eugenics to schooling in the present, and I have not exhausted the list of resemblances. The resilience of particular systems of reasoning suggests that "the problem" is much larger than the existence and persistence of discourses and practices explicitly called "eugenics." As Michel Foucault maintained, interrogating the tactical productivity and the strategical integration of discourses is a critically important scholarly project; I argue that interrogating the systems of reasoning in which they are nested is equally important.[121]

What if different systems of reasoning were in play? How does it become possible to think and imagine in ways other than those I have just described? In a recent NPR *On Point* podcast, Dorothy Butler Gilliam, the first African American female reporter at the *Washington Post*, talked about how her presence changed the stories that the *Post* told. She said that when she began her career, Black newspapers covered different stories or provided different perspectives on stories than White papers did. She stated that as an African American reporter working at a White newspaper, she brought different perspectives and histories to stories, and that she had access to the views of members of communities other than those typically covered by White reporters. She noted, for example, that when she reported on the integration of "Ole Miss" (the University of Mississippi), she "got a different story" than White reporters did.[122] The body does not guarantee or dictate politics, nor does it invariably assure access to alternative discourses; that said, Gilliam's presence opened a window that enabled White readers to see and think differently than they might have otherwise. Her presence on the *Post* staff exemplifies how incremental change at the local level can help effect broader discursive shifts.

Rebranded Eugenics

Rebranding is a third reason why some current discourses and practices resemble eugenics of a century ago. Rebranding is changing the names of groups, journals, activities, or beliefs—removing the word "eugenics"—without altering assumptions, practices, values, or beliefs. Rebranding may have allowed eugenical activities to continue after the term gained a bad reputation; over time, it helped obscure connections between eugenics and the rebranded activities. For example, in 1972, the American Eugenics Society changed its name to the Society for the Study of Social Biology, and in 2010 the group became the Society for Biodemography and Social Biology.[123] Today, the society's journal is called *Biodemography and Social Biology*; from 1969 to 2007 it was called *Social Biology*, and from 1954 to 1968 it was called *Eugenics Quarterly*.[124] The *Embryo Project Encyclopedia* reported that the organization's 1972 name change did *not* reflect a shift in organizational interests or policies, however; it is beyond the scope of my research to determine whether and how these journals and organizations have shifted their focus over time.[125] Nevertheless, new incarnations and the rebranding of eugenics are part of eugenics' history, and Barry Mehler is among the scholars to argue that throughout the years, these new entities have been little more than old wine in new bottles.[126]

In contrast to Nikolas Rose, who distinguished contemporary biomedicine from eugenics, the 2002 report *Human Cloning and Human Dignity*, prepared by the President's Council on Bioethics, raises concerns about the emergence of a new positive eugenics.[127] The council notes that although the contemporary agenda of some who support human cloning may be eugenical, the agenda may be masked:

> Those who favor eugenics and genetic enhancement were once far more open regarding their intentions to enable future generations to enjoy more advantageous genotypes. . . . In the present debate about cloning-to-produce-children, the case for eugenics and enhancement is not made openly, but it nonetheless remains an important motivation for some advocates.[128]

Although the interventional techniques may have changed over time, the goals of some contemporary "therapy" and "enhancement" projects are remarkably similar to those expressed by eugenicists 100 years ago. After acknowledging that current genetic modification efforts may be well intended, the council states that concerns about the emergence of a new eugenics are justified; nevertheless, the council also appears to believe that a clear line of distinction exists between therapy and enhancement:

> The fear of a new eugenics is not, as is sometimes alleged, a concern born of some irrational fear of the future or the unknown. Neither is it born of hostility to technology or nostalgia for some premodern pseudo-golden age of superior naturalness. It is rather born of the rational recognition that once we move beyond therapy into efforts at enhancement, we are in uncharted waters without a map, without a compass, and without a clear destination that can tell us whether we are making improvements or the reverse.[129]

Significantly, in their list of the benefits of cloning that proponents enumerate, the council lists one that echoes the goals of positive eugenics of a century ago: the reproduction of people of great genius, talent, or beauty.[130] Presumably, proponents of cloning would consider musical ability (however defined) to be a kind of talent. The council responded to proponents' arguments by maintaining that the right to have a child does not translate into an unlimited right to decide what kind of child to have.[131]

Education discourse is not exempt from rebranding, some which is evident in research on race differences and intelligence. In a discussion of education and the "new geneism" in Great Britain, David Gillborn argues that "*racial geneism*—the belief that genes shape the nature of ethnic group achievements and inequities—has returned with a vengeance [emphasis in original]."[132] He states that proponents of the genetic basis of IQ are taking a "softly softly" approach, where race is omnipresent but is almost never mentioned.[133] According to Gillborn, "The hereditarians have not changed their mind about race and intelligence—they just don't broadcast it anymore";[134] he maintains that the new geneism bolsters the ideas that inequality is inevitable and that intelligence-based discrimination is justifiable.[135] These ideas would be familiar to and approved by eugenicists such as Seashore. Gillborn says that critics who point to connections between eugenics and current research on the inheritability of IQ or who mention racism run the risk of being denounced or dismissed.[136] He focuses on the work of psychologist

Robert Plomin, a signatory of a letter that appeared in the *Wall Street Journal* in 1994 in defense of *The Bell Curve*.[137] According to Gillborn, Plomin has gone on record saying not only that average IQ scores are stable and different for different races, but that differences in IQ are genetically based.[138] Plomin is a coauthor of *G is for Genes: The Impact of Genetics on Education and Achievement*, a 2013 book that presents some of same arguments that Seashore did; for example, the authors claim that due to genetics, children are not born with the same potential, that it is counterproductive to educate them as if they are, and that geneticists need to team up with educators and policymakers to improve education accordingly.[139] Unlike Seashore, they call for providing more, not fewer, resources to educate children having difficulties in school.[140]

Rebranding also is evident in some current types of research on musical ability. For example, although they do not call themselves eugenicists, some researchers continue to conduct studies of the biological inheritability of musical ability, and some elements of these studies are identical to those found in research of a century ago. Past and present studies of the inheritability of musical ability tend to be connected to each other by the idea that there is a valued, consensually determined entity called musical talent; by a shared, narrow conception of what constitutes this talent; and by the claim that this entity is biologically inheritable. These ideas situate this research in a cultural and historical space shared with eugenics. Furthermore, current studies often echo Seashore's conception of musical talent by equating auditory perception with talent, and like Seashore's work, they measure discrete aspects of auditory perception; in some cases, they even use the Seashore Tests (or tests like Seashore's).[141] Like the work of their predecessors, these recent studies overlook the fact that people who are hard of hearing can and do become highly skilled, successful professional musicians.

A Continuing Research Agenda

Other types of research constitute continuities even though they have not been consciously rebranded. The use of twin studies exemplifies one such continuity. I did not find examples of the use of twins in early-twentieth-century studies of musical talent, but inheritability studies involving twins were common in other research conducted by early-twentieth-century eugenicists. Francis Galton and Edward L. Thorndike were among the early eugenicists to propose or conduct research on twins.[142] Jay Joseph reports that eugenicist Paul Popenoe was the first person to study a set of monozygotic twins; he also states that some recent twin studies were financed by the Pioneer Fund.[143]

Twin studies, especially those in the behavioral sciences, continue to be controversial,[144] yet they remain a staple in inheritability research, some of which focuses on musical talent. One example is "Practice Does Not Make Perfect: No Causal Effect of Music Practice on Music Ability," which appeared in *Psychological Science* in 2014. In this study of more than 10,000 Swedish monozygotic and dizygotic twins between the ages of 27 and 54, researchers set out "to estimate genetic influences on music practice and its covariation with music ability."[145] The researchers used the Swedish Musical Discrimination Test, which measures rhythmic, melodic, and pitch discrimination, to determine participants' musical ability; thus, like Seashore, they equated musical ability with auditory discrimination, and they even described their test as being "similar in construction" to Seashore's.[146] The researchers concluded that practice (presumably the inclination to practice) was biologically inheritable: "Music practice was substantially heritable (40–70 percent). Associations between music practice and music ability were predominantly genetic, and, contrary to the causal hypothesis, nonshared environmental influences did not contribute."[147] Regardless of how they derived their statistics or how they defined "heritable," these researchers produced questionable results simply because they relied on the same narrow, culturally bound understanding of musical ability that Seashore adopted. Furthermore, their test of musical ability, by their own admission, is very similar to Seashore's.

Seashore's long arm of influence is evident in continuing interest in the role of genetics in pitch discrimination; this interest extends beyond the research community. For example, the direct-to-consumer genomics and biotechnology company 23andMe states that based on a person's genetics, sex, and age, it can predict the likelihood that an individual can match pitches; the company states it can do this by checking 529 genetic markers associated with pitch matching.[148] The company makes this assertion as an element of its broader claim that it can provide genetic information about whether a person has genetic variants associated with higher risk of particular diseases, is likely to be a carrier of specific diseases, is likely to exhibit select wellness traits or conditions, and is likely to exhibit twenty-six other general traits.[149] Pitch matching is listed in the general-traits category; unlike the other three categories, which are associated with health, general traits include "fun" genetic information. Among the other traits in this category are mosquito-bite frequency, toe-length ratio, cheek dimples, red hair, and earwax type.[150] I cannot comment on the robustness of 23andMe's science or on the validity of its findings; the findings may confirm that Seashore was on the right track when he stated that pitch discrimination has a genetic component.[151] That said, however, pitch matching only indicates musical ability if it is considered a characteristic of musical ability. Furthermore, Seashore himself stated that pitch discrimination should not be equated with overall musical ability. Not all musical styles and cultures value precise pitch matching; prescribed matching standards may be culturally specific, and some consider an expectation of precise pitch matching to be an ethnocentric, colonizing gesture. Finally, pitch matching tends to be more important in musical contexts where product is more important than participation or process, but thinking about musical production in terms of a quality *product* is not universal.

Thus, my cursory examination of some recent studies of the inheritability of musical talent indicates that the researchers appear to have unquestioningly accepted received understandings of ability derived from eugenicists of the early twentieth century, specifically from Seashore. For example, Tim Spector, one of the authors of a contemporary twin study, was quoted by the media as having said that "if you don't recognise pitch, you are not going to become a great musician"; he also claimed that up to 80 percent of tune deafness is genetic.[152] Elsewhere, in an article titled "Musical Talent Proves to Be Air on a Gene String," *The Independent* reported that Spector believes parents could be wasting their money on music lessons for some children; this statement was followed by a quote from Spector: "If children started life on the lower end of this [talent] scale they are not going to achieve that much, however much parents spend on music lessons. It doesn't mean music lessons are worthless, simply that you have a certain genetic potential."[153] Approximately 100 years ago, Seashore similarly claimed that because musical talent is inherited, parents are wasting money by providing music lessons for some children. Spector, like others conducting similar recent research, appears not to have given much thought to constructs such as musical ability, quality, and greatness. As with early use of the Seashore Tests, in recent research of this ilk, musical talent or ability tends to be equated and conflated with one or a very small number of discrete skills.

Therefore, there are continuities and resemblances between past and present because a host of scholars in subsequent generations followed in Seashore's footsteps. For example, not only did Edwin Gordon develop tests of musical ability that are still for sale today, he suggested that his tests be used by music teachers in the classroom for diagnostic purposes.[154] Students are to be assigned to one of three groups based on their test scores, and instruction is to be accordingly differentiated by group; consistent with the contours of a Gaussian distribution, Gordon recommended that two thirds of the class be assigned to the middle group, one sixth to the top group, and one sixth to the bottom group.[155] These recommendations, although they technically do not lead to elimination, are entirely consistent with Seashore's eugenical goals of identifying quality, measuring it, attributing the highest quality to a select few, and sorting and ordering accordingly in the classroom.

Unapologetic Eugenicists: Where Eugenics is Alive and Well Today

Another reason I see resemblances between past and present is because currently some individuals and groups, including academics and other intellectuals, unapologetically support eugenics and call themselves eugenicists. Consider, for example, Julian Savulescu, an Australian philosopher and bioethicist who is the Uehiro Professor of Practical Ethics at the University of Oxford. Coauthor of the 2012 book *Unfit for the Future: The Need for Moral Enhancement*, Savulescu is a staunch proponent of eugenics.[156] When interviewed by Steve Paulson in 2015 for the National Public Radio program *To the Best of Our Knowledge*, Savulescu assessed the current health of eugenics, proclaiming, "Eugenics is alive and well today," adding that prenatal genetic screening is a type of eugenics.[157] Paulson published segments of the interview in the online journal *Nautilus*, where he stated that Savulescu believes humans have not merely the right but the moral *obligation* to create the best possible humans—to overcome physical, mental, and moral limitations through a multiplicity of means, including genetic modification.[158] Paulson writes, "As for eugenics—creating smarter, stronger, more beautiful babies—he [Savulescu] believes we have an ethical obligation to use advanced technology to select the best possible children."[159] Savulescu claimed that the new eugenics is unlike eugenics of the early twentieth century because the old version was involuntary, racist, and based on the goal of creating a particular kind of society.[160] The new eugenics is different, he claimed, because it is grounded in individual choice.[161] He stated that genetic technology should be used to look for "genes which are correlated with greater advantages or opportunities in life,"[162] and he described some of the traits that he believes should be selected via genetic engineering:

> We have a moral obligation to choose what I've sometimes described as "all-purpose goods." Things like intelligence, impulse control, self-control—some level of empathy or ability to understand other people's

> emotions, some willingness to make self-sacrificial decisions for other people. Those sorts of qualities that we try to instill in children when they're growing up also have some biological bases.
>
> There's huge variation between people in terms of fundamental characteristics and dispositions. When the science of genetics allows us to choose between the range of children that we could have, between those that will have better lives for themselves and be better functioning members of society, we ought to select those embryos rather than just tossing a coin.[163]

In *Unfit for the Future*, Savulescu and his coauthor Ingmar Persson warn that the human race is not sufficiently morally fit to face current and future challenges, notably climate change and global inequality.[164] In an argument reminiscent of eugenic tropes of the early twentieth century, they claim that moral traits—and they mention altruism and a sense of justice—have biological bases.[165] They describe moral enhancement as the process of amplifying in the unfit "those biological factors that by nature are strong in those of us who are morally better."[166] They suggest that one possible way of accomplishing moral enhancement is the selective administration of drugs such as oxytocin.[167] Given statements he made when interviewed by Paulson, it is quite clear that Savulescu also sees genetic engineering as a way to accomplish moral enhancement. Apparently unaware of the complex cultural politics of individual choice, sidestepping the difficulties of identifying what might constitute individual and societal good, and ignoring the fact that he, too, mentions the needs of *society* in his description of what constitutes the good, Savulescu calls himself "the voice of common sense."[168] Like eugenicists of old, he and his coauthor Persson represent themselves as having good intentions, as knowing what constitutes the good, and as constituting the good.

Savulescu is not alone in proudly marching under the banner of eugenics. As I discussed in chapter 7, the White supremacist Richard Lynn does so, too, and promotes a number of current eugenics-related research projects; he continues to claim, for example, that there are race differences in intelligence and musical ability.

Immigration: A Case Study in Resemblances and Connections

Although they do not necessarily reflect the attitudes of all or even most people in the United States, particular strains of current immigration discourse and practice—strains that have come to the fore in the Trump era—bear not-coincidental resemblances to those promulgated by eugenicists of the early twentieth century. As I discussed in previous chapters, early-twentieth-century eugenicists tended to view immigration as a problem, and selective immigration restriction was among the chief goals of eugenics organizations in the United States. In particular, eugenicist Harry Laughlin testified in favor of immigration restriction before a Congressional committee and helped pave the way for passage of the Johnson-Reed Immigration Act of 1924. This highly restrictive law had a profound impact on US immigration for decades. Some analysts maintain that immigration policy reflects the core values—the very heart—of a nation. For example, in an interview broadcast on NPR in 2013, Michael Fix, senior vice president of the Migration Policy Institute, underscored the critical importance of national immigration policy; when asked about immigration reform, he stated that "immigration policy is the DNA of public policy. It's the public policy that sets the country that we will become, not just the country that we are. In that way, it really is a complete expression of our economic, social, political priorities."[169]

Immigration may seem to be a topic far afield from education—music education in particular—but I argue that this is not the case. Immigration policies and practices are contextual elements that have a profound impact on schools, students, and education. They determine and reflect the face of the nation, which means they help decide who a child's classmates will be, and they set the stage for decisions such as which languages are taught and spoken in school. Most importantly, they profoundly affect the lives and welfare of many students. For example, punitive policies such as those supported by the Trump administration can have devastating effects on students who are not documented. According to Coshandra Dillard, increasingly punitive disciplinary practices are part of a school-to-prison pipeline channeling students into the criminal justice system; these practices disproportionately harm students of color and students with disabilities.[170] She states that students currently are being arrested for activities that were not arrest-worthy in the past; significantly, for undocumented immigrants, the pipeline may end in deportation even if the disciplinary action is for a minor infraction and the student exhibited exemplary behavior prior to the precipitating incident.[171] She cites data from the Pew Research Center that estimates that there are about 725,000 undocumented immigrants in US K–12 schools. Thus, resemblances between eugenics of a century ago and current immigration discourse, policies, and practices are germane to discussions of education.

One resemblance between past and present is identifying immigration as a problem of such magnitude that it is precipitating a national crisis. The similarities do not end with the choice of issue, however. Past and present also are connected by argumentation techniques and rhetorical devices, proposed solutions, choice of authoritative sources, funding sources, and reliance on a tight-knit skein of personal relationships to forward specific agendas.

Consider, for example, a shared reliance on fearmongering. In a thinly veiled xenophobic commentary on race and class, eugenicists of the early twentieth century fueled White fears by arguing that particular groups of immigrants posed a threat to the nation. In a May 16, 2018, White House meeting with state and county officials who opposed California's sanctuary-state law, Donald Trump similarly traded in fearmongering in his comments about undocumented immigrants:

> Each of you has bravely resisted California's deadly and unconstitutional sanctuary state laws. You've gone through a lot, too, although it's becoming quite popular what you're doing. A law that forces the release of illegal immigrant criminals, drug dealers, gang members, and violent predators into your communities.
>
> California's law provides safe harbor to some of the most vicious and violent offenders on Earth, like MS-13 gang members putting innocent men, women, and children at the mercy of these sadistic criminals. But we're moving them out of this country by the thousands. MS-13, we're grabbing them by the thousands and we're getting them out. . . .
>
> We have people coming into the country, or trying to come in—and we're stopping a lot of them—but we're taking people out of the country. You wouldn't believe how bad these people are. These aren't people. These are animals. And we're taking them out of the country at a level and at a rate that's never happened before. And because of the weak laws, they come in fast, we get them, we release them, we get them again, we bring them out. It's crazy.[172]

Like statements eugenicists made about immigrants 100 years ago, Trump's comments fueled White fears, and some have argued that this was intentional.

The above quotation from Trump exemplifies other discursive resemblances in addition to fearmongering: anti-immigrant sentiment, an emphasis on differences, and reinforcement of a we/they dichotomy. Perhaps the most significant resemblances are its denial of the full humanity of all people, its reliance on belief in a hierarchy of humans, and its dehumanization of immigrants. The immigrants in question, Trump claimed, are not people at all—they are animals.

According to an article published in the *Los Angeles Times*, statements made by Trump and other opponents of California's sanctuary policies are rife with inaccuracies and distortions, one of them being the false claim that dangerous, violent criminals are being set free due to these policies.[173] *LA Times* reporter Jazmine Ulloa stated that data do not back up the assertion that those protected by these policies prey on their communities; rather, she cited a National Academy of Sciences study that concluded that immigrants are far less likely to commit crimes than people born in the United States.[174] In July 2018, a federal judge rejected the Trump administration's attempt to block two of California's sanctuary laws; the judge put "key parts of a third sanctuary law on hold."[175]

Trump did not mention race or ethnicity in the above passage, but these constructs nevertheless made a thinly veiled appearance in his reference to MS-13, a gang that originated in Los Angeles and is composed largely of Central Americans, notably Salvadorans. Elsewhere, he has not shied away from making racist comments about immigration. For example, early in 2018, the *Washington Post* reported that in a discussion of a bipartisan immigration reform proposal, Trump opposed immigration from what he referred to as "shithole countries"—notably Haiti, El Salvador, and countries in Africa—while simultaneously welcoming more immigration from countries such as Norway.[176] Given that Seashore was a Scandinavian (Swedish) immigrant, Trump presumably was calling for more immigrants like Carl Seashore. Some evidence that Trump's fearmongering was intentional comes from a CNN report stating that White House staffers believed Trump's comments would "resonate" with his base; furthermore, according to CNN, the White House spokesperson did not deny that Trump had made these remarks.[177] To have staff members opining that Trump's statements would resonate with his base implies that these comments were *calculated* to have a particular effect.

White Supremacists, Contemporary Eugenicists, and Trump on Immigration: A Triangle

Not only are there discursive resemblances between Trump's statements and those of prominent eugenicists of the early twentieth century, these resemblances extend to the rhetoric of a third group: contemporary alt-right White supremacists such as Richard Spencer, who have claimed Trump as their hero. For example, Trump's language about people he maintains are not humans resembles what Spencer had said earlier in his famous "Hail Trump" speech, delivered in fall 2016 at the annual meeting of the National Policy Institute. The meeting was held in Washington, DC, shortly after Trump had been elected president. Addressing a room of youngish White men, Spencer gleefully celebrated Trump's recent election; using a manner of address that was strikingly similar to Trump's, Spencer excoriated what he called "the mainstream media":

> Those of us in the alt-right always took president-elect Donald Trump and his chances seriously. . . . Many of us thought all along that he [Trump] could win. The mainstream media, or perhaps we should refer to them in the original German, *lügenpresse* [laughter, applause, hoots], the mainstream media never did. . . . It's not just that they are leftists and cucks. It's not just that many are genuinely stupid. Indeed, one wonders if these people are people at all [scattered laughter] or instead soulless golem animated by some dark power to repeat whatever talking point John Oliver stated the night before. . . . We willed Donald Trump into office. We made this dream our reality. . . . This Trumpean dream is only the beginning.[178]

According to an article published in *Politico Magazine*, right-wing attacks on the "mainstream media" have been underway for decades, long predating Trump and Spencer, and yet Trump has been able to capitalize on the corrosive long-term effects of these attacks, which have become one of the pedal points of his presidency.[179]

In his "Hail Trump" speech, Spencer unapologetically indicated that he is a White supremacist, stating, for example, that "America was, until this past generation, a White country designed for ourselves and our posterity. It is our creation, it is our inheritance, and it belongs to us."[180] He maintained that the press had declared war on Trump and on White America, and he elevated Whites while simultaneously scorning many others: "To be White is to be a striver, a crusader, an explorer, and a conqueror. We build, we produce, we go upward, and we recognize the central lie of American race relations. We don't exploit other groups, we don't gain anything from their presence. They need us and not the other way around"; "Whites do and other groups don't," he claimed.[181] Toward the end of the speech, when he compared Whites to others, he called the latter "despicable creatures":

> Within us [European White men], within the very blood in our veins as children of the sun lies the potential for greatness. That is the great struggle we are called to. We are not meant to live in shame and weakness and disgrace. We were not meant to beg for moral validation from

> some of the most despicable creatures to ever populate the planet. We were meant to overcome, overcome all of it, because that is natural and normal for us.[182]

He closed by shouting, "Hail Trump, hail our people, hail victory"; the crowd responded with cheers, a standing ovation, and a sprinkling of Nazi salutes.[183]

Space does not permit me to include more of Spencer's revelatory speech or to give it the thorough critique it deserves. Nevertheless, because I have spent many years reading eugenics materials from the early twentieth century, his message felt familiar, hitting a host of notes that would have elicited cheers from eugenicists. He based his remarks on the assumed existence of a racial hierarchy, and he infused his speech with racism, anti-Semitism, and anti-immigrant sentiment directed at people of color. Like eugenicists, he used the constructs of natural and normal to justify White supremacy; like eugenicists, he traded in fear of race suicide and spoke of the dangers of degeneracy. By using the term *lügenpresse*, the lying press, which has a long and sordid history in Germany culminating with its use by the Nazis, he consciously aligned himself, and the alt-right generally, with Nazism. The crowd laughed and applauded. Referring to his critics as "cucks" invoked a strong/weak dichotomy that aligned the alt-right with hypermasculinity while simultaneously demeaning others as weak and feminine. Demeaning and dismissing critics, including engaging in acts of humiliation, were among Seashore's tactics. Perhaps the strongest resemblance between Trump, Spencer, and eugenicists, however, was their deployment of dehumanization. Deflecting criticism, in an interview with NBC shortly after the "Hail, Trump" speech, Spencer stated that his comments were intended to be cheeky, exuberant, and ironic: "There's an ironic exuberance to it all. I think that's . . . one of the things that makes the alt-right *fun*, is that we're willing to do things that are a bit cheeky [emphasis mine]."[184] Terrifying is not cheeky.

In an interview with the *New York Times* a few days after Spencer's speech, Trump condemned Spencer's alt-right conference and alt-right groups generally.[185] Nevertheless, contemporary White supremacists tend to agree with Trump on immigration matters, and increasing immigration restrictions was a major theme in Trump's presidential campaign. In June 2015, just a few weeks after Trump announced that he was running for the presidency, NBC severed its business relationship with him in response to statements he had made about Mexican immigrants when he announced his campaign.[186]

Furthermore, Spencer is not the only alt-right White supremacist who lionizes Trump. In an article about online White nationalist memes, the

Southern Poverty Law Center (SPLC) discussed r/The_Donald, a hate-speech platform on Reddit, which describes itself as a "'never-ending rally dedicated to the 45th President'"; its logo is a flag-waving White man wearing a red "Make America Great Again" hat.[187] The SPLC noted that on this site, White nationalists talk about what they call white genocide or the "Great Replacement."[188] The SPLC listed the sources of threat that White nationalists associate with the Great Replacement: "mass immigration, low fertility, miscegenation and abortion."[189] These fears and perceived threats closely resemble those that eugenicists of a century ago referenced in their discussions of race suicide. Significantly, a statement posted on r/The_Donald directly connects White nationalist discourse to eugenics (without ever mentioning eugenics) by referencing the IQ scores of specific groups of immigrants: "'White people have (in the postwar period) failed to recognize that they are a coherent group with group interests. One of those interests is not being systematically displaced from their homelands by violent low IQ third worlders.'"[190] According to the SPLC, White nationalists blame the Great Replacement on Jews and Democrats.[191]

I visited r/The_Donald in November 2018, and at that time, it was dominated by pro-border-wall and anti-immigrant postings. Pro-Trump rhetoric—including forwarded Trump tweets—and progun messages were intermingled with ridicule of the press, universities, professors, feminists, and scientists who warn of climate change. The long list of despised and scorned also included Muslims, Hillary Clinton, Robert Mueller, former president Barack Obama, and people who identify as LGBTQ.[192] Notably, White supremacist sentiment was visible. For example, one posting was the YouTube video "White Panther," which is a critique of the movie *Black Panther*. The posted video criticizes the premises of *Black Panther*, stating that the movie "fails to take into account the huge racial differences in history, culture, biology, and IQ"; at one point the video claims, "White children simply don't matter to the left."[193] One of the many pictures of Donald Trump appearing on the r/The_Donald website featured the caption, "You only hate him cuz hes [*sic*] White." Another posting called him "God Emperor." Pepe the Frog, which has become a White supremacist hate symbol, made frequent appearances on the site. In September 2018, BuzzFeed News reported that r/The_Donald was being aggressively infiltrated by Russian internet trolls.[194] The site was banned in June 2020.

Analyzing the themes that surfaced on r/The_Donald confirms that some discursive elements—including White supremacist and race-based anti-immigrant rhetoric—are virtually identical to those that constituted eugenics discourse of nearly a century ago. Furthermore, as was the case with early-twentieth-century eugenics, the site's discourse is a complex and dynamic assemblage that connects seemingly disparate elements into a mutually supportive whole. Just as it is reductive to say that eugenics of old was all about reproduction, it is reductive to say that r/The_Donald was all about any one subject. Just as there were many different glues holding eugenics together in the early twentieth century, many glues held together the discourses appearing on r/The_Donald. Significantly, the glues of the present closely resemble those of the past.

The Company They Keep: A Contemporary Skein of Relationships

Other resemblances and connections tie contemporary White supremacists to each other, to eugenicists of the early twentieth century, and to the Trump administration. For example, today, as was the case with eugenicists 100 years ago, a number of prominent White supremacists are a part of a tight-knit skein of relationships. The old and the new skeins, in addition to being composed of like-minded individuals who support each other and a common agenda, use similar tactics to achieve their goals, one shared goal being to severely restrict the immigration of some groups.

Financial support from the Pioneer Fund is one element that binds the new skein together; it is an unbroken thread that connects this skein directly to eugenics of old. The Fund is alive and well today, providing support not only for Richard Lynn's research but for a host of other White supremacist projects that may or may not be officially labeled as eugenics. A brief look at the views, activities, and personal relationships of four individuals in the new skein—John Tanton, Jared Taylor, Jason Richwine, and Steve Bannon—reveals not only how these individuals are connected to and support each other, but how they are tied both to eugenics and to the Trump administration.

John Tanton

John Tanton, who died in 2019, was a retired Michigan ophthalmologist who was known as a White supremacist. The SPLC examined Tanton's personal papers in the Bentley Historical Library at the University of Michigan, and reported in 2008 that Tanton had been "at the heart of the white nationalist scene" for decades.[195] The SPLC also revealed that Tanton had shown an interest in eugenics since 1969; in 1996, he founded the Society for Genetic

Education, which by his own admission was grounded on eugenic principles.[196] Aware of eugenics' negative connotations, however, he deliberately chose the term "genetics" for the group's name, the SPLC quoting Tanton as admitting, "'We report ways [eugenics] is currently being done, but under the term genetics rather than eugenics.'"[197]

Consistent with eugenicists of the early twentieth century, Tanton staunchly supported immigration restriction, Aaron Patrick Flanagan calling him the father of the current anti-immigration movement.[198] He also was a fan of John B. Trevor Sr., an architect of the Johnson-Reed Immigration Act of 1924—the law for which eugenicist Harry Laughlin helped lay the foundation.[199]

For decades, Tanton established and furthered pro-English organizations. In 1983, he co-founded U.S.ENGLISH and served as the chair of the board until 1988; U.S.ENGLISH opposes the "drift towards multilingualism in the United States."[200] In 1994, he founded ProEnglish, an organization intent on making English the official language of the United States and on ending bilingual education in schools.[201] He was a long-standing member of ProEnglish's board; in 2019, the ProEnglish website listed him as an emeritus board member.[202] The SPLC noted on January 26, 2018, that ProEnglish's only two staff members had met a few days earlier with a Trump aide to discuss English legislation issues.[203]

According to the SPLC, in 1995, Tanton funded the publication of Peter Brimelow's best seller, *Alien Nation: Common Sense about America's Immigration Disaster*, which is highly critical of US immigration policy and of birthright citizenship; Brimelow also is the founder of the White nationalist hate group VDARE.[204] Brimelow's connections to members of the Trump administration were in the news a few years ago. On August 19, 2018, Robert Costa of the *Washington Post* reported that Trump had fired his speechwriter, Darren Beattie, after the media learned that Beattie had sat on a panel with Brimelow at a Mencken Club conference in 2016; White nationalist Richard Spencer cofounded the club.[205] Two days later, Costa reported that a week earlier, Brimelow had attended a birthday party for Trump's top economic advisor, Larry Kudlow, at Kudlow's home.[206]

One leader in the White nationalist movement with whom Tanton had long-standing connections is Richard Lynn, the SPLC stating that these connections began long before Lynn became head of the Pioneer Fund in 2012. For example, in 1997, Tanton reportedly wrote to Lynn congratulating him on his book *Dysgenics: Genetic Deterioration in Modern Populations*.[207] A year later, Tanton suggested to Harry Weyher, the president of the Pioneer Fund at the time, that the Fund hire Richard Lynn to conduct a "study" of

Barry Mehler.[208] Mehler did some of the groundbreaking research on eugenics that I have cited throughout this book, and Tanton's suggestion was probably part of an attempt to discredit Mehler.

In 1979, Tanton founded the Washington, DC–based Federation for American Immigration Reform (FAIR), a group intent on severely restricting immigration.[209] Calling FAIR a hate group, the SPLC described FAIR's goals:

> FAIR's founder, John Tanton, has expressed his wish that America remain a majority-white population: a goal to be achieved, presumably, by limiting the number of nonwhites who enter the country. One of the group's main goals is upending the Immigration and Nationality Act of 1965, which ended a decades-long, racist quota system that limited immigration mostly to northern Europeans. FAIR President Dan Stein has called the Act a "mistake."[210]

The decades-long racist quota system that the SPLC mentioned was among the legacies of the Johnson-Reed Immigration Act of 1924.

One link between Tanton, FAIR, and eugenics of the early twentieth century is funding; under Tanton's leadership, FAIR accepted more than one million dollars from the Pioneer Fund.[211] According to the SPLC, FAIR has staunchly denied that it has any links to eugenics and has stated that it stopped taking Pioneer Funding in 1994, but Tanton's private papers portray a different, more entangled picture of his relationship to eugenics and the Pioneer Fund.[212] Adding to his established reputation of making racist comments about Jews and Latinos, his papers include correspondence with Holocaust deniers, Ku Klux Klan lawyers, and Harvard professor Samuel Huntington, an immigration critic.[213] The SPLC quoted from a letter to Huntington—a statement that strongly resembles those made in support of early-twentieth-century eugenics:

> "The people who have been the carriers of Western Civilization are well on the way toward resigning their commission to carry the culture into the future. . . . When this decline in numbers is coupled with an aging of the core population . . . it begins to look as if the chances of Western Civilization passing into the history books are very good indeed."[214]

The SPLC also reported that Tanton introduced FAIR leaders to the head of the Pioneer Fund, and that FAIR has been well aware of Tanton's views and activities.[215]

FAIR has been active in shaping recent immigration legislation. For example, according to the SPLC, a 2010 Arizona immigration law, which the SPLC claimed would result in the racial profiling of Latinos, was drafted by Kris Kobach, an attorney with the Immigration Reform Law Institute (IRLI); IRLI is the legal arm of FAIR.[216]

In 1985, Tanton founded the Center for Immigration Studies (CIS), an anti-immigrant think tank that appears on the SPLC's hate group list.[217] He turned to Cordelia Scaife May, heir to the Mellon fortune, for financial backing to help launch CIS;[218] over the years, he returned many times to her and to the influential Colcom Foundation that she founded for anti-immigration funding. For example, according to the SPLC, in 1995 he received money from May to "help fund efforts to draft a legislative solution to end birthright citizenship for undocumented immigrants"; the SPLC also stated that May was a close friend of Tanton's and gave him tens of millions of dollars for his anti-immigration efforts.[219] Other sources have reported even larger donations; for example, in 2015 the *Pittsburgh Post-Gazette* said that the Colcom Foundation had given $23.7 million to FAIR, CIS, and Numbers USA.[220] Numbers USA is an anti-immigrant group established in 1996 by Roy Beck; the *New York Times* reported that Tanton helped Beck found and fund the group.[221] The SPLC stated in 2002 that Tanton had established more than a dozen anti-immigrant groups, and in 2018, it reported that FAIR, CIS, and IRLI—all founded by Tanton—are three of the four "most influential anti-immigrant groups in the country" today.[222]

In the past few years, the media have reported on direct connections between CIS and the Trump administration. For example, according to Laura Reston, writing for the *New Republic* in 2017, Trump got the immigration "statistics" he used in his presidential campaign from CIS; she called CIS "Trump's go-to source for research about migrants and the dangers they pose," and she described CIS data as "anti-immigration screeds" posing as serious research.[223] She reported that CIS also has provided Trump with political cover, noting, for example, that it defended Trump's Muslim ban.[224]

Other media sources indicate that in addition to serving as a data source, CIS has been directly influencing Trump's immigration policy. National Public Radio reported in 2017 that the ideas CIS has been promoting for years have been showing up in Trump's executive orders.[225] The SPLC states that FAIR has influenced Trump's immigration policies as well, and it reports that at least one of Trump's appointees, Julie Kirchner, previously worked for FAIR.[226] In 2017, Kirchner, who is widely known as a staunch anti-immigration activist, was appointed the Citizenship and Immigration

Services Ombudsman in the US Department of Homeland Security. From 2005 to 2015, she worked for FAIR, serving as its executive director for eight of those years.[227] Trump also appointed a former CIS employee and a former CIS Fellow to work in immigration-related positions in his administration. In 2017, Jon Feere became senior advisor to US Immigration and Customs Enforcement (ICE). From 2006 to 2016 he was a legal policy analyst at CIS.[228] In 2018, Ronald Mortensen, whom the SPLC describes as a CIS Fellow, was appointed assistant secretary of state for the Bureau of Population, Refugees, and Migration.[229]

Jared Taylor

Another modern-day White supremacist is Jared Taylor, founder of the New Century Foundation (NCF); he is connected to the early-twentieth-century eugenics movement not merely by shared belief systems but by receipt of Pioneer Fund support. The SPLC describes the NCF as "a self-styled think tank that promotes pseudo-scientific studies and research that purport to show the inferiority of blacks to whites."[230] Taylor also is the former editor of the now-defunct *American Renaissance* magazine.[231] According to the SPLC, he hosts the annual American Renaissance Conference;[232] White supremacist Richard Spencer, whom I discussed earlier in this chapter and in chapter 7, has been among the conference speakers.[233] Aaron Patrick Flanagan, writing for the Center for New Community, reported that Taylor has long promoted the phrase "race-realists" to describe his White supremacist views.[234] This phrase appeared on the Pioneer Fund's website right up until May 2013, the month the site went silent.[235] Echoing sentiments expressed by eugenicists in the 1920s, Taylor reportedly stated in 2005, "When blacks are left entirely to their own devices, Western civilization—any kind of civilization—disappears."[236]

Taylor has made his anti-immigration views widely known. For example, they were on display in his introduction to his edited collection of essays on immigration, *The Real American Dilemma: Race, Immigration, and the Future of America*. This tome was published in 1998 by his own company, New Century Foundation. In it, Taylor states that Gunnar Myrdal's 1944 book *An American Dilemma: The Negro Problem and Modern Democracy*—which he claims has had more influence on American views on race than any other—wrongly claimed that America has a race problem because of White racism and oppression.[237] In his description of what he considers to be the profound but negative effects of Myrdal's ideas, Taylor warns of the deleterious effects of large-scale immigration of non-Whites, and he mourns the potential loss of a White majority:

> Large-scale immigration and racial integration—even forcible integration—have been defended in part because they promote "diversity." A mixture of races, religions, cultures, and even languages is now thought to be an inherently good thing for a country, and if large-scale immigration and high birthrates among non-whites reduce whites to minority status in a few decades, this will simply be the welcome result of having understood the benefits of diversity.[238]

Taylor clearly does not see reducing Whites to minority status as a welcome result of large-scale immigration, however.

His focus on immigration of non-Whites and on birth rates is reminiscent of the race suicide discourse of a century ago. After stating that the contributors to *The Real American Dilemma* believe Myrdal was wrong, he talks about other negative effects of non-White immigration:

> Concentrations of immigrants have brought perplexing social problems to Miami, Los Angeles, and much of Texas, and even the most optimistic boosters of "diversity" are hard pressed to describe exactly what the benefits are or are likely to be.
>
> Many whites are not waiting to find out. They are moving away from areas with large numbers of non-white immigrants to those parts of the country where whites are still a majority. Their behavior suggests the belief that the new, polyglot America will not be an improvement over the old.[239]

In a later chapter, he reiterates another assertion often made by eugenicists of the early twentieth century and similarly fueled by fear of race suicide: the fittest—and Taylor specifies White people—are having too few children.[240]

Taylor claims that race is not a social construct—that "real," constitutional race differences exist, and that these differences are due, at least in part, to genetic differences:

> It is well established that blacks and Hispanics have higher rates of crime, illegitimacy, poverty, and even death rates from most diseases than whites. . . .
>
> There is now a vast body of evidence for an at least partially genetic explanation for group differences in ability and achievement. It is understandable that people should resist this view, with its unpleasant implications of genetic determinism. However, averting our eyes from the evidence has led to dangerous misdiagnoses.[241]

Like eugenicists of the early twentieth century, he places Whites firmly at the top of the racial hierarchy. For example, he claims that unlike other races, Whites and north Asians have built successful societies.[242] He further claims that "for the most part, only whites have been able to make democracy work."[243]

Taylor, like Tanton, is part of the entangled skein of relationships that constitutes contemporary White nationalism. The SPLC reported that Taylor was Tanton's closest friend on the White nationalist scene.[244] Flanagan reported that Taylor sought advice from Tanton in 1990 on how to launch the New Century Foundation.[245] Flanagan also provided names and descriptions of people Taylor described as a distinguished group of truth-tellers who have been axed for telling the truth: Jason Richwine (I will discuss him momentarily); Scott McConnell (Flanagan described him as a member of FAIR's advisory board); Kevin Lamb (Flanagan stated that he worked for Tanton); Peter Brimelow (Flanagan described him as a founder of VDARE and a recipient of funding from both Tanton and the Pioneer Fund), and James Watson.[246] Watson, who was awarded a Nobel Prize in Physiology or Medicine in 1962, served as director, president, and, finally, chancellor of the Cold Spring Harbor Laboratory from 1968 to 2007; significantly, this lab was the base of the Eugenics Record Office from 1910 to 1939. He was relieved of all administrative responsibilities and removed from his position as chancellor in 2007 after having made racist comments about race differences and intelligence; he subsequently quit (or retired from) his job there.[247]

Jason Richwine

Jason Richwine is another figure in the contemporary cluster of like-minded individuals whose work closely resembles race-based eugenics research of the early twentieth century. The SPLC describes him as a "discredited race scientist";[248] he completed his doctoral dissertation, "IQ and Immigration Policy," at Harvard University in 2009. Flanagan reported that recipients and studies funded by the Pioneer Fund figure prominently in the dissertation's reference list.[249] Richwine also cites Jared Taylor's 1992 book *Paved with Good Intentions: The Failure of Race Relations in Contemporary America*.[250] Richwine's dissertation is grounded in hereditarian views of intelligence, and he cites an American Psychological Association summary of twin studies to support the assertion that "a sizable part of the variation in intelligence test scores is associated with genetic differences among individuals."[251] Significantly, he strategically distances himself from the eugenics movement of the early twentieth century by describing early IQ research as crude or bad science. For example, he reviews eugenicist Carl Brigham's 1923 research on IQ, describes some ways Brigham's research is flawed, and states that Brigham's work was grounded in what Richwine refers to as Madison Grant's "bizarre" racial theory.[252] He maintains that his project is different from the early studies, however, in that it has no racial or ethnic policy agenda:

> Nothing in this study suggests that immigrants should be treated on the basis of their group membership. Although the next chapter presents some facts about how IQ varies across countries and ethnic groups, immigrants—and, indeed, all people—should be considered purely as individuals whenever possible. Unlike Brigham's *A Study of American Intelligence*, there is no racial or ethnic policy agenda here. One can deal frankly and soberly with group IQ differences while still subscribing to the classical liberal tradition of individualism.[253]

He apparently assumes that focusing on individuals rather than on groups would protect him from accusations that he has a racial or ethnic agenda. He also appears to have assumed that referring to nations rather than races erases race from the discussion. His dissertation includes tables reporting average IQs in a host of nations; the data are derived from a book Richard Lynn coauthored in 2006 with Tatu Vanhanen, *IQ and Global Inequality*.[254] Richwine claims that Lynn and Vanhanen's research findings are valid, their study reporting significant national differences in average IQ scores: "A metastudy of worldwide IQ by Lynn and Vanhanen (2002), whose updated 2006 data is used in this study, finds that countries differ dramatically in their average IQ, with East Asian countries ranked the highest and sub-Saharan African nations placed at the bottom."[255] He also reports IQ scores of various ethnic and national groups in an effort to establish that while IQ scores of some groups have improved over time, the scores of Mexicans have not.[256] Noting that there are significant average IQ differences between the "white native population" and immigrants,[257] Richwine posits possible reasons for these differences and concludes that genetics is a major factor:

> The U.S. may be attracting immigrants from the low-side of the IQ distribution in their home countries. Second, material deprivation—such as inadequate nutrition, healthcare, and early schooling—could depress immigrant IQ scores. Third, cultural differences that deemphasize education may be a factor. Finally, genetic differences among ethnic groups could contribute to the difference. The chapter assesses

> the plausibility of these explanations, concluding that the material environment and genes probably make the greatest contributions to IQ differences.[258]

Claiming that genes play a significant role in intelligence, Richwine asserts, "There is little evidence that low-IQ countries can fully close the deficit with Europe and East Asia through environmental intervention."[259] He concludes that new immigrants "lack the average cognitive ability that natives possess, and there is little evidence that the difference will go away after a few generations."[260]

Thus, Richwine reached conclusions that eugenicists of the early twentieth century would have applauded, and he is also the coauthor of a Heritage Foundation study used to help defeat the Border Security, Economic Opportunity, and Immigration Modernization Act of 2013 (US Senate bill S. 744).[261] Authored by a bipartisan group that included Chuck Schumer, John McCain, Lindsay Graham, and Marco Rubio, among others, S. 744 was a comprehensive immigration reform bill that would have provided a road to citizenship for an estimated eleven million undocumented immigrants while also significantly increasing spending on border security.[262] The Senate passed the bill, but many conservatives opposed it, and it died in the House of Representatives. Finally, the tightness of the skein of relationships I am describing is illustrated not only by the fact that Richwine cited Taylor in his dissertation but also that Tanton's Center for Immigration Studies has published Richwine's work.[263]

Stephen K. Bannon

Stephen (Steve) K. Bannon is yet another figure who plays a prominent role in the skein of relationships that comprises contemporary White nationalism, and media sources have noted similarities between Bannon's positions on immigration and those held by eugenicists a century ago. Bannon, who was an executive chairman of Breitbart News, served for a short period as Trump's first chief White House strategist and is widely viewed as the engineer of Trump's travel ban on people from seven majority-Muslim states. In an article discussing the ban, Eric Schewe points out that the White supremacy exhibited by right-wing extremists such as Bannon is similar to that seen in "strongly nativist eras such as the 1920s."[264] Schewe states that among the resemblances between the early twentieth century and the present is a shift in the "complexion" of the immigrant population, which in the 1920s precipitated passage of the Johnson-

Reed Immigration Act of 1924; he claims that the Johnson-Reed Act had a profound impact on US immigration for four decades.[265] In his discussion of resemblances between past and present, he mentions eugenics publications from the early twentieth century, including Madison Grant's *The Passing of the Great Race.*[266] He also discusses a 1999 article by Mae M. Ngai, who pointed out that the 1924 immigration law avoided "explicit racial language" and displayed a shift in terminology from race to national origin; Ngai argued that this move "obfuscated" race even though the law was about race.[267] Thus, connectors between past and present include not just Bannon's support of White supremacy, but also Trump's rhetoric and choices of terms—fully on display in the travel ban Bannon engineered—which similarly obfuscate race and religion while permitting them to remain in play.

Bannon's name surfaced in several discussions of a virulently racist, fear-laden White-supremacist book that, according to SPLC investigative reporter Ryan Lenz, has grown in popularity since 2011 among contemporary White nationalists: Jean Raspail's 1973 novel *The Camp of the Saints.*[268] This dystopian book describes White genocide—the destruction of Western civilization by a mass of immigrants of color from India, who are joined in their campaign of annihilation by other immigrants and members of left-wing groups.[269] An excerpt from the novel describes the immigrant mass that has destroyed Western civilization:

> All the kinky-haired, swarthy-skinned, long-despised phantoms; all the teaming ants toiling for the white man's comfort; all the swill men and sweepers, the troglodytes, the stinking drudges, the swivel-hipped menials, the womanless wretches, the lung-spewing hackers; all the numberless, nameless, tortured, tormented, indispensable mass. . . . They don't say much. But they know their strength, and they'll never forget it. If they have an objection, they simply growl, and it soon becomes clear that their growls run the show. After all, five billion growling human beings, rising over the length and breadth of the earth, can make a lot of noise![270]

Thematically and discursively, *The Camp of the Saints* resembles any number of books lauded by eugenicists in the early twentieth century, and the above passage illustrates some of these resemblances: fear of (White) race suicide, racist descriptions of people of color, the perception that the hyperfecundity of the ostensibly unfit has caused White people to be outnumbered, and xenophobic anti-immigrant sentiment. Perhaps most significantly, the passage resembles eugenics because it describes individuals and groups as not fully human—as troglodytes, or as not human at all. Rather than speaking, those in the mass growl like animals. Raspail calls the immigrants ants and thereby does precisely what Rose claims modern biopolitics do not do: he insectifies people.

In 2017, the *HuffPost* quoted Cécile Alduy, a professor at Stanford University and an expert on far-right politics in contemporary France, on *The Camp of the Saints*: "'[This book is] racist in the literal sense of the term. It uses race as the main characterization of characters. . . . It describes the takeover of Europe by waves of immigrants that wash ashore like the plague.' The book, she said, 'reframes everything as the fight to death between races.'"[271]

The Camp of the Saints was first published in English in 1975, and a number of English editions appeared thereafter. Cordelia Scaife May, who also helped fund Tanton's CIS, was a fan of the book, and a number of sources report that she paid for distribution of the second American edition of the novel.[272] The Social Contract Press (a program of US incorporated, founded by John Tranton) republished *The Camp of the Saints* in 1994; in his announcement of this reissue, Tanton stated that the press was "honored" to be responsible for this action.[273]

Bannon referred to *The Camp of the Saints* several times in the months leading up to Trump's election, and the *HuffPost* published links to four audio clips containing these references.[274] One of them is an interview Bannon conducted in October 2015 with Jeff Sessions, Trump's attorney general from 2017 to 2018.[275] Another clip is a January 2016 Breitbart interview that Bannon conducted with Jason Richwine. Richwine, who Bannon introduced as a brilliant Harvard-educated scholar, made the following anti-immigration claims: immigrants are stealing jobs, their access to entitlement programs will drain the nation's coffers, and immigration has tremendous cultural costs. To support the third claim, he stated that the children of immigrants are not assimilating; instead, he argued, they are full of hatred and a desire to kill. Finally, he said that immigrants tend to be left-leaning and that the greatest threat they pose is to conservative values and beliefs, which are in danger of extinction. Bannon closed the interview by calling Richwine "a true patriot."[276]

Bannon and May are only a few of *The Camp of the Saints* fans from the skein of relationships that links the present to eugenics. In a February 2018 issue of the *New Republic*, Sarah Jones noted that Jared Taylor has recommended the book, as has Iowa Congressman Steve King.[277] In January 2019, the *New York Times* described King as a White nationalist and reported on his long-standing alt-right activities, which include demonizing Mexicans, promoting a southern border wall, supporting neo-Nazis, and spreading the Great Replacement theory.[278] In a September 2018 interview with *Unzensuriert*, a web platform associated with the right-wing Austrian Freedom Party, King spoke favorably of *The Camp of the Saints*:

> Why does the left denigrate this book? Why do they say it's a radical, racist book? I read the book, so it was all completely logical to me that this [migration] could come to pass. And that this narrative should be imprinted into everybody's brain: when you are importing people, even importing one single person, you are importing their culture. If you don't import one, ten, or a hundred, but a million: then they will subsume the native culture.[279]

Jones called the book "a veritable fixture on alt-right forums across the internet," mentioned r/The_Donald as one of the sites, and added, "Admiration, or at least cautious respect, for *The Camp of the Saints* seems to be where conservative commentators and politicians align with White nationalists. It offers insight into the true nature of the right's fear of immigration, and shows the extent to which that fear has been normalized."[280] Following Trump's election, K. C. McAlpin penned a defense of *The Camp of the Saints* that was reprinted in the *Social Contract*, a journal published by the Social Contract Press and edited by Tanton from 1990 to 1998. The theme of this issue of the journal was "Malthus Revisited: The Perils of Overpopulation and Globalism," and McAlpin's defense included the proud declaration that the Social Contract Press had been publishing *The Camp of the Saints* since 1994.[281] As I discussed briefly in chapter 2, Galton was heavily influenced by Malthus. Finally, in fall 2019, the Southern Poverty Law Center gained access to leaked emails, written in 2015 and 2016, from Stephen Miller, an immigration hardliner who became White House senior policy advisor in 2017, to Breitbart.[282] The SPLC reports that at the time of the correspondence, Miller was an aide to Senator Jeff Sessions and used a government email account for the messages.[283] In the correspondence, Miller recommended *The Camp of the Saints*, claiming that there are parallels between the plot of the novel and current events in the United States.[284]

I have discussed just a few members of the contemporary group whose research, beliefs, and assertions closely resemble those of eugenicists of the early twentieth century. This contemporary, tight-knit web of relationships is reminiscent of the web that similarly knit eugenicists together a century ago.

As in the early part of the twentieth century, funding from the eugenicist and White supremacist Wickliffe Draper helps support their work, in the contemporary instances via the Pioneer Fund.

Trump, the GOP, Eugenics, and White Supremacy: More Connections

Some of Trump's critics have linked him and his supporters directly to eugenics. In an article appearing in 2017 in the *New Republic*, Sarah Jones argued that Trump has "turned the GOP into the party of eugenics."[285] As partial evidence, she discussed immigration policy, noting that then-Attorney General Jeff Sessions had praised the Immigration Act of 1924.[286] As further evidence of eugenical leanings, she quoted Trump biographer Michael D'Antonio on the topic of inherited superiority. D'Antonio stated that Trump and his family subscribe "'to a racehorse theory of human development. They believe that there are superior people and that if you put together the genes of a superior woman and a superior man, you get a superior offspring.'"[287] Jones noted that the Republican Party is not using the word "eugenics" but is deploying a vision of improvement that "channels the spirit of eugenics" nevertheless:

> If Sir Francis Galton stood before the GOP in 2017 and asked them what they mean by improvement, they'd have ready answers. To Steve Bannon, it is a ban on Muslim refugees trying to enter this country. To Jeff Sessions, it is stricter voting laws that violate the rights of those who are most dependent on the government. To Education Secretary Betsy DeVos, it is an atrophied public school system and a weak Americans with Disabilities Act. To Health and Human Services Secretary Tom Price, it is "high-risk insurance pools" for sick Americans. To Vice President Mike Pence, it is legalized discrimination against LGBT people. And to Speaker Paul Ryan, it is the destruction of the welfare state.[288]

She added that another resemblance between Republican policy and eugenics is the targeting of weakness. Reporting that she has a rare genetic blood disorder, she closed her article with a chilling and bleak assessment:

> Trump makes obvious what I and Americans like me already understood: We are in the same vulnerable position that we have always occupied. This won't change as long as we inhabit a world ruled by

> men who prioritize the free market over human lives. Their ideal society excludes us and every other group ever deemed an obstacle to prosperity. And when they come for us they will call it progress.[289]

Although the free market may not be the source of all problems, Jones's observation about the targeting of those perceived to be weak, both by eugenicists and a host of current national leaders, is on point. Furthermore, she is not the only source to report on Trump's hereditarian stance on ability. In 2015, prior to Trump's election to office, the *Los Angeles Times* published an article by D'Antonio in which he quoted Trump: "'I'm a big believer in natural ability,' Trump told me during a discussion about his leadership traits, which he said came from a natural sense of how human relations work. 'If Obama had that psychology, Putin wouldn't be eating his lunch. He doesn't have that psychology and he never will because it's not in his DNA.'"[290] D'Antonio also quoted Donald Trump Jr.: "'Like him [father Donald], I'm a big believer in race-horse theory. He's an incredibly accomplished guy, my mother's incredibly accomplished, she's an Olympian, so I'd like to believe genetically I'm predisposed to [be] better than average.'"[291]

Certainly one resemblance between early-twentieth-century eugenics and strands of contemporary discourse is the pervasiveness of racism. In an article on the normalization of hate in the Trump era, which appeared in *The Guardian* in 2017, Lois Beckett noted that Trump has "energized fringe racists."[292] According to Ryan Lenz of the Southern Poverty Law Center, whom Beckett quoted, rather than being embarrassed by the moniker, some individuals thrive on being called racists.[293]

Beckett also quoted Marilyn Mayo, a research fellow at the Anti-Defamation League's Center on Extremism, who stated that the alt-right believes they have an ally in Donald Trump.[294] Beckett discussed White supremacists' assertion that the publicity they are receiving during the Trump era—including, ironically, from the left-wing media—is helping their cause. For example, Beckett quoted Andrew Anglin, described as a neo-Nazi internet troll, who claimed that media attention is helping him recruit male teenagers. According to Beckett, Kyle Pope, the editor-in-chief of the *Columbia Journalism Review*, asserted that although they have been around for a long time, extremist groups were not being adequately covered by the mainstream media prior to the rise of Trump, and that the media consequently were surprised by the opinions expressed by these groups and the extent of support for these views.[295]

Resemblances in the Present Moment

I began the final chapter of this book on September 23, 2018, the 611th day of the presidency of Donald Trump. Immigration policies that he has long supported are separating immigrant children from their parents. Multiple media sources report that immigrant children are being caged and that their parents are not being told of their whereabouts. In some systems of reasoning, these actions would be deemed horrifically cruel or not even imaginable. Some conservative leaders see things differently, however. In a June 2018 audio clip broadcast on the NPR program *Morning Edition*, then–US Attorney General Jeff Sessions defended current policy and engaged in distancing, claiming that it is "a real exaggeration" to state that current policies echo Nazi Germany.[296] In the same broadcast, NPR's national political correspondent Mara Liasson reported that fully 27 percent of people in the United States agree with Trump's stance on immigration, an approval rate that rises to 55 percent among Republicans; Liasson adds, "His [Trump's] base loves this."[297] Regardless of Sessions's claims, current immigration policies are remarkably and not coincidentally similar to those forwarded by American eugenicists in the early 1920s. That the United States would even consider such policies and practices today, that 27 percent of the population would approve of them, and that anyone in this country would "love" these cruel and inhumane policies is a strong indication that the systems of reasoning, the desires, and the fears that made eugenics reasonable and rational in the 1920s, are resilient, alive and well in the United States today.

One description of US cultural politics in the Trump era is that "marginal" discourses and practices, which until recently were on their way to extinction, are being cultivated and are flourishing. According to one narrative, what had been inactivated or deactivated—had become a thing of the past—has been reactivated. While it may be true that Trump politics have emboldened and empowered specific groups, and have breathed new life into what some hoped were on the way to extinction, I am not convinced that there ever was an inactivation or deactivation. Furthermore, although Trump has often been described as "the problem," the fact that he was elected points to larger problems. It reflects not merely the robustness of a particular skein of personal relationships, but the robustness of the systems of reasoning that would support his selection and election. That White supremacists have hailed Trump as a hero is more significant than his weak attempts to distance himself from these groups.

The idea that not all humans are of equal worth never went away, nor did impulses to measure, sort, order, and selectively include or exclude. Fear mongering, specifically White racial and ethnic anxiety as manifest in fears of White suicide, never went away. Systematic race genocide, whether effected by imprisonment, death by gun violence, extreme poverty, drug addiction, or mental illness, never went away. Trump politics are an especially fertile medium for particular ideas, allowing them to prosper and be brought to the fore whereas other environments would have been less hospitable. That said, these politics have always been in play in the United States and were nowhere near extinction; Trump politics are an ugly underbelly that has been part of the body all along.

To suggest, however, that the cultural politics of the Trump era are merely continuing business-as-usual is to underestimate the gravity and potentially devastating consequences of the present moment. Pointing out resemblances between the events precipitating the Holocaust and current events in the United States is a treacherous project that no one should undertake lightly. That said, as I have noticed troubling and growing resemblances between eugenics of a century ago and the present, and I have not been the only academic to raise warning flags. In October 2018, noted Holocaust historian Christopher R. Browning published "The Suffocation of Democracy," an essay describing "troubling similarities" between the US present and the interwar period in Europe: isolationism and withdrawal from international organizations and agreements, income disparities with a concentration of wealth at the top, highly restrictive immigration policies, emergency powers that destroy democratic norms, the erosion of organized labor, the old right's installation of a leader they believe they can control while advancing and reaping benefits from their own agenda, division and disarray on the left in the face of a strong conservative alliance, and calculated parliamentary gridlock that diminishes respect for democratic institutions and norms. A major difference between the US present and interwar Europe, Browning states, is that unlike the interwar period in Europe, when authoritarianism was effected by an overt takeover, in the United States today, illiberalism is being accomplished by a *gradual* process of curtailment of rights and protections.[298] In *Ordinary Men: Reserve Police Battalion 101 and the Final Solution in Poland*, Browning discusses what I see as another similarity: an attitude of apathy, indifference, and passivity among the general population.[299] Browning was referring to a gulf that had opened up between the general population and the Jewish minority in Germany during the 1930s, and the apathy he mentions was toward the plight of Jews. A similar attitude of indifference appears to have engulfed a broad swath of the US population at present, however, and the indifference encompasses more than the plight of minorities and immigrants. Prior to reading Browning, I had not noticed all of the resemblances he enumerated, and significantly, he did not mention eugenics or the systems of reasoning that supported it. Nevertheless, his observations provide a broad context within which to consider the eugenical resemblances I have noted. It is also important to remember when making such comparisons that the conditions of possibility that helped create these resemblances began earlier than the 1930s and were not limited to Germany.

I am not saying that history repeats itself, and I am not suggesting that the present is an exact replication of the past. Rather, when Rose and others claim that the biopolitics of the present cannot be called eugenics because there are too many differences, or that eugenics is dead, I counter that although differences clearly exist, the differences the dismissers tend to reference constitute surface chop. Despite and beneath differences, deep, fundamental, and troubling similarities remain that merit fierce interrogation.

Having seemingly moved far afield from education and music education, I pose a question that may be on the minds of my critics: "But what does any of this have to do with education or music education?" My response is simple: everything. Every last thing. By following the entangled strands of past and present, I have demonstrated that education, including music education, is and always has been a part of—not apart from—cultural politics and broader discursive communities and practices, past and present. Thus, events in the US government today that on the surface appear to have nothing to do with the eugenically informed music education research and practice of 100 years ago are inextricably and not-coincidentally connected in complex ways.

Resemblances to Me

Even though I was inclined to distance myself from Seashore by focusing on the ways I am not like him, keeping Seashore's face close to mine enabled me to see resemblances to me and connections to my life. Barry Mehler's description of the typical eugenicist who served on the Advisory Council of the American Eugenics Society hit close to home: middle-class, liberal, progressive, Protestant, White, new professional.[300] There are more resemblances, however; like Seashore, I have lived in the Midwest my whole life, and I attended a private Lutheran college in Minnesota. It is less than an hour's drive from another private Lutheran college, Gustavus Adolphus, Seashore's alma mater. Like Seashore, I have connections to the University of Iowa.

I received a master's degree in music from there in 1978; Himie Voxman, the colleague of Seashore's at Iowa who talked about Seashore's imperiousness, was the director of the School of Music when I was a graduate student. During my doctoral studies at the University of Minnesota, I was not only introduced to the work of Seashore and one of his protégés, the late Edwin Gordon, I met Gordon a number of times. Both Seashore and I spent our academic careers at land-grant universities in the Midwest, where we were surrounded, for the most part, by White people who were mostly interested in classical high art music. I see Madison connections and resemblances as well. For example, from 1913 to 1924, Peter Dykema held the faculty position I held at UW–Madison from 1988 until my retirement in 2019. Together with Seashore's former student Jacob Kwalwasser, he developed a second-generation test of musical talent, the Kwalwasser-Dykema Music Tests. Continuing a research tradition established by Seashore, another of my predecessors, Robert Petzold, was best known for his studies of auditory perception; Petzold was a professor of music education at UW–Madison from 1951 to 1986. Significantly, ideas similar to those eugenicists promulgated about ability, gender, race, and class were familiar to me; they resembled what I was taught as a child. Growing up in a racially diverse, low-income urban neighborhood did not protect me from this toxicity, but it did help lay the groundwork for my realization that I had been told lies. Nevertheless, this project has reminded me that whether I like it or not, I am in the middle of this mess: I am embroiled, implicated, and entangled, and I am not alone.

Gloria Ladson-Billings's discussion of the full social funding of the concept of race came to my mind as I considered this entanglement. Ladson-Billings states that societal investment in the construct of race is so complete that "it is impossible to withdraw it from use even when it does not work to a mainstream advantage."[301] She writes, "The funding of race can . . . [even] occur when the ostensible action is to work against racial categorization or identification."[302] She uses a wood-fired, heated warming bench that she saw in Sweden as an analogy for how the full social funding of race occurs:

> Some sections of the bench were comfortable and the heat was evenly distributed. Other sections were too hot and some sections were cool. What was unique about the bench was [that] the public was both invited to sit on it and encouraged to open the lid at the end of the bench and place another fire log in before leaving. As visitors we benefited from the previous visitors' efforts to keep the bench warm and we maintained that warmth by throwing another log on the fire.

> The way the social funding of race operates reminds me of that bench. It is already "warm" when we enter the society. We are invited to sit upon it and share its benefits and we are encouraged to add fuel as we move on. We did not construct the bench but we take responsibility for maintaining it. Some of us sit on a section of the bench that is cold. We are excluded from the benefits. Others sit on a section that is too hot. We are victimized by the very thing that brings others pleasure. Although the analogy may be crude, I think it helps illustrate the way we may unwittingly participate in a process that we believe benefits us without being aware of the way it regularly and systematically disadvantages others.[303]

Although she views it as a difficult task, she calls on educators to defund the concept of race.[304] Defunding race will, by extension, defund racism. Her description of taking responsibility to fuel the bench reminds me that the ethical demand is not merely to shift from irresponsibility to responsibility, but to reconceptualize responsibility—to what, to whom, why, and how one is responsible.

This probably is the last project of my academic career, and it has been the most discouraging and disillusioning one. I am disappointed but not surprised, and most of all, I am angry. I am angered by the enduring prevalence and growing popularity of hateful ideas and practices, as well as by how outvoted other ways of thinking were in the past and remain to the present. I am angry about the academy's role, past and present, in this hatefulness disguised as wisdom, altruism, and benevolence. I am enraged by the immeasurable damage done by these individuals and ideas. From an early age, I was taught to respect educated people; I aspired to become learned only to spend the last half of my academic career documenting that a learned, White, liberal academic who has been touted as a hero in my field fell far short of his reputation—and that he did not act alone. Furthermore, I am enraged by my own miseducation, which resulted in my own stupidity and blindness. In the music miseducation I received, I was taught about Seashore; only years later, after my formal education had ended, did I learn about W. E. B. Du Bois. From this project, I learned that Seashore dedicated one of his books to William James, and that both G. Stanley Hall and Du Bois were James's students. Once again, I was taught about James and Hall but not Du Bois. To this day, many educators and researchers in music know little or nothing about Du Bois, and I am angry that such miseducation continues. I am enraged by my blindness and by what are probably glaring blindnesses in what I have written in this book, but as with my visual blind spots, although I know they are there, I do not know their precise location. I am angered by the absences, self-serving silences, and "forgetting" that this project has revealed, and I am enraged by my entanglement—my participation—from which I see no escape. Finally, I am enraged by the ethical demand on me—the demand not to dehumanize anyone, not even those with whom I am so very angry. This is a terrible ethical demand; whether the face is Carl Seashore's or Donald Trump's, I am commanded to look at it and to see the person as fully human. Every cell in my body recoils at this demand. Nevertheless, his face is my face; his frailties and immorality are mine. Applying Judith Butler's assertions, I acknowledge that Seashores and Trumps are a part of me and help constitute me.[305]

What have I done and what might I do with my rage? In a recent interview about her new collection of poems, *Taking the Arrow Out of the Heart*, Pulitzer Prize–winning author Alice Walker was asked about the usefulness of anger and about how anger can coexist with peace.[306] Walker called anger a "wakening" and a "fuel," and she advocated for its strategic use as an instrument for change: "I think people might find it useful to figure out a way to channel it [their anger] into the circle of people who you need to change things. . . . Let your anger guide you away from what is dangerous and perilous and toward what is useful."[307] *"Destined to Fail"* is an attempt to channel my anger into just such a circle of people who need to change things: White, left-leaning academics—people like Seashore and people like me. Thus, the primary audience for this book is not those who say, "This is not news to me." This book is for anyone with the stamina and will to wade through it, and it is directed in particular at people like me, privileged White intellectuals, especially those of us involved in education and education reform. Finally, it is for anyone who assumes that then and now, music education is an apolitical endeavor. It is and always has been a profoundly political project.

Seashore's legacy is part of music education's inheritance, my inheritance, and the inheritance of every academic in the United States, although many White academics may not be aware of this or be willing to acknowledge it. Just as the Harrimans and Mellons inherited tainted fortunes, I have inherited and am a part of this tainted history and this tainted present, regardless of my political views. This book is a calling to account, individually and collectively, and in particular, it is a reminder to White people that we need to recognize and take responsibility for the past—for this inheritance—and for the present. What might constitute taking responsibility? What might constitute responsible individual and collective action?

Now What?

I set off on this research journey long ago seeking answers, and I end it with a stream of questions. If histories of the present diagnose the present, what does this project diagnose about now? A question that typically follows a diagnosis also haunts me: "Now what?" I do not have clear answers, but more than at any time in my life, I am convinced that, as the Māori claim, we "walk backwards into the future" (*Kia whakatōmuri te haere whakamua*).[308] I, and we, can only see what has come before, not what lies ahead; what I, and we, do or do not see is governed by what my eyes have been taught to see and not to see. I subscribe to what Lesley Rameka claims is another Māori belief: the past, present, and future are intertwined, and consequently, ancestors walk with us and within us as we walk backward into the future. She explains:

> The past, the present and the future are viewed as intertwined, and life as a continuous cosmic process. Within this continuous cosmic movement, time has no restrictions—it is both past and present. The past is central to and shapes both present and future. . . . The individual carries their past into the future. The strength of carrying one's past into the future is that ancestors are ever present, existing both within the spiritual realm and in the physical, alongside the living as well as within the living.[309]

Carl Seashore and his comrades in eugenics are my ancestors, and they are the ancestors of many others in education and music education. Like all of us, they were complicated, flawed people—no more heroic and no less fully human than we are. If a strength of carrying the past into the future is that our ancestors walk alongside and within us, what can we learn from them? What can Seashore say to us, his children? The historian Tzvetan Todorov reminds us, "The past has lessons for the present, but we must be prepared to hear them."[310] What are we, the descendants, willing to hear? I believe that at the very least, analyzing Seashore can remind academics like me of a few things:

- The importance of respect and universal human regard grounded in the assumption that all people are equals and should be treated as such. Eugenics may be a cautionary tale about what can happen when people individually and collectively believe they are more capable, worthy, and better than others—when they assume that their ideas and cultures are superior to others, best not only for themselves but for everyone else. Seashore clearly saw himself and his friends as superiors destined for greatness and success. He and other eugenicists invoked a higher authority, the "truth of science," to cement the validity of this claim and to confirm their superiority. It is neither natural nor inevitable, however, for people to create hierarchies of humans, to elevate some and degrade others, or even to assume that some humans are more human than others. Racism has stamped the United States from its beginnings, to paraphrase Ibram Kendi, but it is neither natural nor inevitable to think about people in terms of races. Race and racism are neither universal nor eternal, and the beginnings of the United States are not the beginning of time.

- The destructiveness of hate and the power of fear. Irene Butter, a Holocaust survivor interviewed recently for the *1A* podcast "Preserving Stories of Holocaust Survivors," underscored the importance of "refusing to be enemies."[311] Refusing to be enemies does not translate into dismissing the significance of the actions of people like Seashore, or into failing to take responsibility, or into passively accepting annihilation at the hands of others. Rather, it points to the potential productivity of refusing to engage in the power politics of hatred and fear, and of courageously sifting and winnowing through both fears and hopes.
- The value of humility, of acknowledging the limits of knowledge, of listening to our detractors, and of taking critique seriously. Seashore was convinced he was right; he and his accomplices tended to manage and contain criticism by simply dismissing detractors—by ignoring them or attempting to discredit or humiliate them. He surrounded himself with a network of like-minded people who shielded, supported, and promoted each other; doing this effectively created a strong but dangerous barrier that insulated eugenicists from their critics.
- The inadequacy of merely having good intentions. It is clear from the sources I examined that Seashore's intentions were good; the actual effects of the discourses and practices that he promoted were not universally so, however. In many cases, his firm beliefs about what was right did great harm and were flat-out wrong.
- The immeasurable importance of taking ethics seriously and of regularly wrestling with the many ethical dimensions of scholarly activity. This includes keeping abreast of the political landscape of the organizations to which academics belong, and of having the courage to speak up or leave. It also includes monitoring the political agendas of potential research funding sources.

As I have ruminated over Seashore, I also have speculated that the postmodern turn was a needed corrective. Contrary to what some critics have claimed, its endpoint in all instances is not paralysis or moral agnosticism. Rather, it has tended to promote caution, humility, reflexivity, and fierce, never-ending questioning, all of which appear to have been in short supply in the work of eugenicists such as Seashore.

February 2018 marked the beginning of the demolition of the building at the University of Iowa that had borne Seashore's name since 1981.[312] An article published by the University of Iowa describing the demolition stated that its replacement will be called the Psychological and Brain Sciences Building—a name referencing the psychology department Seashore built; the article also noted that psychological and brain sciences is the institution's most popular undergraduate major.[313] My initial response to the article's title, "Paying Homage to Seashore Hall," was to mutter that Seashore and his accessories have received more than their share of homages. I also wondered if choosing a name that continues to pay homage to Seashore, albeit indirectly, is yet another example of rebranding. Overall, I was relieved that Seashore Hall came down, and I optimistically imagine that its removal symbolizes changing times and changing attitudes, although the decision to raze the building probably had nothing to do with changing Seashore's legacy. Attenuating the homages paid to him may be justified and overdue, but Seashore and his legacy should not be forgotten. In short, I do not support demolishing and burying the past along with the building. Rather, I favor a different remembering, recognizing that the past lives on in and is an effect of the present.

I do not have the wisdom or the will to tack a happy ending onto this book, but I will end on a hopeful note—ironically, the very hope in the future that was foundational to eugenics. I do not know what the future holds for music education, education reform, the United States, the human race, or the planet, but this much I do know: the past is not behind us, whoever the "us" may be. It is inside of me and of us. It lives on, in and through the actions of the present, shaping the present—my present and the present of others. According to Hine Waitere, the director of the Indigenous Leadership Centre at Te Whare Wānanga o Awanuiārangi in Whakatāne, New Zealand, another component of walking backward into the future is potential: "I have my back to the future because it has yet to divulge itself—there is always the notion of potential. Culturally we open ancestral houses at dawn in recognition that it is a moment of potential between *to po* (the night) and *te ao hurihuri* (the turning world)."[314]

Thus, the hopefulness with which I end this book lies in the assertion that the *dynamism* of a *turning world* generates potential as we walk backward into the future. I hold fast to the potential of widening possibilities by examining conditions of possibility. Conducting a history of the present is a critical diagnosing that creates the possibility of imagining different futures. As I have demonstrated, eugenics was supported by complex and entangled intersectionalities; imagining different futures will necessarily involve similarly complex unthinking and rethinking. One possible place to begin may be with the polysemic concept of *ubuntu*, which sometimes has been translated from Zulu to mean, "I am because we are," or "We are one." A similar concept is present in a number of African cultures, and so, to some, *ubuntu* may be a familiar, foundational rationale for responsibility. It is part of a very different system of reasoning than that which informs eugenics, however, standing in sharp contrast to the eugenical assertion that all most certainly are *not* one. It also stands in contrast to eugenical conceptions of responsibility. I hope this book will help all of us who are Seashore's descendants and inheritors take individual and collective responsibility for our inheritance. Past, present, resemblances, and responsibility all must matter if all people are to matter *equally*, now and in the future.

Notes

Chapter 1

1. In Seashore's time and to the present, the official name of the institution has been the State University of Iowa. Since 1964, the approved name for everyday usage has been the University of Iowa.

2. Field Secretary, New Haven, CT, to Fair Associations [c. 1930], American Philosophical Society, AES, Am3, 575.06, circulars, titled "Letter from Field Secretary, American Eugenics Association to Fair Associations Asking Education Exhibit Space," image 704, in the "Image Archive on the American Eugenics Movement," DNA Learning Center, Cold Spring Harbor Laboratory, accessed February 10, 2005, www.eugenicsarchive.org/eugenics/view_image.pl?id=704

3. Carl E. Seashore, "Carl Emil Seashore," vol. 1, *A History of Psychology in Autobiography*, ed. Carl Allanmore Murchison (Worcester, MA: Clark University, 1930), 226.

4. Tzvetan Todorov, *Hope and Memory: Reflections on the Twentieth Century* (Princeton, NJ: Princeton University Press, 2003; London: Atlantic, 2014), xx.

5. Walter R. Miles, "Carl Emil Seashore, 1866–1949," vol. 29, *Biographical Memoirs* (New York: Columbia University Press for the National Academy of Sciences, 1956), 263–316.

6. For the eugenics-related citation, see Miles, "Carl Emil Seashore, 1866–1949," 310. There are a few omissions in Miles's list of Seashore's publications.

7. Barry Alan Mehler, "A History of the American Eugenics Society, 1921–1940" (PhD diss., University of Illinois at Urbana-Champaign, 1988), 30, 68, 172n73, 176, 309, 422–23, http://search.proquest.com.ezproxy.library.wisc.edu/docview/303689028?accountid=465

8. Alexander W. Cowan, "Music Psychology and the American Eugenics Movement in the Early Twentieth Century" (MMus thesis, King's College, London, 2016).

9. Alexander W. Cowan, email message to author, April 15, 2019.

10. Adria R. Hoffman, "Competing Narratives: Musical Aptitude, Race, and Equity," in *Palgrave Handbook of Race and the Arts in Education*, eds. Amelia M.

Kraehe, Rubén Gaztambide-Fernández, and B. Stephen Carpenter II (Cham, Switzerland: Palgrave, 2018), 103–17, https://link.springer.com/book/10.1007%2F978-3-319-65256-6

11. Johanna Devaney, "Eugenics and Musical Talent: Exploring Carl Seashore's Work on Talent Testing and Performance," *American Music Review* 48, no. 2 (Spring, 2019): 1–6, http://www.brooklyn.edu/web/aca_centers_hitchcock/AMR_48-2_Devaney.pdf

12. Kim Stanley Robinson, "Ancient Shamans and Roving Neanderthals: Kim Stanley Robinson Imagines Living 30,000 Years Ago," interview by Steve Paulson, *To the Best of Our Knowledge*, Wisconsin Public Radio, September 11, 2015, audio, 10:47, http://archive.ttbook.org/book/kim-stanley-robinson-shamanism

13. Todorov, *Hope and Memory*, 311.

14. Michel Foucault, *The Foucault Reader*, ed. Paul Rabinow (New York: Pantheon Books, 1984), 83.

15. David Garland, "What Is a 'History of the Present?' On Foucault's Genealogies and Their Critical Preconditions," *Punishment & Society* 16, no. 4 (2014): 379.

16. Garland, "What Is a 'History of the Present?'" 367.

17. Garland, "What Is a 'History of the Present?'" 372.

18. John K. Simon, "A Conversation with Michel Foucault," *Partisan Review* 38, no. 2 (1971): 192, http://hgar-srv3.bu.edu/collections/partisan-review/search/detail?id=326091

19. Garland, "What Is a 'History of the Present?'" 372.

20. Kurt Danziger, *Marking the Mind: A History of Memory* (Cambridge, UK: Cambridge University Press, 2008), 12.

21. Todorov, *Hope and Memory*, 311.

22. Thomas S. Popkewitz, *Cosmopolitanism and the Age of School Reform: Science, Education, and Making Society by Making the Child* (New York: Routledge, 2008), 172.

23. Judith Butler, *Parting Ways: Jewishness and the Critique of Zionism* (New York: Columbia University Press, 2012), 9.

24. Emmanuel Levinas, *Ethics and Infinity: Conversations with Philippe Nemo*, trans. Richard A. Cohen (Pittsburgh, PA: Duquesne University Press, 1985), 95.

25. Levinas, *Ethics and Infinity*, 101.

26. Butler, *Parting Ways*, 56.

27. Emmanuel Levinas, *The Levinas Reader*, ed. Seán Hand (Oxford: Basil Blackwell, 1989), 84.

28. Levinas, *Ethics and Infinity*, 97.

29. Judith Butler, *Precarious Life: The Powers of Mourning and Violence* (London: Verso, 2004), xviii.

30. Butler, *Parting Ways*, 56.

31. Butler, *Parting Ways*, 56.

32. Butler, *Precarious Life*, xviii

33. Levinas, *Ethics and Infinity*, 86.

34. Butler, *Parting Ways*, 44.
35. Butler, *Parting Ways*, 47.
36. Zygmunt Bauman, *Modernity and the Holocaust* (Ithaca, NY: Cornell University Press, 1989), 192.
37. Bauman, *Modernity and the Holocaust*, xii.
38. Butler, *Precarious Life*, 16–17.
39. Butler, *Precarious Life*, xviii.
40. Butler, *Parting Ways*, 38.
41. Butler, *Parting Ways*, 60.
42. Levinas, *Ethics and Infinity*, 99.

Chapter 2

1. Carl E. Seashore, "Sectioning Classes on the Basis of Ability," *School and Society* 15, no. 379 (April 1922): 356.
2. Daniel J. Kevles, *In the Name of Eugenics: Genetics and the Uses of Human Heredity* (Berkeley: University of California Press, 1986).
3. Barry Alan Mehler, "A History of the American Eugenics Society, 1921–1940" (PhD diss., University of Illinois at Urbana-Champaign, 1988), http://search.proquest.com.ezproxy.library.wisc.edu/docview/303689028?accountid=465.a
4. Edwin Black, *War against the Weak: Eugenics and America's Campaign to Create a Master Race* (New York: Four Walls Eight Windows, 2003), ix.
5. Alison Bashford and Philippa Levine, eds., *The Oxford Handbook of the History of Eugenics* (Oxford: Oxford University Press, 2010).
6. Stephen Jay Gould, *The Mismeasure of Man* (New York: W. W. Norton, 1996).
7. Steven Selden, *Inheriting Shame: The Story of Eugenics and Racism in America* (New York: Teachers College, 1999).
8. Alexandra Minna Stern, "Gender and Sexuality: A Global Tour and Compass," in *The Oxford Handbook of the History of Eugenics*, ed. Alison Bashford and Philippa Levine (Oxford: Oxford University Press, 2010), 173.
9. Martin S. Pernick, "Eugenics and Public Health in American History," *American Journal of Public Health* 87, no. 11 (November 1997): 1767, https://www.ncbi.nlm.nih.gov/pmc/articles/PMC1381159/pdf/amjph00510-0017.pdf
10. Ellsworth Huntington, *Tomorrow's Children: The Goal of Eugenics* (New York: J. Wiley & Sons, 1935), https://babel.hathitrust.org/cgi/pt?id=mdp.39015034788995;view=1up;seq=7. See Mehler, "History of the American Eugenics," 258–59, for a reference to it as a catechism.
11. Allan Chase, *The Legacy of Malthus: The Social Costs of the New Scientific Racism* (New York: Alfred A. Knopf, 1977), 116, 115.
12. Hans Pols, "Eugenics in the Netherlands and the Dutch East Indies," in *The Oxford Handbook of the History of Eugenics*, ed. Alison Bashford and Philippa Levine (Oxford: Oxford University Press, 2010), 347.
13. Ann G. Winfield, "Eugenic Ideology and Historical Osmosis," in *Cur-*

riculum Studies Handbook: The Next Moment, ed. Erik Malewski (New York: Routledge, 2010), 144.

14. For discussions of Malthus, Gobineau, and Spencer, see Chase, *Legacy of Malthus*, 72–84, 90–92, 105–7.

15. Philippa Levine and Alison Bashford, "Eugenics and the Modern World," in *The Oxford Handbook of the History of Eugenics*, ed. Alison Bashford and Philippa Levine (Oxford: Oxford University Press, 2010), 20.

16. *Oxford English Dictionary Online*, s.v. "gene [n.2]," accessed June 5, 2017, http://www.oed.com/view/Entry/77473?rskey=x1zg4c&result=2#eid

17. Carolyn Beans, "Four Ways Inheritance Is More Complex than Mendel Knew," *Biomedical Beat* (blog), National Institute of General Medical Sciences, March 4, 2016, https://biobeat.nigms.nih.gov/2016/03/four-ways-inheritance-is-more-complex-than-mendel-knew/

18. Nikolas Rose, *The Politics of Life Itself: Biomedicine, Power, and Subjectivity in the Twenty-First Century* (Princeton, NJ: Princeton University Press, 2007), 59.

19. *Oxford English Dictionary Online*, s.v. "eugenics," accessed October 25, 2016, http://www.oed.com/view/Entry/64958?rskey=aT9Gph&result=1#eid

20. Francis Galton, "Eugenics: Its Definition, Scope, and Aims," *American Journal of Sociology* 10, no. 1 (July 1904): 1, http://www.jstor.org/stable/2762125

21. Philippa Levine and Alison Bashford, "Eugenics and the Modern World," 17.

22. Francis Galton, "Hereditary Talent and Character: Part I," *Macmillan's Magazine* 12, no. 68 (June 1865): 157–66, https://search-proquest-com.ezproxy.library.wisc.edu/docview/6069457?accountid=465; Francis Galton, "Hereditary Talent and Character: Second Paper," *Macmillan's Magazine* 12, no. 70 (August 1865): 318–27, http://search.proquest.com.ezproxy.library.wisc.edu/docview/6117693/fulltextPDF/D24741D1A3E54DC9PQ/4?accountid=465; Francis Galton, *Hereditary Genius: An Inquiry into Its Laws and Consequences* (London: Macmillan, 1869), http://galton.org/books/hereditary-genius/1869-FirstEdition/hereditarygenius1869galt.pdf

23. Francis Galton, *Memories of My Life* (New York: E. P. Dutton, 1909), 323, https://archive.org/stream/memoriesmylife01galtgoog#mode/2up/search/323

24. Chase, *Legacy of Malthus*, 98; Philippa Levine and Alison Bashford, "Eugenics and the Modern World," 5.

25. "Eugenics," 1921, Cold Spring Harbor, E.06 Eug-2, Exhibits Book-Second Int. Ex. of Eugenics, p. 15, titled "'Copy of Certificate Awarded for Meritorious Exhibits,' at the Second International Congress of Eugenics," image 543, in the "Image Archive on the American Eugenics Movement," DNA Learning Center, Cold Spring Harbor Laboratory, accessed September 23, 2018, www.eugenicsarchive.org/eugenics/view_image.pl?id=543

26. "Controlling Heredity: The American Eugenics Crusade 1870–1940, International Eugenics Congresses, Eugenics Tree, 1932 [page 510]," Special Collections and Rare Books, University of Missouri, last modified March 16, 2012, https://library.missouri.edu/exhibits/eugenics/congresses.htm

27. Frances Hassencahl suggests that Laughlin and Davenport first met at that meeting. See Frances Janet Hassencahl, "Harry H. Laughlin, 'Expert Eugenics Agent' for the House Committee on Immigration and Naturalization, 1921 to 1931" (PhD diss., Case Western Reserve University, 1970), 54, https://search-proquest-com.ezproxy.library.wisc.edu/docview/302467912?

28. Black, *War against the Weak*, 51.

29. Walter R. Miles, "Carl Emil Seashore, 1866–1949," vol. 29, *Biographical Memoirs* (New York: Columbia University Press for the National Academy of Sciences, 1956), 268.

30. Ann G. Winfield, *Eugenics and Education in America: Institutionalized Racism and the Implications of History, Ideology, and Memory* (New York: Peter Lang, 2007), xvii; Christine Rosen, *Preaching Eugenics: Religious Leaders and the American Eugenics Movement* (Oxford: Oxford University Press, 2004), 6.

31. Philippa Levine and Alison Bashford, "Eugenics and the Modern World," 5.

32. Foucault, *The History of Sexuality*, vol. 1, *An Introduction*, trans. Robert Hurley (New York: Vintage Books, 1990), 140.

33. Philippa Levine and Alison Bashford, "Eugenics and the Modern World," 3.

34. Philippa Levine and Alison Bashford, "Eugenics and the Modern World," 5.

35. Philippa Levine and Alison Bashford, "Eugenics and the Modern World," 13.

36. Philippa Levine and Alison Bashford, "Eugenics and the Modern World," 3–4.

37. Philippa Levine and Alison Bashford, "Eugenics and the Modern World," 9.

38. Philippa Levine and Alison Bashford, "Eugenics and the Modern World," 6.

39. Philippa Levine and Alison Bashford, "Eugenics and the Modern World," 6.

40. Philippa Levine and Alison Bashford, "Eugenics and the Modern World," 6–7.

41. Philippa Levine and Alison Bashford, "Eugenics and the Modern World," 14.

42. Philippa Levine and Alison Bashford, "Eugenics and the Modern World," 11. They quoted Frank Dikötter, "Race Culture: Recent Perspectives on the History of Eugenics," *American Historical Review* 103, no. 2 (April 1998): 467, https://doi.org/10.2307/2649776

43. Philippa Levine and Alison Bashford, "Eugenics and the Modern World," 4.

44. Philippa Levine and Alison Bashford, "Eugenics and the Modern World," 14.

45. Philippa Levine and Alison Bashford, "Eugenics and the Modern World," 11.

46. Philippa Levine and Alison Bashford, "Eugenics and the Modern World," 5.

47. Zygmunt Bauman, *Modernity and the Holocaust* (Ithaca, NY: Cornell University Press, 1989), 89, 13.

48. Bauman, *Modernity and the Holocaust*, 18.

49. Bauman, *Modernity and the Holocaust*, 89.

50. Bauman, *Modernity and the Holocaust*, xii.

51. Bauman, *Modernity and the Holocaust*, 8.

52. Philippa Levine and Alison Bashford, "Eugenics and the Modern World," 9.

53. Philippa Levine and Alison Bashford, "Eugenics and the Modern World," 10.

54. Tzvetan Todorov, *Hope and Memory: Reflections on the Twentieth Century* (Princeton, NJ: Princeton University Press, 2003; London: Atlantic, 2014), 312.

55. Philippa Levine and Alison Bashford, "Eugenics and the Modern World," 12.

56. Philippa Levine and Alison Bashford, "Eugenics and the Modern World," 12.

57. Nikolas Rose, *Politics of Life Itself*, 54.

58. Nikolas Rose, *Politics of Life Itself*, 58.

59. Nikolas Rose, *Politics of Life Itself*, 59.

60. Nikolas Rose, *Politics of Life Itself*, 54.

61. See, for example, Chase, *Legacy of Malthus*, 115.

62. For examples of discussions of membership, see Mehler, "History of the American Eugenics." Mehler provides biographical information about AES members in an appendix to the dissertation. Also the lists maintained by Eugenics Watch: "The American Eugenics Society: Members, Officers and Directors Activities Database," Eugenics Watch, November 8, 2005, http://www.archive.org/details/The_American_Eugenics_Society__Members_Officers_And_Directors_Activites_Database; and Black, *War against the Weak*, 90–95.

63. Mehler, "History of the American Eugenics," 31.

64. Black, *War against the Weak*, 75.

65. Philippa Levine and Alison Bashford, "Eugenics and the Modern World," 13.

66. Daniel J. Kevles, "Here Comes the Master Race," review of *War against the Weak*, by Edwin Black, *New York Times*, October 5, 2003, late edition, sec. 7, 8, https://www.nytimes.com/2003/10/05/books/here-comes-the-master-race.html

67. Kevles, *In the Name of Eugenics*, 73.

68. Kevles, *In the Name of Eugenics*, 73. Christine Rosen confirms that Protestants were the most numerous and most enthusiastic participants in eugenics. See Rosen, *Preaching Eugenics*, 15.

69. Rosen, *Preaching Eugenics*, 4.

70. "Joseph Lewis," Freedom from Religion Foundation, accessed June 7, 2017, https://ffrf.org/news/day/dayitems/item/14432-joseph-lewis

71. Mehler, "History of the American Eugenics," 31.

72. J. B. Eggen was among the outspoken critics of eugenics who also criticized Seashore's work. See J. B. Eggen, "The Fallacy of Eugenics," *Social Forces* 5, no. 1 (September 1926): 104–9, www.jstor.org/stable/3004817. For a sampling of discussions of the opponents of eugenics, see Selden, *Inheriting Shame*, 106–26; Philippa Levine and Alison Bashford, "Eugenics and the Modern World," 19; Kevles, *In the Name of Eugenics*, 113–42; and Black, *War against the Weak*, 99.

73. Black, *War against the Weak*, 99.

74. Rosen, *Preaching Eugenics*, 17; Sharon Mara Leon, "Beyond Birth Control: Catholic Responses to the Eugenics Movement in the United States, 1900–1950," order no. 3142627 (PhD diss., University of Minnesota, 2004), https://search-proquest-com.ezproxy.library.wisc.edu/pqdtglobal/docview/305158996/fulltextPDF/1269932D352428FPQ/1?accountid=465

75. Kevles, *In the Name of Eugenics*, 119.

76. Ann Marie Ryan and Alan Stoskopf, "Public and Catholic School Responses to IQ Testing in the Early 20th Century," *Teachers College Record* 110, no. 4 (2008), https://www.tcrecord.org/content.asp?contentid=14623

77. Winfield, "Eugenic Ideology," 144.

78. Black, *War against the Weak*, 70.

79. [Wilhelm] Frick, "German Population and Race Politics," trans. A. Hellmer, *Eugenical News* 19, no. 2 (March-April 1934): 33.

80. Frick, "German Population and Race," 33–38.

81. Count [Georges Vacher] de Lapouge, "A French View: A Study of National Policies Which Purpose to Influence Eugenical Trends along Definitely Pre-Determined Lines," *Eugenical News* 19, no. 2 (March-April 1934): 39.

82. de Lapouge, "French View," 39.

83. de Lapouge, "French View," 39.

84. de Lapouge, "French View," 39.

85. "Jewish Physicians in Berlin," *Eugenical News* 19, no. 5 (September-October 1934): 126.

86. "Jewish Physicians in Berlin," 126.

87. "Hitler and Race Pride," *Eugenical News* 17, no. 2 (March-April 1932): 60–61.

88. Black, *War against the Weak*, 274.

89. Leon F. Whitney, "Leon Fradley Whitney Autobiography," 1971 [p. 205], Mss.B.W613b, Archives, American Philosophical Society Library, Philadelphia, PA.

90. Black, *War against the Weak*, 318.

91. For further discussion of this flow and a critique of Black, see Kevles, "Here Comes," 8.

92. John Marshall, "Pansies, Perverts and Macho Men: Changing Conceptions of the Modern Homosexual," in *The Making of the Modern Homosexual*, ed. Kenneth Plummer (London: Hutchinson, 1981), 249n6.

93. Ivan Hannaford, *Race: The History of an Idea in the West* (Washington, DC: Woodrow Wilson Center; Baltimore: Johns Hopkins, 1996), 8.

94. Hannaford, *Race: The History*, 187.

95. Hannaford, *Race: The History*, 6.

96. *Oxford English Dictionary Online*, s.v. "race [n.6]," accessed June 27, 2018, http:// www-oed-com.ezproxy.library.wisc.edu/view/Entry/157031?rskey=9PbHku&result=6&isAdvanced=false#eid

97. Hannaford, *Race: The History*, 55.

98. Hannaford, *Race: The History*, 21.

99. Ibram X. Kendi, *Stamped from the Beginning: The Definitive History of Racist Ideas in America* (New York: Nation Books, 2016), 17.

100. Kendi, *Stamped from the Beginning*, 18.

101. Kendi, *Stamped from the Beginning*, 16.

102. Kendi, *Stamped from the Beginning*, 22.

103. Kendi, *Stamped from the Beginning*, 22.

104. Kendi, *Stamped from the Beginning*, 22–23.
105. Kendi, *Stamped from the Beginning*, 23–24.
106. Kendi, *Stamped from the Beginning*, 19.
107. Hannaford, *Race: The History*, 222.
108. Johann Friedrich Blumenbach, "On the Natural Variety of Mankind [*De Generis Humani Varietate Nativa Liber* (1775)]," in *The Anthropological Treatises of Johann Friedrich Blumenbach*, trans. and ed. Thomas Bendyshe (London: Longman, Green, Longman, Roberts, and Green, 1865), 122. Blumenbach also used the classificatory term "mulatto." See p. 112.
109. Galton, "Hereditary Talent and Character: Second Paper," 320.
110. Galton, "Hereditary Talent and Character: Second Paper," 321.
111. Paul Popenoe and Roswell Hill Johnson, *Applied Eugenics* (New York: Macmillan, 1920), 238.
112. Charles W. Mills, *The Racial Contract* (Ithaca, NY: Cornell University Press, 1997), 78.
113. Charles Mills, *Racial Contract*, 56.
114. W. E. Burghardt Du Bois, "Race Relations in the United States," *Annals of the American Academy of Political and Social Science* 140, no. 229 (November 1928): 6, https://www.jstor.org/stable/1016826
115. Du Bois, "Race Relations," 6.
116. Du Bois, "Race Relations," 6.
117. Carl E. Seashore, "Three New Approaches to the Study of Negro Music," *Annals of the American Academy of Political and Social Science* 140, no. 229 (November 1928): 191–92, https://www.jstor.org/stable/1016848
118. Yale S. Nathanson, "The Musical Ability of the Negro," *Annals of the American Academy of Political and Social Science* 140, no. 229 (November 1928): 186–90, https://www.jstor.org/stable/1016847
119. Joseph Peterson, "Methods of Investigating Comparative Abilities in Races," *Annals of the American Academy of Political and Social Science* 140, no. 229 (November 1928): 178–85, https://www.jstor.org/stable/1016846
120. Judith Butler, *Bodies That Matter: On the Discursive Limits of "Sex"* (New York: Routledge, 1993), 3, 6.
121. Butler, *Bodies That Matter*, 9.
122. Butler, *Bodies That Matter*, 1.
123. Butler, *Bodies That Matter*, 2.
124. Butler, *Bodies That Matter*, 16.
125. Butler, *Bodies That Matter*, 16.
126. Butler, *Bodies That Matter*, 16.
127. Butler, *Bodies That Matter*, 8.
128. Butler, *Bodies That Matter*, 1, 9.
129. Ian Hacking, "Making Up People," in *Reconstructing Individualism: Autonomy, Individuality, and the Self in Western Thought*, ed. Thomas C. Heller, Morton Sosna, and David E. Wellbery (Stanford: Stanford University Press, 1986), 222.

130. Hacking, "Making Up People," 222–23.
131. Hacking, "Making Up People," 223.
132. Hacking, "Making Up People," 225.
133. Hacking, "Making Up People," 222.
134. Hacking, "Making Up People," 228.
135. Hacking, "Making Up People," 236.
136. Hacking, "Making Up People," 226.
137. Hacking, "Making Up People," 226.
138. Hacking, "Making Up People," 234.
139. Hacking, "Making Up People," 223.
140. Hacking, "Making Up People," 229.
141. Hacking, "Making Up People," 226.
142. The second vector is the "autonomous behavior of the person so labeled." See Hacking, "Making Up People," 234.
143. "History of Agricultural Statistics," USDA National Agricultural Statistics Service, last modified May 4, 2018, https://www.nass.usda.gov/About_NASS/History_of_Ag_Statistics/
144. See, for example, "Statistics and Eugenics," Dickinson College Wiki, last modified December 9, 2009, http://wiki.dickinson.edu/index.php/Statistics_and_Eugenics
145. For a few representative examples, see Paul Popenoe and Roswell Johnson, *Applied Eugenics*, 238; "Non-Fecundity of the Fit," *Eugenical News* 5, no. 8 (August 1920): 60; and Carl E. Seashore, "Individual and Racial Inheritance of Musical Traits," in *Eugenics, Genetics and the Family, vol. 1, Scientific Papers of the Second International Congress of Eugenics; Held at American Museum of Natural History, New York, September 22–28, 1921* (Baltimore, MD: Williams & Wilkins, 1923; repr., ed. Charles Rosenberg, New York: Garland Publishing, 1985), 237.
146. Georges Canguilhem, *The Normal and the Pathological* (New York: Zone Books, 1989), 119, 203. Canguilhem's quotation about normal being a judgment of value comes from M. Henri Ey, who was quoted in a discussion that followed an article by Eugène Minkowski. See Eugène Minkowski, "A la recherche de la norme en psychopathologie," *L'Évolution-Psychiatrique* 1 (1938): 93.
147. Winfield, *Eugenics and Education*, xvii.
148. Charles White, *An Account of the Regular Gradation in Man, and in Different Animals and Vegetables; and from the Former to the Latter* (London: C. Dilly, 1799), 42, https://archive.org/details/b24924507
149. Charles White, *Account of the Regular Gradation*, 137.
150. Charles Mills, *Racial Contract*, 23.
151. Charles Mills, *Racial Contract*, 23.
152. Charles Mills, *Racial Contract*, 27.
153. Charles Mills, *Racial Contract*, 11.
154. Charles Mills, *Racial Contract*, 11.
155. Charles Mills, *Racial Contract*, 127.
156. Zeus Leonardo and Alicia A. Broderick, "Smartness as Property: A Critical

Exploration of Intersections between Whiteness and Disability Studies," *Teachers College Record* 113, no. 10 (2011): 2206–32, http://www.tcrecord.org.ezproxy.library.wisc.edu/library/content.asp?contentid=16431

157. Thomas S. Popkewitz, *Cosmopolitanism and the Age of School Reform: Science, Education, and Making Society by Making the Child* (New York: Routledge, 2008), 4.

158. Popkewitz, *Cosmopolitanism and the Age*, xiv.

159. Popkewitz, *Cosmopolitanism and the Age*, xiv.

160. Michel Foucault, *Discipline and Punish: The Birth of the Prison*, trans. Alan Sheridan (New York: Vintage Books, 1979), 184.

161. Foucault, *Discipline and Punish*, 184.

162. For a discussion of calculating the value of life, see Nikolas Rose, "Biopolitics in the Twenty First Century: Notes for a Research Agenda," *Distinktion: Scandinavian Journal of Social Theory* 2, no. 3 (2001): 27.

163. Canguilhem, *Normal and the Pathological*, 119. He quotes Ey as found in Minkowski, "A la recherche de la norme," 93.

164. Nikolas Rose, "Biopolitics in the Twenty First Century," 27.

165. Popkewitz, *Cosmopolitanism and the Age*, 40.

166. Leonard Darwin, "The Aims and Methods of Eugenical Societies," in *Eugenics, Genetics and the Family*, vol. 1, *Scientific Papers of the Second International Congress of Eugenics; Held at American Museum of Natural History, New York, September 22–28, 1921* (Baltimore, MD: Williams & Wilkins, 1923; repr., ed. Charles Rosenberg, New York: Garland Publishing, 1985), 7.

167. Philippa Levine and Alison Bashford, "Eugenics and the Modern World," 5.

168. Giorgio Agamben, *State of Exception*, trans. Kevin Attell (Chicago: University of Chicago Press, 2005).

169. Agamben, *State of Exception*, 2.

170. Agamben, *State of Exception*, 6.

171. Agamben, *State of Exception*, 2.

172. "Eugenics," 1921, Cold Spring Harbor, E.06 Eug-2, Exhibits Book-Second Int. Ex. of Eugenics, p. 15, titled "'Copy of Certificate Awarded for Meritorious Exhibits,' at the Second International Congress of Eugenics," image 543, in the "Image Archive on the American Eugenics Movement," DNA Learning Center, Cold Spring Harbor Laboratory, accessed September 23, 2018, www.eugenicsarchive.org/eugenics/view_image.pl?id=543; "Controlling Heredity: The American Eugenics Crusade 1870–1940, International Eugenics Congresses, Eugenics Tree, 1932 [page 510]," Special Collections and Rare Books, University of Missouri, last modified March 16, 2012, https://library.missouri.edu/exhibits/eugenics/congresses.htm

173. Galton, "Eugenics: Its Definition," 5.

174. Rosen, Preaching Eugenics, 4.

175. Rosen, *Preaching Eugenics*, 4–5, 14.

176. Rosen, *Preaching Eugenics*, 5, 8, 9.

177. Rosen, *Preaching Eugenics*, 15.

178. Carl E. Seashore, "Sectioning Classes," 356.

179. "Westminster Confession of Faith [1646] Chapter III: Of God's Eternal Decree," Center for Reformed Theology and Apologetics, accessed September 24, 2014, https://reformed.org/documents/wcf_with_proofs/ (link now goes elsewhere). See Articles 3, 4, and 6.

180. Albert Edward Wiggam, Frederick Osborn, and Leon F. Whitney, "Is Eugenics 'Scientific Calvinism'? Is It Biological Predestination?" *Eugenics* 3, no. 1 (1930): 18.

181. Albert Wiggam, Frederick Osborn, and Leon Whitney, "Is Eugenics 'Scientific Calvinism'?" 18–19.

182. Albert Wiggam, Frederick Osborn, and Leon Whitney, "Is Eugenics 'Scientific Calvinism'?" 19.

183. Albert Wiggam, Frederick Osborn, and Leon Whitney, "Is Eugenics 'Scientific Calvinism'?" 19.

184. Walter Lippmann, "The Abuse of the Tests (IV)," *New Republic* 32, no. 415 (November 15, 1922): 297–98.

185. John White, "Puritan Intelligence: The Ideological Background to IQ," *Oxford Review of Education* 31, no. 3 (September 2005): 423, https://doi.org/10.1080/03054980500222148

186. John White, "Puritan Intelligence," 427.

187. John White, "Puritan Intelligence," 428–36.

188. John White, "Puritan Intelligence," 428–36, 423.

189. John White, "Puritan Intelligence," 424. He quoted himself from John White, "Intelligence—the New Puritanism," *Times Educational Supplement*, October 24, 1969, 4. In the original, he used the word "conceptions" rather than "notions."

190. Mehler, "History of the American Eugenics," 423.

191. See, for example, John White, "Puritan Intelligence," 428, 430.

192. John White, "Puritan Intelligence," 433.

193. John White, "Puritan Intelligence," 426.

194. John White, "Puritan Intelligence," 435.

195. James Boyce, *Born Bad: Original Sin and the Making of the Western World* (Berkeley, CA: Counterpoint, 2015), 10–11, accessed February 7, 2017, ProQuest EBook Central, http://site.ebrary.com/lib/wisconsin/reader.action?docID=11054861; James Boyce, "The Imprint of Original Sin on Western Culture," interview by Steve Paulson, *To the Best of Our Knowledge*, Wisconsin Public Radio, February 5, 2017, audio, 12:21, http://archive.ttbook.org/book/imprint-original-sin-western-culture

196. Boyce, *Born Bad*, 3–4; Boyce, "Imprint of Original Sin."

197. Boyce, *Born Bad*, 4; Boyce, "Imprint of Original Sin."

198. Boyce, "Imprint of Original Sin."

199. Boyce, "Imprint of Original Sin."

200. Rosen, *Preaching Eugenics*, 17.

201. Todorov, *Hope and Memory*, xx.

202. Todorov, *Hope and Memory*, xx.

203. Todorov, *Hope and Memory*, xx.

204. Ilaria Ramelli, *The Christian Doctrine of* Apokatastasis: *A Critical Assessment from the New Testament to Eriugena* (Leiden, Netherlands: Brill, 2013), 819, https://doi-org.ezproxy.library.wisc.edu/10.1163/9789004245709

205. Ramelli, *Christian Doctrine*, 817.

206. Edward T. Oakes, "Christ's Descent into Hell: The *Hopeful* Universalism of Hans Urs von Balthasar," in *"All Shall Be Well": Explorations in Universalism and Christian Theology from Origen to Moltmann*, ed. Gregory MacDonald (Cambridge, UK: James Clarke, 2011), 380. ProQuest Ebook Central. https://ebookcentral.proquest.com/lib/wisc/reader.action?docID=3328652

207. Gregory MacDonald, "Introduction: Between Heresy and Dogma," in *"All Shall Be Well": Explorations in Universalism and Christian Theology from Origen to Moltmann*, ed. Gregory MacDonald (Cambridge, UK: James Clarke, 2011), 10, ProQuest Ebook Central. https://ebookcentral.proquest.com/lib/wisc/reader.action?docID=3328652. MacDonald cites Augustine, *Enchiridion; or Faith, Hope, and Love*, trans. J. F. Shaw, http://www.leaderu.com/cyber/books/augenchiridion.enchiridiontoc.html (link discontinued). I located a similar translation: "It is in vain, then, that some, indeed very many, make moan over the eternal punishment, and perpetual, unintermitted torments of the lost, and say they do not believe it shall be so; not, indeed, that they directly oppose themselves to Holy Scripture, but, at the suggestion of their own feelings, they soften down everything that seems hard, and give a milder turn to statements which they think are rather designed to terrify than to be received as literally true. For 'God,' they say, 'will not forget to be gracious, nor will He, in anger, shut up His tender mercies.'" See Augustine, *The Enchiridion: On Faith, Hope and Love*, ed. Henry Paolucci, trans. J. F. Shaw (Chicago: Henry Regnery, 1961), chapter 112, 129–30.

208. See, for example, Oakes, "Christ's Descent," 384.

209. Richard Bauckham, "Universalism: A Historical Survey," *Themelios* 4, no. 2 (September 1978): 47, https://www.theologicalstudies.org.uk/article_universalism_bauckham.html

210. MacDonald, "Introduction: Between Heresy," 11–12.

211. MacDonald, "Introduction: Between Heresy," 12.

212. Popkewitz, *Cosmopolitanism and the Age*, 4.

213. Carl E. Seashore, "Religious Music in the Public School Choruses," *Music Educators Journal* 28, no. 1 (September-October 1941): 60, http://www.jstor.org/stable/3385847

214. Rosen, *Preaching Eugenics*, 9.

215. Rosen, *Preaching Eugenics*, 17.

216. Foucault, *History of Sexuality*, 102.

217. Galton, "Hereditary Talent and Character: Part I," 165.

218. Todorov, *Hope and Memory*, xx.

219. Tara Fitzpatrick, "The Figure of Captivity: The Cultural Work of the

Puritan Captivity Narrative," *American Literary History* 3, no. 1 (Spring 1991): 4, http://www.jstor.org/stable/489730. See also, for example, the writings of the Latter Day Saints prophet Joseph Smith.

220. "Stirpiculture," *The Circular*, n.s., 2, no. 3 (April 3, 1865): 17.

221. See, for example, Wikipedia, s.v. "Oneida Stirpiculture," accessed May 23, 2016, https://en.wikipedia.org/wiki/Oneida_stirpiculture. See also "Stirpiculture," 17, for an Oneidan reference to stirpiculture; and G., "Improved Breeding by Selection," *The Circular*, n.s., 2, no. 2 (March 27, 1865): 10, for reference to Darwin.

222. Wikipedia, s.v. "Oneida Stirpiculture"; Laurence E. Karp, "Past Perfect: John Humphrey Noyes, Stirpiculture, and the Oneida Community—Part II," *American Journal of Medical Genetics* 12, no. 2 (June 1982): 127, http://onlinelibrary.wiley.com/doi/10.1002/ajmg.1320120202/pdf

223. Mehler, "History of the American Eugenics," 61.

224. Darwin, "Aims and Methods," 7.

225. Darwin, "Aims and Methods," 8.

226. Darwin, "Aims and Methods," 10.

227. Darwin, "Aims and Methods," 10.

228. Darwin, "Aims and Methods," 10.

229. Steven Selden, "Biological Determinism and the Narrative of Adjustment: The High School Biology Textbooks of Truman Jesse Moon, c. 1921–1963," *Curriculum Inquiry* 37, no. 2 (June 2007): 159–96, http://www.jstor.org/stable/30054793

230. Clyde Chitty, *Eugenics, Race and Intelligence in Education* (London: Continuum, 2009), 118, ProQuest Ebook Central, https://ebookcentral.proquest.com/lib/wisc/detail.action?docID=742332

231. Kimberlé Crenshaw, "Demarginalizing the Intersection of Race and Sex: A Black Feminist Critique of Antidiscrimination Doctrine, Feminist Theory and Antiracist Politics," *University of Chicago Legal Forum* (1989): 139–40, https://heinonline-org.ezproxy.library.wisc.edu/HOL/P?h=hein.journals/uchclf1989&i=143

232. Michael Jackson, *At Home in the World* (Durham, NC: Duke University Press, 1995), 149.

233. Michael Jackson, *At Home in the World*, 66.

234. Michael Jackson, *At Home in the World*, 64.

235. Michael Jackson, *At Home in the World*, 122.

236. Michael Omi and Howard Winant, "On the Theoretical Status of the Concept of Race," in *Race, Identity, and Representation in Education*, ed. Cameron McCarthy and Warren Crichlow (New York: Routledge, 1993), 7.

237. Daniel Charles Warrick, "The Establishment of the Study of Fine Arts at the State University of Iowa during the Administration of Walter A. Jessup and Carl E. Seashore" (PhD diss., University of Missouri–Columbia, 1995), 163n42, incorrectly stated that the year of the fire was 1956. The year 1956 was after Seashore's death. University of Iowa archivist David McCarthy located a 1977 letter from his predecessor, Earl Rogers, indicating that a good portion of Seashore's

papers were destroyed in a 1946 fire. For information about the fire, see "Three-Hour Blaze Destroys Portion of East Hall," *Daily Iowan*, 78, no. 202, May 17, 1946, 1, 7.

238. Miles, "Carl Emil Seashore, 1866–1949," 263–316.

Chapter 3

1. Carl E. Seashore, "Carl Emil Seashore," vol. 1, *A History of Psychology in Autobiography*, ed. Carl Allanmore Murchison (Worcester, MA: Clark University, 1930), 229, 236, 238, 239.

2. Carl E. Seashore, "Carl Emil Seashore," 240, 246.

3. Carl E. Seashore, "Carl Emil Seashore," 240, 246. Statistics on Gustavus's second graduating class were provided by archivist Adrianna Darden in an email message to the author, March 4, 2020.

4. Carl E. Seashore, "Carl Emil Seashore," 240–46.

5. Carl E. Seashore, "Carl Emil Seashore," 244.

6. Carl E. Seashore, "Carl Emil Seashore," 247.

7. Carl E. Seashore, "Carl Emil Seashore," 247.

8. Carl E. Seashore, "Carl Emil Seashore," 252.

9. Carl E. Seashore, "Carl Emil Seashore," 252–53; Carl E. Seashore, "Psychology and Life in Autobiography," typed manuscript, pp. 203–7, RG 99.0164, box 2, Carl E. Seashore Papers, Special Collections and University Archives, University of Iowa Libraries, Iowa City, IA; Walter R. Miles, "Carl Emil Seashore, 1866–1949," vol. 29, *Biographical Memoirs* (New York: Columbia University Press for the National Academy of Sciences, 1956), 269.

10. George D. Stoddard, "Carl Emil Seashore: 1866–1949," *American Journal of Psychology* 63, no. 3 (July 1950): 456, www.jstor.org/stable/1418021

11. "Department History—the Iowa Tradition," University of Iowa Department of Psychological and Brain Sciences, accessed December 12, 2018, https://psychology.uiowa.edu/about/department-history%E2%80%94-iowa-tradition

12. "Alumni Register Number, 1847–1911 [College of Liberal Arts]," *Iowa Alumnus* 8, no. 10 (September 1911): 51, https://books.google.com/books?id=MlBGAAAAYAAJ&pg=PA51&lpg=PA51&dq=mary+roberta+holmes+carl+seashore&source=bl&ots=DEJv_GxHpy&sig=mZAkwwfr2cHiFdMKNfdBKZfJwYk&hl=en&sa=X&ei=R7ZxVYKiJI7ZoAT9g4LIDQ&ved=0CCgQ6AEwBDgK#v=onepage&q=mary%20roberta%20holmes%20carl%20seashore&f=false. Her name is listed (apparently incorrectly) as Mabel; she is also listed as Mrs. Carl E. Seashore.

13. Carl E. Seashore, "Carl Emil Seashore," 258–59; Carl E. Seashore, "An Open Letter: Addressed to Women in Graduate Schools," *Journal of Higher Education* 13, no. 5 (May 1942): 240, https://doi.org/10.2307/1974933; Carl E. Seashore, "Psychology and Life," p. 248, RG 99.0164, box 2, Carl E. Seashore Papers.

14. "Department History—the Iowa Tradition."

15. Leonard D. Goodstein, "The Iowa Department of Psychology and the American Psychological Association: A Historical Analysis," in *Psychology at Iowa:*

Centennial Essays, ed. Joan H. Cantor (Hillsdale, NJ: Lawrence Erlbaum, 1991), 53. A 1936 letter to President Jessup suggests that Seashore may not have been completely happy about retiring. See E. A. Gilmore to W. A. Jessup, New York, NY, April 21, 1936, RG 05.01.10, box 30, folder 17, Eugene A. Gilmore Papers, Special Collections and University Archives, University of Iowa, Iowa City, IA.

16. Goodstein, "Iowa Department of Psychology," 54–55; Alan S. Kornspan, "Contributions to Sports Psychology: Walter R. Miles and the Early Studies on the Motor Skills of Athletes," *Comprehensive Psychology* 3, article 17 (2014): 5, https://journals.sagepub.com/doi/pdf/10.2466/32.CP.3.17

17. Carl E. Seashore, "Carl Emil Seashore," 256, 258; Carl E. Seashore, "Psychology and Life," p. 246, RG 99.0164, box 2, Carl E. Seashore Papers; Miles, "Carl Emil Seashore, 1866–1949," 272; Goodstein, "Iowa Department of Psychology," 55; Milton Metfessel, "Carl Emil Seashore, 1866–1949," *Science* 111, no. 2896 (June 30, 1950): 716, http://www.jstor.org/stable/1677658

18. Carl E. Seashore, "Carl Emil Seashore," 256–57; Metfessel, "Carl Emil Seashore, 1866–1949," 716; "Dr. Carl Seashore . . . World Famed Gustavus Graduate Dies," *Greater Gustavus Quarterly* (December 1949): 14; Carl E. Seashore, "Psychology and Life," p. 246, RG 99.0164, box 2, Carl E. Seashore Papers.

19. Carl E. Seashore, "Carl Emil Seashore," 257; Carl E. Seashore, "Psychology and Life," p. 247, RG 99.0164, box 2, Carl E. Seashore Papers; Miles, "Carl Emil Seashore, 1866–1949," 272.

20. "Two Profs Attend Seashore Service," *Gustavian Weekly*, October 28, 1949, 1; Carl E. Seashore, "Psychology and Life," p. 246, RG 99.0164, box 2, Carl E. Seashore Papers; Metfessel, "Carl Emil Seashore, 1866–1949," 716.

21. "Lewin Center Founders," Lewin Center, accessed January 13, 2019, http://www.lewincenter.org/founders.html (site redesigned; see Wayback Machine).

22. Kornspan, "Contributions to Sports," 6; Goodstein, "Iowa Department of Psychology," 55.

23. Sources do not agree on the number of works he wrote, but all estimates are higher than 240 books and articles. Seashore liked to recycle articles—publishing versions of the same essay in multiple sources. Some of these versions were almost identical, and others were quite different. Tracking changes in these versions proved to be an interesting but sometimes challenging project, which was compounded by the fact that he also recycled his work by cutting small sections of one article and pasting them into another quite different article. Furthermore, some of his works were reprinted. These factors may help explain why there are varying reports on the precise size of his oeuvre.

24. For example, he was called giant and a titan in such sources as George W. Crane, "A Tribute" [preface to] *Our Children in the Atomic Age*, by Henry H. Goddard (Mellott, IN: Hopkins Syndicate, 1948), i, http://babel.hathitrust.org/cgi/wayf?target=https%3A%2F%2Fbabel.hathitrust.org%2Fcgi%2Fpt%3Fid%3Dcoo.31924014089894%3Bq1%3Dour%2520children%2520in%2520the%2520atomic%2520age%3Bpage%3Droot%3Bseq%3D9%3Bview%3D1up%3Bsize%3D100%3Borient%3D0. See also Leila Zenderland, *Measuring Minds: Henry Herbert*

Goddard and the Origins of American Intelligence Testing (Cambridge, UK: Cambridge University Press, 1998), 340; Goodstein, "Iowa Department of Psychology," 53; and R. W. Lundin, "Seashore, Carl Emil (1866–1949)," vol. 3, *Encyclopedia of Psychology*, ed. Raymond J. Corsini (New York: John Wiley and Sons, 1984), 279.

25. See Carl E. Seashore, *Pioneering in Psychology*, University of Iowa Studies: Series on Aims and Progress of Research, no. 70 (Iowa City: University of Iowa, 1942), https://babel.hathitrust.org/cgi/pt?id=mdp.39015020052349&view=1up&seq=1; Carl E. Seashore, "Carl Emil Seashore," 259.

26. Miles, "Carl Emil Seashore, 1866–1949," 269.

27. Carl E. Seashore, "The Experimental Study of Mental Fatigue," *Psychological Bulletin* 1, no. 4 (March 15, 1904): 97–101, http://dx.doi.org/10.1037/h0069868

28. Carl E. Seashore, "Communications and Discussions: The Mid-Day Nap," *Journal of Educational Psychology* 1, no. 5 (May 1910): 293–95, doi.org/10.1037/h0070095

29. See Miles, "Carl Emil Seashore, 1866–1949," 272, for further discussion. For example, he did not invent the audiometer but he improved it. See "The American Speech Correction Association Presents the Honors of the Association to Carl Emil Seashore," *Journal of Speech Disorders* 10, no. 1 (March 1945): 2.

30. For example, see Carl E. Seashore, "Some Psychological Statistics: IV. Hearing-Ability and Discriminative Sensibility for Pitch," vol. 2, *The University of Iowa Studies in Psychology*, ed. George T. W. Patrick (Iowa City: University of Iowa, 1899), 55–64, https://books.google.com/books?id=0pRIAAAAYAAJ&pg=PA55&dq=university+of+iowa+studies+in+psychology+hearing+ability&hl=en&sa=X&ved=0CDYQ6AEwAWoVChMIwJy7–4GVxwIVQh4eCh1Wow3b#v=onepage&q=university%20of%20iowa%20studies%20in%20psychology%20hearing%20ability&f=false; and Carl E. Seashore, "Some Psychological Statistics: V. Motor Ability, Reaction-Time, Rhythm, and Time Sense," vol. 2, *The University of Iowa Studies in Psychology*, ed. George T. W. Patrick (Iowa City: University of Iowa, 1899), 64–84, https://books.google.com/books?id=0pRIAAAAYAAJ&pg=PA55&dq=university+of+iowa+studies+in+psychology+hearing+ability&hl=en&sa=X&ved=0CDYQ6AEwAWoVChMIwJy7–4GVxwIVQh4eCh1Wow3b#v=onepage&q=reaction-time&f=false. Consistent with these research interests, he was a member of the Acoustical Society of America. See "American Speech Correction Association," 2.

31. Carl E. Seashore, "Whither Ahead of Science in Music," *Education* 67, no. 3 (November 1946): 152.

32. Carl E. Seashore, *Pioneering in Psychology*, 75.

33. Carl E. Seashore, *Pioneering in Psychology*, 76.

34. Carl E. Seashore, *Pioneering in Psychology*, 76.

35. C. W. Shilling, "The Development of Methods for the Selection of Sound Listening Personnel" (New London, CT: Medical Research Laboratory, U.S. Naval Submarine Base, March 1, 1942), 5–6, Rubicon Research Repository, http://archive.rubicon-foundation.org/7395

36. Scott R. Ross et al., "Detecting Insufficient Effort Using the Seashore Rhythm and Speech-Sounds Perception Tests in Head Injury," *Clinical Neuropsychologist* 20, no. 4 (2006): 798–815, https://doi.org/10.1080/13854040500328477

37. Kelly L. Curtis et al., "Criterion Groups Validation of the Seashore Rhythm Test and Speech Sounds Perception Test for the Detection of Malingering in Traumatic Brain Injury," *Clinical Neuropsychologist* 24, no. 5 (2010): 882–97.

38. M. Paula Roncaglia-Denissen et al., "Enhanced Musical Rhythmic Perception in Turkish Early and Late Learners of German," *Frontiers in Psychology* 4, no. 645 (September 20, 2013), 1–8, https://www.ncbi.nlm.nih.gov/pmc/articles/PMC3778315/

39. Robert A. Leark, Tammy R. Dupuy, Lawrence M. Greenberg, Carol L. Kindschi, and Steven J. Hughes, *T.O.V.A. Professional Manual: Test of Variables of Attention Continuous Performance Test*, ed. no. 8.2–135-ge19058 (Los Alamitos, CA: TOVA, March 28, 2016), 50–51, http://files.tovatest.com/documentation/8/Professional%20Manual.pdf; "The Test of Variables of Attention (T.O.V.A.)," TOVA Company, accessed May 5, 2019, https://www.tovatest.com/

40. "American Speech Correction Association," 2; "Seashore Honored," *Iowa Alumnus* 19, no. 1 (October 1920): 18, https://books.google.com/books?id=E35IAQAAMAAJ&pg=PA18&lpg=PA18&dq=carl+seashore+national+research+council&source=bl&ots=Jr6dotci26&sig=ljYe1eb2Zgcr_KxVq-hwpVLuG3k&hl=en&sa=X&ei=XrtwVYaTO4mQoQSi7oLADQ&ved=0CC0Q6AEwAg#v=onepage&q=carl%20seashore%20national%20research%20council&f=false; Hamilton Cravens, *Before Head Start: The Iowa Station and America's Children* (Chapel Hill: University of North Carolina Press, 1993), 41. However, some sources state he chaired from 1920–21. See Miles, "Carl Emil Seashore, 1866–1949," 292; Barry Alan Mehler, "A History of the American Eugenics Society, 1921–1940" (PhD diss., University of Illinois at Urbana-Champaign, 1988), 423, http://search.proquest.com.ezproxy.library.wisc.edu/docview/303689028?accountid=465; and Carl E. Seashore, "Psychology and Life," p. 76, RG 99.0164, box 2, Carl E. Seashore Papers. The official NRC annual reports stated that he was on the executive committee in 1919, was the vice-chairman in 1920, and was the chairman from 1921 to 1922. See *Fourth Annual Report of the National Research Council* [for 1919] (Washington, DC: Government Printing Office, 1920), 63, https://babel.hathitrust.org/cgi/pt?id=chi.20811221&view=1up&seq=149; *Fifth Annual Report of the National Research Council* [for 1920] (Washington, DC: Government Printing Office, 1921), 77, https://babel.hathitrust.org/cgi/pt?id=chi.20811221&view=1up&seq=231; and *Report of the National Research Council for the Year July 1, 1921–June 30, 1922* (Washington, DC: Government Printing Office, 1923), 80, https://books.google.com/books?id=7bim-5iK8IcC&pg=PA45&lpg=PA45&dq=committee+on+psychology+and+anthropology+NRC+carl+seashore&source=bl&ots=SPfUVb86ut&sig=ACfU3U1qCiWZnVxebeq126–5kZdoBeUXOw&hl=en&sa=X&ved=2ahUKEwiAm6yptrjlAhWCna0KHZ49C98Q6AEwBnoECAgQAQ#v=onepage&q=seashore&f=false

41. Goodstein, "Iowa Department of Psychology," 55, incorrectly states that

Seashore was the first psychologist elected to the NAS. James McKeen Cattell was the first.

42. "American Speech Correction Association," 2.

43. Lundin, "Seashore, Carl Emil (1866–1949)," 279. Miles mentioned an unnamed laboratory textbook. See Miles, "Carl Emil Seashore, 1866–1949," 277.

44. James McKeen Cattell, "The Psychological Corporation," *Annals of the American Academy of Political and Social Science* 110 (November 1923): 165, https://www.jstor.org/stable/1015081. Cattell described Seashore as an elected director. An undated typed manuscript claims that together with Professor Walter Miles, Seashore was one of the originators of the Psychological Corporation, organized as a "Test Construction Agency for Psychologists," but that source may not be trustworthy. See Carl G. Seashore, "Life in the Seashore Family," undated unpublished manuscript, p. iii, RG 99.0164, box 3, Carl E. Seashore Papers, Special Collections and University Archives, University of Iowa Libraries, Iowa City, IA. Humphreys describes Seashore as a collaborator. See Jere T. Humphreys, "Musical Aptitude Testing: From James McKeen Cattell to Carl Emil Seashore," vol. 5, *Sage Directions in Educational Psychology*, ed. Neil J. Salkind (Los Angeles: Sage, 2011), 126, repr. from *Research Studies in Music Education* 10 (1998): 42–53.

45. See, for example, Goodstein, "Iowa Department of Psychology," 53; and Ernest R. Hilgard, "Psychology at Iowa before McGeoch and Spence," in *Psychology at Iowa: Centennial Essays*, ed. Joan H. Cantor (Hillsdale, NJ: Lawrence Erlbaum, 1991), 37–49.

46. George D. Stoddard, preface to *Pioneering in Psychology*, by Carl E. Seashore, University of Iowa Studies: Series on Aims and Progress of Research, no. 70 (Iowa City: University of Iowa, 1942), vii, https://babel.hathitrust.org/cgi/pt?id=mdp.39015020052349&view=1up&seq=1

47. Hilgard, "Psychology at Iowa," 39.

48. Howard H. Kendler, "The Iowa Tradition," in *Psychology at Iowa: Centennial Essays*, ed. Joan H. Cantor (Hillsdale, NJ: Lawrence Erlbaum, 1991), 3.

49. Kendler, "Iowa Tradition," 8.

50. Miles, "Carl Emil Seashore, 1866–1949," 280.

51. Stoddard, "Carl Emil Seashore: 1866–1949," 460; Kendler, "Iowa Tradition," 3; Cravens, *Before Head Start*.

52. Edwin G. Boring, *A History of Experimental Psychology* (New York: D. Appleton-Century, 1929), 646–47.

53. Lundin, "Seashore, Carl Emil (1866–1949)," 279.

54. *Emil's Epilogue*, online newsletter published by the Gustavus Adolphus College Department of Psychological Science, accessed July 22, 2015, https://gustavus.edu/psychology/newsletter/20121012.php

55. James V. Hinrichs, "Carl E. Seashore as Psychologist," in *Multidisciplinary Perspectives on Musicality: Essays from the Seashore Symposium*, ed. Kate Gfeller et al. (Iowa City: University of Iowa School of Music, 2006), 9. In the portion of the quotation I omitted, Hinrichs incorrectly claims that Seashore invented the

audiometer. Seashore may have improved the instrument, but the invention of the audiometer predates him.

56. Carl E. Seashore, "Some Psychological Statistics: IV. Hearing-Ability," 55–64.

57. Carl E. Seashore, "Some Psychological Statistics: V. Motor Ability," 64–84; Carl E. Seashore, "A Voice Tonoscope," vol. 3, *University of Iowa Studies in Psychology*, ed. George T. W. Patrick (Iowa City: University of Iowa, 1902), 18–28, https://books.google.com/books?id=NETWaMam5LMC&pg=RA1-PA145&lpg=RA1-PA145&dq=%22university+of+iowa+studies+in+psychology%22+seashore&source=bl&ots=ZsAhkg0oJi&sig=JmHwRQNo-YvgVrJUU-xGh631kX8&hl=en&sa=X&ved=0CCsQ6AEwBWoVChMIm8rL9Z-VxwIVAXUeCh1Wtwuv#v=onepage&q=tonoscope&f=false

58. Carl E. Seashore, "The Tonoscope and Its Use in the Training of the Voice," *The Musician* no. 11 (1906): 331–32.

59. Carl E. Seashore, "The Measurement of Musical Talent," *Musical Quarterly* 1, no. 1 (January 1915): 129–48, https://www.jstor.org/stable/738047

60. Carl E. Seashore, "How Psychology Can Help the Musician," *Etude* 35, no. 2 (February 1917): 89–90, https://books.google.com/books?id=IpgyAQAAMAAJ&pg=PA89&lpg=PA89&dq=etude++how+psychology+can+help+the+musician&source=bl&ots=tHDoVQu6_g&sig=d7_3e_W1UD8pNiZ_MakBANDHg3A&hl=en&sa=X&ved=0CCEQ6AEwAWoVChMI8pDg88nYxgIVEQySCh3pigIR#v=onepage&q=etude%20%20how%20psychology%20can%20help%20the%20musician&f=false

61. Carl E. Seashore, "Scientific Procedure in the Discovery of Musical Talent in the Public Schools," *Music Supervisors' Journal* 2, no. 3 (January 1916): 10–11, http://www.jstor.org/stable/3383174

62. Carl E. Seashore, "The Psychology of Music. X. Intonation in Violin Performance," *Music Educators Journal* 24, no. 2 (October-November 1937): 23–24, http://www.jstor.org/stable/3385168

63. Miles, "Carl Emil Seashore, 1866–1949," 314.

64. Charles M. Dennis, "For One World," *Music Educators Journal* 33, no. 2 (November-December 1946): 13, https://www.jstor.org/stable/3388394

65. "Necrology, Carl E. Seashore," *Music Educators Journal* 36, no. 2 (November-December 1949): 4, www.jstor.org/stable/3387486

66. The phrase "discerning general readers" comes from the current description of the journal. See "*The Musical Quarterly*: Information for Authors," Oxford University Press, accessed July 10, 2015, http://www.oxfordjournals.org/our_journals/musqtl/for_authors/ms_preparation.html

67. "Preliminary Program: Music Supervisors' National Conference, Saint Louis, Missouri [Front Matter]," *Music Supervisors' Journal* 5, no. 4 (March 1919): 10, http://www.jstor.org/stable/3382284; Carl E. Seashore, "Demonstration of Measurements of Musical Capacity," in *Journal of Proceedings of the Twelfth Annual Meeting of the Music Supervisors' National Conference Held at St. Louis, Missouri,*

March 30–April 4, 1919: 30, https://archive.org/details/journalofproceed005236mbp/page/n35; Carl E. Seashore, "Procedure in the Discovery and the Encouragement of Musical Talent in the Public Schools by Means of Measures of Musical Talent [Address and Discussion]," in *Journal of Proceedings of the Twelfth Annual Meeting of the Music Supervisors' National Conference Held at St. Louis, Missouri, March 30–April 4, 1919*: 30–41, https://archive.org/details/journalofproceed005236mbp/page/n35

68. "Preliminary Program [Front Matter]," 10.

69. W. V. Bingham, "Some Psychological Aspects of Public School Music Instruction," in *Journal of Proceedings of the Ninth Annual Meeting of the Music Supervisors' National Conference Held at Lincoln, Nebraska, March 20–24, 1916*: 97–102, https://archive.org/details/in.ernet.dli.2015.166502/page/n101/mode/2up?q=bingham

70. Charles Benedict Davenport and Morris Steggerda, *Race Crossing in Jamaica* (Washington, DC: Carnegie Institution of Washington, 1929), 3. See also "Studies in Jamaica," *Eugenical News* 11, no. 10 (October 1926): 154.

71. "Program—Twelfth Meeting: St. Louis, Missouri," in *Journal of Proceedings of the Twelfth Annual Meeting of the Music Supervisors' National Conference Held at St. Louis, Missouri, March 30–April 4, 1919*: 11, https://archive.org/details/journalofproceed005236mbp/page/n15

72. Donald K. Routh, *Clinical Psychology since 1917: Science, Practice, and Organization* (New York: Plenum, 1994), 14; "Homecoming," *Iowa Alumnus* 15, no. 3 (December 1917): 72, https://books.google.com/books?id=7xRIAQAAMAAJ&pg=PA72&lpg=PA72&dq=Reuel+H.+Sylvester&source=bl&ots=ALOQ6N-rk3&sig=1RZeK9MUOrVmpNd3iolFS-tB7pc&hl=en&sa=X&ved=0ahUKEwiBwNOUoN7aAhXG8YMKHRLwBa4Q6AEIMTAD#v=onepage&q=Reuel%20H.%20Sylvester&f=false; Reuel H. Sylvester, "Cooperation in Vocational Guidance," *State of Iowa Bulletin of State Institutions* 24, no. 4 (October 1922): 225–29, https://books.google.com/books?id=OzXJAAAAMAAJ&pg=PA225&lpg=PA225&dq=Reuel+H.+Sylvester&source=bl&ots=67GCCI3Ple&sig=DRUgjTjMyFh8A-fGDjQuDrkP1RE&hl=en&sa=X&ved=0ahUKEwiBwNOUoN7aAhXG8YMKHRLwBa4Q6AEILDAB#v=onepage&q=Reuel%20H.%20Sylvester&f=false

73. Reuel H. Sylvester, "The Practical Possibilities of Applied Psychology as Exemplified in the Building of an Army," in *Journal of Proceedings of the Twelfth Annual Meeting of the Music Supervisors' National Conference Held at St. Louis, Missouri, March 30–April 4, 1919*: 28–30, https://archive.org/details/journalofproceed005236mbp/page/n33

74. "Preliminary Program [Front Matter]," 10; "Program—Twelfth Meeting," 11–12; Carl E. Seashore, "Demonstration of Measurements," 30.

75. "Preliminary Program [Front Matter]," 10; "Program—Twelfth Meeting," 12; Carl E. Seashore, "Procedure in the Discovery and the Encouragement," 30–38.

76. "Preliminary Program [Front Matter]," 10; "Program—Twelfth Meeting," 12; Carl E. Seashore, "Procedure in the Discovery and the Encouragement," 38–41.

77. For early examples of these inroads, see Carl E. Seashore, "Scientific Pro-

cedure in the Discovery of Musical Talent," 10–11; Carl E. Seashore, "Vocational Guidance in Music," *Music Supervisors' Journal* 3, no. 2 (November 1916): 18, 20, 22, 24, 26, 28, https://www.jstor.org/stable/3383046; and J. Lawrence Erb et al., "Significant Papers from the M.T.N.A.," *Music Supervisors' Journal* 2, no. 3 (January 1916): 12, 14, http://www.jstor.org/stable/3383175. Also, in 1918, Ginn and Company quoted G. Stanley Hall in a book series advertisement. See "Supervisors of School Music: Hear What Psychologists Say of the Power of Suitable Music [Back Matter]," *Music Supervisors' Journal* 5, no. 1 (September 1918): 31, http://www.jstor.org/stable/3382832

78. Carl E. Seashore, "Procedure in the Discovery and the Encouragement," 34. See also Carl E. Seashore, "An Open Letter to a Professor," *School and Society* 48, no. 1238 (September 17, 1938): 350; repr. with revised title in Carl E. Seashore, *The Junior College Movement* (New York: Henry Holt, 1940) 131–45; Carl E. Seashore, *A Preview to College and Life*, University of Iowa Studies: Series on Aims and Progress of Research, no. 55 (Iowa City: University of Iowa, 1938), 10–11; Carl E. Seashore, "Open Letter: Addressed to Women," 238; "Memorandum on Greetings to the 13th and Last Annual Brain Derby, June 4, 1941," attachment to Carl E. Seashore, Iowa City, IA, to Virgil M. Hancher, Old Capitol, June 9, 1941, RG 05.01.11, box 16, folder 93, Virgil M. Hancher Papers, Special Collections and University Archives, University of Iowa Libraries, Iowa City, IA; and Carl E. Seashore, *A Child Welfare Research Station: Plans and Possibilities of a Research Station for the Conservation and Development of the Normal Child*, Series on Aims and Progress of Research, n.s., vol. 107 (Iowa City, Iowa: The University, 1916), 12–14, https://catalog.hathitrust.org/Record/010551244

79. Erb et al. "Significant Papers," 12, 14.

80. Note that MTNA proceedings were summarized in the *MSJ/MEJ*. See, for example, Erb et al., "Significant Papers," 12, 14, 16, 18, 20, 22, 24, 26, 28.

81. Ian Hacking, *Historical Ontology* (Cambridge, MA: Harvard University Press, 2002), 180; Thomas S. Popkewitz, *Struggling for the Soul: The Politics of Schooling and the Construction of the Teacher* (New York: Teachers College Press, 1998), 10.

82. James Mainwaring, "The Assessment of Musical Ability," *British Journal of Educational Psychology* 17, no. 2 (June 1947): 83, https://doi-org.ezproxy.library.wisc.edu/10.1111/j.2044-8279.1947.tb02214.x

83. Charles Leonhard and Robert W. House, *Foundations and Principles of Music Education* (New York: McGraw-Hill, 1959), 344.

84. Frank W. Pinkerton, "Talent Tests and Their Application to the Public School Instrumental Music Program," *Journal of Research in Music Education* 11, no. 1 (Spring 1963): 76, www.jstor.org/stable/3344533

85. Pinkerton, "Talent Tests and Their Application," 76.

86. Pinkerton, "Talent Tests and Their Application," 76.

87. Pinkerton, "Talent Tests and Their Application," 78.

88. Pinkerton, "Talent Tests and Their Application," 75.

89. Pinkerton, "Talent Tests and Their Application," 78–79.

90. Miles, "Carl Emil Seashore, 1866–1949," 301; Hazel M. Stanton, "Report on Use of Seashore Tests at Eastman School of Music," *Music Supervisors' Journal* 12, no. 4 (March 1926): 22, 24, http://www.jstor.org/stable/3382898

91. Paul R. Lehman, "The Predictive Measurement of Musical Success," *Journal of Research in Music Education* 17, no. 1 (Spring 1969): 16, www.jstor.org/stable/3344180

92. Lehman, "Predictive Measurement," 16.

93. Lehman, "Predictive Measurement," 16.

94. Lehman, "Predictive Measurement," 16.

95. Lehman, "Predictive Measurement," 22.

96. Edwin E. Gordon, "The Legacy of Carl E. Seashore," in *Multidisciplinary Perspectives on Musicality: Essays from the Seashore Symposium*, ed. Kate Gfeller et al. (Iowa City: University of Iowa School of Music, 2006), 60.

97. See, for example, K. Pulli et al., "Genome-Wide Linkage Scan for Loci of Musical Aptitude in Finnish Families: Evidence for a Major Locus at 4q22," *Journal of Medical Genetics* 45, no. 7 (2008): 451–56, http://dx.doi.org/10.1136/jmg.2007.056366; Liisa Ukkola et al., "Musical Aptitude Is Associated with AVPR1A-Haplotpyes," *PLoS ONE* 4, no. 5 (2009), https://doi.org/10.1371/journal.pone.0005534

98. See, for example, Karen Wright, "Top 100 Stories of 2008 #52: Musical Ability Seems to Be 50 Percent Genetic," *Discover Magazine*, December 12, 2008, http://discovermagazine.com/2009/jan/052; and "Finnish Study Shows Musical Aptitude Inherited," TMC News, February 23, 2011, https://www.tmcnet.com/usubmit/2011/02/23/5333381.htm

99. *2019–2020 Catalog: Music Education*, University of Arkansas, accessed November 2, 2019, http://catalog.uark.edu/graduatecatalog/coursesofinstruction/mued/

100. Space does not permit an exhaustive list, but see, for example, James A. Keene, *A History of Music Education in the United States* (Hanover, NH: University Press of New England, 1982), 338; A. Theodore Tellstrom, *Music in American Education, Past and Present* (New York: Holt, Rinehart and Winston, 1971), 201; Leonhard and House, *Foundations and Principles* (1959), 343–44, 362; Charles Leonhard and Robert W. House, *Foundations and Principles of Music Education*, 2nd ed. (New York: McGraw-Hill, 1972), 400–402; Michael L. Mark and Charles L. Gary, *A History of American Music Education*, 3rd ed. (Lanham, MD: Rowman and Littlefield, 2007), 291, 424; Kate Gfeller et al., eds., *Multidisciplinary Perspectives on Musicality: Essays from the Seashore Symposium* (Iowa City: University of Iowa School of Music, 2006); and Ruth Zinar, "Highlights of Thought in the History of Music Education, VIII: Carl Seashore (1866–1949) and the Psychology of Music," *American Music Teacher* 33, no. 3 (January 1984): 44, 46. Also, for some examples of discussion of his tests, see A. Richard Roby, "A Study in the Correlation of Music Theory Grades with the *Seashore Measures of Musical Talents* and the *Aliferis Music Achievement Test*," *Journal of Research in Music Education* 10, no. 2 (Autumn 1962): 137–42, www.jstor.org/stable/3343997; Lehman, "Predictive Measurement," 16–31; Pinkerton, "Talent Tests and Their Application," 75–80; Ruth Wyatt, "A Note on the Use of 'Omnibus' Training to

Validate Seashore's 'Capacity' Hypothesis," *American Journal of Psychology* 52, no. 4 (October 1939): 638–40, https://doi.org/10.2307/1416481; Paul R. Farnsworth, *The Social Psychology of Music* (New York: Dryden, 1958), 235–40; Mary T. Whitley, "A Comparison of the Seashore and the Kwalwasser-Dykema Music Tests," *Teachers College Record* 33, no. 8 (May 1932): 731–51; Edward L. Rainbow and Hildegard C. Froehlich, *Research in Music Education: An Introduction to Systematic Inquiry* (New York: Schirmer Books, 1987), 24, 184; Penelope Nichols-Rothe, "A Short History of the Controversy Surrounding Music Aptitude Testing and the Work of Carl E. Seashore from 1919–1939" (qual. paper, Harvard University, 1987); Gordon, "Legacy of Carl E. Seashore," 51–61; and Humphreys, "Musical Aptitude Testing," 115–29.

101. Russell P. Getz, "1984 and Beyond," *Music Educators Journal* 70, no. 1 (September 1983): 52, www.jstor.org/stable/3401187

102. "Music Educators Hall of Fame: Purpose and Procedures," National Association for Music Education, accessed July 15, 2015, http://www.nafme.org/about/history/music-educators-hall-of-fame/music-educators-hall-of-fame-purpose-and-procedure-2/ (link now goes elsewhere; see Wayback Machine). Known today as the Music Educators Hall of Fame, it originally was called the Music Education Hall of Fame. See Bruce Wilson, Charles L. Gary, and Gary Greene, "Music in Our Schools: The First 150 Years," *Music Educators Journal* 74, no. 6 (February 1988): 2, 90, https://www.jstor.org/stable/3397995

103. Bruce Wilson, Charles Gary, and Gary Greene, "Music in Our Schools," 51.

104. Ramona H. Matthews, "Seashore, Carl E[mil]," *Grove Music Online*, January 20, 2001, https://doi.org/10.1093/gmo/9781561592630.article.25280

105. Gfeller et al., eds., *Multidisciplinary Perspectives.*

106. See, for example, Don D. Coffman, "Seashore's Passion for Measurement," in *Multidisciplinary Perspectives on Musicality: Essays from the Seashore Symposium*, ed. Kate Gfeller et al. (Iowa City: University of Iowa School of Music, 2006), 28–29; Hinrichs, "Carl E. Seashore as Psychologist," 9–10; Gordon, "Legacy of Carl E. Seashore," 51–61; and Estelle R. Jorgensen, "The Seashore-Mursell Debate on the Psychology of Music Revisited," in *Multidisciplinary Perspectives on Musicality: Essays from the Seashore Symposium*, ed. Kate Gfeller et al. (Iowa City: University of Iowa School of Music, 2006), 62–77.

107. Carl G. Seashore, "Life in the Seashore," p. iii, RG 99.0164, box 3, Carl E. Seashore Papers.

108. See, for example, Albrecht Schneider, "Aspects of Sound Recording and Sound Analysis," in *This Thing Called Music: Essays in Honor of Bruno Nettl*, ed. Victoria Lindsay Levine and Philip V. Bohlman (Lanham, MD: Rowman and Littlefield, 2015), 227; Elad Liebman, Eitan Ornoy, and Benny Chor, "A Phylogenetic Approach to Music Performance Analysis," *Journal of New Music Research* 41, no. 2 (2012): 215, http://dx.doi.org/10.1080/09298215.2012.668194 (current online PDF has different pagination); and Eric Clarke, "Empirical Methods in the Study of Performance," in *Empirical Musicology: Aims, Methods, Prospects*, ed. Eric Clarke and Nicholas Cook (New York: Oxford University Press, 2004), 78.

109. "75 Years Ago: 1937," *AMS Newsletter* 42, no. 2 (August 2012): 35, https://cdn.ymaws.com/www.amsmusicology.org/resource/resmgr/files/Newsletter/AMS

Newsletter-2012-8.pdf. For other references to his contributions to musicology, see Miles, "Carl Emil Seashore, 1866–1949," 265; and "American Speech Correction Association," 2, the latter indicating that he was a fellow in the "Musicol. Society" without providing more details.

110. See, for example, Carl E. Seashore and Harold Seashore, "The Place of Phonophotography in the Study of Primitive Music," *Science*, n.s., 79, no. 2056 (May 25, 1934): 485–87, http://www.jstor.org/stable/1659930; Carl E. Seashore, introduction to *Phonophotography in Folk Music*, by Milton Metfessel (Chapel Hill: University of North Carolina Press, 1928), 3–17, https://babel.hathitrust.org/cgi/pt?id=uc1.32106010326780;view=1up;seq=7; Carl E. Seashore, *Psychology of Music* (New York: McGraw-Hill, 1938), 346–59, https://archive.org/details/psychologyofmusi030417mbp; and Carl E. Seashore, "Three New Approaches to the Study of Negro Music," *Annals of the American Academy of Political and Social Science* 140, no. 229 (November 1928): 191–92, https://www.jstor.org/stable/1016848. The following sources discuss the movie project Seashore proposed: Carl E. Seashore, "Cooperation with the Film Industries in the Study of Primitive Music," *Science* 96, no. 2490 (September 18, 1942): 263–65, www.jstor.org/stable/1669751, a similar version of which appeared in Carl E. Seashore, *In Search of Beauty in Music: A Scientific Approach to Musical Esthetics* (New York: Ronald, 1947), 263–65, https://archive.org/details/insearchofbeauty000817mbp; Carl E. Seashore, *Psychology of Music*, 347–48; Carl E. Seashore to Secretary, Motion Picture Academy, Hollywood, CA, May 25, 1943, RG 05.01.11, box 55, folder 52, Virgil M. Hancher Papers, Special Collections and University Archives, University of Iowa Libraries, Iowa City, IA; Archibald MacLeish, Librarian of Congress, Washington, DC, to Carl E. Seashore, Iowa City, IA, June 3, 1943, RG 05.01.11, box 55, folder 52, Virgil M. Hancher Papers, Special Collections and University Archives, University of Iowa Libraries, Iowa City, IA; Carl E. Seashore to Archibald MacLeish, Washington, DC, June 7, 1943, RG 05.01.11, box 55, folder 52, Virgil M. Hancher Papers, Special Collections and University Archives, University of Iowa Libraries, Iowa City, IA; Mrs. Donald Gledhill to Carl E. Seashore, Iowa City, IA, June 9, 1943, RG 05.01.11, box 55, folder 52, Virgil M. Hancher Papers, Special Collections and University Archives, University of Iowa Libraries, Iowa City, IA; and Carl E. Seashore, Iowa City, IA, to Mrs. Donald Gledhill, Hollywood, CA, June 14, 1943, RG 05.01.11, box 55, folder 52, Virgil M. Hancher Papers, Special Collections and University Archives, University of Iowa Libraries, Iowa City, IA.

111. See, for example, Carl E. Seashore, *In Search of Beauty* (1947); Carl E. Seashore, "A Base for the Approach to Quantitative Studies in the Aesthetics of Music," *American Journal of Psychology* 39, no. 1/4 (December 1927): 141–44, https://doi.org/10.2307/1415406; Carl E. Seashore, "Measurements on the Expression of Emotion in Music," *Proceedings of the National Academy of Sciences of the United States of America* 9, no. 9 (September 15, 1923): 323–25, http://www.jstor.org/stable/84312; Miles, "Carl Emil Seashore, 1866–1949," 297–98, 301; Carl E. Seashore and Milton Metfessel, "Deviation from the Regular as an Art Principle," *Proceedings of the National Academy of Sciences of the United States of*

America 11, no. 9 (1925): 538–42, www.jstor.org/stable/84855; Carl E. Seashore, "Meier-Seashore Art Judgment Test," *Science*, n.s., 69, no. 1788 (April 5, 1929): 380, http://www.jstor.org/stable/1652784; and Norman Charles Meier and Carl E. Seashore, *The Meier-Seashore Art Judgment Test* (Iowa City: University of Iowa Bureau of Educational Research and Service, 1929).

112. Francis P. Robinson, "Carl E. Seashore," *Educational Forum* 15, no. 1, pt. 2 (November 1950): 128t.

113. Kathryn M. Kucsan, "Historical Perspectives on Approaches to Aesthetics in Early Music Psychology: The Writings of Carl E. Seashore (1866–1949) and Vernon Lee (1856–1935)" (PhD diss., University of Colorado, 1995).

114. See, for example, Miles, "Carl Emil Seashore, 1866–1949," 285–302; and Laird Addis, "Seashore, Carl Emil," in *The Biographical Dictionary of Iowa* (Iowa City: University of Iowa Press, 2009), http://uipress.lib.uiowa.edu/bdi/DetailsPage.aspx?id=332

115. For further discussion of Seashore's contributions to graduate education at Iowa, see Lewis Lester Jones, "Carl Emil Seashore: Dean of the Graduate College of the University of Iowa, 1908 to 1936, Dean *Pro Tempore*, 1942 to 1946; A Study of His Ideas on Graduate Education" (PhD diss., University of Iowa, 1978), http://search.proquest.com.ezproxy.library.wisc.edu/docview/302883038?accountid=465; and Donald F. Howard, "History of the State University of Iowa: The Graduate College" (PhD diss., University of Iowa, 1947).

116. Addis, "Seashore, Carl Emil."

117. Addis, "Seashore, Carl Emil." See also Leslie B. Sims, "Carl Seashore: A Visionary and Pioneer in Graduate Education," in *Multidisciplinary Perspectives on Musicality: Essays from the Seashore Symposium*, ed. Kate Gfeller et al. (Iowa City: University of Iowa School of Music, 2006), 218–19.

118. "The Flowering of the Valley: Iowa Trains Creative Artists," *Life* 6, no. 23 (June 5, 1939): 54.

119. "Writers' Workshop: History," University of Iowa College of Liberal Arts & Sciences, accessed July 11, 2018, https://writersworkshop.uiowa.edu/about/about-workshop/history

120. See Daniel Charles Warrick, "The Establishment of the Study of Fine Arts at the State University of Iowa during the Administration of Walter A. Jessup and Carl E. Seashore" (PhD diss., University of Missouri–Columbia, 1995), 219.

121. Sims, "Carl Seashore: A Visionary," 220.

122. Seashore is described as such in Don C. Charles, "A Note on Carl Seashore as Country School Teacher," *Journal of the History of the Behavioral Sciences* 5, no. 2 (April 1969): 185, 187, https://doi.org/10.1002/1520-6696(196904)5:2<185::AID-JHBS2300050208>3.0.CO;2-E

123. Addis, "Seashore, Carl Emil."

124. See, for example, Francis Robinson, "Carl E. Seashore," 128t; Daniel Starch, "Carl E. Seashore, 1866–1949," *Journal of Educational Psychology* 41, no. 4 (April 1950): 217–18, https://doi.org/10.1037/h0063517; "In Memoriam—Carl E. Seashore," *Educational Forum* 14, no. 3, pt. 2 (March 1950): 384h; and "From the

Four Corners: A Tribute to. . . . Carl E. Seashore," *NEA Journal: The Journal of the National Education Association* 38, no. 9 (December 1949): 714.

125. Miles, "Carl Emil Seashore, 1866–1949," 294; "American Speech Correction Association," 2; Kendler, "Iowa Tradition," 3.

126. Miles, "Carl Emil Seashore, 1866–1949," 294.

127. "American Speech Correction Association," 1.

128. Miles, "Carl Emil Seashore, 1866–1949," 294.

129. Francis Robinson, "Carl E. Seashore," 128u.

130. Robert S. Harper, "Tables of American Doctorates in Psychology," *American Journal of Psychology* 62, no. 4 (October 1949): 582–83, http://www.jstor.org/stable/1418564. Minton, citing this source, incorrectly reports that Iowa was second during the period from 1919 to 1928. See Henry L. Minton, "The Iowa Child Welfare Research Station and the 1940 Debate on Intelligence: Carrying on the Legacy of a Concerned Mother," *Journal of the History of the Behavioral Sciences* 20, no. 2 (April 1984): 163.

131. See, for example, "The Death of Dean Seashore," *Iowa City Press Citizen*, October 18, 1949, 4; Forest C. Ensign, "Dean Emeritus Carl E. Seashore," *Iowa Alumni Review* 3, no. 1 (December 1949): 8; and "Dean Emeritus Carl E. Seashore Dies at 83," *University of Iowa News Bulletin* 24, no. 6 (November 1949): 1.

132. "Death of Dean Seashore," 4.

133. Miles, "Carl Emil Seashore, 1866–1949," 271.

134. "Chapters," Gordon Institute for Music Learning, accessed May 7, 2019, https://giml.org/chapters/

135. See "American Speech Correction Association," 2, which lists Yale (1935), Gustavus Adolphus (1937), Wittenberg College (1927), University of Pittsburgh (1931), University of Southern California (1935), Augustana College (1939), and the Chicago Musical College (1939). "Dean Emeritus Carl E. Seashore Dies at 83," 1, 6, states he received fewer: five honorary doctorates.

136. "U. of I. Given Bronze Bust of Dr. C. Seashore," *Gustavian Weekly*, November 28, 1939, 1; Carl G. Seashore, "Life in the Seashore," p. iv, RG 99.0164, box 3, Carl E. Seashore Papers; Richard C. Lewis, "Paying Homage to Seashore Hall," *Iowa Now*, November 27, 2017, https://now.uiowa.edu/2017/11/paying-homage-seashore-hall

137. Richard Lewis, "Paying Homage."

138. Margarette Ball Dickson, *One Man and a Dream*, 2nd ed. (Minneapolis: Argus [1937]), 48.

139. Hilgard, "Psychology at Iowa," 40.

140. See, for example, Andrew W. Brown, "The Reliability and Validity of the Seashore Tests of Musical Talent," *Journal of Applied Psychology* 12 (1928): 468–76; James L. Mursell, *The Psychology of Music* (New York: W. W. Norton, 1937; repr., New York: Johnson Reprint, 1970); James L. Mursell, "What about Music Tests?" *Music Educators Journal* 24, no. 2 (October–November 1937): 16–18, www.jstor.org/stable/3385164; Wyatt, "Note on the Use," 638–40; Paul Farnsworth, *Social Psychology of Music*; Robert E. L. Faris, "Reflections on the Ability Dimension in

Human Society," *American Sociological Review* 26, no. 6 (December 1961): 835–43; Jorgensen, "Seashore-Mursell Debate," 62–77; Christian Paul Heinlein, "An Experimental Study of the Seashore Consonance Test," *Journal of Experimental Psychology* 8, no. 6 (December 1925): 408–33, http://dx.doi.org/10.1037/h0069544; Christian Paul Heinlein, "The Affective Characters of the Major and Minor Modes in Music," *Journal of Comparative Psychology* 8, no. 2 (April 1928): 101–42, http://web.b.ebscohost.com.ezproxy.library.wisc.edu/ehost/pdfviewer/pdfviewer?vid=4&sid=710fa1c4-e24e-42af-80f1–3b7aae8ab1cf%40pdc-v-sessmgr06; James L. Mursell, "Measuring Musical Ability and Achievement: A Study of the Correlations of Seashore Test Scores and Other Variables," *Journal of Educational Research* 25, no. 2 (February 1932): 116–26, http://www.jstor.org/stable/27525514; Christian Paul Heinlein, "A Brief Discussion of the Nature and Function of Melodic Configuration in Tonal Memory, with Critical Reference to the Seashore Tonal Memory Test," *Pedagogical Seminary and Journal of Genetic Psychology* 35, no. 1 (1928): 45–61; H. Lowery, "Cadence and Phrase Tests in Music," *British Journal of Psychology* 17, no. 2 (October 1926): 111–18, https://doi.org/10.1111/j.2044-8295.1926.tb00414.x; H. Lowery, "Musical Memory," *British Journal of Psychology* 19, no. 4 (April 1929): 397–404, https://doi.org/10.1111/j.2044–8295.1929.tb00525.x; and D. McCarthy, "A Study of the Seashore Measures of Musical Talent," *Journal of Applied Psychology* 14, no. 5 (October 1930): 437–55, https://psycnet.apa.org/doi/10.1037/h0073360

141. For a few early examples, see Lowery, "Cadence and Phrase," 111–18; and Lowery, "Musical Memory," 397–404.

142. Samuel L. Flueckiger, Some Trends in Music Education," *Music Educators Journal* 25, no. 5 (March 1939): 82, https://www.jstor.org/stable/3385367

143. Shinichi Suzuki, *Ability Development from Age Zero*, trans. Mary Louise Nagata (Athens, OH: Ability Development Associates, 1981), 94.

144. Patricia Shehan Campbell, "Rhythmic Movement and Public School Music Education: Conservative and Progressive Views of the Formative Years," *Journal of Research in Music Education* 39, no. 1 (Spring 1991): 15, www.jstor.org/stable/3344605

145. Jorgensen, "Seashore-Mursell Debate," 63–65.

146. Nichols-Rothe, "Short History," 14.

147. Cravens, *Before Head Start*, 11, 12, 81.

148. Nichols-Rothe, "Short History," 43.

149. See, for example, Milton C. Towner to Dr. Edwin D. Starbuck, Iowa City, IA, November 14, 1924, RG 99.0164, box 2, Carl E. Seashore Papers, Special Collections and University Archives, University of Iowa Libraries, Iowa City, IA; Eddie Baker, New York, NY, to Professor [Edwin D.] Starbuck, September 20, 1926, RG 99.0164, box 2, Carl E. Seashore Papers, Special Collections and University Archives, University of Iowa Libraries, Iowa City, IA; Edwin D. Starbuck to President Walter A. Jessup, September 22, 1926, RG 99.0164, box 2, Carl E. Seashore Papers, Special Collections and University Archives, University of Iowa Libraries, Iowa City, IA; Edwin D. Starbuck to Walter A. Jessup, October 14, 1926,

RG 99.0164, box 2, Carl E. Seashore Papers, Special Collections and University Archives, University of Iowa Libraries, Iowa City, IA; Edwin D. Starbuck to Walter A. Jessup [undated, describing incident on September 21, 1926], RG 99.0164, box 2, Carl E. Seashore Papers, Special Collections and University Archives, University of Iowa Libraries, Iowa City, IA; and Lewis Jones, "Carl Emil Seashore: Dean," 161–71.

150. Towner to Starbuck, November 14, 1924, RG 99.0164, box 2, Carl E. Seashore Papers.

151. Lewis Jones, "Carl Emil Seashore: Dean," 163.

152. Lewis Jones, "Carl Emil Seashore: Dean," 170. See also p. 161.

153. Towner to Starbuck, November 14, 1924, RG 99.0164, box 2, Carl E. Seashore Papers; Baker to Starbuck, September 20, 1926, RG 99.0164, box 2, Carl E. Seashore Papers; Starbuck to Jessup, September 22, 1926, RG 99.0164, box 2, Carl E. Seashore Papers; Starbuck to Jessup, October 14, 1926, RG 99.0164, box 2, Carl E. Seashore Papers; Starbuck to Jessup [undated, describing incident on September 21, 1926], RG 99.0164, box 2, Carl E. Seashore Papers.

154. C. E. Seashore, Iowa City, IA, to [Edwin D.] Starbuck, October 5, 1926, RG 99.0164, box 2, Carl E. Seashore Papers, Special Collections and University Archives, University of Iowa Libraries, Iowa City, IA.

155. Starbuck to Jessup [undated, describing incident on September 21, 1926], RG 99.0164, box 2, Carl E. Seashore Papers.

156. Lewis Jones, "Carl Emil Seashore: Dean," 171–80; Adrian C. North and David J. Hargreaves, *The Social and Applied Psychology of Music* (New York: Oxford University Press, 2008), 25; Himie Voxman, "Some Personal Reflections on Carl E. Seashore," in *Multidisciplinary Perspectives on Musicality: Essays from the Seashore Symposium*, ed. Kate Gfeller et al. (Iowa City: University of Iowa School of Music, 2006), 217.

157. Voxman, "Some Personal Reflections," 216–17.

158. Lewis Jones, "Carl Emil Seashore: Dean," 171–80.

159. Lewis Jones, "Carl Emil Seashore: Dean," 173.

160. See, for example, Metfessel, "Carl Emil Seashore, 1866–1949," 713–17; Lundin, "Seashore, Carl Emil (1866–1949)," 279; "American Speech Correction Association," 1–2; Francis Robinson, "Carl E. Seashore," 128t–128u; George Stoddard, "Carl Emil Seashore: 1866–1949," 456–62; Starch, "Carl E. Seashore, 1866–1949," 217–18; "In Memoriam—Carl E. Seashore," 384h; "From the Four Corners," 714; John S. Kendall, "1891 Gustavus Graduate Dr. Seashore Ranked as One of Top Alumni," Gustavus Adolphus College, accessed January 20, 2005, http://gustavus.edu/academics/psychology/Epilogue/Seashore.html; "Necrology, Carl E. Seashore," 4; Charles, "Note on Carl Seashore," 185–87; Joseph Tiffin, "Carl Emil Seashore: 1866–1949," *Psychological Review* 57, no. 1 (January 1950): 1–2, https://doi.org/10.1037/h0058319; Miles, "Carl Emil Seashore, 1866–1949," 263–316; "Dr. Carl Seashore . . . World Famed," 3, 14; "Pay Last Tributes to 'Dean of Deans': Memorial Services Held Here Sunday for Carl E. Seashore, Who Died October 17," *Iowa City Press Citizen*, October 24, 1949, 11; "Death of Dean Seashore," 4; and Ensign, "Dean Emeritus Carl E. Seashore," 8, 21.

161. In an unpublished autobiography he wrote late in his life, Seashore claimed that he was a charter member of the International Eugenics Society, but I could not find evidence to support this. I believe he meant the American Eugenics Society, of which he was a charter member. There are other errors in the document. For the reference to the International Eugenics Society, see Carl E. Seashore, "Psychology and Life," p. 188, RG 99.0164, box 2, Carl E. Seashore Papers.

162. Harry H. Laughlin, "The Progress of American Eugenics," *Eugenics* 2, no. 2 (February 1929): 4.

163. "New Active Members of Eugenics Research Association," *Eugenical News* 5, no. 7 (July 1920): 53; "Eugenics Research Association—Eighth Annual Meeting," *Eugenical News* 5, no. 7 (July 1920): 52.

164. "Ninth Annual Business Meeting of the Eugenics Research Association: June 24, 1921," *Eugenical News* 6, no. 7–8 (July-August 1921): 56.

165. "New Active Members of Eugenics Research Association," 53.

166. For an in-depth discussion of the American Eugenics Society and its Advisory Council, see Mehler, "History of the American Eugenics."

167. Mehler, "History of the American Eugenics," 61.

168. "Eugenics Society of the United States of America," *Eugenical News* 8, no. 4 (April 1923): 29.

169. For example, Kenny describes one AES member, Clarence G. Campbell, as an "outspoken Nazi sympathizer." See Michael G. Kenny, "Toward a Racial Abyss: Eugenics, Wickliffe Draper, and the Origins of the Pioneer Fund," *Journal of History of the Behavioral Sciences* 38, no. 3 (Summer 2002): 270.

170. Mehler, "History of the American Eugenics," 130.

171. Mehler, "History of the American Eugenics," 130–31.

172. Mehler, "History of the American Eugenics," 135.

173. "The Advisory Council of the Eugenics Committee of the United States of America," *Eugenical News* 8, no. 4 (April 1923): 29.

174. Mehler, "History of the American Eugenics," 132.

175. Mehler, "History of the American Eugenics," 133.

176. Mehler, "History of the American Eugenics," 132.

177. Mehler, "History of the American Eugenics," 68.

178. Field Secretary, New Haven, CT, to Fair Associations [c. 1930], American Philosophical Society, AES, Am3, 575.06, circulars, titled "Letter from Field Secretary, American Eugenics Association to Fair Associations Asking Education Exhibit Space," image 704, in the "Image Archive on the American Eugenics Movement," DNA Learning Center, Cold Spring Harbor Laboratory, accessed February 10, 2005, www.eugenicsarchive.org/eugenics/view_image.pl?id=704

179. Ellsworth Huntington, *Tomorrow's Children: The Goal of Eugenics* (New York: J. Wiley & Sons, 1935), v, https://babel.hathitrust.org/cgi/pt?id=mdp.39015034788995;view=1up;seq=7. Also, see Mehler, "History of the American Eugenics," 258–59, for reference to it as a catechism.

180. Mehler, "History of the American Eugenics," 141.

181. *Organized Eugenics* (New Haven, CT: American Eugenics Society, January 1931), 4, Connecticut State Library Digital Collection, https://cdm15019.conten

tdm.oclc.org/digital/collection/p4005coll11/id/587. The official platform appears on p. x.

182. Mehler, "History of the American Eugenics," 132–33.

183. Carl E. Seashore, "Individual and Racial Inheritance of Musical Traits," in *Eugenics, Genetics and the Family*, vol. 1, *Scientific Papers of the Second International Congress of Eugenics; Held at American Museum of Natural History, New York, September 22–28, 1921* (Baltimore, MD: Williams & Wilkins, 1923; repr., ed. Charles Rosenberg, New York: Garland Publishing, 1985), 231–38.

184. Laughlin, "Progress of American Eugenics," 4.

185. William H. Tucker, *The Funding of Scientific Racism: Wickliffe Draper and the Pioneer Fund* (Urbana: University of Illinois Press, 2002), 27; Mehler, "History of the American Eugenics," 50.

186. Hazel M. Stanton, "An Experimental Investigation of Musical Inheritance," in *Eugenics, Genetics and the Family*, vol. 1, *Scientific Papers of the Second International Congress of Eugenics; Held at American Museum of Natural History, New York, September 22–28, 1921* (Baltimore, MD: Williams & Wilkins, 1923; repr., ed. Charles Rosenberg, New York: Garland Publishing, 1985), 239–42.

187. Bird T. Baldwin, "The Scientific Prediction of the Physical Growth of Children," in *Eugenics in Race and State*, vol. 2, *Scientific Papers of the Second International Congress of Eugenics; Held at American Museum of Natural History, New York, September 22–28, 1921* (Baltimore, MD: Williams & Wilkins, 1923; repr., ed. Charles Rosenberg, New York: Garland Publishing, 1985), 25–29.

188. Preface to *Eugenics, Genetics and the Family*, vol. 1, *Scientific Papers of the Second International Congress of Eugenics; Held at American Museum of Natural History, New York, September 22–28, 1921* (Baltimore, MD: Williams & Wilkins, 1923; repr., New York: Garland Publishing, 1985), ix.

189. Mehler, "History of the American Eugenics," 49.

190. Mehler, "History of the American Eugenics," 50.

191. "Mental and Physical Factors in Programs of Eugenics: A Symposium," *Eugenical News* 33, nos. 3–4 (September-December 1948): 42.

192. "Mental and Physical Factors," 42.

193. "Mental and Physical Factors," 46.

194. "In Praise of Eugenics," *Eugenics* 2, no. 2 (February 1929): 36. Another example of Seashore's opinion being solicited is J. Russell Smith et al., "The Faculty Birth Rate: Should It Be Increased?" *Eugenics* 3, no. 12 (December 1930): 458–60.

195. See, for example, "Vocational Guidance in Music," *Journal of Heredity* 9, no. 2 (February 1918): 66, https://doi-org.ezproxy.library.wisc.edu/10.1093/oxfordjournals.jhered.a111893; "Survey of Musical Ability in Schools," *Journal of Heredity* 8, no. 7 (July 1, 1917): 305, https://doi-org.ezproxy.library.wisc.edu/10.1093/oxfordjournals.jhered.a111819; P[aul] P[openoe], "Musical Ability," review of *The Inheritance of Specific Musical Capacities*, by Hazel M. Stanton, *Journal of Heredity* 13, no. 4 (April 1922): 176, https://doi-org.ezproxy.library.wisc.edu/10.1093/oxfordjournals.jhered.a102196; "Popular Education: Music Tests," *Eugenics* 1, no. 2 (November 1928): 35; "Measuring Musical Capacities," *Eugenical News* 9, no. 8 (August 1924): 71; "The Measurable Elements of Musical Talent," *Eugenical*

News 11, no. 3 (March 1926): 43–44; Morris Steggerda, "Negro-White Hybrids in Jamaica, B.W.I.," *Eugenical News* 13, no. 2 (February 1928): 23; Althea DeBacker, "Student Pedigree-Studies: A German Bard and His Progeny," *Eugenical News* 18, no. 5 (September-October 1933): 106; and "Eugenics Research Association Number: Ninth Annual Meeting," *Eugenical News* 6, nos. 7–8 (July-August 1921): 54.

196. "Popular Education: Music Tests," 35.

197. See, for example, "Survey of Musical Ability," 305; P[openoe], "Musical Ability," 176; and "Vocational Guidance in Music," *Journal of Heredity*, 66.

198. "Eugenics Research Association Number: Ninth Annual Meeting," 54.

199. P[openoe], "Musical Ability," 176.

200. "Measurable Elements of Musical Talent," 43.

201. "Measurable Elements of Musical Talent," 43.

202. "Measurable Elements of Musical Talent," 43–44.

203. "Studies in Jamaica," 154, described the Race Crossing in Jamaica study without mentioning the study's use of the Seashore Tests.

204. DeBacker, "Student Pedigree-Studies," 106.

205. Carl E. Seashore, "The Consulting Psychologist," *Popular Science Monthly* 78 (March 1911): 284–87.

206. Carl E. Seashore, "Consulting Psychologist," 284–85.

207. Carl E. Seashore, "Consulting Psychologist," 286–87.

208. Carl E. Seashore, *Psychology in Daily Life* (New York: D. Appleton, 1914). Use of the term occurs on p. 121, and discussion of generational planning is found on pp. 119–21.

209. Carl E. Seashore, *Psychology in Daily Life*, 122.

210. Carl E. Seashore, *Psychology in Daily Life*, 121.

211. Carl E. Seashore, "The Term 'Euthenics,'" *Science*, n.s., 94, no. 2450 (December 12, 1941): 562, https://www.jstor.org/stable/1668443

212. Carl E. Seashore, *Child Welfare Research Station*, 4.

213. Carl E. Seashore, "Carl Emil Seashore," 229, 231.

214. Carl E. Seashore, "Carl Emil Seashore," 258.

215. Carl E. Seashore, "The Sunny Side of Graduate Work for the Duration," *Journal of Higher Education* 14, no. 6 (June 1943): 289, https://www.jstor.org/stable/1975100. Four versions of this essay exist, three of them published. For the passage in a very similar published version of this article, see Carl E. Seashore, "The Sunny Side of Graduate Work for the Duration," in *Wartime Approaches to Liberal Education: Nine Editorials from* The Daily Iowan ([Iowa City: University of Iowa Publications, 1944?]), 29. See also Carl E. Seashore, "The Sunny Side of Graduate Work," *Daily Iowan*, April 11, 1943, 2, http://dailyiowan.lib.uiowa.edu/DI/1943/di1943-04-11.pdf; and Carl E. Seashore, "The Sunny Side of Graduate Work for the Duration," typed manuscript accompanying Carl E. Seashore to Virgil M. Hancher, March 26, 1943, p. 1, RG 05.01.11, box 55, folder 52, Virgil M. Hancher Papers, Special Collections and University Archives, University of Iowa Libraries, Iowa City, IA.

216. Carl E. Seashore, "The Scope and Function of Euthenics," *Mental Hygiene* 33, no. 4 (October 1949): 594.

217. Carl E. Seashore, "Euthenics, a Design for Living," *Educational Forum* 12, no. 2, pt. 1 (January 1948): 149.

218. Carl E. Seashore, "Carl Emil Seashore," 254.

219. Carl E. Seashore, "Carl Emil Seashore," 259.

220. W. B. Pillsbury, "Biographical Memoir of James McKeen Cattell: 1860–1944," vol. 25, *National Academy of Sciences of the United States of America Biographical Memoirs* (Washington, DC: National Academy of Sciences, 1949), 4, http://www.nasonline.org/publications/biographical-memoirs/memoir-pdfs/cattell-james-m.pdf

221. Seashore published Bingham's work in Carl E. Seashore, ed. and moderator, "Communications and Discussions: Mentality Tests, a Symposium," *Journal of Educational Psychology* 7, no. 4 (April 1916): 230–31. He asked Davenport to send a response via Bingham in Carl E. Seashore, Iowa City, IA, to Charles B. Davenport, Cold Spring Harbor, NY, April 9, 1920, pp. 1–2, MSS.B.D27, box 85, Charles B. Davenport Papers, American Philosophical Society Archives, Philadelphia, PA.

222. Mehler, "History of the American Eugenics," 172, 176.

223. "Freud Centennial History: Psychology, Pedagogy, and School Hygiene, September 6–11, 1909," Clark University, accessed June 23, 2015, https://www.clarku.edu/micro/freudcentennial/history/1909psych.cfm (link discontinued); Seashore's biographer, Walter Miles, stated that the Clark conference helped Seashore envision a mental hospital for the University of Iowa. See Miles, "Carl Emil Seashore, 1866–1949," 281.

224. "Freud Centennial History."

225. See, for example, Mehler, "History of the American Eugenics," 68; and Tucker, *Funding of Scientific Racism*, 23.

226. Ernest R. Hilgard, "Robert Mearns Yerkes: 1876–1956," vol. 38, *Biographical Memoirs* (Washington, DC: National Academy of Sciences, 1965), 391, http://www.nasonline.org/publications/biographical-memoirs/memoir-pdfs/yerkes-robert-m.pdf

227. For more extensive discussion of Yerkes and eugenics, see, for example, Edwin Black, *War against the Weak: Eugenics and America's Campaign to Create a Master Race* (New York: Four Walls Eight Windows, 2003); Stephen Jay Gould, *The Mismeasure of Man* (New York: W. W. Norton, 1996); and Mehler, "History of the American Eugenics."

228. For example, see Carl E. Seashore, Iowa City, IA, to Robert M. Yerkes, Cambridge, MA, October 21, 1911, MS 569, box 43, folder 836, Robert Mearns Yerkes Papers, Manuscripts and Archives, Yale University Library, New Haven, CT; Carl E. Seashore, Iowa City, IA, to Robert M. Yerkes, Cambridge, MA, October 29, 1914, MS 569, box 43, folder 836, Robert Mearns Yerkes Papers, Manuscripts and Archives, Yale University Library, New Haven, CT; Carl E. Seashore, Iowa City, IA, to Robert M. Yerkes, Cambridge, MA, January 19, 1916, p. 2, MS 569, box 43, folder 836, Robert Mearns Yerkes Papers, Manuscripts and Archives, Yale

University Library, New Haven, CT; Carl E. Seashore, Iowa City, IA, to Robert M. Yerkes, Cambridge, MA, November 1, 1916, MS 569, box 43, folder 836, Robert Mearns Yerkes Papers, Manuscripts and Archives, Yale University Library, New Haven, CT; Robert M. Yerkes to Carl E. Seashore, undated, p. 2, MS 569, box 43, folder 836, Robert Mearns Yerkes Papers, Manuscripts and Archives, Yale University Library, New Haven, CT; Robert M. Yerkes to Carl E. Seashore, Iowa City, IA, October 13, 1928, MS 569, box 43, folder 836, Robert Mearns Yerkes Papers, Manuscripts and Archives, Yale University Library, New Haven, CT; Carl E. Seashore, Iowa City, IA, to Robert M. Yerkes, New Haven, CT, November 24, 1931, MS 569, box 43, folder 837, Robert Mearns Yerkes Papers, Manuscripts and Archives, Yale University Library, New Haven, CT; Robert M. Yerkes to C. E. Seashore, November 18, 1931, Iowa City, IA, MS 569, box 43, folder 837, Robert Mearns Yerkes Papers, Manuscripts and Archives, Yale University Library, New Haven, CT; Carl E. Seashore, Iowa City, IA, to Robert M. Yerkes, New Haven, CT, December 12, 1938, MS 569, box 43, folder 837, Robert Mearns Yerkes Papers, Manuscripts and Archives, Yale University Library, New Haven, CT; Robert M. Yerkes to Carl E. Seashore, Iowa City, IA, December 15, 1938, MS 569, box 43, folder 837, Robert Mearns Yerkes Papers, Manuscripts and Archives, Yale University Library, New Haven, CT; Carl E. Seashore, Winter Park, FL, to Robert M. Yerkes, February 15, 1939, MS 569, box 43, folder 837, Robert Mearns Yerkes Papers, Manuscripts and Archives, Yale University Library, New Haven, CT; Robert M. Yerkes to C. E. Seashore, Winter Park, FL, February 16, 1939, MS 569, box 43, folder 837, Robert Mearns Yerkes Papers, Manuscripts and Archives, Yale University Library, New Haven, CT; Carl E. Seashore, Iowa City, IA, to Robert M. Yerkes, New Haven, CT, April 3, 1944 (with attachment), MS 569, box 43, folder 837, Robert Mearns Yerkes Papers, Manuscripts and Archives, Yale University Library, New Haven, CT; Robert M. Yerkes to Carl E. Seashore, Iowa City, IA, May 8, 1944, MS 569, box 43, folder 837, Robert Mearns Yerkes Papers, Manuscripts and Archives, Yale University Library, New Haven, CT; and Robert M. Yerkes to Carl E. Seashore, Iowa City, IA, October 4, 1944, MS 569, box 43, folder 837, Robert Mearns Yerkes Papers, Manuscripts and Archives, Yale University Library, New Haven, CT.

229. Carl E. Seashore to Yerkes, November 24, 1931, MS 569, box 43, folder 837, Robert Mearns Yerkes Papers; Carl E. Seashore to Yerkes, December 12, 1938, MS 569, box 43, folder 837, Robert Mearns Yerkes Papers; Yerkes to Carl E. Seashore, December 15, 1938, MS 569, box 43, folder 837, Robert Mearns Yerkes Papers.

230. Yerkes to Carl E. Seashore, May 8, 1944, MS 569, box 43, folder 837, Robert Mearns Yerkes Papers; Yerkes to Carl E. Seashore, October 4, 1944, MS 569, box 43, folder 837, Robert Mearns Yerkes Papers.

231. Miles, "Carl Emil Seashore, 1866–1949," 295–96.

232. See Wade Pickren, "Robert Yerkes, Calvin Stone, and the Beginning of Programmatic Sex Research by Psychologists, 1921–1930," *American Journal of Psychology* 110, no. 4 (Winter 1997): 603–19, https://www.jstor.org/stable/1423412; and Philip J. Pauly, *Biologists and the Promise of American Life: From Meriwether*

Lewis to Alfred Kinsey (Princeton, NJ: Princeton University Press, 2000), 227–33, for more information on this conference and committee.

233. C. E. Seashore, Washington, DC, to President W. A. Jessup, Iowa City, IA, February 17, 1922, RG 05.01.09, box 94, folder 53, Walter A. Jessup Papers, Special Collections and University Archives, University of Iowa Libraries, Iowa City, IA; C. E. Seashore, Washington, DC, to President W. A. Jessup, Iowa City, IA, March 3, 1922, RG 05.01.09, box 94, folder 53, Walter A. Jessup Papers, Special Collections and University Archives, University of Iowa Libraries, Iowa City, IA; [W. A. Jessup] to Dean C. E. Seashore, Washington, DC, March 15, 1922, RG 05.01.09, box 94, folder 53, Walter A. Jessup Papers, Special Collections and University Archives, University of Iowa Libraries, Iowa City, IA; C. E. Seashore, Washington, DC, to Professor Bird T. Baldwin, Iowa City, IA, March 15, 1922, RG 05.01.09, box 94, folder 53, Walter A. Jessup Papers, Special Collections and University Archives, University of Iowa Libraries, Iowa City, IA.

234. Carl E. Seashore, Iowa City, IA, to Robert M. Yerkes, Cambridge, MA, February 6, 1911, MS 569, box 43, folder 836, Robert Mearns Yerkes Papers, Manuscripts and Archives, Yale University Library, New Haven, CT; Carl E. Seashore, Iowa City, IA, to Robert M. Yerkes, Cambridge, MA, February 22, 1911 (with attachment), MS 569, box 43, folder 836, Robert Mearns Yerkes Papers, Manuscripts and Archives, Yale University Library, New Haven, CT.

235. Yerkes to Carl E. Seashore, undated, p. 1, MS 569, box 43, folder 836, Robert Mearns Yerkes Papers.

236. I could not find strong evidence that two of the individuals named, Woolley and Bronner, were involved in eugenics.

237. Carl E. Seashore to Yerkes, January 19, 1916, p. 1, MS 569, box 43, folder 836, Robert Mearns Yerkes Papers.

238. Robert M. Yerkes to Carl E. Seashore, Iowa City, IA, February 18, 1916, MS 569, box 43, folder 836, Robert Mearns Yerkes Papers, Manuscripts and Archives, Yale University Library, New Haven, CT.

239. Carl E. Seashore, Iowa City, IA, to Robert M. Yerkes, Cambridge, MA, February 23, 1916, MS 569, box 43, folder 836, Robert Mearns Yerkes Papers, Manuscripts and Archives, Yale University Library, New Haven, CT.

240. Carl E. Seashore, "Communications and Discussions: Mentality Tests," *Journal of Educational Psychology* 7, no. 3 (March 1916): 163–66.

241. Carl E. Seashore, ed. and moderator, "Communications and Discussions: Mentality Tests" (April 1916), 229–40; Carl E. Seashore, ed. and moderator, "Communications and Discussions: Mentality Tests, a Symposium," *Journal of Educational Psychology* 7, no. 5 (May 1916): 278–93; Carl E. Seashore, ed. and moderator, "Communications and Discussions: Mentality Tests, a Symposium," *Journal of Educational Psychology* 7, no. 6 (June 1916): 348–60.

242. Robert M. Yerkes to Carl E. Seashore, Iowa City, IA, May 12, 1916, MS 569, box 43, folder 836, Robert Mearns Yerkes Papers, Manuscripts and Archives, Yale University Library, New Haven, CT.

243. Carl E. Seashore, Iowa City, IA, to Robert M. Yerkes, Boston, MA, May 15,

1916, MS 569, box 43, folder 836, Robert Mearns Yerkes Papers, Manuscripts and Archives, Yale University Library, New Haven, CT.

244. Carl E. Seashore, Iowa City, IA, to Robert M. Yerkes, Washington, DC, January 3, 1921 (with attachment), MS 569, box 43, folder 836, Robert Mearns Yerkes Papers, Manuscripts and Archives, Yale University Library, New Haven, CT.

245. Robert M. Yerkes to Carl E. Seashore, Iowa City, IA, January 21, 1921, MS 569, box 43, folder 836, Robert Mearns Yerkes Papers, Manuscripts and Archives, Yale University Library, New Haven, CT.

246. Carl E. Seashore to Yerkes, October 21, 1911, MS 569, box 43, folder 836, Robert Mearns Yerkes Papers.

247. Carl E. Seashore, Iowa City, IA, to Robert Yerkes, New Haven, CT, May 21, 1947 (with attachment), MS 569, box 43, folder 837, Robert Mearns Yerkes Papers, Manuscripts and Archives, Yale University Library, New Haven, CT; Robert M. Yerkes to Carl E. Seashore, Iowa City, IA, May 27, 1947, MS 569, box 43, folder 837, Robert Mearns Yerkes Papers, Manuscripts and Archives, Yale University Library, New Haven, CT.

248. Carl E. Seashore, Iowa City, IA, to Robert Yerkes, New Haven, CT, March 20, 1944 (with attachment), MS 569, box 43, folder 837, Robert Mearns Yerkes Papers, Manuscripts and Archives, Yale University Library, New Haven, CT.

249. Robert M. Yerkes to Carl E. Seashore, Iowa City, IA, March 25, 1944, MS 569, box 43, folder 837, Robert Mearns Yerkes Papers, Manuscripts and Archives, Yale University Library, New Haven, CT; Carl E. Seashore to Yerkes, April 3, 1944, MS 569, box 43, folder 837, Robert Mearns Yerkes Papers. For more information about the proposal, also see Robert M. Yerkes to Carl E. Seashore, Iowa City, IA, April 10, 1944 (with attachment), MS 569, box 43, folder 837, Robert Mearns Yerkes Papers, Manuscripts and Archives, Yale University Library, New Haven, CT; and Carl E. Seashore, Iowa City, IA, to Robert M. Yerkes, New Haven, CT, April 19, 1944, MS 569, box 43, folder 837, Robert Mearns Yerkes Papers, Manuscripts and Archives, Yale University Library, New Haven, CT.

250. Yerkes to Carl E. Seashore, May 12, 1916, MS 569, box 43, folder 836, Robert Mearns Yerkes Papers.

251. Carl E. Seashore to Yerkes, May 15, 1916, MS 569, box 43, folder 836, Robert Mearns Yerkes Papers.

252. Other examples include Carl E. Seashore, Iowa City, IA, to Robert M. Yerkes, New Haven, CT, September 17, 1925, MS 569, box 43, folder 836, Robert Mearns Yerkes Papers, Manuscripts and Archives, Yale University Library, New Haven, CT; Robert M. Yerkes to Carl E. Seashore, Iowa City, IA, September 22, 1925, MS 569, box 43, folder 836, Robert Mearns Yerkes Papers, Manuscripts and Archives, Yale University Library, New Haven, CT; Robert M. Yerkes to Carl E. Seashore, Iowa City, IA, December 4, 1942, MS 569, box 43, folder 837, Robert Mearns Yerkes Papers, Manuscripts and Archives, Yale University Library, New Haven, CT; Robert M. Yerkes to C. E. Seashore, Iowa City, IA, November 10, 1943, MS 569, box 43, folder 837, Robert Mearns Yerkes Papers, Manuscripts and Archives, Yale University Library, New Haven, CT; Robert M. Yerkes to Carl

E. Seashore, Winter Park, FL, February 14, 1944, MS 569, box 43, folder 837, Robert Mearns Yerkes Papers, Manuscripts and Archives, Yale University Library, New Haven, CT; Yerkes to Carl E. Seashore, October 4, 1944, MS 569, box 43, folder 837, Robert Mearns Yerkes Papers; Robert M. Yerkes to Carl E. Seashore, Iowa City, IA, October 19, 1945, MS 569, box 43, folder 837, Robert Mearns Yerkes Papers, Manuscripts and Archives, Yale University Library, New Haven, CT; Robert M. Yerkes to Walter M. Stevenson, New York, NY, May 15, 1947, MS 569, box 43, folder 837, Robert Mearns Yerkes Papers, Manuscripts and Archives, Yale University Library, New Haven, CT; and Yerkes to Carl E. Seashore, May 27, 1947, MS 569, box 43, folder 837, Robert Mearns Yerkes Papers.

253. Carl E. Seashore to Yerkes, September 17, 1925, MS 569, box 43, folder 836, Robert Mearns Yerkes Papers.

254. Yerkes to Carl E. Seashore, September 22, 1925, MS 569, box 43, folder 836, Robert Mearns Yerkes Papers.

255. Carl E. Seashore, Iowa City, IA, to Robert M. Yerkes, New Haven, CT, November 10, 1942, MS 569, box 43, folder 837, Robert Mearns Yerkes Papers, Manuscripts and Archives, Yale University Library, New Haven, CT.

256. Yerkes to Carl E. Seashore, December 4, 1942, p. 1, MS 569, box 43, folder 837, Robert Mearns Yerkes Papers.

257. Yerkes to Carl E. Seashore, February 14, 1944, MS 569, box 43, folder 837, Robert Mearns Yerkes Papers.

258. Yerkes to Carl E. Seashore, October 19, 1945, MS 569, box 43, folder 837, Robert Mearns Yerkes Papers.

259. Yerkes to C. E. Seashore, November 10, 1943, MS 569, box 43, folder 837, Robert Mearns Yerkes Papers.

260. Yerkes to Carl E. Seashore, October 4, 1944, MS 569, box 43, folder 837, Robert Mearns Yerkes Papers.

261. Walter M. Stevenson, New York, NY, to Robert Yerkes, New Haven, CT, May 6, 1947, MS 569, box 43, folder 837, Robert Mearns Yerkes Papers, Manuscripts and Archives, Yale University Library, New Haven, CT.

262. Yerkes to Stevenson, May 15, 1947, MS 569, box 43, folder 837, Robert Mearns Yerkes Papers.

263. C. E. Seashore, Iowa City, IA, to Robert M. Yerkes, New Haven, CT, May 2, 1933, MS 569, box 43, folder 837, Robert Mearns Yerkes Papers, Manuscripts and Archives, Yale University Library, New Haven, CT.

264. C. E. Seashore to Orson D. Munn, New York, NY, May 8, 1933, MS 569, box 43, folder 837, Robert Mearns Yerkes Papers, Manuscripts and Archives, Yale University Library, New Haven, CT.

265. C. E. Seashore to Munn, May 8, 1933, MS 569, box 43, folder 837, Robert Mearns Yerkes Papers.

266. C. E. Seashore to Munn, May 8, 1933, MS 569, box 43, folder 837, Robert Mearns Yerkes Papers.

267. H. M. Parshley, "Sexual Abstinence as a Biological Question: Is Sexual Intercourse a Physiological Necessity?" *Scientific American* 148, no. 5 (May 1933): 283–84, 298–300, www.jstor.org/stable/2496823

268. Robert M. Yerkes to C. E. Seashore, May 13, 1933, Iowa City, IA, MS 569, box 43, folder 837, Robert Mearns Yerkes Papers, Manuscripts and Archives, Yale University Library, New Haven, CT.

269. Carl E. Seashore, Iowa City, IA, to Robert M. Yerkes, New Haven, CT, October 20, 1930, MS 569, box 43, folder 837, Robert Mearns Yerkes Papers, Manuscripts and Archives, Yale University Library, New Haven, CT.

270. Robert M. Yerkes to Carl E. Seashore, Iowa City, IA, October 28, 1930, MS 569, box 43, folder 837, Robert Mearns Yerkes Papers, Manuscripts and Archives, Yale University Library, New Haven, CT.

271. Cravens, *Before Head Start*, 35.

272. C. E. Seashore, Charlottesville, VA, to Mr. [W. A.] Jessup, first undated handwritten letter, ca. 1920, RG 05.01.09, box 61, folder 53, Walter A. Jessup Papers, Special Collections and University Archives, University of Iowa Libraries, Iowa City, IA. Another reference to recruitment of Brigham appeared in C. E. Seashore, Washington, DC, to Mr. [W. A.] Jessup, second undated handwritten letter, ca. 1920, RG 05.01.09, box 61, folder 53, Walter A. Jessup Papers, Special Collections and University Archives, University of Iowa Libraries, Iowa City, IA.

273. C. E. Seashore to Jessup, first undated handwritten letter, ca. 1920, RG 05.01.09, box 61, folder 53, Walter A. Jessup Papers.

274. Mehler, "History of the American Eugenics," 68. For more information on Brigham, see, for example, Black, *War against the Weak*, especially 82–85.

275. Black, *War against the Weak*, 83. For further information on the SATs, see Nicholas Lehmann, *The Big Test: The Secret History of the American Meritocracy* (New York: Farrar, Straus and Giroux, 1999).

276. Carl C. Brigham, *A Study of American Intelligence* (Princeton, NJ: Princeton University Press, 1923), 157–76, https://archive.org/stream/studyofamericani00bri guoft#mode/2up

277. Brigham, *Study of American*, 192.

278. Brigham, *Study of American*, xvii.

279. Carl C. Brigham, "Intelligence Tests of Immigrant Groups," *Psychological Review* 37, no. 2 (March 1930): 164–65.

280. Brigham, "Intelligence Tests of Immigrant," 164.

281. Andrew R. Heinze, *Jews and the American Soul: Human Nature in the Twentieth Century* (Princeton, NJ: Princeton University Press, 2004), 379n9.

282. Black, *War against the Weak*, 85, 83.

283. Mehler, "History of the American Eugenics," 316.

284. Carl E. Seashore, Iowa City, IA, to Robert M. Yerkes, Franklin, NH, August 5, 1922, MS 569, box 43, folder 836, Robert Mearns Yerkes Papers, Manuscripts and Archives, Yale University Library, New Haven, CT; C. E. Seashore, Iowa City, IA, to Robert Yerkes, Washington, DC, August 7, 1923, MS 569, box 43, folder 836, Robert Mearns Yerkes Papers, Manuscripts and Archives, Yale University Library, New Haven, CT; Carl E. Seashore, Iowa City, IA, to Robert M. Yerkes, Franklin, NH, July 17, 1923, MS 569, box 43, folder 836, Robert Mearns Yerkes Papers, Manuscripts and Archives, Yale University Library, New Haven, CT; C.

E. Seashore, Iowa City, IA, to Robert M. Yerkes, New Haven, CT, December 1, 1930, MS 569, box 43, folder 837, Robert Mearns Yerkes Papers, Manuscripts and Archives, Yale University Library, New Haven, CT; C. E. Seashore, Iowa City, IA, to Robert M. Yerkes, New Haven, CT, October 2, 1931, MS 569, box 43, folder 837, Robert Mearns Yerkes Papers, Manuscripts and Archives, Yale University Library, New Haven, CT; Carl E. Seashore to Yerkes, December 12, 1938, MS 569, box 43, folder 837, Robert Mearns Yerkes Papers; Roberta and Carl Seashore, Winter Park, FL, to Friends (Christmas Letter), December 1947, MS 569, box 43, folder 837, Robert Mearns Yerkes Papers, Manuscripts and Archives, Yale University Library, New Haven, CT.

285. See, for example, Carl E. Seashore to Yerkes, August 5, 1922, MS 569, box 43, folder 836, Robert Mearns Yerkes Papers; C. E. Seashore to Yerkes, August 7, 1923, MS 569, box 43, folder 836, Robert Mearns Yerkes Papers; Carl E. Seashore to Yerkes, September 17, 1925, MS 569, box 43, folder 836, Robert Mearns Yerkes Papers; Carl E. Seashore to Yerkes, July 17, 1923, MS 569, box 43, folder 836, Robert Mearns Yerkes Papers; Yerkes to Carl E. Seashore, September 22, 1925, MS 569, box 43, folder 836, Robert Mearns Yerkes Papers; Yerkes to Carl E. Seashore, October 13, 1928, MS 569, box 43, folder 836, Robert Mearns Yerkes Papers; Yerkes to Carl E. Seashore, October 28, 1930, MS 569, box 43, folder 837, Robert Mearns Yerkes Papers; C. E. Seashore to Yerkes, December 1, 1930, MS 569, box 43, folder 837, Robert Mearns Yerkes Papers; C. E. Seashore to Yerkes, October 2, 1931, MS 569, box 43, folder 837, Robert Mearns Yerkes Papers; Carl E. Seashore to Yerkes, November 24, 1931, MS 569, box 43, folder 837, Robert Mearns Yerkes Papers; Carl E. Seashore to Yerkes, December 12, 1938, MS 569, box 43, folder 837, Robert Mearns Yerkes Papers; Yerkes to Carl E. Seashore, December 15, 1938, MS 569, box 43, folder 837, Robert Mearns Yerkes Papers; Carl E. Seashore to Yerkes, November 10, 1942, MS 569, box 43, folder 837, Robert Mearns Yerkes Papers; Yerkes to Carl E. Seashore, December 4, 1942, p. 2, MS 569, box 43, folder 837, Robert Mearns Yerkes Papers; Yerkes to Carl E. Seashore, February 14, 1944, MS 569, box 43, folder 837, Robert Mearns Yerkes Papers; Yerkes to Carl E. Seashore, May 8, 1944, MS 569, box 43, folder 837, Robert Mearns Yerkes Papers; Yerkes to Carl E. Seashore, October 4, 1944, MS 569, box 43, folder 837, Robert Mearns Yerkes Papers; Robert M. Yerkes to Carl Seashore, Iowa City, IA, June 2, 1945, MS 569, box 43, folder 837, Robert Mearns Yerkes Papers, Manuscripts and Archives, Yale University Library, New Haven, CT; Yerkes to Carl E. Seashore, October 19, 1945, MS 569, box 43, folder 837, Robert Mearns Yerkes Papers; and Yerkes to Carl E. Seashore, May 27, 1947, p. 2, MS 569, box 43, folder 837, Robert Mearns Yerkes Papers.

286. Yerkes to Carl Seashore, June 2, 1945, MS 569, box 43, folder 837, Robert Mearns Yerkes Papers.

287. See, for example, Carl E. Seashore to Yerkes, February 23, 1916, MS 569, box 43, folder 836, Robert Mearns Yerkes Papers; and Yerkes to Carl E. Seashore, September 22, 1925, MS 569, box 43, folder 836, Robert Mearns Yerkes Papers.

288. Yerkes to Carl E. Seashore, April 10, 1944, MS 569, box 43, folder 837, Robert Mearns Yerkes Papers; Carl E. Seashore to Yerkes, April 19, 1944, MS 569, box 43, folder 837, Robert Mearns Yerkes Papers.

289. Carl E. Seashore to Yerkes, April 19, 1944, MS 569, box 43, folder 837, Robert Mearns Yerkes Papers.

290. Roberta and Carl Seashore to Friends, December 1947, MS 569, box 43, folder 837, Robert Mearns Yerkes Papers; Roberta and Carl Seashore, Winter Park, FL, to Friends (Christmas Letter) [1948], MS 569, box 43, folder 837, Robert Mearns Yerkes Papers, Manuscripts and Archives, Yale University Library, New Haven, CT.

291. Carl E. Seashore, Lewiston, ID, to the Yerkes Family [undated but between August 17, 1949, and September 25, 1949], MS 569, box 43, folder 837, Robert Mearns Yerkes Papers, Manuscripts and Archives, Yale University Library, New Haven, CT.

292. Carl E. Seashore to the Yerkes Family [undated but between August 17, 1949, and September 25, 1949], MS 569, box 43, folder 837, Robert Mearns Yerkes Papers.

293. Carl E. Seashore to the Yerkes Family [undated but between August 17, 1949, and September 25, 1949], MS 569, box 43, folder 837, Robert Mearns Yerkes Papers.

294. "Dr. Carl Seashore, Psychologist, 83" [unidentified, undated newspaper clipping], MS 569, box 43, folder 837, Robert Mearns Yerkes Papers, Manuscripts and Archives, Yale University Library, New Haven, CT.

295. Garland E. Allen, "Davenport, Charles Benedict," *American National Biography*, February 2000, https://www.anb.org/view/10.1093/anb/9780198606697.001.0001/anb-9780198606697-e-1300392; Allan Chase, *The Legacy of Malthus: The Social Costs of the New Scientific Racism* (New York: Alfred A. Knopf, 1977), 118; "Eugenics Record Office (ERO)," Image Archive on the American Eugenics Movement, DNA Learning Center, Cold Spring Harbor Laboratory, accessed June 24, 2015, http://www.eugenicsarchive.org/html/eugenics/static/themes/20.html

296. Garland Allen, "Davenport, Charles Benedict"; Chase, *Legacy of Malthus*, 118.

297. "Eugenics Record Office (ERO)," Image Archive.

298. Mehler, "History of the American Eugenics," 420.

299. Cera R. Lawrence, "The Eugenics Record Office at Cold Spring Harbor Laboratory (1910–1939)," *Embryo Project Encyclopedia*, April 21, 2011, http://embryo.asu.edu/handle/10776/2091

300. "Eugenics Record Office (ERO)," Image Archive.

301. Ruth Clifford Engs, *The Progressive Era's Health Reform Movement: A Historical Dictionary* (Westport, CT: Praeger, 2003), 119.

302. "The American Eugenics Society, Inc.," *Eugenics* 1, no. 1 (October 1928): opposite 1. For more discussion of Davenport, his views, and the ERO, see, for example, Black, *War against the Weak*; Daniel J. Kevles, *In the Name of Eugenics: Genetics and the Uses of Human Heredity* (Berkeley: University of California Press, 1986; and Kenny, "Toward a Racial Abyss," 263–71.

303. Carl E. Seashore, Iowa City, IA, to Charles B. Davenport, Cold Spring Harbor, NY, January 11, 1919, MSS.B.D27, box 85, Charles B. Davenport Papers, American Philosophical Society Archives, Philadelphia, PA.

304. Carl E. Seashore to Davenport, January 11, 1919, MSS.B.D27, box 85, Charles B. Davenport Papers.

305. Charles B. Davenport to Carl E. Seashore, Iowa City, IA, April 15, 1919 (with attachment), p. 1, MSS.B.D27, box 85, Charles B. Davenport Papers, American Philosophical Society Archives, Philadelphia, PA.

306. Davenport to Carl E. Seashore, April 15, 1919, MSS.B.D27, box 85, Charles B. Davenport Papers.

307. Carl E. Seashore, Iowa City, IA, to Charles B. Davenport, Cold Spring Harbor, NY, April 24, 1919, MSS.B.D27, box 85, Charles B. Davenport Papers, American Philosophical Society Archives, Philadelphia, PA.

308. Charles B. Davenport to Carl E. Seashore, Iowa City, IA, May 2, 1919, MSS.B.D27, box 85, Charles B. Davenport Papers, American Philosophical Society Archives, Philadelphia, PA.

309. See Carl E. Seashore, Iowa City, IA, to Charles B. Davenport, Cold Spring Harbor, NY, May 12, 1919, MSS.B.D27, box 85, Charles B. Davenport Papers, American Philosophical Society Archives, Philadelphia, PA; Carl E. Seashore, Iowa City, IA, to Charles B. Davenport, Cold Spring Harbor, NY, October 4, 1919, MSS.B.D27, box 85, Charles B. Davenport Papers, American Philosophical Society Archives, Philadelphia, PA, which refers to the scale of the project on p. 2; Charles B. Davenport to Carl E. Seashore, Iowa City, IA, October 7, 1919, MSS.B.D27, box 85, Charles B. Davenport Papers, American Philosophical Society Archives, Philadelphia, PA; and Charles B. Davenport to Dr. C. E. Seashore, Iowa City, IA, November 22, 1919, box D27, Charles Benedict Davenport Papers, American Philosophical Society Archives, Philadelphia, PA.

310. Charles B. Davenport to Professor C. E. Seashore, Iowa City, IA, December 16, 1919, box D27, Charles Benedict Davenport Papers, American Philosophical Society Archives, Philadelphia, PA.

311. Carl E. Seashore, Iowa City, IA, to Dr. [Charles B.] Davenport, Cold Spring Harbor, NY, November 17, 1919, MSS.B.D27, box 85, Charles B. Davenport Papers, American Philosophical Society Archives, Philadelphia, PA.

312. Carl E. Seashore to Davenport, April 9, 1920, p. 1, MSS.B.D27, box 85, Charles B. Davenport Papers.

313. Charles B. Davenport to Carl E. Seashore, Washington, DC, April 14, 1920, MSS.B.D27, box 85, Charles B. Davenport Papers, American Philosophical Society Archives, Philadelphia, PA.

314. Carl E. Seashore, Washington, DC, to Charles B. Davenport, Cold Spring Harbor, NY, April 16, 1920, box D27, Charles Benedict Davenport Papers, Archives, American Philosophical Society Library, Philadelphia, PA.

315. "Eugenics Research Association Number: Ninth Annual Meeting," 54.

316. Carl E. Seashore, Washington, DC, to Charles B. Davenport, Cold Spring Harbor, NY, March 4, 1922, box D27, Charles Benedict Davenport Papers, American Philosophical Society Archives, Philadelphia, PA; Charles B. Davenport to Carl E. Seashore, Washington, DC, March 6, 1922, box D27, Charles Benedict Davenport Papers, American Philosophical Society, Philadelphia, PA; Paul G.

Tomlinson, Princeton, NJ, to Charles B. Davenport, Cold Spring Harbor, NY, March 29, 1922, box D27, Charles Benedict Davenport Papers, American Philosophical Society Archives, Philadelphia, PA; Carl E. Seashore, Washington, DC, to Charles B. Davenport, Cold Spring Harbor, NY, March 30, 1922, box D27, Charles Benedict Davenport Papers, American Philosophical Society Archives, Philadelphia, PA; Charles B. Davenport to Paul G. Tomlinson, Princeton, NJ, March 31, 1922, box D27, Charles Benedict Davenport Papers, American Philosophical Society Archives, Philadelphia, PA.

317. Hazel M. Stanton, "The Inheritance of Specific Musical Capacities," *Psychological Monographs* 31, no. 1 (1922): 157, https://books.google.com/books?id=EcZMAAAAYAAJ&pg=PA157&lpg=PA157&dq=psychological+monographs+stanton&source=bl&ots=iF16DIvuj_&sig=BKOODKF4gSp2FlWKAPY_WGSl4co&hl=en&sa=X&ei=wG-MVZDGNdCzoQT9ipCICw&ved=0CCQQ6AEwAA#v=onepage&q=psychological%20monographs%20stanton&f=false

318. Charles B. Davenport to Carl E. Seashore, Iowa City, IA, October 15, 1919, MSS.B.D27, box 85, Charles B. Davenport Papers, American Philosophical Society Archives, Philadelphia, PA. Also, the visit is described in Carl E. Seashore, Iowa City, IA, to Charles B. Davenport, Cold Spring Harbor, NY, October 11, 1919, MSS.B.D27, box 85, Charles B. Davenport Papers, American Philosophical Society Archives, Philadelphia, PA.

319. Charles B. Davenport to Carl E. Seashore, Iowa City, IA, February 15, 1929, MSS.B.D27, box 85, Charles B. Davenport Papers, American Philosophical Society Archives, Philadelphia, PA. A response from Seashore indicates that he was unable to attend but hoped to be present at the next meeting. See Carl E. Seashore, Iowa City, IA, to Charles B. Davenport, Cold Spring Harbor, NY, February 28, 1929, MSS.B.D27, box 85, Charles B. Davenport Papers, American Philosophical Society Archives, Philadelphia, PA.

320. Davenport to Carl E. Seashore, October 15, 1919, MSS.B.D27, box 85, Charles B. Davenport Papers.

321. Carl E. Seashore, Iowa City, IA, to Charles B. Davenport, Cold Spring Harbor, NY, December 24, 1919, MSS.B.D27, box 85, Charles B. Davenport Papers, American Philosophical Society Archives, Philadelphia, PA.

322. Charles B. Davenport to Carl E. Seashore, Iowa City, IA, January 5, 1920, MSS.B.D27, box 85, Charles B. Davenport Papers, American Philosophical Society Archives, Philadelphia, PA.

323. Carl E. Seashore, "Origin of the Term 'Euthenics,'" *Science*, n.s., 95, no. 2470 (May 1, 1942): 455, http://www.jstor.org/stable/1668977

324. "Studies in Jamaica," 154.

325. *Oxford English Dictionary Online*, s.v. "moron [n.2 and adj.]," accessed November 2, 2007, http://www.oed.com/view/Entry/122316?rskey=PomCLj&result=2; Steven A. Gelb, "Social Deviance and the 'Discovery' of the Moron," *Disability, Handicap, and Society* 2, no. 3 (September 1987): 247; Black, *War against the Weak*, 78. For examples of Seashore's use of the term, see Carl E. Seashore, "Sectioning Classes on the Basis of Ability," *School and Society* 15, no. 379 (April 1922):

354; Carl E. Seashore, *Pioneering in Psychology*, 157; Carl E. Seashore, *Psychology of Music*, 57; and Carl E. Seashore, *Learning and Living in College: Psychology of Individual Differences Applied to the Organization and Pursuit of Higher Education; A Study Based upon Experience in the Promotion of the Gifted Student Project in the National Research Council*, University of Iowa Studies: Series on Aims and Progress of Research, vol. 2, no. 1 (Iowa City: The University, 1927), 6.

326. Kevles, *In the Name of Eugenics*, 77.

327. Mehler, "History of the American Eugenics," 68.

328. Kevles, *In the Name of Eugenics*, 78.

329. Zenderland, *Measuring Minds*, 332, 331.

330. Henry H. Goddard, "Forty Years of 'Firsts,'" review of *Pioneering in Psychology*, by Carl. E. Seashore, *Journal of Higher Education* 14, no. 4 (April 1943): 225–26, https://doi.org/10.2307/1975715

331. Carl E. Seashore, "The Master's Key to the Domain of Educational Theory and Practice," *Education Digest* 15, no. 6 (February 1950): 19; repr. fr. *School and Society* 70 (November 26, 1949): 337–38.

332. Carl E. Seashore, "Master's Key," 19.

333. Carl E. Seashore, "Master's Key," 19.

334. Carl E. Seashore, "Master's Key," 20.

335. Miles, "Carl Emil Seashore, 1866–1949," 281.

336. Carl E. Seashore, "Communications and Discussions: Mentality Tests" (March 1916), 163–66.

337. Carl E. Seashore, ed. and moderator, "Communications and Discussions: Mentality Tests" (April 1916), 229.

338. Carl E. Seashore, ed. and moderator, "Communications and Discussions: Mentality Tests" (April 1916), 231–33.

339. Carl E. Seashore, ed. and moderator, "Communications and Discussions: Mentality Tests" (May 1916), 287–93. Defense of the Binet test appears on p. 290.

340. Black, *War against the Weak*, 85.

341. Wikipedia, s.v. "National Research Council (United States)," last modified May 15, 2015, https://en.wikipedia.org/wiki/National_Research_Council_%28United_States%29 (link now goes elsewhere; see Wayback Machine).

342. "Advisory Council of the Eugenics Committee of the United States of America," 29.

343. Carl E. Seashore, "Carl Emil Seashore," 288–89.

344. *Fifth Annual Report of the National Research Council*, 77; *Report of the National Research Council for the Year July 1, 1921*, 80.

345. Cravens, *Before Head Start*, 41.

346. Carl E. Seashore, "Carl Emil Seashore," 289.

347. C. E. Seashore to Dr. Vernon Kellogg, Washington, DC, March 1, 1927, p. 1, RG 05.01.09, box 187, folder 50, Walter A. Jessup Papers, Special Collections and University Archives, University of Iowa Libraries, Iowa City, IA.

348. According to Seashore, the project lasted for six years; he traveled for the final five years and someone else traveled the first year. See Carl E. Seashore, *Pio-*

neering in Psychology, 193. Miles says the project lasted five years. See Miles, "Carl Emil Seashore, 1866–1949," 292.

349. Carl E. Seashore, "Carl Emil Seashore," 290.

350. C. E. Seashore to Kellogg, March 1, 1927, RG 05.01.09, box 187, folder 50, Walter A. Jessup Papers.

351. Vernon Kellogg, Washington, DC, to Walter A. Jessup, Iowa City, IA, January 28, 1925, RG 05.01.09, box 145, folder 49, Walter A. Jessup Papers, Special Collections and University Archives, University of Iowa Libraries, Iowa City, IA. For a list of the schools represented at the conference, see "List of Institutions to be Represented at Honors Courses Conference, University of Iowa, March 17 and 18, 1925, with Names of Delegates," RG 05.01.09, box 145, folder 49, Walter A. Jessup Papers, Special Collections and University Archives, University of Iowa Libraries, Iowa City, IA.

352. Kellogg to Jessup, January 28, 1925, p. 1, RG 05.01.09, box 145, folder 49, Walter A. Jessup Papers.

353. C. E. Seashore, Redlands, CA, to President Walter Jessup, Iowa City, IA, November 28, 1924, RG 05.01.09, box 145, folder 49, Walter A. Jessup Papers, Special Collections and University Archives, University of Iowa Libraries, Iowa City, IA.

354. Vernon Kellogg, Washington, DC, to Walter A. Jessup, Iowa City, IA, March 2, 1925, RG 05.01.09, box 145, folder 49, Walter A. Jessup Papers, Special Collections and University Archives, University of Iowa Libraries, Iowa City, IA.

355. Mehler, "History of the American Eugenics," 204–5.

356. Mehler, "History of the American Eugenics," 82, 135.

357. Seashore states this in the editor's note preceding Hazel M. Stanton, *Measurement of Musical Talent: The Eastman Experiment*, University of Iowa Studies: Studies in the Psychology of Music, n.s. 291, vol. 2 (Iowa City: The University, 1935), 3, https://babel.hathitrust.org/cgi/pt?id=mdp.39015009448773&view=1up&seq=5

358. "Eugenics Research Association Number: Ninth Annual Meeting," 54.

359. Stanton, "Experimental Investigation of Musical Inheritance," 239–42.

360. "Personal Notes," *Eugenical News* 7, no. 1 (January 1922): 4.

361. See, for example, Hazel M. Stanton, "Quantitative Yard-Stick for the Measurement of Musical Capacities," *Eugenical News* 18, no. 4 (July-August 1933): 78–81; and "Measuring Musical Capacities," 71.

362. "Editor's Foreword" by Seashore, in Stanton, *Measurement of Musical Talent*, 3. The Eastman School dismissed Stanton in 1932. See [Arthur J. May and students], "University of Rochester History: Chapter 18; The Birth of a Music Center," Rare Books, Special Collections and Preservation University of Rochester, accessed August 12, 2015, https://rbscp.lib.rochester.edu/2324. On the title page of *Measurement of Musical Talent*, Stanton described herself as a consulting psychologist in music at the Psychological Service Center of New York.

363. Miles, "Carl Emil Seashore, 1866–1949," 301.

364. Carl E. Seashore, *Psychology of Music*, 315.

365. Carl E. Seashore, "Carl Emil Seashore," 274. In 1942, Seashore again quoted Eastman on this topic. See Carl E. Seashore, "Talent," *School and Society* 55, no. 1416 (February 14, 1942): 173.

366. George Eastman, Rochester, NY, to Dr. Carl Emil Seashore, Iowa City, IA, February 15, 1927, RG 05.01.09, box 187, folder 50, Walter A. Jessup Papers, Special Collections and University Archives, University of Iowa Libraries, Iowa City, IA.

367. C. E. Seashore, Washington, DC, to President W. A. Jessup, Iowa City, IA, April 29, 1921 (with attachment), RG 05.01.09, box 76, folder 53, Walter A. Jessup Papers, Special Collections and University Archives, University of Iowa Libraries, Iowa City, IA. For the proposal, see the attachment to the letter: Carl E. Seashore, "Basic Measurements of Music and Speech," pp. 1–7.

368. Carl E. Seashore, "Basic Measurements," p. 6, attachment to C. E. Seashore to President W. A. Jessup, April 29, 1921, 1–7, RG 05.01.09, box 76, folder 53, Walter A. Jessup Papers.

369. C. E. Seashore to Jessup, April 29, 1921, RG 05.01.09, box 76, folder 53, Walter A. Jessup Papers.

370. For more information about Mjøen and his work on eugenics, see, for example, Mehler, "History of the American Eugenics," 53–58; Steven Selden, *Inheriting Shame: The Story of Eugenics and Racism in America* (New York: Teachers College, 1999), 46–48; and Black, *War against the Weak*, 71, 244, 279.

371. C. B. S. Hodson, "Eugenics in Norway," *Eugenics Review* 27, no. 1 (April 1935): 43.

372. Mehler, "History of the American Eugenics," 57–58.

373. Black, *War against the Weak*, 279.

374. Jon Alfred Mjøen, "The Masculine Education of Women and Its Dangers," *Eugenics* 3, no. 9 (September 1930): 323–26.

375. Hodson, "Eugenics in Norway," 43.

376. Hodson, "Eugenics in Norway," 43.

377. Carl E. Seashore, *Psychology of Music*, 309. Seashore cited Fridtjof Mjöen, "Die Bedeutung der Tonhöhenunterschiedsempfindlichkeit für die Musikalität und ihr Verhalten bei der Vererbung," *Hereditas* 7, no. 11 (1926): 161–88; and Jon Alfred Mjöen, *Die Vererbung der musikalischen Begabung* (Berlin: Alfred Metzner, 1934). Note that although Seashore says "Die Bedeutung der Tonhöhenunterschiedsempfindlichkeit für die Musikalität und ihr Verhalten bei der Vererbung" was coauthored by Alfred and Fridtjof, the journal only named one author, Fridtjof. See Fridtjof Mjöen, "Die Bedeutung der Tonhöhenunterschiedsempfindlichkeit," 161.

378. Carl E. Seashore, *Psychology of Music*, 345.

379. Carl E. Seashore, "Musical Inheritance," *Scientific Monthly* 50, no. 4 (April 1940): 355.

380. Jon Mjöen, *Die Vererbung der musikalischen Begabung*, 17, 20, 51.

381. Fridtjof Mjöen, "Die Bedeutung der Tonhöhenunterschiedsempfindlichkeit," 161–88.

382. Jon Alfred Mjøen, "Harmonic and Disharmonic Racecrossings," in *Eugenics in Race and State*, vol. 2, *The Scientific Papers of the Second International Congress of Eugenics; Held at American Museum of Natural History, New York, September 22–28, 1921* (Baltimore, MD: Williams & Wilkins, 1923; repr., ed. Charles Rosenberg, New York: Garland Publishing, 1985), 41–61.

383. Henry Fairfield Osborn, "Address of Welcome," in *Eugenics, Genetics and the Family*, vol. 1, *Scientific Papers of the Second International Congress of Eugenics; Held at American Museum of Natural History, New York, September 22–28, 1921* (Baltimore, MD: Williams & Wilkins, 1923; repr., ed. Charles Rosenberg, New York: Garland Publishing, 1985), 1.

384. Mehler, "History of the American Eugenics," 36; Black, *War against the Weak*, 244.

385. See Miles, "Carl Emil Seashore, 1866–1949," 310, in the publications listed for 1923.

386. Lewis Jones, "Carl Emil Seashore: Dean," 42–43.

387. J. B. Eggen, "The Fallacy of Eugenics," *Social Forces* 5, no. 1 (September 1926): 108, www.jstor.org/stable/3004817

388. Mehler, "History of the American Eugenics," 172.

389. Mehler, "History of the American Eugenics," 176.

390. Mehler, "History of the American Eugenics," 422.

391. Minton, "Iowa Child Welfare Research," 164.

392. Alice Boardman Smuts, *Science in the Service of Children, 1893–1935* (New Haven, CT: Yale University Press, 2006), 130.

393. "The American Eugenics Society: Members, Officers and Directors Activities Database," Eugenics Watch, November 8, 2005, http://www.archive.org/details/The_American_Eugenics_Society__Members_Officers_And_Directors_Activites_Database

394. Alexander W. Cowan, "Music Psychology and the American Eugenics Movement in the Early Twentieth Century" (MMus thesis, King's College, London, 2016); Adria R. Hoffman, "Competing Narratives: Musical Aptitude, Race, and Equity," in *Palgrave Handbook of Race and the Arts in Education*, eds. Amelia M. Kraehe, Rubén Gaztambide-Fernández, and B. Stephen Carpenter II (Cham, Switzerland: Palgrave, 2018), 103–17, https://link.springer.com/book/10.1007%2F978-3-319-65256-6; Johanna Devaney, "Eugenics and Musical Talent: Exploring Carl Seashore's Work on Talent Testing and Performance," *American Music Review* 48, no. 2 (Spring, 2019): 1–6, http://www.brooklyn.edu/web/aca_centers_hitchcock/AMR_48-2_Devaney.pdf

Chapter 4

1. Herman H. Rubin, *Eugenics and Sex Harmony: The Sexes, Their Relations and Problems, Including Recent Fascinating Medical Discoveries, Prevention of Disease, and Special Advice for Common Disorders* (New York: Pioneer Publications, 1946), 130–31.

2. Carl E. Seashore, *The Junior College Movement* (New York: Henry Holt, 1940), 123, https://babel.hathitrust.org/cgi/pt?id=mdp.39015020699834;view=1up;seq=7. Also Carl E. Seashore, "Education for Democracy and the Junior College," *School and Society* 25, no. 643 (April 23, 1927): 473–74. A slightly revised version of this essay was published in Carl E. Seashore, *Learning and Living in College: Psychology of Individual Differences Applied to the Organization and Pursuit of Higher Education; A Study Based upon Experience in the Promotion of the Gifted Student Project in the National Research Council*, University of Iowa Studies: Series on Aims and Progress of Research, vol. 2, no. 1 (Iowa City: The University, 1927), 88–102; and a condensed version was published under the same title in the *Bulletin of the American Association of University Professors* 13, no. 6 (October 1927): 399–404.

3. Carl E. Seashore, *In Search of Beauty in Music: A Scientific Approach to Musical Esthetics* (New York: Ronald, 1947), 366, https://archive.org/details/insearchofbeauty000817mbp/page/n8/mode/2up

4. Carl E. Seashore, *In Search of Beauty* (1947), 366.

5. Donald F. Howard, "History of the State University of Iowa: The Graduate College" (PhD diss., University of Iowa, 1947), 69. On p. 78n70, Howard cites Carl E. Seashore, "The Dean's Function as a Personnel Guide to Students," MS in Office of Graduate College, pp. 2–7.

6. Carl E. Seashore, "Is There Overproduction in Higher Education?" *School and Society* 37, no. 955 (April 15, 1933): 480.

7. Carl E. Seashore, *In Search of Beauty* (1947), 366.

8. "Memorandum on Greetings to the 13th and Last Annual Brain Derby, June 4, 1941," attachment to Carl E. Seashore, Iowa City, IA, to Virgil M. Hancher, Old Capitol, June 9, 1941, RG 05.01.11, box 16, folder 93, Virgil M. Hancher Papers, Special Collections and University Archives, University of Iowa Libraries, Iowa City, IA.

9. Carl E. Seashore and Roberta H. Seashore, "The Aesthetics of Marriage," in *Modern Marriage*, ed. Moses Jung (New York: F. S. Crofts, 1940), 70.

10. Carl E. Seashore and Roberta Seashore, "Aesthetics of Marriage," 70.

11. Carl E. Seashore and Roberta Seashore, "Aesthetics of Marriage," 74.

12. Carl E. Seashore and Roberta Seashore, "Aesthetics of Marriage," 72.

13. Carl E. Seashore and Roberta Seashore, "Aesthetics of Marriage," 72–73.

14. Carl E. Seashore and Roberta Seashore, "Aesthetics of Marriage," 73.

15. Carl E. Seashore and Roberta Seashore, "Aesthetics of Marriage," 73. Carl Seashore quoted Roberta on this subject in Carl E. Seashore, "An Open Letter: Addressed to Women in Graduate Schools," *Journal of Higher Education* 13, no. 5 (May 1942): 240, https://doi.org/10.2307/1974933

16. Carl E. Seashore and Roberta Seashore, "Aesthetics of Marriage," 79–80.

17. Carl E. Seashore, "Education for Democracy," 473.

18. Carl E. Seashore, "Education for Democracy," 474.

19. Carl E. Seashore, *Junior College Movement*, 123.

20. Himie Voxman, "Some Personal Reflections on Carl E. Seashore," in *Multidisciplinary Perspectives on Musicality: Essays from the Seashore Symposium*, ed. Kate Gfeller et al. (Iowa City: University of Iowa School of Music, 2006), 217.

21. Lewis Lester Jones, "Carl Emil Seashore: Dean of the Graduate College of the University of Iowa, 1908 to 1936, Dean *Pro Tempore*, 1942 to 1946; A Study of His Ideas on Graduate Education" (PhD diss., University of Iowa, 1978), 177, http://search.proquest.com.ezproxy.library.wisc.edu/docview/302883038?accountid=465

22. Carl E. Seashore, "Graduate Study: An Address Delivered to the Students in the Colleges of Iowa in 1909," *Bulletin of the State University of Iowa*, n.s., 11 (June 2, 1910): 9.

23. Carl E. Seashore, "Graduate Study: An Address," 3–8.

24. Carl E. Seashore, "Graduate Study: An Address," 8.

25. Carl E. Seashore, "Graduate Study: An Address," 3–4.

26. Carl E. Seashore, "Graduate Study: An Address," 4.

27. Carl E. Seashore, "Graduate Study: An Address," 5.

28. Carl E. Seashore, "Graduate Study: An Address," 7.

29. Carl E. Seashore, "Open Letter: Addressed to Women," 236.

30. Carl E. Seashore, "Open Letter: Addressed to Women," 236.

31. Carl E. Seashore, "Open Letter: Addressed to Women," 237.

32. Carl E. Seashore, "Open Letter: Addressed to Women," 242.

33. Carl E. Seashore, "Open Letter: Addressed to Women," 242.

34. Carl E. Seashore, "Open Letter: Addressed to Women," 236.

35. Carl E. Seashore, "Open Letter: Addressed to Women," 236.

36. Carl E. Seashore, "Open Letter: Addressed to Women," 242.

37. Carl E. Seashore, "Open Letter: Addressed to Women," 237.

38. Carl E. Seashore, "Open Letter: Addressed to Women," 237.

39. Carl E. Seashore, "Open Letter: Addressed to Women," 237.

40. Carl E. Seashore, "Open Letter: Addressed to Women," 237.

41. Carl E. Seashore, "Open Letter: Addressed to Women," 237–38.

42. Carl E. Seashore and Roberta Seashore, "Aesthetics of Marriage," 79.

43. Carl E. Seashore, "Open Letter: Addressed to Women," 239.

44. Carl E. Seashore, "Open Letter: Addressed to Women," 240; Carl E. Seashore and Roberta Seashore, "Aesthetics of Marriage," 72–73.

45. Carl E. Seashore, "Open Letter: Addressed to Women," 240.

46. Carl E. Seashore, "Graduate Study: An Address," 6.

47. Carl E. Seashore, "Open Letter: Addressed to Women," 238–39.

48. Carl E. Seashore, "Open Letter: Addressed to Women," 239–40.

49. Carl E. Seashore, "Open Letter: Addressed to Women," 241.

50. Carl E. Seashore and Roberta Seashore, "Aesthetics of Marriage," 80.

51. Carl E. Seashore, *In Search of Beauty* (1947), 366.

52. Carl E. Seashore, "Graduate Study: An Address," 12.

53. Carl E. Seashore, "Open Letter: Addressed to Women," 241. See also the earlier version: Carl E. Seashore and Roberta Seashore, "Aesthetics of Marriage," 80.

54. Carl E. Seashore, "Open Letter: Addressed to Women," 241.

55. Carl E. Seashore and Roberta Seashore, "Aesthetics of Marriage," 79.

56. Carl E. Seashore and Roberta Seashore, "Aesthetics of Marriage," 80.

57. Carl E. Seashore, "Open Letter: Addressed to Women," 238.

58. Carl E. Seashore, "Open Letter: Addressed to Women," 238.

59. Carl E. Seashore, "Open Letter: Addressed to Women," 238.

60. Carl E. Seashore and Roberta Seashore, "Aesthetics of Marriage," 79.

61. Edwin D. Starbuck to Walter A. Jessup [undated, describing incident on September 21, 1926], RG 99.0164, box 2, Carl E. Seashore Papers, Special Collections and University Archives, University of Iowa Libraries, Iowa City, IA.

62. Starbuck to Jessup [undated, describing incident on September 21, 1926], RG 99.0164, box 2, Carl E. Seashore Papers.

63. Carl E. Seashore, "Graduate Study: An Address," 13.

64. Carl E. Seashore, "Open Letter: Addressed to Women," 238.

65. Carl E. Seashore, "Open Letter: Addressed to Women," 238.

66. Carl E. Seashore, "Carl Emil Seashore," vol. 1, *A History of Psychology in Autobiography*, ed. Carl Allanmore Murchison (Worcester, MA: Clark University, 1930), 255; Carl E. Seashore, "Psychology and Life in Autobiography," typed manuscript, p. 245, RG 99.0164, box 2, Carl E. Seashore Papers, Special Collections and University Archives, University of Iowa Libraries, Iowa City, IA.

67. Carl E. Seashore, *Psychology in Daily Life* (New York: D. Appleton, 1914), 91–92.

68. Carl E. Seashore, *Psychology in Daily Life*, 91–92.

69. See "An Analyzed Rating of Promise for Research in College Students," which was attached to Carl E. Seashore, Iowa City, IA, to Robert M. Yerkes, Washington, DC, January 3, 1921, MS 569, box 43, folder 836, Robert Mearns Yerkes Papers, Manuscripts and Archives, Yale University Library, New Haven, CT.

70. C. E. Seashore to Dr. Vernon Kellogg, Washington, DC, March 1, 1927, p. 2, RG 05.01.09, box 187, folder 50, Walter A. Jessup Papers, Special Collections and University Archives, University of Iowa Libraries, Iowa City, IA.

71. Carl E. Seashore, *A Preview to College and Life*, University of Iowa Studies: Series on Aims and Progress of Research, no. 55 (Iowa City: University of Iowa, 1938), 9–28.

72. Carl E. Seashore, *Preview to College*, 12–13.

73. Carl E. Seashore, *Preview to College*, 12.

74. Carl E. Seashore, *Preview to College*, 12.

75. Carl E. Seashore, *Preview to College*, 12.

76. Carl E. Seashore, *Learning and Living*, 17.

77. Carl E. Seashore, *Learning and Living*, 17.

78. Carl E. Seashore, "Carl Emil Seashore," 246.

79. Claudia Goldin, Lawrence F. Katz, and Ilyana Kuziemko, "The Homecoming of American College Women: The Reversal of the College Gender Gap," *Journal of Economic Perspectives* 20, no. 4 (Fall 2006): 133.

80. Goldin, Katz, and Kuziemko, "Homecoming of American College," 134–36.

81. Goldin, Katz, and Kuziemko, "Homecoming of American College," 136.

82. Goldin, Katz, and Kuziemko, "Homecoming of American College," 135.

83. Carl E. Seashore, "Open Letter: Addressed to Women," 239, 241; Carl E. Seashore and Roberta Seashore, "Aesthetics of Marriage," 80.

84. Carl E. Seashore, *In Search of Beauty* (1947), 363.
85. Carl E. Seashore, *In Search of Beauty* (1947), 364.
86. Carl E. Seashore, *In Search of Beauty* (1947), 364.
87. Carl E. Seashore, *In Search of Beauty* (1947), 364.
88. Carl E. Seashore, *In Search of Beauty* (1947), 365.
89. Carl E. Seashore, *In Search of Beauty* (1947), 365.
90. Carl E. Seashore, *In Search of Beauty* (1947), 366.
91. Carl E. Seashore, *In Search of Beauty* (1947), 363.
92. Carl E. Seashore, *In Search of Beauty* (1947), 367.
93. Walter R. Miles, "Carl Emil Seashore, 1866–1949," vol. 29, *Biographical Memoirs* (New York: Columbia University Press for the National Academy of Sciences, 1956), 281. For a photograph of those attending the conference, see James C. Harris, "Clark University Vicennial Conference on Psychology and Pedagogy," *Archives of General Psychiatry* 67, no. 3 (March 2010): 219, https://doi.org/10.1001/archgenpsychiatry.2010.16
94. For more discussion, see Julia Eklund Koza, "Music and References to Music in *Godey's Lady's Book*, 1830–1877" (PhD diss., University of Minnesota, 1988), especially 302–11.
95. Edward H. Clarke, *Sex in Education; or, A Fair Chance for the Girls* (Boston: James R. Osgood, 1873), https://archive.org/details/sexineducationo01clargoog/page/n6
96. Howard, "History of the State University," 69–70, 201; Lewis Jones, "Carl Emil Seashore: Dean," 171–80. Jones described Seashore as a man of his times on p. 173.
97. See, for example, Adrian C. North and David J. Hargreaves, *The Social and Applied Psychology of Music* (New York: Oxford University Press, 2008), 25; and Paul R. Farnsworth, "The Effects of Role-Taking on Artistic Achievement," *Journal of Aesthetics and Art Criticism* 18, no. 3 (March 1960): 345, http://www.jstor.org/stable/428158. Also Marc Linder, "He Sells Misogynistic Ideas by the Seashore," *Daily Iowan*, March 7, 1997, 4A.
98. See *Oxford English Dictionary Online*, s.v. "race suicide," accessed March 28, 2019, http://www.oed.com/view/Entry/157031?redirectedFrom=%22race+suicide%22#eid27231385; Warren S. Thompson, "Race Suicide in the United States," *Scientific Monthly* 5, no. 1 (July 1917): 22, http://www.jstor.org/stable/22426; and Barry Alan Mehler, "A History of the American Eugenics Society, 1921–1940" (PhD diss., University of Illinois at Urbana-Champaign, 1988), 190, http://search.proquest.com.ezproxy.library.wisc.edu/docview/303689028?accountid=465. Ross, a eugenicist, was fired from Stanford University in 1900 and became a sociology professor at the University of Wisconsin–Madison in 1906.
99. Mehler, "History of the American Eugenics," 190.
100. [Wilhelm] Frick, "German Population and Race Politics," trans. A. Hellmer, *Eugenical News* 19, no. 2 (March-April 1934): 33–38.
101. See, for example, "Our Racial Decay," review of *Race Decadence: An Examination of the Causes of Racial Degeneracy in the United States*, by W. S. Sadler, *Eugenical News* 7, no. 3 (March 1922): 42.

102. C. G. Campbell, "The German Racial Policy," *Eugenical News* 21, no. 2 (March-April 1936): 25.

103. "Population and Its Control: Are the White People Dying Out?" *Eugenical News* 20, no. 1 (January-February 1935): 12–13.

104. "Population and Its Control," 13.

105. Carl E. Seashore, *Junior College Movement*, 123.

106. J. Russell Smith et al., "The Faculty Birth Rate: Should It Be Increased?" *Eugenics* 3, no. 12 (December 1930): 459.

107. Paul Popenoe and Roswell Hill Johnson, *Applied Eugenics* (New York: Macmillan, 1920), 258, 238.

108. "Non-Fecundity of the Fit," *Eugenical News* 5, no. 8 (August 1920): 60. The source quoted from "Class Variation in Fertility [Editorial Notes and Comments]," *New York Medical Journal* 111, no. 24 (June 12, 1920): 1042, https://babel.hathitrust.org/cgi/pt?id=nnc2.ark:/13960/t9v14qw7m;view=1up;seq=1064

109. Paul Popenoe and Roswell Johnson, *Applied Eugenics*, 258.

110. Henry Fairfield Osborn, "Address of Welcome," in *Eugenics, Genetics and the Family*, vol. 1, *Scientific Papers of the Second International Congress of Eugenics; Held at American Museum of Natural History, New York, September 22–28, 1921* (Baltimore, MD: Williams & Wilkins, 1923; repr., ed. Charles Rosenberg, New York: Garland Publishing, 1985), 4.

111. "Eugenics Research Association Number: Ninth Annual Meeting," *Eugenical News* 6, nos. 7–8 (July-August 1921): 49.

112. Paul Popenoe and Roswell Johnson, *Applied Eugenics*, 238–39.

113. Paul Popenoe and Roswell Johnson, *Applied Eugenics*, 246.

114. Frick, "German Population and Race," 33–35.

115. Frick, "German Population and Race," 35.

116. Smith et al., "Faculty Birth Rate," 459.

117. Frick, "German Population and Race," 35.

118. "Eugenics Research Association Number: Ninth Annual Meeting," 49.

119. Frick, "German Population and Race," 33.

120. Henry Osborn, "Address of Welcome," 1.

121. Paul Popenoe and Roswell Johnson, *Applied Eugenics*, 149, 284–85, 299.

122. Paul Popenoe and Roswell Johnson, *Applied Eugenics*, 138.

123. Paul Popenoe and Roswell Johnson, *Applied Eugenics*, 139.

124. Paul Popenoe and Roswell Johnson, *Applied Eugenics*, 138.

125. Paul Popenoe and Roswell Johnson, *Applied Eugenics*, 149.

126. Leonard Darwin, "The Aims and Methods of Eugenical Societies," in *Eugenics, Genetics and the Family*, vol. 1, *Scientific Papers of the Second International Congress of Eugenics; Held at American Museum of Natural History, New York, September 22–28, 1921* (Baltimore, MD: Williams & Wilkins, 1923; repr., ed. Charles Rosenberg, New York: Garland Publishing, 1985), 19.

127. Frick, "German Population and Race," 34.

128. "Racial Fecundity," *Eugenical News* 2, no. 12 (December 1917): 94.

129. Paul Popenoe and Roswell Johnson, *Applied Eugenics*, 173.

130. Frick, "German Population and Race," 36.

131. Charles White, *An Account of the Regular Gradation in Man, and in Different Animals and Vegetables; and from the Former to the Latter* (London: C. Dilly, 1799), 61, https://archive.org/details/b24924507

132. Charles White, *Account of the Regular Gradation*, 71–72.

133. Charles White, *Account of the Regular Gradation*, 60.

134. See Ann Marie Ryan and Alan Stoskopf, "Public and Catholic School Responses to IQ Testing in the Early 20th Century," *Teachers College Record* 110, no. 4 (2008), https://www.tcrecord.org/content.asp?contentid=14623; and Sharon Mara Leon, "Beyond Birth Control: Catholic Responses to the Eugenics Movement in the United States, 1900–1950," order no. 3142627 (PhD diss., University of Minnesota, 2004), https://search-proquest-com.ezproxy.library.wisc.edu/pqdtglobal/docview/305158996/fulltextPDF/1269932D352428FPQ/1?accountid=465. On p. 1, Leon states that opposition from Catholic leadership was strong.

135. Robert M. Yerkes to Carl E. Seashore, Iowa City, IA, May 27, 1947, p. 2, MS 569, box 43, folder 837, Robert Mearns Yerkes Papers, Manuscripts and Archives, Yale University Library, New Haven, CT.

136. Madison Grant, *The Passing of the Great Race, or The Racial Basis of European History* (New York: Charles Scribner's Sons, 1916), 80.

137. Madison Grant, *Passing of the Great Race*, 80.

138. Paul Popenoe and Roswell Johnson, *Applied Eugenics*, 299.

139. Daniel J. Kevles, *In the Name of Eugenics: Genetics and the Uses of Human Heredity* (Berkeley: University of California Press, 1986, 73. See Paul Popenoe and Roswell Johnson, *Applied Eugenics*, 312–16, for another example of a discussion of Asian immigration.

140. Paul Popenoe and Roswell Johnson, *Applied Eugenics*, 301.

141. See Charles Benedict Davenport, *Heredity in Relation to Eugenics* (New York: Henry Holt, 1911), 204–24, https://archive.org/details/heredityinrelati00dave/page/n8, for a representative example of eugenicists' fears of immigrants.

142. Davenport, *Heredity in Relation*, 215–16.

143. Frick, "German Population and Race," 34.

144. Henry Osborn, "Address of Welcome," 1; Leon F. Whitney et al., "Is Eugenics Racial Snobbery? Does It Condemn Whole Peoples?" *Eugenics* 2, no. 2 (February 1929): 20.

145. Edwin Black, *War against the Weak: Eugenics and America's Campaign to Create a Master Race* (New York: Four Walls Eight Windows, 2003), 280–81.

146. Darwin, "Aims and Methods," 19.

147. Paul Popenoe and Roswell Johnson, *Applied Eugenics*, v–vi.

148. Harry H. Laughlin, "The Progress of American Eugenics," *Eugenics* 2, no. 2 (February 1929): 14–15.

149. Mehler, "History of the American Eugenics," 61.

150. Smith et al., "Faculty Birth Rate," 459. See also Frick, "German Population and Race," 37, who advocated having three or four children.

151. Darwin, "Aims and Methods," 13.

152. Ellsworth Huntington, *Tomorrow's Children: The Goal of Eugenics* (New York: J. Wiley & Sons, 1935), 88, https://babel.hathitrust.org/cgi/pt?id=mdp.39015034788995;view=1up;seq=7

153. Darwin, "Aims and Methods," 16.

154. Smith et al., "Faculty Birth Rate," 459.

155. Jon Alfred Mjøen, "The Masculine Education of Women and Its Dangers," *Eugenics* 3, no. 9 (September 1930): 323.

156. Jon Mjøen, "Masculine Education," 324.

157. Jon Mjøen, "Masculine Education," 325.

158. Jon Mjøen, "Masculine Education," 325.

159. Jon Mjøen, "Masculine Education," 325.

160. Jon Mjøen, "Masculine Education," 326.

161. Phyllis Blanchard, Chase Going Woodhouse, and David Snedden, "When Wives Go to Business: Is It Eugenically Helpful?" *Eugenics* 4, no. 1 (January 1931): 19.

162. Blanchard, Woodhouse, and Snedden, "When Wives," 18–19.

163. Anna Garlin Spencer, "Should Married Women Work Outside the Home?" *Eugenics* 4, no. 1 (January 1931): 22.

164. Anna Spencer, "Should Married Women Work?" 24.

165. Alexandra Minna Stern, "Gender and Sexuality: A Global Tour and Compass," in *The Oxford Handbook of the History of Eugenics*, ed. Alison Bashford and Philippa Levine (Oxford: Oxford University Press, 2010), 178, points out that when women took up eugenics, they were almost invariably White women.

166. Melinda Plastas, *A Band of Noble Women: Racial Politics in the Women's Peace Movement* (Syracuse, NY: Syracuse University Press, 2011), 16, ProQuest Ebook Central, https://ebookcentral.proquest.com/lib/wisc/reader.action?docID=3410087

167. Carl E. Seashore, "Carl Emil Seashore," 231.

168. Henry Osborn, "Address of Welcome," 1.

169. Henry Osborn, "Address of Welcome," 3.

170. Darwin, "Aims and Methods."

171. Charles Benedict Davenport, "Research in Eugenics," in *Eugenics, Genetics and the Family*, vol. 1, *Scientific Papers of the Second International Congress of Eugenics; Held at American Museum of Natural History, New York, September 22–28, 1921* (Baltimore, MD: Williams & Wilkins, 1923; repr., ed. Charles Rosenberg, New York: Garland Publishing, 1985), 20–28.

172. Carl E. Seashore, "Carl Emil Seashore," 241.

173. Carl E. Seashore, "Carl Emil Seashore," 258. See also Carl E. Seashore, "Psychology and Life," p. 248, RG 99.0164, box 2, Carl E. Seashore Papers.

174. "Memorandum on Greetings," attachment to Carl E. Seashore to Hancher, June 9, 1941, RG 05.01.11, box 16, folder 93, Virgil M. Hancher Papers.

175. Carl E. Seashore, *Psychology of Music* (New York: McGraw-Hill, 1938), 344–45, https://archive.org/details/psychologyofmusi030417mbp

176. "The Advisory Council of the Eugenics Committee of the United States of America," *Eugenical News* 8, no. 4 (April 1923): 29.

177. Blanchard, Woodhouse, and Snedden, "When Wives," 20.

178. Philip J. Pauly, *Biologists and the Promise of American Life: From Meriwether*

Lewis to Alfred Kinsey (Princeton, NJ: Princeton University Press, 2000), 229; Wade Pickren, "Robert Yerkes, Calvin Stone, and the Beginning of Programmatic Sex Research by Psychologists, 1921–1930," *American Journal of Psychology* 110, no. 4 (Winter 1997): 607, https://www.jstor.org/stable/1423412

179. Pauly, *Biologists and the Promise*, 230.

180. "National Research Council Conference on Sex Problems, October 28–29, 1921" (Washington, DC: National Academy of Sciences, 1921), 23, quoted in Pickren, "Robert Yerkes, Calvin Stone," 608.

181. Pickren, "Robert Yerkes, Calvin Stone," 607.

182. Pickren, "Robert Yerkes, Calvin Stone," 606–7; Pauly, *Biologists and the Promise*, 229–30.

183. Smith et al., "Faculty Birth Rate," 458.

184. Smith et al., "Faculty Birth Rate," 459.

185. Carl E. Seashore, "Carl Emil Seashore," 296.

186. Smith et al., "Faculty Birth Rate," 458.

187. Douglas A. Blackmon, "Silent Partner: How the South's Fight to Uphold Segregation Was Funded Up North—New York Millionaire Secretly Sent Cash to Mississippi via His Morgan Account—'Wall Street Gang' Pitches In," *Wall Street Journal*, June 11, 1999, Eastern edition, A1, http://ezproxy.library.wisc.edu/login?url=http://proquest.umi.com.ezproxy.library.wisc.edu/pqdweb?did=42299728

188. Michael G. Kenny, "Toward a Racial Abyss: Eugenics, Wickliffe Draper, and the Origins of the Pioneer Fund," *Journal of History of the Behavioral Sciences* 38, no. 3 (Summer 2002): 275.

189. Carl E. Seashore, *A Child Welfare Research Station: Plans and Possibilities of a Research Station for the Conservation and Development of the Normal Child*, Series on Aims and Progress of Research, n.s., vol. 107 (Iowa City, Iowa: The University, 1916), 4–5, https://catalog.hathitrust.org/Record/010551244

190. Carl E. Seashore, Iowa City, IA, to Charles B. Davenport, Cold Spring Harbor, NY, December 24, 1919, MSS.B.D27, box 85, Charles B. Davenport Papers, American Philosophical Society Archives, Philadelphia, PA.

191. Charles B. Davenport to Carl E. Seashore, Iowa City, IA, January 5, 1920, p. 2, MSS.B.D27, box 85, Charles B. Davenport Papers, American Philosophical Society Archives, Philadelphia, PA.

192. *Administration and Scope of the Iowa Child Welfare Research Station*, rev. ed., University of Iowa Studies: Aims and Progress of Research, vol. 1, no. 10 (Iowa City: The University, January 1921), 11.

193. *Administration and Scope* (January 1921), 12.

194. Carl E. Seashore, "Individual and Racial Inheritance of Musical Traits," in *Eugenics, Genetics and the Family*, vol. 1, *Scientific Papers of the Second International Congress of Eugenics; Held at American Museum of Natural History, New York, September 22–28, 1921* (Baltimore, MD: Williams & Wilkins, 1923; repr., ed. Charles Rosenberg, New York: Garland Publishing, 1985), 237–38.

195. See Seashore's reference to women and the higher life in Carl E. Seashore, "Open Letter: Addressed to Women," 239.

196. Thomas S. Popkewitz, *Cosmopolitanism and the Age of School Reform: Science, Education, and Making Society by Making the Child* (New York: Routledge, 2008), 4.
197. Madison Grant, *Passing of the Great Race*, 49.
198. Henry Fairfield Osborn, preface to *The Passing of the Great Race, or The Racial Basis of European History*, by Madison Grant (New York: Charles Scribner's Sons, 1916), vii.
199. Laughlin, "Progress of American Eugenics," 14.
200. Katharine Murdoch, "A Study of Differences Found Between Races in Intellect and in Morality [Part II]," *School and Society* 22, no. 569 (November 21, 1925): 659–64.
201. Huntington, *Tomorrow's Children*, 40.
202. Phyllis E. Reske, "Policing the 'Wayward Woman': Eugenics in Wisconsin's Involuntary Sterilization Program," *Wisconsin Magazine of History* 97, no. 1 (Autumn 2013): 19.
203. Huntington, *Tomorrow's Children*.
204. Madison Grant, *Passing of the Great Race*.
205. Mehler, "History of the American Eugenics," 257–58.
206. "The Great Nordic Race," review of *The Passing of the Great Race*, by Madison Grant, *Eugenical News* 2, no. 2 (February 1917): 10–11.
207. "The Color-Races," *Eugenical News* 5, no. 9 (September 1920): 70.
208. Paul Popenoe and Roswell Johnson, *Applied Eugenics*, 301.
209. William H. Tucker, *The Funding of Scientific Racism: Wickliffe Draper and the Pioneer Fund* (Urbana: University of Illinois Press, 2002), 27. See also Leon F. Whitney, "Leon Fradley Whitney Autobiography," 1971 [p. 205]), Mss.B.W613b, Archives, American Philosophical Society Library, Philadelphia, PA.
210. Huntington, *Tomorrow's Children*, 46.
211. Huntington, *Tomorrow's Children*, 46.
212. Huntington, *Tomorrow's Children*, 51.
213. Huntington, *Tomorrow's Children*, 51.
214. Huntington, *Tomorrow's Children*, 51.
215. Huntington, *Tomorrow's Children*, 53.
216. Madison Grant, *Passing of the Great Race*, 46.
217. Madison Grant, *Passing of the Great Race*, 45.
218. "Wisconsin Eugenics Laws," *Eugenical News* 3, no. 5 (May 1918): 38.
219. "Sterilization in Germany," *Eugenical News* 20, no. 1 (January-February 1935): 13.
220. "German Sterilization Progress," *Eugenical News* 19, no. 2 (March-April 1934): 38.
221. For example, see the back covers of several issues published in 1929.
222. C. B. S. Hodson, "Eugenics in Norway," *Eugenics Review* 27, no. 1 (April 1935): 43.
223. Huntington, *Tomorrow's Children*, 54.
224. Madison Grant, *Passing of the Great Race*, 47.
225. Huntington, *Tomorrow's Children*, 95.

226. Paul Popenoe and Roswell Johnson, *Applied Eugenics*, 301–4. They cite Grant on p. 301.

227. Paul Popenoe and Roswell Johnson, *Applied Eugenics*, 307–10.

228. Mehler, "History of the American Eugenics," 182, 184.

229. Paul Popenoe and Roswell Johnson, *Applied Eugenics*, 296.

230. Paul Popenoe and Roswell Johnson, *Applied Eugenics*, 296.

231. Herbert Spencer, "Herbert Spencer on Race Mixture," *Eugenics* 3, no. 2 (February 1930): 63.

232. Black, *War against the Weak*, 261.

233. Paul Popenoe and Roswell Johnson, *Applied Eugenics*, 184.

234. For a discussion of the targeting of Catholics for contraception and sterilization programs, see Ryan and Stoskopf, "Public and Catholic School."

235. Dorothy Roberts, *Killing the Black Body: Race, Reproduction, and the Meaning of Liberty* (New York: Vintage Books, 1999), 56–61.

236. Reske, "Policing the 'Wayward Woman,'" 17.

237. Reske, "Policing the 'Wayward Woman,'" 18.

238. Reske, "Policing the 'Wayward Woman,'" 18, 23.

239. Reske, "Policing the 'Wayward Woman,'" 23.

240. Reske, "Policing the 'Wayward Woman,'" 21.

241. Reske, "Policing the 'Wayward Woman,'" 21.

242. Reske, "Policing the 'Wayward Woman,'" 21.

243. Reske, "Policing the 'Wayward Woman,'" 23. The source Reske cites stated that the women under discussion were "high grade imbecile girls." It is not clear whether they were labeled as such because of their sexual activities or for other reasons. See William N. Bullard, "The Placing Out of High Grade Imbecile Girls," *Boston Medical and Surgical Journal* 160, no. 24 (June 17, 1909): 776.

244. Reske, "Policing the 'Wayward Woman,'" 15.

245. Reske, "Policing the 'Wayward Woman,'" 23.

246. *Oxford English Dictionary Online*, s.v. "promiscuous [adj. and adv.]," accessed October 28, 2018, http://www.oed.com/viewdictionaryentry/Entry/152429

247. Mehler, "History of the American Eugenics," 298.

248. Mehler, "History of the American Eugenics," 61.

249. "Sample Membership Letter in AES Archives, 1922," American Eugenics Society Papers, American Philosophical Society, Philadelphia, PA, quoted in Mehler, "History of the American Eugenics," 61, 62n44. On p. 62n44, Mehler states, "See *Minutes* of the Eugenics Committee of the U.S.A."

250. Mehler, "History of the American Eugenics," 204–5.

251. Mehler, "History of the American Eugenics," 309.

252. For example, see the back covers of several issues published in 1929.

253. For examples of references in *Eugenics* and *Eugenical News*, see Smith et al., "Faculty Birth Rate," 459; "In Praise of Eugenics," *Eugenics* 2, no. 2 (February 1929): 36; "Popular Education: Music Tests," *Eugenics* 1, no. 2 (November 1928): 35; "Mental and Physical Factors in Programs of Eugenics: A Symposium," *Eugenical News* 33, nos. 3–4 (September-December 1948): 46; "The Measurable Elements of

Musical Talent," *Eugenical News* 11, no. 3 (March 1926): 43; "The Eugenics Committee of the United States of America," *Eugenical News* 10, no. 2 (February 1925): 10; "Measuring Musical Capacities," *Eugenical News* 9, no. 8 (August 1924): 71; "Eugenics Society of the United States of America," *Eugenical News* 8, no. 4 (April 1923): 28; "Advisory Council of the Eugenics Committee of the United States of America," 29; "Eugenics Research Association Number: Ninth Annual Meeting," 54; "New Active Members of Eugenics Research Association," *Eugenical News* 5, no. 7 (July 1920): 53; Althea DeBacker, "Student Pedigree-Studies: A German Bard and His Progeny," *Eugenical News* 18, no. 5 (September-October 1933): 106; and Morris Steggerda, "Negro-White Hybrids in Jamaica, B.W.I.," *Eugenical News* 13, no. 2 (February 1928): 23.

254. Henry Osborn, "Address of Welcome," 3.

255. Davenport to Carl E. Seashore, January 5, 1920, p. 1, MSS.B.D27, box 85, Charles B. Davenport Papers.

256. Carl E. Seashore, "The Master's Key to the Domain of Educational Theory and Practice," *Education Digest* 15, no. 6 (February 1950): 19; repr. fr. *School and Society* 70 (November 26, 1949): 337–38.

257. Charles Benedict Davenport and Morris Steggerda, *Race Crossing in Jamaica* (Washington, DC: Carnegie Institution of Washington, 1929), 3.

258. Carl E. Seashore, *Child Welfare Research Station*, 3.

259. Carl E. Seashore, *Child Welfare Research Station*, 4.

260. Carl E. Seashore, *Psychology in Daily Life*, 120–21.

261. Huntington, *Tomorrow's Children*, viii.

262. Mehler, "History of the American Eugenics," 258–59.

263. Huntington, *Tomorrow's Children*, viii.

264. Henry L. Minton, "The Iowa Child Welfare Research Station and the 1940 Debate on Intelligence: Carrying on the Legacy of a Concerned Mother," *Journal of the History of the Behavioral Sciences* 20, no. 2 (April 1984): 160.

265. Minton, "Iowa Child Welfare Research," 164.

266. Minton, "Iowa Child Welfare Research," 164.

267. Minton, "Iowa Child Welfare Research," 164. Minton erroneously cited Carl E. Seashore, *Child Welfare Research Station*, 2, as the source of this quote; it is actually found in Carl E. Seashore, "Plans and Possibilities of a Research Station for the Conservation and Development of the Normal Child," *Iowa Alumnus* 12, no. 4 (January 1915): 17. https://babel.hathitrust.org/cgi/pt?id=uc1.b2872130&view=1up&seq=120

268. Minton, "Iowa Child Welfare Research," 164.

269. Carl E. Seashore, "The Term 'Euthenics,'" *Science*, n.s., 94, no. 2450 (December 12, 1941): 561, https://www.jstor.org/stable/1668443

270. Alice Boardman Smuts, *Science in the Service of Children, 1893–1935* (New Haven, CT: Yale University Press, 2006), 130.

271. Smuts, *Science in the Service*, 130. The 1915 date may not be correct.

272. Wendy Kline, *Building a Better Race: Gender, Sexuality, and Eugenics from the Turn of the Century to the Baby Boom* (Berkeley: University of California Press, 2001), 16.

273. Carl E. Seashore, *In Search of Beauty* (1947), 365.
274. Carl E. Seashore, *Learning and Living*, 104.
275. Carl E. Seashore, "The Individual in Mass Education," *School and Society* 23, no. 593 (May 8, 1926): 574.
276. *Oxford English Dictionary Online*, s.v. "flapper [n.2]," accessed March 14, 2015, http://www.oed.com/view/Entry/71110?rskey=tXiys7&result=3
277. *Oxford English*, s.v. "flapper [n.2]."
278. The *OED* states that the first published use of the term "tramp" meaning a sexually promiscuous woman appeared in 1922; see *Oxford English Dictionary Online*, s.v. "tramp [n.1]," accessed November 3, 2018, http:// www-oed-com.ezproxy.library.wisc.edu/view/Entry/204517?rskey=EqSrdQ&result=1#eid
279. Pickren, "Robert Yerkes, Calvin Stone," 607–8.
280. Allan Chase, *The Legacy of Malthus: The Social Costs of the New Scientific Racism* (New York: Alfred A. Knopf, 1977), 115–16.
281. Carl E. Seashore, "Carl Emil Seashore," 237.
282. Huntington, *Tomorrow's Children*, 51, 53.
283. Kline, *Building a Better Race*, 134.
284. Ian Hacking, "Making Up People," in *Reconstructing Individualism: Autonomy, Individuality, and the Self in Western Thought*, ed. Thomas C. Heller, Morton Sosna, and David E. Wellbery (Stanford: Stanford University Press, 1986), 225.
285. Kline, *Building a Better Race*, 135.
286. Kline, *Building a Better Race*, 137.
287. Kline, *Building a Better Race*, 135–36.
288. Judith Butler, *Bodies That Matter: On the Discursive Limits of "Sex"* (New York: Routledge, 1993), 3.
289. Kline, *Building a Better Race*, 138.
290. Kline, *Building a Better Race*, 139–40. See also Michael Kimmel, *Manhood in America: A Cultural History* (New York: Free Press, 1996), 209.
291. Kline, *Building a Better Race*, 143, 146.
292. Herman Rubin, *Eugenics and Sex Harmony*.
293. Herman Rubin, *Eugenics and Sex Harmony*, 130–31.
294. Herman Rubin, *Eugenics and Sex Harmony*, 129.
295. Herman Rubin, *Eugenics and Sex Harmony*, 129.
296. Herman Rubin, *Eugenics and Sex Harmony*, 129.
297. Herman Rubin, *Eugenics and Sex Harmony*, 129.
298. Herman Rubin, *Eugenics and Sex Harmony*, 130.
299. Herman Rubin, *Eugenics and Sex Harmony*, 130.
300. Herman Rubin, *Eugenics and Sex Harmony*, 129.
301. Herman Rubin, *Eugenics and Sex Harmony*, 130.
302. Herman Rubin, *Eugenics and Sex Harmony*, 130.
303. Herman Rubin, *Eugenics and Sex Harmony*, 130.
304. Herman Rubin, *Eugenics and Sex Harmony*, 130–31.
305. Herman Rubin, *Eugenics and Sex Harmony*, 131.
306. Herman Rubin, *Eugenics and Sex Harmony*, 129–31.

307. Herman Rubin, *Eugenics and Sex Harmony*, 131.
308. Herman Rubin, *Eugenics and Sex Harmony*, 130.
309. Herman Rubin, *Eugenics and Sex Harmony*, 129.
310. Herman Rubin, *Eugenics and Sex Harmony*, 129.
311. Herman Rubin, *Eugenics and Sex Harmony*, 129.
312. Herman Rubin, *Eugenics and Sex Harmony*, 131.
313. Gayle Rubin, "The Traffic in Women: Notes on the 'Political Economy' of Sex," in *Toward an Anthropology of Women*, ed. Rayna R. Reiter (New York: Monthly Review, 1975), 157–210.
314. Kline, *Building a Better Race*, 8.
315. "Eugenics," 1921, Cold Spring Harbor, E.06 Eug-2, Exhibits Book-Second Int. Ex. of Eugenics, p. 15, titled "'Copy of Certificate Awarded for Meritorious Exhibits,' at the Second International Congress of Eugenics," image 543, in the "Image Archive on the American Eugenics Movement," DNA Learning Center, Cold Spring Harbor Laboratory, accessed September 23, 2018, www.eugenicsarchive.org/eugenics/view_image.pl?id=543

Chapter 5

1. For his description of his contributions to education, see Carl E. Seashore, "Carl Emil Seashore," vol. 1, *A History of Psychology in Autobiography*, ed. Carl Allanmore Murchison (Worcester, MA: Clark University, 1930), 269–86.
2. Carl E. Seashore, *The Psychology of Musical Talent* (Boston: Silver, Burdett, 1919), 14–15. See also Carl E. Seashore, "Educational Guidance in Music," *School and Society* 45, no. 1160 (March 20, 1937): 386.
3. Carl E. Seashore, *Vocational Guidance in Music*, University of Iowa Monographs: Aims and Progress of Research, 1st ser., no. 2 (Iowa City: The University, September 1916), 9; Carl E. Seashore, "The Sunny Side of Graduate Work for the Duration," typed manuscript accompanying Carl E. Seashore to Virgil M. Hancher, March 26, 1943, p. 3, RG 05.01.11, box 55, folder 52, Virgil M. Hancher Papers, Special Collections and University Archives, University of Iowa Libraries, Iowa City, IA; Carl E. Seashore, "The Sunny Side of Graduate Work," *Daily Iowan*, April 11, 1943, 2, http://dailyiowan.lib.uiowa.edu/DI/1943/di1943-04-11.pdf; Carl E. Seashore, "The Sunny Side of Graduate Work for the Duration," *Journal of Higher Education* 14, no. 6 (June 1943): 290, https://www.jstor.org/stable/1975100; Carl E. Seashore, "The Sunny Side of Graduate Work for the Duration," in *Wartime Approaches to Liberal Education: Nine Editorials from* The Daily Iowan ([Iowa City: University of Iowa Publications, 1944?]), 30.
4. Carl E. Seashore, "Music," vol. 2, *Handbook of Applied Psychology*, ed. Douglas H. Fryer and Edwin R. Henry (New York: Rinehart, 1950), 684.
5. *Oxford English Dictionary Online*, s.v. "inherit," accessed June 2, 2018, http://www.oed.com/view/Entry/95948
6. *Oxford English*, s.v. "inherit."
7. Stefan Willer, "Sui Generis: Heredity and Heritage of Genius at the Turn of the Eighteenth Century," in *Heredity Produced: At the Crossroads of Biology, Poli-*

tics, and Culture, 1500–1870, ed. Staffan Müller-Wille and Hans-Jörg Rheinberger (Cambridge, MA: MIT Press, 2007), 433.

8. Carl E. Seashore, "The Rôle of Mental Measurement in the Discovery and Motivation of the Gifted Student," *Proceedings of the National Academy of Sciences* 11, no. 9 (September 1925): 544. He used the concept of fitness elsewhere, too. See references to fitness for college work in Carl E. Seashore, "Carl Emil Seashore," 283; and Carl E. Seashore, "Recognition of the Individual," Engineering Society paper [July 1924], p. 3, attachment to Carl E. Seashore, Iowa City, IA, to President Walter A. Jessup, Iowa City, IA, July 16, 1924, RG 05.01.09, box 145, folder 49, Walter A. Jessup Papers, Special Collections and University Archives, University of Iowa Libraries, Iowa City, IA. For references to unfitness for college work, see Carl E. Seashore, *Pioneering in Psychology*, University of Iowa Studies: Series on Aims and Progress of Research, no. 70 (Iowa City: University of Iowa, 1942), 162, https://babel.hathitrust.org/cgi/pt?id=mdp.39015020052349&view=1up&seq=1; and Carl E. Seashore, *The Junior College Movement* (New York: Henry Holt, 1940), 12, https://babel.hathitrust.org/cgi/pt?id=mdp.39015020699834;view=1up;seq=7. For references to fitness for a learned career, see Carl E. Seashore, *Learning and Living in College: Psychology of Individual Differences Applied to the Organization and Pursuit of Higher Education; A Study Based upon Experience in the Promotion of the Gifted Student Project in the National Research Council*, University of Iowa Studies: Series on Aims and Progress of Research, vol. 2, no. 1 (Iowa City: The University, 1927), 5. He said that the Army Tests eliminated the unfit in Carl E. Seashore, "Sunny Side," typed manuscript accompanying a letter dated March 26, 1943, p. 4, RG 05.01.11, box 55, folder 52, Virgil M. Hancher Papers; Carl E. Seashore, "Sunny Side," *Daily Iowan*, 2; and Carl E. Seashore, "Sunny Side," *Journal of Higher Education*, 291. He also said they could be used to rate the fitness of prospective officers; see Carl E. Seashore, *Psychology of Musical Talent*, 257. He referred to the "fit helpmate" in Carl E. Seashore, "An Open Letter: Addressed to Women in Graduate Schools," *Journal of Higher Education* 13, no. 5 (May 1942): 237, https://doi.org/10.2307/1974933; to unfit music teachers in Carl E. Seashore, "Avocational Guidance in Music," *Journal of Applied Psychology* 1, no. 4 (December 1917): 344; and to music students who are unfit to make music a career in Carl E. Seashore, "Youth and Music," *School Review* 48, no. 4 (April 1940): 270–71, http://www.jstor.org/stable/1082068. A manuscript version of this article is found in RG 99.0164, box 2, Carl E. Seashore Papers, Special Collections and University Archives, University of Iowa Libraries, Iowa City, IA.

9. Marouf Arif Hasian Jr., *Eugenics in Anglo-American Thought* (Athens: University of Georgia Press, 1996), 39–40.

10. Hasian Jr., *Eugenics in Anglo-American*, 40. For Hasian Jr.'s source, see Caleb Williams Saleeby, *The Progress of Eugenics* (London: Cassell, 1914), 88, https://babel.hathitrust.org/cgi/pt?id=aeu.ark:/13960/t3fx8j06h;view=1up;seq=12. For more discussion of the connections between the Boy Scouts and eugenics, see Michael Rosenthal, *The Character Factory: Baden-Powell and the Origins of the Boy Scout Movement* (London: Collins, 1986), 150–60.

11. Hasian Jr., *Eugenics in Anglo-American*, 40.

12. For examples of references to the whole person, see Carl E. Seashore, "An Open Letter to a Professor," *School and Society* 48, no. 1238 (September 17, 1938): 349; repr. with revised title in Carl E. Seashore, *The Junior College Movement*, 131–45. Also Carl E. Seashore, *A Preview to College and Life*, University of Iowa Studies: Series on Aims and Progress of Research, no. 55 (Iowa City: University of Iowa, 1938), 10–11; and Carl E. Seashore, *Psychology in Daily Life* (New York: D. Appleton, 1914), 25.

13. Carl E. Seashore, "Open Letter: Addressed to Women," 238.

14. Carl E. Seashore, "Open Letter: Addressed to Women," 238.

15. Seashore discussed morality and moral fitness elsewhere, as well. See, for example, Carl E. Seashore, "Carl Emil Seashore," 230, 242; and Carl E. Seashore, *A Child Welfare Research Station: Plans and Possibilities of a Research Station for the Conservation and Development of the Normal Child*, Series on Aims and Progress of Research, n.s., vol. 107 (Iowa City, Iowa: The University, 1916), 12–16, https://catalog.hathitrust.org/Record/010551244

16. "Memorandum on Greetings to the 13th and Last Annual Brain Derby, June 4, 1941," attachment to Carl E. Seashore, Iowa City, IA, to Virgil M. Hancher, Old Capitol, June 9, 1941, RG 05.01.11, box 16, folder 93, Virgil M. Hancher Papers, Special Collections and University Archives, University of Iowa Libraries, Iowa City, IA.

17. See, for example, Carl E. Seashore, *Child Welfare Research Station*, 4; and Carl E. Seashore, *Psychology of Music* (New York: McGraw-Hill, 1938), 337, https://archive.org/details/psychologyofmusi030417mbp

18. Carl E. Seashore, "Carl Emil Seashore," 252.

19. Carl E. Seashore, "Talent," *School and Society* 55, no. 1416 (February 14, 1942): 171.

20. Carl E. Seashore, "Education for Democracy and the Junior College," *School and Society* 25, no. 643 (April 23, 1927): 469. A slightly revised version of this essay was published in Carl E. Seashore, *Learning and Living in College*, 88–102; and a condensed version was published under the same title in the *Bulletin of the American Association of University Professors* 13, no. 6 (October 1927): 399–404.

21. Carl E. Seashore, *Learning and Living*, 8.

22. Carl E. Seashore, "Graduate Study: An Address Delivered to the Students in the Colleges of Iowa in 1909," *Bulletin of the State University of Iowa*, n.s., 11 (June 2, 1910): 8.

23. Leila Zenderland, *Measuring Minds: Henry Herbert Goddard and the Origins of American Intelligence Testing* (Cambridge, UK: Cambridge University Press, 1998), 247.

24. Madison Grant, *The Passing of the Great Race, or The Racial Basis of European History* (New York: Charles Scribner's Sons, 1916), 47.

25. Ernst Kretschmer, "The Breeding of the Mental Endowments of Genius," *Eugenics* 4, no. 1 (January 1931): 6.

26. Kretschmer, "Breeding of the Mental Endowments," 6.

27. Kretschmer, "Breeding of the Mental Endowments," 7–8.

28. Kretschmer, "Breeding of the Mental Endowments," 11. For a discussion of some eighteenth- and nineteenth-century understandings of genius, see Willer, "Sui Generis," 419–40.

29. Daniel J. Kevles, *In the Name of Eugenics: Genetics and the Uses of Human Heredity* (Berkeley: University of California Press, 1986, 76–77.

30. Carl E. Seashore, "Academic Business," *Education Digest* 11, no. 3 (November 1945): 45; repr. fr. *School and Society* 62 (September 15, 1945): 161–64.

31. Carl E. Seashore, *Preview to College*, 52.

32. Carl E. Seashore, "Academic Business," 45.

33. Carl E. Seashore, "Academic Business," 45.

34. Carl E. Seashore, "Carl Emil Seashore," 227.

35. Carl E. Seashore, "Carl Emil Seashore," 265.

36. Carl E. Seashore, "The Consulting Psychologist," *Popular Science Monthly* 78 (March 1911): 285.

37. Walter R. Miles, "Carl Emil Seashore, 1866–1949," vol. 29, *Biographical Memoirs* (New York: Columbia University Press for the National Academy of Sciences, 1956), 281.

38. Miles, "Carl Emil Seashore, 1866–1949," 280–81.

39. Carl E. Seashore, "Carl Emil Seashore," 267.

40. Carl E. Seashore, "Carl Emil Seashore," 266–67.

41. Carl E. Seashore, "Carl Emil Seashore," 265.

42. Miles, "Carl Emil Seashore, 1866–1949," 281.

43. Carl E. Seashore, "Carl Emil Seashore," 265.

44. Carl E. Seashore, Iowa City, IA, to Virgil M. Hancher, Old Capitol, November 30, 1944, RG 05.01.11, box 103, folder 54, Virgil M. Hancher Papers, Special Collections and University Archives, University of Iowa Libraries, Iowa City, IA.

45. Carl E. Seashore, "Carl Emil Seashore," 265–66.

46. C. E. Seashore, Iowa City, IA, to President W. A. Jessup, Iowa City, IA, January 9, 1923, p. 1, RG 05.01.09, box 114, folder 53, Walter A. Jessup Papers, Special Collections and University Archives, University of Iowa Libraries, Iowa City, IA.

47. C. E. Seashore to Jessup, January 9, 1923, p. 1, RG 05.01.09, box 114, folder 53, Walter A. Jessup Papers.

48. See Miles, "Carl Emil Seashore, 1866–1949," 268, 280.

49. Miles, "Carl Emil Seashore, 1866–1949," 282.

50. Miles, "Carl Emil Seashore, 1866–1949," 280.

51. Miles, "Carl Emil Seashore, 1866–1949," 280.

52. Carl E. Seashore, "Carl Emil Seashore," 268.

53. Carl E. Seashore, "Carl Emil Seashore," 267.

54. Hamilton Cravens, *Before Head Start: The Iowa Station and America's Children* (Chapel Hill: University of North Carolina Press, 1993), 11.

55. Carl E. Seashore, "Carl Emil Seashore," 270.

56. Carl E. Seashore, *Pioneering in Psychology*, 160.

57. Carl E. Seashore, "Carl Emil Seashore," 252–53; Carl E. Seashore, "Psychology and Life in Autobiography," typed manuscript, p. 206, RG 99.0164, box 2, Carl E. Seashore Papers, Special Collections and University Archives, University of Iowa Libraries, Iowa City, IA.

58. Zenderland, *Measuring Minds*, 247.

59. Zenderland, *Measuring Minds*, 247–48.

60. Robert M. Yerkes to Carl E. Seashore, Iowa City, IA, February 18, 1916, MS 569, box 43, folder 836, Robert Mearns Yerkes Papers, Manuscripts and Archives, Yale University Library, New Haven, CT. Yerkes also is quoted in Carl E. Seashore, "Communications and Discussions: Mentality Tests," *Journal of Educational Psychology* 7, no. 3 (March 1916): 163–64.

61. For further discussion, see Zenderland, *Measuring Minds*, 246–47.

62. Yerkes to Carl E. Seashore, February 18, 1916, MS 569, box 43, folder 836, Robert Mearns Yerkes Papers; Carl E. Seashore, "Communications and Discussions: Mentality Tests" (March 1916), 163–64.

63. Carl E. Seashore, "Communications and Discussions: Mentality Tests" (March 1916), 163; Yerkes to Carl E. Seashore, February 18, 1916, pp. 1, 3, MS 569, box 43, folder 836, Robert Mearns Yerkes Papers.

64. Carl E. Seashore, "Communications and Discussions: Mentality Tests" (March 1916), 164.

65. Carl E. Seashore, "Communications and Discussions: Mentality Tests" (March 1916), 165.

66. Carl E. Seashore, ed. and moderator, "Communications and Discussions: Mentality Tests, a Symposium," *Journal of Educational Psychology* 7, no. 4 (April 1916): 229.

67. Carl E. Seashore, ed. and moderator, "Communications and Discussions: Mentality Tests" (April 1916), 229–40. See letters from the following individuals: Angell, 229–30; Haines, 234–37; and Goddard, 231–33. Also Carl E. Seashore, ed. and moderator, "Communications and Discussions: Mentality Tests, a Symposium," *Journal of Educational Psychology* 7, no. 5 (May 1916): 278–93. See letters from the following individuals: Hollingworth, 278, and Goddard, 287–93. Goddard's defense is found on p. 293. Finally, Carl E. Seashore, ed. and moderator, "Communications and Discussions: Mentality Tests, a Symposium," *Journal of Educational Psychology* 7, no. 6 (June 1916): 348–60. See letters from the following individuals: Terman, 348–51; Town, 351–53; Wallin, 353–57; and Whipple, 357–60.

68. Carl E. Seashore, Iowa City, IA, to Robert M. Yerkes, Cambridge, MA, January 19, 1916, p. 2, MS 569, box 43, folder 836, Robert Mearns Yerkes Papers, Manuscripts and Archives, Yale University Library, New Haven, CT; Carl E. Seashore, Iowa City, IA, to Robert M. Yerkes, Cambridge, MA, February 23, 1916, MS 569, box 43, folder 836, Robert Mearns Yerkes Papers, Manuscripts and Archives, Yale University Library, New Haven, CT; Yerkes to Carl E. Seashore, February

18, 1916, MS 569, box 43, folder 836, Robert Mearns Yerkes Papers; Robert M. Yerkes to Carl E. Seashore, undated, MS 569, box 43, folder 836, Robert Mearns Yerkes Papers, Manuscripts and Archives, Yale University Library, New Haven, CT; Robert M. Yerkes to Carl E. Seashore, Iowa City, IA, May 12, 1916, MS 569, box 43, folder 836, Robert Mearns Yerkes Papers, Manuscripts and Archives, Yale University Library, New Haven, CT.

69. This accomplishment was considered to be of sufficient importance to be mentioned in some of his obituaries. See, for example, "SUI's Dean Seashore Dies; Public Service Here Sunday," *Daily Iowan*, October 18, 1949, 1; and "Dean Emeritus Carl E. Seashore Dies at 83," *University of Iowa News Bulletin* 24, no. 6 (November 1949): 6.

70. Carl E. Seashore, *Pioneering in Psychology*, 160–61. For more information about the development of the tests, see Edwin Black, *War against the Weak: Eugenics and America's Campaign to Create a Master Race* (New York: Four Walls Eight Windows, 2003), 80.

71. Miles, "Carl Emil Seashore, 1866–1949," 296.

72. Carl E. Seashore, "Sunny Side," *Journal of Higher Education*, 291. See similar passages in Carl E. Seashore, "Sunny Side," typed manuscript accompanying a letter dated March 26, 1943, p. 4, RG 05.01.11, box 55, folder 52, Virgil M. Hancher Papers; and Carl E. Seashore, "Sunny Side," *Daily Iowan*, 2.

73. Carl E. Seashore, "Sunny Side," typed manuscript accompanying a letter dated March 26, 1943, pp. 3–4, RG 05.01.11, box 55, folder 52, Virgil M. Hancher Papers. See similar passages in Carl E. Seashore, "Sunny Side," *Daily Iowan*, 2; and Carl E. Seashore, "Sunny Side," *Journal of Higher Education*, 290, although in these versions, philosophers are not mentioned. Only professors and graduate students are mentioned in yet another version: Carl E. Seashore, "Sunny Side," in *Wartime Approaches to Liberal Education*, 30.

74. Carl E. Seashore, "Sunny Side," *Journal of Higher Education*, 290. Variant wordings also appeared in Carl E. Seashore, "Sunny Side," *Daily Iowan*, 2; and Carl E. Seashore, "Sunny Side," in *Wartime Approaches to Liberal Education*, 30. The variant wordings indicated that the best were not necessarily sent into combat; however, the statement that many choose to do so was absent from these variants.

75. Mott R. Linn, "College Entrance Examinations in the United States: A Brief History for Counselors . . . ," *Journal of College Admission* 140 (Spring 1993): 8.

76. Charles Benedict Davenport and Morris Steggerda, *Race Crossing in Jamaica* (Washington, DC: Carnegie Institution of Washington, 1929), 42.

77. Black, *War against the Weak*, 82.

78. Black, *War against the Weak*, 83.

79. Harold S. Wechsler, *The Qualified Student: A History of Selective College Admission in America* (New York: John Wiley & Sons, 1977), 7; Linn, "College Entrance Examinations," 6.

80. Linn, "College Entrance Examinations," 6. Linn cites John E. Pomfret, "Colonial Colleges," *Pennsylvania Gazette*, June 1975, 29–35.

81. Wechsler, *Qualified Student*, 7.
82. Linn, "College Entrance Examinations," 7.
83. Linn, "College Entrance Examinations," 8.
84. Wechsler, *Qualified Student*, 97.
85. Linn, "College Entrance Examinations," 8.
86. Wechsler, *Qualified Student*, 105.
87. Carl E. Seashore, "Rôle of Mental Measurement in the Discovery," 543.
88. Wechsler, *Qualified Student*, 24.
89. Carl E. Seashore, "Carl Emil Seashore," 280.
90. Carl E. Seashore, "Carl Emil Seashore," 280–81. This project also is discussed in Carl E. Seashore, *Pioneering in Psychology*, 163–64.
91. According to Giles M. Ruch, 1923–24 was the fourth academic year Iowa used qualifying examinations. If that is the case, then the events Seashore described may have taken place earlier, possibly in 1920. See G. M. Ruch, *A Mental-Educational Survey of 1550 Iowa High School Seniors*, University of Iowa Studies in Education, vol. 2, no. 5 (Iowa City, IA: The University [1923]), 5, https://babel.hathitrust.org/cgi/pt?id=osu.32435028125920&view=1up&seq=3
92. Carl E. Seashore, *Pioneering in Psychology*, 161. See also Carl E. Seashore, "Carl Emil Seashore," 281–82.
93. Carl E. Seashore, *Pioneering in Psychology*, 162.
94. Carl E. Seashore, *Pioneering in Psychology*, 163.
95. Carl E. Seashore, *Pioneering in Psychology*, 164.
96. Wendy Kline, *Building a Better Race: Gender, Sexuality, and Eugenics from the Turn of the Century to the Baby Boom* (Berkeley: University of California Press, 2001), 135.
97. C. E. Seashore, Iowa City, IA, to C. R. Mann, Washington, DC, July 26, 1924, RG 05.01.09, box 145, folder 49, Walter A. Jessup Papers, Special Collections and University Archives, University of Iowa Libraries, Iowa City, IA.
98. Ruch, *Mental-Educational Survey*, 5, 7.
99. Ruch, *Mental-Educational Survey*, 7.
100. Carl E. Seashore, *Pioneering in Psychology*, 162.
101. Carl E. Seashore, "Rôle of Mental Measurement in the Discovery," 543–44. See also Carl E. Seashore, "Recognition of the Individual," pp. 3–4, RG 05.01.09, box 145, folder 49, Walter A. Jessup Papers.
102. Carl E. Seashore, "Carl Emil Seashore," 283.
103. Carl E. Seashore, "Carl Emil Seashore," 283.
104. Carl E. Seashore, "Rôle of Mental Measurement in the Discovery," 544.
105. Carl E. Seashore, "Carl Emil Seashore," 282.
106. Carl E. Seashore, "College Placement Examinations," *School and Society* 20, no. 515 (November 8, 1924): 575; repr. in Carl E. Seashore, *College Placement Examinations*, Washington, DC: National Research Council [1925].
107. Carl E. Seashore, "Rôle of Mental Measurement in the Discovery," 544.
108. Carl E. Seashore, "College Placement Examinations," 575.
109. Carl E. Seashore, "College Placement Examinations," 575. See also Carl E. Seashore, "Rôle of Mental Measurement in the Discovery," 544.

110. Carl E. Seashore, "College Placement Examinations," 575.

111. Carl E. Seashore, "Rôle of Mental Measurement in the Discovery," 544.

112. Carl E. Seashore, "Rôle of Mental Measurement in the Discovery," 544.

113. Carl E. Seashore, "Rôle of Mental Measurement in the Discovery," 544.

114. Carl E. Seashore, "College Placement Examinations," 576. This section of the article also appeared in Carl E. Seashore, *Learning and Living*, 43.

115. Carl E. Seashore, "College Placement Examinations," 577.

116. Carl E. Seashore, "Recognition of the Individual," p. 5, RG 05.01.09, box 145, folder 49, Walter A. Jessup Papers.

117. Carl E. Seashore, "Recognition of the Individual," p. 6, RG 05.01.09, box 145, folder 49, Walter A. Jessup Papers.

118. Carl E. Seashore, "Carl Emil Seashore," 282.

119. Miles, "Carl Emil Seashore, 1866–1949," 297.

120. Carl E. Seashore, "College Placement Examinations," 576.

121. Carl E. Seashore, *Preview to College*, 34.

122. Carl E. Seashore, *Preview to College*, 34–35.

123. Carl E. Seashore, "Editorials: From Vocational Selection to Vocational Guidance," *Journal of Educational Psychology* 8, no. 9 (April 1917): 244–45.

124. Carl E. Seashore, "Editorials: From Vocational Selection," 245.

125. Carl E. Seashore, "Carl Emil Seashore," 295.

126. Carl E. Seashore, Iowa City, IA, to Robert M. Yerkes, Washington, DC, January 3, 1921 (with attachment), MS 569, box 43, folder 836, Robert Mearns Yerkes Papers, Manuscripts and Archives, Yale University Library, New Haven, CT.

127. Carl E. Seashore to Yerkes, January 3, 1921, MS 569, box 43, folder 836, Robert Mearns Yerkes Papers.

128. Carl E. Seashore to Yerkes, January 3, 1921, MS 569, box 43, folder 836, Robert Mearns Yerkes Papers.

129. See "An Analyzed Rating of Promise," attached to Carl E. Seashore to Yerkes, January 3, 1921, MS 569, box 43, folder 836, Robert Mearns Yerkes Papers.

130. Robert M. Yerkes to Carl E. Seashore, Iowa City, IA, January 21, 1921, MS 569, box 43, folder 836, Robert Mearns Yerkes Papers, Manuscripts and Archives, Yale University Library, New Haven, CT.

131. Yerkes to Carl E. Seashore, January 21, 1921, MS 569, box 43, folder 836, Robert Mearns Yerkes Papers.

132. Carl E. Seashore, "Meier-Seashore Art Judgment Test," *Science*, n.s., 69, no. 1788 (April 5, 1929): 380, http://www.jstor.org/stable/1652784; Carl E. Seashore, "Carl Emil Seashore," 278.

133. Norman Charles Meier and Carl E. Seashore, *The Meier-Seashore Art Judgment Test* (Iowa City: University of Iowa Bureau of Educational Research and Service, 1929); Norman Charles Meier, *Aesthetic Judgment as a Measure of Art Talent*, University of Iowa Studies: Series on Aims and Progress of Research, vol. 1, no. 19 (Iowa City: The University, 1926), 7.

134. Carl E. Seashore, "Meier-Seashore Art Judgment Test," *Science*, 380.

135. Meier, *Aesthetic Judgment*, 22.

136. Meier, *Aesthetic Judgment*, 23.

137. Carl E. Seashore, "Carl Emil Seashore," 278.

138. Carl E. Seashore, "Carl Emil Seashore," 279.

139. Carl E. Seashore, "Suggestions for Tests on School Children," *Educational Review* 22 (June 1901): 69–77.

140. Carl E. Seashore, "Carl Emil Seashore," 269, 280.

141. Carl E. Seashore, "Open Letter to a Professor," 352.

142. Carl E. Seashore, "Open Letter to a Professor," 352.

143. Carl E. Seashore, "Open Letter to a Professor," 353.

144. Carl E. Seashore, "Open Letter to a Professor," 353.

145. Miles, "Carl Emil Seashore, 1866–1949," 288.

146. Carl E. Seashore, Iowa City, IA, to Virgil M. Hancher, Old Capitol, November 12, 1941, RG 05.01.11, box 38, folder 94, Virgil M. Hancher Papers, Special Collections and University Archives, University of Iowa Libraries, Iowa City, IA.

147. Carl E. Seashore, *Pioneering in Psychology*, 165.

148. Carl E. Seashore, Iowa City, IA, to President Jessup, October 27, 1924, p. 1, RG 05.01.09, box 145, folder 49, Walter A. Jessup Papers, Special Collections and University Archives, University of Iowa Libraries, Iowa City, IA.

149. Carl E. Seashore to Jessup, October 27, 1924, p. 2, RG 05.01.09, box 145, folder 49, Walter A. Jessup Papers.

150. For further discussion of Lindquist, see, for example, U.S. Congress, Office of Technology Assessment, *Testing in American Schools: Asking the Right Questions, OTA-SET-519* (Washington, DC: US Government Printing Office, February 1992), 122–24, https://www.princeton.edu/~ota/disk1/1992/9236/9236.PDF; and David Holmgren, "Lindquist, Everet Franklin," in *The Biographical Dictionary of Iowa* (Iowa City: University of Iowa Press, 2009), http://uipress.lib.uiowa.edu/bdi/DetailsPage.aspx?id=233

151. Carl G. Seashore, "Life in the Seashore Family," undated unpublished manuscript, p. iii, RG 99.0164, box 3, Carl E. Seashore Papers, Special Collections and University Archives, University of Iowa Libraries, Iowa City, IA.

152. Sam Blumenfeld, "Eugenics, or Scientific Racism, in American Education," *New American*, October 10, 2011, https://www.thenewamerican.com/reviews/opinion/item/10870-eugenics-or-scientific-racism-in-american-education; *Encyclopaedia Britannica Online*, s.v. "James McKeen Cattell, American Psychologist," accessed May 9, 2018, https://www.britannica.com/biography/James-McKeen-Cattell

153. Blumenfeld, "Eugenics, or Scientific Racism"; *Encyclopaedia Britannica*, s.v. "James McKeen Cattell."

154. W. B. Pillsbury, "Biographical Memoir of James McKeen Cattell: 1860–1944," vol. 25, *National Academy of Sciences of the United States of America Biographical Memoirs* (Washington, DC: National Academy of Sciences, 1949), 5, http://www.nasonline.org/publications/biographical-memoirs/memoir-pdfs/cattell-james-m.pdf

155. James McKeen Cattell, "The Psychological Corporation," *Annals of the American Academy of Political and Social Science* 110 (November 1923): 165, https://www.jstor.org/stable/1015081

156. Cattell, "Psychological Corporation," 165.

157. Cattell, "Psychological Corporation," 166.

158. Cattell, "Psychological Corporation," 166–67.

159. Carl E. Seashore to Jessup, October 27, 1924, pp. 2–3, RG 05.01.09, box 145, folder 49, Walter A. Jessup Papers. Through the Extension Division, Seashore also was selling pamphlets and similar materials to other institutions. See, for example, C. E. Seashore, Iowa City, IA, to Administrative Officer Addressed, form letter, August 30, 1926, RG 05.01.09, box 187, folder 50, Walter A. Jessup Papers, Special Collections and University Archives, University of Iowa Libraries, Iowa City, IA.

160. Carl E. Seashore to Jessup, October 27, 1924, p. 5, RG 05.01.09, box 145, folder 49, Walter A. Jessup Papers.

161. Carl E. Seashore, "Sunny Side," *Journal of Higher Education*, 292. See also Carl E. Seashore, "Sunny Side," typed manuscript accompanying a letter dated March 26, 1943, p. 7, RG 05.01.11, box 55, folder 52, Virgil M. Hancher Papers; Carl E. Seashore, "Sunny Side," *Daily Iowan*, 2, which may contain a typographical error and reads "evaluation" not "evolution"; and Carl E. Seashore, "Sunny Side," in *Wartime Approaches to Liberal Education*, 32.

162. Carl E. Seashore, "Carl Emil Seashore," 232.

163. Carl E. Seashore, "Carl Emil Seashore," 231–32.

164. Carl E. Seashore, "Carl Emil Seashore," 232.

165. Carl E. Seashore, "Sunny Side," typed manuscript accompanying a letter dated March 26, 1943, pp. 6–7, RG 05.01.11, box 55, folder 52, Virgil M. Hancher Papers; Carl E. Seashore, "Sunny Side," *Daily Iowan*, 2; Carl E. Seashore, "Sunny Side," *Journal of Higher Education*, 292; Carl E. Seashore, "Sunny Side," in *Wartime Approaches to Liberal Education*, 31–32.

166. Carl E. Seashore, "Sunny Side," *Journal of Higher Education*, 292; Carl E. Seashore, "Sunny Side," in *Wartime Approaches to Liberal Education*, 31.

167. Carl E. Seashore, "Sunny Side," *Journal of Higher Education*, 291–92. Also Carl E. Seashore, "Sunny Side," typed manuscript accompanying a letter dated March 26, 1943, pp. 6–7, RG 05.01.11, box 55, folder 52, Virgil M. Hancher Papers; Carl E. Seashore, "Sunny Side," *Daily Iowan*, 2; Carl E. Seashore, "Sunny Side," in *Wartime Approaches to Liberal Education*, 31–32.

168. Carl E. Seashore, "Sunny Side," typed manuscript accompanying a letter dated March 26, 1943, p. 8, RG 05.01.11, box 55, folder 52, Virgil M. Hancher Papers.

169. Carl E. Seashore, "Carl Emil Seashore," 226–27.

170. Nikolas Rose, "Biopolitics in the Twenty First Century: Notes for a Research Agenda," *Distinktion: Scandinavian Journal of Social Theory* 2, no. 3 (2001): 35; Nikolas Rose, *The Politics of Life Itself: Biomedicine, Power, and Subjectivity in the Twenty-First Century* (Princeton, NJ: Princeton University Press, 2007), 64.

171. Carl E. Seashore, "Sectioning Classes on the Basis of Ability," *School and Society* 15, no. 379 (April 1922): 353–53. See also Carl E. Seashore, "The Individual in Mass Education," *School and Society* 23, no. 593 (May 8, 1926): 569.

172. See also Carl E. Seashore, *Learning and Living*, 7.

173. Carl E. Seashore, "Open Letter to a Professor," 351.

174. Carl E. Seashore, "Open Letter to a Professor," 351.

175. Carl E. Seashore, "Sectioning Classes," 353. See also Carl E. Seashore, *Learning and Living*, 52.

176. Henry Fairfield Osborn, "Address of Welcome," in *Eugenics, Genetics and the Family*, vol. 1, *Scientific Papers of the Second International Congress of Eugenics; Held at American Museum of Natural History, New York, September 22–28, 1921* (Baltimore, MD: Williams & Wilkins, 1923; repr., ed. Charles Rosenberg, New York: Garland Publishing, 1985), 2.

177. Madison Grant, *Passing of the Great Race*, xvi.

178. For a discussion of Hitler's views on Grant's book, see William H. Tucker, *The Funding of Scientific Racism: Wickliffe Draper and the Pioneer Fund* (Urbana: University of Illinois Press, 2002), 27.

179. Allan Chase, *The Legacy of Malthus: The Social Costs of the New Scientific Racism* (New York: Alfred A. Knopf, 1977), 98.

180. Francis Galton, *Hereditary Genius: An Inquiry into Its Laws and Consequences* (London: Macmillan, 1869), 14, http://galton.org/books/hereditary-genius/1869-FirstEdition/hereditarygenius1869galt.pdf

181. See, for example, Carl E. Seashore, "Consulting Psychologist," especially 283–85.

182. Carl E. Seashore, "The Master's Key to the Domain of Educational Theory and Practice," *Education Digest* 15, no. 6 (February 1950): 19; repr. fr. *School and Society* 70 (November 26, 1949): 337–38; Carl E. Seashore, *Pioneering in Psychology*, 158; Carl E. Seashore, "Consulting Psychologist," 289–90; and Carl E. Seashore, "Individual in Mass Education," 569.

183. Carl E. Seashore, "Master's Key," 19. See also, for example, Carl E. Seashore, "Rôle of Mental Measurement in the Discovery," 544; Carl E. Seashore, *Psychology of Musical Talent*, 277, 286; Carl E. Seashore, "The Scope and Function of Euthenics," *Mental Hygiene* 33, no. 4 (October 1949): 598; Carl E. Seashore, *Learning and Living*, 6; Carl E. Seashore, "Carl Emil Seashore," 290; Carl E. Seashore, "Recognition of the Individual," pp. 1, 14, RG 05.01.09, box 145, folder 49, Walter A. Jessup Papers; and Carl E. Seashore, "Educational Guidance in Music," 386.

184. Carl E. Seashore, "Master's Key," 19. He also referenced the visit in Carl E. Seashore, *Learning and Living*, 6–7; and Carl E. Seashore, *Pioneering in Psychology*, 158.

185. Carl E. Seashore, *Learning and Living*, 6–7.

186. Carl E. Seashore, "Master's Key," 20. In Carl E. Seashore, "Recognition of the Individual," pp. 1, 18, RG 05.01.09, box 145, folder 49, Walter A. Jessup Papers, for example, he recommended that the tenet be applied in the Engineering School.

187. Carl E. Seashore, *Learning and Living*, 7.

188. Carl E. Seashore, "Master's Key," 20.

189. See, for example, Paul Popenoe and Roswell Hill Johnson, *Applied Eugenics* (New York: Macmillan, 1920), 188.

190. Kevles, *In the Name of Eugenics*, 78.

191. James L. Mursell, *The Psychology of Music* (New York: W. W. Norton, 1937; repr., New York: Johnson Reprint, 1970), 333.

192. Black, *War against the Weak*, 85.

193. Charles B. Davenport to Carl E. Seashore, Iowa City, IA, January 5, 1920, p. 1, MSS.B.D27, box 85, Charles B. Davenport Papers, American Philosophical Society Archives, Philadelphia, PA.

194. See, for example, Paul Popenoe and Roswell Johnson, *Applied Eugenics*, 149, 172–73.

195. Paul Popenoe and Roswell Johnson, *Applied Eugenics*, 188. The source that Popenoe and Johnson quoted is E. R. Johnstone, "Waste Land Plus Waste Humanity," *Training School Bulletin* 11, no. 4 (June 1914): 60–61, https://books.google.com/books?id=pPBEAQAAMAAJ&pg=PA60&lpg=PA60&dq=johnstone+waste+land+plus+waste+humanity+training+school+bulletin&source=bl&ots=cLqT7YMOhv&sig=ACfU3U2vX6q25ZziEI2AEVTNbnQ7PbltfA&hl=en&sa=X&ved=2ahUKEwimye3F_crnAhWXB50JHXUQDWQQ6AEwAXoECAsQAQ#v=onepage&q=waste%20land%20plus%20waste%20humanity&f=false

196. Paul Popenoe and Roswell Johnson, *Applied Eugenics*, 184.

197. Madison Grant, *Passing of the Great Race*, 45.

198. Chase, *Legacy of Malthus*, 152. The source quoted by Chase is Henry H. Goddard, *The Kallikak Family: A Study in the Heredity of Feeble-Mindedness* (New York: Macmillan, 1916), 108, https://books.google.com/books?id=PjUVAAAAIAAJ&pg=PP1#v=onepage&q&f=false

199. Goddard, *Kallikak Family*, 106–7.

200. Carl E. Seashore, *Learning and Living*, 6.

201. Carl E. Seashore, "Sectioning Classes," 356.

202. Carl E. Seashore, "Open Letter to a Professor," 353.

203. Madison Grant, *Passing of the Great Race*, 45.

204. Thomas S. Popkewitz, *Cosmopolitanism and the Age of School Reform: Science, Education, and Making Society by Making the Child* (New York: Routledge, 2008), 101.

205. Carl E. Seashore, "Recognition of the Individual," p. 14, RG 05.01.09, box 145, folder 49, Walter A. Jessup Papers.

206. Carl E. Seashore, "Master's Key," 19.

207. See, for example, Carl E. Seashore, "Education for Democracy," 469–78.

208. Carl E. Seashore, "Education for Democracy," 470. For his use of the word "privilege," see Carl E. Seashore, *Learning and Living*, 38.

209. Carl E. Seashore, *Junior College Movement*, 2.

210. Carl E. Seashore, "Academic Business," 45.

211. J. Russell Smith et al., "The Faculty Birth Rate: Should It Be Increased?" *Eugenics* 3, no. 12 (December 1930): 459; Carl E. Seashore, "Carl Emil Seashore," 296.

212. Carl E. Seashore, "Education for Democracy," 469.

213. Carl E. Seashore, "Education for Democracy," 470.

214. Carl E. Seashore, *Preview to College*, 18.

215. Carl E. Seashore, *Junior College Movement*, 2.

216. Madison Grant, *Passing of the Great Race*, 5.

217. Madison Grant, *Passing of the Great Race*, 6–7.

218. Madison Grant, *Passing of the Great Race*, 6.

219. Zeus Leonardo and Alicia A. Broderick, "Smartness as Property: A Critical Exploration of Intersections between Whiteness and Disability Studies," *Teachers College Record* 113, no. 10 (2011), http://www.tcrecord.org.ezproxy.library.wisc.edu/library/content.asp?contentid=16431

220. Zeus Leonardo and Alicia Broderick, "Smartness as Property."

221. See Carl E. Seashore, *Learning and Living*, 5; and Carl E. Seashore, "Education for Democracy," 469.

222. Carl E. Seashore, "Education for Democracy," 469.

223. Carl E. Seashore, "Education for Democracy," 469.

224. Carl E. Seashore, *Junior College Movement*, 128.

225. Carl E. Seashore, "Education for Democracy," 469.

226. Carl E. Seashore, "Education for Democracy," 471. See also Carl E. Seashore, "Individual in Mass Education," 570.

227. Carl E. Seashore, "Education for Democracy," 469.

228. Carl E. Seashore, *Junior College Movement*, 4.

229. Carl E. Seashore, *Junior College Movement*, 12.

230. Carl E. Seashore, "Recognition of the Individual," p. 3, RG 05.01.09, box 145, folder 49, Walter A. Jessup Papers.

231. Carl E. Seashore, *Junior College Movement*, 12.

232. Carl E. Seashore, "Education for Democracy," 469.

233. Carl E. Seashore, "Education for Democracy," 471.

234. Carl E. Seashore, "Open Letter to a Professor," 352. See also Carl E. Seashore, "Education for Democracy," 471.

235. Plato, *Republic, Book 3*, 3.415a–3.415c, Perseus Collection, Greek and Roman Materials, accessed August 17, 2017, http://www.perseus.tufts.edu/hopper/text?doc=Perseus%3atext%3a1999.01.0168

236. Plato, *Republic*, Book 3, 3.415c.

237. Allen G. Roper, *Ancient Eugenics: The Arnold Prize Essay for 1918* (Oxford: B. H. Blackwell, 1913), https://archive.org/details/ancienteugenicsa00ropeuoft

238. Carl E. Seashore, *Junior College Movement*, 4.

239. Carl E. Seashore, "Recognition of the Individual," p. 3, RG 05.01.09, box 145, folder 49, Walter A. Jessup Papers. See also Carl E. Seashore, "Individual in Mass Education," 570.

240. Carl E. Seashore, *Junior College Movement*, 4.

241. Carl E. Seashore, *Junior College Movement*, 4.

242. Carl E. Seashore, "Education for Democracy," 469. See also Carl E. Seashore, *Learning and Living*, 8; and Carl E. Seashore, *Junior College Movement*, 1.

243. Carl E. Seashore, *Learning and Living*, 8. See also Carl E. Seashore, "Individual in Mass Education," 570.

244. Carl E. Seashore, "Education for Democracy," 469.

245. See, for example, Carl E. Seashore, "Recognition of the Individual," p. 3, RG 05.01.09, box 145, folder 49, Walter A. Jessup Papers.

246. Carl E. Seashore, *Junior College Movement*, 1–2.
247. Carl E. Seashore, "Education for Democracy," 470.
248. George D. Stoddard, "Carl Emil Seashore: 1866–1949," *American Journal of Psychology* 63, no. 3 (July 1950): 459, www.jstor.org/stable/1418021
249. Carl E. Seashore, "Education for Democracy," 469–78; Carl E. Seashore, *Learning and Living*, 88–102; and Carl E. Seashore, *Junior College Movement*.
250. Carl E. Seashore, *Junior College Movement*, 12.
251. Carl E. Seashore, *Junior College Movement*, 2.
252. Carl E. Seashore, "Education for Democracy," 470.
253. Carl E. Seashore, *Junior College Movement*, 2.
254. Carl E. Seashore, *Junior College Movement*, 2.
255. Carl E. Seashore, "Education for Democracy," 472; Carl E. Seashore, *Junior College Movement*, 12.
256. Carl E. Seashore, "Education for Democracy," 470.
257. Carl E. Seashore, "Education for Democracy," 475.
258. Carl E. Seashore, "Education for Democracy," 472; Carl E. Seashore, *Junior College Movement*, 54–55.
259. Carl E. Seashore, "Education for Democracy," 473–74.
260. Carl E. Seashore, "Education for Democracy," 476, 478.
261. Carl E. Seashore, "Education for Democracy," 473.
262. Carl E. Seashore, *Junior College Movement*, 2.
263. Carl E. Seashore, *Junior College Movement*, 2.
264. Carl E. Seashore, "Education for Democracy," 470.
265. Carl E. Seashore, *Junior College Movement*, 2; Carl E. Seashore, "Education for Democracy," 470.
266. Carl E. Seashore, *Junior College Movement*, 54–55.
267. Carl E. Seashore, *Junior College Movement*, 74–75.
268. Carl E. Seashore, "Education for Democracy," 477.
269. Carl E. Seashore, "Education for Democracy," 470; Carl E. Seashore, *Junior College Movement*, 123.
270. Carl E. Seashore, "Education for Democracy," 470.
271. See Carl E. Seashore, *Junior College Movement*, 123; and Carl E. Seashore, "Education for Democracy," 470.
272. Carl E. Seashore, *Junior College Movement*, 123.
273. *Oxford English Dictionary Online*, s.v. "white trash [n. and adj.]," accessed August 24, 2017, http://www.oed.com/view/Entry/421005?redirectedFrom=white+trash&
274. Matt Wray, *Not Quite White: White Trash and the Boundaries of Whiteness* (Durham, NC: Duke University Press, 2006), 16.
275. Nicole Hahn Rafter, ed., *White Trash: The Eugenic Family Studies, 1877–1919* (Boston: Northeastern University Press, 1988), 74.
276. Carl E. Seashore, "Education for Democracy," 474.
277. Carl E. Seashore, "Education for Democracy," 474.
278. Carl E. Seashore, "Education for Democracy," 474; Carl E. Seashore, *Junior College Movement*, 64–65.

279. Carl E. Seashore, *Junior College Movement*, 64.

280. Carl E. Seashore, *Junior College Movement*, 66.

281. Carl E. Seashore, *Junior College Movement*, 123.

282. Carl E. Seashore, "Education for Democracy," 474.

283. Carl E. Seashore, *Junior College Movement*, 53.

284. Carl E. Seashore, *Junior College Movement*, 53. The source Seashore quoted is Nick Aaron Ford, "The Negro Junior College," *Journal of Negro Education* 5, no. 4 (October 1936): 592, http://www.jstor.org/stable/2292031

285. Carl E. Seashore, *Junior College Movement*, 53.

286. Stephen Jay Gould, *The Mismeasure of Man* (New York: W. W. Norton, 1996), 249–50, 255.

287. Carl C. Brigham, *A Study of American Intelligence* (Princeton, NJ: Princeton University Press, 1923), 192, https://archive.org/stream/studyofamericani00briguoft#mode/2up

288. Brigham, *Study of American*, 192.

289. Virgil M. Hancher to Carl E. Seashore, August 3, 1944, RG 05.01.11, box 103, folder 54, Virgil M. Hancher Papers, Special Collections and University Archives, University of Iowa Libraries, Iowa City, IA.

290. "To Teach Summer Course," *Washington Missourian*, May 11, 1950, 3.

291. "Students' Dissertations in Sociology," *American Journal of Sociology* 53, no. 1 (July 1947): 52, http://www.jstor.org/stable/2770628; "Higher Degrees in Sociology Conferred in 1947," *American Journal of Sociology* 54, no. 1 (July 1948): 58, http://www.jstor.org/stable/2770600; "In Memoriam: Alvin W. Rose," *Arts and Sciences Magazine* (University of Miami) 9, no. 1 (Fall 2008): 29, https://merrick.library.miami.edu/cdm/fullbrowser/collection/asu0242/id/574/rv/compoundobject/cpd/603

292. "In Memoriam: Alvin W. Rose," 29.

293. Carrie Simpson, "On Campus," *New Pittsburgh Courier*, October 21, 1972, national edition, 11. The United Nations Archives has copies of reports that Rose filed while he was in the Congo. See "Folder Experts Reports—Report on Mission to Albertville by Alvin Rose—S-0253-0007-06," United Nations Archives, created April 1–30, 1963, accessed February 15, 2019, https://search.archives.un.org/experts-reports-report-on-mission-to-albertville-by-alvin-rose; and "Folder Technical Assistance—Report on Mission to Albertville by Mr. Alvin Rose, United Nations Senior Social Affairs Consultant—S-0752-0040-08," United Nations Archives, created April 3–9, 1963, accessed February 15, 2019, https://search.archives.un.org/technical-assistance-report-on-mission-to-albertville-by-mr-alvin-rose-united-nations-senior-social-affairs-consultant

294. "News and Announcements," *American Sociological Review* 15, no. 4 (August 1950): 567, https://www.jstor.org/stable/2087320; Mel J. Ravitz, "Sociology and the Political Arena," in *Reminiscences of Wayne: Memoirs of Some Faculty and Staff Members of Wayne State University*, ed. Henry V. Bohm and Paul J. Pentecost (Ann Arbor, MI: Cushing-Malloy, 2000), 22.

295. "In Memoriam: Alvin W. Rose," 29.

296. "News and Events," University of Miami College of Arts and Sciences: Sociology, accessed February 11, 2020, https://sociology.as.miami.edu/news-and-events/index.html

297. "Carnegie Classification of Institutions of Higher Education: Basic Classification Description," Indiana University Center for Postsecondary Research, accessed May 14, 2019, http://carnegieclassifications.iu.edu/classification_descriptions/basic.php

298. Carl E. Seashore, *Learning and Living*, 60.

299. Carl E. Seashore, "Carl Emil Seashore," 284; Carl E. Seashore, *Learning and Living*, 55; Carl E. Seashore, "Recognition of the Individual," p. 7, RG 05.01.09, box 145, folder 49, Walter A. Jessup Papers.

300. Carl E. Seashore, "Recognition of the Individual," p. 7, RG 05.01.09, box 145, folder 49, Walter A. Jessup Papers; Carl E. Seashore, "College Placement Examinations," 578.

301. Carl E. Seashore, "Carl Emil Seashore," 284; Miles, "Carl Emil Seashore, 1866–1949," 289.

302. Carl E. Seashore, *Pioneering in Psychology*, 173. In "Carl Emil Seashore" he also used the word "pioneering" to describe his *efforts*; see p. 285.

303. Carl E. Seashore, *Pioneering in Psychology*, 173.

304. Carl E. Seashore, Iowa City, IA, to Robert M. Yerkes, Cambridge, MA, February 22, 1911 (with attachment), MS 569, box 43, folder 836, Robert Mearns Yerkes Papers, Manuscripts and Archives, Yale University Library, New Haven, CT. He also discussed class experiments and the teaching experiments committee with Yerkes in Carl E. Seashore, Iowa City, IA, to Robert M. Yerkes, Cambridge, MA, February 6, 1911, MS 569, box 43, folder 836, Robert Mearns Yerkes Papers, Manuscripts and Archives, Yale University Library, New Haven, CT; and Carl E. Seashore, Iowa City, IA, to Robert M. Yerkes, Cambridge, MA, October 21, 1911, MS 569, box 43, folder 836, Robert Mearns Yerkes Papers, Manuscripts and Archives, Yale University Library, New Haven, CT. Also W. V. Bingham and W. C. Ruediger, "Proceedings of the Twentieth Annual Meeting of the American Psychological Association and the Seventh Annual Meeting of the Southern Society for Philosophy and Psychology, Washington, DC, December 27, 28, and 29, 1911," *Psychological Bulletin* 9, no. 2 (February 15, 1912): 45, https://psycnet.apa.org/doi/10.1037/h0071836, mentions the report of the committee and the recommendation that it continue.

305. Carl E. Seashore, *Learning and Living*, 55.

306. Carl E. Seashore, "College Placement Examinations," 578.

307. Carl E. Seashore, *Learning and Living*, 55.

308. Miles, "Carl Emil Seashore, 1866–1949," 289–90.

309. Carl E. Seashore, "Rôle of Mental Measurement in the Discovery," 545.

310. Carl E. Seashore, "Recognition of the Individual," p. 8, RG 05.01.09, box 145, folder 49, Walter A. Jessup Papers.

311. Miles, "Carl Emil Seashore, 1866–1949," 290.

312. Carl E. Seashore, "Sectioning Classes," 355.

313. Carl E. Seashore, *Learning and Living*, 56–57.

314. Carl E. Seashore, "Rôle of Mental Measurement in the Discovery," 543; Carl E. Seashore, "Sectioning Classes," 355; Carl E. Seashore, *Learning and Living*, 57.

315. Carl E. Seashore, "Sectioning Classes," 356.

316. Carl E. Seashore, "Sectioning Classes," 357.

317. Carl E. Seashore, *Learning and Living*, 53. Also Carl E. Seashore, "Sectioning Classes," 356.

318. Carl E. Seashore, "Rôle of Mental Measurement in the Discovery," 545.

319. Carl E. Seashore, "Recognition of the Individual," p. 8, RG 05.01.09, box 145, folder 49, Walter A. Jessup Papers.

320. Carl E. Seashore, "Sectioning Classes," 356.

321. Carl E. Seashore, "Rôle of Mental Measurement in the Discovery," 545. See also Carl E. Seashore, "Individual in Mass Education," 572.

322. Carl E. Seashore, "Sectioning Classes," 357.

323. Carl E. Seashore, "Sectioning Classes," 356.

324. Carl E. Seashore, "Recognition of the Individual," p. 8, RG 05.01.09, box 145, folder 49, Walter A. Jessup Papers. For another reference to fair distribution of praise and blame, see Carl E. Seashore, "Sectioning Classes," 356.

325. Carl E. Seashore, *Learning and Living*, 64.

326. Carl E. Seashore, "Sectioning Classes," 358.

327. Lewis Madison Terman et al., *Mental and Physical Traits of a Thousand Gifted Children*, vol. 1, Genetic Studies of Genius (Stanford, CA: Stanford University Press, 1925), 2–3, https://babel.hathitrust.org/cgi/pt?id=mdp.39015001544926&view=1up&seq=9

328. Lewis Madison Terman, "The Mental Hygiene of Exceptional Children," *Pedagogical Seminary* 22, no. 4 (1915): 529–37, https://doi.org/10.1080/08919402.1915.10533983

329. Terman et al., *Mental and Physical Traits*.

330. Leta S. Hollingworth, *Gifted Children: Their Nature and Nurture* (New York: Macmillan, 1926), https://archive.org/details/in.ernet.dli.2015.87120/page/n5

331. Henry H. Goddard, *School Training of Gifted Children* (Yonkers-on-Hudson, NY: World Book, 1928), https://babel.hathitrust.org/cgi/pt?id=mdp.39015008191929&view=1up&seq=5

332. Carl E. Seashore, "The Measurement of Musical Talent," *Musical Quarterly* 1, no. 1 (January 1915): 148, https://www.jstor.org/stable/738047. See also Carl E. Seashore, "Carl Emil Seashore," 289.

333. Carl E. Seashore, *Child Welfare Research Station*, 13.

334. C. E. Seashore to Dr. Vernon Kellogg, Washington, DC, March 1, 1927, RG 05.01.09, box 187, folder 50, Walter A. Jessup Papers, Special Collections and University Archives, University of Iowa Libraries, Iowa City, IA.

335. Terman et al., *Mental and Physical Traits*, vii.

336. Carl E. Seashore, "Carl Emil Seashore," 290.

337. Carl E. Seashore, *Learning and Living*, 53. See also Carl E. Seashore, "Carl Emil Seashore," 290.

338. Carl E. Seashore, "Sectioning Classes," 354.

339. Frederick G. Bonser, *The Reasoning Ability of Children of the Fourth, Fifth, and Sixth School Grades* (New York: Teachers College, Columbia University, 1910), 91, https://archive.org/details/reasoningabilit00bonsgoog/page/n4

340. W. H. Holmes, "Promotion Classes for Gifted Pupils," *Journal of Education* 75, no. 14 (April 4, 1912): 377, www.jstor.org/stable/42819686

341. Holmes, "Promotion Classes," 376–77.

342. Holmes, "Promotion Classes," 378.

343. Madison Grant, *Passing of the Great Race*, 6.

344. Paul Popenoe and Roswell Johnson, *Applied Eugenics*, 149.

345. Carl E. Seashore, "Carl Emil Seashore," 290.

346. Adam S. Cohen, "Harvard's Eugenics Era," *Harvard Magazine*, March-April 2016, http://harvardmagazine.com/2016/03/harvards-eugenics-era. For more information on Lowell's ties to eugenics, see Paul A. Lombardo, "When Harvard Said No to Eugenics: The J. Ewing Mears Bequest, 1927," *Perspectives in Biology and Medicine* 57, no. 3 (Summer 2014): 379–87, http://citeseerx.ist.psu.edu/viewdoc/download?doi=10.1.1.825.1686&rep=rep1&type=pdf

347. Carl E. Seashore, "Recognition of the Individual," pp. 15–16, RG 05.01.09, box 145, folder 49, Walter A. Jessup Papers.

348. Jane Robbins, "The 'Problem of the Gifted Student': National Research Council oEfforts to Identify and Cultivate Undergraduate Talent in a New Era of Mass Education, 1919–1929," vol. 24, *Perspectives on the History of Higher Education: History of Higher Education Annual*, ed. Roger L. Geiger (New Brunswick, NJ: Transaction, 2005), 113.

349. C. E. Seashore to Kellogg, March 1, 1927, RG 05.01.09, box 187, folder 50, Walter A. Jessup Papers.

350. C. E. Seashore to Kellogg, March 1, 1927, p. 2, RG 05.01.09, box 187, folder 50, Walter A. Jessup Papers; Carl E. Seashore, "Carl Emil Seashore," 289, 295.

351. Carl E. Seashore, *Learning and Living*, 5.

352. Miles, "Carl Emil Seashore, 1866–1949," 292.

353. Carl E. Seashore, *Pioneering in Psychology*, 193.

354. Carl E. Seashore, *Pioneering in Psychology*, 193.

355. C. E. Seashore to Kellogg, March 1, 1927, p. 2, RG 05.01.09, box 187, folder 50, Walter A. Jessup Papers.

356. C. E. Seashore to Kellogg, March 1, 1927, p. 2, RG 05.01.09, box 187, folder 50, Walter A. Jessup Papers.

357. C. E. Seashore to Kellogg, March 1, 1927, p. 2, RG 05.01.09, box 187, folder 50, Walter A. Jessup Papers.

358. Carl E. Seashore, *Learning and Living*, 5.

359. Carl E. Seashore, *Pioneering in Psychology*, 193.

360. Carl E. Seashore, *Learning and Living*, 5.

361. Carl E. Seashore, "Carl Emil Seashore," 289; Carl E. Seashore, *Pioneering in Psychology*, 193.

362. Robbins, "'Problem of the Gifted,'" 105.

363. C. E. Seashore to Kellogg, March 1, 1927, pp. 2–3, RG 05.01.09, box 187, folder 50, Walter A. Jessup Papers.

364. C. E. Seashore to Kellogg, March 1, 1927, p. 1, RG 05.01.09, box 187, folder 50, Walter A. Jessup Papers.

365. C. E. Seashore to Kellogg, March 1, 1927, p. 3, RG 05.01.09, box 187, folder 50, Walter A. Jessup Papers.

366. Carl E. Seashore, "Carl Emil Seashore," 289; Carl E. Seashore, *Learning and Living*, 8.

367. C. E. Seashore to Kellogg, March 1, 1927, p. 3, RG 05.01.09, box 187, folder 50, Walter A. Jessup Papers.

368. C. E. Seashore to Kellogg, March 1, 1927, p. 3, RG 05.01.09, box 187, folder 50, Walter A. Jessup Papers; Carl E. Seashore, *Pioneering in Psychology*, 195.

369. Carl E. Seashore, *Pioneering in Psychology*, 194.

370. Carl E. Seashore, *Learning and Living*, 6, 8.

371. Carl E. Seashore, "Carl Emil Seashore," 290. See also Carl E. Seashore, *Learning and Living*, 8.

372. Carl E. Seashore, *Pioneering in Psychology*, 194.

373. Carl E. Seashore, *Learning and Living*, 8.

374. Carl E. Seashore, "Carl Emil Seashore," 290–91; Carl E. Seashore, *Learning and Living*, 9–10.

375. Carl E. Seashore, "Carl Emil Seashore," 290.

376. Carl E. Seashore, "Carl Emil Seashore," 290; Carl E. Seashore, *Pioneering in Psychology*, 195n*.

377. Carl E. Seashore, *Pioneering in Psychology*, 195n*.

378. Carl E. Seashore, *Pioneering in Psychology*, 195n*.

379. Carl E. Seashore, "Carl Emil Seashore," 293.

380. C. E. Seashore, Iowa City, IA, to President Jessup, April 13, 1925, RG 05.01.09, box 145, folder 49, Walter A. Jessup Papers, Special Collections and University Archives, University of Iowa Libraries, Iowa City, IA. He mentioned the trips in C. E. Seashore, Redlands, CA, to President Walter Jessup, Iowa City, IA, November 28, 1924, RG 05.01.09, box 145, folder 49, Walter A. Jessup Papers, Special Collections and University Archives, University of Iowa Libraries, Iowa City, IA. Robbins details these trips and includes the names of other institutions; see "'Problem of the Gifted,'" 105–7.

381. See, for example, Carl E. Seashore, *Pioneering in Psychology*, 195; and Carl E. Seashore, "Carl Emil Seashore," 293.

382. Carl E. Seashore, "Carl Emil Seashore," 293.

383. Carl E. Seashore, "Carl Emil Seashore," 290, 291.

384. Carl E. Seashore, "Carl Emil Seashore," 293.

385. C. E. Seashore to Kellogg, March 1, 1927, p. 4, RG 05.01.09, box 187, folder 50, Walter A. Jessup Papers.

386. Carl E. Seashore, "Carl Emil Seashore," 294.

387. Carl E. Seashore, *Pioneering in Psychology*, 194; Carl E. Seashore, *Learning*

and Living, 5; Carl E. Seashore, "Carl Emil Seashore," 293.

388. Carl E. Seashore, *Pioneering in Psychology*, 196.

389. See Vernon Kellogg, Washington, DC, to Walter A. Jessup, Iowa City, IA, March 2, 1925, RG 05.01.09, box 145, folder 49, Walter A. Jessup Papers, Special Collections and University Archives, University of Iowa Libraries, Iowa City, IA.

390. Miles, "Carl Emil Seashore, 1866–1949," 293. A third byproduct was a series of bulletins issued by the NRC. See Carl E. Seashore, *Pioneering in Psychology*, 196.

391. Robbins, "'Problem of the Gifted,'" 109.

392. Robbins, "'Problem of the Gifted,'" 92, 113.

393. Carl E. Seashore, *Learning and Living*, 105.

394. Carl E. Seashore, *Learning and Living*, 105.

395. See, for example, Vernon Kellogg, Washington, DC, to Walter A. Jessup, Iowa City, IA, January 28, 1925, RG 05.01.09, box 145, folder 49, Walter A. Jessup Papers, Special Collections and University Archives, University of Iowa Libraries, Iowa City, IA; "List of Institutions to be Represented at Honors Courses Conference, University of Iowa, March 17 and 18, 1925,with Names of Delegates," RG 05.01.09, box 145, folder 49, Walter A. Jessup Papers, Special Collections and University Archives, University of Iowa Libraries, Iowa City, IA; and C. E. Seashore to Jessup, November 28, 1924, RG 05.01.09, box 145, folder 49, Walter A. Jessup Papers.

396. Robbins, "'Problem of the Gifted,'" 110.

397. Kellogg to Jessup, January 28, 1925, RG 05.01.09, box 145, folder 49, Walter A. Jessup Papers.

398. Robbins, "'Problem of the Gifted,'" 110.

399. "List of Institutions," RG 05.01.09, box 145, folder 49, Walter A. Jessup Papers. The institutions not in the Midwest are the University of Kentucky and Centre College of Kentucky.

400. Carl E. Seashore, "Carl Emil Seashore," 291.

401. Carl E. Seashore, "Carl Emil Seashore," 270.

402. Carl E. Seashore, "Carl Emil Seashore," 292–93.

403. Miles, "Carl Emil Seashore, 1866–1949," 293.

404. Robbins, "'Problem of the Gifted,'" 114.

405. Carl E. Seashore, "Carl Emil Seashore," 284.

406. Carl E. Seashore, "Recognition of the Individual," p. 17, RG 05.01.09, box 145, folder 49, Walter A. Jessup Papers.

407. Carl E. Seashore, "Graduate Study: An Address," 13.

408. "Graduate Faculty Adopts Radical Changes," *University of Iowa News Bulletin* 4, no. 6 (June 1929): 1.

409. "Graduate Faculty Adopts," 1.

410. "Graduate Faculty Adopts," 1.

411. Carl E. Seashore, *Pioneering in Psychology*, 162.

412. Carl E. Seashore, "Carl Emil Seashore," 291.

413. Carl E. Seashore, *Learning and Living*, 60.

414. See, for example, Carl E. Seashore, "Recognition of the Individual," pp. 16–17, RG 05.01.09, box 145, folder 49, Walter A. Jessup Papers; and Carl E. Seashore, *Learning and Living*, 108–9.

415. Carl E. Seashore, *Learning and Living*, 103.

416. Carl E. Seashore, *Learning and Living*, 103.

417. Carl E. Seashore, *Learning and Living*, 103.

418. Carl E. Seashore, *Learning and Living*, 103–4.

419. Carl E. Seashore, *Learning and Living*, 104.

420. Carl E. Seashore, *Learning and Living*, 109.

421. Carl E. Seashore, *Learning and Living*, 60.

422. Carl E. Seashore, "Recognition of the Individual," pp. 16–17, RG 05.01.09, box 145, folder 49, Walter A. Jessup Papers.

423. Carl E. Seashore, *Learning and Living*, 58.

424. Carl E. Seashore, "Discussion: Intercollegiate Academic Contests," *School and Society* 28, no. 709 (1928): 114.

425. Carl E. Seashore, *Pioneering in Psychology*, 197.

426. Carl E. Seashore, "Discussion: Intercollegiate Academic Contests," 114.

427. Carl E. Seashore, "Discussion: Intercollegiate Academic Contests," 114.

428. Carl E. Seashore, "Discussion: Intercollegiate Academic Contests," 114.

429. Lois M. Quinn, "An Institutional History of the GED," in *The Myth of Achievement Tests: The GED and the Role of Character in American Life*, ed. James Heckman, John Eric Humphries, and Tim Kautz (Chicago: University of Chicago Press, 2014), 62–63. Carl E. Seashore, *Pioneering in Psychology*, 198, also cites the number 1,000.

430. Quinn, "Institutional History," 63.

431. "Lois Jeanne Mayhew Recaptures Title in Iowa 'Brain Derby,'" *Daily Iowan*, June 9, 1937, 1, http://dailyiowan.lib.uiowa.edu/DI/1937/di1937-06-09.pdf

432. "Lois Jeanne Mayhew Recaptures," 1, 6.

433. Carl E. Seashore, *Pioneering in Psychology*, 198.

434. Quinn, "Institutional History," 63. This statistic also was reported by Seashore. See Carl E. Seashore, *Pioneering in Psychology*, 197.

435. See, for example, Holmgren, "Lindquist, Everet Franklin." Seashore mentioned Kirby in Carl E. Seashore, "Iowa Academic Meet," *School and Society* 30, no. 759 (July 13, 1929): 63; and Lindquist in Carl E. Seashore, *Pioneering in Psychology*, 197.

436. See, for example, Quinn, "Institutional History," 62–65.

437. Carl E. Seashore, *Pioneering in Psychology*, 197.

438. Carl E. Seashore, "Iowa Academic Meet," 63.

439. Carl E. Seashore, *Pioneering in Psychology*, 197.

440. "Memorandum on Greetings," attachment to Carl E. Seashore to Hancher, June 9, 1941, RG 05.01.11, box 16, folder 93, Virgil M. Hancher Papers.

441. "Memorandum on Greetings," attachment to Carl E. Seashore to Hancher, June 9, 1941, RG 05.01.11, box 16, folder 93, Virgil M. Hancher Papers.

442. "Memorandum on Greetings," attachment to Carl E. Seashore to Hancher, June 9, 1941, RG 05.01.11, box 16, folder 93, Virgil M. Hancher Papers.

443. "Memorandum on Greetings," attachment to Carl E. Seashore to Hancher, June 9, 1941, RG 05.01.11, box 16, folder 93, Virgil M. Hancher Papers.

444. "Memorandum on Greetings," attachment to Carl E. Seashore to Hancher, June 9, 1941, RG 05.01.11, box 16, folder 93, Virgil M. Hancher Papers.

445. Carl E. Seashore, *Pioneering in Psychology*, 198.

446. Carl E. Seashore, *Pioneering in Psychology*, 198.

447. Carl E. Seashore, *Pioneering in Psychology*, 198n*.

448. Carl E. Seashore, *Pioneering in Psychology*, 198n*.

449. Carl E. Seashore, *Pioneering in Psychology*, 198n**.

450. Carl E. Seashore, "Graduate Study: An Address," 9; Carl E. Seashore, *Learning and Living*, 6.

451. Carl E. Seashore, *Learning and Living*, 103.

452. Carl E. Seashore, "Open Letter to a Professor," 352.

453. See, for example, Carl E. Seashore, "Sectioning Classes," 354, 357–58.

454. Carl E. Seashore, "Sectioning Classes," 354.

455. Carl E. Seashore, "Sectioning Classes," 357.

456. Francis Galton, *Memories of My Life* (New York: E. P. Dutton, 1909), 322, 323, https://archive.org/stream/memoriesmylife01galtgoog#mode/2up/search/323

457. Carl E. Seashore, "Carl Emil Seashore," 227.

458. Carl E. Seashore, "Graduate Study: An Address," 8–9.

459. Carl E. Seashore, "Graduate Study: An Address," 9.

460. Carl E. Seashore, "Open Letter to a Professor," 352.

461. Carl E. Seashore, *Psychology in Daily Life*, 122.

462. Carl E. Seashore, "Recognition of the Individual," p. 3, RG 05.01.09, box 145, folder 49, Walter A. Jessup Papers.

463. Carl E. Seashore, "Academic Business," 47.

464. Carl E. Seashore, "Rôle of Mental Measurement in the Discovery," 545; Carl E. Seashore, "Recognition of the Individual," p. 7, RG 05.01.09, box 145, folder 49, Walter A. Jessup Papers; Carl E. Seashore, "Sectioning Classes," 357.

465. Carl E. Seashore, *Junior College Movement*, 1; Carl E. Seashore, "Education for Democracy," 469.

466. W. M. Hays, "Editorials, Heredity in Man," *American Breeders Magazine* 1, no. 3 (1910): 221, https://babel.hathitrust.org/cgi/pt?id=uma.ark:/13960/t0ft91b2c&view=1up&seq=241; W. M. Hays, "Editorials, Efficiency Records of People," *American Breeders Magazine* 1, no. 3 (1910): 222, https://babel.hathitrust.org/cgi/pt?id=uma.ark:/13960/t0ft91b2c&view=1up&seq=242

467. Madison Grant, *Passing of the Great Race*, 5.

468. Paul Popenoe and Roswell Johnson, *Applied Eugenics*, 149.

469. Paul Popenoe and Roswell Johnson, *Applied Eugenics*, 172–73.

470. Zygmunt Bauman, *Modernity and the Holocaust* (Ithaca, NY: Cornell University Press, 1989), 87, 104.

471. Bauman, *Modernity and the Holocaust*, 15.

Chapter 6

1. For an overview of some of these interests, see Carl E. Seashore, *Psychology of Music* (New York: McGraw-Hill, 1938), https://archive.org/details/psychologyofmusi030417mbp

2. Carl E. Seashore, "Music," vol. 2, *Handbook of Applied Psychology*, ed. Douglas H. Fryer and Edwin R. Henry (New York: Rinehart, 1950), 681.

3. Carl E. Seashore, "Music," 681–86.

4. Carl E. Seashore, "The Measurement of Musical Talent," *Musical Quarterly* 1, no. 1 (January 1915): 129, https://www.jstor.org/stable/738047

5. Carl E. Seashore, "Carl Emil Seashore," vol. 1, *A History of Psychology in Autobiography*, ed. Carl Allanmore Murchison (Worcester, MA: Clark University, 1930), 275.

6. Carl E. Seashore, "Individual and Racial Inheritance of Musical Traits," in *Eugenics, Genetics and the Family*, vol. 1, *Scientific Papers of the Second International Congress of Eugenics; Held at American Museum of Natural History, New York, September 22–28, 1921* (Baltimore, MD: Williams & Wilkins, 1923; repr., ed. Charles Rosenberg, New York: Garland Publishing, 1985), 231.

7. See, for example, Carl E. Seashore, "Individual and Racial Inheritance," 232; Carl E. Seashore, "Measurement of Musical Talent," 130; and Carl E. Seashore, "Musical Inheritance," *Scientific Monthly* 50, no. 4 (April 1940): 352.

8. Carl E. Seashore, "Individual and Racial Inheritance," 235; Carl E. Seashore, "Musical Inheritance," 352–53.

9. He used capacities, for example, in Carl E. Seashore, "Musical Inheritance," 354; Carl E. Seashore, *Vocational Guidance in Music*, University of Iowa Monographs: Aims and Progress of Research, 1st ser., no. 2 (Iowa City: The University, September 1916), 3–4; Carl E. Seashore, "Vocational Guidance in Music," *Music Supervisors' Journal* 3, no. 2 (November 1916): 18, 20, https://www.jstor.org/stable/3383046; and Carl E. Seashore, *Psychology of Music*, 2–5. For examples of his use of traits, see Carl E. Seashore, "Basic Measurements of Music and Speech," p. 4, attachment to C. E. Seashore, Washington, DC, to President W. A. Jessup, Iowa City, IA, April 29, 1921, RG 05.01.09, box 76, folder 53, Walter A. Jessup Papers, Special Collections and University Archives, University of Iowa Libraries, Iowa City, IA; Carl E. Seashore, "Musical Inheritance," 352; and Carl E. Seashore, *Psychology of Music*, 337. For examples of his use of elements, see Carl E. Seashore, "Musical Inheritance," 352; and Carl E. Seashore, "Individual and Racial Inheritance," 235. For examples of this use of factors, see Carl E. Seashore, "Individual and Racial Inheritance," 232; and Carl E. Seashore, *The Psychology of Musical Talent* (Boston: Silver, Burdett, 1919), 7.

10. See, for example, Carl E. Seashore, *Psychology of Musical Talent*, 7–8; Carl E. Seashore, "How Psychology Can Help the Musician," *Etude* 35, no. 2 (February 1917): 89, https://books.google.com/books?id=IpgyAQAAMAAJ&pg=PA89&lpg=PA89&dq=etude++how+psychology+can+help+the+musician&source=bl&ots=tHDoVQu6_g&sig=d7_3e_W1UD8pNiZ_MakBANDHg3A&hl=en&sa=X&ved=0CCEQ6AEwAWoVChMI8pDg88nYxgIVEQySCh3pigIR#v=onepage&q

=etude%20%20how%20psychology%20can%20help%20the%20musician&f=false; and Carl E. Seashore, "Individual and Racial Inheritance," 233–34.

11. Carl E. Seashore, *Psychology of Musical Talent*, 6–7.

12. Carl E. Seashore, *Psychology of Musical Talent*, 7–8.

13. Carl E. Seashore, *Psychology of Musical Talent*, 8.

14. Carl E. Seashore, "Musical Inheritance," 353.

15. Carl E. Seashore, "How Psychology Can Help," 89; Carl E. Seashore, *Psychology of Musical Talent*, 8; Carl E. Seashore, "Individual and Racial Inheritance," 234.

16. Carl E. Seashore, *Psychology of Musical Talent*, 257. See also Carl E. Seashore, *Psychology of Music*, 339.

17. Carl E. Seashore, "Individual and Racial Inheritance," 235.

18. Carl E. Seashore, *Psychology of Music*, 339.

19. Carl E. Seashore, *Psychology of Music*, 57.

20. Carl E. Seashore, *Psychology of Musical Talent*, 69.

21. Carl E. Seashore, "Measurement of Musical Talent," 131–32.

22. Carl E. Seashore, "Measurement of Musical Talent," 130.

23. Carl E. Seashore, "How Psychology Can Help," 89.

24. Carl E. Seashore, "Individual and Racial Inheritance," 233–34.

25. Carl E. Seashore, "Individual and Racial Inheritance," 233–34.

26. Carl E. Seashore, "Musical Inheritance," 354.

27. Carl E. Seashore, "Musical Inheritance," 354.

28. Carl E. Seashore, "Musical Inheritance," 356.

29. Carl E. Seashore, *Vocational Guidance in Music*, University of Iowa Monographs, 3.

30. Carl E. Seashore, "Musical Inheritance," 352.

31. Julia Eklund Koza, "Listening for Whiteness: Hearing Racial Politics in Undergraduate School Music," *Philosophy of Music Education Review* 16, no. 2 (Fall 2008): 151.

32. See, for example, Carl E. Seashore, "Musical Inheritance," 352; Carl E. Seashore, *Psychology of Musical Talent*, 6; and Carl E. Seashore, "Measurement of Musical Talent," 130.

33. Carl E. Seashore, *Psychology of Music*, 2.

34. Carl E. Seashore, *Psychology of Music*, 8.

35. Carl E. Seashore, *Psychology of Music*, 8.

36. Carl E. Seashore, *Psychology of Music*, 2–3.

37. Carl E. Seashore, *Psychology of Music*, 334. For another reference that distinguishes talent from genius, see Carl E. Seashore, "Individual and Racial Inheritance," 232.

38. Julia Eklund Koza, "Music and the Feminine Sphere: Images of Women as Musicians in *Godey's Lady's Book*, 1830–1877," *Musical Quarterly* 75, no. 2 (Summer 1991): 121–22.

39. Carl E. Seashore, "Musical Inheritance," 354.

40. Carl E. Seashore, "Psychology and Life in Autobiography," typed manu-

script, pp. 203–4, RG 99.0164, box 2, Carl E. Seashore Papers, Special Collections and University Archives, University of Iowa Libraries, Iowa City, IA.

41. Kurt Danziger, *Constructing the Subject: Historical Origins of Psychological Research* (Cambridge, UK: Cambridge University Press, 1990), 37.

42. Carl E. Seashore, "Psychology and Life," p. 206, RG 99.0164, box 2, Carl E. Seashore Papers; Johanna Devaney, "Eugenics and Musical Talent: Exploring Carl Seashore's Work on Talent Testing and Performance," *American Music Review* 48, no. 2 (Spring, 2019): 1, http://www.brooklyn.edu/web/aca_centers_hitchcock/AMR_48-2_Devaney.pdf

43. Carl E. Seashore, "Measurement of Musical Talent," 129.

44. Carl E. Seashore, *Psychology of Musical Talent*, 6. For further evidence, see Carl E. Seashore, "Individual and Racial Inheritance," 231; Carl E. Seashore, *Psychology of Music*, 3, 337, 334–45; Carl E. Seashore, "Musical Inheritance," 351; and Carl E. Seashore, "Measurement of Musical Talent," 129.

45. Carl E. Seashore, "Individual and Racial Inheritance," 232.

46. Carl E. Seashore, *Psychology of Music*, 337. For other examples of references to Mendel, see Carl E. Seashore, *Psychology of Musical Talent*, 69; and Carl E. Seashore, *A Child Welfare Research Station: Plans and Possibilities of a Research Station for the Conservation and Development of the Normal Child*, Series on Aims and Progress of Research, n.s., vol. 107 (Iowa City, Iowa: The University, 1916), 4, https://catalog.hathitrust.org/Record/010551244

47. Carl E. Seashore, "Individual and Racial Inheritance," 235–36.

48. Carl E. Seashore, "Individual and Racial Inheritance," 231.

49. Carl E. Seashore, "Individual and Racial Inheritance," 232.

50. Carl E. Seashore, "Individual and Racial Inheritance," 235.

51. Carl E. Seashore, "Musical Inheritance," 351.

52. Carl E. Seashore, "Musical Inheritance," 351.

53. Carl E. Seashore, "Musical Inheritance," 352.

54. Carl E. Seashore, *Psychology of Music*, 3.

55. Carl E. Seashore, "Individual and Racial Inheritance," 232.

56. Carl E. Seashore, "Individual and Racial Inheritance," 233–34.

57. For example, see his assertion about pitch perception in Carl E. Seashore, "Measurement of Musical Talent," 139.

58. Carl E. Seashore, "How Psychology Can Help," 89. See also Carl E. Seashore, *Psychology of Musical Talent*, 4, 273.

59. Carl E. Seashore, "Musical Inheritance," 353.

60. See, for example, Carl E. Seashore, *Psychology of Musical Talent*, 6.

61. Carl E. Seashore, "Avocational Guidance in Music," *Journal of Applied Psychology* 1, no. 4 (December 1917): 342.

62. Carl E. Seashore, *Vocational Guidance in Music*, University of Iowa Monographs, 3.

63. Carl E. Seashore, "Measurement of Musical Talent," 129.

64. Carl E. Seashore, "How Psychology Can Help," 89.

65. Carl E. Seashore, *Psychology of Music*, 5.

66. Carl E. Seashore, *Psychology of Musical Talent*, 6. For other examples, see Carl E. Seashore, "Individual and Racial Inheritance," 232; and Carl E. Seashore, *Psychology of Music*, 2.

67. Carl E. Seashore, "Talent," *School and Society* 55, no. 1416 (February 14, 1942): 171.

68. Carl E. Seashore, *Psychology of Musical Talent*, 6.

69. See also Carl E. Seashore, *Psychology of Music*, 2.

70. Carl E. Seashore, "Music," 681.

71. Carl E. Seashore, "Measurement of Musical Talent," 135.

72. Carl E. Seashore, "Talent," 171.

73. Carl E. Seashore, *Psychology of Music*, 5.

74. Carl E. Seashore, "Musical Inheritance," 352.

75. Stefan Willer, "Sui Generis: Heredity and Heritage of Genius at the Turn of the Eighteenth Century," in *Heredity Produced: At the Crossroads of Biology, Politics, and Culture, 1500–1870*, ed. Staffan Müller-Wille and Hans-Jörg Rheinberger (Cambridge, MA: MIT Press, 2007), 419.

76. Willer, "Sui Generis," 426–27. On p. 426 Willer states that the first chapter was entitled "Descent." An annotated source titles the first chapter "The Family of Bach" and notes that the original had no chapter titles. See the table of contents in Johann Nikolaus Forkel, *Johann Sebastian Bach: His Life, Art, and Work*, trans. and annotated Charles Sanford Terry (London: Constable, 1920); first published as *Ueber Johann Sebastian Bachs Leben, Kunst und Kunstwerke* (Leipzig; Hoffmeister and Kühnel, 1802), https://archive.org/details/johannsebastianb00forkuoft/page/n7

77. Willer, "Sui Generis," 423. Willer quotes Immanuel Kant, *The Critique of Judgement* (1790), trans. James Creed Meredith (Oxford: Oxford University Press, 1952), 168. A similar translation is found in Immanuel Kant, *Critique of the Power of Judgment* (1790), ed. Paul Guyer, trans. Paul Guyer and Eric Matthews (Cambridge: Cambridge University Press, 2000), 186: "Since the talent, as an inborn productive faculty of the artist, itself belongs to nature, this could also be expressed thus: *Genius* is the inborn predisposition of the mind (*ingenium*) *through which* nature gives the rule to art [emphasis in original]."

78. Willer, "Sui Generis," 433.

79. Willer, "Sui Generis," 433.

80. Willer, "Sui Generis," 419.

81. Willer, "Sui Generis," 419.

82. Francis Galton, *Hereditary Genius: An Inquiry into Its Laws and Consequences* (London: Macmillan, 1869), 237–46, http://galton.org/books/hereditary-genius/1869-FirstEdition/hereditarygenius1869galt.pdf. For a family-tree chart, see p. 241.

83. Jere T. Humphreys, "Precursors of Musical Aptitude Testing: From the Greeks through the Work of Francis Galton," *Journal of Research in Music Education* 41, no. 4 (Winter 1993): 320, 322, http://www.jstor.org/stable/3345507

84. W. M. Hays, "Editorials, Efficiency Records of People," *American Breeders Magazine* 1, no. 3 (1910): 222, https://babel.hathitrust.org/cgi/pt?id=uma.ark:/13960/t0ft91b2c&view=1up&seq=242

85. W. M. Hays, "Editorials, Unit Character in Man," *American Breeders Magazine* 1, no. 3 (1910): 223, https://babel.hathitrust.org/cgi/pt?id=uma.ark:/13960/t0ft91b2c&view=1up&seq=243

86. Hays, "Editorials, Unit Character," 223.

87. "Human Pedigrees Detailing the Inheritance of Specific Biological Traits, Inheritance of Musical Talent: Explanatory Notes" [c. 1910], p. 2, Cold Spring Harbor, ERO, titled "'Inheritance of Musical Talent,' Pedigree Chart with Instructions, Eugenics Section, American Breeders Association," image 1770, in the "Image Archive on the American Eugenics Movement," DNA Learning Center, Cold Spring Harbor Laboratory, accessed March 25, 2009, www.eugenicsarchive.org/eugenics/view_image.pl?id=1770

88. "Human Pedigrees Detailing the Inheritance of Specific Biological Traits, Inheritance of Musical Talent" [c. 1910], p. 1, Cold Spring Harbor, ERO, titled "'Inheritance of Musical Talent,' Pedigree Chart with Instructions, Eugenics Section, American Breeders Association," image 1769, in the "Image Archive on the American Eugenics Movement," DNA Learning Center, Cold Spring Harbor Laboratory, accessed November 14, 2018, www.eugenicsarchive.org/eugenics/view_image.pl?id=1769; "Human Pedigrees Detailing the Inheritance of Specific Biological Traits, Inheritance of Musical Talent," 1911, American Philosophical Society, ERO, MSC77, titled "'Human Pedigrees Detailing Inheritance of Specific Biological Traits: Inheritance of Musical Talent,'" Eugenics Section, American Breeders Association, image 84, in the "Image Archive on the American Eugenics Movement," DNA Learning Center, Cold Spring Harbor Laboratory, accessed November 15, 2018, www.eugenicsarchive.org/eugenics/view_image.pl?id=84

89. Charles B. Davenport, Cold Spring Harbor, NY, to Mrs. E. H. Harriman, New York, NY, June 20, 1910, p. 1, American Philosophical Society, Dav, B:D27, Harriman, Mrs. E.H., titled "Charles Davenport Letter to Mrs. E.H. Harriman about Recruitment of First Class," image 421, in the "Image Archive on the American Eugenics Movement," DNA Learning Center, Cold Spring Harbor Laboratory, accessed January 21, 2020, www.eugenicsarchive.org/eugenics/view_image.pl?id=421

90. "Topic: Fitter Family Contests," Image Archive on the American Eugenics Movement, DNA Learning Center, Cold Spring Harbor Laboratory, accessed November 17, 2018, http://www.eugenicsarchive.org/eugenics/topics_fs.pl?theme=8

91. "Topic: Better Baby Contests," Image Archive on the American Eugenics Movement, DNA Learning Center, Cold Spring Harbor Laboratory, accessed November 17, 2018, http://www.eugenicsarchive.org/eugenics/topics_fs.pl?theme=43; "Topic: Fitter Family Contests."

92. "Fitter Families for Future Firesides: A Report of the Eugenics Department of the Kansas Free Fair, 1920–1924, inc.; Foreword," 1924, p. 4, American Philosophical Society, ERO, MSC77, SerVI, Box 4, FF Studies, KS Free Fair, titled "Fitter Families for Future Firesides: A Report of the Eugenics Department of the Kansas Free Fair, 1920–1924," image 196, in the "Image Archive on the American

Eugenics Movement," DNA Learning Center, Cold Spring Harbor Laboratory, accessed November 17, 2018, www.eugenicsarchive.org/eugenics/view_image.pl?id=196

93. "Fitter Families for Future Firesides: A Report of the Eugenics Department of the Kansas Free Fair, 1920–1924, inc.; Foreword," 1924, p. 4, American Philosophical Society, ERO, MSC77, SerVI, Box 4, FF Studies, KS Free Fair, titled "Fitter Families for Future Firesides: A Report of the Eugenics Department of the Kansas Free Fair, 1920–1924," image 196, in the "Image Archive on the American Eugenics Movement," DNA Learning Center, Cold Spring Harbor Laboratory, accessed November 17, 2018, www.eugenicsarchive.org/eugenics/view_image.pl?id=196

94. "Fitter Families Examination," 1925, American Philosophical Society, ERO, MSC77, SerVI, Box 2, FF Studies MA #3, titled "'Average Family' Winner, Fitter Families Contest, Eastern States Exposition, Springfield, MA (1925): Family Examination Summary," image 168, in the "Image Archive on the American Eugenics Movement," DNA Learning Center, Cold Spring Harbor Laboratory, accessed March 25, 2009, www.eugenicsarchive.org/eugenics/view_image.pl?id=168; "Fitter Families Examination," 1925, American Philosophical Society, ERO, MSC77, SerVI, Box 3, FF Studies TX #2, titled "'Large Family' Winner, Fitter Families Contest, Texas State Fair (1925): Family Examination Summary," image 170, in the "Image Archive on the American Eugenics Movement," DNA Learning Center, Cold Spring Harbor Laboratory, accessed March 25, 2009, www.eugenicsarchive.org/eugenics/view_image.pl?id=170; "Fitter Families Examination," 1925, American Philosophical Society, ERO, MSC77, SerVI, Box 3, FF Studies TX #1, titled "'Best Couple,' Fitter Families Contest, Texas State Fair (1925): Family Summary Examination," image 188, in the "Image Archive on the American Eugenics Movement," DNA Learning Center, Cold Spring Harbor Laboratory, accessed March 25, 2009, www.eugenicsarchive.org/eugenics/view_image.pl?id=188

95. "Abridged Record of Family Traits: Father's Father, Father's Mother," 1925, p. 2, American Philosophical Society, ERO, MSC77, SerVI, Box 3, FF Studies TX #2, titled "'Large Family' Winner, Fitter Families Contest, Texas State Fair (1925): Abridged Record of Family Traits," image 179, in the "Image Archive on the American Eugenics Movement," DNA Learning Center, Cold Spring Harbor Laboratory, accessed March 25, 2009, www.eugenicsarchive.org/eugenics/view_image.pl?id=179

96. See, for example, "Fitter Families Examination," 1925, p. 1, American Philosophical Society, ERO, MSC77, SerVI, Box 2, FF Studies MA #1, titled "'Large Family' Winner, Fitter Families Contest, Eastern States Exposition, Springfield (1925): Fitter Families Examination," image 147, in the "Image Archive on the American Eugenics Movement," DNA Learning Center, Cold Spring Harbor Laboratory, accessed March 25, 2009, www.eugenicsarchive.org/eugenics/view_image.pl?id=147; "Abridged Record of Family Traits," 1925, pp. 3–4, 7, American Philosophical Society, ERO, MSC77, SerVI, Box 2, FF Studies MA #1, titled "'Large Family' Winner, Fitter Families Contest, Eastern States Exposition,

Springfield, MA (1925): Abridged Record of Family Traits," images 162–63, 166, in the "Image Archive on the American Eugenics Movement," DNA Learning Center, Cold Spring Harbor Laboratory, accessed March 25, 2009, www.eugenicsarchive.org/eugenics/view_image.pl?id=162; "Fitter Families Examination," 1925, American Philosophical Society, ERO, MSC77, SerVI, Box 2, FF Studies MA #3, titled "'Average Family' Winner, Fitter Families Contest, Eastern States Exposition, Springfield, MA (1925): Family Examination Summary," image 168, in the "Image Archive on the American Eugenics Movement," DNA Learning Center, Cold Spring Harbor Laboratory, accessed March 25, 2009, www.eugenicsarchive.org/eugenics/view_image.pl?id=168; "Fitter Families Examination," 1925, American Philosophical Society, ERO, MSC77, SerVI, Box 3, FF Studies TX #2, titled "'Large Family' Winner, Fitter Families Contest, Texas State Fair (1925): Family Examination Summary," image 170, in the "Image Archive on the American Eugenics Movement," DNA Learning Center, Cold Spring Harbor Laboratory, accessed March 25, 2009, www.eugenicsarchive.org/eugenics/view_image.pl?id=170; "Abridged Record of Family Traits," 1925, pp. 2–3, 5–10, American Philosophical Society, ERO, MSC77, SerVI, Box 3, FF Studies TX #2, titled "'Large Family' Winner, Fitter Families Contest, Texas State Fair (1925): Abridged Record of Family Traits," images 179–80, 182–87, in the "Image Archive on the American Eugenics Movement," DNA Learning Center, Cold Spring Harbor Laboratory, accessed March 25, 2009, www.eugenicsarchive.org/eugenics/view_image.pl?id=179; "Fitter Families Examination," 1925, American Philosophical Society, ERO, MSC77, SerVI, Box 3, FF Studies TX #1, titled "'Best Couple,' Fitter Families Contest, Texas State Fair (1925): Family Summary Examination," image 188, in the "Image Archive on the American Eugenics Movement," DNA Learning Center, Cold Spring Harbor Laboratory, accessed March 25, 2009, www.eugenicsarchive.org/eugenics/view_image.pl?id=188; "Fitter Families Examination," 1927, American Philosophical Society, ERO, MSC77, SerVI, Box 1, FF Studies KS #5, titled "'Medium Family' Winner, Fitter Families Contest, Kansas State Free Fair (1927): Family Examination Summary," image 189, in the "Image Archive on the American Eugenics Movement," DNA Learning Center, Cold Spring Harbor Laboratory, accessed March 25, 2009, www.eugenicsarchive.org/eugenics/view_image.pl?id=189

97. See, for example, Helen Reser, "Student Pedigree-Studies: Inheritance of Musical Ability," *Eugenical News* 20, no. 1 (January-February 1935): 8–9.

98. Alfred Russel Wallace, *Darwinism: An Exposition of the Theory of Natural Selection with Some of Its Applications* (London: Macmillan, 1891), 467. For his critique of eugenics, see Alfred Russel Wallace, *Social Environment and Moral Progress* (New York: Cassell, 1913), 141–46, http://people.wku.edu/charles.smith/wallace/arwbooks/xx_Wallace_Social_Environment_and_Moral_Progress.pdf

99. Carl E. Seashore, "Measurement of Musical Talent," 141–42.

100. Carl E. Seashore, *Psychology of Musical Talent*, 69.

101. Carl E. Seashore, *Psychology of Musical Talent*, 69.

102. Carl E. Seashore, "Individual and Racial Inheritance," 232. He echoed this statement in 1938. See Carl E. Seashore, *Psychology of Music*, 337.

103. Carl E. Seashore, *Psychology of Musical Talent*, 70.

104. Carl E. Seashore, "Musical Inheritance," 356. His obsession with measurement is evident, for example, in a 1921 funding proposal he sent to University of Iowa president Walter Jessup, "Basic Measurements of Music and Speech." See attachment to C. E. Seashore to President W. A. Jessup, April 29, 1921, RG 05.01.09, box 76, folder 53, Walter A. Jessup Papers.

105. Carl E. Seashore, "Carl Emil Seashore," 272.

106. Carl E. Seashore, "Avocational Guidance in Music," 344.

107. Carl E. Seashore, *Vocational Guidance in Music*, University of Iowa Monographs, 3.

108. Carl E. Seashore, "Avocational Guidance in Music," 346.

109. Carl E. Seashore, "Musical Inheritance," 354.

110. Carl E. Seashore, "Avocational Guidance in Music," 346.

111. Carl E. Seashore, "Avocational Guidance in Music," 346.

112. Carl E. Seashore, "Elementary Tests in Psychology," *Journal of Educational Psychology* 7, no. 2 (February 1916): 81.

113. Carl E. Seashore, *Psychology of Musical Talent*, 65.

114. Carl E. Seashore, "Individual and Racial Inheritance," 232.

115. Carl E. Seashore, "Musical Inheritance," 353.

116. Carl E. Seashore, "Musical Inheritance," 353–54.

117. Carl E. Seashore, "Scientific Procedure in the Discovery of Musical Talent in the Public Schools," *Music Supervisors' Journal* 2, no. 3 (January 1916): 10, http://www.jstor.org/stable/3383174; Carl E. Seashore, *Pioneering in Psychology*, University of Iowa Studies: Series on Aims and Progress of Research, no. 70 (Iowa City: University of Iowa, 1942), 75, https://babel.hathitrust.org/cgi/pt?id=mdp.39015020052349&view=1up&seq=1

118. See, for example, Carl E. Seashore, "Elementary Tests in Psychology," 81; Carl E. Seashore, "Measurement of Musical Talent," 130; Carl E. Seashore, "How Psychology Can Help," 89; and Carl E. Seashore, "The Measure of a Singer," *Science*, n.s., 35, no. 893 (February 9, 1912): 207, http://www.jstor.org/stable/1638656

119. Carl E. Seashore, *Pioneering in Psychology*, 75.

120. Carl E. Seashore, "Avocational Guidance in Music," 346.

121. Carl E. Seashore, "Scientific Procedure in the Discovery of Musical Talent," 10.

122. Carl E. Seashore, "Scientific Procedure in the Discovery of Musical Talent," 11.

123. Carl E. Seashore, "Scientific Procedure in the Discovery of Musical Talent," 11.

124. Carl E. Seashore, *Vocational Guidance in Music*, University of Iowa Monographs, 8; Carl E. Seashore, "Avocational Guidance in Music," 346. See also Carl E. Seashore, *A Survey of Musical Talent in the Public Schools Representing the Examination of Children of the Fifth and the Eighth Grades in the Public Schools of Des Moines, Iowa*, 2nd ed., University of Iowa Studies in Child Welfare, vol. 1, no. 2 (Iowa City: The University, February 1924), 7, https://babel.hathitrust.org/cgi/pt?id=mdp.39015009450191&view=2up&seq=1

125. Carl E. Seashore, *Vocational Guidance in Music*, University of Iowa Monographs, 9.

126. Carl E. Seashore, *Pioneering in Psychology*, 75.

127. Carl E. Seashore, "Measurement of Musical Talent," 132–33.

128. Carl E. Seashore, *Psychology of Musical Talent*, 87, 90–91, 108.

129. Carl E. Seashore, "Measurement of Musical Talent," 145.

130. Carl E. Seashore, "Measurement of Musical Talent," 144.

131. Carl E. Seashore, "Measurement of Musical Talent," 144.

132. Carl E. Seashore, "Measurement of Musical Talent," 145.

133. Carl E. Seashore, "Measurement of Musical Talent," 145.

134. Carl E. Seashore, "Measurement of Musical Talent," 145.

135. Carl E. Seashore, *Vocational Guidance in Music*, University of Iowa Monographs, 5–7; Carl E. Seashore, "How Psychology Can Help," 89–90; Carl E. Seashore, *Psychology of Musical Talent*, 19, 21. The graphs in the *Etude* article reported percentiles from different people than those discussed in Carl E. Seashore, *Vocational Guidance in Music*, University of Iowa Monographs, 5–7.

136. Carl E. Seashore, *Psychology of Musical Talent*, 19, 21, 23, 25–26.

137. Carl E. Seashore, *Vocational Guidance in Music*, University of Iowa Monographs, 3.

138. Carl E. Seashore, *Psychology of Music*, 5.

139. See Carl E. Seashore, "Measurement of Musical Talent," 130.

140. Carl E. Seashore, "How Psychology Can Help," 89–90. For another example of this incongruence, see Carl E. Seashore, *Psychology of Musical Talent*, 7–8, 19–26.

141. In an article appearing in the journal *Science* in 1912, Seashore suggested using phonograph recordings to measure singers' capacities for music appreciation, but he did not appear to be referring to the use of recorded sound to measure auditory perception. See Carl E. Seashore, "Measure of a Singer," 206.

142. Walter R. Miles, "Carl Emil Seashore, 1866–1949," vol. 29, *Biographical Memoirs* (New York: Columbia University Press for the National Academy of Sciences, 1956), 300.

143. See Carl E. Seashore, *Manual of Instructions and Interpretations for Measures of Musical Talent* (New York: Columbia Graphophone Educational Department, 1919), https://archive.org/details/manualofinstruct00seasuoft/page/n3. In the 1939 edition, "talent" became "talents." See Edwin E. Gordon, *Introduction to Research and the Psychology of Music* (Chicago: GIA, 1998), 21.

144. For a detailed description of the various versions of the tests, including the 1939 edition; a discussion of their validity and reliability; and a summary of the criticism leveled against them by contemporaneous researchers, see Gordon, *Introduction to Research*, especially 17–37; and Edwin E. Gordon, "The Legacy of Carl E. Seashore," in *Multidisciplinary Perspectives on Musicality: Essays from the Seashore Symposium*, ed. Kate Gfeller et al. (Iowa City: University of Iowa School of Music, 2006), 51–61.

145. Carl E. Seashore, *Manual of Instructions* (1919), 8, 11.

146. Carl E. Seashore, *Manual of Instructions* (1919), 8, 12.

147. Carl E. Seashore, *Manual of Instructions* (1919), 9, 13.
148. Carl E. Seashore, *Manual of Instructions* (1919), 9, 14.
149. Carl E. Seashore, *Manual of Instructions* (1919), 9, 15.
150. Carl E. Seashore, *Manual of Instructions* (1919), 11.
151. Carl E. Seashore, *Manual of Instructions* (1919), 7.
152. Carl E. Seashore, "Procedure in the Discovery and the Encouragement of Musical Talent in the Public Schools by Means of Measures of Musical Talent [Address and Discussion]," in *Journal of Proceedings of the Twelfth Annual Meeting of the Music Supervisors' National Conference Held at St. Louis, Missouri, March 30–April 4, 1919*: 39, https://archive.org/details/journalofproceed005236mbp/page/n35
153. Carl E. Seashore, *Psychology of Musical Talent*, 97–98, 55, 110–11, 158.
154. Carl E. Seashore, *Psychology of Musical Talent*, 282.
155. Carl E. Seashore, *Manual of Instructions and Interpretations for Measures of Musical Talent* (New York: Columbia Phonograph Company, Educational Department [1923]), front cover, 17–18, https://archive.org/details/manualinstructi00seasgoog/page/n1. Note that this version, with penciled-in comments and a copyright date of 1919, has a printed "23" in the lower left-hand corner of the front cover while the original 1919 version has a printed "19" in the same location. An undated version of the manual published by Stoelting Company also includes six subtests; because the manual was acquired by a library in 1935, it must predate the 1939 revision of the tests. See Carl E. Seashore, *Manual of Instructions and Interpretations for Measures of Musical Talent* (Chicago: Charles Stoelting, n.d.), front cover, 1, 13. John Grashel states that the rhythm test was added in 1925 but does not name his source. See John Grashel, "The Measurement of Musical Aptitude in 20th Century United States: A Brief History," *Bulletin of the Council for Research in Music Education*, no. 176 (Spring 2008): 46, http://www.jstor.org/stable/40319432. Gordon stated that the rhythm test was added in 1939 and did not mention the revision appearing in the early 1920s. See Gordon, *Introduction to Research*, 24; and Gordon, "Legacy of Carl E. Seashore," 53. Seashore said that it had been added by 1924. See Carl E. Seashore, "A New Rhythm Apparatus," *Science*, n.s., 59, no. 1519 (February 8, 1924): 147, https://www.jstor.org/stable/1647057. Stating that the rhythm test had recently been added to the set, the penciled-in manual mentioned a published discussion of the standardization of the rhythm test. See Carl E. Seashore, *Manual of Instructions* ([1923]), 17. Zaid Lenoir, who as a student consulted Seashore, used the expanded version of the test in his 1925 master's thesis. See Zaid Delmas Lenoir, "Measurement of Racial Differences in Certain Mental and Educational Abilities" (master's thesis, State University of Iowa, 1925), 22. The rhythm test may not have been readily available, however. Raleigh Moseley Drake reported that he did not use the rhythm test in his 1930 master's degree study because the record had not been available in England for a year. See Raleigh Moseley Drake, "An Experimental Test of the Seashore 'Measures of Musical Talent'" (master's thesis, Boston University, 1930), 2, https://hdl.handle.net/2144/7401
156. Carl E. Seashore, *Manual of Instructions* ([1923]), 17.

157. Gordon, "Legacy of Carl E. Seashore," 51; Gordon, *Introduction to Research*, 21.

158. Carl E. Seashore, *Manual of Instructions* (1919), 4.

159. Carl E. Seashore, *Psychology of Musical Talent*, viii.

160. Miles, "Carl Emil Seashore, 1866–1949," 300.

161. Carl E. Seashore, "Demonstration of Measurements of Musical Capacity," in *Journal of Proceedings of the Twelfth Annual Meeting of the Music Supervisors' National Conference Held at St. Louis, Missouri, March 30–April 4, 1919*: 30, https://archive.org/details/journalofproceed005236mbp/page/n35

162. Carl E. Seashore, "Demonstration of Measurements," 30; Carl E. Seashore, *Manual of Instructions* (1919).

163. "The Measurable Elements of Musical Talent," *Eugenical News* 11, no. 3 (March 1926): 43–44.

164. Carl E. Seashore, *Manual of Instructions* (1919), 6. See also Carl E. Seashore, "Procedure in the Discovery and the Encouragement," 40.

165. See, for example, his discussion of musical imagery and imagination in Carl E. Seashore, *Psychology of Musical Talent*, 211–35.

166. Carl E. Seashore, *Psychology of Musical Talent*, viii–ix.

167. Carl E. Seashore, *Psychology of Musical Talent*, ix.

168. Carl E. Seashore, *Psychology of Musical Talent*, ix.

169. Carl E. Seashore, "Measures of Musical Talent: A Reply to Dr. C. P. Heinlein," *Psychological Review* 37, no. 1 (January 1930): 179. For examples of references to fundamental capacities, see Carl E. Seashore, *Psychology of Music*, 309; Carl E. Seashore, "How Psychology Can Help," 89; Carl E. Seashore, *Vocational Guidance in Music*, University of Iowa Monographs, 3; and Carl E. Seashore, "Three New Approaches to the Study of Negro Music," *Annals of the American Academy of Political and Social Science* 140, no. 229 (November 1928): 192, https://www.jstor.org/stable/1016848

170. Carl E. Seashore, "How Psychology Can Help," 89.

171. Carl E. Seashore, "Carl Emil Seashore," 274.

172. Carl E. Seashore, "Measurement of Musical Talent," 146–47; Carl E. Seashore, "Avocational Guidance in Music," 345. See also Carl E. Seashore, "The Role of a Consulting Supervisor in Music," in *Eighteenth Yearbook of the National Society for the Study of Education* (Part 2), ed. Guy Montrose Whipple (Bloomington, IL: Public School Publishing, 1919), 111, https://babel.hathitrust.org/cgi/pt?id=uc1.10053492963&view=1up&seq=493; and Carl E. Seashore, "Measure of a Singer," 202, 207.

173. Carl E. Seashore, "Measurement of Musical Talent," 147. He also referred to the mission of the psychologist of musical talent in Carl E. Seashore, "Avocational Guidance in Music," 345.

174. Carl E. Seashore, *Vocational Guidance in Music*, University of Iowa Monographs, 3.

175. Carl E. Seashore, *Vocational Guidance in Music*, University of Iowa Monographs, 3.

176. Carl E. Seashore, "Avocational Guidance in Music," 345.

177. Carl E. Seashore, "How Psychology Can Help," 90.

178. Carl E. Seashore, *Vocational Guidance in Music*, University of Iowa Monographs, 4.

179. Carl E. Seashore, "Measurement of Musical Talent," 146.

180. Carl E. Seashore, "How Psychology Can Help," 89.

181. Carl E. Seashore, *Psychology of Musical Talent*, 4. See also Carl E. Seashore, "Avocational Guidance in Music," 343.

182. "Measuring Musical Capacities," *Eugenical News* 9, no. 8 (August 1924): 71.

183. Carl E. Seashore, "Scientific Procedure in the Discovery of Musical Talent," 11; Carl E. Seashore, "How Psychology Can Help," 90; Carl E. Seashore, "Avocational Guidance in Music," 347.

184. Carl E. Seashore, "Avocational Guidance in Music," 347.

185. Carl E. Seashore, *Manual of Instructions* (1919).

186. Carl E. Seashore, *Pioneering in Psychology*, 77, 77n*.

187. Carl E. Seashore, "Demonstration of Measurements," 30; Carl E. Seashore, "Procedure in the Discovery and the Encouragement," 30–41. Compare, for example, pp. 31–34 in the latter source to Carl E. Seashore, *Psychology of Musical Talent*, 272–80.

188. Carl E. Seashore, *Pioneering in Psychology*, 77n*, https://babel.hathitrust.org/cgi/pt?id=mdp.39015020052349&view=1up&seq=1

189. Carl E. Seashore, *Pioneering in Psychology*, 77n*. Elsewhere, he reported that the incident occurred at a meeting of the MTNA. See Carl E. Seashore, "Educational Guidance in Music," *School and Society* 45, no. 1160 (March 20, 1937): 387.

190. Wendy Kline, *Building a Better Race: Gender, Sexuality, and Eugenics from the Turn of the Century to the Baby Boom* (Berkeley: University of California Press, 2001), 135.

191. Carl E. Seashore, "Demonstration of Measurements," 30.

192. Danziger, *Constructing the Subject*, 119.

193. Danziger, *Constructing the Subject*, 120.

194. See, for example, [Eugenics Record Office] Director to John Allen, Norwichtown, CT, November 1, 1919, American Philosophical Society, ERO, MSC77, SerI, Box 46, A:4235, titled "(Eugenic Record Office) Director Letter to John Allen about Participating in a Study of the Inheritance of Musical Ability," image 692, in the "Image Archive on the American Eugenics Movement," DNA Learning Center, Cold Spring Harbor Laboratory, accessed March 25, 2009, www.eugenicsarchive.org/eugenics/view_image.pl?id=692

195. Jon Alfred Mjöen, *Die Vererbung der musikalischen Begabung* (Berlin: Alfred Metzner, 1934), 17, 51; Fridtjof Mjöen, "Die Bedeutung der Tonhöhenunterschiedsempfindlichkeit für die Musikalität und ihr Verhalten bei der Vererbung," *Hereditas* 7, no. 11 (1926): 163, 165, 168, 170–71, 188. Both authors also cited Hazel Stanton. See Jon Mjöen, *Die Vererbung der musikalischen Begabung*, 20, 51; and Fridtjof Mjöen, "Die Bedeutung der Tonhöhenunterschiedsempfindlichkeit," 183–84, 188. John Alfred Mjøen mentioned Charles Davenport and Morris Steggerda's work in *Die Vererbung der musikalischen Begabung*, 8.

196. Hazel M. Stanton, "An Experimental Investigation of Musical Inheritance," in *Eugenics, Genetics and the Family*, vol. 1, *Scientific Papers of the Second International Congress of Eugenics; Held at American Museum of Natural History, New York, September 22–28, 1921* (Baltimore, MD: Williams & Wilkins, 1923; repr., ed. Charles Rosenberg, New York: Garland Publishing, 1985), 239; [Eugenics Record Office] Director to John Allen, Norwichtown, CT, November 1, 1919, American Philosophical Society, ERO, MSC77, SerI, Box 46, A:4235, titled "(Eugenic Record Office) Director Letter to John Allen about Participating in a Study of the Inheritance of Musical Ability," image 692, in the "Image Archive on the American Eugenics Movement," DNA Learning Center, Cold Spring Harbor Laboratory, accessed March 25, 2009, www.eugenicsarchive.org/eugenics/view_image.pl?id=692

197. [Eugenics Record Office] Director to John Allen, Norwichtown, CT, November 1, 1919, American Philosophical Society, ERO, MSC77, SerI, Box 46, A:4235, titled "(Eugenic Record Office) Director Letter to John Allen about Participating in a Study of the Inheritance of Musical Ability," image 692, in the "Image Archive on the American Eugenics Movement," DNA Learning Center, Cold Spring Harbor Laboratory, accessed March 25, 2009, www.eugenicsarchive.org/eugenics/view_image.pl?id=692

198. Carl E. Seashore, *Psychology of Music*, 342–45.

199. See, for example, "Pedigree of Musical Capacity, A Family-Tree Folder Designed Especially for the Genetical Study of Musical Capacity," March 1926, pp. 1–4, Cold Spring Harbor, ERO, ERO Copies of Forms, titled "'Pedigree of Musical Capacity,' Eugenics Record Office Form Including Instructions to Test Sense of Pitch, Intensity, Time, Consonance, Tone, Rhythm," images 1738–41, in the "Image Archive on the American Eugenics Movement," DNA Learning Center, Cold Spring Harbor Laboratory, accessed November 19, 2019, www.eugenicsarchive.org/eugenics/view_image.pl?id=1738. Note the date in the lower left corner of p. 1.

200. Carl E. Seashore, "Musical Inheritance," 354; Carl E. Seashore, "Individual and Racial Inheritance," 236; Carl E. Seashore, *Psychology of Music*, 342.

201. Carl E. Seashore, "Individual and Racial Inheritance," 236.

202. Carl E. Seashore, "Musical Inheritance," 354.

203. Carl E. Seashore, "Individual and Racial Inheritance," 237.

204. Carl E. Seashore, "Individual and Racial Inheritance," 236.

205. Carl E. Seashore, "Individual and Racial Inheritance," 236.

206. Carl E. Seashore, *Psychology of Music*, 341.

207. Carl E. Seashore, *Psychology of Music*, 342.

208. Carl E. Seashore, *Psychology of Music*, 341.

209. Carl E. Seashore, *Psychology of Music*, 341.

210. Carl E. Seashore, "Individual and Racial Inheritance," 237.

211. Carl E. Seashore, "Elementary Tests in Psychology," 82–83.

212. Carl E. Seashore, "Measurement of Musical Talent," 140.

213. Carl E. Seashore, *In Search of Beauty in Music: A Scientific Approach to Musical*

Esthetics (New York: Ronald, 1947), 363–66, https://archive.org/details/insearchof beauty000817mbp/page/n8/mode/2up

214. Carl E. Seashore, "Measurement of Musical Talent," 140.

215. Carl E. Seashore, "Individual and Racial Inheritance," 231.

216. Lester R. Wheeler and Viola D. Wheeler, "The Musical Ability of Mountain Children as Measured by the Seashore Test of Musical Talent," *Pedagogical Seminary and Journal of Genetic Psychology* 43, no. 2 (1933): 352–76, https://doi.org /10.1080/08856559.1933.10532464; Katharine Murdoch, "A Study of Differences Found Between Races in Intellect and in Morality [Part II]," *School and Society* 22, no. 569 (November 21, 1925): 659–64.

217. See, for example, Carl E. Seashore, "Measure of a Singer," 201, 211.

218. Carl E. Seashore, *Psychology of Musical Talent*, 3.

219. Carl E. Seashore, "Measurement of Musical Talent," 148.

220. Danziger, *Constructing the Subject*, 40.

221. Danziger, *Constructing the Subject*, 40–41.

222. Danziger, *Constructing the Subject*, 103.

223. Danziger, *Constructing the Subject*, 104.

224. Ernst Kretschmer, "The Breeding of the Mental Endowments of Genius," *Eugenics* 4, no. 1 (January 1931): 7.

225. Kretschmer, "Breeding of the Mental Endowments," 7.

226. Kretschmer, "Breeding of the Mental Endowments," 9, 7.

227. Carl E. Seashore, *Psychology of Music*, 337.

228. Carl E. Seashore, *Psychology of Music*, 338.

229. Carl E. Seashore, "Individual and Racial Inheritance," 238.

230. Carl E. Seashore, *Psychology of Musical Talent*, 286; Carl E. Seashore, "Measurement of Musical Talent," 146; Carl E. Seashore, "Avocational Guidance in Music," 348; Carl E. Seashore, "Measure of a Singer," 201.

231. Carl E. Seashore, *Psychology in Daily Life* (New York: D. Appleton, 1914), 220. He later quoted himself; see Carl E. Seashore, "Measurement of Musical Talent," 147. See also Carl E. Seashore, "Avocational Guidance in Music," 348.

232. For example, he mentioned their potential use in the music conservatory in Carl E. Seashore, "Measurement of Musical Talent," 147. See also Carl E. Seashore, *Psychology of Musical Talent*, 28.

233. Carl E. Seashore, "Individual and Racial Inheritance," 232. See also Carl E. Seashore, "Measure of a Singer," 210.

234. Carl E. Seashore, "Carl Emil Seashore," 267.

235. Carl E. Seashore, "How Psychology Can Help," 90.

236. Carl E. Seashore, "Music," 686.

237. Carl E. Seashore, *Psychology of Musical Talent*, viii.

238. Carl E. Seashore, *Vocational Guidance in Music*, University of Iowa Monographs, 4.

239. Carl E. Seashore, "How Psychology Can Help," 90.

240. Carl E. Seashore, *Vocational Guidance in Music*, University of Iowa Monographs, 6.

241. Carl E. Seashore, "Carl Emil Seashore," 275.
242. Carl E. Seashore, "Avocational Guidance in Music," 344.
243. Carl E. Seashore, "Avocational Guidance in Music," 344.
244. Carl E. Seashore, "Musical Inheritance," 352.
245. Carl E. Seashore, "Individual and Racial Inheritance," 232; Carl E. Seashore, "Measurement of Musical Talent," 147. For an example of Seashore's use of endowment, see Carl E. Seashore, *Psychology of Musical Talent*, 263.
246. Judith Butler, *Bodies That Matter: On the Discursive Limits of "Sex"* (New York: Routledge, 1993), 1–23.
247. See Butler, *Bodies That Matter*, 1–23, for a discussion of this process, especially p. 3.
248. See, for example, Carl E. Seashore, "Measurement of Musical Talent," 147; and Carl E. Seashore, "Carl Emil Seashore," 272, 275.
249. Carl E. Seashore, *Psychology of Musical Talent*, 285.
250. Carl E. Seashore, "Measurement of Musical Talent," 147.
251. Carl E. Seashore, *Vocational Guidance in Music*, University of Iowa Monographs, 9.
252. Carl E. Seashore, "Scientific Procedure in the Discovery of Musical Talent," 10.
253. Carl E. Seashore, *Vocational Guidance in Music*, University of Iowa Monographs, 10.
254. Carl E. Seashore, "Scientific Procedure in the Discovery of Musical Talent," 10.
255. Carl E. Seashore, "Scientific Procedure in the Discovery of Musical Talent," 11.
256. Carl E. Seashore, *Vocational Guidance in Music*, University of Iowa Monographs, 9; Carl E. Seashore, *Psychology of Musical Talent*, 285.
257. For some examples of his use of the term "dragnet," see Carl E. Seashore, "Music," 684; Carl E. Seashore, *Psychology of Musical Talent*, viii, 27, 282, 285; Carl E. Seashore, *Vocational Guidance in Music*, University of Iowa Monographs, 8; Carl E. Seashore, "Procedure in the Discovery and the Encouragement," 36; Carl E. Seashore, "Educational Guidance in Music," 389; and Carl E. Seashore, "Avocational Guidance in Music," 345, 346, 348.
258. Carl E. Seashore, "Measurement of Musical Talent," 148.
259. Carl E. Seashore, *Vocational Guidance in Music*, University of Iowa Monographs, 10.
260. Carl E. Seashore, *Psychology of Musical Talent*, 24.
261. Carl E. Seashore, *Psychology of Musical Talent*, 24–27.
262. Carl E. Seashore, *Psychology of Musical Talent*, 26–27.
263. Carl E. Seashore, *Psychology of Musical Talent*, 27.
264. He mentioned waste, for example, in Carl E. Seashore, *Psychology of Musical Talent*, 28, 285.
265. Carl E. Seashore, "Youth and Music," *School Review* 48, no. 4 (April 1940):

270, http://www.jstor.org/stable/1082068. A manuscript version of this article is found in RG 99.0164, box 2, Carl E. Seashore Papers, Special Collections and University Archives, University of Iowa Libraries, Iowa City, IA.

266. Carl E. Seashore, *Vocational Guidance in Music*, University of Iowa Monographs, 9; Carl E. Seashore, "Avocational Guidance in Music," 345.

267. Carl E. Seashore, *Psychology of Musical Talent*, 285.

268. Carl E. Seashore, *Psychology of Musical Talent*, 4. See also Carl E. Seashore, "Avocational Guidance in Music," 343.

269. Michael G. Kenny, "Toward a Racial Abyss: Eugenics, Wickliffe Draper, and the Origins of the Pioneer Fund," *Journal of History of the Behavioral Sciences* 38, no. 3 (Summer 2002): 264.

270. Julia Eklund Koza, "The 'Missing Males' and Other Gender Issues in Music Education: Evidence from the *Music Supervisors' Journal*, 1914–1924," *Journal of Research in Music Education* 41, no. 3 (October 1993): 212–32.

271. Julia Eklund Koza, "Music and References to Music in *Godey's Lady's Book*, 1830–1877" (PhD diss., University of Minnesota, 1988), 132–37.

272. Carl E. Seashore, "Educational Guidance in Music," 386.

273. Carl E. Seashore, *Vocational Guidance in Music*, University of Iowa Monographs, 5.

274. Carl E. Seashore, "Musical Inheritance," 352; Carl E. Seashore, "Measurement of Musical Talent," 147.

275. Carl E. Seashore, "Measurement of Musical Talent," 147–48.

276. Carl E. Seashore, "Avocational Guidance in Music," 345, 347.

277. Carl E. Seashore, "Avocational Guidance in Music," 347.

278. Carl E. Seashore, "Educational Guidance in Music," 389.

279. Carl E. Seashore, *Psychology of Musical Talent*, 29.

280. Carl E. Seashore, "Youth and Music," 270–71.

281. Carl E. Seashore, "Avocational Guidance in Music," 345.

282. Carl E. Seashore, "Scientific Procedure in the Discovery of Musical Talent," 11.

283. Carl E. Seashore, "Music," 684.

284. Carl E. Seashore, "Music," 684.

285. Carl E. Seashore, *Psychology of Musical Talent*, 284.

286. Carl E. Seashore, *Psychology of Musical Talent*, 284.

287. See, for example, Carl E. Seashore, "Avocational Guidance in Music," 342; Carl E. Seashore, Iowa City, IA, to President Jessup, October 27, 1924, p. 1, RG 05.01.09, box 145, folder 49, Walter A. Jessup Papers, Special Collections and University Archives, University of Iowa Libraries, Iowa City, IA; Carl E. Seashore, "Carl Emil Seashore," 275; Carl E. Seashore, *Psychology of Musical Talent*, 284; Carl E. Seashore, "Scientific Procedure in the Discovery of Musical Talent," 10; and Carl E. Seashore, "Measure of a Singer," 209–10.

288. Carl E. Seashore, *Vocational Guidance in Music*, University of Iowa Monographs, 4. See also Carl E. Seashore, *Psychology of Musical Talent*, 28.

289. Carl E. Seashore, *Psychology of Musical Talent*, 3.

290. Carl E. Seashore, *Psychology of Musical Talent*, 3.

291. Carl E. Seashore, "Measurement of Musical Talent," 146.

292. Carl E. Seashore, "Scientific Procedure in the Discovery of Musical Talent," 11.

293. Carl E. Seashore, *Psychology of Musical Talent*, 27.

294. Carl E. Seashore, *Vocational Guidance in Music*, University of Iowa Monographs, 3.

295. Carl E. Seashore, *Vocational Guidance in Music*, University of Iowa Monographs, 3.

296. Carl E. Seashore, *Vocational Guidance in Music*, University of Iowa Monographs, 3.

297. Carl E. Seashore, *Vocational Guidance in Music*, University of Iowa Monographs, 4. See also Carl E. Seashore, *Psychology of Musical Talent*, 28.

298. Carl E. Seashore, "Measurement of Musical Talent," 146.

299. Carl E. Seashore, "How Psychology Can Help," 90.

300. Carl E. Seashore, "Procedure in the Discovery and the Encouragement," 36.

301. O. F. Richards et al., "Big Ideas from St. Louis," *Music Supervisors' Journal* 6, no. 1 (September 1919): 6, http://www.jstor.org/stable/3383243. See also Carl E. Seashore, *Psychology of Musical Talent*, 3; and Carl E. Seashore, "Procedure in the Discovery and the Encouragement," 31.

302. O. F. Richards et al., "Big Ideas," 6; Carl E. Seashore, "Procedure in the Discovery and the Encouragement," 31.

303. Carl E. Seashore, *Psychology of Musical Talent*, 67–68.

304. Carl E. Seashore, *Psychology of Musical Talent*, 67.

305. Carl E. Seashore, *Psychology of Musical Talent*, 68.

306. Carl E. Seashore, "Avocational Guidance in Music," 346. See also Carl E. Seashore, *Psychology of Musical Talent*, 283.

307. Carl E. Seashore, "Educational Guidance in Music," 388.

308. Carl E. Seashore, "Avocational Guidance in Music," 346.

309. Carl E. Seashore, "Musical Inheritance," 355.

310. Carl E. Seashore, *Psychology of Musical Talent*, 285; Carl E. Seashore, "Avocational Guidance in Music," 347–48.

311. Carl E. Seashore, "Carl Emil Seashore," 274. Miles also reported that Eastman used the Seashore Tests as a predictive measure and an entrance requirement. See Miles, "Carl Emil Seashore, 1866–1949," 300–301.

312. Hazel M. Stanton, "Report on Use of Seashore Tests at Eastman School of Music," *Music Supervisors' Journal* 12, no. 4 (March 1926): 22, 24, http://www.jstor.org/stable/3382898

313. Carl E. Seashore, "Procedure in the Discovery and the Encouragement," 36–37.

314. "Seashore Test Given," *Gustavian Weekly*, September 12, 1945, 3.

315. Carl E. Seashore, "Avocational Guidance in Music," 348.

316. Carl E. Seashore, "Youth and Music," 269–70.

317. Carl E. Seashore, *Psychology of Musical Talent*, 274.

318. Carl E. Seashore, *Psychology of Musical Talent*, 277. See also Carl E. Seashore, "Procedure in the Discovery and the Encouragement," 33.

319. Carl E. Seashore, *Psychology of Musical Talent*, 277. See also p. 286, and Carl E. Seashore, "Procedure in the Discovery and the Encouragement," 33.

320. Carl E. Seashore, *Psychology of Musical Talent*, 286.

321. Carl E. Seashore, *Psychology of Musical Talent*, 286–88; Carl E. Seashore, "Educational Guidance in Music," 390.

322. Carl E. Seashore, *Psychology of Musical Talent*, 288.

323. Carl E. Seashore, *Psychology of Musical Talent*, 288.

324. Carl E. Seashore, *Psychology of Musical Talent*, 287.

325. Carl E. Seashore, *Psychology of Musical Talent*, 287–88.

326. Carl E. Seashore, *Psychology of Musical Talent*, 286–87.

327. Carl E. Seashore, *Psychology of Musical Talent*, 276.

328. Carl E. Seashore, *Psychology of Musical Talent*, 3.

329. Carl E. Seashore, *Psychology of Musical Talent*, 275. See also Carl E. Seashore, "Procedure in the Discovery and the Encouragement," 32, 37.

330. Carl E. Seashore, *Psychology of Musical Talent*, 275.

331. Carl E. Seashore, "Carl Emil Seashore," 274.

332. Carl E. Seashore, "Carl Emil Seashore," 274.

333. "Preliminary Program: Music Supervisors' National Conference, Saint Louis, Missouri [Front Matter]," *Music Supervisors' Journal* 5, no. 4 (March 1919): 12, http://www.jstor.org/stable/3382284

334. John St. George Joyce, ed., *Story of Philadelphia* (Philadelphia: Rex Printing House, 1919), 517–18, https://babel.hathitrust.org/cgi/pt?id=loc.ark:/13960/t9v129m98;view=1up;seq=7

335. "Opportunities Which the Schools Should Offer the Child of Exceptional Musical Talent: Discussion," in *Journal of Proceedings of the Twelfth Annual Meeting of the Music Supervisors' National Conference Held at St. Louis, Missouri, March 30–April 4, 1919*: 96, https://archive.org/details/journalofproceed005236mbp/page/n101

336. "Opportunities Which the Schools," 96–101.

337. Carl E. Seashore, *Psychology of Musical Talent*, 276.

338. Carl E. Seashore, *Psychology of Musical Talent*, 278.

339. Carl E. Seashore, *Psychology of Musical Talent*, 276–77.

340. Carl E. Seashore, "Youth and Music," 275.

341. Carl E. Seashore, "Youth and Music," 276.

342. "Popular Education: Music Tests," *Eugenics* 1, no. 2 (November 1928): 35.

343. "Popular Education: Music Tests," 35.

344. See, for example, Carl E. Seashore, *Psychology of Musical Talent*, 4. Elsewhere in this source he said that the untalented probably would be better off with less music education, and he claimed that the lowest quarter of an untracked class is abused by the untracked setting. See pp. 275–76.

345. Carl E. Seashore, "Carl Emil Seashore," 274.

346. Carl E. Seashore, *Psychology of Musical Talent*, 286; Carl E. Seashore, "Procedure in the Discovery and the Encouragement," 37.

347. Carl E. Seashore, *Psychology of Musical Talent*, 287.

348. Carl E. Seashore, *Psychology of Musical Talent*, 278.

349. Carl E. Seashore, "Procedure in the Discovery and the Encouragement," 32–33.

350. Carl E. Seashore, *Psychology of Musical Talent*, 263.

351. Carl E. Seashore, "Measurement of Musical Talent," 147–48; see also p. 146.

352. Carl E. Seashore, *Vocational Guidance in Music*, University of Iowa Monographs, 10–11.

353. Carl E. Seashore, "Avocational Guidance in Music," 343. See also Carl E. Seashore, *Psychology of Musical Talent*, 286.

354. See, for example, Carl E. Seashore, "Avocational Guidance in Music," 342–44.

355. Carl E. Seashore, "Measurement of Musical Talent," 146.

356. Carl E. Seashore, *Vocational Guidance in Music*, University of Iowa Monographs, 10.

357. Carl E. Seashore, *Vocational Guidance in Music*, University of Iowa Monographs, 10. See also Carl E. Seashore, "Avocational Guidance in Music," 343–44.

358. "Popular Education: Music Tests," 35.

359. Carl E. Seashore, "Carl Emil Seashore," 274; Carl E. Seashore, "Talent," 173.

360. Carl E. Seashore, "Avocational Guidance in Music," 348.

361. For a reference to conserving energy, see Carl E. Seashore, *Vocational Guidance in Music*, University of Iowa Monographs, 10.

362. Carl E. Seashore, "Talent," 173.

363. Carl E. Seashore, *Psychology of Musical Talent*, 4. See also Carl E. Seashore, "Avocational Guidance in Music," 343.

364. Carl E. Seashore, *Psychology of Musical Talent*, 286.

365. Carl E. Seashore, "Measures of Musical Talent: A Reply to Dr. C. P. Heinlein," 179.

366. Carl E. Seashore, *Psychology of Musical Talent*, 288. See also Carl E. Seashore, "Procedure in the Discovery and the Encouragement," 37.

367. Carl E. Seashore, *Psychology of Musical Talent*, 4.

368. Carl E. Seashore, "Avocational Guidance in Music," 342.

369. Carl E. Seashore, *Psychology of Musical Talent*, 4.

370. Carl E. Seashore, "Procedure in the Discovery and the Encouragement," 31.

371. Carl E. Seashore, "Procedure in the Discovery and the Encouragement," 32.

372. Carl E. Seashore, "Procedure in the Discovery and the Encouragement," 31, 32.

373. Carl E. Seashore, "Procedure in the Discovery and the Encouragement," 32.

374. Carl E. Seashore, "Procedure in the Discovery and the Encouragement," 36–37.

375. Carl E. Seashore, "Procedure in the Discovery and the Encouragement," 32.

376. Carl E. Seashore, *Psychology of Musical Talent*, 263.

377. Carl E. Seashore, *Psychology of Musical Talent*, 257.

378. Carl E. Seashore, *Psychology of Musical Talent*, 275–76.

379. Carl E. Seashore, "Scientific Procedure in the Discovery of Musical Talent," 11.

380. Carl E. Seashore, *Psychology of Musical Talent*, 288; Carl E. Seashore, "Measurement of Musical Talent," 146.

381. "Measurable Elements of Musical Talent," 44. An unsigned three-year contract between Seashore and the Columbia Graphophone Company indicated that Seashore was to receive royalties from 75 percent of the records sold. See undated contract made between Carl E. Seashore and Columbia Graphophone Company, p. 2, RG 99.0164, box 2, Carl E. Seashore Papers, Special Collections and University Archives, University of Iowa Libraries, Iowa City, IA.

382. "Measurable Elements of Musical Talent," 44.

383. "Measures of Musical Talent [Front Matter]," *Music Supervisors' Journal* 6, no. 1 (September 1919): 17, http://www.jstor.org/stable/3383240

384. "Measures of Musical Talent [Front Matter]," 17. A record player on a cart was standard equipment in music classrooms for many years; I used one in my classroom, and I began teaching in 1974.

385. See, for example, "America's Slogan: Freedom, for All, Forever [The Victrola and Victor Records]!" *Music Supervisors' Journal* 5, no. 1 (September 1918): 15, https://babel.hathitrust.org/cgi/pt?id=mdp.39015023355251&view=1up&seq=23, for the Victrola and records. Also "Music Appreciation Material [Columbia Graphophone Company]," *Music Supervisors' Journal* 5, no. 1 (September 1918): 25, https://babel.hathitrust.org/cgi/pt?id=mdp.39015023355251;view=1up;seq=33, for Columbia Records; and "Great Schools of Opera [Front Matter]," *Music Supervisors' Journal* 5, no. 2 (November 1918): 13, http://www.jstor.org/stable/3382352, for the Columbia Grafonola and recordings.

386. See, for example, the Victor Talking Machine Company's full-page 1923 advertisement in the *MSJ*; it features a letter from Frances Clark inviting conference attendees to visit an exhibit promoting music appreciation curricular materials and showcasing Victrola-based instruction: "An Invitation [Front Matter]," *Music Supervisors' Journal* 9, no. 4 (March 1923): 7, http://www.jstor.org/stable/3383049

387. Carl E. Seashore to Virgil M. Hancher, Old Capitol, April 27, 1945 (with attachment), RG 99.0164, box 2, Carl E. Seashore Papers, Special Collections and University Archives, University of Iowa Libraries, Iowa City, IA. In an attachment entitled "Royalties Received from RCA for Seashore Measures of Musical Talent," Seashore indicated that the value of the planned donation of proceeds from the sale of the 1939 version of the Seashore Tests was $1,180.83 (about $16, 844 in 2019 dollars) not including future royalties. For a description of the Memorial Fund, see "The Carl E. Seashore Memorial Fund of the State University of Iowa School of Religion," RG 99.0164, box 2, Carl E. Seashore Papers, Special Collections and University Archives, University of Iowa Libraries, Iowa City, IA.

388. Carl E. Seashore, *Vocational Guidance in Music*, University of Iowa Monographs, 8.

389. Carl E. Seashore, “Procedure in the Discovery and the Encouragement,” 34–35.

390. Carl E. Seashore, “Procedure in the Discovery and the Encouragement,” 30–31.

391. Carl E. Seashore, “Carl Emil Seashore,” 272.

392. Carl E. Seashore, “Carl Emil Seashore,” 272.

393. Lauren Heidingsfelder, “The Slogan of the Century: ‘Music for Every Child; Every Child for Music,’” *Music Educators Journal* 100, no. 4 (June 2014): 47, https://www.jstor.org/stable/43288870

394. Heidingsfelder, “Slogan of the Century,’” 47.

395. Heidingsfelder, “Slogan of the Century,’” 48. Heidingsfelder cites Karl W. Gehrkens, “MENC: Remembering the Early Years,” *Music Educators Journal* 54, no. 2 (October 1967): 60, http://www.jstor.org/stable/3391097

396. Heidingsfelder, “Slogan of the Century,’” 48; Karl W. Gehrkens, “Music for Every Child; Every Child FOR Music,” *Music Supervisors' Journal* 19, no. 5 (May 1933): 31, http://www.jstor.org/stable/3384232

397. Gehrkens, “Music for Every Child,” 31.

398. Gehrkens, “Music for Every Child,” 31.

399. Karl W. Gehrkens, “A Philosophy of Universal Music Education,” *Journal of Research in Music Education* 16, no. 3 (Autumn 1968): 280, www.jstor.org/stable /3344083

400. Karl W. Gehrkens, “Some Questions,” in *Journal of Proceedings of the Sixteenth Annual Meeting of the Music Supervisors' National Conference Held at Cleveland, Ohio, April 9–13, 1923*, ed. George Oscar Bowen (Ann Arbor, MI: University School of Music, 1923), 29, https://archive.org/details/journalofproceed017536m bp/page/n33

401. “Official Program: Music Supervisors' National Conference; Sixteenth Annual Meeting [Back Matter],” *Music Supervisors' Journal* 9, no. 4 (March 1923): 28–30, http://www.jstor.org/stable/3383060; “Program—Sixteenth Meeting,” in *Journal of Proceedings of the Sixteenth Annual Meeting of the Music Supervisors' National Conference Held at Cleveland, Ohio, April 9–13, 1923*, ed. George Oscar Bowen (Ann Arbor, MI: University School of Music, 1923) , 13–21, https://archi ve.org/details/journalofproceed017536mbp/page/n17

402. George Oscar Bowen, “Editorial Comment,” *Music Supervisors' Journal* 11, no. 1 (October 1924): 3, http://www.jstor.org/stable/3383247

403. Carl E. Seashore, *Pioneering in Psychology*, 77.

404. Carl E. Seashore, “Youth and Music,” 273.

405. Carl E. Seashore, “Procedure in the Discovery and the Encouragement,” 31.

406. O. F. Richards et al., “Big Ideas,” 6.

407. Carl E. Seashore, *Vocational Guidance in Music*, University of Iowa Monographs, 10.

408. Carl E. Seashore, “Youth and Music,” 273.

409. Osbourne McConathy, “The Place of Music in the New Educational Program: President's Address,” in *Journal of Proceedings of the Twelfth Annual Meeting of the Music Supervisors' National Conference Held at St. Louis, Missouri, March 30–*

April 4, 1919: 24, https://archive.org/details/journalofproceed005236mbp/page/n29

410. McConathy, "Place of Music," 25.

411. McConathy, "Place of Music," 25.

412. McConathy, "Place of Music," 25.

413. McConathy, "Place of Music," 25.

414. McConathy, "Place of Music," 26.

415. O. F. Richards et al., "Big Ideas," 6.

416. W. Otto Miessner, "Music Democratized," in *Journal of Proceedings of the Twelfth Annual Meeting of the Music Supervisors' National Conference Held at St. Louis, Missouri, March 30–April 4, 1919*: 89–92, https://archive.org/details/journalofproceed005236mbp/page/n93. For the original title of the address, see the conference program on p. 15 of the proceedings.

417. Miessner, "Music Democratized," 89.

418. Miessner, "Music Democratized," 90, 92.

419. Miessner, "Music Democratized," 91.

420. Miessner, "Music Democratized," 92.

421. Miessner, "Music Democratized," 91.

422. O. F. Richards et al., "Big Ideas," 10, 12.

423. Miessner, "Music Democratized," 90.

424. Miessner, "Music Democratized," 90.

425. Miessner, "Music Democratized," 90–91.

426. O. F. Richards et al., "Big Ideas," 10.

427. "History of Miessner Piano Development in Booklet," *Music Trade Review* 77, no. 6 (August 11, 1923): 28, https://mtr.arcade-museum.com/MTR-1923-77-6/index.php?page_no=28; "'I Can See America Go Singing to Her Destiny [Front Matter],'" *Music Supervisors' Journal* 9, no. 5 (May 1923): 9, http://www.jstor.org/stable/3382974?seq=4#page_scan_tab_contents

428. *Music Supervisors' Journal* [Front Matter] 5, no. 4 (March 1919): front cover, https://babel.hathitrust.org/cgi/pt?id=mdp.39015023355251;view=1up;seq=105

429. See *Music Supervisors' Journal* [Front Matter] 5, no. 1 (September 1918): front cover, www.jstor.org/stable/3382824; *Music Supervisors' Journal* [Front Matter] 5, no. 2 (November 1918): front cover, www.jstor.org/stable/3382352; and *Music Supervisors' Journal* [Front Matter] 5, no. 3 (January 1919): front cover, www.jstor.org/stable/3383163

430. *Music Supervisors' Journal* [Front Matter] 6, no. 1 (September 1919): front cover, http://www.jstor.org/stable/3383240

431. *Music Supervisors' Journal* [Front Matter] 10, no. 5 (May 1924): front cover, https://babel.hathitrust.org/cgi/pt?id=mdp.39015008094891&view=1up&seq=507

432. Mary T. Whitley, "A Comparison of the Seashore and the Kwalwasser-Dykema Music Tests," *Teachers College Record* 33, no. 8 (May 1932): 731–51.

433. Jacob Kwalwasser, "The Vibrato: In Phono-Photography" (PhD diss., University of Iowa, 1925), unpaginated acknowledgment page.

434. Paul R. Farnsworth, *The Social Psychology of Music* (New York: Dryden, 1958), 243.

435. Whitley, "Comparison of the Seashore," 731.

436. Whitley, "Comparison of the Seashore," 750.

437. James L. Mursell, "What about Music Tests?" *Music Educators Journal* 24, no. 2 (October-November 1937): 16, www.jstor.org/stable/3385164

438. Mursell, "What about Music Tests?" 16.

439. Mursell, "What about Music Tests?" 16–17.

440. Mursell, "What about Music Tests?" 17.

441. Mursell, "What about Music Tests?" 16.

442. Zygmunt Bauman, *Modernity and the Holocaust* (Ithaca, NY: Cornell University Press, 1989), 89.

443. Bauman, *Modernity and the Holocaust*, 18.

444. Bauman, *Modernity and the Holocaust*, xii.

445. Derek Sivers, "First Follower: Leadership Lessons from a Dancing Guy," February 11, 2010, https://sivers.org/ff. For the original TED talk see Derek Sivers, "How to Start a Movement," TED, February 2010, YouTube video, 2:42, https://www.ted.com/talks/derek_sivers_how_to_start_a_movement

446. Devaney, "Eugenics and Musical Talent," 1; James McKeen Cattell and Livingston Farrand, "Physical and Mental Measurements of the Students of Columbia University," *Psychological Review* 3 (1896): 635–36; and Clark Wissler, "The Correlation of Mental and Physical Tests," *Psychological Review Monograph Supplements* 3, no. 6, whole no. 16 (June 1901), especially 4, 6, 8, 15–17, 21–22, 43, 61.

Chapter 7

1. Carl E. Seashore, *Pioneering in Psychology*, University of Iowa Studies: Series on Aims and Progress of Research, no. 70 (Iowa City: University of Iowa, 1942), 103, https://babel.hathitrust.org/cgi/pt?id=mdp.39015020052349&view=1up&seq=1; Carl E. Seashore, *Psychology of Music* (New York: McGraw-Hill, 1938), 309, https://archive.org/details/psychologyofmusi030417mbp. His statement was a bit more nuanced in Carl E. Seashore, "Musical Inheritance," *Scientific Monthly* 50, no. 4 (April 1940): 354–55.

2. Thomas Russell Garth, *Race Psychology: A Study of Racial Mental Differences* (New York: Whittlesey House, 1931), 155.

3. J. S. P[rice], "Current Literature on Negro Education," review of *Race Psychology in America: A Study of Racial Mental Differences*, by Thomas Russell Garth, *Journal of Negro Education* 2, no. 1 (January 1933): 83, 84, 86, https://www.jstor.org/stable/2292221

4. P[rice], "Current Literature on Negro," 85.

5. Ruth Zinar, "Highlights of Thought in the History of Music Education, VIII: Carl Seashore (1866–1949) and the Psychology of Music," *American Music Teacher* 33, no. 3 (January 1984): 46.

6. Allan Chase, *The Legacy of Malthus: The Social Costs of the New Scientific Racism* (New York: Alfred A. Knopf, 1977), 90.

7. See, for example, Paul Popenoe and Roswell Hill Johnson, *Applied Eugenics* (New York: Macmillan, 1920), 284–92.

8. Henry Fairfield Osborn, "Address of Welcome," in *Eugenics, Genetics and the Family*, vol. 1, *Scientific Papers of the Second International Congress of Eugenics; Held at American Museum of Natural History, New York, September 22–28, 1921* (Baltimore, MD: Williams & Wilkins, 1923; repr., ed. Charles Rosenberg, New York: Garland Publishing, 1985), 2–3.

9. Henry Fairfield Osborn, preface to *The Passing of the Great Race, or The Racial Basis of European History*, by Madison Grant (New York: Charles Scribner's Sons, 1916), viii.

10. "The Great Nordic Race," review of *The Passing of the Great Race*, by Madison Grant, *Eugenical News* 2, no. 2 (February 1917): 10–11.

11. "The Color-Races," *Eugenical News* 5, no. 9 (September 1920): 70.

12. Francis Galton, *Hereditary Genius: An Inquiry into Its Laws and Consequences* (London: Macmillan, 1869), v, http://galton.org/books/hereditary-genius/1869-FirstEdition/hereditarygenius1869galt.pdf

13. Francis Galton, "Hereditary Talent and Character: Second Paper," *Macmillan's Magazine* 12, no. 70 (August 1865): 320, http://search.proquest.com.ezproxy.library.wisc.edu/docview/6117693/fulltextPDF/D24741D1A3E54DC9PQ/4?accountid=465

14. Galton, "Hereditary Talent and Character: Second Paper," 321.

15. Charles Benedict Davenport, *Heredity in Relation to Eugenics* (New York: Henry Holt, 1911), 212–20, https://archive.org/details/heredityinrelati00dave/page/n8; Charles Benedict Davenport and Morris Steggerda, *Race Crossing in Jamaica* (Washington, DC: Carnegie Institution of Washington, 1929), 299. See also Edward Alsworth Ross, *The Old World in the New: The Significance of Past and Present Immigration to the American People* (New York: Century, 1914), especially 24–194, https://archive.org/details/cu31924021182898

16. Harry H. Laughlin, "The Progress of American Eugenics," *Eugenics* 2, no. 2 (February 1929): 15.

17. "Race-Matters," *Eugenical News* 19, no. 1 (January-February 1934): 16–17.

18. Charles White, *An Account of the Regular Gradation in Man, and in Different Animals and Vegetables; and from the Former to the Latter* (London: C. Dilly, 1799), https://archive.org/details/b24924507

19. Henry Osborn, preface to *Passing of the Great Race*, by Madison Grant, ix.

20. Galton, "Hereditary Talent and Character: Second Paper," 326. Also, for example, Alfred Russel Wallace, *Darwinism: An Exposition of the Theory of Natural Selection with Some of Its Applications* (London: Macmillan, 1891), 464, 467.

21. Paul Popenoe and Roswell Johnson, *Applied Eugenics*, 284.

22. Francis Galton, "Ethnological Enquiries on the Innate Character and Intelligence of Different Races" [c. 1909], p. 2, University College London, FG, 138/1, titled "Directions for Responding to a Survey on 'Ethnological Enquiries on the Innate Character and Intelligence of Different Races,' by Francis Galton," image 2090, in the "Image Archive on the American Eugenics Movement," DNA Learning Center, Cold Spring Harbor Laboratory, accessed March 25, 2009, www

.eugenicsarchive.org/eugenics/view_image.pl?id=2090; Wallace, *Darwinism: An Exposition*, 462, 463, 465, 469.

23. Edwin Black, *War against the Weak: Eugenics and America's Campaign to Create a Master Race* (New York: Four Walls Eight Windows, 2003), 29.

24. William Z. Ripley, *The Races of Europe: A Sociological Study* (New York: D. Appleton, 1899; repr., ed. Weston La Barre, New York: Johnson Reprint, 1965), xiii–xv, https://babel.hathitrust.org/cgi/pt?id=uc1.31822007517113;view=1up;seq=5; Madison Grant, *The Passing of the Great Race, or The Racial Basis of European History* (New York: Charles Scribner's Sons, 1916), 17–18.

25. Madison Grant, *Passing of the Great Race*, 23.

26. Leon F. Whitney et al., "Is Eugenics Racial Snobbery? Does It Condemn Whole Peoples?" *Eugenics* 2, no. 2 (February 1929): 20.

27. Paul Popenoe and Roswell Johnson, *Applied Eugenics*, 238.

28. Paul Popenoe and Roswell Johnson, *Applied Eugenics*, 258.

29. Chase, *Legacy of Malthus*, 90.

30. Paul Popenoe and Roswell Johnson, *Applied Eugenics*, 284.

31. Paul Popenoe and Roswell Johnson, *Applied Eugenics*, 291–92.

32. Reginald G. Harris, "Eugenics in South America," *Eugenical News* 7, no. 3 (March 1922): 27–28.

33. Reginald Harris, "Eugenics in South America," 41.

34. "White America," review of *White America: The American Racial Problem as Seen in a Worldwide Perspective*, by Earnest Sevier Cox, *Eugenical News* 9, no. 1 (January 1924): 3.

35. Barry Alan Mehler, "A History of the American Eugenics Society, 1921–1940" (PhD diss., University of Illinois at Urbana-Champaign, 1988), 66–67, http://search.proquest.com.ezproxy.library.wisc.edu/docview/303689028?accountid=465

36. Daniel J. Kevles, *In the Name of Eugenics: Genetics and the Uses of Human Heredity* (Berkeley: University of California Press, 1986), 46.

37. Paul Popenoe and Roswell Johnson, *Applied Eugenics*, 286–89.

38. Paul Popenoe and Roswell Johnson, *Applied Eugenics*, 289.

39. Davenport, *Heredity in Relation*, 216.

40. Davenport, *Heredity in Relation*, 221, 217.

41. Davenport, *Heredity in Relation*, 218–19.

42. Davenport, *Heredity in Relation*, 222.

43. Herbert Spencer, "Herbert Spencer on Race Mixture," *Eugenics* 3, no. 2 (February 1930): 63.

44. Paul Popenoe and Roswell Johnson, *Applied Eugenics*, 301.

45. Paul Popenoe and Roswell Johnson, *Applied Eugenics*, 302.

46. Madison Grant, *Passing of the Great Race*, 69.

47. Galton, "Hereditary Talent and Character: Second Paper," 326.

48. Davenport and Steggerda, *Race Crossing in Jamaica* (1929), 472.

49. Madison Grant, introduction to *The Rising Tide of Color against White World-Supremacy*, by Lothrop Stoddard (New York: Charles Scribner's Sons, 1921), xxxii, https://archive.org/details/risingtideofcolo00stoduoft/page/n7

50. "Color-Races," 70–71.

51. For examples of the use of various terms, see [Wilhelm] Frick, "German Population and Race Politics," trans. A. Hellmer, *Eugenical News* 19, no. 2 (March-April 1934): 34, 38; Carl E. Seashore, *Pioneering in Psychology*, 186; Davenport and Steggerda, *Race Crossing in Jamaica* (1929), including title; Charles Benedict Davenport et al., "Intermarriages between Races: A Eugenic or Dysgenic Force?" *Eugenics* 3, no. 2 (February 1930): 61; Ernst Kretschmer, "The Breeding of the Mental Endowments of Genius," *Eugenics* 4, no. 1 (January 1931): 11; Paul Popenoe and Roswell Johnson, *Applied Eugenics*, 301; and Charles Benedict Davenport, "Report of Committee on Eugenics," *American Breeders Magazine* 1, no. 2 (April, May, June 1910): 127, https://babel.hathitrust.org/cgi/pt?id=uc1.b4528618&view=1up&seq=140

52. Madison Grant, *Passing of the Great Race*, 15.

53. Madison Grant, *Passing of the Great Race*, 14.

54. Madison Grant, *Passing of the Great Race*, 15–16.

55. Madison Grant, *Passing of the Great Race*, 16.

56. Henry Osborn, "Address of Welcome," 3.

57. Frick, "German Population and Race," 38.

58. Paul Popenoe and Roswell Johnson, *Applied Eugenics*, 301.

59. Paul Popenoe and Roswell Johnson, *Applied Eugenics*, 301.

60. Paul Popenoe and Roswell Johnson, *Applied Eugenics*, 292, 293.

61. Reginald Harris, "Eugenics in South America," 42.

62. Kretschmer, "Breeding of the Mental Endowments," 10.

63. Kretschmer, "Breeding of the Mental Endowments," 11.

64. Henry Osborn, "Address of Welcome," 3.

65. Paul Popenoe and Roswell Johnson, *Applied Eugenics*, 296.

66. Paul Popenoe and Roswell Johnson, *Applied Eugenics*, 297.

67. Charles White, *Account of the Regular Gradation*, 117.

68. Charles White, *Account of the Regular Gradation*, 145–56.

69. Herbert Spencer, "Herbert Spencer on Race," 63.

70. Herbert Spencer, "Herbert Spencer on Race," 63.

71. Katharine Murdoch, "A Study of Differences Found Between Races in Intellect and in Morality [Part II]," *School and Society* 22, no. 569 (November 21, 1925): 664.

72. For more details about Alvin Rose, see chapter 5.

73. E. B. Reuter, "The American Mulatto," *Annals of the American Academy of Political and Social Science* 140, no. 229 (November 1928): 37, https://www.jstor.org/stable/1016830

74. Reuter, "American Mulatto," 37–39.

75. Reuter, "American Mulatto," 39–40.

76. Reuter, "American Mulatto," 40–41.

77. Reuter, "American Mulatto," 41–42.

78. Reuter, "American Mulatto," 42.

79. Reuter, "American Mulatto," 42.

80. Reuter, "American Mulatto," 42.

81. Reuter, "American Mulatto," 42.
82. Reuter, "American Mulatto," 42.
83. Reuter, "American Mulatto," 42.
84. Reuter, "American Mulatto," 42–43.
85. Reuter, "American Mulatto," 43.
86. Reuter, "American Mulatto," 43.
87. Henry Osborn, preface to *Passing of the Great Race*, by Madison Grant, ix.
88. Whitney et al., "Is Eugenics Racial Snobbery?" 20.
89. Whitney et al., "Is Eugenics Racial Snobbery?" 20.
90. Whitney et al., "Is Eugenics Racial Snobbery?" 20.
91. Whitney et al., "Is Eugenics Racial Snobbery?" 20.
92. Whitney et al., "Is Eugenics Racial Snobbery?" 20.
93. Whitney et al., "Is Eugenics Racial Snobbery?" 20.
94. Whitney et al., "Is Eugenics Racial Snobbery?" 20.
95. See, for example, Carl E. Seashore, "Music," vol. 2, *Handbook of Applied Psychology*, ed. Douglas H. Fryer and Edwin R. Henry (New York: Rinehart, 1950), 681, for an unclear usage that may be a reference to the whole human race.
96. Carl E. Seashore, "The Term 'Euthenics,'" *Science*, n.s., 94, no. 2450 (December 12, 1941): 562, https://www.jstor.org/stable/1668443
97. Carl E. Seashore, *Introduction to Psychology* (New York: Macmillan, 1923), 276.
98. Carl E. Seashore, *Pioneering in Psychology*, 103.
99. Carl E. Seashore, *In Search of Beauty in Music: A Scientific Approach to Musical Esthetics* (New York: Ronald, 1947), 218, https://archive.org/details/insearchofbeauty000817mbp/page/n8/mode/2up
100. Carl E. Seashore, *In Search of Beauty* (1947), 218.
101. Carl E. Seashore, *In Search of Beauty* (1947), 8.
102. Carl E. Seashore, "Carl Emil Seashore," vol. 1, *A History of Psychology in Autobiography*, ed. Carl Allanmore Murchison (Worcester, MA: Clark University, 1930), 227.
103. See, for example, Carl E. Seashore, *In Search of Beauty* (1947), 299; Carl E. Seashore, *Introduction to Psychology*, 38, 276.
104. Carl E. Seashore, "Cooperation with the Film Industries in the Study of Primitive Music," *Science* 96, no. 2490 (September 18, 1942): 264, www.jstor.org/stable/1669751. A similar version appeared in Carl E. Seashore, *In Search of Beauty* (1947), 294–97; and Carl E. Seashore, *Pioneering in Psychology*, 103.
105. Carl E. Seashore, *Introduction to Psychology*, 38.
106. See, for example, Carl E. Seashore, "Cooperation with the Film," 264; and Carl E. Seashore, *Psychology of Music*, 346.
107. Carl E. Seashore, "The Play Impulse and Attitude in Religion," *American Journal of Theology* 14, no. 4 (October 1910): 512, http://www.jstor.org/stable/3154774
108. Carl E. Seashore, *Pioneering in Psychology*, 103. See also Carl E. Seashore, *In Search of Beauty* (1947), 9.
109. Carl E. Seashore, *Psychology in Daily Life* (New York: D. Appleton, 1914), 41.

110. Carl E. Seashore, "Cooperation with the Film," 264.
111. Carl E. Seashore, *Psychology in Daily Life*, 140–41.
112. Carl E. Seashore, *Psychology in Daily Life*, 140–41.
113. Carl E. Seashore, *Psychology in Daily Life*, 14–15. See also Carl E. Seashore, *Introduction to Psychology*, 276.
114. Carl E. Seashore, *Psychology in Daily Life*, 15. See also Carl E. Seashore, *Introduction to Psychology*, 276.
115. Carl E. Seashore, *Introduction to Psychology*, 38.
116. Carl E. Seashore, "Cooperation with the Film," 264.
117. Carl E. Seashore, "Cooperation with the Film," 264.
118. Thomas Russell Garth and Sarah Rachel Isbell, "The Musical Talent of Indians," *Music Supervisors' Journal* 15, no. 3 (February 1929): 83, www.jstor.org/stable/3382960. See also Garth, *Race Psychology*, 141.
119. Galton, "Hereditary Talent and Character: Second Paper," 320.
120. Carl C. Brigham, *A Study of American Intelligence* (Princeton, NJ: Princeton University Press, 1923), 81–83, 190–91, https://archive.org/stream/studyofamericani00briguoft#mode/2up
121. Brigham, *Study of American*, 190, 192.
122. Bird T. Baldwin, "The Learning of Delinquent Adolescent Girls as Shown by a Substitution Test," *Journal of Educational Psychology* 4, no. 6 (June 1913): 317–32, https://psycnet.apa.org/doi/10.1037/h0069968
123. Morris S. Viteles, "The Mental Status of the Negro," *Annals of the American Academy of Political and Social Science* 140, no. 229 (November 1928): 166–77, https://www.jstor.org/stable/1016845
124. Viteles, "Mental Status of the Negro," 175.
125. Viteles, "Mental Status of the Negro," 174–76.
126. Joseph Peterson, "Methods of Investigating Comparative Abilities in Races," *Annals of the American Academy of Political and Social Science* 140, no. 229 (November 1928): 178, https://www.jstor.org/stable/1016846
127. Peterson, "Methods of Investigating Comparative," 185.
128. Jacob Kwalwasser, "Scientific Testing in Music," *Music Supervisors' Journal* 12, no. 3 (February 1926): 20, www.jstor.org/stable/3383064. Kwalwasser simply referred to "Barden" [*sic*] but the reference probably was to James Bardin, "The Psychological Factor in Southern Race Problems," *Popular Science Monthly* 83 (October 1913): 368–74, https://en.wikisource.org/wiki/Popular_Science_Monthly/Volume_83/October_1913/The_Psychological_Factor_in_Southern_Race_Problems
129. Kwalwasser, "Scientific Testing in Music," 20.
130. Charles H. Thompson, "The Educational Achievements of Negro Children," *Annals of the American Academy of Political and Social Science* 140, no. 229 (November 1928): 208, https://www.jstor.org/stable/1016849
131. E. George Payne, "Negroes in the Public Elementary Schools of the North," *Annals of the American Academy of Political and Social Science* 140, no. 229 (November 1928): 233, https://www.jstor.org/stable/1016851
132. Julia J. Chybowski, "Developing American Taste: A Cultural History of the

Early-Twentieth Century Music Appreciation Movement" (PhD diss., University of Wisconsin-Madison, 2008), 160.

133. Paul Popenoe and Roswell Johnson, *Applied Eugenics*, 283–84.

134. Paul Popenoe and Roswell Johnson, *Applied Eugenics*, 284.

135. Paul Popenoe and Roswell Johnson, *Applied Eugenics*, 306.

136. Paul Popenoe and Roswell Johnson, *Applied Eugenics*, 284n1.

137. For biographical information, see "Reginald G. Harris," Archives at Cold Spring Harbor Laboratory, accessed July 6, 2018, http://library.cshl.edu/personal-collections/reginald-g-harris

138. Reginald G. Harris, "Negro Art as an Indication of Racial Development," *Eugenical News* 8, no. 9 (September 1923): 82.

139. Reginald Harris, "Negro Art," 82.

140. Reginald Harris, "Negro Art," 82.

141. Reginald Harris, "Negro Art," 83.

142. Reginald Harris, "Negro Art," 83.

143. Reginald Harris, "Negro Art," 83.

144. Reginald Harris, "Negro Art," 83.

145. Reginald Harris, "Negro Art," 85.

146. Reginald Harris, "Negro Art," 85.

147. Reginald Harris, "Negro Art," 85.

148. Reginald Harris, "Negro Art," 85.

149. Reginald Harris, "Negro Art," 85.

150. Reginald Harris, "Negro Art," 85.

151. Reginald Harris, "Negro Art," 85–86.

152. Reginald Harris, "Negro Art," 83.

153. Reginald Harris, "Negro Art," 86.

154. Henry Osborn, "Address of Welcome," 2–3.

155. Henry Osborn, "Address of Welcome," 3.

156. Henry Osborn, "Address of Welcome," 3.

157. Carl E. Seashore, *In Search of Beauty* (1947), 298, 303.

158. Carl E. Seashore, *In Search of Beauty* (1947), 303, 298.

159. Carl E. Seashore, *In Search of Beauty* (1947), 303.

160. Carl E. Seashore, *In Search of Beauty* (1947), 298, 303–4.

161. Carl E. Seashore, *In Search of Beauty* (1947), 301.

162. Carl E. Seashore, "Music," 681.

163. For examples of Seashore's discussion of present-primitive music, see Carl E. Seashore, "Cooperation with the Film," 264; and Carl E. Seashore and Harold Seashore, "The Place of Phonophotography in the Study of Primitive Music," *Science*, n.s., 79, no. 2056 (May 25, 1934): 485, http://www.jstor.org/stable/1659930

164. Carl E. Seashore, *In Search of Beauty* (1947), 80.

165. Carl E. Seashore, *Psychology of Music*, 374.

166. Carl E. Seashore, *Psychology of Music*, 347.

167. Carl E. Seashore, *In Search of Beauty* (1947), 303.

168. Carl E. Seashore, introduction to *Phonophotography in Folk Music*, by Milton

Metfessel (Chapel Hill: University of North Carolina Press, 1928), 16, https://babel.hathitrust.org/cgi/pt?id=uc1.32106010326780;view=1up;seq=7

169. Carl E. Seashore, *Psychology of Music*, 347.

170. Carl E. Seashore, *Psychology of Music*, 348–59.

171. Carl E. Seashore and Harold Seashore, "Place of Phonophotography," 485–86.

172. Carl E. Seashore, *Psychology of Music*, 373.

173. Carl E. Seashore, *In Search of Beauty* (1947), 301.

174. Carl E. Seashore, *In Search of Beauty* (1947), 301–2, 305.

175. Carl E. Seashore, *In Search of Beauty* (1947), 305.

176. Carl E. Seashore, *In Search of Beauty* (1947), 302.

177. Carl E. Seashore, *In Search of Beauty* (1947), 301–2.

178. Carl E. Seashore, *In Search of Beauty* (1947), 306.

179. Carl E. Seashore, *In Search of Beauty* (1947), 303.

180. Carl E. Seashore, *In Search of Beauty* (1947), 303.

181. Carl E. Seashore, *In Search of Beauty* (1947), 304.

182. Carl E. Seashore, *In Search of Beauty* (1947), 304.

183. Carl E. Seashore, *In Search of Beauty* (1947), 304.

184. Carl E. Seashore, *In Search of Beauty* (1947), 186–87.

185. Carl E. Seashore, *In Search of Beauty* (1947), 187.

186. Carl E. Seashore, *Psychology of Music*, 375.

187. Carl E. Seashore, *Psychology in Daily Life*, 24. When a revised version of the chapter on play was published in *Introduction to Psychology* in 1923, the section on religion was removed. See Carl E. Seashore, *Introduction to Psychology*, 266–80. For other discussions of religion, see Carl E. Seashore, "Play Impulse," 505–20; and Carl E. Seashore, "The Religion of the Educated Person," *Journal of Higher Education* 18, no. 2 (February 1947): 71–76, http://www.jstor.org/stable/1975910

188. Carl E. Seashore, *Psychology in Daily Life*, 25.

189. Carl E. Seashore, *Psychology in Daily Life*, 27.

190. Yale S. Nathanson, "The Musical Ability of the Negro," *Annals of the American Academy of Political and Social Science* 140, no. 229 (November 1928): 189, https://www.jstor.org/stable/1016847

191. Nathanson, "Musical Ability of the Negro," 189.

192. Nathanson, "Musical Ability of the Negro," 188.

193. Nathanson, "Musical Ability of the Negro," 188.

194. Guy Benton Johnson, "Musical Talent and the Negro," *Music Supervisors' Journal* 15, no. 1 (October 1928): 96, www.jstor.org/stable/3383738 (p. 96 missing from JSTOR).

195. See "Abridged Record of Family Traits," 1925, pp. 2, 9, American Philosophical Society, ERO, MSC77, SerVI, Box 3, FF Studies TX #2, titled "'Large Family' Winner, Fitter Families Contest, Texas State Fair (1925): Abridged Record of Family Traits," images 179, 186, in the "Image Archive on the American Eugenics Movement," DNA Learning Center, Cold Spring Harbor Laboratory, accessed March 25, 2009, www.eugenicsarchive.org/eugenics/view_image.pl?id=179

196. Carl E. Seashore, *Psychology in Daily Life*, 141.

197. Carl E. Seashore, *Psychology of Music*, 373.

198. Carl E. Seashore, *Psychology of Music*, 146.

199. Carl E. Seashore, *In Search of Beauty* (1947), 370.

200. For a discussion of the use of an evolutionary model, see Chybowski, "Developing American Taste," 162–64.

201. Chybowski, "Developing American Taste," 173.

202. Chybowski, "Developing American Taste," 213.

203. Guy Johnson, "Musical Talent and the Negro," 96.

204. Nathanson, "Musical Ability of the Negro," 188.

205. Nathanson, "Musical Ability of the Negro," 188.

206. Chybowski, "Developing American Taste," 166.

207. Nathanson, "Musical Ability of the Negro," 188.

208. "Abridged Record of Family Traits: Father's Father, Father's Mother," 1925, p. 2, American Philosophical Society, ERO, MSC77, SerVI, Box 3, FF Studies TX #2, titled "'Large Family' Winner, Fitter Families Contest, Texas State Fair (1925): Abridged Record of Family Traits," image 179, in the "Image Archive on the American Eugenics Movement," DNA Learning Center, Cold Spring Harbor Laboratory, accessed March 25, 2009, www.eugenicsarchive.org/eugenics/view_image.pl?id=179

209. Carl E. Seashore, *In Search of Beauty* (1947), 370–71.

210. Carl E. Seashore, "Youth and Music," *School Review* 48, no. 4 (April 1940): 270, http://www.jstor.org/stable/1082068. A manuscript version of this article is found in RG 99.0164, box 2, Carl E. Seashore Papers, Special Collections and University Archives, University of Iowa Libraries, Iowa City, IA. Also Carl E. Seashore, "How Psychology Can Help the Musician," *Etude* 35, no. 2 (February 1917): 89, https://books.google.com/books?id=IpgyAQAAMAAJ&pg=PA89&lpg=PA89&dq=etude++how+psychology+can+help+the+musician&source=bl&ots=tHDoVQu6_g&sig=d7_3e_W1UD8pNiZ_MakBANDHg3A&hl=en&sa=X&ved=0CCEQ6AEwAWoVChMI8pDg88nYxgIVEQySCh3pigIR#v=onepage&q=etude%20%20how%20psychology%20can%20help%20the%20musician&f=false

211. Carl E. Seashore, *In Search of Beauty* (1947), 278; Carl E. Seashore, "Three New Approaches to the Study of Negro Music," *Annals of the American Academy of Political and Social Science* 140, no. 229 (November 1928): 191, https://www.jstor.org/stable/1016848

212. Carl E. Seashore, "Cooperation with the Film," 264.

213. Francis P. Robinson, "Carl E. Seashore," *Educational Forum* 15, no. 1, pt. 2 (November 1950): 128t.

214. Carl E. Seashore, *In Search of Beauty* (1947). Other examples include Carl E. Seashore, "Cooperation with the Film," 263–65; Carl E. Seashore, "A Base for the Approach to Quantitative Studies in the Aesthetics of Music," *American Journal of Psychology* 39, no. 1/4 (December 1927): 141–44, https://doi.org/10.2307/1415406; Carl E. Seashore, *Psychology of Music*, 373–82; Carl E. Seashore and Milton Metfessel, "Deviation from the Regular as an Art Principle," *Proceedings of the National*

Academy of Sciences of the United States of America 11, no. 9 (1925): 538–42, www.jstor.org/stable/84855; and Carl E. Seashore, "In Search of Beauty in Music," *Musical Quarterly* 28, no. 3 (July 1942): 302–8, http://www.jstor.org/stable/739259

215. Carl E. Seashore, *Psychology of Music*, 377. See also his defense of experimental aesthetics in Carl E. Seashore, *In Search of Beauty* (1947), 17–25.

216. Carl E. Seashore, *In Search of Beauty* (1947), 18–25.

217. Carl E. Seashore, "Base for the Approach," 144.

218. Norman Charles Meier, *Aesthetic Judgment as a Measure of Art Talent*, University of Iowa Studies: Series on Aims and Progress of Research, vol. 1, no. 19 (Iowa City: The University, 1926), 7, 21.

219. Meier, *Aesthetic Judgment*, 22–23.

220. Carl E. Seashore, "Religious Music in the Public School Choruses," *Music Educators Journal* 28, no. 1 (September-October 1941): 60, http://www.jstor.org/stable/3385847

221. Carl E. Seashore, "Religious Music," 60.

222. Carl E. Seashore, "Religious Music," 60.

223. Carl E. Seashore and Milton Metfessel, "Deviation from the Regular," 540. I could find no information about one singer, "Mr. Welles." If the name was misspelled, however, this may have been tenor John Barnes Wells. Wells was famous and White, although not known for singing opera.

224. Carl E. Seashore and Milton Metfessel, "Deviation from the Regular," 538. For a similar discussion of aesthetics, see Carl E. Seashore, "Base for the Approach," 141–44.

225. Carl E. Seashore and Milton Metfessel, "Deviation from the Regular," 538.

226. Carl E. Seashore and Milton Metfessel, "Deviation from the Regular," 538.

227. Carl E. Seashore and Milton Metfessel, "Deviation from the Regular," 538.

228. Carl E. Seashore and Milton Metfessel, "Deviation from the Regular," 541.

229. Carl E. Seashore and Milton Metfessel, "Deviation from the Regular," 541. For another discussion of vibrato, see Carl E. Seashore, "In Search of Beauty" (1942), 305.

230. Carl E. Seashore and Milton Metfessel, "Deviation from the Regular," 542.

231. Carl E. Seashore and Milton Metfessel, "Deviation from the Regular," 541.

232. Ruth Iana Gustafson, *Race and Curriculum: Music in Childhood Education* (New York: Palgrave, 2009), 127, 135.

233. Chybowski, "Developing American Taste," 168–72.

234. Chybowski, "Developing American Taste," 169.

235. Chybowski, "Developing American Taste," 171–72.

236. Chybowski, "Developing American Taste," 172.

237. Wallace, *Darwinism: An Exposition*, 470, 467.

238. Wallace, *Darwinism: An Exposition*, 467–68.

239. Francis Galton, "Ethnological Enquiries on the Innate Character and Intelligence of Different Races" [c. 1909], p. 2, University College London, FG, 138/1, titled "Directions for Responding to a Survey on 'Ethnological Enquiries on the Innate Character and Intelligence of Different Races,' by Francis Galton,"

image 2090, in the "Image Archive on the American Eugenics Movement," DNA Learning Center, Cold Spring Harbor Laboratory, accessed March 25, 2009, www.eugenicsarchive.org/eugenics/view_image.pl?id=2090

240. "Human Pedigrees Detailing the Inheritance of Specific Biological Traits, Inheritance of Musical Talent: Explanatory Notes" [c. 1910], p. 2, Cold Spring Harbor, ERO, titled "'Inheritance of Musical Talent,' Pedigree Chart with Instructions, Eugenics Section, American Breeders Association," image 1770, in the "Image Archive on the American Eugenics Movement," DNA Learning Center, Cold Spring Harbor Laboratory, accessed March 25, 2009, www.eugenicsarchive.org/eugenics/view_image.pl?id=1770

241. "Human Pedigrees Detailing the Inheritance of Specific Biological Traits, Inheritance of Musical Talent: Explanatory Notes" [c. 1910], p. 2, Cold Spring Harbor, ERO, titled "'Inheritance of Musical Talent,' Pedigree Chart with Instructions, Eugenics Section, American Breeders Association," image 1770, in the "Image Archive on the American Eugenics Movement," DNA Learning Center, Cold Spring Harbor Laboratory, accessed March 25, 2009, www.eugenicsarchive.org/eugenics/view_image.pl?id=1770

242. "Human Pedigrees Detailing the Inheritance of Specific Biological Traits, Inheritance of Musical Talent: Explanatory Notes" [c. 1910], p. 2, Cold Spring Harbor, ERO, titled "'Inheritance of Musical Talent,' Pedigree Chart with Instructions, Eugenics Section, American Breeders Association," image 1770, in the "Image Archive on the American Eugenics Movement," DNA Learning Center, Cold Spring Harbor Laboratory, accessed March 25, 2009, www.eugenicsarchive.org/eugenics/view_image.pl?id=1770

243. Carl E. Seashore, "Youth and Music," 270.

244. Carl E. Seashore, "Youth and Music," 270.

245. Carl E. Seashore, "Youth and Music," 276.

246. Carl E. Seashore, "Youth and Music," 276–77.

247. Carl E. Seashore, "Youth and Music," 277.

248. Carl E. Seashore, "Youth and Music," 277.

249. Carl E. Seashore, "Youth and Music," 277.

250. Garth, *Race Psychology*, 141.

251. Garth, *Race Psychology*, 141.

252. Carl E. Seashore, "Basic Measurements of Music and Speech," p. 3, attachment to C. E. Seashore, Washington, DC, to President W. A. Jessup, Iowa City, IA, April 29, 1921, RG 05.01.09, box 76, folder 53, Walter A. Jessup Papers, Special Collections and University Archives, University of Iowa Libraries, Iowa City, IA; Carl E. Seashore, "Three New Approaches," 191–92; Carl E. Seashore and Harold Seashore, "Place of Phonophotography," 485.

253. Carl E. Seashore to Archibald MacLeish, Washington, DC, May 25, 1943, RG 05.01.11, box 55, folder 52, Virgil M. Hancher Papers, Special Collections and University Archives, University of Iowa Libraries, Iowa City, IA.

254. Carl E. Seashore, introduction to *Phonophotography in Folk Music*, by Milton Metfessel, 16–17.

255. Carl E. Seashore, introduction to *Phonophotography in Folk Music*, by Milton Metfessel, 17.

256. Carl E. Seashore, introduction to *Phonophotography in Folk Music*, by Milton Metfessel, 17.

257. Carl E. Seashore, *Psychology of Music*, 349n*.

258. Carl E. Seashore, *Psychology of Music*, 349, 349n*; Carl E. Seashore, introduction to *Phonophotography in Folk Music*, by Milton Metfessel, 7.

259. Carl E. Seashore, introduction to *Phonophotography in Folk Music*, by Milton Metfessel, 7.

260. Carl E. Seashore, "Basic Measurements," p. 3, attachment to C. E. Seashore to President W. A. Jessup, April 29, 1921, 1–7, RG 05.01.09, box 76, folder 53, Walter A. Jessup Papers.

261. Carl E. Seashore, introduction to *Phonophotography in Folk Music*, by Milton Metfessel, 7, 12, 15.

262. Carl E. Seashore, introduction to *Phonophotography in Folk Music*, by Milton Metfessel, 13–15.

263. Carl E. Seashore, introduction to *Phonophotography in Folk Music*, by Milton Metfessel, 7.

264. Gustafson, *Race and Curriculum*, 127.

265. Milton Metfessel, *Phonophotography in Folk Music: American Negro Songs in New Notation* (Chapel Hill: University of North Carolina, 1928), vii, https://babel.hathitrust.org/cgi/pt?id=uc1.32106010326780;view=1up;seq=7

266. Metfessel, *Phonophotography in Folk Music*, vii.

267. See, for example, Carl E. Seashore, *Psychology of Music*, 356–57; and Carl E. Seashore, *In Search of Beauty* (1947), 281, 284.

268. Carl E. Seashore, "Three New Approaches," 191–92.

269. Carl E. Seashore, *Psychology of Music*, 350, 353–56; Metfessel, *Phonophotography in Folk Music*, 30, 62–63, 86–87, 122.

270. Carl E. Seashore, *Psychology of Music*, 349; Metfessel, *Phonophotography in Folk Music*, 29.

271. Carl E. Seashore, *Psychology of Music*, 351–52.

272. Carl E. Seashore, *Psychology of Music*, 352.

273. Carl E. Seashore, *Psychology of Music*, 352.

274. Carl E. Seashore, *Psychology of Music*, 352.

275. Carl E. Seashore, *Psychology of Music*, 352.

276. Carl E. Seashore, *Psychology of Music*, 352.

277. Metfessel, *Phonophotography in Folk Music*, 57, 81.

278. "History," Hampton University, accessed July 16, 2018, http://www.hamptonu.edu/about/history.cfm

279. Carl E. Seashore, *Psychology of Music*, 356.

280. Carl E. Seashore, *Psychology of Music*, 356.

281. Carl E. Seashore, *Psychology of Music*, 356.

282. Carl E. Seashore, *Psychology of Music*, 356–57.

283. Carl E. Seashore, *Psychology of Music*, 357.

284. Carl E. Seashore, *Psychology of Music*, 357.

285. Carl E. Seashore, *Psychology of Music*, 357.

286. Carl E. Seashore, *Psychology of Music*, 357.

287. Carl E. Seashore, *Psychology of Music*, 357.
288. Carl E. Seashore, *Psychology of Music*, 358.
289. Carl E. Seashore, *Psychology of Music*, 358–59.
290. Carl E. Seashore, *Psychology of Music*, 358.
291. Carl E. Seashore, "Base for the Approach," 141–44.
292. Carl E. Seashore, *Psychology of Music*, 359.
293. Carl E. Seashore, *Psychology of Music*, 359.
294. Carl E. Seashore, *Psychology of Music*, 359.
295. See Carl E. Seashore, *In Search of Beauty* (1947), 279–81, after 281–84, 285–86, 288–89, 290–91, 292–93; and Metfessel, *Phonophotography in Folk Music*, 106–8, 88–90, 69–70, 75–76, 52–53, 72–73.
296. Carl E. Seashore, *In Search of Beauty* (1947), 278.
297. Carl E. Seashore, *In Search of Beauty* (1947), 284.
298. Carl E. Seashore, *In Search of Beauty* (1947), 284.
299. Carl E. Seashore and Harold Seashore, "Place of Phonophotography," 485.
300. *Official Guide Book of the Fair*, published in conjunction with A Century of Progress International Exposition, Chicago, 1933 (Chicago: Cuneo, 1933), 64, 4, http://libsysdigi.library.illinois.edu/oca/Books2008-08/officialguideboo331cent/officialguideboo331cent.pdf
301. *Official Guide Book of the Fair*, 64.
302. Carl E. Seashore and Harold Seashore, "Place of Phonophotography," 485.
303. Carl E. Seashore and Harold Seashore, "Place of Phonophotography," 486.
304. Carl E. Seashore and Harold Seashore, "Place of Phonophotography," 486.
305. Carl E. Seashore and Harold Seashore, "Place of Phonophotography," 486.
306. Carl E. Seashore, "Cooperation with the Film," 263–64.
307. Carl E. Seashore, *Psychology of Music*, 346.
308. Carl E. Seashore, "Cooperation with the Film," 263; Carl E. Seashore, *Psychology of Music*, 347–48.
309. Carl E. Seashore, *Psychology of Music*, 347.
310. Carl E. Seashore, *Psychology of Music*, 348.
311. Carl E. Seashore, *Psychology of Music*, 346.
312. Carl E. Seashore, "Cooperation with the Film," 264.
313. Carl E. Seashore, "Cooperation with the Film," 264.
314. Carl E. Seashore to Secretary, Motion Picture Academy, Hollywood, CA, May 25, 1943, p. 1, RG 05.01.11, box 55, folder 52, Virgil M. Hancher Papers, Special Collections and University Archives, University of Iowa Libraries, Iowa City, IA.
315. Carl E. Seashore, *Psychology of Music*, 348.
316. Carl E. Seashore to Secretary, Motion Picture Academy, May 25, 1943, p. 2, RG 05.01.11, box 55, folder 52, Virgil M. Hancher Papers.
317. Carl E. Seashore, *Psychology of Music*, 348.
318. Carl E. Seashore, *Psychology of Music*, 348.
319. Carl E. Seashore, "Cooperation with the Film," 263, 265.
320. Carl E. Seashore, *Psychology of Music*, 347.

321. Carl E. Seashore, *Pioneering in Psychology*, 108; Carl E. Seashore, "Cooperation with the Film," 263–65; Carl E. Seashore, *In Search of Beauty* (1947), 294–97.

322. Carl E. Seashore, "Cooperation with the Film," 264.

323. Carl E. Seashore, "Cooperation with the Film," 264.

324. Carl E. Seashore, "Cooperation with the Film," 264.

325. Carl E. Seashore, *Psychology of Music*, 349.

326. Carl E. Seashore, *Pioneering in Psychology*, 108; Carl E. Seashore, "Cooperation with the Film," 264. He also described logistics in Carl E. Seashore, *Psychology of Music*, 347.

327. Carl E. Seashore, "Cooperation with the Film," 264. See also Carl E. Seashore, *Psychology of Music*, 347.

328. Carl E. Seashore, "Cooperation with the Film," 264.

329. Carl E. Seashore, *Psychology of Music*, 347.

330. Carl E. Seashore, "Cooperation with the Film," 264; Carl E. Seashore, *Psychology of Music*, 347.

331. Carl E. Seashore, "Cooperation with the Film," 264.

332. Carl E. Seashore, "Cooperation with the Film," 264.

333. Carl E. Seashore, "Cooperation with the Film," 264.

334. Carl E. Seashore, "Cooperation with the Film," 264.

335. Carl E. Seashore, *Pioneering in Psychology*, 108.

336. Carl E. Seashore to Secretary, Motion Picture Academy, May 25, 1943, p. 1, RG 05.01.11, box 55, folder 52, Virgil M. Hancher Papers.

337. Carl E. Seashore to Secretary, Motion Picture Academy, May 25, 1943, RG 05.01.11, box 55, folder 52, Virgil M. Hancher Papers.

338. Carl E. Seashore to Secretary, Motion Picture Academy, May 25, 1943, p. 1, RG 05.01.11, box 55, folder 52, Virgil M. Hancher Papers.

339. Carl E. Seashore to Secretary, Motion Picture Academy, May 25, 1943, RG 05.01.11, box 55, folder 52, Virgil M. Hancher Papers.

340. Carl E. Seashore to MacLeish, May 25, 1943, RG 05.01.11, box 55, folder 52, Virgil M. Hancher Papers.

341. "Marcus Bach Collection, Biography," Brigham Young University, Provo, UT, accessed July 21, 2018, https://lib.byu.edu/collections/marcus-bach-collection/about/biography/

342. Archibald MacLeish, Librarian of Congress, Washington, DC, to Carl E. Seashore, Iowa City, IA, June 3, 1943, RG 05.01.11, box 55, folder 52, Virgil M. Hancher Papers, Special Collections and University Archives, University of Iowa Libraries, Iowa City, IA.

343. MacLeish to Carl E. Seashore, June 3, 1943, RG 05.01.11, box 55, folder 52, Virgil M. Hancher Papers.

344. MacLeish to Carl E. Seashore, June 3, 1943, RG 05.01.11, box 55, folder 52, Virgil M. Hancher Papers.

345. Mrs. Donald Gledhill to Carl E. Seashore, Iowa City, IA, June 9, 1943, RG 05.01.11, box 55, folder 52, Virgil M. Hancher Papers, Special Collections and University Archives, University of Iowa Libraries, Iowa City, IA.

346. "Margaret Herrick, Film History Trailblazer," Academy of Motion Picture Arts and Sciences, September 22, 2015, https://www.oscars.org/news/margaret-herrick-film-history-trailblazer

347. Carl E. Seashore, Iowa City, IA, to Mrs. Donald Gledhill, Hollywood, CA, June 14, 1943, RG 05.01.11, box 55, folder 52, Virgil M. Hancher Papers, Special Collections and University Archives, University of Iowa Libraries, Iowa City, IA.

348. Toni Morrison, *Playing in the Dark: Whiteness and the Literary Imagination* (Cambridge, MA: Harvard University Press, 1992), 17.

349. Morrison, *Playing in the Dark*, 44.

350. Alex Lubin, *Romance and Rights: The Politics of Interracial Intimacy, 1945–1954* (Jackson, MS: University Press of Mississippi, 2005), 51.

351. Carl E. Seashore, "Individual and Racial Inheritance of Musical Traits," in *Eugenics, Genetics and the Family*, vol. 1, *Scientific Papers of the Second International Congress of Eugenics; Held at American Museum of Natural History, New York, September 22–28, 1921* (Baltimore, MD: Williams & Wilkins, 1923; repr., ed. Charles Rosenberg, New York: Garland Publishing, 1985), 231–38. The reference to mate selection appears on p. 238.

352. Carl E. Seashore, "Individual and Racial Inheritance," 231.

353. Carl E. Seashore, *Psychology of Music*, 309.

354. Davenport and Steggerda, *Race Crossing in Jamaica* (1929), 4; Morris Steggerda, "Negro-White Hybrids in Jamaica, B.W.I.," *Eugenical News* 13, no. 2 (February 1928): 21.

355. Davenport and Steggerda, *Race Crossing in Jamaica* (1929), 4; Steggerda, "Negro-White Hybrids in Jamaica," 21.

356. "Galton Society," *Eugenical News* 11, no. 12 (December 1926): 188–89.

357. Charles Benedict Davenport, "Research in Eugenics," in *Eugenics, Genetics and the Family*, vol. 1, *Scientific Papers of the Second International Congress of Eugenics; Held at American Museum of Natural History, New York, September 22–28, 1921* (Baltimore, MD: Williams & Wilkins, 1923; repr., ed. Charles Rosenberg, New York: Garland Publishing, 1985), 27.

358. For an homage to Davenport written by Steggerda, see Morris Steggerda, "Dr. Charles B. Davenport and His Contributions to Eugenics," *Eugenical News* 29, no. 1 (March 1944): 3–10.

359. Davenport and Steggerda, *Race Crossing in Jamaica* (1929), 3.

360. "Galton Society," 188.

361. Black, *War against the Weak*, 305.

362. Morris Steggerda, "Physical Development of Negro-White Hybrids in Jamaica, British West Indies" (PhD diss., University of Illinois at Urbana-Champaign, 1928), http://search.proquest.com.ezproxy.library.wisc.edu/docview/301773996?accountid=465

363. Davenport and Steggerda, *Race Crossing in Jamaica* (1929), 3; "Studies in Jamaica," *Eugenical News* 11, no. 10 (October 1926): 154.

364. "Galton Society," 188.

365. "Studies in Jamaica," 154; Davenport and Steggerda, *Race Crossing in Jamaica* (1929), 4.

366. Davenport and Steggerda, *Race Crossing in Jamaica* (1929), 4.
367. "Studies in Jamaica," 154.
368. Davenport and Steggerda, *Race Crossing in Jamaica* (1929), 299.
369. Davenport and Steggerda, *Race Crossing in Jamaica* (1929), 299.
370. Davenport and Steggerda, *Race Crossing in Jamaica* (1929), 33–42, 299–369.
371. William H. Tucker, *The Funding of Scientific Racism: Wickliffe Draper and the Pioneer Fund* (Urbana: University of Illinois Press, 2002), 31; Davenport and Steggerda, *Race Crossing in Jamaica* (1929), vi–vii, 267–68.
372. "Galton Society," 188.
373. Davenport and Steggerda, *Race Crossing in Jamaica* (1929), 3.
374. "Annual Midwinter Meeting of the Executive Committee of the Eugenics Research Association," *Eugenical News* 11, no. 3 (March 1926): 47.
375. "Studies in Jamaica," 154.
376. Davenport and Steggerda, *Race Crossing in Jamaica* (1929), 5; "Studies in Jamaica," 154.
377. Michael G. Kenny, "Toward a Racial Abyss: Eugenics, Wickliffe Draper, and the Origins of the Pioneer Fund," *Journal of History of the Behavioral Sciences* 38, no. 3 (Summer 2002): 266.
378. Kenny, "Toward a Racial Abyss," 266. On p. 261, Kenny states that his sources are "from the papers of the American Eugenics Society and cited with permission of the American Philosophical Society."
379. Kenny, "Toward a Racial Abyss," 266–67. See also Tucker, *Funding of Scientific Racism*, 30–31.
380. Tucker, *Funding of Scientific Racism*, 30.
381. Douglas A. Blackmon, "Silent Partner: How the South's Fight to Uphold Segregation Was Funded Up North—New York Millionaire Secretly Sent Cash to Mississippi via His Morgan Account—'Wall Street Gang' Pitches In," *Wall Street Journal*, June 11, 1999, Eastern edition, A1, http://ezproxy.library.wisc.edu/login?url=http://proquest.umi.com.ezproxy.library.wisc.edu/pqdweb?did=42299728; Kenny, "Toward a Racial Abyss," 270, 272.
382. Kenny, "Toward a Racial Abyss," 269–70.
383. Tucker, *Funding of Scientific Racism*, 32–33. See also Paul A. Lombardo, "'The American Breed': Nazi Eugenics and the Origins of the Pioneer Fund," *Albany Law Review* 65, no. 3 (February 2002): 766–68, http://search.ebscohost.com/login.aspx?direct=true&AuthType=ip,uid&db=aph&AN=6658610&site=ehost-live&scope=site (link omits pp. 743–44).
384. Tucker, *Funding of Scientific Racism*, 34. See also Kenny, "Toward a Racial Abyss," 271–72; and Lombardo, "'American Breed,'" 749, 780–86.
385. "Pioneer Fund Certificate of Incorporation 1937," Institute for the Study of Academic Racism at Ferris State University, February 1, 1998, https://ferris-pages.org/ISAR/Institut/pioneer/pfund.htm
386. Lombardo, "'American Breed,'" 746–47, 771, 786.
387. Lombardo, "'American Breed,'" 771.
388. Lombardo, "'American Breed,'" 771. On p. 771, Lombardo points out that Laughlin was a conduit, introducing Draper to Nazis. For a discussion of Laughlin's Nazi connections, see pp. 759–65; for Draper's Nazi connections, see pp. 768–74.

389. Lombardo, "'American Breed,'" 749.

390. Kenny, "Toward a Racial Abyss," 280.

391. Lombardo, "'American Breed,'" 786–88; Blackmon, "Silent Partner," A1.

392. Lombardo, "'American Breed,'" 803.

393. Lombardo, "'American Breed,'" 789, 802.

394. Lombardo, "'American Breed,'" 808–9. See also Kenny, "Toward a Racial Abyss," 273–75.

395. Blackmon, "Silent Partner," A1.

396. Tucker, *Funding of Scientific Racism*, 23.

397. "Arthur Jensen," Southern Poverty Law Center, accessed August 6, 2018, https://www.splcenter.org/fighting-hate/extremist-files/individual/arthur-jensen. See also "Pioneer Fund," Southern Poverty Law Center, accessed August 6, 2018, https://www.splcenter.org/fighting-hate/extremist-files/group/pioneer-fund; and Adam Miller, "The Pioneer Fund: Bankrolling the Professors of Hate," *Journal of Blacks in Higher Education* no. 6 (Winter 1994/1995): 60, http://www.jstor.org/stable/2962466

398. "Jean-Philippe Rushton," Southern Poverty Law Center, accessed August 6, 2018, https://www.splcenter.org/fighting-hate/extremist-files/individual/jean-philippe-rushton; Tucker, *Funding of Scientific Racism*, 179, 186, 197, 199, 202–3. For more information about Rushton, see Tucker, especially 197–203. For more information about American Renaissance, see "American Renaissance," Southern Poverty Law Center, accessed August 11, 2018, https://www.splcenter.org/fighting-hate/extremist-files/group/american-renaissance

399. Adam Miller, "Pioneer Fund: Bankrolling," 60–61; Tucker, *Funding of Scientific Racism*, 140–41, 144–48. For more information on Shockley, see Tucker, especially 140–55.

400. "Pioneer Fund," Southern Poverty Law Center; Tucker, *Funding of Scientific Racism*, 80, 110, 139, 159, 163, 167, 169–70. For more information on Pearson, see Tucker, especially 159–79.

401. Lombardo, "'American Breed,'" 745, 750.

402. Bob Herbert, "In America: Throwing a Curve," *New York Times*, October 26, 1994, A27, https://www.nytimes.com/1994/10/26/opinion/in-america-throwing-a-curve.html; Eric Siegel, "The Real Problem with Charles Murray and 'The Bell Curve,'" *Voices* (blog), *Scientific American*, April 12, 2017, https://blogs.scientificamerican.com/voices/the-real-problem-with-charles-murray-and-the-bell-curve/

403. Chip Berlet, "Into the Mainstream," *Intelligence Report*, Southern Poverty Law Center, August 15, 2003, https://www.splcenter.org/fighting-hate/intelligence-report/2003/mainstream; "Pioneer Fund," Southern Poverty Law Center.

404. Kenny, "Toward a Racial Abyss," 277.

405. Blackmon, "Silent Partner," A1.

406. Blackmon, "Silent Partner," A1.

407. Davenport and Steggerda, *Race Crossing in Jamaica* (1929), 364.

408. Davenport and Steggerda, *Race Crossing in Jamaica* (1929), 365.

409. Davenport and Steggerda, *Race Crossing in Jamaica* (1929), 476.

410. See, for example, Davenport and Steggerda, *Race Crossing in Jamaica* (1929), 471–72, 363–64.

411. Charles Benedict Davenport, "Race Crossing in Jamaica," *Scientific Monthly* 27, no. 3 (September 1928): 238, http://www.jstor.org/stable/7978

412. Kenny, "Toward a Racial Abyss," 268.

413. Tucker, *Funding of Scientific Racism*, 31.

414. Tucker, *Funding of Scientific Racism*, 32.

415. Mehler, "History of the American Eugenics," 422.

416. Mehler, "History of the American Eugenics," 422.

417. Charles B. Davenport to Carl E. Seashore, Iowa City, IA, March 25, 1926, MSS.B.D27, box 85, Charles B. Davenport Papers, American Philosophical Society Archives, Philadelphia, PA.

418. Davenport and Steggerda, *Race Crossing in Jamaica* (1929), 3.

419. Charles B. Davenport to Carl E. Seashore, Iowa City, IA, September 22, 1926, MSS.B.D27, box 85, Charles B. Davenport Papers, American Philosophical Society Archives, Philadelphia, PA.

420. Davenport and Steggerda, *Race Crossing in Jamaica* (1929), 299.

421. Davenport and Steggerda, *Race Crossing in Jamaica* (1929), 35–36.

422. Davenport and Steggerda, *Race Crossing in Jamaica* (1929), 300–317. For images of a test sheet used in the study, see "Individual Test Sheet for the Seashore Measurements of the Elements of Musical Ability," 1927, pp. 1–2, National Museum of Health and Medicine, Otis Historical Archives, Steggerda, Box 6 Folder 55, 97 3157, titled "Shortwood College Anthropometric Case: 'Seashore' Measurements of Musical Ability, Conducted by Morris Steggerda for Race Crossing in Jamaica," images 2367–68, in the "Image Archive on the American Eugenics Movement," DNA Learning Center, Cold Spring Harbor Laboratory, accessed March 25, 2009, www.eugenicsarchive.org/eugenics/view_image.pl?id=2367

423. Davenport and Steggerda, *Race Crossing in Jamaica* (1929), 368.

424. Davenport and Steggerda, *Race Crossing in Jamaica* (1929), 316.

425. Davenport and Steggerda, *Race Crossing in Jamaica* (1929), 313.

426. Davenport and Steggerda, *Race Crossing in Jamaica* (1929), 316.

427. Davenport and Steggerda, *Race Crossing in Jamaica* (1929), 302. For similar statements about performance on other portions of the Seashore Tests, see pp. 305, 308, 315–16.

428. See, for example, the discussion of the pitch discrimination test: Davenport and Steggerda, *Race Crossing in Jamaica* (1929), 302. See p. 310 for a similar statement about the harmony results.

429. Davenport and Steggerda, *Race Crossing in Jamaica* (1929), 455–56.

430. Davenport and Steggerda, *Race Crossing in Jamaica* (1929), 455.

431. Davenport, "Race Crossing in Jamaica" (1928), 238.

432. Carl E. Seashore, Iowa City, IA, to Charles B. Davenport, Cold Spring Harbor, NY, October 29, 1929, MSS.B.D27, box 85, Charles B. Davenport Papers, American Philosophical Society Archives, Philadelphia, PA.

433. Carl E. Seashore to Davenport, October 29, 1929, MSS.B.D27, box 85, Charles B. Davenport Papers.

434. Carl E. Seashore to Davenport, October 29, 1929, MSS.B.D27, box 85, Charles B. Davenport Papers.

435. Carl E. Seashore to Davenport, October 29, 1929, MSS.B.D27, box 85, Charles B. Davenport Papers.

436. Charles B. Davenport to Carl E. Seashore, Iowa City, IA, November 1, 1929, MSS.B.D27, box 85, Charles B. Davenport Papers, American Philosophical Society Archives, Philadelphia, PA.

437. Davenport and Steggerda, *Race Crossing in Jamaica* (1929), 4n*.

438. Davenport to Carl E. Seashore, November 1, 1929, MSS.B.D27, box 85, Charles B. Davenport Papers.

439. Carl E. Seashore, Iowa City, IA, to Charles B. Davenport, Cold Spring Harbor, NY, November 5, 1929, MSS.B.D27, box 85, Charles B. Davenport Papers, American Philosophical Society Archives, Philadelphia, PA.

440. Carl E. Seashore, *Pioneering in Psychology*, 179–89. For the reference to race mixtures, see p. 186.

441. "Studies in Jamaica," 154; "Galton Society," 188–89; Steggerda, "Negro-White Hybrids in Jamaica," 21–23.

442. Jon Alfred Mjöen, *Die Vererbung der musikalischen Begabung* (Berlin: Alfred Metzner, 1934), 8.

443. Carl E. Seashore, *Psychology of Music*, 308–9, 345.

444. Carl E. Seashore, "Musical Inheritance," 354–55.

445. Davenport et al., "Intermarriages between Races?" 61.

446. Zaid Delmas Lenoir, "Measurement of Racial Differences in Certain Mental and Educational Abilities" (master's thesis, State University of Iowa, 1925), preface.

447. Lenoir, "Measurement of Racial Differences," 20.

448. Lenoir, "Measurement of Racial Differences," 21, 70, 73. There is an inconsistency in the number of subjects Lenoir reported. The data tables for the Seashore Tests only reported 190 students in each group. See pp. 39, 47.

449. Lenoir, "Measurement of Racial Differences," 81.

450. Lenoir, "Measurement of Racial Differences," 80.

451. Lenoir, "Measurement of Racial Differences," 80.

452. Lenoir, "Measurement of Racial Differences," 82.

453. Lenoir, "Measurement of Racial Differences," 83.

454. Lenoir, "Measurement of Racial Differences," 83.

455. Lenoir, "Measurement of Racial Differences," 83, 76.

456. Daniel T. Kelleher, "The Case of Lloyd Lionel Gaines: The Demise of the Separate but Equal Doctrine," *Journal of Negro History* 56, no. 4 (October 1971): 264, https://www.jstor.org/stable/2716967; "Lorenzo Greene, Lincoln University History Professor, 1933–72," in *Lionel Gaines: The Man, the Mission, the Mystery*, an exhibition organized and presented by the Lincoln University Archives and Ethnic Studies Center, October 1, 2015, section 1, part 17, item 3.2, https://bluetigercommons.lincolnu.edu/lgaines_sec1/17/

457. "Phi Beta Sigma Fraternity, Inc. 1910– . . . A Historical Time Line," Phi Beta Sigma Eastern Region Historical Society, accessed August 14, 2018, http://erhistoricalsociety.tripod.com/id11.html; Distinguished Service Chapter Special Committee, *Distinguished Service Chapter Rules and Guidelines Citation Manual* (Washington, DC: Phi Beta Sigma Fraternity, 2010), 29, http://pbseast.org/wp-content/uploads/2017/12/DSC-Guide-Manual-Approved.pdf; "Zaid Lenoir," memory book posting from Michael Carter, accessed August 14, 2018, http://www.tributes.com/show/Zaid-Lenoir-63194317?active_tab=condolences

458. James W. Endersby and William T. Horner, *Lloyd Gaines and the Fight to End Segregation* (Columbia: University of Missouri Press, 2016), 12; Kelleher, "Case of Lloyd Lionel Gaines," 263–64.

459. Endersby and Horner, *Lloyd Gaines*, 12, 58; Kelleher, "Case of Lloyd Lionel Gaines," 264.

460. Carl E. Seashore, *Psychology of Music*, 308–9. Seashore listed Lenoir's study in the bibliography of *Psychology of Music* but did not refer to it in the body of the book. See source 76 on p. 390.

461. Carl E. Seashore, *Psychology of Music*, 308.

462. Guy Benton Johnson, "The Negro and Musical Talent," *Southern Workman* 56, no. 10 (October 1927): 439–44.

463. Guy Benton Johnson, "A Study of the Musical Talent of the American Negro" (PhD diss., University of North Carolina, 1927); Guy Johnson, "Musical Talent and the Negro," 81, 83, 96.

464. "Guy Benton Johnson Facts," Your Dictionary, 2010, http://biography.yourdictionary.com/guy-benton-johnson (link discontinued).

465. Guy Johnson, "Study of the Musical Talent of the American Negro," ii.

466. Guy Johnson, "Negro and Musical Talent," 439.

467. Guy Johnson, "Study of the Musical Talent of the American Negro," i.

468. Guy Johnson, "Negro and Musical Talent," 439–40; Guy Johnson, "Musical Talent and the Negro," 81, 83.

469. Guy Johnson, "Negro and Musical Talent," 439.

470. Guy Johnson, "Study of the Musical Talent of the American Negro," 1; Guy Johnson, "Musical Talent and the Negro," 83.

471. Guy Johnson, "Negro and Musical Talent," 442.

472. Guy Johnson, "Negro and Musical Talent," 443; Guy Johnson, "Musical Talent and the Negro," 83.

473. Guy Johnson, "Study of the Musical Talent of the American Negro," 79.

474. Guy Johnson, "Study of the Musical Talent of the American Negro," 75–76.

475. Guy Johnson, "Negro and Musical Talent," 442.

476. Guy Johnson, "Negro and Musical Talent," 444.

477. Nathanson, "Musical Ability of the Negro," 186.

478. Nathanson, "Musical Ability of the Negro," 186.

479. Nathanson, "Musical Ability of the Negro," 186.

480. Nathanson, "Musical Ability of the Negro," 186–87.

481. Nathanson, "Musical Ability of the Negro," 187–88.

482. Nathanson, "Musical Ability of the Negro," 189–90.

483. Graham Richards, "Reconceptualizing the History of Race Psychology: Thomas Russell Garth (1872–1939) and How He Changed His Mind," *Journal of the History of the Behavioral Sciences* 34, no. 1 (Winter 1998): 15, https://doi.org/10.1002/(SICI)1520-6696(199824)34:1<15::AID-JHBS2>3.0.CO;2-I

484. Joseph Peterson and Lyle H. Lanier, *Studies in the Comparative Abilities of Whites and Negroes*, Mental Measurement Monographs, no. 5 (Baltimore, MD: Williams and Wilkins, 1929), 125–26.

485. Peterson and Lanier, *Studies in the Comparative*, 128.

486. Peterson and Lanier, *Studies in the Comparative*, 107.

487. Peterson and Lanier, *Studies in the Comparative*, 128.

488. Peterson and Lanier, *Studies in the Comparative*, 130.

489. Peterson and Lanier, *Studies in the Comparative*, 131.

490. Editor's note from Peter Dykema in Garth and Isbell, "Musical Talent of Indians," 83; Graham Richards, "Reconceptualizing the History," 15.

491. Editor's note from Peter Dykema in Garth and Isbell, "Musical Talent of Indians," 83.

492. Garth and Isbell, "Musical Talent of Indians," 83, 86.

493. Garth and Isbell, "Musical Talent of Indians," 85.

494. Garth and Isbell, "Musical Talent of Indians," 87.

495. Garth and Isbell, "Musical Talent of Indians," 86.

496. Garth and Isbell, "Musical Talent of Indians," 86.

497. Compare Garth and Isbell, "Musical Talent of Indians," 83, 85–87, to Garth, *Race Psychology*, 142, 145–48, 155.

498. Garth, *Race Psychology*, 153–54.

499. Garth, *Race Psychology*, 155.

500. Graham Richards, "Reconceptualizing the History," 17–18.

501. Graham Richards, "Reconceptualizing the History," 17, 21.

502. Graham Richards, "Reconceptualizing the History," 17.

503. Lyle H. Lanier, review of *Race Psychology: A Study of Racial Mental Differences*, by Thomas Russell Garth, *American Journal of Psychology* 45, no. 1 (January 1933): 186, https://doi.org/10.2307/1414212

504. Lanier, review of *Race Psychology*, 184–86.

505. Lanier, review of *Race Psychology*, 184.

506. Lanier, review of *Race Psychology*, 186.

507. Seashore misspelled Murdoch's name and incorrectly reported the page numbers of her article. See Carl E. Seashore, *Psychology of Music*, 309, 391.

508. Katharine Murdoch, "A Study of Differences Found Between Races in Intellect and in Morality [Part I]," *School and Society* 22, no. 568 (November 14, 1925): 628–30.

509. Murdoch, "Study of Differences Found Between Races [Part I]," 631.

510. Murdoch, "Study of Differences Found Between Races [Part I]," 632.

511. Murdoch, "Study of Differences Found Between Races [Part II]," 659–60.

512. Murdoch, "Study of Differences Found Between Races [Part I]," 629.

513. Murdoch, "Study of Differences Found Between Races [Part II]," 661.

514. Murdoch, "Study of Differences Found Between Races [Part II]," 662.
515. Murdoch, "Study of Differences Found Between Races [Part II]," 662.
516. Murdoch, "Study of Differences Found Between Races [Part II]," 663.
517. Murdoch, "Study of Differences Found Between Races [Part II]," 663.
518. Murdoch, "Study of Differences Found Between Races [Part I]," 629.
519. Garth, *Race Psychology*, 141.
520. Carl E. Seashore, *Psychology of Music*, 309.
521. Fridtjof Mjöen, "Die Bedeutung der Tonhöhenunterschiedsempfindlichkeit für die Musikalität und ihr Verhalten bei der Vererbung," *Hereditas* 7, no. 11 (1926): 162, 165, 188.
522. Fridtjof Mjöen, "Die Bedeutung der Tonhöhenunterschiedsempfindlichkeit," 166.
523. Fridtjof Mjöen, "Die Bedeutung der Tonhöhenunterschiedsempfindlichkeit," 170–71.
524. Fridtjof Mjöen, "Die Bedeutung der Tonhöhenunterschiedsempfindlichkeit," 173–80.
525. Jon Mjöen, *Die Vererbung der musikalischen Begabung*, 24–35.
526. Jon Mjöen, *Die Vererbung der musikalischen Begabung*, 24, 36–40.
527. Jon Mjöen, *Die Vererbung der musikalischen Begabung*, 17, 20, 51.
528. See, for example, C. B. S. Hodson, "Eugenics in Norway," *Eugenics Review* 27, no. 1 (April 1935): 43–44. Although the article mentioned studies of race crossing conducted in Norway, it did not indicate that the music studies conducted there focused on race crossing.
529. C. T. Gray and C. W. Bingham, "A Comparison of Certain Phases of Musical Ability of Colored and White Public School Pupils," *Journal of Educational Psychology* 20, no. 7 (October 1929): 501, https://doi.org/10.1037/h0073171
530. C. T. Gray and C. W. Bingham, "Comparison of Certain Phases," 506.
531. C. T. Gray and C. W. Bingham, "Comparison of Certain Phases," 502.
532. Raymond Willis Porter, "A Study of the Musical Talent of Chinese Attending Public Schools in Chicago" (PhD diss., University of Chicago, 1931), 1.
533. Porter, "Study of the Musical Talent," 3–5, 10.
534. Porter, "Study of the Musical Talent," 1–2, 16–17, 89.
535. Porter, "Study of the Musical Talent," 94.
536. Porter, "Study of the Musical Talent," 95.
537. Porter, "Study of the Musical Talent," 95.
538. Porter, "Study of the Musical Talent," 5.
539. Kenneth L. Bean, "The Musical Talent of Southern Negroes as Measured with the Seashore Tests," *Pedagogical Seminary and Journal of Genetic Psychology* 49, no. 1 (1936): 244–45, https://doi.org/10.1080/08856559.1936.10533763
540. Bean, "Musical Talent of Southern," 244.
541. Bean, "Musical Talent of Southern," 245.
542. Bean, "Musical Talent of Southern," 246–47.
543. Bean, "Musical Talent of Southern," 245–46.
544. Bean, "Musical Talent of Southern," 247–48.

545. Bean, "Musical Talent of Southern," 248.
546. Bean, "Musical Talent of Southern," 248.
547. Bean, "Musical Talent of Southern," 248–49.
548. Lester R. Wheeler and Viola D. Wheeler, "The Musical Ability of Mountain Children as Measured by the Seashore Test of Musical Talent," *Pedagogical Seminary and Journal of Genetic Psychology* 43, no. 2 (1933): 352–53, 355, https://doi.org/10.1080/08856559.1933.10532464
549. Lester Wheeler and Viola Wheeler, "Musical Ability of Mountain," 352.
550. Lester Wheeler and Viola Wheeler, "Musical Ability of Mountain," 355.
551. Lester Wheeler and Viola Wheeler, "Musical Ability of Mountain," 353, 372.
552. Lester Wheeler and Viola Wheeler, "Musical Ability of Mountain," 372.
553. Lester Wheeler and Viola Wheeler, "Musical Ability of Mountain," 369.
554. Lester Wheeler and Viola Wheeler, "Musical Ability of Mountain," 369.
555. Lester Wheeler and Viola Wheeler, "Musical Ability of Mountain," 372.
556. Lester Wheeler and Viola Wheeler, "Musical Ability of Mountain," 369.
557. Lester Wheeler and Viola Wheeler, "Musical Ability of Mountain," 372.
558. Lester Wheeler and Viola Wheeler, "Musical Ability of Mountain," 372.
559. Lester Wheeler and Viola Wheeler, "Musical Ability of Mountain," 367.
560. Lester Wheeler and Viola Wheeler, "Musical Ability of Mountain," 367.
561. Lester Wheeler and Viola Wheeler, "Musical Ability of Mountain," 372.
562. Helen Elizabeth Sanderson, "Differences in Musical Ability in Children of Different National and Racial Origin," *Pedagogical Seminary and Journal of Genetic Psychology* 42, no. 1 (1933): 103–5, https://doi.org/10.1080/08856559.1933.10534231
563. Sanderson, "Differences in Musical Ability," 104.
564. Sanderson, "Differences in Musical Ability," 107–8.
565. Sanderson, "Differences in Musical Ability," 110.
566. Sanderson, "Differences in Musical Ability," 117.
567. Sanderson, "Differences in Musical Ability," 117.
568. Richard A. C. Oliver, "The Musical Talent of Natives of East Africa," *British Journal of Psychology* 22, no. 4 (April 1932): 334, 337, https://doi.org/10.1111/j.2044-8295.1932.tb00634.x
569. Oliver, "Musical Talent of Natives," 343.
570. Kwalwasser, "Scientific Testing in Music," 18.
571. Kwalwasser, "Scientific Testing in Music," 18.
572. Kwalwasser, "Scientific Testing in Music," 18.
573. Kwalwasser, "Scientific Testing in Music," 18, 20.
574. Kwalwasser, "Scientific Testing in Music," 20.
575. Kwalwasser, "Scientific Testing in Music," 20.
576. Kwalwasser, "Scientific Testing in Music," 18, 20.
577. Kwalwasser, "Scientific Testing in Music," 22.
578. Jacob Kwalwasser, "From the Realm of Guess into the Realm of Reasonable Certainty," *Music Educators Journal* 24, no. 4 (February 1938): 17, http://www.jstor.org/stable/3385448

579. Rosalind Streep, "A Comparison of White and Negro Children in Rhythm and Consonance," *Journal of Applied Psychology* 15, no. 1 (February 1931): 56, http://dx.doi.org/10.1037/h0070190. This may have been Rosalind Streep Langsam, who became a professor at Hunter College.

580. Streep, "Comparison of White," 59, 66.

581. Streep, "Comparison of White," 66.

582. Dorothy van Alstyne and Emily Osborne, "Rhythmic Responses of Negro and White Children Two to Six: With a Special Focus on Regulated and Free Rhythm Situations," *Monographs of the Society for Research in Child Development* 2, no. 4, serial 11 (1937): 2–3, 14; repr. New York: Kraus Reprint, 1966, https://www.jstor.org/stable/1165409

583. van Alstyne and Osborne, "Rhythmic Responses," 54.

584. van Alstyne and Osborne, "Rhythmic Responses," 54.

585. Paul R. Farnsworth, "An Historical, Critical, and Experimental Study of the Seashore-Kwalwasser Test Battery," *Genetic Psychology Monographs: Child Behavior, Animal Behavior, and Comparative Psychology* 9, no. 5 (May 1931): 363.

586. Carl E. Seashore, *Pioneering in Psychology*, 103.

587. Carl E. Seashore, *Psychology of Music*, 309.

588. Carl E. Seashore, "Musical Inheritance," 355.

589. Guy Johnson, "Study of the Musical Talent of the American Negro," 1.

590. Guy Johnson, "Study of the Musical Talent of the American Negro," ii.

591. Guy Johnson, "Negro and Musical Talent," 439.

592. Guy Johnson, "Musical Talent and the Negro," 81.

593. See, for example, C. T. Gray and C. W. Bingham, "Comparison of Certain Phases," 502; and Streep, "Comparison of White," 53.

594. Garth, *Race Psychology*, 149.

595. See, for example, C. T. Gray and C. W. Bingham, "Comparison of Certain Phases," 502.

596. Streep, "Comparison of White," 53.

597. Guy Johnson, "Musical Talent and the Negro," 96.

598. Garth and Isbell, "Musical Talent of Indians," 83, 87; Garth, *Race Psychology*, 141, 155.

599. Lester Wheeler and Viola Wheeler, "Musical Ability of Mountain," 372.

600. Kwalwasser, "Scientific Testing in Music," 18.

601. See, for example, Garth and Isbell, "Musical Talent of Indians," 83.

602. Lenoir, "Measurement of Racial Differences," 5.

603. Garth, *Race Psychology*, 142.

604. Garth, *Race Psychology*, 147.

605. Guy Johnson, "Study of the Musical Talent of the American Negro," 82.

606. Guy Johnson, "Musical Talent and the Negro," 83; Lenoir, "Measurement of Racial Differences," 8.

607. Guy Johnson, "Negro and Musical Talent," 443. He also mentioned this in his dissertation. See Guy Johnson, "Study of the Musical Talent of the American Negro," 77.

608. Guy Johnson, "Negro and Musical Talent," 443. Nathanson also discussed this variability. See Nathanson, "Musical Ability of the Negro," 189.

609. Garth, *Race Psychology*, 143.

610. James L. Mursell, *The Psychology of Music* (New York: W. W. Norton, 1937; repr., New York: Johnson Reprint, 1970), 340.

611. Mursell, *Psychology of Music*, 340.

612. Mursell, *Psychology of Music*, 340.

613. Mursell, *Psychology of Music*, 340.

614. Mursell, *Psychology of Music*, 341.

615. Mursell, *Psychology of Music*, 341.

616. Mursell, *Psychology of Music*, 341.

617. Mursell, *Psychology of Music*, 341.

618. James L. Mursell, "What about Music Tests?" *Music Educators Journal* 24, no. 2 (October-November 1937): 17, www.jstor.org/stable/3385164

619. Mursell, "What about Music Tests?" 16–17.

620. Mursell, "What about Music Tests?" 17–18.

621. Paul R. Farnsworth, *The Social Psychology of Music* (New York: Dryden, 1958), 189.

622. Paul Farnsworth, *Social Psychology of Music*, 188, 218n35.

623. Paul Farnsworth, *Social Psychology of Music*, 189.

624. Paul Farnsworth, *Social Psychology of Music*, 189.

625. Carl E. Seashore to Davenport, October 29, 1929, MSS.B.D27, box 85, Charles B. Davenport Papers.

626. Carl E. Seashore, *Psychology of Music*, 309.

627. Carl E. Seashore, "Musical Inheritance," 355.

628. Carl E. Seashore to Davenport, October 29, 1929, MSS.B.D27, box 85, Charles B. Davenport Papers.

629. Carl E. Seashore, "Three New Approaches," 192.

630. Carl E. Seashore, *Psychology of Music*, 2.

631. Carl E. Seashore, *Psychology of Music*, 3–4.

632. Carl E. Seashore, *Pioneering in Psychology*, 103.

633. Carl E. Seashore, *Pioneering in Psychology*, 103.

634. Graham Richards, "Reconceptualizing the History," 21–22.

635. Carl E. Seashore, *The Psychology of Musical Talent* (Boston: Silver, Burdett, 1919), 115n1.

636. Carl E. Seashore, *Psychology of Musical Talent*, 121. See also pp. 115, 117, 122, 123. In addition, see Carl E. Seashore, "The Sense of Rhythm as a Musical Talent," *Musical Quarterly* 4, no. 4 (October 1918): 507, 508, http://www.jstor.org/stable/737876; and Carl E. Seashore, *Psychology of Music*, 138.

637. Carl E. Seashore, "Sense of Rhythm," 511, 512; Carl E. Seashore, *Psychology of Music*, 143.

638. Carl E. Seashore, "Sense of Rhythm," 513. See also Carl E. Seashore, *Psychology of Musical Talent*, 122.

639. Carl E. Seashore, *Psychology of Musical Talent*, 116; Carl E. Seashore, *Psychology of Music*, 139.

640. Carl E. Seashore, "Sense of Rhythm," 512; Carl E. Seashore, *Psychology of Musical Talent*, 122; Carl E. Seashore, *Psychology of Music*, 143–44.

641. This quotation is from Carl E. Seashore, *Psychology of Music*, 142–43. It is almost identical to the statements appearing in Carl E. Seashore, "Sense of Rhythm," 511; and Carl E. Seashore, *Psychology of Musical Talent*, 120–21. See also Carl E. Seashore, "Play Impulse," 513.

642. For a brief discussion of the belief that waltzing and waltz music were considered by some to be lewd, see Julia Eklund Koza, "Music and References to Music in *Godey's Lady's Book*, 1830–1877" (PhD diss., University of Minnesota, 1988), 160–66.

643. Carl E. Seashore, *Introduction to Psychology*, 277–78; Carl E. Seashore, *Psychology in Daily Life*, 18–19.

644. Michael Golston, "'Im Anfang war der Rhythmus': Rhythmic Incubations in Discourses of Mind, Body, and Race from 1850–1944," *Stanford Electronic Humanities Review Supplement: Cultural and Technological Incubations of Fascism* 5 (December 17, 1996), https://web.stanford.edu/group/SHR/5-supp/text/golston.html

645. Golston, "'Im Anfang.'"

646. Golston, "'Im Anfang.'"

647. Golston, "'Im Anfang.'"

648. Golston, "'Im Anfang.'"

649. Carl E. Seashore, *Psychology of Music*, 146.

650. Estrelda Y. Alexander, *Black Fire: One Hundred Years of African American Pentecostalism* (Downers Grove, IL: IVP Academic, 2011), 21.

651. Alexander, *Black Fire*, 16–17.

652. Alexander, *Black Fire*, 20–21.

653. Alexander, *Black Fire*, 28–29.

654. Alexander, *Black Fire*, 16, 22.

655. Patricia Shehan Campbell, "Rhythmic Movement and Public School Music Education: Conservative and Progressive Views of the Formative Years," *Journal of Research in Music Education* 39, no. 1 (Spring 1991): 13, www.jstor.org/stable/3344605

656. Carl E. Seashore, *Psychology of Music*, 138; Carl E. Seashore, "Sense of Rhythm," 507; and Carl E. Seashore, *Psychology of Musical Talent*, 115–16.

657. Carl E. Seashore, *Psychology of Music*, 356.

658. Carl E. Seashore, *Psychology of Music*, 148.

659. Carl E. Seashore, *Psychology of Music*, 358.

660. Nathanson, "Musical Ability of the Negro," 186.

661. Nathanson, "Musical Ability of the Negro," 186.

662. Guy Johnson, "Study of the Musical Talent of the American Negro," 53.

663. Guy Johnson, "Study of the Musical Talent of the American Negro," 53.

664. Guy Johnson, "Study of the Musical Talent of the American Negro," 53.

665. Guy Johnson, "Study of the Musical Talent of the American Negro," 53.

666. Guy Johnson, "Negro and Musical Talent," 441.

667. Nathanson, "Musical Ability of the Negro," 188.

668. Davenport and Steggerda, *Race Crossing in Jamaica* (1929), 361.

669. Penelope Nichols-Rothe, "A Short History of the Controversy Surrounding Music Aptitude Testing and the Work of Carl E. Seashore from 1919–1939" (qual. paper, Harvard University, 1987), 25–27.

670. Carl E. Seashore, "The Psychology of Music. XI. Two Types of Attitude toward the Evaluation of Musical Talent," *Music Educators Journal* 24, no. 3 (December 1937): 25, www.jstor.org/stable/3385312

671. Nichols-Rothe, "Short History," 27.

672. Carl E. Seashore, "Musical Inheritance," 355.

673. Black, *War against the Weak*, 85.

674. Mehler, "History of the American Eugenics," 31.

675. Miles stated that the quote was from a resolution drafted by William R. Boyd, Chairman of the Finance Committee of the Iowa State Board of Education, and dated September 10, 1946. See Walter R. Miles, "Carl Emil Seashore, 1866–1949," vol. 29, *Biographical Memoirs* (New York: Columbia University Press for the National Academy of Sciences, 1956), 266, 266n1.

676. Charles W. Mills, *The Racial Contract* (Ithaca, NY: Cornell University Press, 1997), 19.

677. Charles Mills, *Racial Contract*, 19.

678. Charles Mills, *Racial Contract*, 19.

679. Gloria Ladson-Billings, "The Social Funding of Race: The Role of Schooling" (working paper, undated pre-2008). A revised and expanded version of this essay appeared in *Peabody Journal of Education* 93, no. 1 (2018): 90–105, https://doi.org/10.1080/0161956X.2017.1403182

680. "Richard Lynn," Southern Poverty Law Center, accessed August 6, 2018, https://www.splcenter.org/fighting-hate/extremist-files/individual/richard-lynn; Richard Lynn, *Eugenics: A Reassessment* (Westport, CT: Praeger, 2001), ix.

681. Lynn, *Eugenics: A Reassessment*, viii–ix.

682. Lynn, *Eugenics: A Reassessment*, 290.

683. "Richard Lynn," Southern Poverty Law Center. See also "Pioneer Fund," Southern Poverty Law Center.

684. "Ulster University Withdraws Status from Prof Richard Lynn," BBC News, April 14, 2018, https://www.bbc.com/news/uk-northern-ireland-43768132

685. "Richard Lynn," Southern Poverty Law Center.

686. Richard Lynn, *Race Differences in Intelligence: An Evolutionary Analysis* (Augusta, GA: Washington Summit, 2006), title page.

687. "White Nationalist," Southern Poverty Law Center, accessed June 3, 2019, https://www.splcenter.org/fighting-hate/extremist-files/ideology/white-nationalist

688. "National Policy Institute: About," National Policy Institute, 2017, accessed August 30, 2018, https://nationalpolicy.institute/whoarewe

689. "The Groups," *Intelligence Report*, Southern Poverty Law Center, January 29, 2010, https://www.splcenter.org/fighting-hate/intelligence-report/2015/groups. The following site says the statement came from a speech made by William Regnery in 2005: Metapedia, s.v. "National Policy Institute," last modified February 23, 2018, https://en.metapedia.org/wiki/National_Policy_Institute

690. Michael Wines and Stephanie Saul, "White Supremacists Extend Their Reach through Websites," *New York Times*, July 5, 2015, A1, https://www.nytimes.com/2015/07/06/us/white-supremacists-extend-their-reach-through-websites.html?_r=0

691. "Alt-Right Leader: 'Hail Trump!'" CNN, November 22, 2016, YouTube video, 2:10, https://www.youtube.com/watch?v=eF72gg9No_U

692. Laura Vozzella, "White Nationalist Richard Spencer Leads Torch-Bearing Protesters Defending Lee Statue," *Washington Post*, May 14, 2017, https://www.washingtonpost.com/local/virginia-politics/alt-rights-richard-spencer-leads-torch-bearing-protesters-defending-lee-statue/2017/05/14/766aaa56–38ac-11e7–9e48-c4f199710b69_story.html?noredirect=on&utm_term=.e96fda1efde1; Perry Stein, "Richard Spencer Hosted an Event at a Maryland Farm. Halfway Through, Everyone Was Kicked Out," *Washington Post*, November 21, 2017, https://www.washingtonpost.com/local/richard-spencer-hosted-an-event-at-a-maryland-farm-halfway-through-everyone-was-kicked-out/2017/11/21/1cd92dfe-9f33–40c4-b6f5-a271a8874c5d_story.html?utm_term=.27337546bf4f

693. Lynn, *Race Differences*, 55–57, 160.

694. Lynn, *Race Differences*, 55. Lynn quoted from Bernard Lewis, *Race and Slavery in the Middle East: An Historical Inquiry* (New York: Oxford University Press, 1990), 94. Lewis, in turn, quoted Ibn Buṭlān, *Risāla fī Shirā' al-Raqīq*, ed. 'Abd al-Salām Hārūn (Cairo, 1373 [*sic*]/1954), 374.

695. Lynn, *Race Differences*, 55.

696. Lynn, *Race Differences*, 55.

697. Lynn, *Race Differences*, 55.

698. Richard Lynn, R. Graham Wilson, and Adrienne Gault, "Simple Musical Tests as Measures of Spearman's g," *Personality and Individual Differences* 10, no. 1 (1989): 25–28, https://doi-org.ezproxy.library.wisc.edu/10.1016/0191–8869(89)90173–6

699. Lynn, *Race Differences*, 57.

700. Lynn, *Race Differences*, 56.

701. Lynn, *Race Differences*, 57.

702. Lynn, *Race Differences*, 57.

703. Lynn, *Race Differences*, 160.

704. Lynn, *Race Differences*, 160.

Chapter 8

1. Carl E. Seashore, "The Term 'Euthenics,'" *Science*, n.s., 94, no. 2450 (December 12, 1941): 561, https://www.jstor.org/stable/1668443; Carl E. Seashore, "Carl Emil Seashore," vol. 1, *A History of Psychology in Autobiography*, ed. Carl Allanmore Murchison (Worcester, MA: Clark University, 1930), 271; Carl E. Seashore, "Euthenics, a Design for Living," *Educational Forum* 12, no. 2, pt. 1 (January 1948): 150n1.

2. *Oxford English Dictionary Online*, s.v. "euthenics," accessed December 1, 2018, http://www.oed.com/view/Entry/65143

3. *Oxford English*, s.v. "euthenics."
4. *Oxford English*, s.v. "euthenics."
5. Carl E. Seashore, "The Scope and Function of Euthenics," *Mental Hygiene* 33, no. 4 (October 1949): 594–95.
6. Carl E. Seashore, "Scope and Function," 594.
7. Carl E. Seashore, "Scope and Function," 596.
8. Carl E. Seashore, "Scope and Function," 595.
9. Carl E. Seashore, "Carl Emil Seashore," 271. See also Carl E. Seashore, "Term 'Euthenics'" (1941); and Carl E. Seashore, "Euthenics, a Design for Living," 149–55.
10. Carl E. Seashore, "Scope and Function," 594.
11. C. G. Campbell, "Eugenics and Euthenics," *Eugenics* 2, no. 9 (1929): 21.
12. C. G. Campbell, "Eugenics and Euthenics," 21–22.
13. C. G. Campbell, "Eugenics and Euthenics," 22.
14. C. G. Campbell, "Eugenics and Euthenics," 22.
15. Charles Benedict Davenport, "Research in Eugenics," in *Eugenics, Genetics and the Family*, vol. 1, *Scientific Papers of the Second International Congress of Eugenics; Held at American Museum of Natural History, New York, September 22–28, 1921* (Baltimore, MD: Williams & Wilkins, 1923; repr., ed. Charles Rosenberg, New York: Garland Publishing, 1985), 27.
16. Carl E. Seashore, "Term 'Euthenics'" (1941), 562; Carl E. Seashore, "Scope and Function," 594.
17. Carl E. Seashore, "Term 'Euthenics'" (1941), 561.
18. "In Praise of Eugenics," *Eugenics* 2, no. 2 (February 1929): 36.
19. Carl E. Seashore, "Euthenics, a Design for Living," 149.
20. Carl E. Seashore, "Scope and Function," 594.
21. Carl E. Seashore, "Origin of the Term 'Euthenics,'" *Science*, n.s., 95, no. 2470 (May 1, 1942): 455–56, http://www.jstor.org/stable/1668977
22. For the draft manuscript, see the attachment to Carl E. Seashore, Iowa City, IA, to Robert Yerkes, New Haven, CT, May 21, 1947, MS 569, box 43, folder 837, Robert Mearns Yerkes Papers, Manuscripts and Archives, Yale University Library, New Haven, CT. For the published article, see Carl E. Seashore, "Euthenics, a Design for Living," 149–55.
23. M. Yerkes to Carl E. Seashore, Iowa City, IA, May 27, 1947, MS 569, box 43, folder 837, Robert Mearns Yerkes Papers, Manuscripts and Archives, Yale University Library, New Haven, CT.
24. Carl E. Seashore, "Euthenics, a Design for Living," 149, 152. Also Carl E. Seashore, "Education for Democracy and the Junior College," *School and Society* 25, no. 643 (April 23, 1927): 474; a slightly revised version was published in Carl E. Seashore, *Learning and Living in College*, University of Iowa Studies: Series on Aims and Progress of Research, vol. 2, no. 1 (Iowa City: The University, 1927), 88–102; and a condensed version was published under the same title in the *Bulletin of the American Association of University Professors* 13, no. 6 (October 1927): 399–404.
25. Carl E. Seashore, "Scope and Function," 598.

26. C. G. Campbell, "Eugenics and Euthenics," 25.

27. C. G. Campbell, "Eugenics and Euthenics," 25.

28. C. G. Campbell, "Eugenics and Euthenics," 25.

29. For more comprehensive discussions of the history of the Station, see Hamilton Cravens, *Before Head Start: The Iowa Station and America's Children* (Chapel Hill: University of North Carolina Press, 1993); Alice Boardman Smuts, *Science in the Service of Children, 1893–1935* (New Haven, CT: Yale University Press, 2006), 117–36; Julia Grant, *Raising Baby by the Book: The Education of American Mothers* (New Haven, CT: Yale University Press, 1998), 115–20; and Carl E. Seashore, *Pioneering in Psychology*, University of Iowa Studies: Series on Aims and Progress of Research, no. 70 (Iowa City: University of Iowa, 1942), 179–89, https://babel.hathitrust.org/cgi/pt?id=mdp.39015020052349&view=1up&seq=1

30. Julia Grant, *Raising Baby*, 116.

31. Cravens, *Before Head Start*, 11.

32. Cravens, *Before Head Start*, 11.

33. Henry L. Minton, "The Iowa Child Welfare Research Station and the 1940 Debate on Intelligence: Carrying on the Legacy of a Concerned Mother," *Journal of the History of the Behavioral Sciences* 20, no. 2 (April 1984): 163.

34. For a discussion of children's living conditions, the child welfare movement, and the US Children's Bureau, see Kriste Lindenmeyer, *"A Right to Childhood": The U.S. Children's Bureau and Child Welfare, 1912–46* (Urbana: University of Illinois Press, 1997). Lindenmeyer discusses Theodore Roosevelt on p. 16.

35. Carl E. Seashore, "Carl Emil Seashore," 271.

36. Carl E. Seashore, "Carl Emil Seashore," 270–71; Walter R. Miles, "Carl Emil Seashore, 1866–1949," vol. 29, *Biographical Memoirs* (New York: Columbia University Press for the National Academy of Sciences, 1956), 283–85.

37. See, for example, Francis P. Robinson, "Carl E. Seashore," *Educational Forum* 15, no. 1, pt. 2 (November 1950): 128t.

38. George D. Stoddard, "Carl Emil Seashore: 1866–1949," *American Journal of Psychology* 63, no. 3 (July 1950): 460, www.jstor.org/stable/1418021

39. Howard H. Kendler, "The Iowa Tradition," in *Psychology at Iowa: Centennial Essays*, ed. Joan H. Cantor (Hillsdale, NJ: Lawrence Erlbaum, 1991), 3.

40. Carl E. Seashore, *A Child Welfare Research Station: Plans and Possibilities of a Research Station for the Conservation and Development of the Normal Child*, Series on Aims and Progress of Research, n.s., vol. 107 (Iowa City, Iowa: The University, 1916), 2, https://catalog.hathitrust.org/Record/010551244

41. Carl E. Seashore, "Carl Emil Seashore," 271.

42. See, for example, Carl E. Seashore, *A Preview to College and Life*, University of Iowa Studies: Series on Aims and Progress of Research, no. 55 (Iowa City: University of Iowa, 1938), 11, 30; Carl E. Seashore, "An Open Letter: Addressed to Women in Graduate Schools," *Journal of Higher Education* 13, no. 5 (May 1942): 238, https://doi.org/10.2307/1974933; Carl E. Seashore, *Child Welfare Research Station*; and Carl E. Seashore, "Education for Democracy," 469.

43. *Administration and Scope of the Iowa Child Welfare Research Station*, rev. ed.,

University of Iowa Studies: Aims and Progress of Research, vol. 1, no. 14, n.s., no. 78 (Iowa City: The University, June 1, 1924), 5.

44. C. E. Seashore, Iowa City, IA, to President W. A. Jessup, Iowa City, IA, January 9, 1923, p. 1, RG 05.01.09, box 114, folder 53, Walter A. Jessup Papers, Special Collections and University Archives, University of Iowa Libraries, Iowa City, IA.

45. C. E. Seashore to Jessup, January 9, 1923, p. 1, RG 05.01.09, box 114, folder 53, Walter A. Jessup Papers.

46. Carl E. Seashore, *Child Welfare Research Station.*

47. Carl E. Seashore, *Child Welfare Research Station*, 3–5.

48. Carl E. Seashore, *Child Welfare Research Station*, 3.

49. Carl E. Seashore, *Child Welfare Research Station*, 3.

50. Carl E. Seashore, *Child Welfare Research Station*, 4.

51. Carl E. Seashore, *Child Welfare Research Station*, 4.

52. Carl E. Seashore, *Child Welfare Research Station*, 4.

53. Carl E. Seashore, *Child Welfare Research Station*, 4–5.

54. Carl E. Seashore, *Child Welfare Research Station*, 4.

55. Carl E. Seashore, *Child Welfare Research Station*, 6.

56. Carl E. Seashore, *Child Welfare Research Station*, 6.

57. Carl E. Seashore, *Child Welfare Research Station*, 7.

58. Carl E. Seashore, *Child Welfare Research Station*, 8.

59. Carl E. Seashore, *Child Welfare Research Station*, 8.

60. Carl E. Seashore, *Child Welfare Research Station*, 9.

61. Carl E. Seashore, *Child Welfare Research Station*, 9.

62. Carl E. Seashore, *Child Welfare Research Station*, 9–10.

63. Carl E. Seashore, *Child Welfare Research Station*, 10.

64. Carl E. Seashore, *Child Welfare Research Station*, 10–11.

65. Carl E. Seashore, *Child Welfare Research Station*, 11.

66. Carl E. Seashore, *Child Welfare Research Station*, 11–12.

67. Carl E. Seashore, *Child Welfare Research Station*, 12.

68. Carl E. Seashore, *Child Welfare Research Station*, 12.

69. Carl E. Seashore, *Child Welfare Research Station*, 12.

70. Carl E. Seashore, *Child Welfare Research Station*, 13.

71. Carl E. Seashore, *Child Welfare Research Station*, 13.

72. Carl E. Seashore, *Child Welfare Research Station*, 14.

73. Carl E. Seashore, *Child Welfare Research Station*, 14.

74. Carl E. Seashore, *Child Welfare Research Station*, 14.

75. Carl E. Seashore, *Child Welfare Research Station*, 15–16.

76. Carl E. Seashore, *Child Welfare Research Station*, 16.

77. Carl E. Seashore, *Child Welfare Research Station*, 18.

78. See, for example, Rima D. Apple, "Constructing Mothers: Scientific Motherhood in the Nineteenth and Twentieth Centuries," *Social History of Medicine* 8, no. 2 (August 1995): 161–78.

79. Michel Foucault, *Discipline and Punish: The Birth of the Prison*, trans. Alan Sheridan (New York: Vintage Books, 1979), 135–38. The quote occurs on p. 138.

80. Michel Foucault, *Power/Knowledge: Selected Interviews and Other Writings, 1972–1977*, ed. Colin Gordon, trans. Colin Gordon et al. (New York: Pantheon, 1980), 39.

81. Foucault, *Discipline and Punish*, 194.

82. Cravens, *Before Head Start*, 35.

83. Bird T. Baldwin, "The Scientific Prediction of the Physical Growth of Children," in *Eugenics in Race and State*, vol. 2, *Scientific Papers of the Second International Congress of Eugenics; Held at American Museum of Natural History, New York, September 22–28, 1921* (Baltimore, MD: Williams & Wilkins, 1923; repr., ed. Charles Rosenberg, New York: Garland Publishing, 1985), 25–29.

84. "Tenth Annual Business Meeting of the Eugenics Research Association, Cold Spring Harbor, June 10, 1922," *Eugenical News* 7, no. 7 (July 1922): 91.

85. "Periodical Literature: *The Popular Science Monthly*, December, 1914. Vol. xxxv, No. 6," review of "The Normal Child: Its Physical Growth and Mental Development," by Bird T. Baldwin, *Eugenics Review* 7, no. 1 (April 1915): 82, https://books.google.com/books?id=xloeAQAAIAAJ&pg=PA82&lpg=PA82&dq=bird++baldwin+eugenics&source=bl&ots=2auUAoCp5p&sig=Rl-ngr7d4JFK0o7__LjrE4V7dj0&hl=en&sa=X&ei=YRw4VeeIFov6oQSltoDYAw&ved=0CCIQ6AEwAQ#v=onepage&q=bird%20%20baldwin%20eugenics&f=false

86. Bird T. Baldwin and Lorle I. Stecher, "Additional Data from Consecutive Stanford-Binet Tests," *Journal of Educational Psychology* 13, no. 9 (December 1922): 556, https://babel.hathitrust.org/cgi/pt?id=mdp.39015075050123&view=1up&seq=586. The studies mentioned in note number 1 came out of the station.

87. Baldwin and Stecher, "Additional Data," 556–60.

88. Cravens, *Before Head Start*, 106, 156.

89. "Professorships at the University of Iowa," *School and Society* 14, no. 340 (July 2, 1921): 7, https://books.google.com/books?id=fLU0AQAAMAAJ&pg=PA7&lpg=PA7&dq=%22Department+of+Eugenics%22++Iowa&source=bl&ots=Ewp9obnK3e&sig=V0cHj4P1S2imsXtVOm_euGfI0H8&hl=en&sa=X&ei=wqg6VY3fDYKooQTKm4GYDg&ved=0CC4Q6AEwBA#v=onepage&q=%22Department%20of%20Eugenics%22%20%20Iowa&f=false

90. Charles B. Davenport to Carl E. Seashore, Iowa City, IA, January 5, 1920, MSS.B.D27, box 85, Charles B. Davenport Papers, American Philosophical Society Archives, Philadelphia, PA.

91. Anne E. Jackson, Iowa City, IA, to Miss Marcella Hotz, Iowa City, IA, March 11, 1920, RG 05.01.09, box 61, folder 53, Walter A. Jessup Papers, Special Collections and University Archives, University of Iowa Libraries, Iowa City, IA.

92. Cravens, *Before Head Start*, 37.

93. *Administration and Scope of the Iowa Child Welfare Research Station*, rev. ed., University of Iowa Studies: Aims and Progress of Research, vol. 1, no. 10 (Iowa City: The University, January 1921), 11; *Administration and Scope* (June 1, 1924), 12–13.

94. *Administration and Scope* (January 1921), 12.

95. *Administration and Scope* (June 1, 1924), 2; *Administration and Scope* (January 1921), 2.

96. *Administration and Scope* (January 1921), 11.

97. *Administration and Scope* (January 1921), 11; *Administration and Scope* (June 1, 1924), 12.

98. *Administration and Scope* (June 1, 1924), 12.

99. B. T. Baldwin and P. W. Whiting, Memorandum to Dean [Carl E.] Seashore, "The Dog as Material for Genetic Investigations of Psychical and Physical Traits," October 3, 1922, p. 1, attachment to Dean [Carl E. Seashore], Iowa City, IA, to Dr. J. C. Merriam, Washington, DC, October 7, 1922, RG 05.01.09, box 114, folder 53, Walter A. Jessup Papers, Special Collections and University Archives, University of Iowa Libraries, Iowa City, IA.

100. Dean [Carl E. Seashore] to Merriam, October 7, 1922 (with attachment), RG 05.01.09, box 114, folder 53, Walter A. Jessup Papers.

101. Samuel T. Orton, Iowa City, IA, to President W. A. Jessup, Iowa City, IA, November 1, 1924, p. 1, RG 05.01.09, box 145, folder 49, Walter A. Jessup Papers, Special Collections and University Archives, University of Iowa Libraries, Iowa City, IA.

102. Orton to Jessup, November 1, 1924, pp. 1–2, RG 05.01.09, box 145, folder 49, Walter A. Jessup Papers.

103. *Administration and Scope* (June 1, 1924), 12–13.

104. *Administration and Scope* (June 1, 1924), 13.

105. *Administration and Scope* (June 1, 1924), 12.

106. *Administration and Scope* (January 1921), 5.

107. Carl E. Seashore, *Pioneering in Psychology*, 179.

108. Carl E. Seashore, *Pioneering in Psychology*, 186.

109. Carl E. Seashore, Iowa City, IA, to Charles B. Davenport, Cold Spring Harbor, NY, December 24, 1919, MSS.B.D27, box 85, Charles B. Davenport Papers, American Philosophical Society Archives, Philadelphia, PA.

110. Davenport to Carl E. Seashore, January 5, 1920, MSS.B.D27, box 85, Charles B. Davenport Papers.

111. Davenport to Carl E. Seashore, January 5, 1920, p. 2, MSS.B.D27, box 85, Charles B. Davenport Papers.

112. Davenport to Carl E. Seashore, January 5, 1920, p. 2, MSS.B.D27, box 85, Charles B. Davenport Papers.

113. Carl E. Seashore, "Euthenics, a Design for Living," 149. See also a reference to the good life on p. 154.

114. Carl E. Seashore, "Euthenics, a Design for Living," 149.

115. Carl E. Seashore, "Euthenics, a Design for Living," 149, 150.

116. Carl E. Seashore, "Euthenics, a Design for Living," 150.

117. Carl E. Seashore, "Euthenics, a Design for Living," 149, 150–54. More support for teaching euthenics is found in Carl E. Seashore, "Education for Democracy," 474.

118. Carl E. Seashore, "Euthenics, a Design for Living," 149.

119. Carl E. Seashore, "Euthenics, a Design for Living," 150.

120. Carl E. Seashore, "Euthenics, a Design for Living," 150–51.

121. Carl E. Seashore, "Euthenics, a Design for Living," 151.

122. Carl E. Seashore, "Euthenics, a Design for Living," 152.

123. Carl E. Seashore, "Euthenics, a Design for Living," 152.

124. Carl E. Seashore, "The Sunny Side of Graduate Work for the Duration," typed manuscript accompanying Carl E. Seashore to Virgil M. Hancher, March 26, 1943, p. 8, RG 05.01.11, box 55, folder 52, Virgil M. Hancher Papers, Special Collections and University Archives, University of Iowa Libraries, Iowa City, IA. This reference did not appear, however, in Carl E. Seashore, "The Sunny Side of Graduate Work," *Daily Iowan*, April 11, 1943, 2, http://dailyiowan.lib.uiowa.edu/DI/1943/di1943-04-11.pdf; Carl E. Seashore, "The Sunny Side of Graduate Work for the Duration," *Journal of Higher Education* 14, no. 6 (June 1943): 289–92, https://www.jstor.org/stable/1975100; or Carl E. Seashore, "The Sunny Side of Graduate Work for the Duration," in *Wartime Approaches to Liberal Education: Nine Editorials from* The Daily Iowan ([Iowa City: University of Iowa Publications, 1944?]), 29–32.

125. Smuts, *Science in the Service*, 132. See also, for example, Minton, "Iowa Child Welfare Research," 164.

126. Minton, "Iowa Child Welfare Research," 170.

127. Minton, "Iowa Child Welfare Research," 164; Smuts, *Science in the Service*, 130.

128. Daniel J. Kevles, *In the Name of Eugenics: Genetics and the Uses of Human Heredity* (Berkeley: University of California Press, 1986, 142.

Chapter 9

1. Michel Foucault, *The History of Sexuality*, vol. 1, *An Introduction*, trans. Robert Hurley (New York: Vintage Books, 1990), 27.

2. Michele Norris, *The Grace of Silence: A Memoir* (New York: Pantheon Books, 2010), especially 57–60, 70–72, 97–101.

3. Norris, *Grace of Silence*, 60.

4. Norris, *Grace of Silence*, 168, and caption to photo number 5 in insert between pp. 96 and 97.

5. Norris, *Grace of Silence*, 168.

6. Norris, *Grace of Silence*, 166–67.

7. Norris, *Grace of Silence*, 168.

8. Norris, *Grace of Silence*, 168.

9. For an in-depth discussion of the concept of the full social funding of race, see Gloria Ladson-Billings, "The Social Funding of Race: The Role of Schooling" (working paper, undated pre-2008). A revised and expanded version of this essay appeared in *Peabody Journal of Education* 93, no. 1 (2018): 90–105, https://doi.org/10.1080/0161956X.2017.1403182

10. Foucault, *History of Sexuality*, 27.

11. José Medina, "The Meanings of Silence: Wittgensteinian Contextualism and Polyphony," *Inquiry* 47, no. 6 (2004): 563, http://dx.doi.org/10.1080/00201740410004304

12. Medina, "Meanings of Silence," 566.

13. Foucault, *History of Sexuality*, 102.

14. Eugenicist Herbert Spencer Jennings, for example, severed ties with the Eugenics Society. See Elazar Barkan, "Reevaluating Progressive Eugenics: Herbert Spencer Jennings and the 1924 Immigration Legislation," *Journal of the History of Biology* 24, no. 1 (Spring 1991): 105, www.jstor.org/stable/4331159

15. Michael Omi and Howard Winant, "On the Theoretical Status of the Concept of Race," in *Race, Identity, and Representation in Education*, ed. Cameron McCarthy and Warren Crichlow (New York: Routledge, 1993), 7.

16. See Ladson-Billings, "Social Funding," for more discussion of the concept of the full social funding of race.

17. Walter R. Miles, "Carl Emil Seashore, 1866–1949," vol. 29, *Biographical Memoirs* (New York: Columbia University Press for the National Academy of Sciences, 1956), 310.

18. Adria R. Hoffman, "Competing Narratives: Musical Aptitude, Race, and Equity," in *Palgrave Handbook of Race and the Arts in Education*, eds. Amelia M. Kraehe, Rubén Gaztambide-Fernández, and B. Stephen Carpenter II (Cham, Switzerland: Palgrave, 2018), 103–17, https://link.springer.com/book/10.1007%2F978-3-319-65256-6

19. Alexander W. Cowan, "Music Psychology and the American Eugenics Movement in the Early Twentieth Century" (MMus thesis, King's College, London, 2016); Johanna Devaney, "Eugenics and Musical Talent: Exploring Carl Seashore's Work on Talent Testing and Performance," *American Music Review* 48, no. 2 (Spring, 2019): 1–6, http://www.brooklyn.edu/web/aca_centers_hitchcock/AMR_48-2_Devaney.pdf

20. Tracey Hunter-Doniger, "The Eugenics Movement and Its Impact on Art Education in the United States," *Arts Education Policy Review* 118, no. 2 (2017): 83–92, https://doi.org/10.1080/10632913.2015.1051256; Bethsaida Nieves, "Making of Race: Movements in the Colonialization and Production of Difference in Puerto Rico's Education at the Turn of the Twentieth Century" (PhD diss., University of Wisconsin–Madison, 2019); Peter Woods, "Operationalizing Aesthetics within the Eugenics Movement: Cautionary Implications for Aesthetic Education" (paper presentation, Annual Meeting of the American Educational Research Association, Toronto, Canada, April 8, 2019). Singleton is a doctoral candidate at the University of Georgia.

21. For more discussion of sounds and silences in music education, see Julia Eklund Koza, "In Sounds and Silences: Acknowledging Political Engagement," *Philosophy of Music Education Review* 15, no. 2 (Fall 2007): 168–76.

22. Koza, "In Sounds and Silences," 168.

23. Koza, "In Sounds and Silences," 168.

24. David G. Myers, *Psychology: Eighth Edition in Modules*, 8th ed. (New York: Worth, 2006).

25. Myers, *Psychology: Eighth Edition*, inside front and back covers.

26. Myers, *Psychology: Eighth Edition*, 443. The quote from Terman appeared in Lewis Madison Terman, *The Measurement of Intelligence: An Explanation of and a Complete Guide for the Use of the Stanford Revision and Extension of the Binet-Simon*

Intelligence Scale (Cambridge, MA: Riverside, 1916), 7, https://archive.org/details/measurementofint008006mbp/page/n9

27. Myers, *Psychology: Eighth Edition*, 444.

28. Myers, *Psychology: Eighth Edition*, 444.

29. David G. Myers and C. Nathan DeWall, *Myers' Psychology for the AP Course*, 3rd ed. (New York: Bedford, Freeman & Worth, 2018), inside front cover.

30. Myers and DeWall, *Myers' Psychology*, 634.

31. See Myers, *Psychology: Eighth Edition*, 458–59, for some references to these individuals; also pp. R-48, R-55, and R-67. For references to Lynn in the 2018 textbook, see Myers and DeWall, *Myers' Psychology*, pp. 636, 655, and R-50; to Herrnstein, see pp. 285 and R-36; and to Rushton, pp. 316 and R-70. Charles Murray is not mentioned in the 2018 textbook.

32. David Blight, "Historian Says '12 Years' Is a Story the Nation Must Remember," interview by Terry Gross, *Fresh Air*, NPR, October 24, 2013, audio, 25:06, https://www.npr.org/templates/transcript/transcript.php?storyId=240491318

33. Blight, "Historian Says."

34. Blight, "Historian Says."

35. Norris, *Grace of Silence*, xiv.

36. Norris, *Grace of Silence*, xiii, xii.

37. Norris, *Grace of Silence*, 174.

38. Julia Eklund Koza, "Someday They Will Dance," *Women and Music: A Journal of Gender and Culture* 16 (2012): 110–11.

39. Carl E. Seashore, *The Junior College Movement* (New York: Henry Holt, 1940), 53, https://babel.hathitrust.org/cgi/pt?id=mdp.39015020699834;view=1up;seq=7

40. Virgil M. Hancher to Carl E. Seashore, August 3, 1944, RG 05.01.11, box 103, folder 54, Virgil M. Hancher Papers, Special Collections and University Archives, University of Iowa Libraries, Iowa City, IA.

Chapter 10

1. Barry Alan Mehler, "A History of the American Eugenics Society, 1921–1940" (PhD diss., University of Illinois at Urbana-Champaign, 1988), 69, http://search.proquest.com.ezproxy.library.wisc.edu/docview/303689028?accountid=465

2. Graham Richards, "Reconceptualizing the History of Race Psychology: Thomas Russell Garth (1872–1939) and How He Changed His Mind," *Journal of the History of the Behavioral Sciences* 34, no. 1 (Winter 1998): 23, https://doi.org/10.1002/(SICI)1520-6696(199824)34:1<15::AID-JHBS2>3.0.CO;2-I. For an example of Garth's early support of eugenics, see Thomas Russell Garth, "Race and Psychology," *Scientific Monthly* 23, no. 3 (September 1926): 243, 245, https://www.jstor.org/stable/7525

3. Edwin Black, *War against the Weak: Eugenics and America's Campaign to Create a Master Race* (New York: Four Walls Eight Windows, 2003), 85.

4. Daniel J. Kevles, *In the Name of Eugenics: Genetics and the Uses of Human Heredity* (Berkeley: University of California Press, 1986, 119–20, 122, 134–35; Philippa Levine and Alison Bashford, "Eugenics and the Modern World," in *The Oxford Handbook of the History of Eugenics*, ed. Alison Bashford and Philippa Levine (Oxford: Oxford University Press, 2010), 19.

5. Carlos X. Rodriguez, "Culture, Society and Musicality: Beyond Seashore's Model of the Musical Mind," in *Multidisciplinary Perspectives on Musicality: Essays from the Seashore Symposium*, ed. Kate Gfeller et al. (Iowa City: University of Iowa School of Music, 2006), 139.

6. Jaap Kunst, *Ethno-Musicology: A Study of Its Nature, Its Problems, Methods and Representative Personalities to Which Is Added a Bibliography*, 2nd ed. (Hague, Netherlands: Martinus Nijhoff, 1955), 9.

7. Kunst, *Ethno-Musicology*, 22–23.

8. See, for example, Kunst, *Ethno-Musicology*, 10–19. Also Jaap Kunst, *De Inheemse muziek in Westelijk Nieuw-Guinea*, Koninklijke Vereeniging Indisch Instituut, Amsterdam, Mededeling no. 43, Afdeling Culturele en Physische Anthropologie no. 38 (Amsterdam: Indisch Instituut, 1950).

9. bell hooks [Gloria Watkins], *Black Looks: Race and Representation* (Boston: South End Press, 1992), 21, 62.

10. Charles W. Mills, *The Racial Contract* (Ithaca, NY: Cornell University Press, 1997), 11.

11. See, for example, Philippa Levine and Alison Bashford, "Eugenics and the Modern World," 3–4, 8–10.

12. Nikolas Rose, *The Politics of Life Itself: Biomedicine, Power, and Subjectivity in the Twenty-First Century* (Princeton, NJ: Princeton University Press, 2007), 54.

13. Nikolas Rose, *Politics of Life Itself*, 51.

14. Nikolas Rose, *Politics of Life Itself*, 73.

15. Nikolas Rose, *Politics of Life Itself*, 55.

16. Nikolas Rose, *Politics of Life Itself*, 58.

17. Nikolas Rose, *Politics of Life Itself*, 54.

18. Nikolas Rose, *Politics of Life Itself*, 57.

19. Nikolas Rose, *Politics of Life Itself*, 56, 58, 62. For example, he includes race on pp. 56 and 62 but not on p. 58.

20. Nikolas Rose, *Politics of Life Itself*, 75, 55, 69.

21. Nikolas Rose, *Politics of Life Itself*, 58, 62.

22. Nikolas Rose, *Politics of Life Itself*, 55.

23. Nikolas Rose, *Politics of Life Itself*, 62.

24. Nikolas Rose, *Politics of Life Itself*, 62.

25. Nikolas Rose, *Politics of Life Itself*, 64.

26. Nikolas Rose, *Politics of Life Itself*, 63.

27. Nikolas Rose, *Politics of Life Itself*, 59.

28. Nikolas Rose, *Politics of Life Itself*, 60.

29. Nikolas Rose, *Politics of Life Itself*, 64. On p. 58 he is more specific, stating that the "four terms that delineated eugenics" do not characterize molecular biopolitics.

30. Nikolas Rose, *Politics of Life Itself*, 69.

31. Nikolas Rose, *Politics of Life Itself*, 63.

32. Nikolas Rose, *Politics of Life Itself*, 64.

33. Nikolas Rose, "Biopolitics in the Twenty First Century: Notes for a Research Agenda," *Distinktion: Scandinavian Journal of Social Theory* 2, no. 3 (2001): 26; Nikolas Rose, *Politics of Life Itself*, 62.

34. Nikolas Rose, *Politics of Life Itself*, 62.

35. Nikolas Rose, *Politics of Life Itself*, 58.

36. Nikolas Rose, *Politics of Life Itself*, 73.

37. Nikolas Rose, *Politics of Life Itself*, 69.

38. Nikolas Rose, *Politics of Life Itself*, 64.

39. Nikolas Rose, *Politics of Life Itself*, 63.

40. Nikolas Rose, *Politics of Life Itself*, 70.

41. Nikolas Rose, *Politics of Life Itself*, 75.

42. Nikolas Rose, *Politics of Life Itself*, 70.

43. Nikolas Rose, *Politics of Life Itself*, 66.

44. Nikolas Rose, *Politics of Life Itself*, 69.

45. Nikolas Rose, *Politics of Life Itself*, 51.

46. Nikolas Rose, *Politics of Life Itself*, 70.

47. Nikolas Rose, *Politics of Life Itself*, 70, 58, 64.

48. Carl E. Seashore, "Individual and Racial Inheritance of Musical Traits," in *Eugenics, Genetics and the Family*, vol. 1, *Scientific Papers of the Second International Congress of Eugenics; Held at American Museum of Natural History, New York, September 22–28, 1921* (Baltimore, MD: Williams & Wilkins, 1923; repr., ed. Charles Rosenberg, New York: Garland Publishing, 1985), 231.

49. Carl E. Seashore, *Psychology in Daily Life* (New York: D. Appleton, 1914), 121.

50. "Eugenics," 1921, Cold Spring Harbor, E.06 Eug-2, Exhibits Book-Second Int. Ex. of Eugenics, p. 15, titled "'Copy of Certificate Awarded for Meritorious Exhibits,' at the Second International Congress of Eugenics," image 543, in the "Image Archive on the American Eugenics Movement," DNA Learning Center, Cold Spring Harbor Laboratory, accessed September 23, 2018, www.eugenicsarchive.org/eugenics/view_image.pl?id=543

51. Nikolas Rose, *Politics of Life Itself*, 58–59.

52. Nikolas Rose, *Politics of Life Itself*, 59.

53. For a discussion of Bauman and Agamben, see Nikolas Rose, *Politics of Life Itself*, 56–58.

54. Nikolas Rose, *Politics of Life Itself*, 55.

55. Steven Singer, "Standardized Testing Creates Captive Markets," *Gadfly on the Wall* (blog), April 8, 2017, https://gadflyonthewallblog.com/2017/04/08/standardized-testing-creates-captive-markets/

56. Valerie Strauss, "Five Reasons Standardized Testing Isn't Likely to Let Up," *Washington Post*, March 11, 2015, https://www.washingtonpost.com/news/answer-sheet/wp/2015/03/11/five-reasons-standardized-testing-isnt-likely-to-let-up/?noredirect=on&utm_term=.c240c6ce5176. The *Post* did not report the source of these data.

57. *Music Education Catalog: Music Education for Life; Early Childhood through College* (Chicago: GIA Publications, 2018), 375.

58. *Music Education Catalog*, 375.

59. Edwin E. Gordon, "Musical Aptitude Profile (Grades 5–12)," GIA Publications, Inc., accessed January 11, 2019, https://www.giamusic.com/products/P-musicaptitudeprofile.cfm

60. One recent study supporting gifted education is Carolyn M. Callahan et al., "What Works in Gifted Education: Documenting the Effects of an Integrated Curricular/Instructional Model for Gifted Students," *American Educational Research Journal* 52, no. 1 (February 2015): 137–67, https://www.jstor.org/stable/24546724

61. "WCATY Mission," Board of Regents of the University of Wisconsin System, accessed December 12, 2018, https://wcaty.wisc.edu/mission/

62. "WCATY Eligibility," Board of Regents of the University of Wisconsin System, accessed December 18, 2018, https://wcaty.wisc.edu/eligibility/

63. Kevles, *In the Name of Eugenics*, 141–42.

64. "Lewin Center Founders," Lewin Center, accessed January 13, 2019, http://www.lewincenter.org/founders.html (site redesigned; see Wayback Machine).

65. *Organized Eugenics* (New Haven, CT: American Eugenics Society, January 1931), 1, Connecticut State Library Digital Collection, https://cdm15019.contentdm.oclc.org/digital/collection/p4005coll11/id/587

66. Nikolas Rose, *Politics of Life Itself*, 57.

67. Charles White, *An Account of the Regular Gradation in Man, and in Different Animals and Vegetables; and from the Former to the Latter* (London: C. Dilly, 1799), 42, https://archive.org/details/b24924507

68. Edwin E. Gordon, *Learning Sequences in Music: Skill, Content, and Patterns; A Music Learning Theory* (Chicago: GIA, 1993), 3, 2; Edwin E. Gordon, *Learning Sequences in Music: Skill, Content, and Patterns; A Music Learning Theory, Study Guide*, G-2345SG (Chicago, IL: GIA Publications, 1997), 25.

69. Gordon, *Learning Sequences in Music: Skill, Content, and Patterns; A Music Learning Theory*, 2, 3; Gordon, *Learning Sequences in Music: Skill, Content, and Patterns; A Music Learning Theory, Study Guide*, 26.

70. Gordon, *Learning Sequences in Music: Skill, Content, and Patterns; A Music Learning Theory*, 2; Gordon, *Learning Sequences in Music: Skill, Content, and Patterns; A Music Learning Theory, Study Guide*, 25.

71. Gordon, *Learning Sequences in Music: Skill, Content, and Patterns; A Music Learning Theory*, 2; Gordon, *Learning Sequences in Music: Skill, Content, and Patterns; A Music Learning Theory, Study Guide*, 25.

72. Gordon, *Learning Sequences in Music: Skill, Content, and Patterns; A Music Learning Theory, Study Guide*, 26.

73. Gordon, *Learning Sequences in Music: Skill, Content, and Patterns; A Music Learning Theory*, 4–7; Gordon, *Learning Sequences in Music: Skill, Content, and Patterns; A Music Learning Theory, Study Guide*, 25–26.

74. Gordon, *Learning Sequences in Music: Skill, Content, and Patterns; A Music Learning Theory*, 1.

75. Gordon, *Learning Sequences in Music: Skill, Content, and Patterns; A Music Learning Theory*, 1.

76. Gordon, *Learning Sequences in Music: Skill, Content, and Patterns; A Music Learning Theory*, 1.

77. See Catherine Mills, "Biopolitics, Liberal Eugenics, and Nihilism," in *Giorgio Agamben: Sovereignty and Life*, eds. Matthew Calarco and Steven DeCaroli (Stanford, CA: Stanford University, 2007), especially pp. 181–85, for a discussion of normal as conceptualized by Foucault, Agamben, and Canguilhem.

78. Howard Gardner and Thomas Hatch, "Multiple Intelligences Go to School: Educational Implications of the Theory of Multiple Intelligences," *Educational Researcher* 18, no. 8 (November 1989): 5. For further discussion of the debate, see Leila Zenderland, *Measuring Minds: Henry Herbert Goddard and the Origins of American Intelligence Testing* (Cambridge, UK: Cambridge University Press, 1998), 247–48. See also Carl E. Seashore, "Communications and Discussions: Mentality Tests," *Journal of Educational Psychology* 7, no. 3 (March 1916): 163–66; Carl E. Seashore, ed. and moderator, "Communications and Discussions: Mentality Tests, a Symposium," *Journal of Educational Psychology* 7, no. 4 (April 1916): 229–40; and Carl E. Seashore, ed. and moderator, "Communications and Discussions: Mentality Tests, a Symposium," *Journal of Educational Psychology* 7, no. 5 (May 1916): 278–93, which exemplify the early debate.

79. Gardner and Hatch, "Multiple Intelligences," 5.

80. Gardner and Hatch, "Multiple Intelligences," 5.

81. Gardner and Hatch, "Multiple Intelligences," 6.

82. Adam G. Harry, "America's Got Talent? Interrogating Students' Constructions of Musical Ability" (PhD diss., University of Wisconsin–Madison, 2018).

83. Harry, "America's Got Talent?" iv. See also pp. 73–77, 157.

84. Shinichi Suzuki, *Ability Development from Age Zero*, trans. Mary Louise Nagata (Athens, OH: Ability Development Associates, 1981), 94.

85. Suzuki, *Ability Development*, 94.

86. Ellen Winner, "The Miseducation of Our Gifted Children," Davidson Institute, 1996, http://www.davidsongifted.org/Search-Database/entry/A10316

87. Winner, "Miseducation of Our Gifted."

88. Chester E. Finn and Brandon L. Wright, *Failing Our Brightest Kids: The Global Challenge of Educating High-Ability Students* (Cambridge, MA: Harvard Education Press, 2015), 1, 3, 10.

89. Chester Finn and Brandon Wright, *Failing Our Brightest*, 4.

90. Chester Finn and Brandon Wright, *Failing Our Brightest*, 1, 9.

91. Chester Finn and Brandon Wright, *Failing Our Brightest*, 6.

92. Callahan et al., "What Works," 137–67.

93. Callahan et al., "What Works," 138–43.

94. Nikolas Rose, *Politics of Life Itself*, 63.

95. Nikolas Rose, *Politics of Life Itself*, 63.

96. *A Nation at Risk: The Imperative for Educational Reform; A Report to the Nation and the Secretary of Education, United States Department of Education* (Washington, DC: National Commission on Excellence in Education, April 1983),

https://www.edreform.com/wp-content/uploads/2013/02/A_Nation_At_Risk_1983.pdf

97. Scott A. Sandage, *Born Losers: A History of Failure in America* (Cambridge, MA: Harvard University Press, 2005), 4, ProQuest EBook Central, https://ebookcentral.proquest.com/lib/wisc/reader.action?docID=3300274&ppg=4

98. Scott A. Sandage, "Scott Sandage on 'Born Losers,'" interview by Anne Strainchamps, *To the Best of Our Knowledge*, Wisconsin Public Radio, March 5, 2006, audio, 9:00, http://archive.ttbook.org/listen/6248

99. Carl E. Seashore, "The Master's Key to the Domain of Educational Theory and Practice," *Education Digest* 15, no. 6 (February 1950): 19; repr. fr. *School and Society* 70 (November 26, 1949): 337–38.

100. Giorgio Agamben, *Homo Sacer: Sovereign Power and Bare Life*, trans. Daniel Heller-Roazen (Stanford, CA: Stanford University Press, 1998), 139.

101. Agamben, *Homo Sacer*, 142.

102. *The House I Live In*, directed by Eugene Jarecki (New York, NY: Virgil Films and Entertainment, 2013), DVD, 108 min.

103. *House I Live In*.

104. *House I Live In*.

105. Arthur Jensen, "A Conversation with Arthur Jensen (Part II)," interview by *American Renaissance*, *American Renaissance* 3, no. 9 (September 1992): 5.

106. Zygmunt Bauman, *Modernity and the Holocaust* (Ithaca, NY: Cornell University Press, 1989), 89.

107. I am referring here to Bauman's description of society as a garden. See Bauman, *Modernity and the Holocaust*, 18.

108. Bauman, *Modernity and the Holocaust*, 17.

109. Bauman, *Modernity and the Holocaust*, 18.

110. Bauman, *Modernity and the Holocaust*, 99.

111. Bauman, *Modernity and the Holocaust*, 102.

112. Bauman, *Modernity and the Holocaust*, 103.

113. Bauman, *Modernity and the Holocaust*, 153–54.

114. Shoko Yoneyama and Asao Naito, "Problems with the Paradigm: The School as a Factor in Understanding Bullying (with Special Reference to Japan)," *British Journal of Sociology of Education* 24, no. 3 (2003): 315, https://doi.org/10.1080/01425690301894

115. Yuseon An and Jiyeon Kang, "Relationship between Organizational Culture and Workplace Bullying among Korean Nurses," *Asian Nursing Research* 10, no. 3 (September 2016): 234–39, https://doi.org/10.1016/j.anr.2016.06.004

116. Giorgio Agamben, *State of Exception*, trans. Kevin Attell (Chicago: University of Chicago Press, 2005).

117. Tzvetan Todorov, *Hope and Memory: Reflections on the Twentieth Century* (Princeton, NJ: Princeton University Press, 2003; London: Atlantic, 2014), xx.

118. Carl E. Seashore, "The Sunny Side of Graduate Work for the Duration," *Journal of Higher Education* 14, no. 6 (June 1943): 289, https://www.jstor.org/stable/1975100; Carl E. Seashore, "The Sunny Side of Graduate Work," *Daily Iowan*,

April 11, 1943, 2, http://dailyiowan.lib.uiowa.edu/DI/1943/di1943-04-11.pdf; Carl E. Seashore, "The Sunny Side of Graduate Work for the Duration," in *Wartime Approaches to Liberal Education: Nine Editorials from* The Daily Iowan ([Iowa City: University of Iowa Publications, 1944?]), 29. A similar passage is found in Carl E. Seashore, "The Sunny Side of Graduate Work for the Duration," typed manuscript accompanying Carl E. Seashore to Virgil M. Hancher, March 26, 1943, p. 1, RG 05.01.11, box 55, folder 52, Virgil M. Hancher Papers, Special Collections and University Archives, University of Iowa Libraries, Iowa City, IA.

119. Carl E. Seashore, "Sunny Side," *Journal of Higher Education*, 290; Carl E. Seashore, "Sunny Side," *Daily Iowan*, 2; Carl E. Seashore, "Sunny Side," in *Wartime Approaches to Liberal Education*, 30. See also Carl E. Seashore, "Sunny Side," typed manuscript accompanying a letter dated March 26, 1943, p. 3, RG 05.01.11, box 55, folder 52, Virgil M. Hancher Papers.

120. Todorov, *Hope and Memory*, 20.

121. Michel Foucault, *The History of Sexuality*, vol. 1, *An Introduction*, trans. Robert Hurley (New York: Vintage Books, 1990), 102.

122. Dorothy Butler Gilliam, "'Trailblazer' Dorothy Butler Gilliam's 'Fight to Make the Media Look More Like America,'" interview by Meghna Chakrabarti, *On Point* podcast, WBUR, January 8, 2019, audio, 47:19, https://www.wbur.org/onpoint/2019/01/08/trailblazer-dorothy-butler-gilliam-media-diversity-washington-post

123. Rachel Gur-Arie, "American Eugenics Society (1926–1972)," *Embryo Project Encyclopedia*, last modified July 4, 2018, https://embryo.asu.edu/pages/american-eugenics-society-1926–1972; "American Eugenics Society 1945–2012," p. 1, SCRIBD, last modified June 3, 2012, https://www.scribd.com/doc/97130973/American-eugenics-society-1945–2012. Sources do not agree on when the first name change occurred. The latter source states (incorrectly, I believe) that it took place in 1973.

124. "*Biodemography and Social Biology*: Publication History," Taylor & Francis Group, accessed December 7, 2018, https://www.tandfonline.com/loi/hsbi20

125. Gur-Arie, "American Eugenics Society (1926–1972)."

126. Mehler, "History of the American Eugenics," 118–27.

127. *Human Cloning and Human Dignity: The Report of the President's Council on Bioethics* (New York: PublicAffairs, 2002), 120.

128. *Human Cloning and Human Dignity*, 121.

129. *Human Cloning and Human Dignity*, 123.

130. *Human Cloning and Human Dignity*, 88.

131. *Human Cloning and Human Dignity*, 93.

132. David Gillborn, "Softly, Softly: Genetics, Intelligence and the Hidden Racism of the New Geneism," *Journal of Education Policy* 31, no. 4 (2016): 366, http://dx.doi.org/10.1080/02680939.2016.1139189

133. Gillborn, "Softly, Softly," 366.

134. Gillborn, "Softly, Softly," 382.

135. Gillborn, "Softly, Softly," 368.

136. Gillborn, "Softly, Softly," 370.

137. "Mainstream Science on Intelligence," *Wall Street Journal (1923–Current File)*, December 13, 1994, A18, http://search.proquest.com.ezproxy.library.wisc.edu/docview/904944036?accountid=465

138. Gillborn, "Softly, Softly," 374.

139. Kathryn Asbury and Robert Plomin, *G Is for Genes: The Impact of Genetics on Education and Achievement* (Chichester, West Sussex, UK: Wiley Blackwell, 2014), 5–6, 11–12, https://onlinelibrary-wiley-com.ezproxy.library.wisc.edu/doi/book/10.1002/9781118482766

140. Asbury and Plomin, *G Is for Genes*, 6.

141. See, for example, K. Pulli et al., "Genome-Wide Linkage Scan for Loci of Musical Aptitude in Finnish Families: Evidence for a Major Locus at 4q22," *Journal of Medical Genetics* 45, no. 7 (2008): 451–56, http://dx.doi.org/10.1136/jmg.2007.056366; and Liisa Ukkola et al., "Musical Aptitude Is Associated with AVPR1A-Haplotpyes," *PLoS ONE* 4, no. 5 (2009), https://doi.org/10.1371/journal.pone.0005534. Both studies used portions of the Seashore Tests. Dennis Drayna et al., "Genetic Correlates of Musical Pitch Recognition in Humans," *Science* 291, no. 5510 (March 9, 2001): 1969–72, https://search-proquest-com.ezproxy.library.wisc.edu/docview/213581689/F9A59576DBE84623PQ/73?accountid=465, examined error detection in melodies.

142. Francis Galton, "The History of Twins, as a Criterion of the Relative Powers of Nature and Nurture," *Fraser's Magazine* 12, no. 71 (November 1875): 566–76, https://search-proquest-com.ezproxy.library.wisc.edu/docview/2645576/F0671B2C90084B23PQ/4?accountid=465; Edward L. Thorndike, "Measurement of Twins," *Journal of Philosophy, Psychology and Scientific Methods* 2, no. 20 (September 28, 1905): 547–53, http://www.jstor.org/stable/2011451

143. Jay Joseph, *The Trouble with Twin Studies: A Reassessment of Twin Research in the Social and Behavioral Sciences* (New York: Routledge, 2015), 253–56. For a critical analysis of histories of twin studies, see Thomas Teo and Laura C. Ball, "Twin Research, Revisionism and Metahistory," *History of the Human Sciences* 22, no. 5 (December 2009): 1–23, https://www.researchgate.net/publication/43344186_Twin_Research_Revisionism_and_Metahistory

144. For an example of a recent critique of these studies, which itself has come under fire, see Joseph, *Trouble with Twin*.

145. Miriam A. Mosing et al., "Practice Does Not Make Perfect: No Causal Effect of Music Practice on Music Ability," *Psychological Science* 25, no. 9 (September 2014): 1,796, www.jstor.org/stable/24543915. Another example of a music-related twin study is Drayna et al., "Genetic Correlates," 1969–72.

146. Mosing et al., "Practice Does Not," 1,798.

147. Mosing et al., "Practice Does Not," 1,795.

148. "Ability to Match Musical Pitch," 23andMe, Inc., accessed December 10, 2018, https://medical.23andme.com/wp-content/uploads/2018/08/Ability-to-Match-Musical-Pitch.pdf

149. "Explore 23andMe Genetic Reports," 23andMe, Inc., accessed December 10, 2018, https://medical.23andme.com/reports/

150. "Traits Reports," 23andMe, Inc., accessed December 10, 2018, https://medical.23andme.com/reports/#traits

151. For a discussion of potential shortcomings of 23andMe, and an opinion on the FDA's decision to rein in 23andMe, see Linnea M. Baudhuin, "The FDA and 23andMe: Violating the First Amendment or Protecting the Rights of Consumers?" *Clinical Chemistry* 60, no. 6 (June 2014): 835–37, http://clinchem.aaccjnls.org/content/clinchem/60/6/835.full.pdf

152. David Derbyshire, "Melody Gene 'Is the Key to Music Ability,'" *The Telegraph*, March 9, 2001, http://www.telegraph.co.uk/news/uknews/1325655/Melody-gene-is-the-key-to-music-ability.html

153. Lorna Duckworth, "Musical Talent Proves to Be Air on a Gene String," *The Independent*, March 9, 2001, https://advance-lexis-com.ezproxy.library.wisc.edu/document/teaserdocument/?pdmfid=1516831&crid=ba315dc3–4ad7–4e2e-8923–301ceb4ece6a&pddocfullpath=%2Fshared%2Fdocument%2Fnews%2Furn%3AcontentItem%3A42HV-8TW0–00SH-812S-00000–00&pddocid=urn%3AcontentItem%3A42HV-8TW0–00SH-812S-00000–00&pdcontentcomponentid=8200&pdteaserkey=h1&pditab=allpods&ecomp=sp79k&earg=sr0&prid=0103974c-70e1–434c-8076–7d1d0573b682

154. Edwin E. Gordon, *Learning Sequences in Music: A Contemporary Music Learning Theory* (Chicago: GIA, 2007), 288.

155. Gordon, *Learning Sequences in Music: A Contemporary Music Learning Theory*, 288.

156. Ingmar Persson and Julian Savulescu, *Unfit for the Future: The Need for Moral Enhancement* (Oxford: Oxford University, 2012).

157. Julian Savulescu, "The Moral Argument for Human Cloning, Genetic Enhancement," interview by Steve Paulson, *To the Best of Our Knowledge*, Wisconsin Public Radio, October 18, 2015, audio, 12:43, http://archive.ttbook.org/book/moral-argument-human-cloning-genetic-enhancement

158. Julian Savulescu, "The Philosopher Who Says We Should Play God," interview by Steve Paulson, *Nautilus*, September 3, 2015, http://nautil.us/issue/28/2050/the-philosopher-who-says-we-should-play-god

159. Savulescu, "Philosopher Who Says."

160. Savulescu, "Moral Argument."

161. Savulescu, "Moral Argument."

162. Savulescu, "Moral Argument."

163. Julian Savulescu, "As a Species, We Have a Moral Obligation to Enhance Ourselves," interview by TED Guest Author, TED, February 19, 2014, https://ideas.ted.com/the-ethics-of-genetically-enhanced-monkey-slaves/

164. Persson and Savulescu, *Unfit for the Future*, 104–5.

165. Persson and Savulescu, *Unfit for the Future*, 109.

166. Persson and Savulescu, *Unfit for the Future*, 112.

167. Persson and Savulescu, *Unfit for the Future*, 118.

168. Savulescu, "Philosopher Who Says."

169. For Fix's comments, see Rachel Martin, "What Visa Changes Say about U.S. Immigration Priorities," *Weekend Edition Sunday*, NPR, May 5, 2013, audio,

5:17, https://www.npr.org/2013/05/05/181293112/what-visa-changes-say-about-u-s-immigration-priorities

170. Coshandra Dillard, "The School-to-Deportation Pipeline," *Teaching Tolerance*, no. 60 (Fall 2018): 43.

171. Dillard, "School-to-Deportation Pipeline," 43.

172. "Remarks by President Trump at a California Sanctuary State Roundtable," The White House, May 16, 2018, https://www.whitehouse.gov/briefings-statements/remarks-president-trump-california-sanctuary-state-roundtable/

173. Jazmine Ulloa, "No, California's 'Sanctuary State' Law Does Not Allow the Release of Dangerous Criminals to the Streets," *Los Angeles Times*, April 6, 2018, https://www.latimes.com/politics/la-pol-ca-sanctuary-state-criminals-explained-20180406-htmlstory.html

174. Ulloa, "No, California's 'Sanctuary State.'"

175. Josh Gerstein and Ted Hesson, "Judge Largely Rejects Trump Bid to Block California Sanctuary Laws," *Politico*, July 5, 2018, https://www.politico.com/story/2018/07/05/trump-sanctuary-cities-ruling-695286; Sudhin Thanawala and Don Thompson, "Trump Loses Effort to Block 2 California Sanctuary Laws," *Chicago Sun Times*, July 5, 2018, https://chicago.suntimes.com/2018/7/5/18459016/trump-loses-effort-to-block-2-california-sanctuary-laws

176. Josh Dawsey, "Trump Derides Protections for Immigrants from 'Shithole' Countries," *Washington Post*, January 12, 2018, https://www.washingtonpost.com/politics/trump-attacks-protections-for-immigrants-from-shithole-countries-in-oval-office-meeting/2018/01/11/bfc0725c-f711-11e7-91af-31ac729add94_story.html?utm_term=.f8673fd27b10

177. Eli Watkins and Abby Phillip, "Trump Decries Immigrants from 'Shithole Countries' Coming to US," CNN, last modified January 12, 2018, https://www.cnn.com/2018/01/11/politics/immigrants-shithole-countries-trump/index.html

178. Richard Spencer, "Richard Spencer—NPI 2016, Full Speech," Red Ice TV, recorded November 19, 2016, at the 2016 National Policy Institute Conference in Washington, DC, YouTube video, 32:37, https://www.youtube.com/watch?v=Xq-LnO2DOGE (link discontinued).

179. Tim Alberta, "The Deep Roots of Trump's War on the Press: Long Before Cries of 'Fake News,' There Was Brent Bozell and His Media Research Center," *Politico Magazine*, April 26, 2018, https://www.politico.com/magazine/story/2018/04/26/the-deep-roots-trumps-war-on-the-press-218105

180. Richard Spencer, "Richard Spencer—NPI 2016."

181. Richard Spencer, "Richard Spencer—NPI 2016."

182. Richard Spencer, "Richard Spencer—NPI 2016."

183. Richard Spencer, "Richard Spencer—NPI 2016."

184. Hallie Jackson and Tim Stelloh, "White Nationalist Alt-Righter Claims 'Hail Trump' Comments Were 'Ironic,'" NBC News, November 21, 2016, https://www.nbcnews.com/politics/white-house/white-nationalist-alt-righter-claims-hail-trump-comments-were-ironic-n687021

185. Jonah Engel Bromwich, "Donald Trump's *New York Times* Interview in 12

Tweets," *New York Times*, November 22, 2016, https://www.nytimes.com/2016/11/22/us/politics/donald-trump-times-tweets.html?login=smartlock&auth=login-smartlock

186. David Bauder, "NBC to Trump: You're Fired," *Wisconsin State Journal*, June 30, 2015, B6.

187. Justin Ward, "Day of the Trope: White Nationalist Memes Thrive Online," in *Hate and Extremism in 2018* (Montgomery, AL: Southern Poverty Law Center, 2018), 23.

188. Ward, "Day of the Trope," 25.

189. Ward, "Day of the Trope," 24.

190. SirTossAside in Ward, "Day of the Trope," 24.

191. Ward, "Day of the Trope," 25.

192. "R/The_Donald: The_Donald Is a Never-Ending Rally Dedicated to the 45th President of the United States, Donald J. Trump," Reddit, accessed November 28, 2018, https://www.reddit.com/r/The_Donald/ (site banned on June 29, 2020).

193. "White Panther," Way of the World, February 16, 2018, YouTube video, 18:02, https://www.youtube.com/watch?v=AmgxftI4O20

194. Ryan Broderick, "Reddit's Largest Pro-Trump Subreddit Appears to Have Been Targeted by Russian Propaganda for Years," *Buzzfeed News*, September 24, 2018, https://www.buzzfeednews.com/article/ryanhatesthis/reddits-largest-pro-trump-subreddit-appears-to-have-been

195. Heidi Beirich, "John Tanton's Private Papers Expose More Than 20 Years of Hate," *Intelligence Report*, Southern Poverty Law Center, November 30, 2008, https://www.splcenter.org/fighting-hate/intelligence-report/2008/john-tanton%E2%80%99s-private-papers-expose-more-20-years-hate

196. Beirich, "John Tanton's Private Papers."

197. Beirich, "John Tanton's Private Papers."

198. Aaron Patrick Flanagan, "Flocking Together: Jason Richwine & the Legacy of the Pioneer Fund's 'Race Realism,'" Center for New Community, May 15, 2013, accessed October 1, 2013, http://imagine2050.newcomm.org/2013/05/15/flocking-together-jason-richwine-the-legacy-of-the-pioneer-funds-race-realism/ (site discontinued).

199. Beirich, "John Tanton's Private Papers."

200. "The Board of Directors," ProEnglish, accessed March 28, 2019, https://proenglish.org/the-board-of-directors/; Peter Strescino, "U.S. English Chief Resigns Her Position," *Pueblo Chieftain*, October 18, 1988, 1A.

201. "Board of Directors," ProEnglish; "Our Mission," ProEnglish, accessed March 28, 2019, https://proenglish.org/our-mission/

202. Beirich, "John Tanton's Private Papers"; "Board of Directors," ProEnglish.

203. Stephen Piggott, "Anti-Immigrant Hate Group ProEnglish Visits White House," *Hatewatch* (blog), Southern Poverty Law Center, January 26, 2018, https://www.splcenter.org/hatewatch/2018/01/26/anti-immigrant-hate-group-proenglish-visits-white-house

204. "A Renewed Attack on the 14th Amendment," in *Hate and Extremism in*

2018 (Montgomery, AL: Southern Poverty Law Center, 2018), 17; "VDARE," Southern Poverty Law Center, accessed December 2, 2018, https://www.splcenter.org/fighting-hate/extremist-files/group/vdare

205. Robert Costa, "Trump Speechwriter Fired amid Scrutiny of Appearance with White Nationalists," *Washington Post*, August 19, 2018, https://www.washingtonpost.com/politics/trump-speechwriter-fired-amid-scrutiny-of-appearance-with-white-nationalists/2018/08/19/f5051b52-a3eb-11e8-a656–943eefab5daf_story.html?utm_term=.c20c34e08ff6. In a Twitter post dated August 20, 2018, Spencer claimed that he had cofounded the Club. See also Alex Amend, "*Daily Caller* News Foundation Reporter Cancels Scheduled Appearance at Influential White Nationalist Gathering," *Hatewatch* (blog), Southern Poverty Law Center, September 14, 2018, https://www.splcenter.org/hatewatch/2018/09/14/daily-caller-news-foundation-reporter-cancels-scheduled-appearance-influential-white

206. Robert Costa, "Trump Adviser Larry Kudlow Hosted Publisher of White Nationalists at His Home," *Washington Post*, August 21, 2018, https://www.washingtonpost.com/politics/trump-adviser-larry-kudlow-hosted-publisher-of-white-nationalists-at-his-home/2018/08/21/f418a76c-a55e-11e8–8fac-12e98c13528d_story.html?utm_term=.0016d3de9e3d

207. Beirich, "John Tanton's Private Papers."

208. Beirich, "John Tanton's Private Papers."

209. Flanagan, "Flocking Together"; "Federation for American Immigration Reform," Southern Poverty Law Center, accessed October 6, 2018, https://www.splcenter.org/fighting-hate/extremist-files/group/federation-american-immigration-reform

210. "Federation for American Immigration."

211. Beirich, "John Tanton's Private Papers." Also Flanagan, "Flocking Together"; and "SPLC Exposes Racist Origins of New Arizona Law," *SPLC Report*, 40, no. 2, Summer 2010, 5.

212. Beirich, "John Tanton's Private Papers."

213. Beirich, "John Tanton's Private Papers."

214. Beirich, "John Tanton's Private Papers."

215. Beirich, "John Tanton's Private Papers."

216. "SPLC Exposes Racist Origins," 1, 5.

217. "Center for Immigration Studies," Southern Poverty Law Center, accessed October 6, 2018, https://www.splcenter.org/fighting-hate/extremist-files/group/center-immigration-studies; Joel Rose, "Mark Krikorian, Who Urges Cutting Immigration, Gains Relevance in Trump Era," *All Things Considered*, NPR, April 10, 2017, audio, 3:53, https://www.npr.org/2017/04/10/523311475/mark-krikorian-who-urges-cutting-immigration-gains-relevance-in-trump-era

218. Laura Reston, "Where Trump Gets His Fuzzy Border Math," *New Republic*, March 10, 2017, https://newrepublic.com/article/140951/trump-gets-fuzzy-border-math

219. "Renewed Attack on the 14th," 17.

220. Chris Potter and Mark Roth, "Pittsburgh's Colcom Foundation Plays Major Role in Immigration-Control Debate," *Pittsburgh Post-Gazette*, February 14, 2015, https://www.post-gazette.com/news/environment/2015/02/15/Pittsburgh-s-Colcom-Foundation-plays-major-role-in-immigration-control-debate/stories/201502150072

221. Julie Hirschfeld Davis, "Genial Force behind Bitter Opposition to Immigration Overhaul," *New York Times*, December 3, 2014, https://www.nytimes.com/2014/12/04/us/politics/roy-h-beck-quietly-leads-a-grass-roots-army.html

222. "John Tanton Is the Mastermind behind the Organized Anti-Immigration Movement," *Intelligence Report*, Southern Poverty Law Center, June 18, 2002, https://www.splcenter.org/fighting-hate/intelligence-report/2002/john-tanton-mastermind-behind-organized-anti-immigration-movement; "Renewed Attack on the 14th," 17.

223. Reston, "Where Trump Gets."

224. Reston, "Where Trump Gets."

225. Joel Rose, "Mark Krikorian."

226. Brett Barrouquere, "Tied Tightly to Trump, Anti-Immigration Group FAIR Takes to the Capital—and Airwaves—Once Again," *Hatewatch* (blog), Southern Poverty Law Center, September 4, 2018, https://www.splcenter.org/hatewatch/2018/09/04/tied-tightly-trump-anti-immigration-group-fair-takes-capital-%E2%80%94-and-airwaves-%E2%80%94-once-again

227. "Julie Kirchner," United States Department of Homeland Security, last modified May 10, 2017, https://www.dhs.gov/person/julie-kirchner

228. "Jon Feere," LinkedIn, accessed October 6, 2018, https://www.linkedin.com/in/jonfeere/. For more information on Kirchner and Feere, see Maria Santana, "Hard-Line Anti-Illegal Immigration Advocates Hired at 2 Federal Agencies," CNN, April 12, 2017, https://www.cnn.com/2017/04/11/politics/trump-administration-immigration-advisers/index.html

229. "U.S. Immigration and Customs Enforcement Acting Director to Speak at Hate Group Event Tomorrow," *Hatewatch* (blog), Southern Poverty Law Center, June 4, 2018, https://www.splcenter.org/hatewatch/2018/06/04/us-immigration-and-customs-enforcement-acting-director-speak-hate-group-event-tomorrow

230. "American Renaissance," Southern Poverty Law Center, accessed August 11, 2018, https://www.splcenter.org/fighting-hate/extremist-files/group/american-renaissance

231. Flanagan, "Flocking Together"; "Jared Taylor," Southern Poverty Law Center, accessed October 7, 2018, https://www.splcenter.org/fighting-hate/extremist-files/individual/jared-taylor

232. "Jared Taylor," Southern Poverty Law Center.

233. Richard Spencer, "Facing the Future as a Minority," recorded at the eleventh American Renaissance Conference (April 5–7, 2013), published on YouTube on September 16, 2017, YouTube video, 44:22, https://www.youtube.com/watch?v=yCv7Vaziylc

234. Flanagan, "Flocking Together."

235. "Controversies: Setting the Record Straight," Pioneer Fund, Inc., April 3, 2013, accessed October 14, 2018, https://web.archive.org/web/20130403132941/http:/www.pioneerfund.org:80/Controversies.html (site discontinued; Wayback Machine link included).

236. Flanagan, "Flocking Together."

237. Jared Taylor, introduction to *The Real American Dilemma: Race, Immigration, and the Future of America*, ed. Jared Taylor (Oakton, VA: New Century Foundation, 1998), 1–2.

238. Taylor, introduction to *Real American Dilemma*, 2.

239. Taylor, introduction to *Real American Dilemma*, 2.

240. Jared Taylor, "Race and Nation," in *The Real American Dilemma: Race, Immigration, and the Future of America*, ed. Jared Taylor (Oakton, VA: New Century Foundation, 1998), 43.

241. Taylor, introduction to *Real American Dilemma*, 3.

242. Taylor, "Race and Nation," 49.

243. Taylor, "Race and Nation," 51.

244. Beirich, "John Tanton's Private Papers."

245. Flanagan, "Flocking Together."

246. Flanagan, "Flocking Together."

247. Marilyn Simons and Bruce Stillman, "Statement by Cold Spring Harbor Laboratory Addressing Remarks by Dr. James D. Watson in '*American Masters: Decoding Watson*,'" Cold Spring Harbor Laboratory, January 11, 2019, https://www.cshl.edu/statement-by-cold-spring-harbor-laboratory-addressing-remarks-by-dr-james-d-watson-in-american-masters-decoding-watson/; Amy Harmon, "In DNA Era, New Worries about Prejudice," *New York Times*, November 11, 2007, http://www.nytimes.com/2007/11/11/us/11dna.html?_r+1&ex=1195448400&en=b01d056

248. Stephen Piggott and Alex Amend, "More than an Occasional Crank: 2,012 Times the Center for Immigration Studies Circulated White Nationalist Content," *Hatewatch* (blog), Southern Poverty Law Center, May 23, 2017, https://www.splcenter.org/hatewatch/2017/05/23/more-occasional-crank-2012-times-center-immigration-studies-circulated-white-nationalist

249. Flanagan, "Flocking Together."

250. Jason Richwine, "IQ and Immigration Policy" (PhD diss., Harvard University, 2009), 63, 156, http://search.proquest.com.ezproxy.library.wisc.edu/docview/304890816?accountid=465

251. Richwine, "IQ and Immigration," 11.

252. Richwine, "IQ and Immigration," 18–21.

253. Richwine, "IQ and Immigration," 21.

254. Richwine, "IQ and Immigration," 135–41.

255. Richwine, "IQ and Immigration," 27–28. The quote is on p. 27, and Richwine's validity claims are on pp. 27–28.

256. Richwine, "IQ and Immigration," 65.

257. Richwine, "IQ and Immigration," iii.

258. Richwine, "IQ and Immigration," 4.

259. Richwine, "IQ and Immigration," 69.

260. Richwine, "IQ and Immigration," 59.

261. Flanagan, "Flocking Together."

262. "A Guide to S.744: Understanding the 2013 Senate Immigration Bill," American Immigration Council, July 10, 2013, https://americanimmigrationcouncil.org/research/guide-s744-understanding-2013-senate-immigration-bill; Bob Ortega, "Immigration Bill Could Be Windfall for Ariz. Economy," *USA Today*, April 18, 2018, https://www.usatoday.com/story/news/nation/2013/04/18/arizona-economy-immigration-bill/2094461/

263. Richwine, "IQ and Immigration," 63, 156. See also Piggott and Amend, "More than an Occasional."

264. Eric Schewe, "The Historic Echoes of Trump's Immigration Ban," *JSTOR Daily*, February 7, 2017, https://daily.jstor.org/the-historic-echoes-of-trumps-immigration-ban/

265. Schewe, "Historic Echoes."

266. Schewe, "Historic Echoes."

267. Mae M. Ngai, "The Architecture of Race in American Immigration Law: A Reexamination of the Immigration Act of 1924," *Journal of American History* 86, no. 1 (June 1999): 88, https://www.jstor.org/stable/2567407

268. Lenz is quoted in Sarah Jones, "The Notorious Book that Ties the Right to the Far Right," *New Republic*, February 2, 2018, https://newrepublic.com/article/146925/notorious-book-ties-right-far-right

269. For examples of summaries and critique of the book, see Paul Blumenthal and J. M. Rieger, "This Stunningly Racist French Novel Is How Steve Bannon Explains the World," *HuffPost*, last modified March 6, 2017, https://www.huffingtonpost.com/entry/steve-bannon-camp-of-the-saints-immigration_us_58b75206e4b0284854b3dc03; Ruth Conniff, "The War on Aliens: The Right to Call the Shots," *The Progressive* 57, no. 10 (October 1993): 22–26, 28–29; and Sarah Jones, "Notorious Book."

270. Jean Raspail, *The Camp of the Saints*, trans. Norman Shapiro (New York: Charles Scribner's Sons, 1975), 294–95.

271. Blumenthal and Rieger, "This Stunningly Racist."

272. Brendan O'Connor, "The Eugenicist Doctor and the Vast Fortune behind Trump's Immigration Regime," Splinter, July 5, 2018, https://splinternews.com/the-eugenicist-doctor-and-the-vast-fortune-behind-trump-1827322435, states that May donated the money in1983. *HuffPost* is another source reporting that this occurred in 1983; see Blumenthal and Rieger, "This Stunningly Racist." However, the second edition, published by the Institute for Western Values, came out in 1982. The earliest reference I found to May's donation is Strescino, "U.S. English Chief," 1A. See also Priscilla Falcon and Patricia J. Campbell, "The Politics of Language and the Mexican American: The English Only Movement and Bilingual Education," in *Racism and the Underclass: State Policy and Discrimina-*

tion against Minorities, ed. George W. Shepherd Jr. and David Penna (New York: Greenwood, 1991), 150; James Crawford, *Hold Your Tongue: Bilingualism and the Politics of "English Only"* (Reading, MA: Addison-Wesley, 1992), 158, 160; and Reston, "Where Trump Gets." Also Conniff, "War on Aliens," 24, reports that May paid for the first US *reprint*.

273. John Tanton, "*The Camp of the Saints* Revisited," *Social Contract* 5, no. 2 (Winter 1994–95): 83, https://www.thesocialcontract.com/artman2/publish/tsc0502/article_410.shtml

274. Blumenthal and Rieger, "This Stunningly Racist." *Newsweek* also reported on Bannon referencing *The Camp of the Saints*. See Chantal Da Silva, "Is Trump's Military Strategy Based on Anti-Immigration Fantasy Novel 'Camp of the Saints'?" *Newsweek*, April 4, 2018, https://www.newsweek.com/did-trump-base-military-strategy-anti-immigration-fantasy-novel-camp-saints-871306

275. Jeff Sessions, "'The American People Are Angry Alright . . . at the Politicians'—Senator Jeff Sessions," interview by Stephen K. Bannon, SiriusXM News & Issues October [4 or 5], 2015, accessed December 6, 2018, audio, 22:44, https://soundcloud.com/siriusxm-news-issues/the-american-people-are-angry

276. Jason Richwine, interview by Stephen K. Bannon, *Breitbart News Daily*, Breitbart, January 6, 2016, audio, 6:43, https://soundcloud.com/breitbart/breitbart-news-daily-jason-richwine-january-6–2016

277. Sarah Jones, "Notorious Book."

278. Trip Gabriel, "Before Trump, Steve King Set the Agenda for the Wall and Anti-Immigrant Politics," *New York Times*, January 10, 2019, https://www.nytimes.com/2019/01/10/us/politics/steve-king-trump-immigration-wall.html

279. Steve King, "Steve King: Bring Pride Back to Austria," interview by Caroline Sommerfeld, *Unzensuriert*, September 2, 2018, https://www.unzensuriert.at/content/0027654-restore-western-civilization-world-interview-steve-king

280. Sarah Jones, "Notorious Book."

281. K. C. McAlpin, "'The Camp of the Saints' Revisited: Modern Critics Have Justified the Message of a 1973 Novel on Mass Immigration," *Social Contract* 27, no. 4 (Summer 2017): 53, https://www.thesocialcontract.com/pdf/twentyseven-four/tsc_27_4_mcalpin.pdf

282. Michael Edison Hayden, "Stephen Miller's Affinity for White Nationalism Revealed in Leaked Emails," *Hatewatch* (blog), Southern Poverty Law Center, November 12, 2019, https://www.splcenter.org/hatewatch/2019/11/12/stephen-millers-affinity-white-nationalism-revealed-leaked-emails

283. Hayden, "Stephen Miller's Affinity."

284. Hayden, "Stephen Miller's Affinity."

285. Sarah Jones, "Trump Has Turned the GOP into the Party of Eugenics," *New Republic*, February 15, 2017, https://newrepublic.com/article/140641/trump-turned-gop-party-eugenics

286. Sarah Jones, "Trump Has Turned the GOP."

287. Sarah Jones, "Trump Has Turned the GOP."

288. Sarah Jones, "Trump Has Turned the GOP."

289. Sarah Jones, "Trump Has Turned the GOP."

290. Michael D'Antonio, "Op-Ed: Donald Trump Believes He Was Born to Be King," *Los Angeles Times*, December 3, 2015, https://www.latimes.com/opinion/op-ed/la-oe-1203-dantonio-trump-race-horse-theory-20151203-story.html

291. D'Antonio, "Op-Ed: Donald Trump."

292. Lois Beckett, "How Leftwing Media Focus on Far-Right Groups Is Helping to Normalize Hate," *The Guardian*, March 5, 2017, https://www.theguardian.com/world/2017/mar/05/left-wing-media-far-right-normalize-hate-trump

293. Beckett, "How Leftwing Media."

294. Beckett, "How Leftwing Media."

295. Beckett, "How Leftwing Media."

296. Mara Liasson, "Politics in the News: Immigration and the Southern Border Crisis," *Morning Edition*, NPR, June 19, 2018, https://www.npr.org/2018/06/19/621269617/politics-in-the-news-immigration-and-the-southern-border-crisis

297. Liasson, "Politics in the News."

298. Christopher R. Browning, "The Suffocation of Democracy," *New York Review of Books*, October 25, 2018, https://www.nybooks.com/articles/2018/10/25/suffocation-of-democracy/

299. Christopher R. Browning, *Ordinary Men: Reserve Police Battalion 101 and the Final Solution in Poland* (New York: Harper Perennial, 1998), 200.

300. Mehler, "History of the American Eugenics," 68.

301. Gloria Ladson-Billings, "The Social Funding of Race: The Role of Schooling" (working paper, undated pre-2008), 6. A revised and expanded version of this essay appeared in *Peabody Journal of Education* 93, no. 1 (2018): 90–105, https://doi.org/10.1080/0161956X.2017.1403182

302. Ladson-Billings, "Social Funding," 8.

303. Ladson-Billings, "Social Funding," 12–13.

304. Ladson-Billings, "Social Funding," 2.

305. See Judith Butler, *Parting Ways: Jewishness and the Critique of Zionism* (New York: Columbia University Press, 2012), 60.

306. Alice Walker, "What to Do with an Arrow in Your Heart," interview by Shannon Henry Kleiber, *To the Best of Our Knowledge*, Wisconsin Public Radio, December 1, 2018, audio, 14:10, https://www.ttbook.org/interview/what-do-arrow-your-heart

307. Walker, "What to Do."

308. Lesley Rameka, "*Kia Whakatōmuri Te Haere Whakamua*: 'I Walk Backwards into the Future with My Eyes Fixed on My Past,'" *Contemporary Issues in Early Childhood* 17, no. 4 (2016): 387, https://doi.org/10.1177/1463949116677923

309. Rameka, "*Kia Whakatōmuri*," 387.

310. Todorov, *Hope and Memory*, xxi.

311. Joshua Johnson, "Preserving Stories of Holocaust Survivors," *1A* podcast, produced by Amanda Williams, November 8, 2018, audio, 35:24, https://the1a.org/shows/2018-11-08/preserving-stories-of-holocaust-survivors

312. Ethan Fickau, "Seashore Hall Demolition Begins," KCRG-TV9, February 21, 2018, https://www.kcrg.com/content/news/Seashore-Hall-demolition-begins-474715123.html

313. Richard C. Lewis, "Paying Homage to Seashore Hall," *Iowa Now*, November 27, 2017, https://now.uiowa.edu/2017/11/paying-homage-seashore-hall

314. Hine Waitere, email message to author, November 8, 2018.

Bibliography

"Ability to Match Musical Pitch." 23andMe, Inc. Accessed December 10, 2018. https://medical.23andme.com/wp-content/uploads/2018/08/Ability-to-Match-Musical-Pitch.pdf

Addis, Laird. "Seashore, Carl Emil." In *The Biographical Dictionary of Iowa*. Iowa City: University of Iowa Press, 2009. http://uipress.lib.uiowa.edu/bdi/DetailsPage.aspx?id=332

Administration and Scope of the Iowa Child Welfare Research Station. Revised edition. University of Iowa Studies: Aims and Progress of Research, vol. 1, no. 10. Iowa City: The University, January 1921.

Administration and Scope of the Iowa Child Welfare Research Station. Revised edition. University of Iowa Studies: Aims and Progress of Research, vol. 1, no. 14, n.s., no. 78. Iowa City: The University, June 1, 1924.

"The Advisory Council of the Eugenics Committee of the United States of America." *Eugenical News* 8, no. 4 (April 1923): 29–30.

Agamben, Giorgio. *Homo Sacer: Sovereign Power and Bare Life*. Translated by Daniel Heller-Roazen. Stanford, CA: Stanford University Press, 1998.

Agamben, Giorgio. *State of Exception*. Translated by Kevin Attell. Chicago: University of Chicago Press, 2005.

Alberta, Tim. "The Deep Roots of Trump's War on the Press: Long before Cries of 'Fake News,' There Was Brent Bozell and His Media Research Center." *Politico Magazine*, April 26, 2018. https://www.politico.com/magazine/story/2018/04/26/the-deep-roots-trumps-war-on-the-press-218105

Alexander, Estrelda Y. *Black Fire: One Hundred Years of African American Pentecostalism*. Downers Grove, IL: IVP Academic, 2011.

Allen, Garland E. "Davenport, Charles Benedict." *American National Biography*. February 2000. https://www.anb.org/view/10.1093/anb/9780198606697.001.0001/anb-9780198606697-e-1300392

"Alt-Right Leader: 'Hail Trump!'" CNN. November 22, 2016. YouTube video, 2:10. https://www.youtube.com/watch?v=eF72gg9No_U

"Alumni Register Number, 1847–1911 [College of Liberal Arts]." *Iowa Alumnus* 8, no. 10 (September 1911): 21–98. https://books.google.com/books?id=MlBGAAAAYAAJ&pg=PA51&lpg=PA51&dq=mary+roberta+holmes+carl+seashore&source=bl&ots=DEJv_GxHpy&sig=mZAkwwfr2cHiFdMKNfdBKZfJwYk&hl=en&sa=X&ei=R7ZxVYKiJI7ZoAT9g4LIDQ&ved=0CCgQ6AEwBDgK#v=onepage&q=mary%20roberta%20holmes%20carl%20seashore&f=false

Amend, Alex. "*Daily Caller* News Foundation Reporter Cancels Scheduled Appearance at Influential White Nationalist Gathering." *Hatewatch* (blog). Southern Poverty Law Center, September 14, 2018. https://www.splcenter.org/hatewatch/2018/09/14/daily-caller-news-foundation-reporter-cancels-scheduled-appearance-influential-white

"The American Eugenics Society, Inc." *Eugenics* 1, no. 1 (October 1928): opposite p. 1.

"The American Eugenics Society: Members, Officers and Directors Activities Database." Eugenics Watch. November 8, 2005. http://www.archive.org/details/The_American_Eugenics_Society__Members_Officers_And_Directors_Activites_Database

"American Eugenics Society 1945–2012." SCRIBD. Last modified June 3, 2012. https://www.scribd.com/doc/97130973/American-eugenics-society-1945-2012

"American Renaissance." Southern Poverty Law Center. Accessed August 11, 2018. https://www.splcenter.org/fighting-hate/extremist-files/group/american-renaissance

"The American Speech Correction Association Presents the Honors of the Association to Carl Emil Seashore." *Journal of Speech Disorders* 10, no. 1 (March 1945): 1–2.

"America's Slogan: Freedom, for All, Forever [The Victrola and Victor Records]!" *Music Supervisors' Journal* 5, no. 1 (September 1918): 15. https://babel.hathitrust.org/cgi/pt?id=mdp.39015023355251&view=1up&seq=23

"Annual Midwinter Meeting of the Executive Committee of the Eugenics Research Association." *Eugenical News* 11, no. 3 (March 1926): 46–48.

An, Yuseon, and Jiyeon Kang. "Relationship between Organizational Culture and Workplace Bullying among Korean Nurses." *Asian Nursing Research* 10, no. 3 (September 2016): 234–39. https://doi.org/10.1016/j.anr.2016.06.004

Apple, Rima D. "Constructing Mothers: Scientific Motherhood in the Nineteenth and Twentieth Centuries." *Social History of Medicine* 8, no. 2 (August 1995): 161–78.

"Arthur Jensen." Southern Poverty Law Center. Accessed August 6, 2018. https://www.splcenter.org/fighting-hate/extremist-files/individual/arthur-jensen

Asbury, Kathryn, and Robert Plomin. *G Is for Genes: The Impact of Genetics on Education and Achievement*. Chichester, West Sussex, UK: Wiley Blackwell, 2014. https://onlinelibrary-wiley-com.ezproxy.library.wisc.edu/doi/book/10.1002/9781118482766

Augustine. *The Enchiridion: On Faith, Hope and Love*, edited by Henry Paolucci. Translated by J. F. Shaw. Chicago: Henry Regnery, 1961.

Augustine. *Enchiridion; or Faith, Hope, and Love*. Translated by J. F. Shaw.

http://www.leaderu.com/cyber/books/augenchiridion.enchiridiontoc.html (link discontinued).

Baldwin, Bird T. "The Learning of Delinquent Adolescent Girls as Shown by a Substitution Test." *Journal of Educational Psychology* 4, no. 6 (June 1913): 317–32. https://psycnet.apa.org/doi/10.1037/h0069968

Baldwin, Bird T. "The Scientific Prediction of the Physical Growth of Children." In *Eugenics in Race and State*, vol. 2, *Scientific Papers of the Second International Congress of Eugenics; Held at American Museum of Natural History, New York, September 22–28, 1921*, 25–29. Baltimore, MD: Williams & Wilkins, 1923. Reprint, edited by Charles Rosenberg. New York: Garland Publishing, 1985.

Baldwin, Bird T., and Lorle I. Stecher. "Additional Data from Consecutive Stanford-Binet Tests." *Journal of Educational Psychology* 13, no. 9 (December 1922): 556–60. https://babel.hathitrust.org/cgi/pt?id=mdp.39015075050123&view=1up&seq=586

Bardin, James. "The Psychological Factor in Southern Race Problems." *Popular Science Monthly* 83 (October 1913): 368–74. https://en.wikisource.org/wiki/Popular_Science_Monthly/Volume_83/October_1913/The_Psychological_Factor_in_Southern_Race_Problems

Barkan, Elazar. "Reevaluating Progressive Eugenics: Herbert Spencer Jennings and the 1924 Immigration Legislation." *Journal of the History of Biology* 24, no. 1 (Spring 1991): 91–112. www.jstor.org/stable/4331159

Barrouquere, Brett. "Tied Tightly to Trump, Anti-Immigration Group FAIR Takes to the Capital—and Airwaves—Once Again." *Hatewatch* (blog). Southern Poverty Law Center, September 4, 2018. https://www.splcenter.org/hatewatch/2018/09/04/tied-tightly-trump-anti-immigration-group-fair-takes-capital-%E2%80%94-and-airwaves-%E2%80%94-once-again

Bashford, Alison, and Philippa Levine, eds. *The Oxford Handbook of the History of Eugenics*. Oxford: Oxford University Press, 2010.

Bauckham, Richard. "Universalism: A Historical Survey." *Themelios* 4, no. 2 (September 1978): 47–54. https://www.theologicalstudies.org.uk/article_universalism_bauckham.html

Bauder, David. "NBC to Trump: You're Fired." *Wisconsin State Journal*, June 30, 2015, B6.

Baudhuin, Linnea M. "The FDA and 23andMe: Violating the First Amendment or Protecting the Rights of Consumers?" *Clinical Chemistry* 60, no. 6 (June 2014): 835–37. http://clinchem.aaccjnls.org/content/clinchem/60/6/835.full.pdf

Bauman, Zygmunt. *Modernity and the Holocaust*. Ithaca, NY: Cornell University Press, 1989.

Bean, Kenneth L. "The Musical Talent of Southern Negroes as Measured with the Seashore Tests." *Pedagogical Seminary and Journal of Genetic Psychology* 49, no. 1 (1936): 244–49. https://doi.org/10.1080/08856559.1936.10533763

Beans, Carolyn. "Four Ways Inheritance Is More Complex than Mendel Knew." *Biomedical Beat* (blog). National Institute of General Medical Sciences, March 4, 2016. https://biobeat.nigms.nih.gov/2016/03/four-ways-inheritance-is-more-complex-than-mendel-knew/

Beckett, Lois. "How Leftwing Media Focus on Far-Right Groups Is Helping to

Normalize Hate." *The Guardian*, March 5, 2017. https://www.theguardian.com/world/2017/mar/05/left-wing-media-far-right-normalize-hate-trump

Beirich, Heidi. "John Tanton's Private Papers Expose More Than 20 Years of Hate." *Intelligence Report*. Southern Poverty Law Center, November 30, 2008. https://www.splcenter.org/fighting-hate/intelligence-report/2008/john-tanton%E2%80%99s-private-papers-expose-more-20-years-hate

Berlet, Chip. "Into the Mainstream." *Intelligence Report*. Southern Poverty Law Center, August 15, 2003. https://www.splcenter.org/fighting-hate/intelligence-report/2003/mainstream

Bingham, W. V. "Some Psychological Aspects of Public School Music Instruction." In *Journal of Proceedings of the Ninth Annual Meeting of the Music Supervisors' National Conference Held at Lincoln, Nebraska, March 20–24, 1916:* 97–102. https://archive.org/details/in.ernet.dli.2015.166502/page/n101/mode/2up?q=bingham

Bingham, W. V., and W. C. Ruediger. "Proceedings of the Twentieth Annual Meeting of the American Psychological Association and the Seventh Annual Meeting of the Southern Society for Philosophy and Psychology, Washington, DC, December 27, 28, and 29, 1911." *Psychological Bulletin* 9, no. 2 (February 15, 1912): 41–92. https://psycnet.apa.org/doi/10.1037/h0071836

"*Biodemography and Social Biology*: Publication History." Taylor & Francis Group. Accessed December 7, 2018. https://www.tandfonline.com/loi/hsbi20

Black, Edwin. *War against the Weak: Eugenics and America's Campaign to Create a Master Race*. New York: Four Walls Eight Windows, 2003.

Blackmon, Douglas A. "Silent Partner: How the South's Fight to Uphold Segregation Was Funded Up North—New York Millionaire Secretly Sent Cash to Mississippi via His Morgan Account—'Wall Street Gang' Pitches In." *Wall Street Journal*, June 11, 1999, Eastern edition, A1. http://ezproxy.library.wisc.edu/login?url=http://proquest.umi.com.ezproxy.library.wisc.edu/pqdweb?did=42299728

Blanchard, Phyllis, Chase Going Woodhouse, and David Snedden. "When Wives Go to Business: Is it Eugenically Helpful?" *Eugenics* 4, no. 1 (January 1931): 18–20.

Blight, David. "Historian Says '12 Years' Is a Story the Nation Must Remember." Interview by Terry Gross. *Fresh Air*, NPR, October 24, 2013. Audio, 25:06. https://www.npr.org/templates/transcript/transcript.php?storyId=240491318

Blumenbach, Johann Friedrich. "On the Natural Variety of Mankind [*De Generis Humani Varietate Nativa Liber* (1775)]." In *The Anthropological Treatises of Johann Friedrich Blumenbach*, translated and edited by Thomas Bendyshe, 65–141. London: Longman, Green, Longman, Roberts, and Green, 1865.

Blumenfeld, Sam. "Eugenics, or Scientific Racism, in American Education." *New American*, October 10, 2011. https://www.thenewamerican.com/reviews/opinion/item/10870-eugenics-or-scientific-racism-in-american-education

Blumenthal, Paul, and J. M. Rieger. "This Stunningly Racist French Novel Is How Steve Bannon Explains the World." *HuffPost*. Last modified March 6, 2017.

https://www.huffingtonpost.com/entry/steve-bannon-camp-of-the-saints-immigration_us_58b75206e4b0284854b3dc03

"The Board of Directors." ProEnglish. Accessed March 28, 2019. https://proenglish.org/the-board-of-directors/

Bonser, Frederick G. *The Reasoning Ability of Children of the Fourth, Fifth, and Sixth School Grades*. New York: Teachers College, Columbia University, 1910. https://archive.org/details/reasoningabilit00bonsgoog/page/n4

Boring, Edwin G. *A History of Experimental Psychology*. New York: D. Appleton-Century, 1929.

Bowen, George Oscar. "Editorial Comment." *Music Supervisors' Journal* 11, no. 1 (October 1924): 3–4, 6, 8. http://www.jstor.org/stable/3383247

Boyce, James. *Born Bad: Original Sin and the Making of the Western World*. Berkeley, CA: Counterpoint, 2015. Accessed February 7, 2017. ProQuest EBook Central. http://site.ebrary.com/lib/wisconsin/reader.action?docID=11054861

Boyce, James. "The Imprint of Original Sin on Western Culture." Interview by Steve Paulson. *To the Best of Our Knowledge*, Wisconsin Public Radio, February 5, 2017. Audio, 12:21. http://archive.ttbook.org/book/imprint-original-sin-western-culture

Brigham, Carl C. "Intelligence Tests of Immigrant Groups." *Psychological Review* 37, no. 2 (March 1930): 158–65.

Brigham, Carl C. *A Study of American Intelligence*. Princeton, NJ: Princeton University Press, 1923. https://archive.org/stream/studyofamericani00briguoft#mode/2up

Broderick, Ryan. "Reddit's Largest Pro-Trump Subreddit Appears to Have Been Targeted by Russian Propaganda for Years." *Buzzfeed News*. September 24, 2018. https://www.buzzfeednews.com/article/ryanhatesthis/reddits-largest-pro-trump-subreddit-appears-to-have-been

Bromwich, Jonah Engel. "Donald Trump's *New York Times* Interview in 12 Tweets." *New York Times*, November 22, 2016. https://www.nytimes.com/2016/11/22/us/politics/donald-trump-times-tweets.html?login=smartlock&auth=login-smartlock

Brown, Andrew W. "The Reliability and Validity of the Seashore Tests of Musical Talent." *Journal of Applied Psychology* 12 (1928): 468–76.

Browning, Christopher R. *Ordinary Men: Reserve Police Battalion 101 and the Final Solution in Poland*. New York: Harper Perennial, 1998.

Browning, Christopher R. "The Suffocation of Democracy." *New York Review of Books*, October 25, 2018. https://www.nybooks.com/articles/2018/10/25/suffocation-of-democracy/

Bullard, William N. "The Placing Out of High Grade Imbecile Girls." *Boston Medical and Surgical Journal* 160, no. 24 (June 17, 1909): 776–79.

Buṭlān, Ibn. *Risāla fī Shirā' al-Raqīq*, edited by 'Abd al-Salām Hārūn. Cairo, 1373 [*sic*]/1954.

Butler, Judith. *Bodies That Matter: On the Discursive Limits of "Sex."* New York: Routledge, 1993.

Butler, Judith. *Parting Ways: Jewishness and the Critique of Zionism*. New York: Columbia University Press, 2012.

Butler, Judith. *Precarious Life: The Powers of Mourning and Violence*. London: Verso, 2004.

Callahan, Carolyn M., Tonya R. Moon, Sarah Oh, Amy P. Anzano, and Emily P. Hailey. "What Works in Gifted Education: Documenting the Effects of an Integrated Curricular/Instructional Model for Gifted Students." *American Educational Research Journal* 52, no. 1 (February 2015): 137–67. https://www.jstor.org/stable/24546724

Campbell, C. G. "Eugenics and Euthenics." *Eugenics* 2, no. 9 (1929): 21–25.

Campbell, C. G. "The German Racial Policy." *Eugenical News* 21, no. 2 (March-April 1936): 25–29.

Campbell, Patricia Shehan. "Rhythmic Movement and Public School Music Education: Conservative and Progressive Views of the Formative Years." *Journal of Research in Music Education* 39, no. 1 (Spring 1991): 12–22. www.jstor.org/stable/3344605

Canguilhem, Georges. *The Normal and the Pathological*. New York: Zone Books, 1989.

"Carnegie Classification of Institutions of Higher Education: Basic Classification Description." Indiana University Center for Postsecondary Research. Accessed May 14, 2019. http://carnegieclassifications.iu.edu/classification_descriptions/basic.php

Cattell, James McKeen. "The Psychological Corporation." *Annals of the American Academy of Political and Social Science* 110 (November 1923): 165–71. https://www.jstor.org/stable/1015081

Cattell, James McKeen, and Livingston Farrand. "Physical and Mental Measurements of the Students of Columbia University." *Psychological Review* 3 (1896): 618–48.

"Center for Immigration Studies." Southern Poverty Law Center. Accessed October 6, 2018. https://www.splcenter.org/fighting-hate/extremist-files/group/center-immigration-studies

"Chapters." The Gordon Institute for Music Learning. Accessed May 7, 2019. https://giml.org/chapters/

Charles, Don C. "A Note on Carl Seashore as Country School Teacher." *Journal of the History of the Behavioral Sciences* 5, no. 2 (April 1969): 185–87. https://doi.org/10.1002/1520-6696(196904)5:2<185::AID-JHBS2300050208>3.0.CO;2-E

Chase, Allan. *The Legacy of Malthus: The Social Costs of the New Scientific Racism*. New York: Alfred A. Knopf, 1977.

Chitty, Clyde. *Eugenics, Race and Intelligence in Education*. London: Continuum, 2009. ProQuest Ebook Central. https://ebookcentral.proquest.com/lib/wisc/detail.action?docID=742332

Chybowski, Julia J. "Developing American Taste: A Cultural History of the Early Twentieth- Century Music Appreciation Movement." PhD diss., University of Wisconsin–Madison, 2008.

Clarke, Edward H. *Sex in Education; or, A Fair Chance for the Girls*. Boston: James R. Osgood, 1873. https://archive.org/details/sexineducationo01clargoog/page/n6

Clarke, Eric. "Empirical Methods in the Study of Performance." In *Empirical Musicology: Aims, Methods, Prospects*, edited by Eric Clarke and Nicholas Cook, 77–102. New York: Oxford University Press, 2004.

"Class Variation in Fertility [Editorial Notes and Comments]." *New York Medical Journal* 111, no. 24 (June 12, 1920): 1042. https://babel.hathitrust.org/cgi/pt?id=nnc2.ark:/13960/t9v14qw7m;view=1up;seq=1064

Coffman, Don D. "Seashore's Passion for Measurement." In *Multidisciplinary Perspectives on Musicality: Essays from the Seashore Symposium*, edited by Kate Gfeller, Don D. Coffman, Carlos X. Rodriguez, and David J. Nelson, 28–29. Iowa City: University of Iowa School of Music, 2006.

Cohen, Adam S. "Harvard's Eugenics Era." *Harvard Magazine*, March-April 2016. http://harvardmagazine.com/2016/03/harvards-eugenics-era

"The Color-Races." *Eugenical News* 5, no. 9 (September 1920): 70–71.

Conniff, Ruth. "The War on Aliens: The Right to Call the Shots." *The Progressive* 57, no. 10 (October 1993): 22–26, 28–29.

"Controlling Heredity: The American Eugenics Crusade 1870–1940, International Eugenics Congresses, Eugenics Tree, 1932 [page 510]." Special Collections and Rare Books, University of Missouri. Last modified March 16, 2012. https://library.missouri.edu/exhibits/eugenics/congresses.htm

"Controversies: Setting the Record Straight." Pioneer Fund, Inc. April 3, 2013. Accessed October 14, 2018. https://web.archive.org/web/20130403132941/http:/www.pioneerfund.org:80/Controversies.html (site discontinued; Wayback Machine link included).

Costa, Robert. "Trump Adviser Larry Kudlow Hosted Publisher of White Nationalists at His Home." *Washington Post*, August 21, 2018. https://www.washingtonpost.com/politics/trump-adviser-larry-kudlow-hosted-publisher-of-white-nationalists-at-his-home/2018/08/21/f418a76c-a55e-11e8–8fac-12e98c13528d_story.html?utm_term=.0016d3de9e3d

Costa, Robert. "Trump Speechwriter Fired amid Scrutiny of Appearance with White Nationalists." *Washington Post*, August 19, 2018. https://www.washingtonpost.com/politics/trump-speechwriter-fired-amid-scrutiny-of-appearance-with-white-nationalists/2018/08/19/f5051b52-a3eb-11e8-a656–943eefab5daf_story.html?utm_term=.c20c34e08ff6

Cowan, Alexander W. "Music Psychology and the American Eugenics Movement in the Early Twentieth Century." MMus thesis, King's College, London, 2016.

Crane, George W. "A Tribute." [Preface to] *Our Children in the Atomic Age*, by Henry H. Goddard, i–ii. Mellott, IN: Hopkins Syndicate, 1948. http://babel.hathitrust.org/cgi/wayf?target=https%3A%2F%2Fbabel.hathitrust.org%2Fcgi%2Fpt%3Fid%3Dcoo.31924014089894%3Bq1%3Dour%2520children%2520in%2520the%2520atomic%2520age%3Bpage%3Droot%3Bseq%3D9%3Bview%3D1up%3Bsize%3D100%3Borient%3D0

Cravens, Hamilton. *Before Head Start: The Iowa Station and America's Children*. Chapel Hill: University of North Carolina Press, 1993.

Crawford, James. *Hold Your Tongue: Bilingualism and the Politics of "English Only."* Reading, MA: Addison-Wesley, 1992.

Crenshaw, Kimberlé. "Demarginalizing the Intersection of Race and Sex: A Black Feminist Critique of Antidiscrimination Doctrine, Feminist Theory and Antiracist Politics." *University of Chicago Legal Forum* (1989): 139–67. https://heinonline-org.ezproxy.library.wisc.edu/HOL/P?h=hein.journals/uchclf1989&i=143

Curtis, Kelly L., Kevin W. Greve, Raven Brasseux, and Kevin J. Bianchini. "Criterion Groups Validation of the Seashore Rhythm Test and Speech Sounds Perception Test for the Detection of Malingering in Traumatic Brain Injury." *Clinical Neuropsychologist* 24, no. 5 (2010): 882–97.

D'Antonio, Michael. "Op-Ed: Donald Trump Believes He Was Born to Be King." *Los Angeles Times*, December 3, 2015. https://www.latimes.com/opinion/op-ed/la-oe-1203-dantonio-trump-race-horse-theory-20151203-story.html

Danziger, Kurt. *Constructing the Subject: Historical Origins of Psychological Research*. Cambridge, UK: Cambridge University Press, 1990.

Danziger, Kurt. *Marking the Mind: A History of Memory*. Cambridge, UK: Cambridge University Press, 2008.

Darwin, Leonard. "The Aims and Methods of Eugenical Societies." In *Eugenics, Genetics and the Family*, vol. 1, *Scientific Papers of the Second International Congress of Eugenics; Held at American Museum of Natural History, New York, September 22–28, 1921*, 5–19. Baltimore, MD: Williams & Wilkins, 1923. Reprint, edited by Charles Rosenberg. New York: Garland Publishing, 1985.

Da Silva, Chantal. "Is Trump's Military Strategy Based on Anti-Immigration Fantasy Novel 'Camp of the Saints'?" *Newsweek*, April 4, 2018. https://www.newsweek.com/did-trump-base-military-strategy-anti-immigration-fantasy-novel-camp-saints-871306

Davenport, Charles Benedict. *Heredity in Relation to Eugenics*. New York: Henry Holt, 1911. https://archive.org/details/heredityinrelati00dave/page/n8

Davenport, Charles Benedict. Papers. Archives, American Philosophical Society Library, Philadelphia, PA.

Davenport, Charles Benedict. "Race Crossing in Jamaica." *Scientific Monthly* 27, no. 3 (September 1928): 225–38. http://www.jstor.org/stable/7978

Davenport, Charles Benedict. "Report of Committee on Eugenics." *American Breeders Magazine* 1, no. 2 (April, May, June 1910): 126–29. https://babel.hathitrust.org/cgi/pt?id=uc1.b4528618&view=1up&seq=140

Davenport, Charles Benedict. "Research in Eugenics." In *Eugenics, Genetics and the Family*, vol. 1, *Scientific Papers of the Second International Congress of Eugenics; Held at American Museum of Natural History, New York, September 22–28, 1921*, 20–28. Baltimore, MD: Williams & Wilkins, 1923. Reprint, edited by Charles Rosenberg. New York: Garland Publishing, 1985.

Davenport, Charles Benedict, Ales Hrdlicka, Louis I. Newman, Melville J. Herskovits, Frank H. Hankins, and C. M. Goethe. "Intermarriages between Races: A Eugenic or Dysgenic Force?" *Eugenics* 3, no. 2 (February 1930): 58–62.

Davenport, Charles Benedict, and Morris Steggerda. *Race Crossing in Jamaica*. Washington, DC: Carnegie Institution of Washington, 1929.

Davis, Julie Hirschfeld. "Genial Force behind Bitter Opposition to Immigration

Overhaul." *New York Times*, December 3, 2014. https://www.nytimes.com/2014/12/04/us/politics/roy-h-beck-quietly-leads-a-grass-roots-army.html

Dawsey, Josh. "Trump Derides Protections for Immigrants from 'Shithole' Countries." *Washington Post*, January 12, 2018. https://www.washingtonpost.com/politics/trump-attacks-protections-for-immigrants-from-shithole-countries-in-oval-office-meeting/2018/01/11/bfc0725c-f711-11e7-91af-31ac729add94_story.html?utm_term=.f8673fd27b10

"Dean Emeritus Carl E. Seashore Dies at 83." *University of Iowa News Bulletin* 24, no. 6 (November 1949): 1, 6.

"The Death of Dean Seashore." *Iowa City Press Citizen*, October 18, 1949, 4.

DeBacker, Althea. "Student Pedigree-Studies: A German Bard and His Progeny." *Eugenical News* 18, no. 5 (September-October 1933): 106–8.

de Lapouge, Count [Georges Vacher]. "A French View: A Study of National Policies Which Purpose to Influence Eugenical Trends along Definitely Pre-Determined Lines." *Eugenical News* 19, no. 2 (March-April 1934): 39–40.

Dennis, Charles M. "For One World." *Music Educators Journal* 33, no. 2 (November-December 1946): 13. https://www.jstor.org/stable/3388394

"Department History—the Iowa Tradition." University of Iowa Department of Psychological and Brain Sciences. Accessed December 12, 2018. https://psychology.uiowa.edu/about/department-history%E2%80%94-iowa-tradition

Derbyshire, David. "Melody Gene 'Is the Key to Music Ability.'" *The Telegraph*, March 9, 2001. http://www.telegraph.co.uk/news/uknews/1325655/Melody-gene-is-the-key-to-music-ability.html

Devaney, Johanna. "Eugenics and Musical Talent: Exploring Carl Seashore's Work on Talent Testing and Performance." *American Music Review* 48, no. 2 (Spring, 2019): 1–6. http://www.brooklyn.edu/web/aca_centers_hitchcock/AMR_48-2_Devaney.pdf

Dickson, Margarette Ball. *One Man and a Dream*. 2nd ed. Minneapolis, MN: Argus [1937].

Dikötter, Frank. "Race Culture: Recent Perspectives on the History of Eugenics." *American Historical Review* 103, no. 2 (April 1998): 467–78. https://doi.org/10.2307/2649776

Dillard, Coshandra. "The School-to-Deportation Pipeline." *Teaching Tolerance*, no. 60 (Fall 2018): 42–45.

Distinguished Service Chapter Special Committee. *Distinguished Service Chapter Rules and Guidelines Citation Manual*. Washington, DC: Phi Beta Sigma Fraternity, 2010. http://pbseast.org/wp-content/uploads/2017/12/DSC-Guide-Manual-Approved.pdf

Drake, Raleigh Moseley. "An Experimental Test of the Seashore 'Measures of Musical Talent.'" Master's thesis, Boston University, 1930. https://hdl.handle.net/2144/7401

Drayna, Dennis, Ani Manichaikul, Marlies de Lange, Harold Snieder, and Tim Spector. "Genetic Correlates of Musical Pitch Recognition in Humans." *Science* 291, no. 5510 (March 9, 2001): 1969–72. https://search-proquest-com.ezproxy.library.wisc.edu/docview/213581689/F9A59576DBE84623PQ/73?accountid=465

"Dr. Carl Seashore . . . World Famed Gustavus Graduate Dies." *Greater Gustavus Quarterly* (December 1949): 3, 14.

Du Bois, W. E. Burghardt. "Race Relations in the United States." *Annals of the American Academy of Political and Social Science* 140, no. 229 (November 1928): 6–10. https://www.jstor.org/stable/1016826

Duckworth, Lorna. "Musical Talent Proves to Be Air on a Gene String." *The Independent*, March 9, 2001. https://advance-lexis-com.ezproxy.library.wisc.edu/document/teaserdocument/?pdmfid=1516831&crid=ba315dc3–4ad7–4e2e-8923–301ceb4ece6a&pddocfullpath=%2Fshared%2Fdocument%2Fnews%2Furn%3AcontentItem%3A42HV-8TW0–00SH-812S-00000–00&pddocid=urn%3AcontentItem%3A42HV-8TW0–00SH-812S-00000–00&pdcontentcomponentid=8200&pdteaserkey=h1&pditab=allpods&ecomp=sp79k&earg=sr0&prid=0103974c-70e1–434c-8076–7d1d0573b682

Eggen, J. B. "The Fallacy of Eugenics." *Social Forces* 5, no. 1 (September 1926): 104–9. www.jstor.org/stable/3004817

Emil's Epilogue. Online newsletter published by the Gustavus Adolphus College Department of Psychological Science. Accessed July 22, 2015. https://gustavus.edu/psychology/newsletter/20121012.php

Endersby, James W., and William T. Horner. *Lloyd Gaines and the Fight to End Segregation*. Columbia: University of Missouri Press, 2016.

Engs, Ruth Clifford. *The Progressive Era's Health Reform Movement: A Historical Dictionary*. Westport, CT: Praeger, 2003.

Ensign, Forest C. "Dean Emeritus Carl E. Seashore." *Iowa Alumni Review* 3, no. 1 (December 1949): 8, 21.

Erb, J. Lawrence, Carl E. Seashore, F. W. Wodell, P. W. Dykema, Waldo S. Pratt, T. Carl Whitmer, Will Earhart, and Frederic Lillebridge. "Significant Papers from the M.T.N.A." *Music Supervisors' Journal* 2, no. 3 (January 1916): 12, 14, 16, 18, 20, 22, 24, 26, 28. http://www.jstor.org/stable/3383175

"The Eugenics Committee of the United States of America." *Eugenical News* 10, no. 2 (February 1925): 10–11.

Eugenics, Genetics and the Family, vol. 1, *Scientific Papers of the Second International Congress of Eugenics; Held at American Museum of Natural History, New York, September 22–28, 1921*. Baltimore, MD: Williams & Wilkins, 1923. Reprint, edited by Charles Rosenberg. New York: Garland Publishing, 1985.

"Eugenics Record Office (ERO)." Image Archive on the American Eugenics Movement, DNA Learning Center, Cold Spring Harbor Laboratory. Accessed June 24, 2015. http://www.eugenicsarchive.org/html/eugenics/static/themes/20.html

"Eugenics Research Association—Eighth Annual Meeting." *Eugenical News* 5, no. 7 (July 1920): 52–53.

"Eugenics Research Association Number: Ninth Annual Meeting." *Eugenical News* 6, nos. 7–8 (July-August 1921): 49–56.

"Eugenics Society of the United States of America." *Eugenical News* 8, no. 4 (April 1923): 28–29.

"Explore 23andMe Genetic Reports." 23andMe, Inc. Accessed December 10, 2018. https://medical.23andme.com/reports/

Falcon, Priscilla, and Patricia J. Campbell. "The Politics of Language and the Mexican American: The English Only Movement and Bilingual Education." In *Racism and the Underclass: State Policy and Discrimination against Minorities*, edited by George W. Shepherd Jr. and David Penna, 145–58. New York: Greenwood, 1991.

Faris, Robert E. L. "Reflections on the Ability Dimension in Human Society." *American Sociological Review* 26, no. 6 (December 1961): 835–43.

Farnsworth, Paul R. "The Effects of Role-Taking on Artistic Achievement." *Journal of Aesthetics and Art Criticism* 18, no. 3 (March 1960): 345–49. http://www.jstor.org/stable/428158

Farnsworth, Paul R. "An Historical, Critical, and Experimental Study of the Seashore-Kwalwasser Test Battery." *Genetic Psychology Monographs: Child Behavior, Animal Behavior, and Comparative Psychology* 9, no. 5 (May 1931): 291–393.

Farnsworth, Paul R. *The Social Psychology of Music*. New York: Dryden, 1958.

"Federation for American Immigration Reform." Southern Poverty Law Center. Accessed October 6, 2018. https://www.splcenter.org/fighting-hate/extremist-files/group/federation-american-immigration-reform

Fickau, Ethan. "Seashore Hall Demolition Begins." KCRG-TV9. February 21, 2018. https://www.kcrg.com/content/news/Seashore-Hall-demolition-begins-474715123.html

Fifth Annual Report of the National Research Council [for 1920]. Washington, DC: Government Printing Office, 1921. https://babel.hathitrust.org/cgi/pt?id=chi.20811221&view=1up&seq=231

Finn, Chester E., and Brandon L. Wright. *Failing Our Brightest Kids: The Global Challenge of Educating High-Ability Students*. Cambridge, MA: Harvard Education Press, 2015.

"Finnish Study Shows Musical Aptitude Inherited." TMC News. February 23, 2011. https://www.tmcnet.com/usubmit/2011/02/23/5333381.htm

Fitzpatrick, Tara. "The Figure of Captivity: The Cultural Work of the Puritan Captivity Narrative." *American Literary History* 3, no. 1 (Spring 1991): 1–26. http://www.jstor.org/stable/489730

Flanagan, Aaron Patrick. "Flocking Together: Jason Richwine & the Legacy of the Pioneer Fund's 'Race Realism.'" Center for New Community. May 15, 2013. Accessed October 1, 2013. http://imagine2050.newcomm.org/2013/05/15/flocking-together-jason-richwine-the-legacy-of-the-pioneer-funds-race-realism/ (site discontinued).

"The Flowering of the Valley: Iowa Trains Creative Artists." *Life* 6, no. 23 (June 5, 1939): 54–58.

Flueckiger, Samuel L. "Some Trends in Music Education." *Music Educators Journal* 25, no. 5 (March 1939): 18–19, 81–83. https://www.jstor.org/stable/3385367

"Folder Experts Reports—Report on Mission to Albertville by Alvin Rose—S-0253-0007-06." United Nations Archives. Created April 1–30, 1963, accessed

February 15, 2019. https://search.archives.un.org/experts-reports-report-on-mission-to-albertville-by-alvin-rose

"Folder Technical Assistance—Report on Mission to Albertville by Mr. Alvin Rose, United Nations Senior Social Affairs Consultant—S-0752-0040-08." United Nations Archives. Created April 3–9, 1963, accessed February 15, 2019. https://search.archives.un.org/technical-assistance-report-on-mission-to-albertville-by-mr-alvin-rose-united-nations-senior-social-affairs-consultant

Ford, Nick Aaron. "The Negro Junior College." *Journal of Negro Education* 5, no. 4 (October 1936): 591–94. http://www.jstor.org/stable/2292031

Forkel, Johann Nikolaus. *Johann Sebastian Bach: His Life, Art, and Work.* Translated and annotated by Charles Sanford Terry. London: Constable, 1920. First published as *Ueber Johann Sebastian Bachs Leben, Kunst und Kunstwerke.* Leipzig; Hoffmeister and Kühnel, 1802. https://archive.org/details/johannsebastianb00forkuoft/page/n7

Foucault, Michel. *Discipline and Punish: The Birth of the Prison.* Translated by Alan Sheridan. New York: Vintage Books, 1979.

Foucault, Michel. *The Foucault Reader*, edited by Paul Rabinow. New York: Pantheon Books, 1984.

Foucault, Michel. *The History of Sexuality*, vol. 1, *An Introduction.* Translated by Robert Hurley. New York: Vintage Books, 1990.

Foucault, Michel. *Power/Knowledge: Selected Interviews and Other Writings, 1972–1977*, edited by Colin Gordon. Translated by Colin Gordon, Leo Marshall, John Mepham, and Kate Soper. New York: Pantheon, 1980.

Fourth Annual Report of the National Research Council [for 1919]. Washington, DC: Government Printing Office, 1920. https://babel.hathitrust.org/cgi/pt?id=chi.20811221&view=1up&seq=149

"Freud Centennial History: Psychology, Pedagogy, and School Hygiene, September 6–11, 1909." Clark University. Accessed June 23, 2015. https://www.clarku.edu/micro/freudcentennial/history/1909psych.cfm (link discontinued).

Frick, [Wilhelm]. "German Population and Race Politics." Translated by A. Hellmer. *Eugenical News* 19, no. 2 (March-April 1934): 33–38.

"From the Four Corners: A Tribute to. . . . Carl E. Seashore." *NEA Journal: The Journal of the National Education Association* 38, no. 9 (December 1949): 714.

G. "Improved Breeding by Selection." *The Circular*, n.s., 2, no. 2 (March 27, 1865): 10.

Gabriel, Trip. "Before Trump, Steve King Set the Agenda for the Wall and Anti-Immigrant Politics." *New York Times*, January 10, 2019. https://www.nytimes.com/2019/01/10/us/politics/steve-king-trump-immigration-wall.html

Galton, Francis. "Eugenics: Its Definition, Scope, and Aims." *American Journal of Sociology* 10, no. 1 (July 1904): 1–25. http://www.jstor.org/stable/2762125

Galton, Francis. *Hereditary Genius: An Inquiry into Its Laws and Consequences.* London: Macmillan, 1869. http://galton.org/books/hereditary-genius/1869-FirstEdition/hereditarygenius1869galt.pdf

Galton, Francis. "Hereditary Talent and Character, Part 1." *Macmillan's Magazine* 12, no. 68 (June 1865): 157–66. http://galton.org/essays/1860–1869/galton-1865-hereditary-talent.pdf

Galton, Francis. "Hereditary Talent and Character: Second Paper." *Macmillan's Magazine* 12, no. 70 (August 1865): 318–27. http://search.proquest.com.ezproxy.library.wisc.edu/docview/6117693/fulltextPDF/D24741D1A3E54DC9PQ/4?accountid=465

Galton, Francis. "The History of Twins, as a Criterion of the Relative Powers of Nature and Nurture." *Fraser's Magazine* 12, no. 71 (November 1875): 566–76. https://search-proquest-com.ezproxy.library.wisc.edu/docview/2645576/F0671B2C90084B23PQ/4?accountid=465

Galton, Francis. *Memories of My Life*. New York: E. P. Dutton, 1909. https://archive.org/stream/memoriesmylife01galtgoog#mode/2up/search/323

"Galton Society." *Eugenical News* 11, no. 12 (December 1926): 188–90.

Gardner, Howard, and Thomas Hatch. "Multiple Intelligences Go to School: Educational Implications of the Theory of Multiple Intelligences." *Educational Researcher* 18, no. 8 (November 1989): 4–10.

Garland, David. "What Is a 'History of the Present?' On Foucault's Genealogies and Their Critical Preconditions." *Punishment & Society* 16, no. 4 (2014): 365–84.

Garth, Thomas Russell. "Race and Psychology." *Scientific Monthly* 23, no. 3 (September 1926): 240–45. https://www.jstor.org/stable/7525

Garth, Thomas Russell. *Race Psychology: A Study of Racial Mental Differences*. New York: Whittlesey House, 1931.

Garth, Thomas Russell, and Sarah Rachel Isbell. "The Musical Talent of Indians." *Music Supervisors' Journal* 15, no. 3 (February 1929): 83, 85–87. www.jstor.org/stable/3382960

Gehrkens, Karl W. "MENC: Remembering the Early Years." *Music Educators Journal* 54, no. 2 (October 1967): 59–60. http://www.jstor.org/stable/3391097

Gehrkens, Karl W. "Music for Every Child; Every Child FOR Music." *Music Supervisors' Journal* 19, no. 5 (May 1933): 31. http://www.jstor.org/stable/3384232

Gehrkens, Karl W. "A Philosophy of Universal Music Education." *Journal of Research in Music Education* 16, no. 3 (Autumn 1968): 278–81. www.jstor.org/stable/3344083

Gehrkens, Karl W. "Some Questions." In *Journal of Proceedings of the Sixteenth Annual Meeting of the Music Supervisors' National Conference Held at Cleveland, Ohio, April 9–13, 1923*, edited by George Oscar Bowen, 28–38. Ann Arbor, MI: University School of Music, 1923. https://archive.org/details/journalofproceed017536mbp/page/n33

Gelb, Steven A. "Social Deviance and the 'Discovery' of the Moron." *Disability, Handicap, and Society* 2, no. 3 (September 1987): 247–58.

"German Sterilization Progress." *Eugenical News* 19, no. 2 (March-April 1934): 38.

Gerstein, Josh, and Ted Hesson. "Judge Largely Rejects Trump Bid to Block California Sanctuary Laws." *Politico*, July 5, 2018. https://www.politico.com/story/2018/07/05/trump-sanctuary-cities-ruling-695286

Getz, Russell P. "1984 and Beyond." *Music Educators Journal* 70, no. 1 (September 1983): 52–54. www.jstor.org/stable/3401187

Gfeller, Kate, Don D. Coffman, Carlos X. Rodriguez, and David J. Nelson, eds.

Multidisciplinary Perspectives on Musicality: Essays from the Seashore Symposium. Iowa City: University of Iowa School of Music, 2006.

Gillborn, David. "Softly, Softly: Genetics, Intelligence and the Hidden Racism of the New Geneism." *Journal of Education Policy* 31, no. 4 (2016): 365–88. http://dx.doi.org/10.1080/02680939.2016.1139189

Gilliam, Dorothy Butler. "'Trailblazer' Dorothy Butler Gilliam's 'Fight to Make the Media Look More Like America.'" Interview by Meghna Chakrabarti. *On Point* podcast, WBUR, January 8, 2019. Audio, 47:19. https://www.wbur.org/onpoint/2019/01/08/trailblazer-dorothy-butler-gilliam-media-diversity-washington-post

Goddard, Henry H. "Forty Years of 'Firsts,'" review of *Pioneering in Psychology*, by Carl. E. Seashore. *Journal of Higher Education* 14, no. 4 (April 1943): 225–26. https://doi.org/10.2307/1975715

Goddard, Henry H. *The Kallikak Family: A Study in the Heredity of Feeble-Mindedness*. New York: Macmillan, 1916. https://books.google.com/books?id=PjUVAAAAIAAJ&pg=PP1#v=onepage&q&f=false

Goddard, Henry H. *School Training of Gifted Children*. Yonkers-on-Hudson, NY: World Book, 1928. https://babel.hathitrust.org/cgi/pt?id=mdp.39015008191929&view=1up&seq=5

Goldin, Claudia, Lawrence F. Katz, and Ilyana Kuziemko. "The Homecoming of American College Women: The Reversal of the College Gender Gap." *Journal of Economic Perspectives* 20, no. 4 (Fall 2006): 133–56, A1–A4.

Golston, Michael. "'Im Anfang war der Rhythmus': Rhythmic Incubations in Discourses of Mind, Body, and Race from 1850–1944." *Stanford Electronic Humanities Review Supplement: Cultural and Technological Incubations of Fascism* 5 (December 17, 1996). https://web.stanford.edu/group/SHR/5-supp/text/golston.html

Goodstein, Leonard D. "The Iowa Department of Psychology and the American Psychological Association: A Historical Analysis." In *Psychology at Iowa: Centennial Essays*, edited by Joan H. Cantor, 51–59. Hillsdale, NJ: Lawrence Erlbaum, 1991.

Gordon, Edwin E. *Introduction to Research and the Psychology of Music*. Chicago: GIA, 1998.

Gordon, Edwin E. *Learning Sequences in Music: A Contemporary Music Learning Theory*. Chicago: GIA, 2007.

Gordon, Edwin E. *Learning Sequences in Music: Skill, Content, and Patterns; A Music Learning Theory*. Chicago: GIA, 1993.

Gordon, Edwin E. *Learning Sequences in Music: Skill, Content, and Patterns; A Music Learning Theory, Study Guide*. G-2345SG. Chicago, IL: GIA Publications, 1997.

Gordon, Edwin E. "The Legacy of Carl E. Seashore." In *Multidisciplinary Perspectives on Musicality: Essays from the Seashore Symposium*, edited by Kate Gfeller, Don D. Coffman, Carlos X. Rodriguez, and David J. Nelson, 51–61. Iowa City: University of Iowa School of Music, 2006.

Gordon, Edwin E. "Music Aptitude Profile (Grades 5–12)." GIA Publications, Inc.

Accessed January 11, 2019. https://www.giamusic.com/products/P-musicaptitudeprofile.cfm

Gould, Stephen Jay. *The Mismeasure of Man*. New York: W. W. Norton, 1996.

"Graduate Faculty Adopts Radical Changes." *University of Iowa News Bulletin* 4, no. 6 (June 1929): 1–3.

Grant, Julia. *Raising Baby by the Book: The Education of American Mothers*. New Haven, CT: Yale University Press, 1998.

Grant, Madison. Introduction to *The Rising Tide of Color against White World-Supremacy*, by Lothrop Stoddard, xi–xxxii. New York: Charles Scribner's Sons, 1921. https://archive.org/details/risingtideofcolo00stoduoft/page/n7

Grant, Madison. *The Passing of the Great Race, or The Racial Basis of European History*. New York: Charles Scribner's Sons, 1916.

Grashel, John. "The Measurement of Musical Aptitude in 20th Century United States: A Brief History." *Bulletin of the Council for Research in Music Education*, no. 176 (Spring 2008): 45–49. http://www.jstor.org/stable/40319432

Gray, C. T., and C. W. Bingham. "A Comparison of Certain Phases of Musical Ability of Colored and White Public School Pupils." *Journal of Educational Psychology* 20, no. 7 (October 1929): 501–6. https://doi.org/10.1037/h0073171

"The Great Nordic Race," review of *The Passing of the Great Race*, by Madison Grant. *Eugenical News* 2, no. 2 (February 1917): 10–11.

"Great Schools of Opera [Front Matter]." *Music Supervisors' Journal* 5, no. 2 (November 1918): 13. http://www.jstor.org/stable/3382352

"The Groups." *Intelligence Report*. Southern Poverty Law Center, January 29, 2010. https://www.splcenter.org/fighting-hate/intelligence-report/2015/groups

"A Guide to S.744: Understanding the 2013 Senate Immigration Bill." American Immigration Council. July 10, 2013. https://americanimmigrationcouncil.org/research/guide-s744-understanding-2013-senate-immigration-bill

Gur-Arie, Rachel. "American Eugenics Society (1926–1972)." *Embryo Project Encyclopedia*. Last modified July 4, 2018. https://embryo.asu.edu/pages/american-eugenics-society-1926–1972

Gustafson, Ruth Iana. *Race and Curriculum: Music in Childhood Education*. New York: Palgrave, 2009.

"Guy Benton Johnson Facts." Your Dictionary. 2010. http://biography.yourdictionary.com/guy-benton-johnson (link discontinued).

Hacking, Ian. *Historical Ontology*. Cambridge, MA: Harvard University Press, 2002.

Hacking, Ian. "Making Up People." In *Reconstructing Individualism: Autonomy, Individuality, and the Self in Western Thought*, edited by Thomas C. Heller, Morton Sosna, and David E. Wellbery, 222–36. Stanford: Stanford University Press, 1986.

Hancher, Virgil M. Papers. Special Collections and University Archives, University of Iowa Libraries, Iowa City, IA.

Hannaford, Ivan. *Race: The History of an Idea in the West*. Washington, DC: Woodrow Wilson Center; Baltimore: Johns Hopkins, 1996.

Harmon, Amy. "In DNA Era, New Worries about Prejudice." *New York Times*, November 11, 2007. http://www.nytimes.com/2007/11/11/us/11dna.html?_r+1&ex=1195448400&en=b01d056

Harper, Robert S. "Tables of American Doctorates in Psychology." *American Journal of Psychology* 62, no. 4 (October 1949): 579–87. http://www.jstor.org/stable/1418564

Harris, James C. "Clark University Vicennial Conference on Psychology and Pedagogy." *Archives of General Psychiatry* 67, no. 3 (March 2010): 218–19. https://doi.org/10.1001/archgenpsychiatry.2010.16

Harris, Reginald G. "Eugenics in South America." *Eugenical News* 7, no. 3 (March 1922): 17–42.

Harris, Reginald G. "Negro Art as an Indication of Racial Development." *Eugenical News* 8, no. 9 (September 1923): 82–86.

Harry, Adam G. "America's Got Talent? Interrogating Students' Constructions of Musical Ability." PhD diss., University of Wisconsin–Madison, 2018.

Hasian Jr., Marouf Arif. *Eugenics in Anglo-American Thought*. Athens: University of Georgia Press, 1996.

Hassencahl, Frances Janet. "Harry H. Laughlin, 'Expert Eugenics Agent' for the House Committee on Immigration and Naturalization, 1921 to 1931." PhD diss., Case Western Reserve University, 1970. https://search-proquest-com.ezproxy.library.wisc.edu/docview/302467912?

Hayden, Michael Edison. "Stephen Miller's Affinity for White Nationalism Revealed in Leaked Emails." *Hatewatch* (blog). Southern Poverty Law Center, November 12, 2019. https://www.splcenter.org/hatewatch/2019/11/12/stephen-millers-affinity-white-nationalism-revealed-leaked-emails

Hays, W. M. "Editorials, Efficiency Records of People." *American Breeders Magazine* 1, no. 3 (1910): 222. https://babel.hathitrust.org/cgi/pt?id=uma.ark:/13960/t0ft91b2c&view=1up&seq=242

Hays, W. M. "Editorials, Heredity in Man." *American Breeders Magazine* 1, no. 3 (1910): 221–22. https://babel.hathitrust.org/cgi/pt?id=uma.ark:/13960/t0ft91b2c&view=1up&seq=241

Hays, W. M. "Editorials, Unit Character in Man." *American Breeders Magazine* 1, no. 3 (1910): 223. https://babel.hathitrust.org/cgi/pt?id=uma.ark:/13960/t0ft91b2c&view=1up&seq=243

Heidingsfelder, Lauren. "The Slogan of the Century: 'Music for Every Child; Every Child for Music.'" *Music Educators Journal* 100, no. 4 (June 2014): 47–51. https://www.jstor.org/stable/43288870

Heinlein, Christian Paul. "The Affective Characters of the Major and Minor Modes in Music." *Journal of Comparative Psychology* 8, no. 2 (April 1928): 101–42. http://web.b.ebscohost.com.ezproxy.library.wisc.edu/ehost/pdfviewer/pdfviewer?vid=4&sid=710fa1c4-e24e-42af-80f1–3b7aae8ab1cf%40pdc-v-sessmgr06

Heinlein, Christian Paul. "A Brief Discussion of the Nature and Function of Melodic Configuration in Tonal Memory, with Critical Reference to the Seashore Tonal Memory Test." *Pedagogical Seminary and Journal of Genetic Psychology* 35, no. 1 (1928): 45–61.

Heinlein, Christian Paul. "An Experimental Study of the Seashore Consonance Test." *Journal of Experimental Psychology* 8, no. 6 (December 1925): 408–33. http://dx.doi.org/10.1037/h0069544

Heinze, Andrew R. *Jews and the American Soul: Human Nature in the Twentieth Century*. Princeton, NJ: Princeton University Press, 2004.

Herbert, Bob. "In America: Throwing a Curve." *New York Times*, October 26, 1994, A27. https://www.nytimes.com/1994/10/26/opinion/in-america-throwing-a-curve.html

"Higher Degrees in Sociology Conferred in 1947." *American Journal of Sociology* 54, no. 1 (July 1948): 57–62. http://www.jstor.org/stable/2770600

Hilgard, Ernest R. "Psychology at Iowa before McGeoch and Spence." In *Psychology at Iowa: Centennial Essays*, edited by Joan H. Cantor, 37–49. Hillsdale, NJ: Lawrence Erlbaum, 1991.

Hilgard, Ernest R. "Robert Mearns Yerkes: 1876–1956," vol. 38, *Biographical Memoirs*, 383–425. Washington, DC: National Academy of Sciences, 1965. http://www.nasonline.org/publications/biographical-memoirs/memoir-pdfs/yerkes-robert-m.pdf

Hinrichs, James V. "Carl E. Seashore as Psychologist." In *Multidisciplinary Perspectives on Musicality: Essays from the Seashore Symposium*, edited by Kate Gfeller, Don D. Coffman, Carlos X. Rodriguez, and David J. Nelson, 9–10. Iowa City: University of Iowa School of Music, 2006.

"History." Hampton University. Accessed July 16, 2018. http://www.hamptonu.edu/about/history.cfm

"History of Agricultural Statistics." USDA National Agricultural Statistics Service. Last modified May 4, 2018. https://www.nass.usda.gov/About_NASS/History_of_Ag_Statistics/

"History of Miessner Piano Development in Booklet." *Music Trade Review* 77, no. 6 (August 11, 1923): 28. https://mtr.arcade-museum.com/MTR-1923-77-6/index.php?page_no=28

"Hitler and Race Pride." *Eugenical News* 17, no. 2 (March-April 1932): 60–61.

Hodson, C. B. S. "Eugenics in Norway." *Eugenics Review* 27, no. 1 (April 1935): 41–44.

Hoffman, Adria R. "Competing Narratives: Musical Aptitude, Race, and Equity." In *Palgrave Handbook of Race and the Arts in Education*, edited by Amelia M. Kraehe, Rubén Gaztambide-Fernández, and B. Stephen Carpenter II, 103–17. Cham, Switzerland: Palgrave, 2018. https://link.springer.com/book/10.1007%2F978-3-319-65256-6

Hollingworth, Leta S. *Gifted Children: Their Nature and Nurture*. New York: Macmillan, 1926. https://archive.org/details/in.ernet.dli.2015.87120/page/n5

Holmes, W. H. "Promotion Classes for Gifted Pupils." *Journal of Education* 75, no. 14 (April 4, 1912): 376–79. www.jstor.org/stable/42819686

Holmgren, David. "Lindquist, Everet Franklin." In *The Biographical Dictionary of Iowa*. Iowa City: University of Iowa Press, 2009. http://uipress.lib.uiowa.edu/bdi/DetailsPage.aspx?id=233

"Homecoming." *Iowa Alumnus* 15, no.3 (December 1917): 70–72. https://books.google.com/books?id=7xRIAQAAMAAJ&pg=PA72&lpg=PA72&dq=Reuel+H.+Sylvester&source=bl&ots=ALOQ6N-rk3&sig=1RZeK9MuOrVmpNd3iolFS

-tB7pc&hl=en&sa=X&ved=0ahUKEwiBwNOUoN7aAhXG8YMKHRLwBa4Q6AEIMTAD#v=onepage&q=Reuel%20H.%20Sylvester&f=false

hooks, bell [Gloria Watkins]. *Black Looks: Race and Representation*. Boston: South End Press, 1992.

The House I Live In. Directed by Eugene Jarecki. New York, NY: Virgil Films and Entertainment, 2013. DVD, 108 min.

Howard, Donald F. "History of the State University of Iowa: The Graduate College." PhD diss., University of Iowa, 1947.

Human Cloning and Human Dignity: The Report of the President's Council on Bioethics. New York: PublicAffairs, 2002.

Humphreys, Jere T. "Musical Aptitude Testing: From James McKeen Cattell to Carl Emil Seashore," vol. 5, *Sage Directions in Educational Psychology*, edited by Neil J. Salkind, 115–29. Los Angeles: Sage, 2011. Reprinted from *Research Studies in Music Education* 10 (1998): 42–53.

Humphreys, Jere T. "Precursors of Musical Aptitude Testing: From the Greeks through the Work of Francis Galton." *Journal of Research in Music Education* 41, no. 4 (Winter 1993): 315–27. http://www.jstor.org/stable/3345507

Hunter-Doniger, Tracey. "The Eugenics Movement and Its Impact on Art Education in the United States." *Arts Education Policy Review* 118, no. 2 (2017): 83–92. https://doi.org/10.1080/10632913.2015.1051256

Huntington, Ellsworth. *Tomorrow's Children: The Goal of Eugenics*. New York: J. Wiley & Sons, 1935. https://babel.hathitrust.org/cgi/pt?id=mdp.39015034788995;view=1up;seq=7

"'I Can See America Go Singing to Her Destiny [Front Matter].'" *Music Supervisors' Journal* 9, no. 5 (May 1923): 9. http://www.jstor.org/stable/3382974?seq=4#page_scan_tab_contents

"Image Archive on the American Eugenics Movement." DNA Learning Center, Cold Spring Harbor Laboratory. http://www.eugenicsarchive.org/eugenics/list_topics.pl

"In Memoriam: Alvin W. Rose." *Arts and Sciences Magazine* (University of Miami) 9, no. 1 (Fall 2008): 29. https://merrick.library.miami.edu/cdm/fullbrowser/collection/asu0242/id/574/rv/compoundobject/cpd/603

"In Memoriam—Carl E. Seashore." *Educational Forum* 14, no. 3, pt. 2 (March 1950): 384h.

"In Praise of Eugenics." *Eugenics* 2, no. 2 (February 1929): 36.

"An Invitation [Front Matter]." *Music Supervisors' Journal* 9, no. 4 (March 1923): 7. http://www.jstor.org/stable/3383049

Jackson, Hallie, and Tim Stelloh. "White Nationalist Alt-Righter Claims 'Hail Trump' Comments Were 'Ironic.'" NBC News. November 21, 2016. https://www.nbcnews.com/politics/white-house/white-nationalist-alt-righter-claims-hail-trump-comments-were-ironic-n687021

Jackson, Michael. *At Home in the World*. Durham, NC: Duke University Press, 1995.

"Jared Taylor." Southern Poverty Law Center. Accessed October 7, 2018. https://www.splcenter.org/fighting-hate/extremist-files/individual/jared-taylor

"Jean-Philippe Rushton." Southern Poverty Law Center. Accessed August 6, 2018. https://www.splcenter.org/fighting-hate/extremist-files/individual/jean-philip pe-rushton

Jensen, Arthur. "A Conversation with Arthur Jensen (Part II)." Interview by *American Renaissance*. *American Renaissance* 3, no. 9 (September 1992): 1, 3–5.

Jessup, Walter A. Papers. Special Collections and University Archives, University of Iowa Libraries, Iowa City, IA.

"Jewish Physicians in Berlin." *Eugenical News* 19, no. 5 (September-October 1934): 126.

Johnson, Guy Benton. "Musical Talent and the Negro." *Music Supervisors' Journal* 15, no. 1 (October 1928): 81, 83, 96. www.jstor.org/stable/3383738 (p. 96 missing from JSTOR).

Johnson, Guy Benton. "The Negro and Musical Talent." *Southern Workman* 56, no. 10 (October 1927): 439–44.

Johnson, Guy Benton. "A Study of the Musical Talent of the American Negro." PhD diss., University of North Carolina, 1927.

Johnson, Joshua. "Preserving Stories of Holocaust Survivors." *1A* podcast, produced by Amanda Williams, November 8, 2018. Audio, 35:24. https://the1a.org/shows /2018-11-08/preserving-stories-of-holocaust-survivors

Johnstone, E. R. "Waste Land Plus Waste Humanity." *Training School Bulletin* 11, no. 4 (June 1914): 60–63. https://books.google.com/books?id=pPBEAQAAM AAJ&pg=PA60&lpg=PA60&dq=johnstone+waste+land+plus+waste+humani ty+training+school+bulletin&source=bl&ots=cLqT7YMOhv&sig=ACfU3U2 vX6q25ZziEI2AEVTNbnQ7PbltfA&hl=en&sa=X&ved=2ahUKEwimye3F _crnAhWXB50JHXUQDWQQ6AEwAXoECAsQAQ#v=onepage&q=was te%20land%20plus%20waste%20humanity&f=false

"John Tanton Is the Mastermind behind the Organized Anti-Immigration Movement." *Intelligence Report*. Southern Poverty Law Center, June 18, 2002. https:// www.splcenter.org/fighting-hate/intelligence-report/2002/john-tanton -mastermind-behind-organized-anti-immigration-movement

Jones, Lewis Lester. "Carl Emil Seashore: Dean of the Graduate College of the University of Iowa, 1908 to 1936, Dean *Pro Tempore*, 1942 to 1946; A Study of His Ideas on Graduate Education." PhD diss., University of Iowa, 1978. http:// search.proquest.com.ezproxy.library.wisc.edu/docview/302883038?accountid =465

Jones, Sarah. "The Notorious Book that Ties the Right to the Far Right." *New Republic*, February 2, 2018. https://newrepublic.com/article/146925/notorious -book-ties-right-far-right

Jones, Sarah. "Trump Has Turned the GOP into the Party of Eugenics." *New Republic*, February 15, 2017. https://newrepublic.com/article/140641/trump-tu rned-gop-party-eugenics

"Jon Feere." LinkedIn. Accessed October 6, 2018. https://www.linkedin.com/in/jo nfeere/

Jorgensen, Estelle R. "The Seashore-Mursell Debate on the Psychology of Music Revisited." In *Multidisciplinary Perspectives on Musicality: Essays from the Seashore*

Symposium, edited by Kate Gfeller, Don D. Coffman, Carlos X. Rodriguez, and David J. Nelson, 62–77. Iowa City: University of Iowa School of Music, 2006.

Joseph, Jay. *The Trouble with Twin Studies: A Reassessment of Twin Research in the Social and Behavioral Sciences*. New York: Routledge, 2015.

"Joseph Lewis." Freedom from Religion Foundation. Accessed June 7, 2017. https://ffrf.org/news/day/dayitems/item/14432-joseph-lewis

Joyce, John St. George, ed. *Story of Philadelphia*. Philadelphia: Rex Printing House, 1919. https://babel.hathitrust.org/cgi/pt?id=loc.ark:/13960/t9v129m98;view=1up;seq=7

"Julie Kirchner." United States Department of Homeland Security. Last modified May 10, 2017. https://www.dhs.gov/person/julie-kirchner

Kant, Immanuel. *The Critique of Judgement* (1790). Translated by James Creed Meredith. Oxford: Oxford University Press, 1952.

Kant, Immanuel. *Critique of the Power of Judgment* (1790), edited by Paul Guyer. Translated by Paul Guyer and Eric Matthews. Cambridge: Cambridge University Press, 2000.

Karp, Laurence E. "Past Perfect: John Humphrey Noyes, Stirpiculture, and the Oneida Community—Part II." *American Journal of Medical Genetics* 12, no. 2 (June 1982): 127–30. http://onlinelibrary.wiley.com/doi/10.1002/ajmg.1320120202/pdf

Keene, James A. *A History of Music Education in the United States*. Hanover, NH: University Press of New England, 1982.

Kelleher, Daniel T. "The Case of Lloyd Lionel Gaines: The Demise of the Separate but Equal Doctrine." *Journal of Negro History* 56, no. 4 (October 1971): 262–71. https://www.jstor.org/stable/2716967

Kendall, John S. "1891 Gustavus Graduate Dr. Seashore Ranked as One of Top Alumni." Gustavus Adolphus College. Accessed January 20, 2005. http://gustavus.edu/academics/psychology/Epilogue/Seashore.html

Kendi, Ibram X. *Stamped from the Beginning: The Definitive History of Racist Ideas in America*. New York: Nation Books, 2016.

Kendler, Howard H. "The Iowa Tradition." In *Psychology at Iowa: Centennial Essays*, edited by Joan H. Cantor, 1–17. Hillsdale, NJ: Lawrence Erlbaum, 1991.

Kenny, Michael G. "Toward a Racial Abyss: Eugenics, Wickliffe Draper, and the Origins of the Pioneer Fund." *Journal of History of the Behavioral Sciences* 38, no. 3 (Summer 2002): 259–83.

Kevles, Daniel J. "Here Comes the Master Race," review of *War against the Weak*, by Edwin Black. *New York Times*, October 5, 2003, late edition, sec. 7, 8. https://www.nytimes.com/2003/10/05/books/here-comes-the-master-race.html

Kevles, Daniel J. *In the Name of Eugenics: Genetics and the Uses of Human Heredity*. Berkeley: University of California Press, 1986

Kimmel, Michael. *Manhood in America: A Cultural History*. New York: Free Press, 1996.

King, Steve. "Steve King: Bring Pride Back to Austria." Interview by Caroline Sommerfeld. *Unzensuriert*, September 2, 2018. https://www.unzensuriert.at/content/0027654-restore-western-civilization-world-interview-steve-king

Kline, Wendy. *Building a Better Race: Gender, Sexuality, and Eugenics from the Turn of the Century to the Baby Boom*. Berkeley: University of California Press, 2001.

Kornspan, Alan S. "Contributions to Sports Psychology: Walter R. Miles and the Early Studies on the Motor Skills of Athletes." *Comprehensive Psychology* 3, article 17 (2014): 1–11. https://journals.sagepub.com/doi/pdf/10.2466/32.CP.3.17

Koza, Julia Eklund. "In Sounds and Silences: Acknowledging Political Engagement." *Philosophy of Music Education Review* 15, no. 2 (Fall 2007): 168–76.

Koza, Julia Eklund. "Listening for Whiteness: Hearing Racial Politics in Undergraduate School Music." *Philosophy of Music Education Review* 16, no. 2 (Fall 2008): 145–55.

Koza, Julia Eklund. "The 'Missing Males' and Other Gender Issues in Music Education: Evidence from the *Music Supervisors' Journal*, 1914–1924." *Journal of Research in Music Education* 41, no. 3 (October 1993): 212–32.

Koza, Julia Eklund. "Music and the Feminine Sphere: Images of Women as Musicians in *Godey's Lady's Book*, 1830–1877." *Musical Quarterly* 75, no. 2 (Summer 1991): 103–29.

Koza, Julia Eklund. "Music and References to Music in *Godey's Lady's Book*, 1830–1877." PhD diss., University of Minnesota, 1988.

Koza, Julia Eklund. "Someday They Will Dance." *Women and Music: A Journal of Gender and Culture* 16 (2012): 97–112.

Kretschmer, Ernst. "The Breeding of the Mental Endowments of Genius." *Eugenics* 4, no. 1 (January 1931): 6–11.

Kucsan, Kathryn M. "Historical Perspectives on Approaches to Aesthetics in Early Music Psychology: The Writings of Carl E. Seashore (1866–1949) and Vernon Lee (1856–1935)." PhD diss., University of Colorado, 1995.

Kunst, Jaap. *De Inheemse muziek in Westelijk Nieuw-Guinea*. Koninklijke Vereeniging Indisch Instituut, Amsterdam, Mededeling no. 43, Afdeling Culturele en Physische Anthropologie no. 38. Amsterdam: Indisch Instituut, 1950.

Kunst, Jaap. *Ethno-Musicology: A Study of Its Nature, Its Problems, Methods and Representative Personalities to Which Is Added a Bibliography*. 2nd ed. Hague, Netherlands: Martinus Nijhoff, 1955.

Kwalwasser, Jacob. "From the Realm of Guess into the Realm of Reasonable Certainty." *Music Educators Journal* 24, no. 4 (February 1938): 16–17. http://www.jstor.org/stable/3385448

Kwalwasser, Jacob. "Scientific Testing in Music." *Music Supervisors' Journal* 12, no. 3 (February 1926): 18–24. www.jstor.org/stable/3383064

Kwalwasser, Jacob. "The Vibrato: In Phono-Photography." PhD diss., University of Iowa, 1925.

Ladson-Billings, Gloria. "The Social Funding of Race: The Role of Schooling." Working paper, undated pre-2008. A revised and expanded version of this essay appeared in *Peabody Journal of Education* 93, no. 1 (2018): 90–105. https://doi.org/10.1080/0161956X.2017.1403182

Lanier, Lyle H. Review of *Race Psychology: A Study of Racial Mental Differences*, by

Thomas Russell Garth. *American Journal of Psychology* 45, no. 1 (January 1933): 183–86. https://doi.org/10.2307/1414212

Laughlin, Harry H. "The Progress of American Eugenics." *Eugenics* 2, no. 2 (February 1929): 3–16.

Lawrence, Cera R. "The Eugenics Record Office at Cold Spring Harbor Laboratory (1910–1939)." *Embryo Project Encyclopedia*. April 21, 2011. http://embryo.asu.edu/handle/10776/2091

Leark, Robert A., Tammy R. Dupuy, Lawrence M. Greenberg, Carol L. Kindschi, and Steven J. Hughes. *T.O.V.A. Professional Manual: Test of Variables of Attention Continuous Performance Test*. Ed. no. 8.2-135-ge19058. Los Alamitos, CA: TOVA, March 28, 2016. http://files.tovatest.com/documentation/8/Professional%20Manual.pdf

Lehman, Paul R. "The Predictive Measurement of Musical Success." *Journal of Research in Music Education* 17, no. 1 (Spring 1969): 16–31. www.jstor.org/stable/3344180

Lehmann, Nicholas. *The Big Test: The Secret History of the American Meritocracy*. New York: Farrar, Straus and Giroux, 1999.

Lenoir, Zaid Delmas. "Measurement of Racial Differences in Certain Mental and Educational Abilities." Master's thesis, State University of Iowa, 1925.

Leon, Sharon Mara. "Beyond Birth Control: Catholic Responses to the Eugenics Movement in the United States, 1900–1950." Order No. 3142627. PhD diss., University of Minnesota, 2004. https://search-proquest-com.ezproxy.library.wisc.edu/pqdtglobal/docview/305158996/fulltextPDF/1269932D352428FPQ/1?accountid=465

Leonardo, Zeus, and Alicia A. Broderick. "Smartness as Property: A Critical Exploration of Intersections between Whiteness and Disability Studies." *Teachers College Record* 113, no. 10 (2011): 2206–32. http://www.tcrecord.org.ezproxy.library.wisc.edu/library/content.asp?contentid=16431

Leonhard, Charles, and Robert W. House. *Foundations and Principles of Music Education*. New York: McGraw-Hill, 1959.

Leonhard, Charles, and Robert W. House. *Foundations and Principles of Music Education*. 2nd ed. New York: McGraw-Hill, 1972.

Levinas, Emmanuel. *Ethics and Infinity: Conversations with Philippe Nemo*. Translated by Richard A. Cohen. Pittsburgh, PA: Duquesne University Press, 1985.

Levinas, Emmanuel. *The Levinas Reader*, edited by Seán Hand. Oxford: Basil Blackwell, 1989.

Levine, Philippa, and Alison Bashford. "Eugenics and the Modern World." In *The Oxford Handbook of the History of Eugenics*, edited by Alison Bashford and Philippa Levine, 3–24. Oxford: Oxford University Press, 2010.

"Lewin Center Founders." Lewin Center. Accessed January 13, 2019. http://www.lewincenter.org/founders.html (site redesigned; see Wayback Machine).

Lewis, Bernard. *Race and Slavery in the Middle East: An Historical Inquiry*. New York: Oxford University Press, 1990.

Lewis, Richard C. "Paying Homage to Seashore Hall." *Iowa Now*, November 27, 2017. https://now.uiowa.edu/2017/11/paying-homage-seashore-hall

Liasson, Mara. "Politics in the News: Immigration and the Southern Border Crisis." *Morning Edition*, NPR, June 19, 2018. https://www.npr.org/2018/06/19/621269617/politics-in-the-news-immigration-and-the-southern-border-crisis

Liebman, Elad, Eitan Ornoy, and Benny Chor. "A Phylogenetic Approach to Music Performance Analysis." *Journal of New Music Research* 41, no. 2 (2012): 215–42. http://dx.doi.org/10.1080/09298215.2012.668194 (current online PDF has different pagination).

Lindenmeyer, Kriste. *"A Right to Childhood": The U.S. Children's Bureau and Child Welfare, 1912–46*. Urbana: University of Illinois Press, 1997.

Linder, Marc. "He Sells Misogynistic Ideas by the Seashore." *Daily Iowan*, March 7, 1997, 4A–5A.

Linn, Mott R. "College Entrance Examinations in the United States: A Brief History for Counselors. . . ." *Journal of College Admission* 140 (Spring 1993): 6–16.

Lippmann, Walter. "The Abuse of the Tests (IV)." *New Republic* 32, no. 415 (November 15, 1922): 297–98.

"Lois Jeanne Mayhew Recaptures Title in Iowa 'Brain Derby.'" *Daily Iowan*, June 9, 1937, 1, 6. http://dailyiowan.lib.uiowa.edu/DI/1937/di1937-06-09.pdf

Lombardo, Paul A. "'The American Breed': Nazi Eugenics and the Origins of the Pioneer Fund." *Albany Law Review* 65, no. 3 (February 2002): 743–830. http://search.ebscohost.com/login.aspx?direct=true&AuthType=ip,uid&db=aph&AN=6658610&site=ehost-live&scope=site (link omits pp. 743–44).

Lombardo, Paul A. "When Harvard Said No to Eugenics: The J. Ewing Mears Bequest, 1927." *Perspectives in Biology and Medicine* 57, no. 3 (Summer 2014): 374–92. http://citeseerx.ist.psu.edu/viewdoc/download?doi=10.1.1.825.1686&rep=rep1&type=pdf

"Lorenzo Greene, Lincoln University History Professor, 1933–72." In *Lionel Gaines: The Man, the Mission, the Mystery*, an exhibition organized and presented by the Lincoln University Archives and Ethnic Studies Center. October 1, 2015. Section 1, part 17, item 3.2. https://bluetigercommons.lincolnu.edu/lgaines_sec1/17/

Lowery, H. "Cadence and Phrase Tests in Music." *British Journal of Psychology* 17, no. 2 (October 1926): 111–18. https://doi.org/10.1111/j.2044–8295.1926.tb00414.x

Lowery, H. "Musical Memory." *British Journal of Psychology* 19, no. 4 (April 1929): 397–404. https://doi.org/10.1111/j.2044–8295.1929.tb00525.x

Lubin, Alex. *Romance and Rights: The Politics of Interracial Intimacy, 1945–1954*. Jackson, MS: University Press of Mississippi, 2005.

Lundin, R. W. "Seashore, Carl Emil (1866–1949)," vol. 3, *Encyclopedia of Psychology*, edited by Raymond J. Corsini, 279. New York: John Wiley and Sons, 1984.

Lynn, Richard. *Eugenics: A Reassessment*. Westport, CT: Praeger, 2001.

Lynn, Richard. *Race Differences in Intelligence: An Evolutionary Analysis*. Augusta, GA: Washington Summit, 2006.

Lynn, Richard, R. Graham Wilson, and Adrienne Gault. "Simple Musical Tests as Measures of Spearman's g." *Personality and Individual Differences* 10, no. 1 (1989): 25–28. https://doi-org.ezproxy.library.wisc.edu/10.1016/0191–8869(89)90173–6

MacDonald, Gregory. "Introduction: Between Heresy and Dogma." In *"All Shall Be Well": Explorations in Universalism and Christian Theology from Origen to Moltmann*, edited by Gregory MacDonald, 1–25. Cambridge, UK: James Clarke, 2011. ProQuest Ebook Central. https://ebookcentral.proquest.com/lib/wisc/reader.action?docID=3328652

"Mainstream Science on Intelligence." *Wall Street Journal (1923–Current File)*, December 13, 1994, A18. http://search.proquest.com.ezproxy.library.wisc.edu/docview/904944036?accountid=465

Mainwaring, James. "The Assessment of Musical Ability." *British Journal of Educational Psychology* 17, no. 2 (June 1947): 83–96. https://doi-org.ezproxy.library.wisc.edu/10.1111/j.2044–8279.1947.tb02214.x

"Marcus Bach Collection, Biography." Brigham Young University, Provo, UT. Accessed July 21, 2018. https://lib.byu.edu/collections/marcus-bach-collection/about/biography/

"Margaret Herrick, Film History Trailblazer." Academy of Motion Picture Arts and Sciences. September 22, 2015. https://www.oscars.org/news/margaret-herrick-film-history-trailblazer

Mark, Michael L., and Charles L. Gary. *A History of American Music Education*. 3rd ed. Lanham, MD: Rowman and Littlefield, 2007.

Marshall, John. "Pansies, Perverts and Macho Men: Changing Conceptions of the Modern Homosexual." In *The Making of the Modern Homosexual*, ed. Kenneth Plummer, 133–54. London: Hutchinson, 1981.

Martin, Rachel. "What Visa Changes Say about U.S. Immigration Priorities." *Weekend Edition Sunday*, NPR, May 5, 2013. Audio, 5:17. https://www.npr.org/2013/05/05/181293112/what-visa-changes-say-about-u-s-immigration-priorities

Matthews, Ramona H. "Seashore, Carl E[mil]." *Grove Music Online*. January 20, 2001. https://doi.org/10.1093/gmo/9781561592630.article.25280

[May, Arthur J., and students]. "University of Rochester History: Chapter 18; The Birth of a Music Center." Rare Books, Special Collections and Preservation University of Rochester. Accessed August 12, 2015. https://rbscp.lib.rochester.edu/2324

McAlpin, K. C. "'The Camp of the Saints' Revisited: Modern Critics Have Justified the Message of a 1973 Novel on Mass Immigration." *Social Contract* 27, no. 4 (Summer 2017): 53–54. https://www.thesocialcontract.com/pdf/twentyseven-four/tsc_27_4_mcalpin.pdf

McCarthy, D. "A Study of the Seashore Measures of Musical Talent." *Journal of Applied Psychology* 14, no. 5 (October 1930): 437–55. https://psycnet.apa.org/doi/10.1037/h0073360

McConathy, Osbourne. "The Place of Music in the New Educational Program:

President's Address." In *Journal of Proceedings of the Twelfth Annual Meeting of the Music Supervisors' National Conference Held at St. Louis, Missouri, March 30–April 4, 1919*: 24–28. https://archive.org/details/journalofproceed005236mbp/page/n29

"The Measurable Elements of Musical Talent." *Eugenical News* 11, no. 3 (March 1926): 43–44.

"Measures of Musical Talent [Front Matter]." *Music Supervisors' Journal* 6, no. 1 (September 1919): 17. http://www.jstor.org/stable/3383240

"Measuring Musical Capacities." *Eugenical News* 9, no. 8 (August 1924): 71.

Medina, José. "The Meanings of Silence: Wittgensteinian Contextualism and Polyphony." *Inquiry* 47, no. 6 (2004): 562–79. http://dx.doi.org/10.1080/00201740410004304

Mehler, Barry Alan. "A History of the American Eugenics Society, 1921–1940." PhD diss., University of Illinois at Urbana-Champaign, 1988. http://search.proquest.com.ezproxy.library.wisc.edu/docview/303689028?accountid=465

Meier, Norman Charles. *Aesthetic Judgment as a Measure of Art Talent.* University of Iowa Studies: Series on Aims and Progress of Research, vol. 1, no. 19. Iowa City: The University, 1926.

Meier, Norman Charles, and Carl E. Seashore. *The Meier-Seashore Art Judgment Test.* Iowa City: University of Iowa Bureau of Educational Research and Service, 1929.

"Mental and Physical Factors in Programs of Eugenics: A Symposium." *Eugenical News* 33, nos. 3–4 (September–December 1948): 42–51.

Metfessel, Milton. "Carl Emil Seashore, 1866–1949." *Science* 111, no. 2896 (June 30, 1950): 713–17. http://www.jstor.org/stable/1677658

Metfessel, Milton. *Phonophotography in Folk Music: American Negro Songs in New Notation.* Chapel Hill: University of North Carolina, 1928. https://babel.hathitrust.org/cgi/pt?id=uc1.32106010326780;view=1up;seq=7

Miessner, W. Otto. "Music Democratized." In *Journal of Proceedings of the Twelfth Annual Meeting of the Music Supervisors' National Conference Held at St. Louis, Missouri, March 30–April 4, 1919*: 89–92. https://archive.org/details/journalofproceed005236mbp/page/n93

Miles, Walter R. "Carl Emil Seashore, 1866–1949," vol. 29, *Biographical Memoirs*, 263–316. New York: Columbia University Press for the National Academy of Sciences, 1956.

Miller, Adam. "The Pioneer Fund: Bankrolling the Professors of Hate." *Journal of Blacks in Higher Education* no. 6 (Winter 1994/1995): 58–61. http://www.jstor.org/stable/2962466

Mills, Catherine. "Biopolitics, Liberal Eugenics, and Nihilism." In *Giorgio Agamben: Sovereignty and Life*, edited by Matthew Calarco and Steven DeCaroli, 180–202. Stanford, CA: Stanford University, 2007.

Mills, Charles W. *The Racial Contract.* Ithaca, NY: Cornell University Press, 1997.

Minkowski, Eugène. "A la recherche de la norme en psychopathologie." *L'Évolution-Psychiatrique* 1 (1938): 67–95.

Minton, Henry L. "The Iowa Child Welfare Research Station and the 1940 Debate on Intelligence: Carrying on the Legacy of a Concerned Mother." *Journal of the History of the Behavioral Sciences* 20, no. 2 (April 1984): 160–76.

Mjöen, Fridtjof. "Die Bedeutung der Tonhöhenunterschiedsempfindlichkeit für die Musikalität und ihr Verhalten bei der Vererbung." *Hereditas* 7, no. 11 (1926): 161–88.

Mjöen, Jon Alfred. *Die Vererbung der musikalischen Begabung*. Berlin: Alfred Metzner, 1934.

Mjøen, Jon Alfred. "Harmonic and Disharmonic Racecrossings." In *Eugenics in Race and State*, vol. 2, *The Scientific Papers of the Second International Congress of Eugenics; Held at American Museum of Natural History, New York, September 22–28, 1921*, 41–61. Baltimore, MD: Williams & Wilkins, 1923. Reprint, edited by Charles Rosenberg. New York: Garland Publishing, 1985.

Mjøen, Jon Alfred. "The Masculine Education of Women and Its Dangers." *Eugenics* 3, no. 9 (September 1930): 323–26.

Morrison, Toni. *Playing in the Dark: Whiteness and the Literary Imagination*. Cambridge, MA: Harvard University Press, 1992.

Mosing, Miriam A., Guy Madison, Nancy L. Pedersen, Ralf Kuja-Halkola, and Fredrik Ullén. "Practice Does Not Make Perfect: No Causal Effect of Music Practice on Music Ability." *Psychological Science* 25, no. 9 (September 2014): 1795–1803. www.jstor.org/stable/24543915

Murdoch, Katharine. "A Study of Differences Found Between Races in Intellect and in Morality [Part I]." *School and Society* 22, no. 568 (November 14, 1925): 628–32.

Murdoch, Katharine. "A Study of Differences Found Between Races in Intellect and in Morality [Part II]." *School and Society* 22, no. 569 (November 21, 1925): 659–64.

Mursell, James L. "Measuring Musical Ability and Achievement: A Study of the Correlations of Seashore Test Scores and Other Variables." *Journal of Educational Research* 25, no. 2 (February 1932): 116–26. http://www.jstor.org/stable/27525514

Mursell, James L. *The Psychology of Music*. New York: W. W. Norton, 1937. Reprint, New York: Johnson Reprint, 1970.

Mursell, James L. "What about Music Tests?" *Music Educators Journal* 24, no. 2 (October-November 1937): 16–18. www.jstor.org/stable/3385164

"*The Musical Quarterly*: Information for Authors." Oxford University Press. Accessed July 10, 2015. http://www.oxfordjournals.org/our_journals/musqtl/for_authors/ms_preparation.html

"Music Appreciation Material [Columbia Graphophone Company]." *Music Supervisors' Journal* 5, no. 1 (September 1918): 25. https://babel.hathitrust.org/cgi/pt?id=mdp.39015023355251;view=1up;seq=33

Music Education Catalog: Music Education for Life; Early Childhood through College. Chicago: GIA Publications, 2018.

"Music Educators Hall of Fame: Purpose and Procedures." National Association for Music Education. Accessed July 15, 2015. http://www.nafme.org/about/history/music-educators-hall-of-fame/music-educators-hall-of-fame-purpose-and-procedure-2/ (link now goes elsewhere; see Wayback Machine).

Music Supervisors' Journal [Front Matter] 5, no. 1 (September 1918): front cover. www.jstor.org/stable/3382824

Music Supervisors' Journal [Front Matter] 5, no. 2 (November 1918): front cover. www.jstor.org/stable/3382352

Music Supervisors' Journal [Front Matter] 5, no. 3 (January 1919): front cover. www.jstor.org/stable/3383163

Music Supervisors' Journal [Front Matter] 5, no. 4 (March 1919): front cover. https://babel.hathitrust.org/cgi/pt?id=mdp.39015023355251;view=1up;seq=105

Music Supervisors' Journal [Front Matter] 6, no. 1 (September 1919): front cover. http://www.jstor.org/stable/3383240

Music Supervisors' Journal [Front Matter] 10, no. 5 (May 1924): front cover. https://babel.hathitrust.org/cgi/pt?id=mdp.39015008094891&view=1up&seq=507

Myers, David G. *Psychology: Eighth Edition in Modules*. 8th ed. New York: Worth, 2006.

Myers, David G., and C. Nathan DeWall. *Myers' Psychology for the AP Course*. 3rd ed. New York: Bedford, Freeman & Worth, 2018.

Nathanson, Yale S. "The Musical Ability of the Negro." *Annals of the American Academy of Political and Social Science* 140, no. 229 (November 1928): 186–90. https://www.jstor.org/stable/1016847

"National Policy Institute: About." The National Policy Institute. 2017. Accessed August 30, 2018. https://nationalpolicy.institute/whoarewe

"National Research Council Conference on Sex Problems, October 28–29, 1921." Washington, DC: National Academy of Sciences, 1921. Quoted in Wade Pickren. "Robert Yerkes, Calvin Stone, and the Beginning of Programmatic Sex Research by Psychologists, 1921–1930." *American Journal of Psychology* 110, no. 4 (Winter 1997): 608. https://www.jstor.org/stable/1423412

A Nation at Risk: The Imperative for Educational Reform; A Report to the Nation and the Secretary of Education, United States Department of Education. Washington, DC: National Commission on Excellence in Education, April 1983. https://www.edreform.com/wp-content/uploads/2013/02/A_Nation_At_Risk_1983.pdf

"Necrology, Carl E. Seashore." *Music Educators Journal* 36, no. 2 (November-December 1949): 4. www.jstor.org/stable/3387486

"New Active Members of Eugenics Research Association." *Eugenical News* 5, no. 7 (July 1920): 53.

"News and Announcements." *American Sociological Review* 15, no. 4 (August 1950): 565–68. https://www.jstor.org/stable/2087320

"News and Events." University of Miami College of Arts and Sciences: Sociology. Accessed February 11, 2020. https://sociology.as.miami.edu/news-and-events/index.html

Ngai, Mae M. "The Architecture of Race in American Immigration Law: A

Reexamination of the Immigration Act of 1924." *Journal of American History* 86, no. 1 (June 1999): 67–92. https://www.jstor.org/stable/2567407

Nichols-Rothe, Penelope. "A Short History of the Controversy Surrounding Music Aptitude Testing and the Work of Carl E. Seashore from 1919–1939." Qualifying paper, Harvard University, 1987.

Nieves, Bethsaida. "Making of Race: Movements in the Colonialization and Production of Difference in Puerto Rico's Education at the Turn of the Twentieth Century." PhD diss., University of Wisconsin–Madison, 2019.

"Ninth Annual Business Meeting of the Eugenics Research Association: June 24, 1921." *Eugenical News* 6, no. 7–8 (July-August 1921): 56.

"Non-Fecundity of the Fit." *Eugenical News* 5, no. 8 (August 1920): 60.

Norris, Michele. *The Grace of Silence: A Memoir*. New York: Pantheon Books, 2010.

North, Adrian C., and David J. Hargreaves. *The Social and Applied Psychology of Music*. New York: Oxford University Press, 2008.

Oakes, Edward T. "Christ's Descent into Hell: The *Hopeful* Universalism of Hans Urs von Balthasar." In *"All Shall Be Well": Explorations in Universalism and Christian Theology from Origen to Moltmann*, edited by Gregory MacDonald, 382–99. Cambridge, UK: James Clarke, 2011. ProQuest Ebook Central. https://ebookcentral.proquest.com/lib/wisc/reader.action?docID=3328652

O'Connor, Brendan. "The Eugenicist Doctor and the Vast Fortune behind Trump's Immigration Regime." Splinter. July 5, 2018. https://splinternews.com/the-eugenicist-doctor-and-the-vast-fortune-behind-trump-1827322435

Official Guide Book of the Fair. Published in conjunction with A Century of Progress International Exposition, Chicago, 1933. Chicago: Cuneo, 1933. http://libsysdigi.library.illinois.edu/oca/Books2008–08/officialguideboo331cent/officialguideboo331cent.pdf

"Official Program: Music Supervisors' National Conference; Sixteenth Annual Meeting [Back Matter]." *Music Supervisors' Journal* 9, no. 4 (March 1923): 28–30. http://www.jstor.org/stable/3383060

Oliver, Richard A. C. "The Musical Talent of Natives of East Africa." *British Journal of Psychology* 22, no. 4 (April 1932): 333–43. https://doi.org/10.1111/j.2044–8295.1932.tb00634.x

Omi, Michael, and Howard Winant. "On the Theoretical Status of the Concept of Race." In *Race, Identity, and Representation in Education*, edited by Cameron McCarthy and Warren Crichlow, 3–10. New York: Routledge, 1993.

"Opportunities Which the Schools Should Offer the Child of Exceptional Musical Talent: Discussion." In *Journal of Proceedings of the Twelfth Annual Meeting of the Music Supervisors' National Conference Held at St. Louis, Missouri, March 30–April 4, 1919*: 96–101. https://archive.org/details/journalofproceed005236mbp/page/n101

Organized Eugenics. New Haven, CT: American Eugenics Society, January 1931. Connecticut State Library Digital Collection. https://cdm15019.contentdm.oclc.org/digital/collection/p4005coll11/id/587

Ortega, Bob. "Immigration Bill Could Be Windfall for Ariz. Economy." *USA*

Today, April 18, 2018. https://www.usatoday.com/story/news/nation/2013/04/18/arizona-economy-immigration-bill/2094461/

Osborn, Henry Fairfield. "Address of Welcome." In *Eugenics, Genetics and the Family*, vol. 1, *Scientific Papers of the Second International Congress of Eugenics; Held at American Museum of Natural History, New York, September 22–28, 1921*, 1–4. Baltimore, MD: Williams & Wilkins, 1923. Reprint, edited by Charles Rosenberg. New York: Garland Publishing, 1985.

Osborn, Henry Fairfield. Preface to *The Passing of the Great Race, or The Racial Basis of European History*, by Madison Grant, vii–ix. New York: Charles Scribner's Sons, 1916.

"Our Mission." ProEnglish. Accessed March 28, 2019. https://proenglish.org/our-mission/

"Our Racial Decay," review of *Race Decadence: An Examination of the Causes of Racial Degeneracy in the United States*, by W. S. Sadler. *Eugenical News* 7, no. 3 (March 1922): 42.

Parshley, H. M. "Sexual Abstinence as a Biological Question: Is Sexual Intercourse a Physiological Necessity?" *Scientific American* 148, no. 5 (May 1933): 283–84, 298–300. www.jstor.org/stable/2496823

Pauly, Philip J. *Biologists and the Promise of American Life: From Meriwether Lewis to Alfred Kinsey*. Princeton, NJ: Princeton University Press, 2000.

"Pay Last Tributes to 'Dean of Deans': Memorial Services Held Here Sunday for Carl E. Seashore, Who Died October 17." *Iowa City Press Citizen*, October 24, 1949, 11.

Payne, E. George. "Negroes in the Public Elementary Schools of the North." *Annals of the American Academy of Political and Social Science* 140, no. 229 (November 1928): 224–33. https://www.jstor.org/stable/1016851

"Periodical Literature: *The Popular Science Monthly*, December, 1914. Vol. xxxv, No. 6," review of "The Normal Child: Its Physical Growth and Mental Development," by Bird T. Baldwin. *Eugenics Review* 7, no. 1 (April 1915): 82. https://books.google.com/books?id=xloeAQAAIAAJ&pg=PA82&lpg=PA82&dq=bird++baldwin+eugenics&source=bl&ots=2auUAoCp5p&sig=Rl-ngr7d4JFK0o7__LjrE4V7dj0&hl=en&sa=X&ei=YRw4VeeIFov6oQSltoDYAw&ved=0CCIQ6AEwAQ#v=onepage&q=bird%20%20baldwin%20eugenics&f=false

Pernick, Martin S. "Eugenics and Public Health in American History." *American Journal of Public Health* 87, no. 11 (November 1997): 1767–72. https://www.ncbi.nlm.nih.gov/pmc/articles/PMC1381159/pdf/amjph00510-0017.pdf

"Personal Notes." *Eugenical News* 7, no. 1 (January 1922): 4.

Persson, Ingmar, and Julian Savulescu. *Unfit for the Future: The Need for Moral Enhancement*. Oxford: Oxford University, 2012.

Peterson, Joseph. "Methods of Investigating Comparative Abilities in Races." *Annals of the American Academy of Political and Social Science* 140, no. 229 (November 1928): 178–85. https://www.jstor.org/stable/1016846

Peterson, Joseph, and Lyle H. Lanier. *Studies in the Comparative Abilities of Whites and Negroes*. Mental Measurement Monographs, no. 5. Baltimore, MD: Williams and Wilkins, 1929.

"Phi Beta Sigma Fraternity, Inc. 1910– . . . A Historical Time Line." Phi Beta

Sigma Eastern Region Historical Society. Accessed August 14, 2018. http://erhistoricalsociety.tripod.com/id11.html

Pickren, Wade. "Robert Yerkes, Calvin Stone, and the Beginning of Programmatic Sex Research by Psychologists, 1921–1930." *American Journal of Psychology* 110, no. 4 (Winter 1997): 603–19. https://www.jstor.org/stable/1423412

Piggott, Stephen. "Anti-Immigrant Hate Group ProEnglish Visits White House." *Hatewatch* (blog). Southern Poverty Law Center, January 26, 2018. https://www.splcenter.org/hatewatch/2018/01/26/anti-immigrant-hate-group-proenglish-visits-white-house

Piggott, Stephen, and Alex Amend. "More than an Occasional Crank: 2,012 Times the Center for Immigration Studies Circulated White Nationalist Content." *Hatewatch* (blog). Southern Poverty Law Center, May 23, 2017. https://www.splcenter.org/hatewatch/2017/05/23/more-occasional-crank-2012-times-center-immigration-studies-circulated-white-nationalist

Pillsbury, W. B. "Biographical Memoir of James McKeen Cattell: 1860–1944," vol. 25, *National Academy of Sciences of the United States of America Biographical Memoirs*, 1–16. Washington, DC: National Academy of Sciences, 1949. http://www.nasonline.org/publications/biographical-memoirs/memoir-pdfs/cattell-james-m.pdf

Pinkerton, Frank W. "Talent Tests and Their Application to the Public School Instrumental Music Program." *Journal of Research in Music Education* 11, no. 1 (Spring 1963): 75–80. www.jstor.org/stable/3344533

"Pioneer Fund." Southern Poverty Law Center. Accessed August 6, 2018. https://www.splcenter.org/fighting-hate/extremist-files/group/pioneer-fund

"Pioneer Fund Certificate of Incorporation 1937." Institute for the Study of Academic Racism at Ferris State University. February 1, 1998. https://ferris-pages.org/ISAR/Institut/pioneer/pfund.htm

Plastas, Melinda. *A Band of Noble Women: Racial Politics in the Women's Peace Movement*. Syracuse, NY: Syracuse University Press, 2011. ProQuest Ebook Central. https://ebookcentral.proquest.com/lib/wisc/reader.action?docID=3410087

Plato. *Republic, Book 3*. Perseus Collection, Greek and Roman Materials. Accessed August 17, 2017. http://www.perseus.tufts.edu/hopper/text?doc=Perseus%3atext%3a1999.01.0168

Pols, Hans. "Eugenics in the Netherlands and the Dutch East Indies." In *The Oxford Handbook of the History of Eugenics*, edited by Alison Bashford and Philippa Levine, 347–62. Oxford: Oxford University Press, 2010.

Pomfret, John E. "Colonial Colleges." *Pennsylvania Gazette*, June 1975, 29–35.

P[openoe], P[aul]. "Musical Ability," review of *The Inheritance of Specific Musical Capacities*, by Hazel M. Stanton. *Journal of Heredity* 13, no. 4 (April 1922): 176. https://doi-org.ezproxy.library.wisc.edu/10.1093/oxfordjournals.jhered.a102196

Popenoe, Paul, and Roswell Hill Johnson. *Applied Eugenics*. New York: Macmillan, 1920.

Popkewitz, Thomas S. *Cosmopolitanism and the Age of School Reform: Science, Education, and Making Society by Making the Child*. New York: Routledge, 2008.

Popkewitz, Thomas S. *Struggling for the Soul: The Politics of Schooling and the Construction of the Teacher*. New York: Teachers College Press, 1998.

"Popular Education: Music Tests." *Eugenics* 1, no. 2 (November 1928): 35.

"Population and Its Control: Are the White People Dying Out?" *Eugenical News* 20, no. 1 (January-February 1935): 12–13.

Porter, Raymond Willis. "A Study of the Musical Talent of Chinese Attending Public Schools in Chicago." PhD diss., University of Chicago, 1931.

Potter, Chris, and Mark Roth. "Pittsburgh's Colcom Foundation Plays Major Role in Immigration-Control Debate." *Pittsburgh Post-Gazette*, February 14, 2015. https://www.post-gazette.com/news/environment/2015/02/15/Pittsburgh-s-Colcom-Foundation-plays-major-role-in-immigration-control-debate/stories/201502150072

"Preliminary Program: Music Supervisors' National Conference, Saint Louis, Missouri [Front Matter]." *Music Supervisors' Journal* 5, no. 4 (March 1919): 8, 10, 12, 14. http://www.jstor.org/stable/3382284

P[rice], J. S. "Current Literature on Negro Education," review of *Race Psychology in America: A Study of Racial Mental Differences*, by Thomas Russell Garth. *Journal of Negro Education* 2, no. 1 (January 1933): 83–87. https://www.jstor.org/stable/2292221

"Professorships at the University of Iowa." *School and Society* 14, no. 340 (July 2, 1921): 7. https://books.google.com/books?id=fLU0AQAAMAAJ&pg=PA7&lpg=PA7&dq=%22Department+of+Eugenics%22++Iowa&source=bl&ots=Ewp9obnK3e&sig=V0cHj4P1S2imsXtVOm_euGfI0H8&hl=en&sa=X&ei=wqg6VY3fDYKooQTKm4GYDg&ved=0CC4Q6AEwBA#v=onepage&q=%22Department%20of%20Eugenics%22%20%20Iowa&f=false

"Program—Sixteenth Meeting." In *Journal of Proceedings of the Sixteenth Annual Meeting of the Music Supervisors' National Conference Held at Cleveland, Ohio, April 9–13, 1923*, edited by George Oscar Bowen, 13–21. Ann Arbor, MI: University School of Music, 1923. https://archive.org/details/journalofproceed01753 6mbp/page/n17

"Program—Twelfth Meeting: St. Louis, Missouri." In *Journal of Proceedings of the Twelfth Annual Meeting of the Music Supervisors' National Conference Held at St. Louis, Missouri, March 30–April 4, 1919*: 11–16. https://archive.org/details/journalofproceed005236mbp/page/n15

Pulli, K., Kai Karma, R. Norio, P. Sistonen, H. H. H. Göring, and Irma Järvelä. "Genome-Wide Linkage Scan for Loci of Musical Aptitude in Finnish Families: Evidence for a Major Locus at 4q22." *Journal of Medical Genetics* 45, no. 7 (2008): 451–56. http://dx.doi.org/10.1136/jmg.2007.056366

Quinn, Lois M. "An Institutional History of the GED." In *The Myth of Achievement Tests: The GED and the Role of Character in American Life*, edited by James Heckman, John Eric Humphries, and Tim Kautz, 57–108. Chicago: University of Chicago Press, 2014.

"Race-Matters." *Eugenical News* 19, no. 1 (January-February 1934): 16–17.

"Racial Fecundity." *Eugenical News* 2, no. 12 (December 1917): 94.

Rafter, Nicole Hahn, ed. *White Trash: The Eugenic Family Studies, 1877–1919*. Boston: Northeastern University Press, 1988.

Rainbow, Edward L., and Hildegard C. Froehlich. *Research in Music Education: An Introduction to Systematic Inquiry*. New York: Schirmer Books, 1987.

Rameka, Lesley. "*Kia Whakatōmuri Te Haere Whakamua*: 'I Walk Backwards into the Future with My Eyes Fixed on My Past.'" *Contemporary Issues in Early Childhood* 17, no. 4 (2016): 387–98. https://doi.org/10.1177/1463949116677923

Ramelli, Ilaria L. E. *The Christian Doctrine of* Apokatastasis: *A Critical Assessment from the New Testament to Eriugena*. Leiden, Netherlands: Brill, 2013. https://doi-org.ezproxy.library.wisc.edu/10.1163/9789004245709

Raspail, Jean. *The Camp of the Saints*. Translated by Norman Shapiro. New York: Charles Scribner's Sons, 1975.

Ravitz, Mel J. "Sociology and the Political Arena." In *Reminiscences of Wayne: Memoirs of Some Faculty and Staff Members of Wayne State University*, edited by Henry V. Bohm and Paul J. Pentecost, 15–25. Ann Arbor, MI: Cushing-Malloy, 2000.

"Reginald G. Harris." Archives at Cold Spring Harbor Laboratory. Accessed July 6, 2018. http://library.cshl.edu/personal-collections/reginald-g-harris

"Remarks by President Trump at a California Sanctuary State Roundtable." The White House. May 16, 2018. https://www.whitehouse.gov/briefings-statements/remarks-president-trump-california-sanctuary-state-roundtable/

"A Renewed Attack on the 14th Amendment." In *Intelligence Report: Hate and Extremism in 2018*, 16–19. Montgomery, AL: Southern Poverty Law Center, 2018.

Report of the National Research Council for the Year July 1, 1921–June 30, 1922. Washington, DC: Government Printing Office, 1923. https://books.google.com/books?id=7bim-5iK8IcC&pg=PA45&lpg=PA45&dq=committee+on+psychology+and+anthropology+NRC+carl+seashore&source=bl&ots=SPfUVb86ut&sig=ACfU3U1qCiWZnVxebeq126-5kZdoBeUXOw&hl=en&sa=X&ved=2ahUKEwiAm6yptrjlAhWCna0KHZ49C98Q6AEwBnoECAgQAQ#v=onepage&q=seashore&f=false

Reser, Helen. "Student Pedigree-Studies: Inheritance of Musical Ability." *Eugenical News* 20, no. 1 (January-February 1935): 8–9.

Reske, Phyllis E. "Policing the 'Wayward Woman': Eugenics in Wisconsin's Involuntary Sterilization Program." *Wisconsin Magazine of History* 97, no. 1 (Autumn 2013): 14–27.

Reston, Laura. "Where Trump Gets His Fuzzy Border Math." *New Republic*, March 10, 2017. https://newrepublic.com/article/140951/trump-gets-fuzzy-border-math

Reuter, E. B. "The American Mulatto." *Annals of the American Academy of Political and Social Science* 140, no. 229 (November 1928): 36–43. https://www.jstor.org/stable/1016830

"Richard Lynn." Southern Poverty Law Center. Accessed August 6, 2018. https://www.splcenter.org/fighting-hate/extremist-files/individual/richard-lynn

Richards, Graham. “Reconceptualizing the History of Race Psychology: Thomas Russell Garth (1872–1939) and How He Changed His Mind.” *Journal of the History of the Behavioral Sciences* 34, no. 1 (Winter 1998): 15–32. https://doi.org/10.1002/(SICI)1520–6696(199824)34:1<15::AID-JHBS2>3.0.CO;2-I

Richards, O. F., Osbourne McConathy, Carl E. Seashore, T. P. Giddings, O. E. Robinson, Charles H. Farnsworth, Theresa Wild, Howard C. Davis, W. Otto Miessner, J. Lawrence Erb, C. H. Miller, Peter Christian Lutkin, Marshall M. Bartholomew, and O. F. Lewis. “Big Ideas from St. Louis.” *Music Supervisors' Journal* 6, no. 1 (September 1919): 5–8, 10, 12, 14, 16, 18. http://www.jstor.org/stable/3383243

Richwine, Jason. Interview by Stephen K. Bannon. *Breitbart News Daily*, Breitbart, January 6, 2016. Audio, 6:43. https://soundcloud.com/breitbart/breitbart-news-daily-jason-richwine-january-6–2016

Richwine, Jason. “IQ and Immigration Policy.” PhD diss., Harvard University, 2009. http://search.proquest.com.ezproxy.library.wisc.edu/docview/304890816?accountid=465

Ripley, William Z. *The Races of Europe: A Sociological Study*. New York: D. Appleton, 1899. Reprint, edited by Weston La Barre. New York: Johnson Reprint, 1965. https://babel.hathitrust.org/cgi/pt?id=uc1.31822007517113;view=1up;seq=5

Robbins, Jane. “The ‘Problem of the Gifted Student’: National Research Council Efforts to Identify and Cultivate Undergraduate Talent in a New Era of Mass Education, 1919–1929,” vol. 24, *Perspectives on the History of Higher Education: History of Higher Education Annual*, edited by Roger L. Geiger, 91–124. New Brunswick, NJ: Transaction, 2005.

Roberts, Dorothy. *Killing the Black Body: Race, Reproduction, and the Meaning of Liberty*. New York: Vintage Books, 1999.

Robinson, Francis P. “Carl E. Seashore.” *Educational Forum* 15, no. 1, pt. 2 (November 1950): 128t–128u.

Robinson, Kim Stanley. “Ancient Shamans and Roving Neanderthals: Kim Stanley Robinson Imagines Living 30,000 Years Ago.” Interview by Steve Paulson. *To the Best of Our Knowledge*, Wisconsin Public Radio, September 11, 2015. Audio, 10:47. http://archive.ttbook.org/book/kim-stanley-robinson-shamanism

Roby, A. Richard. “A Study in the Correlation of Music Theory Grades with the *Seashore Measures of Musical Talents* and the *Aliferis Music Achievement Test*.” *Journal of Research in Music Education* 10, no. 2 (Autumn 1962): 137–42. www.jstor.org/stable/3343997

Rodriguez, Carlos X. “Culture, Society and Musicality: Beyond Seashore's Model of the Musical Mind.” In *Multidisciplinary Perspectives on Musicality: Essays from the Seashore Symposium*, edited by Kate Gfeller, Don D. Coffman, Carlos X. Rodriguez, and David J. Nelson, 138–39. Iowa City: University of Iowa School of Music, 2006.

Roncaglia-Denissen, M. Paula, Maren Schmidt-Kassow, Angela Heine, Peter Vuust, and Sonja A. Kotz. “Enhanced Musical Rhythmic Perception in Turkish Early and Late Learners of German.” *Frontiers in Psychology* 4, no. 645 (September 20, 2013): 1–8. https://www.ncbi.nlm.nih.gov/pmc/articles/PMC3778315/

Roper, Allen G. *Ancient Eugenics: The Arnold Prize Essay for 1918*. Oxford: B. H. Blackwell, 1913. https://archive.org/details/ancienteugenicsa00ropeuoft

Rose, Joel. "Mark Krikorian, Who Urges Cutting Immigration, Gains Relevance in Trump Era." *All Things Considered*, NPR, April 10, 2017. Audio, 3:53. https://www.npr.org/2017/04/10/523311475/mark-krikorian-who-urges-cutting-immigration-gains-relevance-in-trump-era

Rose, Nikolas. "Biopolitics in the Twenty First Century: Notes for a Research Agenda." *Distinktion: Scandinavian Journal of Social Theory* 2, no. 3 (2001): 25–44.

Rose, Nikolas. *The Politics of Life Itself: Biomedicine, Power, and Subjectivity in the Twenty-First Century*. Princeton, NJ: Princeton University Press, 2007.

Rosen, Christine. *Preaching Eugenics: Religious Leaders and the American Eugenics Movement*. Oxford: Oxford University Press, 2004.

Rosenthal, Michael. *The Character Factory: Baden-Powell and the Origins of the Boy Scout Movement*. London: Collins, 1986.

Ross, Edward Alsworth. *The Old World in the New: The Significance of Past and Present Immigration to the American People*. New York: Century, 1914. https://archive.org/details/cu31924021182898

Ross, Scott R., Steven H. Putnam, Scott R. Millis, Kenneth M. Adams, and Rebecca A. Krukowski. "Detecting Insufficient Effort Using the Seashore Rhythm and Speech-Sounds Perception Tests in Head Injury." *Clinical Neuropsychologist* 20, no. 4 (2006): 798–815. https://doi.org/10.1080/13854040500328477

Routh, Donald K. *Clinical Psychology since 1917: Science, Practice, and Organization*. New York: Plenum, 1994.

"R/The_Donald: The_Donald Is a Never-Ending Rally Dedicated to the 45th President of the United States, Donald J. Trump." Reddit. Accessed November 28, 2018. https://www.reddit.com/r/The_Donald/ (site banned on June 29, 2020).

Rubin, Gayle. "The Traffic in Women: Notes on the 'Political Economy' of Sex." In *Toward an Anthropology of Women*, edited by Rayna R. Reiter, 157–210. New York: Monthly Review, 1975.

Rubin, Herman H. *Eugenics and Sex Harmony: The Sexes, Their Relations and Problems, Including Recent Fascinating Medical Discoveries, Prevention of Disease, and Special Advice for Common Disorders*. New York: Pioneer Publications, 1946.

Ruch, G. M. *A Mental-Educational Survey of 1550 Iowa High School Seniors*. University of Iowa Studies in Education, vol. 2, no. 5. Iowa City, IA: The University [1923]. https://babel.hathitrust.org/cgi/pt?id=osu.32435028125920&view=1up&seq=3

Ryan, Ann Marie, and Alan Stoskopf. "Public and Catholic School Responses to IQ Testing in the Early 20th Century." *Teachers College Record* 110, no. 4 (2008): 894–922. https://www.tcrecord.org/content.asp?contentid=14623

Saleeby, Caleb Williams. *The Progress of Eugenics*. London: Cassell, 1914. https://babel.hathitrust.org/cgi/pt?id=aeu.ark:/13960/t3fx8j06h;view=1up;seq=12

"Sample Membership Letter in AES Archives, 1922." American Eugenics Society Papers, American Philosophical Society, Philadelphia, PA. Quoted in Barry Alan Mehler, "A History of the American Eugenics Society, 1921–1940." PhD diss., University of Illinois at Urbana-Champaign, 1988, 61, 62n44. http://search.proquest.com.ezproxy.library.wisc.edu/docview/303689028?accountid=465

Sandage, Scott A. *Born Losers: A History of Failure in America*. Cambridge, MA: Harvard University Press, 2005. ProQuest EBook Central. https://ebookcentral.proquest.com/lib/wisc/reader.action?docID=3300274&ppg=4

Sandage, Scott A. "Scott Sandage on 'Born Losers.'" Interview by Anne Strainchamps. *To the Best of Our Knowledge*, Wisconsin Public Radio, March 5, 2006. Audio, 9:00. http://archive.ttbook.org/listen/6248

Sanderson, Helen Elizabeth. "Differences in Musical Ability in Children of Different National and Racial Origin." *Pedagogical Seminary and Journal of Genetic Psychology* 42, no. 1 (1933): 100–119. https://doi.org/10.1080/08856559.1933.10534231

Santana, Maria. "Hard-Line Anti-Illegal Immigration Advocates Hired at 2 Federal Agencies." CNN. April 12, 2017. https://www.cnn.com/2017/04/11/politics/trump-administration-immigration-advisers/index.html

Savulescu, Julian. "As a Species, We Have a Moral Obligation to Enhance Ourselves." Interview by TED Guest Author. TED, February 19, 2014. https://ideas.ted.com/the-ethics-of-genetically-enhanced-monkey-slaves/

Savulescu, Julian. "The Moral Argument for Human Cloning, Genetic Enhancement." Interview by Steve Paulson. *To the Best of Our Knowledge*, Wisconsin Public Radio, October 18, 2015. Audio, 12:43. http://archive.ttbook.org/book/moral-argument-human-cloning-genetic-enhancement

Savulescu, Julian. "The Philosopher Who Says We Should Play God." Interview by Steve Paulson. *Nautilus*, September 3, 2015. http://nautil.us/issue/28/2050/the-philosopher-who-says-we-should-play-god

Schewe, Eric. "The Historic Echoes of Trump's Immigration Ban." *JSTOR Daily*. February 7, 2017. https://daily.jstor.org/the-historic-echoes-of-trumps-immigration-ban/

Schneider, Albrecht. "Aspects of Sound Recording and Sound Analysis." In *This Thing Called Music: Essays in Honor of Bruno Nettl*, edited by Victoria Lindsay Levine and Philip V. Bohlman, 224–38. Lanham, MD: Rowman and Littlefield, 2015.

Seashore, Carl E. "Academic Business." *Education Digest* 11, no. 3 (November 1945): 45–48. Reprinted from *School and Society* 62 (September 15, 1945): 161–64.

Seashore, Carl E. "Avocational Guidance in Music." *Journal of Applied Psychology* 1, no. 4 (December 1917): 342–48.

Seashore, Carl E. "A Base for the Approach to Quantitative Studies in the Aesthetics of Music." *American Journal of Psychology* 39, no. 1/4 (December 1927): 141–44. https://doi.org/10.2307/1415406

Seashore, Carl E. "Carl Emil Seashore," vol. 1, *A History of Psychology in Autobiography*, edited by Carl Allanmore Murchison, 225–97. Worcester, MA: Clark University, 1930.

Seashore, Carl E. *A Child Welfare Research Station: Plans and Possibilities of a Research Station for the Conservation and Development of the Normal Child*. Series on Aims and Progress of Research, n.s., vol. 107. Iowa City, Iowa: The University, 1916. https://catalog.hathitrust.org/Record/010551244

Seashore, Carl E. "College Placement Examinations." *School and Society* 20, no. 515 (November 8, 1924): 575–78. Reprinted in Carl E. Seashore, *College Placement Examinations*. Washington, DC: National Research Council [1925].

Seashore, Carl E. "Communications and Discussions: Mentality Tests." *Journal of Educational Psychology* 7, no. 3 (March 1916): 163–66.

Seashore, Carl E., ed. and moderator. "Communications and Discussions: Mentality Tests, a Symposium." *Journal of Educational Psychology* 7, no. 4 (April 1916): 229–40.

Seashore, Carl E., ed. and moderator. "Communications and Discussions: Mentality Tests, a Symposium." *Journal of Educational Psychology* 7, no. 5 (May 1916): 278–93.

Seashore, Carl E., ed. and moderator. "Communications and Discussions: Mentality Tests, a Symposium." *Journal of Educational Psychology* 7, no. 6 (June 1916): 348–60.

Seashore, Carl E. "Communications and Discussions: The Mid-Day Nap." *Journal of Educational Psychology* 1, no. 5 (May 1910): 293–95. doi.org/10.1037/h0070095

Seashore, Carl E. "The Consulting Psychologist." *Popular Science Monthly* 78 (March 1911): 283–90.

Seashore, Carl E. "Cooperation with the Film Industries in the Study of Primitive Music." *Science* 96, no. 2490 (September 18, 1942): 263–65. www.jstor.org/stable/1669751. A similar version appeared in Carl E. Seashore, *In Search of Beauty in Music: A Scientific Approach to Musical Esthetics*, 294–97. New York: Ronald, 1947. https://archive.org/details/insearchofbeauty000817mbp

Seashore, Carl E. "Demonstration of Measurements of Musical Capacity." In *Journal of Proceedings of the Twelfth Annual Meeting of the Music Supervisors' National Conference Held at St. Louis, Missouri, March 30–April 4, 1919*: 30. https://archive.org/details/journalofproceed005236mbp/page/n35

Seashore, Carl E. "Discussion: Intercollegiate Academic Contests." *School and Society* 28, no. 709 (1928): 114.

Seashore, Carl E. "Editorials: From Vocational Selection to Vocational Guidance." *Journal of Educational Psychology* 8, no. 9 (April 1917): 244–45.

Seashore, Carl E. "Educational Guidance in Music." *School and Society* 45, no. 1160 (March 20, 1937): 385–93.

Seashore, Carl E. "Education for Democracy and the Junior College," *School and Society* 25, no. 643 (April 23, 1927): 469–78. A slightly revised version was published in Carl E. Seashore, *Learning and Living in College*, University of Iowa Studies: Series on Aims and Progress of Research, vol. 2, no. 1, 88–102. Iowa City: The University, 1927. A condensed version was published under the same title in the *Bulletin of the American Association of University Professors* 13, no. 6 (October 1927): 399–404.

Seashore, Carl E. "Elementary Tests in Psychology." *Journal of Educational Psychology* 7, no. 2 (February 1916): 81–86.

Seashore, Carl E. "Euthenics, a Design for Living." *Educational Forum* 12, no. 2, pt. 1 (January 1948): 149–55.

Seashore, Carl E. "The Experimental Study of Mental Fatigue." *Psychological Bulletin* 1, no. 4 (March 15, 1904): 97–101. http://dx.doi.org/10.1037/h0069868

Seashore, Carl E. "Graduate Study: An Address Delivered to the Students in the Colleges of Iowa in 1909." *Bulletin of the State University of Iowa*, n.s., 11 (June 2, 1910): 3–13.

Seashore, Carl E. "How Psychology Can Help the Musician." *Etude* 35, no. 2 (February 1917): 89–90. https://books.google.com/books?id=IpgyAQAAMAAJ&pg=PA89&lpg=PA89&dq=etude++how+psychology+can+help+the+musician&source=bl&ots=tHDoVQu6_g&sig=d7_3e_W1UD8pNiZ_MakBANDHg3A&hl=en&sa=X&ved=0CCEQ6AEwAWoVChMI8pDg88nYxgIVEQySCh3pigIR#v=onepage&q=etude%20%20how%20psychology%20can%20help%20the%20musician&f=false

Seashore, Carl E. "Individual and Racial Inheritance of Musical Traits." In *Eugenics, Genetics and the Family, vol. 1, Scientific Papers of the Second International Congress of Eugenics; Held at American Museum of Natural History, New York, September 22–28, 1921*, 231–38. Baltimore, MD: Williams & Wilkins, 1923. Reprint, edited by Charles Rosenberg. New York: Garland Publishing, 1985.

Seashore, Carl E. "The Individual in Mass Education." *School and Society* 23, no. 593 (May 8, 1926): 569–76.

Seashore, Carl E. "In Search of Beauty in Music." *Musical Quarterly* 28, no. 3 (July 1942): 302–8. http://www.jstor.org/stable/739259

Seashore, Carl E. *In Search of Beauty in Music: A Scientific Approach to Musical Esthetics*. New York: Ronald, 1947. https://archive.org/details/insearchofbeauty000817mbp/page/n8/mode/2up

Seashore, Carl E. Introduction to *Phonophotography in Folk Music*, by Milton Metfessel, 3–17. Chapel Hill: University of North Carolina Press, 1928. https://babel.hathitrust.org/cgi/pt?id=uc1.32106010326780;view=1up;seq=7

Seashore, Carl E. *Introduction to Psychology*. New York: Macmillan, 1923.

Seashore, Carl E. "Iowa Academic Meet." *School and Society* 30, no. 759 (July 13, 1929): 63.

Seashore, Carl E. "Is There Overproduction in Higher Education?" *School and Society* 37, no. 955 (April 15, 1933): 478–82.

Seashore, Carl E. *The Junior College Movement*. New York: Henry Holt, 1940. https://babel.hathitrust.org/cgi/pt?id=mdp.39015020699834;view=1up;seq=7

Seashore, Carl E. *Learning and Living in College: Psychology of Individual Differences Applied to the Organization and Pursuit of Higher Education; A Study Based upon Experience in the Promotion of the Gifted Student Project in the National Research Council*. University of Iowa Studies: Series on Aims and Progress of Research, vol. 2, no. 1. Iowa City: The University, 1927.

Seashore, Carl E. *Manual of Instructions and Interpretations for Measures of Musical Talent*. Chicago: Charles Stoelting, n.d.

Seashore, Carl E. *Manual of Instructions and Interpretations for Measures of Musical Talent*. New York: Columbia Graphophone Educational Department, 1919. https://archive.org/details/manualofinstruct00seasuoft/page/n3

Seashore, Carl E. *Manual of Instructions and Interpretations for Measures of Musical Talent*. New York: Columbia Phonograph Company, Educational Department [1923]. https://archive.org/details/manualinstructi00seasgoog/page/n1

Seashore, Carl E. "The Master's Key to the Domain of Educational Theory and Practice." *Education Digest* 15, no. 6 (February 1950): 19–21. Reprinted from *School and Society* 70 (November 26, 1949): 337–38.

Seashore, Carl E. "The Measurement of Musical Talent." *Musical Quarterly* 1, no. 1 (January 1915): 129–48. https://www.jstor.org/stable/738047

Seashore, Carl E. "Measurements on the Expression of Emotion in Music." *Proceedings of the National Academy of Sciences of the United States of America* 9, no. 9 (September 15, 1923): 323–25. http://www.jstor.org/stable/84312

Seashore, Carl E. "The Measure of a Singer." *Science*, n.s., 35, no. 893 (February 9, 1912): 201–12. http://www.jstor.org/stable/1638656

Seashore, Carl E. "Measures of Musical Talent: A Reply to Dr. C. P. Heinlein." *Psychological Review* 37, no. 1 (January 1930): 178–83.

Seashore, Carl E. "Meier-Seashore Art Judgment Test." *Science*, n.s., 69, no. 1788 (April 5, 1929): 380. http://www.jstor.org/stable/1652784

Seashore, Carl E. "Music," vol. 2, *Handbook of Applied Psychology*, edited by Douglas H. Fryer and Edwin R. Henry, 681–86. New York: Rinehart, 1950.

Seashore, Carl E. "Musical Inheritance." *Scientific Monthly* 50, no. 4 (April 1940): 351–56.

Seashore, Carl E. "A New Rhythm Apparatus." *Science*, n.s., 59, no. 1519 (February 8, 1924): 146–47. https://www.jstor.org/stable/1647057

Seashore, Carl E. "An Open Letter: Addressed to Women in Graduate Schools." *Journal of Higher Education* 13, no. 5 (May 1942): 236–42. https://doi.org/10.2307/1974933

Seashore, Carl E. "An Open Letter to a Professor." *School and Society* 48, no. 1238 (September 17, 1938): 349–56. Reprinted with revised title in Seashore, Carl E. *The Junior College Movement*, 131–45. New York: Henry Holt, 1940.

Seashore, Carl E. "Origin of the Term 'Euthenics.'" *Science*, n.s., 95, no. 2470 (May 1, 1942): 455–56. http://www.jstor.org/stable/1668977

Seashore, Carl E. Papers. Special Collections and University Archives, University of Iowa Libraries, Iowa City, IA.

Seashore, Carl E. *Pioneering in Psychology*. University of Iowa Studies: Series on Aims and Progress of Research, no. 70. Iowa City: University of Iowa, 1942. https://babel.hathitrust.org/cgi/pt?id=mdp.39015020052349&view=1up&seq=1

Seashore, Carl E. "Plans and Possibilities of a Research Station for the Conservation and Development of the Normal Child." *Iowa Alumnus* 12, no. 4 (January 1915): 16–17. https://babel.hathitrust.org/cgi/pt?id=uc1.b2872130&view=1up&seq=120

Seashore, Carl E. "The Play Impulse and Attitude in Religion." *American Journal of Theology* 14, no. 4 (October 1910): 505–20. http://www.jstor.org/stable/3154774

Seashore, Carl E. *A Preview to College and Life*. University of Iowa Studies: Series on Aims and Progress of Research, no. 55. Iowa City: University of Iowa, 1938.

Seashore, Carl E. "Procedure in the Discovery and the Encouragement of Musical Talent in the Public Schools by Means of Measures of Musical Talent [Address and Discussion]." In *Journal of Proceedings of the Twelfth Annual Meeting of the*

Music Supervisors' National Conference Held at St. Louis, Missouri, March 30–April 4, 1919: 30–41. https://archive.org/details/journalofproceed005236mbp/page/n35

Seashore, Carl E. *Psychology in Daily Life*. New York: D. Appleton, 1914.

Seashore, Carl E. *Psychology of Music*. New York: McGraw-Hill, 1938. https://archive.org/details/psychologyofmusi030417mbp

Seashore, Carl E. "The Psychology of Music. X. Intonation in Violin Performance." *Music Educators Journal* 24, no. 2 (October-November 1937): 23–24. http://www.jstor.org/stable/3385168

Seashore, Carl E. "The Psychology of Music. XI. Two Types of Attitude toward the Evaluation of Musical Talent." *Music Educators Journal* 24, no. 3 (December 1937): 25–26. www.jstor.org/stable/3385312

Seashore, Carl E. *The Psychology of Musical Talent*. Boston: Silver, Burdett, 1919.

Seashore, Carl E. "The Religion of the Educated Person." *Journal of Higher Education* 18, no. 2 (February 1947): 71–76. http://www.jstor.org/stable/1975910

Seashore, Carl E. "Religious Music in the Public School Choruses." *Music Educators Journal* 28, no. 1 (September-October 1941): 60. http://www.jstor.org/stable/3385847

Seashore, Carl E. "The Role of a Consulting Supervisor in Music." In *Eighteenth Yearbook of the National Society for the Study of Education* (Part 2), edited by Guy Montrose Whipple, 111–23. Bloomington, IL: Public School Publishing, 1919. https://babel.hathitrust.org/cgi/pt?id=uc1.l0053492963&view=1up&seq=493

Seashore, Carl E. "The Rôle of Mental Measurement in the Discovery and Motivation of the Gifted Student." *Proceedings of the National Academy of Sciences* 11, no. 9 (September 1925): 542–45.

Seashore, Carl E. "Scientific Procedure in the Discovery of Musical Talent in the Public Schools." *Music Supervisors' Journal* 2, no. 3 (January 1916): 10–11. http://www.jstor.org/stable/3383174

Seashore, Carl E. "The Scope and Function of Euthenics." *Mental Hygiene* 33, no. 4 (October 1949): 594–98.

Seashore, Carl E. "Sectioning Classes on the Basis of Ability." *School and Society* 15, no. 379 (April 1922): 353–58.

Seashore, Carl E. "The Sense of Rhythm as a Musical Talent." *Musical Quarterly* 4, no. 4 (October 1918): 507–15. http://www.jstor.org/stable/737876

Seashore, Carl E. "Some Psychological Statistics: IV. Hearing-Ability and Discriminative Sensibility for Pitch," vol. 2, *The University of Iowa Studies in Psychology*, edited by George T. W. Patrick, 55–64. Iowa City: University of Iowa, 1899. https://books.google.com/books?id=0pRIAAAAYAAJ&pg=PA55&dq=university+of+iowa+studies+in+psychology+hearing+ability&hl=en&sa=X&ved=0CDYQ6AEwAWoVChMIwJy7-4GVxwIVQh4eCh1Wow3b#v=onepage&q=university%20of%20iowa%20studies%20in%20psychology%20hearing%20ability&f=false

Seashore, Carl E. "Some Psychological Statistics: V. Motor Ability, Reaction-Time, Rhythm, and Time Sense," Vol. 2, *The University of Iowa Studies in Psychology*, edited by George T. W. Patrick, 64–84. Iowa City: University of Iowa, 1899.

https://books.google.com/books?id=0pRIAAAAYAAJ&pg=PA55&dq=university+of+iowa+studies+in+psychology+hearing+ability&hl=en&sa=X&ved=0CDYQ6AEwAWoVChMIwJy7-4GVxwIVQh4eCh1Wow3b#v=onepage&q=reaction-time&f=false

Seashore, Carl E. "Suggestions for Tests on School Children." *Educational Review* 22 (June 1901): 69–82.

Seashore, Carl E. "The Sunny Side of Graduate Work." *Daily Iowan*, April 11, 1943, 2. http://dailyiowan.lib.uiowa.edu/DI/1943/di1943-04-11.pdf

Seashore, Carl E. "The Sunny Side of Graduate Work for the Duration." *Journal of Higher Education* 14, no. 6 (June 1943): 289–92. https://www.jstor.org/stable/1975100

Seashore, Carl E. "The Sunny Side of Graduate Work for the Duration." In *Wartime Approaches to Liberal Education: Nine Editorials from* The Daily Iowan. 29–32. [Iowa City: University of Iowa Publications, 1944?].

Seashore, Carl E. *A Survey of Musical Talent in the Public Schools Representing the Examination of Children of the Fifth and the Eighth Grades in the Public Schools of Des Moines, Iowa.* 2nd ed. University of Iowa Studies in Child Welfare, vol. 1, no. 2. Iowa City: The University, February 1924. https://babel.hathitrust.org/cgi/pt?id=mdp.39015009450191&view=2up&seq=1

Seashore, Carl E. "Talent." *School and Society* 55, no. 1416 (February 14, 1942): 169–73.

Seashore, Carl E. "The Term 'Euthenics.'" *Science*, n.s., 94, no. 2450 (December 12, 1941): 561–62. https://www.jstor.org/stable/1668443

Seashore, Carl E. "Three New Approaches to the Study of Negro Music." *Annals of the American Academy of Political and Social Science* 140, no. 229 (November 1928): 191–92. https://www.jstor.org/stable/1016848

Seashore, Carl E. "The Tonoscope and Its Use in the Training of the Voice." *The Musician* no. 11 (1906): 331–32.

Seashore, Carl E. "Vocational Guidance in Music." *Music Supervisors' Journal* 3, no. 2 (November 1916): 18, 20, 22, 24, 26, 28. https://www.jstor.org/stable/3383046

Seashore, Carl E. *Vocational Guidance in Music.* University of Iowa Monographs: Aims and Progress of Research, 1st ser., no. 2. Iowa City: The University, September 1916.

Seashore, Carl E. "A Voice Tonoscope," vol. 3, *University of Iowa Studies in Psychology*, edited by George T. W. Patrick, 18–28. Iowa City: University of Iowa, 1902. https://books.google.com/books?id=NETWaMam5LMC&pg=RA1-PA145&lpg=RA1-PA145&dq=%22university+of+iowa+studies+in+psychology%22+seashore&source=bl&ots=ZsAhkg0oJi&sig=JmHwRQNo-YvgVrJUU-xGh631kX8&hl=en&sa=X&ved=0CCsQ6AEwBWoVChMIm8rL9Z-VxwIVAXUeCh1Wtwuv#v=onepage&q=tonoscope&f=false

Seashore, Carl E. "Whither Ahead of Science in Music." *Education* 67, no. 3 (November 1946): 152–56.

Seashore, Carl E. "Youth and Music." *School Review* 48, no. 4 (April 1940): 268–77. http://www.jstor.org/stable/1082068

Seashore, Carl E., and Milton Metfessel. "Deviation from the Regular as an Art Principle." *Proceedings of the National Academy of Sciences of the United States of*

America 11, no. 9 (1925): 538–42. www.jstor.org/stable/84855

Seashore, Carl E., and Harold Seashore. "The Place of Phonophotography in the Study of Primitive Music." *Science*, n.s., 79, no. 2056 (May 25, 1934): 485–87. http://www.jstor.org/stable/1659930

Seashore, Carl E., and Roberta H. Seashore. "The Aesthetics of Marriage." In *Modern Marriage*, edited by Moses Jung, 70–80. New York: F. S. Crofts, 1940.

"Seashore Honored." *Iowa Alumnus* 19, no. 1 (October 1920): 18. https://books.google.com/books?id=E35IAQAAMAAJ&pg=PA18&lpg=PA18&dq=carl+seashore+national+research+council&source=bl&ots=Jr6dotci26&sig=ljYe1eb2Zgcr_KxVq-hwpVLuG3k&hl=en&sa=X&ei=XrtwVYaTO4mQoQSi7oLADQ&ved=0CC0Q6AEwAg#v=onepage&q=carl%20seashore%20national%20research%20council&f=false

"Seashore Test Given." *Gustavian Weekly*, September 12, 1945, 3.

Selden, Steven. "Biological Determinism and the Narrative of Adjustment: The High School Biology Textbooks of Truman Jesse Moon, c. 1921–1963." *Curriculum Inquiry* 37, no. 2 (June 2007): 159–96. http://www.jstor.org/stable/30054793

Selden, Steven. *Inheriting Shame: The Story of Eugenics and Racism in America*. New York: Teachers College, 1999.

Sessions, Jeff. "'The American People Are Angry Alright . . . at the Politicians'—Senator Jeff Sessions." Interview by Stephen K. Bannon. SiriusXM News & Issues, October [4 or 5], 2015, accessed December 6, 2018. Audio, 22:44. https://soundcloud.com/siriusxm-news-issues/the-american-people-are-angry

"75 Years Ago: 1937." *AMS Newsletter* 42, no. 2 (August 2012): 35. https://cdn.ymaws.com/www.amsmusicology.org/resource/resmgr/files/Newsletter/AMSNewsletter-2012–8.pdf

Shilling, C. W. "The Development of Methods for the Selection of Sound Listening Personnel." New London, CT: Medical Research Laboratory, U.S. Naval Submarine Base, March 1, 1942. Rubicon Research Repository. http://archive.rubicon-foundation.org/7395

Siegel, Eric. "The Real Problem with Charles Murray and 'The Bell Curve.'" *Voices* (blog). *Scientific American*, April 12, 2017. https://blogs.scientificamerican.com/voices/the-real-problem-with-charles-murray-and-the-bell-curve/

Simon, John K. "A Conversation with Michel Foucault." *Partisan Review* 38, no. 2 (1971): 192–201. http://hgar-srv3.bu.edu/collections/partisan-review/search/detail?id=326091

Simons, Marilyn, and Bruce Stillman. "Statement by Cold Spring Harbor Laboratory Addressing Remarks by Dr. James D. Watson in '*American Masters: Decoding Watson*.'" Cold Spring Harbor Laboratory. January 11, 2019. https://www.cshl.edu/statement-by-cold-spring-harbor-laboratory-addressing-remarks-by-dr-james-d-watson-in-american-masters-decoding-watson/

Simpson, Carrie. "On Campus." *New Pittsburgh Courier*, October 21, 1972, national edition, 11.

Sims, Leslie B. "Carl Seashore: A Visionary and Pioneer in Graduate Education." In

Multidisciplinary Perspectives on Musicality: Essays from the Seashore Symposium, edited by Kate Gfeller, Don D. Coffman, Carlos X. Rodriguez, and David J. Nelson, 218–21. Iowa City: University of Iowa School of Music, 2006.

Singer, Steven. "Standardized Testing Creates Captive Markets." *Gadfly on the Wall* (blog). April 8, 2017. https://gadflyonthewallblog.com/2017/04/08/standardized-testing-creates-captive-markets/

Sivers, Derek. "First Follower: Leadership Lessons from a Dancing Guy." February 11, 2010. https://sivers.org/ff

Sivers, Derek. "How to Start a Movement." TED. February 2010. YouTube video, 2:42. https://www.ted.com/talks/derek_sivers_how_to_start_a_movement

Smith, J. Russell, C. C. Little, Edward Alsworth Ross, H. H. Newman, Carl E. Seashore, Kerr D. Macmillan. "The Faculty Birth Rate: Should It Be Increased?" *Eugenics* 3, no. 12 (December 1930): 458–60.

Smuts, Alice Boardman. *Science in the Service of Children, 1893–1935*. New Haven, CT: Yale University Press, 2006.

Spencer, Anna Garlin. "Should Married Women Work Outside the Home?" *Eugenics* 4, no. 1 (January 1931): 21–25.

Spencer, Herbert. "Herbert Spencer on Race Mixture." *Eugenics* 3, no. 2 (February 1930): 63.

Spencer, Richard. "Facing the Future as a Minority." Recorded at the eleventh American Renaissance Conference (April 5–7, 2013). Published on YouTube on September 16, 2017. YouTube video, 44:22. https://www.youtube.com/watch?v=yCv7Vaziylc

Spencer, Richard. "Richard Spencer—NPI 2016, Full Speech." Red Ice TV. Recorded November 19, 2016, at the 2016 National Policy Institute Conference in Washington, DC. YouTube video, 32:37. https://www.youtube.com/watch?v=Xq-LnO2DOGE (link discontinued).

"SPLC Exposes Racist Origins of New Arizona Law." *SPLC Report*, 40, no. 2, Summer 2010, 1, 5.

Stanton, Hazel M. "An Experimental Investigation of Musical Inheritance." In *Eugenics, Genetics and the Family, vol. 1, Scientific Papers of the Second International Congress of Eugenics; Held at American Museum of Natural History, New York, September 22–28, 1921*, 239–42. Baltimore, MD: Williams & Wilkins, 1923. Reprint, edited by Charles Rosenberg. New York: Garland Publishing, 1985.

Stanton, Hazel M. "The Inheritance of Specific Musical Capacities." *Psychological Monographs* 31, no. 1 (1922): 157–204. https://books.google.com/books?id=EcZMAAAAYAAJ&pg=PA157&lpg=PA157&dq=psychological+monographs+stanton&source=bl&ots=iF16DIvuj_&sig=BKOODKF4gSp2FlWKAPY_WGSl4co&hl=en&sa=X&ei=wG-MVZDGNdCzoQT9ipCICw&ved=0CCQQ6AEwAA#v=onepage&q=psychological%20monographs%20stanton&f=false

Stanton, Hazel M. *Measurement of Musical Talent: The Eastman Experiment*. University of Iowa Studies: Studies in the Psychology of Music, n.s. 291, vol. 2. Iowa City: The University, 1935. https://babel.hathitrust.org/cgi/pt?id=mdp.39015009448773&view=1up&seq=5

Stanton, Hazel M. "Quantitative Yard-Stick for the Measurement of Musical Capacities." *Eugenical News* 18, no. 4 (July-August 1933): 78–81.

Stanton, Hazel M. "Report on Use of Seashore Tests at Eastman School of Music." *Music Supervisors' Journal* 12, no. 4 (March 1926): 20, 22, 24, 26. http://www.jstor.org/stable/3382898

Starch, Daniel. "Carl E. Seashore, 1866–1949." *Journal of Educational Psychology* 41, no. 4 (April 1950): 217–18. https://doi.org/10.1037/h0063517

"Statistics and Eugenics." Dickinson College Wiki. Last modified December 9, 2009. http://wiki.dickinson.edu/index.php/Statistics_and_Eugenics

Steggerda, Morris. "Dr. Charles B. Davenport and His Contributions to Eugenics." *Eugenical News* 29, no. 1 (March 1944): 3–10.

Steggerda, Morris. "Negro-White Hybrids in Jamaica, B.W.I." *Eugenical News* 13, no. 2 (February 1928): 21–23.

Steggerda, Morris. "Physical Development of Negro-White Hybrids in Jamaica, British West Indies." PhD diss., University of Illinois at Urbana-Champaign, 1928. http://search.proquest.com.ezproxy.library.wisc.edu/docview/301773996?accountid=465

Stein, Perry. "Richard Spencer Hosted an Event at a Maryland Farm. Halfway Through, Everyone Was Kicked Out." *Washington Post*, November 21, 2017. https://www.washingtonpost.com/local/richard-spencer-hosted-an-event-at-a-maryland-farm-halfway-through-everyone-was-kicked-out/2017/11/21/1cd92dfe-9f33-40c4-b6f5-a271a8874c5d_story.html?utm_term=.27337546bf4f

"Sterilization in Germany." *Eugenical News* 20, no. 1 (January-February 1935): 13.

Stern, Alexandra Minna. "Gender and Sexuality: A Global Tour and Compass." In *The Oxford Handbook of the History of Eugenics*, edited by Alison Bashford and Philippa Levine, 173–91. Oxford: Oxford University Press, 2010.

"Stirpiculture." *The Circular*, n.s., 2, no. 3 (April 3, 1865): 17.

Stoddard, George D. "Carl Emil Seashore: 1866–1949." *American Journal of Psychology* 63, no. 3 (July 1950): 456–62. www.jstor.org/stable/1418021

Stoddard, George D. Preface to *Pioneering in Psychology*, by Carl E. Seashore, vii. University of Iowa Studies: Series on Aims and Progress of Research, no. 70. Iowa City: University of Iowa, 1942. https://babel.hathitrust.org/cgi/pt?id=mdp.39015020052349&view=1up&seq=1

Strauss, Valerie. "Five Reasons Standardized Testing Isn't Likely to Let Up." *Washington Post*, March 11, 2015. https://www.washingtonpost.com/news/answer-sheet/wp/2015/03/11/five-reasons-standardized-testing-isnt-likely-to-let-up/?noredirect=on&utm_term=.c240c6ce5176

Streep, Rosalind. "A Comparison of White and Negro Children in Rhythm and Consonance." *Journal of Applied Psychology* 15, no. 1 (February 1931): 53–71. http://dx.doi.org/10.1037/h0070190

Strescino, Peter. "U.S. English Chief Resigns Her Position." *Pueblo Chieftain*, October 18, 1988, 1A–2A.

"Students' Dissertations in Sociology." *American Journal of Sociology* 53, no. 1 (July 1947): 49–60. http://www.jstor.org/stable/2770628

"Studies in Jamaica." *Eugenical News* 11, no. 10 (October 1926): 154.

"SUI's Dean Seashore Dies; Public Service Here Sunday." *Daily Iowan*, October 18, 1949, 1.

"Supervisors of School Music: Hear What Psychologists Say of the Power of Suitable Music [Back Matter]." *Music Supervisors' Journal* 5, no. 1 (September 1918): 31. http://www.jstor.org/stable/3382832

"Survey of Musical Ability in Schools." *Journal of Heredity* 8, no. 7 (July 1, 1917): 305. https://doi-org.ezproxy.library.wisc.edu/10.1093/oxfordjournals.jhered.a111819

Suzuki, Shinichi. *Ability Development from Age Zero*. Translated by Mary Louise Nagata. Athens, OH: Ability Development Associates, 1981.

Sylvester, Reuel H. "Cooperation in Vocational Guidance." *State of Iowa Bulletin of State Institutions* 24, no. 4 (October 1922): 225–29. https://books.google.com/books?id=OzXJAAAAMAAJ&pg=PA225&lpg=PA225&dq=Reuel+H.+Sylvester&source=bl&ots=67GCCI3Ple&sig=DRUgjTjMyFh8A-fGDjQuDrkP1RE&hl=en&sa=X&ved=0ahUKEwiBwNOUoN7aAhXG8YMKHRLwBa4Q6AEILDAB#v=onepage&q=Reuel%20H.%20Sylvester&f=false

Sylvester, Reuel H. "The Practical Possibilities of Applied Psychology as Exemplified in the Building of an Army." In *Journal of Proceedings of the Twelfth Annual Meeting of the Music Supervisors' National Conference Held at St. Louis, Missouri, March 30–April 4, 1919*: 28–30. https://archive.org/details/journalofproceed005236mbp/page/n33

Tanton, John. "*The Camp of the Saints* Revisited." *Social Contract* 5, no. 2 (Winter 1994–95): 83. https://www.thesocialcontract.com/artman2/publish/tsc0502/article_410.shtml

Taylor, Jared. Introduction to *The Real American Dilemma: Race, Immigration, and the Future of America*, edited by Jared Taylor, 1–10. Oakton, VA: New Century Foundation, 1998.

Taylor, Jared. "Race and Nation." In *The Real American Dilemma: Race, Immigration, and the Future of America*, edited by Jared Taylor, 43–55. Oakton, VA: New Century Foundation, 1998.

Tellstrom, A. Theodore. *Music in American Education, Past and Present*. New York: Holt, Rinehart and Winston, 1971.

"Tenth Annual Business Meeting of the Eugenics Research Association, Cold Spring Harbor, June 10, 1922." *Eugenical News* 7, no. 7 (July 1922): 91.

Teo, Thomas, and Laura C. Ball. "Twin Research, Revisionism and Metahistory." *History of the Human Sciences* 22, no. 5 (December 2009): 1–23. https://www.researchgate.net/publication/43344186_Twin_Research_Revisionism_and_Metahistory

Terman, Lewis Madison. *The Measurement of Intelligence: An Explanation of and a Complete Guide for the Use of the Stanford Revision and Extension of the Binet-Simon Intelligence Scale*. Cambridge, MA: Riverside, 1916. https://archive.org/details/measurementofint008006mbp/page/n9

Terman, Lewis Madison. "The Mental Hygiene of Exceptional Children." *Pedagogical*

Seminary 22, no. 4 (1915): 529–37. https://doi.org/10.1080/08919402.1915.1053 3983

Terman, Lewis Madison, Bird T. Baldwin, Edith Bronson, James C. DeVoss, Florence Fuller, Florence L. Goodenough, Truman Lee Kelley, Margaret Lima, Helen Marshall, Albert H. Moore, A. S. Raubenheimer, G. M. Ruch, Raymond L. Willoughby, Jenny Benson Wyman, Dorothy Hazeltine Yates. *Mental and Physical Traits of a Thousand Gifted Children*, vol. 1, Genetic Studies of Genius. Stanford, CA: Stanford University Press, 1925. https://babel.hathitrust.org/cgi/pt?id=mdp.39015001544926&view=1up&seq=9

"The Test of Variables of Attention (T.O.V.A.)." The TOVA Company. Accessed May 5, 2019. https://www.tovatest.com/

Thanawala, Sudhin, and Don Thompson. "Trump Loses Effort to Block 2 California Sanctuary Laws." *Chicago Sun Times*, July 5, 2018. https://chicago.suntimes.com/2018/7/5/18459016/trump-loses-effort-to-block-2-california-sanctuary-laws

Thompson, Charles H. "The Educational Achievements of Negro Children." *Annals of the American Academy of Political and Social Science* 140, no. 229 (November 1928): 193–208. https://www.jstor.org/stable/1016849

Thompson, Warren S. "Race Suicide in the United States." *Scientific Monthly* 5, no. 1 (July 1917): 22–35. http://www.jstor.org/stable/22426

Thorndike, Edward L. "Measurement of Twins." *Journal of Philosophy, Psychology and Scientific Methods* 2, no. 20 (September 28, 1905): 547–53. http://www.jstor.org/stable/2011451

"Three-Hour Blaze Destroys Portion of East Hall." *Daily Iowan*, 78, no. 202, May 17, 1946, 1, 7.

Tiffin, Joseph. "Carl Emil Seashore: 1866–1949." *Psychological Review* 57, no. 1 (January 1950): 1–2. https://doi.org/10.1037/h0058319

Todorov, Tzvetan. *Hope and Memory: Reflections on the Twentieth Century*. Princeton, NJ: Princeton University Press, 2003. Republished, London: Atlantic, 2014.

"Topic: Better Baby Contests." Image Archive on the American Eugenics Movement, DNA Learning Center, Cold Spring Harbor Laboratory. Accessed November 17, 2018. http://www.eugenicsarchive.org/eugenics/topics_fs.pl?theme=43

"Topic: Fitter Family Contests." Image Archive on the American Eugenics Movement, DNA Learning Center, Cold Spring Harbor Laboratory. Accessed November 17, 2018. http://www.eugenicsarchive.org/eugenics/topics_fs.pl?theme=8

"To Teach Summer Course." *Washington Missourian*, May 11, 1950, 3.

"Traits Reports." 23andMe, Inc. Accessed December 10, 2018. https://medical.23andme.com/reports/#traits

Tucker, William H. *The Funding of Scientific Racism: Wickliffe Draper and the Pioneer Fund*. Urbana: University of Illinois Press, 2002.

2019–2020 Catalog: Music Education. University of Arkansas. Accessed November 2, 2019. http://catalog.uark.edu/graduatecatalog/coursesofinstruction/mued/

"Two Profs Attend Seashore Service." *Gustavian Weekly*, October 28, 1949, 1.

Ukkola, Liisa, Päivi Onkamo, Pirre Raijas, Kai Karma, and Irma Järvelä. "Musical

Aptitude Is Associated with AVPR1A-Haplotpyes." *PLoS ONE* 4, no. 5 (2009). https://doi.org/10.1371/journal.pone.0005534

Ulloa, Jazmine. "No, California's 'Sanctuary State' Law Does Not Allow the Release of Dangerous Criminals to the Streets." *Los Angeles Times*, April 6, 2018. https://www.latimes.com/politics/la-pol-ca-sanctuary-state-criminals-explained-20180406-htmlstory.html

"Ulster University Withdraws Status from Prof Richard Lynn." BBC News. April 14, 2018. https://www.bbc.com/news/uk-northern-ireland-43768132

"U. of I. Given Bronze Bust of Dr. C. Seashore." *Gustavian Weekly*, November 28, 1939, 1.

U.S. Congress, Office of Technology Assessment. *Testing in American Schools: Asking the Right Questions, OTA-SET-519*. Washington, DC: United States Government Printing Office, February 1992. https://www.princeton.edu/~ota/disk1/1992/9236/9236.PDF

"U.S. Immigration and Customs Enforcement Acting Director to Speak at Hate Group Event Tomorrow." *Hatewatch* (blog). Southern Poverty Law Center, June 4, 2018. https://www.splcenter.org/hatewatch/2018/06/04/us-immigration-and-customs-enforcement-acting-director-speak-hate-group-event-tomorrow

van Alstyne, Dorothy, and Emily Osborne. "Rhythmic Responses of Negro and White Children Two to Six: With a Special Focus on Regulated and Free Rhythm Situations." *Monographs of the Society for Research in Child Development* 2, no. 4, serial 11 (1937): i-iv, 1–63. Reprint, New York: Kraus Reprint, 1966. https://www.jstor.org/stable/1165409

"VDARE." Southern Poverty Law Center. Accessed December 2, 2018. https://www.splcenter.org/fighting-hate/extremist-files/group/vdare

Viteles, Morris S. "The Mental Status of the Negro." *Annals of the American Academy of Political and Social Science* 140, no. 229 (November 1928): 166–77. https://www.jstor.org/stable/1016845

"Vocational Guidance in Music." *Journal of Heredity* 9, no. 2 (February 1918): 66. https://doi-org.ezproxy.library.wisc.edu/10.1093/oxfordjournals.jhered.a111893

Voxman, Himie. "Some Personal Reflections on Carl E. Seashore." In *Multidisciplinary Perspectives on Musicality: Essays from the Seashore Symposium*, edited by Kate Gfeller, Don D. Coffman, Carlos X. Rodriguez, and David J. Nelson, 216–17. Iowa City: University of Iowa School of Music, 2006.

Vozzella, Laura. "White Nationalist Richard Spencer Leads Torch-Bearing Protesters Defending Lee Statue." *Washington Post*, May 14, 2017. https://www.washingtonpost.com/local/virginia-politics/alt-rights-richard-spencer-leads-torch-bearing-protesters-defending-lee-statue/2017/05/14/766aaa56–38ac-11e7–9e48-c4f199710b69_story.html?noredirect=on&utm_term=.e96fda1efde1

Walker, Alice. "What to Do with an Arrow in Your Heart." Interview by Shannon Henry Kleiber. *To the Best of Our Knowledge*, Wisconsin Public Radio, December 1, 2018. Audio, 14:10. https://www.ttbook.org/interview/what-do-arrow-your-heart

Wallace, Alfred Russel. *Darwinism: An Exposition of the Theory of Natural Selection with Some of Its Applications*. London: Macmillan, 1891.

Wallace, Alfred Russel. *Social Environment and Moral Progress*. New York: Cassell, 1913. http://people.wku.edu/charles.smith/wallace/arwbooks/xx_Wallace_Social_Environment_and_Moral_Progress.pdf

Ward, Justin. "Day of the Trope: White Nationalist Memes Thrive Online." In *Hate and Extremism in 2018*, 22–25. Montgomery, AL: Southern Poverty Law Center, 2018.

Warrick, Daniel Charles. "The Establishment of the Study of Fine Arts at the State University of Iowa during the Administration of Walter A. Jessup and Carl E. Seashore." PhD diss., University of Missouri–Columbia, 1995.

Watkins, Eli, and Abby Phillip. "Trump Decries Immigrants from 'Shithole Countries' Coming to US." CNN. Last modified January 12, 2018. https://www.cnn.com/2018/01/11/politics/immigrants-shithole-countries-trump/index.html

"WCATY Eligibility." Board of Regents of the University of Wisconsin System. Accessed December 18, 2018. https://wcaty.wisc.edu/eligibility/

"WCATY Mission." Board of Regents of the University of Wisconsin System. Accessed December 12, 2018. https://wcaty.wisc.edu/mission/

Wechsler, Harold S. *The Qualified Student: A History of Selective College Admission in America*. New York: John Wiley & Sons, 1977.

"Westminster Confession of Faith [1646] Chapter III: Of God's Eternal Decree." Center for Reformed Theology and Apologetics. Accessed September 24, 2014. https://reformed.org/documents/wcf_with_proofs/ (link now goes elsewhere).

Wheeler, Lester R., and Viola D. Wheeler. "The Musical Ability of Mountain Children as Measured by the Seashore Test of Musical Talent." *Pedagogical Seminary and Journal of Genetic Psychology* 43, no. 2 (1933): 352–76. https://doi.org/10.1080/08856559.1933.10532464

White, Charles. *An Account of the Regular Gradation in Man, and in Different Animals and Vegetables; and from the Former to the Latter*. London: C. Dilly, 1799. https://archive.org/details/b24924507

White, John. "Intelligence—the New Puritanism." *Times Educational Supplement*, October 24, 1969, 4.

White, John. "Puritan Intelligence: The Ideological Background to IQ." *Oxford Review of Education* 31, no. 3 (September 2005): 423–42. https://doi.org/10.1080/03054980500222148

"White America," review of *White America: The American Racial Problem as Seen in a Worldwide Perspective*, by Earnest S. Cox. *Eugenical News* 9, no. 1 (January 1924): 3.

"White Nationalist." Southern Poverty Law Center. Accessed June 3, 2019. https://www.splcenter.org/fighting-hate/extremist-files/ideology/white-nationalist

"White Panther." Way of the World. February 16, 2018. YouTube video, 18:02. https://www.youtube.com/watch?v=AmgxftI4O20

Whitley, Mary T. "A Comparison of the Seashore and the Kwalwasser-Dykema Music Tests." *Teachers College Record* 33, no. 8 (May 1932): 731–51.

Whitney, Leon F. "Leon Fradley Whitney Autobiography," 1971. Mss.B.W613b. Archives, American Philosophical Society Library, Philadelphia, PA.

Whitney, Leon F., John M. Cooper, Sidney S. Tedesche, and Roswell Hill Johnson. "Is Eugenics Racial Snobbery? Does It Condemn Whole Peoples?" *Eugenics* 2, no. 2 (February 1929): 20–21.

Wiggam, Albert Edward, Frederick Osborn, and Leon F. Whitney. "Is Eugenics 'Scientific Calvinism'? Is It Biological Predestination?" *Eugenics* 3, no. 1 (1930): 18–19.

Willer, Stefan. "Sui Generis: Heredity and Heritage of Genius at the Turn of the Eighteenth Century." In *Heredity Produced: At the Crossroads of Biology, Politics, and Culture 1500–1870*, edited by Staffan Müller-Wille and Hans-Jörg Rheinberger, 419–40. Cambridge, MA: MIT Press, 2007.

Wilson, Bruce, Charles L. Gary, and Gary Greene. "Music in Our Schools: The First 150 Years." *Music Educators Journal* 74, no. 6 (February 1988): 25–101. https://www.jstor.org/stable/3397995

Wines, Michael, and Stephanie Saul. "White Supremacists Extend Their Reach through Websites." *New York Times*, July 5, 2015, A1. https://www.nytimes.com/2015/07/06/us/white-supremacists-extend-their-reach-through-websites.html?_r=0

Winfield, Ann G. "Eugenic Ideology and Historical Osmosis." In *Curriculum Studies Handbook: The Next Moment*, edited by Erik Malewski, 142–67. New York: Routledge, 2010.

Winfield, Ann G. *Eugenics and Education in America: Institutionalized Racism and the Implications of History, Ideology, and Memory*. New York: Peter Lang, 2007.

Winner, Ellen. "The Miseducation of Our Gifted Children." Davidson Institute. 1996. http://www.davidsongifted.org/Search-Database/entry/A10316

"Wisconsin Eugenics Laws." *Eugenical News* 3, no. 5 (May 1918): 38–39.

Wissler, Clark. "The Correlation of Mental and Physical Tests." *Psychological Review Monograph Supplements* 3, no. 6, whole no. 16 (June 1901): 1–62.

Woods, Peter. "Operationalizing Aesthetics within the Eugenics Movement: Cautionary Implications for Aesthetic Education." Paper presented at the Annual Meeting of the American Educational Research Association, Toronto, Canada, April 8, 2019.

Wray, Matt. *Not Quite White: White Trash and the Boundaries of Whiteness*. Durham: Duke University Press, 2006.

Wright, Karen. "Top 100 Stories of 2008 #52: Musical Ability Seems to Be 50 Percent Genetic." *Discover Magazine*, December 12, 2008. http://discovermagazine.com/2009/jan/052

"Writers' Workshop: History." University of Iowa College of Liberal Arts & Sciences. Accessed July 11, 2018. https://writersworkshop.uiowa.edu/about/about-workshop/history

Wyatt, Ruth. "A Note on the Use of 'Omnibus' Training to Validate Seashore's 'Capacity' Hypothesis." *American Journal of Psychology* 52, no. 4 (October 1939): 638–40. https://doi.org/10.2307/1416481

Yoneyama, Shoko, and Asao Naito. "Problems with the Paradigm: The School as a Factor in Understanding Bullying (with Special Reference to Japan)." *British Journal of Sociology of Education* 24, no. 3 (2003): 315–30. https://doi.org/10.1080/01425690301894

"Zaid Lenoir." Memory book posting from Michael Carter. Accessed August 14, 2018. http://www.tributes.com/show/Zaid-Lenoir-63194317?active_tab=condolences

Zenderland, Leila. *Measuring Minds: Henry Herbert Goddard and the Origins of American Intelligence Testing*. Cambridge, UK: Cambridge University Press, 1998.

Zinar, Ruth. "Highlights of Thought in the History of Music Education, VIII: Carl Seashore (1866–1949) and the Psychology of Music." *American Music Teacher* 33, no. 3 (January 1984): 44, 46.

Index

NOTE: The following abbreviations have been used in this index: AES (American Eugenics Society); ERO (Eugenics Record Office); ERA (Eugenics Research Association); ICWRS (Iowa Child Welfare Research Station); NRC (National Research Council).